WOMAN'S OWN

COOK BOOK

PUBLISHED FOR NEWNES BOOKS
by THE HAMLYN PUBLISHING GROUP LTD.,
HAMLYN HOUSE · 42 THE CENTRE · FELTHAM
MIDDLESEX

LONDON · NEW YORK · SYDNEY · TORONTO

© George Newnes Limited, 1964

Sixth Impression 1971

ISBN 0 600 40336 X

Printed and bound in England by
Hazell Watson & Viney Ltd, Aylesbury, Bucks

CONTENTS

CONTENTS

CONTENTS

COLOUR ILLUSTRATIONS

ANYONE CAN BE A GOOD COOK

*The secret of success is chiefly attention
to detail—partly an adventurous spirit*

An ideal menu for a bride's first dinner party: Shrimp Cocktails followed by Baked Ham
with Pineapple, Brussels Sprouts, Chestnuts and Duchess Potatoes, Plum Meringue and Coffee

SOME people have naturally cool hands for pastry; a flair for making a sponge as light as a feather; the knack of turning out a perfect soufflé; or a way with sauces. So the idea arises that a good cook has some special faculty, like the born gardener's "green fingers" that make everything grow.

It is probably nothing more than that time-honoured definition of genius: "An infinite capacity for taking pains." And, since anyone can—if she will—take pains, it follows logically that everyone is *potentially* a good cook.

These simple rules will help you achieve your aim, whether you are a young bride or a busy mother with so many hungry mouths to feed that there is little time for experimenting.

1. Use a good recipe and follow it exactly, weighing or measuring the ingredients accurately. Even if you have made dozens of Yorkshire Puddings from memory, try making one by a new recipe just for once. The essence of good cooking is never to get set in your ways.

2. Be brave and original. Make the best of the wonderful variety of exciting and unusual foods now available. Perhaps you once enjoyed a Chinese meal at a restaurant or loved the food you had on a

Serve roast duck surrounded by orange slices and crisp lettuce leaves, and you will build a reputation as a hostess with ideas

A good cook never scorns the simple, cheap foods, but gives them a millionaire appearance, like these baked potatoes stuffed with cheese (below)

holiday in Spain? Well, then, try your hand at cooking the Chinese or the Spanish way. Never let anyone convince you that you have to be a professional chef to make choux pastry or ice a wedding cake. If you have the courage to try, you will almost certainly find what nonsense such warnings are.

3. Equip your kitchen with the basic necessities, add only the gadgets you are *sure* will really help you, as and when you can afford them, and do keep an open mind about new ideas and inventions. For instance, the quick mixing method for pastry and cakes, made possible by the introduction of the vegetable fat shortenings, has improved many people's cooking out of all recognition, particularly those who were apt to skimp on the creaming of cake mixtures and pastry mixing. Tomorrow's new idea may eliminate the weak spot in *your* cooking.

4. Do not scorn simple dishes or inexpensive ingredients. A really good cook can make the cheapest cuts look and taste delicious—and that must be your aim. Remember that the appearance of a dish is every bit as important as its vitamin content and its flavour, for it is the appeal to the eye that tempts the appetite.

The simplest garnish will transform an otherwise ordinary meal into a sumptuous repast; the way you present a dish can alter its whole value. What could be cheaper or easier to prepare for supper than potatoes baked in their jackets and stuffed with cheese? And what could be less inspiring to behold? But not if you do them this way:

Stuffed Potatoes with Eye Appeal

Split the skins of the nicely baked potatoes downwards from a central point to look like petals, scoop out the floury inside, mix it well with butter, plenty of grated cheese, salt, pepper and a little milk or cream, then put it back inside the potato shells and heat through. Garnish with sprigs of parsley and serve with whole uncooked tomatoes, for a colourful and tasty meal.

When you dish up roast duck, surround it on the dish with slices of fresh, peeled orange and lettuce leaves; the contrast in flavour as well as colour is memorable, the kind of little detail that marks you out as a hostess of ideas.

Mince Tart en Surprise

Another little trick that never fails is to serve a well-known and popular dish with a surprise trimming. Mince Tart en Surprise is a good example. You make a flat mince tart, flavouring the mincemeat with rum or brandy, if possible. Leave it to cool and, just before serving, spoon a family brick of vanilla ice cream over the mincemeat. Make the meringue by whisking 2 egg-whites until very stiff, then folding in 3 oz. castor sugar with a metal spoon. Pipe or spoon the meringue over the flan, making sure that the ice cream is entirely covered. " Flash" cook in a very hot oven for 2 to 3 minutes only, until the meringue is just tinged with golden brown. You can vary this with an apple or banana filling, but the mincemeat is particularly good.

5. Do not attempt too much in the early stages of training to be a good cook. If you do, you will only get flustered and worried and things will go unexpectedly wrong.

There is nothing against the mere male learning to be a good cook too— and he need not look as scared as Danny Kaye

It is a mistake to experiment with a lot of fancy, complicated dishes when entertaining Always try them out on the family circle first, to make sure. The ideal meal for a bride entertaining her first guests would be a cold first course which can be put on the table in advance, a main course that can be dished up and kept hot ready to be brought to table without fuss, and a simple sweet. Here is a suggested menu:

Lobster Cocktails (see Hors d'œuvres and Appetisers)
Baked Ham with Pineapple (see Cookery in the United States)
Sprouts and Chestnuts
Duchess Potatoes (see Vegetables)
Plum Meringue

For the **Plum Meringue,** put a large can of red plums, or 1½ lb. fresh South African plums, lightly stewed in a little water and 2 dessertspoonfuls sugar, into a fireproof glass dish. Bring ⅓ pint of plum juice to the boil. Mix 2 teaspoonfuls cornflour to a smooth paste with juice or water, blend with the heated juice, return to the pan and stir until it clears and thickens slightly. Pour over plums and cool. Beat 2 egg-whites until stiff, fold in 2 dessertspoonfuls castor sugar, pile meringue on top of cooled fruit, bake in a slow oven for 20 to 30 minutes until meringue is slightly browned.

One sure way to cookery success is to make an old and tried
favourite with a surprise trimming. This is Mince Tart en Surprise,
with an ice cream and meringue top

ENTERTAINING

If you have no room for a formal sit-down dinner party, you can still invite your friends to a wine and cheese evening, a fork luncheon or just for tea

MODERN entertaining has become so adaptable that it can be made to fit any household or flatlet.

A golden rule for all hostesses should be: "The less help available, the simpler the meal." A worried, preoccupied hostess only communicates her feelings to her guests. In fact, it is far better to give your guests bread and cheese and beer or wine, plus your whole attention, than an elaborate meal which has obviously worried you to death in its planning.

The sort of entertaining which gives the hostess most work is, of course, the formal luncheon or dinner party. If the housewife has to prepare everything herself, or with very little help, it is best to choose dishes that can be cooked, as far as possible, beforehand. If there is a refrigerator, dishes made the day before can be kept fresh and sweet.

An electric hot plate in the dining room is very useful when one is single-handed. The first course can be put on the table before the guests come into the room, the second on the hot plate. Then, if the sweet is a cold one, the hostess need only put each course as it is finished on a trolley, which can be wheeled away when the meal is over.

Earthenware and fireproof dishes, in which the food can be served as well as cooked, save washing up and look very attractive.

Aim at simplicity in table decorations: shining glass, well-polished silver and a bowl of flowers (low enough to allow the guests to see each other's faces) are all that is required.

SUGGESTED MENUS FOR A FORMAL LUNCHEON OR DINNER PARTY

(A few recipes marked with an * are given after these menus, the others will be found in their respective chapters.)

Hors d'œuvres
Grilled steak maître d'hôtel
Chip potatoes and cauliflower
Fruit flan and cream
Cheese and biscuits
Coffee

Grapefruit
Blanquette of veal and mushrooms or
Fish à la Meunière*
Mashed potatoes and green peas
Pineapple fritters or fresh asparagus
Cheese and biscuits
Coffee

Eggs en cocotte with asparagus tips
(or chopped mushrooms or green peas)
Cutlets en casserole with carrots
Mashed potatoes and peas, beans, or
Brussels sprouts
Strawberries or raspberries (frozen, if out of season) with cream
Cheese and biscuits
Coffee

Grapefruit or foie gras
Beef en daube with new potatoes, peas and young carrots or baby marrows
Green salad
Lemon meringue pie
Cheese
Coffee

(*Hot weather meal*)
Melon or iced consommé
Sole Véronique with new potatoes and French beans
Vanilla ice cream with hot chocolate sauce
Cheese
Coffee

Taramasalata (see Cookery in Greece) or smoked cod's roe
Roast duck, roast potatoes, green peas and apple sauce
Orange salad
Fresh pineapple and cream
Cheese
Coffee

An ideal cold buffet supper for Boxing Day. On the hot-plate is a bowl of creamy soup. Foods are: savoury biscuits topped with gherkin slices; French bread with slices of cheese; a fruit flan; sausage rolls; cheese straws; a fruit cup; pears with ice cream. Note the olives, cherries and cocktail sausages speared on sticks round the candles

Hors d'œuvres
Pheasant, partridge or grouse
(according to season)
Chip potatoes and salad
Pear or peach melba
Coffee

Melon
Tournedos of beef
Mashed potatoes and green peas
Vanilla soufflé
Coffee

Foie gras
(served with very thin, crisp, hot toast and
fresh butter)
Chicken Maryland*
Chip potatoes and cauliflower
Melon (or pineapple) en surprise*
Coffee

Do not forget to provide some form of packet crispbread, as well as ordinary bread, and have barley water, lemonade, orange squash or cider for those who do not drink wine.

Remember, too, that not only is fresh fruit appreciated inwardly; it is also a delight to the eye.

Asparagus, if in season, should be served after the poultry or meat course.

An excellent extra course to take its place can be made by mixing together almost any kind of fresh vegetables in a white sauce (such as tiny carrots, green peas and beans).

Informal Luncheons and Dinners

Informal meals can be as long or as short as you like, and can include the many delicious dishes which are not suitable for more formal occasions, such as steak and kidney pie, joints, or poultry; and for the sweet course the more substantial type of pudding. Serving and setting should be carefully thought out. Even the most informal meal should look attractive.

Recipes

Fish à la Meunière (suitable for small soles, whiting or trout or larger fish in slices)

Melt enough clarified butter in an earthenware dish (in which the fish can be served) to half cover the fish. Make small cuts in each side of the fish, dip into seasoned flour and brown well on one side before turning it over on to the other. Just before serving, add a very little finely chopped parsley and a squeeze of lemon juice.

13

A cantaloup melon is equally good served in this way. Pineapple or melon-flavoured ice cream can be used instead of ordinary cream.

BUFFET MEALS AND FORK LUNCHES

The "stand up and help yourself" meal is a popular form of modern entertaining particularly suitable for small premises. A wide variety of different foods should be attractively dis-

If you serve Stilton at the end of a meal, treat it with reverence—wrap it in a clean table napkin and accompany it with port and walnuts

For informal entertaining, there is nothing better than a cheese and beer or wine party. Beer and Cheddar are natural soul-mates—and throw in plenty of crusty bread and pickled onions for good measure

Chicken Maryland

Cut a young bird into joints, brush each piece over with melted butter, season, and roll in flour and breadcrumbs. Put into a well-buttered dish and bake in the oven for about $\frac{1}{2}$ hour, basting frequently with butter. Serve with a sauce made from the giblets. Fried bananas go excellently with this dish.

Pineapple (or Melon) en Surprise

Take a ripe pineapple, cut a slice off the bottom so that it stands firmly on a dish, then cut off the head low enough to enable the contents to be removed with a sharp knife. Put aside the head with the leaves intact.

Cut out the inside (keeping the juice carefully), chop it into neat pieces and mix with it any fresh fruit in season, as you would do for a fruit salad. Add the juice and put the mixture back into the pineapple. Just before serving, add plenty of fresh cream. Replace the top.

played on a long, narrow buffet table, with piles of clean plates and spoons and forks (no other cutlery should be necessary if the right foods are chosen) at intervals. The guests are then invited to help themselves. A big tureen of steaming soup, a bowl of hot risotto or a flat dish full of sizzling sausages on a hot-plate makes a pleasant change from an entirely cold buffet.

COCKTAIL AND SHERRY PARTIES

This is one of the easiest ways of entertaining people to whom one owes hospitality, because a large number of close friends and casual acquaintances can be asked together. Indeed, one of the first rules for a successful cocktail or sherry party seems to be that it should be as crowded as possible.

Though sherry is more popular and less extravagant than cocktails, the best plan is to provide both, plus lemonade, barley water, grapefruit, pineapple or tomato juice or iced coffee for those who prefer soft drinks.

Six o'clock is the usual time for such a party, and as many of your guests, if they happen to be going on to a theatre or cinema afterwards, will cut out dinner, provide plenty of "eats." (See chapter on Party Snacks and Sandwiches.)

The Drinks

Have a good supply of cocktails ready mixed in a large jug before your guests arrive. For an average party of twenty, a bottle of dry sherry together with one of a sweeter type will be enough, with a bottle of gin and one each of French and Italian vermouth for the cocktails. Recipes for making these will be found in the chapter on Mixed Drinks.

Sweet cocktails are generally served with a maraschino cherry on a stick in each glass, dry ones with green olives.

If the party is a very large one, it is some-times possible to arrange with your wine merchant that any unopened bottles of spirits can be returned.

INVITATION FOR TEA AND CARDS

Many women find that a Bridge or Canasta tea is an easy and pleasant way of entertaining their women friends. Start your party about three o'clock, play for an hour, then have tea, and there will probably be time for another hour's play afterwards.

Tea is a simple affair, but make it look as attractive as you possibly can. Have tiny hot scones in the winter and small, dainty sandwiches all the year round. There are many attractive fancy cutters to be bought which add very much to the appearance of sandwiches. Bridge rolls are easily filled and easy to handle. Choose small cakes, and provide China as well as Indian tea, with slices of lemon for those who prefer it to milk with China tea. Dishes of sweets or chocolates may be placed so that they can easily be reached during play, and there should be plenty of cigarettes and ashtrays.

Cocktails or sherry are often served just before the party breaks up.

Serve asparagus as a separate course, just after the meat or poultry, accompanied by melted butter, which is nicest if you keep it really hot over a spirit lamp or night-light hot-plate

15

HORS D'ŒUVRES AND APPETISERS

Make your savoury delicacies interesting, dainty and good
to eat—or serve piquant fruit juice to start the meal

HORS D'ŒUVRES—originally side dishes "outside the works" (so to say) of a formal dinner—have long been established as appetisers at the beginning of a meal, often taking the place of the soup course.

Their purpose is to whet the appetite, not to allay it; they should therefore be piquant in flavour and attractively served in small portions. All kinds of fish, meat, vegetables and fruit, well seasoned and dressed, go to the making of these savoury delicacies, generally served cold. Imagination has plenty of scope in the combination of ingredients and their decoration with colourful morsels. Canapés—choice bits mounted on bread sliced and cut into small squares or circles the size of a penny and then toasted or fried—are popular.

Fruit or fruit juices fairly tart in flavour are frequently served at the beginning of a meal in place of a variety of hors d'œuvres. Suggestions for these, rather a class apart, are given first.

FRUIT APPETISERS

Avocado Pear.—This is served raw, unskinned, cut in half lengthwise, the seeds removed and with a vinaigrette sauce sprinkled into the hollow. It looks its best on a cool lettuce leaf, but the avocado pear should not be put into a refrigerator.

Grapefruit.—This is often served halved in its skin. Cut the grapefruit in half and remove the seeds. Using a sharp knife, separate each section from its membrane, or remove the membrane between the sections altogether. Cut round and under the sections to detach them from the skin. Cut out the core. Sprinkle with sugar and chill before serving in grapefruit glasses or on plates. Decorate with a glacé cherry at the centre.

Grapefruit and Orange.—Mix equal quantities of grapefruit and orange pulp cut into small pieces. Sprinkle with lemon juice and sugar. Chill and serve in grapefruit glasses.

Melon (Cantaloup).—Allow a good thick segment for each person. Take out the seeds carefully, chill and serve with or without sugar, or with ground ginger.

Melon (Honeydew).—Serve in sections 2 or 3 in. wide, prepared as for Cantaloup.

Melon (Water).—Cut the pulp into small balls. Sprinkle with lemon juice and sugar; chill and serve in glasses, decorated with small sprigs of fresh mint.

Orange Juice (Iced).—Strain the juice and serve in small glasses set in cracked ice on plates.

Orange and Mint.—Choose small and preferably sour oranges. Remove the skin from the sections (using scissors) and chill. Serve in glasses, sprinkled liberally with lemon juice, icing sugar and finely chopped mint.

Pineapple and Strawberries. — Mix halved strawberries with an equal amount of diced pineapple in glasses; pour over a mixture of one-third lemon juice to two-thirds orange juice, sweetened.

Strawberry and Cherry Cocktail.—Combine strawberry juice with an equal quantity of icing sugar, sharpened to taste with lemon juice, and pour over stoned cherries and some chopped almonds. Serve very cold in cocktail glasses.

Tomato Juice Cocktail.—Mix together ½ pint of tomato juice, 1 tablespoonful each of lemon juice and vinegar, 2 teaspoonfuls of sugar, 1 teaspoonful of grated onion, ½ teaspoonful of Worcester sauce, a pinch of celery salt and a piece of bay leaf. Let it stand for a while, then strain through muslin, chill, and serve in small glasses.

HORS D'ŒUVRES VARIETIES

Fish

Anchovies.—Wash to remove the brine in which they have been preserved. Fillet,

Photo: Canned Foods Advisory Bureau

APPETISERS : **1. Rounds of beetroot on luncheon meat, carrot and luncheon meat on mashed pilchard. 2. Peas and an anchovy on mashed herring and onion, paprika and meat on scrambled egg. 3. Sieved hard-boiled egg on pilchard with beet. 4. Tomato and luncheon meat rounds; asparagus on cream cheese and onion.**

THREE-COURSE DINNER COOKED IN A PRESSURE COOKER

Tomato Soup, followed by Braised Pigeons with cauliflower and potatoes, with Steamed Canary Puddings as a sweet—all cooked quickly and well in a Presto 508B Pressure Cooker.

First prepare and cook the soup—pressure cooking time 3 minutes at 15 lb. pressure.

Then rinse cooker. Pre-heat base, add fat and brown pigeons well on all sides. Add water and pressure-cook birds for 9 minutes at 15 lb. pressure. Cool cooker and place cooking rack over birds. Add cauliflower and potatoes (halved lengthwise so that they take same time as cauliflower) in separators and cook for 6 minutes. Cool cooker. Dish up pigeons and vegetables and garnish as required.

Place 1 pint boiling water in cooker and put individual dariole moulds two-thirds full of sponge mixture on rack in cooker. Steam gently for 10 minutes, then cook at 15 lb. pressure for 10 minutes—while eating the first two courses. Let cooker cool and serve.

For full details and recipes, see chapter on Pressure Cooking, page 272.

SIMPLE BUT APPETISING—above, minced meat in a pastry flan case; below, fried lamb cutlets attractively served in a ring of creamed potatoes with green peas has eye appeal

Photo: Canned Foods Advisory Bureau

IN THE PARTY SPIRIT

It is a great art—and the secret of success as a hostess—to be able to produce at short notice a meal that looks as if it had taken hours of painstaking preparation and which positively invites the guests to stay and enjoy it. Imagination is the essential factor. Here is a tasty meal most attractively served, yet made from the supplies in any well-stocked store cupboard. The recipes for Cold Meat Mould, seen above garnished with a fresh salad, and Forgotten Dessert are to be found in the chapter on Emergency Meals, which begins on page 232

and arrange the fillets attractively, adding a little oil, alone or on lettuce. Garnish with chopped parsley, capers, hard-boiled egg. The fillets, which can be bought already prepared, are also a useful garnish for other dishes.

Anchovy Butter (see also French Cookery).—Pound six or seven anchovies with $\frac{1}{4}$ lb. of butter; season and put through a sieve. Serve very cold on small biscuits or rounds of prepared bread.

Anchovy Canapés.—Use anchovy butter, or pounded anchovies, or anchovy paste bought already prepared. Season with lemon juice and pile on the prepared bread. Decorate with hard-boiled egg slices.

Caviare.—This is the epicure's dish. Caviare, or salted sturgeon's roe, should be kept very cold. Serve it from the pot in which it is bought—placed on a folded napkin with shavings of ice—with Cayenne and quarters of lemon; or in halved hard-boiled eggs from which the yolks have been removed.

Caviare Canapés.—Cover one-half of the prepared pieces of bread with the caviare, topped by a ring of hard-boiled egg-white, and cover the remainder with minced raw onion, topped by a little sieved hard-boiled egg-yolk.

Fish Mayonnaise. — Arrange cooked white fish or salmon, flaked or cut into short lengths, on lettuce. Coat with mayonnaise and decorate with fillets of anchovy, sliced hard-boiled eggs, cold sliced potatoes, capers, parsley, etc.

Herrings (Salt).—Remove the excess salt by soaking in cold water for several hours. Fillet, and let the fillets, cut into narrow diagonal strips, stand for about 6 hours in vinegar with pepper and sliced onion.

Lobster in Aspic.—Set the lobster pieces in aspic with slices of hard-boiled egg, cooked peas, etc., using small moulds. Turn out when set and serve on lettuce, decorated with parsley.

Lobster or Crab Canapés. — Pile chopped cooked fish, seasoned with lemon juice and Worcester sauce, on small rounds of prepared bread or biscuits, and decorate with pieces of pickled beetroot and olives; or mix with cream, season with salt and Cayenne, and decorate with parsley.

Oysters.—These are served alone, with no other hors d'œuvres dishes offered. Serve on the half-shell, allowing five or six oysters to each person, with a quarter-lemon and thin brown bread and butter.

Oyster Cocktail.—Put four or five oysters into each glass and pour over a dressing prepared (for six persons) from 3 tablespoonfuls tomato ketchup, 4 tablespoonfuls lemon juice, 2 tablespoonfuls vinegar, 2 teaspoonfuls horseradish, 1 teaspoonful salt and $\frac{1}{4}$ teaspoonful tabasco sauce.

Prawns or Shrimps.—Arrange round the edge of a wineglass containing crushed ice, or round half a cut lemon, cut side downwards, with their tails tucked underneath; or serve very cold, shelled, sprinkled with lemon juice, with brown bread and butter, or on a lettuce leaf coated with mayonnaise.

Prawn Canapés.—Pound shelled prawns in a mortar with lemon juice, oil and small chilli peppers, and pile on small rounds of prepared bread.

Prawn or Lobster Cocktail.—Place shredded lettuce in glasses and fill up with chopped or sliced prawns or lobster. Cover with whisked mayonnaise sauce with

Prawn or Lobster Cocktail, with its sharp dressing, is served in individual glasses

Mixed hors d'œuvres looks attractive in a special dish with separate compartments
for olives, tomato salad, anchovy eggs, vegetable salad and cod's roe

tomato ketchup and a little Worcester sauce added and top with lettuce leaf and whole prawn or piece of lobster.

Rollmops.—These pickled rolled fillets of herrings can be bought in Continental stores ready to serve.

Smoked Salmon.—Slice very thinly and serve with lemon, Cayenne pepper and thin brown bread and butter.

Sardines.—Serve whole, sprinkled with lemon juice and a little oil, and decorated with parsley; or remove skin and backbones, add lemon juice, mash with a fork and mount on small rounds of prepared bread; or mix with an equal quantity of butter, adding lemon juice and Cayenne.

Shrimps (Potted).—Buy prepared; or put picked shrimps into a pot with salt, pepper and nutmeg to taste; cook in moderate oven for 10 minutes, cool, then seal with softened butter on top. Serve in tiny individual jars with hot toast and lots of butter.

Tunny Fish.—Slice the fish thinly. Dress with oil and lemon juice or vinegar; decorate with chopped parsley and capers.

Meat Pastes, Sausages

Meat pastes can be served straight from the pot or in small chunks, eaten with bread or toast, or are used, with garnishes, to make *canapés* or small sandwiches. French, German, Belgian and Dutch specialities can be bought—the most noted (and expensive) being the Strasbourg *pâté de foie gras* (pure goose liver). The French *pâté maison*, generally a goose liver mixed with some pork, varies, according to the maker.

Calf's Liver Paste.—Slowly cook $\frac{1}{4}$ lb. of chopped calf's liver with an equal amount of diced fat bacon in an ounce of butter, adding finely chopped parsley, salt, pepper and a teaspoonful of mixed spice. Drain off the fat, pound in a mortar, add a teaspoonful of anchovy essence, and sieve. Press into small pots and let them stand in a cool oven for $\frac{1}{2}$ hour. Then pour melted butter over the tops of the pots.

Chicken Liver Paste.—Mash together to a paste $\frac{1}{4}$ lb. of cooked chicken livers and 2 oz. of finely chopped onion, fried in butter or chicken fat. Season with pepper, salt and mustard.

Pâté de foie gras Canapés.—Thin the paste with cream, add Cayenne pepper and salt; pile on rounds of prepared bread, garnish with parsley.

Sausages.—Liver sausage, cold pork sausage, salami and other boiled or smoked Continental sausages are useful. Remove skin, cut into very thin slices, arrange in rows on a dish, garnish with parsley, radishes, gherkins, olives, or make into small decorated sandwiches. Tiny cooked sausages can be served on their own.

Eggs

Hard-boiled eggs may be served alone, with a dressing, or stuffed, or in aspic, or as a decoration. When used whole or halved cut a small piece off the end so that the egg will stand.

Halved Eggs.—Mask with mayonnaise or chaudfroid sauce. Decorate with chopped parsley.

Chopped Eggs.—Chop or slice, mix with dressing, and decorate.

Anchovy Eggs.—Halve hard-boiled eggs. Take out the yolks and pound with anchovies or anchovy sauce, butter and seasoning. Fill the egg-whites with the mixture, using a warm knife, and decorate with chopped parsley, capers, pieces of egg, small pieces of tomato, or green or red peppers.

Egg and Onion.—Remove the yolks from hard-boiled eggs; mix with a little oil, vinegar and seasoning; then add the egg-white, chopped, and chopped spring onions. Serve piled in little mounds or as canapés, with garnishes.

Devilled Eggs.—Mash the yolks from halved hard-boiled eggs with butter, vinegar, mustard and seasoning, and refill the egg-whites. Or pound the yolks with butter, anchovy essence, Cayenne and salt.

Egg with Anchovies.—Arrange anchovy fillets on small lettuce leaves, place pieces of hard-boiled egg on top (or chopped white and sieved yolk), with finely chopped parsley and seasoning. Moisten with oil.

Egg and Devilled Ham Canapés.—Mince ham with gherkin, Cayenne, salt,

Some hors-d'œuvre suggestions attractively presented on modern pottery plates with wooden accessories—Fresh Haddock Mayonnaise, Parsley Tomatoes, Asparagus, and, above, Shrimps and Dressed Cucumber

anchovy essence; mix with chopped hard-boiled egg, and place on rounds of prepared bread.

Plovers' Eggs (when in season).—Hard-boil and shell the eggs. Group in a nest of watercress or chopped lettuce, dressed with oil and vinegar.

Vegetables and Fruit

Asparagus Tips.—Cook (see Chapter on Vegetables) and serve with French dressing.

Beans.—Mix cooked butter beans with oil and vinegar dressing while still warm. Sprinkle with chopped parsley or gherkins. Combine cooked French beans with chopped apple and mix with salad dressing.

Beetroot.—Slices of cooked beetroot are particularly useful for decorations, cut into rings, stars and other fancy shapes.

Beetroot and Onion.—Soak thin slices of cooked beetroot and raw onion in dressing, then arrange on dish, the onion on top. Sprinkle with chopped mint.

Beetroot (Stuffed).—Cut thick slices into small rounds and scoop out the centre. Stuff with chopped celery, onion, grated Brussels sprouts, or fish, etc., moistened with salad dressing. Garnish with parsley.

Cauliflower.—Arrange cooked sprigs dressed with mayonnaise in a dish and decorate with anchovy fillets curled round them.

Celery.—Shred it into matchstick lengths or cut into slices and serve with salad dressing or mayonnaise.

Celery with Cheese.—Mix cream cheese with cream and mayonnaise. Pepper well, and add chopped celery.

Cucumber.—Slice very thinly, sprinkle with salt and leave to stand for a while. Drain and dress with vinegar, sugar and pepper, or salad dressing. Sprinkle with chopped parsley.

Gherkins and Salted Nuts.—An attractive platter can be made up with salted almonds or peanuts; gherkins (sweet or sour) and perhaps pickled peaches.

Olives (Black or Green).—Drain off the pickle and serve them plain (whole or stoned), stuffed, or as a garnish.

Olive Canapés (1).—Mix finely chopped olives, watercress, lettuce, parsley with paprika and mayonnaise, and pile on small rounds of brown bread and butter. Or mix the chopped olives with chopped nuts, apples, cream cheese and mayonnaise. Or place small slices of garlic sausage on rounds of fried bread. Pile chopped olives on top.

Olive Canapés (2).—Use Spanish olives, which are the larger kind. Stone them and stuff with various mixtures, allowing the stuffing to show at the top, e.g. cream some butter and flavour it with anchovy essence to use as a filling, or pound together hard-boiled egg-yolk, butter, *foie gras* and seasoning. Spread some of the mixture on small rounds of fried bread, or place a beetroot or egg-white ring on the prepared bread, and stand the stuffed olives on top

Olive and Anchovy Sandwiches.—Make tiny sandwiches filled with finely chopped olives mixed with an equal amount of anchovy paste and some butter.

Peppers (Green and Red).—Slice green and red peppers finely and serve in alternate layers on a crisp lettuce leaf with French dressing or mayonnaise.

Potato Salad.—Cook small potatoes in their skins and peel and slice while still warm. Add finely chopped onion, salt and pepper. Mix with mayonnaise. Sprinkle with chopped parsley or mint.

Radishes.—Cut off the roots and scrape around the top, but leave a leaf or two by which the radish can be held. Serve while fresh, standing in a very little water. Or make radish "flowers" for decorations by cutting petal shapes from the root end to just below the stalk and placing in water (the "petals" will open out in about 1 hour).

Tomatoes.—Plunge into boiling water, then into cold, to remove skin easily. Slice, and serve with French dressing or with alternate thin slices of dressed onion. Sprinkle with chopped parsley. Or alternate with slices of hard-boiled egg and dress with mayonnaise. Garnish with chopped parsley and paprika.

Tomatoes (Stuffed).—Cut out the centre and drain. Cut a small piece off the base so that the tomato will stand. Fill with dressed chopped vegetables, or fish, prawns, etc., pounded butter, lemon juice and seasoning.

Tomato and Green Pepper.—Skin and slice the tomatoes, add small strips of green pepper (raw) and chopped onion. Dress with oil, vinegar and seasoning, and garnish with chopped parsley.

SOUPS

*The first course sets the tone of a meal—choose consommé to
stimulate appetite, a thick soup to satisfy it*

STOCK is the basis of most soups and many sauces. Stock-making is a very simple process, with

Six Stock-Making Rules

(1) Always use a large, strong, clean saucepan with a close-fitting lid and preferably small handles so that it can be put into the oven.

(2) Ingredients for stock must be fresh, but meat and bones may be used again for a second stock. Cut meat into small pieces, chop bones up small, remove all fat. Peel and wash vegetables and cut into pieces.

(3) Start with cold water to extract the flavour from meat and bones, bring slowly to the boil, skimming off scum as it forms, then simmer slowly with the lid on.

(4) Vegetables, since they require only about half as long to cook as meat, should be put in half-way through the total cooking time.

(5) Strain stock while hot through a sieve into a basin and leave to cool. Do not remove the fat from the top until you are ready to use the stock, because a layer of fat keeps out the air and so acts as a preservative. To remove fat,

loosen it round the edge of the basin with a knife, and lift off.

(6) Stock is best made the day before you want to use it. It should not be kept for long, particularly in hot weather. If it contains vegetables, it must be boiled up daily. Water in which vegetables have been boiled may be added to stock, but *not* thickened gravy.

There are six kinds of stock:

(1) *Brown Stock,* made from the bones and meat of beef.

(2) *White Stock,* made from meat and bones of chicken, veal, rabbit or turkey, with vegetables and seasoning.

(3) *Clear Brown Stock for Clear Soup,* made from shin of beef, with or without a knuckle of veal.

(4) *Fish Stock.*

(5) *Vegetable Stock.*

(6) *Second Stock,* made by boiling up meat a second time.

Brown Stock

This should be made, if possible, the day before it is required. Allow a quart of cold water and half a teaspoonful of salt to a pound of beef bones (cooked or uncooked),

21

adding any scraps of meat available, with the fat carefully removed. Bring slowly to the boil, skimming often, and simmer very slowly, with the lid on, for 4–5 hours. Half-way through cooking time, add a few slices of carrot, turnip, onion and a bouquet garni consisting of sprigs of thyme, parsley, mace, marjoram and a bay leaf tied up in a muslin bag (dried herbs will do if fresh are not available). Allow to cool. Strain into a basin, removing fat before use.

White Stock

Allow a quart of cold water to a pound of knuckle of veal. Cut up meat and bones, cover with water, add a teaspoonful of salt and bring slowly to the boil. Skim often and simmer very slowly for 5 hours. Half-way through cooking time, add a slice each of turnip and onion, a small stick of celery and a bunch of mixed herbs, 3 or 4 peppercorns, a bay leaf and 3 or 4 cloves tied up in a muslin bag. Be sparing with the vegetables or the stock will not be a good colour. Strain through a hair sieve or fine cloth into a bowl. Stand in a cool place and remove fat when cold and stock is required for use.

Clear Brown Stock for Clear Soup

Allow a quart of cold water and a teaspoonful of salt to a pound of shin of beef (meat and bones together, or a mixture of beef and knuckle of veal). Break up bones, slice the meat thinly, removing fat. Put into pan with the water and salt and bring slowly to the boil. Simmer very gently, skimming regularly, for 3 hours. Then add one small carrot, one small onion and a stick of celery all cut up small, and a bouquet garni (as for Brown Stock). Simmer for a further 2 hours, then strain through a fine cloth or hair sieve.

Fish Stock

Fish stock, unlike other kinds of stock, should be used the day it is made. Allow a quart of cold water and a teaspoonful of salt to a pound of white fish, bones and trimmings, which *must* be absolutely fresh. Mackerel, salmon, herring and other strongly flavoured fishes are not suitable. Wash fish well in cold salted water and bring to the boil. Skim thoroughly and simmer for 20 minutes, then add a sliced onion, a bay leaf, a stick of celery cut into pieces and a bouquet garni (see under Brown Stock). Cook very gently for $\frac{1}{2}$ hour, strain, and the stock is ready for immediate use.

Vegetable Stock

Allow a quart of cold water to a pound of mixed vegetables (turnips, onions, celery, parsley stalks, leeks, carrots, as available). Wash, peel and slice the vegetables and fry them lightly in 1 oz. melted fat for about 10 minutes, without browning them. Add water and bring to the boil, adding 2 or 3 peppercorns, 2 or 3 cloves and bouquet garni (see under Brown Stock). Simmer with the lid on for 2 or 3 hours, then strain.

NOTE: If vegetable stock is not available, the next best thing for soups or gravies is the water in which vegetables have been boiled.

Second Stock

This is made by returning to the stock-pot meat and/or bones already used for stock-making, together with the same quantity of cold water as previously used. Odd scraps of left-over meat (cooked or uncooked) may be added. Bring slowly to the boil and simmer for 3 or 4 hours, strain and use for sauces and purées.

Soup Quantities

Allow $\frac{1}{2}$ pint of soup per person; somewhat less (say 1–1$\frac{1}{2}$ gills) if soup forms one course of a substantial meal.

TO SERVE WITH SOUP

Squares of dry toast or fried dice of bread may be served with all vegetable and meat soups which have no individual garnish. Alternatives are Rice Krispies or Puffed Rice, warmed and crisped in the oven. A little sherry (about 2 tablespoonfuls to a quart) improves the flavour of most soups. Grated Parmesan cheese is another delicious addition.

Quaker Soup Drops

These make an excellent addition to clear soups. The following quantities make enough drops for 3 pints of soup.

1 oz. plain flour	1 teaspoonful melted
1 egg	butter or margarine
$\frac{1}{2}$ oz. One-Minute	1 teaspoonful minced
Quaker Oats	parsley
$\frac{1}{2}$ teaspoonful	$\frac{1}{4}$ teaspoonful baking
Worcester sauce	powder
$\frac{1}{4}$ gill tepid water	Salt and pepper

Sift flour into a basin with salt and pepper to taste. Hollow out centre and add melted fat and yolk of egg. Make into a batter with the water and stir in the Quaker Oats, parsley and Worcester sauce. Set aside for about ½ hour. Just before using, fold in the beaten egg-white and baking powder to make a mixture thin enough to drop easily from the spoon. Pour mixture gently through a coarse colander over the saucepan of gently simmering soup. Cover and simmer for about 5 minutes, then serve. (If less soup is used, reduce the quantity of drops accordingly.)

CLEAR SOUPS

Consommé (Clear Soup) (for 4–5)

1 *quart clear brown stock*	2 *tablespoonfuls sherry*
¼ *lb. gravy beef*	*Vegetables, according*
Whites and shells of 2 eggs	*to taste, to flavour*
	Seasoning

Remove all traces of fat from the stock, then, while still cold, pour on to the broken egg-shells, meat and vegetables cut up small, in a large saucepan. Add the beaten egg-whites and heat slowly, whisking till the scum rises. Then stop whisking and bring to the boil. When scum reaches nearly to the top of the pan, reduce heat and simmer gently for 30 minutes.

Strain through a clean cloth, season, add sherry and bring to required temperature for serving.

Consommé à la Jardinière

Make the consommé as above and garnish with tiny diced pieces of carrot and turnip, or green peas and little sprigs of cauliflower first cooked till tender.

Iced Consommé

Make consommé as above, chill, and serve in cups.

Consommé Julienne

Make consommé as above. Shred a carrot and a turnip into strips 1–1½ in. long and not more than ⅛ in. thick, cook in salted water till tender, then add to consommé just before serving.

Consommé au Riz

Make consommé as above. Boil 1 oz. rice in a pint of salted water till the grain feels soft when it is pressed between the finger and thumb. Strain and pour cold water over the rice. Add to consommé and bring to the boil before serving.

A good vegetable soup can be reinforced by the addition of extra rice and peas or beans boiled separately, flavoured with a little Cayenne pepper

Consommé Royal

This is a clear soup served with a garnish of savoury custard. For a quart of consommé, made as above, you need for the custard garnish:

1 *gill clear stock*   1 *egg*
Seasoning

Beat the egg with the stock and season well. Put into a well-greased basin over a saucepan of slowly boiling water and steam gently until firm, but do *not* allow custard to boil. Cool, then turn out on to a plate and cut into fancy shapes. Put these in a hot tureen and pour the hot consommé over them. Serve promptly.

As a variation, ½ tablespoonful of grated Parmesan cheese may be added to the egg and stock before steaming.

Consommé Portugais

Make consommé as above. Garnish with a raw tomato diced small, 8 prunes stoned and cut into circles, and a leek cut into 1½ in. strips and cooked until tender in salted water.

Consommé Tomate

Add ½ lb. tomatoes cut into quarters when vegetables are added, then proceed as for consommé above.

Tomato Soup (Clear) (for 6–7)

2 *lb. ripe tomatoes*	1 *onion*
½ *lb. lean beef*	1 *turnip*
3 *pints good stock*	6 *peppercorns*
Bouquet garni (see	*Whites and shells of*
Brown Stock)	*2 eggs*
Pepper, salt and sugar	½ *gill cold water*
to taste	

Cut the tomatoes, onion and turnip in quarters and put them into a saucepan with the bouquet garni, peppercorns and stock. Mince the beef finely and mix with it the cold water. Put this with the vegetables. Whip the egg-whites, crush the shells and add to the rest of the ingredients in the saucepan. Bring slowly to the boil, whisking all the time. Simmer for 30 minutes, strain through a cloth, then return to the saucepan, reheat, season and dissolve in it one lump of sugar. Serve with slightly whipped cream or grated Parmesan cheese, according to taste.

THICK VEGETABLE SOUPS

The basis of these soups is either Brown or White Stock. In the absence of stock, milk or the liquid in which vegetables have been boiled can be used as a substitute.

Artichoke Soup (for 6–7)

2 *lb. Jerusalem arti-*	1 *oz. butter*
chokes	1 *oz flour*
1 *onion*	½ *pint milk*
1 *stick celery*	*A few bacon rinds*
1 *quart white stock*	*Seasoning*
Lemon juice	¼ *pint cream*
	(optional)

Wash, peel and slice the vegetables, squeezing lemon juice over the artichokes to keep their colour. Melt the butter in a saucepan and toss the vegetables in it for about 5 minutes, with the lid on, shaking to prevent them from getting brown or sticking. Pour on cold stock, add bacon rinds cut small and seasoning, bring to the boil and simmer gently until all vegetables are soft and tender. Put through a hair sieve, return to the pan, adding the milk mixed to a smooth paste with the flour. Bring to the boil, stirring continually. Boil for 5 minutes.

A ¼ pint of cream, added after it has cooled slightly, lifts this soup right into the luxury class. Reheat, but do not allow to boil again.

Brown Vegetable Soup (for 4–5)

1 *small head of celery*	2 *oz. flour*
2 *small onions*	1 *quart brown or*
2 *small carrots*	*bone stock*
2 *small potatoes*	*Salt and pepper*
2 *small tomatoes*	*Bouquet garni (as for*
2 *oz. dripping*	*Brown Stock)*

Wash, peel and cut the vegetables up small. Fry the onions in the hot dripping until slightly browned. Add flour, stirring well into the fat, then stock, bouquet garni and all the vegetables and bring to the boil, stirring constantly. Simmer about 1½ hours until vegetables are quite tender. Sieve, reheat and season to taste. Serve with croûtons of fried bread.

Carrot Soup (for 4–5)

1 *lb. carrots*	1 *oz. butter*
1 *quart white or*	½ *pint milk*
vegetable stock	1 *dessertspoonful fine*
Sprig of parsley	*oatmeal or cornflour*
Salt and pepper	

Wash and scrape the carrots well, then grate them on a coarse grater. Wash, dry

24

White vegetable soup, thick and creamy, makes a welcoming first course on a cold night

and break the parsley into small pieces. Fry the parsley lightly in the butter, then add the grated carrot and "sweat" in the fat, shaking the pan frequently to prevent burning. Add the stock and simmer for about 45 minutes until the carrot is tender. Mix the oatmeal or cornflour to a paste with the milk, add to the soup with seasoning and cook for 5 minutes.

Celery Soup (for 4)

1 head of celery	1 onion
1 oz. butter	½ pint milk
1½ pints white stock	1 oz. cornflour
Bay leaf	Pepper and salt
Bacon rinds or ham bone	Bouquet garni (as for Brown Stock)

Wash and shred the celery. Melt the butter in a saucepan and cook the celery, sliced onion and bay leaf for about 15 minutes, with the lid on, shaking occasionally to prevent burning. Add the stock, chopped bacon rinds, seasoning and bouquet garni, bring to the boil and simmer gently until the celery is soft. Put through a sieve, return to the saucepan and reheat.

Make a smooth paste with the cornflour and milk, and stir it into the soup. Bring to the boil and serve.

Cucumber Soup (for 4–5)

2 large cucumbers	½ pint milk
	1 oz. butter
1 quart white stock	2 egg-yolks
Pepper and salt	

Peel the cucumbers, take out seeds, cut into slices. Melt the butter and in it fry the sliced cucumbers lightly, without browning them. Add stock, bring to the boil and simmer until the cucumber is tender. Rub through a hair sieve and return to pan, season with salt and pepper. Beat the egg-yolks, stir them into the milk, then gradually add the milk and egg mixture to the cucumber purée, stirring. Reheat, but do not allow to boil.

Haricot Bean Soup (for 5–6)

8 oz. haricot beans	A few bacon rinds
1 onion	1 gill milk
1 stick of celery	½ oz. butter
1 quart white stock	Blade of mace
Pepper and salt	

Wash the beans thoroughly, soak in water overnight, then rinse well, put with blade of mace, cut up celery, bacon rinds and sliced onion into a pan with the butter and cook for a few minutes. Add the stock, cold, and bring to the boil. Simmer gently for about 2 hours, stirring now and again.

Rub through a sieve, then return to the pan, adding the milk and pepper and salt, stirring well all the time.

Tomato Soup (for 3–4)

1 lb. fresh or tinned tomatoes	1 oz. butter or margarine
2 oz. ham or bacon	Bay leaf
3 shallots	Pepper and salt
1 pint white stock, or ½ pint milk and ½ pint water	½ oz. finest sago 2 lumps sugar

Put the chopped bacon or ham, the bay leaf and sliced shallots into a saucepan with the butter and simmer slowly for 5 minutes, stirring carefully. Add the tomatoes and cook slowly for about 20 minutes. Rub through a sieve and put back into the saucepan. Add the stock. Bring to the boil. Then add the sago and sugar and simmer for 5 minutes. Season and serve with croûtons.

THICK MEAT SOUPS AND BROTHS

Kidney Soup (for 5–6)

½ lb. ox kidney	Small turnip and carrot
1 quart brown or bone stock	Large onion
1 oz. flour	Pepper and salt
1 oz. dripping	Mushroom trimmings or 1 tablespoonful mushroom ketchup
Bouquet garni (see Brown Stock)	
Glass of sherry (optional)	

Wash and cut the kidney into pieces, removing all fat. Wash and peel the vegetables, cut them up and fry them with the kidney in the hot fat until brown. Add the stock and bring to the boil. Skim well. Simmer very gently for two hours. Rub the kidney and vegetables through a sieve and put back in the saucepan. Make the flour into a paste with a very little water and pour into the stock, stirring well. Add bouquet garni and boil for a few minutes. Season, add mushroom trimmings or mushroom ketchup and, if liked, a glass of sherry just before serving.

Mulligatawny Soup (for 4–5)

1 quart brown stock	1 oz. dripping
2 onions	1 teaspoonful lemon juice
1 carrot	1 tablespoonful curry powder
1 turnip	
1 oz. flour	
1 apple	1 dessertspoonful shredded coconut
1 teaspoonful chutney	

Cut the vegetables up into small pieces and fry quickly in the dripping until brown; stir in the flour and curry powder, fry for a few minutes, stirring all the time, then add the stock, the apple (peeled, cored and chopped small) and the coconut. Simmer for 1–2 hours, and sieve. Put back into the pan and heat. Add the chutney and lemon juice at the end.

A dish of boiled rice should be served with this soup.

Oxtail Soup (for 8–10)

1 oxtail	Bouquet garni (see Brown Stock)
2 quarts brown stock	6 peppercorns
1 turnip	3 cloves
1 carrot	¼ teaspoonful celery salt
Salt and pepper	
2 oz. dripping	
1 oz. flour	

Wash the tail well, wipe, break up into pieces and fry with the vegetables, peeled and cut small, in dripping until brown. Add stock, celery salt, peppercorns, cloves and bouquet garni tied up in a muslin bag. Simmer gently for about 3–4 hours, season and strain, putting back the smaller pieces of the tail. Reheat and thicken with the flour made into a paste with warm water, adding a little browning if necessary. The larger pieces of meat from the tail can be served as a main dish with vegetables.

Pot-au-Feu (for 4–5)

1 lb. shin of beef	1 cabbage
1 quart of water	2 oz. sago or tapioca
1 leek	Bouquet garni (see Brown Stock)
1 parsnip	
1 carrot	Blade of mace
Stick of celery (or a few celery seeds)	6 peppercorns
1 turnip	Salt to taste
	A few cloves

Wipe the meat and tie it with tape so that it does not lose its shape. Put in a saucepan or casserole with the water. Bring to the boil, add salt to taste and skim well. Simmer for ½ hour.

Wash, peel and cut up the vegetables except the cabbage, and add, together with the bouqet garni, peppercorns, mace and cloves tied up in a muslin bag. Simmer gently for 1½ hours.

Clean the cabbage, cut it in half and tie together with a piece of tape. Add it to the liquid and simmer gently till tender. Take out the meat, untie it and put on a hot dish surrounded by the vegetables. The cabbage should be served separately.

Strain the liquid through a colander, using some for gravy. Leave the rest to get cold, and when it is required, take off the fat, bring it to the boil and throw in the sago or tapioca. Cook gently till transparent. Serve.

Chicken Broth (for 6)

Carcase of 1 chicken (and any available chicken left-overs)	1 oz. rice or pearl barley
1 small carrot	Bouquet garni (see Brown Stock)
1 small turnip	Salt and pepper
1 small onion	1 teaspoonful chopped parsley
1 stick of celery	
3 pints water	

Break the carcase into pieces, peel, wash and cut up the vegetables and put them all in a large pan with the water, the washed rice or barley and the bouquet garni. Bring slowly to the boil and simmer gently for 2 hours. Strain, reheat and add the chopped parsley and seasoning just before serving.

Mock Turtle Soup (for 7–8)

½ calf's head
2 oz. lean ham
Bouquet garni (see Brown Stock)
Juice of ½ lemon
1 carrot
1 turnip
2 onions
1 stick celery
2 quarts water
1 oz. cornflour
2 tablespoonfuls sherry
Salt and Cayenne pepper

Wash and blanch the head by covering it with cold water and bringing it to the boil, chop it in pieces and put into a pan with the bouquet garni, ham diced small, and water. Bring slowly to the boil, skim, and simmer gently for at least 2 hours. Then take out the head and simmer the peeled and cut-up vegetables in the stock for 2 hours. Strain, leave till cold to remove all fat from the top. Finally, reheat the stock, thicken it with the cornflour made into a paste with a little water. Add sherry, lemon juice, salt and Cayenne,

and serve garnished with little cubes of the meat from the head.

Rabbit Broth (for 4)

1 rabbit	Salt and pepper
1 large onion	1 oz. flour
1 quart boiling water	1 oz. dripping

Cut the rabbit into pieces and blanch. Wipe thoroughly. Sprinkle with flour and fry in the dripping until brown. Add the boiling water and the onion chopped fine. Season and simmer for 2 hours. Thicken with the flour mixed to a smooth paste with a little water, bring to the boil, stirring well, and cook for 2–3 minutes. Take out the rabbit, cutting off a few small pieces of the meat and adding them to the broth as a garnish. Serve the rest as a main dish.

CREAM SOUPS

Asparagus Soup (for 4–5)

30 heads of asparagus	¼ pint cream (optional)
1 quart vegetable stock or vegetable water	Seasoning

Cut the tips off the asparagus heads and keep them for garnishing. Clean and cut

Grated Parmesan cheese is a delicious addition to many soups

27

the stalks into pieces and bring to the boil with the stock. Simmer for 1 hour, then rub through a hair sieve and heat the purée once more to boiling point. Add seasoning to taste, and the asparagus tips, and cook slowly until the tips are tender—about 10 minutes. Just before serving, add cream, if liked, and reheat, but do not allow to boil. Serve with croûtons of fried bread.

Barley Cream Soup (for 4–5)

2 oz. pearl barley	1 onion
1 quart white stock	1 carrot
1 oz. butter or margarine	Stick of celery
	¼ pint cream or milk
Salt and pepper	Nutmeg

Wash and blanch the pearl barley by covering it with cold water and bringing it to the boil, then straining and rinsing it in cold water. Melt the butter in a pan and cook the washed, peeled and sliced vegetables in it for 2–3 minutes, with the lid on, shaking to prevent them sticking. Add the barley, stock, salt and pepper to taste, bring to the boil and simmer for 2 hours. Sieve. Add cream, a little grated nutmeg and reheat without boiling.

Brussels Sprouts Soup (1) (for 4–5)

1 lb. Brussels sprouts	½ pint milk
1 quart white stock	Pepper and salt
1 level dessertspoonful finest sago	Green colouring

Wash sprouts, taking off old leaves, and cook in boiling salted water until tender but not "mushy." Drain and rub through a sieve. Bring the stock, milk and sago to the boil. Add the sprout purée, pepper and salt, a few drops of colouring and whisk up. Serve hot, but do not boil again.

Brussels Sprouts Soup (2) (for 4–5)

1 lb. Brussels sprouts	2 oz. butter
1 quart stock	1 oz. flour
Pepper and salt	A little cream

Melt the butter in a saucepan, add the flour and mix well together, then add the stock. Boil Brussels sprouts in salted water till just tender, preserving the colour, and rub through a fine hair sieve. Add to the boiling stock and season. A dash of cream added just before serving is a great improvement.

Cabbage Soup (for 3–4)

1 small cabbage	½ pint milk
1 small onion	½ oz. cornflour
1 pint white stock	Chopped parsley
Pepper and salt	

Wash the cabbage, removing the stalk and all coarse outside leaves. Drain, chop finely, plunge into boiling salted water and boil for 5 minutes. Drain and add to the stock with the chopped onion, bring to the boil and simmer gently for 20 minutes.

Make a paste with the cornflour and milk, and add, stirring all the time until soup boils. Season to taste and add the chopped parsley at the last moment before serving.

Cauliflower Soup (for 5–6)

1 good-sized cauliflower	1 pint white stock
	1 oz. cornflour
1 pint milk	Chopped parsley
Pepper and salt	1 tablespoonful cream (optional)

Remove the outer leaves from the cauliflower, wash and cut into small pieces. Plunge into salted boiling water and boil hard until tender enough to rub through a hair sieve. Drain and sieve. Bring the stock to the boil. Make the cornflour into a smooth paste with a little of the milk and add to the stock, stirring well. Bring to the boil, add the cauliflower purée, the remainder of the milk, pepper and salt and, at the last minute, the chopped parsley.

A tablespoonful of cream added before serving greatly improves this soup.

Chestnut Soup (for 3–4)

½ lb. chestnuts	Pinch of celery salt
1 pint white stock	Cayenne pepper and salt
1 gill milk	
1 gill cream	1 oz. flour

Shell the chestnuts by scoring them with a cross, then roasting until the skins crack and come off easily. Take off inner brown skin—if necessary, by plunging shelled chestnuts into boiling water—then mash slightly and put into a pan with stock. Simmer until tender enough to rub through a sieve—about 1½ hours. Make a paste with the flour and milk, add with the seasoning, heat, but do not allow to boil. Add the cream just before serving.

Cream of Onion Soup (for 6–7)

1 quart milk	1 tablespoonful brown or wholemeal flour
6 large onions	
2 oz. butter	2 egg-yolks
A little salt	
A little cream	

28

Small squares of toast can be served with vegetable or meat soups

Peel, scald and slice the onions, and cook them lightly in the melted butter for ½ hour. Heat the milk. Add the dry flour to the onions, stirring constantly for 3 minutes. Then turn the mixture into the milk and cook for 15 minutes. Strain, reheat and add salt. Beat the egg-yolks with the cream, then stir into the soup. Cook for a few minutes, stirring constantly and not allowing to boil. (If cream is not available, milk can be used instead, in which case add a tablespoonful of butter at the same time.)

Fish Soup (1) (for 6–7)

2 pints fish stock	1 oz. butter or mar-
I oz. cornflour	garine
Pepper and salt	Dessertspoonful
½ pint milk	chopped parsley

Melt the butter or margarine in a saucepan and add the cornflour, stirring to a smooth paste. Pour on the stock and bring to the boil, stirring all the time. Add the milk and boil again. Season with salt and pepper, and at the last moment add the chopped parsley.

Fish Soup (2) (for 5–6)

To vary the above soup, make a fish stock without vegetable flavouring, allowing 1 quart of water and a teaspoonful of salt to a pound of white fish bones and trimmings.

Make 1 oz. cornflour into a smooth paste with 1 gill milk, add to the stock, stirring all the time as it comes to the boil. Season to taste and simmer gently for 5 minutes. Beat 1 egg, pour it into a hot tureen, and at once add the soup, stirring well. Serve with fried dice of bread.

Leek and Potato Soup (for 5–6)

2 leeks	2 or 3 potatoes
1 oz. flour	1 quart water
½ pint milk	1 onion
Salt and pepper	1 oz. butter

Melt the butter in a saucepan, stir in the flour and cook for a few minutes, then gradually add the milk, stirring as it comes to the boil. Add the water, the potatoes, peeled and cut up, and the leeks and onion cut small. Bring to the boil and simmer gently for 20–30 minutes until the vegetables are tender. Put through a coarse sieve, pressing the vegetables through, return to the saucepan, reheat, season and serve. (If the soup is too thick, thin it with a little more milk.)

Lobster or Oyster Soup (for 4–5)

½ pint can lobster or	2 oz. flour
oysters	½ gill milk
1 quart fish stock	Juice of ½ lemon
	Seasoning

29

Strain the liquid from the can into the stock. Bring. to the boil, add the flour blended to a smooth paste with the milk, boil for 5 minutes, stirring all the time. Then add lobster or oysters, lemon juice and seasoning.

If fresh oysters are used, remove the beards and stew for 5 minutes in a little water. Strain, and add to stock.

Mushroom Soup (for 4)

½ lb. mushrooms	2 oz. flour
2 oz. butter	½ pint milk
1 tablespoonful	Bouquet garni (see
vinegar	Brown Stock)
Salt and pepper	

Cover the washed but not peeled mushrooms with cold water and a tablespoonful of vinegar. Bring slowly to the boil and simmer gently until mushrooms are soft enough to be rubbed through a sieve. Return the resulting purée to the pan and keep hot. Now melt the butter, stir the flour into it and gradually add the milk, stirring all the time. Season with salt and pepper and a bouquet garni tied up in a muslin bag. Bring to the boil and boil for 3 minutes, then add the mushroom purée. Stir well and serve hot with fried croûtons.

Lentil or Split Pea Soup (for 3–4)

½ lb. split peas or	1 oz. butter or mar-
lentils	garine
1 onion	1½ pints water (or
Small carrot	part water from
Small turnip	ham or boiling
Bacon rinds to flavour	bacon)
A few outer leaves of	¼ pint milk
celery	Salt and pepper

Wash and soak the dried peas or lentils overnight in the cold water. Next day, bring to the boil with the cut up bacon rinds and simmer for 1 hour. Wash. peel and slice the vegetables and add, cooking until they are soft. Put through a sieve, or mash with a wooden spoon. Replace in the saucepan with the milk, reheat, stirring all the time. put in the margarine or butter and pepper and salt and serve.

If water from ham or bacon boiling is used, omit salt.

Potage Maigre (for 4–5)

1 quart water	1 fairly large slice of
Medium-sized cab-	bread
bage	2 oz. butter
Pepper and salt	½ lb. potatoes, sliced
1 onion	in thin rounds

Boil the water in a saucepan. Add the butter (not margarine) and let it melt. Put in the potatoes.

Shred the cabbage, chop the onion and cut up the bread in very small cubes and add them to the potatoes, with pepper and salt. Boil all together for ½ hour.

Potato Soup (for 5–6)

1 lb. potatoes	1 teaspoonful salt
1½ pints milk	Pinch of pepper
½ pint white stock	1 teaspoonful
1½ oz. butter, mar-	chopped parsley
garine or dripping	1 medium onion
1 oz. cornflour	

Boil the potatoes, strain and mash in the usual way. Scald the milk with the sliced onion in it. Add the stock, most of the milk and the butter to the mashed potatoes, and stir well. Mix the cornflour to a paste with a little of the milk and pour into the hot soup, stirring well. Simmer for 3 minutes, add the seasoning, and sprinkle chopped parsley on top at the last minute. Serve with fried dice of bread.

Spinach Soup (for 3–4)

1 lb. spinach	½ pint milk
1 pint white stock	1 teaspoonful corn-
1 oz. butter or mar-	flour
garine	Pepper and salt

Wash the spinach in several lots of water, then cook in its own moisture and rub through a sieve. Bring the stock to the boil. Make the cornflour into a smooth paste with the milk, add it to the stock and again bring to the boil. Then add the butter or margarine and seasoning. At the last moment, add the purée of spinach and remove from the fire the moment it boils or the colour of the soup will be spoiled. Serve with Puffed Rice heated in the oven.

A little cream greatly improves the flavour.

White Vegetable Soup (for 4)

1 moderate-sized	Pinch of dried herbs
carrot, turnip and	1 oz. cornflour
onion	1½ pints white stock
1 parsnip or swede	or vegetable water
1 stick of celery	½ pint milk
1 leek	Pepper and salt

Wash, peel and cut the vegetables into small dice; bring to the boil with the stock or water, herbs, and a pinch of salt. Simmer gently for ½ hour. Then add the cornflour mixed to a smooth paste with the milk, and stir well while it thickens. Add seasoning.

FISH

There are more fish in the sea than many housewives have ever tried
—a wonderful chance for originality

FISH is not only a good and digestible item of diet, but one of the few remaining natural foods still available to us over-civilised human beings. Its food value is high, being a splendid source of protein. A pound of herrings more than equals a pound of red meat in food value and, though herrings are the most nutritious of all, other fish rank high in the estimation of the nutrition experts.

There are so many different kinds of fish —with infinitely varied flavours, textures and characteristics—yet in the choice of no other basic food are people inclined to be so conservative. Cod, haddock, plaice, sole and herring are not by any means the only delicacies to be found on the fish-monger's slab.

Whiting, so delicious cooked with their "tails in their mouths"; mackerel, King George V's favourite, with the distinctive flavour that is just as good whether eaten hot or "soused" in vinegar; brill, that looks rather like turbot but is always far cheaper and available most of the year round; the colourful red mullet—these are but a few of the lesser-known fish the adventurous housewife will want to introduce into her menus.

When Fish is in Season

(*a*) **Sea Fish.** All kinds can safely be eaten all the year round, but the following list shows those which are at their best in certain seasons:

Bream (Sea)	June to November
Brill	All the year
Coal Fish (Coley)	September to May
Cod	September to May
Conger Eel	June to March
Flounder	January to March
Gurnet	July to March
Haddock (Fresh)	May to January
Hake	July to January
Halibut	July to April
Herring	June to February

John Dory	January to March
Lemon Sole	December to April
Mackerel	April to November
Mullet, Grey	August to April
Mullet, Red	May to July
Plaice	May to January
Skate	October to May
Smelt	September to March
Sole	March to January
Sprat	November to February
Turbot	March to December
Whitebait	March to July
Whiting	December to March
Witch Sole	August to March

(*b*) **Freshwater Fish** must not be caught between March 14th and June 16th, the breeding season. These are the commonest varieties:

Barbel	Loach
Bleak	Minnow
Bream (Freshwater)	Perch
Carp	Pike
Chub	Rainbow Trout
Dace	Roach
Eel	Rudd
Grayling	Tench
Gudgeon	

NOTE: Fresh salmon (home-caught) has a close season from August 31st to February 1st, but imported salmon is available all the year round. Freshwater trout (home-caught) has a close season from September 30th to March 1st, but imported trout is available all the year round.

(*c*) **Shell Fish**

Crab is at its best from April to June.

Lobster (close season in Scotland June 1st to September 1st) is in best supply in the summer months.

Oysters—Natives and Deep Sea Oysters are in season from September 1st to June 14th. Foreign Oysters are available all the year round.

Prawns—all the year round, but most abundant in summer.

Escallop—best quality from November to March.

Mussel—in season from end of July to April; at their best August to November.

How to Shop for Fish

Fish in its prime should be stiff and firm, plentifully covered with fresh-looking scales and with bright, colourful eyes. There should be nothing dry or flabby about it. Colouring should be bright—such as the spots on plaice, the scales and fins of herring, cod or mackerel, the shell of a crab.

All sorts of factors, including the time of year, the weather, etc., affect the price of fish. Cod may therefore be cheapest one day, haddock another, and it pays to ask your fishmonger's advice. Herring is always good value, whether you buy it fresh, salted, smoked, pickled or canned.

If the fishmonger fillets a fish for you, ask him to give you the skin and bones. These are good for making a stock, which in turn will make a delicious sauce to go with the fish.

Keeping Fish Fresh

Never leave fish wrapped up in paper. When you get home, unwrap it promptly and put in the refrigerator in a covered container or polythene bag, or on a plate covered loosely but securely with muslin wrung out in vinegar and water. This is particularly important in hot weather and when there are flies about. Fresh fish should always be cooked the day it is bought.

Preparing Fish for Cooking

Even when fish is bought cleaned and filleted, it should be washed thoroughly under the cold tap and wiped inside and out with a clean damp cloth. The scales can be removed by scraping from the tail to the head with a sharp knife.

Sole, plaice, etc., to be cooked whole, should have their heads and fins cut off, and the belly, just behind the head, cleaned out thoroughly. Remember to keep the trimmings and use them for stock. Scraps of cooked fish should also be kept, as there are many ways of using them.

A fillet may be skinned by placing it on a board, skin downwards. Grasp the tail and, with a knife, roll the flesh back off the skin from tail-end to head.

Fried Fish

This is the most popular way of cooking fish, and the following method is one that cannot go wrong. First wash, dry and sprinkle fish with salt, then dip it in egg. Next, dip it into hard breadcrumbs (bought in packets or baked in the oven till crisp). Heat the frying pan slightly and *then* put in enough fat to cover the pan to a depth of $\frac{1}{4}$ in. When a faint blue smoke appears and *not* before, lay the fish gently into the fat. Turn it over when the bottom half is

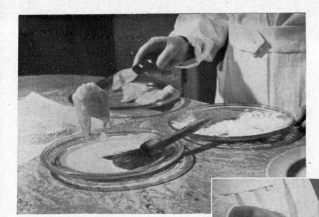

For perfect fried fish: Wash, dry, sprinkle with salt, then dip in egg (left)

Next, coat the fillets in seasoned flour, shaking off the surplus (below)

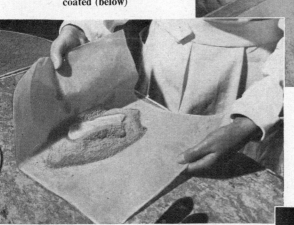

Put breadcrumbs on a sheet of kitchen paper, place fish on top and shake until well coated (below)

For deep frying always use a basket, have the fat really hot and do not cook too much at once (below)

Chip potatoes, the traditional English accompaniment to fried fish, should be cooked in a basket in deep fat

brown and cook the other side. Lift on to crumpled kitchen paper and drain off the fat.

NOTE: Keep a special frying pan for fish and nothing else. If necessary, tie a label marked "Fish" on the handle to deter other members of the family from using it for anything else. Clean the fish frying pan out with a small handful of dry salt—no water or anything else is necessary. The salt will leave it clean and sweet for next time. Also start a deep-fat frier for fish and chips. Keep the fat well strained and you can use it over and over again.

The cooking time naturally varies enormously, thick fish steaks requiring much longer than thin fillets. For this reason, large fish and fish steaks should be fried in a little fat; fillets or small fish, such as whitebait, in deep fat.

Baked Fish

Most suitable way of cooking whole round white fish, such as haddock or whiting, or for thick cuts.

Wash and wipe the fish with a clean cloth, season well, squeeze a few drops of lemon juice over them, stuff if liked. Place the fish in a buttered baking tin or casserole, cover with greased paper and bake in a moderate oven. When cooked, the skin will crack or the flesh come away from the bones easily when tested with a skewer. Whole fish, the size of a herring, take between 10 and 15 minutes, others in proportion, according to size.

Boiled Fish

Boiling is advisable only when large fish or thick pieces are to be cooked. A fish kettle is the best for this purpose, as the drainer makes it easy for the fish to be lifted out without breaking. If you have no fish kettle, use an ordinary saucepan and tie up the fish in a pudding cloth.

Put into hot but not actually boiling water with 1 dessertspoonful of salt and 1 tablespoonful of vinegar or lemon juice to every quart of water and, if possible, a bouquet garni. The water should just cover the fish, no more.

Exceptions to this are: (1) salmon, which on account of its tough skin should be put into gently boiling water, and (2) mackerel, which should be put into tepid water because of its delicate skin.

Allow about 6 minutes to each pound of fish and 6 minutes over. Thick cuts of fish, such as salmon or cod, need 10 minutes to the pound and 10 minutes over. Fish is done when it comes away from the bone at the slightest pressure; fillets when a liquid like thick cream comes out of them.

Steamed Fish

Steaming is preferable to boiling because more of the flavour is retained, but it takes almost twice as long. Thin slices or fillets of fish should always be steamed, never boiled.

Rub whole flat fish or fish cut in large pieces with a cut lemon to preserve the colour.

Wash and wipe the fish well, season, squeeze a little lemon juice over, wrap in greased paper and put in a steamer over boiling water.

Fish can also be steamed between two greased plates over a saucepan of boiling water, or in a moderate oven. Allow 10–15 minutes. This way preserves all the delicate flavour.

Poached Fish

An excellent method for smoked haddock and small whole fresh fish.

Half fill a shallow pan (a frying pan will do very well) with water flavoured with salt and vinegar (proportions 1 dessertspoonful salt and 1 tablespoonful vinegar to each quart of water), bring to the boil, put in fish and cook gently (for times, see under Boiled Fish above).

Grilled Fish

Grilling is particularly suitable for fillets or slices of fish and is, incidentally, more digestible than frying. Wipe the fish thoroughly with a clean cloth, soak in a plate of olive oil or brush over with melted butter before putting under the hot grill. Slash the skin of small whole fish in several places. Baste white fish with melted fat.

Fish Stock (see Soup-making, p. 22)

Brill Supreme

Cut a small brill into fillets; skin them and sprinkle with chopped egg and breadcrumbs. Cook in margarine. Serve with grilled tomatoes and, if possible, croquettes of rice. A Béarnaise sauce is ideal, but tartare will do almost as well.

COD AND SIMILAR WHITE FISH RECIPES

American Cod

In a well-greased deep casserole, place alternate layers of buttered bread, seasoning, flaked cod, partly boiled onions and raw tomatoes. On the top layer place bread dotted with knobs of butter. Soak whole in milk (each ½ pint beaten with 1 egg). Cover dish well and cook in moderate oven until set (about 1 hour).

Baked Cod with Mushrooms (for 4)

1 lb. cold boiled flaked cod fillet	¾ pint seasoned white sauce
Juice of ½ lemon	2 oz. sliced cooked mushrooms
Breadcrumbs	
Mashed potatoes	Butter or margarine

Mix the fish with the white sauce, adding the lemon juice and mushrooms. Place the mixture in a well-buttered casserole, cover with breadcrumbs and dot with knobs of butter or margarine. Decorate the edges with a border of mashed potatoes, using a star tube. Cook in fast oven until browned.

Casserole of Cod, Haddock or Plaice (for 4)

1 lb. cod, haddock or plaice (whichever is cheapest and best)	Salt and pepper
	½ lb. parboiled potatoes
2 medium-sized onions, sliced	4 tomatoes
	2 oz. margarine
Chopped parsley	

Skin, bone and cut the fish into pieces about 1 in. square. Arrange in a shallow well-greased ovenproof dish and surround with quartered parboiled potatoes, whole skinned tomatoes and sliced onions. Season with salt and pepper, dot with margarine and bake in moderate oven until cooked, basting with melted margarine. Sprinkle with chopped parsley before serving.

Cod and Mushroom Scallops (for 4)

1 lb. fresh cod fillets	2 oz. mushrooms
1 gill milk	Salt, pepper and a little grated cheese
1 oz. margarine	
½ oz. flour	Breadcrumbs

Poach the cod gently in the milk and a little water. Separately cook the mushrooms, sliced, in half the margarine. When cooked, drain the fish and mushrooms, saving the fish liquor for sauce. Flake the fish, mix with mushrooms and pack fairly tightly into individual scallop shells. Make a roux with the flour and remaining margarine, gradually add the liquor from the fish, season, return to heat and cook until the sauce thickens. Spoon sparingly over the fish and mushroom mixture, scatter breadcrumbs and grated cheese on top, dot with margarine and heat in a fast oven.

Cod Fillets Portugaise

Cod fillets	1 Spanish onion
2 or 3 tomatoes	1 oz. butter
1 oz. grated cheese	Salt and pepper

Place fillets in a greased fireproof dish. Slice onion very thinly and place on top with sliced tomatoes. Sprinkle over salt and pepper and grated cheese, top with butter in small pieces. Bake 20–30 minutes.

Cod Fillets with Mushroom Stuffing (for 4)

4 cod fillets (middle cut about 1 in. thick)	
Salt and pepper	
1 egg-yolk	
4 oz. white bread (without crust)	
1½ oz. margarine	
1 tablespoonful chopped parsley	
Finely grated rind of 1 lemon	
A little milk	4 mushrooms

Crumble bread into bowl, pour over enough milk to moisten and leave to soak. Squeeze any surplus milk out of bread so that it is fairly dry, stir in chopped parsley, lemon rind and egg-yolk, season with salt and pepper. Wash mushrooms, keep tops on one side. Chop stalks finely and add to stuffing.

Wipe fish with damp cloth. Stuff the centres, wrapping the side pieces firmly round stuffing, tie with string. Put into fireproof dish or baking tin, sprinkle with pepper and salt. Brush over fillets and mushroom tops with melted margarine. Cover fish with greaseproof paper and bake in moderate oven for 20–30 minutes. After first 10 minutes, put the mushrooms in beside the fish. Serve hot with green peas.

COOK'S TIP

FOR GOOD LOOKING FISH

Before frying, dry the fish, dip in milk and roll in coating made from 1 heaped tablespoonful cornflour, ½ level teaspoonful salt and ¼ level teaspoonful pepper. (Tested in the experimental kitchen of Brown & Polson Ltd.)

Codfish in Golden Sauce (for 4)

1 lb. cooked cod fillet	1 oz. butter or mar-
½ pint milk	garine
1 tablespoonful made	1 oz. flour
or French mustard	1 tablespoonful
(thick consistency)	vinegar
3–4 medium, cooked,	½ level tablespoonful
diced potatoes	sugar
Croûtons	Salt and pepper

Flake the fish into small pieces. Melt butter or margarine in a saucepan; add flour and stir over low heat for a few seconds. Remove saucepan from heat. Gradually add the milk and stir well until smooth. Bring slowly to the boil, stirring all the time, and cook gently for 5 minutes. Remove from heat, stir in the mustard, vinegar and sugar. Mix well. Add the potatoes and flaked cod fillet; season with salt and pepper. Heat through. Serve garnished with croûtons of fried bread.

Cod Mornay (for 4)

4 cod fillets	2 oz. grated cheese
½ pint Mornay sauce (see Sauces chapter)	

Cover the bottom of a serving dish with some of the Mornay sauce, arrange on this the cod fillets, poached and well drained, cover with more of the sauce, sprinkle with grated cheese and brown quickly.

Cod Oriental (for 2)

¼ lb. fresh and firm	1 tablespoonful olive
cod	oil
Bay leaf	Squeeze of lemon
Salt and pepper	juice
Boiled rice	Chopped parsley

Wash and dry the cod and cut it into small chunks, about 1½ in. square. Put these into a basin containing the olive oil blended with the lemon juice, salt and pepper, and a bay leaf. Leave to marinade for ½ hour or so, then skewer the pieces and grill, under a hot grill, turning frequently, until they are lightly browned. Serve on a bed of rice, with sliced tomato and chopped parsley to garnish. Even better served with savoury rice—cooked rice tossed in hot fat with cooked strips of bacon and onion and a suspicion of garlic.

Cod Puffs (for 2–3)

8 oz. cooked flaked	1 oz. melted mar-
cod fillet	garine or butter
2 eggs	Onion or lemon juice
Salt and pepper	to taste
6 oz. mashed potatoes	

Mix fish with eggs, add potatoes, melted margarine or butter, salt and pepper. A teaspoonful of onion or lemon juice may be added to taste. Mix all the ingredients well and drop from a spoon into hot deep fat. Cook until browned and serve with egg or tomato sauce.

Cod with Cheese and Potatoes (for 3–4)

¾ lb. cod fillets	¾ lb. potatoes
3 oz. grated cheese	¼ pint well-seasoned
2 tomatoes	white sauce
2 tablespoonfuls	1 oz. margarine
breadcrumbs	

Partly cook the cod in a little salted water and parboil the potatoes. Grease a fireproof dish and arrange alternate layers of flaked cod, finely sliced potato and grated cheese in it. Pour over the white sauce, making certain all the crevices are filled up. Cover with sliced tomato, dot with margarine and sprinkle the breadcrumbs on top. Bake in a moderate oven for about 30 minutes.

Cod with Mushroom Sauce (for 4)

4 medium-sized cod	½ pint scalded milk
fillets	½ pint water
4 oz. chopped mush-	2 oz. butter
rooms	2 oz. flour
1 oz. chopped onion	Salt and pepper

Place the onion and mushrooms in the water and cook for 3 minutes. Add butter and flour, stirring continuously. Add the scalded milk and heat all to boiling point. Season to taste and pour over the fish in a well-greased baking dish. Bake in moderate oven for 30 minutes.

Cod with Spinach (for 3–4)

1 lb. flaked cod fillet	Few drops olive oil
½ lb. chopped cooked	2 sliced onions
spinach	⅔ pint milk
1 oz. flour	Breadcrumbs
Salt, pepper, nutmeg	Fat for frying

Gently fry onions until slightly browned. Add spinach, stirring constantly. Still stirring, slowly add the flour and warmed milk. Season with salt, pepper and nutmeg. Simmer for 15 minutes. Into a casserole dish put a layer of prepared spinach, covering this with a layer of fish, repeating the layers until spinach and fish are used up, and finishing with spinach. Sprinkle with breadcrumbs and a few drops of olive oil. Bake in a moderate oven for 30 minutes until golden brown.

FISH

Cod's Roe

This is often bought ready boiled, but to cook a whole fresh roe, place in enough boiling salted water to cover, with a tablespoonful of vinegar. Boil for 20–30 minutes, according to size. Cool, then cut into thick slices and fry in hot shallow fat.

Cold Fish Savoury (for 4)

½ lb. cooked cod fillets	Cayenne pepper
¼ pint milk	4 squares of buttered toast
Anchovy essence	Hard-boiled egg
Vinegar	Parsley

Flake the fish. Moisten with the milk. Season to individual taste with anchovy essence, vinegar and Cayenne pepper. Pile when cold on the squares of buttered toast. Sprinkle with the chopped hard-boiled egg and finely chopped parsley.

Coquilles au Colin (for 3–4)

½ lb. cooked boned fish	1 large dessertspoonful flour
2 oz. butter	2 dessertspoonfuls grated Gruyère cheese
2 oz. mushrooms	
Salt and pepper	
About ¾ pint milk	A few shrimps
4 scallop shells	

Make a white sauce with the butter and flour and the heated milk (see chapter on Sauces). Peel and cut up the mushrooms, and add them with salt and pepper to the sauce. Cook for 10 minutes, then add the shelled shrimps and at the last moment the grated cheese. Be sparing with the salt because of the shrimps.

Butter four scallop shells, half-fill them with fish, then pour over the sauce and sprinkle a little grated cheese over each shell. Top with a small piece of butter and put under a hot grill until brown.

Coquilles of Cod (for 4)

½ lb. flaked cooked cod	4 well-scrubbed and dried scallop shells (obtainable from fishmongers for a few pence)
Anchovy essence, if liked	
1 or 2 hard-boiled eggs	½ lb. macedoine of vegetables
A little mayonnaise	
Chopped parsley	

Coat the inside of the scallop shells with a little mayonnaise, flavoured, if liked, with anchovy. Put in a layer of seasoned macedoine of vegetables, then a layer of flaked cooked cod. Border with chopped hard-boiled egg and chopped parsley.

Fish fillets, deep-fried an appetising golden shade, are served with crisp potato balls

Cottage Crab (for 4)

1 lb. cod fillets	2 eggs
Lettuce	1 oz. margarine
Cucumber	Pepper
2 oz. shrimps	Made mustard
Sliced cucumber to garnish	

Steam the cod fillets, flake them and leave to cool. Wash and dry lettuce, slice cucumber and chop shrimps. Melt the margarine in a saucepan, add the beaten eggs, season with pepper and a little made mustard. Stir together over a gentle heat until the mixture thickens. Leave to cool. Arrange a ring of lettuce leaves around a dish. Pile the flaked fish inside them and top with the egg mixture. Garnish with a ring of sliced cucumber.

Fish and Bacon Casserole

In the bottom of individual casserole dishes sprinkle fried sliced onions and cooked bacon strips. Lay a slice of fresh cod fillet in each casserole, sprinkle with salt and pepper and cover with sliced cooked potatoes. Fill the casserole with fish stock. Cook gently in a slow oven.

Fish and Macaroni Pie (for 3–4)

1 filleted fresh had-dock	1 tablespoonful grated cheese
2 oz. macaroni	½ oz. butter
1 teaspoonful made mustard	½ oz. flour
	¼ pint milk
Pepper and salt	

Break the macaroni into small pieces and boil it. Put a layer of macaroni into a well-greased pie dish, then a layer of flaked seasoned fish. Fill the pie dish with alternate layers until almost full. Then pour over it white sauce made from the butter, flour, mustard and milk.

Sprinkle grated cheese on top and bake in a moderate oven until brown on top (about ½ hour).

Fish and Potato Rolls

To each half-teacupful of cooked fish, add the same quantity of mashed potato, a small piece of butter, pepper, salt and just a flavouring of mace. Work the mixture into a stiff paste with a beaten egg, and make into little rolls 3 in. long, with flat ends. Flour well, egg-and-breadcrumb, and fry in deep fat until a golden brown. Garnish with parsley and lemon, and serve with melted butter.

Fishcakes

½ lb. cold boiled cod	¼ lb. mashed potatoes
1 egg	Streaky bacon
Seasoning	Browned bread-crumbs

Mash the fish, add mashed potatoes, season, bind with an egg and roll in crisp breadcrumbs. Shape into round flat cakes. Put a few strips of streaky bacon in a cold frying pan and cook gently till some of the fat is fried out. Then put in codfish cakes and brown in the bacon fat.

Fishcakes Creole

1 lb. cooked cod fillet	Parsley or crisp sprigs of watercress
1 tablespoonful melted margarine	1 large onion
6 oz. fine bread-crumbs	A small piece of garlic
½ teaspoonful dried thyme	3 sprigs of chopped parsley
Egg and breadcrumbs	

Flake the cod very finely. Mix into it the margarine and breadcrumbs. Chop the onion and garlic together very finely, add the chopped parsley and thyme, then mix well with the fish, adding a little milk if the mixture tends to fall apart. Shape into smallish, flat, round cakes and coat with egg and breadcrumbs. Fry in shallow fat. Garnish with parsley or watercress.

Fish Casserole (for 4)

A 3-oz. can of lobster	1 lb. fresh fillet of cod
4 oz. margarine	2 oz. raw chopped onion
A 16-oz. can lobster soup	4 oz. plain flour
¼ pint milk	Salt and pepper to taste
4 oz. grated cheese	

Cut the raw cod into pieces 1 in. square. Roll in the flour and lightly brown very quickly in the margarine in a frying pan. Put the partly cooked fish into a casserole, flake lobster, add all ingredients except cheese, and mix well. Finally, sprinkle cheese on top. Bake in a moderate oven for 40 minutes. Serve very hot with peas and mashed potatoes.

Fish Custard

Cold cooked fish	Pepper and salt
Shallot	Milk and eggs for
A few chopped capers	custard

Flake the fish, removing any bones, and put some into a buttered pie dish. Sprinkle pepper and salt over it, a little chopped caper and a very little chopped shallot. Add more layers of fish and seasoning until

Fried fillets garnished with mixed vegetables, sliced lemon, tomato and sprigs of parsley

all is used. Make a custard, allowing 3 eggs to a pint of milk. Pour it carefully over the fish and bake in a slow oven (standing the dish in a tin with a little water in it) until a delicate brown.

Fish Cutlets (for 3–4)

¼ lb. cooked fish	1 teaspoonful
½ oz. butter	chopped parsley
½ oz. flour	1 teaspoonful
½ gill milk or fish	anchovy essence
stock	Egg, breadcrumbs
1 egg-yolk	and fat for frying
Pepper and salt	

Remove the skin and any bones from the fish and flake it up finely. Add the parsley, anchovy essence and pepper and salt. Melt the butter in a saucepan, stir in the flour and add the milk or fish stock, stirring until the mixture thickens and draws away from the side of the saucepan. Remove from the heat and put in the fish and the beaten egg-yolk. Turn the mixture out on to a plate to get cold, then make it into neat cutlets, using a little flour if necessary. Egg-and-breadcrumb them and fry in deep fat until golden brown. Drain well and garnish with fried parsley and slices of lemon.

Fish Hotpot (for 3–4)

1 lb. cod fillets	2 oz. grated cheese
Marrow (about 1 lb.)	2–3 tablespoonfuls
1 lb. new potatoes	cider or milk
2 stalks celery (or	Garlic
2 peppers)	Browned bread-
1 oz. butter or mar-	crumbs (or corn-
garine	flakes)
Salt and pepper	

Cut fillets into eight or ten even-sized pieces. Peel marrow, remove seeds and cut into sections. Cut potatoes into rounds ⅛ in. thick. Finely dice celery or peppers. Mix vegetables and divide into three portions.

Rub casserole with cut garlic and then grease with butter or margarine. Put a layer of marrow, potato and celery or peppers at the bottom, then *half* the fish. Add salt, pepper and 1 oz. grated cheese, another layer of vegetables, then remaining fish, seasoning and cider or milk. Add remaining cheese, then the vegetables and, finally, browned breadcrumbs or cornflakes. Dot on top with pats of butter or margarine. Bake in a moderate oven for 1 hour.

Fish Mousse (for 3–4)

1 lb. cooked whiting or fresh haddock	½ pint white sauce
1 teaspoonful powdered gelatine	2 egg-whites
	1 tablespoonful cream
	Pepper and salt

Make the white sauce with fish stock if possible and dissolve the gelatine in it. Pound the fish and add to the sauce, with seasoning to taste, the cream and, lastly, the well-whisked egg-whites. Beat lightly and put in a soufflé mould. Serve cold with salad and cold tomato sauce.

Fish Omelet

Flake finely about 2 oz. cooked fish. Season, add a little cream, work it into a paste, heat and put aside in a warm place. Make a plain omelet and fold the fish into it just before dishing it up.

Fish Patties or Vol-au-Vent

Make some patty cases (see Pastry chapter). Use any cooked fish, flaked into small pieces and moistened with some good fish sauce. Season well, add a squeeze of lemon juice or a little grated rind, a beaten egg-yolk and, if possible, a little cream. Heat the mixture and pile into the patty cases. Put on the lids and heat the patties in the oven for 2 or 3 minutes. If liked, a few shelled chopped shrimps may be added to the mixture.

Fish Pie (1) (for 3–4)

½ lb. cooked white fish (cold)	Grated lemon rind
1 gill anchovy sauce	1 tomato
1 teaspoonful chopped parsley	1 lb. potatoes (cooked)
1 hard-boiled egg	Pepper and salt
	Butter

Make anchovy sauce (see Sauces), stir in flaked fish, chopped parsley, cut-up egg, lemon rind, pepper and salt. Grease a pie dish, put in the mixture, then some slices of tomato and cover with mashed potato. Put a few pieces of butter on top and bake for ¾ hour.

NOTE: Uncooked fish should be steamed before being added to the sauce.

Fish Pie (2) (for 4)

¾ lb. cooked cod fillet	1 lb. cooked potatoes (mashed)
½ pint thick white sauce	¾ oz. butter or margarine
2 hard-boiled eggs (finely chopped)	A little hot milk
1 level dessertspoonful chopped capers	Salt and pepper
	Good pinch grated nutmeg

Skin and flake the cod. To the white sauce add the fish, eggs and capers. Season with salt and pepper. Put into a pie dish. Melt the butter in a saucepan and add the potatoes, salt, pepper, nutmeg and sufficient hot milk to give a fairly soft creamy consistency. Beat well and pile on top of the fish. Smooth the surface, "rough up" with a fork, brush with egg or milk and brown in a moderate oven for approximately 25 minutes.

Garnish with lemon wedges and parsley.

Fish Pie—Russian Style (for 4)

½ lb. flaky pastry	1 chopped hard-boiled egg
1 filleted haddock or codling	2 tablespoonfuls white sauce
Grated lemon rind	
Pepper and salt	

(This recipe is at its best when made with flaky pastry, but is almost as good made with short. Though haddock is its proper constituent, a codling makes a reasonable substitute.)

Cut the fish into small pieces and mix with the other ingredients for the filling. Roll the pastry into a square, trim and lay the filling in the centre. Fold the pastry to the centre, decorate with pastry leaves. Place on a greased baking sheet and bake in a hot oven for 30–40 minutes or until the pastry is golden brown.

Fish Pudding (for 3–4)

½ lb. cooked fish	1 gill milk
2 oz. breadcrumbs	Pepper and salt
1 egg	Chopped parsley
Anchovy essence	

Break up the fish into small pieces, add the breadcrumbs, pepper and salt, parsley, anchovy essence, the beaten egg and, lastly, the milk. Put the mixture into a greased basin, cover with greased paper and steam for 1 hour. Serve with anchovy or tomato sauce.

Fish Soufflé (for 3–4)

2 oz. butter	Pepper and salt
2 oz. flour	2 or 3 eggs (separated)
1 tablespoonful anchovy essence	About a gill of milk
5 oz. white fish	1 tablespoonful cream

Melt the butter and add the flour, anchovy essence and seasoning, stirring well. Then add the egg-yolks and milk. Continue stirring over the fire until the mixture is about to boil, then take it off. Stir in the finely pounded white fish and the cream. When well blended, stir in the well-beaten

40

egg-whites lightly, pour into a buttered soufflé dish and bake for about ½ hour.

Fish Surprises (for 4)

½ lb. uncooked cod fillet	Lemon wedges and parsley for garnish
2 level tablespoonfuls finely chopped parsley	Strained juice of 1 lemon
2 rounded tablespoonfuls flour	Grated rind of ½ lemon
Salt and pepper	4 level tablespoonfuls butter or margarine

Skin the fillet and reduce it to a fine, smooth consistency by mashing well with two forks. Add lemon rind, parsley and seasoning. Beat the butter or margarine to a smooth paste with the flour. Work in the fish and other ingredients. Add the lemon juice. Divide the now firm and pliable mixture into from six to eight pieces. Shape on a lightly floured board into fish balls or cakes. Fry in hot fat and serve garnished with lemon wedges and parsley.

Fish Timbales (for 3–4)

1 lb. cooked white fish	2 egg-whites
White sauce	Pepper and salt

Make some white sauce (see Sauces chapter), using fish stock and cornflour. Add seasoning and then put in the fish, pounded up. Lastly, fold in the well-beaten whites. Butter some timbale moulds, fill almost full with the mixture, twist a piece of buttered paper over the top, steam for 20 minutes, then turn out carefully.

Fresh Haddock (Stuffed)

Wash and dry the haddock. Make sufficient veal stuffing (see Poultry and Game chapter) to fill, and then sew up with a needle and thread. Put in a tin with some dripping or butter. Cover with a piece of buttered paper and then another tin, and bake for 30 minutes or according to size, basting well. Serve with brown sauce.

NOTE: Cod or hake can also be stuffed and baked.

Grilled Haddock Marinade

For each person, take half a large fillet of haddock. Prepare a marinade of olive oil (or melted margarine), a dash of lemon juice, salt and pepper, and a bay leaf, the quantity depending on the number of fillets. Leave the fillets to marinade for ½ hour or more, then grill, turning to ensure thorough cooking, until lightly browned. Serve on a hot dish, with maître d'hôtel butter (see Cookery in France), served separately.

Haddock baked with Egg Sauce

Cut fillets of haddock into pieces, season

Grilled or fried trout, are cooked whole in olive oil, brought to the table with lemon slices in their mouths and garnished with parsley

strongly with salt, pepper and paprika, and place in generously buttered baking dish with strips of fat bacon on top and between them. Cover with a piece of greaseproof paper and bake slowly for about 1 hour. Make white sauce with 1 oz. butter or margarine, 2 dessertspoonfuls flour and a breakfastcupful of milk. When thick and smooth, add chopped hard-boiled egg and a teaspoonful of capers and pour over fish. Sprinkle with freshly chopped parsley and serve in baking dish.

Haddock stuffed with Grapes (for 2–3)

1¼ lb. fresh haddock	½ lb. white grapes
1 oz. breadcrumbs	½ oz. melted butter
1 egg	8 squashed grapes
Browned bread-	½ tumbler of fish
crumbs	stock or water
Mixed herbs	Salt and pepper

Ask the fishmonger to cut off the head of the haddock, open fish on belly side and remove backbone. Peel grapes and remove pips. Make stuffing with breadcrumbs, herbs, seasoning, melted butter, squashed grapes and egg for binding to soft consistency. Spread out cleaned fish, run a double row of halved grapes along one side, cover with stuffing, top with halved grapes. Sew up the fish. Place in a well-greased fireproof dish, pour in fish stock or water and juice that has run out of the grapes. Season fish, break a walnut of margarine over it. Bake in a moderate oven for 25 minutes, keeping basted. Remove cotton, peel off top skin, sprinkle fish and bind cooking liquor with browned breadcrumbs, add remaining grapes to sauce.

Kedgeree (see Breakfast Dishes)

Miracle Fish Salad

1 lb. cod fillets	Lime juice (prefer-
3 tablespoonfuls	ably unsweetened)
olive oil	1 tablespoonful white
Salt, pepper, sugar	vinegar
Watercress	

Flake the fish and place it in lime juice (just enough to cover). Leave for about 8 hours in a cool place—not the refrigerator —when it will look and taste "cooked." Pour off the juice, make a French dressing with the oil, and a tablespoonful of vinegar to a teaspoonful of the lime juice. Season well. Dress the watercress with this and

pile the fish up in the middle of it. If preferred, mayonnaise can be used instead of the French dressing.

Quick Creamed Cod on Toast (for 4)

1 lb. smoked cod	1 oz. flour
fillets	1 oz. margarine
½ pint milk	4 slices buttered toast

Poach the cod gently for 15–20 minutes. Melt the margarine in a stout saucepan, add the flour and blend well. Gradually pour on milk, away from heat, stirring all the time, return to heat and bring to the boil, still stirring. Make four slices of buttered toast and, meanwhile, flake the cooked and drained fish into the sauce. Stir it gently to heat right through. Spoon this mixture on to the hot buttered slices of toast and serve at once. If liked, garnish with slices of hard-boiled egg or sieved hard-boiled yolk.

Robin Hood Curry (for 4)

(Named, not after the famous outlaw, whose staple diet was venison, but after the lovely little fishing village and holiday resort nestling below the Yorkshire cliffs.)

1 lb. flaked cod	1 oz. margarine
1 small onion, finely	2 level teaspoonfuls
chopped	curry powder
1 small apple, finely	1 rounded table-
chopped	spoonful plain flour
½ pint water or fish	1 teaspoonful salt
stock	1 tablespoonful
1 tablespoonful	chutney
sultanas	

Melt the fat and fry the apple and onion lightly. Add curry powder and flour and fry for a minute or two, stirring well, gradually stir in the liquid, then add salt, sultanas and chutney. Bring to the boil and simmer gently for 20–30 minutes. Add the flaked fish and simmer for another 10 minutes. Serve boiled rice separately.

Savoury Baked Fish (for 4)

1 lb. cod or haddock	½-pint tin tomato,
Breadcrumbs	mushroom or
2 oz. margarine	onion soup

Cut the fish up into four thick slices and put these into a fireproof dish. Pour the soup over the fish—it should just cover the fish; if it does not, add water. Sprinkle generously with breadcrumbs, add dabs of margarine and bake in a moderate oven for 20 minutes.

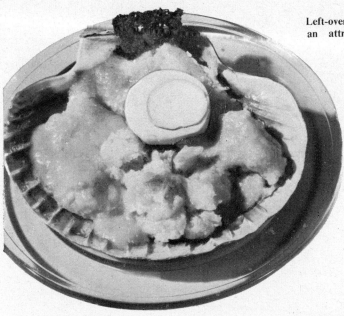

Left-over fish can be used to make an attractive dish, served in scallop shells

dish. Sprinkle pepper and salt over it. Put the butter in pieces on the top and bake in a moderately hot oven for 10 minutes, basting well. Take out, add the chopped mushrooms and cream, and cook for 10 minutes more. Finally, stir the beef extract into the liquor and finish in the oven, basting once or twice.

Shattuck Haddock

Cut fish into fillets and lay them in a fireproof dish, lined with butter or margarine. Sprinkle with salt and pepper, and arrange on top of the fish five or six thick slices of peeled tomato. Bake in a hot oven for ½ hour, basting frequently with its own liquor.

Spiced Cod

2 lb. cod fillet	1 egg-white
1 pint water	Clove of garlic
3 tablespoonfuls vinegar	A few peppercorns
1 clove	Chopped parsley
1 onion (sliced)	Batter
	Salt and pepper
Fat for frying	

Flake cod and put into a large dish. In a separate dish mix water, vinegar, garlic, peppercorns, parsley, onion and clove, and pour over fish. Leave for 1½ hours, then remove fish, dry in a clean cloth, dip in well-seasoned batter and thinly whipped egg-white. Fry in very hot fat to a rich golden colour. Serve with egg sauce (see Sauces chapter).

HALIBUT

Halibut à la Suisse (for 3–4)

1 lb. halibut	2 oz. mushrooms
2 oz. butter	2 tablespoonfuls cream
½ teaspoonful beef extract	Pepper and salt

Wipe the fish and put it in a buttered

Halibut with Tomatoes (Baked) (for 3–4)

1 lb. halibut	3 tomatoes
1 oz. melted butter	1 very small onion
2 tablespoonfuls cream	Pinch of castor sugar
	Fat for frying
Pepper and salt	

Wipe the fish and skin it; put it in a buttered dish and sprinkle pepper and salt on top. Pour over the melted butter and cook in a moderately hot oven for about 20 minutes. Meanwhile, fry the onion, sliced very finely, in a little fat until it is golden brown, take out the fish, put slices of tomato on top with a pinch of sugar, then the onion, and lastly the cream. Put back in oven for 10 minutes.

HERRINGS, BLOATERS, KIPPERS AND MACKEREL

Baked Herrings and Tomatoes (for 4)

2 level teaspoonfuls dry mustard	2 teaspoonfuls vinegar
4 herrings cleaned and boned	8 oz. tomatoes skinned and sliced
1 small onion, very finely sliced	½–1 teaspoonful salt
¼ level teaspoonful pepper	1 tablespoonful stock or water

Mix the mustard and vinegar together. Open the herrings out flat and, if large, cut each into three pieces. Spread with the mustard mixture. Arrange the onion, herrings and tomatoes in alternate layers in an ovenproof dish, seasoning each layer. Add

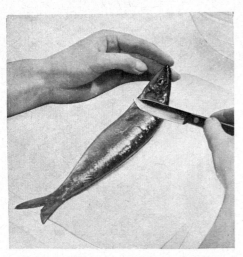

To prepare a herring: (1) With a sharp knife, cut off the head and tail and scale the fish

(2) Make a shallow cut along the backbone, beginning at the head end

the stock and bake in a moderate oven ¾ hour. Serve hot.

Baked Stuffed Herrings (for 4)

4 herrings	1 teaspoonful
½ teacupful bread-	chopped parsley
crumbs	1 small onion
Salt and pepper	½ teaspoonful butter

Clean and wash herrings and remove heads. Split open and remove backbones. To make the stuffing, chop the onion very finely and add breadcrumbs, parsley and seasoning. If the fish have roes, mix two with the stuffing and this will bind it, otherwise use a little beaten egg. Sprinkle the inside of each herring with salt and pepper and spread a portion of the stuffing down the centre. Roll up and tie with cotton or pierce with a small wooden skewer. Cook in a buttered fireproof dish covered with greaseproof paper for 15 minutes. Remove paper and allow to brown.

Goodwood Herrings (for 6)

6 fresh herrings	6 tomatoes
4 tablespoonfuls	1 tablespoonful mar-
breadcrumbs	garine or dripping
1 small minced onion	½ teaspoonful grated
1 tablespoonful	lemon rind
chopped parsley	A pinch of dried
Small wooden	thyme
skewers	Salt and pepper

Scale, clean and behead the herrings, but leave in the roes. Twist the fish head to tail and fasten with a tiny wooden skewer or cocktail stick. Slice the top off each

tomato with a sharp knife Keep the slice Scoop out the inside of each, discard the hard core, keep the pulp. Put bread-crumbs, herbs, onion, lemon, salt and pepper into a basin and add enough tomato pulp to moisten. Fill each tomato with this mixture, put a tiny piece of margarine on top and replace the covers. Set a tomato in the centre of each curled herring. Put in a greased fireproof dish and cook for 20 minutes in a fairly hot oven. Serve in the dish in which they are cooked.

Grilled Bloaters

Bloaters
A little margarine or dripping for frying roes

Break off the heads of the fish, split open the backs and remove roes and backbone. Toss roes in a little hot margarine or dripping in a small pan until golden brown. Heat grill, grease the grid and place fish on it with insides to the heat. When browned, turn over and grill the backs. Serve very hot with the roes.

Grilled Herrings with Lemon

1 herring per person   Lemon juice
A little butter

Scale and clean the fish, then wipe with a clean cloth. Skewer the heads and tails together. Brush each with a very little butter and grill quickly under a very hot grill until brown. Squeeze on the lemon juice and serve at once.

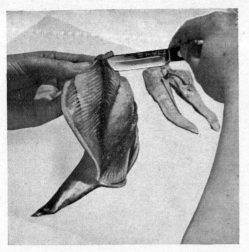

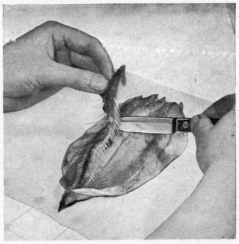

(3) Remove roe, if any, and insert knife under backbone

(4) Flatten out fish and lift backbone. Small bones should come away at the same time

Grilled Kippers

Kippers
Pepper
Lemon juice
Margarine or butter

Wipe each kipper with a damp cloth and cut off the head. Heat the grill and put the kippers on the hot grid, skin side uppermost, and grill for 1 minute. Turn kippers, place a pat of margarine or butter on top and cook for a further 5–6 minutes. Sprinkle with pepper and, if liked, a squeeze of lemon juice. Serve at once.

(5) Separate hard roes from soft, and handle as little as possible. Roes can be cooked with the herrings or kept for use as a separate dish

Herrings à la Maître d'Hôtel (for 4)

4 *large herrings*
2 *teaspoonfuls finely*
  chopped parsley
Salt and pepper
1 *dessertspoonful*
  olive oil
Juice of ½ lemon
½ *pint white sauce*
  Cayenne

Scale, clean and wash the herrings. Cut off the heads, split them down the back, and remove the backbone and as many small bones as possible. Put them on a flat dish and sprinkle with salt, pepper and the oil. Leave for 1 hour, basting frequently. Grill until golden brown. Prepare a good white sauce, not too thick (see Sauces chapter). Stir in the parsley and lemon juice, season well with salt and a few grains of Cayenne and serve cold.

Herrings fried in Oatmeal (see chapter on Cookery in Scotland).

Herrings, Lowestoft Style

Scale, clean and behead the fish. Make a strong brine by putting 2 handfuls of common salt into 1½ pints of water. Bring to the boil, put in the fish and let the water gallop for 6 minutes. The flesh will be firm and full of flavour and not at all mushy, because the heavy brine prevents the water from soaking into it. Can be eaten hot, or served cold with salad.

Herring Pie (for 4–5)

½ lb. grated raw potato	¼ teaspoonful nutmeg
½ lb. grated raw apple	1 onion (chopped)
2 teaspoonfuls lemon juice	Salt and pepper
	4 herrings, boned
	6 oz. pastry

Grease a shallow dish and arrange half the potato, apple and onion on it. Sprinkle on the nutmeg, seasoning and lemon juice. Lay the herrings on top. Cover with remainder of the potato, apple and onion mixture. Roll out pastry and cover dish. Bake in a hot oven for 30 minutes.

Herrings with Mustard Sauce

Wipe the fish with a clean cloth, split open, then egg-and-breadcrumb them. Fry in a little butter, cut side downwards first, for 7 to 8 minutes. Serve with mustard sauce (see chapter on Sauces).

Jugged Kippers

Roll up kippers, put them into a jug and pour on enough fast-boiling water to cover them. Cover the jug and let it stand in a warm place for 5 minutes, then take out fish, drain and serve with a pat of butter. NOTE: This method avoids cooking smells.

Kipper Creams (for 3)

2 large kippers	Pinch of nutmeg
Pepper	2 egg-yolks
3 or 4 tablespoonfuls top of milk	1 egg-white
	Lemon juice

Cover kippers with boiling water and leave for a few minutes. Drain, remove skin and bones, and mash. Beat up the yolks and white of egg, add fish, pepper, nutmeg, a squeeze of lemon juice and, lastly, the milk. Put into lightly buttered individual fireproof dishes and cook in a cool oven for 20–25 minutes, until golden brown and set.

Mackerel (Fried)

Wipe the fish well with a clean cloth, split open and egg-and-breadcrumb them. Fry in a little butter, cut-side down first, for 7–8 minutes. Serve with maître d'hôtel butter (see Cookery in France)

Mackerel with Apple or Gooseberry Sauce

Wash the fish, cut off the heads and wipe with a clean cloth. (Do not wash after the heads are cut off as the flavour will be spoilt.) Score in two or three places and put small pieces of butter on the fish. Put under a hot grill and cook for 15 minutes, turning half-way. (The fish can be split open if preferred.) Serve with apple or gooseberry sauce or with pats of maître d'hôtel butter (see Cookery in France).

Marinated Herrings

Soak salt herrings in water for 24 hours, changing the water several times. Clean, bone and skin the herrings and dry them with a cloth. Roll fillets in flour and fry quickly in margarine. Put into glazed or ovenproof dish, add bay leaves, spices and pepper. Cover with cold boiled vinegar and leave for 2–3 days.

Marinated Mackerel or Herrings (for 3–4)

3 or 4 fish	12 peppercorns
¼ pint vinegar	Bay leaf
¼ pint water	Pepper and salt

Wash and clean the fish, put into a deep dish, head to tail. Pour over them the vinegar and water; then add the peppercorns, bay leaf and seasoning. Bake in a slow oven for about 1 hour, allow to cool, and serve cold.

Pickled Herrings (see chapter on Cookery in Scotland)

Savoury Herrings (for 4)

4 herrings	Juice of 1 lemon
1 tablespoonful chutney	Salt and pepper
	¼ oz. margarine

Scale, clean and bone the herrings and open them out flat. Sprinkle with salt and pepper, spread with a little chutney and fold together again. Place in a well-greased baking dish, sprinkle with the lemon juice and cover with a greased paper. Bake in a moderate oven for 10 minutes, then remove the paper and cook for a further 5 minutes until brown. NOTE: There is no fishy smell when herrings are cooked by this method.

Summer Kippers

Wrap kippers in greaseproof paper or put in a covered casserole and bake for 10 minutes.

PILCHARDS

Paprika Pilchards (for 4)

4 pilchards	Potatoes
Porridge oats	About ½ pint milk
½ oz. margarine	1 tablespoonful
1 dessertspoonful	paprika
flour	Salt and pepper
1 dessertspoonful	1 tablespoonful
tomato purée	evaporated milk

Butter a baking dish and cover the bottom with very thin slices of peeled potatoes. Dust with pepper and salt, then put on another layer of potatoes. Salt and pepper these, and sprinkle a few raw porridge oats over them. Heat a small cup of milk with margarine and pour over the potatoes. Cover the dish and bake for at least 1 hour, basting twice. Remove cover, place the cleaned and decapitated pilchards on the potatoes. Blend the paprika, flour, salt, pepper, tomato purée and evaporated milk, add ¼ pint milk and any liquid in the dish and bring to the boil, stirring carefully. Pour the sauce over the fish, replace in the oven and cook for a further ½ hour, basting at frequent intervals.

PLAICE

Fried Fillets of Plaice, Whiting, Haddock, etc.

See p. 32 for instructions on how to fry fish.

Fillets of Plaice (Grilled)

Heat the grill thoroughly and brush the fillets of plaice (two for each person) with oil to which has been added some chopped herbs, preferably fennel or thyme. Sprinkle the fillets with lemon juice and grill them slowly, first on one side and then on the other, brushing them occasionally with the herb - flavoured oil. Serve alone or with mornay or tartare sauce (see Sauces), or maître d'hôtel butter.

Fish in Batter

1 lb. fish
1 large egg
½ pint milk
¼ lb. flour
A dash of pepper and nutmeg
1 oz. dripping
Pinch of salt

Place dripping in a pie dish or meat tin. Wash and dry fish, cut into about eight pieces and arrange in dish. Cover with greaseproof paper and put into the oven for fat to get hot. Make the rest of the ingredients into a Yorkshire pudding batter (see Puddings and Sweets) and, when the fat is really hot, remove greaseproof paper, pour the batter into the tin and bake for about 40 minutes.

Fillets of Plaice (Steamed)

Wipe the fillets, season them and fold them over once. Then put them in a well-buttered tin with a very little milk. Cover with a piece of greased paper, put another tin on top and steam in a slow oven for about 10 minutes.

Make some white sauce, add to it the liquor from the fish and serve separately.

Fillets of Plaice with Shrimp Sauce (for 2–3)

Medium-sized plaice (filleted)	1 tablespoonful salt
Juice of a lemon	Shrimp sauce (see Sauces chapter)

Have the plaice cut into four fillets, roll each one up and pass a wooden skewer through them all. Put them in a deep pie dish, cover with cold water, squeeze in the juice of a lemon, add the salt, put the dish in the oven with a plate on top and bake until the fish is quite done.

Drain, remove the skewers and arrange the fillets neatly in an upright position. Pour the hot sauce over them and serve at once.

RED MULLET

Red Mullet (Grilled)

Cut off fins and tails of fish, scrape lightly, wash well and wipe with a cloth.

Score the sides of the fish, season with plenty of salt and pepper and a generous sprinkling of lemon juice. Smear with olive oil and put on a very hot grill. The fish should be accompanied by steamed potatoes (new, if possible) and by melted or anchovy butter.

COOK'S TIP

FISHY SMELLS quickly disappear from utensils used for cooking and eating fish if wiped with soft paper, then rinsed in cold water. A little mustard in the washing-up water also removes odour

Red Mullet à la Crème (for 4)

4 small red mullet	1 teaspoonful olive
1 teaspoonful corn-	oil
flour	1 teaspoonful
1 tablespoonful butter	butter
6 tablespoonfuls	3 tablespoonfuls
cream or top of	sherry
milk	

Salt, pepper and lemon juice

Cut off the fins and tails, scrape lightly and wipe with a cloth. Season through the gills with salt, pepper and lemon juice. Melt the tablespoonful of butter and olive oil and, when hot, fry the fish in it for 5 or 6 minutes on each side. Remove and keep warm. Add the extra butter to what is left in the pan and blend in the cornflour. Add the cream, season with salt, pepper and lemon juice, and stir in the sherry. Cook for a few minutes till smooth and serve over the fish.

Red Mullet au Gratin (for 2–3)

2 red mullet	½ teaspoonful
4 button mushrooms	chopped onion
1 tablespoonful	Grated rind of ½ a
sherry	lemon
1 teaspoonful mush-	1 tablespoonful
room ketchup	browned bread-
2 oz. butter	crumbs
1 teaspoonful	Parsley and lemon
chopped parsley	slices to garnish

Pepper and salt

Wash the fish, cut off their heads and fins, then dry with a clean cloth. Grease a dish with some of the butter, sprinkle over it half the onion, mushrooms, lemon rind and chopped parsley. Score the fish across once or twice and put them on top. Season, and add the rest of the chopped ingredients. Add sherry and ketchup, sprinkle on breadcrumbs, cut the remainder of the butter into small pieces and place on top, and bake in a moderate oven for about 20 minutes. Garnish with parsley and slices of lemon.

Red Mullet in Paper Cases (for 4)

4 small red mullet	Salt, pepper, lemon
3 tablespoonfuls	juice
butter	1 tablespoonful
1 tablespoonful	chopped parsley
finely minced	1 teaspoonful
shallot	chopped fennel (if
	available)

Cut off the fins and tails with kitchen scissors, but do not empty the fish as the liver is considered a delicacy. Scrape lightly, and wipe with a clean cloth. Season through the gills with salt, pepper and lemon juice. Work the parsley and shallot —and fennel if used—into the butter and spread the creamed mixture on the fish. Wrap each fish loosely but securely in a square of oiled greaseproof paper and cook in a fairly hot oven for about 15 minutes until tender. Serve the fish in their wrappers, but accompany with anchovy butter or a home-made tomato sauce or simply with cut lemon. (Chopped shrimps or anchovy fillets can be creamed into the butter with which the mullet are spread before baking, with excellent results).

Red Mullet Meunière (for 4)

4 small red mullet	1 tablespoonful
½ teaspoonful olive	butter
oil	Good squeeze of
1 dessertspoonful	lemon juice
chopped parsley	Parsley and lemon
Flour	slices to garnish

Salt and pepper

Trim and wipe the fish, and season well. Roll lightly in a little flour. Heat the butter and oil together and, when hot, fry the fish in it for about 10 minutes, turning once. Add the lemon juice and parsley to the pan, and another tablespoonful of butter; pour over the fish and serve simply garnished with sprigs of parsley and slices of lemon.

For a more elaborate dish, pound 4 anchovy fillets (previously soaked for several hours in water to remove the salt) with 1 sardine and 2 tablespoonfuls of butter, a tablespoonful of chopped parsley and a squeeze of lemon juice, and add this to the butter in the pan.

Red Mullet Venetian

Fry the mullet in oil. Serve surrounded by button mushrooms and stuffed olives with Sauce Venitienne: Reduce 8 tablespoonfuls of Tarragon vinegar and a good dessertspoonful of finely chopped shallot or chives by a good half and add it to ¾ pint of good white sauce.

SALMON

Salmon (Boiled)

Clean the fish and carefully scrape off the scales, then poach it *very* gently in salted water or court bouillon over a low heat so that it never quite boils. Allow 10 minutes per pound of fish plus an extra 10 minutes, at the end of which it should be a good even pink shade right through and

A special occasion fish dish: lightly poached trout, served cold, covered with green mayonnaise and decorated with red pimento to give a bizarre effect

will flake easily. If using frozen salmon, add a tablespoonful of olive oil to the cooking water; this eliminates any danger of excessive dryness.

Boiled salmon to be served cold should be left to cool in the water in which it was cooked and served with mayonnaise (see Salads chapter) or tartare sauce (see Sauces) and a cucumber salad.

Salmon (Baked)

Brush the piece of salmon well all over with melted butter or olive oil, season with salt and pepper, wrap up in greased paper and bake in a fairly hot oven, allowing about 1 hour for a piece of fish weighing about 1½ lb.

Salmon (Steamed)

Clean and scale the fish, then dip in boiling water for a few seconds to seal in the flavour and preserve the colour. Cook very gently over boiling water in a fish kettle, allowing about 20 minutes to the pound and 20 minutes over. Serve as for Boiled Salmon.

Salmon Steaks (Grilled)

Scrape off the scales with a very sharp knife and either marinade the steaks in olive oil for ½ hour or spread them well with butter on both sides. Grill them until both sides are golden. Serve with sliced lemon, pats of maître d'hôtel butter (see Cookery in France) or tartare sauce, fresh green peas or cucumber salad.

Salmon Steaks (Steamed)

Scrape off scales with a very sharp knife. Put the steaks in a casserole with a tablespoonful of water, a pinch of salt and a few lumps of butter. Cover first with greaseproof paper and then with the lid of the casserole, and cook in a moderate oven until the fish comes easily away from the bone.

Salmon Mousse (see p. 40)

SARDINES

Sardines Fried in Batter

Drain the sardines well on paper to remove the oil, skin them, remove heads and tails. Make fritter batter (see p. 123), dip the sardines in, one at a time, and fry in deep fat until brown. Serve with lemon and bread and butter.

49

SHELL FISH

Cockles and Mussels

Wash several times in clean water, sprinkle with salt and boil for about 10 minutes or until the shells open. Remove black weed from mussels. Steam off liquid. Serve with vinegar.

Dressed Crab (for 4)

1 *cooked crab*	1 *tablespoonful*
Chopped parsley	*mayonnaise or*
Green salad	*French dressing*
1 *oz. breadcrumbs*	(*see Salads chapter*)
Pepper and salt	

Remove the flesh from the large claws and the meat from the shell (being careful to discard the fingers or gills stuck to the sides of the shell, the bag or sac near the head and the green intestines). Mix the ingredients together, wash and dry the shell and fill with the mixture. Serve on a bed of green salad garnished with parsley and the small claws.

Lobster

Lobster is nearly always sold cooked. A good lobster is heavy in proportion to its size.

If uncooked, tie up the claws, wash, and plunge head down into boiling water. Cook for 35–45 minutes.

To prepare for table, break off the big claws and crack them carefully. Cut down the back with a sharp knife from head to tail, and remove the inside and the spongy-looking gills. Arrange the pieces of the body and the large claws on a dish and garnish with the small claws and salad. Serve with tartare sauce (see Sauces chapter), mayonnaise or French dressing (see Salads chapter).

Lobster au Gratin (for 4–5)

1 *good-sized lobster*	*Breadcrumbs*
1 *teaspoonful*	1 *tablespoonful flour*
chopped shallot	½ *pint milk*
1 *oz. butter*	*Cayenne pepper*
Chopped parsley	*Anchovy essence*
1 *tablespoonful*	1 *egg-yolk*
cream	*Butter*

Cut the lobster in half, dividing the head from the body, and take out all the meat, saving the shells. Cut the meat in slices.

Put a teaspoonful of chopped shallot in a saucepan with the butter and cook for a few minutes, add the flour, mixing well, and the milk, stir continually and let it boil gently for 5 minutes.

Add the lobster, seasoned with Cayenne pepper, chopped parsley and anchovy essence, put the saucepan back on the fire and stir until it boils. Remove from fire and stir in the egg-yolk and the cream. Fill the shells with the mixture, sprinkle breadcrumbs on top, dot with butter and bake in the oven for 20 minutes.

Lobster in the American Style (Homard à l'américaine) (see chapter on Cookery in France)

Lobster Mornay (as served at the Ivy Restaurant, London)

Take the cooked lobster off the shell and steep in white cream sauce (Béchamel) with grated Parmesan cheese. Replace lobster in shell and cover with sauce, sprinkle grated cheese over the top and place in a moderate oven or under the grill until golden brown.

Lobster Neuberg (see chapter on Cookery in the U.S.A.)

Lobster Thermidor (see chapter on Cookery in the U.S.A.)

Oyster Patties

Make puff pastry patties (see Pastry).

Beard and scald the oysters, cut them up into three or four pieces, put into a sauce made with cornflour, Cayenne pepper and salt, lemon juice and cream, and heat through. If the patties are to be served hot, put some of the mixture into each patty, put on the lids, and heat for 2 or 3 minutes in the oven. If they are to be served cold, let the mixture get cold before filling the patties.

Scalloped Oysters

Scald the oysters in their own liquor. Take them out, beard them and strain. Put in scallop shells and between each layer of oysters sprinkle a few breadcrumbs seasoned with pepper, salt and a little nutmeg. Top with small pieces of butter and enough breadcrumbs to make a smooth surface to cover the oysters. Bake in a quick oven for 5 minutes.

Scalloped Scallops

Wash the scallops, wipe them, remove the beards and black part, then cut up into three or four pieces. Stew in a little milk with pepper and salt, remove the scallops, thicken the liquor with flour made into a smooth paste, replace the scallops and re-heat. Butter the shells, scatter bread-crumbs over them and put in enough of the mixture just to cover. Scatter some more breadcrumbs over each, put a small piece of butter on top and brown in the oven.

Scallops (for 2–3)

6 scallops	Fat for frying
Pepper and salt	Flour
Egg and breadcrumbs	

Scallops must be absolutely fresh to be wholesome. Open the shells and remove the beards and any black parts, leaving only the yellow and white part to be eaten. Wash, dry and scatter seasoned flour over them, then egg-and-breadcrumb and fry in deep fat for 3–4 minutes. Drain well and serve in shells, garnished with parsley and cut lemon.

Scampis (Dublin Bay Prawns) Frits (as served at the Ivy Restaurant, London)

(1) Pass the prawns in milk and flour and fry in deep fat until golden. May be served with Tartare or Tomato Sauce or lemon.

(2) Pass the prawns in flour, milk and breadcrumbs and fry in deep fat until golden. Serve with sauces as above.

(3) *Meunière*. Pass the prawns in flour. Pour oil into frying pan, cook the scampis in it until a golden colour. Serve with lemon juice, golden (melted) butter to which parsley is added, and season to taste.

SKATE

Skate (for 3–4)

1 lb. skate	1½ oz. grated cheese
4 oz. breadcrumbs	1 gill white sauce

Boil the fish in salted water until it comes away easily from the bones, drain well and flake up. Put a layer of fish into a greased fireproof dish, cover with breadcrumbs and a good sprinkling of cheese. Continue these layers until all are used up, then pour over the well-seasoned sauce and bake in a fairly hot oven until brown on top—about 30 minutes.

SMELTS

Smelts (for 2)

6 smelts	Butter
Seasoning	1 dessertspoonful
Egg and breadcrumbs	chopped parsley

Wipe the fish, split them open and season

Red Mullet, cooked in greaseproof paper, are served in their wrappers

them. Then egg-and-breadcrumb them and fry in a little butter until a golden brown. Sprinkle chopped parsley over them and serve with anchovy sauce, black butter or melted butter (see Sauces).

SOLE

Sole au Parmesan

Fillets of sole	Cheese sauce
Pepper, salt and	Grated cheese
Cayenne	

Wipe the fillets, roll up and put in a well-buttered tin with a little pepper and salt, and bake for 15 minutes. Make cheese sauce (see Sauces and use fish stock instead of milk) and add a little Cayenne. Pour the sauce over the fish and sprinkle grated cheese over the top. Finish either under a hot grill or in the oven.

NOTE: Fillets of any other white fish can be cooked in the same way.

Sole Béchamel

Cook in the same way as for Sole au Parmesan (see previous recipe), but serve with Béchamel sauce (see Sauces) in place of cheese sauce. Use fish stock, if possible, for the sauce instead of milk.

Sole Duglère (as served at the Ivy Restaurant, London)

Place sole in a casserole and smother with chopped shallots, parsley and tomatoes, a little white wine or lemon juice and cook in the oven. When cooked, take fish up. To make sauce, bring what remains in the dish to the boil (adding a little fish stock if too thick), reduce slightly, then add a little cream or top of the milk, butter and seasoning.

Sole Véronique (for 4)

4 *large fillets of sole*	2 *oz. butter*
(lemon will do)	4 *tablespoonfuls*
1 *shallot*	*white wine or dry*
2 *tablespoonfuls*	*cider*
white sauce	½ *lb. white grapes*
Salt and pepper	

Peel the grapes and take out the pips. Lay the fillets of sole flat in a frying pan, dot with half the butter, sprinkle with salt and pepper and finely chopped shallot and pour over them the wine or cider. Cover and poach very gently for about 10 minutes. Dish up and keep hot while you stir the white sauce and rest of the butter into the liquor in the pan. Stir over a low heat until piping hot and creamy. At the last minute stir in the prepared grapes and pour over the fish, serving immediately.

SPRATS

Salt Fried Sprats

Wash sprats. Heat a heavy iron frying pan. Sprinkle fairly generously with salt and put the sprats in over a moderate heat. When brown on one side, turn and brown on the other. Serve immediately on really hot plates with sliced lemon.

TROUT

Trout

This fish may be grilled, fried, baked or boiled. Freshwater trout should be thoroughly washed in salted water to get rid of the muddy taste.

Trout (Boiled)

Poach very gently over a low heat in salted water or a court bouillon containing white wine When cooked, drain thoroughly, then arrange the fish on a hot dish. Garnish with Hollandaise or gooseberry sauce (see Sauces) and serve boiled potatoes with it.

Trout in Court Bouillon

In a court bouillon made from white wine, seasoned with onion, parsley, thyme, bay leaf, salt and pepper, simmer the trout very gently. When done, remove from liquid and leave to cool. Serve cold, preferably quite plain but, if desired, with a sauce made from a little of the liquor in which the fish were cooked, blended with butter and flour and reduced by half.

Trout (Baked)

Drain and dry the fish after cleansing, then put in a greased fireproof dish and sprinkle with pepper and salt, chopped parsley and shallot. Pour over plenty of melted butter and lemon juice, and bake in a moderate oven for 20–25 minutes, according to size of fish. Serve with black butter sauce (see Sauces).

Trout (Fried)

Clean, wash and dry some small trout and fry in olive oil. Sprinkle with lemon juice and serve with slices of lemon.

Trout (Grilled)

Score the prepared trout on both sides, brush them liberally with olive oil and grill for 3 or 4 minutes on each side. Serve hot with tartare sauce (see Sauces chapter).

TURBOT

Turbot

The delicate flavour of this fish is best preserved by either boiling or, better still, steaming. It should be rubbed over with lemon to preserve its colour, and on no account should it be overcooked. Garnish with parsley and lemon and serve a good sauce with it.

NOTE: An excellent way to steam turbot is to put it between two dishes with a little milk and butter and cook it slowly in the oven.

(Brill can be cooked in the same way as turbot.)

WHITEBAIT

Whitebait (Fried)

Wash the whitebait, drain in a colander, then put on a cloth and turn over and over until the fish are quite dry. Put some seasoned flour on a piece of paper and toss the fish in it. Put them in a strainer and shake off any surplus flour. Have some deep fat ready, put a few fish at a time in the frying basket and plunge the basket into the boiling fat for about 2 minutes. Take out, put on paper and keep hot. Reheat the fat between each frying. When all are cooked, put the whole lot back in the basket and plunge them back in the fat for 1 minute. They should be a very light brown and quite crisp. Drain well on paper, and serve with lemon slices and brown bread and butter.

WHITING

Whiting au Parmesan

Wipe the fillets and put them on a greased tin in the oven with some pepper and salt and a tablespoonful of milk. Cover with greased paper and put another tin on top. Cook for a few minutes. Make cheese sauce (see Sauces chapter) with grated Parmesan cheese and pour it over the fillets. They can either be put under the grill to finish or back into the oven.

Whiting Bercy

Butter a dish, sprinkle it with chopped shallot and parsley, and lay the fish on this. Season with salt and pepper, moisten with cider and cook in the oven with frequent bastings. Dish up the whiting, reduce the cooking liquor by half, thicken it, pour it over the fish and boil quickly.

Whiting Colbert

Open the fish down the centre of the back and remove the backbone after breaking it near the head and tail. Season, egg-and-breadcrumb, and fry in deep fat. Serve covered with maître d'hôtel butter (see Cookery in France).

Whiting with Caper Sauce

Wipe the fish with a dry cloth, put the tails into the mouths and fasten with skewers, egg-and-breadcrumb them and fry a rich brown. Drain well and serve with caper sauce.

NOTE: Whiting can also be steamed or put between two dishes in the oven with a little milk or butter.

Most luxurious of all fish dishes is steamed salmon, here seen decorated with endive and slices of lemon colourfully topped with beetroot and cucumber

MEAT

Choose it with skill, cook it with loving care and serve it elegantly—
for it is the basis of most main meals

IT is a well known fact that tough meat is not always the butcher's fault and that wrong cooking can ruin the choicest cuts. It is equally true that the best cooking in the world can do little to help if the meat itself is at fault. For that reason it is essential that every housewife who wants her meat course to be successful should know something about how to choose meat wisely. Here are the guiding principles.

CHOOSING MEAT

General

Meat, one of the most valuable sources of protein in our diet, consists mainly of fibres bound together by a tough substance known as connective tissue. The parts of the animal which are in most active use during its lifetime—such as the legs and neck—have more connective tissue and are therefore tougher than cuts from less active portions of its anatomy. They therefore need longer, slower cooking.

Too recently killed—and therefore too fresh—meat always tends to be tough. The best way to make it tender is to steep it in a marinade of vinegar (with or without olive oil), flavoured with spices and herbs, or to add lemon juice, vinegar, wine or cider during cooking. There are also several good proprietary meat tenderisers on the market which achieve the same result.

Imported meat which is still frozen must be carefully thawed, preferably in a warm kitchen. During this process it will change colour: this is only the effect of defrosting and does not mean the meat is not good. There is very little difference—except in price—between home-killed and good imported meat. When well cooked, imported joints have the same flavour, tenderness and nourishment.

Beef should be bright red in colour, well covered with firm, white fat and the flesh firm to the touch. If it is to be tender, it should be well hung before cooking and, whether kept in a cool larder or in a refrigerator, should always stand at room temperature for an hour or more before cooking. There is as much food value in the cheaper cuts as the expensive ones, but the cheaper ones need longer, more careful cooking. The diagram facing p. 64 shows from which parts of the animal the main cuts of beef come; here is a guide to cooking them.

Roasting Joints of Beef.—Sirloin, rib, aitchbone, sometimes silverside, brisket, topside, flank (thick end), baron of beef (2 sirloins together).

Grill or Fry.—Fillet or rump steak.

Salt and Boil.—Silverside, brisket.

Braise/Stew. — Aitchbone or top rib, silverside, flank, hock, brisket, shin, oxtail, blade and chuck.

For Soups and Gravies.—Hock, neck, shin, oxtail.

Mutton should be a dull red, firm and fine in grain. The fat should be white and hard. It is more easily digested than beef and should also be hung well before it is cooked.

Lamb is pink rather than red, the fat being firm and of a clear whitish colour, the bone at the joint in chops being reddish. It is also more digestible than beef, but should not be hung for long.

Turn to the diagram facing p. 64 to see where the joints of mutton and lamb are located on the animal. Now to cook them:

Roasting Joints of Mutton and Lamb.— Leg, loin, saddle of mutton, shoulder, best end of neck.

Fry, Grill or Bake.—Loin chops and cutlets, lamb's kidneys and liver.

Boil.—Leg.

Stew.—Scrag, breast, loin, lamb's tongue, lamb's kidneys, lamb's liver, sweetbreads.

Veal, the flesh of a calf, should be pinkish

With roast mutton, either hot or cold, the perfect contrast in flavour is a tart red currant jelly

white, not so firm as beef and the fat slightly pink. The flesh should on no account feel clammy to the touch or be flabby. Unlike the pinkish veal known in Britain, Continental veal is almost pure white—being the flesh of milk-fed calves. Veal requires longer cooking than other meats and is less easily digested.

See diagram facing p. 65 for the joints of veal, which are best cooked as follows:

Roasting Joints.—Fillet or loin, leg, shoulder, best end.

Stew.—Breast, knuckle, calf's tongue.

Grill or Fry.—Chops or cutlets, fillet, calf's liver, calf's kidneys.

Pork fat should be white but the lean varies in colour according to the age of the animal. In a young pig it is practically white, while in an older one it is pink. The flesh should be finely grained and firm to touch. When cooked, the pork fat should be white, *never* pink. It is important that pork should be absolutely fresh and cooked very thoroughly—and slowly. If cooked too quickly, it will be tough and indigestible, and it is not in any case as easily digested as beef or mutton.

Turn to illustration facing p. 65 for diagrams showing where joints of both pork and bacon are cut from the pig. Here is the general cooking guide:

Roasting Joints of Pork.—Leg, spare rib, chine, loin, blade.

Salt and Boil.—Chine, pig's head.

Boil.—Belly, hand, tongue, pig's feet.

Grill or Fry.—Chops.

Stew.—Pig's fry.

Pickle.—Pig's cheeks (bath chaps).

Bacon and Ham

Bacon is the name for the back and sides and ham for the hind legs of a pig when they have been salted, cured and, perhaps, also smoked. Bacon that is salted and dried only is known as green bacon.

The fat should be a clear white and the lean firm, with a thick rind. The best way to test the condition of a whole uncooked ham is to run a long thin carving knife right in as far as the bone; if the blade point smells fresh and pleasant when withdrawn, the ham is nice and fresh. Most hams require soaking overnight before they are boiled.

The diagram facing p. 65 shows from

55

which part of the pig the various pieces of bacon come. This is the cooking guide:

Boiling Joints of Bacon.—Gammon hock, loin, collar.

Grill or Fry (Rashers).—Gammon, streaky, back, collar, long loin.

Venison, the flesh of the deer, must be kept for some time to attain its proper game flavour and must therefore be chosen with great care to make certain it is fresh. The safest test is that suggested for ham— to plunge a long thin-bladed knife into the joint close to the bone. If the tip of the blade smells sweet when withdrawn, the venison is in good condition.

Roasting Joints of Venison.—Leg and loin (separately or together as the haunch), fillet.

Grill or Fry.—Chops.

Stew or Broil.—Steak, best end of neck, breast.

For Pie or Pasty.—Neck or breast.

TO PREPARE MEAT FOR COOKING

All meat should be thoroughly wiped with a damp cloth before cooking. Salted meats should first be soaked in cold water for about 4 hours. If in hot weather meat develops a slight smell, wipe it with a cloth dipped in vinegar and wrung out.

COOKING MEAT

Meat may be boiled, braised, pot roasted, stewed, grilled, fried or roasted.

Boiling

Fresh meat should be put into boiling water, cooked rapidly for about 5 minutes, then simmered gently. Salted meat should be covered with cold or tepid water, brought slowly to the boil and simmered. The minimum of water—just enough to cover—ensures the best flavour, and a bouquet garni, some peppercorns and/or an onion stuck with half a dozen cloves should be included. When the water has boiled, skim, put a lid on the pan and cook until it is possible to run a fine skewer easily through the meat. Cooking times are difficult to give in general terms, as so much depends on the meat and the dish to be made. An average of 20 minutes to the pound plus 20 minutes over is a good rough guide for beef and mutton; 25–30 minutes per pound for pork, bacon and ham (minimum 45 minutes), 30 minutes per pound and 30 minutes over for salt beef.

Small joints do not lend themselves so well to boiling as larger ones and easily get overcooked and tough. The water must never be allowed to boil fast or the meat will be tasteless as well as hard. For a tender joint with a full rich flavour, simmer gently. Keep the liquid for soups and gravies.

Braising

This is an excellent way of cooking cheaper and less tender cuts. First brown the meat in enough melted fat to cover the bottom of the pan; then brown some mixed diced vegetables—carrots, onions, parsnips, turnips and potatoes—and drain off all surplus fat. Season to taste, add a bouquet garni, put the meat on top of the vegetables in the saucepan or casserole, pour in about half a pint of stock or water, cover with a tight-fitting lid and simmer very gently, either in the oven or over a low heat until the meat is tender. This method is ideal for small joints, kidneys, cutlets, fillets, sweetbreads, etc.

Pot Roasting

This is a very similar method to braising except that no liquid is used, the meat being cooked in a saucepan in fat only. A very strong saucepan is necessary or it will burn. Brown the meat—and the vegetables, if these are to be cooked with the joint— exactly as for braising. Leave the surplus liquid fat in the saucepan with the meat, put on a tight-fitting lid and cook very slowly till tender, allowing 40–45 minutes per pound, according to the thickness of the meat.

Stewing

This is often the busy housewife's refuge when she has little time to spare and a meal to cook for the family. Once a stew is prepared, it needs little or no attention—except to see that it never actually boils. This is all-important—to keep it simmering gently only. A stew cooks equally well on the top of the stove in a saucepan with a well-fitting lid or in a covered fireproof dish or casserole in the oven. The cheaper cuts of meat can be cooked slowly in this way until they are tender, preferably with not too much liquid and plenty of vegetables and seasonings. Allow between 2 and 3 hours. When done, the gravy should be thick and rich.

Grilling

One of the most delicious ways of cooking meat, it is also one of the quickest. For this reason it is suitable only for the best thin cuts, such as lamb or pork chops, fillets of beef, steaks, kidneys, sausages, bacon and ham. First, make sure that the grill is red hot when you start cooking the meat. Next, grease and warm the grid. Spread the meat lightly on both sides with butter or let it stand for a few minutes on a plate in olive oil. Season it, put it on the heated and greased grid, and let it sizzle gently until one side is cooked. Turn it with two knives or plastic meat tongs, but never with a fork because, if the meat is punctured, the juices will run out and much of the goodness and flavour be lost. Cook the other side, basting with the liquid fat.

The time required varies according to the thickness of the meat but, roughly, steak should take 8–20 minutes (depending on thickness and also on whether it is preferred well- or under-done); cutlets 7–10 minutes, kidneys about 8 minutes, bacon rashers between 3 and 5 minutes (according to thickness), sausages about 10 minutes.

Frying

This is a tasty way of cooking meat, whether it is deep- or shallow-fried, but much less digestible than grilling. Oil, lard, vegetable fat or clarified dripping may be used and should be heated until a faint blue smoke rises from the pan. (Beyond this point it will smoke and burn, and the fat become unsuitable for further use. The test of a high-quality frying fat or oil is that it can be heated to at least 360° F. before it begins to smoke or burn.)

For deep-fat frying, a deep but not too wide and very solid saucepan is needed and a frying basket that will fit into it easily. Meat to be fried is usually covered either with flour and egg and breadcrumbs, or batter. If in flour and egg and breadcrumbs, it should be put into the basket

For crisp crackling like this, get your butcher to score the pork, then baste it frequently while roasting. And don't forget the apple sauce!

and lowered into the hot fat, which should nearly half-fill the pan. Meat coated in batter should be lowered straight into the pan and not put into a frying basket because the batter tends to stick to the wires; as it cooks, it rises to the top and can be easily taken out with a fish slice or ladle.

Do not try to fry too much at a time, as this reduces the temperature of the fat. Remember to heat up the fat again to the point where the faint blue haze appears before putting in another batch for cooking. When the meat is cooked, drain well on kitchen paper and keep hot.

Shallow-frying is the method used for food not encased in batter or flour, egg and breadcrumbs. A frying pan is used and only just enough clean, moisture-free fat (vegetable oil or fat, lard or clarified dripping) to cover the bottom. Heat until the faint blue haze appears, then put in the meat, brown it on one side and turn it for the other side to brown. Allow the same times as for grilling. When shallow-frying fat bacon, heat the pan well but do not use any fat; just put in the rashers and cook them in their own fat.

Of the two methods, deep-fat frying, though it needs far more fat to begin with, is the more economical since the same fat can be used again and again, provided it is kept in good condition. After use and when it has cooled a little, it should be run through a strainer into a jar.

To clarify fat.—Fat that has become brown and discoloured or contains particles of food can be clarified for future use. Put the fat into a saucepan and cover it with water. Bring to the boil, stir in a pinch of bicarbonate of soda and pour into a clean basin and leave to cool. When cold, the fat will rise and form a cake on top. Lift this off, scrape away any sediment from underneath, wipe the fat and put aside for future use. If required for frying, melt the fat again in a saucepan and heat until it stops bubbling—an indication that no more water remains in it. Cool and store for frying.

To render fat.—Any scraps of fat from beef, mutton, pork or veal may be used. Remove skin, flesh and discoloured parts, then cut the fat up small, put into a strong saucepan and cover with cold water. Simmer, without a lid on the pan, for several hours, stirring from time to time, until the remaining liquid is clear yellow. Cool, strain through a cloth and use for all frying.

Roasting

(1) Put the joint on a rack in a baking tin with the fat side upwards and some pieces of dripping on top. Stand this tin in a larger tin and put a little water in the lower one, filling it up when necessary. The steam from the water helps to keep the joint moist and prevents it from shrinking. Cover the meat with greased paper—partly to prevent it from getting scorched and partly to keep the oven clean. The oven should be very hot for the first 10 minutes, moderate for the rest of the cooking time. Allow roughly 20 minutes for each pound of meat and 20 minutes over for beef and mutton; say, 25 minutes to the pound and 25 minutes over for veal and pork. Baste frequently, particularly if the joint is lean, or to provide good crackling on a joint of pork. Basting is not so necessary when the joint is cooked in a covered roasting tin.

(2) Large joints are better cooked at a moderate temperature throughout and the cheaper cuts should always be roasted slowly at low temperature.

To Make Gravy

Drain off the fat from the baking tin, leaving only the sediment, and put the tin over a low heat, add a little pepper and salt and some stock or vegetable water, and stir well. Serve it clear with beef and mutton.

To thicken the gravy, leave a tablespoonful of the liquid fat with the sediment, stir in a tablespoonful of flour and cook for 5 minutes until brown, stirring frequently, then add stock or vegetable water and seasoning, together with a little browning if liked.

BEEF

Beef à la Mode (for 4)

2 lb. lean beef	3 oz. butter or dripping
Stock	ping
Bouquet garni	Pepper and salt to
A few button onions	taste
and mushrooms	6 small carrots

Wash and peel vegetables and halve mushrooms and carrots. Fry the meat

MEAT

quickly and lightly on all sides in the melted butter or dripping, turning it with tongs or knives (not a fork, to avoid piercing it and letting the juices escape). Add stock, not quite to cover the meat, also the vegetables and bouquet garni and seasonings. Simmer gently for 2–3 hours until meat is really tender; cool and skim fat from gravy; reheat and serve hot from casserole.

Beef Olives (for 4–5)

1 lb. lean beefsteak cut very thin in small slices	1 oz. butter or dripping
½ pint stock	Pepper and salt
1 dessertspoonful mushroom ketchup	1 oz. flour
	Veal stuffing (see Poultry chapter)
1 onion	

Make some veal stuffing. Put the slices of meat on a board and spread them with stuffing, keeping it well away from the edges. Roll them and put them four deep on a skewer or tie them up separately with cotton. Shake a little flour over them. Melt the butter and, when hot, fry the sliced onion until brown. Put the onion into a casserole, then fry the meat until brown and add it to the onion.

Make some thick gravy in the frying pan with the flour and stock, season and strain it over the olives. Put the casserole either in a moderate oven or over a slow flame and cook for 2 hours or more until the meat is tender. Add the mushroom ketchup just before serving. Garnish with shredded cooked carrot and turnip in little heaps, sprinkling chopped parsley over them.

NOTE: Cold under-done beef can also be made into olives, but in this case fry the onions only, add the olives to the gravy and cook over a low heat or in the oven for 30 minutes, then serve.

Beef Roll (for 4–5)

1 lb. fresh minced beef	1 dessertspoonful flour
2 bacon rashers, chopped	1 gill stock
	Pepper and salt
2 oz. breadcrumbs	Pinch of dried herbs
	1 egg

Mix the dry ingredients together in a basin and add the stock and beaten egg. Bind the mixture together and form into a roll on a floured board, pressing the edges well together. Scald a pudding cloth, flour it and put the roll in it, tying it securely. Steam for 1½ hours and serve cold.

A hot beef roll can be baked or steamed. If baked, cover with greased paper and baste well. Serve with brown or tomato sauce.

Beef Stew (Economical) (for 4–5)

1 lb. shin or thick flank of beef or oxtail or oxcheek	1 level tablespoonful flour
¼ pint water or brown stock	Pinch of herbs, if desired
Seasoned flour	Onion, carrot and turnip
	Fat for frying

Wipe the meat, cut it into small pieces, roll it in seasoned flour and fry quickly in a saucepan or casserole in just enough fat to prevent it burning. Then add the water or stock and the cut-up vegetables and herbs, bring to the boil and simmer very gently for about 2 hours.

Make a smooth paste with the flour and a little water, and add, stirring well, just before the stew is done. Simmer gently for 5 minutes.

If dumplings (see Pastry chapter) are served, give them 20 minutes' cooking and then remove them, putting them on a hot-plate while you stir in the flour. Then replace them if the stew is to be served in a casserole, or put them with the stew on a hot dish.

Boiled Beef and Dumplings

Silverside, thick flank, brisket, aitch-bone or round of beef	Carrots, turnips and onions

Weigh the meat and rinse it well. Allow 20 minutes for each pound and 20 minutes over. Put the meat into enough warm water to cover it and bring it slowly to the boil. Skim, then simmer very gently, adding the sliced vegetables ½ hour before the end. Suet dumplings (see Pastry chapter) may be added, and these will take 20 minutes to cook. Serve a little of the liquid in a sauce boat.

Braised Beef (for 5–6)

2 lb. round, shin, thick flank or rib of beef (boned, rolled and skewered) or oxtail or oxcheek	2 oz. butter or dripping
	Onion, carrot, turnip, parsnip, celery, as desired
	Pepper and salt
About 1 gill water	

Wipe the meat and tie it into shape. Melt the fat in a deep casserole or saucepan. Peel and cut up the vegetables and put them in with the seasoning. When they are hot, add the meat and the water. Put a piece of greased paper under the lid and cook in a slow oven for at least 2 hours.

Casserole of Beef (for 4–5)

1 lb. lean beefsteak	¼ pint stock (or water with a little Marmite)
1 large onion	
1 carrot	
1 turnip	Seasoning
Small head of celery	1 oz. butter or dripping
1 tablespoonful flour	

Cut the steak into fair-sized pieces and dip in the seasoned flour. Heat the butter in a frying pan, slice the onion and fry it quickly until brown. Put it into a casserole, then fry the meat quickly until brown and place it on top of the onion. Slice the other vegetables and put them on the meat. Pour in the stock. Brown the flour in the remaining fat in the frying pan, add enough water or stock to make it into a paste and

cook until it thickens. Strain it into the casserole and cook in a slow oven, or on the hot-plate, for at least 1½ hours. A half-teaspoonful of anchovy essence or two or three cloves add very much to the flavour. Boiled macaroni, separately cooked, may be placed round the dish when serving.

Grilled Fillets of Beef or Steak
(Tournedos)

Cut the meat into neat rounds about 1½ in. thick, season and grill for about 8 minutes, using plenty of butter or olive oil and turning once. (For grilling see p. 57.) The fillets can be served on a bed of mashed potatoes, or any green vegetable, and garnished with a little shredded horse-radish on each fillet, or a pat of maître d'hôtel butter (see chapter on Sauces). Serve with a good gravy.

A more elaborate way is to fry some croûtes of bread exactly the size of the fillets and serve the fillets on these, topped with a mushroom and a little butter. A scrape of horseradish may also be added.

Grilled Steak

Always beat steaks hard on both sides with a rolling pin or large wooden spoon before cooking. Then grill as described earlier in this chapter, adapting the time according to whether it is liked under- or well-done. Steak may be slashed three or four times across the top and a piece of butter inserted in each. Serve with vegetables according to taste, and garnish with grilled tomatoes, mushrooms and fresh watercress.

Jugged Beef (for 7–8)

2 lb. thick lean beef-steak	Port, claret or marsala
2 rashers of fat bacon	2 tablespoonfuls flour
1 large onion, peeled and sliced	Rind of half a lemon, 4 cloves, bay leaf, bunch of herbs (in muslin bag)
1 pint stock or water	
2 oz. butter or dripping	
1 carrot	1 tablespoonful red currant jelly
Forcemeat balls (see chapter on Poultry)	

Cut the meat into 1-in. cubes and roll in flour. Cut the bacon into cubes. Melt the butter or dripping in a frying pan and, when hot, fry the onion until brown. Put it into a deep casserole or saucepan. Then fry the meat and bacon until brown and add them to the casserole with the stock, the carrot (cut in half), and the lemon rind, cloves, etc., tied up in a muslin bag.

Specially cooked and photographed in the Creda kitchens

An appetising way of serving Haricot Mutton, garnished with small whole onions and rosettes of mashed potato. With it go chicory and young carrots in white sauce and green peas

Make some thick gravy in the frying pan with a little stock or water and flour and strain it into the casserole. Simmer gently for 2 hours, or cook in a moderate oven.

Make forcemeat balls, roll them in breadcrumbs and fry until brown. Put them in the casserole 10 minutes before serving. At the last moment, add the wine as desired and the red currant jelly. Serve with red currant jelly.

Oxtail

Wash the tail well, divide into pieces, then dry. Proceed as for Casserole of Beef (see previous page), but allow a quart of stock or water instead of three-quarters of a pint and cook slowly for 3–4 hours

or longer, if necessary, until the tail is quite tender and the meat comes easily off the bones.

Ox Tongue

Ox tongue	*1 turnip*
1 large onion	*Bunch of herbs in a*
1 large carrot	*muslin bag*
Salt	

Trim the tongue, cleaning the root thoroughly, and let it soak in cold water for 1 hour, or up to 24 hours if the tongue has been smoked and hung for some time. Then put it on its side in a saucepan in tepid water, with the herbs, and bring slowly to the boil. Skim well, and simmer gently for 3 hours, or until tender. Cut up

61

the vegetables and put them in with the tongue for the last $\frac{3}{4}$ hour. Take out the tongue and skin it, then place it on a warm dish and use the vegetables as a garnish.

Serve with caper, Cumberland or parsley sauce (see chapter on Sauces). If to be served cold, press tightly into a round tin only just big enough to take it. Leave to get quite cold, then turn out of tin.

Pressed Beef

4 lb. brisket	A few peppercorns,
1 dessertspoonful salt	2 bay leaves, blade
A pinch of mixed	of mace, a few all-
spice	spice, $\frac{1}{2}$ teaspoonful
Large onion	mixed herbs (tied
Carrot	up in a muslin bag)
Turnip	

For the glaze

1 teacupful stock	1 teaspoonful
Browning	powdered gelatine

Wipe the meat well, rub in the salt and the mixed spice, and leave it in a bowl for 12 hours, turning it once during that time. Put it into a saucepan, just cover with tepid water, add the vegetables, cut up, and the herbs in muslin bag, and bring to the boil. Simmer very slowly for about 2 hours or until the bones can be easily removed. Take out the meat, remove the bones and turn the meat on to a dish. Put another dish on top and heavy weights on this. Leave to get cold. Strain off a cupful of the liquor, add a teaspoonful of powdered gelatine and a little browning to colour it. Stir it well until the gelatine is dissolved. Allow to cool, then pour it over the meat. Before the glaze hardens, garnish the beef either with hard-boiled eggs cut into patterns, or with sprinkles of heaped chopped parsley, or with the remains of the gelatine made darker and cut into fancy shapes.

Roast Beef

Sirloin or ribs of beef are the best joints for roasting, but round of beef, aitchbone or thick flank can also be cooked in this way. They should, however, have longer cooking and frequent basting (see Roasting, p. 58).

Serve with Yorkshire pudding (see Puddings chapter) and horseradish sauce.

Vienna Steaks (for 3-4)

1 lb. lean beefsteak	Very small pinch of
1 rasher of bacon	spice
1 very small onion	1 level tablespoonful
Egg or milk to bind	flour
Pepper and salt	Fat for frying

Mince the beef, bacon and onion, and mix with the spice, seasoning and enough egg or milk to bind. Make into small cakes about 1 in. thick, flour lightly and fry in a very little hot fat, browning quickly on both sides. Then cover the pan and cook very slowly for $\frac{1}{4}$ hour. Serve with thick brown gravy or tomato sauce and either chip or cone potatoes and small tomatoes baked whole.

MUTTON AND LAMB

Boiled Lamb or Mutton

Leg or middle neck can be boiled (see p. 56). Serve either with caper or onion sauce.

Braised Shoulder of Mutton

Shoulder of mutton	1 pint hot water
Onion, carrot,	Pepper and salt
parsnip, turnip,	Bunch of herbs
celery	2 oz. butter or drip-
1 tablespoonful flour	ping

Remove the bone from the meat, or get the butcher to do this. Wipe the meat and tie it into shape. Melt the fat in a deep baking tin or very large casserole and put in the cut-up vegetables, herbs, and pepper and salt. Cook for a few minutes. Put the mutton in a quick oven for 10 minutes, then place it on top of the vegetables, pour over the water and put a piece of greased paper over the meat. Cover with lid or another tin and cook in a slow oven for at least 3 hours, removing the lid for the last $\frac{1}{2}$ hour. Take out the meat, strain off the gravy and put the vegetables round the meat. Then thicken the gravy with the flour and serve separately. Red currant jelly or cranberry sauce should also be served with this dish.

Cutlets—Mutton or Lamb (Fried)

Best end of neck	Dripping or butter
Pepper and salt	Egg and breadcrumbs

Get the butcher to saw off the chine bone; it is then quite easy to separate the cutlets. Wipe the meat and divide up the cutlets, cutting off the end bones. Trim away any superfluous fat and make them as good a shape and as much of a size as possible. Season, brush over with beaten egg, dip in fine breadcrumbs and stand for a few minutes on a piece of paper in a dish or tin. Melt the fat until the blue smoke rises, then put in the cutlets and cook for about 10 minutes, or until they are a nice brown on both sides. Drain well before serving.

The usual way of serving is to prop them up round a heap of mashed potatoes or green vegetables with the bones all the same side, or arrange them in the middle and put a ring of mashed potatoes round. Garnish with green peas, baked tomatoes or mushrooms, and serve with brown onion, piquant or tomato sauce (see chapter on Sauces).

Cutlets—Mutton or Lamb (Grilled)

Prepare as for frying, but instead of egg and breadcrumbs, either spread with butter on both sides or stand in olive oil on a plate for a few minutes, turning them over once (for grilling, see p. 57).

Haricot Mutton (for 4–5)

1 lb. best end of neck or middle neck	2 oz. haricot beans
1 oz. flour	1 onion
1 oz. butter or dripping	1 small carrot
	Pepper and salt
	¾ pint stock (or water)

Soak the beans overnight, put them into cold water and boil gently until soft. Keep them hot. Prepare the meat by cutting off the fat and dividing into small pieces. Melt the butter in a saucepan or casserole and try the sliced onion until pale brown. Take it out and keep hot, then fry the meat and, when brown, remove. Put the flour in the pan and brown it, then add the stock and seasoning and bring to the boil, skimming well. Put the meat and onion back, and the sliced carrot, and simmer gently for 1½ hours. To serve, put the meat on a hot dish, season the sauce and pour over it, and add the beans either in small heaps or at either end. Sprinkle them with parsley. Garnish with any seasonable vegetables.

Hotpot (for 5–6)

1½ lb. best end or middle neck of mutton	1 onion
	2 sheep's kidneys
	1 oz. flour
1½ lb. potatoes	Pepper and salt
½ pint warm stock or water	1 tablespoonful mushroom ketchup
1 oz. dripping	

Cut meat into neat pieces and brown in the hot dripping; then put in a casserole or deep fireproof dish, and sprinkle with salt

For a really substantial and very appetising meal, serve a poached egg on top of a grilled steak, with fresh green peas and beans and new potatoes

and pepper. Brown the sliced onion in the dripping, add it to the casserole, and season. Next, brown the cut-up kidneys, season and add them. Cut half the potatoes into thick slices and the other half into quarters, and put the sliced ones on top of the kidneys. Make a thick gravy with the stock and flour in the frying pan; add the ketchup and strain over the potatoes. Then add the potato quarters and a few pieces of dripping on top. Put on the lid and cook in a moderate oven for 2 hours, removing the lid for the last ½ hour so that the potatoes may brown. Serve in the dish in which it is cooked. Mushrooms may be added if desired.

Irish Stew (for 5–6)

2 lb. middle neck or scrag end of mutton	1 lb. onions
2 lb. potatoes	About ½ pint water
	Pepper and salt

Wipe the meat and cut it up. Peel and cut up the potatoes and onions. Put into a saucepan alternate layers of potatoes, meat, onions and, lastly, potatoes. Add the water and pepper and salt, and simmer very gently for 2 hours.

Ragoût of Mutton (for 5–6)

1½ lb. middle neck	1 bay leaf
Onion, parsnip, turnip	2 oz. dripping or butter
1 pint water	1 tablespoonful mushroom ketchup or a few mushrooms
1 tablespoonful pearl barley soaked overnight	
Pepper and salt	

Wipe and cut up the meat. Brown it in the dripping in a frying pan, then put into a casserole. Dice the vegetables, fry them and put into the casserole with the water, bay leaf, pearl barley, pepper and salt, and ketchup or mushrooms. Bring to simmering point. Cover with a well-fitting lid and cook in a slow oven or on the hot-plate for 2 hours.

Roast Mutton or Lamb

Leg, loin, neck (best end), shoulder or stuffed breast can all be roasted (for roasting, see p. 58).

Serve with mint sauce or red currant jelly.

NOTE: Be careful to serve a shoulder the right way for carving. If you are not certain, put a fork in to find which is the fleshy part, allowing for a deep cut; this part should be farthest away from the carver.

Stuffed Roast Shoulder of Mutton

Take out the bone, wipe the meat well and season. Make some veal stuffing (see Poultry chapter) and put it in the middle of the mutton. Then tie it into shape with a piece of string, or sew it up. Weigh the meat, and roast in the usual way. When about to serve, take off the string or remove stitches.

NOTE: Leg of mutton or breast can also be stuffed and roasted.

PORK, BACON AND HAM

Boiled Bacon

Cover the bacon, in a saucepan, with cold water and bring slowly to the boil. Remove scum as it rises and simmer gently until skin comes off easily. Leave to cool in the cooking water (which, if not too salt, may be used for soups and gravies), remove skin, cover with browned breadcrumbs and serve either reheated or cold.

Boiled Ham

Soak the ham overnight, then put in a saucepan of warm water and bring slowly to the boil, letting it simmer very gently until it is tender. Allow 25 minutes to the pound and 25 minutes over. Test with a skewer or by seeing if the rind comes away easily. If overcooked, the meat will shrink away from the bone. Leave in cooking water until nearly cold, then take out and skin. Sprinkle with baked breadcrumbs and a little moist brown sugar.

To Bake.—Boil as above, but remove from heat just before the ham is cooked, stand in water until nearly cold, then skin and stick with cloves, cover with brown sugar and breadcrumbs, and bake in a moderate oven for 1 hour.

Brawn (for 5–6)

Half a pig's head (pickled)	1 teaspoonful dried herbs, 12 peppercorns (in a muslin bag)
2 onions	
1 tablespoonful chopped parsley	

Put the head in warm salted water for a few hours, and then clean thoroughly with a brush. Put it into enough warm water to cover, with the onions (whole) and the herbs in a bag, and bring to the boil. Sim-

HOW TO BUY MEAT

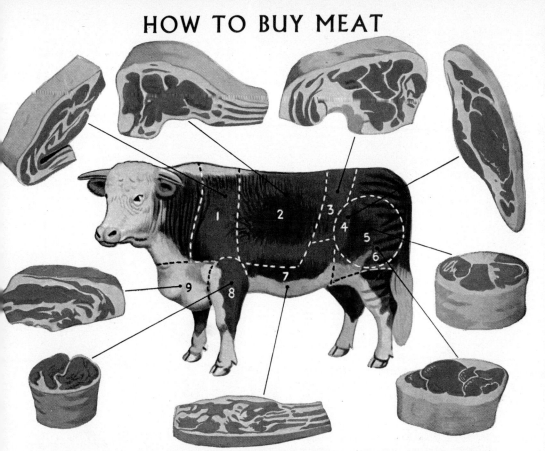

Choose **BEEF** with the help of the diagram above ; the flesh should be rich red and the fat white and firm.
1. Chuck, a cheap cut, needs slow cooking.   2. Ribs are good for roasting.   3. Sirloin is a fine but expensive
joint.   4. Rump—steak for grilling or frying.   5. Silverside will roast, is perfect for traditional boiled beef.
6. Topside; pot roast or cook in casserole.   7. Flank, a cheap cut, for pies and stews.   8. Shin is cheap; use for
beef tea.   9. Brisket is good salted and boiled.

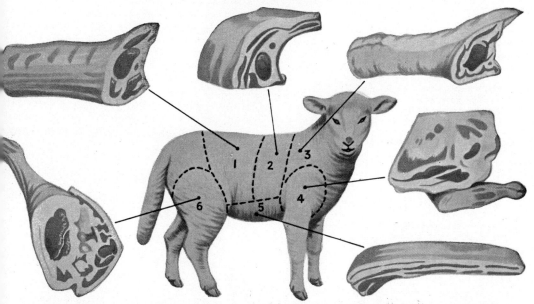

LAMB comes in the following joints, shown above; its flesh should be pink, the fat creamy white and firm.
1. Loin roasts well.   2. Best end of neck, a good roasting joint.   3. Neck makes excellent stews.   4. Shoulder
is a fat but very tasty joint to roast.   5. Breast, the cheapest cut, is good for stewing; can also be boned, stuffed
and roasted.   6. Leg may be roast or boiled.

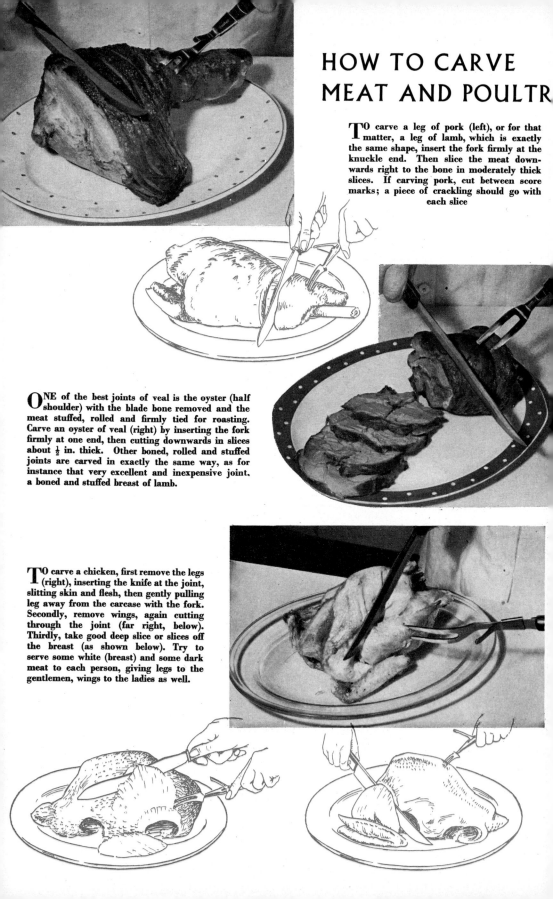

HOW TO CARVE MEAT AND POULTR

TO carve a leg of pork (left), or for that matter, a leg of lamb, which is exactly the same shape, insert the fork firmly at the knuckle end. Then slice the meat downwards right to the bone in moderately thick slices. If carving pork, cut between score marks; a piece of crackling should go with each slice

ONE of the best joints of veal is the oyster (half shoulder) with the blade bone removed and the meat stuffed, rolled and firmly tied for roasting. Carve an oyster of veal (right) by inserting the fork firmly at one end, then cutting downwards in slices about $\frac{1}{2}$ in. thick. Other boned, rolled and stuffed joints are carved in exactly the same way, as for instance that very excellent and inexpensive joint, a boned and stuffed breast of lamb.

TO carve a chicken, first remove the legs (right), inserting the knife at the joint, slitting skin and flesh, then gently pulling leg away from the carcase with the fork. Secondly, remove wings, again cutting through the joint (far right, below). Thirdly, take good deep slice or slices off the breast (as shown below). Try to serve some white (breast) and some dark meat to each person, giving legs to the gentlemen, wings to the ladies as well.

Wield the knife with skill and your meat will go much farther and look and taste better

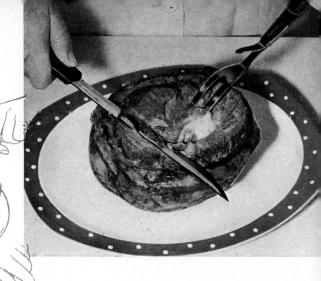

The "Prestige" carving knife and fork are used in all photographs on these two pages, except the veal and the rolled rib of beef, which are carved with the "Prestige" steak slicer

RIB of beef, boned and rolled, is carved across the round (above) in thin slices with a flat knife. To carve an unboned sirloin (diagrams left), first turn over and carve undercut (fillet) down to bone in $\frac{1}{4}$-in. slices. Turn over and slice top meat down to the bone in even slices.

TO carve neck of lamb (right), insert fork firmly between the bones to hold joint upright. Then separate the cutlets between the bones, using a sharp knife.

TO carve shoulder of lamb (below right), put fork firmly near knuckle and tilt joint up. Make deep cuts through the meaty "flap" right down to the bone, carving fairly thick wedge-shaped slices. Then turn joint over (below) and slice meat horizontally from the blade bone. Serve each person with a slice of each cut. Note that, generally speaking, beef is sliced very thin, while it is correct to carve both lamb and veal in quite thick slices. All meat should be cut *across* the grain, except the undercut of a sirloin.

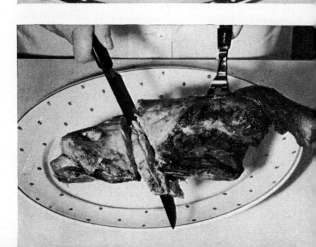

HOW TO BUY MEAT

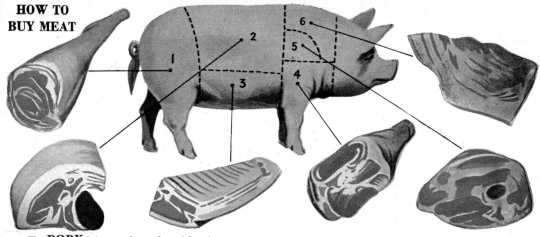

The **PORK** joints to choose from (above) are:
1. Leg, roast or boil. 2. Loin, roast whole or divide into chops and grill. 3. Belly, boil or braise. 4. Hand, salt, boil and serve cold. 5. Blade bone is best braised. 6. Spare rib, either roast whole or cut into chops and grill or fry. Note—ask the butcher to score all pork for roasting.

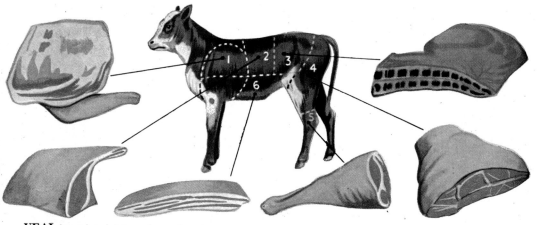

VEAL is cut into joints as shown above:
1. Shoulder, roast either whole or cut in half. 2. Best end of neck, roast or cut into cutlets and fry. 3. Loin provides thin slices for escallops, chops for frying; or stuff and roast. 4. Fillet, good but expensive, is usually fried in slices. 5. Knuckle is cheaper; stew or braise. 6. Breast, a cheap cut, for stewing.

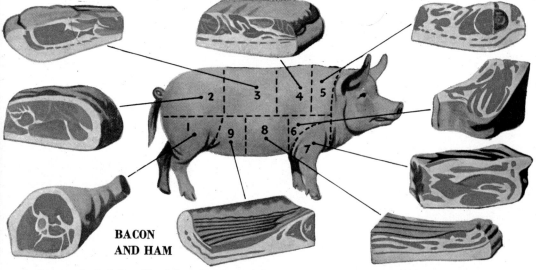

BACON AND HAM

1. Gammon hock, boil and/or bake. 2. Gammon, fry, or boil whole. 3. Long back, best rashers. 4. Prime collar, boil. 5. End of collar, inexpensive; boils well. 6. Slipper, lean; good for boiling. 7. Fore hock, cheaper; good for boiling. 8. Thick streaky, cheaper rashers. 9. Flank, cheaper, with a lot of fat.

mer very gently until the bones can be removed. Take out the meat and, when cool enough, remove the bones. Let the liquor boil rather fast meanwhile, and put in the bones when removed from the head. Cut up the meat into small squares and take out any gristle or skin. Put the squares together with the chopped parsley into a mould (it should be three parts full), then pour in enough strained scalding liquor to fill it to the top. Leave until cold to set. It should be a firm jelly.

Curried Sausages (for 4–5)

1 lb. pork sausages	1 apple
1 oz. butter	1 onion
Curry powder to	Squeeze of lemon
taste	juice
½ oz. rice flour	Salt
Breadcrumbs	1 teaspoonful
Boiled rice	chopped chutney
1 pint stock	

Skin the sausages and cut them in half, then roll in breadcrumbs and fry until brown. Peel and slice the onion and apple. Melt the butter and, when hot, fry the apple and onion, then add the rice flour, curry powder and salt, stirring well, and cook gently for 5 minutes. Add the stock slowly and bring to the boil. Put the sausages and chopped chutney in the sauce and reheat, adding a squeeze of lemon juice right at the end. Serve the sausages on a hot dish surrounded by boiled rice and pour the sauce over them.

Mock Goose (for 3–4)

1 lb. pork sausages,	Sage
skinned	1 lb. mashed potatoes
1 onion	Pepper and salt

Break up the sausages with a fork and put alternate layers of sausage and potatoes, seasoned with chopped onion, sage, pepper and salt into a fireproof dish. Bake until brown and serve with apple sauce.

Pig's Feet

Cover the feet with water, put in a small handful of salt and simmer gently for 6–8 hours. Leave to cool but, while still warm, press out the bones gently with the hand and leave until the following day. Dip in egg and breadcrumbs and fry until a good brown.

Pork Chops

Fried.—Trim each chop into a neat shape, removing nearly all the fat, season

and sprinkle a little flour over them. The fat trimmings can be used to fry them in (for frying, see p. 57). Serve with apple or gooseberry sauce or fry sliced apples and serve round them.

Baked or Grilled.—They may also be baked in a moderate oven and should take about ½ hour; or they can be grilled (see p 57).

Roast Pork

Either leg, loin or spare rib is best for roasting. Get the butcher to score the rind well (for roasting, see p. 57). Serve with apple or gooseberry sauce.

Roast Pork (Stuffed)

Bone the pork. Make sage and onion stuffing (see Poultry chapter), put it in, roll the meat up and tie it firmly. Serve with apple or gooseberry sauce.

Sausages

Fried.—Put the sausages in a tin and pour over them enough almost boiling water to cover them; let them remain in it for 3 minutes. Then take them out, wipe and dry thoroughly, and puncture the skins with a fork. Fry them in a very little fat until they are a good brown, turning frequently. Do not cook them too quickly. Drain well and serve on a bed of mashed potatoes.

Grilled.—Sausages to be grilled should be brushed with fat in the usual way and put under a hot griller. Pork sausages are excellent served with apple sauce, sliced fried apples or bananas.

Toad-in-the-Hole

Make a Yorkshire pudding batter mixture (see Puddings chapter) and leave to stand for at least ½ hour. Melt a little fat in a baking tin and get it really hot in the oven, pour in the batter and then put in the sausages, or skin sausages, put them into the hot fat and pour batter on top. Bake in a moderate oven for 30 minutes.

VEAL

Blanquette of Veal (for 3–4)

1 lb. fillet of veal	1 gill of stock
2 oz. butter	2 or 3 cloves
Pepper and salt	Button mushrooms or
1 bay leaf	small whole toma-
1 tablespoonful flour	toes

Coat the fillet with flour. Melt the butter

in a frying pan and fry the veal until golden brown on both sides. Put the meat and butter into a casserole, add the stock, cloves, bay leaf and seasoning. Put on the lid and simmer for 1½ hours. Add the mushrooms or tomatoes a quarter of an hour before the end. Take out the meat and the mushrooms or tomatoes. Strain the liquor and pour it over the meat. If it is too thick, add a little water and heat it.

Fricassée of Veal (for 3–4)

1 lb. fillet of veal	Half a lemon
1 onion, sliced	Pepper and salt
1 egg-yolk	1 oz. butter
6 peppercorns	1 tablespoonful flour
Pinch of dried herbs	1 gill milk
½ pint water	

Cut the meat into neat pieces and put in a saucepan, with the warm water, and bring it to the boil. Add the herbs, onion, peppercorns, lemon peel and seasoning, and simmer very gently for about 1½ hours. Take up the veal, strain off the stock and make it into a creamy white sauce with the butter, flour and milk (see Sauces chapter). Bring to the boil and cook for 5 minutes. Take off the fire and stir in the beaten egg-yolk and a teaspoonful of lemon juice. Put the meat in the sauce and reheat without boiling. Garnish with rolls of bacon (grilled on a skewer) or grilled rashers, or with fried diamonds or crescents of bread, segments of lemon and small, whole, fried or grilled mushrooms.

Ragoût of Veal (or Rabbit) (for 3–4)

1 lb. lean meat	1 oz. butter
(breast or fillet)	½ pint stock
1 tablespoonful flour	Salt and pepper
Pinch of mixed spice	1 bay leaf
1 large onion	Thyme
Garlic, if desired	Parsley
4 or 5 carrots	Grate of nutmeg

Wipe the meat and cut it into neat pieces. Melt the butter and fry the meat until golden brown, being careful it does not burn. Take it out of the saucepan and keep hot. Make a thick sauce with the flour and stock. Add salt, pepper, mixed spice, herbs, onion (whole), garlic, carrots cut in rounds, and a grate of nutmeg. Put the meat back in the saucepan and cook slowly for 1½ hours, keeping the lid on. Take out the onion and garlic, put the meat on a hot dish with the carrots and strain the sauce over it. Rabbit may be substituted for the meat.

Stewed Knuckle of Veal (for 4–5)

1 turnip	2 or 3 lb. knuckle of
Hot water	veal
¼ lb. rice	1 tablespoonful
2 onions	chopped parsley
1 carrot	Pepper and salt
Squeeze of lemon	Small dumplings
juice	(see Pastry chapter)

Wipe the meat with a damp cloth. Put it into a saucepan with enough hot water to cover, bring to the boil and skim. Put in the chopped onions, carrot and turnip, and seasoning, and simmer slowly for 1½ hours. Add the rice (well washed) for the last ½ hour of the cooking. Small dumplings should be added during the last 10 minutes. Add a squeeze of lemon juice right at the end. Put the meat on a hot dish, surrounded by the rice and vegetables, and sprinkle with chopped parsley, or serve with parsley sauce.

Stuffed Veal

Boned breast (or fillet	Lemon juice
or loin) of veal	Veal stuffing (see
Pepper and salt	Poultry chapter)

Put the meat flat on a board, the skin side underneath, and rub with a little lemon juice. Then season, spread the stuffing over it, roll it up, skewer and tie securely. Trim the ends if necessary. Put in a baking tin and roast in the usual way.

NOTE: It is quite simple to bone the meat if you cannot get the butcher to do it. Simply spread it flat on the table and, with a short, sharp knife, prise out the bones, taking excess fat too. These can be used separately for a stew, casserole or soup.

Veal Cutlets (for 3–4)

1 lb. fillet of veal	½ pint brown, mush-
1 egg	room or tomato
Breadcrumbs	sauce (see Sauces
A little lemon juice	chapter)
and rind	2 oz. dripping
Chopped parsley	Rolls of bacon
Boiled potatoes	Pepper and salt

Cut the veal into neat rounds or ovals and, if necessary, beat them until they are a good shape. Squeeze a little lemon juice over them. Break the egg on a plate, beat it and add the chopped parsley, seasoning, lemon juice and rind. Dip the cutlets into this mixture and then roll them in the breadcrumbs, pressing them on well. Leave to stand until dry. Meanwhile, make whichever sauce is preferred and mash

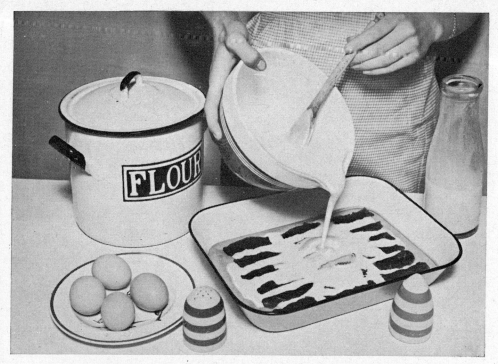

Toad-in-the-Hole consists of a Yorkshire pudding batter poured over sausages, which are nicer if skinned; or you can make it with small chops instead of sausages

some freshly cooked potatoes. Put a few small rolls of thin slices of bacon on a skewer and cook in the oven. Melt the dripping in a frying pan and, when hot, fry the cutlets until they are brown on both sides. Cook fairly slowly and allow between 10 and 12 minutes. Drain well. To serve, pile them on a heap of mashed potatoes, peas or spinach and garnish with lemon and bacon rolls. Serve the sauce separately.

Veal Galantine (for 6 or more)

1 lb. veal (breast or shoulder)	4 oz. breadcrumbs
½ lb. ham or bacon	2 hard-boiled eggs
Rind of half a lemon, grated	1 tablespoonful chopped parsley
	Egg to bind

For the glaze

1 cupful stock	Meat extract
1 teaspoonful powdered gelatine	

Mince the veal and ham, and make it into a firm dough with the breadcrumbs, parsley, lemon rind and egg to bind. Put it on a wet board and press it out flat, then lay the hard-boiled eggs, cut in thick slices, down the centre and fold over, pressing the edges well together. Scald a pudding cloth,

flour it and put the roll in, tying it loosely. Steam for 1½ hours.

For the glaze.—Make a cupful of stock with any meat extract and add a teaspoonful of powdered gelatine. Stir it well until the gelatine is dissolved. Cool, and put it over the galantine.

Veal in Tomato Sauce (for 3–4)

1 lb. lean veal	2 oz. sausage or chopped ham
1 oz. butter or some olive oil	Salt and pepper
1 onion	3 tablespoonfuls tomato purée
1 small carrot	
Stick of celery	Flour

Put the butter or oil into a saucepan and add the meat (whole), the vegetables (cut up), the sausage (cut in small pieces) and the seasoning. Cook until brown, being careful not to burn. Pour in the tomato purée and sprinkle in a little flour. Stir in some hot water now and again, and simmer the mixture gently until the veal is tender. Serve meat separately with potatoes or other vegetables, the sauce being served with macaroni and grated Parmesan cheese as a first course.

Veal Marengo (for 3-4)

1 *lb. lean veal (breast or fillet)*	1 *dessertspoonful tomato ketchup*
1 *dessertspoonful oil*	*Pinch of dried herbs*
1 *oz. butter*	1 *dessertspoonful flour*
1 *onion*	½ *pint stock or water*
1 *shallot*	*Salt and pepper*
Little garlic, if desired	2 *or* 3 *cloves*

Mushrooms, small onion, dessertspoonful of sherry, if desired

Wipe and cut the meat into pieces, put in a saucepan and fry quickly in the oil and butter, moving it about to prevent burning. Take out the meat and keep hot; then fry the onion and add to the meat. Make a thick sauce with the flour and the stock in the saucepan. Replace the meat and onion, and add salt, pepper, herbs, minced shallot, garlic, tomato ketchup and cloves, cover and simmer gently for 1½ hours. If liked, mushrooms may be added ¼ hour before the cooking is finished.

Arrange the meat on a dish, surrounded by the mushrooms. Strain the sauce and pour over the dish, or serve with small onions put in ½ hour before the end of the cooking. A dessertspoonful of sherry added to the sauce improves the flavour.

OFFAL

Brains

Baked.—Soak the brains well in warm salted water until they are quite clean, then drop in boiling water and boil for 2 minutes. Drain well. Next coat them with egg and breadcrumbs and put in a greased baking tin with some fat bacon on top and bake in the oven until a pale brown. They should take about 20 minutes. Serve with grilled tomatoes or tomato sauce.

Braised.—Soak the brains well in warm salted water until they are quite clean. Slice an onion and put it in a saucepan. Put the brains on the onion, with a little pepper and salt, and a gill of milk. Put a piece of greased paper under the lid and simmer very slowly for about 20 minutes. Take out the brains and put on a warm dish. Thicken the liquor with a little cornflour and simmer for 5 minutes. Remove the onion, add some chopped parsley and pour the sauce over the brains.

Fried.—Soak the brains well in warm salted water until they are quite clean, then drop them in boiling salted water and boil for 2 minutes. Take up carefully and drain well. When cool, flour, egg-and-bread-crumb them, and fry in deep fat until brown. Drain and serve with gravy. Grilled tomatoes are an excellent addition.

Calf's Liver

Fried.—Wash and dry the liver, and cut into slices. Remove the rinds from a few rashers of bacon and fry the rashers. Keep the bacon hot while you fry the liver in the bacon fat for 10-15 minutes, according to the thickness of the slices. Put on a hot dish with the rashers on top. Brown a little flour in the fat, add water and cook for 5 minutes, then season well and pour round the liver.

Grilled.—Wash the liver, dry and cut into slices, put on a plate with a little olive oil and seasoning, and leave for 10 minutes or so, turning the slices over after about 5 minutes. Then put under the hot grill and cook for about 7 minutes.

Fried brains make a delicious and nourishing dish. Serve with grilled tomatoes and garnish with parsley

Fricasée of Veal in a creamy white sauce, colourfully garnished with bacon rolls, mushrooms, parsley, lemon butterflies and diamond-shaped croûtons

Casserole of Liver

Wash and dry the sliced liver and coat it lightly with seasoned flour. Cut the rinds off some thin bacon rashers. Peel and slice one or two onions thinly. Cover the bottom of a casserole with a layer of bacon, then put in layers of onions and liver, continuing alternately until all are used up, ending with bacon. Just cover with hot stock or water, cover and cook in a slow oven for about an hour or until liver is tender.

Kidneys (Devilled) (for 2–3)

4 kidneys	Pinch of salt
1 oz. butter or drip-	Pinch of sugar
ping	1 teaspoonful Har-
1 teaspoonful dry	vey's or Worcester
mustard	sauce and 1 of
	mushroom ketchup

Put the kidneys in very hot water for 2 or 3 minutes, then drop them into cold water. Remove the skins; cut them almost through and lay open. Fry in a little butter or dripping (or brush over with melted butter, season and grill). Take out the kidneys and put on a hot dish. Make a sauce with the mustard, salt, sugar, Harvey's sauce and mushroom ketchup, and put a little in each kidney's centre and shut it up, or else add a little stock and make a thinner sauce to serve separately. Serve with little rolls of grilled bacon on croûtons, or on grilled sliced tomatoes.

Kidneys (Grilled)

Put the kidneys into very hot water for 2 or 3 minutes, then drop them into cold water. This prevents them from curling during cooking. Remove the skin, cut almost through and lay open. Brush over with melted butter, season and grill. Serve each on a croûton of bread with a small pat of maître d'hôtel butter (see French Cookery), closing the kidney on the butter. Sprinkle with a little chopped parsley. They can also be served with grilled tomatoes, bacon or flat mushrooms on the bread, and the kidney on top.

Kidneys and Onions (for 4)

4 large onions	4 kidneys
Stock	1 glass of rum

Carefully peel the onions and scoop out enough of the centres to take a kidney each. Cut a slice off the top of each for a lid. Wash the kidneys and stuff each onion with a kidney, top with the lid, put into a casserole, and half cover with stock. Simmer, with the lid on, for 2 hours, until the kidney is tender and, about 3 minutes before it is cooked, add a glass of rum.

Mock Turtle (for 4–5)

Half a calf's head	Forcemeat balls (see
Small piece of veal	Poultry chapter)
Vegetables	Flour
Mixed herbs	Butter
½ pint mixed sherry	Seasoning
and port	

Wash the head thoroughly and leave to soak. Then boil it with the vegetables, herbs and veal. Take the head out when done and strain off the stock. Next day, cut the meat into square pieces. Put the stock on to boil. Fry some flour in a little butter. When brown, put it into a basin and gradually mix with some of the boiling stock. Then put all back in the pan and bring to the boil. Season with Cayenne, salt and a little Harvey's sauce. Put in the meat and forcemeat balls and reheat. Remove from fire and add mixed sherry and port. Do not let it boil after the wine is added.

Stuffed Heart (Sheep's or Lamb's)

Soak the heart in warm salted water until thoroughly clean. Then take away the pipes from the top and cut through the division in the middle. Stuff with veal stuffing (see Poultry chapter). Tie a piece of greased paper over the stuffing and bake in a very slow oven, either in a casserole with the lid on or in a covered baking tin, for 1–1½ hours. Put plenty of dripping over the heart and baste occasionally. Serve with red currant jelly.

NOTE: Ox heart can also be cooked in the same way, but takes 2 hours. It should be partly steamed first to get the best results.

Sweetbreads

Baked.—Soak in warm salted water for ½ hour, then drop into fast-boiling salted water for 2 minutes. Take out and dry well. Dip in egg and breadcrumbs, or flour them. Put some fat bacon on top, cover with a piece of greased paper and bake in a slow oven for 30 minutes, or according to size.

NOTE: Calves' or lambs' sweetbreads may be cooked in this way, but lambs' sweetbreads take less time.

Braised.—Clean the sweetbreads as above. Slice an onion and a carrot, and put them in a saucepan with the sweetbreads on top, a little pepper and salt, and a gill of milk. Put a piece of greased paper under the lid and simmer very slowly for 40 minutes. Take out the sweetbreads and put on a warm dish. Thicken the liquor with a little cornflour and let it simmer for 5 minutes, put in some button mushrooms, cooked separately in a little stock. Take out the mushrooms and put them round the sweetbreads. Remove the onion and carrot. At the last moment, add a little cream and a beaten egg-yolk to the sauce. Stir well and add a little chopped parsley. Pour the sauce over the sweetbreads and serve.

Tripe and Onions (for 4–5) (see also chapter on English Counties)

1 lb. dressed tripe	1 oz. butter
2 onions	1 tablespoonful flour
1 gill milk	1 pint milk (or milk
Chopped parsley	and water)
Pepper and salt	

Wash the tripe well. Put into cold water and bring to the boil, drain and cut into neat pieces. Put in a saucepan with the pint of milk and simmer for 1½ hours, adding the onions, sliced, for the last ½ hour. Take out the tripe and keep it hot. Make the flour into a paste with the remaining milk added to the liquor, stirring well. Bring to the boil, add the seasoning and butter, and cook for 5 minutes. Pour the sauce over the tripe, and sprinkle with little chopped parsley before serving.

Tripe with Bacon (for 4–5)

1 lb. cooked tripe	Grated rind of half a
4 rashers of bacon	lemon
1 onion, chopped	1 gill of milk
Chopped parsley	1 dessertspoonful
Pepper and salt	cornflour
Milk to cover	Mashed potato

Cut the tripe into strips and put a piece of bacon, some chopped onion, parsley, lemon rind and seasoning on each. Roll up and tie firmly. Put in a saucepan with enough cold milk just to cover, bring to the boil and simmer gently for 20 minutes. Take out the tripe and keep hot. Make a sauce with the liquor and the cornflour made into a paste with the milk. Let it simmer gently for 5 minutes. Put the mashed potato on a dish, arrange the rolls on it and pour over the sauce. Sprinkle with chopped parsley and serve.

POULTRY AND GAME

*How to choose, cook and serve the Christmas turkey, a boiling fowl or
one of the many delicious game birds, with their stuffings and garnishes*

IT is most important when choosing
poultry to be able to tell whether a bird
is young or old. One method of cooking
may be excellent for a little poussin. An
older bird will only be satisfactory if
cooked in quite a different way. Here,
therefore, are the points to bear in mind
when choosing and buying poultry.

Chickens are roughly of three kinds:
(1) *Poussins*, weighing 1–2 lb. each, aged
7–12 weeks, usually roasted and served
whole; or cut into quarters and fried or
grilled.
(2) *Spring Chickens, Fowls and Cockerels*
—the larger type (from 3 lb. upwards)
suitable for roasting. A fowl (hen
weighing up to about 8 lb.) is also excellent for fricassée or casseroles.
(3) *Boiling Hens*—for fricassée, casserole
or boiling.
No chicken, whatever its age, should
have a gamy smell, however slight. The
flesh should be firm, with enough fat to
make the bird nice and plump. Wings and

breast bone should be pliable, feet soft and
rather moist. The older a chicken is, the
harder and dryer its feet and the stiffer its
breast bone.

Duck (or Duckling) can sometimes
weigh as much as 7 lb., but is liable to be
tough if more than 12 months old. A
young bird can be recognised by its bright
yellow feet and bill, which get darker as the
bird grows older. The bill should also be
pliable, the flesh white and the breast feel
nicely meaty.

Wild Duck (or Mallard) is distinguished
by its red bill.

Goose must be under 2 years old at the
very most. Choose for the table a bird
with some down on its legs and with soft
and pliable feet and bill.

Green Goose is a young bird, not more
than 6 months old, and is served roast, but
unstuffed.

Turkey should have black legs, white
flesh, pliable cartilage at the end of the
breast bone, and a broad plump breast.
Though a cock may weigh as much as

20 lb. at only 9 months, the best turkey to choose is a hen of about 7–9 months old. As a general rule, the hens are tenderer and more economical than the cocks, which have heavy bones.

Pigeons.—Both tame pigeons and the larger wild variety should, when young and good for the table, have pinkish legs and claws, well-covered limbs and breasts, and not too dark-coloured skin. They should be eaten fresh.

Game Birds are usually sold unplucked and it is therefore more difficult to judge their condition. Points to look for are soft feet and smooth, pliable legs. In young birds the feathers under the wing and on the breast are soft and downy and the spurs rounded. The breast should be hard and plump.

It is impossible to lay down hard and fast rules as to the length of time game should be hung, because tastes vary so much, and what strikes some as unpleasantly high will prove almost tasteless to others. The birds should always be hung from the neck, unplucked and undrawn, in a cool larder with a good current of air circulating round them. When a feather can be pulled easily from the tail, the birds have hung long enough.

It is also important to know the times of year when it is permissible to shoot the various game birds.

Grouse is in season from August 12th to December 10th.

Hare is in season from August 1st to end of February.

Partridge is in season from September 1st to January 31st.

Pheasant is in season from October 1st to January 31st.

Plover is in season from September 1st to March 1st.

Ptarmigan is in season from August 20th to December 20th.

Snipe is in season from August 12th to January 31st.

Wild Duck is in season from August 12th to January 31st.

Wild Goose is in season from August 1st to March 15th.

Woodcock is in season from August 12th to January 31st.

Quail and *Wood Pigeon* are in season all the year round.

Guinea Fowl is in season when game is not. The flesh tends to dryness, but it can be cooked in any way suitable for a chicken: well larded and roasted, or stewed being the two favourite methods.

Hare and *Rabbit.*—Hares should be hung (not paunched) in a cool place in a good current of air for at least a week, according to the weather. They must be very well cooked and the flesh should not be reddish in colour.

Tame rabbits have a more delicate flavour and are much tenderer than wild ones, have an almost white flesh and take less time to cook. Many people, however, favour the stronger flavour of the wild variety. But wild or tame, the flesh of a rabbit suitable for the table should be quite stiff and without any discoloration. If young, the teeth are small and white and the claws long and pointed. In an older rabbit, the teeth are long and yellow and the claws round and rough. Rabbits should be cooked and eaten fresh.

Preparing Poultry and Game

Poultry and game are now nearly always purchased ready for the table. In the country, however, there may be occasions when the housewife is required to pluck, draw and truss a bird herself, so here are instructions on how to do it.

To Pluck and Singe.—Holding the bird firmly with its neck facing your right, pull out the feathers one at a time, grasping them firmly between the finger and thumb, taking care not to damage the skin. Singe the bird all over with a lighted taper to remove stubs of old feathers.

To Draw.—Cut off the head and neck close to the body but leaving the skin loose. Remove the crop and windpipe, bend and snap off legs just below the joint, then pull out, one at a time, the eight tendons in each leg (if not removed, these will make the bird tough). Put the forefinger inside the bird and loosen the heart, etc., inside the breast, working the finger from left to right. Then lay the bird on its back and make a crossways slit just above the tail. You should then have an opening large enough to allow the insides to be first loosened with the fingers and then drawn away in one mass. Cut the gall bladder away from the liver, being very careful not to break the gall bladder, as this would give a bitter taste to the flesh;

slit the gizzard and remove inner skin and contents. Wash the gizzard, liver and neck well and put aside to make gravy. Wash a fowl under the cold tap and then in cold salted water; wipe out game with a damp cloth.

To Truss for Roasting.—For a roasting fowl, break the long bones above the spur, twist and draw out the sinews. Stuff the bird at the neck end and fold the skin over. Then press the legs forward at the knee joints to the breast bone, turn the wings in and under, and put a trussing needle threaded with string through the wing joint, the leg and the body, drawing it out at the other side through leg and wing. Cross the string on the back, wind round the legs and tail and tie firmly.

To Truss a Fowl for Boiling.—First cut the skin at the knee joints, twist off feet and legs, draw out sinews from the thighs; then, with a finger in the neck end and a thumb against the knee joint, push the legs upwards inside the loosened skin and fold in the lower end of the bird to make a compact shape. Truss with needle and string as for roast fowl.

To Joint.—Any large bird, such as a chicken, can conveniently be divided into twelve pieces as follows:

First cut off legs at thigh joints, then cut each leg into two portions at knee joints, making *four pieces.*

Repeat the process with the wings, making another *four pieces.*

Remove the breast whole, by cutting through the ribs with a pair of scissors, and divide this lengthwise into *two pieces.*

The underneath of the bird can also be divided down the middle lengthwise and gives another *two pieces.*

To Stuff.—After the contents of the bird's inside have been removed and it has been well washed out, stuffing may be put in at either or both ends, and then stitched in with thread, which is, of course, removed before serving.

To Cook Poultry and Game

Larding.—To improve the flavour and overcome the tendency of many birds to dryness, they are often larded. Long thin strips of very hard fat bacon (lardoons) are inserted into the flesh, with the ends sticking out.

A less satisfactory but quicker alternative is to put rashers of fat bacon on the breast of a bird before roasting. A knob of margarine or butter may also be inserted right inside a small bird or fowl to prevent the flesh from becoming too dry during cooking.

Chicken (Boiled)

1 *boiling fowl*	*Salt, pepper, pepper-*
Cloves, if liked	*corns, parsley,*
1 *onion*	*thyme*
	1 *bay leaf*

Place a trussed fowl, with a small onion and a bay leaf inside it, in a large saucepan with a tight-fitting lid, add other ingredients and cover with boiling water. Simmer, with the lid on, but do *not* boil, until the chicken is tender (1½ hours or more, according to size and age of bird). Serve with rice moistened with the chicken liquor and garnish with chopped parsley.

Chicken (Fried)

1 *spring chicken*	1½ *gills milk*
divided into	4 *oz. flour*
quarters	1 *egg*
	Salt and pepper

First steam the chicken until very nearly but not quite tender. Meanwhile, make the other ingredients into a batter. Stand for ½ hour, then dip the pieces of chicken in it and deep-fry them (see Meat chapter) till golden brown (about 10–12 minutes).

Chicken (Roast)

Put the trussed bird on a rack in a baking tin, with some slices of fat bacon, or pieces of dripping, over the breast, cover it with greased paper and put into a hot oven for a few minutes, then lower the heat and cook until tender. A

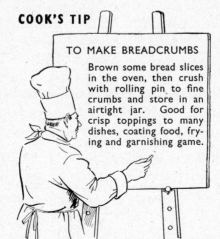

COOK'S TIP

TO MAKE BREADCRUMBS

Brown some bread slices in the oven, then crush with rolling pin to fine crumbs and store in an airtight jar. Good for crisp toppings to many dishes, coating food, frying and garnishing game.

small chicken should take about ¾ hour, a heavier one 1 hour, whereas an older bird may take up to 1½ hours. Baste occasionally. Remove the paper just before the bird is cooked, baste well and brown. Sausages or rolls of bacon may be served with the chicken, which should be garnished with watercress and accompanied by bread sauce.

Put the giblets in a little water, with an onion and a pinch of salt, simmer gently while the chicken is cooking, and use the liquor to make the gravy. Before serving, take out the skewers and remove the string.

NOTE: If the bird is over a year old, it is better to steam it for about 1 hour and then roast it slowly, basting frequently.

Chicken (Steamed)

Put the chicken in a piece of greased paper and place it in a steamer over boiling water. Cook until tender. Allow 1–2½ hours according to age and size. The giblets should be put in the boiling water, as they will make excellent stock which can be used in making thick Béchamel, egg, lemon or parsley sauce to serve with the chicken.

NOTE: In the absence of a steamer, a fowl can be steamed in a colander with a lid on top over a saucepan.

Chicken en Casserole (for 5–6)

1 chicken (4–5 lb.)	1 oz. butter
2½ pints of water	1 tablespoonful flour
3 rashers of bacon	1 or 2 hard-boiled
1 lb. raw sausage	eggs, broken up
meat	Pinch of dried thyme
Pepper and salt	Boiled rice
Breadcrumbs	

Joint a fowl and cook very slowly in 2½ pints of water for about 2 hours, until it is quite tender and easily separated from the bone. Line a 3-pint casserole with well-boiled rice. Put in the chicken, cut into small pieces, the rashers of bacon cut up small and fried, the sausage meat in bits, and the hard-boiled eggs cut up. Thicken the stock, which should measure 1–1½ pints, with the flour, season, and add a tiny pinch of dried thyme. Strain into the casserole and bake for 1 hour. Take off the lid of the casserole, put some browned breadcrumbs and a few dabs of butter on the top, and return to the oven without the lid for 5 minutes or so. Then serve. A very little onion can be added if liked.

Chicken Fricassée (for 4–5)

A young chicken	2 oz. butter
1 onion	1 dessertspoonful
1 egg-yolk	cornflour
6 peppercorns, pinch	1 pint white stock, or
of dried herbs (in	milk and water
muslin bag)	A squeeze of lemon
Pepper and salt	juice
A little milk	

Cut the chicken into joints and remove as much of the skin as possible. Put in a saucepan with the stock, onion, herbs, peppercorns and seasoning, and simmer very gently for ¾ hour. Remove the chicken and keep it hot. Strain off the liquor. Put the stock back into the pan, make a paste with the cornflour and a little milk, and add it to the stock, stirring all the time. Bring to the boil and simmer for 5 minutes. Remove from the heat and add the beaten yolk, butter and a squeeze of lemon juice. Reheat without boiling. Pour the sauce over the chicken and serve with grilled rolls of bacon, or decorate with slices of lemon. If liked, fried bread cut into fancy shapes can be served with it.

NOTE: If cooked chicken is used, simmer the stock, onion, herbs, peppercorns and seasoning together for about 20 minutes, then strain the liquor and make the sauce. Add the chicken and reheat without letting it boil.

Duck (Roast)

Stuff with sage and onion (see p. 76) and roast in the same way as chicken, allowing ¾–1 hour. Serve with apple sauce.

Game (Grouse, Pheasant, Partridge, Snipe, Plover, Ptarmigan, Wild Goose) (Roast)

Cook exactly as for chicken, the time varying with the size and variety:

Grouse and pheasant, 40–50 minutes.
Partridge, ptarmigan, 25–35 minutes.
Snipe, plover, 15–20 minutes.
Wild goose, 15 minutes per lb.

Serve with fried crumbs and bread sauce and garnish with watercress.

To fry crumbs.—Fry 4 oz. fresh breadcrumbs in ½ oz. clarified butter over a gentle heat until brown. Drain and serve.

Goose (Roast)

Stuff with sage and onion (see p. 76) and cook in the same way as chicken, allowing 2–2½ hours. Serve with brown gravy and either apple or cranberry sauce.

Specially cooked and photographed in the Creda kitchens

A piquant Orange Salad is the perfect accompaniment to wild duck, served with peas, creamed potatoes, apple sauce and gravy

Guinea Fowl (Roast)

Roast as for chicken.

Turkey (Roast)

Cook in the same way as chicken, but stuff with chestnut or veal stuffing or sausage meat (see p. 76), and serve with brown gravy and bread or cranberry sauce. Allow 15 minutes to the pound and 15 minutes over.

Salmi of Pheasant (or any Cold Game)

Cut a roast pheasant into neat pieces (see Jointing, p. 73). Make thick brown sauce with trimmings of the bird and some vegetables. Put the pieces of pheasant into the

sauce and reheat without letting it boil. A few stewed prunes and a tablespoonful of sherry or marsala add greatly to the flavour. Serve with red-currant jelly.

Jugged Hare (for 10–12)

A hare	1 tablespoonful red-
Bacon rinds or bone	currant jelly
1 large onion	1 stick of celery
1½ pints water	2 tablespoonfuls flour
2 oz. butter or drip-	Rind of half a lemon,
ping	4 cloves, 1 bay leaf,
1 carrot	bunch of herbs (tied
Port, claret or	up in muslin bag)
marsala	Veal stuffing

Wash and cut up the hare, and flour the pieces. Melt the butter in a frying pan and

75

when hot, fry the sliced onion until brown. Put into a deep casserole or saucepan. Then fry the meat until brown, add to the casserole with the carrot, cut in half, the celery, cut up, and the lemon rind, cloves, etc., in a muslin bag, add the bacon rinds and, lastly, the water. Make some thick gravy in the frying pan with a little stock or water and flour, and strain it into the casserole. Simmer gently for 2 hours on the hot plate, or in a moderate oven. Make forcemeat balls (see below), roll in breadcrumbs and fry until brown, then put into the casserole 10 minutes before dishing up. Just before serving, remove the carrot, celery, bacon rinds and herbs, add the wine as desired and a tablespoonful of red-currant jelly. Serve with red-currant jelly.

Stewed Rabbit (for 4–5)

1 rabbit	Pepper and salt
2 large onions, sliced	1 tablespoonful flour
2 fresh, streaky pork	1 oz. butter
rashers	½ pint milk
½ pint water	

Wash, dry and cut the rabbit into neat pieces. Put first the rabbit, then the pork and lastly the onions into the saucepan, add the milk, water and seasoning. Bring to the boil and simmer gently for 1¼ hours.

Take up the meat and onions and put them on a hot dish. Strain off the liquor and make it into a sauce with the flour, butter and a little milk. Bring to the boil and cook for 5 minutes. Pour the sauce over the rabbit and serve. A few button mushrooms put in ¼ hour before the rabbit is cooked add greatly to the flavour.

STUFFINGS AND GARNISHES

Chestnut Stuffing (sufficient for medium-sized turkey)

2 lb. chestnuts, par-boiled	1 rasher of bacon
Liver of turkey, par-boiled	2 oz. butter
	Pepper and salt

To parboil the chestnuts, cut a slit in the skins, plunge into boiling water and leave to soak for 20 minutes. Then put them in the oven to crisp the skins, after which they should peel easily. Mince the chestnuts, liver and bacon. Add the butter,

warmed, and the seasoning, and mix well together.

Liver Forcemeat

½ lb. liver (cooked)	A little stock
2 oz. fat bacon	2 oz. breadcrumbs
1 small onion	Salt and pepper
A grate of nutmeg	

Mince the liver and bacon, add the finely chopped onion, the breadcrumbs soaked in a little stock, seasoning and nutmeg. Add more stock, if necessary, to moisten the mixture so that it will bind.

This forcemeat can be used to stuff game or chicken.

Sage and Onion (sufficient for 2 ducks or a goose)

4 onions	4 oz. breadcrumbs
1 dessertspoonful powdered sage or 6 leaves of fresh sage	1 oz. butter
	Egg to bind
	Pepper and salt
	Stock or water

Peel the onions, chop finely and simmer in a little water or stock until tender. Add the sage (chopped or powdered), breadcrumbs, butter, pepper and salt, and stir well. Then add enough beaten egg to bind. If preferred, this can be served in a sauce boat instead of as a stuffing, in which case omit the egg and add instead enough stock to make it into a purée.

Sausage Stuffing (sufficient for medium turkey)

1 lb. sausage meat	2 oz. breadcrumbs
½ teaspoonful mixed herbs	1 teaspoonful chopped parsley
1 egg	

Break up the sausage meat with a fork, mix in other ingredients and bind with egg.

Veal (or Forcemeat) Stuffing (sufficient for 2 chickens or rabbits or a turkey)

4 oz. breadcrumbs	1 dessertspoonful chopped parsley
1 oz. chopped suet	Milk or egg to bind
Grated rind of ½ lemon	Chopped ham as desired
Pepper and salt	
Pinch of dried herbs	

Put all the dry ingredients in a basin, mix them well, and then add enough milk or beaten egg to make into a stiff paste which will bind together very firmly.

NOTE: May be used for fish as well as meat and poultry.

Aspic Jelly

1½ pints water
¼ pint mixed vinegars
  (Tarragon and
  French wine)
Small carrot, onion
  and turnip
A few peppercorns
Small piece of celery
Rind and juice of half a lemon
2½ oz. sheet gelatine
Egg-white and egg-shell

Cut the vegetables into small pieces. Put all the ingredients, except the egg, into a stewpan and stir until the gelatine is dissolved. Add the egg-shell and the egg-white and whisk well until it forms thick scum on the top. Boil well and then draw to side for 20 minutes. Pour gently through a jelly bag or cloth.

Aspic jelly is used to make cold savoury dishes containing meat, game, poultry, fish, vegetables and/or hard-boiled eggs in moulds. Line a mould (or small individual ones) with aspic jelly, add chopped cooked meats, etc., fill up with jelly and put in cool place to set. It should be firm enough to turn out for serving.

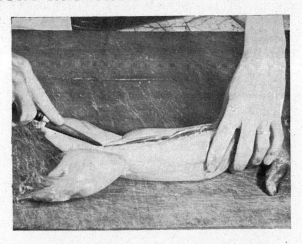

To bone a rabbit: (1) Slit along each side of backbone from neck end and remove meat

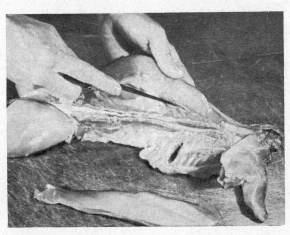

(2) Remove saddle portions, keeping knife close to bone, and sever backbone where back legs join body (above)

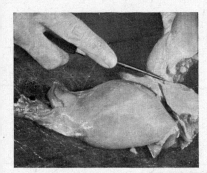

(3) Cut away leg portions, removing as much meat as possible with each (above)

(4) Ease out leg bones, starting at point nearest body, scraping meat from bone as you pull it (right)

Aspic Jelly (Quick Method)

1 teaspoonful
  Marmite
½ pint water
2 level teaspoonfuls
  powdered gelatine
Seasoning
1 teaspoonful lemon
  juice
1 dessertspoonful
  Tarragon vinegar

Heat the water, add the Marmite, seasoning and gelatine, and stir well until the gelatine is dissolved and the mixture clear. Then remove from the fire, add the lemon juice and vinegar, and stir well.

SAVOURY PIES
AND PUDDINGS

*Combined with a pastry or suet crust, either meat or
poultry makes a substantial and tasty main course*

Beef or Mutton Patties (for 5–6)

8 oz. rough puff or puff pastry	Beaten egg

Filling for Beef Patties

6 oz. fresh meat (minced) A little chopped kidney Pepper and salt Stock to moisten	To be mixed together

Filling for Mutton Patties

6 oz. fresh mutton (cut very small) 1 teaspoonful chopped onion 1 teaspoonful chopped parsley Pinch of mixed herbs Pepper and salt Chopped mushroom Stock to moisten	To be mixed together

Make a rough puff or puff pastry (see Pastry chapter) and grease patty pans. Roll out to about $\frac{1}{4}$ in. thick and leave for 5 minutes to allow for shrinking. Then cut out rounds to fit the patty pans, allowing two rounds for each. Put one into the bottom of each pan, and fill with meat mixture. Moisten the edges and put on the tops, pressing them firmly together. Nick up the edges with the back of a fork and make a hole in the centre. Decorate with small pastry leaves.

Bake the patties for about 45 minutes, lowering the heat after the pastry has risen well. Brush with beaten egg 10 minutes before they are to come out. Test with a skewer before removing them from the oven.

Chicken or Veal Patties (for 4–5)

8 oz. rough puff or puff pastry

Filling for Chicken Patties

4 oz. cooked chicken, cut very fine 1 oz. ham or bacon, cut very fine Squeeze of lemon juice A little cream to moisten	pounded together

Filling for Veal Patties

4 oz. cooked veal, cut into small dice A little grated lemon rind 1 oz. ham or bacon, cut into small dice 1 hard-boiled egg, if liked (chopped) Pepper and salt White stock	well mixed together

Make patty cases as for Beef or Mutton Patties. Mix together either the chicken or veal filling, heat it and then pile it into the patty cases. Put on the lids and put the patties into the oven for 2 or 3 minutes to heat through.

Cornish Pasty (see Recipes from English Counties)

Egg and Bacon Pie (for 4)

8 oz. potato or short-crust pastry (see Pastry chapter) 2 tablespoonfuls milk	4 large or 6 small rashers bacon 2 eggs Salt and pepper

Line a pie plate with half the potato or shortcrust pastry. Cut the bacon rashers into slices and scatter over the pastry. Then pour on the eggs lightly beaten with the milk and seasoning, cover with a pastry lid and bake in a hot oven for 25–30 minutes. Serve hot or cold.

Mutton Pudding (for 6–8)

2 lb. best end or middle neck mutton Onion	Chopped parsley Pepper and salt Stock or water $\frac{1}{2}$ lb. suet crust
A few mushrooms	

Grease a pudding basin and get ready a pudding cloth. Slice the meat away from the bones and cut into small pieces. Make suet crust and roll it until it is large enough to line the basin, leaving enough to cover the top. Put in the meat, chopped onion and parsley in layers, and season. Then add a few mushrooms and fill with white stock or water. Moisten the edge of the suet crust and put on the top, pressing the edges well together. Put a piece of greased paper over it, then the pudding cloth, and steam over boiling water for about $2\frac{1}{2}$ hours.

Pork Pie (for 4–5)

$\frac{3}{4}$ lb. lean pork 2 tablespoonfuls hot stock or water	Salt and pepper Hard-boiled egg Egg for coating
Pinch of sage	
$\frac{1}{2}$ lb. hot-water pastry (see Pastry chapter)	

**Raised Pork Pie, the top ornamented with pastry whirls, makes a delicious cold
main dish—so do Beef or Mutton, Chicken or Veal patties**

Cut meat into small pieces and season it.

Line a tin with the pastry while it is warm, leaving enough for the top. Fill the tin with the pork and hard-boiled egg cut in slices, and sprinkle in the sage. Pour in 2 tablespoonfuls of hot water or stock. Moisten the edge of the pie and put on the cover, making a hole in the centre. Decorate with pastry leaves. Brush the pie with egg-yolk and bake in hot oven for 1½ hours.

Add some good stock flavoured with onion (if there are any bones, put them in a stewpan and let them simmer for this) while the pie is cooling.

NOTE: The most suitable tin for making pork pies is a collar tin, the sides of which open on a hinge kept in place by a skewer, thus enabling one to take out the pie very easily. Failing this, use a cake tin with a movable bottom.

Rabbit Pie (for 6–8)

1 rabbit	Grated lemon rind
1 hard-boiled egg	Pepper and salt
Rolls of bacon	Rough puff or short-
Chopped parsley	crust pastry
Stock or water	

Wash the rabbit thoroughly, dry and cut up. Put layers of rabbit, bacon and slices of hard-boiled egg into a pie dish with a pie funnel, and sprinkle each layer with parsley, lemon rind and seasoning. Half fill the dish with stock or water.

Roll out rough puff or shortcrust pastry (see Pastry chapter) to the size of the pie dish (it should be about $\frac{1}{2}$ in. thick). Cut a strip wide enough to fit the edge of the dish; wet the edge and put the strip on. Then moisten the strip and put on the top. Trim round the edge and decorate as desired. Cut a hole in the centre so that the steam can escape, and decorate round the hole. Bake in a very hot oven until the pastry has risen (about 20 minutes), then lower the heat and give it another hour, covering the pie with greased paper. Paint the crust with egg just before the end, raising the heat enough to brown it. Unless the rabbit is a young one, it is advisable to stew and cool it first.

Sausage and Bacon Pudding (for 5–6)

1 lb. sausages	1 dessertspoonful
3 rashers lean bacon	flour
1 onion	White stock or water
1 apple	$\frac{1}{2}$ lb. suet crust
Pinch of dried herbs	(see Pastry chapter)
Pepper and salt	

Grease a pudding basin and get ready a pudding cloth. Cut up the sausages into short pieces and roll the bacon. Make suet crust and roll it out until it is large enough to line the basin, keeping back enough to cover the top. Put in the sausages, bacon, thinly sliced onion and apple, and dried herbs in layers, sprinkling a little flour and seasoning in between each. Fill the basin three parts full with stock or water. Moisten the edge of the suet crust and put on the top, pressing the edges well together. Put a piece of greased paper over it, then the pudding cloth and steam over boiling water for $2\frac{1}{2}$–3 hours.

Sausage Rolls

Sausages	Flaky pastry
Egg-yolk	(see Pastry chapter)

Dip the sausages in boiling water and remove skins with a knife. Cut each in half and roll into shape, using a little flour. Roll out the pastry to $\frac{1}{4}$ in. thick. Cut into squares about 5 in. wide. Place a roll of sausage in the centre of each. Damp all round the edges with beaten egg. Fold the pastry round the sausage and press the edges well together. Trim the edges with a sharp knife. Brush with egg-yolk. Cut three slashes on the top of each sausage roll. Place on a floured baking sheet and bake in a hot oven for 20 minutes.

Savoury Suet Roll

Roll suet crust (see Pastry chapter) into an oblong on a floured board. Make one end slightly wider than the other. Put some chopped bacon, a little chopped parsley, a very small onion, chopped finely, and seasoning on the crust, spreading it to within an inch of the edge. Moisten the edges all round and then roll it up, the narrow end towards the wider one, pressing it firmly as you roll. Put the roll into a scalded, floured pudding cloth, steam for $2\frac{1}{2}$ hours and serve with a good gravy.

Steak and Kidney Pie (for 5–6)

1 lb. rump or beef	Flour
steak	Seasoning
1 kidney (calf's or	8 oz. rough puff or
sheep's)	shortcrust pastry
1 gill water or stock	Egg

Wipe the meat, skin the kidney and cut into small pieces; then dip them into the flour and seasoning. Put the pieces into a pie dish with a pie funnel in the middle and add water or stock. Make rough puff or shortcrust pastry (see Pastry chapter) and proceed as for rabbit pie. Put a piece of greased paper over the pie, bake in a very hot oven until the pastry has risen (about 20 minutes), then lower the heat and cook slowly for about 2 hours, reducing the heat gradually all the time.

NOTE: If beefsteak is used, it is advisable to cook the meat partly first, simmering it very slowly, and then allow it to cool before putting on the pastry. Add the kidney just before you put the crust on, and cook the pie for 1 hour.

Beat an egg and paint the surface of the pie about 10 minutes before you take it out of the oven, increasing the heat to brown. Before serving, add a little hot stock or water. If the pie is to be served cold, add a very little gelatine to the liquid before putting it through the funnel.

For supper or buffet parties, outdoor picnics or TV evenings, sausage rolls are
always popular—and they are quick and easy to make, too

Steak and Kidney Pudding (for 4–5)

1 lb. beefsteak	½ lb. suet crust
1 kidney (ox, calf's or sheep's)	A little water or unsalted stock
A little flour	Seasoning

Grease a pudding basin and get ready a
pudding cloth. Wipe the meat and skin the
kidney, and cut into small pieces. Dip into
the flour and seasoning. Roll out suet crust
(see Pastry chapter) until large enough to
line the basin, leaving enough to cover the
top. Put in the meat, adding a very little
water or unsalted stock. Moisten the edge
of the suet crust and put on the top, pressing the edges well together. Put a piece of
greased paper over it, then the pudding
cloth, and steam it over boiling water for 3
hours. Either turn on to a hot dish or serve
in the basin with a napkin tied round it.
Before serving, cut a small hole in the crust
and add a little hot stock or water through
a paper funnel, replacing the piece of crust.

Veal and Ham Pie (for 7–8)

1½ lb. fillet of veal	2 eggs
4 oz. bacon or ham	1 gill white stock or water
Grated rind of half a lemon	¼ lb. rough puff pastry or shortcrust
Teaspoonful chopped parsley	Salt and pepper

Hard-boil the eggs. Cut the meat into
small pieces; put the salt and pepper,
chopped parsley and lemon rind on a plate
and dip the pieces in. Put alternate layers
of veal, ham and eggs into a pie dish and
add the stock or water.

Make the pastry (see Pastry chapter) and
proceed as for rabbit pie, but cook for 1½
hours only. If preferred, the veal can be
partly cooked first and then allowed to
cool, in which case ½ hour's baking will be
enough.

Vol-au-Vent of Chicken, Meat or Game

Make some patty or Vol-au-Vent cases
from puff pastry (see Pastry chapter). For
the filling any cooked chicken, game or
well-flavoured meat may be used. Flake it
into small pieces and moisten with a rich
white sauce. Season well, add a squeeze
of lemon juice or a little grated lemon rind,
a beaten egg-yolk and, if possible, a little
cream. Heat the mixture, then pile into the
scooped-out patty cases. Put on the lids of
the cases and heat the patties through in the
oven for 2 or 3 minutes. If liked, a little
chopped parsley or chives or other savoury
flavourings may be added to the mixture.

COLD MEAT AND MADE-UP DISHES

There are many tasty ways of using up the remains of a joint

COLD joints are sometimes not very appetising to look at, especially if they have suffered at the hands of an unskilled carver. If they are to be served as they are, it is a good plan to cut the meat into neat slices beforehand, and arrange them on a dish with little bunches of watercress, slices of tomato, celery tops, endive, etc., according to the season. Serve with potatoes baked in their jackets, an attractive salad and a home-made chutney.

Twice-cooked meat loses much of its nutritive value, so when you come to warm up the remnants of joints, remember that the less they are cooked the better. They merely need heating.

Corned Beef Hash (for 5–6)

1 lb. can of corned beef	1¼ lb. cold boiled potatoes
Milk or cream	Pepper and salt

Mix well together the beef and potatoes, chopped small, then season. Put the mixture into a hot, buttered frying pan, moisten with milk or cream, stir well, then spread evenly over the pan and cook very slowly over low heat for 40–45 minutes. (It is safer to use an asbestos mat if the pan is on a direct flame.) Then turn the hash and fold on to a hot dish. Garnish with parsley.

Croquettes

Cold cooked beef, veal or mutton	Flour and egg and breadcrumbs
Equal quantity of cold mashed potatoes	Milk, egg or gravy to bind
Fat for frying	1 or 2 onions
	Chopped parsley
Pepper and salt	

Mince the meat and add it to the mashed potatoes. Cut the onion into slices and fry until brown. Then add them to the mixture with a little chopped parsley, pepper and salt, and enough egg, milk or gravy to make a firm dough. Shape into rounds, ovals or rolls, and sprinkle well with flour,

then roll in egg and breadcrumbs. Fry in deep fat until brown, and serve with brown or piquant sauce (see Sauces Chapter).

Curried Beef, Chicken, Mutton or Veal (for 5–6)

1 lb. cooked chicken, beef, mutton or veal	Boiled rice
	1 teaspoonful chutney
1 oz. butter or dripping	½ pint cold stock or water
1 onion	1 tablespoonful flour
Curry powder to taste	Juice of half a lemon
Pinch of spice	1 dessertspoonful tomato ketchup
1 small apple	Salt

Cut the meat into small pieces. Melt the butter in a saucepan, add the sliced onion and apple, and fry until brown. Stir in the sieved curry powder, flour and spice, and cook for a few minutes. Then add the stock, salt and ketchup, bring to the boil and skim. Simmer for 20 minutes. Add the chopped meat, lemon juice and chutney, and reheat without boiling. A few slices of banana, or some chopped sultanas, or a little grated orange peel can be added according to taste. Serve with boiled rice.

NOTE: If uncooked meat is used, fry the meat first, and after it is added to the curry simmer slowly for 1–1½ hours in a double saucepan.

Ghiac (for 3–4)

1 lb. cooked meat	1 large round of bread
1 large egg	
Sauce to flavour	Pepper and salt
Breadcrumbs	Gravy, stock or soup

Mince the meat, a quarter of which should be fat. Put the bread in a basin, pour hot gravy, stock or soup over it, soak, then beat smooth. Beat the egg and add to the meat with a little sauce to flavour, and seasoning. Mix with the bread. Put the mixture into a greased oblong tin and bake in a moderate oven for 1 hour. Leave to settle for a few minutes, turn on

Left-overs can be turned into tasty dishes, like these made in the Creda kitchens. Top: Roman Pie filled with peas and carrots, Fish Pie and a Sweet Mould made from left-over fruit and custard. Centre: Duchesse Flan—asparagus and egg in cheese sauce. Left: Shepherd's Pie. Right: Meat Rissoles

to a hot dish, sprinkle with breadcrumbs and brown under the grill. Serve with hot gravy.

Ham Cake (for 5–6)

This is an excellent way of using up the remains of a ham.

1½ lb. ham, fat and lean	1 large slice of bread
	½ pint milk
1 egg	

Pound the ham in a mortar or mince it as finely as possible. Boil the bread in the milk, and beat it and the ham well together. Lastly, add the beaten egg. Put the mixture into a mould and bake until it is a rich brown.

Ham Mousse (for 4–5)

½ lb. lean ham	1 gill cream
About ½ pint savoury stock	(unsweetened condensed milk can be used)
2 small teaspoonfuls powdered gelatine	Pinch of Cayenne pepper
Aspic jelly to garnish	

Put the ham through the mincer twice.

Melt the gelatine in a little stock. Strain the rest of the stock on to the minced ham and add the seasoning. Pour in the gelatine and cream and whip together until smooth and frothy. Put the purée into a plain soufflé mould and smooth it down very lightly. Garnish with aspic jelly.

If the mousse is to be turned out of the mould, add another teaspoonful of powdered gelatine and put some slices of hard-boiled egg at the bottom of the mould. When turned out, garnish with aspic jelly.

Chicken, pheasant or veal mousse can be made in the same way, garnished with green peas or baby carrots, and mayonnaise sauce served as a dressing.

Hasty Pie (for 4–5)

1 lb. minced cold meat	1 onion
	1 lb. hot potatoes
Cooked parsnips, carrots, leek, celery, etc.	Pepper and salt
	Gravy
	1 oz. butter
Dripping	

83

Fry the sliced onion in the butter. Line a greased pie dish with mashed potato and then put alternate layers, well seasoned, of onion, minced meat and chopped vegetables. Add some gravy to moisten. Top with a layer of mashed or quartered potatoes and a little oiled dripping, and bake in a moderate oven for $\frac{3}{4}$ hour.

Jombalayah (for 3–4)

4 oz. Patna rice	Cayenne pepper and
4 oz. cooked ham	salt
1 lettuce	

Wash the rice and put it into a large pan of quickly boiling salted water. Boil until tender, steam and dry well. Chop the ham into small pieces, season it, and add it to the rice when cold. Serve on lettuce leaves, as cold as possible.

Rissoles (for 4–5)

1 lb. cold beef, mutton or veal, chopped small or minced	Flour, egg and bread-crumbs for coating
$\frac{1}{2}$ teaspoonful pounded onion	2 oz. breadcrumbs
	1 oz. melted butter
	1 egg-yolk
Salt and pepper	Egg, milk or gravy to
Worcester sauce	bind
	Fat for frying

Season the meat with the salt and pepper, Worcester sauce and pounded onion; add the breadcrumbs, melted butter, and enough egg, milk or gravy to bind, and form into rounds. Flour them, roll in egg and breadcrumbs, and fry in deep fat until brown. Drain well and serve with tomato sauce.

Savoury Cake (for 3–4)

1$\frac{1}{2}$ lb. boiled potatoes	1 egg
$\frac{1}{2}$ lb. minced mutton	$\frac{1}{2}$ pint stock
1$\frac{1}{2}$ oz. butter	$\frac{1}{2}$ oz. flour
1 teaspoonful mush-room ketchup	1 tablespoonful browned bread-crumbs
Salt and pepper	

Put the potatoes through a sieve. Add $\frac{1}{2}$ oz. melted butter, salt and egg-yolk, and mix well. Butter the inside of a deep cake tin. Put in the breadcrumbs and cover the sides and bottom with potato, pressing it well in. Brush the inside and edge of potato lining with beaten egg-white and bake until a nice brown.

Turn out, then carefully turn over on to a dish so that the opening faces upwards. Keep hot. Melt the remainder of the butter in a pan; add the flour and brown well. Add stock, seasoning and ketchup, and bring to the boil. Add meat and heat through; then pour it into the potato cake. Serve with gravy.

Croquettes are always a family favourite. They can be shaped into rolls, rounds or ovals, according to taste

Savoury Mince (for 5–6)

1½ *lb. cold mutton*
½ *oz. gelatine*
1 *teacupful of water*
¼ *pint brown stock*
A few button mush-
  rooms
Pepper and salt
2 *or 3 tomatoes (or*
  a small can of
  tomato purée)
2 *lb. potatoes*
1 *egg*
1 *oz. butter*
Flour

Mince the meat. Dissolve the gelatine in the warm water. Put a few mushrooms into the stock and cook until tender. Boil the tomatoes to pulp in another saucepan, sieve, and add the juice and the pulp (or the purée if fresh tomatoes are not used) to the stock. Add the mince and the dissolved gelatine, and season with pepper and salt. Stand the pan on the side of the stove where it will keep hot without boiling. Boil the potatoes, drain and mash well with a fork; whisk in the butter, the beaten egg and add a sprinkling of flour. Beat the mixture well and arrange it as a border round a dish and bake in a moderate oven. When golden brown, pour in the mince and serve.

Minced cold chicken or turkey makes a good filling for little open patties—excellent for cold supper on Boxing Day

Shepherd's Pie (for 5–6)

1 *lb. cold meat*   *Dripping*
1 *lb. hot potatoes*   *Pinch of dried herbs*
Gravy   *Salt and pepper*
          Small onion, minced

Grease a pie dish, and put in the meat (minced or chopped very fine), the minced onion, dried herbs, pepper and salt, and some good rich gravy. Spread the mashed potatoes over the top, put slices of tomato on top, dot with dripping and heat well in a hot oven until brown.

A layer of sliced tomatoes can be added between the meat and the potatoes.

Taffy Sole (1) (for 3–4)

½ *lb. any kind of cold*   2 *eggs*
  meat, chopped fine   *Pepper, salt, and a*
2 *oz. butter*   *little chopped*
Gravy or cream   *parsley*

Mix all together with a cupful of gravy or cream. Butter a small tin, put the mixture in it and bake for ½ hour. Turn out and serve with or without gravy.

Taffy Sole (2) (for 5–6)

½ *lb. rice stewed in*   ½ *lb. minced meat,*
  brown gravy   *seasoned with salt*
1 *egg*   *and pepper*

Mix all together and bake for 1 hour in a mould. Serve with brown gravy. A little grated ham improves.

Stew the rice in white stock—using veal, stewed rabbit or chicken.

SAUCES

*These finishing touches are the art of cookery—they will
brighten up a homely dish or add distinction to an elaborate one*

SAUCES are, as it were, the finishing
touches to the dish they accompany and,
therefore, a very important part of the
menu. It is no exaggeration to say that
they can either make or mar a meal. A
well-made appetising sauce will brighten
up many a homely dish and add piquancy
to more elaborate ones.

A perfect sauce proves its creator a true
artist, so extra time devoted to this branch
of cooking is well spent.

This chapter contains simple and inexpensive recipes for sauces likely to be used
in the ordinary household from day to day.
In many cases we also suggest how and
with what to serve them.

But for the truly ambitious cook there
are many more sauces, both more exotic
and sometimes considerably more extravagant, to be found in the chapters on Cookery at Home and Abroad.

Sauces may be sweet or savoury, made
with milk or stock; thickened with flour,
cornflour, arrowroot or eggs; and served
thick or thin, hot or cold. But infinite as
the variety is, there are certain basic principles of sauce-making.

(1) Smoothness is essential, so always stir
    well; continuously when making and
    blending a roux.
(2) Flour, if used in sauce, must be
    cooked for 2 or 3 minutes to avoid a
    pasty taste. When using cornflour in-
    stead of flour, remember it is bulkier,
    so a little less is needed.
(3) If using stock for sauces, first skim off
    fat and strain it thoroughly: a sauce
    may be rich but never greasy.
(4) Rich sauces are slowly simmered for a
    long time, then strained through a
    tammy cloth, which should be boiled
    after use and kept scrupulously clean.

Roux

Basis of many sauces is a roux, made by
stirring equal quantities of flour or cornflour and butter together over a moderate
heat until thoroughly blended. This is
called a *White Roux* when cooked without
being coloured; a *Blond Roux* when
cooked to a pale fawn shade, and a *Brown
Roux* when allowed to turn slightly brown.

Reducing

To "reduce" a sauce, strain it, bring to
the boil and boil hard over a quick heat in
a shallow pan till the required quantity of
liquid has "boiled away," leaving what remains very much richer and better.

White Sauce

1 oz. butter or mar- Pepper and salt
  garine ½ pint milk or white
1 oz. flour or corn-   stock
  flour

Melt the butter, add sieved flour very
slowly, stirring all the time, and cook over
moderate heat for a few minutes till
smooth, without colouring. Remove from
the fire, beat in the milk or stock gradually
with a whisk or wooden spoon. Put it back
on the fire and bring to the boil, stirring all
the time. Season and cook for 5 minutes.

NOTE. If you want a thick coating sauce,
allow a little more flour and an equal quantity of fat. For a thin sauce, double the
liquid. If your sauce has a tendency to be
lumpy, use cornflour instead of flour.

This foundation can be used for the following sauces for which you will find
recipes in this chapter:

Anchovy, Béarnaise, brain, caper,
cheese, egg, horseradish, mustard, onion,
oyster, parsley, shrimp and Velouté.

SAUCES—SAVOURY

Admiral's Sauce (for 4) (Served with boiled fish)

½ pint melted butter 2 pounded anchovies
1 teaspoonful chopped Some fine slices of,
  capers   lemon peel
3 chopped shallots or Salt and pepper
  chives

Simmer all ingredients over a low heat
till the anchovies disintegrate. Remove

A good sauce can make or mar a dish. Sole Caprice is only baked fillets served in a thick, creamy white sauce, garnished with grapes and almonds

lemon peel and add salt and pepper as required.

Anchovy Sauce (for 4)

½ pint white sauce
Pepper and salt

1 teaspoonful anchovy essence (or more according to taste)

Make a white sauce (see p. 86), omitting seasoning, and, when cooked, add anchovy essence and pepper and salt to taste.

Apple Sauce (for 4) (Served with pork)

1 lb. apples (sharp cookers are best)
½ oz. butter
½ gill water

Grated rind of half a lemon
1 tablespoonful brown sugar

Wash and slice, but do not peel the apples, and cook with the water, lemon rind and sugar till they become pulp, stirring from time to time. Put through a sieve, reheat, and add the butter.

Béarnaise Sauce (for 4) (Served with grilled steak)

2 egg-yolks
3 tablespoonfuls chopped shallots or onions
1 tablespoonful cream or a little butter

1 dessertspoonful Tarragon vinegar
1 gill malt vinegar
1 gill white sauce (see p. 86)
Salt and pepper

Boil the shallots or onions in the malt vinegar, and strain. Stir the onion-flavoured vinegar into the white sauce, bring to boiling point, then remove pan from heat and add the beaten yolks. Season, and add the Tarragon vinegar and cream or butter last thing before serving.

Béchamel Sauce (for 4) (see also French Cookery)

½ pint milk
1 small onion or shallot
Small piece of carrot
Piece of celery
1 bay leaf

1 clove
5 peppercorns
1 oz. flour
1 oz. butter
¼ gill of cream
Salt

Bring the milk to the boil with the vegetables, bay leaf, clove and peppercorns, and leave to stand for 5 minutes with the lid on, then strain. Make a white sauce in the usual way (see p. 86) with the flour, butter and flavoured milk. Bring to the boil and simmer for 10–15 minutes. Finally, add the salt and cream.

Black Butter Sauce (for 3–4)

This can be served with grilled fish or baked skate or trout. It is also very good with French beans or with old broad beans which have to be skinned.

2 oz. fresh butter   Salt and pepper
        Vinegar to taste

Melt the butter and heat till it is a good brown, but not burned. Add the vinegar and seasoning and reheat, stirring well, but do not allow to boil.

Bolognese Sauce (see Italian Cookery)

Brain Sauce (for 3–4) (Served with calf's or sheep's head)

½ pint white sauce   1 teaspoonful lemon
(see p. 86)   juice
Sheep's brains   Chopped parsley

Wash the brains thoroughly and simmer in a little salted water for 10 minutes. Strain, rub through a hair sieve and stir with the lemon juice and chopped parsley into the white sauce.

Bread Sauce (for 3–4) (Served with roast poultry)

Small onion   1 oz. butter
½ pint milk   Salt and pepper
2 oz. breadcrumbs   2 peppercorns
        2 cloves

Simmer the onion, cut in half and stuck with the cloves, with the peppercorns and a pinch of salt in the milk for about 30 minutes. Strain, and put the milk back into the saucepan. Bring to the boil, stir in the breadcrumbs slowly and heat to boiling point again. Add butter and seasoning.

Brown Sauce (for 6)

1 carrot   Lemon juice
2 oz. butter   1 pint stock
1½ oz. flour   1 onion
1 tomato   2 mushrooms
        Salt and pepper

Peel and slice vegetables, and fry onion and carrot in melted butter until brown Stir in flour, cook to a pale brown colour, then add mushrooms, tomato, lemon juice and stock and bring to the boil, stirring continuously. Simmer for 10 minutes, skim off fat, season and strain.

Caper Sauce (for 4) (Served with boiled mutton or fish)

½ pint white sauce   1 tablespoonful
(see p. 86)   capers
1 teaspoonful of the caper vinegar or lemon
        juice

Make the white sauce and, when cooked, add the capers, chopped; remove from fire and stir in the vinegar or lemon juice.

Celery Sauce (for 4)

1 small head white   ½ pint milk
    celery   1 oz. butter or 1 table-
1 small onion   spoonful cream
1 oz. flour   Seasoning to taste

Mix the flour to a paste with a little of the milk. Peel the onion. Wash and cut the celery, including leaves, into small pieces and cook both in the rest of the milk until tender. Remove onion and rub celery through a sieve. Put the purée back into the pan and add the flour paste, stirring well. Bring to the boil and cook for 5 minutes. Add seasoning and cream or butter.

Cheese Sauce (for 4)

½ pint white sauce   2 tablespoonfuls grated
(see p. 86)   cheese (either good
Made mustard to   dry Cheddar and a
    taste   little Parmesan or all
A little butter   Parmesan)

Make a thin white sauce, using only about half the usual quantity of flour. Put in the grated cheese, mustard and butter. Stir till the cheese is dissolved.

Cranberry Sauce (for 4)

An American favourite served with turkey, roast pork, ragoût of mutton, veal cutlets, or salmi of pheasant. (See also Cookery in the United States.)

½ pint water   4 oz. brown sugar
        1 lb. cranberries

Wash the cranberries and stew in the water till they turn to pulp, stirring frequently. Add brown sugar, stir till dissolved, then beat up well with a metal whisk.

Cumberland Sauce

2 tablespoonfuls red   2 tablespoonfuls
    currant jelly   vinegar
½ teaspoonful   A few chopped glacé
    mustard   cherries
1 lemon and 1 orange   Salt and pepper
½ gill water   ½ gill port wine

Peel lemon and orange carefully, shred the skins and boil for 5 minutes in the water. Cool and strain. Add the juice of the lemon and orange and other ingredients. Let the sauce stand from morning to evening, on ice if possible. If bottled and tied down, it will keep for several days. Do not strain.

Curry Sauce (for 3–4)

½ pint vegetable stock
1 small onion
1 tomato
1 oz. flour
Pepper and salt
1½ oz. dripping
1 carrot
1 apple
1 teaspoonful curry powder
A few drops of lemon juice

Heat the dripping and fry the sliced onion and carrot lightly in it, then stir in the sieved flour and curry powder, with the lemon juice, and cook gently for a few minutes, stirring all the time. Add the stock slowly, then the sliced tomato and the apple, peeled and sliced, and seasoning to taste. Bring to the boil and simmer gently for about 10 minutes. Strain and reheat.

Demi Glacé Sauce

½ pint Espagnole sauce (see below)
¼ pint meat gravy
1 teaspoonful meat glaze (see French Cookery)

Boil sauce, gravy, and glaze together for about 15 minutes to reduce. Strain and serve.

Egg Sauce (for 4) (Served with steamed fish)

½ pint white sauce (see p. 86)
2 hard-boiled eggs

Make ½ pint white sauce and add the eggs, chopped finely; or put eggs through a coarse sieve before adding.

Espagnole Sauce

2 oz. lean ham or bacon
1 small onion
1 carrot
1 pint brown stock
2 oz. flour
Bouquet garni
Salt and pepper
2 oz. butter

Photographs taken in the Experimental Kitchen of Brown & Polson Ltd.

How to make a white sauce, step by step: (1) Melt 1 oz. butter in a small saucepan over a low heat. (2) Add 1 level tablespoonful cornflour and stir until well blended. (3) Pour on ½ pint of milk gradually, stirring all the time, bring gently to the boil and boil for 3 minutes. (4) When the sauce is thick and smooth, add seasonings or flavouring as required

Melt butter and lightly fry in it the onion, carrot and ham, and cut into small pieces. Stir in flour and cook till light brown on low heat. Add bouquet garni and then the stock gradually, bring to boil and simmer very gently for about 1½ hours, skimming at intervals. Strain through tammy and either serve with 2 tablespoonfuls of sherry added at the last minute or use as basis for other sauces, such as Poivrade.

Gooseberry Sauce (for 4) (Serve with roast pork, mackerel, or white fish)

½ pint green goose- berries	Pepper and salt
	¼ gill cold water
1 oz. butter	½ teaspoonful arrow-
1 dessertspoonful granulated sugar	root
	A little water

Top and tail and wash the gooseberries and put them with the sugar into the water. Simmer till they are soft enough to rub through a fine sieve. Mix the arrowroot with a very little cold water into a smooth paste and add, stirring well, to the boiling pulp. Cook for 3 minutes. Season, and lastly beat in the butter.

Green Sauce

Leaves of parsley, Tarragon and fennel	Mayonnaise (see Salads)

Wash, dry and mince the herbs, add a little cold water and pass through a hair sieve or tammy. Add to a well-seasoned mayonnaise.

Hollandaise Sauce (see also French Cookery)

2 egg-yolks	Juice of ½ lemon (or 1
Salt and pepper	tablespoonful Tar-
2 oz. butter	ragon vinegar)

Melt half the butter, either in the top of a double boiler or in a basin over boiling water. Beat egg-yolks well and add to butter with lemon juice and seasoning. Keep water boiling gently and stir until sauce thickens, being careful it does not curdle, and adding the rest of the butter at the last minute.

Horseradish Sauce (for 3–4)

1 tablespoonful grated horseradish	¼ pint white sauce (see p. 86)
1 teaspoonful granu- lated sugar	1 tablespoonful cream (if liked)
Pinch of salt and pepper	A very little made mustard
1 tablespoonful vinegar	

Put all the ingredients into a bowl and beat well with a fork. This sauce keeps for some time if put into a corked bottle.

Marmite Sauce (for 4)

Excellent for children; serve with vegetables or poached eggs.

½ pint vegetable water	1 tablespoonful flour
	Teaspoonful Marmite
1 oz. butter	Pepper and salt to taste

Make the flour into a smooth paste with a little water, and pour it slowly into the hot vegetable water. Add the Marmite, butter and seasoning, bring to the boil, and cook for 5 minutes.

Mayonnaise (see Salads and French Cookery)

Green Mayonnaise: Add a little parsley or spinach juice.

Red Mayonnaise: Add a little beetroot juice.

Melted Butter (for 4–5) (Serve with asparagus)

2 oz. butter	Squeeze of lemon juice

Melt the butter very slowly, so that it does not lose its creamy appearance. Add a squeeze of lemon juice if liked.

Mint Sauce (for 4–5) (Serve with roast lamb)

2 tablespoonfuls chopped mint	A little boiling water
	1 gill vinegar (or half
2 dessertspoonfuls sugar (or to taste)	vinegar and half lemon juice)

Wash and strip mint leaves from stalks and chop finely. Pour boiling water over mint and sugar, barely enough to cover. Leave to stand till cold. Add the vinegar, or vinegar and lemon juice.

Mornay Sauce

Add grated Parmesan or other hard cheese to Béchamel sauce (see p. 87).

Mushroom Sauce

½ pint Béchamel sauce (see p. 87)	1 oz. butter
	¼ lb. mushrooms

Wash, peel and slice mushrooms and cook them lightly in the butter. Add to the Béchamel sauce the mushrooms and, strained, the butter in which they were cooked.

Mustard Sauce (Served with grilled herrings)

Make a white sauce (see p. 86), adding 1 teaspoonful dry mustard at the same time as the flour.

Onion Sauce (for 3–4) (Serve with boiled mutton)

2 or 3 onions	½ pint white sauce
Cream	(see p. 86)

Cook the onions in salted boiling water till tender, drain and chop finely. Add to the white sauce and reheat, adding a dash of cream just before serving.

Oyster Sauce (for 5–6)

¼ pint white sauce (see p. 86)
Pinch of Cayenne
1 doz. oysters
Squeeze of lemon juice

Beard the oysters and cut each up into three or four pieces, being careful to save the liquor in the shells. Blanch them in the liquor. Add the oysters, the liquor, a pinch of Cayenne and a squeeze of lemon juice to the white sauce. Reheat, without allowing to boil.

Parsley Sauce (for 4)

½ pint white sauce	1 dessertspoonful
(see p. 86)	chopped parsley

When the white sauce is cooked and still boiling, stir in the parsley.

Piquant Sauce

To brown sauce (see p. 88) add a tablespoonful of vinegar and, if liked, some chopped gherkins and capers.

Poivrade Sauce (for 4)

½ pint brown	1 oz. lean ham
sauce (see p. 88)	6 peppercorns
1 oz. butter	Herbs (parsley,
1 carrot	thyme, etc.)
1 small onion	

Gently fry the sliced carrot and onion with the diced ham and herbs in butter, add crushed peppercorns, pour on the

COOK'S TIP

MAKE RICHER GRAVY

To 1 tablespoonful of fat add 1 dessertspoonful 'Patent' Cornflour. Cook for a few minutes, add ½ pint stock, boil for 1 minute, season

sauce, bring to the boil and simmer for 10 minutes. Skim well, season, add sherry, if liked, and strain through tammy.

Poulette Sauce (for 5–6)

2 oz. butter	Salt and pepper
2 oz. flour	Bouquet garni
1 pint white stock	2 egg-yolks
Cream and lemon juice, if liked	
2 or 3 mushrooms (optional)	

Make as for a thick white sauce. Remove from heat, beat in the egg-yolks and flavourings. 2 or 3 chopped mushrooms are also delightful cooked in this sauce.

Shrimp Sauce (for 3–4) (Served with turbot or halibut)

1 oz. butter or margarine
A few drops of lemon juice
1 blade of mace and 1 bay leaf
1 oz. flour
2 or 3 drops anchovy essence
1 gill picked shrimps
½ pint milk and water
Salt and pepper

Cook the shrimp shells in milk and water with a blade of mace and a bay leaf, and use the liquor to make a white sauce with the flour and butter. Season well, then add the picked shrimps, anchovy essence and lemon juice, stir thoroughly and reheat.

Soubise Sauce (for 3–4)

½ pint Béchamel	1½ lb. onions
sauce (see p. 87)	1 tablespoonful cream
½ pint milk	or butter
2 cloves	Salt and pepper

Peel and cut onions into pieces and simmer till soft in milk with salt, pepper and cloves. Meanwhile, gently simmer Béchamel sauce till reduced to half. Sieve onions, mix with the Béchamel, and add cream or butter just before serving.

Supreme Sauce (for 4)

½ pint Velouté sauce	Juice of ½ lemon
(see next page)	½ oz. butter
2 well-beaten egg-yolks	

Add egg-yolks, lemon juice and butter

cut up in small pieces to the sauce before serving.

Sweet and Sour Sauce

1 tablespoonful corn-flour	1 tablespoonful sugar
1 tablespoonful malt vinegar	1 tablespoonful soy sauce (dark)
1½ cups water	1 tablespoonful tomato sauce

Place all the ingredients except the tomato sauce in a pan and cook over a slow heat, stirring all the time, until it has the consistency of treacle; add the tomato sauce. This sauce can be made in advance and re-heated when needed and is excellent with Belly of Pork.

Tartare Sauce (for 4)

1 pint mayonnaise (see Salads chapter)	1 tablespoonful chopped gherkins
1 tablespoonful chopped parsley	1 tablespoonful chopped capers

Mix all ingredients well together and serve cold.

Tomato Sauce (1) (for 4–5)

1 lb. tomatoes (fresh or canned	2 small lumps of sugar
Bacon bone or rinds	1 oz. butter
1 small onion	Seasoning
¼ pint milk or white stock	

Melt the butter in a saucepan and add the sliced tomatoes, bacon rinds or bone. sugar and onion, peeled and cut up. Cook very slowly till tender, stirring well. Rub through a sieve and thin with milk or stock. Season and serve.

Tomato Sauce (2) (for 4) (Serve with boiled macaroni or rice)

6 large tomatoes	1 tablespoonful flour
3 oz. butter	Large pinch of salt
2 tablespoonfuls grated Parmesan cheese	1 tablespoonful chopped onion

Stew and rub the tomatoes through a sieve. Cook the chopped onion in the butter for a few minutes, then add the cheese, flour and salt. Mix well together and, when the mixture boils, add the tomato purée. Bring it to the boil again.

Velouté Sauce (1) (for 4)

The classical French recipe for this sauce, including a fowl, is given in the chapter on French Cookery. For a small family it can be made from the following ingredients:

2 oz. butter	1 pint water
2 medium carrots	2 onions
3 or 4 peeled mushrooms	½ pint white sauce (see p. 86)
Bouquet garni	Salt and pepper

Fry sliced carrots and onions lightly over low heat without browning, gradually adding water, seasoning and mushrooms. Simmer gently for 30 minutes, skimming carefully. Strain through tammy, bring to boiling point again and stir in white sauce.

Velouté Sauce (2)

A very simple Velouté sauce can be made by adding 1 teaspoonful lemon juice to ½ pint white sauce (see page 86) made from white stock (see Soup chapter).

Vinaigrette Sauce (for 4) (Served with asparagus or calf's head)

3 tablespoonfuls olive oil	Chopped capers, gherkins, parsley, shallots, Tarragon, chervil and chives, according to taste
1 tablespoonful wine vinegar	
Salt and pepper	

Mix herbs and seasoning with vinegar, then gradually blend in the oil, beating thoroughly.

BUTTERS

Anchovy Butter (see also French Cookery chapter)

2 oz. butter	2 or 3 anchovy fillets (or dessertspoonful anchovy essence)
Lemon juice	
Pepper	

Warm and beat the butter with a wooden spoon till it is the consistency of thick cream, drop in the anchovies or essence, beating all the time. A squeeze of lemon juice and some pepper greatly improves the flavour.

Brandy or Rum Butter (Hard Sauce) (Served with Christmas pudding)

2 oz. butter	2 oz. castor sugar
Brandy or rum to taste	

Slightly warm the butter and beat to a cream with the sugar. Add brandy or rum to taste and put in a cool place till required.

Honey Butter (Served on steamed puddings)

1 oz. honey	4 oz. butter

Beat the butter to a cream, then add the honey (melted) and mix thoroughly.

Maître d'hôtel Butter (see French Cookery chapter)

SAUCES—SWEET

Exactly the same principles apply to sweet sauces, the seasoning being omitted and sugar and the desired flavouring added instead. For instance, lemon or orange sauce can be made by adding a little juice to sweetened white sauce.

If you want something a little richer than the ordinary white sauce, use a little more butter or beat in the yolk of an egg, being careful first to remove your sauce from the fire, as it will curdle if it boils. Cream or unsweetened condensed milk may also be added.

If flavouring with brandy, rum or sherry, put it in right at the end, sherry particularly being very liable to curdle sauce.

Apricot Sauce (for 4)

12 *fresh apricots*
1 *glass Madeira*
Demerara sugar to taste

Halve apricots, remove and break stones, peel and pound kernels and stew together in a little water till fruit is really soft. Then add Madeira and sugar, and stir well over moderate heat until sauce is reduced to syrup. Pass through a sieve before serving.

Brandy Sauce (for 4) (Served with plum pudding)

1 *dessertspoonful cornflour*	1 *egg-yolk*
½ *pint milk*	1 *oz. butter*
Sugar to taste	*A wineglassful of brandy*

Make the cornflour into a smooth paste with a little of the milk. Heat the rest of the milk with the sugar and, when boiling, pour it over the cornflour. Return to saucepan, bring to the boil, and cook for 5 minutes. Remove from the heat and, when it is no longer boiling, add the beaten egg-yolk, butter and brandy. Stir con-

Caper Sauce, with its characteristically sharp taste, gives piquancy to boiled mutton or fish

tinuously over a low heat, or, better still, in a double boiler, until it thickens, not letting it boil or it will curdle.

Rum or sherry can be used instead of brandy.

Chocolate Sauce (Plain) (for 4–5)

½ *pint milk*	3 *teaspoonfuls cocoa*
1 *level teaspoonful cornflour or custard powder*	*Vanilla essence*
	A little butter

Mix the cocoa and the cornflour or custard powder into a smooth paste with a little of the milk. Bring the rest of the milk to the boil, then stir in the paste. Bring to the boil again, simmer for 5 minutes, stirring well, add a few drops of vanilla essence and, lastly, the butter.

Chocolate Sauce (Rich) (for 4–5)

½ pint milk
¼ level teaspoonful cornflour or custard powder

¼ lb. chocolate
Vanilla essence or vanilla stick
A little cream or butter

Stir the chocolate with 2 tablespoonfuls of the milk and the stick of vanilla until it boils. Add the rest of the milk (keeping back just enough to make the cornflour or custard powder into a paste) and bring to the boil. Add the paste, stirring all the time, and bring to the boil again. Cook for 5 minutes. Remove from heat and, if a stick of vanilla was not used, add a few drops of vanilla essence.

If desired, a little cream or butter can be added to make it richer.

Coffee Sauce (for 4)

½ pint black coffee
1 oz. Demerara sugar
1 tablespoonful cream
1 egg-yolk

1 dessertspoonful arrowroot or cornflour
Pinch of salt

Mix the arrowroot or cornflour to a smooth paste with a very little water. Heat the coffee, sugar and salt to boiling point, and pour on to the paste, stirring well. Put back into the saucepan, bring to the boil and cook for 3 minutes. Just before serving, stir in the cream and beaten egg-yolk. Serve hot, but do not allow to boil or the egg may curdle.

Custard Sauce (1) (for 3–4) (May be served hot or cold)

2 or 3 egg-yolks
½ pint milk
1 oz. castor sugar

Rind of a lemon, or stick of vanilla, or sherry to flavour, according to taste

Bring milk and lemon rind or vanilla nearly to the boil and pour into well-beaten egg-yolks. Strain back into pan (top of double boiler for preference), add sugar and stir until it thickens, then remove quickly from heat. If liked, stiffly beaten egg-white may be whisked into the sauce when it is cool. If flavoured with sherry, put this in at the last minute when cooked.

Custard Sauce (2) (for 3–4)

1 egg
½ pint of milk
1 oz. castor sugar

1 level teaspoonful cornflour
Flavouring

Put the milk and sugar on to boil, keeping back enough milk to mix the cornflour to a smooth paste. Add the beaten egg to cornflour paste, then pour the milk slowly in, stirring well. Put back in the saucepan and bring almost to boiling point. Add flavouring as desired.

German Sauce (for 3–4)

¼ pint sherry
3 egg-yolks

1 oz. castor sugar

Whisk all the ingredients together over a moderate heat until the mixture turns frothy, without curdling.

Ginger Sauce (for 3–4)

½ small teaspoonful ground ginger
½ pint water
Lemon juice
1 dessertspoonful cornflour

1 tablespoonful Golden Syrup
1 oz. butter
Crystallised ginger, chopped

Mix the cornflour and ground ginger together into a paste with a little of the water. Bring the rest of the water to the boil with the syrup, then stir in the paste. Cook for 5 minutes, adding the butter towards the end, and add a little chopped crystallised ginger and a squeeze of lemon juice just before serving.

Hard Sauce (see Brandy Butter, p. 92)

Jam Sauce (for 3–4) (Served with sponge puddings)

3 tablespoonfuls of any jam
½ pint water

1 teaspoonful cornflour
1 teaspoonful lemon juice

Make the cornflour into a smooth paste with a little of the water. Boil the jam with the rest of the water and pour it on to the paste. Return to the saucepan and boil for 5 minutes, add lemon juice and strain through a coarse sieve.

Lemon or Orange Sauce (for 3–4)

½ pint white sauce, unseasoned (see p. 86)

1 lemon or orange
4 oz. granulated sugar

Make some white unseasoned sauce, putting the rind of the fruit into the milk to flavour. Add sugar, bring to the boil, remove from the fire and, after a minute or two, add the lemon or orange juice.

Marmalade Sauce (for 3–4)

1 tablespoonful marmalade
1 teaspoonful cornflour
1 gill water

1 dessertspoonful lemon juice
1 tablespoonful Golden Syrup

Bring marmalade, syrup, lemon juice and most of the water to the boil. Mix the cornflour to a smooth paste with a little water and stir into the mixture, cook for 5 minutes, stirring all the time, then serve.

Melba or Raspberry Sauce (for 5–6)
(Served with ice cream)

½ lb. fresh, canned or frozen raspberries
½ oz. cornflour
½ pint water
2 oz. castor sugar
(Raspberry jam may be substituted for the fruit, the sugar then being omitted)

Stew the fruit till soft, pass through a fine sieve, then simmer the pulp with the sugar for 10 minutes very slowly. Mix cornflour to a smooth paste with a little water, stir in and boil for 2 or 3 minutes.

Moussaline Sauce (Sweet) (for 3–4)

3 egg-yolks
2 egg-whites
½ gill cream
Lemon juice
1 oz. sugar
A few drops vanilla

Whisk egg-yolks, cream, sugar and flavourings together in a double boiler over gently boiling water until mixture becomes thick and frothy. Mix in the stiffly beaten egg-whites and serve.

Rum Sauce (for 4)

1 egg-yolk
2 dessertspoonfuls Jamaica rum
2 dessertspoonfuls icing sugar
1 egg-white, stiffly beaten
1 small bottle double cream, whipped
Grated lemon rind

Beat egg-yolk with rum and sugar. Add beaten egg-white, whipped cream and lemon rind.

Sabayon Sauce (for 3–4)

3 egg-yolks
1 oz. castor sugar
1 gill Madeira or Marsala wine

Whisk egg-yolks and sugar in upper part of a double boiler over gently boiling water till frothy. Add wine gradually, stirring all the time, and strain.

Treacle Sauce (for 5–6)

1 gill water
8 oz. treacle or syrup
1 oz. butter
1 level dessertspoonful arrowroot
Lemon juice

Mix the arrowroot into a paste with a little of the water, bring the rest of the water, syrup (or treacle) and butter to the boil. Add the paste and cook for 3 minutes. Add a squeeze of lemon juice.

Wine Foam Sauce (for 3–4)

1 egg
1 dessertspoonful sugar
¼ pint sherry or Marsala
A strip of lemon peel

Put all the ingredients into a double boiler over gently boiling water, warming the sherry or Marsala slightly first. Whisk well until frothy. Remove peel and serve.

Christmas dinner would be incomplete without Hard Sauce, known in some parts of the country as Brandy Butter, but just right to bring out the flavour of a good rich plum pudding

VEGETABLES

How to cook and serve these important foods as tastily as they do on the Continent—and introducing some that may be new to you

THE French and, indeed, most Continental peoples are far better vegetable cooks than the British. The reason is not difficult to find. In France, Holland, Belgium and other Continental countries vegetables are regarded as important foods, quite often worthy of being served as a separate dish and always chosen for their absolute freshness. See chapters on Cookery at Home and Abroad.

There really is no excuse to-day for watery cabbage, sad, tasteless carrots and soapy potatoes. These are three of the cheapest vegetables on the market. They are full of valuable vitamins and, when properly cooked, taste absolutely delicious.

Yet, according to the dieticians, most families would do better if, instead of serving up the vegetables and throwing away the water in which they were cooked, they reversed the process, drinking the water and letting the vegetables go. For there is no sense in eating food after all the goodness has been boiled out of it—which is what happens to many vegetables in the hands of over-zealous cooks. Therefore:

Never overcook vegetables.—When boiling them, use no more water than is absolutely necessary, cover the pan (unless otherwise instructed) and do not let them go off the boil. As a general rule, vegetables grown *above* the ground should be plunged into water that is already boiling and cooked fast; those from *below* ground put into cold water and cooked slowly. Cooking time depends chiefly upon the age of the vegetables, very young ones taking the least time.

Do not use soda to preserve colour.—A pinch of sugar does just as well and neither destroys the vitamins nor makes the vegetables indigestible.

Cook vegetables in their skins to get the best—and the nicest flavour—out of them. Either serve them like that or peel them after cooking. If you must peel vegetables before cooking, do it as thinly as possible, because the best part lies just below the skin.

Save the vegetable water for soups, stews and sauces.

Always serve vegetables as soon as they are cooked. If they are kept hot or reheated the vitamins are destroyed.

Boiling vegetables is the quickest method of cooking them. Very little of their value or flavour will be lost if you remember to choose a small pan with a close-fitting lid, to use the very minimum of water and to avoid overcooking. Just before serving, drain well and put them back in the pan or into a warmed casserole with a little butter or margarine and return to the stove for a few minutes, shaking the pan to prevent them sticking. Alternatively, drain the vegetables just *before* they are completely cooked and finish them in a casserole in the oven with a lump of butter.

Stewing or Steaming are ideal methods for getting the full value from vegetables. Both methods naturally take longer than boiling—allow about twice as long- -but the result is delicious and not extravagant if you choose days when you have the oven on or are using a saucepan on top of which a steamer can be put.

Put the vegetables into salted boiling water for a few seconds only. Drain them well and, while still hot, put them with a little butter or margarine and salt into a warmed casserole or fireproof dish with a well-fitting lid. Put the casserole either into the oven or in a steamer over a saucepan, whichever fits in with your other cooking.

Vegetables stewed or steamed are particularly useful as a separate course, an economical catering idea which is not nearly as popular as it deserves to be. A meal beginning with a substantial soup, followed by at least two well cooked and tasty vegetables and ending with a satisfying sweet course makes a welcome change from the ordinary lunch or dinner menu.

When fresh vegetables are both scarce

and *expensive*, you can get a variety of frozen or canned vegetables, both of which taste excellent and also retain their valuable vitamins, provided they are cooked according to the instructions on the package (see chapter on Emergency Meals).

Left-over vegetables, as well as the water in which they have been cooked, are well worth keeping. They can be used to garnish soups or, cut up small, are useful in salads.

Artichokes (Green or Globe)

Allow one per person. Cut off the stalks close to the leaves and take off outer leaves; trim the points if discoloured. Wash well and soak in cold water for at least ½ hour. Drop, head downwards, into plenty of salted boiling water to which a little lemon juice has been added and boil for 40–45 minutes. When cooked, the leaves should come out easily. Drain and serve hot with melted butter or white sauce or cold with salad dressing. The leaves are pulled out one at a time, dipped in the sauce or dressing and eaten.

A basket of freshly gathered vegetables is transformed into a delicious cooked dish. A small marrow is served whole, surrounded by young green peas, cauliflower, new potatoes, tomatoes, broad beans, carrots, asparagus and onions

Artichokes (Jerusalem)

Boiled.—(1) Wash, peel and put the artichokes for a few minutes into cold water to which a little lemon juice has been added, to preserve their colour. Drain and put them into boiling salted water with a squeeze of lemon juice and cook for 30–35 minutes. Drain when tender, and serve with white or parsley sauce.

(2) Prepare as for the first method, then put the artichokes into a *very* little boiling salted water with a squeeze of lemon juice and cook for a few minutes, then add an equal quantity of boiled milk. Simmer until the artichokes are tender. Drain and either serve with a sauce made from the milk and water in which they were cooked and a little cornflour and butter, or pour some warmed and well mixed cream and butter over them

and sprinkle with chopped parsley.

Fried.—Wash, pare and slice the artichokes thinly. Fry immediately in very hot fat. Drain, and serve piping hot.

Asparagus

Cut the white skin off the lower end of the stalks, wash well and trim the stalks to an even length. Tie into a bundle and stand upright, tips upwards, in well-salted boiling water. Cook until tender (between 25 and 40 minutes, according to size of stalks). If liked, a sprig of fresh mint may be added to the cooking water. Drain, untie bundle and lay flat on dish with stems parallel. Serve hot with melted butter or Béchamel sauce. Cold cooked asparagus may also be

97

served with a French dressing of olive oil and lemon juice or vinegar (see Salads).

Aubergine (Egg-plant)

Fried.—Peel off the deep violet-coloured skin, slice across about $\frac{1}{2}$ in. thick, dip in seasoned flour and brown for about 20 minutes in a little fat. Serve hot—excellent with fried or grilled bacon.

Baked.—Wash, but do not peel. Slice the aubergines in half lengthwise, making a few incisions in the skin with a sharp knife and put them, outside downwards, into a well greased casserole. Dot with fat and bake in a hot oven for 20–25 minutes.

Stuffed.—See Greek Cookery chapter.

Bananas

Baked.—Choose firm but ripe bananas, peel and put either whole or halved lengthwise in a buttered casserole, dot with butter or dripping and bake in a moderate oven for 10–15 minutes until soft.

Scalloped.—See page 105.

Beetroot

To boil, wash well, being careful not to damage the outside skin (the beet would then lose its colour). Boil gently until soft —the time varies considerably. Young beets take from 30 to 45 minutes, old ones anything from 2 to 3 hours.

To serve hot, peel immediately, slice thinly, sprinkle with lemon juice or dress with parsley sauce, melted butter or white sauce.

To serve cold, remove the outer skin when cooked and cooled, cut into convenient slices, serve with lemon juice, vinegar or French dressing (see Salads).

Broad Beans

Shell and drop the beans into enough salted, fast-boiling water to cover them. Boil gently until soft (15–30 minutes, according to age), drain, add a knob of butter and some chopped parsley or serve with parsley sauce.

Broccoli

Cut off the stalks and coarse outside leaves, wash thoroughly, then cook in boiling salted water until just tender (about 15 minutes). Drain well and serve with melted butter (with or without lemon juice) or white sauce.

Brussels Sprouts

Remove outer leaves and wash well. Drop into boiling salted water and cook fast until tender but *not* mushy (10–15 minutes), then drain thoroughly and serve hot. Properly cooked sprouts should be whole and just crisp. Alternatively, drain and dry the sprouts just *before* they are completely cooked, then either return them to the saucepan or put them into a warmed casserole with a little butter or margarine, salt and pepper. Either toss them gently in the pan over a moderate flame until they are quite hot, but without allowing them to fry, or heat them through in the casserole in the oven.

Cabbage

Choose the freshest possible cabbage and cook it with care just before serving. Trim off hard stalk and discoloured and damaged leaves, but remember the outside green leaves contain more food value—and are far tastier—than the heart, so don't throw them away. Wash thoroughly and leave, head downwards, in salted cold water for 15–20 minutes to remove insects; but do *not* soak for any longer than that. Cut cabbage into four or more pieces, according to its size, and plunge into boiling salted water (just enough to cover it). Cook without the lid on until tender but *not* mushy (about 10–15 minutes). Drain well, pressing out all the moisture, add a piece of butter or margarine when putting into the serving dish and serve immediately.

Another method is to shred the cabbage finely; just cover the bottom of a saucepan with boiling salted water, put in cabbage and cover with a tight-fitting lid. Cook for 3–5 minutes, shaking the pan once or twice, by which time the water should have boiled away. Add a lump of butter or margarine and toss over heat until melted. Grate a little nutmeg on top before serving.

Cabbage cooked in this way keeps its colour, and there are no cooking smells.

Carrots

Wash well and scrape. Cook whole if young; slice old ones lengthwise or dice them small. Cook in boiling salted water with a lump of sugar in it. Young carrots take from 15 to 20 minutes, old ones from $\frac{3}{4}$ to 1 hour. Drain and put back into the pan or into a warmed casserole with a good knob of butter or margarine, salt and pepper. Serve hot, garnished with parsley.

If you are using the oven, you can cook carrots in a covered casserole with a good knob of butter or margarine, salt and pepper—and just enough water to prevent them from sticking.

Cold cooked carrots may be reheated by frying lightly in butter, or used cold in salads.

Cauliflower

Remove the outer leaves, cut off stalk, wash well and soak in cold, well salted water for ½ hour to eliminate insects. Then plunge head downwards into salted boiling water and cook until soft. It should take about 20 minutes if young, up to 30 minutes for older ones. Drain well and serve whole, garnished with white sauce, or divide into individual flowerets and cover with breadcrumbs fried brown in butter. Alternatively, sprigs of cooked cauliflower may be covered with white sauce, breadcrumbs and (if liked) grated cheese, dotted with butter or margarine and browned under the grill; or they may be dipped in batter and fried.

Celeriac

Peel the roots and cut in pieces. Cook in boiling salted water until tender, drain and serve hot with melted butter or cold with oil and vinegar.

Celery

Boiled. — Wash a head of celery and scrape the outside sticks well. Cut into 3- or 4-in. pieces. Cover with salted boiling water or milk and water and simmer until just tender (about 1 hour). Drain well and serve with a white or cheese sauce made from the liquid.

Braised.—Wash and scrape the sticks and

cut into 3-in. pieces. Dry well. Cook slowly in butter, either in a frying pan or a casserole in the oven, until the celery is tender and a nice brown. Remove and keep hot. Add either a very little water or some stock to the cooking liquid, season and pour over the celery.

To serve raw.—Wash the celery, cut off very rough outside sticks (and keep for cooking) then cut either into quarters lengthwise or separate into individual sticks. The green tops as well as the heart are eaten raw and are excellent in salads. Celery is also served raw with cheese. To keep it fresh and crisp, stand in cold water.

Chestnuts

Roasted.—Slit the chestnuts with a pointed knife, then roast until done, peel while hot and serve promptly with butter.

Boiled.—Slit the chestnuts, cover with cold water and bring to the boil. Drain and peel while still hot. Then simmer the peeled chestnuts until tender in salted water or milk and water. Serve hot with butter.

Chicory

Wash, but do not leave in water longer than necessary. If chicory has to be kept, wrap it in a moist cloth to prevent the light and air from turning its leaves brown. Cook

A sprinkling of finely chopped parsley or chives and a dab of butter make all the difference to a dish of tiny new potatoes, green peas and young broad beans

the heads whole. Grease the bottom of the pan with butter or margarine or good-quality fat and put the chicory in. Dissolve 1 teaspoonful of salt in 2 tablespoonfuls of water, add the juice of 1 lemon and pour over the chicory. Put a saucer or small plate on the chicory to press it down, put on the lid and bring to the boil. Boil for about $\frac{1}{2}$ hour, drain well and serve hot with a few knobs of butter.

Chicory is also excellent eaten raw, either alone or as part of a salad.

NOTE: The lemon juice is essential to keep chicory a good colour.

Corn on the Cob (or Indian Corn)

Remove husk and silk, and drop the cobs into a pan of fast-boiling salted water, preferably with a teaspoonful of sugar in it. Cook for about 6 minutes and serve, just as it is, with lots of butter and salt and pepper. Alternatively, scrape the seeds from the cobs and gently warm them in a pan with a little butter and seasoning, shaking to prevent them sticking.

Cucumber

Boiled.—Peel thinly and cut lengthwise, removing seeds. Cook in enough boiling salted water to cover until soft (about 10 minutes). Drain, keeping the liquid to make a sauce.

Fried.—Peel and wipe, cut into small slices. Dry in a cloth, season and dip in egg and breadcrumbs. Fry till brown, and drain.

French Beans

French beans should be young and tender enough to be cooked whole. Simply nip off the ends and peel off the string right round the pod. Wash and plunge them into boiling salted water with a teaspoonful of sugar to bring out the flavour. When young, they should not need more than 12–15 minutes to cook. As soon as they are tender, drain, then put them back in the hot pan or a warmed casserole with a good knob of butter or margarine, pepper and salt. Serve hot. Older ones must be sliced before cooking, boiled for about 20 minutes, and may be served with a tomato or Hollandaise sauce (see Sauces chapter).

Kale or Turnip Tops

Remove tough leaves and thick stalks,

To make Stuffed Cabbage: Wash and trim cabbage, cut off stalk and remove outside leaves. Line a basin with a clean cloth and arrange leaves inside. Cut cabbage in four, slice finely, place in a saucepan with 2 oz. margarine and cook slowly for about $\frac{1}{2}$ hour, stirring often

wash well and cook in boiling salted water for 15–20 minutes. Drain and serve with butter, salt and pepper.

Kohl Rabi

Peel, wash and cut into cubes. Simmer in a little boiling salted water until tender (about 20 minutes). Drain and serve with white sauce.

Leeks

Boiled.—Cut off the roots, remove coarse outer leaves and wash very thoroughly under running water, splitting if necessary to get out the earth and mud. Put into boiling salted water and cook gently until tender (about 20–25 minutes). Drain well and pour over them either melted butter, seasoned with salt and pepper, or white sauce.

Cooked in Milk.—Proceed as above, but take the leeks out of the boiling water after a few minutes and cook them slowly in milk. When tender, drain and use the milk to make a sauce with a little butter and flour, flavouring with cheese if liked.

Lettuce

Boiled.—Wash well, removing damaged leaves and stalk. Plunge into enough salted boiling water to cover, and cook for 12–18

When the cabbage is soft and golden, add 2 teaspoonfuls chopped parsley, 1 onion chopped fine, and seasoning. Continue cooking for 10 minutes. Add 2 tablespoonfuls fresh breadcrumbs, 1 egg, and place in cabbage leaves

Tie up the cloth and cook in a pan of boiling salted water for 1 hour. Serve on a hot dish sprinkled with crumbs fried golden brown in a little margarine, with tomato sauce, small browned onions and sauté potatoes as a garnish

minutes, according to size and age. When tender, drain, chop, season well and add a small piece of butter. Serve either alone or on slices of fried bread.

Marrow

Baby marrows and courgettes have the most delicate flavour and hardly any seeds. They should be cooked whole, unpeeled, in a pan with a tightly fitting lid containing a very little salted water, a knob of butter or margarine, salt and pepper. Bring to the boil and simmer gently till tender (about 10–15 minutes). Serve with the liquor poured over them or with melted butter.

Larger marrows must be peeled, have their seeds removed and be cut into slices. Then boil gently for about 20 minutes, drain and serve with white or cheese sauce made from the water in which the marrow was cooked.

Mushrooms

Fried.—Remove stalks, peel and, if large, cut into pieces. Melt a little butter in a frying pan. Dredge mushrooms with flour and cook for about 5 minutes or until tender, with a little salt and pepper. Serve on toast or with crisp bacon rashers.

Stewed.—Peel, wash and remove stalks

from mushrooms. If large, cut into pieces. Put about 2 oz. butter into a casserole or saucepan and fry the mushrooms in it for a few minutes. Add seasoning and a few drops of lemon juice. Put on the lid and simmer very slowly for about 10 minutes or until tender, stirring now and again. Make a smooth paste with 1 teaspoonful of cornflour and 1 gill of stock or milk; add this, stirring gently, bring to the boil and cook slowly for a few minutes. Sprinkle with parsley and serve hot.

Nettles

Only young nettles should be used. Wash them thoroughly in several changes of water, then cook as for spinach, without any additional water, stirring occasionally to prevent them sticking. Either rub through a sieve or chop finely. Reheat, season well and add a small piece of butter.

Onions

Always peel onions under cold water and wash the knife and your hands in *cold* water afterwards to get rid of the smell.

Boiled.—Peel and cover with cold salted water and boil until tender. Drain well and serve either with a good knob of butter or with white sauce.

Fried.—Slice finely and fry gently until

golden brown. Drain on paper and serve hot.

Baked.—Place the onions (whole) in a well greased baking tin and cook in a moderate oven for about 1 hour or until tender.

Casseroled.—Small whole onions should be used. Peel them and put into a covered casserole with some butter or dripping and seasoning. Cook gently for about 2 hours.

Parsnips

Boiled.—Wash and scrape, cut lengthwise in quarters, then across into $\frac{1}{2}$-in. thick slices. Boil in enough salted water to cover until soft but firm (about 10–15 minutes). Drain and put into a casserole or back into the pan with a little butter or margarine and seasoning, and sauté a light brown. Sprinkle with chopped parsley before serving.

Baked.—Wash, peel and cut lengthwise into quarters, removing the hard core from the centre. Then either steam for 45 minutes or 1 hour and finish off in a baking tin with a little dripping and seasoning until nicely brown, or roast in the tin with meat or poultry, basting from time to time with seasoned dripping.

Mashed.—Wash, peel, cut into small pieces and boil in salted water until soft. Drain, rub through a sieve, then put the purée back in the pan with a little butter and heat through gently, stirring in a little cream or top of the milk and seasoning just before serving.

Peas (Green)

Shell and rinse in cold water. Put the peas into just enough salted boiling water to cover them, add a few leaves of mint and a pinch of sugar. Boil, uncovered, slowly until soft when tested between the finger and thumb (about 10 minutes for young peas, 20–25 minutes for older ones). Drain thoroughly and return to the pan or a warmed casserole with a little butter or margarine and seasoning. Serve.

Peppers

These are known as Spanish Peppers (or Pimento), Long, Green or Red Peppers (or Capsicum) according to their shape and colour.

Fried.—Split the peppers lengthwise down the middle and take out seeds. Plunge into boiling salted water, leave for 5 minutes, drain, then toss in butter and seasoning for about 5 minutes. Alternatively, the slices of peppers may be dipped in egg and breadcrumbs and fried crisp and golden in deep fat.

Stuffed.—Cut tops off the peppers and remove seeds. Boil for 2 minutes, then pour cold water over them, stuff with a mixture of minced meat and seasoning or macaroni and cheese. Put back the tops and bake in a moderate oven in a well-greased casserole, basting from time to time with the liquor.

Potatoes

Baked.—Thoroughly wash and dry some good large potatoes, prick the skins with a fork and bake them in a moderate oven for between 40 and 80 minutes, according to size, or until they feel soft when gently squeezed. Serve at once or the potatoes will get hard and shrivelled—and keep them hot, if necessary, by wrapping them in a hot cloth, never in the oven. Split them open along one side with a fork, put a knob of butter or margarine and a sprinkling of salt and pepper (preferably Cayenne) inside, and serve at once.

Baked and Stuffed.—Wash and dry thoroughly, prick the skins with a fork and bake in a moderately hot oven until soft, time depending on age and size of potatoes. When done, split skins lengthwise, scoop out the contents, add butter, seasoning and a little milk or cream, flavoured, if liked, with grated cheese, chopped parsley or diced fried bacon and onion. Put the mixture back into the skins and return to a hot oven or brown under a hot grill for 5–10 minutes.

Boiled (old).—Either scrub clean, if to be cooked in their skins, or, if not, peel as thinly as possible (the best flavour is to be found just below the skin), put into a saucepan of cold salted water, bring to the boil and cook gently until very nearly soft, taking care not to break them. Drain, peel if cooked in their skins, then stand them in the dry saucepan on one side of the stove for a few minutes with the lid on. A few seconds before serving, remove the lid to allow the steam to escape, leaving them dry and floury. Cooking time varies tremendously, according to the variety, age and size, but 20–30 minutes is about average. Choose potatoes of uniform size, or cut up the large ones.

Boiled (*new*).—Wash well and rub with a rough cloth to remove skin, or scrape with a sharp knife. Put into boiling salted water with a sprig of mint and simmer gently until done (about 20 minutes), drain and then replace for a few minutes in the pan at the side of the stove to dry. Put with a small piece of butter or margarine into a casserole or hot vegetable dish, and serve. A little chopped parsley scattered over new potatoes glistening with golden butter makes them look and taste delicious.

Fried.—Wash, peel and cut the potatoes in slices, straws or any shapes you like, throwing them into cold water until you are ready to use them. Then drain and dry thoroughly with a clean cloth. Put them into hot deep fat (butter, fat or oil may be used), preferably in a frying basket, and fry till they are a rich brown. Cook only a few at a time and do them slowly, tossing them about to prevent them from sticking. Drain well and put in a warm place on soft paper. When all are ready, put them back in the basket, boil up the fat and plunge them in for about 2 minutes. Drain and season.

Mashed.—Boil old potatoes (see oppo-site) till tender, drain and peel or, if peeled first, cook till just tender and drain. Either rub through a coarse sieve or beat well with a fork, then put back in the pan over the heat, add a good knob of butter or margarine, salt and pepper, and beat well with a wooden spoon, thin to the right creamy consistency with a little hot milk. Serve garnished with a sprinkling of chopped parsley.

New Potatoes with Orange.—Slice some large new potatoes, put them in layers in a casserole and between each layer grate a little orange peel. Add plenty of salt to give the dish sharpness, just cover with milk and cook for half an hour in a fairly hot oven till the top is brown like Lancashire Hot Pot. If liked, you can chop a little garlic into the dish low down between layers.

Puffed.—Cut the potatoes into slices about $\frac{1}{8}$ in. thick and fry, preferably in a frying basket, in hot deep fat, removing them just *before* they brown. Cook a few at a time and toss to prevent them from sticking. When all are done, return them to

Mushrooms, always a favourite among vegetables, will go much farther if they are stuffed with a savoury mixture bound with an egg

the basket, boil up the fat again and plunge the basket into it. Repeat this process twice. Drain well and serve.

Roast.—Peel large potatoes thinly and cut into halves or quarters. Put into the baking tin with meat, either under or around the joint. Baste well with dripping. Turn when brown on one side and season with pepper and salt. Allow about 1–1½ hours for potatoes to roast a nice rich brown.

Sauté.—Wash, peel, cut in slices and parboil some old potatoes. Drain well, then toss them in a frying pan with a little butter until a pale brown. Turn and cook the other side, keeping the pan moving constantly to prevent burning. Season and garnish with chopped parsley before serving.

Steamed (old).—Wash and put the potatoes, preferably unpeeled, into the steamer over a saucepan of fast boiling water. Just before they are tender, peel and put them back in the steamer, pour away the boiling water from underneath, cover the potatoes with a cloth and the steamer lid, and leave them to finish cooking on the side of the stove in their own steam.

Potatoes Anna.—Wash, peel and slice the potatoes into thin rings, toss them into cold water for 10 minutes, then drain and dry them thoroughly. Into a round, deep, well buttered casserole put a layer of the potato rings, season well with salt and pepper, dot with butter, then put in another layer of potatoes, season and dot with butter, and so on until the dish is nearly full. Bake in a hot oven for 1 hour, after which the potatoes should be a nice pale brown and able to be turned out of the mould.

Potato Cakes.—Mix some mashed potatoes (see p. 103) into a thick paste with a little flour and a pinch of salt. Roll the paste out on a pastry board, cut into rounds or triangles and fry in butter until brown on both sides. Drain well and serve hot. May be eaten with a meat dish or as a sweet, sprinkled with sugar.

Potato Cones.—Put some hot mashed potatoes (see p. 103) into a saucepan with a little butter, salt and pepper. Then add a beaten egg-yolk and, if possible, a little cream. Stir the mixture well. Beat in the egg-white after removing from the fire. Flour a board, shape the mixture into cones and brown in a quick oven.

Potato Croquettes.—Mash some hot potatoes (see previous page). When cool, season and add an egg-white, well beaten, and just enough flour to make the mixture hold together. Form into balls, roll in flour, coat with egg and breadcrumbs, and fry in deep fat to a light brown. Drain well and serve hot.

This mixture can also be made into cottage loaves or little rolls and baked in a quick oven. In this case, pour a little oiled butter over them before putting in to bake, to glaze surface.

Duchess Potatoes.—Cook and mash 1 lb. of potatoes. Add one or two egg-yolks, 1 oz. of butter, about a tablespoonful of cream, salt, pepper and a little nutmeg, if liked. Pipe this creamy mixture into the shape of rosettes on a greased baking tin, brush with egg and bake in a hot oven until well browned.

Runner Beans

Cut off the ends and remove the strings, then slice the beans diagonally into long thin strips, using a sharp knife. Put them straight into a saucepan of cold water. Bring to the boil and cook fast, uncovered, for about 15 minutes, or until the beans are tender. Drain and put into a hot dish with a piece of butter or margarine and seasoning and serve hot.

Salsify

Wash and scrape well, adding a little lemon juice to the water to preserve the colour. Cook in boiling salted water with a little lemon juice until tender (about 30–40 minutes). Drain and serve hot with white sauce or tossed in butter in a frying pan until nicely browned, then seasoned with pepper, salt and a squeeze of lemon. Salsify can also be served cold with a good French dressing (see Salads chapter).

Sea Kale

Wash well, separating the stalks, and tie in bundles or break into small pieces and place in sufficient salted boiling water with a squeeze of lemon juice just to cover. Simmer gently until soft (about 30 minutes) with the lid off. Drain well and serve with melted butter or white sauce.

Sorrel

Remove the stalks, wash in several changes of water till absolutely clean, then

MEET A NEW VEGETABLE DISH

BANANA SCALLOPS

Here's a new and exciting way of serving bananas—cooked, hot and crisply fried—instead of potatoes, to go with a meat, fish or vegetarian dish. Delicious with boiled cauliflower

Banana Scallops (for 4)

4 firm bananas
Melted fat or salad oil
1½ teaspoonfuls salt
1 egg, slightly beaten, or ¼ cupful
    undiluted evaporated milk
½ cupful cornflake crumbs, bread or biscuit
    crumbs

Salt egg or milk slightly. Peel bananas and slice crosswise into pieces ¾–1 in. thick. Dip into egg or milk. Drain. Roll in crumbs, and fry in the hot fat for about 1½–2 minutes, or until brown and tender. To deep-fry, have deep frying saucepan ½–⅔ full of melted fat or oil. To shallow-fry, have 1 in. of melted fat or oil in frying pan. Heat fat until a 1-in. cube of bread will brown in about 40 seconds. Drain well and serve hot as a vegetable.

---

cook in just sufficient water to cover the bottom of the pan, with salt sprinkled over, until tender (about 10–15 minutes). Stir frequently. Drain and chop finely.

Spinach

Wash carefully in several different waters, discarding the coarse and discoloured leaves. Put into a saucepan and cook in the moisture adhering to it, without adding any other liquid, stirring to prevent sticking, for about 15 minutes or until nice and soft. Drain very thoroughly, squeezing the excess moisture out, then chop. Put back into the pan or into a warmed casserole with a good knob of butter or margarine and seasoning, and reheat.

Spinach Purée.—Cook as above, then rub through a sieve. Reheat, adding a little butter, pepper and salt.

Creamed Spinach.—Proceed as for Spinach Purée (above), then stir in a little cream till it is the desired consistency.

Swedes

Peel, slice and cook in salted boiling water until tender. Drain and mash with butter and seasoning.

Tomatoes

Baked or Grilled: Cut the tomatoes in half, sprinkle with salt and pepper, put a little oiled butter or a dab of margarine, bacon fat or dripping on each, and either grill or bake in a moderate oven for about 10–15 minutes.

Turnips

Peel and dice, then cook in salted boiling water until tender (young ones will need about 15 minutes, old 45 minutes or even more). Drain and mash or rub through a sieve with a wooden spoon—or keep in dice if small and young—and return to the saucepan or a warmed casserole with a little butter or margarine, seasoning and milk. Reheat and serve.

Turnip Tops (see Kale)

SALADS

The most useful dish on the menu, a salad is at home with most foods, hot or cold—or by itself

AT any time of the year, from January to December, you can serve a delicious, tempting, health-giving salad every day—and it need not be expensive either. The Victorian conception of a little wilted lettuce, a few slices of tomato and cucumber, and some beetroot soaked in vinegar was a depressing dish at any time and, fortunately, only made its appearance on hot summer days, as an accompaniment to cold meat. Now salads provide the most wonderful opportunity for the imaginative housewife to introduce variety—in flavours and colour—into her family's meals.

We know from the dieticians that we get the *full* flavour and value out of fruit and vegetables only if we eat them raw. Once you put those theories into practice, your palate proves how right the experts are. Raw vegetable salads are appetising and a sure way of getting sufficient vitamin C into the daily diet, for all green leaves and, to a lesser extent, edible roots and blanched stems, supply this vitamin in abundance. They are also richly endowed with such important alkaline elements as potassium, calcium, iron, magnesium and sodium, all of which are essential to health—and very conducive to beauty.

Getting a salad into the menu every day need not present any problems. There is no nicer start to a meal than crisp green lettuce, sliced raw tomato, grated raw vegetables or fruits, served with an appetising dressing. As an accompaniment to a main dish, or to follow it; as a course on its own or a garnish with fish, meat or poultry—salad is at home anywhere in the meal.

It is fun to make almost as much of a ritual of the salad bowl as Victorian menfolk used to make out of passing the port. Prepare the green ingredients beforehand and bring them to the table, beautifully crisp and dry, in a big wooden bowl, then mix your dressing to your liking and toss the salad thoroughly and lovingly with a wooden spoon and fork.

Practically every vegetable that is more often cooked can just as well be eaten raw if it is properly prepared—and preferably when young and tender. When the more conventional salad ingredients are scarce, expensive or unobtainable, there is always an alternative. Lettuce can be replaced by that favourite of Continental housewives, cornsalad, or, cheaper still, by the crisp heart of a white or red cabbage finely chopped, or the tender inside leaves of raw spinach. Nearly all the culinary herbs—chives, mint, parsley, marjoram, thyme, etc.—are delicious in salads, and so are nasturtium and dandelion leaves. You can put all kinds of fruit—fresh, tinned, dried or cooked—into salads, and so make a dish that is a meal in itself.

WINTER INGREDIENTS

Here are just a few of the amazing variety of vegetables usually obtainable in the U.K. between November and March (the most difficult time for salads), all of which are excellent raw:

Jerusalem artichokes, cabbage, beetroot, carrots, cornsalad (or lamb's lettuce), garlic, leeks, onions, parsnips, winter radishes, shallots, swedes, watercress, beet-spinach, celery, celeriac, dandelion, endive, land-cress, chives, turnips, Brussels sprouts, chicory, seakale.

These and many other ingredients can be combined in innumerable different ways, though a salad should contain a well-blended mixture of a few things, rather than too many at once.

The chief rules for good salad-making are:

(1) Everything must be crisp, cool, dry. Don't dress a green salad until the last minute before serving; green leaves wilt quickly under oil. The exceptions are the salads you marinate in a French dressing—Potato, Russian, Fish, for example.

(2) If you cut up vegetables, make them small enough to eat easily, but large enough to keep their identity.

Dressing the salad with oil and vinegar, perfectly blended, should be done slowly, carefully, lovingly—preferably at the table, as a ritual

(3) Choose the ingredients with an eye to contrast in flavour, colour and texture —and arrange attractively.

Green vegetables, such as lettuce, watercress, endive, etc., should be very carefully handled or they will lose their crispness. If they are inclined to be limp, plunge them into fresh cold water for 20 minutes before using, but never soak them for longer. A tablespoonful of Milton should be added to a quart of water to cleanse thoroughly, and will not make the greens taste if washed off in clean water. Salad greens not required for immediate use should be put, unwashed, into a tightly covered receptacle, such as a saucepan, or wrapped in a damp cloth or put into a polythene bag in a cold place (but not near the freezing compartment of the refrigerator).

Lettuce and Batavia Endive.—Remove discoloured outside leaves and cut off root stump. Plunge into cold water, separating the leaves and opening up the heart. Wash thoroughly at least twice in fresh cold water, then shake well in a salad basket or colander to remove excess moisture, and finally toss lightly in a clean dry cloth.

Curly Endive.—Prepare as for lettuce, but remember the dark green outer leaves have a characteristic bitter taste not liked by everyone. If in doubt, remove these.

Watercress is now mostly grown in running water under perfectly hygienic conditions and sold in bundles with the grower's name attached. Even so, it sometimes has little quite harmless insects, so wash it in several waters, the first containing a tablespoonful of Milton to the quart, remove decayed leaves and all fibrous matter or straggly roots. Dry well.

Cornsalad.—Remove roots and rinse in cold water. Dry.

Mustard and Cress.—To remove all the black seeds and wash properly, hold a handful of the cress in one hand under a running tap so that the seeds get washed away. Or put the cress into a bowl of cold water and swish the water round and round, so that the seeds travel out, leaving the cress free.

Radishes.—Wash in cold water, do not peel or scrape, and dry with a cloth. Young ones may be served with their green tops on, larger ones are better sliced, some of the smaller leaves being used separately.

Spring Onions.—Cut away root fibres, peel off outside skin and remove a little of the green tops. Wash in cold water and serve either whole or sliced.

Celery.—Wash carefully, cutting away discoloured and coarse parts but keeping these for use cooked or for soup. Use both the crisp white stalks and the tender green leaves in salad. To make a very attractive garnish, take a stick of celery and with a sharp knife cut about five or six parallel slits downwards one-third of its length. Put into water and leave for an hour or two, when the ends will all curl back. Both ends may be curled in this way.

Cucumber should be rinsed in cold water and cut, unpeeled, into chunks. This is less likely to cause indigestion than when it is eaten peeled and sliced very thin so that the valuable vitamins, etc., in the skin are lost, and it is often not properly masticated.

Cabbage.—Choose a firm white or red cabbage, cut away the outer leaves, which can be cooked, and use the heart only for salad. Cut out the hard core, wash well in cold water, leave for 10 or 15 minutes (but not more) in salted cold water to remove insects, then shake off surplus moisture and slice thinly or shred with a sharp knife.

Brussels Sprouts.—Prepare as for cabbage.

Spinach, Nasturtium Leaves and Herbs.—Wash well in cold salted water, shaking dry afterwards.

Root Vegetables (artichokes, carrots, young turnips, parsnips, etc.) should be scrubbed, scraped rather than peeled, and either grated or cut into very thin strips.

NOTE: They must be grated at the last minute, just before serving, or they will lose their attractive colour and much of their vitamin content.

Cooked Vegetables (carrots, peas, potatoes, for instance) are a pleasant addition to many salads. They must be very firm so that they can be diced or cut into fancy shapes. Potatoes intended for salad should be boiled in their skins and peeled afterwards.

SERVING SALADS

Salads may be served in a glass, china or wooden bowl, in small individual dishes or on dinner plates. The arrangement is most important. No dish has more "eye-appeal" than a good salad. Avoid overcrowding and never let leaves project over the edge of the plate.

You can make an attractive effect by arranging the top layer of a salad in different coloured quarters. Hard-boiled egg-whites and yolks chopped very fine, green peas, diced beetroot, sprigs of parsley, celery tops, diced cucumber, capers, grated raw carrot, nuts, segments of apple, orange or grapefruit, fluted slices of bananas, a few black or green grapes or olives, some dates, can all be used to make a fascinating colour scheme as well as a tasty and nourishing salad. But remember—it's contrast that makes a good effect.

DRESSINGS

Light French dressing (or Vinaigrette) is best with green salads. Heavier dressings, such as cream salad dressing or a rich mayonnaise, are good with more substantial salad dishes. But the question of which dressing for which salad is very much a matter of taste.

Remember, whichever you choose, never to mix the dressing with a green salad until just before serving—or the greens will wilt—and always use a wooden spoon for mixing.

For recipes for dressings see end of chapter.

FRUIT AND VEGETABLE SALADS

Apple, Cabbage and Celery Salad

Shred the heart of a white cabbage finely, cut up some celery, peel and dice one or two apples. Mix with cream salad dressing.

Banana and Nut Salad

Peel bananas and cut them in three. Then cut each piece in half lengthways and roll in chopped walnuts (or any other nuts). Arrange the banana pieces on lettuce and pour over some French dressing.

Banana Vegetable Salad

Wash and dry one or more varieties of fresh crisp greens and arrange in a bowl previously rubbed with garlic (if liked). Add long strips of ripe banana, garnish with celery curls, onion, radish roses, wedges of tomato or strips of carrot. Serve with French dressing.

Beetroot and Egg Salad

Lettuce	Radishes
Beetroot or tomato	Hard-boiled egg

Arrange some whole inner leaves of lettuce on a dish. Put a few slices of beetroot or tomato on each and a slice of hard-boiled egg on top. Garnish with radish flowers.

Celery and Nut Salad

Chop some walnuts and dice some celery and mix well together. Serve with French dressing.

Celery, Cabbage and Nut Salad

Head of celery	Small cabbage or
Chopped walnuts	lettuce

Clean the celery and dice it. Shred the lettuce or cabbage finely, using only the inside. Mix together, sprinkle with the chopped nuts and serve with cream salad dressing.

Celery and Potato Salad

4 medium-sized
   potatoes cooked in
   their skins, peeled
   and cut in cubes
Celery tips
Stick of celery cut
   into small pieces
Apple, peeled, cored
   and sliced
French dressing

Mix the potato, apple and celery together with French dressing. Garnish with celery tips.

Cream Cheese Salad

Work together salad dressing and enough cream cheese to bind the mixture. Make into small balls on a wet board with a wet knife and roll in chopped nuts. Serve on lettuce or mustard and cress, and decorate with grated raw carrot, chopped parsley or slices of tomato.

Cream Cheese and Pineapple Salad

Pineapple rings
Cream cheese
Salad dressing
Lettuce
Cress

Make cream cheese balls by working enough cream cheese into salad dressing for the mixture to bind, and then rolling it on a wet board with a wet knife. Put some lettuce leaves on a dish with pineapple rings on top and put a cream cheese ball into the centre of each. Arrange the cress in between the rings.

Cucumber and Sour Cream Salad

Into a cup of sour cream stir 6 finely chopped spring onions or chives. Slice the cucumber and toss in the dressing.

Date Salad

Dates	Lettuce
Chopped stoned raisins	Cream cheese
	Chopped almonds

Stone the dates and stuff them with a mixture of raisins, cream cheese and

Star Salad has slices of hard-boiled egg and beetroot on a bed of grated cheese and lettuce

chopped almonds. Serve on lettuce or any green salad with French dressing.

Egg and Green Pea Salad

Hard-boiled eggs	Mayonnaise
Green peas	Lettuce
(cooked)	Cream cheese balls

Wash the lettuce and arrange the leaves whole in a dish. Cut the eggs in half lengthwise, scoop out the yolks and fill the eggs with green peas mixed with mayonnaise. Arrange the eggs on the lettuce. Mix the yolks with a little cream cheese and enough mayonnaise to bind and roll into balls. Garnish with these.

English Salad

Tomatoes	Lettuce
Cucumber	Watercress
Spring onions	Hard-boiled egg
Beetroot	Radishes

Prepare the lettuce and watercress and place some of it in a salad bowl. Add alternate layers of tomato, cucumber, spring onion and beetroot, cut into thin slices. Garnish with radishes and quarters of hard-boiled egg. Serve with French dressing or cream salad dressing.

Fluted Banana Fruit Salad (for 1)

½ peach, apricot or pear (fresh or canned)	1 ripe banana Salad greens Berries

Place half a peach, apricot or pear in a lettuce cup (made by cutting out the stem from a small lettuce, then letting the water from the cold tap run inside, forcing open the leaves) on a plate. Arrange a half-circle of fluted banana slices (see picture opposite), garnish with berries and sprigs of greens. Serve with French or cream dressing.

Frozen Salad (for 10–12)

1 tablespoonful lemon juice	6 oz. cream cheese
2 tablespoonfuls mayonnaise	2 tablespoonfuls crushed pineapple
1 teaspoonful salt	½ cupful chopped walnuts
½ cupful maraschino cherries (quartered)	3 ripe bananas, cubed
1 cupful whipped cream	Salad greens

Add lemon juice and salt to mayonnaise and stir into cheese. Add pineapple, cherries, nuts and fold in cream. Then add bananas. Turn into refrigerator tray and freeze until firm. Garnish with salad greens.

Green Salad

A green salad is best served by itself. It may consist of lettuce, cress, endive or chicory, well washed and dried. Serve with a dressing made from 3 tablespoonfuls of olive oil, 1 tablespoonful vinegar, salt and pepper, and a little finely chopped parsley, chives, tarragon or a hint of garlic, according to taste. Excellent to follow a hot meat or poultry dish.

Melon Ball Salad (for 1)

1 ripe banana	Melon balls
	Salad greens

Peel and cut banana lengthwise into halves. Place the halves cut side up, side by side, in centre of plate. Place a few melon balls at each end, garnish with crisp salad greens and serve with mayonnaise.

Mixed Fruit and Vegetable Salad

2 bananas	Nuts
Orange	A small cucumber
Lettuce	2 tomatoes
	Watercress

Arrange some whole inner leaves of lettuce on a dish. Peel the bananas and slice them and the cucumber. Peel the orange and remove the pith. Slice it thinly and remove the pips. Slice the tomatoes. Arrange these four ingredients in quarters and garnish with a little watercress and a few walnuts.

Orange Salad

Peel and quarter the oranges, removing the white pith and the pips. Season with salt, pepper and a little lemon juice mixed together with a little olive oil. Garnish with watercress. Serve with guinea fowl or wild duck.

Orange Tomato Aspic Salad

1 dessertspoonful gelatine	¾ cupful canned tomato soup
1 breakfastcupful orange juice	Lettuce
Dash of Cayenne	½ cupful chopped celery
¼ teaspoonful salt	

Soak gelatine in ½ cupful orange juice for 5 minutes. Dissolve over hot water. Add rest of orange juice and mix well. Add soup and seasoning. Chill. When mixture thickens, add celery, pour into small greased cups and leave to set. Serve on a couple of crisp lettuce leaves on small individual plates.

Delicious with beef pot roast, jugged

Fluted bananas add a professional touch—you do it by running the prongs of a fork down the banana

hare or stew with a rich dark gravy. An orange salad also makes rich meat dishes easier to digest as well as more enjoyable to eat.

Pineapple and Banana Salad (for 1)

2 slices canned pine-
apple
Salad greens
1 ripe banana

Place a ring of pineapple round each end of a peeled banana. Garnish with crisp salad greens and, if liked, strawberries. Serve with mayonnaise.

Potato Salad (Cold)

Cut freshly cooked, peeled cold potatoes (cooked in their skins) into cubes and add some chopped parsley or chives. Mix the potato cubes well with vinaigrette. Sprinkle with a little chopped parsley.

Potato Salad (Hot)

Peel and slice some freshly cooked cold potatoes into a fireproof dish. Season with salt and pepper, a little chopped parsley

and some chives. Carefully blend 2 tablespoonfuls wine vinegar with 4 tablespoonfuls olive oil, add the juice of a lemon and heat this dressing to boiling point. Pour over the potatoes, cover, and gently heat in the oven. Serve hot.

Russian Salad

Cooked peas, beans, carrots, potatoes
Mayonnaise

Cut vegetables into small dice and mix well with mayonnaise. To decorate the top, divide into squares and garnish each section differently: one with chopped egg-yolk, one with chopped white, one with peas and one with beans.

Stuffed Tomato Salad

Cut off a thin slice from the top of each tomato. Remove the seeds and pulp, and put a little salt in each. Allow them to stand for a time upside down. Then fill and serve on lettuce.

Tomatoes prepared in this way can be stuffed with all kinds of fillings, including the following:

Pineapple Banana Salad—a whole banana slipped through two pineapple rings garnished with fruit or green salad

Cucumber cut in cubes, and mixed with mayonnaise.

Chopped apple and celery mixed with mayonnaise.

Sardines, boned and cut up, mixed with tomato and mayonnaise.

Cream cheese and French dressing worked together.

Tomato and Pineapple Salad

Tomatoes	Lettuce
Crushed pineapple	Mayonnaise

Put some lettuce in a shallow bowl. Cut the tomatoes into quarters without quite cutting through. Remove the pips and fill the centres with crushed pineapple (or pineapple cubes chopped very finely) mixed with mayonnaise, and place them on the lettuce.

Tomato Salad

4 tomatoes	Chopped chives or
1 tablespoonful wine	spring onion
vinegar	Pinch of salt and
2 tablespoonfuls	pepper
olive oil	Parsley and shredded
	celery

Scald the tomatoes to remove the skins. Peel and slice thinly and arrange them in a dish with the chopped chives or onion sprinkled over. Blend the oil and vinegar, and season. Garnish with parsley and celery shredded finely.

Vegetarian Salad Lunch

Arrange on individual plates freshly grated raw carrot, swede, beetroot, white turnip, grated cheese or cream cheese, milled nuts, shredded fresh herbs (mint, parsley, marjoram). Serve with French dressing and wholemeal bread, butter and Marmite.

Waldorf Banana Salad (for 4–6)

1 diced unpeeled red	Crisp lettuce or other
apple	salad greens
½ cupful mayonnaise	½ cupful diced celery
or salad dressing	2 sliced ripe bananas
	Walnut halves

Mix together apple, celery, mayonnaise or salad dressing, and lightly add banana slices. Arrange on lettuce. Garnish with greens and nuts.

CHICKEN AND FISH SALADS

Chicken Salad

Cooked chicken	Beetroot
Lettuce	Capers
Cress	Mayonnaise

Slice the meat and put it in the centre of

For a summer main dish, prawns and hard-boiled eggs in aspic, served with salad

Salmon Salad Tropical is an exotic dish combining fruit, fish and green salad. You can ring the changes by using chicken or tuna fish instead of salmon

the dish and cover with mayonnaise. Arrange the lettuce and cress round the chicken. Cut the beetroot into small dice and place in groups on top of the sauce, and garnish with capers in between.

Fish Salad

Any cold cooked fish   Mayonnaise
Cooked potatoes   Cress
           Cucumber

Flake the fish and put it in a dish with slices of potato and cucumber. Pour some mayonnaise over and surround with cress.

Lobster (or Crab) Salad

Lobster (canned or   French dressing or
   freshly boiled)   mayonnaise
Lettuce   Beetroot
        Seasoning

Shred the lobster finely. Wash the lettuce and arrange it in a dish with the lobster. Season well with pepper and salt. Arrange slices of beetroot round and cover with either French dressing or mayonnaise.

Salmon Salad

Cooked salmon (fresh   Radishes
   or canned)   Pepper and salt
New potatoes   French dressing

Flake and season the salmon, then pile it in a dish and pour over it a little French dressing. Slice the potatoes thinly, pour dressing over them, season, and arrange them round the salmon with an outer ring of small radishes with a little of their green left on.

Salmon Salad Tropical (for 4–6)

1 cupful diced ripe   1 tablespoonful pre-
   banana   pared mustard
1 cupful diced pine-   1½ cupfuls flaked
   apple   salmon
2 tablespoonfuls   1½ teaspoonfuls salt
   chopped sweet   1 tablespoonful
   pickle   mayonnaise
½ cupful diced celery   Lettuce

Mix together lightly and arrange on the lettuce. Garnish with sprigs of parsley, etc.

QUICK MAIN COURSE SALADS

Avocado Pear and Cottage Cheese Salad

1 *large ripe avocado pear*	1 *small onion, chopped fine*
1 *lb. firm tomatoes*	¼ *lb. cottage cheese*

Peel avocado, remove seed and chop up finely. Skin and cut the tomatoes up small and put in salad bowl with the avocado, the cheese and onion. Serve with a dressing made by mixing thoroughly together:

3 *dessertspoonfuls olive oil*	1 *dessertspoonful lemon juice or white wine vinegar*
1 *teaspoonful white pepper*	
A speck of Cayenne	

This is a slightly exotic salad that can be served equally well by itself or with such meats as a pot roast, escallop of veal or boiled ham.

Ham and Tomato Salad

Cut some cold boiled ham or boiled bacon off the bone and put it through a mincer. Mix with enough good mayonnaise to make into a thick paste. Add roughly chopped cucumber. Scoop out large firm tomatoes with a teaspoon and stuff them with the ham mixture. Place on a bed of watercress and serve with half a hard-boiled egg, a few radishes and a freshly sliced banana with a squeeze of lemon juice.

Hot Weather Salad Cooler

This is a dish very popular in many parts of the world for its refreshing flavour and because it is nourishing and healthful, as well as very quick and easy to prepare.

All you need are a few inches per person of fresh cucumber, pared and roughly cut into ½-in. cubes, one or two firm, ripe tomatoes cut into quarters and then across, and a bottle of yoghourt scooped out on to the plate with the salad. Serve either with a few young spring onions or just a fine grating of freshly ground black pepper.

10-Minute Tomato Salad

Hard-boil one or two eggs per person for 10 minutes in just boiling water. Cool quickly in cold water. Skin one or two tomatoes per person. Thinly slice a cucumber. Prepare the salads on individual plates, starting with a wide border of cucumber slices with black pepper grated over them. Cover the centre of the plate with thick slices of tomato sprinkled with chopped parsley or chives, top with the hard-boiled egg cut lengthwise into four quarters and arranged to look like flower petals. In the centre put rolled anchovy fillets, boned and mashed sardines, or a few olives or capers (for a contrast in flavour and colour). Squeeze fresh lemon juice over the salad and serve with a good mayonnaise and plenty of fresh crusty bread and butter.

SALAD DRESSINGS

Cream Salad Dressing

1 *tablespoonful mustard*	1 *teaspoonful salt*
2 *tablespoonfuls lemon juice*	1 *cupful whipped cream*

Put the mustard and salt in a basin, add the lemon juice and 2 tablespoonfuls of cream. Beat the rest of the cream stiffly and then add the mixture, beating well until it is quite stiff.

French Dressing (1)

½ *gill vinegar*	*Salt and pepper*
	1 *gill olive oil*

Mix the vinegar, oil, and salt and pepper together. Beat well, or shake in a covered container till thoroughly mixed. Chill. Shake before using.

To vary French dressing.—Use lemon juice instead of vinegar; or add a little dry mustard; or a little finely chopped shallot.

French dressing is used for plain green salads. It can be made at the last moment and should be mixed with the salad just before serving.

French Dressing (2)

Make some French dressing with olive oil and lemon juice and add to it a little Worcester sauce, dry mustard and a very little onion juice. Shake the ingredients well together before using.

Mayonnaise (see also Cookery in France)

The thought of making mayonnaise often frightens busy people because of the idea still prevailing that it is such a slow process. Certainly the oil must be poured in in a very thin stream, but it is not necessary to put it in drop by drop after the first few minutes. The mixture should be stirred smoothly and quickly the whole time with a wooden spoon or a wire whisk until so stiff that it can only be stirred with difficulty. Vinegar is then added to thin it.

Mayonnaise Sauce (1)

1 egg-yolk	1–2 tablespoonfuls
Salt and pepper	vinegar or lemon
½ teaspoonful made	juice
mustard	½ pint best salad oil

Put the egg-yolk into a bowl with the mustard and seasoning. Pour the oil in drop by drop at first, then in a very thin stream, stirring smoothly and quickly all the time. Add sufficient vinegar to make the sauce of the required consistency.

Mayonnaise sauce keeps for a short time. It should be added just before serving.

Mayonnaise Sauce (2)

2½ teaspoonfuls plain	2 tablespoonfuls
flour	dried egg (dry)
1 teaspoonful salt	½ pint vinegar
4 dessertspoonfuls	4 teaspoonfuls
salad oil	mustard
½ teaspoonful pepper	½ teacupful sugar
	1 pint fresh milk

Mix the flour and seasonings with oil, add sugar, dried egg, milk and vinegar. Bring gently to the boil, stirring all the time. This mayonnaise keeps well for some time if bottled.

Piquant Dressing

1 cupful thick or	¼ teaspoonful paprika
sour cream	(optional)
⅛ teaspoonful pepper	¼ teaspoonful grated
1 tablespoonful	lemon rind
bottled horseradish	2 teaspoonfuls sugar
4 teaspoonfuls lemon	½ teaspoonful pre-
juice	pared mustard, or
¾ teaspoonful salt	⅛ teaspoonful dry
	mustard

Whip cream until fluffy but not stiff. Fold in salt, pepper, paprika, horseradish, lemon rind, lemon juice, sugar and mustard. If sour cream is used, the lemon juice should be reduced to 3 teaspoonfuls.

Salad Dressing

Pinch of salt and	1 tablespoonful flour
pepper	1½ tablespoonfuls
1 teaspoonful dry	melted butter
mustard	1 egg
1½ tablespoonfuls	1 teacupful boiling
sugar	milk
¼ teacupful vinegar	

Mix the dry ingredients together and then add the egg, slightly beaten. Next, add the melted butter and then the hot milk. Stir well over boiling water until it thickens without boiling. Take off and add the vinegar slowly. When cold, store in well-corked jar. It will keep for weeks.

The secret of a good mayonnaise is to be lavish with the olive oil and sparing with the vinegar. For extra piquancy, add chopped home-grown chives or other flavourings, according to individual taste

PUDDINGS AND SWEETS

The sweet course is most important—particularly
if there are children or men in the family

A WIDE repertoire of sweet dishes is a necessity in any household where there are children. The sweet course is very often a favourite with the men, too. Fortunately, the variety of ways in which the chief pudding ingredients can be used to produce different results is almost unlimited.

Here, first of all, are a few general hints on pudding making.

Boiled and Steamed Puddings

A steamed pudding is always lighter than a boiled one. Whichever you are making, be sure to have the water boiling at the right moment. A scalded floured pudding cloth should be put over the top of the basin when cooking a boiled pudding; for a steamed one, a double piece of greased paper.

Soufflés

Moulds for steamed or baked soufflés should be well buttered first, and then a double band of paper, wide enough to come above the tin and to reach half-way down it, should be buttered and tied round the outside of the tin, the single edge being at the top and the double edge below. A round of greased paper should be cut to cover the top.

Baked soufflés are served in the dish they are baked in, the paper being removed. They *must* be served the moment they leave the oven, or they will "flop." Steamed soufflés are turned out.

Cold Puddings

Moulds for cold puddings should be rinsed under the tap before they are used. When the mixture is to be turned out, put the mould into hot water for a minute or two to loosen it.

INGREDIENTS

In these recipes, plain flour is used unless otherwise stated, and the necessary amount of baking powder, or bicarbonate of soda, given. If self-raising flour is substituted, the baking powder must be omitted. Where bicarbonate of soda is to be used, it is best to use plain flour.

Sultanas and currants should be thoroughly cleaned before use. The quickest way to do this is to put them on a wire sieve, sprinkle them with flour, and rub them well over the sieve with your hand. Look them over carefully and remove any stalks that remain. Raisins, unless already prepared, should always be stoned.

HOT PUDDINGS

American Banana Fritters

Melted fat or oil	3 or 4 firm bananas
¼ cupful flour	Fritter batter (p. 123)

Peel bananas, cut into three or four diagonal pieces and roll in flour. Dip in batter, completely coating each banana piece. Fry in hot fat for 4–6 minutes, turning frequently to brown evenly. Serve very hot with fruit sauce.

Apple and Raisin Pudding (for 5–6)

8 oz. rice	Sugar
1 pint water	Butter
Pinch of salt	1½ lb. apples
4 oz. raisins	

Boil the rice in the water until nearly done but not too soft, strain, and add a pinch of salt and a small piece of butter while the rice is hot, stirring well. Peel and core the apples and cut into slices; clean and stone raisins and mix with the apples. Butter a pie dish, put in alternate layers of rice and apple and raisin mixture, sprinkling each fruit layer with sugar, and finishing with a layer of apples on top. Put the butter in small pieces on the top and bake in a moderate oven for ¾ hour.

Apple Cake with Lemon Sauce (for 4)

½ lb. self-raising flour	1 egg
½ teaspoonful salt	About ⅓ pint milk
1½ oz. butter or margarine	4 cooking apples
2 dessertspoonfuls sugar	Cinnamon
	Lemon juice

Mix and sift dry ingredients. Work in butter or margarine with tips of fingers,

116

or two knives, add milk with well-beaten egg and mix quickly with knife. Dough must be soft enough to spread in tin. Put into buttered shallow baking tin—square, oblong or 9-in. flan tin. Have the apples ready—pared, cored and cut in quarters— and when dough has spread, press apples into dough in parallel rows. Sprinkle with sugar and cinnamon and a few drops of lemon juice. Bake in hot oven for ½ hour. Serve hot or cold with lemon sauce.

Lemon sauce

¼ pint boiling water	Rind and juice of 3
¼ lb. sugar	medium lemons
1 oz. butter	1 teaspoonful corn-
	flour

Mix the sugar and cornflour. Add boiling water gradually, stirring all the time. Cook for 8–10 minutes. Add lemon juice, rind and butter. Serve hot.

Apple Charlotte (1) (for 4–6)

4 oz. breadcrumbs	Juice and rind of 1
2 lb. cooking apples	lemon
2 oz. brown sugar	2 tablespoonfuls
Butter	syrup
1 tablespoonful water	

Stew the apples, peeled, cored and sliced, gently in a little water with the sugar. Grease a pie dish and sprinkle some breadcrumbs over the bottom. Then add alternate layers of apples and breadcrumbs, finishing with breadcrumbs.

Heat the lemon juice, syrup, water and lemon rind, and pour over the mixture. Put a few pieces of butter on top and bake in a moderate oven for about ½ hour.

Apple Charlotte (2) (for 4–6)

Slices of stale bread	3 oz. clarified butter
2 lb. cooking apples	1 oz. margarine
Juice and rind of half	2 oz. brown sugar
a lemon	

Cut up the apples but do not core or peel them; stew with the lemon juice, rind, sugar, margarine and a very little water, then rub through a sieve. Take a soufflé tin or round fireproof dish and cut two rounds of bread to fit the top and bottom, and fingers of bread to fit round the sides. Dip the bread into clarified butter and line the tin with it. (To clarify butter, melt it in a pan over a gentle heat, remove any scum that rises, pour off the clear liquid and throw away the sediment.)

Apple Meringues—the apples are baked, filled with mincemeat, topped with meringue and served with chocolate sauce

Pour in the apple purée, put on the bread lid, cover with a piece of buttered paper, put a plate on top to weight it down and bake in a moderate oven till the bread is crisp and brown (about 45 minutes). Either turn out on to a dish or serve in the casserole sprinkled with castor sugar.

Apple Dumplings with Suet Crust

Peel some good baking apples thinly, core them and fill the centres with castor sugar.

Make suet crust (see Pastry section) and roll it out on a floured board. Cut into rounds large enough to cover the apples. Put an apple on each round, moisten the edges of the pastry and bring them together, covering the apple completely. Turn over on to a greased tin and bake in a moderate oven for 30-40 minutes.

Apple Meringue (for 4-5)

1 lb. apples, peeled and cored	2 eggs
	Sugar to taste

For the shortbread

6 oz. butter	8 oz. flour
	1 oz. sugar

Rub the butter into the sieved flour, add the sugar, and work into a dough. Roll into a round, press up the edges with the fingers, prick the centre and bake in a moderate oven for 25-30 minutes. Put the apples, peeled and cored, into a saucepan with a very little water and boil to a pulp. Add sugar and 2 egg-yolks. Put the apple mixture on the shortbread, beat the egg-whites stiff and pile on top. Brown in a cool oven.

Apple Meringues with Chocolate Sauce (for 4)

4 apples	Mincemeat
1 egg-white	2 oz. castor sugar

Peel and core apples. Place in a fireproof dish and fill centres with mincemeat. Bake in a moderate oven until soft. Whisk egg-white until stiff, fold in sugar, pile on top of each apple and brown lightly in a cool oven.

For the chocolate sauce

2 oz. block chocolate	2 oz. sugar
1 teaspoonful cocoa	¼ pint water
1 egg-yolk	1 teaspoonful strong
¼ teaspoonful vanilla	black coffee

Put chocolate, cocoa, sugar and water into a pan and bring to the boil. When dissolved, simmer until consistency of thin cream (about 15-20 minutes). Fold in vanilla, coffee and, finally, the egg-yolk, gradually. Beat thoroughly, but do not reheat before serving.

Apple Soufflé (for 4-5)

1½ pints milk	1 oz. butter
1 oz. castor sugar	1 lb. apples
1 teacupful rice	2 eggs

Boil the rice in the milk until tender, then add the butter and the egg-yolks, without allowing to boil. Stew the apples with sugar to taste and put them at the bottom of a buttered pie dish with the rice on top. Bake in a cool oven until set. Beat the egg-whites to a stiff froth, fold in the sugar, pile on top of the soufflé and bake till golden brown. This may be eaten hot or cold.

Apricot Upside-down Cake (for 4-5)

1½ lb. fresh apricots	½ lb. soft light brown
1 oz. butter	sugar (pieces)
Sponge cake batter	

Wash apricots in colander and remove stems. Drain, and cut in half, removing stones. Butter large, thick, iron frying pan very generously and sprinkle with the brown sugar. Place apricots closely all over the sugared pan, keeping the cut side up. Now make sponge cake batter:

2 eggs, separated	4 oz. flour
½ lb. sugar (less 1 tablespoonful)	1½ level teaspoonfuls baking powder (or
3 tablespoonfuls boiling water	½ teaspoonful if self-raising flour is
¼ teaspoonful lemon juice	used)
	¼ teaspoonful salt

Beat yolks until thick and light. Gradually add half the sugar, the boiling water and lemon juice, and beat. Whip egg-whites until stiff but not dry, and add the rest of the sugar gradually. Combine with yolks. Fold in flour, mixed and sifted with baking powder and salt. Spread batter over the apricots and bake in moderate oven for about ½ hour. When done, turn on to large plate upside down and serve with sweetened whipped cream handed separately. Can also be served plain.

Australian Pudding (for 8-10)

1 lb. flour	4 oz. raisins
8 oz. suet	8 oz. sugar
4 oz. currants	Salt
Pinch of mixed spice	A little grated lemon
2 oz. candied peel	rind
1 teaspoonful bicarbonate of soda	½ pint milk and water

Sift the flour, add the suet, fruit, peel chopped finely, lemon rind, sugar, salt and spice. Mix well together. Warm the milk and water and pour on to the soda so that it froths up well. Pour at once into the dry ingredients and stir thoroughly. Put into a greased basin (it should come only two-thirds of the way up because it rises), cover with a double piece of greased paper and steam for 3 hours, or bake for 1½ hours in a moderate oven.

Baked Alaska (see Soufflé Omelets, p. 129)

Baked Bananas

Peel bananas. Place in a well-greased baking tray. Sprinkle with brown sugar. Bake in a moderate oven for 15–18 minutes or until tender. Serve with fruit sauce. (Baked bananas may also be served as a vegetable if sprinkled with salt instead of sugar before baking.)

Baked Banana Custard (for 4)

3 eggs	Nutmeg or cinnamon
3 bananas	1 oz. castor sugar
1 pint milk	

Break eggs separately into a basin, add sugar and beat thoroughly, then add the pulp of the bananas and the milk. Pour this into one large or two small buttered pie dishes, grate over a little nutmeg or powdered cinnamon and bake in a moder-ately heated oven (in a tin containing water) for about 35 minutes. Dish up and serve hot.

Baked Bread Pudding (for 3–4)

4 oz. baked bread-crumbs	1 pint milk
1 tablespoonful sugar	3 oz. currants
1 tablespoonful Golden Syrup	½ oz. chopped lemon peel
Pinch of salt	½ teaspoonful mixed spice
1 egg	

Heat the milk and pour it over the bread-crumbs. Add all the other ingredients, ex-cept the syrup, which must be mixed in last. Stir the mixture well. Put into a greased pie dish and bake in a hot oven for 1 hour.

Baked Custard (for 3–4)

1 pint milk	Flavouring (vanilla
Sugar to taste	essence, lemon,
2 eggs	orange or almond)

Beat the eggs, milk and sugar together,

Chocolate Crumble Pudding, with a crisp top, is very easy to make

and add flavouring as desired. Pour the mixture into a buttered pie dish and stand it in a tin of water in a moderate oven to prevent curdling. Add a cupful of cold water to the tin in about 20 minutes. Cook in a very slow oven for 30–40 minutes.

Banana Apple Betty (for 6)

2 tart apples, pared and cored	¾ cupful sugar
½ teaspoonful cinna-mon	3 firm bananas, peeled
	3 cupfuls soft bread-crumbs
¼ teaspoonful salt	

Slice apples and cut bananas crosswise into ½-in. pieces. Mix sugar, cinnamon and salt with crumbs. Place alternate layers of crumbs and fruit in a well buttered baking dish, using crumbs for top and bottom layers. Cover baking dish and bake in a moderate oven about 40 minutes. Un-cover. Bake 5 minutes longer or until crumbs are browned. Serve hot, with cream, custard or fruit sauce.

Banana Stuffed Pancakes (for 4)

These are made with the usual pancake batter (p. 126), but are folded in three round a spoonful of banana filling, and served either with a smooth vanilla sauce or a hot jam sauce.

For the banana filling

2 *large ripe bananas*	1 *dessertspoonful*
A *good squeeze of*	*sugar*
lemon juice	

Mash bananas, mix in sugar and lemon juice to taste. Put 2 or 3 teaspoonfuls in centre of each pancake and fold ends over.

For the vanilla sauce

½ *oz. butter*	¾ *pint boiling water*
1 *tablespoonful flour*	¼ *cupful sugar*
1 *teaspoonful vanilla*	

Melt butter, add flour and stir over low heat until it bubbles. Do not brown. Add boiling water with sugar and cook until smooth and thick. Add vanilla, strain and serve hot.

Banana Pancakes Flambées

Roll pancakes round banana filling as for Banana Stuffed Pancakes and place side by side on silver entrée dish or decorative shallow fireproof dish. Heat 3 tablespoonfuls dark Jamaica rum in saucepan and pour over filled pancakes to moisten thoroughly and flavour. Set light to rum and serve.

Batter Pudding (Steamed) (for 4)

4 *oz. flour*	½ *pint milk*
2 *eggs*	*Pinch of salt*

Sieve the flour and salt into a basin. Make a well in the centre and break the eggs into it; add a little of the milk and mix it in well. When half the milk is in, beat well for 10 minutes, then add the rest, still beating. Leave for 1 hour. Grease a mould, pour the mixture in, cover with a double piece of greased paper and steam for 1½ hours. Serve with Golden Syrup or jam.

Bread and Butter Pudding (for 4)

3 *oz. stale bread*	*Grated lemon rind*
Butter	1 *pint milk*
Sultanas	2 *eggs*
	Sugar to taste

Cut some thin slices of stale bread, remove the crusts, cut into neat squares and butter. Put about half the bread and butter into a buttered pie dish, then a handful of sultanas and a little grated lemon rind, then the rest of the bread, with a few sultanas on top. Beat the eggs, add them to the milk, with sugar to taste, and pour this mixture into the pie dish. Leave to soak for ½ hour, then put into a tin of water and bake in moderate oven for 30 minutes

Bread Pudding

Stale bread	*Currants*
Suet or dripping	*Brown sugar*
Sultanas	*Pinch of spice*
	Chopped peel

Put some stale bread in a basin and pour boiling water over it. Let it stand for a few minutes, then squeeze dry. Beat some dripping or suet into the bread, add sultanas, currants, sugar, spice and peel to taste, and mix well. Grease a pie dish, sprinkle the sides and bottom with brown sugar, and put in the mixture. Bake in a moderate oven till brown (about 45 minutes), then turn out on to a dish. If liked, this pudding can be steamed instead, but in this case an egg should be added.

Cabinet Pudding (for 6–7)

5 *oz. sponge fingers*	2 *oz. glacé cherries*
or cakes	1 *pint milk*
3 *oz. sugar*	*Rum or Madeira*
4 *oz. sultanas*	3 *eggs*

Soak the sultanas and cherries in a little rum or Madeira, stirring well with a fork. Butter and sugar a pudding basin, then line it with sponge fingers cut in pieces. Arrange the remainder in alternate layers with the cherries and sultanas and sugar. Make a custard with the milk and eggs (see Caramel Custard below) and pour in slowly so that the fingers get well soaked. Steam for 1 hour and serve with custard or any sweet sauce.

Caramel Custard (for 3–4)

2 *oz. loaf sugar*	2 *whole eggs and 2*
½ *gill cold water*	*egg-yolks*
Squeeze of lemon	½ *pint milk*
juice	*Flavouring*
	Sugar

To make the caramel: Cook the loaf sugar, water and lemon juice until golden brown, shaking the pan now and again. Pour quickly into a dry hot soufflé tin and tilt the tin so that the caramel runs over the bottom and sides. Leave to cool. *For the custard:* Beat the eggs with the sugar and add the milk, warmed to blood heat, and flavouring to taste, then strain it into the

Chocolate Rainbow Pudding—pink, brown and yellow—topped with custard is popular with children of all ages

soufflé tin. Cover with a double piece of greased paper and steam *very* slowly for about 50 minutes or till the custard is set and firm; or bake in a moderate oven, standing the tin in another tin containing water. Turn out on to a hot dish. Caramel custard can also be served cold, and should then be left to cool before turning out.

Castle Puddings (for 4–5)

2 oz. butter	1 egg
2 oz. sugar	Pinch of baking
2 oz. flour	powder

Beat the butter and sugar to a cream, add the egg and then the flour and baking powder, sieved together. Mix well. Grease and half fill some small moulds and steam for about 30 minutes, or bake in a quick oven for 15–20 minutes. Serve with ginger, jam or treacle sauce.

Chocolate Pudding (for 3–4)

2 oz. chocolate powder	Pinch of salt
½ pint milk	2 eggs
2 oz. breadcrumbs	2 oz. butter
2 oz. ground rice	2 oz. sugar
	Vanilla essence

Beat the butter and sugar together until creamy. Separate the whites and yolks of the eggs and add the well beaten yolks to

the mixture. Sieve the dry ingredients together and stir lightly into the mixture. Then add the milk and, lastly, the stiffly beaten egg-whites and vanilla essence. Put into a greased mould, cover with a double piece of greased paper and steam for 1½ hours. Serve with custard.

Chocolate Almond Pudding with Orange Sauce (for 4–5)

4 oz. castor sugar	4 oz. flour
3 oz. margarine	1 teaspoonful almond
3 eggs	essence
2 oz. ground rice	1 teaspoonful baking
4 oz. drinking choco-	powder
late	Pinch of salt

Cream margarine and sugar, and beat in egg-yolks. Blend chocolate with a little water and add with dry ingredients and flavouring. Fold in stiffly-whipped egg-whites. Turn into a greased basin, and steam for 1½–1¾ hours.

For the orange sauce

Juice and rind of 1 large orange	1 level teaspoonful arrowroot or corn-
¼ pint water	flour
1 oz. sugar	

Blend arrowroot or cornflour with a little cold water. Boil sugar, juice and grated rind with remaining water and pour over

121

arrowroot. Return to pan, bring to boil, stirring until it thickens.

Chocolate Crumble Pudding (for 6)

For the chocolate pudding

1 pint milk	2 oz. sugar
1½ oz. cornflour	1 oz. cocoa

For the crumble top

4 oz. plain flour	1 oz. sugar
2 oz. margarine	Pinch of salt

Blend cocoa, cornflour and sugar together with a little of the cold milk. Boil remainder of the milk and pour over blended mixture. Return to pan and cook until thickened. Pour into pie dish and allow skin to form.

To make crumble.—Rub fat into flour and stir in sugar and pinch of salt. Spread on top of the chocolate pudding and bake in moderate oven until golden brown.

Chocolate Rainbow Pudding (for 4)

5½ oz. flour	1½ teaspoonfuls bak-
½ oz. custard powder	ing powder
Pinch of salt	¼ teaspoonful vanilla
3 oz. sugar	essence
3 oz. margarine	¼ pint milk
1 teaspoonful cocoa	Carmine

Cream the fat and sugar, add the sifted flour, salt, baking powder and custard powder, and mix with milk to a soft, dropping consistency. Add vanilla essence. Divide into three. With carmine, colour one-third pink, add cocoa to another third. Put the three mixtures into a greased pudding basin in scattered spoonfuls. Cover with greased paper and steam for 2 hours. Serve with custard.

Chocolate Meringue Pudding (for 4)

2 oz. breadcrumbs	1 or 2 eggs
½ pint milk	1 oz. drinking choco-
1 oz. sugar	late
1 oz. margarine	
(2 oz. castor sugar to each egg-white for	
meringue)	

Bring sugar, chocolate and margarine to the boil with the milk, pour on to the breadcrumbs in a basin. Cool slightly and add egg-yolks. Place in greased pie dish and bake in moderate oven until set.

For meringue.—Whisk egg-whites until stiff and fold in castor sugar lightly. Pile on top of pudding. Place on low shelf in slow oven and bake until golden brown.

Christmas Pudding (for about 20)

2 lb. raisins	2 lb. chopped suet
2 lb. currants	2 oz. chopped
2 lb. sultanas	almonds
1 lb. breadcrumbs	½ teaspoonful salt
1 lb. flour	½ gill sherry
¼ lb. mixed peel	½ gill brandy
1 lb. brown sugar	A little milk
2 teaspoonfuls bak-	Juice of 2 lemons
ing powder	Grated nutmeg
6 eggs	½ teaspoonful ginger

Clean fruit, removing all stalks. Sift and mix all dry ingredients together. Stir in the beaten eggs, the sherry, brandy and lemon juice. Add enough milk to make the mixture a fairly stiff consistency. Put into greased basins with a piece of greased paper on the top and then a scalded pudding-cloth. Steam for 8 hours, or according to size. Reboil for several hours when the pudding is to be eaten.

NOTE: This quantity makes about 12 lb. The time required for cooking the puddings naturally depends on their size. Puddings of 1–2 lb. would not require so long.

Coffee Crumble (for 4–6)

¾ oz. cornflour	1 oz. margarine
1 teaspoonful cocoa	2 tablespoonfuls
1 tablespoonful coffee	quick porridge oats
essence or black	2 tablespoonfuls
coffee	breadcrumbs or
½ pint milk	biscuit crumbs
2 oz. sugar	

Blend cornflour and cocoa with a little of the milk. Heat remainder of the milk and coffee together. Pour on to the cornflour mixture. Return to the pan and boil for 3 minutes, stirring all the time. Add 1½ oz. sugar and pour into a fireproof dish. Cream margarine with the remainder of the sugar. Add porridge oats and breadcrumbs. Mix well and spread on top of the coffee cream. Put into hot oven for about 10 minutes.

Cottage Pudding (for 3–4)

4 oz. cooked potatoes	2 eggs
1 pint of milk	2 oz. sugar

Mash the potatoes, add the sugar, eggs and, lastly, the milk. Mix well together. Grease a pie dish, pour in the mixture and bake in a moderate oven for ¾ hour.

Curate's Pudding (for 3–4)

6 tablespoonfuls	2 or 3 tablespoonfuls
mashed potatoes	milk
4 oz. sugar	2 eggs
2 oz. butter	1 lemon
1 saltspoonful salt	

Cream the butter and sugar together until thick and smooth, add the eggs and beat well. Add the juice and grated rind of the lemon, then the salt and milk, and mix in the potato. Pour into a greased pie dish and bake for 30–35 minutes in a moderate oven.

Date Pudding (for 3–4)

8 oz. stoned dates	2 oz. flour
4 oz. brown bread-crumbs	3 oz. shredded suet
½ teaspoonful baking powder	1 tablespoonful Golden Syrup
	Milk

Cut up the dates and mix with the dry ingredients and the Golden Syrup. Add enough milk to make into a fairly stiff mixture and put into a greased basin; cover with a double piece of greased paper and steam for 2–2½ hours.

Fig Pudding (for 4–6)

8 oz. breadcrumbs	2 eggs
8 oz. figs	Scrape of nutmeg
6 oz. shredded suet	½ pint milk
6 oz. sugar	

Chop the figs very finely and mix with the breadcrumbs, sugar, suet and nutmeg. Add the beaten eggs and the milk. Put the mixture into a greased basin, cover with a double piece of greased paper and steam for 3 hours. Serve with wine foam sauce.

French Pancakes (for 4–6)

2 oz. flour	2 oz. sugar
2 oz. butter	2 eggs
Pinch of baking powder	1 gill milk
	Jam

Grease some flat, round tins. Cream the butter and sugar, add the beaten egg-yolks, then the flour, baking powder and milk, and lastly fold in the whipped whites. Pour the mixture into the tins and bake in a moderate oven for about 10 minutes, when the pancakes should be well risen and brown. Turn out on to a hot dish, sandwich the pancakes together with hot jam and sprinkle with castor sugar.

Fritter Batter (for 6–7)

4 oz. flour	Pinch of salt
1 gill tepid water	1 egg

Separate the egg-white from yolk. Sieve the flour and salt into a basin, make a well in the centre and drop in the yolk. Add the water, mixing it in gradually with a wooden spoon. Work in the flour well and leave to stand. Lastly, whip the egg-white to a stiff froth and fold it in. This batter can be used for either sweet or savoury fritters. Sprinkle sugar over sweet fritters, and add a pinch of Cayenne pepper and salt to savoury ones.

Chocolate Meringue Pudding—the base is mainly breadcrumbs, milk, chocolate and egg-yolk, very quickly prepared

Fruit Fritters

Apples, bananas, oranges, pineapple, apricots, etc., all make excellent fritters. Canned fruit can also be used, but it should be well drained first. For batter recipe, see previous page.

Sprinkle the slices, sections or chunks of fruit with castor sugar and dip them in the batter. Have some hot fat ready (it should be at least 2 in. deep), and drop in a few fritters. Leave enough room for them to swell. Brown one side, then turn and brown the other, lowering the heat a little. When they puff out and become crisp, lift them out and let the fat drain away. Then put them on kitchen paper to finish draining and sprinkle with plenty of castor sugar. Arrange in a neat pile on a d'oyley and eat at once.

Frying Batter (for 6–7)

4 oz. flour	1 oz. oiled butter or
1 gill tepid water	salad oil
Pinch of salt	

Sieve the flour and salt into a bowl, make a well in the centre, add the butter or oil and warm water gradually, beating well with a wooden spoon. Leave for at least 1 hour before using. A stiffly beaten white of egg can be folded into the mixture just before using.

Ginger Pudding (for 3–4)

2 oz. flour	2 tablespoonfuls
4 oz. breadcrumbs	Golden Syrup
3 oz. shredded suet	1 teaspoonful ground
½ teaspoonful baking	ginger (or more,
powder	according to taste)
Chopped ginger, if	Milk
available	

Mix the dry ingredients in a basin, add the Golden Syrup, and, lastly, enough milk to make a fairly firm mixture. Put into a greased basin, cover with a double piece of greased paper and steam for 2–2¼ hours.

NOTE: A little chopped ginger adds greatly to the flavour of this pudding.

Grainger Pudding (for 6)

2 oz. ground rice	1 egg
1 pint milk	1 teaspoonful almond
2 oz. margarine	essence
2 oz. sugar	Apricot jam
2 oz. drinking choco-	Coconut or blanched
late	almonds

Sprinkle ground rice and chocolate on to warm milk in saucepan, bring to the boil and cook until thick. Add sugar, margarine and almond essence and, finally, beaten egg. Pour into greased pie dish and cover with apricot jam. Coat with coconut or blanched almonds and bake in moderate oven for 15–20 minutes.

Half-pay Pudding (for 4–5)

3 oz. shredded suet	½ teaspoonful baking
3 oz. breadcrumbs	powder
3 oz. flour	3 oz. sultanas
1 tablespoonful	3 oz. currants
Golden Syrup	1½ gill milk
Pinch of mixed spice	

Mix all the dry ingredients together, stir in the syrup and, lastly, the milk. Beat well and put the mixture into a buttered basin. Cover with a double piece of greased paper and steam for 3 hours.

Hasty Pudding (for 3–4)

1 pint milk	1 oz. butter
4 tablespoonfuls flour	Sugar to taste

Bring the milk to the boil. Mix the flour to a thick paste with cold water, and add it gradually to the milk, stirring the whole time. Add the butter and sugar, and continue stirring till the mixture thickens (about 10–15 minutes). Serve with Golden Syrup, jam or brown sugar.

Jubilee Pudding (for 3–4)

4 oz. flour	1 whole egg and 1
3 oz. butter and mar-	white
garine mixed	4 oz. currants
2 tablespoonfuls sugar	A little peel, if liked
¼ teaspoonful bicar-	Milk
bonate of soda	

Cream the butter and sugar together, add the beaten eggs, then the dry ingredients mixed together, and enough milk to make a thickish batter. Put the mixture into a greased basin with a double piece of greased paper on top, and steam for 1½ hours. Serve with treacle or wine foam sauce.

Kitchen Pudding (for 7–8)

1 lb. flour	1 teaspoonful bak-
8 oz. dripping	ing powder
4 oz. stoned raisins	A little milk
A little moist sugar	

Sieve the flour and the baking powder, and rub in the dripping. Add the moist sugar and the raisins, and stir well. Mix with a little milk until fairly stiff, sprinkle a little Demerara sugar on top and bake in a moderate oven until brown (about 45 minutes). It should be very light and crisp.

Almond flavoured Lafayette Puddings are cooked in dariole moulds. Hot chocolate custard
is poured on top

Lafayette Puddings (for 4)

3 oz. ground almonds	4 oz. castor sugar
4 oz. flour	1 teaspoonful baking
2 oz. breadcrumbs	powder
2 eggs	2 oz. glacé cherries
4 oz. margarine	Milk to mix

Grease 8 dariole moulds. Sieve flour
and baking powder together. Add ground
almonds and breadcrumbs. Cream margarine and sugar together. Beat in the
eggs. Add the dry ingredients and milk if
necessary. Lastly, add the glacé cherries,
quartered, and mix well. Fill the moulds
three-quarters full. Cover with greased
paper. Steam for 40 minutes to 1 hour.
Serve with chocolate custard sauce:

For the chocolate sauce

½ pint milk	1 egg
½ oz. drinking choco-late	2 teaspoonfuls sugar

Put the milk and sugar on to boil,
sprinkle in the drinking chocolate and stir
until dissolved. Beat the egg lightly with a
fork. When the milk is almost boiling, pour
on to the beaten egg and whisk for a few
minutes. Pour mixture into a jug and stand
in a saucepan of boiling water, or cook in a
double saucepan, until the custard
thickens.

Lemon Pudding (for 3–4)

4 oz. breadcrumbs	2 oz. moist sugar
1 oz. flour	Grated rind of 1
½ teaspoonful bak-ing powder	lemon
2 oz. shredded suet	1 egg
	¼ gill milk

Mix all the dry ingredients together with
the lemon rind. Add the beaten egg and
milk, and stir the mixture well. Put into
a greased mould, cover with a double piece
of greased paper and steam for 2 hours.
Serve with lemon sauce, using the juice of
the lemon.

Marmalade Pudding (for 3–4)

2 oz. breadcrumbs	2 oz. castor sugar
2 oz. flour	1 egg
2 oz. shredded suet	¼ teaspoonful baking
Grated rind of 1	powder
lemon	½ gill milk
2 tablespoonfuls marmalade	Sauce

Mix all the dry ingredients together, siev-
ing the flour and baking powder. Add the
marmalade, egg and milk. If the mixture
is too stiff, add a little more milk. Put mixture into a greased basin, cover with a
double piece of greased paper and steam
for 2½ hours.

To make the sauce.—Peel a lemon very

thinly and cut the peel into short strips. Boil these in water until soft, then add 2 tablespoonfuls of sugar and 2 teaspoonfuls of cornflour made into a paste with a little water. Stir well and simmer for about 3 minutes. Remove from fire and add 2 teaspoonfuls of lemon juice. Dish up the pudding and serve with the sauce.

Milk Pudding (for 2–4)

2 oz. rice, sago or tapioca	½ oz. butter
	1 pint milk
1 tablespoonful sugar	Pinch of salt

Just cover the cereal with water and let it stand for 5 minutes. Strain off water, and put the cereal in a greased pie dish with the sugar, butter, salt and milk. Let it soak for about 1 hour. Then stir it well and cook slowly in a cool oven for 2 hours, stirring well after ½ hour.

The above recipe makes a pudding of medium thickness; more or less cereal should be used to vary the consistency according to taste. An egg can be added if desired, in which case the cereal should be boiled in the milk first and the egg added when cool. Then bake in the oven for 20 minutes.

Mysterious Pudding (for 4–5)

2 eggs and their weight in flour, fresh butter and moist sugar	1 teaspoonful marmalade
	A level teaspoonful bicarbonate of soda

Separate the egg-whites from the yolks. Cream the butter and sugar, add the yolks, then the flour, soda and marmalade. Fold in the beaten whites. Pour into a basin or mould, which the mixture should only half fill since it rises very much. Steam for 1¼ hours.

Nuremberg Pudding (for 6–7)

¼ pint Golden Syrup	½ teaspoonful bicarbonate of soda
8 oz. flour	
4 oz. shredded suet	1 oz. candied peel
1 gill milk	1 egg

Mix the milk and the syrup together. Add the suet to the sieved flour and chopped peel. Then beat in the egg and, lastly, add the milk, syrup and soda. Put either into small greased moulds or into a large one and steam for ½ hour or 2½ hours as the case may be. Serve with Golden Syrup.

Oatmeal Pudding (for 3–4)

4 oz. coarse oatmeal	2 oz. shredded suet
½ pint milk	Nutmeg
2 oz. currants	Sugar to taste
	Small egg

Boil the milk and pour it on the oatmeal. Let it stand till the next day. Then add the other ingredients and bake in a slow oven for 2 hours.

Orange Pudding (for 4–5)

3 oranges	1 oz. butter
1¼ pints milk	3 oz. sugar
1½ oz. cornflour	2 eggs
	Pinch of salt

Peel the oranges, cut in pieces and place in a buttered dish. Mix cornflour with a little of the milk. Boil remainder of milk, add to the cornflour paste and cook for 10 minutes, stirring constantly. Add the butter and a pinch of salt. Sprinkle a little sugar over the oranges. Mix the rest of the sugar with the yolks of the eggs, and add to the milk and cornflour mixture. Stir for a minute or two longer over the fire without boiling. Pour over the oranges and bake for 10 minutes. Beat the egg-whites stiffly, fold in a little castor sugar, pile on top and return to cool oven for about 10 minutes, to set and tinge a very pale brown.

Pancakes (for 7–8)

8 oz. flour	2 eggs
Butter or lard for frying	1 pint milk
	Pinch of salt

Sift the flour and salt into a basin, make a well in the centre and pour into it the beaten eggs. Mix with a wooden spoon, adding half the milk a little at a time and stirring in the flour from the sides gradually to keep the mixture a smooth creamy consistency. When all the flour is mixed in, beat well for 10 minutes and stir in the remaining milk. Pour the batter into a jug. It can be used at once, or may be left to stand uncovered, but not for more than 1½–2 hours.

In a thick-based frying pan (preferably an omelet pan), heat the butter or lard and pour it off into a cup, leaving just enough to coat the pan thinly. Heat until a thin film of blue smoke can be seen, then pour in a little batter, tilting the pan so that an even coating is obtained. Cook until the surface of the batter is dry—which

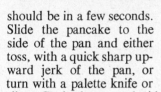

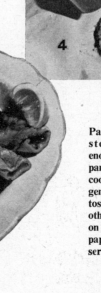

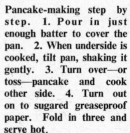

should be in a few seconds. Slide the pancake to the side of the pan and either toss, with a quick sharp upward jerk of the pan, or turn with a palette knife or slice. Cook the second side for about $\frac{1}{2}$ minute, until slightly browned. Invert pancake on to sugared paper and sprinkle with lemon juice and castor sugar. Fold in three and keep warm while making the other pancakes. Serve with castor sugar and quarters of lemon.

Pancakes may also be served with hot jam or fruit inside, or flat with hot jam or fruit spread on them, the pancakes then being placed one on top of the other.

Pancake-making step by step. 1. Pour in just enough batter to cover the pan. 2. When underside is cooked, tilt pan, shaking it gently. 3. Turn over—or toss—pancake and cook other side. 4. Turn out on to sugared greaseproof paper. Fold in three and serve hot.

Pudding à la Margot (for 3–4)

3 slices of bread ⅛ in.   Butter
   thick   Jam
        Whisky or brandy

For the sauce

2 oz. butter   3 tablespoonfuls
1 tablespoonful corn-   sugar
   flour   1 pint water

Spread the slices of bread lightly with butter and thickly with jam. Put them on top of one another in a pudding dish and pour over them a glass of brandy or whisky. When it has soaked in, fill up with melted butter sauce made as follows:

Make a paste with the cornflour, the sugar and a little water. Boil the rest of the water with the butter and pour it over the paste, stirring well. Pour this sauce over the slices of bread and bake in a moderate oven till the pudding is a nice brown.

Queen's Pudding (for 3–4)

½ pint milk   2 egg-yolks
2 oz. breadcrumbs   2 oz. sugar
Rind of ½ lemon   1 oz. butter
    3 tablespoonfuls jam

For the meringue
2 oz. castor sugar and 2 egg-whites

Heat the milk with the lemon rind, remove the peel and pour milk over the breadcrumbs. Add the sugar and the butter, and leave to soak for about 30 minutes. Then add the beaten yolks. Butter a pie dish, pour in the mixture and bake in a moderate oven for ½ hour, or until set. Take out the pudding, spread the top with jam and pile on the stiffly beaten egg-whites into which 2 oz. sugar have been folded. Sprinkle the top with castor sugar and put the pudding back into the oven until the meringue is slightly brown.

NOTE: This pudding can also be made with any dry biscuit or cake crumbs.

Roly-poly Pudding, with Jam, Treacle or Mincemeat (for 4)

8 oz. flour   ½ teaspoonful baking
3 or 4 oz. shredded   powder
   suet   Water or milk
     Pinch of salt

Sieve the flour, baking powder and salt, add the suet and mix well. Add enough water or milk to make a firm rather dry dough. Roll the crust into an oblong on a floured pastry board, making one end a little wider than the other. Spread with jam, Golden Syrup or mincemeat to within 1 in. of the edge (if syrup is used, scatter a tablespoonful of breadcrumbs over it). Moisten the edges of the crust and roll up from the narrow end, pressing it down as you roll. Scald and flour a pudding-cloth and put the roly-poly, wrapped in greased paper, in it. Fold over the cloth and tie the ends firmly, or bring them together in the middle and pin with a safety-pin. Boil for 1½ hours.

Roly-poly Pudding with Sultanas and Currants

Proceed as above, but add to the dry ingredients 3 oz. sultanas, 3 oz. currants, 2 oz. sugar and 1 oz. chopped peel. Omit the jam, treacle or mincemeat.

St. Cross Pudding (for 3–4)

6 oz. flour   2 eggs
4 oz. sugar   1 teaspoonful baking
2 oz. lard   powder
2 tablespoonfuls milk Jam

Rub 1 oz. lard into the flour, add the sugar and baking powder, then the eggs well beaten and, lastly, the milk. Melt the other ounce of lard in the pie dish and add a thick layer of jam; then pour in the mixture and bake in a moderate oven for ¾–1 hour.

Snowdon Pudding (for 5–6)

12 oz. breadcrumbs   Raisins
8 oz. moist sugar   1½ small lemons
      3 eggs

For the sauce

½ pint water   Rind and juice of 1½
8 oz. lump sugar   lemons

Mix the breadcrumbs, sugar, juice and grated rind of the lemons well together. Then add the well-beaten eggs and beat. Line a greased basin with raisins and pour in the mixture. Steam for 2½ hours.

To make the sauce.—Cut the lemon rind into very thin strips and boil in the water until soft; add the lump sugar and boil until quite clear. Add the lemon juice and pour over the pudding.

Soufflé à la Vanille (for 3–4)

4 oz. sugar   5 egg-yolks
1½ oz. flour   4 egg-whites
1½ oz. butter   ½ pint milk
     Vanilla essence

Heat the milk, sugar, butter and a few drops of vanilla essence together. Make a smooth paste with the flour and a little milk, add this to the hot milk, stirring well. Cook for 2 minutes, then cool. Beat in the egg-yolks and, when quite cool, fold in the stiffly beaten whites. Pour the soufflé into a buttered, sugared dish which should not be more than three-quarters full. Cook in a moderate oven for 20–25 minutes and serve immediately.

Soufflé Omelet (for 1–2)

2 eggs	½ oz. butter
Pinch of salt	Flavouring

Separate the egg-yolks from the whites. Get ready a buttered pan. Whisk the yolks and add desired flavouring (vanilla, lemon, etc.). Then whisk the whites very stiffly, adding a pinch of salt, fold into the yolks and pour the mixture into the hot buttered pan and let it cook for about 4 minutes over a moderate flame. Do not stir. Take it off and put it under the hot grill for 2 or 3 minutes until slightly firm. Cut a slit almost across and put in your filling (hot jam, hot fruit purée, etc.); then fold over carefully and slide on to a hot dish. Sprinkle with a little castor sugar and serve *at once*.

This omelet can also be served unfilled, in which case it should be accompanied by a chocolate, ginger or treacle sauce.

Chocolate Mousse makes a delicious cold sweet for summer meals

Vanilla ice cream is the foundation of this Chocolate Sundae

Soufflé Omelet (Baked) (for 3–4)

5 eggs	2 or 3 oz. sugar
	Vanilla

Separate the egg-yolks from the whites. Beat the yolks with sugar for 20 minutes. Beat the whites separately for 10 minutes (just before serving). When the time to serve has arrived, stir the yolks and whites lightly together and put the mixture on to a flat dish and into a *very* hot oven for 3–5 minutes, when the soufflé should have risen at least 5 in. and be well browned. Sprinkle with castor sugar and serve immediately.

NOTE: This soufflé mixture can be poured over a block of ice-cream to make a **Baked Alaska**. The oven must be *very* hot to cook the soufflé before the ice melts and the ice must be completely covered with the soufflé mixture.

Sponge Pudding (for 3–4)

4 oz. flour	¼ teaspoonful baking
3 oz. butter and mar-	powder
garine mixed	A little milk
2 oz. sugar	1 tablespoonful
1 whole egg and 1	Golden Syrup
egg-white	Fruit

Cream the fat and sugar together, add the beaten eggs, the flour and the baking powder. Then add sufficient milk to make a thickish batter. Lastly, add the Golden Syrup. Put the mixture into a greased basin with a double piece of greased paper on top and steam for 1½ hours. Serve with treacle sauce.

NOTE: Chocolate powder or ground ginger can be used as a flavouring for this pudding if liked. If chocolate is used, add a few drops of vanilla and omit the syrup.

Suet Pudding with Fresh or Bottled Fruit (for 4–5)

½ lb. flour	½ teaspoonful baking
4 oz. shredded suet	powder
Water or milk	Fruit
Pinch of salt	Sugar to taste

Sieve flour, baking powder and salt, and add suet, mixing well together. Add enough water or milk to make a firm dough, roll out the crust on a floured board, keeping back enough for the lid, and line a greased basin with it. Put in the fruit and sugar. Moisten the edges of the crust and put on the lid, pressing it firmly. Cover with a double piece of greased paper and steam for 2½ hours.

Ten-minute Dumplings (for 4–5)

4 oz. breadcrumbs	2 oz. sugar
4 oz. shredded suet	2 eggs
4 oz. currants	Salt and nutmeg
Milk (if required)	

Mix the dry ingredients together, add the beaten eggs and a little milk (if required), and make into about ten firm dumplings. Boil for 10 minutes, and serve with lemon sauce.

Toffee Pudding (for 4–5)

12 oz. bread, cut in	8 oz. Demerara sugar
squares	8 oz. Golden Syrup
4 oz. butter	Milk

Put the sugar, butter and syrup into a frying pan, and boil until golden brown. Dip the squares of bread in milk, then put into pan and let them get really hot. Pile them up on a hot dish and serve, if possible, with whipped cream.

Treacle Layer Pudding (for 5–6)

8 oz. flour	Water or milk
½ teaspoonful baking	Pinch of salt
powder	Treacle
3–4 oz. shredded suet	Breadcrumbs
Rind of ½ lemon	

Sieve the flour, baking powder and salt, add the suet and mix well. Add enough water or milk to make a firm, rather dry dough. Divide the crust in half and roll out one half to line the basin. Cut off enough from the remaining half to make the lid, then roll out the rest thinly. Put in some treacle, with a sprinkling of breadcrumbs and grated lemon rind. Cut out a round of crust large enough to cover the treacle, moisten the edge and join on to the paste lining. Continue until the basin is full, finishing with the lid.

Cover with double greased paper and then the pudding cloth. Steam for 2½–3 hours.

Treacle Sponge (for 5–6)

8 oz. flour	½ teaspoonful bicar-
4 oz. shredded suet	bonate of soda
1 egg	1 teacupful milk
1 teaspoonful ground	1 teacupful Golden
ginger	Syrup

Sieve the flour and the ginger, and add the shredded suet. Beat in the egg, add the syrup and most of the milk, leaving just enough to dissolve the bicarbonate of soda. Mix thoroughly, and at the last moment stir in the soda in the warmed milk. Put into a greased basin and cover with a double piece of greased paper. Steam for 2½ hours.

Victoria Pudding (for 4–5)

3 egg-yolks and 2 egg-	4 oz. butter
whites	4 oz. powdered
4 oz. castor sugar	biscuits
Jam	

Beat the egg-yolks, add the sugar, the melted butter and powdered biscuit. Mix well together. Beat the egg-whites very stiffly and fold into the mixture. Put some jam in the bottom of small buttered moulds and fill with the mixture. Bake in a moderate oven for 30 minutes, then turn out carefully.

Yorkshire Pudding (for 4–6)

8 oz. flour	1 pint milk
2 eggs	Pinch of salt

Sieve the flour and salt into a basin. Make a well in the centre and break the eggs into it; add a little of the milk and mix it in well. When half the milk is in, beat well for 10 minutes, then add the rest of the milk, still beating. The batter should stand for at least 1 hour before it is used. Add about a tablespoonful of cold water at the last minute for a really light pudding. Get a little fat really hot before pouring in the batter then bake in a moderate oven for 30 minutes, raising the heat just enough to brown it at the end.

COLD PUDDINGS

Apple Snow (for 3–4)

1½ lb. apples
2 tablespoonfuls castor sugar
2 egg-whites

Strip of lemon rind
Whipped cream and red currant jelly

Cut the apples up, without either peeling or coring, and stew with the lemon rind in a very little water (just enough to prevent them sticking to the pan) on moderate heat until soft. Rub through a sieve and leave to cool, then beat in the sugar and fold in the stiffly beaten whites. Arrange in a dish and decorate with whipped cream and red currant jelly. A few chopped pistachio nuts are an excellent addition.

Australian Jelly (for 3–4)

2 oz. sago
½ pint milk
Lemon essence

½ pint water
1 tablespoonful Golden Syrup
Cochineal

Soak the sago in the water for 1 hour, then boil until transparent, add the milk and syrup, and cook for 2 or 3 minutes. Add flavouring and colouring. Pour into a wetted mould and leave till cold before turning out.

Charlotte Russe (for 4–5)

Sponge finger biscuits
Cherries

Angelica
Jelly

For the vanilla cream

½ pint cream
1 gill milk
½ oz. powdered gelatine

½ gill water
Castor sugar to taste
Vanilla essence

Line the sides of a soufflé mould closely with the biscuits so that no spaces are left between. Pour in a thin layer of coloured jelly and, when almost set, arrange some cherries and angelica in it. Next make the vanilla cream as follows: Slightly whip the cream, add the sugar, milk and vanilla. Dissolve the gelatine in the water (warmed), and when cool, add it to the mixture. Stir till it begins to set, then pour into the mould. Leave to get quite cold and set firm. Turn out carefully and serve with apricot jam sauce poured round the pudding.

For a hot day—Fruit Chocolate Marshmallow served in parfait glasses

Chestnut Surprise

Wash some chestnuts, cut a slit in the skins and boil till they are soft enough to peel. If they are put in the oven for a minute or two, the skins will come off more easily. Flavour a small quantity of milk with vanilla, add a little sugar and boil the chestnuts in it until they are perfectly soft. Pass through a sieve, after which they should look like vermicelli. Serve topped or surrounded with custard or whipped cream.

Chestnut Cream (for 4)

1 lb. peeled chestnuts (about 1½ lb. unpeeled)
2 tablespoonfuls cream

2 oz. sugar
¼ lb. chocolate
2 oz. butter
1 orange

Cook chestnuts slowly and pass them through a sieve to make purée (see recipe above). Melt chocolate in a little water and add to it the butter and sugar, stirring until well mixed. While the purée is still warm, stir the two mixtures together. Pour into glasses and leave for 24 hours in a cold place. Decorate with orange segments and whipped cream.

Chocolate Blancmange (for 3–4)

1 tablespoonful cocoa
or grated chocolate
1½ tablespoonfuls
castor sugar
1 pint milk
Butter
Vanilla essence
1½ tablespoonfuls
cornflour

Mix the cocoa, sugar and cornflour into a smooth paste with some of the milk. Boil the rest of the milk and pour it on to the paste, stirring well, then return to the saucepan and bring to the boil. Simmer gently for 6 minutes, stirring well all the time. Add vanilla essence to taste and a little butter. Pour into a mould and turn out when set.

Chocolate Cream (for 4–5)

1 quart milk
½ lb. grated choco-
late
5 or 6 lumps of sugar
2 tablespoonfuls
potato flour (or
3 or 4 egg-yolks)

Dissolve the chocolate in a small quantity of milk, stirring the whole time, till it is a smooth paste. Then add the potato flour, which has been mixed with a little cold water (or the beaten yolks), and the sugar. Add the rest of the milk and bring to the boil. If eggs are used, reheat without boiling. Turn into glass dish or custard glasses.

Chocolate Jelly (for 4–5)

1 quart milk
1 oz. castor sugar
6 tablespoonfuls
grated chocolate
¾ oz. powdered gela-
tine
Vanilla essence

Dissolve the gelatine in the milk, then add the grated chocolate and the sugar and cook for 10 minutes, stirring all the time. Allow to cool, beat well with a whisk and add the vanilla essence. Pour into a wetted mould and leave to set. Turn out carefully.

Chocolate Mayonnaise (for 5–6)

4 small sponge cakes
½ lb. chocolate
4 eggs
A little sherry

Flake the chocolate into a basin and dissolve over hot water. Cut the sponge cakes in half across, put them at the bottom of a soufflé dish and pour a little sherry over them. When the chocolate has melted, move from the hot water and stir in the beaten egg-yolks. Whip the whites stiffly and fold them into the chocolate, then pour the mixture over the sponge cakes and leave to stand for 12 hours.

Chocolate Mousse (1) (for 4)

1 pint milk
1 oz. cornflour or
custard powder
¼ pint evaporated milk
or cream
1 oz. cocoa
Sugar to taste
Vanilla essence
3 tablespoonfuls hot
water
¼ oz. gelatine

Wet a mould or individual cups. Dissolve the gelatine in the hot water. Blend the cornflour and cocoa with a little milk. Put the remainder on to boil. When boiling, pour on to the cornflour mixture, return to saucepan to cook for 2–3 minutes, stirring continuously. Sweeten and add the essence. Cool slightly. Pour the evaporated milk into a basin and whisk until thick, then fold immediately into the chocolate mixture. Pour into wetted mould and leave to set.

NOTE: Evaporated milk will thicken more easily and quickly when whisked if it is previously boiled in its tin for about 20 minutes, then thoroughly chilled for an hour or two, preferably in the refrigerator, before being opened.

Chocolate Mousse (2) (for 4)

¼ lb. plain chocolate   4 eggs

Melt the chocolate gently over hot water. Separate the egg-whites from the yolks and stir yolks into melted chocolate. Beat the whites until stiff and fold into the mixture. Pour into wetted moulds and leave to set.

Decorate with whipped cream.

Chocolate Soufflé (for 4–5)

1½ gills cream
1 oz. castor sugar
¼ oz. powdered gela-
tine
2 eggs
1½ oz. grated choco-
late
Warm water and milk

Separate the egg-whites from the yolks. Whisk the yolks with the sugar over hot water until the consistency of thick cream is reached. Dissolve the gelatine in a little warm water, the grated chocolate in a little milk and strain both into the beaten yolks. Whip the cream and add. Lastly, beat the egg-whites to a stiff froth and fold lightly into the mixture. Pour into a soufflé dish and stand in a cold place.

Chocolate Sundae

Vanilla ice cream
Apricot jam syrup
Chopped nuts
Chocolate sauce
Bananas or pears
Cream

Place ice cream in glasses and coat with

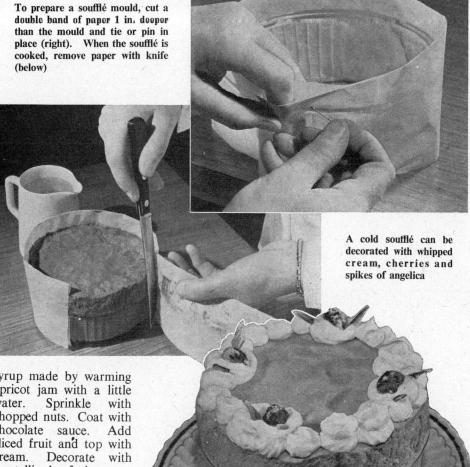

To prepare a soufflé mould, cut a double band of paper 1 in. deeper than the mould and tie or pin in place (right). When the soufflé is cooked, remove paper with knife (below)

A cold soufflé can be decorated with whipped cream, cherries and spikes of angelica

syrup made by warming apricot jam with a little water. Sprinkle with chopped nuts. Coat with chocolate sauce. Add sliced fruit and top with cream. Decorate with crystallised fruit, preserved ginger, etc.

Chocolate Trifle (for 4)

Small sponge fingers
Chopped nuts
Fruit in season
½ pint chocolate sauce
½ pint whipped cream
Juice from fruit

Arrange sponge fingers around the bottom and sides of either individual sundae glasses, waxed cases or a large glass bowl and moisten thoroughly with fruit juice. Leave to soak for 30 minutes in the juice. Then sprinkle on the chopped nuts and arrange fruit on top. Pour on chocolate sauce as evenly as possible and put in a refrigerator or other cold place to set. When cold, decorate with cream.

Cider Jelly (for 3–4)

½ pint cider   *½ pint water*
½ oz. powdered gela-   *2 tablespoonfuls*
tine   *sugar*

Put the gelatine into a saucepan with the water and the sugar and heat sufficiently to dissolve the gelatine, then strain into the cider and pour into a wetted mould. Turn out when set.

Coffee Cream (for 3–4)

½ pint milk	2 oz. sugar
2 eggs	¾ oz. powdered gela-
½ pint coffee (strained)	tine

Separate the egg-whites from the yolks. Soak the gelatine with the milk, coffee and sugar for 15 minutes. Then heat slowly, without boiling. Stir until the gelatine is dissolved, take off the fire and cool a little, then pour gradually on to the egg-yolks and beat well. Beat the whites to a stiff froth and fold into the mixture. Pour into a soufflé dish and leave to set.

Coffee Pudding (for 4–5)

1 gill strong coffee	4 eggs
5 oz. sugar	1 pint milk
	Small pinch of salt

Boil the milk and leave it to cool a little. Beat the eggs and sugar together and add the milk and salt, then the coffee. Strain the mixture into a pie dish, stand in a tin with boiling water half way up the dish and cook in a moderate oven until quite firm. Leave to cool and, when cold, sprinkle with castor sugar.

Cold Soufflé (for 3–4)

1 pint milk	½ oz. powdered gela-
Thinly peeled rind of	tine
1 lemon	1 oz. sugar
2 eggs	Cream

Stir the milk, lemon rind, gelatine and sugar over the fire until the gelatine is dissolved and the flavour extracted from the lemon. Leave to cool a little, then strain over the beaten egg-yolks and put back in the saucepan. Cook for 5 minutes, stirring all the time, without boiling. Stand in cold water to cool, fold in a little whipped cream and the stiffly beaten egg-whites and pour the mixture into a prepared soufflé dish to set. Decorate with whipped cream.

Cream Cheese (Petit Gervais)

Stand a pint of milk in a temperature of about 70° F. overnight or till solid. Drain through muslin for about 4–6 hours, and turn into a dish. This can be eaten as a sweet with fresh cream or strawberries, or as a cheese with salt and pepper, on biscuits or bread.

Custard

2 eggs	½ pint milk
	½ oz. sugar

Beat together the eggs, sugar and milk and pour the mixture into a well-buttered basin or individual moulds and cover with greaseproof paper. Stand on a folded cloth in a saucepan containing enough water to come not more than half way up the basin or moulds. Simmer gently over a low heat for 30–35 minutes for a large custard, 15–20 minutes for small individual ones.

Date Chocolate Flan (for 4)

2 oz. margarine	6 oz. stale cake
3 teaspoonfuls sugar	crumbs
3 teaspoonfuls	6 oz. dates
Golden Syrup	2 bananas
3 teaspoonfuls cocoa	Cream
powder	

Cream margarine, sugar and syrup. Add cocoa and cake crumbs, knead well together. Press mixture into a flan ring, place upside down on the plate to be used for serving. Remove ring when mixture is set. Arrange stoned dates and sliced bananas alternately and decorate with whipped cream.

Empress Rice Pudding (for 4)

3 oz. rice	1 pint milk
3 oz. sugar	1 oz. butter
Stick of vanilla	4 leaves of gelatine
1½ oz. fruit preserve	1 gill whipped cream
	A little Kirsch

Boil the rice in the milk with sugar, butter and vanilla. When well cooked and creamy, dissolve gelatine leaves in a little milk, mix with the fruit preserve steeped in Kirsch and add the whipped cream. Pour into mould and chill in refrigerator for about 2 hours. Turn out and serve with a Sabayon sauce.

Fruit Blancmange (for 3–4)

1 lb. juicy fruit	2 tablespoonfuls
Water	cornflour
	Sugar to taste

Stew the fruit with a little water and put through a sieve. Add water to bring the pulp to ¾ pint and sweeten to taste. Mix cornflour with ¼ pint of cold water, and add it to the fruit. Boil for 3 minutes, stirring all the time. Pour into a wetted mould and turn out when cold.

Fruit Chocolate Marshmallow

3 oz. marshmallows	1 level teaspoonful
¼ pint hot drinking	gelatine
chocolate made	Pineapple
with water	Pineapple jelly
¼ pint evaporated milk	Cream

Dissolve marshmallows in hot chocolate. Add gelatine and stir well until dissolved. Whip milk and add to chocolate. When cool and beginning to set, whisk well again. Place pineapple in base of parfait glasses. Fill nearly to the top with chocolate marshmallow. Finish with chopped pineapple jelly, cream and pineapple pieces. (For quick method of whipping evaporated milk, see Chocolate Mousse recipe.)

Fruit Mousse

1 *packet lemon or orange jelly*	¼ *pint nearly boiling water*
Grated peel and juice of 1 orange	¼ *pint evaporated milk*

Melt the jelly in the hot water. Add the orange juice and grated peel, and leave to cool. Whisk the evaporated milk until it becomes thick and doubles its quantity. (For quick method see Chocolate Mousse recipe.) Fold in the jelly mixture and whisk well. Leave to cool, but when it begins to set whisk well again, then turn into a mould and leave for several hours to set firm.

NOTE: There are many variations of this recipe. It can be made with orange jelly and a fresh orange or with all lemon, with black currant jelly or, for a very special one, with a tin of black currant purée and 1 oz. gelatine instead of packet jelly. It can be made equally well with ¼ pint strong black coffee and 1 oz. gelatine.

Fruit Mould (Danish) (for 4–5)

1 *lb. raspberries*	2 *tablespoonfuls*
1 *lb. red currants*	*potato flour*
Sugar to taste	

Cover the fruit with water and simmer gently until soft. Strain, and put the juice in a pan on the fire with sugar to taste. Mash up the potato flour with a little cold juice, add this and simmer until the mixture stiffens. Pour into a wetted mould. Serve cold with cream and sugar.

Fruit Russe

Make a Genoese Cake (see Cakes) and when cold, scoop out a large circle in the middle and fill with alternate layers of any sweetened stewed fruit (fresh or canned) and cream, keeping back the juice. The fruit should be stewed with very little water. Decorate with angelica, cherries or any crystallised fruit and whipped cream.

Garden Fancies will appeal to children. The fern-decorated orange cases are filled with blancmange and topped with fresh fruit

Garden Fancies (for 4)

4 *large oranges*	1 *oz. cornflour*
1 *egg-yolk*	¼ *oz. butter*
1 *oz. sugar*	*A pinch of salt*
½ *oz. chopped glacé*	*Grated rind of* 1
cherries	*orange*
1 *pint milk*	

Cut a slice off the top of each orange and, using stainless steel scissors, remove insides (which can be kept for fruit salad). Scrub outsides of oranges and with cement glue arrange foliage on the outsides. Leave to dry. Make a blancmange with the milk, cornflour and sugar and, when thickened and still hot, add the butter and beaten egg-yolk. Reheat, without boiling, for 2 minutes, add grated rind of an orange, salt and glacé cherries and pour immediately into the orange cases. Allow to cool and, just before serving, decorate the tops with any fruit available, or, if preferred, with piped cream. Arrange on a bed of leaves for serving. Keep the orange cases—they can be used again.

Gâteau de Pommes (for 3–4)

¼ *lb. loaf sugar*	½ *pint water*
Grated rind of small	1 *lb. apples, peeled*
lemon	*and cored*

Boil the sugar and water until it becomes sugary again. Then add the apples and the lemon rind and boil again until quite stiff, stirring carefully. Put into a mould and, when cold, turn out and serve with custard or cream.

Ginger Cream (for 3–4)

½ *oz. powdered gela-*	2 *tablespoonfuls*
tine	*ginger syrup*
1 *gill hot water*	¼ *pint cream*
2 *oz. castor sugar*	3 *oz. preserved ginger*

Dissolve the gelatine in the hot water. Whip the cream and the sugar together till stiff, then add the gelatine and water (just warm), the ginger syrup and preserved ginger cut small. Stir gently until it begins to set, then pour into a mould. It must be stirred until it is poured into the mould, or the gelatine and sugar will sink to the bottom and spoil the appearance.

Gooseberry Fool (for 6–7)

2 *lb. gooseberries*	½ *pint custard or*
8 *oz. sugar*	*cream*
	1 *gill water*

Stew the gooseberries in the water with the sugar until soft, then put through a fine sieve. Cool, add the custard or cream and beat together well. Serve with cream, either in custard glasses or in a dish.

NOTE: Any fresh, soft fruit can be used instead of gooseberries.

Gottespeiss (for 4)

4 *oz. stale bread-*	4 *oz. cup chocolate*
crumbs	1 *oz. chopped nuts*
4 *oz. Demerara sugar*	*(for decoration)*
½ *pint cream*	

Place breadcrumbs, cream, sugar and made cup chocolate in that order in layers in glass bowl or individual dishes, finishing with a layer of cream. Decorate with chopped nuts and a circle of dry cup chocolate.

Honeycomb Pudding (for 4–5)

1 *quart milk*	2 *oz. loaf sugar*
3 *eggs*	1 *teaspoonful vanilla*
½ *oz. powdered gela-*	*essence*
tine	

Separate the egg-whites from the yolks. Dissolve the gelatine in a little warm milk, add the sugar, the rest of the milk and the beaten yolks and stir over a gentle heat until it thickens like a custard. Then take the saucepan off the fire, leave to cool, fold in the stiffly beaten whites. Add the vanilla essence and pour into a wetted mould. Turn out when set.

Hungarian Soufflé (for 4–5)

5 *eggs*	3 *tablespoonfuls cold*
14 *lumps of sugar*	*water*
5 *sheets gelatine*	

Cook the sugar in the water until it browns, to form caramel. Whip the whites of the eggs well. Then pour in the gelatine dissolved in a little water, stirring gently, and add the boiling sugar. Keep whisking well all the time. Pour into a well-wetted mould and leave to set.

For the sauce, boil some more caramel, as above, add it to the egg-yolks with a little cold milk, whisking all the time until it thickens and is free of lumps. When the mould is cold, turn out and pour this sauce over.

Jamaica Rum Sponge

Sponge fingers	3 *dessertspoonfuls*
1 *lemon jelly and a*	*Jamaica rum*
little extra	4 *oz. pink marsh-*
¼ *pint evaporated*	*mallows*
milk	*Glacé cherries*
Just under ½ *pint hot*	*Hazel nuts*
water.	

Sponge cakes with chocolate cream make this nut-coated Party Dessert which tastes as nice as it looks

Dissolve the jelly in a little less than half a pint of hot water and leave to cool but not to set. Make a little extra jelly and dip the sponge fingers into it, arranging them round a wetted mould. Whisk milk until it thickens (for method, see Chocolate Mousse recipe), add jelly a little at a time. Gradually add the rum. Whisk until beginning to set, then stir in cherries, nuts and marshmallows (cut in four). Fill up mould and leave to set.

For a simpler variation of this sweet, use quarter slices of bananas alternately with sponge fingers and thin slices of banana instead of the nuts, marshmallows and cherries.

Lemon Jelly (for 4–5)

½ pint cold water	1-in. stick cinnamon
½ pint boiling water	and 2 cloves
1 oz. powdered gela-	12 oz. loaf sugar
tine	Whites and shells of 2
Rind and juice of 4	eggs
lemons	Sherry (optional)

Put the gelatine in the cold water, add the rind of the lemons, the cinnamon and cloves. Stand for a few minutes, then pour on the boiling water and stir until the gelatine is dissolved. Add the juice of the lemons, the sugar and the slightly beaten whites. Then add the egg-shells washed and crushed, and bring the mixture to the boil, whisking all the time. Simmer very gently for 3 minutes, then remove from the heat and stand for 5 minutes. Scald a jelly bag and pour the jelly mixture slowly through it When nearly cold, put into a wetted mould. A little sherry can be added if desired.

Orange jelly can be made in the same way, substituting orange juice and rind for the lemons and omitting the cinnamon and cloves.

Wine jelly can be made in the same way, using ½ pint wine instead of the ½ pint cold water.

Lemon Pudding (for 5)

2 eggs	6 oz. sugar
Juice and rind of 1	2 dessertspoonfuls
lemon	flour
½ pint hot milk	¼ teaspoonful salt

Beat egg-yolks, beat in sugar, lemon juice and flour, and add scalded milk. Fold in stiffly beaten egg-whites, lemon rind and salt. Pour into buttered custard cups. Stand these in hot water in dripping-pan and bake in moderate oven for 45 minutes. Serve cold.

Lemon Sponge (for 3–4)

½ pint boiling water	2 egg-whites
½ oz. powdered gelatine	Juice and rind of 2 lemons
2 oz. sugar	

Put the lemon rind in the boiling water and leave for 5 minutes. Strain, dissolve the gelatine in the water and add the lemon juice and sugar. Stand until cold. Whisk well and fold in the stiffly beaten egg-whites, whisking until the mixture is firm enough for a spoon to stand upright in it. Pour into a glass dish. Serve cold with custard.

Maraschino Prunes (for 4–5)

8 oz. stewed prunes	1 pint custard
½ wineglassful maraschino	2 oz. loaf sugar
	A little water
Cream	

Stone the prunes and soak them in a soufflé dish with the maraschino. Cover with the custard. Boil the sugar and a little water until pale brown, then pour over the custard and prunes and leave to set. Crack the caramel and cover with whipped cream just before serving.

Meringues

6 egg-whites	9 oz. castor sugar
Whipped cream for filling	3 oz. granulated sugar

NOTE: for every egg-white used allow 1½ oz. castor sugar and ½ oz. granulated sugar. Meringues can be coloured by adding cochineal, coffee essence or cocoa.

Grease a flat baking tin. Line with greaseproof paper and brush this lightly with olive oil. Add another layer of paper and oil this too. Mix the sugars. Beat the egg-whites until stiff so that when the basin is turned upside down they will not move. Add one quarter of the sugar and whisk again. Fold in remainder of sugar with a metal spoon. Put the mixture into an icing pump or forcing bag with plain nozzle and pipe on to the tin in rounds. Alternatively, shape with a dessertspoon, smooth surface with a palette knife and slip out with the help of a second dessertspoon. Dust well with castor sugar and bake in a *very* cool oven for 2–3 hours until crisp. Remove meringues, turn upside down and press centres gently. Return to oven until quite dry.

An alternative method is to leave the meringues in a warm airing cupboard overnight. This ensures that they remain white and obviates the use of the oven.

Mocha Cream (for 4–5)

6 small sponge cakes	3 egg-yolks
½ teacupful strong coffee	4 oz. butter
	3 oz. castor sugar

Cream the butter and sugar together, then add the coffee and the beaten yolks, slowly. Line a plain mould with the sponge cakes cut in slices, pour in some of the mixture, then add more sponge cakes. Continue until the mould is full. Put a saucer on top, with a heavy weight on it. Stand until next day, then turn out and serve with whipped cream.

Orange Baskets

Make and cool an orange jelly. Cut oranges in half, scoop out the insides and keep for orangeade or fruit salad. Fill skins with jelly and leave to set. Cover the jelly with whipped cream and decorate with thin slices of crystallised orange or glacé cherries. Make handles of thin strips of angelica.

Overturned Chocolate Cream (for 4)

1 pint milk	5 oz. chocolate powder
2 oz. castor sugar	
6 eggs	

Bring the milk to the boil and add chocolate powder. In a basin, beat the sugar energetically with the whole eggs, and pour in the milk and chocolate. Turn into a mould, cook in a slow oven in a bain-marie (or stand the mould in a tin containing water) until well set. Leave to cool, and turn out.

Party Dessert

Sponge cakes	Angelica
Chocolate butter cream	Cream
	Nuts
Warm drinking chocolate	Cherries

Split the sponge cakes and sandwich them together with the chocolate cream (for recipe, see Regency Gâteau). Cut into slices, dip in warm chocolate and pack into a dish or basin. Stand for ½ hour, turn out and coat with cream and nuts, decorate with halved glacé cherries and spikes of angelica.

Pudding à la Royal (for 4–5)

½ pint whipped cream
½ pint milk
3 eggs
7 sheets of gelatine
3 oz. brown bread-crumbs
Sugar and vanilla to taste

Make a custard with the milk, sugar, vanilla and eggs and, when cold, add the whipped cream. Add the dissolved gelatine and breadcrumbs. Stir lightly and pour into a wetted mould. When cold, turn out and serve with whipped cream or custard and fruit.

Prune Caramel (for 3–4)

½ lb. prunes
¼ lb. brown sugar
Piece of stick cinnamon
½ cupful milk or thin cream
2 eggs
1 pint cold water

Soak the prunes overnight in the cold water, then cook them gently with the sugar and cinnamon for 2 hours. Put through a hair sieve, take out the cinnamon, add the eggs, well beaten, and the milk or cream, and pour the mixture into a mould previously lined with burnt sugar (see Caramel Custard recipe). Steam for ½ hour. When cold, turn out and serve with whipped cream.

Prune Mould (for 3–4)

1 lb. prunes
Rind and juice of a lemon
Powdered gelatine
1 pint water
2 oz. brown sugar

Wash the prunes and soak with the lemon rind in the water overnight. Cook them with the sugar until soft. Put through a sieve. Allow ½ oz. gelatine to a pint of prune purée. Dissolve the gelatine in a little water and add, together with the lemon juice, to the purée. Stir until it begins to thicken, then pour into a wetted mould. When set, turn out and decorate with blanched almonds and whipped cream.

Raspberry Sponge (for 5–6)

1 oz. powdered gelatine
½ pint water
8 oz. sugar
2 egg-whites
8 oz. raspberry syrup (or jam)
1 pint boiling water
Juice of a lemon

Dissolve the gelatine in ½ pint of water, then add the pint of boiling water. When

Regency Gâteau, a delicious party sweet, in which the flavours of coffee and chocolate are combined

139

cool, add the sugar and raspberry syrup (or jam), the juice of the lemon and the beaten egg-whites. Whisk until stiff. Serve cold with cream.

Regency Gâteau

Marie biscuits	Chocolate butter
Cold coffee	cream
Whipped cream (for	Nuts
decoration)	

Use the plate on which the sweet will be served. Fill a piping bag, using a vegetable pipe, with chocolate butter cream or chocolate flavoured cream or custard. Dip several biscuits into the coffee, just long enough to take off the crispness. Place about six biscuits close together on the plate. Cover with cream from the piping bag. Repeat layers of biscuits and cream alternately. Decorate with whipped cream, nuts and piping of chocolate cream.

Butter Cream.—This is a simple filling which can be flavoured to suit many recipes.

3 oz. butter or mar-	6 oz. sieved icing
garine	sugar
1–2 teaspoonfuls milk or water	

Cream margarine and sugar until soft and light. Beat in liquid gradually. Add flavouring to taste. Chocolate flavour— 1 oz. drinking chocolate, a few drops of vanilla essence. Other flavours: Peppermint—a few drops of peppermint essence and green colouring. Walnut—½ oz. chopped walnuts and a teaspoonful coffee essence or strong black coffee.

Russian Cream (for 5–6)

2 oz. sugar	½ oz. powdered gela-
1 pint milk	tine
½ pint whipped cream	Chopped glacé
2 oz. ground rice	cherries
	Flavouring

Wet the ground rice with a little milk. Put the rest of the milk and the sugar on to boil, then stir in the ground rice, gradually, and continue stirring for about 8 minutes. Then draw the saucepan to one side. Dissolve the gelatine in a little warm milk and pour it into the rice, stirring well. When sufficiently cool, add the whipped cream and mix lightly together. Flavour with vanilla or a liqueur, and pour into a mould which has already been decorated with preserved cherries chopped small. Leave to set and serve cold.

NOTE: If liked, omit the cherries in the mould, colour the mixture with cochineal and decorate with chopped pistachio nuts.

Strawberry or Raspberry Cream (for 5–6)

1 pint strawberries	3 oz. castor sugar
(or raspberries)	½ oz. powdered gela-
1 gill water	tine
½ pint double cream	

Prepare the fruit and put it into a basin, sprinkle with the sugar and stand for 1 hour, then rub through a sieve. Dissolve the gelatine in the warm water, and add the fruit purée. Whip the cream until quite stiff, then add the fruit and gelatine, stirring well together. Pour the mixture into a wetted mould to set.

Summer Pudding

This pudding can be made with any soft, fresh fruit, such as raspberries, black currants, etc., or with canned, quick-frozen or bottled fruit. Fresh or quick-frozen fruit must first be stewed with a little water and sugar to taste. Cut some stale bread in slices to fit the top and bottom of a pudding basin and then pieces to go round the sides. Dip the bread in the fruit juice and line the basin with it. Pour in the hot fruit and put a round of bread on top as a lid. Put a plate on top with a weight on it and let the pudding stand for the night. Turn out and serve with custard or cream.

NOTE: Summer Pudding can also be made with sponge cakes instead of bread.

Sweet Chestnut Mousse

25 chestnuts	3 oz. vanilla sugar
1 pint cream	1 egg-white

Cook and peel the chestnuts and put through a sieve to make a purée. Stir over moderate heat with the sugar until very smooth. Add the whipped cream and the egg-white. Pour into a mould, chill for about 3 hours. Turn out on to a folded napkin.

Tapioca Cream (for 3–4)

¼ oz. gelatine	1 tablespoonful
1 pint milk	tapioca
1 tablespoonful sugar	1 tablespoonful cream

Dissolve the gelatine in a little milk. Bring the rest of the milk to the boil and, while boiling, stir in the tapioca. Boil for 5–10 minutes. Add the sugar and cream, then stir in the gelatine. When nearly cold, put into wetted mould to set.

Tonito Pudding (for 4–5)

8 oz. castor sugar
¼ oz. gelatine
1 pint water
4 eggs
Rind and juice of a
    lemon
Cream

Separate the egg-whites from the yolks. Melt the gelatine in the warmed water and boil. Cool a little, then pour on to the sugar, lemon and yolks. Stir well. When nearly cold, whip the whites stiffly, fold them into the mixture and put into a glass dish with whipped cream on top.

Trifle

Cut some sponge cakes in half lengthwise and sandwich them together again with jam, arranging them neatly in a glass dish. Put some ratafia biscuits on top and stick blanched split almonds into the sponge cakes. Pour over them a wineglassful of sherry or fruit syrup made either with fresh fruit stewed and strained, or jam diluted with hot water and strained or from a can of fruit. Cover with a good cold custard and stand overnight. Before serving, decorate with almonds, angelica, "hundreds and thousands," glacé cherries or crystallised fruit, according to taste, and small piles of whipped cream.

Rice cooked in milk and flavoured with either rum or vanilla is the basis of Winter Sport. It can be served in individual dishes and decorated either with sliced bananas and Maltesers, or with grated chocolate and almond rolls

Winter Sport

1 pint milk	½ level teaspoonful salt
2 oz. sugar	
2 bananas	1 tablespoonful Jamaica rum or a few drops vanilla flavouring
2 oz. rice	
1 oz. sultanas	
1 oz. chopped walnuts	

Wash rice. Cook gently in a double saucepan with the sugar, milk and salt for approximately 1½ hours. Cool thoroughly, stir in diced bananas, walnuts and sultanas. Add the rum or vanilla flavouring, and mix well. Turn into individual dishes and decorate with sliced bananas and Maltesers, or with grated cup chocolate and almond rolls. Serve with cream or custard.

Puddings and sweets requiring pastry will be found in the Pastry chapter immediately following.

All photographs in Puddings and Sweets Chapter by Cadbury Bros., except those on pages 127, 133, 135 and 141.

PASTRY

The secret of a light hand with pastry is very simple —"Keep Cool"

Making Flaky Pastry: dab small pieces of fat on the rolled-out dough—

SUCCESS in pastry making depends on two essentials: the minimum of handling, and keeping everything as cool as possible at all stages. If you observe these two basic rules, you will soon gain a reputation for "a light hand with pastry."

You will need a mixing bowl big enough to get both hands into; kitchen scales; a flour sifter (failing that, the flour may be passed through a fine sieve); a kitchen knife; a rolling pin, and either a pastry board or a large cool surface on which to roll the pastry.

Ingredients, as well as your hands and the utensils you use, should be as cool as possible. Use really cold water for mixing, keep flour and fat in a very cool place (the fat preferably in the refrigerator), roll the pastry out on a cold surface, such as an enamel topped table or a marble slab, and choose one of the modern rolling pins made of cool glass or china. (In an emergency, a pint milk bottle, well washed and rinsed in cold water, makes an excellent rolling pin.)

The only handling necessary is when you rub the fat into the flour, and this should be done with a light touch and hands freshly washed, rinsed in cold water and thoroughly dried, using the tips of the fingers only. Remember, the more air there is in the pastry, the lighter it will be, so don't press or roll it hard.

Butter, lard, vegetable fat, clarified dripping and margarine are all suitable for different kinds of pastry. Lard and vegetable fat make the shortest pastry; half lard, half vegetable fat is a good general-purpose mixture. Baking powder is not necessary,

and plain flour should be used in preference to self-raising.

The amount of water required varies according to what flour is used. The lighter and finer the flour, the more water it will take. If you use too much water, the pastry may be tough.

Flour the board and the rolling pin so that the pastry does not stick. Be very sparing with the flour you sprinkle over the pastry, as too much dry flour spoils its appearance and toughens it.

The cooking of pastry is as important as the making. The oven must be hot enough to prevent the fat melting and running out before the starch grains in the flour have had time to burst and absorb it. It should be cooked quickly and the oven door must not be opened until it is very nearly done.

There are several different kinds of pastry:

(1) *Short Pastry* is the quickest and easiest, and should be used at once.

(2) *Flaky Pastry* can be kept for several days provided the weather is cold. In any case it should be made at least an hour before you intend to use it.

(3) *Puff Pastry* requires more time in the making. It can be used the day it is made, or, if the weather is cold or if put in a refrigerator, it will keep, wrapped in well-greased paper.

(4) *Rough Puff Pastry* should be left for at least ½ hour before it is used or, if

142

Spry Cookery Centre photographs

Then, having folded the dough in three, seal the edges with the rolling pin

wrapped in well-greased paper, it will keep for several days in cold weather.

(5) *Potato Pastry* is economical and excellent for jam puffs, tarts or pies.

(6) *Choux Pastry*, which is made in an entirely different way from the other kinds, is used for continental pastries such as éclairs, cream buns, etc.

(7) *Biscuit Pastry*, often used as an alternative to short pastry for flans.

(8) *Hot Water Pastry* for raised meat pies.

(9) *Suet Crust* for steamed and boiled puddings.

Short Pastry (Used for flans, tarts and pies)

8 oz. flour	¼ teaspoonful salt
4 oz. lard or 3½ oz. vegetable fat	Cold water for mixing

Sift flour and salt. Cut fat into small pieces and rub it lightly into the flour with the fingertips until the mixture looks like fine breadcrumbs. Then add just sufficient very cold water to make a dry dough, mixing it in with a knife. Lightly flour the board and rolling pin and roll out the pastry, being careful not to put any weight on the rolling pin, neither kneading nor handling the pastry more than is absolutely necessary, and always rolling in the same direction. The thickness is a matter of taste, but pastry should never be more than ¼ in. thick or there is a danger of the outside getting brown before the inside is properly cooked. Trimmings left over can be gathered together in layers, without kneading or pressure, and lightly rolled out again.

For a Fruit or Jam Tart on a Plate.—Line the greased pie-plate with short pastry, trimming round the edges. Put in fruit or jam cold, damp edges of the pastry and cover with another layer of pastry. Brush with milk and sprinkle lightly with sugar.

For a Flan Case.—Grease the flan tin or ring and sprinkle it lightly with flour, then line with the short pastry. Trim edges. Put a piece of greaseproof paper inside the flan with a little rice or a few breadcrumbs on it (this is known as "baking blind") and cook in a moderate oven (400° F.) until the pastry begins to brown, then remove rice and paper and return to oven for a few minutes. Flan case is then ready for filling.

Flaky Pastry (Used for pies, tarts, sausage rolls, patties, etc.)

8 oz. flour	6 oz. lard or 5 oz. vegetable fat
½ teaspoonful salt	
Cold water for mixing	

Put the flour and salt in a basin and rub in one-third of the fat until it has the appearance of fine breadcrumbs. Mix to a stiff dough with a little cold water, using a knife for mixing. Roll out on a floured board into an oblong piece. Cut half the remainder of the fat into small pieces and scatter them over two-thirds of the paste. Flour well and fold the paste in three, sealing the edges neatly with the rolling pin. Leave for 10 minutes. Turn the paste round so that the sides become the ends and roll out again, then add the rest of the fat in the same way as before. Flour, fold in three, turn and roll out again. Leave for 10 minutes. Fold in three once more and, if possible, put away in a cool place in a covered basin for 1 hour or more. Roll out before using and bake in a hot oven.

NOTE: When using up trimmings of this pastry, always put them one on top of the other and beat together with a rolling pin before rolling out, to preserve the flaky effect.

Puff Pastry (Used for patty and vol-au-vent cases, etc.)

Equal quantities of best quality flour and butter	Cold water for mixing Pinch of salt

Sieve the flour and salt, and mix to a springy dough with the water. Roll out on a floured board and leave for 15 minutes. Squeeze the butter in a floured cloth or beat it with a butter pat on a slab to get out the moisture, and flatten it to about 1 in. thickness. Put the butter in one piece in the middle of the pastry, then fold the pastry up over it, first at the two ends, then at the sides, pressing the edges with the rolling-pin to seal in the air. Leave for 15 minutes or more, then roll into a long, narrow strip, fold in four again and leave for another 15 minutes. Repeat four times, allowing the pastry to rest—covered with a clean cloth—for 15 minutes between each turn. Finally, roll into the required shape.

Rough Puff Pastry (Used for meat pies which have to be in the oven for a long time, also fruit pies and patties)

8 oz. flour	3 oz. lard or vegetable
½ teaspoonful salt	fat
Cold water to mix	(Use less fat in hot
3 oz. butter or	weather)
margarine	

Chop the fats into the sieved flour, using two knives and keeping it in fairly large pieces. Add the salt and enough water to bind the dough, the pieces of fat still remaining whole. Do not use the hands at all, but mix the water in with a knife. Turn on to a floured board and roll out four times, folding in three and leaving to rest for 15 minutes each time. Put away in a cool place for at least ½ hour before rolling out for use.

Potato Pastry (May be used for meat pies, jam puffs, tarts and pies)

9 oz. flour	1 teaspoonful baking
2 oz fat	powder
2 oz. cooked mashed	Cold water to mix
potato	Pinch of salt

Sieve the flour, salt and baking powder, and rub in the fat finely; then work in the mashed potato. When smooth, mix to a stiff dough with a very little cold water. Roll out and bake in a hot oven.

Choux Pastry (Used for éclairs, cream buns and continental pastries)

1 gill water	3 eggs
Pinch of salt and	2¼ oz. flour
sugar	1¼ oz. butter

Bring the butter and water to the boil, with the pinch of salt and sugar. Sieve the flour and shoot it into the pan. Stir over a low heat until the mixture leaves the bottom of the pan quite clean. Remove from heat and allow to cool, then gradually mix in the beaten eggs, one at a time. Beat well and flavour as required.

Biscuit Crust (Used for fruit flans)

4½ oz. flour	2 oz. butter or
1 egg-yolk	margarine
1 oz. castor sugar	Pinch of salt

Beat the butter and sugar to a cream, add the egg-yolk and work in the sieved flour and salt. Place flan ring on a baking sheet. Roll out pastry and line the ring with it. Cover the pastry with a piece of grease-proof paper and spread beans or rice on it to keep the pastry in shape. Bake blind in a hot oven for 20 minutes. Remove the paper and beans or rice. Allow the pastry to dry off in the oven for 2 or 3 minutes, then put to cool.

Hot Water Pastry (For raised meat pies)

¼ lb. flour	2 oz. lard or vegetable
½ gill milk	fat
½ gill water	Pinch of salt

Put the sieved flour and salt into a basin. Boil the lard, water and milk together, and pour it into the middle of the flour. Mix well with a knife. Knead the dough until it is smooth. Use while warm and line a basin, using the hands to mould it.

Suet Crust (Used for steamed or boiled meat or sweet puddings and dumplings) (for 4–5)

8 oz. flour	3 or 4 oz. shredded
Pinch of salt	suet
Water or milk	½ teaspoonful baking
	powder

Sieve the flour, baking powder and salt, add the suet with enough water or milk to make a firm but rather dry dough.

NOTE: If desired, 6 oz. flour and 2 oz. breadcrumbs can be used instead of 8 oz. flour for sweet puddings.

PASTRY SWEET DISHES

Almond Cheese Cakes (for 5–6)

8 oz. flaky pastry	Grated rind of quar-
2 oz. ground almonds	ter of lemon
2 oz. butter	1 drop almond
2 oz. castor sugar	essence
1 whole egg and	1 drop maraschino
1 egg-yolk	(or sherry or
Raspberry jam	brandy)

Line patty pans with the pastry and put a drop of raspberry jam in the bottom of each. Cream the butter and sugar, add the

A sure favourite with children and grown-ups alike—Chocolate Meringue Pie is easy to make but looks most professional

egg and yolk, unbeaten. Add the rest of the ingredients and beat well. Put a spoonful of the mixture into each tartlet. Cook in a hot oven until risen and brown. Finish off in a cooler oven until the pastry is cooked through (about 25 minutes altogether).

Apple Dumplings (for 4–5)

8 oz. short pastry   6 medium-sized
Castor sugar   apples

Peel the apples and cut out the cores. Fill the centres with castor sugar. Roll the pastry ⅛ in. thick and cut out six circles large enough to cover the apples. Put an apple on each and work the dough over the apple, pressing the edges (slightly moistened) together. Brush with cold water and sprinkle with castor sugar, or paint with a little milk. Bake in a moderately hot oven until the apples are tender and the pastry crisp.

Apple Tart (Open) (for 3–4)

6 oz. short pastry   Apples and brown
Raspberry jam   sugar

Grease a deep pie plate and line it with pastry, then spread a thin layer of raspberry jam, a layer of thinly sliced apples sprinkled with brown sugar, and bake until the apples are cooked and the pastry just brown.

Apricot Flan (for 4–5)

For the crust

½ oz. butter   ½ teaspoonful baking
4 oz. flour   powder (unless self-
1 egg   raising flour is
1 tablespoonful milk   used)
            1½ teaspoonfuls sugar

For the filling

1½–2 lb. fresh apricots   ½ teaspoonful cinna-
¼–½ lb. sugar (accord-   mon or grated nut-
   ing to taste)   meg
3 dessertspoonfuls top   1 egg-yolk
   of milk, or cream

Sieve flour and mix in dry ingredients.

145

Blend in butter with finger-tips. Add egg and milk, and mix. Toss on slightly floured board and pat or roll $\frac{1}{4}$ in. thick. Cover a large, well-greased flan tin (round or oblong) with the pastry, and place on it stoned, halved apricots (hollow side up) in neat rows. Sprinkle thickly with sugar and spice. Beat egg-yolk, mix with top of milk or cream, and drip over fruit. Bake in a hot oven until fruit is soft and crust well browned underneath.

Banana and Golden Syrup Tart (for 4–5)

8 oz. short pastry	1 tablespoonful
2 bananas	Golden Syrup
1 oz. grated breadcrumbs	

Line a deep sandwich tin with some of the pastry. Pour on Golden Syrup and spread all over. Cut bananas into thin rounds and cover the syrup with them, and top with breadcrumbs. Roll out the remaining pastry thinly and cover the whole with it, pressing the edges together after trimming round the tin. Bake in a moderate oven for 15 minutes. Serve hot or cold.

Chocolate Amber Pudding (for 6–8)

6 oz. short pastry	2 oz. drinking chocolate
1 lb. apples	
3 oz. sugar	2 egg-yolks
1 oz. margarine	2 tablespoonfuls water

For the meringue

4 oz. castor sugar	2 egg-whites

Line a pie plate with pastry. Peel, core and slice apples, and stew until soft with sugar and water. Add the margarine, drinking chocolate and egg-yolks. Beat well. Put apple mixture into pastry case and bake in moderate oven for 20–25 minutes until pastry is done. About 10 minutes before pudding is cooked, whisk egg-whites until stiff, fold in sugar lightly and pile on to the pudding. Bake in slow oven until meringue is set.

Chocolate Flan (for 6–8)

6 oz. short pastry or	1 oz. cornflour
biscuit crust	1 oz. sugar
$\frac{1}{2}$ oz. cocoa	$\frac{3}{4}$ pint milk

Line a 7-in. flan tin with the pastry and bake blind. Mix cocoa and cornflour to a paste with a little of the milk. Bring remainder of milk to the boil with sugar, pour on to paste, then return to saucepan and bring to the boil again, stirring all the time. Cook for 2 minutes, then pour into cooked flan case and leave to cool. Decorate with piped cream or mock cream.

Chocolate Meringue Pie (for 6–8)

6 oz. short pastry	$\frac{1}{2}$ pint milk
$\frac{1}{2}$ oz. cocoa	2 oz. cornflour
2 egg-yolks	1 tablespoonful sugar
$\frac{1}{2}$ oz. margarine	

For the meringue

3 oz. castor sugar	2 egg-whites

Line an 8-in. flan ring with the pastry and bake blind. Blend the cornflour and cocoa to a smooth paste with a little of the milk, bring remainder of milk to the boil and pour on, with the sugar. Allow to cool, then add margarine and egg-yolks and pour into cooked flan case. Bake in moderate oven for 20–25 minutes until firm. Whip egg-whites until stiff, fold in sugar and pile on chocolate. Bake in a cool oven until set, and serve hot or cold

Cornish Treacle Tart

Short pastry	Golden Syrup
Breadcrumbs	Grated lemon rind

Line a greased enamel pie plate with pastry and cut out another round to go on top. Sprinkle breadcrumbs over pastry, pour Golden Syrup over, then more breadcrumbs and a little grated lemon rind. Moisten pastry edges and put on the top, pressing it down gently. Nick the edges with the back of a fork. Bake in a moderately hot oven for about 40 minutes. Be careful that the tart is not too full or the mixture will ooze out.

Custard Tarts (for 5–6)

8 oz. short pastry	1 pint milk
3 eggs	Sugar to taste
	Grated nutmeg

Line small fireproof dishes with the pastry, prick at the bottom and bake lightly, then take out of the oven. Make a custard with the milk and eggs, add sugar to taste and fill the tarts. Grate a little nutmeg on each. Put back in oven and bake slowly until the custard is set.

Eccles Cakes (for 6–7)

8 oz. flaky or rough	1 oz. castor sugar
puff pastry	1 oz. butter
4 oz. currants	$\frac{1}{2}$ oz. chopped peel

Melt the butter in a pan and add the sugar, currants and peel. Roll out the pastry and cut into rounds. Place a little of the mixture on each round. Moisten the edges of the pastry and draw it all together

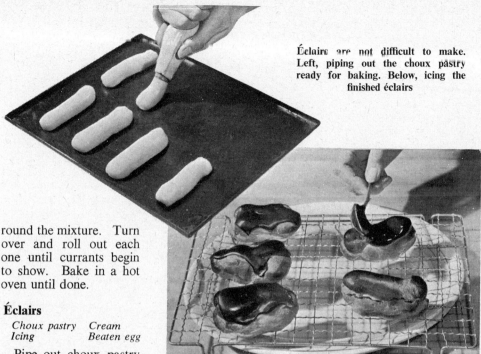

Éclairs are not difficult to make. Left, piping out the choux pastry ready for baking. Below, icing the finished éclairs

round the mixture. Turn over and roll out each one until currants begin to show. Bake in a hot oven until done.

Éclairs

Choux pastry   Cream
Icing   Beaten egg

Pipe out choux pastry into an éclair tin or on to a baking tin, making éclairs the required size, brush with beaten egg and bake in a quick oven for about 30 minutes. Be very careful of draughts while they are cooking. When cooked, leave to cool, then make an incision in the side, near the bottom, take out the soft part of the centre and fill with whipped cream, sweetened and flavoured with vanilla if liked. Spread chocolate or coffee glacé icing on top.

NOTE: For the piping, use either a forcing bag or a metal syringe. The éclairs before going into the oven should be about ¾ in. wide and 3–4 in. long. Put them into an oven of about 400° F. for the first 10 minutes, then reduce the heat to 350° F.

Éclair Delights

Make éclairs as above, but fill with a mixture of whipped cream and chopped fruit (cherries, grapes, orange, etc.). Coat with chocolate icing made from a 2-oz. block of plain chocolate, 4 oz. icing sugar, 2 tablespoonfuls milk and water, and a few drops of vanilla essence; decorate with piped whipped cream and fruit.

Fruit Flan

Canned or fresh   Biscuit crust
* stewed fruit*
For the syrup
¼ oz. arrowroot   ¼ pint juice
*   1 tablespoonful sugar*

Boil the sugar and juice. Put the arrowroot in a basin and mix with a little liquid. Pour the hot syrup on to it and bring the whole mixture to the boil, stirring until it thickens. Colour the mixture, according to what fruit is used, arrange the fruit, cut in slices if large, in the bottom of the flan. When the syrup is cool, pour it evenly over the fruit.

NOTE: If canned fruit is used, its own syrup will provide the liquid and no sugar is needed. If oranges are used, make syrup with orange juice and water.

Fruit Pie (for 4–5)

8 oz. short pastry   4 oz. sugar (or to
2 lb. fruit   taste)
*   Water*

Prepare the fruit and put in a quart sized pie dish with sugar, a little water and a pie funnel or inverted egg cup in the middle. Roll out the pastry a little larger than the

147

pie dish. Cut off a strip to line the edge of the dish. Moisten the edge and put on the strip. Then moisten the pastry and put on the top, pressing well together and nicking the edges with the back of a fork. Make a ½-in. slit in the centre of the pastry to let the steam out. Bake in a moderately hot oven for 35–45 minutes, lowering the heat once the pastry has risen.

NOTE: Do not stretch the pastry when putting it on or it will shrink away from the edge as it cooks. The dish should be well filled with fruit or the pastry will collapse.

The cooking time varies according to what fruit is used.

Fruit pies can also be made on an enamel plate with the fruit between two rounds of pastry (see Cornish Treacle Tart).

Gâteau Saint Honoré aux Oranges (for 5–6)

Short pastry made from 3 oz. flour, 1½ oz. fat, pinch of salt and water to mix	Choux pastry made from 2 oz. flour, 1 oz. margarine, ½ gill water, 1 egg, pinch of salt

For the filling and decoration

Mandarin oranges Pistachio nuts	Cream

For the chocolate icing

3 oz. icing sugar ½ oz. margarine 1 tablespoonful water	1 dessertspoonful cocoa

Roll short crust pastry into a large, round, place on a greased tin and prick well. Using a star pipe, pipe a ring of choux pastry round the short pastry to form a border, and pipe about nine separate stars on to the tin. Bake in a fairly hot oven for about 30 minutes. Leave until cold.

To make the chocolate icing.—Boil margarine, water and cocoa together and stir to a smooth paste. Remove from heat, stir in icing sugar, and beat until smooth.

Ice the separate choux stars, decorate with pistachio nuts and fix into position with cream round the ring of pastry. Mix oranges and cream together and fill the centre of the case with this mixture, building up with stars of cream and the choux stars. Decorate with sections of mandarin orange.

Grape Boats (for 6)

6 oz. plain flour Pinch of salt 1 small egg-yolk ½ lb. white grapes	3 oz. margarine 1 teaspoonful castor sugar A little water for mixing

For the glaze

3 tablespoonfuls sieved apricot jam	3 tablespoonfuls castor sugar
3 tablespoonfuls water	

Sieve flour and salt together, rub in fat with the finger-tips. Mix to a stiff paste with the egg-yolk and a little cold water, add sugar, knead very lightly and roll out thinly. Line twelve boat-shaped tartlet tins (4½-in. size) with the pastry, pricking at the bottom with a fork. Stand tins on a baking sheet, bake in a hot oven for 12–15 minutes. Remove from tins and, when cold, put three grapes in each. Coat grapes with apricot glaze and leave to set.

To make the glaze.—Boil together for a few minutes the jam, sugar and water until the syrup is of the consistency to thicken lightly when tested on a plate.

Grape and Apple Sauce Pie (for 4–5)

2 cups washed grapes 2 cups apple sauce 2 tablespoonfuls quick-cooking tapioca Whipped cream for topping	8 oz. sugar ¼ pint water 9-in. pastry flan shell, made with short pastry or biscuit crust

Cook grapes for about 10 minutes in a little water in a covered saucepan over moderate heat. Rub through strainer, add sugar, apple sauce, water and return to heat. Stir in tapioca and cook until clear. Leave to cool, then turn into the pastry shell. Top with whipped cream just before serving.

Grape Chiffon Pie (for 4–5)

1 packet raspberry or strawberry jelly ½ pint whipped cream 1½ teacupfuls washed grapes (peeled and stoned) Just under 1 pint water	1 egg-white 4 oz. castor sugar 1 egg-yolk 9-in. pastry case, made from short pastry or biscuit crust

Make the jelly, using just under 1 pint hot water, leave to cool and, when almost set, whisk until light. Beat the egg-white until stiff and fold into the whipped cream. Combine the jelly and cream mixtures by stirring lightly together; add sugar to the grapes and fold into jelly and cream mixture. Brush over the pastry case with egg-yolk, to prevent it becoming soggy, and put the mixture into it. Decorate the top with whole grapes and chill until firm.

Gâteau Saint Honoré aux Oranges is a delicious party sweet made of choux pastry, cream and mandarin oranges

Jalousie (Venetian Blind)

Puff pastry
Beaten egg
Chopped apples and sugar

Roll out the pastry to the length of the baking tin and cut into two strips, 3 or 4 in. wide. Place one strip on the tin and paint all round the edge with beaten egg. Put the apple and sugar down the middle of the pastry, piling it fairly high but keeping it ½ in. away from the edges. Fold the other strip of pastry in half sideways and cut the folded side evenly with a knife to within ½ in. of the other side; cuts should be about 1 in. apart. Unfold the strip, which will now resemble a Venetian blind, and place it over the strip on the tin, pressing the sides down well together. Paint all over with egg. Decorate the edges by nicking with the blunt side of a knife. Bake in a hot oven. When cooked, scatter sugar all over and return to the oven for 1 minute to glaze.

Jam, Lemon Curd or Treacle Tart

Short pastry
Jam, lemon curd, or Golden Syrup and breadcrumbs

Grease an enamel plate and line it with pastry. Fill the centre with jam or lemon curd, or Golden Syrup mixed with breadcrumbs. Decorate with narrow strips of pastry twisted and stretched across the tart. Nick the edge with the back of a fork and bake in a fairly hot oven for about 15 minutes, taking care that the filling does not burn or get too dark.

Jam Puffs

Flaky pastry
Raspberry jam

Roll out the pastry and cut it into 4- or 5-in. squares. Put a little jam in the centre of each square. Wet round the edges with beaten egg. Fold each square diagonally and press down the edges. Brush the tops with cold water and sprinkle with sugar. Bake in a hot oven until light brown (about 20 minutes).

Jam Roly-poly

Roll short pastry into an oblong, making one end slightly wider than the other. Spread jam evenly over it, leaving 1 in. all round, moisten the edges and roll up, starting at the narrower end. Press gently as you do so. Bake in a moderately hot oven for about 45 minutes.

Jam Tartlets

Short pastry   *Jam or lemon curd*

Roll out the pastry, cut into rounds with a crinkly cutter and line patty pans with it. Put a small teaspoonful of jam or lemon curd in each. Cook in a hot oven for 10 minutes.

Mille Feuilles

Puff pastry   *Browned almonds*
Apricot jam   *Pistachio nuts*
Whipped cream   *(chopped)*
Glacé icing

Roll out the pastry fairly thin and divide into four strips about 4 in. wide. Leave for $\frac{1}{4}$ or $\frac{1}{2}$ hour. Prick very well all over with a fork. Bake on a baking sheet in a hot oven until brown. When cold, trim into shape and spread one strip with apricot jam, place another strip on top and spread with whipped cream; add another strip and spread with jam. Place the fourth strip on the top, cut into fingers, and ice. Decorate with pipings of cream, pistachio nuts and almonds.

Mince Pies

Flaky or short pastry   Mincemeat

Roll out pastry and cut into rounds. Grease patty pans and line with half the rounds of pastry. Put 1 or $1\frac{1}{2}$ teaspoonfuls mincemeat in each, damp edges all round with cold water, put remaining rounds of pastry on top, press down well together all round the edges. Paint tops of mince pies with cold water and sprinkle with sugar. With a skewer, prick a hole through the pastry in the centre of each mince pie. Bake in a hot oven for 20 minutes.

Pastry Fingers

Take any flaky or short pastry left over, roll it out and spread jam over half of it. Moisten the edges of the lower half, fold over top half, brush over with cold water and sprinkle with castor sugar. Bake in a moderate oven. When cooked, cut into squares or fingers. Eat either hot or cold.

Patty Cases

Roll out puff pastry to a little more than $\frac{1}{4}$ in. in thickness. Let it stand in a cold place for a few minutes. Then cut rounds with either a plain or crinkly cutter about $2\frac{1}{2}$ in. across. Take a smaller cutter ($1\frac{1}{2}$ in. across) and cut a round in the centre of half the large rounds for the lids. Damp the edges of the larger rounds with cold water or beaten egg and put the rings on top. Put the patties on a baking tin and prick the middles with a fork to prevent them rising. Brush with beaten egg and bake for 20–25 minutes in a hot oven. Scoop out a little of the soft part from the centre when they are cooked.

The small rings, or lids, should be put on another tin, brushed over with egg and baked for 10–12 minutes. If the patties are to be served hot, fill them with the warm filling, put on the lids and then heat in the oven for 2 or 3 minutes.

Patty Cases for Vol au Vent

Proceed as for patty cases above, but roll out the pastry to about $\frac{3}{4}$ in. thick, keeping it very even. Bake the cases for about 30 minutes in a hot oven (400° F.) until the sides are firm but the pastry not turning brown. About 10 minutes before cooking is complete, brush the lids with egg. For suitable vol-au-vent fillings see Fish, Meat and Poultry sections.

Viennese Grape Tart (for 6–8)

8 oz. plain flour   Water for mixing
1 dessertspoonful   5 oz. margarine
   castor sugar   Most of 1 egg-yolk
             For the filling
5 oz. castor sugar $\frac{1}{2}$ lb. white grapes
Grated rind of half a $2\frac{1}{2}$ oz. ground
   lemon   almonds
             2 egg-whites

Rub fat into flour with fingertips, mix to a stiff paste with the egg-yolk and a very little cold water. Add sugar, knead lightly and roll out thinly, using rather more than half to line a deep 8-in. sandwich tin.

Mix sugar, ground almonds, lemon rind and egg-whites into a softish paste, beating for a minute. Fill pastry case with this, then press into it at intervals the grapes, previously washed and stoned. Cover with a trellis of pastry strips, brush with egg-yolk diluted with water. Bake in a slow oven for 1 hour. When cool, remove from tin, serve cold, dredged with sifted icing sugar.

Alternatively, desiccated coconut and a little almond essence may be used instead of ground almonds.

FRUIT

*Cooked or raw, tropical or
home-grown, there is a fruit
for every occasion and
every taste*

A S with everything else,
there is an art in pre-
paring and serving fruit,
whether raw or cooked.
Nothing looks more appetising than half a grapefruit,
nicely chilled, with a cherry
in the centre. A simple dish
of stewed or baked apples
can be delicious if perfectly
cooked and attractively presented.

Preparing Fruit

Whether the fruit is
bought from a greengrocer
or—far better—picked from
your own trees or bushes,
discard quite ruthlessly any
that is damaged or over-ripe.
Examine fruit carefully to

At any time of the year a bowl of fresh fruit makes
a perfect table decoration

see that the skins are unbroken—and soft
fruits (the berries, for example) particularly
for grubs and insects. The best way to
clean soft fruits is to put them in a colander
and then plunge it into a bowl of cold
water. Drain thoroughly and remove
damaged or unsound fruit.

The quickest and easiest way to prepare
currants is to run a fork down the stalks
so that the berries fall off into a bowl.
Gooseberries need to be topped and tailed,
and this can be done quite quickly with an
old pair of small scissors.

Stewed Fruit

Calculate ½ pint of water to each pint of
fruit, adding sugar according to taste.

Freshly peeled fruits (such as apples,
soft pears, grapefruit, oranges, rhubarb)
and soft fruits (such as raspberries, logan-

berries, blackberries, gooseberries, cherries, white and red currants) should be
stewed in syrup. Allowing ½ pint of water
for each pound of fruit, boil the water with
2–4 oz. sugar per ½ pint (according to
sweetness of fruit and to personal taste),
cook for 3 or 4 minutes, then add the
washed and prepared fruit. Simmer gently
until cooked, the time varying according to
the type of fruit. Rhubarb, for example,
needs only a minute or two in the hot
syrup.

Incidentally, those who find rhubarb too
acid should try cooking it this way. Wash
and cut the sticks of rhubarb into 1-in.
lengths, discarding the leaves but keeping
as much of the red part as possible. Put
into a saucepan and just cover with cold
water. Bring quickly to the boil, remove
immediately from the heat and drain off all

the water. Return the rhubarb to the pan, add cold water and sugar to taste (or syrup made as above) in the correct proportions and cook in the usual way.

Hard pears and black currants, which have hard skins, should be put into cold water with the sugar, brought to the boil and simmered very gently until done.

Apples retain their flavour best if cooked in their skins this way: Wash the apples well, then cut them up quite roughly into chunks, removing any bruised or damaged parts but leaving the skins and cores. Put them into a saucepan with a *very* little cold water (only just enough to cover the bottom and prevent them from sticking) and bring gently to the boil. Simmer until they become frothy and feel quite soft when tried with a fork. Remove from the heat and rub through a fine sieve. The resulting apple purée has all the flavour from the skins and is often quite sweet enough without any additional sugar. It is delicious served hot, with a tiny pat of butter stirred in with a little brown sugar, honey or Golden Syrup; or cold as a sweet with cream or as the basis of Apple Snow.

Baked Fruit

Apples, pears, bananas and grapefruit can be baked whole, with excellent results. The apples should be cooked whole, cored but not peeled, and may then have the space filled with brown sugar, dates, or a mixture of stoneless raisins and sugar. Cut round the skin with a sharp knife to prevent bursting. Place them in a buttered fireproof dish with about a tablespoonful of water and a small knob of butter, and bake until just soft to the touch but not bursting through their skins. Grapefruit and pears are better cut in half before they are baked in the same way.

Halved grapefruit are also delicious grilled and served hot.

Baked bananas are appetising as a vegetable (particularly with bacon) or as a dessert with cream or a hot fruit sauce. Peel the bananas, place them in a well-buttered baking pan, brush well with butter and sprinkle with salt. Bake in a moderate oven for 15–18 minutes or until tender (that is, easily pierced with a fork).

Dried Fruit

Dried fruit, such as apple rings, apricots, peaches, prunes, pears and figs, should be well washed and soaked overnight. Then bring to the boil in the water in which they have been soaked, with sugar to taste. They need very little cooking once they have come to the boil.

Out-of-Season Fruits

Frozen and canned fruits in great variety are now available at reasonable prices and are extremely useful for fruit salads, flans and tarts. South African apricots, peaches and grapes coming in the English winter are also a great boon.

Apple Porcupines (for 3–4)

4 *apples*	*Sugar*
Jelly or jam	*Water*
Whipped cream	*Almonds*

Wipe, core and peel the apples (whole). Boil together enough sugar and water (in the proportion of 4 oz. sugar to $\frac{1}{2}$ pint water) to cover the apples and a little over. Cook the syrup for 7 minutes, then put in the whole apples and simmer them until soft. Skim occasionally. Take out and cool the apples. Then fill with either jelly or apricot jam, and stick with blanched split almonds. Serve in the syrup and decorate with whipped cream.

Apple Salad (for 2–3)

1 *lb. ripe eating*	2 *oz. preserved ginger*
apples	4 *oz. red currant jelly*
	Whipped cream

Peel and core the apples and slice them finely. Put them in a dish and cover with the preserved ginger, cut into very thin shavings. Warm the red currant jelly until it runs. Cool it a little, then pour over the apples and ginger. Just before serving, whip some cream and decorate with it.

Baked Bananas (1) (for 4–5)

6 *bananas*	3 *oz. brown sugar*
2 *tablespoonfuls*	2 *tablespoonfuls*
melted butter	*lemon juice*

Peel the bananas, cut them in half lengthwise and put them in a fireproof dish. Brush well with butter, sprinkle with sugar and lemon juice, and bake slowly for about 20 minutes, basting occasionally.

Or, instead of the sugar, pour $\frac{3}{8}$ cupful of molasses or maple syrup over the bananas before baking. Cook in the same way and serve hot, garnished with hot toasted almonds.

Baked Bananas (2) (for 4–5)

6 bananas   3 oz. sugar
Sherry to cover   Arrowroot

Peel the bananas and cut them in half lengthwise. Let them soak in a little sherry for ½ hour, then put them into a fireproof dish, sprinkle 2 oz. sugar over them, add a little water and bake

Prepare bananas for baking by brushing with melted butter (above). They can be served as a sweet or vegetable (left)

some whipped cream, slices of banana covered with grated chocolate, then some whipped cream and more jam. Finish with cream and decorate with cherries and angelica.

in a moderate oven for about 20 minutes. Put the sherry into a saucepan, add the rest of the sugar and a little arrowroot mixed to a paste with cold water, and simmer until it thickens. Pour over the bananas and serve.

Banana Ambrosia (for 6–8)

2 oranges   1½ cupfuls shredded
3 bananas   coconut
¼ cupful icing sugar

Peel oranges and cut crosswise into thin slices. Peel and slice bananas. Arrange alternate layers of oranges and bananas in a serving dish on a bed of coconut and sugar. Repeat the layers until all ingredients are used. Chill.

Banana Creams (The Quick Sweet)

A spoonful of jam   Grated chocolate
Slices of banana   Whipped cream
Cherries and angelica

Fill champagne or sundae glasses with the following layers: a spoonful of jam,

Banana Cream Whip (for 4–6)

2 to 3 bananas   ½ cupful whipped
1 tablespoonful   cream
  lemon juice   ¼ cupful sugar
      ⅛ teaspoonful salt

Mash the peeled bananas and mix in the lemon juice, sugar and salt. Fold in whipped cream. Chill and serve within 1 hour, garnished with sliced bananas.

Banana Custard

Peel some bananas and cut them in half lengthwise. Spread the halves with raspberry jam and put together again. Put them in a dish and pour custard over them.

Black-eyed Susan

1 large orange per   Blackberries or
  person   chopped dates to
Fruit salad dressing   garnish

Peel one large sweet orange for each serving. Remove as much as possible of the white pith and separate into segments.

Arrange in a circle like marguerite petals on a small plate for individual service. Put a small mound of fresh blackberries or chopped dates in the centre and pour over dressing made as follows: Stir well, or shake thoroughly in a tightly screwed glass jar, the juice of one orange, the juice of half a lemon and honey to taste. (This is excellent on any fresh fruit salad.)

Combination Fruit Plate (for 1)

1 *sweet red-skinned*   1 *ripe banana*
  apple (*unpeeled*)   2 *or* 3 *strawberries*
1 *orange*   (*optional*)

Cut unpeeled apple lengthwise into four thin wedges and remove core. Peel orange and slice crosswise. Cut two slices into halves. Peel and slice banana. Arrange three rows of fruit on a plate with strawberries on top as shown below.

Compôte of Apples (for 2–3)

1 *lb. apples*   4 *oz. loaf sugar*
½ *pint water*   *Lemon juice*

Put the sugar, water and a few drops of lemon juice into a casserole and boil quickly for 10 minutes. Peel, core and quarter the apples, put into boiling syrup and cook slowly in the oven until tender, being careful they do not break. Take out the apples, boil the syrup a little longer to reduce it, and then pour it over the apples. Serve with cream.

NOTE: A little white wine, sherry or kirsch is a great improvement to this compôte.

Fruit Jelly

Make lemon, orange or wine jelly and pour into a mould into which have been put slices of banana, strawberries, raspberries, grapes, apricots, peaches, stoned raisins, etc.

An even more delicious fruit jelly can be made with the syrup from a can or bottle of fruit. Dissolve either gelatine or a packet jelly (of the same flavour as the fruit) in ¼ to ½ pint of hot water and make up to a pint with the fruit syrup. Particularly suitable fruits are gooseberries, currants, plums or cherries.

Apple, orange, banana, decorated with strawberries, make this individual serving of Combination Fruit Plate

Orange, grapes and banana "trimmed" with walnuts make a colourful sweet

Fruit Salad

All fruit used in the making of fruit salads should be ripe, but never over-ripe, and absolutely sound. Oranges should have all the white pith removed and, of course, the pips. Plums should be well wiped, cut in half and stoned. If the skin is coarse, they should be peeled. Other fruit, such as bananas, apples, etc., should be peeled and cut in neat small pieces.

When canned fruit is used, the syrup is excellent as a dressing. A little sherry, Madeira, brandy or liqueur may be added as desired.

To make a syrup, allow 4 oz. sugar to $\frac{1}{2}$ pint of water (this should be enough to cover 1 lb. of fruit) and boil together for 10 minutes. Let the syrup cool and then pour it over the salad and mix well. Always let a salad stand for some hours, if possible, to allow the syrup to soak in well, but do not add raw apple until the last moment, as it turns brown. Serve chilled, or as cold as possible.

A few shredded almonds, chopped walnuts or a little shredded coconut can also be added. Small meringue cases filled with cream are very good served with fruit salads, or a handful of ratafia biscuits put over the top just before serving is an excellent addition.

Fruit Salad for a Party (for 30)

6 oranges	Chopped walnuts
1 grapefruit	3 bananas
1-lb. can peaches	$\frac{1}{2}$ lb. grapes
1 small bottle or can gooseberries	2 oz. Golden Syrup
	$\frac{1}{2}$-lb. can pineapple

Simmer the finely cut rinds of 3 oranges in a very little water with the Golden Syrup for quite $\frac{1}{2}$ hour. Cut up all the fruit (except the grapes and gooseberries) into small pieces and pour the syrup over them, together with that from the canned fruit. Let the whole remain covered for 6 hours before serving. Serve very cold with cream.

NOTE: This is a most delicious salad and suitable for children's parties, wedding receptions, etc.

Suggestions for other Fruit Salads:

Oranges, bananas, pineapple cubes, maraschino cherries.

Pear Condé is a famous sweet. The fruit, covered with apricot jam sauce, stand on a bed of rice and whipped cream

Oranges, stoned dates, stoned raisins and chopped nuts.

Cubes of avocado pear and fresh pineapple, and grapefruit segments, in pineapple syrup (made from the pineapple juice, sweetened with honey and a dash of lemon juice).

Pineapple chunks and seedless grapes in pineapple juice.

Fresh pineapple slices and fresh strawberries.

Diced cantaloup melon, strawberries, sliced pears.

Bananas, peaches and raspberries.

Apples, pears and loganberries.

Halved plums and loganberries.

New Baked Apples

Apples	Brown sugar
Slices of bread ½-in. thick	Marmalade
	Butter

Core, but do not peel, the apples and cut round with a very sharp knife under the skin to allow them to expand. Fill with butter, marmalade and brown sugar. Spread the bread with butter, marmalade and brown sugar, and put an apple on each slice. Put them in a buttered fire-proof dish not too close together and add lumps of butter and a few dessertspoonfuls of marmalade. Pour in a little water and sprinkle the apples well with brown sugar.

Bake for ½ hour or longer, basting frequently. Serve in the dish in which they are cooked.

Orange Fantasy (for 4)

(Recipe by Luigi of the Savoy Hotel Grill Room, London)

4 oranges (large "navel" ones)
1 cupful sugar
2 tablespoonfuls Grand Marnier
1 cupful water

Peel oranges carefully, removing as much of the white pith as possible. Cut peel of 1 orange (with white pith removed) into very fine longish strips. Soak in a little Grand Marnier liqueur while you prepare syrup by boiling 1 cupful of water with 1 cupful of sugar for 5 minutes. Now cook peel in syrup over low flame till fairly tender. Cool. Slice oranges in quarters and add juice to syrup. Stir well and add the rest of the Grand Marnier. Put sliced oranges in a glass bowl and pour over the peel and syrup. Serve very cold.

Orange Mousse (for 10)

2 cupfuls double cream	2 cupfuls orange pulp cut in small pieces and drained
¼ lb. confectioner's sugar	1 teaspoonful vanilla essence
⅛ teaspoonful salt	

Whip cream, sugar and salt together until stiff. Add fruit and vanilla and mix well. Chill, and then freeze in ice-cube compartment, turning refrigerator on to very cold so as to freeze as fast as possible. Serve with whipped cream and wafers or petit-fours.

Oranges with Coconut

| Oranges | Finely grated coconut |
| Sugar | |

Peel some oranges, taking away all the pith, and cut them into slices on a plate so that none of the juice is wasted. Put some in a deep bowl and sprinkle with finely grated coconut and sugar; put in more layers until the bowl is full, the top layer being coconut and sugar. Stand for 1–2 hours so that the orange and coconut get well blended. Serve with cream if liked.

Oranges, Whole

Soak oranges for 24 hours, then boil until tender. Cut a hole in the top and take out all the pulp and pips. Make a syrup, allowing 1 oz. sugar for each orange, put the pulp in the syrup and fill the oranges with it. Decorate with glacé cherries, angelica or split almonds.

Pear Condé (for 4–6)

4–6 pears	Double cream
1 cupful sugar	1 cupful rice (boiled)
Apricot jam	1½ cupfuls water
Rum or rum essence	

Rinse cooked rice thoroughly by placing in strainer and pouring plenty of hot water through it. Allow to cool in strainer or colander. Peel the pears thinly and cook until tender, but still firm, in syrup made by boiling the sugar and water for 5 minutes. Prepare apricot sauce by heating the jam with just enough water to make a thin, smoothly flowing sauce, and add a

drop or two of rum or rum essence. Whip the cream and mix about half of it with the cold rice. Place rice in serving dish, stand cooked cold pears on top, stalks up, pour sauce over and pipe the remainder of the whipped cream round the edge of the dish.

Pears à la Alexandra (for 3–4)

Canned Bartlett pears	½ pint lemon jelly
Whipped cream	1 pint thick custard

Make a thick custard, allowing 4 eggs to a pint of milk, and adding sugar to taste. Pour it into the bottom of a glass dish. Make the jelly and, when cool but still liquid, pour over the custard. Arrange the pears in quarters on top and pipe the whipped cream over them. Decorate with glacé cherries and angelica.

Stewed Pears

Hard stewing pears	Sugar to taste
Water to cover	Strip of lemon peel
2 or 3 cloves	

Peel, quarter and core the pears, and put them in a saucepan with enough cold water to cover them. Add the lemon, sugar and cloves, bring to the boil and simmer gently until soft. When they turn pink, boil more rapidly, to deepen the colour.

Chilled melon cut in half and filled with mixed fruit salad looks gay on a summer dinner party table

ICES

Four mouth-watering sundaes—you can make them all from home-made ice cream, combined with whipped cream and various fruits

ICES are always a popular item on the menu, especially with the children and at parties. They are really very simple to make at home and are also nutritious.

When making ices it is important to remember that freezing takes away from the sweetness of the mixture, so more sugar is required. Too little sugar will make the mixture freeze too hard and too much will prevent it freezing properly.

Colouring should be used sparingly, as crude colours make ices look unattractive.

To avoid ices that have ice splinters in them and are coarse in texture, take them out of the freezing tray when half-frozen, turn into a chilled basin and beat well, adding some lightly whipped cream, egg-white or evaporated milk.

Generally speaking, the best results are obtained by switching the freezing control to the coldest freezing-point to start with, allowing the mixture from 1–1½ hours'

freezing before taking it from the tray and beating it with cream, egg-white or evaporated milk until light and frothy. If the mixture is a rich one, it should be put back in the tray with the control left at freezing; a less rich and thinner mixture should have the control at half-freeze. In either case, when the ice is frozen to the right consistency the switch should be turned back to normal.

When using evaporated milk as a substitute for cream, measure the amount you need, put it in the top of a double saucepan over boiling water (or in to tin in a saucepan of boiling water) and heat to scalding point, then turn into a basin and chill quickly. Whip and add to the ice cream.

WATER ICES

Water ices need a syrup made of sugar and water as a foundation. To this syrup either fruit purée or fruit juice can be added. A little wine or liqueur added to a water ice is a great improvement.

Syrup for Water Ices

1 *pint water*   ½ *lb. sugar*
Juice of half a lemon

Put the water and sugar into a saucepan, bring to the boil and boil for 10 minutes, skimming when necessary. Add the lemon juice and strain through a jelly bag.

Lemon or Orange Water Ice

½ pint syrup (as opposite)
½ pint lemon or orange juice
1 egg-white
Rinds of 2 lemons or oranges

Pour the syrup, while still hot, over the thinly peeled fruit rinds, leave to cool and then add the fruit juice. Strain through a jelly bag. When half-frozen, whip in the stiffly beaten egg-white and freeze until ready for the table.

Raspberry or Strawberry Water Ice

1 pint raspberries or strawberries
4 oz. sugar
1 gill water
Lemon juice

Sprinkle the sugar over the raspberries or strawberries, let them stand for 2 hours, then mash them, squeeze through muslin, add the water and a squeeze of lemon juice and freeze.

Ice Lollies

These prime favourites with the children can be made at home in special "lolly"-shaped containers. Use any of the above recipes for water ices or, alternatively, make a strong, sweet lemon or orangeade, pour it into the containers, put a cocktail stick in each—and when you take them out of the freezing compartment of the refrigerator you will have most professional lollies.

ICE CREAMS

Though they are generally known as ice *creams*, cream need not form part of the foundation. Custard made with eggs and milk or cornflour is generally used. If a richer ice is desired, a little cream can be added, or if a very rich ice is wanted half cream and half custard makes a delicious mixture. Remember that if cream is used, the same proportion of sugar must be used as if only custard were employed—i.e. 3 oz. to 1 pint.

Basic Ice Cream (1)

1 pint milk
2 egg-yolks
3 oz. sugar

Bring the milk and sugar almost to the boil. Beat the egg-yolks well and add to the milk, stirring all the time. Put the mixture in the top of a double saucepan over hot water and stir until it thickens. Leave to get quite cold before freezing.

Basic Ice Cream (2)

1 pint milk
1 oz. cornflour
¼ pint thick cream (or evaporated milk)
3 oz. sugar
2 eggs
Vanilla flavouring as liked

Pineapple water ice, above, is delightfully refreshing, a pleasant change from the more usual ice cream

Hot chocolate sauce makes a wonderful contrast served with vanilla ice cream

Mix the cornflour with a little of the milk, heat the remainder of the milk with the sugar in a double saucepan, then add to the cornflour and stir in double saucepan until the mixture thickens. Cook gently for about 8 minutes, then remove from heat and leave to cool. Beat the eggs, then gradually stir in the mixture, add flavouring and cream, cool thoroughly, then freeze.

Chocolate Ice Cream (1)

1 *pint custard*	1 *gill cream, if liked*
Vanilla essence	3 *oz. grated chocolate*
A little water	

Make a custard and let it cool. Dissolve the chocolate in a little water and add it to the custard. Then add a few drops of vanilla essence and mix well. Add the cream, which should be lightly whipped, and freeze.

Chocolate Ice Cream (2)

Boil together 1 gill evaporated milk, 1 gill water and 4 oz. castor sugar. Put 1½ dessertspoonfuls powdered gelatine to soak in 1 tablespoonful of cold water. Then dissolve it in the hot syrup. Stir in 4 oz. grated chocolate until dissolved. When cool, add ½ teaspoonful vanilla essence, 1 gill chilled evaporated milk and the same quantity whipped enough to hold its shape, and stir thoroughly. Freeze until of the right consistency, stirring now and again in the tray.

Coffee Ice Cream

Make a custard as for Chocolate Ice Cream (1), but use equal parts of milk and strong black coffee. Cream can be added if desired.

Fruit Ice Cream

1 *pint vanilla ice cream (see next page, or buy in block)*	2 *oz. each glacé cherries, angelica or any crystallised fruit, according to taste*

Cut the fruit up small and beat it into the vanilla ice cream, then turn into freezing-tray and freeze.

Maraschino Ice Cream

1 *wineglassful Maraschino*	1 *pint vanilla ice cream*
1 *oz. castor sugar*	

Beat the cream until stiff, stir in sugar and Maraschino and freeze.

Neapolitan Ice Cream

This consists of three or more different coloured and flavoured ice creams frozen together in layers—pink (strawberry), white (vanilla), green (Maraschino or peppermint) and chocolate being the most popular combination.

Peach Melba

Make vanilla ice cream (see next page) and put a spoonful each into the necessary number of sundae glasses. Peel fresh peaches, quarter them and put two quarters into each glass. Pour over them either raspberry purée or raspberry jam (sieved if liked) and cover the top with whipped cream.

NOTE: When fresh peaches are not available, canned ones may be used instead.

Pear Melba

Make as for Peach Melba, but use fresh ripe or canned pears instead.

Peppermint Ice Cream

2 *tablespoonfuls crème de menthe*	1 *pint ice cream*

Before freezing the plain ice cream, stir in the crème de menthe, mixing thoroughly. This is a wonderfully refreshing hot weather dish.

Raspberry Ice Cream

Put ½ lb. raspberry jam into a gravy strainer and pour on to it ¾ pint milk. Press the jam against the sides of the strainer with the back of a wooden spoon until only the seeds of the jam remain. Stir the mixture well, then freeze hard. Half an hour before serving, turn into a chilled basin and beat well; return to the refrigerator until needed.

Strawberry or Raspberry Ice Cream

½ *pint strawberry or raspberry pulp*	1 *egg-white*
1 *pint milk*	10–12 *oz. sugar*
	½ *pint cream*
Juice of a lemon	

To make the pulp, clean and stalk about 1 lb. fruit, sprinkle with sugar and leave to stand for about 2 hours, then rub through a hair sieve.

Boil the milk, add the rest of the sugar and let it get nearly cold. Then add the fruit pulp, the lemon juice and, lastly, the stiffly

The perfect "important occasion" sweet—an Ice Pudding made in a special mould from any kind of home-made ice cream, preferably in a variety of flavours and colours

whipped cream. Partially freeze the mixture, then beat in the stiffly whipped eggwhite and continue to freeze.

NOTE: If canned fruit is used, put it through a sieve and use a little of the syrup, but reduce the quantity of sugar.

Vanilla Ice Cream (1)

3 gills milk	1 whole egg and 2
1 gill cream or	yolks
evaporated milk	1 tablespoonful
½ teaspoonful vanilla	sherry (optional)
essence	2 oz. castor sugar

Heat the milk and sugar without boiling. Beat the egg and yolks, stir in the milk, mix well and put back in the saucepan. Then cook over a gentle heat until the mixture thickens without letting it boil. Stir all the time. Pour into a basin and leave until cool. When cold, put into the freezing tray and, when half frozen, turn into a chilled basin and add the sherry, vanilla, cream or evaporated milk whipped just enough to hold its shape. Beat well, return to the tray and continue freezing until ready, then turn the control back to

normal. Excellent served with hot chocolate sauce (see Sauces).

Vanilla Ice Cream (2)

1 pint custard	1 gill cream if desired
	Vanilla essence

Make custard and let it cool, add vanilla essence to taste and the whipped cream, and freeze.

NOTE: If cream is used, a little more sugar is needed when making the custard.

ICE PUDDINGS

Special moulds with lids are required for these. The mould should be placed in the freezing compartment for 15 minutes before it is used. Cut a piece of greaseproof paper ½ in. larger than the lid of the mould, grease it on both sides, fill the mould with half-frozen ice cream, cover with greased paper, put on lid and freeze until firm. When ready, dip mould in cold water, take off lid and paper, turn pudding on to a chilled dish and decorate as liked.

Any kind of ice cream may be used for puddings.

Tomato Cheese Surprises make savoury mouthfuls. Serve them on crisp chicory leaves, garnished with watercress and sliced hard-boiled egg

SAVOURIES

Round off a good dinner with a tasty dish that is well seasoned and piping hot—and serve it in small quantities

SAVOURIES, coming as they do, at the end of a meal, must be particularly appetising to be appreciated. Two things are essential: (1) definite and distinctive flavour, so be generous with the seasoning; and (2) they should be served really piping hot, if possible straight from the grill or oven. This is not always possible, but savouries suffer more than other dishes from being kept hot, especially those served on croûtes. **Croûtes,** that is, fingers or rounds of fried or toasted bread, form the basis of many savouries.

In addition to the recipes in this chapter, see also those under the heading "Lunch and Supper Dishes" for slightly more substantial savouries which could be served after a light main course.

Anchovy Toast

Fry some croûtes, spread with anchovy paste and garnish with a little chopped parsley.

Angels on Horseback

Oysters	*Squeeze of lemon*
Rolls of fat bacon	*juice*
Anchovy essence	*Cayenne pepper*
Croûtes	*Anchovy paste*

Get ready some fried croûtes, spread them with anchovy paste and keep them hot. Beard the oysters and lay them on slices of fat bacon with a dash of anchovy essence, a squeeze of lemon juice and a sprinkling of Cayenne. Roll up the bacon and fasten with a skewer or cocktail stick.

Fry quickly on both sides in hot fat, or grill, and serve on the croûtes.

Buck Rarebit

Make Welsh Rarebit (see p. 164) and put a poached egg on top of each serving.

Cheese Aigrettes (for 6–7)

1 gill water	*2 eggs*
1 oz. butter or mar-	*2 oz. flour*
garine	*2 oz. grated cheese*
Pepper and salt	

Put the water and the butter into a saucepan and bring to the boil. Shake in the flour and stir all the time until the mixture comes away from the sides. Then stir in the cheese, still beating, until the mixture is smooth. Add a pinch of pepper and salt. Cool a little, then beat in the eggs one at a time and continue beating until smooth. Break the mixture into little rocky lumps and drop into deep boiling fat, cook slowly at first, increasing the heat towards the end. Allow 10–15 minutes. Drain well on paper and sprinkle with a little grated cheese before serving.

Cheese d'Artois (for 5–6)

6 oz. flaky or short	*1 egg-white*
pastry	*3 oz. grated cheese*
1 oz. butter or mar-	*Cayenne pepper*
garine	*Salt and pepper*
2 egg-yolks	*A little made mustard*

Make pastry (see Pastry chapter). Put the cheese into a basin, add yolks and melted butter, then seasoning, and stir in the stiffly beaten egg-white. Roll out the pastry thinly. Spread the mixture on half the pastry. Moisten the edges with beaten egg and fold over the other half of the pastry. Mark across in squares or strips. Brush with beaten egg and sprinkle with cheese. Bake in a hot oven for 10–15 minutes and cut where marked.

Cheese Savouries (for 6–7)

2 oz. flour	2 oz. grated Parmesan
2 oz. butter or mar-	cheese
garine	Salt and Cayenne
A little water	

For the filling

¼ teacupful cream	1 tablespoonful
Cayenne	Parmesan cheese

Sift the flour and seasoning together and rub in the butter. Add the grated cheese and mix well. Mix to a stiff dough with a little water. Put the mixture on a floured board and roll out. Line some small greased boat-shaped tins and bake "blind" in the oven until a golden brown. Allow to cool.

For the filling.—Whip the cream and fold in the Parmesan cheese; add a pinch of Cayenne, pile the mixture into the shapes and garnish with green salad. Serve cold.

Chicken Liver on Toast

Uncooked chicken	Fat for frying
liver	Pepper
Rashers of fat bacon	Croûtes

Get ready some fried croûtes and keep them hot. Cut uncooked chicken liver into neat pieces, roll them in slices of fat bacon with a pinch of pepper and fasten each with a skewer or cocktail stick. Fry quickly on both sides in hot fat and serve on croûtes.

Cod's Roe

Smoked cod's roe	Capers
Egg-yolk	Butter
A little milk	Pepper
Fried croûtes	

Fry the croûtes, drain and keep hot. Soak the roe in water for 1 hour to soften it, then dry and slice. Warm it in a little butter, add the beaten yolk, a little milk and pepper. Reheat without boiling. Serve on the croûtes and garnish with a few capers.

Cod's Roe on Potato Cakes

Cold, cooked, fresh	A little cream
cod's roe	Pepper and salt
Potato cakes	Capers

Cut up the roe and mix it with the cream and a pinch of pepper and salt, and heat in a saucepan. Make flat potato cakes (see chapter on Vegetables), fry them until brown and put some of the cod's roe on each. Garnish with a few capers.

Devilled Biscuits

Water biscuits	A very little dry
Grated cheese	mustard
Butter	A pinch of Cayenne

Mix some butter and a very little dry mustard together and spread the biscuits thickly with it, adding a pinch of Cayenne. Cover thickly with grated cheese and put under the griller or in the oven for a few minutes until brown.

Haddock Croûtes (for 3–4)

2 tablespoonfuls cold,	Chopped parsley
cooked smoked	Chopped gherkins
haddock, flaked	1 dessertspoonful
½ oz. butter	cream
Cayenne	1 egg-yolk
Croûtes	

Prepare some fried croûtes and keep them hot. Melt the butter and add the haddock, cream, Cayenne and gherkins. Stir in the yolk and heat, without boiling. Pile neatly on the croûtes and sprinkle with chopped parsley.

Herring Roes on Toast

Herring roes	Butter
Flour	Pepper
Croûtes	

Two savoury flavours combine to make **Sardine Welsh Rarebit Fingers** specially tasty for the last course of a meal

Put the roes in salt water to clean them, then drain and pour boiling water over them to make them curl up. Drain again. Put a pinch of pepper in some flour and sprinkle the flour lightly over the roes. Prepare croûtes and keep them hot. Fry the roes in a little butter for 3 or 4 minutes, then put them on the croûtes and garnish with chopped parsley or chopped hard-boiled egg-yolk.

Sardines on Toast

Sardines	1 tablespoonful milk
Croûtes	or cream
1 egg-yolk	3 drops Tarragon
½ oz. butter	vinegar
	Pepper

Bone the sardines, fold together again and put in the oven to warm. Fry croûtes and keep hot. Mix the egg-yolk, butter, vinegar, pepper and milk or cream in a saucepan, stirring to a smooth batter, without boiling. Put the sardines on the croûtes and pour the mixture over them. Garnish with a little chopped parsley or a small piece of tomato.

Sardine Welsh Rarebit Fingers (for 6)

4 whole slices of toast	12 sardines
covered with Welsh	Sprigs of parsley or
Rarebit (see recipe	watercress
(1) next column)	Paprika pepper

Lay 3 sardines side by side on each slice of Welsh Rarebit and heat through under the grill. Cut into fingers and sprinkle decoratively with the paprika pepper. Serve hot, garnished with parsley or watercress

Scotch Woodcock

Croûtes	½ oz. butter
Anchovy paste	1 tablespoonful milk
1 egg-yolk	or cream
	Pepper

Fry croûtes, make a dent in the middle of each, spread with anchovy paste and keep hot. Mix the egg-yolk, butter, pepper and milk or cream in a saucepan and stir to a smooth batter without boiling. With a teaspoon, fill the hollows in the croûtes with the mixture and sprinkle with chopped parsley or put a curled anchovy on each.

Stuffed Mushrooms

Cup mushrooms	Chopped parsley
Chopped ham or liver	Butter
Breadcrumbs	Pepper and salt
A very little chopped	A little milk or stock
onion	Croûtes

Wash the mushrooms and remove the skin and stalks. Mix together the ham, breadcrumbs, onion, parsley and seasoning, and bind with a little milk or stock. Fill the mushrooms with the mixture and put a small piece of butter on top of each. Put the mushrooms on a buttered tin in a moderate oven and bake for 15–20 minutes. Prepare fried croûtes and serve the mushrooms, hot, on these.

Tomato Cheese Surprises (for 4)

8 small firm tomatoes	Seasoned flour
2 oz. grated cheese	Brown breadcrumbs
Salt	Vegetable fat for
Cayenne pepper	frying
	1 egg

Skin the tomatoes and remove the cores. Stuff tightly with the grated cheese seasoned well with salt and Cayenne. Roll in seasoned flour. Dip in egg and coat well with breadcrumbs. Fry in hot vegetable fat for 2–3 minutes until a golden brown. Serve cold garnished with chicory or watercress.

Venetian Toasts (for 3–4)

1 egg-yolk	Pinch of dried herbs
2 tablespoonfuls	Butter
minced ham	Pepper
	Croûtes

Mince the ham very finely, add a pinch of herbs and pepper. Heat in a saucepan with a little butter and the egg-yolk. Pile it on croûtes and serve at once. A little minced chicken liver can be added.

Welsh Rarebit (1) (for 5–6)

12 oz. grated Cheddar	Cayenne and salt
cheese	2 oz. margarine
Made mustard to	4 tablespoonfuls milk
taste	Buttered toast

Put the cheese and margarine into a basin and mix well. Add milk and seasoning and mix to a stiff paste. Spread the mixture smoothly on buttered toast and place under the griller until light brown.

Welsh Rarebit (2) (for 5–6)

4 oz. grated cheese	1 oz. melted butter
Made mustard to	1 tablespoonful milk
taste	Buttered toast
	Cayenne and salt

Stir the butter, milk, cheese, mustard and seasoning in a saucepan until it thickens, then pour smoothly over the toast and put under the griller for a few minutes until brown.

NOTE: The cheese should not be allowed to go stringy. If it does, add 2 teaspoonfuls of fine breadcrumbs and stir well.

CHEESE

Among the finest home-produced English cheeses are Cheddar, Wensleydale, Stilton, Leicester and Caerphilly

The delight of the gourmet, cheese completes a perfect meal—and is one of the most nutritive and concentrated of foods

CHEESE has a history going back for more than twenty centuries—it formed part of the diet of Greek athletes in classical times, and poets from Homer onwards have sung its praises. In our day there is such a variety available, especially from the Continent, that selection becomes a fascinating occupation in itself.

Cheese is one of the most nutritive and concentrated forms of food: the fat and protein content of about a gallon of milk is found in one pound of cheese, and an ounce of cheese has nearly twice the amount of body-building protein of an ounce of meat. For those needing a high percentage of protein and calcium in their diet, such as children and old people, cheese is an invaluable and easily digested food. It is also economical because, being so highly concentrated, it is best eaten in small quantities.

A piece of cheese, with bread, biscuit or fruit, is the perfect last or next to the last course of a meal.

The simplest cheese is made by draining the whey from the curds of naturally soured milk (pasteurised milk, by the way, will not sour correctly), and this soft cream cheese must be eaten fresh, not more than three or four days after it is made. In general, cheese is made from the curd of milk formed as the result of the addition of rennet. The curds are sometimes scalded, sometimes not. The whey is drained off and, in hard or semi-hard cheeses, the curds are pressed into traditional and characteristic shapes. The cheeses are then set aside to ripen, the ripening period varying from a few days to many months. In a large number of varieties moulds are introduced into the cheese to produce, during the ripening process, blue-veining or other characteristics. Some cheeses are flavoured with herbs.

The varieties arise from differences in the quality of the milk used—from skimmed milk to full cream—and in the cheese-making processes.

Buying and Keeping

For domestic use, it is best to buy cheese in small quantities, and, when buying, to ask the supplier whether it is ready for immediate eating, as it may be displayed for sale not quite ripe. A cheese reaches a definite peak of maturity, and after that has been passed, deterioration may begin, in some cheeses, within two days; others will keep for months.

A cut piece of cheese must be kept moist unless you wish to dry it for grating; it should be wrapped in a damp cloth and kept in a covered dish, or it can be kept in a polythene bag. If you wish to store a whole cheese, the rind should be left exposed to the air and turned over frequently. Any mould on it should be scraped off, the cheese rubbed dry and then rubbed with oil or melted fat. Once it is cut, the cut surface should be protected with greaseproof paper.

165

Varieties

Over a hundred varieties of cheese are available in the U.K. Of these, only a tenth are home produced. The greatest number of cheeses imported from the Continent come from France; others come from Italy, Switzerland, Holland, Denmark, and there are cheeses, too, from Norway, Sweden and Germany. A great deal of cheese, mostly Cheddar in type, comes from the Commonwealth. In addition, there are the popular processed cheeses, attractively packed in tinfoil and easy to keep.

Cheeses, like wines, bear the names of their places of origin, where they have been made for centuries on the local farms. There is still considerable small-scale production of regional cheeses, particularly in France, but in all countries production of the well-known cheeses is now mostly large-scale.

In the U.K., "farmhouse" cheese, which used to be sold in the ancient local "Cheese Fairs," is often sought nostalgically. Although still available, the supply is steadily declining. There are fewer than 120 farmhouse cheese producers to-day; in 1939 there were 1,120. The shift to large-scale production is partly due to planned milk marketing and the attendant development of cheese factories; partly to the fact that farmers' daughters are no longer content with their traditional tasks in the dairy. (In the old days a Cheshire farmer looking out for a wife would ask a girl to lift the heavy lid of the parish chest. If she could do this, she was considered strong enough for the cheese-making.) The cheeses made by the women of the farmer's family were taken for sale to the local Cheese Fairs.

Nevertheless, the characteristics of a regional cheese are retained in large-scale production, which has the advantages of modern machinery; and the cheeses are carefully tested and graded.

The following are some of the well-known cheeses of different countries. Most are generally obtainable, but in case of difficulty write direct to Thomas Marsh (Leadenhall) Ltd., Leadenhall Market, London, E.C.3, who import cheeses from all parts of the world and who supplied the cheeses shown in the photographs on pages 168 and 169.

U.K. CHEESES

Caerphilly

Though Welsh in origin, Caerphilly now comes from the West Country, chiefly Somerset. It has a mild tangy flavour, is rather flaky in texture, not hard, though firm in body. It ripens quickly and is ready for consumption in 10 to 14 days after manufacture. After 3 or 4 weeks it begins to deteriorate.

Cheddar

The best known of all English cheeses. Half the cheese made in the U.K. is Cheddar (some of it actually made in its place of origin), and so is most of the cheese imported from Canada, Australia and New Zealand. It is a firm, smooth cheese, close in texture and clean and mellow in flavour, of high nutritive value. Its colour should be uniform and the rind unbroken. Among its virtues are its good keeping qualities. It is a cheese used most commonly for cooking; buy it for the table but harden it by exposure to air for grating.

The largest cheese ever made was among Queen Victoria's wedding presents: a Cheddar weighing 11 cwt. and standing more than 9 ft. high.

Cheshire

The most ancient of English cheeses. Though Cheshire-type cheese comes from as far afield as Holland and New Zealand, the main centre of production is still in or near Cheshire, where the salty soil is responsible for its distinctive piquant flavour. The body is firm, not hard, and flaky in texture. A Cheshire cheese has the same height as diameter, with square edges.

Derby

A flat-shaped cheese, uniformly white and of close, smooth texture; clean and mild in flavour.

Dunlop

A Scottish cheese from Ayrshire; flattish in shape, flaky in texture.

Gloucester and Double Gloucester

The single Gloucester is good for toasting. The Double Gloucester is better known—an enriched Cheshire kind of cheese, with a mellow, distinctive flavour.

Lancashire

A little-known cheese, differing from other hard-pressed varieties in that, when three years old, it can be spread like butter. It is notably good for toasting when ripe.

Leicestershire

Not well known outside the Midlands, and formerly an exclusive farmhouse product. It is red-brown in colour inside and rather crumbly. It keeps well. Recommended to be eaten with apple pie.

Stilton

The "King of Cheeses," and world famous. A semi-hard, double-cream, blue-veined cheese, which, though now produced on a large scale in the Midlands, still retains its character and is made by highly skilled enthusiasts—it is a difficult cheese to produce. Its fame spread in the old days when travellers staying at the Bell Inn, Stilton, on the Leicestershire border, took away pieces of this admirable cheese. A fully matured Stilton has a clean, mild flavour and is velvety—or of a flaky open texture. The body should be uniformly creamy white, apart from the blue-grey mould radiating from the centre. The coat should be thin, moist, slightly wrinkled and drab coloured. It takes six months or even more to ripen, and should be eaten when fully ripe. There is also a quick-ripening *White Stilton*, without blueing.

Stilton cheeses used to be put under a wine tap to absorb a few drops every day, and port is sometimes added now if the cheese has become too dry.

Wensleydale

A rich, creamy soft cheese, delicately blue-veined, and sweet. The ripe cheese should have a greyish-white skin, clearly showing the pressure marks of its bandage. There is also a creamy *White Wensleydale*, with no blue-veining, which is eaten fresh and sold in cheeses from $\frac{1}{2}$ lb. to 14 lb. in weight. It was formerly little known outside the Yorkshire dales, where the formula was first introduced by the Abbots of the Abbey of Jervaulx, but it now has a wide reputation.

English Cream Cheeses

These unheated and unpressed cheeses, which spread like butter, must be eaten within four days of manufacture, as they deteriorate quickly.

FRENCH CHEESES

The following are the most celebrated and most easily obtainable of more than 400 varieties of French regional cheeses.

Throughout Scandinavia cheese is eaten at almost every meal. Above, a selection from Denmark includes Danish Blue, Samsoe, Esrom, and other types

Bleu d'Auvergne

A fine quality whole milk blue-mould cheese, uncooked and unpressed, either crustless, or with a very light crust.

Brie

A famous whole milk, inoculated, soft cheese, flat and round in shape, named after La Brie province east of Paris, but now made in other parts also. It is uncooked and unpressed, and is best bought in small quantities as deterioration begins within 48 hours after it has passed its peak of maturity. Sections can be bought in light wooden boxes. There are three varieties: *Brie de Coulommiers* (or simply *Coulommiers*), *Brie de Melun* and *Brie de Meaux*, the last being one of the most celebrated French cheeses.

Camembert

The French cheese best known in England is made mainly in Normandy, but elsewhere also on a considerable scale, and even in other countries. It is rich and soft, uncooked and unpressed, with a dark rind and pale yellow inside. Like Brie, it begins to deteriorate within 48 hours of reaching maturity. It is best eaten when beginning to go soft; later the mould with which it is inoculated decomposes the casein further, and an exceedingly strong smell is produced. It is usually exported in small boxes.

Cantal

A hard whole milk cheese, somewhat sharp in flavour; red or white. It is similar to the English Cheddar.

Carré de l'Est

A soft cheese, similar to Camembert.

Demi-Sel

A whole milk soft cheese sold in quarter pounds. Made mostly in Normandy.

Demi-Suisse

A highly perishable soft cheese made from pure double cream, which should be eaten within three days of arrival by air from Normandy.

Le Port du Salut (or Port-Salut)

The "veritable fromage" is made by the Trappist monks in the Abbey of that name at Entrammes (Mayenne), though production goes on now in a much wider field. It is medium solid, round and flat, mild in flavour, and of great repute. The factory-produced Port-Salut is heavier and thicker than the hand-made Abbey production.

Munster

A semi-hard whole milk cheese with a dark red rind, made in the Munster valley in Alsace and in other parts of that area.

Pont l'Evêque

This yellow, semi-hard, fermented cheese is still produced exclusively on farms of the Pont l'Evêque district of Normandy, where its production is more than a thousand years old.

From Switzerland come Emmenthal, Petit Gruyère (in sections) and Geska. Norway provides Gjetost and Germany Limburger

France produces (left to right, top row): Carré de l'Est, Port Salut, Tome de Savoie, Demi-Sel. Centre: Pont l'Evêque, Bleu d'Auvergne, Demi-Suisse, Brie and Roquefort. Bottom row: Camembert, Saint Paulin, Coulommiers

Roquefort

French law lays it down that Roquefort Cheese can be made only from ewe's milk, and the genuine Roquefort, with a world-wide reputation, bears a label of a red sheep in an oval. The cheeses are matured in the natural limestone caves at Roquefort in the Cevennes, where the unique atmospheric conditions produce a flavour which, it is claimed, cannot be reproduced in the many Roquefort imitations made elsewhere. As sheep's milk is extremely rich, Roquefort cheese has a great nutritive value. If kept covered in a refrigerator, it will remain unspoiled for a long time.

Saint Paulin

A mild and creamy "Le Port du Salut"-type cheese, round and flat in shape.

Tome de Savoie au Raisin

This cheese from Haute Savoie is fermented in vats in which the local wine is made, so acquiring its characteristic flavour. It is a round, flat cheese, its rind coated with the skins and stones of black grapes, and consequently a dark purple colour.

ITALIAN CHEESES

Bel Paese

A well-known cheese, 4 lb. in weight, soft, creamy and mild in flavour, with very small holes, from the plains of North Lombardy.

Burrini

Gourd-shaped and rich in fats, as it is filled with a kind of butter. It is served cut into small portions.

Caciocavelli

A pear-shaped hard cheese of strong flavour, with a glazed rind. It will keep indefinitely. Used grated in cooking.

Gorgonzola

This celebrated semi-hard, blue-veined cheese takes its name from a village near Milan, and its principal place of production is still in that region. It is made, however, elsewhere on a considerable scale, and there is a Danish "Gorgonzola." There are two types: the conventional 20-lb. cheese, and a small "mountain Gorgonzola" which is not mass-produced and is of better quality.

Parmesan

A very hard cheese of fine flavour from Parma, used chiefly for grating. (It can be bought in tins already grated or, more economically, in a piece for grating at home.)

Sardo

A black, very hard cheese from Sardinia, used grated for culinary purposes.

SWISS CHEESES

Emmenthal (Emmentaler)

A hard cheese very similar to the famous Gruyère but with bigger "eyes" or holes, milder and somewhat softer. Most of the Emmenthal in the U.K. is sold under the name of Gruyère. It is made near

Berne and elsewhere, not only in Switzerland.

Gruyère

The premier Swiss cheese and world famous. A cooked hard cheese, pale yellow, smooth and firm, distinguished by the large "eyes" with which it is honeycombed and by its characteristic and agreeable odour and flavour. It comes from the Canton of Friburg, but is made also in many other parts. (There is a French Gruyère.)

Petit Gruyère

Processed Gruyère sold in tin-foil-wrapped sections.

Schabzieger (Geska)

A very hard and highly flavoured cheese, green in colour, used chiefly for grating, and sold in small cones. It is made from skimmed milk, cooked with herbs and matured for several months.

DUTCH CHEESES

There is a long-standing Government control on the genuineness and composition of Dutch cheeses, and every cheese for export bears a Government mark as a guarantee.

Edam

A globe-shaped cheese about 4 lb. in weight, with a polished red rind and a smooth, deep yellow interior; mild in flavour.

Gouda

A famous cheese, round and flat with a polished yellow rind; about 10 lb. in weight. There is also a small size. Genuine Gouda is rich in fat, made from whole milk on about 5,000 farms in the provinces of southern Holland and Utrecht.

GERMAN CHEESE

Limburger

The most famous of all German cheeses; a semi-hard, whole milk cheese, highly flavoured and strong smelling, from the Hartz mountains.

SCANDINAVIAN CHEESES

Crème Chantilly (Hablé)

A national speciality of Sweden made from pasteurised cream. It is sold in wedge-shaped boxes, wrapped in tin-foil and should be kept under mild refrigeration.

Danish Blue

The speciality cheese of Denmark; a smooth, creamy cheese with a network of blue-green veins and a mellow aromatic flavour.

Danish Fynbo

A semi-hard cheese made from whole milk, similar to Samsoe (see below) but milder.

Esrom (Danish Port-Salut)

An imitation of the French Port-Salut and less expensive. Mild and creamy.

Samsoe

A firm, pressed cheese, taking its name from the Danish island of Samsoe, made from whole milk; mild and creamy with a nutty flavour. It keeps well.

Gjetost

A national speciality of Norway; a semi-hard cheese with a delicate caramel flavour, sold in oblong blocks; made from mixed goat's and cow's milk. It should be served cut wafer thin.

PROCESSED CHEESES

These cooked cheeses are comparatively new to the U.K. market, but their development has been rapid. They are extremely popular and there are many varieties. Wrapped in tin-foil in small portions, they are attractively boxed and can be kept for long periods. Both English and Continental processed cheeses are obtainable everywhere.

SERVING CHEESE

Cheese is usually served at the end of the meal. Some people, however, prefer to have it before the sweet. This has one big advantage: the cheese comes to table while there is still red wine left from the meat course, and this goes excellently with it. If it is taken after the sweet (which is served with a white wine), port should be handed with the cheese.

Serve cheeses on a wooden board, with a wooden-handled cheese knife. Those in the photograph of Swiss cheeses are obtainable from the Civil Service Stores, London.

BREAKFAST DISHES

Start the day well with a nourishing meal, well cooked and nicely served

A cheerful breakfast cloth and matching napkins, in fine Irish linen, with checks of scarlet, green and white.

A GOOD breakfast is essential for anyone with a day's work to do. Children at play or school, who burn up a tremendous amount of energy running about, the breadwinner who goes off to office or factory—*and* the housewife herself—will all feel fitter and get less tired if a good foundation is laid at the breakfast table. It need not be the traditional eggs and bacon necessarily. Fish, porridge and cereals are all suitable.

Here are a few suggestions. Other recipes for breakfast foods come under Egg Dishes (see p. 174) and Fish (see p. 31).

Bacon for Boiling

Good bacon has red lean and white firm fat. Thick streaky is the best cut, but for small pieces the flank is excellent and cheaper. Since bacon is often salt, it is a good plan to soak it in warm water for 1 or 2 hours before cooking. Then remove the rusty parts and scrape the rind and underside with a sharp knife to get it as clean as possible. Put into a saucepan of cold water and bring slowly to the boil, skimming as the scum rises to the surface. Simmer gently until thoroughly cooked (allow 45 minutes per pound). When cooked, the rind should strip off quite easily. Cover the top with bread-raspings.

Bacon, Baked

Remove the rinds and put the rashers into a tin so that they overlap each other; cook in a moderate oven until the fat is transparent—about 10–15 minutes, according to the thickness of the rashers.

Bacon, Fried

Cut off the rinds with kitchen scissors or a sharp knife and put with the rashers into a frying pan, warm slowly, and then fry until the fat is transparent and as crisp as liked. (If the lean looks very dry and there is only a little fat, add a teaspoonful of dripping to the pan when frying.)

Bacon, Grilled

Remove rinds with kitchen scissors and put the rashers on previously warmed griller under hot grill. Cook until as crisp as desired.

Bacon and Apple

Allow a moderate-sized apple to 2 rashers of bacon. Wipe and core the apples without peeling them, cut into slices ¾ in. thick. Grill or fry the bacon first, remove from the pan and keep hot, then fry or grill the sliced apple in the bacon fat. Put on to a hot dish, sprinkle the apple lightly with sugar and add a scrape of nutmeg, then arrange the rashers on top.

Bacon and Bananas

Allow 1 banana to 2 rashers of bacon. Peel and cut in half lengthwise. Grill or fry the bacon, keep hot, and grill or fry the bananas in the bacon fat. Serve hot.

Bacon and Kidneys

Fry or grill the bacon and put aside to keep hot. Fry or grill the kidneys, previously washed and cored, in the bacon fat, turning them over once; when the red gravy flows freely, arrange on the bacon. Brown a teaspoonful of sieved flour in the fat, stir in a very little stock and bring to the boil. Season well and pour over the kidneys.

Bacon and Macaroni (for 2–3)

2 oz. macaroni	2 oz. bacon rashers
Pepper and salt	½ pint stock
Scrape of nutmeg	½ oz. butter

Break the macaroni into small pieces, put into quickly boiling salted water and boil for 5 minutes, then drain. Put the macaroni into the boiling stock and simmer gently until tender. Cut the bacon into small pieces and fry, then add the drained macaroni, the butter, nutmeg and seasoning. Mix over a gentle heat until the macaroni is brown, turn on to a hot dish.

Bacon and Tomatoes

Fry or grill the bacon, remove and keep hot. Slice the tomatoes, skinned if liked, and cook in the bacon fat until thoroughly hot, then arrange round the bacon, sprinkle with salt and pepper and serve.

Bacon may also be served with sausages, fried or grilled, with eggs, fried, scrambled or boiled, and fried bread.

Eggs (see chapter on Egg Dishes, p. 174)

Finnan Haddock

Put smoked haddock into cold water and soak for some hours. When required, simmer very gently in milk and water until quite tender; drain and cut into neat squares. Put on to a hot dish with a small piece of butter on each, sprinkle with pepper and keep hot while you lightly poach some eggs. Slide an egg on to each square and serve at once.

Haddock à la Reine (for 4)

4 oz. boiled rice	Smoked haddock
3 hard-boiled eggs	(cooked)
Seasoning	1 oz. butter
	Fried bread

Fry half the well drained dry rice in the hot butter. When thoroughly hot, add 2 chopped egg-whites, seasoning and the flaked-up haddock. Stir until thoroughly heated through, then pile up on a hot dish, put the rest of the rice (heated) round, and garnish with the remaining hard-boiled egg cut in slices and 2 egg-yolks sprinkled over the fish, etc. Arrange fried bread round

and put the fish in the oven for a few minutes to make sure it is thoroughly hot.

Herrings (see Scottish and Fish chapters)

Kedgeree (for 4–5)

6 oz. cooked fish	2 hard-boiled eggs
(any fish will do,	1 egg
but smoked	2 oz. butter
haddock is best)	2 chillies or pinch of
4 oz. boiled rice	Cayenne pepper
Seasoning	

Flake the fish smoothly. Chop the hard-boiled eggs and chillies. Melt the butter in a pan and, when hot, add the fish, rice, eggs and chillies (or Cayenne), and heat thoroughly. Beat the egg, stir it in, adding seasoning if necessary, reheat and serve.

Kippers (see also chapter on Fish Dishes)

Put the kippers into boiling water for a minute or two, remove and dry. Heat a small quantity of fat in a frying pan, put in the kippers, cover with a lid and cook until tender; or grill on a warmed griller.

Porridge (see also Scottish section)

This may be made of any of the varieties of flaked oats which cook quickly, or with oatmeal, coarse, medium or fine. Allow 2 tablespoonfuls to a pint of salted water, bring the water to the boil, sprinkle in the oatmeal, stirring so that it does not form lumps, boil and stir for 5 minutes.

Coarse oatmeal needs at least 2 hours' cooking in a double saucepan—the longer it is cooked the more digestible it will be. Medium oatmeal should simmer for at least 1 hour. When using fine oatmeal it is advisable to mix it to a smooth paste with cold water and then add it to the boiling water, otherwise it is apt to go lumpy. Add more boiling water, if necessary, during the cooking process. Porridge should be of a pouring consistency.

Salmon Cakes (for 4–5)

8 oz. tinned salmon	Anchovy sauce
Salt and pepper	Lemon juice
3 tablespoonfuls	6 oz. mashed potato
breadcrumbs	1 egg
Fat for frying	

Flake the salmon, removing any skin or bones, and mix with the potato. Add a few drops of lemon juice, seasoning to taste, and moisten with anchovy sauce. Form into balls, flatten them slightly, brush over with beaten egg and toss in the bread-crumbs. Fry in hot deep fat.

Specially cooked and photographed in the Creda kitchens

A cooked breakfast will ensure a good day's work and play. This tempting array provides a suggestion for every day of the week : grilled herrings; fish rissoles on tomatoes; scrambled eggs; bacon and tomato on sausage meat; kidney, sausage, tomato and mushrooms; sausage, bacon, eggs and tomato; and sausages wrapped in pancakes. Grapefruit, hot or cold, can be served as a first course

EGG DISHES

Tasty and nourishing, they are a stand-by for any meal, from breakfast to supper

EGG dishes have three great points in their favour. They are quick to prepare, they are very nourishing, and they often save the situation in an emergency. A golden rule in every household should be: Never be short of eggs.

As everyone knows, there are all sorts and conditions of eggs, from new-laid to cooking eggs. Nothing but really new-laid eggs should be used for boiling, poaching, scrambling or frying, as the slightest suggestion of staleness is very disagreeable.

A simple test to find out whether an egg is new-laid or not is to put it into a pint of water containing 1 oz. salt. If it sinks to the bottom, it is absolutely fresh. If it is more than 3 days old, it floats. If 2 or 3 days old, it neither sinks to the bottom nor floats, but hovers in between.

Here are a few more facts about eggs.

The yolk of an egg is rich in vitamins and salts, the white is nourishing and very easily digested.

The colour of the shell makes no difference to the food value of the egg. An egg with a white shell is just as good as one with a brown shell.

Eggs between 2 and 4 days old are best for beating. Put in a pinch of salt and beat them in a draught.

Ducks' eggs are stronger flavoured and richer than hens', but less digestible. They must always be cooked for 10 minutes.

Eggs put down in waterglass will keep for a year. If eggs are plentiful in the spring and the price therefore low, it is undoubtedly an economy to preserve them for the winter, but the eggs must be *fresh*, not more than 24 hours old and infertile. They should be wiped over before being put into the waterglass.

The easiest way to break an egg is to give it a sharp tap in the middle with a knife, or to tap the edge of a cup or bowl with the egg, whichever is more convenient. Then widen the crack with both thumbs and let the egg slide out into a cup or bowl.

When using several eggs, break them separately into a cup or basin. Otherwise a stale one may spoil them all.

To separate white from yolk, crack the egg as described above, hold half of the shell in each hand over a basin and pour the egg gently from one to the other so that the white runs into the basin. Be careful not to break the egg-yolk, and when the white has been separated put it into another cup or bowl.

The commonest ways of cooking eggs are:

Soft-boiled (1)

Plunge the egg into a pan of fast-boiling water and cook according to taste: 3 minutes (very soft); $3\frac{1}{2}$ minutes (average light); 4 minutes (medium-hard) or $4\frac{1}{2}$ minutes (firm).

Soft-boiled (2)

Cover the egg with cold water and bring slowly to the boil. The moment the water boils, remove from the heat.

Hard-boiled

Put the egg into boiling water and boil for 10 minutes—not more or the egg will be discoloured. Put immediately into cold water to cool.

Coddled

Put the egg into a pan of boiling water, cover the pan and reduce the heat so that the water does not boil again. Leave eggs 4 minutes for soft; 6–7 minutes for medium; 15–20 for hard.

Poached

Break the egg carefully into a cup. Unless a special poacher is used, put a teaspoonful of vinegar and a pinch of salt into a frying pan half-full of water, slide in the egg, keeping the white together with a spoon. Simmer gently until the egg is set and the white opaque, spooning water over the egg. Remove with a slice, drain and serve on hot buttered toast.

Fried

Use as small a pan as possible. Heat some lard or butter, and when the blue smoke rises, slide in the egg and draw off heat for a minute. Then replace over a very low heat and fry until set, shaking the pan to prevent the egg sticking. A plate

put over the frying pan helps the top to set. Remove with a slice and drain well.

Steamed

Grease an individual fireproof dish and break an egg into it. Stir the yolk and white together, add a pinch of salt, put the dish in a saucepan with enough boiling water to come half-way up, and steam until set.

Scrambled

Allow to each egg $\frac{1}{2}$ oz. butter or margarine and 1 tablespoonful milk. Melt the butter in a saucepan and add the slightly beaten eggs, milk and a little pepper and salt. Stir until nearly set. Remove from the heat and serve on hot buttered toast.

Anchovy Eggs

Hard-boil the eggs, shell them and cut in half. Take out the yolk and mix it with anchovy essence and cream or oiled butter. Mash with a fork on a plate, then put the mixture back in the whites, garnish with mustard and cress or watercress, and put a few capers on top of each half. Serve with brown bread and butter.

Eggs in Bread Sauce look attractive served in the dish in which they are cooked. A border of green peas adds a pleasing note of colour contrast

Curried Eggs (for 3–4)

4 hard-boiled eggs	Squeeze of lemon
1 oz. butter	juice
Curry powder to taste	1 teaspoonful
½ oz. rice flour	chopped chutney
Boiled rice	Salt
1 apple and 1 onion	½ pint stock

Melt the butter and, when hot, fry the sliced apple and onion, then add the rice flour, curry powder and salt, and cook for 5 minutes, stirring well. Stir in the stock and bring to the boil. Cut the eggs into halves or quarters and put them in the sauce with the chopped chutney and re-heat. Add a squeeze of lemon juice right at the end. Serve on a dish, surrounded by the rice, and pour the sauce over.

Devilled Eggs (for 4–5)

6 eggs	2 tablespoonfuls
Pinch of castor sugar	cream
A little mustard	1 tablespoonful
Cayenne and salt	vinegar
Parsley and thyme	

Hard-boil the eggs, cut them in half and take out the yolks. Pound until very fine and add to them the sugar, mustard, Cayenne, salt, cream and vinegar. Mix well together with a little chopped parsley and thyme, and fill the whites. Serve cold, garnished with mustard and cress or watercress.

Eggs à la Béchamel

Poach eggs in good white or brown stock and serve in Béchamel sauce (see Sauces chapter). Garnish with chopped gherkins, capers or parsley.

Egg and Bacon Fritters

Poach the required number of eggs and leave to get cold. Drain and roll each in a thin slice of bacon. Dip in batter and fry. Serve with fried parsley.

Eggs and Cheese

Hard-boil the eggs and chop them. Pour cheese sauce into a greased fireproof dish, put in the eggs and sprinkle Parmesan cheese over them. Then put the dish under the griller or in the oven until brown on top.

Egg Cutlets (for 3–4)

3 hard-boiled eggs	1 teaspoonful
1 oz. butter	chopped parsley
1 tablespoonful flour	Pepper and salt
1 gill milk	½ teaspoonful
2 oz. breadcrumbs	anchovy essence
Egg and breadcrumbs for coating	Fat for frying

Make a thin paste with a little of the milk and the flour. Heat the rest of the milk and pour in the paste, stirring well, and add the butter. Boil gently for 5 minutes. Then add the eggs, chopped finely, the breadcrumbs, seasoning, chopped parsley and anchovy essence, and mix well. Put the mixture on a plate and, when cool enough, make into cutlets. Flour, roll in egg and breadcrumbs, and fry in deep fat until a good brown. Drain well and serve with anchovy sauce (see Sauces chapter).

NOTE: Tomato ketchup can be used instead of anchovy. In this case serve the cutlets with tomato sauce; alternatively, add 2 oz. chopped ham and serve with brown or tomato sauce.

Eggs en Cocotte

Eggs	Pepper and salt
Butter	A little cream

Butter the required number of small fireproof cocotte dishes, break eggs into them, put a little cream on each egg, and a sprinkle of pepper and salt. Bake in a moderate oven for 6–8 minutes, according to taste. A little grated cheese can be sprinkled over the top, or some chopped ham or tomato purée placed at the bottom.

Eggs in Bread Sauce

Put hot bread sauce (for recipe see Sauces chapter) into a fireproof dish. Break eggs into a cup and slide them one at a time into the bread sauce, being careful the yolks do not break. Sprinkle a little grated cheese over the eggs and bake for about 10 minutes.

Eggs in Mustard Sauce

Hard-boiled eggs (hot)	Grated cheese
Cream	Mustard sauce (see Sauces chapter)

Make mustard sauce, and add a little cream to it. Cut hard-boiled eggs into slices and put them in a fireproof dish. Sprinkle half the cheese over them and then pour in the mustard sauce. Sprinkle the rest of the cheese over it and brown under the griller or in the oven.

Egg Mayonnaise (1)

Hard-boiled eggs	Ham, crab or
Mayonnaise	lobster

Cut the eggs lengthwise: Take out the yolks and mash with a fork on a plate.

For a mushroom-filled omelet place the cooked mushrooms across the centre of the omelet when it has just set

Then tilt the pan and, with a fork or palette knife, fold the omelet carefully in half without breaking it

Fill the whites with chopped ham, crab or lobster. Pour mayonnaise sauce over them and sprinkle the yolk on the top. Garnish with strips of cucumber cut very small, or beetroot or peas, and serve surrounded by mustard and cress.

Have a warm plate ready, slide the omelet on to it, serve—and eat it—immediately

Egg Mayonnaise (2)

As an alternative to hard-boiled eggs, which some people find indigestible, poach the eggs and let them get cold. Serve on a bed of lettuce with mayonnaise on top.

Eggs on Spinach

Cook spinach (see Vegetable chapter) and make it into a purée. Hard-boil eggs, cut them into quarters and arrange on the spinach. Serve with fried croûtons of bread.

NOTE: Hot poached eggs can also be served on a bed of spinach purée; quick-frozen or canned spinach may be used instead of fresh.

Eggs stuffed with Cheese (for 3-4)

4 hard-boiled eggs	White sauce
2 tablespoonfuls Parmesan cheese (grated)	A very little made mustard
1 teaspoonful vinegar	Salt and pepper Melted butter

Cut the eggs in half. Scoop out the yolk, and add to it the cheese, vinegar, mustard, seasoning and enough melted butter to make a firm mixture. Roll it into balls to fit into the whites. Serve either hot or cold. If served hot, make white sauce, place the eggs in it and reheat in a casserole in the oven.

Eggs stuffed with Chicken or Veal (for 3-4)

4 hard-boiled eggs	Chopped chicken or veal (cooked)
Salt and pepper	Peas, beetroot and carrot (cooked)
Mayonnaise sauce	
Salad	

Cut the eggs in half. Scoop out the yolk and add to it the chopped dice of chicken or veal, green peas, dice of beetroot and carrot, and seasoning. Make mayonnaise sauce (see Salad chapter) and toss the yolk, etc., lightly in it. Fill the whites with the mixture and serve on a bed of salad.

Eggs with Cheese and Breadcrumbs
(for 3–4)

4 eggs	½ oz. butter
1 gill thin cream	1 teaspoonful
Breadcrumbs	chopped parsley
2 oz. grated cheese	Salt and pepper

Break the eggs carefully and put them into a well-buttered fireproof dish. Whip the cream slightly and season it with salt and pepper, then pour it over the eggs and sprinkle over it the chopped parsley, grated cheese, breadcrumbs and small pieces of butter. Cook in a moderate oven until the eggs are just set and serve at once.

Fricasséed Eggs (for 3–4)

1 tablespoonful	Squeeze of lemon
chopped onion	juice
1 oz. butter	1 teacupful of milk
Pinch of ground	A little flour
ginger	Pepper and salt
Fried bacon	4 eggs

Fry the onion in the butter until golden brown, sprinkle in a little flour, pinch of ginger, pepper and salt, and cook for 3 minutes, stirring all the time. Add the milk slowly and bring to the boil. Remove from fire, and add a squeeze of lemon juice. Hard-boil and slice eggs, pour sauce over them and serve with fried bacon.

Omelets

Making an omelet is not really difficult —provided the rules are carefully followed.

(1) Keep a special pan (preferably not an aluminium one) for omelets and never use it for anything else. Instead of washing the pan after use, wipe it clean with kitchen paper.
(2) Always fry in *butter*.
(3) Serve *immediately* the omelet is cooked, before it falls flat.

French Omelet (for 2–3)

3 eggs	1 tablespoonful
Pepper and salt	cold water
	1 oz. butter

Beat the eggs well with the water and a pinch of pepper and salt, using a rotary beater if possible—the more it is beaten the lighter the omelet will be. Well butter the pan and, when very hot but not quite smoking, pour in the mixture and reduce the heat. Run a knife round the edge and underneath so that the mixture does not stick, and tilt the pan to allow the still-liquid part to run under and get evenly cooked. When just set, fold over quickly with a knife and slide on to a hot dish. *Serve at once.*

Omelets with the same Foundation but with Different Flavours

Mixed Herbs.—Add a good pinch of mixed herbs and a teaspoonful of very finely chopped onion to the mixture before pouring it into the pan.

Cheese.—Add 2 tablespoonfuls of grated Parmesan cheese to the mixture before pouring it into the pan.

Ham.—Add 2 tablespoonfuls of finely chopped ham to the mixture before pouring it into the pan.

Mushroom.—Either add 2 tablespoonfuls of very finely chopped cooked mushrooms to the mixture before pouring it into the pan, or cook shredded mushrooms in a little butter, cream or white sauce and put across centre of omelet just before folding over.

Kidney.—Fry minced kidney and add to the omelet just before it is turned over.

Soufflé Omelet

3 eggs (separated)	1 tablespoonful
Pepper and salt	cold water
(if savoury)	1 oz. butter

Beat egg-yolks, and add water and seasoning. Beat whites until very stiff and fold into yolks. Either fry as for French omelet until outer surface begins to crisp and then finish in a very hot oven or under hot grill, or cook entirely in a very hot oven, in a buttered pan, for 10 minutes. Serve instantly.

Varieties of Flavouring for Soufflé Omelet

Jam.—Make soufflé omelet without salt and pepper and fold in hot jam, sprinkle with sugar and put under hot grill for 1 or 2 minutes to melt sugar.

Rum.—Fill soufflé omelet with hot apricot jam, pour warm rum over and set it alight. Serve with ice-cold cream.

Poached Eggs with Mushrooms

Make toast and cut it into rounds. Fry flat mushrooms, put them on the buttered toast and keep hot. Put a poached egg on each and place in a fireproof dish. Make cheese or mushroom sauce (see Sauces chapter) and pour on the eggs, sprinkle with cheese and brown under the grill.

Savoury Custards (for 2–3)

3 eggs	½ gill cream
1 gill strong well-flavoured white stock	Chopped chive
	Shallot
	Grated ham or tongue

Beat the eggs well. Add the cream and the stock. Season with a finely chopped chive, shallot, and chopped, grated or shredded ham or tongue. Mix well. Pour the mixture into small buttered moulds. Steam for 10 minutes. Turn out on to a dish and serve with or without gravy as preferred. Garnish with little heaps of French beans or carrots.

Scotch Eggs (for 5–6)

1 lb. sausage meat	Breadcrumbs and flour
4 hard-boiled eggs	
Fat for frying	1 egg (for coating)

Hard-boil the eggs, shell and dry them. Sprinkle with flour and cover with sausage meat. Roll in egg and breadcrumbs, and fry in deep fat until golden brown. Drain well, cut in half and serve hot with brown gravy or tomato sauce, or cold with salad.

Scrambled Eggs with Bacon or Ham

Allow 1 egg, ½ oz. butter or margarine, and 1 tablespoonful of milk for each person. Heat the diced bacon or ham in a saucepan with the butter, add the slightly beaten egg and milk, and stir until nearly set. Remove from the fire and serve on hot buttered toast.

Scrambled Eggs with Cheese (for 4)

2 oz. butter	1 teaspoonful chopped parsley chives and shallots
6 oz. Gruyère cheese, grated	
1 wineglassful dry white wine	A little grated nutmeg
4 eggs	

Melt the butter and cheese slowly over a moderate flame, then add the wine, herbs and nutmeg. Bring slowly to the boil, stir in the egg-yolks separately and finally the well-beaten whites. Stir until the mixture thickens like scrambled egg and serve on toast.

Scrambled Eggs with Tomato

Allow 1 egg per person. Skin tomatoes, cut them up and cook in a little butter and add them to the lightly beaten eggs. Melt a little butter or margarine in the saucepan, add the egg and tomato mixture with a little pepper and salt. Stir until nearly set. Remove from the fire and serve on hot buttered toast.

Scotch Eggs, covered with sausage meat and fried till crisp and golden, are equally tasty hot or cold

LUNCH AND SUPPER DISHES

*Some ideas to provide enough nourishment for the
family at the lighter of the two main meals in the day*

IN addition to the following recipes, consult also the chapters on Egg Dishes and Vegetarian Cookery.

Cauliflower au Gratin

1 cauliflower	White sauce
3 oz. grated cheese	Browned bread-
A little margarine	crumbs

Wash the cauliflower well, cutting away most of the stalk, and soak in cold water. Cook until tender, drain well (keeping the water for the sauce), break up the flowers into fair-sized pieces and put them in a fireproof dish. Make the sauce (see Sauces chapter), using half milk and half cauliflower water, add half the cheese and stir well. Pour sauce over cauliflower, sprinkle remainder of cheese on top, cover with browned breadcrumbs, dot with margarine and brown under grill.

Cheese Fondue (for 6)

1½ cupfuls fresh breadcrumbs	2 eggs (separated)
1½ cupfuls grated cheese	1½ cupfuls milk
	1 tablespoonful butter, melted
¼ teaspoonful salt	

Soak breadcrumbs in milk. Add cheese, beaten egg-yolks, salt and melted butter. Fold in stiffly beaten egg-whites. Pour into a greased baking dish, place in a pan of hot water and oven-poach in a moderate oven for about 40 minutes.

Cheese Pudding (for 3–4)

1 oz. butter	Pinch of mustard and
2 oz. breadcrumbs	salt
½ pint milk	2 oz. grated cheese
1 egg (separated)	

Heat the milk, stir in the butter, breadcrumbs, mustard and salt, and add the cheese and beaten egg-yolk. Whip the egg-white to a stiff froth and fold in lightly. Pour the mixture into a well-greased pie dish and bake for 15–20 minutes.

Cheese Puffit (for 6–8)

12 ½-in. slices stale bread	½ lb. cheese, sliced
4 eggs	¼ pint milk
¼ teaspoonful salt	Dash of pepper and paprika

Arrange slices of bread and cheese in alternate layers in a greased baking dish. Beat eggs slightly, add milk and seasonings, and pour over the bread and cheese. Cover and keep in the refrigerator until ready to bake. Place in a pan of hot water and oven-poach in a moderate oven until set (about 45 minutes). If thoroughly chilled before baking, the puffit will puff up like a soufflé.

Cheese Soufflé (for 4–6)

1 oz. butter	2 eggs
1 gill milk	2 oz. Parmesan
1 dessertspoonful cornflour	cheese
	Cayenne and salt

Melt the butter in a pan. Add cornflour and seasoning and then the milk. Boil for 3 minutes, stirring well. Cool slightly. Separate the egg-whites from the yolks and beat in the yolks and the cheese. Whip the whites until they are very stiff and fold into the sauce. Put into a prepared and well-buttered soufflé dish, and bake in a moderate oven for 20–25 minutes until risen and light brown. Serve at once.

Cheese Vegetable Rarebit (for 6)

1 cupful tomato juice	Toast
1½ teaspoonfuls dry mustard	1 tablespoonful fat
Salt and pepper to taste	2 teaspoonfuls Worcester sauce
3 cupfuls grated cheese	2 cupfuls cooked vegetables or spaghetti
1 egg	

Heat tomato juice, fat, mustard, Worcester sauce, salt and pepper in top of double boiler. Add well-beaten egg and cook until mixture thickens (about 3 minutes). Add grated cheese and stir until melted. Arrange hot vegetables on toast, pour sauce on top and serve at once.

Galette au Nouilles (for 3–4)

6 oz. macaroni	2 oz. grated Gruyère
2 eggs	cheese
A little minced ham	2 oz. butter

Cook the macaroni in boiling, salted water for about ¼ hour, drain well, add half the butter while the macaroni is hot, mixing well, and finally add the Gruyère and minced ham. Beat the eggs and add them to the macaroni. Melt the rest of the butter in a saucepan, put in the mixture and brown the galette on one side. Turn it on to a plate for a moment, put a small piece of butter in the saucepan, replace the galette and brown the other side. Serve alone or with tomato sauce (see Sauces chapter).

Grilled tomatoes on toast, topped with melted Cheddar cheese or cheese sauce and a crisp bacon rasher, are a perfect light meal

Gnocchi of Semolina
(for 4–5)

1 pint milk
6 oz. semolina
1½ oz. butter
1½ oz. grated Parmesan cheese
2 eggs
Salt

Cook the semolina in the milk, take it off the fire, add seasoning, half the butter, half the cheese, and then the eggs. Mix well. Spread about 1 in. thick on a plate. When firm, cut into almond-shaped pieces. Pile the gnocchi on a dish, sprinkling the layers with the rest of the cheese and the butter in tiny pieces, but not putting any on the top layer. Lastly, brown in the oven and serve hot, either alone or as an accompaniment to meat.

Macaroni à la Forge

Cook macaroni until tender in a good stock made the day before. Drain and put into a fireproof dish with plenty of grated Gruyère and Parmesan cheese, a good piece of butter and some grated breadcrumbs. Bake in the oven until brown.

Celery cut in 1-in. lengths and cooked till tender in salted water can be used instead of macaroni.

Macaroni Cheese (for 3–4)

4 oz. macaroni
Pepper, salt and, if liked, paprika
1 teacupful of milk
4 oz. grated Cheddar cheese
1 oz. butter or fat bacon

Put the macaroni into boiling, salted water and cook until just tender (about 10 minutes). Drain well and put in a fireproof dish with layers of grated cheese, seasoning each layer. Add a teacupful of milk, sprinkle grated cheese on top and dot either with lumps of butter or with sliced bacon or garnish with Cheese Balls. To make them, combine 1½ oz. Cheddar cheese with 3 teaspoonfuls browned breadcrumbs and a little Cayenne; form into balls. Bake in a moderate oven until slightly brown (20–30 minutes).

Rice Croquettes (for 4–5)

4 oz. rice
4 oz. grated cheese
Breadcrumbs
1 egg
1 tablespoonful tomato purée
Pepper and salt
Fat for frying

Wash the rice well, boil in a very little water (adding more if necessary) until soft. Put the rice, the grated cheese, tomato purée, pepper and salt into a basin and add enough egg to bind. When cool, make into croquettes. Roll them in breadcrumbs and fry in deep fat for 5 minutes. Serve with cheese or tomato sauce. (For recipes see Sauces chapter).

Rice, Macaroni or Spaghetti with Tomato Sauce (for 6–7)

1 lb. rice	Small onion
1½ oz. butter	A little stock
2 tablespoonfuls	Pinch of nutmeg
grated cheese	Tomato sauce
1 egg-yolk	(see Sauces chapter)
Large pinch of salt	

Put the rice, butter and onion, finely chopped, into a saucepan with enough stock to make the rice swell. Simmer for 25 minutes, stirring and adding more stock as needed. When the rice is well filled out and quite soft, stir in the cheese, nutmeg and salt. Just before taking it off the fire, add the egg-yolk. The tomato sauce may be stirred into the rice or served separately.

NOTE: If macaroni or spaghetti is used, it should be cooked in boiling salted water until quite soft (between 15 and 20 minutes—the time varies with the quality).

Risotto (see Italian Cookery chapter)

Savoury Pie (for 4–5)

1 breakfastcupful	2 oz. melted
brown breadcrumbs	margarine
2 cooked potatoes	1 teacupful vegetable
1 tomato, sliced	stock
Spanish onion, par-	Pinch of salt
boiled and sliced	1 tablespoonful
finely	soaked tapioca
1 teaspoonful mixed	1 oz. ground nuts or
herbs	grated cheese
¼ lb. cooked rice	Butter

Grease a pie dish and line it with half the breadcrumbs, keeping the rest for the top. Mix together all the other ingredients except the stock and butter and put into the pie dish. Pour the stock over them and then sprinkle over the breadcrumbs. Put small pieces of butter on the top and bake in the oven for ½ hour.

Savoury Rice

Cook rice slowly in stock until very tender, then put it into a shallow fireproof dish and cover with a good layer of grated cooking cheese. Bake until the top is a nice golden brown. If liked, the rice can be flavoured all through with layers of cheese, finishing with a sprinkling of cheese on the top.

Savoury Rice with Onion

Cook rice in good stock until tender. Melt a little butter, slice up a large onion and fry it until brown. Put the rice and onion in layers in a greased fireproof dish, with a pinch of mixed herbs and a little pepper and salt. Put lumps of butter or margarine on top and bake in the oven until brown (about ½ hour).

Sole Ribbons (for 2)

1 medium filleted sole	1 dessertspoonful
Beaten egg	seasoned flour
Browned bread-	Vegetable fat shorten-
crumbs	ing for frying
A little Cayenne pepper	

Wash and dry the fillets and skin. Cut lengthways into ¼–½-in. ribbons. Roll in seasoned flour, dip in beaten egg and coat with breadcrumbs. Fry in hot vegetable fat shortening for 3–4 minutes. Sprinkle with Cayenne and serve with potato chips.

Spaghetti with Tomatoes (for 3–4)

1 small onion	4 oz. spaghetti
1 lb. fresh cooked or	Bacon bone or rinds
canned tomatoes	2 oz. butter
Tomato purée	Salt and pepper

Put the spaghetti, bacon bone or rinds and onion into boiling water and cook for 15–20 minutes. Drain well and remove the rinds or bone and onion. Then add the tomatoes (sieved), the purée and the seasoning. Reheat in the saucepan with the butter. Serve, preferably with grated Parmesan cheese.

Stuffed Potatoes

1 large potato per	Pepper and salt
person	Grated cheese
Butter	A little milk

Wash the potatoes thoroughly, but do not peel them; dry, prick with a fork and bake in a hot oven until soft. Slit each one in half lengthwise and, with a fork, scoop out the floury part. Add to it the butter, pepper and salt, a little milk, some grated cheese and mash together. Return the mixture to the shells, sprinkle a little cheese on top and put in a hot oven or under the grill for 5–10 minutes.

NOTE: As alternative stuffings, instead of cheese, try hot green peas with a little butter; finely chopped fried onion, minced meat or bacon. Tomato purée may be used instead of the milk.

Stuffed Vegetable Marrow

1 medium-sized	Sausage meat or
marrow	minced meat or
Pepper and salt	veal stuffing
A little milk	Chopped parsley
Gravy	

Stand the tomatoes in a basin of boiling water for 1 or 2 minutes, remove the skins, dry, and cut in half. Put some of the tomatoes into a greased fireproof dish, then put in half the butter, a pinch of pepper and salt, and sprinkle in half the breadcrumbs and cheese. Add the rest of the tomatoes, butter, breadcrumbs and cheese, and bake in a quick oven for about 15 minutes.

(Above) Sole Ribbons— a new variation on the fried fish theme—are tasty with lemon and parsley garnish

(Right) An old and tried favourite — Macaroni Cheese, with cheese balls on the top—goes well with fairy toast

Photographs in this chapter taken at the Spry Cookery Centre

Wash and peel the marrow. If young, cut off one end and with a long - handled spoon scoop out the pips and the pulpy part. If not so young, cut lengthwise, peel and remove the seeds. Put the meat into a basin with the parsley and a little pepper and salt. Stir it together and bind with a little milk. Then put the stuffing into the marrow and either put the top on again, cover with greased paper and tie securely, or put the halves together and tie firmly in several places. Place the marrow in a tin greased with dripping or butter. Cover it with a piece of greased paper and put a tin over it. Bake in a moderate oven until the marrow is quite tender; it will take 1–1½ hours, according to the size and age of the marrow. Baste it occasionally. Serve with gravy.

Tomatoes au Gratin (for 3–4)

1 lb. tomatoes	2 heaped tablespoon-
2 oz. breadcrumbs	fuls grated cheese
1 oz. butter	Pepper and salt

Vegetable Marrow au Gratin (for 3–4)

8 oz. marrow (when	1 gill water
prepared)	2 oz. butter
3 oz. grated cheese	3 oz. breadcrumbs

Wash and peel the marrow and cut it up. Simmer with 1 oz. butter and the water until tender. Put alternate layers of marrow with the liquid and cheese and breadcrumbs into a greased fireproof dish, finishing with a layer of breadcrumbs, etc. Dot with butter. Bake for about 10 minutes.

Vegetable Pie (for 4–5)

1 lb. mashed potatoes	1 lb. cooked turnips,
1 oz. butter	carrots, parsnips
2 tomatoes	and onion
½ pint gravy or stock	Pepper and salt

Put the vegetables (except potatoes) in a greased fireproof dish in layers, pour over the gravy; season. Top with the potatoes and dot with butter. Bake for 30 minutes.

CAKES

For special parties or tea after school there's nothing quite so popular as home-made cake—and it's nourishing too

CAKE-MAKING is one of the pleasantest forms of cookery, and nothing gives a cook a greater feeling of satisfaction than a perfectly made and perfectly baked cake.

There are three main methods used in cake-mixing:

(1) Beating the sugar and eggs together with an egg whisk until the mixture is thick and creamy, and then folding in the flour lightly. This method is used for sponge cakes and usually no shortening is needed.

(2) Beating the sugar and butter (or other fat) together until the mixture is light in colour and creamy. The longer they are beaten, the better the cake. Scrape the sides of the basin with a palette knife at intervals to ensure that all the mixture is well beaten.

In cold weather, when the fat is very hard, the basin may be stood in warm water for a minute or two, but the butter must never be allowed to melt or become oily.

The eggs (or the yolks only) should be beaten and added separately, the mixture being beaten hard the whole time. Add them slowly, with a little flour in between, to prevent curdling. The main bulk of the flour and the baking powder are added last. In some recipes the egg-whites are kept until the end, when they must be whisked stiffly enough to stay in the bowl when it is turned upside down, then folded in. This makes cakes very light.

This method is used for all rich cakes.

(3) Rubbing the butter (or other fat) lightly into the flour with the tips of the fingers and thumb until the mixture is like fine breadcrumbs. In hot weather, rinse the hands in cold water first. The eggs and any other liquid are added at the end.

This method is used for plain cakes, pastry and scones.

Shortening

Good margarine and/or one of the branded vegetable shortenings can be substituted for butter when necessary, with excellent results. Lard or cooking fat often successfully combine with butter or margarine.

Eggs

Preserved eggs can be used for all cakes except where the whites have to be beaten stiffly, when new-laid eggs must be used. Remember to break each egg into a cup and not straight into the mixture when one "doubtful" egg may spoil all the ingredients.

Sugar

Castor sugar should be used for biscuits and sponges, granulated for other cakes. Soft brown sugar gives fruit cakes a very good dark colour.

Flour

Never mix new flour with the old in the bin. It is best to use plain flour and add the necessary baking powder or soda. Always sieve flour and baking powder before use; the more air it contains, the lighter the cake will be.

Baking Powder

Whether bought or home-made, baking powder must be kept in a tin with a tight-fitting lid. To make it at home, put equal parts of bicarbonate of soda, cream of tartar and ground rice through a sieve seven times to get them well mixed. Put away in a tin, and stir well before using.

Dried Fruit

All dried fruit should be well cleaned before use. Put on a sieve, sprinkle with flour and rub well. This will remove many of the stalks; the fruit should then be carefully looked over. Washed fruit must be thoroughly dried before use. Raisins and dates should be stoned if necessary, and glacé cherries cut in halves or quarters.

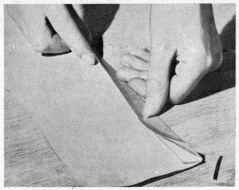

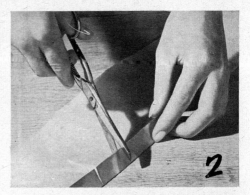

THE SECRET OF LIGHT CAKES

Give them the Air

Whether a cake is delightfully light—or sad and heavy—depends more than anything upon the amount of air and carbon dioxide it contains. Though these are not listed in the ingredients in cake recipes, you introduce air when you sieve the flour (and the more you sieve it, the more air you get into it), when you beat the eggs and, finally, when you beat the mixture (hence the need to beat really thoroughly). The equally important carbon dioxide is produced when you add either (a) baking powder, which contains a balanced mixture of alkali and acid, or (b) bicarbonate of soda combined with something acid, such as cream of tartar, treacle, sour milk, etc.

So when you make a sponge cake, which should be the lightest, airiest of all cakes, be sure to aerate the mixture as much as you possibly can—by beating the eggs well before you lightly fold in, first the

Preparing a cake tin. Cut a strip of greaseproof paper long enough to go round tin and 2 in. deeper. Fold up ½ in. along bottom edge (1); nick with scissors (2); place in tin, pressing well against sides (3); cut a circle to fit bottom and grease them both (4); pour in cake mixture and make a well in centre before baking (5)

(A) Incorrect recipe balance gives insufficient aeration; (B) correct balance gives perfect cake

sugar and then the flour (well-sieved, of course).

Recipe Balance

Another secret of successful cake making is to follow a good recipe accurately and always watch carefully that the various ingredients are in the right proportions.

For instance, you won't make your cake lighter simply by increasing the quantity of baking powder, but only by getting the exact amount in relation to the other ingredients. The richer the cake and the more fruit it contains, the less baking powder it needs. In the case of a really rich Christmas cake, for instance, no baking powder at all should be used, since the ingredients themselves are sufficient to form the structure of the cake. For this reason, plain flour should always be used for rich cakes so that the amount of the raising agent can be varied.

The research scientists of Messrs George Borwick & Sons, Ltd., the baking powder manufacturers, have prepared the following table showing how the quantities of baking powder should be varied **per pound of flour** with the amount of fruit in semi-rich and rich cakes:

	Semi-rich
No fruit	*2½ level teaspoonfuls*
8 oz. fruit	*1½ level teaspoonfuls*
12 oz. fruit	*1¼ level teaspoonfuls*
16 oz. fruit	*1 level teaspoonful*

	Rich
No fruit	*2 level teaspoonfuls*
8 oz. fruit	*1¼ level teaspoonfuls*
12 oz. fruit	*¾ level teaspoonful*
16 oz. fruit	*No baking powder*

Provided you keep the balance of the ingredients the same, you can adapt and improve standard recipes to please yourself.

Chief points of recipe balance that must be remembered are these: an egg is a toughening agent and fat a shortening one, so they must stay in step. Increase eggs and fat, remember to reduce baking powder. If you reduce the egg content, you must also reduce the quantity of fat, or the cake may collapse. If you increase the fat to make the cake richer, you must also increase the egg content and reduce the baking powder.

When about to Make a Cake

(1) Light the oven in good time so that it is hot enough when the cake is ready to go in. Until you get to know your own oven, allow about 10 minutes for a gas oven, 15 minutes for electric.

(2) Prepare your cake tin. To do this, melt a little lard or olive oil and paint the sides and bottom of the tin well (keep a pastry brush for the purpose); cut a strip of greaseproof paper to go round the side and about 2 in. deeper so that it will stick up above the top of the tin; fold up ½ in. at the bottom edge and nick all round with scissors (this will make it lie flat at the bottom of the tin); cut greaseproof paper to fit the bottom of the tin, grease all the paper, and press down well. The cake will not be a good shape unless the paper fits neatly. Fill tins no more than two-thirds full to allow for rising.

For rich fruit cakes, which have to be in the oven a long time, put a double layer of paper, greasing the first one well.

Small crinkly paper cases or well-greased tins can be used for little cakes.

Alternatively, you can put the tin or tins, unlined and ungreased, into the oven to get hot. Take out when the cake mixture is quite ready. Turn it

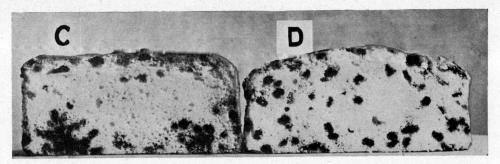

(C) Incorrect balance gives coarse texture, flat top and fallen fruit; (D) the cake as it should be

into the hot tin and return immediately to the oven.

(3) Next, weigh the ingredients carefully. Then make your cake.

Cake-baking

To the inexperienced cook, this is the most difficult part of cake-making. If the oven is too hot, a hard crust forms on the cake and the inside cannot rise properly; if it is too slow, the cake becomes dry and does not rise properly.

As a general guide, here is a chart of the required heats:

Bread, scones and pastry . . .	450° F.
Small cakes and Swiss roll . . .	400° F.
Genoese, Madeira, sponges . . .	370° F.
Small fruit cakes	340° F.
Large, rich, fruit cakes	320° F.
Biscuits	330° F.

In the recipes for sandwiches, small cakes, etc., that follow in this section, the time has been given. In the case of larger cakes, however, this varies so much according to the size of the tin used that it is not possible to be precise. Remember that the thicker the cake, the longer it will take to cook. When a large cake has risen and begun to set on the top, the heat can be lowered a little, but cakes should never be moved once in the oven and the door should be closed gently. Sponge cakes are best left alone.

Some ovens are apt to burn cakes at the top or bottom, even when the heat is correct. If this happens, put some kitchen salt or silver sand on a baking sheet under the cakes. Water in the bottom of a gas oven will help to prevent burning and prevent the cake getting too dry.

To test whether a cake is cooked, touch the top lightly with the tip of the finger. If

the cake is done, the surface should spring back once the finger is removed. If you hear a little crunch as you touch the cake, it is not quite done. To test a large, rich, fruit cake, it is best to put a heated fine-steel knitting needle right through the middle. Then draw it out carefully. If the cake is done, the needle will be quite clean.

When the cake is done, lift it out of the tin by the paper, or turn it gently on to the hand and put it on a rack or sieve, out of the draught, to cool. If it sticks, stand the tin on a damp cloth for 10 minutes and it will come out easily. When quite cold, put it in a tin until wanted.

Cake Failings and How to Avoid Them

Everybody makes occasional mistakes and nobody achieves perfection without a good deal of practice, so there is no need to be disheartened if your first attempts at cake-making are not absolutely up to your own self-imposed standards. Try again— and again—carefully following the basic rules already given. And here are some of the misfortunes that beset the cake-maker, with their probable causes:

(1) *Fruit sinking* to the bottom is nearly always due to too much baking powder, occasionally to too much liquid making the batter too slack to support the fruit. Use plain (not self-raising) flour, and measure the baking powder very carefully according to the richness of the cake and the amount of fruit it contains (see table of baking powder quantities opposite). If you use an electric mixer, over-creaming of the fat and sugar is a possible contributory cause, but not if you cream by hand.

(2) *Heavy cake* is usually the result of too

much flour, fat or liquid, or baking too slowly.

(3) *Sinking in the middle* is usually a sign of too much raising agent in the mixture, too hot an oven, or slamming the oven door before the cake has had time to set.

NOTE: The door should never be opened until the cake has been in the oven for 15 minutes.

(4) *Coarse texture* may be due to the fat, sugar and eggs not being creamed enough at the beginning, too much baking powder, or too slow an oven.

(5) *Excessive dryness* is often the result of too stiff a mixture or baking at too low a temperature or for too long.

Icing Cakes: For recipes and instructions see separate chapter.

PLAIN CAKES

Chocolate Cake

6 oz. plain flour	Vanilla essence
1 oz. cocoa	4 oz. sugar
1 teaspoonful baking	2 eggs
powder	Milk or water to mix
4 oz. margarine	Pinch of salt

Grease a 6-in. cake tin. Cream the margarine and sugar until white and fluffy. Beat in the eggs gradually. Stir in the sieved flour, cocoa, baking powder and pinch of salt with enough liquid to make a soft dropping consistency. Add a few drops of vanilla essence to flavour. Bake in a moderate oven for $\frac{3}{4}$–1 hour.

Chocolate Coconut Cake

1½ oz. desiccated	4 oz. plain flour
coconut	1 level dessertspoon-
¼ pint milk	ful cocoa
4 oz. margarine	Pinch of salt
6 oz. sugar	1 teaspoonful baking
2 eggs	powder

Soak the coconut in the milk for ½ hour. Cream fat and sugar, add the lightly beaten eggs and then the coconut and milk. Stir in the well-sieved dry ingredients, mix well and turn into a greased lined tin 10 in. by 8 in. Bake in a moderate oven for 30–40 minutes. When cold, decorate the top as desired, or cut into fingers.

Chocolate Swiss Roll

2 eggs	1 tablespoonful warm
1½ oz. flour	water
2 oz. castor sugar	1 oz. grated sweetened
1 teaspoonful baking	chocolate
powder	

Grease a Swiss roll tin, line with greaseproof paper and then grease the paper well. Separate the whites from the yolks of the eggs. Beat the yolks and the sugar together until the mixture is creamy. Then add the warm water, and immediately after that the chocolate. Whisk the whites stiffly, and add alternately with the sieved flour and baking powder, folding them in lightly. Put the mixture in the tin and bake in a hot oven for about 12 minutes. Turn out on to a piece of greaseproof paper well sprinkled with icing sugar, trim the edges and roll it up. Then put it on a rack to cool.

When quite cold, unroll and fill with whipped cream or vanilla butter icing.

Coconut Cake

6 oz. flour	3 oz. desiccated coco-
3 oz. butter	nut
4 oz. castor sugar	1 small teaspoonful
A little milk	baking powder
2 small eggs	

Cream the butter and sugar, and add the beaten eggs gradually. Then add the flour, baking powder and the coconut and, lastly, a little milk. Put the mixture into a prepared cake tin and bake in a moderate oven for about 1¼ hours.

Cornflour Cake

4 oz. cornflour	1 teaspoonful baking
1 oz. flour	powder
2 oz. castor sugar	1 egg
2 oz. butter	A little milk

Cream the butter and sugar, and add the egg beaten with a little milk. Then add the sieved cornflour, flour and baking powder. Put into a prepared cake tin and bake in a moderate oven for about 1 hour.

Eggless Cake

8 oz. plain flour	3 oz. sugar
3 oz. margarine	1 teaspoonful
Pinch of salt	vanilla essence
4 teaspoonfuls baking	About ¼ pint milk
powder	and water

Mix flour, baking powder and salt. Rub in the fat, add the sugar and vanilla and mix to a dropping consistency with the milk and water. Turn into a greased 7-in. tin and bake in a moderate oven for $\frac{3}{4}$ to 1 hour.

Honey Cake

8 oz. flour	3 oz. sugar
4 oz. honey	1 teaspoonful baking
2 eggs	powder
3 oz. butter	

Cream the butter and sugar, and add the beaten eggs gradually. Beat in the honey and, lastly, add the sieved flour and baking powder. Put into a prepared shallow cake tin and bake in a moderate oven for about 45 minutes.

Madeira Cake

8 *oz. flour*	1 *teaspoonful baking*
5 *oz. butter*	*powder*
5 *oz. sugar*	*Grated rind of a*
4 *eggs*	*lemon or orange*

Cream the butter and sugar until white and fluffy, and add the beaten eggs gradually, alternating with the flour, baking powder and fruit rind all sieved together. If the mixture is too dry, moisten to dropping consistency with a little milk. Put into a prepared cake tin and bake in a moderate oven for about 1¼ hours. After about 25 minutes put two pieces of lemon peel on top.

Marble Cake

6 *oz. self-raising flour*	*Pinch of baking*
4 *oz. margarine*	*powder*
4 *oz. sugar*	*Pinch of salt*
2 *eggs*	*Vanilla essence*
½ *oz. cocoa*	*Green colouring*
Milk or water to mix	

Grease a 6-in. cake tin. Cream the margarine and sugar until light and fluffy. Beat in the eggs gradually, then stir in the sieved flour and salt, add vanilla essence to flavour and enough milk or water to make a soft dropping consistency. Take out one-third of the mixture, place on a saucer and colour green. Take out half of remaining mixture, place on saucer. Add cocoa and pinch of baking powder, together with liquid. Using teaspoons, place alternate colours in cake tin. Bake in a moderate oven for ¾–1 hour.

Sponge Cake

3 *eggs*	½ *teaspoonful baking*
4 *oz. castor sugar*	*powder*
	4 *oz. flour*

Prepare a tin by first brushing it over thoroughly with melted butter. Then mix equal small quantities of sieved flour and castor sugar; put it into the tin and shake the tin well until both sides and bottom are well coated. Then shake out any superfluous flour and sugar. Beat the eggs and sugar together until the mixture is thick and creamy (quite ½ hour). Then fold in the sieved flour and baking powder very lightly, using a metal spoon.

Put the mixture into the tin and bake *at once* in a hot oven for 20 minutes. Do not touch the mixture once it is in the tin.

Chocolate Madeleines are coated with melted jam, desiccated coconut and grated chocolate

Swiss Roll

3 eggs	Small pinch of baking
2½ oz. flour	powder
3½ oz. castor sugar	Icing sugar and jam

Grease a Swiss roll tin, line with grease-proof paper and then grease the paper well. Beat the eggs and sugar together until the mixture is thick and creamy, then lightly fold in the flour and the baking powder, sieved well together, using a metal spoon. Pour the mixture into the tin and bake in a hot oven for about 10 minutes. While it is cooking, get ready a piece of greaseproof paper a little larger than the tin and sprinkle it well with icing sugar. Also heat some jam. Turn the cake on to the paper, trim the edges and spread rather thinly with the hot jam. Roll up quickly.

Vanilla Cake

4 oz. butter	½ teacupful milk
2 eggs	6 oz. sugar
1 teaspoonful baking	12 oz. flour
powder	Vanilla essence

Separate the yolks and whites of the eggs. Beat the butter to a cream, then stir in the sugar and the well-beaten egg-yolks. Beat the mixture well, then fold in the egg-whites whisked stiff. Sift flour and baking powder together and stir it gradually into the mixture, adding the milk and a few drops of vanilla essence. Bake in a well-greased tin in a moderate oven for about 1 hour.

Victoria Sandwich

2 eggs, their weight in	½ teaspoonful baking
butter, sugar and	powder
flour	Jam for filling

Cream the butter, add sugar and cream well again. Add the beaten eggs gradually and then the flour and baking powder, well sieved together. Put the mixture into two greased sandwich tins and bake in a fairly quick oven for 20 minutes. When cold, spread with raspberry jam and put together.

SMALL CAKES

Chocolate Buns

4 oz. butter	Pinch of baking
2 oz. grated chocolate	powder
2 tablespoonfuls milk	4 oz. castor sugar
2 eggs	3 oz. flour
	Pinch of salt

Cream the butter and sugar, and add the grated chocolate dissolved in the warmed milk. Beat in the eggs slowly, then add the flour, baking powder and salt sieved together. Put the mixture into greased bun tins and bake in a hot oven for 15–20 minutes. Either leave plain, or ice with chocolate glacé icing, and decorate with cherries and angelica or desiccated coconut.

Chocolate Cream Crunchies

6 oz. self-raising flour	Vanilla essence
2 oz. cornflour	6 oz. margarine
2 oz. cornflakes	3 oz. sugar
1 oz. drinking choco-	1 egg
late	Pinch of salt

Cream the margarine and sugar, then gradually beat in the egg. Stir in sieved dry ingredients, vanilla, and the cornflakes. If soft, leave to become firm. Mould into balls the size of walnuts, place on a greased tin and bake in a moderate oven for about 15 minutes. When cold, sandwich together with suitable filling, such as peppermint butter cream.

Chocolate Lemon Buns

7 oz. flour	Lemon curd
1 teaspoonful baking	1 oz. cocoa
powder	3 oz. margarine
4 oz. sugar	Milk to mix

Rub the fat into the sieved flour. Add the cocoa, sugar and baking powder. Mix to a stiff dough with milk. Turn on to floured board and shape into a sausage of 2-in. diameter. Cut into rounds ½ in. thick and neaten with a knife. Place on greased baking sheet and make hole in centre of each with thumb. Fill each hole with lemon curd, sprinkle with sugar and bake in a hot oven for 15–20 minutes. (These quantities make about 14 buns.)

Chocolate Macaroon Tartlets

Short pastry	3 oz. ground almonds
1 oz. grated chocolate	4 oz. castor sugar
1 egg	Vanilla essence

Roll out pastry, cut into rounds with a crinkly cutter and line greased patty pans with it. Mix together the ground almonds and the castor sugar. Beat the egg and add it to the mixture. Melt the chocolate and add with a few drops of vanilla essence. Put some of the mixture into each of the patty pans and bake in a fairly quick oven for 15–20 minutes.

Cream or butter icing can be used to sandwich together these dainty Chocolate Shells

Chocolate Madeleines

2 eggs	1½ oz. margarine
2 oz. castor sugar	Pinch of salt
2 oz. self-raising flour	Desiccated coconut,
Vanilla essence	grated chocolate
¼ oz. cocoa	and jam

Grease about nine dariole moulds. Melt the fat. Whisk eggs and sugar until thick, add vanilla. Lightly fold in sieved flour, cocoa and salt alternately with the melted fat. Quickly half-fill the moulds and bake in a hot oven for approximately 11 minutes. Turn on to a wire tray to cool. Decorate by coating with a little melted jam and rolling in desiccated coconut and grated chocolate.

Chocolate Melting Moments

2 oz. margarine	2 oz. sugar
1 egg	½ oz. cocoa
3½ oz. self-raising flour	Rolled oats

Cream the fat and the sugar until light and fluffy. Gradually beat in the egg. Stir in cocoa and flour. Damp hands and roll mixture into walnut-sized balls. Toss in the oats. Place on greased tray, flatten slightly and bake in a moderate oven for 15–20 minutes. (Makes about 9 cakes.)

Chocolate Shells

3 oz. fat	3 oz. castor sugar
1 small egg	4 oz. self-raising flour
1 oz. cocoa	Whipped cream

Cream fat and sugar until light and fluffy. Gradually add the lightly beaten egg, then stir in the sieved flour and cocoa. Using a forcing bag with a star nozzle, pipe small shell shapes on to a greased baking sheet, adding a dessertspoon of milk if too stiff. Bake in a moderately hot oven for 10–15 minutes. Cool on a wire tray and sandwich together with cream. (Makes about 6 cakes.)

Chocolate Swiss Tarts

4 oz. margarine	1 oz. cocoa
3 oz. self-raising flour	Whole nuts for
Vanilla essence	decoration
1 oz. icing sugar	

Cream the fat and sugar until light and fluffy. Add the essence and mix in the sieved flour and cocoa until thoroughly blended. Using a large star pipe, force into baking cases with a spiral motion. Place nut in centre of each and bake on a baking sheet in a moderate oven for about 30 minutes. (These quantities make about 6 tarts.)

Coconut Buns

6 oz. flour	2 oz. desiccated coco-
1 egg	nut
2 oz. castor sugar	¼ teaspoonful baking
1½ oz. butter	powder

Rub the butter into the sieved flour and baking powder, add the sugar and then the coconut. Beat the egg and add it gradually. Take two forks and put the mixture in rocky drops on a greased baking sheet. Bake for 10 minutes in a fairly hot oven.

Gingerbread Slab

12 oz. self-raising	8 oz. treacle
flour	3 oz. chopped peel
4 oz. butter	4 oz. sugar
3½ oz. preserved	½ gill milk
ginger	1 teaspoonful bicar-
2 eggs	bonate of soda
½ oz. ground ginger	

Sieve the flour and mix with sugar and ginger. Rub in the butter, then add the peel and preserved ginger cut in small pieces. Beat the eggs into the treacle and add to the mixture. Dissolve the soda in the warmed milk and add. Then mix all well together. Put the mixture in a flat tin and bake in a moderate oven for about 45 minutes. Cut up when cold.

Orange Buns

4 oz. butter	½ teaspoonful baking
4 oz. sugar	powder
4½ oz. flour	Grated rind of an
2 eggs	orange

Beat the butter and sugar to a cream, add the orange rind, then the beaten eggs gradually, and lastly the flour and baking powder. Put the mixture into small, round, greased tins and bake for about 12 minutes in a fairly hot oven. Either leave plain or ice with orange glacé icing and decorate with crystallised orange slices, or strips of angelica and crystallised flower petals.

Queen Cakes

2 oz. butter	1 oz. sultanas
2 oz. sugar	1 egg
3 oz. flour	Pinch of baking
1 oz. cherries (or peel)	powder

Cream the butter and sugar until light and fluffy, add the beaten egg and then the dry ingredients. Bake in a hot oven, in

well-greased small fancy tins or in crinkly paper cases, for 10 minutes.

NOTE: Finish off either by scattering a few chopped almonds on the top or putting half a cherry on each before baking; or, when cold, ice with white glacé icing and decorate with a cherry and a little angelica.

Ring Doughnuts (see also Bread chapter)

4 oz. flour	1 teaspoonful baking
1 oz. castor sugar	powder
1 oz. butter	Pinch of spice
1 egg	A little milk

Rub the butter into the flour, then sieve in the sugar, baking powder and spice. Beat the egg and add it with enough milk to make a light stiff dough. Put the dough on a floured board and roll it out to about ½ in. in thickness. Cut into rounds and remove the centres with a smaller cutter, leaving the ring about ½ in. in width. Fry in deep fat until a good brown and dredge with castor sugar.

Rock Cakes

12 oz. flour	Milk (if required)
1 teaspoonful baking	4 oz. currants
powder	1 oz. chopped peel
3 oz. butter	3 oz. sugar
1 egg	Good pinch of spice
Nutmeg	

Rub the butter into the sieved flour. Add all the dry ingredients. Beat the egg and add it and a little milk if necessary, but the mixture must be dry. Stir with a spoon, keeping it rough. Put little heaps on a floured tin and bake in a moderate oven for 15 minutes.

Yorkshire Parkin

8 oz. self-raising flour	1 oz. chopped peel
8 oz. oatmeal	4 oz. butter
8 oz. treacle	1 teaspoonful ground
4 oz. sugar	ginger
1 egg	2 teaspoonfuls bicar-
1 gill milk	bonate of soda
Pinch of salt	

Rub the butter into the sieved flour, then add the rest of the dry ingredients, the treacle, milk and beaten egg. Mix well together. Put the mixture in a prepared shallow tin and cook in a slow oven for about 2 hours. When cool, cut into squares.

NOTE: Parkin will keep for some time in an airtight tin.

CACTUS CAKES—a chocolate macaroon mixture decorated with green marzipan

MARBLE CAKE in three colours, topped with decorative feather icing

Photographs by Cadbury Bros.

CAKES

ICED CAKES

For icing recipes, see separate chapter.

Battenberg Cake

6 oz. margarine	¼ teaspoonful baking
6 oz. sugar	powder
6 oz. plain flour	Pinch of salt
3 eggs	1 oz. cocoa
Vanilla essence	Milk to mix
Lemon curd or jam	

Grease and line two 4 in. × 8 in. loaf tins. Cream margarine and sugar until light and frothy, then beat in the eggs, a little at a time. Add the dry ingredients, except cocoa, and enough milk to make a soft dropping consistency. Divide the mixture in half, adding cocoa to one and vanilla essence to the other. Bake in separate tins in a moderate oven for about 20–25 minutes.

When cool, cut each cake in half, lengthways. Sandwich a vanilla strip to a chocolate strip, using lemon curd or jam, put a thin layer of lemon curd or jam on top and then the remaining two strips, so that the vanilla strip is on top of the chocolate and the chocolate on top of the vanilla. Cover all over with almond paste, mark out a trellis pattern on the top and, if liked, decorate with glacé cherries and angelica.

Caramel Gâteau

2 eggs	2 teaspoonfuls cocoa
3 oz. sugar	2½ oz. plain flour
Pinch of salt	

For the filling

2 oz. butter or margarine	3 oz. icing sugar
	Vanilla essence
1 level tablespoonful cocoa	1–2 teaspoonfuls milk or water

For the icing

4 oz. brown sugar	Pinch of cream of tartar
2 tablespoonfuls water	1 small egg-white

Grease and line three 6-in. sandwich tins. Whisk eggs and sugar together, beating over bowl of hot water until thick and foamy; remove, continue beating until cold. Then fold in sieved flour and salt lightly. Divide mixture into three equal parts, add cocoa to one part. Bake 20 minutes in fairly hot oven. Cool on wire tray. Sandwich together with butter icing, the chocolate one in the middle.

To make the caramel icing, put the sugar and water into a strong saucepan with a pinch of cream of tartar and boil for 4 minutes, then pour gradually on to the lightly whisked egg-white and continue to whisk until thick. Pour over the cake and allow to set. Decorate with chocolate drops.

Battenberg Cake, in two colours and coated with almond paste, is a long-established favourite

Colour Page opposite:
Chocolate Swiss Roll, Dundee Cake, Scones, Madeleines, Marble Cake, Preserved Ginger Cake

Cherry Trellis Cake

3 eggs	3 oz. plain flour
3 oz. castor sugar	Pinch of salt
	1 oz. cocoa

For the butter cream

3 oz. margarine	2 oz. glacé cherries
4½ oz. icing sugar	2 teaspoonfuls milk
	Vanilla essence

Grease and line three 6-in. sandwich tins. Whisk eggs and sugar together, over a bowl of hot water, until thick and foamy; remove, continue beating until cold. Lightly fold in sieved flour, cocoa and salt. Divide between the tins and bake 20 minutes in fairly hot oven. Cool on wire tray, sandwich cakes together with cherry butter cream, made by creaming margarine and adding the other ingredients. Coat sides with plain butter cream, roll in sugar. Decorate top in trellis design, add halved cherries.

Chocolate Cake (Rich)

6 oz. flour	Vanilla essence
6 oz. sugar	Pinch of salt
6 oz. margarine	1 teaspoonful baking
3 eggs	powder
	1½ oz. cocoa

Grease and line a 7-in. cake tin. Separate egg-yolks from whites. Cream the fat and sugar until light and fluffy, add the egg-yolks gradually, stir in the sieved dry ingredients and add flavouring. Then, quickly, add stiffly beaten egg-whites. Bake in a moderate oven (middle shelf) for 1¼ hours. Cool, decorate with chocolate icing.

Chocolate Cakes

3 oz. sugar	5 oz. self-raising flour
2½ oz. margarine	½ oz. cocoa
1 egg	Pinch of salt
A few drops of vanilla	3 tablespoonfuls milk
essence	

Grease and line a Swiss roll tin 9½ in. × 7 in. Cream the margarine and sugar until light and fluffy, then beat in the egg gradually. Add dry ingredients, milk to mix to a smooth dropping consistency, and vanilla. Bake in a moderate oven for 20–25 minutes. Cool before icing, then cut into slices.

Chocolate Gâteau

2 eggs	¾ oz. cocoa
2 oz. sugar	1½ oz. melted butter
2 oz. plain flour	or margarine
Pinch of salt	Cream and jam

Grease and line a Swiss roll tin 11 in. × 7 in. Whisk the eggs and sugar together until light and foamy, then lightly fold in the sieved flour, cocoa and salt alternately, with the melted fat. Pour quickly into the tin and bake in hot oven for about 8 minutes. Turn on to a wire tray to cool. When cool, cut into four and sandwich the pieces together with cream. Coat the sides with cream or jam and nuts or chocolate vermicelli. Ice the top with chocolate icing and decorate as desired.

Chocolate Japs

2 egg-whites	Small pinch of cream
8 oz. castor sugar	of tartar
	4 oz. ground almonds

Whisk egg-whites and cream of tartar until very thick, then whisk in 4 oz. sugar. Mix in the remaining sugar and ground almonds, blending thoroughly. Using a plain ½-in. nozzle, pipe rounds on to a greased, floured baking sheet and bake in a moderate oven for about 25 minutes. Allow to cool, then, using a 2-in. plain cutter, cut into circles. Sandwich together with chocolate butter icing, spread the sides with butter icing and coat with chocolate vermicelli or crumbs made from the cake trimmings. Cover the tops with icing and decorate as desired.

Chocolate Log

2 oz. plain flour	2 eggs
2 oz. sugar	1 oz. cocoa
	Pinch of salt

Grease and line a Swiss roll tin. Whisk the eggs and sugar together until thick and foamy, then lightly fold in the sieved flour, cocoa and salt. Bake in hot oven for about 7–8 minutes. Turn on to sugared paper over a damp cloth and roll up. When cold, unroll, spread with butter icing and roll up again. Cover the outside of the cake with chocolate butter icing and mark with a fork so that it looks like a log.

Chocolate Macaroon Fancies

4 oz. ground almonds	4 oz. castor sugar
1 oz. margarine	2 egg-whites
(melted)	Blanched almonds
	2½ oz. cocoa

Grease a baking sheet, or line it with rice paper. Whip the egg-whites until stiff, then fold in the dry ingredients and the margarine. Place in small heaps, or pipe, on baking sheet, and bake in a slow to moderate oven until firm (about 15 minutes). Cool on wire tray, then sandwich together in

Caramel Gâteau is a three-layer sponge—the middle layer chocolate-flavoured —filled with butter icing

twos with butter cream and coat tops with chocolate glacé icing. Put a split blanched almond on top of each. (These quantities make 14 macaroons.)

Chocolate Mushroom Cake

2 oz. margarine	Milk to mix
2 oz. sugar	3 oz. self-raising flour
1 egg	½ oz. cocoa
Pinch of salt	Apricot jam

Grease and line a 6-in. sandwich-tin, preferably one with sloping sides. Cream fat and sugar together until white and fluffy, then add beaten egg gradually, beating well in between each addition. Stir in the sieved dry ingredients, keeping the mixture a soft dropping consistency by adding milk as necessary. Bake in a moderate oven for 20–25 minutes, turn out and cool on a wire tray. When cold, brush the bottom and sides with a little melted apricot jam. Make almond icing, set aside a small piece for the "stalk," then roll the remainder into a circle to fit the bottom and sides of cake and press into place. Spread the top with chocolate butter icing, mark with a fork to look like mushroom gills, and place "stalk" in position.

Chocolate Sandwich Cake

Proceed as for Chocolate Cake (see Plain Cakes) but bake, in two 6-in. greased sandwich tins, in a moderate oven for 20 minutes. When cool, sandwich together with chocolate butter icing, spread butter icing smoothly over the top and decorate with a piped border, or as desired.

Alternative Flavours

(1) Mocha Cake—add 1 tablespoonful coffee essence or strong black coffee.
(2) Chocolate Date Cake—add 3 oz. chopped dates.
(3) Chocolate Coconut Cake—add 1 oz. desiccated coconut.

Chocolate Walnut Cake

4 oz. margarine	4 oz. self-raising flour
4 oz. sugar	2 eggs
2 oz. cup chocolate	Pinch of salt
	Milk to mix

Grease and line a 7-in. cake tin. Heat oven to moderate and use middle shelf. Cream the margarine and sugar until white and fluffy, then add well-beaten eggs gradually. Fold in sieved flour and salt and, lastly, add the chocolate. If necessary, add a little milk to make a soft dropping consistency. Bake for 35–40 minutes, until well risen and firm to the touch, and turn on to a wire tray to cool. Cover the top with chocolate glacé icing and decorate with walnuts.

Coffee Cake

2 oz. butter	1¼ teaspoonfuls bak-
3 oz. brown sugar	ing powder
6 oz. flour	1 dessertspoonful
1 egg and 1 egg-yolk	coffee essence

For the sauce

¼ pint milk	3 oz. castor or granu-
	lated sugar

Put the milk and white sugar in a pan, heat until the sugar is dissolved, and leave to cool.

Cream the butter and brown sugar, add the beaten eggs gradually, and beat in well. Fold in the flour and baking powder, add the sauce and, lastly, the coffee essence. Bake in a fairly hot oven for about 1 hour.

Ice on top with coffee glacé icing or coffee butter icing; or cut the cake across once or twice and fill with coffee butter icing and ice all over with coffee glacé icing. Decorate with walnuts. If coffee butter icing is used for the top, put a little in a forcing bag with a rose squeezer and pipe designs on the top.

Coffee Nougatine

Make a coffee cake as above and, when it is cold, cut it open and fill with coffee butter icing. Spread the butter icing all over the cake as smoothly as possible and scatter chopped browned almonds over it.

Genoese Cake

4 oz. butter	¼ teaspoonful baking
4 oz. sugar	powder
2 eggs	4½ oz. flour
½ oz. ground rice	Jam

Cream the butter and sugar until light and fluffy. Then add the beaten eggs gradually and beat well. Put in the flour, ground rice and baking powder and, when it is well mixed, turn into a prepared tin and bake in a fairly quick oven for about 1 hour. When cold, cut in half and put a layer of either apricot, raspberry or strawberry jam in the middle and ice the top with meringue icing flavoured with a little sieved jam and coloured to match the jam.

Genoese Slab for Small Iced Cakes

4 eggs	3 oz. flour
4 oz. castor sugar	Pinch of baking
2 oz. melted butter	powder

Beat the eggs and sugar with a whisk over hot water until the mixture is thick and creamy. Then whisk until cold. Add the sieved flour, baking powder and melted butter. Put the mixture into a greased, lined flat tin and smooth down. The mixture should not be more than ½ in. deep before it is cooked. Bake in a hot oven for 15–20 minutes.

When the slab is cold, turn it upside-down and trim the edges. Beat up meringue icing, flavour and colour as desired, and spread it smoothly over the slab. With a sharp knife, cut into strips of suitable size and cut each strip into different shapes—diamonds, triangles, squares and fingers. Do this as quickly as possible or the icing will begin to set and will crack. Decorate according to taste.

Alternatively, cut the cake into strips before icing, and ice the strips in different colours.

If liked, some of the slab can be cut through and filled with jam. Scatter icing sugar on the top and cut into squares.

Another alternative is to flavour the slab with orange rind and ice it with orange glacé icing.

Hungarian Cake

6 oz. self-raising flour	3 eggs
5 oz. castor sugar	2 teaspoonfuls strong
4 oz. margarine	black coffee
Pinch of salt	A little milk

Grease and line an 8-in. cake tin. Cream the margarine and sugar until light and fluffy, and beat in the eggs gradually. Stir in dry ingredients and the coffee, with a little milk if necessary to make a dropping consistency. Bake in a moderate oven for 1¼ hours. When cool, split across and sandwich together with chocolate butter. Ice with chocolate glacé icing.

Neapolitan Cake

5 oz. margarine	A little milk if
5 oz. sugar	necessary
2 eggs	Glacé and butter
8 oz. plain flour	icings
1 teaspoonful baking	Nuts
powder	Cherries
	Angelica

Hungarian Cake, right, is a coffee-flavoured sponge with chocolate icing

For Christmas, a Chocolate Log made like a Swiss Roll looks seasonable and attractive

Beat the sugar and butter to a cream and add the beaten eggs, then the grated orange rind. Fold in the flour and baking powder, sieved together. Put into a prepared cake tin and bake in a fairly quick oven for about 1 hour.

When cool, ice with orange glacé icing. One or two fillings of orange curd can be put in if desired. Decorate with crystallised orange slices.

Orange Sandwich

2 eggs and their weight in butter, sugar and flour	¼ teaspoonful baking powder
	Grated rind of ½ orange

Beat the butter and sugar to a cream, add the beaten eggs, then the orange rind and, lastly, the sieved flour and baking powder. Put into two greased sandwich tins and bake in a fairly quick oven for 20 minutes. When cool, but not cold, spread orange glacé icing on both pieces of sandwich and put them together. When the sandwich is completely cold and the icing has set, ice the top with orange glacé icing and decorate with crystallised orange slices and angelica.

For colouring	
1 dessertspoonful cocoa	Cochineal

Cream margarine and sugar until light and fluffy, beat in eggs and fold in sieved flour and baking powder. Mix with milk to a soft dropping consistency. Divide into three portions and colour one with the cocoa and another with the cochineal. Put into three well-greased sandwich tins and bake in a moderate oven for 15–20 minutes. Turn out on to a wire tray and, when cool, sandwich together with butter icing and coat with glacé icing. Decorate as desired with nuts, cherries and angelica.

Orange Cake

5 oz. butter	½ teaspoonful baking
6 oz. sugar	powder
6 oz. flour	3 eggs
1 orange	

Queen Mary's Birthday Cake

6 egg-yolks	2 oz. melted butter
4 oz. castor sugar	2 egg-whites
	3 oz. flour

For the chocolate ganache filling

½ pint cream	8 oz. grated choco-
6 oz. sugar	late

Whisk together the egg-yolks, whites and sugar in a bowl over hot water until light and thick. Lightly stir in the melted butter and sieved flour, pour the mixture into two prepared round cake tins and bake in a moderate oven for about 30 minutes. Turn out and leave on a wire tray to cool.

To make the filling.—Cook the cream, sugar and chocolate together in a heavy saucepan. Leave for 1 hour to cool, then cut each of the cakes across in half and spread with the ganache so that you have a four-layer sandwich. Coat the cake with the remainder of the ganache, which by this stage has almost set.

Tiger Cakes

4 oz. flour	4 oz. margarine
½ oz. castor sugar	A little water

For the decorations
Caramel

4 oz. loaf sugar	¼ gill water

Mocha icing

Coffee flavoured	Chopped nuts
butter cream	

Rub the fat into the flour and add sugar. Mix to a stiff paste with a little water, then roll out ¼ in. thick and cut into small rounds. Place on a greased tray and bake in a moderate oven until pale brown. When cool, sandwich together with mocha icing, coat sides also with mocha icing and roll in chopped nuts. Pipe icing round the top edge of each cake. Make caramel by dissolving sugar slowly in water and when clear boiling until golden colour. Put a little caramel on top of each cake. (Quantities given make about 9 cakes.)

Walnut or Hazelnut Cake

4½ oz. butter	3 eggs
6 oz. sugar	¼ teaspoonful baking
7½ oz. flour	powder
2¼ oz. chopped wal-	¾ teaspoonful salt
nuts (or hazelnuts)	Milk

Cream the butter and sugar until light and fluffy, and gradually add the beaten eggs. Put all the dry ingredients together and add them to the mixture. Lastly, add the milk. Put into a prepared cake tin and bake in a fairly quick oven for about 1¼ hours. Ice all over, or just on top, with white meringue icing.

CAKES THAT CAN BE ICED OR PLAIN

Cherry Cake

8 oz. flour	1 teaspoonful baking
4 oz. sugar	powder
4 oz. butter	4 oz. cherries
2 eggs	1 oz. chopped
A little milk	almonds

Cream the butter and sugar, and add the beaten eggs gradually. Cut the cherries in half and add them with the almonds. Then put in the flour and baking powder sieved together and, lastly, a little milk. Put the mixture into a prepared tin and bake in a moderate oven for about 1¼ hours. If desired, ice with white meringue icing and decorate with cherries and angelica.

Golden Cake

3 oz. butter or mar-	6 oz. self-raising flour
garine	½ gill milk
3 egg-yolks	¼ teaspoonful vanilla
Pinch of salt	essence or grated
6 oz. castor sugar	rind of orange

Cream fat and sugar until fluffy. Beat in egg-yolks, one at a time. Sift dry ingredients and mix in alternately with the milk and essence. Bake for 1 hour in a moderate oven. This cake is equally good eaten as it is or iced with American frosting or orange icing, according to the flavouring used.

Pineapple Cake

6 oz. flour	1 oz. glacé pineapple
2 oz. butter	cubes
3 oz. sugar	½ teaspoonful baking
1 egg	powder
	A little milk

Cream the butter and sugar, and add the beaten egg. Then mix in the sieved flour and baking powder, a little milk and, lastly, the pineapple cut in small pieces. Put the mixture into a prepared cake tin and bake in a fairly quick oven for about 1 hour. If desired, ice with pineapple glacé icing and put in a pineapple filling.

Preserved Ginger Cake

6 oz. butter	4 eggs
6 oz. sugar	4 oz. preserved ginger
10 oz. flour	4 oz. mixed peel
1 teaspoonful baking powder	½ teaspoonful ground ginger
Rind of ½ lemon	

Cream the butter and sugar, and add the beaten eggs gradually. Sieve the flour and baking powder, and add the peel and ginger chopped small, the grated lemon rind and the ground ginger. Then add all these to the mixture and mix them in well. Put into a prepared cake tin and bake in a fairly quick oven for about 1¼ hours. If desired, ice with white meringue icing and decorate with preserved ginger and angelica.

PARTY GATEAUX

Banana Shortcake

Plain round sponge cake	2–3 teaspoonfuls sugar
Small carton of double cream	2 or 3 ripe bananas
A little grated orange peel	1 egg-white (optional)

Whip the cream with the sugar and orange peel and, if desired, add a stiffly beaten egg-white (this makes the cream fluffier, and also makes it go further). Cut the sponge cake right across (as for a sandwich) and, just before serving, fill with sliced bananas and cream. Top with remainder of cream.

Chocolate Banana Gâteau

2 oz. plain flour	1 oz. cocoa
2 oz. sugar	Pinch of salt
2 eggs	1 oz. melted margarine
Whipped cream and sliced bananas	

For the jam glaze	
2 tablespoonfuls apricot jam	1 tablespoonful water
1 tablespoonful sugar	1 teaspoonful lemon juice

Grease a flan tin and heat up oven to hot. Whisk the eggs and sugar until thick and foamy, then fold in lightly the sieved flour, cocoa and salt. Add melted fat, folding in quickly. Pour into prepared tin and bake for 8–9 minutes. Leave to cool, then fill with sliced bananas and pour glaze over. The glaze is made by boiling all the ingredients together until reduced. Then

Tiger Cakes are coated with mocha icing and nuts, and topped with caramel

remove from heat, sieve, and leave to cool a little before using. When set, pipe a decoration of whipped cream round the edge.

Chocolate Pear Gâteau

Canned or fresh ripe pears cut in quarters	1 pint orange jelly ½ pint whipped cream Chopped nuts
	Angelica

For the sponge base

2 eggs	2 oz. plain flour
2 oz. sugar	1 oz. cocoa
	Pinch of salt

Grease and sugar a sponge flan tin. Whisk eggs and sugar together until thick and frothy, fold in sieved flour, cocoa and salt. Pour immediately into tin and bake in moderate oven for 10–15 minutes. When cooked, turn out and leave to cool. Make orange jelly and pour slowly over sponge until sponge is moist, then leave to set. Prepare pears either by simmering in a pink syrup until faintly pink, or by painting on pink colouring with a small brush. Mix a little of the cream with a little chopped pear and pile on to the sponge base. Arrange remaining pears in quarters on top and pipe cream round the edge. Decorate with chopped nuts and angelica.

Fruit Basket

3 eggs	3 oz. plain flour
3 oz. castor sugar	Pinch of salt
½ oz. cocoa	Cherries and cream
Chocolate icing	for filling

Grease and line three 6-in. sponge sandwich tins. Heat up oven to hot. Whisk eggs and sugar together until thick and foamy, then lightly fold in the sieved flour, cocoa and salt. Divide equally between the three tins and bake for 10 minutes. Cool on a wire tray, then sandwich two of the cakes together with a little fruit and cream. Coat the sides of the cake with cream and sprinkle with chocolate vermicelli or cup chocolate. Cut a circle out of the third cake, to make the lid, and cover with chocolate icing. Put the third cake on top of the other two, coating the sides as before, and fill with fruit and cream. Place the lid on top and decorate with stars of cream and cherries.

Gâteau Suprême

3 eggs	½ oz. cocoa
3 oz. castor sugar	3 oz. plain flour
	Pinch of salt

For the butter cream

3 oz. margarine	2 teaspoonfuls milk or
4½ oz. icing sugar	water
	Vanilla essence

For the praline

3 oz. castor sugar	3 oz. whole almonds

Proceed as for Fruit Basket (previous recipe) making three sponge cakes.

To make the praline.—Put ingredients into a thick saucepan and melt on a low heat. Stir frequently when sugar has melted and is turning colour until it caramels well and the almonds appear to be roasted. Turn out on to a greased tin and leave until cold and set. Break into pieces and grind or pound to a powder. Keep in an airtight tin until wanted.

Add 3 tablespoonfuls of praline to half the butter cream and sandwich the cakes together with this mixture. Coat the sides with plain butter cream and roll in praline. Decorate the top with cream and marzipan fruits, or as desired.

FRUIT AND RICHER CAKES

Cherry Cake (Rich)

8 oz. plain flour	1½ level teaspoonfuls
6 oz. castor sugar	baking powder
Pinch of salt	6 oz. margarine
1 tablespoonful	3 eggs
lemon juice	4 oz. glacé cherries

Heat the oven to very moderate, and grease and line a 7-in. cake tin. Wash and dry the cherries thoroughly, then cut into quarters and toss in a little flour. Sieve together the flour, baking powder and salt. Cream the fat and sugar thoroughly, until soft and pale cream in colour. Add the eggs one at a time, with a little of the sieved flour mixture after each one, and beat well. Fold in the remaining flour mixture, together with the lemon juice, using a metal spoon. Fold in the quartered cherries, mix thoroughly, but do not beat. Turn into the prepared tin and smooth the top. Bake for 2 hours. Remove from oven and, after 5 minutes, remove from tin and cool on a wire tray.

Dundee Cake

4½ oz. butter	½ teaspoonful baking
6 oz. brown sugar	powder
6 oz. flour	Pinch of salt
6 oz. sultanas	Pinch of spice
3 oz. currants	3 eggs
3 oz. mixed peel (chopped)	Almonds for top

Fruit Basket, for a special party, can be served either as a cake or sweet

Cream the butter and sugar until light and fluffy, add the beaten eggs gradually, and then the dry ingredients, sifted and mixed together. Stir in the fruit, previously prepared and cleaned, put the mixture into a cake tin, doubly lined with ungreased greaseproof paper, scatter the almonds on the top and bake in a moderate oven for about 2¼ hours.

Empire Cake

6 oz. flour	2 oz. chopped peel
4 oz. butter	3 eggs
4 oz. sugar	Small ½ teaspoonful
4 oz. sultanas	baking powder and
2 oz. currants	mixed spice
1 oz. chopped almonds	Grated lemon rind

Sift dry ingredients, with exception of the sugar, and clean and prepare fruit. Cream the butter and sugar together until light and fluffy, gradually add the beaten eggs, then the other ingredients. Put the mixture in a cake tin lined with 2 layers of ungreased greaseproof paper and bake in a moderate oven for about 1¼ hours. This cake may be iced with almond paste and royal icing.

Family Cake (Eggless and inexpensive)

8 oz. flour	1 oz. chopped lemon
4 oz. soft brown sugar	peel, if liked
4 oz. sultanas	½ teaspoonful bicar-
4 oz. margarine	bonate of soda
½ teaspoonful mixed	1 teaspoonful vinegar
spice or nutmeg	¼ gill milk

Rub the margarine into the flour and add the sugar, fruit and spice or nutmeg. Mix together the milk, soda and vinegar, and stir immediately into the mixture. Put into a prepared cake tin and bake in a quick oven, lowering the heat when the cake has risen (about 1½ hours altogether).

Gingerbread (1)

6 oz. flour	1 egg
1 dessertspoonful	2 oz. Golden Syrup
ground ginger	2 oz. black treacle
Pinch of salt	1 tablespoonful mar-
2 oz. butter	malade
2 oz. moist brown	½ teaspoonful bicar-
sugar	bonate of soda
A little milk	

Sieve the flour, salt and ginger into a basin. Put the butter, sugar, syrup, treacle and marmalade into a saucepan and stir over a gentle heat until liquid. Then pour into the dry ingredients and beat well. Add the well-beaten egg and then the soda dissolved in a little hot milk. Beat well and pour into a greased, shallow cake tin. Bake for about 1 hour in a slow oven.

Gingerbread (2) (Eggless)

9 oz. flour	1 teaspoonful baking
½ teaspoonful salt	powder
¼ lb. treacle or syrup	1 teaspoonful ground
2 tablespoonfuls	ginger
margarine	1 gill sour milk

Sift the flour thoroughly with the baking powder, salt and ginger. Melt the margarine until it has the consistency of oil. Stir the treacle and sour milk together until well mixed, then beat them into the flour mixture until really smooth. Add the melted fat and turn into a well-greased shallow tin. Bake in a moderate oven for about 1 hour. Can be eaten cold as a cake, but is best served hot with plenty of butter.

Honey Fruit Cake

8 oz. flour	1 teaspoonful cinna-
3½ oz. margarine or	mon
fat	2 oz. sugar
4 oz. dried fruit	1 teaspoonful bicar-
(currants, sultanas,	bonate of soda
etc.)	2 tablespoonfuls
¼ pint milk	honey

Sieve the flour and cinnamon and rub in the fat, then add the sugar and dried fruit, cleaned and prepared. Dissolve the bicarbonate of soda in the milk, stir in the honey and gradually pour this mixture into the dry ingredients, stirring thoroughly. Put into a well-greased tin and bake in a moderate oven for 15 minutes, reduce the heat when the cake begins to brown and cook for a further 50–60 minutes. It should be firm when pressed in the centre and golden brown in colour.

Housekeeper's Cake

8 oz. flour	1 teaspoonful baking
4 oz. granulated sugar	powder
4 oz. currants	2 oz. chopped mixed
4 oz. lard and mar-	peel
garine, mixed	A little spice
2 small eggs	A little milk

Sieve together the flour, baking powder and spice, and rub in the lard and margarine. Then add the currants, sugar and peel. Beat the eggs and add them to the mixture. Lastly, add a little milk. Put into

a prepared cake tin, sprinkle some castor sugar on top and bake in a moderate oven for about 1 hour.

Lunch Cake

12 oz. flour	2 oz. lard
2 oz. butter	2 oz. chopped peel
3 eggs	8 oz. currants
1 teaspoonful ground	6 oz. sugar
ginger	2 teaspoonfuls
½ oz. caraway seeds	baking powder
	A little milk

Rub the butter and lard into the well-sieved flour and baking powder. Add all the dry ingredients. Separate the egg-yolks from the whites, add a little milk to the yolks, then stir into the mixture. Beat the whites to a stiff froth and fold them in lightly. Put the mixture in a prepared cake tin and bake in a slow oven for about 1½ hours.

Marmalade Cake

8 oz. self-raising flour	Vanilla essence
2 eggs	1 oz. lard or vege-
1 tablespoonful	table fat
Golden Syrup	3 oz. margarine
1 tablespoonful	3 oz. sugar
marmalade	Mixed fruit as liked
	Pinch of salt

Cream the sugar and fats very thoroughly together, add the salt, syrup and marmalade. Beat the eggs. Sift the flour and add to the mixture alternately with the eggs, beating well. Stir in the fruit (sultanas, raisins, currants, chopped dates, glacé cherries, mixed peel, according to taste and availability) and flavouring. Bake in a well-greased, unlined tin in a moderate oven for about 1 hour 20 minutes.

Nut and Chocolate Lump Cake

4 oz. margarine	2 eggs
4 oz. sugar	2 oz. drinking choco-
4 oz. flour	late
2 oz. chopped nuts	1 teaspoonful baking
4 oz. plain or milk	powder
block chocolate	1 dessertspoonful
broken into pea-	coffee essence
sized pieces	

Cream the margarine and sugar together until frothy. Beat the eggs in gradually. Stir in the well-sieved dry ingredients with sufficient liquid to make a dropping consistency. Finally, fold in the nuts and broken chocolate. Turn into a prepared cake tin and bake in a moderate oven for 50–60 minutes.

Plum Cake

12 *oz. flour*	4 *oz. treacle*
6 *oz. butter*	8 *oz. raisins*
4 *eggs*	8 *oz. currants*
1 *teaspoonful bicar-*	4 *oz. chopped mixed*
bonate of soda	*peel*
A little milk	4 *oz. brown sugar*

Cream the butter and sugar together until frothy, then add the treacle and, after that, the beaten eggs gradually, then the sieved flour and cleaned and prepared fruit. Dissolve the soda in a little warm milk and add to the mixture at once. Stir well. Put the mixture into a prepared cake tin and bake in a moderate oven for $1\frac{1}{2}$–$1\frac{3}{4}$ hours.

Raisin Cake

8 *oz. brown sugar*	1 *lb. flour*
4 *eggs*	8 *oz. stoned raisins*
8 *oz. currants*	$\frac{1}{2}$ *teacupful milk*
1 *teaspoonful bicar-*	1 *teaspoonful mixed*
bonate of soda	*spice*
	8 *oz. butter*

Rub the butter into the sieved flour and add the rest of the dry ingredients. Then add the beaten eggs and, lastly, the milk. Bake in a moderate oven for about $1\frac{3}{4}$ hours.

Seed Cake

3 *eggs*	4 *oz. flour*
3 *oz. butter*	4 *oz. sugar*
2 *teaspoonfuls cara-*	*Small* $\frac{1}{2}$ *teaspoonful*
way seeds	*baking powder*

Separate the egg-yolks from the whites.

Beat the butter and sugar to a cream, then add one egg-yolk and a third of the flour and baking powder sieved together. Add another yolk and more flour, and so on until all the flour is in. Lastly, add the cara way seeds. Whisk up the egg-whites to a stiff froth and fold them in at the end. Put the mixture into a prepared cake tin and bake in a moderate oven for about 1 hour.

Spicy Topped Fruit Cake

8 *oz. plain flour*	2 *eggs*
4 *oz. lard and mar-*	4 *oz. sugar*
garine mixed	*Grated rind of*
4 *oz. dried fruit*	1 *lemon*
$1\frac{1}{2}$ *teaspoonfuls*	$\frac{1}{2}$ *teaspoonful vanilla*
baking powder	*essence*

Water for mixing

For spicy top

3 *oz. flour*	1 *teaspoonful mixed*
$1\frac{1}{2}$ *oz. sugar*	*spice*

$1\frac{1}{2}$ *oz. margarine*

Rub the fats into the well sieved flour and baking powder till it looks like fine breadcrumbs. Add sugar, lemon rind and fruit, then beaten eggs, vanilla and enough water to make a soft dropping consistency. Put into a well greased cake tin. For the spicy top, mix flour, spice and sugar, rub in fat and sprinkle on top of cake before baking. Bake in moderate oven for about $1\frac{1}{2}$ hours.

Photographs of cakes on pages 189, 191, 193, 195, 197, 199, 201 *and* 203 *by Cadbury Bros.*

Gâteau Suprème is coated in butter icing, then rolled in praline

HOW TO MIX A
CAKE
IN THREE MINUTES

1. Sieve flour, baking powder and sugar into a large mixing bowl

2. Add fat in a lump, unbeaten eggs and water

3. Beat for 1 minute with wooden spoon till ingredients are well mixed

WITH the vegetable fat shortenings now on the market, an entirely new method of quick cake-mixing has revolutionised cooking. Speed is the keynote of this new technique—and you really can mix the ingredients, add liquid, pour into the baking tin and put the cake in the oven all inside three minutes.

The method shown here is the one specially devised in the Spry Cookery Centre to be used with Spry and is called "Lightning Mix." The Trex method is somewhat similar, except that the manufacturers advocate cutting the fat into small pieces before mixing, and there are minor variations in recipe proportions.

These quick-mix methods are equally suitable for large and small cakes and baked puddings. The great advantage is that the busy housewife can prepare a cake or pudding in a fraction of the time normally required.

4. Turn into a greased sandwich tin lined with greaseproof paper on the bottom

5. The baked sandwich, after 30 to 35 minutes in a moderate oven

CAKES FOR SPECIAL OCCASIONS

Weddings, Christenings, Easter and Christmas—they all call for celebration cakes of their own

INSTRUCTIONS for making the various kinds of icing mentioned in this chapter will be found in the following chapter on "Icings and Fillings."

Birthday Cake

10 oz. butter	4 oz. chopped peel
10 oz. sugar	4 oz. ground almonds
10 oz. flour	1 eggcupful rum
6 eggs	½ teaspoonful baking
8 oz. sultanas	powder
4 oz. currants	

Beat the butter and sugar to a cream, then add the beaten eggs one by one, beating well. Add a little flour with the last two or three eggs if the mixture shows any signs of curdling. Put all the other dry ingredients together and add them to the mixture gradually; half-way through, add the rum. Stir the mixture thoroughly so that everything is well blended. Put the mixture into a cake tin, greased and doubly lined with greaseproof paper, and bake in a slow oven until thoroughly cooked through (about 1½ hours). When cold, cover with almond paste, and when this is thoroughly dry and firm (after a day or two), ice either with American icing, decorating at once, or with royal icing. When the icing is set, suitable wording such as "A Happy Birthday," or a child's name, can be written on top in coloured royal icing. Sugar roseholders in different colours and tiny candles to match can be bought from any good confectioner or grocer.

NOTE: Birthday cakes need not necessarily be fruit cakes. It is entirely a matter of taste. A large chocolate or orange cake is popular with children, and in this case use chocolate or orange glacé icing.

Christening Cake

8 oz. butter	½ gill brandy
8 oz. castor sugar	¼ teaspoonful almond
12 oz. sultanas	essence
12 oz. currants	8 oz. chopped peel

"The key of the door" is the theme of this gay 21st birthday cake iced in two colours

12 oz. flour	½ teaspoonful baking
5 eggs	powder
2 oz. chopped	1 dessertspoonful
almonds	black treacle

Cream the butter and sugar. Beat the eggs and add them slowly, beating well. Add a little flour towards the end, if the mixture shows any signs of curdling. Mix all the dry ingredients together and add them to the mixture, putting in the almond essence, treacle and brandy alternately with the sifted flour. Stir well, so that all the ingredients are well blended. Put the mixture into a well greased, doubly lined cake tin and bake in a slow oven until thoroughly cooked (about 3 hours).

Christening cakes should be iced with royal icing and decorated with formal pipings. A sugar cradle with a tiny doll inside or a sugar stork holding a cradle can be bought from any good confectioner and should be placed in the centre of the cake.

Christmas Cake

8 oz. flour	4 oz. glacé cherries
8 oz. butter	A little rum or
8 oz. dark sugar	brandy
8 oz. currants	½ teaspoonful baking
8 oz. sultanas	powder

4 *oz. orange peel (chopped fine)*
4 *oz. lemon peel (chopped fine)*
1 *oz. ground almonds*
½ *teaspoonful cinnamon*
¼ *teaspoonful mixed spice*
4 *eggs*

Cream the butter and sugar. Add the beaten eggs one at a time, beating well. Add a little flour with the last egg or two, if the mixture shows any signs of curdling. Put all the other dry ingredients together, and add

The traditional white Royal Icing, with lettering and decorations piped on, always looks right on a Christmas Cake

them to the mixture. Put in the rum half-way through. Stir the mixture well so that all the ingredients are well blended. Put the mixture into a well greased doubly lined cake tin and bake in a slow oven until thoroughly cooked (about 3 hours).

NOTE: **This cake should be made at least 3 weeks before Christmas as it improves with keeping.**

A Christmas cake can be iced in several different ways.

First put on a layer of almond paste, then ice with royal icing in one of the following ways:

(1) Coat with royal icing and, when set, decorate with formal pipings and finish off with marzipan berries, silver balls, angelica leaves, etc., etc.; or with a Father Christmas, Esquimaux, Polar bears, etc.

(2) Coat the top and decorate in the same way as above. Put a paper frilling of whatever colour is desired round the sides; white and gold or white and silver look very attractive.

(3) Beat up the royal icing extra stiff (double the ordinary amount will be required)

Even a beautiful three-tiered Wedding Cake can be made and iced at home—or you can compromise by making your own cake and having it professionally iced

For an Easter Sunday tea party, the traditional Simnel Cake, topped and sandwiched together with almond paste, has spring chicks and coloured eggs as decoration

and lay it thickly and roughly all over the cake. Do not smooth it down. Instead, take a fork and with it rough up the icing all over the cake until it resembles a wind-blown snowdrift. Make the points of icing all go in the same direction to make it look more realistic. Put red marzipan berries unevenly between the points of icing and finish off with tiny diamond shapes of angelica, two to each berry. This is a very attractive decoration and makes a change from the usual extremely formal icing.

Simnel or Easter Cake

8 oz. butter	½ teaspoonful baking
8 oz. sugar	powder
12 oz. flour	1 dessertspoonful
6 oz. sultanas	black treacle
6 oz. currants	Almond paste
4 eggs	6 oz. chopped peel

Beat the butter and sugar to a cream. Beat the eggs and add them gradually to the mixture, beating well. Put all the dry ingredients together and add them to the mixture, stirring thoroughly. Add the treacle half-way through. Cut a round of almond paste the size of the cake tin. Put half the cake mixture into the tin. Then put in the round of almond paste and press down well. Put in the rest of the cake mixture and bake in a moderate oven until thoroughly cooked (about $1\frac{3}{4}$ hours). (If a plainer cake is required, omit the almond paste filling.)

When cold, put another round of almond paste on the top, sticking it on with a little melted Golden Syrup. Cut a strip about 1 in. wide, or according to the size of the cake, and put it round the edge, first painting it with a little beaten egg-yolk to make it stick. Mark the strip with a fork. Then paint the whole top lightly with egg-yolk and put the cake in a very hot oven until the almond paste is a golden brown. Take out of the oven and cool on a rack.

When quite cold, place Easter decorations in the centre—small sugar eggs, fondant sweets, chickens, etc.

Wedding Cake (Three-tiered)

1 lb. 3 oz. butter	12 eggs
$\frac{1}{4}$ lb. 3 oz. castor sugar	$9\frac{1}{2}$ oz. chopped almonds
2 lb. 6 oz. currants	$1\frac{3}{4}$ gills rum
2 lb. 6 oz. sultanas	1 lb. 3 oz. chopped peel
$9\frac{1}{2}$ oz. glacé cherries	

$9\frac{1}{2}$ oz. raisins	$1\frac{1}{2}$ tablespoonfuls black treacle
$\frac{1}{2}$ teaspoonful almond essence	$\frac{1}{4}$ teaspoonful mixed spice
2 teaspoonfuls baking powder	$\frac{1}{4}$ teaspoonful cinnamon
1 lb. $12\frac{1}{2}$ oz. flour	

Cream the butter and sugar. Add the beaten eggs gradually, beating well, and adding flour towards the end if the mixture shows any signs of curdling. Put all the dry ingredients together and add them slowly to the mixture, stirring well. Put in the almond essence, the treacle and the rum alternately with the flour. Mix well so that all the ingredients are well blended. Put the mixture into well greased, doubly lined cake tins (10-in., 8-in. and 6-in.) and bake in a slow oven until thoroughly cooked.

NOTE: **Wedding cake should be made at least a month before it is needed as it improves greatly with keeping.**

To Ice a Wedding Cake.—Wedding cakes are usually made in two or three tiers. First, cover each cake thickly with almond paste, then coat smoothly with royal icing and put each cake on a thick silver board a little wider than the cake.

When the coating is absolutely hard, decorate with formal pipings rather more elaborately than for other cakes, and ornament with wedding favours which can be bought from any good confectioner—sugar doves, little silver shoes, silver horseshoes, small sprays of orange blossom, etc.—arranging them round the edge only of the tops of the cakes and round the sides. Leave the centres of the cakes bare.

For a wedding cake in tiers, small sugar pillars are necessary. Put them towards the centre of the cake and then build it up. The small cake on top should be finished off with a central ornament such as a small silver vase filled with sprays of orange blossom.

Centrepiece of a Valentine's Day party is this sponge sandwich, with lemon curd inside and a fluffy pink icing trimmed with a heart in button sweets

ICINGS AND FILLINGS

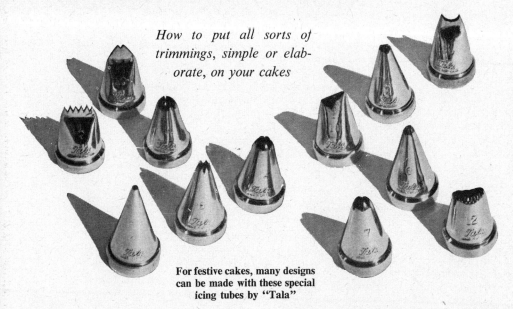

How to put all sorts of trimmings, simple or elaborate, on your cakes

For festive cakes, many designs can be made with these special icing tubes by "Tala"

ICING and decorating is the most fascinating part of cake-making, providing ample scope for originality in appearance and flavours.

Much practice is needed to become expert at icing, but some kinds are much easier than others. Butter icing is, perhaps, the easiest to begin on, as it is soft and does not set quickly. Glacé and meringue icing are also within the scope of the beginner.

Royal icing is in a class by itself, as it is used only for Christmas, wedding and such special occasion cakes. This will set into any shape and therefore lends itself to elaborate designs.

Almond Paste

10 *oz. sugar (half icing and half castor)*
1 *teaspoonful vanilla essence*
1 *teaspoonful rum (optional)*
8 *oz. ground almonds*
1 *teaspoonful sherry (optional)*
1 *teaspoonful lemon juice*
8 *drops of almond essence*
Egg to mix (about 1)

Sieve the two sugars well and mix with the almonds and flavourings and enough egg to bind thoroughly. Knead with the hands, adding the moisture very gradually, as the oil in the almonds comes out with working. Knead till it forms a dough. When rolling, sprinkle icing sugar on board.

Almond paste is used chiefly on rich fruit cakes and also for Simnel cakes.

Trim the cake neatly before putting on the almond paste and brush it lightly with a little warm apricot jam or Golden Syrup.

Make whatever quantity of almond paste you require. Roll it out to the required thickness and mark it in a circle the edge of the tin in which the cake was baked. Cut round this mark with a sharp knife and apply paste to the top of the cake, smoothing with a palette knife or ordinary knife dipped into hot water. Press it down well and roll it flat with the rolling pin.

If desired, the sides of the cake can also be coated with almond paste. Roll it out and cut it into strips of the depth of the cake and stick them to the sides of the cake with a little melted Golden Syrup. Flatten and smooth with a rolling pin or knife, particularly where the strips join.

If the cake is also to have a white icing, the almond paste must be really smooth and the cake a good shape. Leave for 2 or 3 days in a warm, dry place for the almond paste to dry out and harden.

When making a Simnel cake, which has no white icing on top, the almond paste should be scored with a fork to form a pattern, brushed with egg-yolk and lightly browned under the grill or in a quick oven.

American Frosting

8 oz. loaf or granulated sugar	A little lemon juice and vanilla
1 egg-white	A pinch of cream of tartar
1 gill water	

Dissolve the sugar in the water, without letting it boil, add the cream of tartar, then boil to 240° F., testing, if possible, with a sugar thermometer—or until it spins a thread when dropped from a spoon (about 10 minutes on a moderate flame).

Beat the egg-white until it is very stiff and pour the syrup slowly into it, whisking hard all the time. Add the flavouring and beat until the icing will pile up without spreading. Then spread quickly on the cake before it sets. When set, it should be crisp outside and soft inside. This is a delicious icing for fruit cakes, but it is rather tricky to make, so follow the instructions carefully.

Butter Icing (1)

6 oz. sieved icing sugar	4 oz. fresh butter

Beat the butter with a wooden spoon until it has the consistency of thick cream, then gradually mix in the sugar until thick and creamy.

For Chocolate Butter Icing.—Grate some unsweetened chocolate (about a tablespoonful) into a saucer and stand it in a warm place, but away from direct heat, until the chocolate is quite dissolved. Pour it into the butter icing and beat it in well.

For Coffee Butter Icing.—Add a tablespoonful of strong black coffee or, if liked, coffee essence to the butter icing and beat well.

For Orange or Lemon Butter Icing— Grate the rind of an orange or lemon and mix with the sieved sugar before adding it to the butter.

For Vanilla Butter Icing.—Flavour the butter icing with a little vanilla essence.

Butter icing must be really cold and hard when used and should be spread as smoothly as possible over the cake with a small palette knife.

If used for decorating purposes, put some into a forcing bag or syringe, using whichever icing head you like (a rose squeezer is always effective), and pipe little roses or a border or whatever you please, working quickly, as the warmth of the hand tends to soften the icing.

This icing is very rich and should therefore be used as a filling or topping for a *plain* cake.

Butter Icing (2)

2 oz. butter or margarine	1–2 teaspoonfuls milk A few drops of
3 oz. icing sugar	vanilla essence

Beat fat and sieved sugar together until white and creamy, add vanilla essence and beat in milk very gradually.

Chocolate Icing

2-oz. block of plain chocolate	2 tablespoonfuls milk and water
4 oz. icing sugar	Vanilla essence

Chop the chocolate coarsely and put it into a basin with the milk and water. Stand the basin in a saucepan of hot water, and when the chocolate has melted, stir in the well sieved icing sugar and vanilla essence, then beat thoroughly.

Glacé Icing

1 lb. icing sugar	3½ tablespoonfuls warm water

Sieve the sugar to eliminate all lumps. Put the warm water in a basin and add the icing sugar gradually, beating all the time with a wooden spoon. The basin should be placed over warm water, but the icing should not be allowed to get more than lukewarm or it may be lumpy and dull. When ready for use it should be of the consistency of thick sauce that will flow over and coat the back of the spoon.

This icing is inclined to be transparent, but a second coat can always be put on if necessary. If it is too soft, add a little more sugar.

Spread evenly over the cake with a small palette knife as soon as it is made. Add decorations while the icing is soft. The cake should then not be moved until the icing is quite set or it will crack.

For Chocolate Glacé Icing.—Warm the icing a little and add a few drops of vanilla essence and grated unsweetened chocolate until the icing is well flavoured and a good colour. If too thick, add a *very* little water.

For Coffee Glacé Icing.—Use strong black coffee instead of warm water when mixing the icing.

For Orange or Lemon Glacé Icing.— Make the icing with orange or lemon juice instead of water and colour it with a few

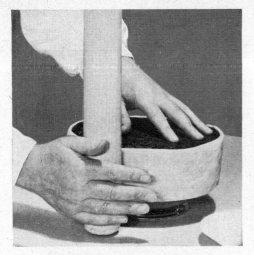

Applying Almond Icing to the side of the cake. Joins are neatened with a rolling pin

To flatten the top when putting on Royal Icing, hold a metal rule or palette knife straight, with both hands, and draw the edge of the blade right across

drops of orange or lemon vegetable colouring.

For Pineapple Glacé Icing.—Take a small can of crushed pineapple, strain off the juice and use it instead of water for making the icing. Use the pineapple pulp, mixed well with castor sugar, for pineapple filling.

For Raspberry or Strawberry Glacé Icing.—Strain off the syrup from a small can of fruit and use it instead of water for making the icing. Keep fruit for raspberry or strawberry filling.

Meringue Icing

Slightly beat an egg-white and gradually add to it sieved icing sugar. When fairly stiff, add a tablespoonful of water and put the basin over warm water. Beat the icing hard and add more icing sugar until it is of the same consistency as thick sauce. Continue beating for about 10 minutes, when it should be thick and creamy. Never let it get more than lukewarm.

This is the best icing for a slab cake which is to be cut up into small iced cakes because it sets slowly. It can be coloured or flavoured as desired.

Royal Icing

2 *egg-whites*   1 *teaspoonful lemon*
1 *lb. icing sugar*   *juice*

(These quantities will make sufficient icing to coat and decorate a moderate-sized

Smooth Royal Icing round the side of the cake with a damp palette knife. Stand the cake on a turntable, if possible

cake, up to about 8 in. in diameter and 3 in. deep. For larger cakes, increase the quantities in the proportions of 8 oz. icing sugar for each egg-white.)

Sieve the icing sugar at least three times and put two-thirds of it into a bowl, keeping the remainder to be added later. Whisk the egg-whites very lightly and add, a little at a time, to the sugar, beating hard with a wooden spoon. Add the lemon juice, a few drops at a time, and continue beating,

211

working in the remaining sugar by degrees. The icing should be beaten really hard for about 10 minutes, until it is so stiff that the wooden spoon will stand up in it without falling.

Royal icing sets harder and keeps better than any other and is therefore used for large, rich, fruit cakes for special occasions such as Christmas, birthdays, christenings and weddings.

Always keep the basin of royal icing covered with a damp cloth and in a cool place.

How to Use Royal Icing

(1) *Coating.*—Beat up the quantity of royal icing required and make sure the cake is smooth and even on top. Place the cake, preferably covered with almond paste, on an upturned plate or inverted cake tin and spread the icing evenly all over the cake. Smooth it over the top and round and round the sides until it is quite even. A good way to get it smooth is to dip a palette knife in hot water, shake off the drops and give a last sweep all over the icing with the hot wet knife. A turning board can be used to stand the cake on if available.

Now leave the cake all night or until the icing is absolutely set and hard. (This takes longer in wet weather.) Before the icing hardens, trim it round the bottom with a knife. It is a good plan to put the cake on a silver board, as it looks nice and is much easier to handle. For a wedding cake, two coats are usually put on in this way and each coat *must* dry thoroughly before the next one is put on.

(2) *Decorating.*—Beat up some royal icing as stiffly as possible. Choose the icing head you wish to use. (A rose squeezer is very popular and is most effective. A shell squeezer is also attractive and not difficult to use.) Put it in the end of an icing syringe or forcing bag and fill up the bag or syringe with icing.

Now squeeze any patterns you choose all over the cake in any design you fancy. It is best for a beginner to practise on the back of a plate until even patterns can be produced.

If desired, the icing can be coloured. Pink piping on a white-coated cake is very effective. By using a head with a small plain hole at the end, any wording can be written on the top of the cake.

The pipings must be ornamented before they set. Silver balls are always an attractive addition.

If the cake is on a silver board, squeeze a pattern of icing all round the bottom of the cake where it joins the board, to finish it off.

For a simpler form of trimming, use coloured edible cake decorations, glacé cherries, angelica, crystallised fruits, coloured fondants, crystallised rose or violet petals, nuts, coloured coffee sugar, real or artificial flowers.

FILLINGS

The simplest sponge or other plain cake can be raised to the party class with the addition of a good filling. The butter icing recipes given under Icings can be used equally well as fillings, and here are some alternative suggestions.

Apple Filling

2 *good-sized eating apples*	1 *lemon*
	8 *oz. granulated sugar*
Sherry (optional)	

Wash, peel and core the apples and grate them into a saucepan, add the strained lemon juice and grated rind, and then the sugar. Bring slowly to the boil, stirring well, then cook gently for 5 minutes, stirring all the time. Add a very little sherry if liked. Leave the mixture to get cold, then spread it on one half of the cake and press the other half on top.

Banana Filling

2 *or 3 bananas*	2 *tablespoonfuls*
Cream	*apricot jam*

Put the bananas through a hair sieve and mix the apricot jam with the purée. Whip up a little cream and fold into the mixture. Spread on one half of the cake and put the other half on top, pressing together well.

Chocolate Filling

4 *oz. plain chocolate*	2 *oz. butter*
8 *oz. icing sugar*	2 *oz. carton of cream*

Melt the chocolate and the butter together in the top of a double boiler or in a basin over a saucepan of boiling water. Sift the icing sugar well, then stir it into the mixture, together with about half the cream. Leave over the hot water for 10 minutes, then beat in as much more cream as required to make it the right consistency.

Coffee Candy Filling

Make butter icing, using 3 oz. icing sugar and 2 oz. butter and flavour with coffee essence. Spread on half the cake, then sprinkle crushed sugar candy on top. Spread the other half of the cake very lightly with coffee icing and put the halves together, pressing well.

Confectioners' Cream

> ¼ teacupful cold milk
> 1 dessertspoonful cornflour
> 1 teaspoonful lemon juice
> 1 egg-yolk
> 3 oz. castor sugar

Make the cornflour into a

To ice a birthday cake, pipe decorative borders on with a star tube (above), then write the owner's name with a thread tube (left). Note the right way to hold the icing syringe

smooth paste with the milk and add the sugar. Put into a saucepan and stir over a gentle heat till it thickens. Allow to cool, then add the beaten yolk and, lastly, the strained lemon juice. Stir well and put aside to get quite cold. Then spread on one half of the cake and press the other half on top.

Prune and Almond Filling

> 8 oz. granulated sugar   ½ gill prune liquid
> 2–3 oz. chopped   2 egg-whites
>   almonds   1 tablespoonful sherry
>   4 oz. prunes

Wash the prunes and put to soak overnight in cold water, then cook in the same water until tender. Take ½ gill of the juice and put into a saucepan with the sugar, heating slowly while the sugar dissolves. Then boil to 245° F. (or until a drop or two tested in cold water forms a soft ball between the finger and thumb). Have ready the egg-whites beaten to a stiff froth and slowly add the boiling syrup to them, beating all the time. Lastly, add the stoned chopped prunes and the chopped almonds, together with the sherry. Spread on each half of the cake and press lightly together.

Raspberry Filling

Whip some cream and spread each half of the cake with it. Crush some fresh raspberries in a basin with a little castor sugar and spread over one half, put the other half on top and press gently together. This filling can also be made with frozen or, if necessary, canned strawberries. As a variation, raspberries may be substituted for the strawberries.

BISCUITS

So quick to make, and they go perfectly with coffee or tea at any time of the day

Afghans

8 oz. flour	1 tablespoonful cocoa
7 oz. butter	1 tablespoonful coco-
3 oz. sugar	nut
2 oz. cornflakes	

Cream butter and sugar thoroughly together. Add well-sifted flour, cocoa and coconut, then the cornflakes. Mix thoroughly, then put spoonfuls of the mixture on to a well-greased baking tray—at a good distance apart as they spread surprisingly—and bake in a moderate oven for 15–20 minutes. When cold, ice with chocolate icing (see Cake Icings chapter).

Almond Fingers

Short pastry	Macaroon paste
Raspberry jam	Chopped almonds

Roll the pastry out fairly thin and cut it into long rectangles. Spread each very thinly with raspberry jam, keeping it well away from the edge. Then put on a layer of macaroon paste and sprinkle with chopped almonds.

Bake on a baking sheet in a moderate oven until the pastry is cooked and the macaroon paste firm and set. Cool; then, with a sharp knife, cut into fingers.

Australian Shortbread

8 oz. rolled oats	2 oz. white sugar
4 oz. butter	A little salt

Cream the butter and sugar, and add the oats and salt. Put the mixture into a greased flat tin and flatten it down well. Bake in a moderate oven for 20 minutes. Stand until almost cold, and then cut into rather broad fingers.

Banana Oatmeal Biscuits

1½ cupfuls flour	3 oz. margarine
½ teaspoonful baking	1 cupful sugar
powder	1 egg
1 teaspoonful salt	1 cupful mashed ripe
¾ teaspoonful	bananas
cinnamon	1¼ cupfuls rolled oats
½ cupful chopped nuts	

Sift together the flour, baking powder, salt and cinnamon. Beat the margarine until creamy, add the sugar gradually and continue beating until the mixture is light and fluffy. Add the egg and beat well, then add bananas, rolled oats and nuts, and mix thoroughly. Add the flour mixture and blend well. Drop by teaspoonfuls on to a greased baking tray, keeping the spoonfuls about 1½ in. apart. Bake in a moderate oven for about 15 minutes. (These quantities make about 3½ dozen biscuits.)

Bourbon Biscuits

2 oz. plain flour	1 oz. cocoa
2 oz. margarine	1 egg
2 oz. sugar	A few drops of
2 oz. semolina	vanilla essence

For the filling

½ oz. margarine	1 heaped tablespoon-
1 teaspoonful cocoa	ful icing sugar

Cream the fat and sugar together and beat in the egg a little at a time. Sieve the flour and cocoa, and mix with the semolina. Lightly knead the dry ingredients into the creamed mixture, then add vanilla essence and a little water, if necessary, to make a firm dough. Roll out and with a knife cut into fingers (about 24). Prick, and sprinkle with granulated sugar before baking. Place on a greased tin and bake in a moderate oven for about 20 minutes until crisp. Turn on to a cake rack and leave until cold.

To make the filling.—Melt the margarine, and sieve the sugar and cocoa together. Mix the cocoa and sugar with the melted margarine a little at a time and use at once to sandwich the biscuits together.

Brandy Snaps (see also Scottish Cookery chapter)

2 oz. flour	2 oz. butter
2 oz. castor sugar	Pinch of ground
2 oz. Golden Syrup	ginger

Melt the butter in a saucepan, add the sugar, syrup, sieved flour and ginger, stirring well over the heat until smooth. Have ready a greased tin and put teaspoonfuls of the mixture on it, far apart. Bake in a moderate oven for 6–8 minutes until golden brown and lacey in appearance. Then take out quickly, leave for a minute to cool a little, take up each in turn on a palette knife and put round a greased rolling-pin for a few seconds until it starts to set, then

Bourbon Biscuits, one of the nicest of the chocolate varieties, are easily
made and sandwiched together with butter icing

A vegetable star pipe is used to give these Chocolate Cream Fingers this professional appearance

quickly take off and curl round the finger. Store in an airtight tin until needed, otherwise they will get very sticky. When quite cold, fill with whipped cream.

Butterscotch Cookies

12 oz. plain flour	8 oz. brown sugar
4 oz. margarine or fat	1 teaspoonful vanilla
½ teaspoonful salt	essence
1 egg	Chopped nuts
4 teaspoonfuls baking	(optional)
powder	

Beat the egg, then mix with it the sugar, vanilla and fat melted to an oily consistency. Mix thoroughly. Sift the dry ingredients together, stir into the sugar and egg mixture, and knead into a stiff, rather dry dough (no additional moisture must be used). Shape into a roll about 1½ in. in diameter. Leave for at least 1 hour, then cut into slices about ½ in. thick and bake on a greased tray in a moderate oven for about 20 minutes. Space well out on the baking tray, as they tend to spread.

Cheese Biscuits

3 oz. butter	Pinch of salt and
2 oz. grated cheese	pepper
About 4 oz. flour	

Cream the butter and cheese, add the salt, pepper and flour. Work in sufficient flour to make a firm dough. Then roll out on a floured board and cut into rounds. Prick before putting them in the oven. Bake on a baking sheet until pale brown (about 15 minutes).

Chocolate Biscuits

8 oz. flour	1½ dessertspoonfuls
4 oz. castor sugar	chocolate powder
4 oz. butter	1 small egg

Rub the butter into the flour, chocolate powder and sugar. Beat the egg, add to the mixture and knead it into a dough. Roll out on a board and cut into small rounds just under ¼ in. thick. Put the rounds on a baking sheet and bake in a moderate oven for about 20 minutes until quite firm.

When cold, put them together in pairs with vanilla butter icing and ice with chocolate glacé icing (see Cake Icings chapter).

Chocolate Cream Fingers

5 oz. flour	1 egg
3 oz. margarine	A few drops vanilla
3 oz. sugar	essence
1 oz. cocoa	Pinch of salt
Milk or water to mix	

Cream the fat and sugar until light and fluffy. Beat in the egg. Sieve dry ingredients into this and mix to a very stiff dropping consistency with liquid and vanilla essence. Using a vegetable star pipe in a forcing bag, pipe in lengths on to a greased baking sheet. Bake in a hot oven for 10–15 minutes. Leave to cool, then sandwich together with pink or white butter cream, dust with icing sugar or dip the ends in chocolate icing (see chapter on Icings).

Chocolate Drops

2 eggs	1 oz. cocoa
2 oz. castor sugar	A few drops vanilla
Pinch of salt	essence
2 oz. plain flour	1 teaspoonful milk

Heat the oven to moderate; grease and lightly flour a baking sheet. Whisk the eggs and sugar until thick and creamy; add milk and vanilla, then fold in the sieved dry ingredients. Drop in small teaspoonfuls well apart on to the tin. Bake until firm. Cool on a wire tray and, when cold, sandwich together in twos with whipped cream or butter cream (see Icings). Dust the tops with icing sugar and decorate as desired.

Chocolate Macaroons

4 oz. ground almonds	2½ oz. drinking
1 oz. margarine	chocolate
4 oz. castor sugar	2 egg-whites
Blanched almonds	

Grease a baking sheet or line with rice paper. Whip the egg-whites until stiff, then fold in the dry ingredients and melted margarine. Place in small heaps on baking sheet, putting a blanched almond on each. Bake in a slow to moderate oven until firm (about 20 minutes). (These quantities make about 10 macaroons.)

Chocolate Shortbread Biscuits

4 oz. flour	3 oz. sugar
4 oz. butter or mar-	1 oz. ground rice
garine	1 tablespoonful cocoa

Rub the fat into the flour and add dry ingredients. Knead all together to a smooth dough then roll into a round ½ in. thick. Crimp the edges with fingers and thumb. Place on a baking sheet, prick well and mark into nine triangular sections. Bake in a moderate oven until firm (about 1 hour).

Chocolate Whirls

4 oz. flour	1 egg-yolk
2 oz. margarine	Pinch of salt
2 oz. sugar	1 tablespoonful milk
1 dessertspoonful	to mix
cocoa	

Grease a baking sheet. Rub the margarine into the sieved flour and salt, then

Macaroons are not difficult to make. These are a change because they
are flavoured with chocolate

add the sugar. Divide the mixture in half, and to one half add the cocoa and sufficient beaten egg-yolk and milk to form a stiff dough. Roll out both pieces and place one on top of the other. Roll up as for Swiss roll, then cut into slices. Place slices on a greased tray and bake in a hot oven for 15 minutes.

Coconut Pyramids

8 oz. desiccated coco-	3 egg-whites
nut	4 oz. castor sugar

Mix the sugar and coconut together, then fold them into the stiffly beaten egg-whites until the mixture is dry and crumbly. Colour half the mixture pink. Using a fork, pile into pyramids on a greased tin and bake in a fairly slow oven until set (about 30–40 minutes).

Easter Biscuits

6 oz. flour	Pinch of mixed spice
3 oz. butter	½ oz. chopped peel
1½ oz. currants	3 oz. castor sugar
Half an egg	Small pinch of salt

Cream the butter and sugar, and add the beaten egg; then add the other ingredients and knead into a dough. Put on a floured board and roll out to about ¼ in. thick. Cut into rounds with a crinkly cutter and put on a baking sheet. Brush with egg-white, dredge with sugar and bake in a moderate oven until pale brown (about 15 minutes).

Fancy Biscuits

8 oz. flour	4 oz. butter
4 oz. sugar	Half an egg

Rub the butter into the flour and sugar, and add the beaten egg. Knead the mixture into a firm dough, roll it on a floured board and cut into small rounds just under ¼ in. thick. Put on a baking sheet and bake in a moderate oven for about 20 minutes until quite firm. When cold, put together in pairs with lemon curd or raspberry jam and ice the tops with pink or yellow glacé icing or meringue icing (see Icings chapter).

Ginger Biscuits

8 oz. flour	1 dessertspoonful
3 oz. butter	ground ginger
4 oz. castor sugar	1 dessertspoonful
Small pinch of soda	black treacle
	Half an egg

Beat the butter and sugar to a cream and add the beaten egg. Next, add the dry ingredients, adding the treacle half-way.

Knead the mixture into a dough, roll out as thinly as possible on a floured board and cut into rounds with a plain large cutter. Bake in a moderate oven until brown and set (about 10 minutes).

Golliwogs (Shrewsbury biscuit mixture)

2 oz. fat	4 oz. plain flour
2 oz. sugar	Egg-yolk to mix
	Vanilla essence

Cream fat and sugar, and beat in egg. Add vanilla essence and gradually fold in the flour. Knead lightly to a stiff consistency, roll thinly on a floured board and cut out rounds with a 3-in. plain cutter. On half the circles, cut out "faces." Bake in a moderate oven for 7–10 minutes until firm and pale yellow, but *not* brown.

Make white glacé icing, take out 1 teaspoonful (to be used for the eyes), take out another teaspoonful and colour pink (to be used for mouths), and to the remainder add cocoa and a little water to make a coating consistency. Cover the top biscuits with the chocolate-coloured icing, and sandwich to plain biscuits with butter cream or apricot jam. Fill in the eyes with white icing and the mouths with pink, and add tiny dollops of chocolate to the eyes. (For icings see Icings chapter.)

Hungarian Chocolate Biscuits

4 oz. margarine	4 oz. self-raising flour
2 oz. castor sugar	1 oz. cocoa
½ teaspoonful vanilla essence	Pinch of salt

For the filling
Chocolate butter cream, rum flavoured
(see Icings)

Cream the margarine, sugar and vanilla essence. Sieve the flour, cocoa and salt into the mixture, then roll into balls the size of a walnut and place on a greased baking sheet. Flatten with a fork dipped in water and bake in a moderate oven for 12 minutes. Cool, sandwich together in pairs with the filling and dust tops with icing sugar.

Macaroons

2 oz. ground almonds	1½ egg-whites (not whipped)
½ oz. ground rice	
4 oz. castor sugar	Rice paper
Almonds for tops	Almond essence, if liked

Line a tin with rice paper. Mix all the ingredients together, put the mixture in a

Golliwog faces are fun for a children's party. The foundation is a Shrewsbury Biscuit mixture

These fancy biscuit cutters from the Bex range of kitchen equipment are in gay colours and cannot rust. With a set of six different shapes you can make most attractive biscuits

forcing bag and squeeze out on to the rice paper in small heaps far apart. Put an almond on the top of each and bake in a moderate oven for 20 minutes.

Nut Biscuits

8 oz. flour
4 oz. castor sugar
4 oz. butter
Half an egg
Small pinch of salt
2 oz. chopped hazel-nuts or walnuts

Rub the butter into the flour, add the rest of the dry ingredients and then the beaten egg. Knead the mixture into a firm dough and roll it out on a floured board until it is about ¼ in. thick. Cut into rounds with a crinkly cutter. Put on a baking sheet and bake in a moderate oven until pale brown (about 15 minutes).

Oatcakes (see also Scottish Cookery)

4 oz. fine oatmeal
4 oz. coarse oatmeal
8 oz. white flour
2½ oz. lard
1 teaspoonful salt
Pinch of bicarbonate of soda
Hot water

Rub the lard into the flour and oatmeals. Add the soda and salt, and mix to a dough with hot water. Roll out very thin, cut into triangles and bake on a floured baking sheet in a moderate oven for about 20

minutes, turning them over half-way through.

Oatmeal Biscuits

4 oz. flour
2 oz. butter
1 egg
2 oz. fine oatmeal
1 oz. castor sugar

Mix the dry ingredients. Add the melted butter and the beaten egg with a little milk if the mixture is too dry. Roll out and cut into rounds, and bake on a floured baking sheet in a moderate oven until pale brown (about 15 minutes).

Orange and Chocolate Biscuits

4 oz. margarine
4 oz. castor sugar
6 oz. flour
1 oz. drinking chocolate
1 oz. rice flour
1 egg
1 teaspoonful grated orange rind
Pinch of salt
Pinch of cinnamon

Cream margarine and sugar, beat in egg gradually. Stir in flour and salt. Divide into two portions. Into one, stir rice flour and orange rind, and into the other, drinking chocolate and a pinch of cinnamon. Roll out each piece of dough ⅛ in. thick on a floured board. Cut into shapes and place on a greased baking sheet. Bake in a moderately hot oven for about 12 minutes. When cold, sandwich together with orange butter cream (see Icings chapter) or orange curd.

Parkin Biscuits

4 oz. flour	1 teaspoonful ground
4 oz. oatmeal	ginger
1 oz. butter	½ teaspoonful
4 oz. black treacle	bicarbonate of soda

Mix all the dry ingredients in a basin, melt the butter and treacle together, and stir in. Knead the mixture well, put on a floured board and roll out. Cut into rounds with a crinkly cutter. Bake on a baking sheet in a fairly slow oven until firm and set (about 20 minutes).

Shortbread Biscuits (see also Scottish Cookery)

8 oz. flour	6 oz. butter
4 oz. sugar	2 oz. ground rice

Beat the butter and sugar to a cream, add the flour and ground rice. Knead into a firm dough, roll on a floured board and cut into shapes with fancy cutters. Prick with a fork. Bake in a moderate oven for about 20 minutes, then take out and sprinkle with castor sugar.

Shrewsbury Biscuits

3 oz. butter	1 egg
3 oz. castor sugar	6 oz. flour
1 lemon	

Cream the butter and sugar, and add the beaten egg. Then add the flour, the grated lemon rind and 6 drops of the juice. Knead the mixture well and roll out thinly. Cut into rounds and bake for 10 minutes until they are a pale lemon colour.

Spice Biscuits (1)

3 oz. butter	1 tablespoonful
2 oz. sugar	treacle
6 oz. flour	1 teaspoonful ground
1 teaspoonful	ginger
cinnamon	½ teaspoonful
1 tablespoonful syrup	bicarbonate of soda

Beat the sugar and butter to a cream, warm the treacle and syrup, and mix together. Then add the flour, ginger, cinnamon and soda, and knead into a dough. Roll out on a well-floured board and cut into rounds. Bake in a fairly slow oven until firm and set (about 20 minutes).

Spice Biscuits (2)

2 oz. fat	2 oz. margarine
1 dessertspoonful	2 teaspoonfuls mixed
Golden Syrup	spice
2 oz. sugar	6 oz. flour

Bring fats and syrup to boiling point in a saucepan. Mix the dry ingredients together, pour in the hot fat and syrup, and mix well. Take a teaspoonful at a time and put well apart on to a greased baking sheet, flattening at the top with a fork. Bake in a moderate oven until nicely brown (about 20 minutes).

Biscuit photographs in this chapter by Cadbury Bros.

Orange and Chocolate Biscuits cut into fancy shapes and sandwiched together with orange butter cream or orange curd

HOME-MADE SWEETS

Let the children help to make— as well as eat—these wholesome luxuries

For Nut Fondants, just dip the shelled nuts in fondant mixture (above), put them on a slab, decorate the tops (left) and leave to set

SWEET-MAKING is an attractive hobby, and home-made sweets, if well made, are far nicer and more original than bought ones. If going in for sweet-making at all seriously, it is as well to buy the proper equipment: a sweet thermometer, a set of steel bars and a marble slab. These are particularly useful for toffee, fudge and caramel. The thermometer can be put into the mixture while it is boiling. Fudge should boil to 240° F., caramel to 255° F. and toffee to 300° F.

The steel bars are for setting the candy. They should be arranged on the slab to enclose a square or an oblong of the size required. The inner side of the bars and the enclosed part of the slab should be well greased with olive oil; a pastry brush is best for the purpose. When ready, the hot candy should be poured between the bars. When cool, the bars can be removed and the candy cut up.

If, however, sweets are only to be made occasionally, the following test can be used. Drop a little of the candy into some cold water and then roll it between the fingers; fudge will form a soft ball when done, caramel a hard ball and toffee will crack when tested. Instead of steel bars, well-oiled tins or dishes can be used.

Everything used for sweet-making must be scrupulously clean, and it is a good plan to keep a special aluminium saucepan for the purpose. Enamel should not be used as it is inclined to chip. An upturned enamel tray or an enamel slab can be used instead of the marble slab.

Boiling sweets should be stirred occasionally to prevent them sticking to the bottom of the pan and burning, but the stirring must be as gentle as possible or the mixture will go sugary. If a thermometer is used, the mixture can be stirred by gently dragging it across the bottom of the pan.

In the following pages you will find recipes for different kinds of sweets. After having practised on these, you can try to invent original ones of your own.

Caramel

1 lb. castor sugar	4 tablespoonfuls
½ pint cream	glucose
½ pint milk	4 oz. unsweetened
2 oz. butter	cooking chocolate

Grate the chocolate. Put the butter, sugar, cream, milk and glucose into a pan,

221

After cooling, fondants can de dipped in melted coating chocolate to make chocolate creams

heat and stir them until the sugar is dissolved, then simmer gently for 10 minutes. Add the grated chocolate and boil quite hard, stirring gently all the time, until the temperature is 255° F. (or until the caramel will form a hard ball when tested in cold water). Take off the fire and, when the bubbles have settled, pour at once into an oiled tin (or on to an oiled slab between bars). As soon as it is cold, cut into neat squares with a sharp knife.

Chocolate Coconut Truffles

4 tablespoonfuls castor sugar	2 tablespoonfuls milk
1 tablespoonful cocoa or drinking chocolate	5 oz. coconut
	2 oz. margarine
	Vanilla or coffee essence

Put the sugar, milk and margarine in a pan and dissolve over a gentle heat. Remove from heat, add cocoa, essence and coconut, and mix well. Form into balls and roll in dry coconut. Leave to harden. (These quantities make 12 truffles.)

Chocolate Drops

4 oz. plain chocolate	6 oz. dates
2 oz. raisins	¼ teaspoonful cinnamon
A few drops of lemon juice	

Flake the chocolate and melt it over hot water. Add fruit (stoned and chopped fine), cinnamon and lemon juice. Remove from heat and beat with a wooden spoon until it thickens. Take out in spoonfuls, roll in balls in a mixture of grated chocolate and castor sugar.

Chocolate Krispies

7 tablespoonfuls Rice Krispies	1 oz. vegetable fat shortening
1 tablespoonful syrup	1 heaped tablespoonful drinking chocolate

Melt fat and syrup slowly in a saucepan, add chocolate and heat thoroughly. Remove from heat and, using a metal spoon, fold in Rice Krispies, making sure that they are well coated. Place in small spoonfuls on a lightly greased baking sheet and leave until cold.

Chocolate Krackolates

7 tablespoonfuls Corn Flakes	1 level tablespoonful cocoa
1 tablespoonful icing or castor sugar	1 tablespoonful syrup
1 oz. vegetable fat shortening	2 tablespoonfuls coconut or 1 tablespoonful grated orange peel

Melt fat and syrup slowly in a saucepan, but do not boil. Add cocoa, remove from heat and stir in sugar. With a metal spoon, quickly fold in the Corn Flakes and coconut (or orange peel), until well coated. Place in small spoonfuls on a lightly greased baking sheet and leave to cool.

Coconut Ice

1 lb. granulated sugar	½ gill cold water and milk mixed
6 oz. desiccated coconut	Cochineal

Using a large pan, dissolve the sugar in the milk and water, then boil fast to 240° F. (or until the mixture will form a soft ball when tested in cold water). Take if off the fire, add the coconut and stir until the mixture thickens.

Pour half into an oiled tin (or on to an oiled slab between bars). Colour the remainder pink and pour it on top of the white ice. When cool, cut into fingers.

NOTE: For Chocolate Coconut Ice add 1 dessertspoonful cocoa and a little vanilla essence instead of pink colouring.

Coconut Ice always comes in two colours—chocolate and vanilla here make a change from the usual pink and white

Porcupines are baked sweetmeats containing dates, nuts and coconut and are substantial enough to appear on the tea table

Date Truffles

1 box of dates	4 oz. plain chocolate
Marzipan (see	Chocolate vermicelli
opposite page)	

Remove stones from dates and replace with rolls of marzipan. Dip dates in melted chocolate, then roll in chocolate vermicelli and place in paper sweet cases.

Fondants

2 lb. sugar	1 dessertspoonful
¼ pint water	glucose

Soak sugar and water for 1 hour and bring gently to the boil, adding glucose and boil to 237° F., then leave until bubbles disappear. Pour on to a damped slab to cool; work with spatula until smooth, then put into a pan with a little water and flavouring and warm gently, without boiling, until liquid. Pour into a cool tin or, preferably, into dry, ribbed moulds and leave to set. Or dip shelled hazel nuts in the liquid mixture and leave to set.

Fudge (Chocolate)

1 gill milk	1 lb. granulated sugar
1 gill cream	2 oz. grated, un-
2 oz. butter	sweetened chocolate

Put the milk, cream, butter and sugar into a pan and bring to the boil. Add the chocolate and boil for 15–20 minutes until it is 240° F. (or will form a soft ball when tested in cold water). Stir gently at intervals to prevent burning.

Take off the fire and let the bubbles settle. Beat against the sides with a spatula until the mixture granulates. Then pour it quickly into an oiled tin (or on to an oiled slab between bars). When cold, cut into squares.

Fudge (Coffee)

1 lb. granulated sugar	1 dessertspoonful
1 gill milk	coffee essence or
1½ oz. butter	strong black coffee

Make in exactly the same way as chocolate fudge, adding the coffee flavouring after taking the mixture off the fire and before beating it. It will need rather more beating than chocolate fudge to make it granulate, owing to the extra liquid.

Fudge (Walnut)

2 lb. granulated sugar	2 oz. butter
3 oz. grated, unsweet-	½ pint chopped
ened chocolate	walnuts
Pinch of cream of	1 teaspoonful vanilla
tartar	essence
½ pint milk	

Make in exactly the same way as chocolate fudge, adding the walnuts, cream of tartar and vanilla after taking the mixture off the fire and before beating it.

Glacé Fruits

For the syrup

½ lb. granulated	¼ level teaspoonful
sugar	cream of tartar
¼ pint water	

Stir sugar and water together until sugar is dissolved. Add cream of tartar. Boil to 290° F. (or until it cracks when tested in cold water). Dip each separate fruit—or, in the case of grapes, small bunch—into the hot syrup so that it is completely coated. Place on an oiled slab and leave until dry and quite cold. If the syrup begins to set hard, it can be brought back to the right consistency if stood over hot water.

Suitable fruits are cherries, figs, segments or peel of grapefruit, lemons and oranges, prunes. They should be firm and not too ripe, and must first have stalks and stones removed.

Lemon Creams

1 egg-white	Icing sugar
1 lemon	Yellow vegetable
A little crystallised	colouring
lemon peel	

Sieve plenty of icing sugar on to a piece of paper. Slightly beat the egg-white in a basin and gradually stir in the icing sugar. When thick and creamy, add the lemon juice and grated lemon rind and continue stirring in icing sugar until the mixture forms a dough. (Just before this, add the colouring until the mixture is pale lemon colour.) Roll out the dough on a sugared board and cut into rounds with a small cutter. Line a rack with greaseproof paper, scatter some sieved icing sugar on it and put the creams on the rack. Press down a small square of crystallised lemon peel on the top of each and leave them to set.

Marrons Glacés

2 lb. chestnuts

For the syrup

½ pint water	3 tablespoonfuls
1 lb. sugar	vanilla essence

Make slits in the chestnuts with a sharp knife and plunge them into boiling water and boil for 10 minutes. Cool and peel,

LIGHT AND COLOUR ON THE DINNER TABLE

LIGHT and colour are important and closely related factors in the artistic preparation and serving of food. A soft mellow light from two candles on the table, augmented by more candles or shaded wall lamps in the room, creates a leisured atmosphere of gracious living. This soft lighting combines with a beautiful traditional table setting to suggest an intimate dinner-party for four. Some people, however, insist on being able to "see what they are eating." The clear bright light from a hanging chandelier or from lightly shaded wall lamps shows up to full advantage a strongly contrasted colour scheme, like the modern table setting photographed below. Here the keynote is freshness, and clear bright colours invite one to linger and enjoy the meal to come.

Above: a fine Irish linen damask cloth in the chrysanthemum design by York Street, which has been popular for over a hundred years, makes a lovely setting for fine china, gleaming silver, good food and wine

It's a modern idea to mix and match your table linen. Left: table cloth and napkins are Hunter Green Irish linen scalloped in white, the placemats in terra-cotta edged with white, from Waring & Gillow. Try vivid colours with white, dove grey, pale blue or primrose yellow

Sweets you can make even when you're short of sugar! Chocolate Krispies are sweetened with syrup

being careful to remove the inside skin as well. Boil sugar, vanilla and water until it is white and roughens round the edge of the pan. Put the chestnuts in the syrup and simmer very gently for about 15 minutes, not letting it boil. Leave the chestnuts to soak in the syrup for 24 hours, then take them out and drain. Add more sugar to syrup and boil until really thick. Return chestnuts to hot syrup, simmer for 5 minutes at most and leave to cool. Take chestnuts out of syrup and stand to dry on a cake tray.

Marzipan

1 lb. loaf sugar	12 oz. ground
1 gill water	almonds
3 oz. icing sugar	2 egg-whites

Dissolve the loaf sugar in the water and boil to 240° F. (or until it forms a soft ball when tested in cold water). Draw the pan aside and, when slightly cooled, add the ground almonds and egg-whites. Stir by the side of the fire for a few minutes. Then turn on to a sugared slab and add the icing sugar, working it in with a spatula until the mixture is cool enough to handle. Knead until quite smooth. When cold, wrap up the marzipan in greaseproof paper and store in a tin until required.

Marzipan (Uncooked)

½ lb. ground almonds	¼ lb. castor sugar
¼ lb. icing sugar	Almond essence
2 egg-whites	

Mix the almonds with the carefully crushed and sifted icing sugar and the castor sugar. Add essence and the well-beaten egg-whites, a little at a time, using as much as is needed to make a firm dough. Use in the same way as cooked marzipan.

Marzipan Potatoes and Fruits

Model some marzipan into shapes like new potatoes. Prick them with a skewer to resemble eyes and roll them in fine chocolate powder.

NOTE: Marzipan can be coloured as desired by dabbing it with vegetable colouring or essence, and kneading it on a board sprinkled with icing sugar. (Little oranges, apples and lemons can be made in this way.)

Marzipan Stuffed Fruits

Glacé cherries, cut in half, may be filled with uncoloured, stoned prunes and dates with coloured marzipan.

Mint Cake

1 lb. granulated sugar	2 teaspoonfuls
1 gill milk	peppermint essence
	(or a few drops oil
	of peppermint)

Boil the sugar and milk to 240° F. (or until a soft ball is formed when tested in cold water). Take off the fire and add the peppermint. Beat hard until the mixture thickens. Pour into an oiled tin (or on to an oiled slab between bars). When cold, cut into squares with a sharp knife. For brown mint cake, use Demerara sugar.

Neapolitan Bars

Using half the quantity of marzipan made above, divide into three, colouring one green and one pink with vegetable colourings. Roll out into three strips. On the pink one spread some chocolate filling; put the plain marzipan on top; spread some vanilla filling on that and finish with green marzipan. Cut into slabs and leave to cool. (For chocolate and vanilla fillings, see chapter on Icings.)

Nougat

9 oz. granulated sugar	1 egg-white
1½ oz. glucose	1 oz. chopped walnuts
½ gill water	1 oz. chopped glacé
½ teaspoonful vanilla	cherries
essence	1 oz. chopped
½ teaspoonful brandy	blanched almonds
or rum	½ teaspoonful lemon
½ oz. angelica (cut up	juice
small)	Rice paper

Line a tin, or bars and slab, with rice paper. Dissolve the sugar and glucose in the water in a pan and boil to 240° F. (or until the mixture forms a soft ball when tested in cold water). Meantime, beat the egg-white very stiff in a basin. Pour half the syrup gradually on to it, whisking all the time.

Boil the rest of the syrup to 270° F. (or to a very hard ball) and then add to it the beaten mixture and all the other ingredients. Stir for a few minutes until the mixture is firm and white, and then put it in the prepared tin. Put a piece of rice paper on the top and press down until it sticks to the nougat. When cold, cut into bars.

Peppermint Creams

2 egg-whites	Oil of peppermint
1 teaspoonful water	(or peppermint
Icing sugar	essence)

Sieve plenty of icing sugar. Slightly beat the egg-whites and gradually add the icing sugar, beating hard. When fairly thick, add the water and a few drops of oil of peppermint (or 2 teaspoonfuls of essence). Continue adding sugar until the mixture will knead on a sugared board. Roll out and cut into rounds. Place on sugared paper to set.

Porcupines

6 oz. chopped dates	1 oz. margarine
3 oz. chopped nuts	1½ oz. cocoa
2 oz. sugar	Egg
Desiccated coconut	

Cream margarine and sugar. Stir in dry ingredients and bind with egg. Roll into balls the size of a walnut. Coat with coconut. Bake in a slow oven for 10 minutes.

Toffee (Plain)

1 lb. granulated sugar	1 large dessertspoon-
4 oz. butter	ful glucose
1 gill water	

Put the sugar, water and glucose into a pan and heat until completely dissolved. Boil for about 10 minutes. Add the butter and boil to 300° F. (or until it will crack when tested in cold water). Let the bubbles settle. Then pour out at once into an oiled tin (or on to an oiled slab between bars). When cold, cut into squares.

Treacle Toffee

12 oz. Demerara	Pinch of cream of
sugar	tartar
4 oz. butter	8 oz. black treacle
¼ gill water	

Dissolve the sugar, butter and treacle in the water and bring to the boil. Add the cream of tartar and boil to 260° F. (or until a hard ball is formed when tested in cold water). Pour into an oiled tin (or on to an oiled slab between bars) and cut up as soon as it is cool. Put into an airtight tin.

Turkish Delight

1 lb. loaf sugar	1 oz. gelatine
Icing sugar	2 oz. almonds
1½ gills water	

Put the gelatine to soak in ½ gill cold water. Blanch the almonds and chop them rather coarsely. Dissolve the sugar in 1 gill water and then boil to 240° F. (or until it will make a soft ball when tested in cold water). Meanwhile, bring the gelatine to the boil, add it to the mixture with the nuts and pour into an oiled tin. When cold, cut into squares and roll in icing sugar.

Date Truffles are stuffed with marzipan and coated with chocolate—a delicious mixture of flavours

BREAD, BUNS AND SCONES

*Even the staff of life is not too hard to make at home
—and scones are really quick bakes*

BREAD making at home is thought by some to take more time than a modern housewife has to spare, while kneading is believed to be unduly hard work. But it is, in fact, no more tiring than beating a batch of cakes, and while the dough is rising one can get on with other work. It is necessary to bake only once a week, as home-made bread keeps well for a week.

YEAST RECIPES

Compressed yeast can be bought from bakers and should be ordered as required. If kept moist and at blood heat, its cells multiply and let off gases which give bread its light, porous consistency. Too much heat kills the yeast, while too little prevents its action. It should be kept in a cool place until wanted, then creamed with a little sugar, to start it working, before the warmed liquid is added to it.

The basins used for mixing bread, the flour and the milk or water should always be warmed to blood heat. While the dough is rising, it should be covered with a cloth and put in a warm place (but away from direct heat), either in front of or over the oven. It should be left until it has risen to twice its original size.

The kneading is extremely important, as it distributes the yeast and its gases evenly through the bread.

Bread (White)

3½ lb. flour
2 teaspoonfuls salt
1 tablespoonful sugar
1 oz. yeast
3 oz. lard
1½ pints milk and water (half and half)

Rub the lard into the sifted flour. Cream the yeast with the sugar and add to it the milk and water heated to blood heat. Make a hole in the centre of the warmed flour and pour in the milk and yeast. Scatter a little flour over the top and sprinkle the salt round the edge away from the yeast and milk. Stand to rise in a warm place for 20 minutes. Mix the flour by hand to a dough till there is no dry flour left. Clean the hand with flour and knead for 5 minutes. Stand to rise in a warm place, covered with a cloth, for 1½–2 hours, when the dough should have doubled itself. Knead for 15 minutes. Then form into loaves and put in warm well-greased bread tins, or make into desired shape and put on a warm baking tin. (For a Coburg loaf mark the top with a cross just before baking.) Put in a warm place for 10 minutes. Bake in a hot oven for 30 minutes and reduce the heat gradually until done. Bread is ready when it feels firm and sounds hollow if tapped.

Bread (Brown)

This can be made in exactly the same way, using wholemeal instead of white flour.

Fruit Bread

To each 1 lb. of dough made as above, knead in 1 oz. sugar and 2 oz. currants. Put into greased tins and leave in a warm place until doubled in size. Then bake at

Doughnuts—either the ring or the round variety—are fried in deep fat, then well drained before rolling in sugar

400° F. for 10 minutes, reducing to 300° F. for 35–40 minutes.

Bread Rolls

1¼ lb. flour	1 oz. sugar
1 oz. yeast	1 teaspoonful salt
½ pint milk	3 oz. fat

Warm the milk, and melt the fat in it, then add sugar and salt, and leave to cool. When lukewarm, stir in the yeast and flour, mix well, turn into greased pan and leave to double itself. Knead, leave to rise, form into shapes required (round balls, knots, twists or crescents) and bake on a floured baking sheet at 425° F. for 15–20 minutes.

Bridge Rolls

1 lb. flour	½ pint water
2 oz. lard	1 egg
½ oz. yeast	Salt
1 teaspoonful sugar	

Rub the fat into the flour and make a well in the middle. Cream the yeast with the sugar and pour lukewarm water over it. Then add the mixture to the flour. Set to rise for 30 minutes in a warm place. Then add the egg and a little salt, and mix well. Stand to rise again for 1½ hours. Put on a saucepan of water to boil. Knead the dough and cut it in half. Cut up and form into oval rolls. Put them on a baking

sheet and stand over the steam from the boiling water for ½ hour. Bake in a very hot oven for 10–15 minutes.

NOTE: Be careful of draughts while the rolls are rising.

Doughnuts

1 lb. flour	½ pint milk
2 oz. butter	2 eggs
½ oz. yeast	Jam
½ teaspoonful salt	½ teaspoonful sugar

Rub the butter into the flour, add the salt, then warm. Cream the yeast with the sugar. Make a hole in the centre of the flour, pour in the warm milk and well beaten eggs. Then add the yeast. Mix to a light dough and leave to rise in a warm place for 1 hour. Roll out on a floured board and cut into rounds ¼ in. thick. Put a little jam on alternate rounds. Moisten the edges, cover with another round and press the edges together. Put in tart tins in a warm place for 20–30 minutes Fry in deep fat, drain well and roll in castor sugar.

Lardy Cake (Buckinghamshire recipe)

1 lb. dough (which has just finished rising)	3 oz. currants
	Pinch of spice
	3 oz. sugar
6 oz. lard	

Knead the dough and flatten it out with a rolling pin. Then spread it with lard, sprinkle the currants and sugar over it, and a pinch of spice. Roll the dough up, flatten it out again and slash it on the top with a knife. Put in a greased tin and let it stand in a warm place for 10 minutes. Then bake in a fairly quick oven for about 45 minutes, lowering the heat well towards the end.

NOTE: Lardy Cake should be eaten the day it is made.

Spiced Loaf

1 lb. flour	A little chopped peel, if liked
3 oz. lard	
3 oz. sugar	½ teaspoonful mixed spice
½ oz. yeast	
6 oz. sultanas	Not quite ½ pint milk

Dissolve the fat in the milk and heat to blood heat. Cream the yeast with a little sugar and add it to the milk. Pour this mixture into the warmed flour, sugar, sultanas, chopped peel and spice, and mix well. It should be a very soft dough. Set it in a warm place for 1½ hours, then knead well, keeping the hands dry with a little flour. Put into a bread tin and set it in a warm place again until it is well risen

What could possibly be more appetising than a batch of freshly baked loaves of all shapes and sizes, served with lots of fresh butter? These were specially baked and photographed in the Creda kitchens

Bake in a moderate oven for 40 minutes. Mix together a dessertspoonful of milk and a teaspoonful of castor sugar, take out the loaf, brush it over with this mixture and put it back in the oven for a few minutes.

Tea Cakes

8 oz. flour	½ oz. yeast
½ teaspoonful salt	About a gill of milk
1 teaspoonful sugar	or milk and water
1 oz. lard or butter	

Rub the lard into the sifted flour and warm slightly. Then add the sugar. Cream the yeast with a little extra sugar and pour some of the warm milk into it. Then pour this mixture into the centre of the flour. Add the salt round the edge away from the yeast. Scatter flour over the yeast lightly. Let it stand in a warm place for 10 minutes. Add the rest of the milk and mix to a light dough and knead well. Put in a warm place to rise, covering the bowl over with a cloth. Leave until risen to double its size. Knead again, divide into three, roll and shape into round tea cakes. Prick each one with a fork. Put them on a warmed, greased tin, covered with a cloth, and stand in a warm place to rise, for 10 minutes. Then bake in a quick oven for about 12 minutes. Brush with butter and put back in the oven for 1 minute.

NOTE: To test if they are done, tap them. If cooked, this should make a hollow sound.

Tea Cakes (with Currants)

Make in the same way as tea cakes (above). When the dough has risen to double its size, knead in 1 oz. currants and ½ oz. sugar and work in well. Allow to rise again. Then cut into three and roll into rounds. Stand the rounds on a warm tin, covered with a cloth, to rise (about 20 minutes). Then bake in a quick oven for about 12 minutes. Brush with butter and put back in the oven for 1 minute.

Currant Buns or Bun Men

½ lb. flour	2 oz. margarine
Pinch of salt	1 egg
½ oz. yeast	⅛ pint tepid water
1 oz. sugar	2 oz. currants
½ teaspoonful mixed spice	

Rub fat into well sifted flour and salt. Make a well in the centre and stir in the egg. Add the yeast and sugar mixed together with the water. Knead well and leave to rise till it has doubled in quantity. Then knead the currants and spice very lightly into the dough on a floured board. Shape into eight round balls or bun men, put on to a greased baking tray, allow to prove for about 10 minutes, then bake in a hot oven for 5 minutes, reducing temperature to moderate for another 5 minutes.

While the buns are baking, put a tablespoonful of sugar into a little water, add ½ pint milk, boil hard for 2 or 3 minutes, then cool. While the buns are still hot, paint them lightly with this glaze.

SODA BREAD

Soda bread makes a change from yeast bread and is very quick to make as it can be baked at once. Soda scones should be eaten fresh, but if any are left over, they can be toasted and served hot the next day.

Soda Bread (Brown) (1)

8 oz. flour	About ½ pint sour milk or buttermilk
8 oz. wholemeal flour	
1 teaspoonful salt	1 level teaspoonful bicarbonate of soda
2 teaspoonfuls sugar	

Sieve all the dry ingredients together and mix with milk or buttermilk. Knead to a dough, then roll out and cut into two large loaves or four smaller ones. Put on a floured baking sheet and bake in a very hot oven for about 20 minutes.

Soda Bread (Brown) (2)

Use the same quantities as for Soda Bread (Brown) (1). Rub 3 oz. butter, lard or dripping into the flour, then sieve in the other dry ingredients and mix with buttermilk or milk. Instead of rolling out the dough, make it moister by adding a little more sour milk or buttermilk, put in a greased cake or bread tin and bake in a very hot oven.

Soda Bread (White)

Make in the same way as Brown Soda Bread (1) or (2) above, but use all white flour.

Steamed Bread

1 lb. wholemeal flour	1 dessertspoonful cream of tartar
1 tablespoonful brown sugar	1 teaspoonful bicarbonate of soda
½ teaspoonful salt	
½ pint milk	

Sieve together all the dry ingredients, then add the milk. Put the dough into a greased 4-lb. stone jam jar, with a piece of greased paper on top. Steam for 2 hours.

Fruit Tea Bread

1¼ cupfuls sifted flour	1 cupful mashed ripe bananas (2 to 3 bananas)
2 teaspoonfuls baking powder	
¼ teaspoonful bicarbonate of soda	⅔ cupful sugar
⅓ cupful vegetable fat	2 eggs, well beaten
	½ teaspoonful salt

Sift together the flour, baking powder, bicarbonate of soda and salt. Beat the fat in a mixing bowl until creamy, then gradually add the sugar and continue beating until light and fluffy. Add eggs and beat well, then add the flour mixture alternately with bananas, a small amount at a time, mixing after each addition only enough to moisten the dry ingredients. Turn into a greased loaf pan ($8\frac{1}{2} \times 4\frac{1}{2} \times 2\frac{1}{2}$ in.) and bake in a moderate oven for about 1 hour 10 minutes or until bread is done.

Variations can be made by adding to the egg mixture:

(1) 1 cupful finely chopped dried apricots. (If the apricots are very dry, soak them in warm water until soft. Drain and dry well before using.)
(2) ½ cupful coarsely chopped nuts.
(3) 1 cupful finely chopped dried prunes (if very dry, treat as apricots above).
(4) 1 cupful seedless raisins.
(5) 1 cupful mixed candied fruit, ¼ cupful raisins and ½ cupful chopped nuts.

SCONES

Drop Scones (see also Scottish cookery)

4 oz. flour	½ teaspoonful cream of tartar
Half an egg	
1 dessertspoonful Golden Syrup	½ teaspoonful bicarbonate of soda
Milk to mix	Pinch of salt

Sieve together the flour, cream of tartar, soda and salt. Make a hole in the middle, drop in the beaten egg and the Golden Syrup. Mix to a stiff batter with milk, added gradually. Grease and heat a girdle.

Drop the mixture on it in tablespoonfuls. Brown on one side, then turn over and cook on the other side. Keep hot in a soft cloth. Butter and serve hot.

Plain Scones (1)

8 oz. flour	½ teaspoonful cream
1½ oz. butter	of tartar
1 teaspoonful castor	Buttermilk or sour
sugar	milk to mix
½ teaspoonful bicar-	Pinch of salt
bonate of soda	

Sieve the dry ingredients and rub in the butter. Add enough buttermilk to make a spongy dough. Turn on to a floured board, knead lightly and roll out. Cut in rounds and put them on a hot girdle. Cook steadily until well risen and a very pale brown. Then turn over and cook the other side.

NOTE: These scones may be baked in a quick oven for 10–15 minutes.

Plain Scones (2)

8 oz. flour	Pinch of salt
1 teaspoonful baking	1 oz. butter or lard
powder	Half an egg
½ gill milk	

Rub the butter into the flour, then add the baking powder and salt. Beat the egg,

Just an ordinary currant bun mixture, but they win all hearts at tea if shaped into little men

add it, and then the milk. Knead the mixture into a dough and put on a floured board. Roll out 1 in. thick, cut into rounds and bake in a hot oven for 10–15 minutes.

Potato Scones

Boil some potatoes and, when cooked, drain off the water, and put the potatoes through a masher on to a floured board. Add a pinch of salt, and work in as much sifted flour as will make the mixture into a stiff dough. Roll out, sprinkle with flour and cut into rounds or triangles. Grease and heat a girdle and put the rounds on it. Brown on one side, turn over with a palette knife and brown the other side. Serve hot.

Sultana Scones

8 oz. flour	Milk to bind
2 oz. granulated sugar	2 oz. sultanas
1 oz. butter	Small egg
½ teaspoonful cream	½ teaspoonful bicar-
of tartar	bonate of soda

Rub the butter into the flour and add the rest of the dry ingredients. Then add the beaten egg and enough milk to make the mixture into a dough. Roll out on a floured board and cut into large rounds. Then cut each round in half. Paint with a little beaten egg and bake in a hot oven for about 15–20 minutes.

You can make a fascinating variety of fruit-flavoured tea breads, combining banana with nuts, raisins, prunes, etc.

231

EMERGENCY MEALS

*When unexpected guests arrive, the clever housewife
turns to her store cupboard to save the situation*

THESE days no practical housewife need be stumped by the arrival of unexpected guests for Sunday dinner—or unduly put out when her husband telephones on early closing day to say he is bringing the boss home for dinner. You really can buy—and safely store for long periods in quite a small space in your emergency cupboard—the necessary ingredients for a banquet or a simple picnic meal, all in cans, jars, tubes and packets.

If you can manage the initial outlay, you can always invest in a jar of chicken breasts, a tin of whole chicken, some cans of pâté de foie gras, perhaps something really exotic like a jar of grapes in wine.

But without being as extravagant as that, you can call an emergency cupboard excellently stocked if it contains the following:

Soups.—Several cans and packets in different flavours—excellent to flavour dull meat and fish dishes.

Meat.—Cans of luncheon meat, chicken, stewed steak, kidneys, tongue; Ravioli.

Fish.—Cans of herrings, tuna, salmon.

Vegetables.—Canned peas, corn, tomatoes, mixed vegetables, beans, asparagus tips, carrots, celery, beetroot. Packets of "Swel" prepared (dried) vegetables.

Fruits.—Canned strawberries, peaches, fruit salad, pineapple, apple purée.

Oddments for Trimmings.—Carton of Parmesan cheese. Small can tomato juice. Cans of evaporated (unsweetened) and condensed (sweetened) milk and cream. Jar of horseradish cream. Tubes of French mustard and tomato purée.

You can supplement these emergency rations with some of the excellent quick-frozen foods now on the market which are easy and quick to cook or heat.

SOUPS

With some canned and packet soups in the store cupboard you can always start a meal off well. The obvious thing is to serve canned soup "neat"; but you can make more subtle flavours by adroit mixing.

Remember that canned soups are best turned out of the can before heating, as they are nearly always concentrated and need diluting. Milk added to a thick soup increases its nutritive value and improves the creamy texture and flavour. Never heat canned soups more than is necessary.

Here are some ideas for flavour experiments. Once you start, you will no doubt think out many of your own:

(1) Combine a can of Scotch broth with an equal quantity of milk or milk and water. Season and sprinkle liberally with chopped parsley.

(2) Combine a can of consommé with the same quantity of water or clear stock. After heating, add a dessertspoonful of sherry and some shredded carrots, and sprinkle with sieved hard-boiled egg-yolk.

(3) Mix a can of chicken soup with a can of asparagus or onion soup and a can measure of milk. Season and add a half-teaspoonful of fresh thyme and simmer for a few minutes. Add fresh chopped chives just before serving.

(4) Add a can measure of milk to a can of tomato soup. Season as desired. Heat through and, on serving, add some very thinly sliced raw onion and a tablespoonful of fried croûtons to each portion.

(5) Mix a can of kidney soup with an equal quantity of bone stock and a cupful of cooked spaghetti. Season as desired and serve very hot.

(6) Combine a can of mushroom soup with a can of onion soup and a can measure of milk or water. Season and heat. Serve sprinkled with grated Parmesan cheese.

Another use for canned soups.—When you want to give a dish a distinctive and exciting flavour and have not the time—or the raw ingredients—to make a special sauce, try using canned chicken, celery, onion or mushroom soups in place of cream sauces.

This hors d'œuvre doesn't look like a last-minute concoction, but it could not be quicker or easier to prepare from a can of smoked herring fillets

HORS D'ŒUVRES

Herring and Horseradish

Flake up the flesh of some canned herring. Mix with horseradish sauce to taste and spread in sandwiches or on tiny pieces of toast (see Sauces chapter for horseradish sauce, or it can be bought in jars).

Herring Fillets as Hors d'œuvres

1 can smoked herring fillets	1 very small onion or shallot
1 hard-boiled egg	Chopped parsley

Remove the fillets carefully from the tin and drain them. Arrange in an hors d'œuvres dish or on plates. Scatter with a few very fine rings of onion. Chop white and yolk of egg separately and arrange in lines between the fillets. Garnish with chopped parsley.

Hot Savoury Bouchées

6 oz. rough puff or flaky pastry (see Pastry chapter)	1 teaspoonful chopped parsley
1 tablespoonful cream or top of milk	1 small can soft herring roes
	Lemon rind and juice
	Salt and pepper

Bake some small puff pastry cases. Drain all liquid from the roes, mash them lightly with a fork and mix with the cream or top of milk. Put into a small pan and heat very gently, stirring all the time. Add chopped parsley, the grated rind of half a lemon and a teaspoonful of lemon juice. Season well and, when quite hot, fill the pastry cases and serve at once.

Marine Puffs

6 oz. rough puff pastry (see Pastry chapter)	Salt and pepper
	1 small can fresh herrings in tomato sauce
½ teaspoonful lemon juice	
A little milk or beaten egg	

Roll the pastry into an oblong ¼ in. thick and cut in half. Remove bones and tails from the herrings, flake them and add salt and pepper and lemon juice to taste. Spread the fish on one piece of pastry and cover with the other. Brush top with milk or beaten egg and cut into fingers. Bake in a very hot oven for 25 minutes. (These quantities make about 12 puffs.)

A tasty dish made from your "iron rations"—Herring and Corn Fritters are both satisfying and appetising

FISH DISHES

Friday Dish (for 2)

1 *small can herrings*	1 *small can tomato or*
2 *oz. cooked rice*	*mushroom soup*
1 *tablespoonful*	1 *oz. grated cheese*
breadcrumbs	*Salt and pepper*

If the herrings are packed in tomato sauce, use tomato soup. If they are packed in their own juice, use mushroom soup.

Remove the skin and backbones from the fish and flake them. Mix with the cooked rice and add salt and pepper to taste. Pour over sufficient soup to make a moist consistency. Turn into a fireproof dish and sprinkle with cheese and breadcrumbs. Bake in a hot oven for 20–25 minutes.

Herring and Corn Fritters (for 3–4)

1 *small can herrings*	1 *small can whole*
in tomato sauce	*kernel corn*
2 *tablespoonfuls flour*	*Fat for frying*
1 *egg*	*Salt and pepper*

Sift the flour into a bowl and make into a batter with the egg. Remove tails and centre bones from the fish and flake it. Add fish, tomato sauce and drained corn to the batter. Season with salt and pepper and drop tablespoonfuls of the mixture into smoking hot fat. Fry golden brown and serve at once.

Herring Milanaise (for 4)

1 *can herring in*	¼ *lb. macaroni or*
tomato sauce	*spaghetti*
1 *oz. butter or mar-*	2 *oz. grated or thinly*
garine	*sliced cheese*

Cook the macaroni in salted water, drain well, add the butter or margarine and stir gently. Drain the herring, make it very hot and place on a hot dish. Add the tomato sauce to the macaroni at the last moment, add the cheese and garnish round the herring.

NOTE: Rice may be used in place of macaroni or spaghetti if preferred.

Herring Roll (for 4)

6 *oz. short crust*	1 *can herrings*
pastry (see Pastry	*Salt and pepper*
chapter)	*Lemon juice*
Milk or egg	

Remove tails and centre bones and flake the fish. Add salt, pepper and lemon juice to taste. Roll the pastry into an oblong shape, spread the fish over it, bringing it well to the edges. Damp the edges, roll up and seal the ends. Brush the top with milk or beaten egg. Bake in a hot oven for 30 minutes.

Herring Tyrolienne (for 3)

1 egg-yolk	½ teaspoonful salt
2 tablespoonfuls salad oil	½ teaspoonful French mustard
1 tablespoonful vinegar or lemon juice	1 small teaspoonful each Tarragon, finely chopped spring onion and chervil
1 can herring in tomato	
Pepper	

Put the egg-yolk into a basin with the salt, pepper and mustard. Using a small whisk, mix well and stir in, very gradually, the salad oil. Add the tomato sauce from the herring and the Tarragon, onion and chervil. If too rich, stir in vinegar or lemon juice. Pour this sauce over the herring and serve with sliced or diced beetroot.

Mock Oyster Pie (for 3)

1 large can soft herring roes	2 oz. breadcrumbs
1 egg	½ pint milk
Salt and pepper	1 oz. melted margarine

Mash the herring roes and mix them with the breadcrumbs. Place in a greased pie dish. Beat the egg and add the milk, melted margarine, ¼ teaspoonful salt and pepper to taste. Pour this custard over the fish mixture. Allow to stand 20 minutes. Bake in a moderate oven for 25 minutes or until the custard is set.

Scalloped Herring Mornay

1 can herring in tomato	White sauce (see Sauces chapter)
Grated cheese	Cold mashed potato

Remove backbone from the herring and break up the fish with a fork in the tomato sauce. Add a small quantity of white sauce to bind, and pile the mixture into scallop shells. Surround with a border of mashed potatoes, sprinkle with grated cheese and heat under the grill until golden brown.

Soft Roes and Bacon (for 4)

16 oz. can soft roes	2 tablespoonfuls plain flour (approx.)
4 oz. bacon rashers	
1 lb. mashed potatoes	Parsley

Fry the bacon and keep hot. Roll the roes in the flour and fry in the bacon fat. Meanwhile, make a bed of the mashed

You can whip these up between the warning 'phone call and the guests' arrival—Supper Cakes served with grilled tomatoes

235

potatoes and arrange the roes and bacon on top. Garnish with parsley. Serve with canned baked beans.

Spiced Pilchards (for 4)

1 large can pilchards	4 tablespoonfuls
2 tablespoonfuls	vinegar
water	Liquor from canned
2 oz. finely	fish
chopped onion	½ teaspoonful mixed
½ oz. chopped parsley	herbs

Drain the liquor from the can and, if the dish is to be served hot, warm the fish in the oven while making the sauce. To make the sauce, simmer the onion, herbs, vinegar, water and fish liquor together for 3–5 minutes, then add chopped parsley and pour the sauce over the fish. Serve hot with canned tomatoes and mashed potatoes or cold with salad and mashed potatoes.

Stuffed Herring (for 4)

1 large can herring in	Parsley
tomato	1 dozen capers
1 onion	1 egg
3 tablespoonfuls	1 oz. melted butter or
breadcrumbs	margarine
Pinch of salt	Pinch of pepper
	Made mustard

Mix the breadcrumbs and melted butter or margarine with the chopped capers, parsley and onion. Add seasoning and about ½ teaspoonful made mustard and mix in the beaten egg. Remove fish carefully from the tin, fill with stuffing and bake.

Supper Cakes (for 4)

1 small can fresh	1 teaspoonful
herrings	chopped parsley
Salt and pepper	Browned bread-
1 small egg	crumbs
1 lb. cooked potatoes	Fat for frying

Remove tails and centre bones, and flake the fish. Mash the potato and mix it lightly with the fish, parsley, pepper and a very little salt. Turn on to a floured board and form into flat cakes. Coat with beaten egg and crumbs. Fry in hot shallow fat until golden brown on both sides.

Tuna Moulds (for 3–4)

7 oz. can tuna fish	1½ tablespoonfuls
8 oz. can peas	gelatine
¼ pint liquor from the	1 teaspoonful salt
peas and water	2 teaspoonfuls
1 dessertspoonful	chopped parsley
anchovy essence	½ teaspoonful pepper
	Colouring, if desired

Dissolve the gelatine in the hot water and vegetable liquor. Roughly chop the tuna fish and mix it with the rest of the ingredients. Add colouring, if desired. Rinse out 8 dariole moulds with cold water and fill them with the mixture. Allow to set, then turn out. Serve with salad.

MEAT DISHES

Bacon and Bean Pie (for 4)

16 oz. can baked	½ teaspoonful pepper
beans	4 oz. streaky bacon
1 oz. chopped onion	1 teaspoonful salt
1 lb. potatoes	Milk

Cook and mash potatoes with a little milk and seasoning. Cut bacon into strips, fry it and the onion until lightly browned, then mix with the beans, add seasoning, pour into a casserole and cover with the mashed potatoes. Bake in a fairly hot oven for 20–30 minutes. Serve hot, with canned spinach.

Casserole of Pork (for 4)

1 can pork luncheon	¼ lb. each cooked
meat	carrot, turnip, and
2 small onions	macaroni
Vegetable stock	1 bay leaf
	Fat for frying

Chop the onions and fry in fat until brown. Place in bottom of casserole, then add layers of vegetables, macaroni and diced meat. Add bay leaf. Moisten well with vegetable stock or gravy made with vegetable extract. Cook slowly until well heated through.

Chicken Soufflé (for 3–4)

10 oz. can chicken	½ pint milk
(or other canned	1 teaspoonful salt
meat)	2 oz. plain flour
2 oz. margarine	2 eggs (separated)
1 tablespoonful	1 tablespoonful
chopped onion	chopped parsley
	¼ teaspoonful pepper

Melt the margarine in a saucepan, add flour, then milk mixed with any chicken liquor from the can and cook until smooth. Remove from heat, add beaten egg-yolks, seasoning, onion, parsley, chopped chicken and, finally, fold in the stiffly whipped egg-whites. Pour mixture into a greased casserole dish. Bake in a moderate oven for approximately 45 minutes. Serve immediately, with canned garden peas and new potatoes tossed in butter.

A delicious cold buffet made entirely from canned goods. The main dish is vegetables in aspic, followed by Gâteau St. Honoré à la Crême and Cheese Dreams

Cold Meat Mould (for 4)

8 oz. can luncheon meat	1 teaspoonful sherry
12 oz. can diced carrots	Pepper and salt
	8 oz. can peas
¼ pint vegetable liquor	¼ oz. aspic jelly crystals
Lettuce leaves	1 hard-boiled egg
	Mayonnaise

Mix the liquor from peas and carrots together and, if it is not quite ¾ pint, make up with water. Heat the liquor and dissolve aspic crystals in it. Cut meat into small cubes and dice hard-boiled egg. Rinse out mould in cold water, pour in a little aspic jelly and arrange some of the peas in a pattern. Allow to set. Mix meat, egg, peas, a third of the carrots, sherry and seasoning with the remainder of the jelly, and when it begins to "jell" pour into the mould and allow to set. To serve, turn out on to lettuce leaves and mix remainder of the diced carrots with 3 tablespoonfuls mayonnaise and arrange as a garnish round the mould.

Corned Beef Cakes (for 4)

8 oz. canned corned beef	1 oz. raw onion (chopped)

Pepper and salt
8 oz. cooked mashed potato

Flour, egg, breadcrumbs and fat for frying

Mix all ingredients together and shape into cakes. Roll them in flour and then in egg and, finally, breadcrumbs. Fry in hot, shallow fat. Serve with tomato sauce (see Sauces chapter).

Kidney Omelet (for 4)

2 oz. butter or margarine	6 eggs
2 tablespoonfuls cold water	Salt and pepper to taste

For the filling
8 oz. can stewed kidneys

Beat the eggs well together, add the cold water and season to taste. Melt a knob of butter in the frying pan and, when fairly hot, pour in a quarter of the egg mixture. Tilt the pan backwards and forwards, allowing the uncooked egg to run to the sides of the pan and at the same time keeping the omelet moving until just set. The kidneys, which should have been seasoned and heated in a separate pan, are then placed on one half of the omelet. Fold over the other half and turn on to a hot dish. Make three more omelets in the same way. Serve immediately with canned broad beans and duchesse potatoes.

Netherlands Puffs (for 3–4)

2 cupfuls finely chopped Dutch luncheon meat

For the batter

2 oz. flour	½ pint milk
1 egg	Salt

Make a Yorkshire pudding batter (see Puddings chapter), add the meat, divide the mixture into well-greased patty pans and bake for about 15 minutes in a hot oven.

Quick Salad Platter (for 4)

8 oz. can mixed vege-tables in mayon-naise	8 oz. can garden peas
	8 oz. can diced carrots
	8 oz. can sliced beet-root
8 oz. can pork luncheon meat	2 hard-boiled eggs
2 large tomatoes	Chopped parsley

Cut the tomatoes in half, hollow out the centres and fill with the diced vegetables in mayonnaise. Arrange down the centre of the dish. Cut the luncheon meat in slices and the eggs in halves, and arrange at opposite ends of the dish. Place the rest of the canned foods in rows on the dish. Cover the eggs with a little mayonnaise and garnish the whole with chopped parsley.

Risotto (for 4)

2 oz. margarine	Salt and pepper to taste
2 oz. chopped onion	
6–8 oz. canned lun-cheon meat (diced)	Pinch of mixed herbs
6 oz. Patna rice	1 pint meat stock or water

Heat margarine in a saucepan, add onion, rice and mixed herbs, cook until lightly browned, then add salt and pepper and about a quarter of the stock. Cook for about 20 minutes, adding remainder of liquid at intervals as it is absorbed. When rice is tender, add diced meat and cook for a further 5 minutes. Serve very hot.

Spaghetti with Bolognaise or Napolitaine Sauce (for 4)

1 lb. spaghetti	Grated Parmesan cheese
Knobs of butter	
Salt	

Make the sauce first because it takes longer.
Boil spaghetti in plenty of fast-boiling water for 18–20 minutes, stirring with a fork occasionally. Keep on the firm side but do not overcook. Drain very well, and place on a dish. Add knobs of butter and grated Parmesan cheese. Toss and mix well together; season. Serve at once with one of the following sauces separately:

Bolognaise Sauce

4 oz. finely chopped meat	Salt and pepper
	Chopped parsley
1 capsule tomato purée	½ chopped onion
	Olive oil

Heat a little olive oil in a saucepan, add the chopped onion, fry briskly until golden. Add meat and fry briskly for 2 or 3 minutes. Empty tomato purée into a cup, dilute with warm water and stir until dissolved, then pour into the saucepan. Season; cook slowly for 1 hour. Add chopped parsley.

Napolitaine Sauce

Prepared in the same way as the Bolognaise Sauce, but without the meat.

Steak and Mushroom Pie (for 4)

8 oz. flaky pastry (see Pastry chapter)	16 oz. can stewed steak
2 oz. chopped onion	4 oz. sliced mush-rooms
1 tablespoonful plain flour	4 tablespoonfuls cold water
Salt and pepper to taste	

Empty the can of stewed steak into a pie dish, add remainder of ingredients, place pie funnel in centre of mixture and cover with flaky pastry. Bake in a hot oven until pastry is cooked (about 30–40 minutes). Serve with canned celery hearts and new potatoes.

VEGETABLES AND VEGETARIAN DISHES

Carrots au Gratin (for 4)

½ pint white sauce (see Sauces chapter)	3 or 4 tablespoonfuls grated cheese
Salt and pepper	4 teacupfuls of boiling water
2 oz. "Swel" carrots	
Breadcrumbs	

Soak the carrots in boiling water for 1 hour. Bring to the boil and cook until tender (about 15–20 minutes). Strain and keep hot in a baking dish, while making the white sauce with the liquid in which the carrots were cooked. Season the sauce well, add half the grated cheese, pour over carrots, sprinkle remaining cheese and the breadcrumbs on top, and brown under the grill or in a hot oven. Serve hot.

A real party dish—Charlotte Russe, one of the most luxurious of all sweets, yet made from "emergency stores"

Cheese Dreams (for 2–3)

8 oz. can asparagus	8 oz. processed
Fingers of toast	cheese
A little butter	Cayenne pepper

Butter the toast, place asparagus on each piece and cover with a thin slice of cheese. Place under the grill and leave until the cheese just starts to melt. Sprinkle with Cayenne pepper and serve very hot.

Creamed Beetroot (for 4)

½ pint white sauce (see Sauces chapter)	2 oz. "Swel" beet-root dice
Salt and pepper	1 tablespoonful vinegar
Small pinch of ground cloves or grated nutmeg	Chopped parsley to garnish
4 teacupfuls of boiling water	

Soak the beetroot in water and vinegar for 4 hours (or overnight). Bring to the boil in the soaking water and cook until tender (about 20–30 minutes). Make white sauce, season and add ground cloves or nutmeg and vinegar, then add the cooked beetroot. Serve hot, garnished with chopped parsley.

Mixed Vegetable Fritters (for 4)

2 oz. "Swel" mixed vegetables	4 teacupfuls boiling water
Seasoning	Fat for frying

For the batter

4 oz. flour	½ teacupful milk
	1 egg

Pour the water on to the vegetables and leave to soak for 1 hour. Bring to the boil and cook for 5 minutes, season and strain.

Make batter (see Pudding chapter) and add vegetables. Drop in dessertspoonfuls into hot fat and fry until golden brown. Drain, serve hot with fried bacon. This quantity makes about 18 fritters.

Onion Savoury (for 4)

2 oz. "Swel" onion	White sauce (made
3 teacupfuls milk and	with 2 oz. flour and
water	2 oz. margarine)
2 tablespoonfuls	½ oz. "Swel" carrots
chopped nuts or	2 tablespoonfuls
grated cheese	white breadcrumbs
Salt	

Soak the carrots in 1 teacupful boiling water. After 1 hour add the onion, 2 tea-cupfuls milk and water, and salt to taste. Bring to the boil and simmer for 15 minutes or until tender. Strain, and use the liquid to make the white sauce. Put the vegetables into a pie dish, cover with sauce, sprinkle the top with breadcrumbs and chopped nuts or grated cheese. Heat thoroughly in a hot oven until crisp and brown, or brown under the grill. Serve with fried potatoes.

Spaghetti and Egg Croquettes (for 4)

16 oz. can spaghetti	Browned bread-
in tomato	crumbs
2 oz. plain flour	2 oz. chopped raw
1 tablespoonful	onion
chopped parsley	2 hard-boiled eggs
1 beaten raw egg	Fat for frying

Empty the spaghetti into a saucepan, add onion and flour, and cook until the mixture thickens, then add diced egg and chopped parsley. Turn out on to a plate to cool. When nearly cold, divide mixture into equal-sized sections and shape into croquettes on a floured board; then dip each one into beaten egg, then breadcrumbs. Fry in very hot deep fat for a few seconds only. (If not removed quickly, the croquettes will split.) Serve hot with canned carrots tossed in melted butter or margarine and new potatoes.

Vegetable Cheese Flan (for 3–4)

8 oz. short pastry	12-oz. can mixed
6 oz. grated cheese	vegetables
¼ pint vegetable liquor	2 oz. margarine
and milk mixed	2 oz. plain flour
2 teaspoonfuls salt	¼ teaspoonful pepper

Make a sauce with the margarine and flour, adding strained vegetable liquor and milk, salt, pepper, half the cheese and vegetables. Pour this mixture into uncooked pastry case, sprinkle remainder of cheese on top. Bake in a hot oven for 30–40 minutes.

Vegetable Patties (for 4)

1 oz. "Swel" mixed	Browned bread-
vegetables	crumbs
4 oz. cooked mashed	2 teacupfuls boiling
potatoes	water
Beaten egg	Fat for frying

Pour the water on to the vegetables and leave to soak for 1 hour. Bring to the boil and cook until tender, then strain. Mix the vegetables with the potato and bind with half the beaten egg. When cool enough to handle, form into patties, coat with egg and breadcrumbs, and fry in hot fat until golden brown. Drain, and serve hot.

SWEETS

Apple Charlotte (for 4)

16 oz. can of sweet-	¼ lemon (grated rind
ened apple purée	and juice)
or slices	2 oz. castor sugar
½ teaspoonful cinna-	4–6 oz. thinly sliced
mon	bread (without
2 oz. margarine	crust)

Melt the margarine and use a pastry brush to brush it lightly over each side of the sliced bread. Line a dish with some of the prepared bread, pour in the apple with the other ingredients added, cover the top of the mixture with remaining slices of bread. Bake in a moderate oven for about 1 hour or until bread is brown and crisp. Serve hot or cold.

Charlotte Russe (for 4)

8 oz. can peaches or	8 oz. can evaporated
apricots	milk
¼ pint lemon jelly	2 tablespoonfuls
2 tablespoonfuls hot	gelatine
water	¼ pint fresh milk
1½ oz. sugar	2 tablespoonfuls
1 tablespoonful rum	sherry
1 doz. (approx.)	½ teaspoonful vanilla
sponge fingers	essence

Rinse out a charlotte russe mould with cold water. Pour in the lemon jelly about ¼ in. deep and arrange the drained fruit in a pattern on it and allow the jelly to set. Then place sponge fingers all round the inside of the mould. Dissolve gelatine in the hot water. Heat fresh milk and sugar together and add dissolved gelatine, vanilla essence, sherry and rum. Allow this mixture to stand until just beginning to set. Fold in the whipped evaporated milk and pour the mixture into the mould and allow

Strawberries and raspberries have a magic all their own that few people can resist. The very sight of these top favourite summer fruits served out of season positively makes the mouth water. Nowadays, however, though their season is short, we can always get the frozen ones and very good they are. Below, whole strawberries fill a mound of meringue and decorate a pie, while sliced ones top a mousse. The little glasses contain Raspberry Sabayon, each one with a raspberry on the top.

Vegetarian dishes need not be dull and stodgy—far from it! Not a scrap of meat has been used in any of the appetising foods you can see on these two pages, any of which would make a satisfying main dish for a family lunch or supper. Above, a flan case filled with a savoury mixture of cheese and sweet corn, a smoked fish chowder, a casserole of tuna fish with crushed potato crisps on top—just a few ideas to start you thinking up some unusual dishes of your own.

The clever use of spices, herbs and unusual ingredients makes these meatless dishes tasty and exciting. For instance, mashed banana, sweet cicely and sour cream add piquancy to the macaroni dish at the top and it's garnished with onion rings. Scooped-out slices of garlic-flavoured French bread are filled with egg scrambled with tinned crab, white wine and curry powder. Shredded cabbage is curried and served with an attractive savoury egg garnish. Try these on the family and they won't miss meat!

Despite the wonderful array of cakes to be seen in the bakers' windows, freshly made, home-baked ones still taste better, invariably earn enthusiastic praise from your family and visitors—and what a wonderful feeling of satisfaction when you take a freshly baked cake out of the oven! Left are two favourites that never lose their appeal—German Pound Cake and Simnel Cake (to be eaten at Easter).

Photographs: Radiation New World Ltd.

Home bread-making is back in fashion again. Many modern housewives have discovered that yeast bakery is not difficult or unduly time-consuming. Make it once a week and you will always have nice fresh bread —if the family allow it to last that long! A hot loaf or a batch of clover rolls (right) will be an irresistible temptation to men as well as children! Want to start right away? Then see p. 227.

it to set in a very cool place. To serve, turn out and garnish with any left-over jelly or fruit.

Forgotten Dessert (for 4)

16 oz. can straw- berries	¼ teaspoonful vanilla essence
6 oz. castor sugar	6 oz. can evaporated
½ oz. gelatine	milk
	3 egg-whites

Whip egg-whites until they are very stiff, fold in castor sugar and vanilla essence. Grease a plate with olive oil and spread the meringue about ¼ in. thick over the bottom but pile it high around the sides. Heat the oven to approx. 400° F., place meringue in the oven and turn off the heat. Leave for at least 6 hours. Drain juice from the strawberries, heat and dissolve gelatine in it, cool, then just as it begins to set, fold in the stiffly whipped evaporated milk. Allow to set, then pile it into the meringue "plate." Garnish on top with the strawberries.

Jelly Fluff (for 4)

1 pint packet jelly	1 pint canned fruit
8 oz. can fruit	juice
	2 egg-whites

Dissolve the jelly in the heated fruit juice, which can be a mixture of juice from the can of fruit together with any left over from another can of fruit. When beginning to set, fold in the stiffly beaten egg white and fruit, pour into a jelly mould and leave to set. To serve, turn out of the mould.

Rhubarb Ring (for 4–5)

2 16-oz. cans rhubarb (drained)	8 oz. short pastry (see Pastry chapter)

For the sauce

2 teaspoonfuls red jam	2 teaspoonfuls corn- flour
	½ pint fruit juice

Roll out the pastry into an oblong about 15 in. by 6 in. Cover with the rhubarb and roll up, having moistened the edges of the pastry to secure the roll firmly. Form into a ring, moisten each end again and secure firmly. Slash the roll at 1-in. intervals around outer edge. Place on a tin and bake in a moderate oven for about 40 minutes.

For the sauce.—Mix the cornflour with a little juice. Boil remainder with jam, add to the cornflour mixture, boil and pour over ring.

Rhubarb Ring is an unusual dessert. If you have no rhubarb in the cupboard, make a Cherry Ring instead—it's just as good

VEGETARIAN CATERING

Proving for those who still have doubts that there are many tasty alternatives to fish, flesh and fowl

SOME clarification appears to be necessary concerning the meaning of the term "vegetarian," since some people seem to believe that vegetarians eat fish, though they do not eat flesh foods. Some even believe that poultry can be classified as a vegetarian food. Others, going to the opposite extreme, think that a strict vegetarian not only refuses flesh, fish and fowl but all dairy produce as well, i.e. milk, cheese, butter, eggs, etc.

The definition of the word, as used by the Vegetarian Societies, has always implied the exclusion of flesh, fish and fowl from the diet, with or without the addition of dairy produce. The majority of vegetarians in the U.K. to-day do include dairy produce in their diet, which is sometimes called "lacto-vegetarian." The few strict vegetarians who do not take dairy produce now use the term "vegan" to differentiate their dietary from that of ordinary vegetarians.

As there are certain dangers involved in adopting a "vegan" diet unless the subject is very carefully studied and applied, the material here presented concerns itself only with the diet in which dairy produce is included.

Newcomers to the vegetarian way of living are frequently anxious to know how to balance their diet correctly so that their health may not suffer as a result of the change. Such concern is natural in view of the fact that, until recently, orthodox medical and scientific opinion has frowned upon the fleshless diet.

Circumstances affecting food supplies in recent years—namely the two world wars and the tremendous increase in world population—have brought such a degree of pressure to bear on this aspect of life that traditional beliefs have had to be reconsidered and are now shown to be incorrect in the light of recent scientific research. Over a century of organised vegetarianism in the U.K. has brought with it concrete evidence, not only that one can remain healthy, but that with reasonable care one's health, if it has previously been impaired, can often be improved by such a diet.

The majority of vegetarians favour a diet consisting of 50 per cent. raw salads and fruit with 50 per cent. conservatively cooked vegetables—both accompanied by an adequate portion of carbohydrate (energy-giving) foods and protein (body-building) foods.

CARBOHYDRATES

There is a tendency to overdo the consumption of carbohydrates, especially in the early days of changing over to vegetarianism, because of a false belief that larger quantities are needed to take the place of the foods eliminated from the diet. The carbohydrates consist of starchy foods and sugars, many of which suffer from the modern tendency to "process" them. If genuine wholewheat bread is obtainable or made at home, this provides an excellent foundation food which is very satisfying and is claimed by some to be the most nearly perfect human food, containing carbohydrates, protein, fat, mineral salts and certain vitamins.

The sugar to be preferred is the natural Barbados or genuine Demerara, both of which are usually obtainable at Health Food Stores. Honey is an excellent food.

PROTEINS

While, as indicated above, there are certain vegetarians who do not use dairy produce such as milk, cheese and eggs, it is usually inadvisable to make too sweeping a change in one's diet. The normal alternatives to take the place of flesh, fish and fowl will therefore be cheese, eggs, nut kernels and pulse foods (beans, peas and lentils).

There is frequently anxiety about suitable *quantities* of foods, even among those

To appeal to the eye as well as the palate, cauliflower attractively arranged
with green peas and spaghetti

who have never worried about the amount of meat and other protein foods formerly taken. The requirements of individuals will always vary considerably, according to temperament and such circumstances as occupation, etc. It cannot be emphasised too strongly, however, that it is very dangerous just to eliminate fish, flesh and fowl from the diet. Adequate amounts of alternative protein foods, of good quality, must be included if health and vigour are to be maintained, and part of these should be in the form of dairy produce. **As a rough guide, at least 2–4 ounces of protein should be included in each day's diet —a proportion at each main meal.**

The growing child requires the larger amount of body-building (protein) food, and this is, of course, seen to be reasonable when its specific purpose is understood. The adult body requires protein mainly for purposes of *renewal* of tissue. Vegetarians believe that more harm may well be done by excessive anxiety about the quantities required than is likely to result from too much or too little being taken. The human organism is amazingly adaptable, so do not fear to experiment within reasonable limits, as the normally healthy body has numerous devices which safeguard it.

Of the alternative foods, **cheese** contains a good proportion of protein (quite equal to good-quality meat) and has a considerable fat content. It can be used just as it is, or it can form the basis of many very palatable cooked dishes.

Eggs are handy for a quick meal and also add appreciably to the protein content of cooked dishes in which the other ingredients may be somewhat deficient, as in the case of some of the pulse foods.

Most **nut kernels** provide a good balance of protein, carbohydrate and fat, and have the advantage that they can be used as purchased, either whole or milled, with salads or fruit. They also form a good basis for innumerable fried, baked or steamed savouries, which can be very appetising when served with seasonable, conservatively cooked fresh vegetables, or cold with salads.

The pulse foods, with the exception of the soya bean, provide only a small amount of protein in relation to their bulk *when cooked*. Analysis of the raw beans, peas or lentils shows a good percentage of protein but, because they absorb a large amount of water in cooking, the protein content after cooking is relatively small. The addition of eggs or cheese to such dishes increases their value as protein foods.

Soya flour, although not possessing an outstanding flavour, is rich in excellent protein and can therefore be used with advantage in conjunction with other tastier foods.

Dried milk powder is also a valuable addition to dishes requiring more protein.

FATS

The vegetarian need experience no difficulty over the fat content of the diet. The nut and pure vegetable fats available in place of the ordinary cooking fats are excellent, and are so rich in pure oils that rather less of them should be used when making pastry or cakes. The vegetarian margarines are also excellent and contain no whale oil, being manufactured exclusively from vegetable and nut oils.

All the nuts contain appreciable quantities of readily assimilable oils and, if more is required, olive oil or nut oil is easily obtainable.

FLAVOURINGS

Herbs, either dried or, preferably, fresh, can be used with advantage in the making of savoury dishes. Sprigs of freshly picked herbs also add considerably to the attractiveness of raw salads. When using dried herbs, the flavour is greatly improved if they are steeped in a small quantity of boiling water for a little while before use.

MENTAL ATTITUDE TO FOOD

This matters a great deal and affects the body's assimilation. At times of emotional stress or strain, it is advisable not to eat until the body and mind can be relaxed.

The vegetarian should truly be able to enjoy his food, for he takes it as fresh and full of vitality as it is possible to get it, and he has the happy knowledge that no human being has been engaged in slaughtering animals for food on his behalf. Vegetarian foods are in themselves attractive, full of colour, fragrance and variety of flavour.

ALTERNATIVES TO MEAT EXTRACTS

There are several well-known yeast extracts on the market which can be used in place of meat extracts in making gravies, soups and stews, as well as in other ways. Among the better known are Marmite and Yeastrel.

A useful tip for improving the flavour of gravies is to cook the yeast extract slightly in the fat before adding thickening and stock or water. This gives a fuller and better flavour to the gravy.

SOUPS

Almost any ordinary soup recipe can be easily adapted to fit the requirement of vegetarian catering. Vegetable stock can take the place of meat stock and yeast extracts, such as Marmite and Yeastrel, that of meat extracts as flavouring agents, at the same time adding appreciable amounts of vitamin B. A further excellent flavouring agent, of entirely vegetable origin, is Vesop, which is in liquid form.

The flavour of most vegetable soups is considerably enhanced if the vegetables are cut up small and "sweated" for about 15–20 minutes in vegetarian margarine before adding liquids. The lid of the saucepan should be kept on and the heat low during this part of the process.

SAVOURIES

These provide the main protein contribution to vegetarian menus and are therefore of supreme importance. They must not merely appeal to the palate or to the eye—although they should do both of these things—but must contain adequate protein foods. If there is any doubt as to the sufficiency of proteins in a meal, add either an egg or, where suitable, some grated cheese.

A selection of dishes based on nut

kernels, pulses, cheese and eggs follows. The chapter on Egg Dishes provides further variations, the only necessary alterations being that the fat used should be vegetarian and the "filling" of the omelets, for example, be in harmony with vegetarian requirements.

VEGETARIAN SWEETS

Most recipes for the sweet course can be readily adapted for vegetarians by the substitution of vegetarian fats in place of lard, etc. Also wholemeal flour can be used in place of white flour for those who prefer it.

In place of gelatine, agar-agar (which is a form of seaweed) can be used for making jellies and for thickening purposes. This not only serves a ultilitarian purpose, but also adds organic iodine and other mineral elements to the diet.

In general, vegetarians prefer fresh fruit.

Raw Fruit Porridge (Bircher muesli)

Raw fruit porridge is a whole-year-round dish. It can be made from nearly all fruits and is very good with apples grated with core and peel.

During spring when no fresh fruit is available, the dish should be made from dried fruit (prunes, apple rings, pears, apricots) or from grated raw carrots. During summer and autumn a large choice of soft and stone fruit gives ample variety.

The Basic Mixture per person is the same for every fruit.

1 dessertspoonful medium oatmeal, 1 tablespoonful sweetened condensed milk or milk (top of the milk) or 1 teaspoonful nut cream (diluted with water to a whitish consistency). Sweeten with honey or brown sugar to taste. Juice of half fresh lemon.

Soak oats, covered with water, for 12–24 hours. Mix condensed milk (or nut cream or sweetened milk) with lemon juice, add to the oats and stir well. Then add fruit pulp and stir well again. Serve at once with sprinkled milled nuts if available. If it has to be kept for some time before serving, cover it well.

Fruit Pulp—per person

Dried Fruit. 3½ oz. dried fruit soaked for 12–24 hours or more until the stones come easily from the prunes; stone and

Tomatoes stuffed with a mixture of grated cheese, breadcrumbs and beaten egg, and topped with parsley

either chop finely or pass through a mincer or emulsifier

Carrot. 3 oz. raw carrots peeled and grated into the basic mixture. Mix quickly to prevent loss of colour. Carrot muesli has to be prepared with special care as carrots have not the flavour of fruit. It requires more sweetening and lemon flavour. If available, add 2 oz. raw rhubarb juice. (Raw rhubarb juice can be made in a juice extractor or by grating washed and wiped unpeeled rhubarb on a two-way grater into a bowl, covered with a piece of butter muslin. Then squeeze butter muslin and add juice to the mixture. This gives a better flavour and is a rich source of vitamin C, so necessary in spring.

Soft Fruit. 5 oz. soft fruit, selected, washed and mashed with a plated fork or wooden masher—e.g. strawberries, raspberries, loganberries, bilberries, red and blackcurrants, blackberries, etc.

Stone Fruit. 5 oz. stone fruit, washed, stoned and chopped or passed through a mincer or emulsifier — e.g. cherries, peaches, apricots, plums, greengages, damsons, etc.

Apple. One big or two small apples, washed and wiped: take off stalks, tops and brown spots, and then grate with core and peel into bowl with the mixture. Mix quickly and well to prevent browning.

Protein Stock

2 oz. haricot beans	2 oz. split peas
1 onion	1 carrot
¼ teaspoonful celery salt	Some parsley, herbs, pepper and salt
3 cloves	A blade of mace

Soak the dried vegetables overnight, and in the morning add the other ingredients. Cover with 4 pints of water, bring to the boil and then simmer for 4 hours. Strain into a bowl and use as required. The yield is about 2¾–3 pints and the stock will keep very well.

Savoury Sandwich Spread

½ pint haricot beans	2 oz. fine wholewheat breadcrumbs
2 oz. grated cheese	
Pepper and salt	2 oz. vegetarian margarine
Nutmeg	
Paprika	Protein stock

Soak the beans overnight, and the next morning drain and wash them and put them into a fireproof casserole with enough protein stock to cover them. Cover and cook gently in a slow oven until soft, then pass the beans through a mincer and, while they are still hot, beat in the cheese, margarine and breadcrumbs. Season with pepper, salt and nutmeg, adding, if liked, a little paprika. Press the mixture into scrupulously clean dry pots and run a little melted margarine over the top to seal.

Store until needed. This should keep for a reasonable time, but should be watched for signs of mould.

VARIOUS MAIN DISHES

Almond and Potato Croquettes

6 oz. milled almonds	1 egg
3 cupfuls mashed potatoes	2 tablespoonfuls grated raw onion
2 dried and crushed shredded wheat sections	1 teaspoonful mixed dried herbs
½ cupful finely minced parsley	Pepper and salt
	Grated cheese for sprinkling

Mix all the ingredients except the cheese, shape the mixture into large egg-size balls, arrange these on a well-greased baking dish, sprinkle a little grated cheese over each, bake for 30 minutes in a moderate oven.

Cheese Delight (for 4–6)

2 eggs, well beaten	2 oz. wholemeal flour
2 oz. vegetarian margarine	1 breakfastcupful cold water
2 oz. grated cheese	Salt and pepper

Season the flour with salt and pepper, and add the cold water very gradually, mixing to a smooth cream. Melt the margarine in a saucepan and add the flour mixture. Stir and boil for 5 minutes. Stir in the grated cheese and remove from the heat. Add the well-beaten eggs and pour into a well-greased baking dish.

Bake for 30 minutes.

Serve with green beans, either hot, or cold as a salad.

Green Bean Salad

Cook some prepared French or runner beans. Drain them well and, while still warm, marinade them in a French dressing made from equal parts of oil and vinegar. Add some chopped chives or onion and stand for 1 hour.

Serve on a bed of lettuce.

Angel in the Snow—the egg
is separated and the white
beaten before grilling—is an
excellent dish for an invalid

Cheese and Onion Pie

6 oz. pastry
2 large onions
2 eggs
1 cupful milk
1 oz. vegetarian
   margarine
3 oz. grated cheese
Salt and pepper

Make some pastry, using 6 oz. wholewheat flour, etc., and line a 9-in. pie plate with it. Slice the onions into thin rings and cook gently in margarine. Do not let them brown. Boil milk, beat in the eggs and most of the cheese and season to taste. Put the onions in the pastry case, pour over the milk mixture and sprinkle cheese on top. Bake in a slow oven for 40–45 minutes.

Serve with thin slices of onion and cucumber marinaded for 1 hour in a French dressing.

Haricot, Leek and Mushroom Pie

½ lb. mushrooms
2 cupfuls pulped
   baked haricot
   beans (good-quality
   canned baked beans
   are suitable)

6 plump leeks
1 cupful breadcrumbs
1 egg
1 oz. fat
1 oz. flour
Pepper and salt

Clean and cut leeks into 1-in. lengths, cover with water, simmer for 30 minutes. Meanwhile, prepare and slice mushrooms, simmer in another saucepan with water to cover for 20 minutes. Make thick sauce of the fat, flour and leek and mushroom cooking waters. Mix cooked leeks and mushrooms and put into a well-greased pie dish. Pour in the sauce. Cover with a "crust" made by mixing the bean pulp, beaten egg, breadcrumbs and seasoning. Dot with fat. Bake for ½ hour in moderately hot oven.

Leeks and Fruit with Curry Sauce

4 large leeks
¼ pint curry sauce

4 dried bananas (or
   prunes or dried
   figs)

Wash leeks and cut in half lengthwise. Cook in a little water until tender, then drain well, keeping the water to make the curry sauce. Grease a fireproof casserole, put in a layer of leeks, another of bananas (or other fruit) cut lengthwise, topping with one of the leeks. Make curry sauce (see p. 249) and pour over leeks. Cover with lid and put in oven for 30 minutes. Serve with mashed potatoes and hard-boiled eggs.

Brown Gravy

1 teaspoonful Yeastrel
   or Marmite
1 oz. wholemeal flour

1 oz. margarine
½ pint stock
Seasoning

Brown margarine in saucepan, add Yeastrel or Marmite, flour, and mix well. Gradually stir in stock, stirring until it boils, season and simmer for 5 minutes.

Nut Roast with Chestnut Stuffing

¼ lb. hazel nuts or
   cashews
6 oz. wholemeal
   breadcrumbs
2 onions

1 oz. vegetarian mar,
   garine
Seasoning
Gravy

Mill nuts, mix with breadcrumbs and seasoning. Cut onion finely, fry to a golden brown. Place onion on top of mixture, pour over about 6 tablespoonfuls gravy, mix into a stiff dough. Form into roll, cut through centre lengthwise, place chestnut stuffing on inner side, replace top half of roast, smooth with knife. Bake in hot oven for 30 minutes.

Chestnut Stuffing

¾ lb. chestnuts	2 oz. breadcrumbs
1 onion	Seasoning

Place chestnuts in a saucepan with cold water, bring to the boil, peel. Cook chestnuts in ½ pint water, strain, mash, add fried onion, breadcrumbs and seasoning, so that the mixture becomes stiff.

Nut Roast

¼ lb. slightly roasted ground cashew or hazel nuts	1 lb. boiled, mashed potatoes
1 teacupful vegetable stock, milk or water	1 small grated onion
	2 dessertspoonfuls fat
	1 teaspoonful Yeastrel
1 egg	Salt to taste
Grated cheese	

Beat the egg, pour over the mashed potatoes, mix well with the onion and fat. Dissolve the Yeastrel in the liquid, mix with all the other ingredients, put into a buttered fireproof dish. Sprinkle with grated cheese, put dots of fat on top, bake in a moderate oven for 30 minutes, until golden brown.

Serve with Brown Gravy (see previous page for recipe).

Onions stuffed with Nuttolene

2 large Spanish onions	1½ teaspoonfuls curry powder
1 small can Nuttolene	Salt to taste
Fat for frying	

Boil onions until tender. Allow to cool and drain, then scoop out centres.

Mash Nuttolene with a fork on a wooden board, then fry in a little fat to bring out the flavour. Mix in a bowl with the scooped-out onion chopped up small, the curry powder and salt. If the mixture appears dry, add a little milk or water. Stuff the onions with the mixture and place in a greased fireproof dish; if any mixture is left over, place round the onions. A dessertspoonful of grated cheese will improve the flavour. Place in hot oven and lower the heat. Bake in a moderate oven for ½ hour, and serve with mashed potatoes.

Never use fat with mashed potatoes if you want them to be light; use milk only and beat well.

Red Cabbage with Chestnuts

1 medium-sized red cabbage	2 tablespoonfuls sugar
2 large apples	1½ lemons
1 oz. cooking fat	½ lb. chestnuts
¼ stick of cinnamon	A little salt
2 cloves	1 pint vegetable liquid
2 small onions	1 oz. margarine

Wash the cabbage in warm water and cut very fine with a knife or vegetable shredder. Wash and dry apples and cut into quarters. Melt cooking fat in a saucepan and add to it prepared cabbage and apples. Cook for about 5–10 minutes. Add cinnamon, sugar and juice of the lemons, one whole onion and cloves, and stew for another 20 minutes. The cabbage should be soft but not sticky when cooked. If a little more liquid is required, use vegetable stock.

Wash chestnuts and cut a cross in each one, bake until half cooked, then peel quickly. Put chestnuts, margarine and one cut-up onion into saucepan and cook for 5 minutes. Add liquid and salt and simmer slowly until chestnuts start to fall to pieces. If a little milk is added at the end, it gives a creamy flavour. Chestnuts are served with the red cabbage, and can also be served as a separate vegetable with salad, but not with potatoes.

Roast Nutmeat

4 oz. mixed milled nuts	1 cupful well-boiled rice
4 oz. milled peanuts	1 cupful brown breadcrumbs
1 egg	½ teaspoonful dried thyme
1 large cupful fried chopped onion	¼ pint vegetable cooking water
1 clove garlic, finely minced	
Pepper and salt	

Mix all the ingredients thoroughly. Pack into well-greased baking dish. Bake in a moderate oven for 45 minutes.

NOTE: See that the onions are finely chopped and fry them slowly until well browned before adding to the mixture. Serve with stuffed tomatoes, peas, gravy.

Stuffed Tomatoes

Cut a slice from the top of each tomato, carefully remove a little of the pulp so as to leave firm cases. Mix the pulp with an equal amount of grated cheese, breadcrumbs and beaten egg; season with pepper and salt and add a grate of nutmeg. Fill the cases with the mixture. Bake in hot oven for 15 minutes, using a well-greased earthenware dish.

NOTE: Roll surplus stuffing into tiny balls.

Gravy

Drain the fat from the pan in which onions are fried, pour ½ pint of vegetable cooking water into pan, simmer for 5 minutes, stir in a coffeespoonful of extract and a few drops of gravy browning. Serve hot, seasoned to taste.

Savoury Egg Pastry

Short pastry to line six patty dishes	½ cupful of milk
3 eggs	½ onion
1 tablespoonful flour	Parsley and chives or sage
1 tomato	A little salt

Mix the eggs gradually into the flour, add the milk and stir well. Add the peeled, chopped onion, finely cut tomato, chopped herbs and salt. Line patty dishes with pastry, pour in egg mixture and bake in a slow oven for about 20 minutes. The pastry will be ready when the top is light golden brown.

Savoy and Apple Savoury with Curry Sauce

Savoy cabbage
Curry sauce
2 apples
3 medium-sized leeks

Choose a firm savoy and quarter it after washing. (Do not soak vegetables in water but wash them quickly.) Steam the savoy for about 20 minutes, then cool and cut into thick slices. Place in a greased fireproof casserole, then add a layer of thin slices of apple and a layer of leeks, washed and cut lengthwise in four. Cover again with savoy, pour on curry sauce and cook in a moderate oven for 30 minutes.

Curry Sauce

1 level dessertspoonful fat	2 heaped teaspoonfuls sugar
2 round dessertspoonfuls wholemeal flour	1 level teaspoonful salt
1 heaped teaspoonful curry powder	½ pint vegetable stock or water

Melt fat, add flour and curry, cook gently, stirring, till yellowish. Add liquid, boil, put in sugar and salt, simmer for 10 minutes.

Lentil cutlets can be made into a variety of shapes and served with potatoes and peas or carrots and spaghetti

Spaghetti Rondelles

4 oz. long, unbroken spaghetti	1 small onion
2 oz. grated cheese	1 oz. margarine
½ cupful tomato pulp	Seasoning
	1 egg

Boil the spaghetti in plenty of water, slightly salted, for 25 minutes. Drain thoroughly, and turn into a fresh saucepan containing the melted margarine. Cook over gentle heat, stirring with a wooden spoon for 3 or 4 minutes. Stir in the grated onion, the cheese, tomato pulp, beaten egg and seasoning. Cook gently for a few minutes, then stand in a cool place for ½ hour. Deposit little bun-shaped rondelles of the spaghetti upon a well-greased baking tin. Bake in a hot oven for 20 minutes. Serve hot with sprouts and butter mint sauce.

Butter Mint Sauce

1 oz. flour	1 tablespoonful chopped fresh mint
1 oz. margarine	
½ pint milk	1 teaspoonful butter
Seasoning	

Melt margarine in a saucepan, stir in flour, gradually add milk, simmer for 5 minutes, season to taste, stir in mint and butter just before serving.

Spinach and Mushroom

1 lb. spinach	½ pint white sauce, made with wholemeal flour
¼ lb. mushroom stalks	
Salt to taste	

Wash and steam spinach; chop up finely. Chop mushroom stalks. Pour a little water into a saucepan, barely covering the bottom, and add a dessertspoonful of oil. (Fats are more easily digested when treated in this way.) Add the mushroom stalks and leave over a small flame until tender. Make white sauce, add the spinach and mushroom to it and simmer for another 10 minutes.

Garnish with fried wholemeal bread and hard-boiled egg; or make a hole in the centre and fill this with scrambled egg. (An economical method is to add a little flour and milk before scrambling in a frying pan.) Sprinkle with cheese or grated nuts.

Stuffed Steamed Cabbage (for 4)

1 cabbage	1 egg, beaten
2 large onions	2 oz. vegetarian margarine
6 oz. wholemeal breadcrumbs	Salt and pepper

Remove the outside leaves from the cabbage and wash them well. Chop the centre part, wash and drain it thoroughly, melt the margarine and cook the cabbage gently in it for a few minutes. Mince the onion and mix together the cabbage, onion and breadcrumbs. Season with salt and pepper, and bind with the beaten egg.

Place a pudding cloth in a basin, then arrange the outside leaves and fill with the mixture. Cover and steam for 1 hour.

Serve with a good brown sauce flavoured with nutmeg, and baked potatoes.

Tomato and Mushroom Patties

Enough puff or short pastry to make six patties

For the filling

3 large tomatoes	1 oz. cooking fat or margarine
½ lb. mushrooms	
1 small onion	Salt or herbs to taste

Wash and dry the tomatoes and mushrooms and cut into slices. Peel onion and cut into small cubes. Melt the cooking fat in a saucepan and fry onions light brown. Add mushrooms and stew for about 10 minutes. After that, add tomatoes and stew for about 5 more minutes. Add a little salt or chopped herbs to taste.

Drain off all liquid which can be used for the gravy. Roll out pastry and cut out large round pieces. Put the mixture on one side of the round pastry piece and cover with the other side of the pastry, thus making a half-circle. Press sides of the pastry together. Brush with egg or water and bake for 20 minutes in moderate oven.

Tomato Sauce

½ lb. tomatoes	1 oz. flour
1 onion	¼ pint stock
1 oz. margarine	½ teaspoonful sage
Seasoning	

Finely chop onion, fry golden brown in the margarine, add tomatoes, sage and seasoning. Sift in flour, add stock, stirring all the time. Put through strainer and re-boil.

Vegetable Medley with Brown Sauce

1 lb. potatoes	3 oz. swedes
6 oz. carrots	4 oz. onions
Frying fat	

Dice the carrot and swede, cover with water, boil until tender. Meanwhile, slice and slowly fry the onions until coloured. Cut the prepared potatoes into Brazil-nut sections. Place the *cooked* carrot and swede, fried onions, and the cut *raw*

Stuffed potatoes for cold-weather meals. If small, slice top and use as lid

potatoes, seasoned, in a well-greased casserole, cover and bake (or simmer on asbestos mat) for 1 hour or until the potatoes are quite done.

NOTE: For an exotic dish, add 6 or 7 soaked prunes, a tablespoonful of nut fat and a teaspoonful of brown sugar prior to final cooking. Serve with Brown Sauce.

Brown Sauce

1 oz. fat	1 small teaspoonful
1 oz. flour	Marmite
¼ pint vegetable	Few drops gravy
cooking water	browning
	Pepper and salt

Melt the fat in a saucepan, stir in the flour and cook gently for 3 minutes. Gradually add half the liquid, stir in the browning and Marmite, add rest of liquid, season to taste, simmer for 2 minutes.

Vegetable Roast

½ lb. lentils	4 oz. mashed potato
½ lb. onions	1 tablespoonful
3 oz. wholemeal	chopped parsley
breadcrumbs	Salt and pepper

Soak the lentils, drain them and cook in 2 pints water with the onions chopped finely. Pour off any surplus liquor and mix in the breadcrumbs, potato and parsley. Season with pepper and salt to taste, and place the mixture in a well-greased baking dish. Put a few flakes of margarine on top and bake in a moderate oven for 30 minutes until golden brown.

Serve with baked jacket potatoes, spinach, apple sauce and a good brown gravy made from the reserved liquor and some Marmite.

Vegetable Sausage Rolls

Enough puff or short pastry to make six sausage rolls

For the filling

1 carrot	2 potatoes
1 parsnip	Marjoram
1 leek	Thyme
1 onion	A little salt
A few cabbage leaves	1 tablespoonful oats
Frying fat	Marmite (optional)

Clean, peel and cook all the vegetables with a little water, put through the mincer. Mix with the chopped thyme and marjoram and salt, add the oats. If a little

Marmite is added, it improves the taste. Make small sausages out of this mixture and fry, then put away to cool. Roll out the pastry and make squares big enough to cover the fried sausages. Brush tops of the rolls with egg or water and bake for about 20 minutes in moderate oven.

Walnut Roast with Parsley Stuffing

½ lb. milled walnuts	*2 oz. vegetarian margarine*
½ lb. wholemeal breadcrumbs (fresh)	*¼ teaspoonful powdered sage*
1 large onion	*Seasoning*

Make exactly as Nut Roast with Chestnut Stuffing (see p. 247), but stuff with Parsley Stuffing.

Parsley Stuffing

4 oz. fresh wholemeal breadcrumbs	*½ teaspoonful thyme*
2 oz. grated or melted margarine	*2 tablespoonfuls chopped parsley*
Seasoning	*Grated rind of ½ lemon*

Mix all ingredients together and bind with thick gravy.

SAVOURY EGG DISHES

In addition to the following recipes, see also the chapter on Egg Dishes for all the well-known recipes enjoyed equally by vegetarians and non-vegetarians.

Angels in the Snow

4 slices wholewheat bread	*4 large eggs*
Butter or vegetarian margarine	*Pepper and nutmeg*
	¼ teaspoonful salt

Toast four slices of wholewheat bread, leaving one side more lightly browned than the other, and butter this side.

Separate the eggs, putting each yolk by itself in a cup. Put the whites together in a basin, add the salt and a pinch each of pepper and nutmeg, and beat until stiff but not dry. Spread the beaten egg-whites over the four pieces of toast, taking care to touch the sides, and drop a yolk exactly in the centre of each.

Brown lightly under the grill and serve. The egg-white may be scattered with grated cheese if liked.

This is an excellent dish for an invalid.

Eggs in Onion Sauce

4–8 eggs	*Watercress*
1 large onion	*1 tablespoonful wholewheat flour*
1 teaspoonful salt	
Mashed potatoes	*¼ teaspoonful pepper*
¾ pint milk	

Chop the onion and cook it in the milk with the pepper and salt until soft. Blend the flour with ½ cupful cold water and use this to thicken the sauce. Bring to the boil again and simmer for 5–8 minutes until cooked. Meanwhile, poach the eggs lightly until the whites are just set. When the eggs are ready, make a border of mashed potatoes on an oval dish, arrange the eggs in the centre and pour the onion sauce over the top. Trim with the best part of the watercress and serve.

Savoury Rice with Eggs

4 oz. rice	*¾ pint milk*
1 large onion	*4–8 eggs*
2 oz. fat for frying	*4 large tomatoes*
2 teaspoonfuls horse-radish cream	*3 oz. grated dry cheese*
1 tablespoonful wholewheat flour	*Salt*

Chop the onion and fry it in the fat until brown. Add the rice and stir until the grains are opaque. Put the rice-onion mixture into a pan with ¾ pint boiling water and 1 teaspoonful salt, bring to the boil, then simmer gently until soft and the water is absorbed. Add more water during cooking if it becomes too dry.

Meanwhile, hard-boil or poach the eggs and keep them warm. Boil the milk, pour it on to the flour mixed with a little water, and return it to the pan. Stir in the grated cheese, horseradish and 1 teaspoonful salt and cook for 5–6 minutes. Cut the eggs into quarters, and halve and grill the tomatoes. Put a ring of rice on an oval dish, pile the eggs in the centre. Pour the cheese sauce over the eggs and surround the mound with grilled tomatoes. A few chopped stuffed olives may be added to the rice if liked.

Vegetarian Scotch Eggs

4 hard-boiled eggs	*¼ teaspoonful pepper*
2 uncooked eggs	*2 oz. mushrooms*
2 teaspoonfuls chopped parsley	*5 oz. wholewheat breadcrumbs*
2 oz. butter or vegetarian margarine	*1 large onion*
	1 teaspoonful salt

Shell and dry the hard-boiled eggs, chop the onion finely and beat the two uncooked eggs. Skin and chop the mushrooms into small pieces. Melt the butter or margarine in a pan and cook the chopped onion in it until soft, but not brown. Add the mushrooms and cook gently until they are done.

Then remove the pan from the heat, mix in 2 oz. of the breadcrumbs and the parsley, season with pepper and salt, and bind with some of the beaten egg. Divide the mixture into four parts and use it to coat the hard-boiled eggs. It will not stick unless the eggs are quite dry. Stand for a few minutes and then coat with egg and breadcrumbs. Fry in deep fat and serve cold with horseradish cream. Green bean salad is excellent with this dish.

DISHES MADE FROM PULSES

Bean Roast with Tomatoes

½ lb. butter beans or haricots	1 teaspoonful mixed herbs
1 onion	1 tablespoonful chopped parsley
¼ lb. margarine	
2 eggs	1 lb. small ripe tomatoes
¼ lb. breadcrumbs	
Seasoning	

Soak beans overnight, then cook in slightly salted water together with the onion, peeled and sliced, until beans are soft.

Mash and put beans and onion in basin, then add 2 oz. of the margarine, the well-beaten eggs, breadcrumbs, herbs and seasoning. Mix well together. Turn on to a floured board, shape into a neat block and dredge with flour. Place on well-greased baking tin with remainder of margarine in small lumps on top. Place tomatoes round the savoury (whole).

Bake for about ½ hour in a medium oven, basting occasionally. When nicely browned, serve with a brown gravy (see p. 247) and apple sauce (see chapter on Sauces). If preferred, this roast can be eaten cold with salad.

Croquettes

1 pint haricot or butter beans or red lentils	Powdered sage or thyme
	1 dessertspoonful lemon juice
2 oz. margarine	
Seasoning	

Soak the beans or lentils overnight, then cook in slightly salted water until easy to mash. Dry well and sieve. Melt the margarine in a saucepan, add bean or lentil purée, powdered sage or thyme, lemon juice (if desired) and a seasoning of salt and pepper to taste. Mix well together, heat for a few minutes carefully, then set aside to cool. Shape into croquettes, brush with egg and roll in breadcrumbs; fry to a golden brown in deep fat. Drain and serve hot, garnished with parsley.

NOTE: The flavour of the above may be varied by the addition of 2 oz. chopped, fried peanuts.

Stuffed eggs, orange segments and lettuce, are the main ingredients of this salad, with cress for decoration

253

Cutlets

¾ lb. cooked, sieved lentils, beans or split peas	½ lb. mashed potatoes Salt and pepper to taste
1 teaspoonful chopped sage or thyme	2 medium-sized onions

Mix the purée with the mashed potatoes and add the onions (either chopped and fried or boiled, drained and chopped) together with herbs and seasoning as desired. Moisten the mixture, if necessary, with a little stock used in cooking the pulses. Shape as desired, either flour or dip in egg and breadcrumbs, and fry a golden brown in hot fat.

Family Hot-pot

Potatoes (peeled)	Baked beans in tomato sauce
Carrots (cleaned and sliced)	¼ lb. mushrooms (if desired)
Celery (cleaned and cut)	Marmite gravy
Onions (peeled and sliced)	Herbs and seasoning, as required
Grated cheese	Margarine for frying

Cook onion rings until lightly browned in margarine. Into a fair-sized baking-tin slice a layer of potatoes, then a layer of onions and other vegetables, followed by a layer of baked beans. Season as required. Cover again with a layer of sliced potatoes, add Marmite gravy on top of vegetables, and scatter grated cheese over the top. Bake in fairly hot oven until vegetables are well cooked—about 2 hours. Serve very hot, with a green vegetable.

If preferred, canned peas can be used in place of baked beans. Sliced tomatoes can also be added.

Lentil Soufflés

½ pint lentils	1 oz. flour
1 oz. margarine	¼ pint vegetable stock or Marmite gravy
½ small onion (chopped)	2 egg-whites

Prepare lentils by washing and cooking until soft in slightly salted water. Drain and, when dry, put through a sieve.

Melt margarine in saucepan, add onion and cook until tender; then add flour, cook slightly (stirring) before adding stock or gravy. Boil and cook for a few moments, then add to lentils, mixing all together. Whisk egg-whites until stiff and fold carefully into the lentil mixture.

Three-parts fill small, greased, fireproof dishes with the mixture, and bake for about 15 minutes in a fairly hot oven. Serve immediately they are ready. Very nice with chipped potatoes and spinach.

Peasant Lentil Dish

½ pint red lentils	1 peeled and chopped onion
2 oz. margarine or nut fat	1 tablespoonful flour
Salt and pepper	

Cook lentils until easy to mash, dry and put through a sieve. Melt fat in saucepan, add chopped onion, and fry until slightly browned; then add flour, cooking for a minute or two before adding gradually about ½ pint of water. Boil up, stirring all the time, and cook for 15 minutes or longer. Add lentil purée and seasoning, and continue to cook for a further 15 minutes. Serve very hot with any vegetables.

Savoury Bean Roll

2 breakfastcupfuls canned beans in tomato sauce	½ lb. grated cheese Breadcrumbs (preferably wholemeal)

Mash the beans, add the grated cheese, together with sufficient breadcrumbs to make a fairly stiff mixture. Shape into a loaf or roll, place in a baking tin and bake in a moderate oven for about ½ hour; baste occasionally with Nutter or Suenut melted in a little water. Serve with vegetables and brown gravy or with tomato sauce.

MEATLESS STEAK DISHES

Meatless Steaks, attractively packed in large or small cans, ready for use, do not contain nuts, but are made from gluten of wheat which has a protein value twice as high as nuts. Apart from their high food value, they look and taste good.

Curried Meatless Steaks

1 large can Meatless Steaks	1 dessertspoonful or more curry powder
2 large onions	2 tomatoes
2 oz. margarine	1 sweet apple
3 teaspoonfuls Vesop	1 dessertspoonful sultanas

Chop onions. Fry in margarine. Add curry powder and continue cooking for several minutes till blended. Add tomatoes, Vesop and fruit. Cook till onions are tender. Add steaks with liquid from can and simmer for 15 minutes.

Serve with plain boiled rice or Pulao (see

Radish roses and watercress are used to decorate a salad of diced mixed vegetables and macaroni

next page) and sweet mango chutney. It is essential to use as little liquid as possible in curries and to rely on fruit and vegetables for thickening. Flour should never be used.

Hungarian Goulash

1 large can Meatless Steaks	1½ oz. margarine
1 tablespoonful tomato purée	Small pinch caraway seeds
1 medium onion	2 teaspoonfuls Vesop
12 small new potatoes	1½ pints water
1 teaspoonful paprika	1 dessertspoonful flour

Slice onion thinly. Fry in saucepan, then add paprika, tomato purée, caraway seeds, Vesop and flour blended in liquid from can and water. Simmer for 10 minutes. Add steaks and new potatoes, cooked in their jackets and skinned. Simmer again gently for 15 minutes. Serve with tiny wholemeal dumplings.

Meatless Steak and Mushroom Pudding

6 oz. wholemeal pastry	1 medium-sized onion
1 small can Meatless Steaks	2 teaspoonfuls Vesop
	2 teaspoonfuls flour
4 oz. mushrooms	1 oz. margarine
	½ pint stock or water

Chop onion and fry in saucepan. Wipe and slice mushrooms and stems. Add to onion and cook for 5 minutes. Blend in flour, Vesop and liquid from steaks made up to ½ pint with stock or water. Allow to cool. Line greased basin with thin pastry. Cut steaks into medium-sized pieces and arrange in the pastry-lined basin. Pour over sauce. Cover with pastry, loosely tie and steam for 1 hour.

The same ingredients arranged in pie-dish, covered with pastry and baked, make a very good pie.

Meatless Steaks Jardinière

1 can Meatless Steaks	2 teaspoonfuls Vesop
12 tiny onions	¾ pint stock or water
1 oz. margarine	Mixed cooked vegetables
1 dessertspoonful flour	

Skin onions and fry without breaking until well browned. Carefully remove from fat. Stir flour into remaining fat. Add liquid from can, Vesop and stock. Cook for about 5 minutes until sauce is smooth and thick. Add steaks and onions. Simmer very gently for 10 minutes. Serve with border of diced mixed vegetables with carrots and peas to add colour.

Pulao

1 medium-sized onion	3 cardamom seeds
1 large cupful well-washed rice	and cloves
	1 bay leaf
2 oz. butter or margarine	Salt

Cut onion finely and fry till brown. Add rice, herbs and seasoning. Cook till rice is pale brown colour. Add water to cover 1 in. above rice level. Cover and cook over gentle heat till all moisture is absorbed and rice grains separate. Shake pan from time to time but do not stir.

Savoury Pasties

12 oz. wholemeal pastry	1 large parboiled potato
1 small can Meatless steaks	1 medium-sized onion
1 oz. margarine	2 teaspoonfuls Vesop

Chop and fry onion. Add cut-up steaks, liquid from can, Vesop and 3 tablespoonfuls water. Simmer gently for 5 minutes. Add potato cut into small dice and leave mixture to cool. Roll pastry thinly and cut into four even-sized pieces. Place steak mixture on pastry and form into pasties. Bake in brisk oven for about 20 minutes till pastry is crisp and well browned.

POTATO DISHES

Potatoes are an important part of vegetarian diet. During the winter they are even more important than during warm weather: their high calorific value—375 calories per lb.—as well as their vitamin C content help to maintain fitness. To get the best value out of them, bake in their skins, a method with many variations.

Bircher Potatoes

2 lb. of potatoes	A little caraway seed
A little salt	Oil or margarine

Scrub potatoes until absolutely clean, dry with a towel. Grease a baking tin with either liquid margarine or oil, sprinkle with salt and caraway seeds and bake till tender. If you do not care for caraway seed, use salt only. The potatoes taste quite different from ordinary baked potatoes and are very nourishing.

Potato Delights

This makes a very good main dish eaten with vegetables. Boil 2 lb. potatoes in their skins. When cold, cut them into thick slices and put a piece of Cheddar cheese on each slice. Put on a greased baking sheet and bake in a hot oven until the cheese melts.

Potatoes in Béchamel

2 lb. potatoes	1 egg
2 oz. grated cheese	Pinch of grated
½ pint milk	nutmeg
1 oz. margarine	A little margarine for
1 tablespoonful flour	the top

Parboil the potatoes in their skins. Cut them into thick slices and put them into a greased fireproof dish.

Make the sauce as follows: melt the margarine and add flour and milk. Bring to boil and stir well until it is thick and smooth, which takes about 1–2 minutes. Let it stand covered until cool. Add cheese, nutmeg, egg-yolk and stiffly beaten egg-white. If the sauce is too thick, add a little water or milk. Pour it over the potatoes, put a few dabs of margarine on top and bake for about 40 minutes. Serve with a salad.

Potatoes with Cream Cheese

2 lb. potatoes	Parsley or chives
¼ lb. cream cheese (preferably home-made)	Fat for greasing dish
	Pinch of salt

Parboil the potatoes and cut into slices. Grease a fireproof dish and put into it alternate layers of potatoes and cream cheese mixed with parsley or chives finely chopped. Salt the potatoes slightly. Finish off with a layer of potatoes. Bake for 20 minutes.

Stuffed Potatoes

Scrub the potatoes and, if large, cut them into halves. If they are small, cut only a piece off like a lid. It can be put over the stuffing. Make a hollow in each potato and fill it with the following mixture:

For the stuffing

1 oz. margarine	Finely chopped
1 oz. grated cheese	parsley, or dried
Brown breadcrumbs	herbs reconstituted with hot water

Cream the margarine and add the other ingredients. Stuff the potatoes and bake for about ¾ hour.

UNCOOKED MEALS

In a balanced diet one should have at least 50 per cent. of the day's food raw, either a whole uncooked meal or half a lunch or supper uncooked and the other half cooked. But uncooked salad does not mean shredded carrots one day and tomato salad with lettuce the next, or the usual variety (cooked beetroot, two slices of cucumber and four slices of tomatoes). This is, of course, insufficient. An adequate uncooked meal consists of a fruit or vegetable cocktail, a salad consisting of a fruit, root and leaf vegetable; and a small sweet uncooked or unbaked.

Tomatoes, cucumbers and marrows are considered fruit vegetables. During winter time, when tomatoes and cucumbers are very expensive and marrows unobtainable, ordinary fruit can be used in salads. Cabbage, celery, leeks and spinach are leaf vegetables.

Spring onions or ordinary onions finely chopped, parsley, mint, chives, sage, thyme, etc., make excellent dressings when mixed with home-made mayonnaise or lemon and olive oil. For something very appetising, mix raw, grated horseradish roots with a little lemon juice and mayonnaise, and pour this dressing over grated, raw beetroots or red cabbage.

Here are recipes for an uncooked meal. All ingredients are for 6 people.

Tomato Cocktail

Wash raw tomatoes, cut into small pieces, put through a strainer and mix the juice with a little lemon juice and, if liked, a little brown sugar.

Grapefruit Salad

2 *medium-sized grapefruit*	3 *oranges*
4 *apples (Bramleys or any other not-too-sweet kind)*	1 *large tablespoonful whipped cream*
	2 *glacé or other cherries*

Peel the grapefruit and oranges and cut into segments, wash the apples (do *not* peel), dry and cut into segments, mix fruit together, top with cream and decorate with cut-up cherries.

Summer salad with sliced hard-boiled egg, cucumber and tomato contains plenty of nourishment

Shredded Beetroots with Herb Sauce

2 *large beetroots*	1 *teaspoonful*
2 *tablespoonfuls*	*chopped herbs (any*
olive oil	*kind) mixed with a*
½ *lemon*	*tablespoonful of*
	home-made mayon-
	naise

Wash the beetroots and soak in cold water for a few hours, grate on Bircher Grater, mix with lemon and olive oil. Pour the mixed herbs and mayonnaise (see Salads chapter) over beetroots.

Green Cabbage Salad with Roasted Cashew Nuts

¼ *head of medium-*	½ *lemon*
sized cabbage	2 *tablespoonfuls of*
¼ *lb. roasted cashew*	*home-made mayon-*
nuts	*naise (see Salads)*

Wash and soak cabbage in cold water. Cut cabbage very fine with knife or grate on a coarse grater. Grind cashew nuts finely and mix with grated cabbage, add lemon juice and mayonnaise. Mix well.

Decorate the salads with lettuce and cress. Great care should be taken to make them look as attractive as possible. A good colour scheme which pleases the eye makes a meal much more attractive than the knowledge that it is rightly balanced.

Fruit Medleys

About 1½ *cupfuls of*	1 *teaspoonful lemon*
mixed fruit (raisins,	*juice*
sultanas, prunes,	1 *tablespoonful of*
figs, dates)	*thin cream (top of*
¼ *lb. grated almonds*	*the milk or milk is*
or other nuts	*sufficient)*
2 *teaspoonfuls brown*	
sugar	

Wash the fruit in warm water, put through mincer, mix all ingredients together into a fairly stiff mixture, form little balls and roll them in grated nuts.

Bircher Pudding

2 *or* 3 *carrots*	2 *oz. ground almonds*
2 *tablespoonfuls*	*A few drops of lemon*
brown sugar	*juice*
2 *tablespoonfuls of*	1 *cupful of cornflakes*
cream (or top of	*or any other flakes*
the milk)	1 *large apple*

Peel and soak the carrots for a few hours in cold water, grate on a very fine grater. Wash and dry apple, grate finely. Mix grated carrots and apple with almonds, sugar, lemon juice, cream and cornflakes. Press into little pudding basins and put in a cold place for 30 minutes. Turn out on a plate and either top with cream or pour milk over the pudding.

The uncooked meal can be supplemented by cooked or baked potatoes in their skins or by Bircher Potatoes (see p. 256).

SALAD IDEAS
by IVAN BAKER

A leading authority on vegetarian cookery and catering and the author of many books on the subject, Mr. Baker also contributed the recipes for Almond and Potato Croquettes; Haricot, Leek and Mushroom Pie; Roast Nutmeat; Stuffed Tomatoes; Spaghetti Rondelles; Butter Mint Sauce, and Vegetable Medley with Brown Sauce.

Tomato, minced onion or capers, olive oil and lemon.

Watercress, diced orange, oil and lemon, garnish with little heaps of diced beet.

Finely shredded raw cabbage, small dice of preserved cucumber, a little chopped onion, oil and lemon. Toss well. Chill. Serve.

Sliced celery heart, diced apple, walnut halves, sour cream dressing (see below).

Core a large pear, fill with cream cheese previously moistened with mayonnaise. Chill, peel, slice, serve on endive.

Freshly grated raw carrot centre, thin outer ring of finely grated swede flavoured with onion juice. Mustard and cress garnish.

Potato salad made with diced, freshly boiled jacket potatoes, dressed with lemon then oil, while warm, then tossed carefully with a little chopped onion and seasoning.

Russian salad made by mixing 1 cupful canned peas, 1 cupful small diced cooked carrot, 1 cupful small diced cooked potato, ½ cupful diced cooked swede, oil and lemon, then mayonnaise dressing.

Sliced hard-boiled egg, diced tomato, sliced preserved cucumber, diced cooked beet, oil and lemon. Garnish with cress and diced grapefruit or orange.

Sliced chicory, cleaned, soaked sultanas arranged on prepared endive. Garnish with black and green olives and cress sprigs.

Sour Cream Dressing. Stir 2 tablespoonfuls lemon juice into 5 tablespoonfuls unsweetened evaporated milk.

(See also the main Salads chapter for many recipes suitable also for Vegetarians.)

INVALID COOKERY

To tempt flagging appetites, food must look specially inviting

Photo: Electrolux

A perfect tray for the sick-room—piping hot beef tea is followed by ice-cold jellied chicken and a cream sweet, all attractively served

THE appearance of food is nearly as important as its flavour and never more so than when it is prepared for the sick-room. Invalids' appetites need tempting, and a daintily arranged tray will often mean that the meal is eaten with relish instead of merely being picked at. As far as is possible, all food intended for the sick-room should be prepared the day it is to be eaten. Most foods look far more appetising served in individual dishes, glasses, etc. A golden rule is never to overload an invalid's plate or tray. Nothing is more likely to discourage a capricious appetite, so make the portions small and attractive to look at and you may be rewarded with a request for a second helping.

Be sparing with seasoning and fats; grill, steam or bake rather than fry, and serve hot food really hot and cold food really cold.

SOUPS FOR INVALIDS

Beef Tea (now used chiefly to promote appetite)

1 lb. lean shin of beef   1 pint lukewarm
Pinch of salt   water

Cut the meat into very small pieces, removing all fat, and put it, with the water and salt, into a double saucepan over boiling water. Cover and simmer for at least 2 hours. If to be used at once, strain and take off the fat with a piece of soft paper. Otherwise, stand in a cool place uncovered and remove the fat when cold.

Beef and Sago Broth

1 lb. gravy beef   1 quart water
1 oz. sago   1 egg-yolk
            Salt to taste

Cut up the meat finely and stew it very slowly in the water for 3 hours. Meanwhile, soak the sago in ¼ pint water for 30 minutes and cook in the top of a double boiler until clear. Strain off the beef tea, return to saucepan and add salt and sago. Cook gently for 30 minutes. Remove from the heat. Beat the egg-yolk in a basin, add a little of the broth, stir well and then pour into the broth. Reheat but do not allow to boil.

Chicken Broth

Use the liquor from a boiled fowl, add the chicken bones and bring to the boil, then simmer for 2 or 3 hours. Strain through a sieve, remove all fat and season to taste. If liked, add a very little cooked rice. To make the broth more nourishing, add a beaten egg-yolk and a tablespoonful of cream to ½ pint of the strained liquor and reheat without boiling.

Soups made from good stock, if not greasy or too highly flavoured, and milk soups are also suitable for invalids, but those containing much vegetable should be

Junket is an ideal sweet for an invalid—
nourishing and easy to eat

avoided as possibly indigestible. (See Soup chapter for Consommé, Kidney Soup, Tomato Soup, Barley Cream Soup and Rabbit Broth.)

FISH

Avoid the strongly flavoured varieties. Most suitable are sole, plaice, whiting, cod, fresh haddock, halibut and turbot. All fish for invalids should be steamed, poached, baked or grilled, but *not* fried.

Steamed Fillet of Fish (sole, plaice or other white fish)

Wash the fish, lay it on a well-buttered plate, lightly peppered and salted, with another plate on top. Steam for 20–30 minutes over a pan of boiling water. Decorate with a little chopped parsley and serve hot.

Poached Fish

A whole sole on the bone or fillets of sole, plaice or other white fish may be placed in a frying pan, completely covered with fish stock or milk and water, very lightly seasoned with salt and pepper, and

gently simmered until tender. It should take about 10 minutes per lb.

Fish Cream (2 helpings)

4 oz. fresh haddock	½ oz. butter
1 tablespoonful milk	1 egg
½ oz. breadcrumbs	Squeeze of lemon
Salt and pepper	juice
½ gill cream	

Wipe the fish and shred it finely, removing bones and skin. Melt the butter in a saucepan, add the egg-yolk, milk and breadcrumbs. Cook until thick, without boiling, add to the fish, mix well together and rub through a fine sieve. Add seasoning, lemon juice, cream and egg-white, stiffly beaten. Turn into a greased basin, cover with greased paper and steam very gently for about 40 minutes. Turn out carefully and serve at once.

Fish in Custard (1–2 helpings)

2 fillets of sole or plaice	1 gill milk
Pepper and salt	1 small egg
	Water biscuit

Beat up the egg with the milk and the biscuit crushed to powder, then add seasoning to taste. Put the fillets one on top of the other in a greased fireproof dish, season and heat in a hot oven. When the fillets are hot, add the custard mixture and continue cooking until the fish is done and the custard set, then lift the fillets carefully from the dish and put on a hot plate with the flakes of custard on top.

Soufflé Pudding

About 1 lb. cod fillet	2 or 3 egg-whites
1 teacupful milk or evaporated milk	Salt, pepper and a squeeze of lemon juice
2 tablespoonfuls soft breadcrumbs	Parsley

Skin the cod and chop as finely as possible. Mix with the breadcrumbs, milk and seasonings, including the lemon juice. Fold in the stiffly beaten egg-whites and pour carefully into a greased soufflé dish or casserole. Either steam for about 1¼ hours, then put under a hot grill for a few minutes to brown the top, or bake for 1 hour in the centre of a very moderate oven. Garnish with sprigs of parsley

OTHER MAIN DISHES

Chicken, rabbit, eggs and various kinds of offal, such as brains and sweetbreads, are more digestible than meat and therefore more suitable for invalids.

Brain Scallop (1 helping)

Set of brains (calf's or sheep's)	1 gill white sauce
1 teaspoonful chopped parsley	Few drops of lemon juice
Breadcrumbs	½ oz. butter

Wash the brains several times in salted water, then carefully remove the skin. Plunge into boiling water for 2–3 minutes to blanch, then drain carefully. Simmer in the white sauce for 20 minutes, add the parsley and lemon juice, and put into a greased scallop shell. Sprinkle with breadcrumbs, put the butter in tiny pieces on top and brown either under a hot grill or in a quick oven.

Chicken Panada

Take a lean chicken, wash well and boil gently until the bones can be removed, then return the flesh to the liquor and cook gently until tender. Strain off the liquor. Put the meat twice through the mincer, add a little of the liquor to thin it, and serve either hot or cold, according to taste.

Egg Dishes (see separate chapter, pp. 174–179)

Invalid's Chop (1 helping)

Mutton or lamb chop	2 tablespoonfuls stock
½ oz. breadcrumbs	or water
Buttered toast	Pepper and salt

Shred the meat off the bone and put into a saucepan with the breadcrumbs, stock or water and seasoning. Simmer gently for 10 minutes, then serve on hot buttered toast.

Rabbit Cream (1 helping)

2 oz. raw rabbit
¼ oz. breadcrumbs
½ egg-white
Pepper and salt
¼ oz. butter
¼ gill milk
¼ gill cream

Put the milk, butter and breadcrumbs into a saucepan and heat until the butter melts and the breadcrumbs

swell. Put the rabbit four times through the mincer, then add to the milk, etc. Beat the egg-white to a stiff froth and fold lightly into the mixture. Add the cream and seasoning. Three-parts fill little dariole moulds with the mixture, cover with greased paper and stand in a saucepan with boiling water half-way up the sides. Put on the lid of the pan and steam gently for 40 minutes, then turn out and serve.

SWEETS

Arrowroot Pudding (1–2 helpings)

1 tablespoonful arrowroot	Brandy to taste ½ pint milk
1 teaspoonful castor sugar	Small egg

Mix the arrowroot to a smooth paste with a little of the milk, boil the rest with the sugar and pour on to the arrowroot, stir well, return to the pan and cook for 5 minutes, stirring continuously. Take off the heat, add the well-beaten egg and brandy, pour into a small, warm, greased pie dish and put into a quick oven for a few minutes to brown the surface.

Bread and Milk (1 helping)

1 slice of bread	Pepper and salt
½ pint milk	or sugar

Remove crust and cut the bread into squares. Boil the milk, pour over the bread, cover and leave for a minute or two. Add a dash of salt and pepper or sugar, according to taste, and serve at once.

NOTE: If liked, half a teaspoonful of meat extract or Marmite can be dissolved

Brains or sweetbreads are more digestible than meat and may be served in cream sauce

in the boiling milk before it is poured over the bread.

Caudle (1 helping)

½ pint gruel	Glass of brandy
1 egg-white	Grated lemon rind
Scrape of nutmeg	Sugar to taste.

To make the gruel, mix together 1 oz. medium oatmeal and ½ pint water, stand for 1 hour, then stir and strain into a saucepan. Stir over the fire until boiling, then simmer gently for 15 minutes, with the brandy, nutmeg, lemon rind and sugar to taste. Let the mixture cool, then fold in the stiffly beaten egg-white.

Cornflour Soufflé (1–2 helpings)

½ pint milk	1 egg
Grated rind of	½ oz. cornflour
¼ lemon	½ oz. castor sugar

Mix the cornflour to a smooth paste with a little of the milk, boil the rest and pour on to the paste, stirring at the same time. Return to the pan and cook for 5 minutes, stirring all the time. Let it cool a little, then add the sugar, lemon rind and beaten egg-yolk and stir well. Whip the egg-white stiffly and fold into the mixture as lightly as possible. Turn into a greased pie dish and bake in a fairly slow oven until a pale brown. Serve at once.

Egg Jelly (3–4 helpings)

½ pint water	1½ oz. castor sugar
Rind and juice of a	¼ oz. powdered gelatine
lemon	
2 eggs	Sherry to taste

Heat the water, lemon rind, sugar and gelatine without boiling until the gelatine is dissolved and the flavour of the lemon rind extracted. Strain, then add the lemon juice and the beaten eggs and heat, carefully stirring all the time without boiling. When the mixture is thick and creamy, add the sherry and pour into a wetted mould to set.

Junket

½ pint fresh milk	Vanilla essence, or
1 tablespoonful sugar	dessertspoonful
1 teaspoonful rennet	black coffee to
Nutmeg	flavour

Follow instructions on the packet or bottle containing the rennet (or junket powder) for exact quantity to use, but remember more rennet is needed with pasteurised milk.

Stir in the rennet when the milk has been heated just to blood temperature—tested with your finger—and then remove from heat. Add flavouring and sugar and stand in glasses to cool. Serve cold with a little nutmeg grated on top.

Milk Jelly (3–4 helpings)

1 pint milk	½ oz. powdered gelatine
Rind of half lemon	tine
1½ oz. castor sugar	

Put the ingredients into a saucepan and stir over a low heat for 10 minutes or so until the sugar and gelatine have dissolved. Do not let the mixture boil. Take out the lemon rind. Pour the mixture into a basin, stirring now and again until it is the consistency of thick cream. Then pour into small wetted moulds and leave to set.

INVALID DRINKS

Barley Water

1½ pints boiling water	2 oz. pearl barley
Rind of a lemon	1 oz. loaf sugar

Wash the barley in cold water and put into a saucepan, cover with cold water and bring to the boil. Then strain and put the barley back into the pan and add the sugar. Peel the lemon thinly so that none of the white pith is removed, put the peel with the barley and sugar and add 1½ pints of boiling water, then simmer gently for about 15 minutes. Strain into a jug and serve cold.

NOTE: If liked, the juice of the lemon can be added when the barley water is cold.

Black Currant Tea

1 teaspoonful lemon	½ pint boiling water
juice	1 dessertspoonful
1 teaspoonful castor	black currant jam
sugar	or purée

Put the jam or purée, sugar and lemon juice into a jug, pour on the boiling water and stir well. Cover with a plate and stand on the hot-plate for 15–20 minutes, then strain.

Serve hot to relieve colds.

Egg Flip (for 1)

½ pint milk	1 oz. castor sugar
1 egg	Sherry or brandy

Dissolve the sugar in the milk. Beat the egg well and stir the milk on to it, add sherry or brandy and pour into a glass.

THE VERSATILE PASTA FAMILY

How to recognise good quality and how to cook the many
varieties so that they are tasty, nourishing—and not fattening

MARCO POLO, it is rumoured, first introduced noodles to the Western world after one of his visits to China. True or not, it is a fact that pasta has now become the staple diet of the Italians, as well as being accepted all over the world as an economical and nutritious food.

Dozens of different kinds of pasta are to be bought in London's Soho, and the best are made from the same basic ingredient, durum wheat. This is a hard, glutinous wheat which is washed and then finely ground to meal, the husk and other rough parts being removed. Most important in the production of pasta is the selection of the finest wheat and the drying of the paste, which ensures that the finished product will be of the right colour and consistency when cooked.

Among the types most popular in the U.K. are macaroni, spaghetti, vermicelli, noodles, shells, bows, macaroni alphabets, and even animal shapes for children's soup. Incidentally, all these varieties are actually made in Britain, and since the finest-quality wheats are in many cases Empire-grown, these products have many advantages over their imported counterparts. The longer varieties should not break when being lifted from the pot after cooking, and other types should retain their shape.

The characteristics of a first-class macaroni or spaghetti are that it should be a creamy pale amber in colour, of a smooth appearance, and free from mottled specks or similar discolorations. It should break with a clean snap, leaving fresh glossy ends, and when cooked should be firm, non-sticky and have retained its shape.

Right Cooking Method

The most readily available type of paste product in the U.K. is macaroni, which may be used in any dish where pasta is required. It has a high protein content and is rich in energy-giving carbohydrates. Its low fibre content makes it readily assimi-lated without any irritating effects on the digestive system, and it is thus suitable for both children and invalids.

An excellent standby in the kitchen, easily and quickly prepared, pasta should not be spoiled by bad cooking. It should always be plunged into plenty of salted, fast-boiling water, and removed while still firm, and not after it has been stewed to a pulp. Time of cooking varies with individual products—about 8 minutes for quick-cooking varieties, and 15–25 minutes for stick or thicker types.

Many people steer clear of pasta because they believe it to be "fattening," but, in fact, most of the free starch is removed after cooking, by placing the pasta in a colander and running hot water through it. This rinsing is essential for perfection of taste and texture if the pasta is being served with a sauce and not being cooked in with the main ingredients.

Need Not Boil Over

A useful hint in the cooking of pasta is to add a spoonful of olive oil or a knob of margarine to the cooking water to prevent it from boiling over. To give your spaghetti or macaroni a glossy appearance, toss it in a little fat after cooking. This also helps to drive off excess water.

Pasta, and particularly macaroni, is the most versatile of foods, and can be served with meat, fish or cheese as a main dish; as an accompaniment to the main dish; in soups and in sweets. Cold macaroni, blended with a sauce, can make a substantial addition to salads.

The recipes that follow give some idea of the uses to which pasta may be put. Spaghetti or noodles can often be substituted for macaroni, if so desired.

SOUPS

A Hint for all Soups ...

Cook a handful of macaroni, drain well, toss in 1 oz. melted fat and leave to become cold. Add to soup before serving, and it will be found that the delicious nutty flavour of the pasta is retained and the texture remains firm.

Noodle Soup—Spanish Style (for 4)

1 *pint stock*	1 *dessertspoonful*
4 *oz. cooked noodles*	*flour*
1 *small onion*	*Salt and pepper to*
1 *small can pimento*	*taste*
Fat for frying	

Chop onion finely, fry golden brown in fat. Stir in flour, cook for 5 minutes over low heat, stirring all the time. Add stock and noodles, and boil for 5 minutes. Chop pimento coarsely, add to the soup with salt and pepper and boil for 1 minute.

Shrimp and Macaroni Soup (for 4)

1 *pint shrimps*	½ *pint stock*
4 *oz. macaroni*	1 *small onion*
½ *pint cider*	*chopped*
1 *teaspoonful*	1 *teaspoonful*
Worcester sauce	*chopped parsley*
Salt and pepper to	2 *oz. margarine or*
taste	*butter*

Cook onion in margarine until soft, add shrimps and parsley, cook for 5 minutes, add cider and stock. Bring to the boil, add macaroni, season and boil until cooked. A teaspoonful of Worcester sauce may be added before serving.

Genoese Soup (for 4–6)

8 *oz. macaroni or*	2 *bay leaves or*
noodles	*marjoram leaves*
1 *quart stock, or 1*	2 *tablespoonfuls*
quart water and 3	*grated cheese*
meat cubes	*Salt and pepper to*
1 *egg*	*taste*

Bring the stock, or water and meat cubes, to the boil and add the bay or marjoram leaves and the macaroni. Cook for 5 minutes. Mix the egg with 2 tablespoonfuls of the soup, season and boil for 1 minute, remove the herbs, sprinkle cheese on top and serve at once.

MEAT AND FISH DISHES

Oxtail Suprême

½ *lb. macaroni or*	1 *chopped carrot*
noodles	1 *cupful beer or*
1 *oxtail*	*cider*
2 *oz. fat from oxtail*	*Salt and pepper*
½ *lb. tomatoes*	2 *bay leaves*
1 *teaspoonful paprika*	1 *small can processed*
2 *onions*	*peas*

Cut oxtail into pieces, removing surplus fat. Fry in the fat until browned, stir in

paprika, fry for another 5 minutes. Add sliced tomatoes, sliced onions and carrot. Stir well, add beer or cider, salt and pepper and bay leaves. Simmer in oven or on hot plate for 2 hours. Cook macaroni or noodles in plenty of well-salted boiling water (only 7 minutes if quick-cooking variety) and drain well. Toss in a little butter or margarine, mix with the peas, arrange round edge of large warmed serving dish, pour oxtail mixture into centre, then warm through in oven.

Sausage and Tomato Macaroni (for 4–6)

8 *oz. macaroni*	¼ *pint thick tomato*
½ *lb. sausages*	*sauce or purée*
2 *medium-sized*	6 *chopped olives*
onions	*(optional)*
½ *saltspoonful pepper*	1 *teaspoonful salt*
Fat for frying	

Put macaroni on to cook. Cut the sausages into 1-in. pieces and fry. Remove from pan and fry the chopped onions in the fat until a delicate brown. Return sausages to pan, add the tomato sauce or purée and the chopped olives, if used. Drain the macaroni and fold in the sausages, onions, etc., and season with salt and pepper. Place in a greased pie dish and bake in a slow oven for 15–20 minutes.

Spaghetti Italienne (for 4)

This is a basic recipe which can be used for any type of pasta.

½ *lb. spaghetti (or*	2 *tablespoonfuls*
other pasta)	*tomato purée*
1 *tablespoonful flour*	1 *onion*
½ *pint water*	*Tomato sauce*
4 *oz. grated cheese*	*Fat for frying*

Cook spaghetti for 15 minutes (if quick macaroni is used, cook for 8 minutes). Blend flour with a little cold water from ½ pint. Boil rest of water, add to flour, stirring constantly. Re-boil, add tomato purée. Season and simmer for 3 minutes. Cook chopped onion gently in fat. Add tomato sauce, grated cheese and spaghetti, well drained. Serve with grated cheese served separately.

Macaroni and Fish in Scallop Shells (for 4)

4 *deep scallop shells*	1 *cupful cooked fish,*
1 *cupful cooked*	*lobster or shrimps*
macaroni	½ *cupful white sauce*
2 *tablespoonfuls*	*(see Sauces chapter)*
butter	1 *lightly beaten egg*
2 *tablespoonfuls grated cheese*	
(½*-pint cups used throughout*)	

Sausage and Tomato Macaroni is a tasty and satisfying lunch or supper dish—particularly good if garnished, as here, with stuffed olives

Butter the four shells. Mix the hot macaroni with the butter and cheese, and partly fill each shell with this mixture. Place the fish, shredded, on the bed of macaroni, cover with the white sauce mixed with the egg, sprinkle with a little cheese and bake for 10 minutes in a hot oven.

Macaroni Fish Loaf
(for 5–6)

6 oz. quick macaroni
1 lb. white fish, flaked and boned
1 dessertspoonful lemon juice
1 teaspoonful grated onion
$\frac{1}{3}$ pint milk
2 eggs
Salt and pepper
Slices of cucumber
2 slices lemon
2 tablespoonfuls breadcrumbs

Macaroni Fish Loaf is both cool and decorative for a summer meal—and ideal for a picnic, with its fresh garnish of sliced cucumber and ornamental lemon slices

Cook macaroni for 8 minutes. Drain. Mix with milk, fish, lemon juice, grated onion and eggs, lightly beaten. Season to taste. Grease loaf tin, sprinkle with breadcrumbs and bake for 40 minutes in a moderate oven. Cool, turn out of tin and garnish with slices of cucumber and rounds of lemon peel.

SAVOURY DISHES

Macaroni Cheese (for 4)

Cheese and pasta are often combined in cooking, and of the many dishes known in the U.K., perhaps macaroni cheese is the most popular. There are many variations of this dish, and the following are two basic recipes which can be amended according to taste.

4 oz. quick macaroni	¼ teaspoonful paprika
2 oz. cornflour	3–4 oz. grated cheese
½ pint milk	Dash Yorkshire
¼ teaspoonful	relish
mustard powder	Pinch salt
Knob of margarine	Breadcrumbs

Cook macaroni until tender. Drain, keeping liquor. Blend the cornflour with a little milk taken from ½ pint, add rest of milk to ½ pint macaroni liquor and boil. Stir into blended cornflour, return to pan, simmer for 3 minutes, stirring constantly. Add margarine, mustard powder and paprika, Yorkshire relish and salt. Add grated cheese. Stir, add macaroni, reheat gently without overcooking cheese. Pour into fireproof dish, sprinkle with mixed breadcrumbs and grated cheese, dot with margarine and brown under grill. Garnish with chopped parsley and triangles of toast, if desired.

Savoury Cheese Macaroni (for 4)

8 oz. macaroni	3 eggs
½ oz. butter or	1 teaspoonful salt
margarine	Pinch Cayenne
4 oz. bacon	pepper
4 oz. grated cheese	

Cook macaroni in plenty of boiling, salted water. Drain and turn into a heated dish. Dot with butter or margarine and keep warm. Cut the bacon across into thin strips, add the beaten eggs and seasoning, and scramble until the mixture begins to thicken. Add to the macaroni with the 4 oz. grated cheese, and give the macaroni a good stir. Garnish and serve at once. Serve a bowl of grated cheese separately.

Macaroni with Chestnuts (for 4)

4 oz. macaroni	3 tablespoonfuls
8 oz. chestnuts	cream or top of
Salt and pepper	milk
2 oz. grated cheese	2 oz. margarine

Cook the macaroni and drain well. Slit skins of chestnuts and boil for 20 minutes, remove outer and inner skins and chop roughly. Mix chestnuts and macaroni, season with salt and pepper, and put in a greased baking dish. Sprinkle with grated cheese and dot with margarine. Add the cream or top of milk and bake in a moderate oven for 20 minutes.

DESSERTS

Apricot Macaroni Meringue (for 4–5)

2 oz. macaroni	1 small can of apricots
6 eggs	½ pint milk
1 dessertspoonful	1 dessertspoonful
cornflour	sugar

Cook macaroni until tender, and strain. Chop apricots and fold through macaroni. Make a custard by beating the egg-yolks, then stirring into the heated milk, blended with the cornflour. Cook gently without boiling until mixture thickens. When thick, fold into macaroni. Beat the egg-whites until very stiff, adding sugar. Pile on top of mixture and cook in hot oven until meringue is set and just turned in colour. About 15 minutes. Serve hot.

Noodle Omelet

3 tablespoonfuls milk	3 eggs, lightly beaten
½ teaspoonful salt	3 cupfuls cooked
3 tablespoonfuls	noodles
butter or margarine	Fat for frying
	Sugar

Add milk and seasoning to eggs. Sauté the noodles in butter or margarine until lightly browned, then pour in egg mixture and mix. Heat a little fat in omelet pan, pour in noodle mixture and when set fold in half. Dust with sugar and serve immediately.

Noodles with Cream Cheese (for 4)

½ lb. noodles	6 oz. cream or cottage
2 tablespoonfuls	cheese
warm water	3 dessertspoonfuls
½ teaspoonful	sugar
cinnamon	3 oz. sultanas

Add noodles to plenty of salted boiling water and cook until tender. Soak sultanas in boiling water for 15 minutes. Mix cheese with warm water, sugar and cinnamon.

Macaroni Cheese may not sound exciting but there are many variations; here is a delicious one, crisp and brown on top, served with triangles of toast

Add to drained noodles, together with sultanas, previously dried in a cloth.

Macaroni and Date Charlotte (for 4)

3 oz. macaroni	1 pint milk
1 tablespoonful sugar	2 eggs
	4 oz. chopped dates

For sprinkling

2 oz. margarine	1 teaspoonful sugar
2 oz. breadcrumbs	Grated nutmeg

Cook the macaroni and drain well. Add the sugar and milk, and simmer for 5 minutes. Remove from the heat and add the slightly beaten eggs, stirring well. Put the chopped dates in a well-greased pie dish; pour in the macaroni mixture. Melt the margarine in a saucepan, add the crumbs, teaspoonful of sugar and the grated nutmeg. Stir until the margarine has been absorbed by the crumbs, then spread on top of the macaroni. Bake for 20 minutes in a hot oven, or until the top is browned.

SALAD SAUCES

Here are three basic sauces for use with cold macaroni in salads.

Tomato-Onion Sauce

Simmer 1 large, coarsely chopped onion in 1 cupful of water, with salt, pepper and a dash of sugar. When tender, add 1 small can tomato purée. Blend 1 heaped teaspoonful flour with a little water and thicken sauce. Mix well with macaroni. Serve cold.

Creamy Cheese Sauce

Blend 1 teaspoonful cornflour with 1 cupful evaporated milk. Put in saucepan with 1 cupful grated sharp cheese, salt and pepper. Simmer until cheese is melted, stirring constantly. Add some finely chopped spring onions and mix with macaroni. Serve cold.

Celery Cheese Sauce

Drain the macaroni and keep hot. Mix 1 large cupful grated cheese with $\frac{1}{2}$ cupful macaroni water. Bring to the boil, season with pepper and a teaspoonful of celery salt. Mix with hot macaroni. Cool before serving.

THE DECORATION OF FOOD

*Dyed Easter eggs . . . tomato men . . . a sandwich tower . . .
rainbow-hued jellies and heraldic gingerbread*

THERE are two important principles to be considered in cooking: pleasing the palate and pleasing the eye. One achieves the first by means of the second. Not nearly enough attention is paid to the presentation of food.

It is so easy to make even the dullest dish look attractive. For example, fish is in itself very decorative, yet *steamed plaice* has, for many of us, the most unpleasant associations. But try this way of presenting it: Before cooking, rub the white sides of the fish with lemon to bleach them. Lightly steam the fillets, leaving them in their black skins. Lay them alternately on your dish—one black, one white, etc., so that you get a pattern of light and dark which compels interest. Choose brightly coloured vegetables and arrange them round the fish.

Use of Colour

We have certain inherent feelings towards colour in food which are most important when considering its presentation. Dark colours are often associated unconsciously in our minds with dirt, and we hardly ever colour food blue or green. Green is the colour of nature, but it is also the colour of poison.

Always try to include at least one example of naturally decorative food, such as sliced tomatoes or fried egg, when arranging each meal. Keep a bunch of parsley at hand. It looks more interesting in its natural state. Chives are also a useful decoration, and a sprinkling of chopped watercress is to be thoroughly recommended on almost any type of unsweetened dish. It adds a most distinctive flavour and

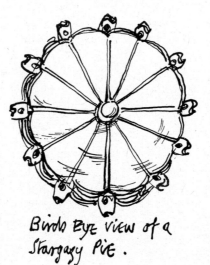

Birds Eye View of a Stargazy Pie.

an attractive dash of dark green to any dish. A subtle visual effect can also be achieved by using Cayenne pepper instead of the ordinary kind.

Pies are the easiest dishes to decorate. The reason for their particular shapes is usually very practical. A Cornish Pasty has a join along the top because it was considered less likely to spill the gravy that way when it was baked in the old Cornish hearth ovens. Certain pie fillings have traditional decorations. Apple pies, for example, are traditionally covered with wide strips of lattice which should be "nailed" together with cloves.

Stargazy Pie is an interesting-looking dish for a Buffet Supper. It is an old recipe and was originally made from pilchards, but any fish of a similar shape will do, and even sprats could be used as a filling for tiny individual pies. It was considered wasteful to cover the fish-heads with pastry, but if they were cut off, the rich oil would be lost. So the fish were laid, tails together, heads outwards like the spokes of a wheel, on a round dish and covered with a circle of pastry, leaving their heads bare. You can add your own decoration by cutting the remainder of the pastry into thin strips and laying them on the pastry cover to form the spokes of the wheel.

Decorating with Pastry

Pastry lends itself very well to all sorts of designs and patterns. You can plait and twist to your heart's content. Try decorating your next pie with enormous pastry flowers. Cut out of the remains of the pie pastry three sets of petals, each set a little

268

larger than the previous one. For a medium-sized pie, the largest petals should be 3 in. long. Arrange the petals to form a flower, working in layers inwards and curving the petals slightly to make them look natural. Make several flowers for a large pie.

Decorated Easter eggs are easily made by drawing an original design on a hard-boiled egg with a piece of sharpened candle wax. Dip the egg into cochineal or some other harmless dye and the wax will form a white pattern on the coloured ground. This is the Czechoslovakian method. The Caucasian way is to tie the hard-boiled eggs in different coloured scraps of material and boil them again for a few minutes. Remove from the saucepan and unwrap them when they have cooled and you will discover the most beautiful multi-coloured marbled eggs. Finally, polish them with goose fat to make them glow.

Salad Ideas

Here are a few ideas to help with salads: Chop your lettuce into long thin slices. It looks more unusual, and it goes farther too. Serve a small plate of lettuce salad with the main dish as they do on the Continent. To keep it from becoming limp and discoloured, always cut lettuce with a steel knife. Leave the rind on the cucumber; it is easier to digest and looks much more at-

Radishes and a Tomato Man.

An Easter Egg.

tractive. Cut patterns on radishes; this is easier to do than it looks. Sprinkle capers and slices of raw pimento over your salad.

Making tomato men is a good way of keeping children busy. Choose a few very large firm tomatoes and slice off the tops. Scoop out enough of the inside to allow a hard-boiled egg to sit firmly on each tomato. Fix the remainder of the tomato on each egg to make a hat and secure with a cocktail stick. Mark out the face and hair with black peppers and make legs and arms with celery stalks.

Celery in a jug on the table looks more attractive if the ends are curled. This you can do by drawing the point of a skewer through, from the top, dividing the celery into strips for about 5 in.

Open sandwiches provide a great many

opportunities for ingenuity. Cut with a pastry cutter into various shapes or roll them up and secure with cocktail sticks. Cut the crusts neatly off and sink them trellis-wise in extra rich sandwich spread. Make squares, Battenberg fashion, of closed or open sandwiches.

A good idea for parties is a Sandwich Tower. Buy a cylindrical loaf and carefully cut the whole into sandwiches with different-coloured fillings. Cut each sandwich in half and then build up the tower—one sandwich on top of another. Pass a wide ribbon underneath and tie at the top with a huge bow.

Although Chaudfroid of Chicken looks complicated, it is in actual fact quite easy to make at home. It was discovered accidentally by the Mareschal of Luxembourg, who was called away from table for some time. When he returned, he ate the food which had got cold and was so delighted with its taste that he had it served that way in future. It is made by cooking a chicken and making $\frac{3}{4}$ pint of white sauce and $\frac{1}{4}$ pint of aspic jelly. Cut the white flesh of the chicken into large pieces and lay them on a rack. Add the aspic jelly to the sauce, and when it is smooth but not set, pour over the chicken; decorate with slices of hard-boiled egg, ham, tomatoes, cucumber, etc., cut into shapes. When the chicken has set, coat each portion with liquid aspic jelly and arrange on a bed of the remainder of the chicken (boned), mixed with a salad and seasoned.

Choosing the right china in which to present your dishes is equally important. Dark colours and over-patterned dishes rarely show the food to advantage. Contemporary china is excellent for casual decoration, but traditionally decorative foods look their best on silver dishes; so do jellies and sweets, which also look very attractive served in cut-glass bowls or individual dishes.

Old Jelly Moulds

It is sad that the use of moulds has declined. If you have any old-fashioned ones in good condition, do use them. They were made in much more interesting shapes then than they are to-day. To get the best results for multi-coloured jellies, cut a piece of cardboard to fit the middle of the mould very closely and pour different-coloured jellies down the sides. Wait for them to set, remove the cardboard and fill the remainder with yet another colour.

Make cakes and puddings in moulds which should be well buttered before filling. Here is a delicious recipe which should be made in a Continental-type mould with a hole in the centre:

Take $\frac{1}{2}$ lb. shelled walnuts, 8 tablespoonfuls of castor sugar, 8 eggs and 3 tablespoonfuls home-made bread-crumbs, vanilla and a little rum or brandy. Beat the egg-yolks and the sugar to a white creamy consistency and add the walnuts, breadcrumbs and vanilla and mix thoroughly. Whip the egg-whites until stiff, add to the mixture and pour into the mould. Bake in a cool oven for about $\frac{3}{4}$ hour. Dilute a sherry glass of rum or brandy with a tumbler of water, add sugar to taste and bring to the boil. While both the cake and the rum are still hot, pour slowly over the cake.

Old fashioned Jelly moulds and an Orange Basket.

Flower Pie and Curled Celery.

Just before serving, whip double cream with sugar and fill the hole and surround the cake, sprinkle with cinnamon and decorate with roasted walnut halves.

Now that so many people have electric mixers, it is much easier to make the complicated sweets that used to take hours to whisk by hand. Here is a beautiful-looking one: Pulp and sweeten ½ dozen apples. Whisk six egg-whites and add two tablespoonfuls of sugar. Mix the two together until stiff. To make the outside crisp, put in the oven for 2 minutes to harden. Garnish with tarragon leaves and slices of sugared fruit.

Try arranging fresh fruit with moss and tiny fern leaves as a centrepiece for the table. Orange baskets are great favourites with children. Mark out, on half of each orange, a diamond pattern. On the other half mark the handle, which should be ½ in. wide and include the stalk end of the fruit. Scoop out the inside and cut your pattern with a sharp-pointed knife and push out the unwanted pieces from the inside with the flat end of a spoon. Fill the baskets with jelly and garnish with glacé cherries and angelica speared on cocktail sticks.

Here is an American recipe for Gingerbread. Warm ½ lb. of treacle and stir in ¼ lb. of butter. Mix and sift together 4 tablespoonfuls of sugar, a pinch of mixed spice, 3 teaspoonfuls of ginger, finely sliced lemon rind and 1 lb. of flour and stir into the treacle and butter. Dissolve 1 teaspoonful of bicarbonate of soda in a tablespoonful of warm cream, add to the mixture and stir well. Roll out about ½ in. thick and cut into large heraldic and fleur-de-lys shapes. Lay them on a greased tin and bake for 15 minutes in a moderate oven. Decorate with cloves.

Given at Tournaments

The oldest gingerbread was not a cake, but a solid slab of honey, baked flour and ginger. In medieval days it was a popular gift, rather like expensive chocolates today. It was given at tournaments and appropriately it seems to have been designed to imitate armour, being coloured a deep tawny brown shade, polished with egg-white and decorated with clusters of six small box leaves to form a fleur-de-lys and gilt-headed cloves driven in like nails. A wonderful chance to revive, even if only in gingerbread, the glory of pageantry.

For a decorative summer drink, peel a pineapple, cut into thin slices, place in a bowl, cover with castor sugar and leave for a few hours. Bring the peel to the boil in a little water, skim and pour over pineapple. Add 6 oz. sugar and a bottle of wine and chill. Just before drinking add a bottle of soda water or—for the millionaire touch—champagne.

PRESSURE COOKERY

*This modern method saves time and fuel and
preserves the vitamins and flavour in your food*

PRESSURE cookery, which is growing steadily in popularity, has so many advantages that it is surprising any housewife can still lack the courage to try it for herself. At first, however, it does seem a trifle alarming to have to deal with a pan that whistles or hisses and has to be cooled under the cold tap before you can take off the lid. But the reward is a tremendous saving in time, fuel, space and food values. Once you take to a pressure cooker, you will hate the idea of being without one.

But first let us consider the advantages of pressure cookers. These, briefly, are:
(1) The full natural flavour and colour of the food are retained.
(2) Because cooking is quick, at a great heat, and the food is not in direct contact with the water, the all-important minerals and vitamins are preserved.
(3) Time saved averages between ½ hour and 1 hour per main meal, a great consideration for modern housewives, particularly those with outside jobs. For example, a steak and kidney pudding, which would take between 4 and 5 hours in the ordinary way, can be cooked in a pressure cooker in 60 minutes.

NOTE: Cooking time saved is also an economy in fuel. Generally speaking, any dish can be pressure cooked in from one-fifth to one-third the usual time.
(4) Where kitchen space is limited to one gas ring or hotplate, a whole meal can be cooked in one utensil.
(5) Different kinds of foods, even those as highly flavoured as onions, can be cooked in the same cooker at the same time as a pudding or fruit without the slightest danger of contamination.

On the other hand, there is no room for slap-dash guesswork cookery. With a pressure cooker you *must*:
(1) Obey the instructions to the letter and master the perfectly simple principles before you start.

(2) Time each dish exactly and resist the temptation to allow "a minute or two extra" because you can't believe it could possibly be done in the time the book says. Do that, and the bones in an Irish stew would, in a few minutes, turn out quite porous so that you could scrunch them up like sugar, while Brussels sprouts or cabbage would be reduced to a wet mush.
(3) Not expect the impossible. Obviously a pressure cooker will not actually bake, fry or roast, but it *will* do practically anything else, including making the toughest and cheapest cuts of meat deliciously tender in a surprisingly short time. And you can always pop the meat into a very hot oven or under a hot grill for a few minutes to "crisp" the outside like a genuine roast.

Not a New Idea

The idea of pressure cooking is not a new one, and the principles are known to have been applied in the days of the first Queen Elizabeth. John Evelyn, writing in 1682 in his famous Diary, describes a wonderful supper he ate cooked in what he calls "Monsieur Papin's digestors," and from what he says these must have been the ancestors of our present-day pressure cookers.

Since that time enormous progress has been made. The principle of pressure cooking is, nevertheless, a very simple one. At 15-lb. pressure, which is used for everyday cooking, the temperature inside the cooker rises to 250° F., whereas the highest temperature you can obtain in an open saucepan is boiling point, 212° F. Furthermore, all the steam is confined inside the cooker instead of evaporating into the air.

There are various different makes and sizes of pressure cooker on the market, but, generally speaking, the working principle is the same. If you decide to buy one, your best plan is to go to some big store, which is certain to have the latest models, and

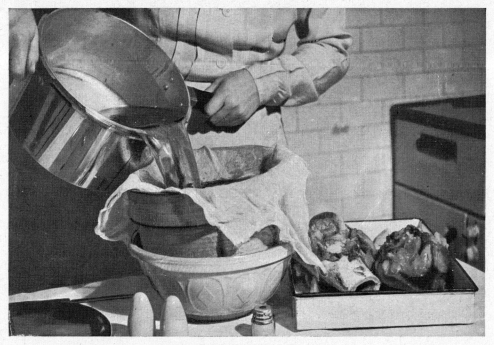

With a pressure cooker stock-making is easy, even from a small quantity of bones.
After cooking, strain the stock in the usual way

inspect them for yourself. What size you choose must, of course, be largely governed by the number of people for whom you cook. The smaller types of cooker are designed to give a pressure of 15 lb. a square inch, or about 250° F. Many of these are so designed that they can be taken straight to table once pressure has been reduced. In some types a spare lid is supplied for this purpose. The larger cookers, suitable for very large numbers, or for bottling fruit and vegetables, have a pressure gauge which registers pressure from 5 to 40 lb.

A family of four can get constant use from a 6-quart and a 7-pint pressure cooker, and a larger family would get the same service from 8-quart and 7-pint sizes. With two pressure cookers for a large family, or a large-sized cooker for a small family, a whole meal can be prepared in less than half the normal cooking time, thus cutting the fuel costs drastically.

30-minute Dinner

Here is a full dinner menu cooked in half an hour:

Fricassee of Veal
Potatoes
Carrots
Apple Charlotte

Fricassee of Veal

1 lb. fillet veal	½ tablespoonful
1 small onion	lemon juice
4 small mushrooms	Dried herbs to taste
6 peppercorns	(blade of mace,
1 oz. margarine ·	bay leaf, thyme,
1 oz. flour	parsley, marjoram)
½ pint stock or water	

Cut veal in small cubes. Place in cooker with mushrooms and sliced onion. Add stock or water, lemon juice and herbs tied in a muslin bag.

Prepare **Apple Charlotte** by mixing together 3 oz. breadcrumbs, 2 oz. sugar, ½ teaspoonful cinnamon and the grated rind of a lemon. Flavour 3 sliced apples with lemon juice. Put alternate layers of crumb mixture and fruit in a well-greased bowl. Pour 2 oz. margarine over the mixture and cover with two thicknesses of greased white paper. Tie securely. Stand the pudding bowl on the rack in the cooker with the veal. Bring to 15-lb. pressure (according to the manufacturer's specific instructions) and cook for 10 minutes.

Meanwhile, scrape and wash medium-sized new potatoes and new carrots.

After 10 minutes' cooking time, reduce pressure by cooling cooker. Open cooker and add salted vegetables. Close cooker and again bring to 15-lb. pressure. Cook for 5 minutes. Reduce pressure, remove lid and dish up vegetables and pudding. Add prepared thickening (margarine and flour) to veal, and cook for 5 minutes without replacing cooker cover. A little milk may also be stirred in.

Alternatively, if you have two cookers, use the larger one for the veal and apple charlotte, the second for the vegetables alone.

By pressure cooking this meal, a busy woman saves at least an hour's cooking time. Normal cooking methods take 80–90 minutes. She has cut her fuel bill by a third, and all the vitamins in the food remain, for none have been lost by evaporation or dilution in water.

Important points to remember are:

(1) **Safety.** You are enlisting the aid of a powerful force which should be treated with respect and intelligence, but every cooker is fitted with a safety device which operates automatically if too much pressure is building up, and releases it. In the smaller cookers these small safety-plugs are quite easy to replace.

(2) **Loading.** Never fill your cooker more than two-thirds full of food. In the case of liquids, such as soups, do not more than half fill. Allow for swelling in the case of such foods as rice, or pulse vegetables. On no account should food ever be allowed to touch the lid of the pressure cooker. A pudding basin used inside the cooker should never be more than two-thirds full, so that the pudding can rise; for milk puddings, only half full or the milk may boil over into the surrounding water. Cover steamed puddings with two thicknesses of greased paper. Use the rack supplied with your cooker when cooking green vegetables by themselves; when making stews, on the other hand, you do not need it.

(3) **Liquids.** The amount of liquid necessary for pressure cookery depends on the length of the cooking time, not on the quantity of food to be cooked. The amount given may seem very inadequate to the beginner, but it should never be exceeded. The small amount is due to the fact that in pressure cookery there is little or no evaporation.

The amount of liquid varies with the kind of pressure cooker, so it is important to follow the manufacturer's instructions carefully on this point. One general rule, however, applies to all models—for steamed puddings, use 2–2½ pints of water to allow for the pre-steaming period before the pressure control is adjusted, which is required to enable the pudding to rise. When making soups, stews or other dishes containing liquid, only the amount to be actually served with the finished dish should be put into the cooker—provided this is not less than the minimum required for the type of cooker.

NOTE: For milk puddings, allow 3 oz. grain to 1 pint liquid, instead of the usual 2 oz.

(4) **Seasoning.** Be sparing with seasoning. The speed of pressure cookery means that the natural mineral content of the food is retained and less seasoning is therefore needed. It is advisable for this reason, generally speaking, to add seasoning after cooking is finished. Alternatively, salt may be sprinkled on the prepared, washed and drained vegetables before putting them in the cooker.

(5) **Thickening and Gravies.** When gravy or stock is to be thickened, as for example when braising meat, the flour, mixed to a smooth paste with water or stock, should be added at the end of the pressure cooking and cooked in the open pan. If thickened beforehand it might, during the rapid cooking process, stick to the bottom of the pan.

(6) **Bringing to Pressure.** Fix the lid of your cooker firmly into position and put on a high heat until a steady flow of steam comes out of the vent pipe. This means that the water inside the cooker is boiling, turning into steam and has driven out all the air.

(7) **Controlling Pressure.** When the steady flow of steam comes from the vent pipe, adjust the pressure control and leave on high heat until the required pressure is reached. You will know this has happened when there is a continual slight hiss of steam from the vent pipe, or on some models it is recorded on a gauge. Then reduce the heat to "low"—just enough to

Braised Steak and Vegetables, a dish that takes a long time to cook in the oven, will take 20 minutes at the very most in a pressure cooker—and taste delicious. Prepare the ingredients in the usual way (left), brown them in the open cooker first, then bring to pressure

maintain the pressure—and *start timing*. On an electric hotplate, the heat may be switched right off if the cooking time is less than 10 minutes; if longer, it should be turned down to "low." When using electricity, it is sometimes necessary to pull the pressure cooker partly off the hotplate to control the pressure.

(8) **Reducing Pressure.** The cooker cannot be opened while it still contains pressure, owing to the force exerted against the pan and the lid. So never attempt to force off the lid; if it does not come off easily, that means there is still pressure inside and it requires further cooling.

There are two ways of cooling, depending on what is being cooked. Quick cooling, when cold water is run over the sides of the cooker for about 30 seconds, or the cooker is plunged into a basin of cold water, is the best for vegetables. It does not make the food cold, as it only reduces the temperature to boiling point.

Gradual cooling, by moving the cooker from the stove and leaving it in a cool place for between 5 and 20 minutes (according to the contents), is best for meat, poultry, puddings, soups, stews, or when bottling or sterilising fruit in glass jars. Steamed puddings will collapse if the pressure is reduced too quickly, meat may become dry and glass jars are liable to crack.

(9) **Cooking Several Things Together.** To cook together foods requiring differing times, you can either (*a*) part-cook those with the longest cooking times, (*b*) cut them up smaller, or (*c*) put in the other foods later on in the cooking time. For instance, to cook halved potatoes (8 minutes) with green peas (2–3 minutes), put in the potatoes, add water, pressure-cook for 6 minutes, then cool quickly, open and add peas, close cooker again, bring back to pressure and cook for another 2 minutes. Cool and serve.

"Steamed" Cakes

If you do not want to have your oven on for cake baking, there are certain types of cakes, such as "boiled" fruit cake and gingerbread, which can be steamed in the cooker. It is advisable to put the cake, once you have taken it out of the cooker, under a fairly hot grill for a few minutes to dry off the top. Never fill your cake tin more than two-thirds full, and cover the top of the tin with a double piece of greaseproof paper.

Adapting Favourite Recipes for Pressure Cooking

One of the most exciting aspects of pressure cooking is learning how to adapt famous and exotic recipes—or your own favourites—to the new time- and fuel-saving method. It is surprisingly easy and, though it may take a little experimenting at first, it is well worth it. Once you have the timing correct, the dish will turn out exactly the same over and over again, and in a fraction of the time required by the old method. Soups and casseroles, and such long-cooking, one-dish meals, are an excellent way to start.

There are a few things to remember when working out recipes for pressure-cooking methods:

Time.—In experimenting with cooking time, it is better to err on the side of under cooking rather than over cooking. If, when you open the cooker, the food is a little underdone, it is easy to process for a few minutes more. Roughly speaking, the cooking time should be cut by 66–75 per cent.

Liquid.—Reduce the amount of liquid in the recipe, starting with only a little more than you want in the finished dish. If you used the normal amount of liquid, you would probably end up with a soup instead of a stew. You need to allow ¼ pint for every 15 minutes' cooking time in all cookers except the Presto, from which there is absolutely no loss by evaporation.

Seasoning.—As you use less liquid, there will be less to dilute the seasoning, so use less until you have tried out the recipe.

Fat.—Reduce the quantity of fat for browning meat, poultry and game by about one-half.

If you are at all familiar with pressure cooking you will find that, though you may be testing a recipe for the first time, you will have plenty of clues. You may never have cooked Bœuf Bourguignon, for instance, but you will certainly be familiar with the timing for beef stew. Thus you will know that the timing for cooking cubed beef must be the same in both recipes, and though they taste quite different, the difference lies in the use of wine and herbs in the one and not in the way they are cooked.

Here's our conversion for:

Beef Stew (Ordinary cooking)

1½ lb. steak	3 stalks celery
2 oz. fat	2 oz. dried peas
1½ pints stock	1 oz. flour
1 large onion	Salt and pepper

Soak peas overnight. Cube meat, slice onion, dice celery. Brown ingredients in casserole, add stock, bring to boil and sim-

mer gently for at least 1 hour. Season and thicken gravy with flour.

Beef Stew (Pressure cooking)

1½ lb. steak	3 stalks celery
1 oz. fat	2 oz. dried peas
¾ pint stock	1 oz. flour
1 large onion	Salt and pepper

Soak peas overnight. Cube meat, slice onion, dice celery. Preheat pressure cooker, add fat. Brown meat in it. Add vegetables, stock and seasoning. Close and bring to 15-lb. pressure. Cook for 15–20 minutes. Open cooker and thicken. Cook for 3 minutes in open cooker.

Bœuf Bourguignon (French recipe adapted to pressure cooking)

1½ lb. steak	8 small onions
1 oz. fat	Parsley, bay leaf,
¾ pint liquid (¼ pint	thyme, clove of
stock + ½ pint	garlic all in muslin
burgundy)	bag
Salt, pepper and flour	

Cube meat. Dust with seasoned flour. Preheat pressure cooker, add fat. Brown meat. Add onions, liquid and herbs. Close and bring to 15-lb. pressure. Cook for 15–20 minutes. Open cooker and remove muslin herb bag.

STOCK

The speed of pressure cookery makes it well worth while to make stock with quite a small quantity of bones. Here is a recipe using only 2 lb.

Bone Stock

2 lb. bones—marrow	1 quart of water
if possible	1 turnip
2 onions	1 small stick of celery
1 carrot	1 or 2 cloves
Seasoning	

Wash the bones and break up if large. Put into the cooker with the rest of the ingredients and bring slowly to the boil. Skim, then put on the lid and bring to pressure. Reduce the heat and pressure-cook for 45 minutes. When cold, lift off any fat on the top.

MEAT

A joint that has been pressure cooked can be given the authentic crisp appearance of a roast if you place it in a hot oven or under the grill for a few minutes just before serving.

The following table gives a guide to cooking times for meat, as used in stews, casseroles or braises:

Beef, lamb or mutton, veal: cut 1 in. thick, 10–15 minutes.
Pork: cut 1 in. thick, 15–20 minutes.
Beef, lamb or mutton: cut 2 in. thick, 20–25 minutes.
Veal: cut 2 in. thick, 18–20 minutes.
Pork: cut 2 in. thick, 25–30 minutes.

Average times for joints of meat are as follows:

Beef: 8–10 minutes per lb.
Lamb or mutton: 10–12 minutes per lb.
Pork and veal: 12–15 minutes per lb.

MAIN DISHES

Boiled Beef with Dumplings

2–2½ lb. silverside
2 carrots, sliced
1 turnip, sliced
2 onions, sliced
Salt and pepper
1 pint water

Prepare meat and place in pressure cooker with sliced vegetables, seasoning and water. Cook at 15-lb. pressure for 20–25 minutes. Let cooker cool slowly. Drop small dumplings (see Pastry chapter) into the hot liquid and cook for 10 minutes in open pressure cooker.

Braised Pheasant

1 pheasant
1 oz. fat
1 stick celery
1 onion
Stock
½ oz. bacon
1 carrot
1 turnip
Herbs
Salt and pepper

For the stuffing

1 sliced onion
1 cut celery stalk
1 shredded apple
Salt and pepper

Wash and dry bird well. Stuff with a mixture of celery, onion and apple, mixed with salt and pepper to taste. Skewer bird firmly. Preheat open pressure cooker, add fat and brown bird lightly on all sides. Remove bird from pan. Now fry the bacon lightly in the fat and add the thickly sliced vegetables. Fry lightly. Season and add herbs. Just cover with stock (taking care to add at least the minimum quantity of liquid needed for your pressure cooker). Lay the bird on top of the bed of vegetables and close cooker. Bring to 15-lb. pressure and cook for 18–20 minutes. Let cooker cool of its own accord.

Calf's Liver with Herbs

2 lb. liver, cut ½ in. thick
1½ oz. fat
¼ pint white wine or stock
1 teaspoonful chopped parsley
1 teaspoonful chopped chives
Juice of half a lemon
Salt, pepper and flour

Dredge liver in sifted flour, season to taste with salt and pepper. Preheat open pressure cooker and melt fat in it. Brown liver on all sides. Add wine or stock. Close cooker, bring to pressure and cook at 15-lb. pressure for 8 minutes. Cool. Remove liver to warmed dish. Add herbs and lemon juice to liquid in cooker and boil for a few minutes in open cooker. Pour over liver and serve.

Carrots in a Blanket

2 lb. veal cut ½ in. thick (beef may be used instead of veal)
6 carrots
2 teaspoonfuls salt
4 or 5 medium-sized potatoes
2 tablespoonfuls flour
1 teaspoonful paprika
2 tablespoonfuls fat
¼ teaspoonful pepper
¼ pint water

Cut meat in thin strips the width of a bacon rasher. Quarter carrots. Wrap a strip of meat round each carrot segment and fasten with a skewer. Season with salt and pepper and roll in combined flour and paprika. Preheat cooker, melt fat in it, brown

To clear strained stock for clear soups, add the white and shell of an egg, then bring to the boil and whisk well

277

rolls on all sides. Place potatoes round and on top of rolls. Add ¼ pint water. Close cooker. Cook at 15-lb. pressure for 8–10 minutes. Let cooker cool.

Devilled Neck of Lamb

2 lb. neck of lamb	1 teaspoonful dry
1 oz. fat	mustard
1 onion, sliced	2 teaspoonfuls salt
2 stalks celery,	¼ teaspoonful pepper
chopped	¼ pint vinegar
¼ pint stock	

Preheat pressure cooker, add fat. Brown meat well on all sides. Add vegetables and brown lightly. Mix mustard and seasoning with vinegar and add to meat and vegetables. Bring to 15-lb. pressure and cook for 15 minutes. Cool cooker slowly.

Fricassee of Rabbit

1 rabbit	½ tablespoonful
1 onion, sliced	lemon juice
4 small mushrooms	Bouquet garni
1 oz. fat	6 peppercorns
¼ pint milk	Salt
½ pint stock or water	1 oz. flour

Soak, wash, dry and joint rabbit. Place in cooker with mushrooms and onion and gently fry in the fat. Add stock, bouquet garni, lemon juice and seasonings. Cook at 15-lb. pressure for 15 minutes. Let cooker cool. Thicken with flour and milk and cook for 3–4 minutes without replacing cover.

Hungarian Beef Goulash

2 lb. stewing steak	1 teaspoonful Tarra-
1 oz. flour	gon vinegar
1 oz. fat	1 teaspoonful mar-
2 bay leaves	joram
1 lb. onions, shredded	1 teaspoonful
1 teaspoonful paprika	chopped capers
¼ pint dry sherry	
¼ pint stock or water } or ½ pint stock	
Parsley	

Cut beef in 1-in. cubes and dredge with flour. Preheat pressure cooker, add fat. Brown meat well on all sides. Add onion and seasonings. Blend well, add liquid. Cook at 15-lb. pressure for 15 minutes. Let cooker cool. Open cooker, remove parsley and bay leaves. If an extra bright red colour is required, heat a nut of butter and add 1 teaspoonful paprika and 2 tablespoonfuls wine. Bring quickly to boiling point and pour over goulash when served. Traditionally, goulash should be served with noodles (3–4 minutes at 15-lb. pressure).

Jugged Hare

1 hare	1 tablespoonful red
1 rasher of bacon	currant jelly
1 oz. fat	Pepper and salt
1 sliced carrot	Bouquet garni
1 onion stuck with	1½ oz. flour
cloves	¼ pint red wine
¾ pint stock	

Skin, paunch and joint hare (see Poultry and Game chapter), retaining blood, liver, heart and kidney. Preheat cooker, add fat, and brown hare and bacon in it. Add stock, seasoning, herbs and prepared vegetables. Close cooker, bring to 15-lb. pressure and cook for 30 minutes. Meanwhile, prepare and fry forcemeat balls, using cooked minced liver and kidney of hare. Cool cooker when cooking time is up, remove bouquet garni and stir in blended flour to thicken stock. Bring to boil and cook in open cooker for 3–4 minutes. Now remove onion, stir in strained blood, wine and jelly. Reheat gently. Serve with forcemeat balls (see Poultry chapter).

Porcupine Meatballs

1 lb. minced raw beef	3 stalks celery,
3 oz. rice, uncooked	chopped
1 teaspoonful salt	1 green pepper, sliced
1 teaspoonful pepper	1 tablespoonful sugar
1 tin tomato soup	¼ teaspoonful dry
1 oz. fat	mustard
1 onion, sliced in	1 gill hot water
rings	1 teaspoonful salt

Mix beef, rice, salt, pepper and a quarter of the tomato soup. Form into eight balls. Preheat open cooker, melt fat in it. Brown meatballs well. Dissolve the salt, dry mustard and sugar in the hot water and the remainder of the soup. Pour over meatballs. Add prepared onion, celery and green pepper. Close cooker and cook at 15-lb. pressure for 20 minutes. Cool cooker. Serve meatballs in sauce.

Salmi of Grouse

2 grouse	Seasoning
2 oz. mushroom	¼ pint cider
stalks	¼ pint stock or water
1 oz. fat	Bouquet garni
1 onion, sliced	½ oz. flour

Joint grouse. Preheat open cooker, melt fat. Brown joints all over. Add onion, chopped mushrooms, bouquet garni, seasoning and stock. Add broken-up carcases and giblets if available. Cook at 15-lb. pressure for 10 minutes. Strain off stock. Blend flour with stock and cider, and bring to boil. When cooked, lay joints of grouse in the thin sauce, discard vegetables and carcases. Cook for further 10 minutes at 15-lb. pressure. Cool.

Shrimp Creole

1 oz. fat	½ teaspoonful sugar
3 stalks celery, chopped	4 oz. shrimps
	2 oz. rice
1 onion, sliced	¼ teaspoonful chilli powder
½ pint tomato juice	
½ tablespoonful vinegar	Salt

Preheat cooker and melt fat in it. Lightly brown onion and celery, add salt, chilli powder, tomato juice, vinegar, sugar and rice. Stir well to mix. Close cooker and bring to 15-lb. pressure. Cook for 10 minutes. Cool cooker. Open and add shrimps. Stir in open cooker till heated through.

Shrimp-stuffed Cucumber

4 small, stubby cucumbers	¼ pint thick white sauce (see Sauces)
3 oz. chopped shrimps	¼ pint water

Peel cucumbers, cut in half lengthwise and scrape out seeds, thus forming boat-shaped segments. Combine shrimps with white sauce and fill "boats" with the mixture. Place on rack in cooker with ¼ pint water. Close cooker. Cook at 15-lb. pressure for 3 minutes. Cool. Serve with wholemeal bread.

Spanish Rice

6 slices bacon, minced	2 teaspoonfuls paprika
2 onions, sliced	
1 clove garlic (optional)	2 oz. rice
	½ lb. tomatoes and ½ pint stock or water (or tin of tomatoes)
1 green pepper (sliced)	
2 teaspoonfuls salt	

Preheat open cooker, add bacon. Slightly brown onion, garlic, green pepper. Add washed rice and fry till just coloured. Add tomatoes, stock and seasoning. Cook at 15-lb. pressure for 10 minutes. Cool cooker, stir well and serve.

Spiced Pot Roast

2 lb. brisket beef	½ teaspoonful cinnamon
2 onions, sliced	
2 carrots, sliced	Salt, pepper, 2 cloves
½ lb. tomatoes, peeled	1 oz. fat
½ pint vinegar	

Preheat cooker, add fat and brown meat. Add halved tomatoes, sliced vegetables, seasonings and vinegar. Cook at 15-lb.

Vegetable marrow, filled with a savoury stuffing, is a delicious supper dish that lends itself particularly well to quick preparation in a pressure cooker

pressure for 25 minutes. Let cooker cool. Remove meat and crisp in oven. (If your pressure cooker has an indicator weight from which no steam escapes during cooking time, use only 4 tablespoonfuls vinegar.)

Steak and Kidney Pudding (Pressure-cooking time: 60 minutes)

For the pastry

6 oz. flour	2½ oz. shredded suet
1 teaspoonful baking powder	½ teaspoonful salt Water to mix

For the filling

1 lb. stewing beef	¼ lb. kidney
1 onion	Salt and pepper
¼ pint stock or water	½ oz. fat
2½ pints water in cooker	

Cube meat and slice onion. Preheat open cooker and melt fat in it. Brown meat thoroughly, then brown onion lightly. Add stock or water and seasoning. Cook at 15-lb. pressure for 15 minutes. Let cooker cool.

Prepare suet crust (see Pastry) and line a pudding basin which fits easily into the cooker. Fill pastry-lined basin with the meat and gravy already cooked. Cover with a top of suet crust. Cover basin with two thicknesses of greased paper or aluminium foil. Place basin on rack in cooker with 2½ pints water. Allow steam to flow gently from vent pipe for 15 minutes. Then bring to 15-lb. pressure and cook for a further 30 minutes. Let cooker cool.

Stuffed Marrow (Pressure-cooking time, including preparation: 20 minutes)

1 marrow	1 oz. melted fat
4 oz. cooked meat, minced	4 mushrooms
1 chopped onion	2 sprigs parsley
Salt and pepper	1 oz. breadcrumbs
	1 beaten egg
¼ pint water	

Peel and cut marrow into 6-in. slices, scooping out all the seeds. Make stuffing by mixing all the ingredients together. Fill each slice of marrow with stuffing. Pour ¼ pint water into a 7-pint size pressure cooker (or ½ pint water for larger cookers), place marrow slices on rack, close cooker, bring to 15-lb. pressure and pressure-cook for 5 minutes. Quick-cool the cooker and serve.

Stuffed Peppers or Capsicums

1 lb. peppers	Cooked Spanish Rice
¼ pint water	(see previous page)

Slice off the top of each pepper and re-move seeds. Place in pressure cooker on rack with ¼ pint water. Cook at 15-lb. pressure for 5 minutes. Cool cooker. Stuff each pepper with prepared rice. Place peppers in a flat dish, add a little fat, and brown in a hot oven or under the grill.

Tuna Fish Casserole

1 can tuna fish	1 teaspoonful salt
1 cupful peas	¼ teaspoonful pepper
2 tablespoonfuls margarine	1 onion, sliced
	Toasted breadcrumbs
3 tablespoonfuls flour	Paprika
½ pint milk	¼ pint water in cooker

Make white sauce by melting margarine and blending in flour, adding milk and stirring until at boiling point. Season. Grease a dish or ring mould which fits easily into the cooker. Flake tuna fish and fill the mould with alternate layers of fish, onion, peas, crumbs and sauce. Repeat layers. Sprinkle top with paprika. Cover with two thicknesses of greased paper, securely tied. Place on rack in cooker with water. Cook at 15-lb. pressure for 10 minutes. Cool. This dish can be crisped and browned under the grill after cooking, if desired.

Vegetable Chop-Suey

1½ oz. fat	¼ pint stock
1 onion, sliced	1 teaspoonful salt
6 stalks celery, cut up, with leaves	4 hard-boiled eggs, chopped
1 green pepper, sliced	2 oz. mushrooms
	Soy or Chinese sauce

Preheat open cooker and melt fat in it. Fry onion. Add stock, vegetables and seasoning. Close cooker and cook for 3 minutes at 15-lb. pressure. Cool cooker. Stir in eggs and sauce. Serve over rice (cooked 8–10 minutes at 15-lb. pressure) or noodles (3–4 minutes at 15-lb. pressure).

QUICK ONE-DISH MEALS

These will save time in preparing, in cooking, in serving and in dish washing. All can be cooked without the help of a pressure cooker, but they will then take much longer.

Porridge

3 heaped tablespoonfuls oatmeal or quick porridge oats	¾ pint water
	½ teaspoonful salt

Bring water to boil in open cooker, add salt, then stir in oatmeal, continue stirring

280

Because it cooks at such intense heat and the water never touches the food, you can cook a custard pudding, sprouts, carrots—and even onions—all at once without fear of contamination

until quite smooth. Cover and *bring slowly to pressure over low heat*. Pressure cook as follows:

Quick porridge oats: 3 minutes.
Fine oatmeal: 10 minutes.
Medium oatmeal: 15 minutes.
Coarse oatmeal: 20 minutes.

Reduce pressure with cold water and stir before serving.

NOTE: The pressure cooker must never be more than half full when porridge is being cooked.

Surprise Casserole

1½ lb. pork sausages	Medium can of
3 onions, sliced	creamed corn
6 potatoes, sliced	2 teaspoonfuls salt
1 dessertspoonful fat	¼ teaspoonful pepper
½ pint tomato juice	

Preheat pressure cooker, add fat and brown sausages. Pour off excess fat. In bottom of cooker place alternate layers of potato, onion and corn. Season each layer. Place sausages on top and pour tomato juice over. Cook at 15-lb. pressure for 5 minutes. Cool quickly and serve.

Six-layer Dinner

1 lb. potatoes, sliced	1 lb. tomatoes,
½ head celery,	skinned
chopped	2 teaspoonfuls salt
½ lb. minced beef	¼ teaspoonful pepper
2 onions, chopped	1 dessertspoonful fat
1 green pepper, sliced	½ pint water or stock

Preheat pressure cooker and melt fat. Add layers of ingredients in order as above. Season each layer. Pressure cook at 15-lb. pressure for 7 minutes. Cool cooker and serve.

Pork and Bean Dinner

6 oz. dried beans	1 medium onion,
½ lb. diced pork	sliced
1 oz. brown sugar	2 tablespoonfuls
1 teaspoonful salt	mushroom ketchup
½ teaspoonful mustard	½ pint tomato juice
¼ pint water	

Soak beans overnight, then drain. Preheat pressure cooker and brown diced pork. Add beans, sugar, salt, mustard, onion, ketchup, tomato juice and water (enough to cover beans). Close cooker, bring to 15-lb. pressure and cook for 10–20 minutes, depending on type of bean. Let cooker cool slowly.

COOKING VEGETABLES

Fresh, frozen or dried vegetables can all be cooked with excellent results in a pressure cooker.

Fresh Vegetables should be prepared in the normal way, roots being diced, greens and cabbage shredded and cauliflower, for example, divided into flowerets. Several different vegetables can be cooked simultaneously, each retaining its individual flavour. Where there is a difference in the cooking times of vegetables to be cooked together (for instance, potatoes which take 8 minutes and sliced cabbage which only requires 2–3 minutes), those requiring longer cooking can be cut in smaller pieces or pressure cooked for a short time before the others are added.

Always use ½ pint of water in the cooker when cooking fresh vegetables and put it in the cooker first. Place the vegetables on the trivet or in the separators and sprinkle ¼ flat teaspoonful of salt over them. Reduce pressure by the quick method of running cold water over the outside or standing the cooker in a bowl of cold water.

Be sure to keep the liquid in which vegetables have been pressure cooked. It is a valuable basis for soups, sauces and gravies.

The following guide gives the approximate times needed to cook various vegetables after pressure has been reached:

Artichokes (Jerusalem) cut in halves or quarters, according to size: 3–4 minutes.
Beans, Broad: 2–4 minutes.
Beans, Green: 2–4 minutes.
Beetroot (small): 15 minutes. (Larger beetroot require up to 1 pint of water and 40 minutes cooking time.)
Broccoli, Sprouting: 2–3 minutes.
Brussels Sprouts (whole): 2–4 minutes.
Cabbage (sliced): 2–3 minutes.
Carrots (diced): 3–4 minutes.
Carrots (new—whole): 5–6 minutes.
Cauliflower (in flowerets): 2–3 minutes.
Celery (sliced): 3–5 minutes.
Leeks: 3–5 minutes.
Onions (quartered or sliced): 3–4 minutes.
Onions (whole): 10 minutes.
Parsnips (sliced): 3–4 minutes.
Peas: 1–3 minutes.
Potatoes (medium-sized whole): 8 minutes.
Potatoes (new): 6–8 minutes.
Swedes (cubed): 3–5 minutes.
Spinach: 1 minute.
Tomatoes (whole): 2–3 minutes.
Turnips (cubed): 3–5 minutes.
Vegetable Marrow (sliced, with skin left on if young and tender): 3–4 minutes.

Frozen Vegetables should be partly thawed or, if still frozen, broken up, then cooked in ¼ *pint boiling water only*, either on the trivet or in the separators and with salt to taste.

Approximate cooking time for frozen vegetables after pressure has been reached are as follows:

Asparagus: 3½ minutes.
Brussels Sprouts: 3 minutes.
Cauliflower: 3½ minutes.
Mixed Vegetables: 5 minutes.
Peas: 3 minutes.
Runner or French Beans: 2 minutes.
Spinach: 2 minutes.

Dried Vegetables and Pulses, such as lentils and haricot beans (both a valuable source of proteins), should first be soaked in boiling water, with ½ teaspoonful of salt to every ½ pint of water, for 2 hours. *Then cook in 2 pints of water to every pound* of dried vegetables or pulses, pouring the appropriate amount of water into the cooker first and taking care that, with the vegetables in, the pan is not more than half full. *Bring to pressure slowly over a low heat* instead of the usual high heat; after cooking, reduce pressure the slow way, at room temperature for 5–10 minutes, then run cold water over the cooker for a few seconds before raising the lever.

Here are approximate cooking times after pressure has been reached for the chief dried vegetables and pulses:

Butter Beans, small Haricot Beans: 15–20 minutes.
Lentils: 10–20 minutes.
Peas: 15 minutes.
Pearl Barley: 20 minutes.
Rice: 10–15 minutes.
Split Peas: 10–15 minutes.

Celery with Cheese

Place sticks of washed celery on the rack in pressure cooker with ¼ pint water. Cook for 3 minutes at 15-lb. pressure. Meanwhile, make a thick cheese sauce. Pour over the cooked celery and serve with wholemeal bread.

Alternatively, arrange cooked celery stalks on grill plate. Fill each stalk with grated cheese and a few raisins. Cover with a little butter and cook for 1 minute under the grill.

Cauliflower or Leeks and Cheese

All vegetables have greater flavour and

food value when cooked by pressure because none of the vitamins or mineral salts are lost in the cooking liquid. Try cauliflower (5 minutes at 15-lb. pressure) or leeks (3 minutes) with a similar cheese sauce.

PUDDINGS

Ordinary recipes for steamed puddings can be used when cooking puddings in your pressure cooker, but it is generally advisable when using the smaller cookers to steam the mixture in the normal way for at least 20 minutes of the whole boiling time. This can be done quite simply, because, until the lid is fixed in position and the pan sealed, you can treat your pressure cooker just like an ordinary saucepan. This preliminary cooking means that the pudding rises well before it is subjected to pressure. Fill your basin not more than three-quarters full, and cover with a piece of greased paper and a pudding cloth. Stand in the cooker on the rack and pour in sufficient *boiling* water to come half way up the basin, put on the lid and steam normally for 20 minutes, then bring to pressure and cook for the necessary length of time. Time needed for the whole process is one-third of what you would allow if steaming the pudding in the normal way.

Christmas Pudding

4 oz. sultanas	1 teaspoonful mixed spice
4 oz. raisins	
2 oz. currants	½ teaspoonful ground cinnamon
2 oz. mixed peel	
1 oz. chopped nuts	½ wineglassful brandy (optional)
1 lemon	
3 oz. shredded suet	½ gill milk
1 oz. flour	2 eggs
4 oz. soft breadcrumbs	4 oz. soft brown sugar
½ teaspoonful grated nutmeg	2½ pints water in cooker
	Pinch of salt

Prepare fruit. Add to sifted dry ingredients, which should be well mixed together. Add grated rind of the lemon and sugar. Mix thoroughly. Mix with beaten eggs, brandy (if used) and milk. Turn into a well-greased pudding basin and cover with two thicknesses of greased paper, tied in position. Put basin on rack in cooker, in which 2½ pints water have been heated. Close cooker; let steam flow gently through vent pipe for 20 minutes before adding pressure control. Bring to 15-lb. pressure and cook for 1½ hours. Let pressure reduce of its own accord.

To reheat home-made or shop-bought

Sponge puddings and suet mixtures are best pressure cooked in small individual moulds covered with greased paper or aluminium foil and securely tied

Christmas pudding, place the pudding, in its mould, on the rack with 1 pint boiling water. Bring to 15-lb. pressure and cook for 15–20 minutes. That will save a lot of time on the day.

If, however, you have a favourite Christmas pudding recipe which you want to adapt to pressure cooking, just cut the cooking time by 75 per cent. Also pre-steam the pudding for 20 minutes before bringing to pressure, then cook at 15-lb. pressure.

"Baked" Custard

2 eggs	Vanilla or almond
¼ pint milk	flavouring or
2 tablespoonfuls	grated orange or
sugar	lemon peel
½ pint of water for cooking	

Beat eggs and sugar, scald milk, add flavouring and mix with the eggs. Pour into a greased pint-sized mould, cover with one layer of greaseproof paper, stand on trivet in cooker, add water. Cover and bring to pressure and pressure cook for 5 minutes. Reduce pressure at room temperature, turn out custard and either serve hot with jam or caramel sauce, or cold with thick cream and fresh or stewed fruit.

If desired, custard can be made in individual moulds, and will then only need to cook for 2½ minutes.

JAMS, JELLIES AND MARMALADES

For jams and jellies, a pressure cooker provides a short-cut on the pre-cooking of the fruit. Because this part of the process is done in the steam-tight pressure cooker, there is no evaporation or loss of flavour. All your favourite recipes can be adapted, and the recipes given here merely serve to show the general procedure. There are two important points to remember.

(1) **Do not fill your cooker more than half-full.**

(2) **Always cook jam in an open cooker once you have added the sugar.**

Gooseberry Jam

2 lb. gooseberries	2 lb. sugar
¼ pint water	

Wash, top and tail fruit. Place in cooker with water. Close cooker, bring to 15-lb. pressure and cool at once. Open cooker, stir in sugar until dissolved and boil for 10

minutes *without replacing lid*. Pot into warm jars and seal at once. Yield: 4 lb. jam.

Times for pre-cooking fruits for jam-making

Apricots: 3 minutes at 15-lb. pressure. Cool at once.

Black Currants: 3 minutes at 15-lb. pressure. Cool at once.

Cherries: 5 minutes at 15-lb. pressure. Cool at once.

Damsons: 5–10 minutes at 15-lb. pressure, depending on type, size, ripeness. Cool at once.

Plums: 5 minutes at 15-lb. pressure. Cool at once.

Raspberries: Bring to 10-lb. pressure. Cool at once.

Rhubarb: Bring to 10-lb. pressure. Cool at once.

Strawberries: Bring to 10-lb. pressure. Cool at once.

Blackberry and Apple Jelly

2 lb. blackberries	¼ pint water
Juice of 1 lemon	1 lb. sugar to each
2 large cooking apples	pint of juice

Pick over and wash blackberries. Slice apples, but do not peel or core. Place fruit in cooker with juice and water. Process at 10-lb. pressure for 3 minutes. Cool. Turn contents into jelly bag and strain overnight. Measure juice and place in cooker, adding 1 lb. sugar to each pint juice. Bring to boil in open cooker, stirring all the time, and boil rapidly until jelly sets when tested. Pot and seal at once.

Seville Orange Marmalade

2 lb. Seville oranges	4 lb. sugar
1 lemon	1 pint water

Wash and shred the fruit. Tie pips and some of the pith in muslin and place in pressure cooker with fruit and water. Close cooker, bring to 15-lb. pressure and cook for 15 minutes. Let cooker cool. Open cooker, add sugar and stir until dissolved. Boil in open pressure cooker until a set is obtained.

Any citrus fruit, or combination of fruits, may be used for marmalade. Far less water is needed when you make your marmalade in a pressure cooker, because you do not lose liquid by evaporation.

For **Chunky Marmalade** the recipe above should be used, but the fruit should be sliced thickly, and the fruit and sugar boiled in the open pressure cooker until dark.

After 10 minutes pre-steaming and 10 minutes at pressure, out come these perfect cherry sponge puddings (right)

In a medium or large pressure cooker, you can safely do two layers of pudding moulds at a time (below), provided there is space between the top ones and the lid

water and process for 10 minutes at 15-lb. pressure. Let cooker cool. Remove muslin bag, add sugar and boil quickly until a set is obtained (about 10 minutes).

Sweet Orange Marmalade

1 lb. oranges
1 lemon
3 lb. sugar
1½ pints water

Wash fruit. Slice thinly, tie pips in muslin and place in cooker with water. Bring to 15-lb. pressure and cook for 10 minutes. Let cooker cool. Open cooker, add sugar and stir until dissolved. Boil fast in open cooker until a set is obtained.

Lemon Marmalade

2 lb. lemons   5 lb. sugar
          1½ pints water

Wash and peel the lemons very finely. Shred the peel, remove pith from fruit and tie with the pips in muslin. Cut up the flesh and place with muslin bag and contents in the cooker with water. Close cooker, bring to 15-lb. pressure and cook for 10 minutes. Let cooker cool. Open cooker, stir in the sugar until dissolved and boil in open cooker until a set is obtained.

Grapefruit and Lemon Marmalade

4 lemons   3 lb. sugar
2 grapefruit   1 pint water

Shred the peel of the fruit. Remove most of the grapefruit pith and tie with all the pips in muslin. Put in pressure cooker with

Spiced Bramble Jelly

3 lb. blackberries   1 teaspoonful mixed
½ pint water   nutmeg, cinnamon
1 lb. sugar to each   and mace
pint of juice

Wash fruit and place on rack in pressure cooker with water and spices. Close cooker, bring to 10-lb. pressure and cook for 2 minutes. Cool. Strain overnight in a jelly bag. Next day, measure juice and place in cooker with appropriate amount of sugar. Boil in open pressure cooker until jelly sets when tested.

In true country fashion, the pulp in the jelly bag is not wasted. Make it into:

The time-saving way of bottling fruit in a pressure cooker—first pack the jars with fruit leaving ½ in. headspace, then pour on hot syrup or water and close

Spiced Bramble Cheese

Rub the fruit pulp through a wire sieve, and to each pound of pulp add ¾ lb. sugar. Leave to soak for some hours. Add the juice and grated rind of 1 lemon. Boil together, stirring constantly, and pot and seal while still hot.

Apple and Plum Cheese

3 *lb. apples (windfalls*   ¼ *pint water*
   will do)   ¾ *lb. sugar to each*
1 *lb. plums*   *pint of pulp*

Slice apples, do not peel or core. Place with plums on rack in pressure cooker with water. Cook at 15-lb. pressure for 1 minute. Cool. Sieve fruit and measure pulp. Add sugar in proportion to the pulp and boil in open pressure cooker until a set is obtained. Pot and seal.

Sloe and Apple Cheese is made in the same way, adding a little extra sugar if the sloes are very tart.

Hips and haws are the delight of every country child—and a valuable source of vitamin C. These recipes show how to make full use of them.

Haw Sauce

1½ *lb. haws*   1 *oz. salt and* 1 *tea-*
½ *pint vinegar*   *spoonful pepper*
        4 *oz. sugar*

Wash haws and place on rack in pressure cooker with vinegar. Pressure cook for 10 minutes at 15-lb. pressure. Cool. Sieve haws and return to cooker with sugar and seasonings. Boil in open cooker for 10 minutes, then pot and seal.

Haw Jelly

1 *lb. sugar and juice*   3 *lb. haws*
  of 1 *lemon to each*   1 *pint water*
  pint of juice

Wash haws and place on rack in pressure cooker with water. Cook for 10 minutes at 15-lb. pressure. Cool. Pour into jelly bag and leave to strain. Next day, measure juice and add proportionate amounts of lemon juice and sugar. Bring to boil in open cooker and boil until jelly sets when tested. Pot and seal at once.

Haw sauce and haw jelly are excellent with all meats.

Hip and Apple Jam

1 *lb. rose hips*	¾ *pint water*
1 *lb. apples*	¾ *lb. sugar*

Place hips in cooker with ½ pint water, cook at 15-lb. pressure for 15 minutes. Cool. Strain through jelly bag. Next day, place the sliced apples in cooker with ¼ pint water and bring to 10-lb. pressure. Cool at once. Mash apples to a pulp, add hip juice and sugar, and boil rapidly until a set is obtained.

Pear Catsup

2 *lb. pears*	½ *teaspoonful each of*
4 *oz. sugar*	*pepper, cinnamon*
¼ *pint vinegar*	*and ground cloves*
1 *teaspoonful salt*	

Place pears in cooker with vinegar and process at 15-lb. pressure for 3–5 minutes, depending on type of pear. Rub through sieve. Add remaining ingredients and boil gently in open pressure cooker until thickened. Pot and seal.

FRUIT BOTTLING

Particular delight of the thrifty housewife is a stock of home bottled fruit on her pantry shelves, ready for the winter months. Here's the way the pressure-cooking method of home bottling works out step by step.

(1) Use only jars in perfect condition, rejecting any that are chipped or cracked. Wash in soapy water, rinse in hot water and leave in clean hot water until ready for use.

(2) Select fresh, young and tender fruit, firm but ripe. Grade to size. Clean and prepare as necessary.

(3) Fill jars with fruit, leaving ½-in. head space.

(4) Cover with hot syrup or water. Barely cover fruits which make a lot of their own juice when cooking.

Thin syrup—8 oz. sugar—1½ pints liquid	water
Medium syrup—8 oz. sugar—1 pint liquid	or
Thick syrup—8 oz. sugar—½ pint liquid	juice

(5) Work out air bubbles with a clean knife, or by tapping jars on board. Wipe all seeds or pulp from top of jars.

(6) Adjust closures on jars. If using screw-top jars, screw up band tightly, then release a quarter-turn.

(7) Turn rack upside down in cooker and put in 2 pints hot water.

After anything from 3 to 7 minutes (according to the fruit being bottled) at 5-lb. pressure, you leave to cool, then remove jars to a wooden board and tighten lids. The cooker is the Presto 706B

(8) Stand jars on rack, but do not allow them to touch each other. Pack with newspaper if necessary, or run up a rubber band on each jar.

(9) Stand cooker on high heat. Fix lid. Allow steam to flow through vent pipe for 1 minute.

(10) Fix indicator weight or pressure-control weight. Bring to 5-lb. pressure. Start counting processing time. Do not let pressure fluctuate, as this may cause liquid to be forced from the jars.

(11) When processing time is up, remove cooker from heat. Allow pressure to reduce at room temperature. Do not cool by either of the quick-cooling cold-water methods, as this will cause glass jars to crack.

(12) When all pressure is reduced, open cooker. Remove jars to wooden board or cloth surface, away from draughts. Tighten screw bands. (If jars are still bubbling, wait till all movement ceases before lifting out of cooker.)

Leave for 24 hours. Test seal, wipe jars clean, label and date. Store in cool, dry place.

All fruit bottling should be done at 5-lb. pressure. The following table gives processing time in minutes for different fruits after 5-lb. pressure has been reached.

Apples	4	Cherries	5
Apricots	7	Currants	3
Blackberries	4	Damsons	5
Gooseberries	3	Plums	4
Loganberries	3	Raspberries	3
Peaches	7	Rhubarb	3
Pears	7	Strawberries [1]	3
Pineapple (slices)	4		

[1] Strawberries should be hulled, brought to simmering point in enough medium syrup barely to cover. Leave overnight to soak. Next day, reheat. Pack into jars. Cover with syrup. Process in usual way at 5-lb. pressure.

VEGETABLE PRESERVING

Vegetables cannot be bottled safely and easily like fruits. Certain bacteria, which in fruit are killed by the combination of moderate heat and natural fruit acids, cannot be destroyed in vegetables except at very high temperatures. These organisms may be present in bottled vegetables which look and smell perfectly fresh. There is no way of detecting them, but they are quite capable of causing acute food poisoning.

The *only* way to bottle vegetables with a reasonable degree of safety is by using a pressure cooker with a reliable pressure gauge which will maintain a pressure of at least 10 lb. and a temperature of 240° F. Smaller models without a pressure gauge are *not* to be recommended for this purpose.

CAKES

Basic Cake Recipe

4 oz. margarine or butter	6 oz. flour
4 oz. sugar	1 teaspoonful baking powder
2 eggs	2 tablespoonfuls milk

1½ pints boiling water

Flavouring

2 heaped tablespoonfuls cocoa, or
3 oz. glacé cherries, or
Grated rind of 1 lemon or orange, etc.

Cream margarine and sugar, beat eggs, then add them gradually to mixture alternately with the sifted flour and baking powder (and cocoa if making chocolate cake). Stir in milk and fruit (if used), then put mixture into well-greased cake tin and cover with two thicknesses of greaseproof paper. Put tin on trivet in cooker with boiling water. Put lid on cooker and, with pressure control lever up, steam on low heat for 15 minutes. Then put pressure control lever down and pressure cook for 40 minutes. Reduce pressure gradually at room temperature, take out cake and put it under a hot grill for 2 or 3 minutes to crisp and brown the top.

SPECIAL BABY FOODS

Strained and puréed vegetables and fruits can be prepared in the pressure cooker.

Strained Spinach

Wash thoroughly and remove stalks, etc., from spinach. With trivet in cooker, put in spinach, add ¼ pint water, cover, bring to pressure and pressure cook for 2 minutes. Reduce pressure with cold water, dish up and sieve spinach.

Vegetable Purée

Dice the vegetables (either carrots alone or mixed carrot, potato, tomato, etc.) and put them into the cooker containing the trivet. Add ¼ pint water. Cover and bring to pressure and pressure cook for 5 minutes. Reduce pressure with cold water. Dish up and sieve the vegetables, diluting with stock from the pressure cooker.

PARTY SNACKS AND SANDWICHES

For the cocktail, sherry or tea party, food should be dainty and good to look at as well as to eat

THERE is no easier way of returning hospitality than with a cocktail, sherry or afternoon tea party. The success of such entertaining depends very largely on the array of attractive-looking "eats" provided. (See a l s o Chapters on Entertaining and Cocktails, Cups and Punches.) Cocktail or sherry party snacks can include tiny cooked sausages (each with a little stick so that it can be eaten in the fingers), small cooked new potatoes and minute sausage rolls, as well as the ever popular olives, potato crisps, gherkins, little onions and salted almonds.

Plain biscuits can be spread with caviare, anchovy, sardines, shrimps or prawns, and there are many suggestions for canapés in the chapter on Hors d'œuvres. Literally, a canapé is a slice of bread fried in butter, but often crisp pastry diamonds and squares are used instead. You can give your canapés a professional touch by brushing them over lightly with aspic jelly, then adding the savoury mixture (flaked cooked haddock, sliced gherkin and sliced tomato is one suggestion) and finally spooning a small quantity of the jelly on top.

Savoury Suggestions

Open savoury tarts are also excellent for cocktail parties. Various mixtures can be used for the filling, but here is one worth trying (the quantities given are sufficient for about nine or ten tartlets). You will need a cupful of cold, flaked haddock, cod or other white fish. Make $\frac{1}{2}$ pint well seasoned white sauce, using $\frac{3}{4}$ oz. flour, $\frac{3}{4}$ oz. butter and the liquor in which the fish was cooked, and, while it is still hot, stir in a teaspoonful of gelatine dissolved in cold water. Mix in the fish carefully, line the tartlets with strips of skinned tomato and, when the fish mixture is cool to the jellying point, place generous spoonfuls in the tartlets. Dust with paprika and garnish with

A tasty platter for a party contains thin slices of Pumpernickel and Gruyère cheese, with curls of butter

289

either parsley, a slice of tomato topped with pimento-stuffed olive, or chopped caper and a little parsley, or sprinkle with fennel.

Another idea is to serve very tiny fish croquettes—either round ones or cork-shaped—impaled on cocktail sticks.

Cheese Straws

4 oz. plain or self-raising flour	1 egg-yolk
Pinch of salt	2 oz. Cheddar cheese (or 1 oz. Cheddar and 1 oz. Parmesan)
Dash of Cayenne pepper	
2 oz. vegetable fat shortening	1 tablespoonful water

To make the cheese pastry, sieve the flour, salt and Cayenne pepper together, then rub in the vegetable fat shortening until the mixture resembles breadcrumbs. Stir in the finely grated cheese and bind with the egg-yolk and water. Knead lightly and roll out to a square $\frac{1}{4}$ in. thick. Trim the edges with a knife and cut into strips 3 in. wide, then into straws $\frac{1}{4}$ in. wide. Gather the scraps together, roll out and cut into rounds with a 3-in. cutter. Cut out the centres with a smaller cutter to make rings. Place rings and straws on a baking sheet and bake near the top of a hot oven for 7–10 minutes. Cool on a cake rack. Place the straws in the rings for serving. (Makes 70–80 straws.)

Photos on this page taken at the Spry Cookery Centre

Those with a sweet tooth will like these crisp Poinsettias as a change from savouries

Poinsettias

4 oz. flaky pastry	A little icing sugar
2 oz. finely chopped almonds	A few glacé cherries

Roll out the flaky pastry (see Pastry chapter) to $\frac{1}{2}$ in. thickness. Cut into $2\frac{1}{2}$-in. squares. Place the squares on a baking sheet and cut 1 in. in from each corner towards the centre. Fold alternate corners into the centre in pinwheel fashion. Press gently in the centre. Decorate with small pieces of glacé cherry and a few almonds. Bake near the top of a hot oven for 10–15 minutes. Dust with icing sugar and serve as a biscuit with cocktails, sherry, fruit or fruit fools. (Makes approximately 14 Poinsettias.)

SANDWICHES

Ribbon Sandwiches

Cut three or more slices of bread about $\frac{1}{4}$ in. thick. Alternate layers of brown and

Cheese Straws, in neat little bundles slipped through pastry rings, make delicious cocktail savoury snacks

Cocktail sausages and tiny sausage rolls, ribbon sandwiches, miniature vol-au-vents and an assortment of canapés and open tarts, specially made in the Creda kitchens

white bread can be used, if liked. Fill them, using creamed butter, wrap in a damp cloth and put a weight on them. Cut, just before serving, to the size required.

Fillings for Ribbon Sandwiches
(1) Alternate layers of tongue and grated Gruyère cheese.
(2) Alternate layers of chopped cucumber and anchovy essence, with a little cream to mix, and salmon mixed with cream and chopped white of egg.
(3) Alternate layers of chicken and ham, and lettuce.

Rolled Sandwiches

Use fairly new bread, cut in thin slices, remove crusts, spread with creamed butter and any filling liked. Roll up the slices and fasten with cocktail sticks. These are good for wrapping round little sausages or, particularly if brown bread is used, round sticks of canned asparagus.

Suggested Fillings for Sandwiches
Savoury:
Anchovy essence mixed with creamed butter, a very little grated horseradish and a squeeze of lemon juice.
Chicken.
Cream cheese and watercress.
Cucumber moistened with mayonnaise.
Foie gras purée.
Grated cheese.
Grated Gruyère cheese with chopped nuts, Cayenne and salt.
Ham.
Cold scrambled eggs (much easier to spread and so less wasteful than hard-boiled), anchovy paste, a few drops of vinegar and a pinch of mustard, mixed with creamed butter.
Cold scrambled eggs and pickles chopped finely.
Cold scrambled eggs and sliced tomato
Lettuce and tomato.
Sardines (skinned, boned and mashed),

291

sieved hard-boiled egg-yolks, a pinch of Cayenne and salt, a squeeze of lemon juice and olive oil to bind.

Tomato and cucumber.

Tongue.

Sweet:

Dates and nuts chopped finely.
Figs and nuts chopped finely.
Chopped nuts and honey.
Banana and marmalade.
Dates with orange juice.
Cream cheese and strawberry jam.
Sliced banana with raspberry jam.

Crispbread Sandwiches

Butter two pieces of crispbread. Chop some stoned raisins and dates and sandwich them together with this.

Cucumber and Chive Sandwiches

2 tablespoonfuls salad oil	⅛ teaspoonful pepper
1 tablespoonful vinegar or lemon juice	1 cucumber
	1 teaspoonful chives, chopped
¼ tablespoonful salt	6 tablespoonfuls butter
¼ teaspoonful dry mustard	1½ teaspoonfuls paprika
10 *thin slices bread*	

Combine salad oil, vinegar or lemon juice, salt, mustard and pepper. Blend well. Peel cucumber, slice thinly and marinate in the French dressing for ½ hour. Add chopped chives. Blend butter and paprika together. Spread on slices of bread. Spread 5 slices with layer of cucumber and cover with remaining slices. Cut into desired shape.

Devilled Sandwiches

2 oz. almonds	1 dessertspoonful cream
A little cream cheese	
1 tablespoonful chopped pickle	Pinch of salt and Cayenne
Butter	

Blanch the almonds, shred them, and fry in a little butter until pale brown, stirring all the time. Mix together the other ingredients, except the cream cheese, and pour the mixture over the nuts. Cook for 2 minutes, stirring well. Leave to cool. Beat the cream cheese until soft, then season. Spread it on water biscuits, sprinkle the nuts, etc., on top and cover with more biscuits spread with cream cheese.

Savoury Sandwiches

1 tablespoonful cream	Cream cheese
1 tablespoonful apple chutney	1 tablespoonful chopped nuts
	Brown bread
Butter	

Watercress and cream cheese is an excellent mixture for sandwich filling—both tasty and nutritious. It is invariably a favourite with adults and children alike

The simplest sandwiches go up in the world if you use fancy cutters and a dash of imagination. Here you see "wheel" shapes and mushrooms, made from white bread cut thin and a dark-coloured filling for contrast

Put the cream cheese, cream, chutney and chopped nuts into a basin and mix them well together, working in the cheese. Butter some brown bread, spread some of the mixture on it, and put another piece of buttered bread on top. Cut into any shape required.

Open Sandwiches

Top a thin slice or round of wholemeal bread or toast with halibut, cod or haddock creamed with a thick white wine or cider sauce, place on a crisp inner leaf of lettuce and garnish with two twisted anchovy fillets and a dusting of parsley.

A layer of watercress, three thin slices of tomato in oil and vinegar dressing, a dessertspoonful of curried white fish garnished with chopped banana or finely chopped sweet apple.

Halve hard-boiled eggs lengthwise, mash the yolks with a teaspoonful of vinegar, a tablespoonful of oil and a dash of Worcester sauce (to each two eggs). Work in a dessertspoonful of cold flaked fish and season well with chutney, pepper and curry powder. Heap in the egg-whites, grill lightly and serve on rounds of toast.

Jellied Open Sandwiches

For open sandwiches glazed with aspic jelly, the bread should be cut into different shapes, then fried, toasted or lightly buttered and the savoury mixture put on top. To make the glaze, use 1 oz. aspic jelly crystals per pint of water or canned vegetable liquor. Pour it on when it is just setting. Here are some suggestions:

Sliced canned luncheon meat, hard-boiled egg, peas and carrots.

A small roll of ham, carrots cut into shapes, peas, capers, etc.

Slice of canned cheese, tomato, anchovy fillets, peas, etc.

Sliced Vienna sausages, stuffed olives,. capers.

Brislings or sild, carrots, peas, hard-boiled eggs, etc.

More ideas for open sandwiches will be found in the chapters on Sweden and Denmark.

293

There is no secret, no mystery, only common sense in the very simple art of—

MAKING GOOD COFFEE

Turkish coffee is the only kind that should be boiled. Serve it, thick and rich, from a long-handled jug (above)

Right, a streamlined model that makes filter coffee by the infusion method

Arabia about 1,200 years ago —when a goat-herd was startled to observe the liveliness of his goats after they had eaten the berries of a certain bush. To-day, the beans from these berries invigorate and cheer the heart all over the globe.

Choice of Coffee

East Africa, the West Indies, India, the Belgian Congo and Brazil are the main coffee-growing areas. As coffee acquires different characteristics, according to the climate and soil in which it is grown, choice is a matter of experiment and taste. Some cling to, say, Costa Rica, Kenya, Brazil or Mocha. But a blend of two or more varieties may be preferred. If you buy from a skilled blender, local conditions—climate and type of water—will have been taken into consideration in relation to flavour. It is best to consult reliable coffee suppliers and try out the varieties.

Many households run two or more coffees at the same time—perhaps a mild coffee for breakfast, a pungent, invigorating one at midday, a smooth, full coffee after dinner.

Degree of Roasting

The raw green coffee beans are roasted to drive off moisture and to break down the cells so that the oils which provide the aroma and flavour can be released. In medium roasting, the oils are not fully released, so that, before grinding, medium-roast coffee remains fresher for longer than high roast. The degree of roasting naturally affects the colour and flavour. A lightly roasted, lightly coloured bean will be mild-flavoured; a medium one stronger; and a highly roasted bean will give a dark-coloured, more aromatic and pungent, even bitter, coffee.

A WORLD of pleasant associations surrounds coffee: lingering over an after-dinner coffee with friends, pausing in one's work for a stimulating cup, having coffee and watching the passers-by at a table outside a Continental café, catching the delicious aroma wafted from a shop when coffee is being roasted—what could be more agreeable? Coffee goes with good humour, hospitality and civilised living.

It is worth making coffee well. In the U.K. the popularity of coffee has increased enormously since the middle of the century. Yet one still hears people sigh that they wish they "could make good coffee like So-and so" or talk longingly about the coffee they had on their holiday abroad—as though coffee making were an innate gift on the Continent but a mystery hidden from most on the other side of the Channel. Yet it is not a difficult art, and there is an infinite variety of efficient and beautiful coffee making equipment on the market.

Coffee is said to have been discovered in

Grinding

Nothing can beat coffee ground just before use. Air is the enemy. It absorbs the oils from the ground coffee, replacing them with moisture, so that freshness is lost. The shorter the time between grinding and brewing, the better the coffee will be. The advantages of grinding at home are obvious.

Vast and fearsome were the grinding machines of our forebears. To-day, coffee mills for the home kitchen are neat and elegant. The *"Mokkaffee"* and *"Peugeot"* box mills, for example, adjustable to the grind required, are useful for the small household. The *"Mokkaffee"* wall mill, for attachment to larder door or dresser, and similarly adjustable, has a practically airtight buff porcelain glass coffee catcher. Even the traveller is catered for—with a handy, small, round, metal-box type mill. An electric grinder produces fresh coffee in a few seconds at the press of a switch.

Good coffee deserves a lovely service. Thistle design on Flemish green by Spode-Copeland is perfect on a silver tray in a Regency room

The mesh size of the filter you use may decide whether you need a coarse, medium or fine grind. Finely ground coffee is more economical. A fine ground is essential for use with Espresso machines.

If your supplier is grinding the beans for you, indicate the grind required. Ask for "Espresso grind" for that type of machine. For Turkish coffee, the beans should be pulverised.

Storing

As exposure to air means loss of strength, it is best to buy in small quantities. In a screw-topped container with a rubber ring, coffee can be kept reasonably fresh for the following periods:

Medium roasted beans . .	12–14 days
High roasted beans . .	7–10 days
Medium roasted ground .	5 days
High roasted ground . .	3–4 days
Turkish or pulverised . .	1 day

Chicory

Although the addition of chicory to coffee is not much favoured by connoisseurs, many people add it because they like the flavour it imparts, or for reasons of economy. It makes the resultant brew darker. Chicory can be bought by the pound, roasted and ground all ready, and added in the proportion of a teaspoonful of chicory to a dessertspoonful of ground coffee.

Packed Brands

Although there is more real satisfaction in choosing one's coffee and grinding shortly before use, one can by-pass the process by buying coffee, roasted and

The Russell Hobbs electric coffee pot (with matching basin and jug) makes coffee to your personal taste by means of a time-control selector

ground, in tins, preferably vacuum-packed. Here the air is extracted and replaced by the natural gas of coffee to keep its freshness. Once the tin has been opened, the coffee should be used up in less than ten days, or the flavour and aroma will be lost.

The "instant" coffees in tins, which consist of pulverised coffee to be dissolved in boiling water, are useful for quick cups or for picnics.

BREWING THE COFFEE

General Principles

Use four heaped dessertspoonfuls of ground coffee for each pint of water. Less coffee than this is needed in the Espresso method, and more for Turkish coffee.

Use freshly boiled water, starting from freshly drawn cold water. Do not use water that has been heated before.

Do not let the coffee itself boil, as this spoils the flavour. Turkish coffee is the only exception here.

Serve the coffee as soon as possible after it is ready. Do not let it stand on the grounds for any length of time, or it will become bitter. If it must be kept for a time, strain it into a pot from which it can be served and keep it hot—without letting it boil.

Coffee can be reheated, but with loss of flavour. Again, do not let it boil. If you are using milk with the coffee,

serve it hot or cold, but, when heating it, do not allow it to form a skin or boil Boiled milk will spoil the flavour of the coffee.

Wash the equipment after each use and rinse with clear hot water. Do not use soda.

There are four main methods of making coffee: by infusion, percolation, pressure and suction.

Infusion

Under this heading comes coffee made in a jug, pot or saucepan.

Measure the coffee into a warmed china jug. Pour on fresh boiling water, stir well, and let it stand for one minute. Draw a spoon over the surface to skim off the coffee grounds standing on top. Let it stand for another four minutes, and then pour it through a strainer into another warmed china jug and serve quickly.

In the *"Melior"* coffee pot, the coffee is infused in the pot and then a metal rod, which comes through the lid and holds a filter inside, is pressed down, so that the grounds are trapped while the coffee is served.

The saucepan method is to put a measured quantity of coffee and water in a saucepan and place on heat. Stir it well and bring just to boiling point and no more—it must not boil. Remove from heat, stir again, cover tightly and let it stand in a warm place for five minutes. Then strain into a warmed jug or pot.

Percolation

This covers coffee made by the great variety of filter or drip methods and in percolators.

The French *café filtre* consists of an earthenware pot with a lower chamber, from which the coffee is served, and an upper chamber with a lid and a fine filter at its base. A perforated disc or filter paper is sometimes fitted over this.

Put the required amount of coffee into the upper section, spreading it evenly over the filter disc or paper (if this is used). Pour boiling water to the required amount over it, cover and let it stand in a warm place until dripping is completed. Then remove the upper section and serve the coffee.

A French way is to stand the pot in a pan of water which is kept hot. The coffee in the upper section is first damped with boiling water and allowed to stand for five minutes. Then boiling water is poured on in small quantities every two or three minutes for about a quarter of an hour.

The one-cup filters, a familiar sight in French cafés, have their own charm. You just sit at table and wait for the coffee in the filter chamber to drip through into the cup in front of you.

The Italian *"Napolitana"* is a modern and ingenious coffee pot which produces excellent filter coffee and has the added delight of having to be turned completely upside-down. Made of thick aluminium with copper top and bottom, it is one complete unit—i.e. the water is boiled in it. It is in three separate sections. Water is put into the straight-handled section, which is placed on the heat. The ground coffee is placed in the container at one end of the middle section; the perforated cap is fitted on to it and clipped down. The other end of this section is open. It is then lowered gently into the first section (it slides in), the container being uppermost. The third section (from which the coffee will be served) is inverted over the top. When the water boils, the machine is removed from the heat and the whole turned upside-down. It then stands for a time until the water has percolated through the coffee into the "jug" section.

Percolators with a central pipe and a glass top are familiar coffee-making machines. Put the required amount of fresh cold water into the percolator and bring to the boil. Then remove from the heat and place the required amount of coffee into the strainer in the upper part of the pot. Cover, return to the heat and allow the water to bubble up through the tube and percolate gently through the coffee for six to eight minutes. Then remove strainer and serve.

Percolators, however, have a great disadvantage in that the coffee gets boiled in the container, and if the process is continued too long very bad coffee results. An electric percolator is, however, a very quick and easy method for busy people.

The Russell Hobbs electric coffee pot, with its good-looking ceramic body, is equipped with a time-control selector and a special "keep hot" device.

Pressure

In the Italian *Espresso*, coffee is "expressed" under pressure. Cold water is placed in the boiler section of the machine, which is heated. Just before boiling point, the water expands and wets the finely ground coffee in a cage, forming an obstacle to the water which, at boiling point, forces its way through the coffee. The coffee resulting is collected in a pot underneath or

One-cup filters, coffee cup (left), or breakfast cup size (right), work on the infusion method.
You just sit and wait till your cup is full

in an upper chamber or direct into a cup. The process is quick—taking about four to seven minutes from start to finish. It is also economical. Very finely ground or pulverised coffee is used in the proportion of 1 teaspoonful of coffee to each cup of water, or $\frac{1}{2}$ oz. of coffee to just a little over $\frac{1}{2}$ pint of water (for six demi-tasses).

The machines on the market are admirable in design and finish, and made of an alloy which does not affect flavour or colour. They have the advantage of being unbreakable. Most makes can be obtained either fitted for electric heating or non-electric—in which case the machine is placed directly on the heat.

The *Espresso* method gives an intensely strong brew, especially good for after-dinner black coffee.

Some details are given below of several machines of this type available. The list is, however, not comprehensive.

In the attractive *"Columbia,"* cold water is placed in the machine's lower chamber. Into this is fitted the funnel filter, in which the ground coffee is placed. Over this goes a filter disc, and the collector or top chamber is screwed on to the boiler. The machine is then placed on the heat, and in due course the coffee gushes from the aperture at the upper end of the small pipe standing in the collector. It is retained here, and served.

In the *"Vesuviana"* and *"Trimel"* makes, the expanding water travels over a bridge and is forced through the coffee in a cage. The coffee resulting is collected in a pot underneath. The *"Trimel"* is non-electric only.

The *"Aquilas"* is very suitable for a quick brew direct into glass or cup. It is electric or non-electric; the latter design is for heating by liquid or solid methylated spirit, and is useful for camping conditions.

Suction or Vacuum

This is the principle of coffee-making apparatus, such as *"Cona," "S.L.R.," "Silex"* and *"Whitecross."*

The all-glass vacuum coffee maker is familiar and long-established. To sit at table and watch the proceedings inside the glass bowl is a leisurely after-dinner pleasure in itself. Admirable coffee results, as the water is boiling when it comes in contact with the ground coffee, but the brew itself does not boil.

In the *"Cona,"* the lower bowl containing cold water is placed over the heat at the base. Then the filter and the measured amount of coffee (6 dessert spoonfuls of medium ground to $1\frac{1}{2}$ pints of water) are put in the upper bowl, which is inserted in a vacuum-maker with a vented stem. When the coffee has risen into the upper bowl (except for a small quantity which must remain below), the coffee is allowed to infuse for about two minutes. The infused coffee drains into the lower bowl and, when all has passed through, the upper bowl is removed and the coffee served.

The *"Cona" Rex* is a modern streamlined version of the equipment, which can be carried in one hand. There is a wide variety of attractive models in the Cona range. Some are efficiently heated by means of a tiny spirit lamp and others are powered by electricity.

Turkish Coffee is in a class by itself, as this is the only instance in which boiling the coffee is correct procedure. There are special cooking pots available for its making. Pulverised coffee must be used—about a tablespoonful for each demi-tasse.

Put the coffee and an equal amount of granulated sugar into the pot, add cold water and bring to the boil.

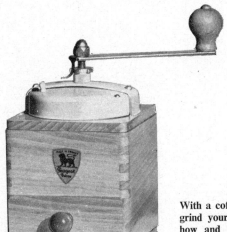

With a coffee mill you can grind your own beans just how and when you want them—and be sure your coffee is absolutely fresh

A cup of strong black coffee and a liqueur—the perfect end to a wonderful meal, graciously served. The Irish linen dinner mats are navy and pale blue embroidered with a wheat design

Stir it gently, take it from the heat, stir again, and replace on heat. Do this several times in succession, until the coffee is thick and foamy. Add a few drops of aromatic water, such as rosewater, and serve at once without milk or cream. As this is very strong coffee, the smallest cups are used.

SERVING THE COFFEE

Black Coffee is usually served after dinner. It should be strong, freshly made and in small cups. Sugar is added according to taste. The French like to add a liqueur-glass of brandy to each cup.

Café au lait

With a pot of coffee in one hand and a pot of hot milk in the other, pour an equal amount of coffee and milk into each cup. It is a breakfast drink, served in large cups or bowls.

Vienna Coffee

Drop whipped cream on strong black coffee in the cup—the result is delicious. It is often served with small cakes.

Iced Coffee

Serve strong coffee, cooled, with cracked ice in tall glasses, and top with whipped cream or ice-cream.

COFFEE FOR FLAVOURING IN COOKING

Make coffee in the usual way, but with less water, as the brew should be as intense as possible.

We are indebted to the Algerian Coffee Stores, Ltd., Old Compton Street, London, W.1, for much useful information regarding coffee making and for all photographs of equipment (except the *Atomic*). They are the sole retailers of the "*Columbia*" and "*Trimel*" machines.

299

A GOOD CUP OF TEA

*It revives the weary, soothes the nervy and is a joy
to most people on all occasions and at all times*

THROUGHOUT the U.K.—and in many other Eastern and Western countries—tea-drinking is almost a ritual. There is magic in a cup of tea. It revives the weary, soothes the nervy and is in demand on all occasions and at all times. This world-wide fame and much of the satisfaction derived from a good cup of tea is due to the untiring, conscientious work of British tea firms.

A housewife can go to almost any large or small grocer in any part of the U.K. and buy a known brand of tea, at a reasonable price, from which she can be certain to obtain a good brew, provided she and the grocer observe the rules.

Tea firms spend much time, thought and money in producing the right teas, and the right blends, to suit individual palates and varying water supplies. The big national tea firms produce and supply different blends of tea for the hard- and soft-water districts, and the right kind is automatically supplied by the grocers.

Family grocers who blend their own teas take the quality of the local water supply into consideration. Small leaf tea infuses more quickly than large leaf, and is most suitable for use with hard water, which gives a slower infusion. Large leaf can be used satisfactorily in any medium- or soft-water district.

Sometimes no fewer than twenty different teas are used to make up one blend. The quality and flavour of that blend must be constant over the years, and it is, to a great extent, the job of the tea taster to keep it so. When the stock of one tea which is included in a blend runs out, it must be replaced by another which gives exactly the same result. This is not easy, because the buds and leaves gathered from one plantation at different times vary considerably. Samples are sent to the buyers so that the tea can be tasted and judged before it is auctioned in Mincing Lane.

Tea tasting methods are strictly controlled and are the same throughout the trade. First, a sample of each tea is weighed in a highly sensitive scale, using a piece of metal equal in weight to a silver sixpence. The tea is then brewed with carefully measured boiling water, and infused for 6 minutes, strained and tasted warm. Anyone with a normally sensitive palate can become a tea taster, but so far

Tea at breakfast time tastes better from a fine cup. This Spode Stone China service is "Gloucester" patterned in blue on a delicate grey and shaped after a traditional Chinese design

Visitors enjoy afternoon tea—made as it should be made—at the
Ceylon Tea Centre in London

very few women have taken up this career. After this stage, the blending, cutting of the leaf where necessary, weighing, packaging and labelling are done by machinery.

Treatment of the Dry Leaf.—Tea, particularly in the dry state in which it is imported, is very easily contaminated by other flavours. Up to the time when it leaves the tea firms, it is carefully isolated in wooden boxes lined with tinfoil. When it reaches the grocer, and later the housewife, it should continue to be isolated from anything with a strong smell or flavour. Take note of the way the tea packets are treated at the grocers. If they are stored next to soap, cheese, chocolate, etc., go elsewhere to buy your tea.

When it arrives home, undo the package and tip the leaves into a tin with a close-fitting lid. Most well-made, labelled kitchen canisters are satisfactory. Before using a new tin, store some old dry leaves in it for several days to remove the metallic smell. When the empty tin smells of tea, it is ready for use. Never put new leaves on to old, and never mix different brands or types. Paper may affect the flavour of tea after a time, so it should not be stored in the packet. More important still, sealed or opened packets must never be left among other foods on larder shelves or in the kitchen, even for a few hours.

Temperature for storage is not important, and tea can keep in good condition in an airtight, moisture-proof canister hanging on the kitchen wall. Provided conditions are right, tea can be stored satisfactorily in the home for as long as six months or more.

The Kettle.—The kind of kettle used for boiling the water is important. Enamel or tin-lined metal is best. Aluminium alloy is not as good until it has become furred, so that the water does not come into contact with the metal. A new aluminium kettle should be seasoned by steam treatment for 1 hour, or by boiling water in it for 2 hours. This seasoning can be destroyed by scouring. Rinse the kettle with cold water, but do not scour.

The Water.—Fill the kettle with freshly-drawn cold water. Heat it till boiling—

that is until steam pours from the spout and the surface of the water is covered with bubbles. Pour immediately on to the tea leaves. A perfect infusion is not obtained with water below boiling point, nor with water that has either stood cold or been warmed slowly, nor water that has been kept boiling even for a few minutes.

Hard and Soft Water.—Infusion of the leaves takes longer in hard than in soft water, and the right blend should be chosen to suit the water. Medium water that is neither very hard nor very soft is the best for tea-making. Tea experts do not recommend the use of artificial softeners, such as bicarbonate of soda, or water-softening plant. Softened water produces a darker-coloured brew, but destroys a great deal of the flavour. Time the infusion and be patient when using hard water—for instance, in London 6 minutes' infusing may be needed, in Manchester 3 minutes, to produce the same result with the same tea.

The Teapot.—Pottery or china is the best material for teapots. Silver or silver-plate come second. Other metals can be used if they are tin or enamel-lined, or well-seasoned as described for the kettle. Teapots should be washed and dried after use.

The "T.T." teapot, invented by Dr. John Tutin and Dr. J. Lockwood Taylor, and on the market since 1954, is designed to economise in the amount of tea used.

The teapot departs from traditional design by having a built-in detachable "hot-water jug." A 1-pint cylindrically-shaped container with a tube fitted to the base is placed in a 2-pint earthenware teapot of orthodox appearance, suspended from a ridge just below the rim. A space remains between the bottom of the tube and the inside of the base of the teapot.

To make tea, you take out the container and warm the teapot, place one scoop of tea in the pot, replace the container, fill the pot with boiling water and allow the usual time for brewing. Infusion takes place in the space between the container and the walls of the pot. As the tea is poured, it is automatically replaced by hot water from the container, which re-infuses the tea. Six good-strength cups of tea can be obtained before refilling with more hot water.

Making the Tea.—Make the pot really hot with plenty of boiling water. Tip out the water. Measure in the tea, allowing 1 *level* caddy spoon per person, and 1 extra (a caddy spoon is slightly larger than a teaspoon). Take the pot to the kettle and pour on the *boiling* water. The amount of water needed varies according to the tea used, and to personal taste.

To obtain the full flavour of the tea it must be made strong enough, but strength of flavour has nothing to do with colour. Cover the pot with a cosy or some kind of insulating jacket, and leave to infuse for about 5 minutes. The full value will be extracted from the leaves in that time. Longer infusing simply produces a darker colour and extracts more tannin, which gives a bitter flavour. The ideal way is to remove the leaves after 5 or 6 minutes, and for this method the specially prepared tea-bags, sold by many grocers, are convenient.

It is better to add the maximum quantity of boiling water to the leaves all at once than to add half or three-quarters of the amount needed, and the rest later.

Pouring the Tea.—There is no golden rule about the addition of milk to tea. Pouring it into the tea usually gives an appearance of strength. Most tea experts favour putting milk in the cup first, and then pouring in the tea slowly. This gives more even mixing and is unlikely to separate the milk. Boiled milk affects the flavour.

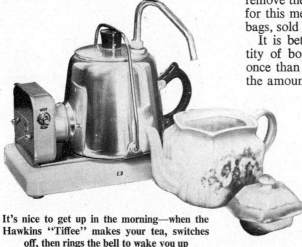

It's nice to get up in the morning—when the Hawkins "Tiffee" makes your tea, switches off, then rings the bell to wake you up

COCKTAILS, CUPS AND PUNCHES

Showing you how to mix your drinks the right way

Juleps and cobblers are popular summer evening drinks—served ice cold in frosted glasses with fruit, cherries, olives or sprigs of mint on top

IT is said that in early Roman times a physician invented a mixed drink of wine, lemon juice and a few pinches of dried adders, which was regarded as a splendid apéritif. This recipe may not appeal to all now—but it gives the modern cocktail a history.

The cocktail is a short mixed drink, drunk as an appetiser before lunch or dinner. Popularised at first in America, it became familiar between the two world wars. Before that there were the apéritifs and the long mixed drinks—the wine cup and punch—which are still as popular as ever, with all their modern variations — cobblers, slings, highballs, etc.

The "cup" is not an appetiser, but an alternative to wine, drunk sometimes with the meal, or convivially at leisure during the evening, perhaps in the garden. As the purpose of the cocktail is to whet the appetite, it should not be too sweet (though some are), and should be cold, preferably iced. The cup, on the other hand, is usually sweet, often with plenty of fruit in it, and may be ice cold or piping hot.

The cocktail should be mixed just before it is served and (except for the effervescent and a few other kinds) have a short, sharp shaking. It should not be allowed to stand long—this is detrimental to its quality. It belongs to the age of speed. The cup, on the other hand, goes back to an age of leisure. Its concoction is slow and deliberate; it may need to stand for a while; and, far from being violently shaken, it is comfortably stirred.

There is wide scope for imagination and originality in the making of every kind of mixed drink. Although there is a vast range of accepted recipes, there is pleasure to be had in experimentation and in concocting one's own. Variety is all.

COCKTAILS, CUPS AND PUNCHES

APÉRITIFS

To whet the appetite before a meal the well-known French trade-named apéritifs, already mixed, are often served iced, without further addition (except soda water, if desired), e.g. *Amer Picon* (a "bitter"), *Byrrh* (red wine basis), *Dubonnet* (red wine basis), *Lillet* (white wine basis), *St. Raphaël* (white wine basis), *Pernod* (aniseed basis).

Sherry and French and Italian vermouth are also served neat as apéritifs.

COCKTAILS

The cocktail is a mixture of any kind of wine or spirit with any other wine or spirit or liqueur or fruit juice, usually shaken in a special shaker with crushed ice. There are over 5,000 kinds of named cocktails. Most of the recipes given here are for the more familiar and popular ones. The professional cocktail mixer has a great range of bottles on which to draw, but the amateur at home can in fact make good cocktails with very limited resources. As a minimum: from a bottle of French vermouth, a bottle of Italian vermouth, a bottle of gin and a bottle of fruit juice or fruit syrup, one could produce ten varieties.

A cherry can be added most appropriately to a sweetish cocktail (e.g. one made with Italian vermouth), not to a dry one (e.g. made with French vermouth), with which an olive goes well.

For cocktail mixing at home the following items are desirable: two cocktail shakers (one for highly flavoured mixtures and one for milder kinds), a mixing glass (for cocktails needing to be stirred, not shaken, e.g. dry martinis, Manhattans), a corkscrew and bottle opener, spirit measures, bottles of bitters (a few drops of Angostura bitters will do wonders), a strainer, bar spoons and a fruit knife, cherry sticks and drinking straws, a supply of clean, clear ice, and cocktail glasses (which hold 2 or 3 liquid ounces). Also cherries, olives, orange and lemon slices and cut-up peel.

The success of a cocktail depends on a balance of flavours, without one unduly overshadowing the rest. It is advisable, therefore, to use a spirit measure in following a recipe. Fill your shaker no more than four-fifths full of ice and ingredients, and shake it shortly and sharply. Strain your cocktails into chilled glasses if possible.

(If you prefer to have a professional cocktail bartender at your private party, the services of one can be supplied through the United Kingdom Bartenders' Guild, 5, Blenheim Street, London, W.1.)

Alexander. (An old and well-known cocktail. Iced, it is served before dinner; without ice it is an after-dinner drink.) One-third brandy, one-third crème de caçao, one-third fresh cream. Shake and strain.

Bronx. One-half dry gin, one-sixth each of French vermouth, Italian vermouth and orange juice. Shake and strain.

Dubonnet. One-half Dubonnet, one-half dry gin. Stir and strain. Place a pared piece of lemon rind on top.

Manhattan. Two-thirds rye whisky, one-third Italian vermouth and a dash of Angostura bitters. Stir and strain; add a cherry to each cocktail.

Martini (*Dry*). (The best known and most popular cocktail of all. A good appetiser; very potent.) One-half French vermouth, one-half gin.

There are variations, e.g. two-thirds gin, one-third French vermouth, a dash of orange bitters; a twist of lemon peel added.

Martini (*Sweet*). One-half Italian vermouth, one-half gin. Again there are variations depending on taste.

Old Fashioned. (This is served in the tumbler known as the "Old Fashioned" glass.) A glass of whisky (Bourbon, Rye or Scotch), a lump of sugar saturated with Angostura bitters and enough water to dissolve it. A lump of ice. Decorate with orange or lemon slice and a cherry, and serve it with a spoon for stirring.

Orange Cocktail. Half a cocktail glass of Raphaël, half of orange juice, one large spoonful of curaçao, dash of Angostura bitters. Shake and strain. Serve with slice of orange.

Sidecar. (Very popular.) One-third brandy, one-third Cointreau, one-third lemon juice. Shake and strain. (Or, one-half brandy and one-quarter each of Cointreau and lemon juice.)

White Lady. Similar to *Sidecar*, but with gin instead of brandy,

HOW TO SERVE THE DRINKS

Cocktails

Mix just before serving, give a short, sharp shaking with crushed ice, do not stand for long. Serve before a meal, very cold. Pour into small, shallow glasses from the shaker. Add (if liked) a cherry if sweet; an olive if dry. For recipes see chapter beginning on page 303.

Sherry

Decant and serve at room temperature in small deep glasses either before a meal, with the soup, or as a between-meals drink. If served in the all-purpose glass approved by the Wine and Food Society and shown on page 314, serve only one-third full.

Table Wines

RED go with meat and game. Open the bottle two or three hours before the meal and stand in the dining-room so that it is at room temperature. Serve in a rounded bulb-shaped glass, never more than two-thirds full.

WHITE accompany fish, poultry, white meats and sweets. Serve from the bottle, chilled but not frozen. Glasses the same or slightly smaller than those for Red wines.

Champagne

The wine for celebrations, champagne may be drunk at any time, with or without food. Serve chilled, the bottle standing in a bucket of ice. Open when required, wrap the bottle in a napkin and pour into thin saucer-shaped glasses or champagne goblets.

Brandy

Serve at the end of the meal, with coffee, pouring a *very* little into the bottom of a large, preferably warmed, balloon glass, which should be cradled in the palms of the hands to warm the brandy.

Liqueurs

Serve in miniature glasses in small quantities with coffee at the end of dinner. Alternatively, Port may be served at the end of the meal—in a glass much the same shape as a sherry glass but slightly larger.

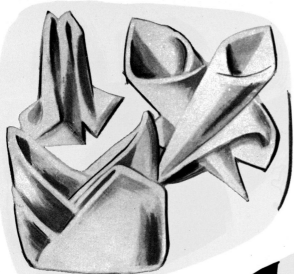

"DINNER

The etiquette of entertaining is not really formidable, but the rules are well worth following and based on practical common sense

FULL-SIZED white table napkins are essential for a formal lunch or dinner-party. Easiest fancy shape is the Mitre, above. Just fold the napkin in half twice, then fold it diagonally, bring the base points of the triangle together and slip one inside the other.

Prepare grapefruit by first slicing in half crossways, then cutting with a curved knife round the edge where the pith joins the fruit. Use a straight knife to loosen the sections. Top each half with a glacé cherry.

CUTLERY is always arranged so that one works from the outside inwards. The place setting, left, is laid with fish-eaters for hors d'œuvres on the outside, then a spoon for soup, a small knife for butter, and a knife and fork for the main course. Dessert spoon and fork are laid across the top. Right, another style provides for soup, fish, main course, dessert and cheese.

S SERVED"

SEATING the guests can be quite a problem. Host and hostess sit at opposite ends of the table and, when numbers permit, the two sexes are placed alternately, husbands and wives being separated whenever possible, and the chief male guest sitting at the hostess's right, the chief woman guest on the host's right. In the case of a party of eight, this obviously is impossible. The hostess's end of the table then remains as it should and adaptations are made at the host's end, as shown below.

CHIEF duties of the host are pouring out the wine and carving. Many couples carve in the kitchen and bring the food in on a hotplate. But if the host carves at table, the hostess or a helper passes round the plates, serving the ladies first, handing vegetables and sauces at the guests' left for them to help themselves.

THE WINE-PRODUCING DISTRICTS OF FRANCE

From each region come wines named *after the local châteaux and sub-districts*

FRANCE, the greatest wine-growing and wine-drinking country in the world, produces a wonderful variety of wines. You will find on a wine list, either at your wine merchant's or in a restaurant, that the various types are grouped together under the name of their district of origin—Bordeaux, Champagne, Alsace, Languedoc, etc.

Under the general heading of Bordeaux, for example, come many wines bearing the names of the châteaux and the sub-districts of the region of Bordeaux, such as Graves, Médoc and St. Emilion. The wines of Alsace, on the other hand, are mostly named after the grapes from which they are made.

For a festive occasion—a wine or fruit cup in a sparkling green glass bowl shaped like a giant goblet. The ladle has a lip that prevents spilling, and the matching glasses complete the set, from Liberty, London

Speciality Cocktails

Peter, famous cocktail barman at l'Apéritif Grill, London, recommends experimenting in cocktail mixing. The following are among his own prize-winning recipes with which he has won silver cups in European and world international cocktail-mixing competitions.

First Lady. One-third lemon gin, one-third peach brandy, one-third pineapple juice, two dashes of maraschino. Serve with a cherry.

Rye Lane. One-third rye whisky, one-third curaçao, one-third orange juice, two dashes Crème de Noyau (or almond essence).

Torino. One-quarter lemon gin, one-quarter mandarin liqueur, one-quarter Italian vermouth, one-quarter passionfruit juice.

COBBLERS

These are warm weather drinks, American in origin.

Whisky Cobbler. Fill a goblet with cracked ice. Add 2 oz. whisky, one teaspoonful sugar, four dashes curaçao. Stir and decorate with a slice of lemon and any other fruit; also a sprig of mint if desired. Serve with straws.

Rum, brandy or gin can be used instead of whisky.

Wine Cobbler (any wine). Fill 7 oz. wineglass with cracked ice. Add 3 oz. wine, a teaspoonful of sugar and four dashes curaçao. Stir and decorate with fruit and sprig of mint. Serve with straws.

Sherry Cobbler. Thinly slice two oranges and a lemon and place in bowl with pieces of pineapple in layers with a cupful each of fine sugar and shaved ice. Add two cupfuls of cold water and one cupful of sherry; also other fruit for decoration. Stir and serve in goblets with some fruit in each.

COLLINS, COOLERS, SLINGS, HIGHBALLS

These are also long, warm weather drinks. There are many variations of each, but these are standard recipes.

Tom Collins. A famous drink, served in tall glasses and well iced. Place cracked ice in glass, add 2 oz. gin, a teaspoonful of sugar and juice of half a lemon. Stir and fill to the top with water or soda water. Decorate with a slice of lemon. Rum, brandy or whisky can be used instead of gin.

Rum Cooler. 2 oz. rum, juice of half a lemon or one lime, four dashes of grenadine. Shake well with a lump of ice and strain into a tall glass; fill with soda water.

Highball. 1½ oz. brandy, gin, rum or whisky in a tumbler with a lump of ice. Fill with soda water or dry ginger ale and squeeze lemon rind on top.

Gin Sling. (Slings are served in tumblers topped with a slice of lemon.) 2 oz. gin, a teaspoonful of sugar dissolved in water or grenadine, a lump of ice. Fill up with water and stir. This is the basic recipe. Cherry brandy, benedictine, lemon juice are sometimes used in making slings, and brandy, rum or whisky used in place of gin.

CUPS

The "Wine Cup" is generally a summer drink, mixed in a large bowl and served from a glass jug. The main ingredient is usually wine, with the addition of spirits, liqueurs, varied fruits, soda water and ice. A cup should look attractive and interesting—there is plenty of room here for one's own initiative, especially in the choice of fruit, as almost any kind can be used.

Gin, rum, lager beer or cider can provide the basis of a "cup" instead of wine, Or an apéritif can be used.

Whatever the ingredients, the "cup" should be well chilled, but not allowed to become over diluted with melting ice. When soda water is used it should be added at the last moment.

Strain it into the glasses to avoid pips, etc., and place pieces of fruit in the glasses —or not—as desired.

Apricot-quina Cup. Cut six ripe apricots into cubes and steep in sugar with half a wineglass of St. Raphaël for 12 hours in a jug. Then add half a bottle of St. Raphaël and serve with ice and soda water.

Celebration Toast (*Claret Cup*). Ingredients sufficient for 14 glasses: one bottle claret, one bottle soda water, one glass sherry, sugar to taste. Fruit, mint, lemon rind, grated nutmeg.

Pare rind of lemon and place in bowl. Add a little sugar and pour on one wineglassful of sherry. Add the claret. Decorate with fruit and mint and add more sugar if necessary. Add the nutmeg. Allow to stand for an hour. Strain and ice. Serve with soda water (or dry champagne).

Champagne Cup. (1) (Quantities to provide 40 glasses.) Place four lumps of sugar saturated with Angostura bitters in a large bowl with two sliced oranges and a wineglassful of brandy. Add four bottles of champagne. Let it stand for 20 minutes. Serve with an ice cube floating in each glass and add soda water.

(2) (For four persons.) To a quart of champagne add a wineglassful of brandy, a liqueurglassful each of maraschino and Grand Marnier and two liqueurglassfuls of curaçao, with a tablespoonful of fine sugar Add cracked ice and slices of orange, lemon and pineapple; decorate with sprigs of mint.

Cider Cup. (For four persons.) To a quart of cider add a liqueurglassful each of maraschino, curaçao and brandy (*or* a sherryglassful of sherry, half that quantity of brandy and juice of half a lemon, with sugar to taste). Add any fruits desired, and a couple of sprigs of mint or borage or a sprig of verbena—and cracked ice. Strain.

Cool Sunshine. (Quantities to provide 15 glasses.) To a bottle of white burgundy (Macon Blanc) add pears, oranges and apples, peeled but not cut too small. Allow to stand for 2 hours. Immediately before serving add a wineglassful of brandy and one-third of a wine bottle full of soda water. Serve well iced.

Cooli. (Quantities to provide 12 glasses.) Stir together a bottle of Graves, Clos du Rey, and a liqueurglassful of orange curaçao with a sliced peeled apple. Let it stand for about 2 hours. Add half a wine bottle full of soda water just before serving, and serve well iced.

Coronet. (Quantities to provide 14 glasses.) Place pears, apples or peaches, peeled and cut up, in a bowl with two wineglassfuls of port. Leave in a cool place for 3 hours: then add one bottle of red burgundy (Beaujolais), half a pint of still lemon squash (diluted with water and

Cocktails for two or for a party call for this Martini Mixer, elegant glass stirring rod and long-stemmed glasses, from Liberty, London

sliced crystallised ginger and a cupful of sliced pineapple. Stir in also half a sliced orange and half a sliced lemon. Add a sprig of bruised mint and let stand for 1 or 2 hours. Just before serving add two large bottles of aerated lemonade. Serve with cracked ice.

Rhine Maiden. (Quantities to provide 10 glasses.) Pour a bottle of hock on peeled grapes in a bowl and allow to stand for 2 hours. Then add soda water; ice and serve immediately, leaving fruit in the bowl.

Rose Belle Cup. (Quantities to provide 10 glasses.) Stir well together a bottle of vin rosé, one-third of a wine bottle full of soda water or lemonade and sugar to taste. Serve well iced.

Pride of Oporto. (Quantities to provide 30 glasses.) Squeeze into a bowl the juice of one lemon. Add half a gill of orange curaçao and a bottle of dry tawny port. Decorate with thin slices of lemon and leave for 20 minutes. Top each glass when serving with cold soda water.

Lager Beer Cup. To the juice of four lemons and the pared rind of two in a bowl add a cupful of water, two sherry glasses of sherry and two bottles of lager. Add sugar to taste and a grating of nutmeg.

(For wine cup (hot) see *Mulled Wine* and *Punches* on next page.)

not too sweet). Do not add orange or lemon.

Golden Rod. (Quantities to provide 14 glasses.) Pour a bottle of Alsatian wine into a bowl of peeled grapes, sliced melon and other fruits; leave for half an hour. Add sugar to taste and serve well iced with fizzy lemonade.

Midsummer Revel. (Quantities to provide 8 glasses.) Pour a bottle of white burgundy on to cut-up melon and halved peeled peaches (fresh or tinned) in a bowl and leave for 3 hours. Add a liqueurglassful of maraschino and serve iced.

My Cup. (Quantities to provide 36 glasses.) Stir four bottles of red Algerian wine (Belorah) and one bottle tawny port with a quarter cupful of sugar in a large bowl. Add a cupful of lemon or orange juice or squash, half a cupful of finely

MINT JULEP

This is a very old drink. Crush together in a large tumbler four to six sprigs of fresh mint and half a tablespoonful of fine sugar, with one tablespoonful of water, until the sugar is dissolved and the flavour extracted from the mint. Add 2 oz. of whisky and fill the tumbler with crushed ice. Stir well. When the outside of the glass is frosted, decorate with mint and serve with straws.

A julep is also made using iced champagne instead of whisky, with less mint and sugar and a slice of orange and a cherry added.

MULLED WINE

This hot, spiced drink calls for a cold winter's night as its setting. The less-expensive wines can be used effectively.

Boil to a syrup in half pint water 3 oz. of sugar with a pinch each of cinnamon, ginger and powdered cloves (or nutmeg and cinnamon). Add this to a pint of wine (port, claret, Algerian) and heat to just below boiling point, stirring slowly. Serve while hot, with a twist of pared orange peel in each glass. Or bring the wine almost to boiling point and then add the spices, sugar and boiling water.

PICK-ME-UPS AND SUSTAINING DRINKS

Cold

Brandy Flip. Shake well together one egg, one teaspoonful of sugar and 2 oz. brandy. Strain into a 5-oz. wineglass and grate nutmeg on top.

Rum, whisky, sherry, claret or port can be used instead of brandy.

Pick-me-up Cocktail. Shake well together a cocktail glass of brandy and one of milk, one teaspoonful of sugar with a dash of Angostura bitters. Strain into a tumbler and add soda water.

Prairie Oyster. (A famous non-alcoholic pick-me-up.) Put a teaspoonful each of Worcester sauce and tomato catsup into a wineglass and drop in the yolk of an egg, without breaking it. Add two dashes of vinegar and a sprinkle of pepper.

Hot

Blue Blazer. (A stimulating spectacle as well as drink.) Put 2 oz. Scotch whisky into a metal mug with a teaspoonful of powdered sugar, and a similar quantity of boiling water into another metal mug. Put a lighted match to the whisky, and when it blazes up pour it quickly into the boiling water; then pour it all back and to and fro five or six times—rapidly—so that the blaze is continuous. When it dies down, serve the drink in a small tumbler with a twist of pared lemon peel on top.

Grog. (The old universal remedy.) Place 2 oz. rum in a tumbler with a lump of sugar, the juice of half a lemon, two cloves and a small stick of cinnamon. Fill the glass with boiling water.

Hot Egg Nogg. Beat an egg with a teaspoonful of sugar and pour into a tumbler with 1 oz. brandy and 1 oz. rum. Fill up with hot milk and grate nutmeg on top. (The milk could be cold, and sherry or other wine used instead of spirits.)

Hot Toddy. To 1½ oz. gin, rum or whisky, add one teaspoonful of sugar, two cloves, a small stick of cinnamon and a slice of lemon. Add boiling water. Serve in a small tumbler or an "old-fashioned" glass.

PUNCHES

Rum is the traditional basic ingredient of punch. The punchbowl, in which the host mixed the drink at table before his expectant guests, was a feature particularly of eighteenth-century England. Punch was made hot or cold. For cold punch lime juice was preferred to lemon juice.

Hot

Ale Punch. Bring almost to boiling point in a large pan: a quart of old ale, quarter pint each of gin, rum and whisky, one sliced lemon, a pinch each of ground cinnamon, cloves and nutmeg, adding a pint of boiling water and sugar to taste. Strain for serving into a bowl and decorate with a few more thin lemon slices.

Buckingham Palace Punch (recipe by Monsieur René Poussin, former Buckingham Palace Chef)

1 bottle dark Jamaica rum	Juice and grated rind of 3 lemons
1 bottle brandy	Pinch of cinnamon
2½ bottles water	Pinch of cloves
2½ oz. lump sugar	Bare ½ grated nutmeg

Put lemon, spices, sugar and water in saucepan and boil for 5 minutes. Add rum and brandy. As soon as hot, strain through muslin and serve.

M. Poussin uses an old Victorian silver wine-cooler for a punch bowl. You could also use a large fruit bowl, a soup tureen or a jug.

Guy Fawkes' Grog

1 bottle red wine	1 pint water
½ pint Jamaica rum	Juice and rind of 1
1 glassful brandy	lemon
1 stick of cinnamon	

Place all ingredients in a large saucepan and heat slowly. Strain and serve very hot with slices of lemon.

Jamaica Fizzer

Juice of ½ lemon	2 measures Jamaica
1 teaspoonful sugar	rum
1 measure brandy	

Dissolve sugar in a little boiling water. Add lemon juice, brandy and Jamaica rum and top with boiling water.

Portwine Punch (Negus). Rub a quarter pound of loaf sugar on lemon rind until yellow and place in a large jug; add juice of one lemon, a grating of nutmeg, a pint of port (one of the less expensive kinds would do well) and a quart of boiling water. Stir, let it stand, covered, and serve.

The Rum Banger. Dissolve $\frac{1}{4}$ lb. sugar in a pint of milk. Add the yolks of 2 eggs beaten together. Add a pint of Jamaica rum. Serve very hot but do not boil.

Rum Punch. Heat a quarter pint of rum with a quart of beer, spices, sugar, lemon slices and hot water. (See *Ale Punch.*)

Cold

Brandy Punch (per goblet). Pour 2 oz. brandy and four dashes of curaçao on to shaved ice. Add fruit and mint and stir well, then finish with ginger ale.

Planter's Punch. (1) The traditional recipe is: one of sour (lime), two of sweet (sugar) three of strong (rum), four of weak (water and ice).

(2) (Per tumbler.) Stir together a single measure of rum, one teaspoonful of grenadine, juice of half a lemon. Add lemon and orange slices and soda water.

Non-alcoholic

Fruit Punch. (1) Thinly slice three peeled oranges and place in a bowl with two sliced bananas, a handful of green grapes and a handful of stoned cherries. Pour over a syrup made by boiling 1 lb. sugar and one quart water together for 5 minutes. Add the juice of three lemons and three oranges and let it stand for an hour in a cool place. Then add a pint of ginger ale, half pint of cold tea, a quart of soda water and cracked ice.

(2) Rub quarter pound sugar over lemon and orange peel until yellow and add to a cupful of pineapple pulp with juice, half cupful of orange juice, quarter cupful of lemon juice and one pint of grape juice. Add a small pinch of salt, a grating of nutmeg and a few sprigs of mint. Stir and let it stand, covered, for an hour in a cool place. Strain over cracked ice and add soda water.

A special Christmas Punch Set by Spode-Copeland for convivial entertaining. The 10-in. wide bowl, six cups and a ladle are decorated with Christmas trees, holly and mistletoe

HOME-MADE DRINKS

Home-made drinks are always popular and, incidentally, are very wholesome. Black currant syrup or raspberry vinegar, taken in hot water last thing at night, helps to soothe a cold. Summer drinks, such as lemonade or orangeade, should, whenever possible, have ice cubes added just before serving. Iced tea and coffee are also delicious hot weather drinks.

Black Currant Syrup

6 lb. black currants   12 bruised cloves (in
6 lb. Demerara sugar   muslin bag)

Prepare the black currants. Put cloves in a large jar and fill up with alternate layers of sugar and currants. Cover tightly to exclude all air. Leave for 6 weeks, then draw off liquid and bottle. Keep corked until the syrup is needed.

Ginger Beer

2 lemons   ½ oz. cream of tartar
1 oz. bruised ginger   1 lb. sugar
1 gallon cold water   ½ oz. yeast on toast

Put the rinds of the lemons into a large saucepan with the ginger, cream of tartar and sugar. Pour the cold water over them and bring to the boil, then leave until lukewarm. Spread the yeast on the toast and let it float on top of the liquid. Cover with a cloth and leave for 24 hours, then strain and bottle. Store in a cool place. It will be ready for use in 2 or 3 days.

Iced Russian Tea

Allow three teaspoonfuls of China tea containing a good proportion of Orange Pekoe for every pint required, infuse with rapidly-boiling fresh water, stand for 10 minutes, strain very clear, then put in the fridge or on ice until very cold. Half a gill of Jamaica rum is enough for a half-pint glass, and the sugar (if liked) should be melted first. Put plenty of ice in the glass, add a slice of lemon stuck with one clove, then pour in the cold tea. For a minty flavour, dust a good supply of fresh sprigs with sugar, place them on top of the lemon slice, and pour the tea through them. This beverage can be prepared in a big glass jug, but it is not advisable to keep the tea too long in the refrigerator.

Lemonade

Rinds of 2 lemons   Juice of 4 lemons and
Rind of 1 orange   2 oranges
1 quart boiling water   Sugar to taste

Put the fruit rinds and juice into a jug and pour the boiling water on top. Add sugar and water, or soda water, to taste.

Lemon or Orange Squash

To every glassful of cold water, or soda water, allow the juice of half a lemon or orange and a dessertspoonful of castor sugar. Stir well.

Orangeade

4 or 5 oranges   1 oz. citric acid dis-
4 lb. loaf sugar   solved in a cupful
2½ pints cold, boiled   of hot water
water

Rub the sugar against the rind of the oranges, being careful that no pith or juice gets mixed in. (The lumps will turn orange colour.) Pour the cold, boiled water over the sugar, add the dissolved acid (cold) and leave for 2 or 3 days for the sugar to dissolve, stirring occasionally. When the sugar has dissolved, strain the orangeade through a muslin and bottle it. Wax the corks with sealing wax.

Raspberry Vinegar

3 lb. raspberries   1 quart white wine
Sugar   vinegar

Remove stalks from raspberries and put 1 lb. into a china bowl. Pour vinegar over them and leave overnight. Next day, strain off liquor, pour it on to 1 lb. fresh raspberries, and leave overnight. Next day, strain again and pour liquor on to last pound of fresh raspberries. Leave overnight, then strain through a cloth damped with vinegar. Allow 1 lb. of loaf sugar to every pint of juice, put in a preserving pan, heat, and stir until the sugar has dissolved; then simmer very gently for 20 minutes, skimming at the end. Bottle when cold. When using, allow 1 or 2 tablespoonfuls of the vinegar to a glass of water.

NOTE: Strawberry, red currant or black currant vinegar can be made in the same way.

Sloe Gin

3 pints sloes   ⅛ oz. bitter almonds
1 lb. castor sugar   2 quarts gin

Wipe the sloes, remove stalks and prick them here and there with a needle. Put into a stone jar with the gin and sugar and the blanched almonds, cork tightly and shake well. Continue to shake well twice a week. Strain through muslin and bottle in a stone jar, corking securely.

THE BEGINNER'S GUIDE TO WINE

Some practical pointers for the inexperienced on the choice of wines at reasonable prices and how to serve them

THE inexperienced housewife who knows little about wine—except that she has perhaps enjoyed it in a restaurant or at someone else's house—should start her own wine buying by asking the advice of a *reputable* and experienced wine merchant. These are easier to find than might be imagined, and it is simple enough to recognise those who really know their job. The wine merchant who does not take a real interest in his customer's problems (probably because he has not the knowledge or experience to advise her) should be left strictly alone. In such circumstances the best plan is to write direct to one of the old-established wine merchants for help and advice, explaining exactly what the wines are wanted for (for instance, a dance, wedding reception, special dinner party, or just for ordinary consumption at home) and giving some indication of what she is prepared to pay.

There is no reason why wine should be an expensive luxury. You can get a very pleasant bottle of any kind except champagne for under 10s. Since about six good glasses can be got out of one bottle, this should be enough for dinner for four people. Serve two different wines (a white wine with the fish or the sweet and a red wine with the meat), and for an outlay of under £1 you can turn an ordinary meal into a truly festive occasion.

Wines and Foods that Go Together

Now to consider the wines to choose. The general principle is simple enough: with delicately flavoured dishes, serve delicate (white) wines; with more robust food, the full-blooded red wines. In other words,
white wines go with white meats (shellfish, fish, veal, poultry, etc.) and sweets; red wines with meat and game; while poultry can be accompanied either by red or white, according to taste. The white wines that go best with fish, cold poultry, etc., are the dry ones, such as Hock, Moselle, White Burgundy or Graves. Sweet white wines, such as Sauternes, should be served with the sweet course.

UNDERSTANDING THE WINE LIST

You will find on a wine list that the various types of wine are grouped together under the name of the district from which they come.

Bordeaux, for example, includes not only wines sold as Red Bordeaux and White Bordeaux, but an amazing variety bearing the names of the Châteaux and the sub-districts of the region.

The wines of Margaux and St. Julien are of a light character, while the wines of Pauillac, St. Estephe and St. Emilion are more full and fruity. For example, in the wine merchant's list you will see:

Red Bordeaux (or Claret)
Château Talbot St. Julien.
Château Lafite, Pauillac.

White Bordeaux
Graves (medium dry and dry).
Cerons (dry).
Sauternes (sweet).
Barsac (sweet).
Lupiac (medium sweet).
St. Croix du Mont (medium sweet).

Burgundy is another wonderful province of France from which come:

Red Burgundies
Beaujolais Mâcon.
Beaune. Corton, Savigny, Pommard.
Chambertin. Nuits Saint-Georges,
    Romaneé, Volnay.

White Burgundies
Meursault, Montrachet, Pouilly-Fuisse.
Chablis.

Alsace

The wines of *Alsace* are of the Hock and Moselle type. Most are named after the grape from which they are produced. Among the best-known are:

Sylvaner (dry).
Riesling (dry).
Gewurstraminer and Traminer.

The wines of Alsace should be served cool or chilled. They may be taken as an apéritif, served most successfully with hors d'œuvre, fish, etc.

Champagne From the Champagne countryside comes the wine for celebrations, a wine to be drunk at any time, with or without food, preferably slightly chilled.

France, the greatest wine-growing and wine-drinking country in the world, produces many other delightful wines, but for the beginner these are enough to be going on with. With the wines of Bordeaux, Burgundy, Alsace and Champagne—plus Chianti (white or red) and Vermouth from Italy; Sherry from Spain; Hock and Moselle from Germany, and Port from Portugal—to choose from, there is no limit to your possible fame as a hostess.

Though there is no need whatever for the ordinary wine-drinker to set up as an authority on vintages, it is important to know something about them, if only because they cause such apparent diversity in price. The following chart, which has been prepared by the Wine and Food Society, should be used as guidance when considering the choice of wines, but not as a hard-and-fast rule. Remember only the connoisseurs amongst your friends are likely to appreciate a 1959 champagne or a 1952 burgundy. Most of them would be just as happy with a less distinguished and much less expensive wine. On the other hand, an intelligent interest in vintages will repay the enthusiastic amateur. With the help of a good wine merchant you should be able to buy, for no more than about 10s. a bottle, a wine of a good vintage and can then let it mature for a few years.

Year	Port	Claret	Burgundy	Rhone	Rhine & Moselle	Sauternes	White Burgundy	Champagne
1941	4	2	2	3	2	0	1	4
1942	6	3	3	5	5	4	4	5
1943	5	5	5	6	5	6	6	5
1944	4	4	2	3	3	4	2	3
1945	7	6	7	6	6	7	6	6
1946	5	3	4	4	4	3	5	3
1947	7	7	7	7	6	7	7	7
1948	7	6	5	4	5	4	5	4
1949	4	7	6	6	7	5	6	6
1950	6	6	4	6	5	4	6	3
1951	3	3	3	4	2	3	3	2
1952	4	6	7	7	6	6	6	7
1953	5	7	6	6	7	7	7	7
1954	5	4	4	5	3	3	4	3
1955	7	6	6	7	5	6	6	7
1956	2	3	2	5	3	4	3	4
1957	5	5	5	4	5	3	5	2
1958	5	5	4	6	5	5	4	5
1959	3	7	6	6	7	7	7	7
1960	7	4	5	5	5	4	3	4
1961	4	6	6	5	5	5	6	6
1962	5	6	5	6	6	6	5	6

0 = no good   7 = the best

Vintage Chart for the years 1941 to 1962, prepared by the Wine and Food Society and reproduced here by their permission

Commonwealth Wines

With the exception of Moselle, Champagne, Chianti, and a few others, practically all types of wine are now produced in the countries of the Commonwealth, notably South Africa and Australia. They are considerably cheaper and often quite as good as their European counterparts, but the only way to discover the ones *you* like is by the old method of trial and error. However, you certainly need not feel ashamed of serving a South African sherry or an Australian burgundy simply because of their origin.

Beautiful glass adds beauty to the dinner table. Above, comport, champagne and goblet in intaglio design in Stuart crystal

Christmas Dinner

Since most families start serious wine-buying at Christmas time, here is a suggested menu, showing a choice of the right wines to serve with various courses.

Apéritif: Dry Sherry, Alsatian Riesling, Champagne or young Moselle.

With the Turkey: Claret or Champagne.
If *Goose* or *Duck:* Claret or Burgundy.
With the Christmas Pudding: Champagne or Advocat (as sauce).
With Cheese (if served): Burgundy or Port.

Boxing Day Buffet Supper

With Cold Chicken, Turkey, etc.: Moselle or Alsatian wine.

Casual Christmas Entertaining

For a friendly drink at 11 a.m. or a small informal party just before lunch, with cocktail savouries and biscuits, serve dry sherry instead of cocktails.

Dinner Party Menu

Smoked Salmon with White Burgundy
(Pouilly or Chablis)
Steak with Burgundy or Claret
Cheese and Coffee with Cognac

Here is a basic list of the wines and foods that go well together. Like the Vintage Chart, it is to be treated as guidance only—and certainly not as a menu for an outsize feast!

Hors d'Œuvres: Pale Dry Sherry, Vodka or Akvavit.
Oysters: Chablis, Champagne, Moselle.
Soup: Madeira, Sherry, Marsala.

A lovely example of cut decoration in Stuart crystal—a goblet, cocktail glass and claret glass

Fish: Hock, Moselle, White Burgundy.

Entrée: Chianti, Claret.

Roast: Burgundy.

Poultry: Claret, Champagne.

Sweet: Sauternes, Barsac.

Cheese: Port, Old Brown Sherry. Burgundy also goes well with certain cheeses, notably Port Salut and Brie.

Coffee: Cognac. Liqueurs.

After Dinner with Nuts: Port.

Party Planning

When ordering champagne for a wedding reception, dance or dinner party, quantities should be calculated on this basis:

At a wedding reception, allow 1 bottle for every 3 people. At a dance, allow 1 bottle for every 2 people. For drinking toasts, allow 15 bottles for 100 people.

Table wines should be delivered two or three days before use, but your wine merchant will advise according to vintage and type of wine.

Approved by the Wine and Food Society as the perfect all-purpose wine glass, it is equally suitable for champagne, claret or sherry. Made by Elfverson; obtainable from Heal's, London

The general storage rule is that wines should lie down and spirits stand up; that all wines should be kept in an even temperature of about 58° to 60° Fahrenheit. Red wine should be opened two or three hours before serving and left in the dining-room, so that it is served at room temperature. Do *not* heat it up in hot water or in front of the fire. White wines should be served chilled but not frozen.

When drawing the cork from a wine bottle, first remove capsule, wipe the neck of the bottle clean, and put the corkscrew into the cork *straight*. If a red wine, cover mouth of bottle with a piece of muslin to prevent dirt entering while it is standing to come to room temperature.

Wine Glasses

Rows of elegant wine glasses of all sizes from liqueur to champagne look beautiful on a well-laid dinner table. But for the small family of limited means who want to experiment with wines, it is good to know that a glass has been designed from which everything, with the exception of liqueurs, can be drunk. You simply vary the quantities—serving it only one-third full of sherry, for instance. Sherry, white and red wines, champagne, even brandy can be served in this beautifully shaped all-purpose wineglass.

And here, as a grand finale, are a couple of good recipes for party punches:

Spiced Rum Punch

> 1 *bottle rum*
> $\frac{1}{6}$ *bottle orange squash*
> $\frac{1}{6}$ *bottle sherry*
> *Pinch grated nutmeg*
> $\frac{1}{6}$ *bottle brandy*
> $\frac{1}{3}$ *pint strong cold tea*
> *Stick of cinnamon*
> 4 *cloves*

Heat all the ingredients slowly and thoroughly without boiling.

Hot Spiced Burgundy

Place in a saucepan a bottle of Burgundy (reasonable price). Heat slowly but do not boil. Add 10 cloves, $\frac{1}{4}$ lb. brown sugar, pinch of cinnamon. Serve hot with grated nutmeg.

OPEN-AIR EATING

All food tastes better out of doors, but a good picnic takes planning

A most inviting picnic lunch—raised pork pies, baby sausages on sticks, Scotch eggs, followed by cherry tarts and jelly

PICNIC—all over the world and despite English summers—the word holds a thrill. Most people are quite prepared to risk a dull day for the pleasure of eating out of doors, since fresh air seasoning turns even plain fare into something almost classic.

What Sort of Picnic?

There are several ways of going on an outing that includes lunch and/or tea in the open.

The picnic by car can be fairly elaborate if wished; transport of food and equipment is easy and can even include the pressure cooker.

The walker, cyclist and motor-cyclist must necessarily plan picnic meals that are both light to carry and non-bulky.

A picnic meal in the garden can be prepared beforehand and carried out at the time, or it can be cooked out, barbecue-fashion. The following are victuals and drink suggestions suitable for all categories of picnic.

FOOD FOR LUNCHES

Savouries

Sandwiches are ever popular, and many helpful ideas for fillings have been given in a previous chapter. Here are some suggestions for alternative food:

Stuffed Rolls.—The small, crisp dinner rolls from the baker make a pleasant change from sandwiches. They should be split two-thirds open, some of the soft bread scooped out and the rolls buttered, then stuffed. Try: (1) finely chopped hard-boiled egg and chopped celery bound with mayonnaise; (2) Gouda or Edam cheese grated and bound with tomato ketchup; (3) cold, cooked fish, flaked, mixed with finely chopped celery or chives, a squeeze of lemon juice and bound with mushroom or tomato ketchup. Garnish with a few sprigs of watercress.

Sausage or Sardine Rolls.—Small succulent rolls of this type, home-made, are sure favourites. Plain shortcrust pastry is preferable to a richer paste, and the sausage meat can be seasoned with a good pinch of mace as well as salt and pepper. Tail the sardines and drain thoroughly on kitchen paper before rolling in pastry.

Savoury Bread Rolls, the long kind, can have a variety of fillings. Split and butter, then fill with: (1) a cooked sausage spread with mustard; (2) long, thick sticks of cheese with a dash of salad cream or sweet chutney: (3) lengths of tender grilled steak or ham with mustard seasoning.

Scotch Eggs and Hard-boiled Eggs are easily eaten in the fingers and as tasty cold as hot. (For Scotch Eggs recipe see chapter on Egg Dishes.)

Cheese and Bacon Savouries are good— roll rashers of cooked bacon round sticks of cheese and fasten with cocktail sticks or wrap in lettuce leaves.

Ham Horseshoes

8 oz. plain flour	5–6 tablespoonfuls
Pinch of salt	water
5 oz. vegetable fat	½ lb. sliced cooked
shortening	ham

Sieve the flour and salt. Divide the shortening into four portions and rub one portion into the flour. Add the water and mix to a smooth non-sticky dough. If any flour is unabsorbed add another teaspoonful of water until the dough is smooth. Sprinkle with flour, form into an oblong shape with the fingers, and turn on to a floured board. Cover with a damp cloth and leave to rest for 30 minutes. Roll out to an oblong 11 × 6 in. Dab small pieces of the second portion of shortening evenly over the top two-thirds of the dough, leaving a margin of ½ in. all round. Fold the bottom third of the pastry upwards, and the top third down to cover it. Brush off surplus flour, seal the open edges with a rolling pin, and turn the pastry half-way round to the left. Roll out again to a strip 11 × 6 in. Add the third portion of shortening, fold the pastry in three, seal, give a half turn and roll again. Repeat once again with the remaining portion of shortening. Roll out, fold and seal for the fourth time without any shortening. Leave covered for 30 minutes in a cool place. Finally, roll out to an oblong 15 × 10 in. with the edges trimmed. Divide into six squares of equal size. Cut across each square to form triangles. Place a piece of ham on each triangle and, working from the longest edge towards a point, roll up the pastry with the ham inside. Damp the corner and secure. Shape gently into horseshoes, place on a baking sheet. Brush with beaten egg or milk and bake in a very hot oven for 15–20 minutes. (Makes 12 horseshoes.)

Aspic Savouries.—A variety of delicacies can be prepared in individual moulds or ramekins and travel well. Packeted aspic jelly saves time in preparation. Shrimps, prawns, cubes of chicken, beef, veal or pork, sliced egg are some suggestions for setting in the jelly, and the well-drained contents of a tin of macedoine of vegetables can also be added for extra interest and flavour.

Accessories for Savouries.—Plain bread and butter sandwiches go well with aspic savouries.

Tomatoes combine with almost any savoury, but should be firm so that they can be eaten like apples.

Chunks of peeled or unpeeled cucumber and sticks of celery stand travel and are cool and juicy. For perfect transit, pack tomatoes in a tin box and cucumber and celery in tall jars with screw caps.

Lettuce included in sandwiches and rolls is liable to arrive limp and faded-looking, but keeps crisp if packed into a vacuum jar.

Sweets

These need not be limited to a tinful of small cakes or a large cake, which in any case are best kept for tea.

Fruit Jellies can be made in dariole moulds or individual waxed cases, sets of which can be bought at good stationers. Choose a refreshing jelly, such as lime or lemon, and combine with tinned orange slices, apricots cut in convenient pieces, or fruit salad. For something a little more subtle, combine fresh grapes, halved and pipped, with strawberry jelly, or put fresh grapefruit in pineapple jelly.

Plate Tarts.—If these are replaced in their baking tins after cooling and packed in a round cake tin for travelling, they will do so without damage. Firm fillings should be chosen—bakewell, syrup or jam, or firm fruit such as apple, peach or pear, or pineapple finished with a light glaze (see Pastry chapter).

Table-creams, Jelly-creams. — Packet varieties made with milk come in attractive flavourings, can be made in individual cases, or set in a coloured basin (if you have a car for transport) and served from it.

Mousse and Meringue.—One enterprising hostess filled small oblong waxed cases with chocolate mousse and topped each with half a coffee meringue; packed firmly in a 4-lb. biscuit tin, they emerged unruffled at the picnic and were a great success.

Ice Cream is perfectly possible if you invest in a vacuum jar. Buy the ice as near starting time as possible, or en route, and press it well down into the jar, out of its wrappings.

Thirst Quenchers

Juicy oranges are perhaps the simplest way of carrying liquid refreshment, and if the skins are prepared beforehand by quartering with a sharp knife, they peel easily when needed. Juicy plums are light to carry and refreshing for the odd corners in a one-person lunch box, and transport by car allows for a melon or pineapple to be carried for thirst quenching.

Fruit drinks and milk in parchment cartons are lighter and less bulky than bottled drinks and can be taken through straws. Iced coffee or tea can be carried in vacuum flasks.

FOOD FOR TEAS

As a change from sandwiches and in addition to cake, some of the following suggestions may appeal:

Small cheese scones, split and buttered beforehand; plain scones made with finely chopped walnuts; or brown scones spread with watercress butter.

Sweet scone suggestions: buttered currant and sultana scones; brown scones spread with butter and crystallised honey; home-made plain, sweet buns split, lightly buttered and filled with sliced bananas. A little red jam could be added for extra flavour.

A tinful of small iced cakes in paper cups is more interesting than a whole cake. If a firm icing is used, they travel well. And a tinful of crisp, home-made biscuits is a good finish for a tea-time meal.

Have plenty of tea in flasks, and milk and fruit drinks in cartons if there are children who don't take tea.

NOTE: Much of the "flavour" of vacuum flask tea can be avoided if the tea is poured into the flasks through a fine strainer so that no tea leaves enter, and corks should be covered with greaseproof paper before use. Milk should always be carried separately and added to the tea when it is poured out. With iced tea serve a slice of lemon instead of milk.

COOKING OUT

Cooking in the backyard is gaining favour: fun for the family weekends, when the weather calls for picnic meals, and grand for entertaining when a summer evening picnic party in your garden can make you a name as a good hostess.

Build the oven firmly of bricks or stones, a back and two sides of a square, and place a grill on top—a discarded rack from the oven is good for this purpose. The open front should face the prevailing wind; the height of the oven should be about four bricks. For fuelling, in general use soft woods for quick cooking—boiling and frying; hard woods for longer processes—roasting, steaming and baking.

Sausages, ribs, chops, kabobs and steaks can be cooked on the grill; hamburger or rissoles, ham or bacon and eggs in a frying pan; potatoes, plain or stuffed, baked in the hot ashes.

The Pressure Cooker

This is an intriguing way of producing a hot meal with the minimum of effort if you travel by car and can carry cooker (with or without a primus stove). Here is a

Ham Horseshoes make a tasty main dish for a lunch out of doors, served with an ice-cold drink

317

tested idea from the Pressure Cooking Advice Bureau:

Macaroni with Meat Balls

1 *lb. minced beef*	2 *tins tomatoes (or*
1 *chopped onion*	1 *lb. fresh tomatoes*
8 *oz. packet of*	*and* 1 *pint water)*
macaroni	*Salt and pepper to*
	taste

Home preparations.—Season beef and form into small balls. Preheat the pressure cooker, add a little fat and brown the meat. Now add onion, tinned tomatoes (or fresh skinned tomatoes and water) and seasoning Pack the macaroni separately.

When you are ready for your picnic meal, mix the macaroni in with the other ingredients. Bring to the boil, stirring occasionally. Now close the cooker, exhaust all air and bring to 15 lb. pressure. Cook for 12 minutes. Let the cooker cool gradually.

Alternatively, the meal can be cooked at home and will stay hot in the cooker for a maximum of 4 hours, after which reheating will be necessary. In the latter case, the pressure cooker should not be quick-cooled and should not be opened before the food is served.

Wrap the cooker in several newspapers to insulate it.

No creamed foods or chicken dishes should be precooked and left before being used. But there are many other good dishes (such as a beef stew) that can be cooked at home and kept hot for the picnic.

PACKING AND EQUIPMENT

Picnics should be great fun; but they can be an awful bore if their preparation means first scrimmaging round for suitable tins, enough old cups and mugs for drinks, and a vacuum flask that has been used through the winter for holding turps— yes, we have two men friends guilty of this crime! It's well worth collecting adequate equipment and *keeping it for picnic purposes only,* so that it is always ready and in good condition.

A fitted basket or case is an excellent foundation providing, usually, four cups, two flasks, sugar and milk containers, and a light metal sandwich box. It's useful, too, to invest in a small, light fibre suitcase to hold extra equipment and food.

Ideas for further equipment are: plastic spoons for sweets and small plastic plates for savouries; extra sandwich tins for other foods; travelling salt and pepper pots; extra polythene bottles for milk (those supplied in picnic sets are not usually big enough). If you are going to produce anything like a raised pie or galantine, calling for knives and forks and large plates, look around in sports shops and camp equipment departments of large stores for folding sets of knife and fork. These are quite reasonable, much less bulky than household cutlery—and it doesn't matter so much if they get lost. Sets of various sized cardboard plates can be bought at good stationers, and can be used several times if greaseproof paper is put under the food. Cardboard cups or beakers are good for cold drinks, but tend to give a characteristic flavour to hot tea or coffee.

Further aids to comfort and convenience: a vacuum flask of warm water and a plastic envelope holding one or more face flannels and guest towels—a boon for dealing with sticky fingers and young mouths after eating. And carry a simple first-aid kit against insect bites, burns (if you are cooking out) and children's tumbles at play.

So much for equipment. Now here are one or two packing tips: damped greaseproof paper or large lettuce leaves, washed and shaken nearly dry, make excellent wrappers for keeping sandwiches fresh in their tins.

Use newspaper in preference to other paper for packing round cakes or individual sweets, as it holds firmly without being hard. It will also keep an ice cream brick cold for up to two hours.

Sets of polythene bags are hygienic, useful for holding such items as shelled hard-boiled eggs and Scotch eggs as they are water- and greaseproof, and one can be used finally for the collection of all leftovers and used paper.

Vacuum containers are made now in great variety and can be used to transport hot or cold drinks, hot soup, ice cream or ice cubes for cocktails. Expenditure on several of these items is not therefore an extravagance.

Happy eating-out days to you all.

CAMP COOKERY

*The secret of preparing out of doors three good meals a
day that are substantial enough for lusty holiday appetites*

CAMPING has grown greatly in popularity in recent years. Every, summer thousands spend their holidays and weekends enjoying sunshine and fresh air amid natural surroundings, free from the routine of their normal daily lives.

Food is an ever-present necessity, however, in camp as elsewhere. To provide good meals without devoting too much time to the process, it is essential to find out beforehand something about the most suitable equipment and the different techniques required.

Choosing a Stove

Those whose experience of cooking in the open is confined to boiling a kettle over a methylated spirit stove on a windy day, or over a fitful blaze of damp twigs, may regard the preparation of complete meals as an operation far beyond their capabilities. Though this is quite a mistaken idea, you must have the proper equipment. For serious cooking, spirit stoves of any description are not suitable on account of their slowness, susceptibility to draughts and the amount of fuel consumed. On the other hand, wood fires will give good heat if you know how to make and use them properly, but have many obvious disadvantages, and for the small family unit have long been superseded by one of the many types of portable stove burning Calor gas, paraffin or petrol.

To digress a moment, there is nothing quite like a wood fire in camp for warmth and sociability, especially when twilight falls and the air begins to cool. But it is best kept for that purpose, and then only when sufficient dead wood can be found (no breaking down of living trees). The camp-site owner's permission to light a fire must first be obtained and a suitable place agreed. Wood fires are not permitted on some camp sites.

319

Cooking by Gas

The simplest method is undoubtedly with Calor gas, which provides a flame that won't blow out in the wind and requires no pumping or priming.

You can get either a portable boiling ring, which gives 24 hours' continuous burning with the burner full on, or a double boiler unit capable of heating the water for tea and frying eggs at the same time. Both are small enough to be stowed away in a car or trailer and both operate from one portable gas cylinder.

Pressure Stoves

Both paraffin and petrol pressure stoves originated in Sweden, and several reliable types, of Swedish and British manufacture, are available. The air-pressure type, which burns paraffin, is probably the most popular. There are several different pattern burners, but the principle of operation in all paraffin pressure stoves is the same: the burner must be preheated beforehand in order to vaporise the rising paraffin before the stove will burn properly.

This is achieved by burning a small quantity of methylated spirit poured into a small circular cup at the base of the burner or, better still, by using two or three small pieces of broken-up solid-fuel tablet as sold for use with some picnic stoves. The solid fuel is safer and has the added advantages that it is more compact, will not spill and a week's supply may easily be carried in a small tin.

The tank of the stove is fitted with a filler cap, in the centre or side of which is the air-valve screw, a pump for forcing air into the tank and a burner or, in upright collapsible types, a hole into which the burner is screwed, which is closed by a screw plug when the stove is dismantled.

A metal draught shield is usually supplied to confine the heat of the priming fuel around the burner during the preheating process. The air-valve screw must be open while this is taking place, but is screwed down just before the priming fuel becomes exhausted. You then push the pump lightly once or twice, light the burner and the stove should burn with a blue flame and slight hissing sound. When the stove is burning properly, without spitting, a few more strokes of the pump will bring the

flame and the heat up to full power, and may be repeated as necessary.

For camp use, "roarer" pattern burners are best as they are less susceptible to draughts than the "silent" pattern.

If the stove fails to light properly the first time, and, instead of the blue hissing flame, paraffin begins to rise and, possibly, becomes ignited by the remains of the priming fuel, the air-valve screw must be released immediately and the preheating procedure repeated. The ignited paraffin must not be allowed to burn on in the false hope that it may make the stove burn correctly, particularly if the stove is near the tent or other inflammable material.

Provided the burner nipple hole is not blocked, failure to light properly is usually caused by either too little priming fuel, closure of the air valve and pumping too soon, or cool draughts. As a protection against draughts, a windshield in one form or another is essential and consists of three sides of material to fit around the stove, with the central, closed side at the back facing the direction of the prevailing wind. Best for mobile camping is a length of cotton material divided into three sections by metal rods or canes which can be stuck in the turf around the stove. Such windshields can be purchased or made at home.

If these operations sound somewhat complicated to the uninitiated, in practice the knack is quickly acquired, even by children, provided they are old enough to be trusted with matches.

When the stove is alight, the size and heat of the flame may be controlled by judicious use of the air-release screw. By simply unscrewing this and leaving it open, the stove may be extinguished.

Cooking by Petrol

The other types of stove most widely used for camp cookery burn petrol. They have increased greatly in popularity in recent years, particularly among motorists with their ready-to-hand fuel supply. Care must be taken, however, to ensure that the type of stove purchased will burn *all kinds* of petrol, including leaded petrol as generally used in private motor vehicles. Some petrol stoves, mostly small sizes, but including *all* those designed for either paraffin *or* petrol, will only work efficiently with *un*leaded petrol, which has to be obtained specially from a garage.

Although petrol stoves in themselves are perfectly safe —most are fitted with a safety valve—the usual caution in handling petrol must be observed when refilling.

Petrol stoves differ from paraffin ones in these essentials:

(1) Petrol stoves are not fitted with a pressure release valve screw, for the obvious reason that undoing the screw to extinguish the stove would release petrol vapour, which is extremely inflammable and highly dangerous. (This is the chief reason why petrol should never be used in a stove designed only for paraffin.) In place of the screw valve, a positive on-and-off tap is always fitted, which can also be used for controlling the size and heat of the flame.

(2) No preheating is required except in the smaller sizes, and then only a little, easily applied with a match or two, or a small piece of solid fuel.

With all types of vapour stoves the tiny hole from which the igniting gas escapes must be kept clear of dirt and obstruction. Some stoves are fitted with self-pricking burners, but the majority are not and a supply of prickers (the correct size for the stove) should always be kept at hand. Since the nipple hole is liable to become enlarged with constant use and so impair the efficiency of the stove, it is wise to carry spare nipples and a nipple key.

Stoves of each type are supplied in various sizes, ranging from $\frac{1}{3}$-pint petrol and $\frac{1}{2}$-pint paraffin to about 2 pints in either (quantities refer to tank capacity). Single- and double-burner types are available, the latter mostly in compact folding ranges which are immediately ready for use when opened.

The smaller sizes (up to 1 pint) are suitable for a single camper; the 1-pint alone or 1-pint plus $\frac{1}{2}$-pint for two people. For

Most suitable methods for camp cookery are frying and boiling, whether over a wood fire or on a special stove

three or more, two stoves of at least 1-pint capacity, or a double-burner stove, are really necessary.

Cooking Equipment

For use with camping stoves, special aluminium saucepans have been designed without fixed handles but with a slot to take a detachable handle which fits all sizes.

NOTE: Always remove the handle when a pan has been placed on or lifted from the stove. With it on, it is so easy to tip the pan over.

These saucepans are made in about eight sizes, ranging from approximately 1-pint to $4\frac{1}{2}$-pints capacity. Each size "nests" in the next larger. Frying pans, also, without handles, are available in different sizes and can be matched to the largest saucepan, and so will act as a cover to the set of pans for ease in carriage. Separate light lids,

321

with lifting rings, are also obtainable for all pans.

Aluminium plates are most suitable for camp use, as they are light, unbreakable, easily cleaned and carried. Several types of screw-top containers, in aluminium and polythene (unbreakable), can be obtained for carrying different kinds of food and condiments—tea, sugar, jam, etc. For butter and fats, glass or plastic-lined screw-top aluminium containers are best.

The transparent food bags sold for sandwich lunches and storing food in the refrigerator are ideal for all kinds of eatables that do not require a tin. Excluding air, they really do keep the food fresh.

Cups and saucers in unbreakable polythene are best for camp use. Aluminium cups should be avoided; they burn the lips if used for hot liquids.

Large aluminium cans with lids and handles are useful for water and milk, but the wide-necked polythene jars, with screw-tops, are probably better for milk. Water, of course, may also be fetched in the familiar type camp bucket and basin, but there is no need for these items to be of heavy canvas material to be efficient. Quite suitable items in good lightweight fabric, or even in plastic, can be purchased. They bulk small for ease in carriage when not in use.

A fish slice, no matter how small, for dishing up fried foods should not be forgotten; nor the swab and nylon pot scourer or brush for the inevitable washing up. Soap powder should be carried in a screw-top tin; cardboard easily gets damp and soggy in the open.

Although most meals cooked in camp will no doubt consist of boiled, stewed or fried foods in their many varieties, a small oven for camp use is on the market. One type measures 11 by 11 by 9 in. high and is suitable for most stoves.

Steamers are also obtainable, and for those who like toast for breakfast, there is a round, flat, gauze toaster specially for use with camp stoves which is quite efficient. If there are three or more people to cook for, a pressure cooker is invaluable (see chapter on Pressure Cookery).

Planning Meals

When meals are planned, the limiting factors are the capacity of stove or stoves and the size and number of saucepans available. It is, however, quite easy to cook a meal of two courses on one stove; a third

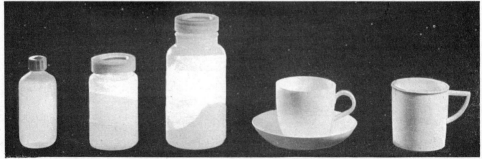

For carrying milk and other liquids, also for cups and beakers, the best material is 'Polythene' which is unbreakable, tasteless, stainless and can be sterilised in boiling water. (Camtors)

Photo by the Camping Club of Great Britain and Ireland

A windshield, consisting of three sides of material, is essential to protect the stove from draughts. Equipment shown above includes (right), a lightweight camp bucket for water, also aluminium cooking and eating utensils, the saucepans with detachable handles

may be added by the ambitious—by simply changing the pans about and keeping one hot on top of another. For example, when preparing breakfast, the water for tea should first be heated and covered with a plate. The porridge can then be cooked and placed on top of the saucepan containing the hot water, close to the stove, while the bacon and/or eggs are fried. When that is done, the porridge can be warmed for a few seconds and, while it is being eaten, the water for the tea brought to the boil, with the bacon, etc., covered by a plate, keeping warm on top. The same procedure can be followed for other meals. The important thing to remember is that dishes which will not spoil by being reheated, or partly cooked first and finished later, should always be cooked first and put back for reheating just before serving the meal.

If two stoves are in operation, it is, of course, much easier, but even then it is advisable to heat a pan of hot water first. It is always necessary in camp cookery to time the operations so that the courses are ready to be served hot as they are wanted.

Tea can be made quite successfully in a saucepan and strained into the cups, though a light aluminium teapot really is an improvement if it can be carried. Another very desirable extra is a tea cosy. A pan of tea that has cooled off will not spoil if it is warmed up on the stove, provided it does not simmer or boil.

Choice of Equipment

When buying equipment, it is advisable to consult one of the firms specialising in lightweight camping equipment, most of which issue very comprehensive catalogues.

For more information about camping in general or to meet other campers, enquiry should be made to The Camping Club of Great Britain and Ireland, 35 Old Kent Road, London, S.E.1, who cater for all forms of camping and caravanning, issue a list of camp sites to members, supply specialist information, and arrange camping fixtures in Great Britain and camping tours abroad.

ONE-ROOM CHEF

*Living alone in limited space, with the minimum of cooking
facilities, is no excuse for not having proper meals*

ONE-ROOMERS of all ages and both
sexes can and should eat well by their
own hand.

At the outset, limited space and inadequate equipment tend to cast a deep depression over the whole idea, but that can
be altered, and a boiled egg and a "cuppa"
need not be the sole repertoire for an evening meal.

The elderly and not-so-active need light,
nourishing meals; men and women, after
work, need equally nourishing but more
substantial meals and, above all, those
that are quickly cooked.

The right equipment and a small but
adequate store cupboard are essentials; so,
too, is a collection of quickly cooked
recipes to start with.

Equipment

The most important item, naturally, is
the cooker.

Personal experience of bed-sitters is of
one miniature gas-ring, wobbly, situated in
the hearth by the gas-fire and in close proximity to the wooden surround of the mantelpiece. This sort of arrangement does
dampen one's zest for home cooking, but
no landlord will mind something better
being installed, if it is not at his expense,
and it really is well worth drawing on
savings to get that something better. What
you don't spend on meals out will soon
close the savings gap.

Bed-sitterites are well catered for by gas
and electric appliance manufacturers. You
can choose the Big Baby Belling electric
cooker, which stands only 36 in. high
(42 in. to the top of the splash plate), is
21 in. wide and 16 in. deep. It won't take
up much space, but will enable you to cook
a full scale dinner for five or six people in
its roomy oven, with combined grill-boiler,
on which you can cook on top while you
grill or toast underneath. It can stand on a
table or be supplied with a stand and it
boasts a plate-warming cupboard that
could do double duty in emergencies as an
airer!

The Belling and several other small

electric cookers suitable for one-room
living can be plugged in anywhere as they
work off any 13- or 15-amp power point.

Much smaller and costing a lot less are
the various gas hotplates, most of which
have two boiling burners, a grill and a
spillage tray. It's amazing what a variety
of hot dishes can be prepared on these.

Then there are the rapidly growing number of electric "cook on the table" appliances—frypans, skillets, combined cooker-fryers and pressure cookers. These are
smart and streamlined, usually with oven-glass or metal lids.

Three Presto automatic cooking appliances can all be operated by one electric
control unit. So you can buy, say, the frypan and control master unit first, then add
the pressure cooker, and finally the cooker-fryer (which boils, stews, steams, braises,
deep-fries and comes with its own chip
basket).

Apart from the cooker, dual-purpose
utensils are worth considering. The three-section saucepan or frypan can perform
wonders in cooking a whole meal for
one.

Steamers and double saucepans are good
friends to small-space cooks, and so is the
self-basting roasting tin. A Dutch oven is
invaluable, and this, by the way, provides
the genuine means of roasting—*in front* of
a hot fire. For this purpose, a gas fire
capable of fierce heat is best.

Two strong enamel plates, dinner size,
are most useful for cooking over a pan
of hot water. And oven-glass ramekins
should not be forgotten, nor a clearly
marked oven-glass measuring jug, showing
cups as well as fluid ounces.

The pressure cooker, of course, is a
boon and the chapter on Pressure Cookery
may be consulted for further information.

The Store Cupboard

It is at last possible to buy small sizes
of a good variety of canned foods.

Suggestions for your store cupboard are:
small-size steak and kidney puddings
(ample for one, enough for two); pork

luncheon meat loaf (Dutch brands are delicious hot or cold, as are good brands of ham and beef loaf); small cans of macaroni cheese; filled ravioli paste, the small size of *pink* salmon makes a tasty meal and is not prohibitive, compared with red salmon. Tuna fish, too, is delicious, and keep in hand a can or two and some packets and cubes of interesting soup. (See also chapter on Emergency Meals.)

Some vegetables, particularly peas, baked beans and macédoine of vegetables, come in handy small cans and so do a variety of fruits, evaporated milk and cream. Small canned steamed puddings and creamed rice are also available.

Frozen foods come to the rescue in many emergencies. When you are right out of ideas for dinner and can investigate the contents of one of the frozen food cabinets in good shops and stores everywhere, you might choose fish fingers or chops and peas with a mousse for the sweet course. Eating this way is apt to be expensive, but can be a blessing when, in the mood for entertaining, you want some, say, out-of-season vegetable or fruit to lift your meal out of the ordinary.

Delicatessen shops are another useful source of ideas for preparing quick meals. Various ingredients for all kinds of salads can usually be bought, and save much preparation. If you have a small oven, packets of ready-mixed puff or short pastry may be bought, needing only to be rolled out at home and made up into sweet or savoury dishes. Unfilled, cooked vol-au-vent cases can be filled at home and gently heated for a savoury supper, and there is a wide variety of cooked meats and packet meals needing no cooking.

The Argyll Gas Hotplate is small enough for the tiniest one-room flatlet but has two highly efficient boiling burners and a high-speed grill, is fitted with push-in safety taps. (Stoves Ltd.)

COLLECTED RECIPES

Light Savouries

Quick Cod.—About ½ lb. cod fillet. Wash, dry and place on enamel plate over a pan of boiling water. Pour a little milk over fish, add a nut of butter and pepper and salt to taste. Cover with another plate or the saucepan lid, and cook for about 15 minutes or until fish is cooked right through. Drain off the liquor and use to make white sauce (see Sauces chapter), or flavour the sauce with finely chopped parsley, sprinkle the fish with a little grated cheese and put under the grill long enough to melt and brown the cheese.

Masked Egg and Spinach.—Prepare about ¼ pint white sauce in the top half of a double saucepan, using the heat from the boiling water in the bottom half of the pan; flavour lightly with tomato ketchup or grated cheese. Cook spinach separately in the water that clings to the leaves after washing. A few minutes before it is ready, put an egg to soft-boil in the bottom half of the double saucepan. Drain and season the spinach, place on a warmed dinner plate. Shell the egg when cooked, place on the spinach and mask both with the sauce.

Savoury Scramble.—Boil water in bottom pan of double saucepan. Dice a slice of luncheon meat or cold, boiled ham, and put into inner pan with 2 tablespoonfuls milk and a knob of butter or margarine.

The Big Baby Belling electric cooker stands on a table or its own stand. Combined grill-boiler gives maximum efficiency—and clothes can be aired in the plate-warming cupboard!

Heat gently until fat is melted. Remove pan and stir in a well-beaten egg seasoned to taste. Return to outer pan and cook until mixture "scrambles." Turn on to crisp, buttered toast.

Cheese Custard.—Mix a small, lightly beaten egg with $\frac{1}{2}$ cupful warm milk. Mix separately in small basin or soufflé dish $1\frac{1}{2}$ tablespoonfuls each of grated cheese and breadcrumbs, season to taste and sprinkle over the custard. Cover securely with greaseproof paper, place in pan of cold water to come half-way up basin and bring gradually to the boil, lid on pan, to set custard. Boil for about 20 minutes. If you have a small oven, bake in moderate heat to set egg.

Stuffed Onion.—Choose a large onion, Spanish if possible, peel, cross-cut the root end lightly and cook in boiling salted water until tender but still firm. Set the pan aside for the moment. Remove some of the centre of the onion and chop up with a little left-over meat, peas, beans or tomato; season and bind with a little tomato or mushroom ketchup. Pile into centre of onion, put onion into small basin, top with piece of butter or margarine, and put back over pan, lid off, and bring to boil until onion is thoroughly heated through. Or serve stuffed onion (or stuffed baked apple) with a hot curry sauce.

Variation.—A quicker onion dish is to boil the onion, drain, place on a warmed dinner plate, top with a piece of butter and plenty of grated cheese and eat with brown bread or toast.

More Substantial Savouries

One-man Grill.—Toast a large slice of bread on one side only. On the untoasted side put $\frac{1}{4}$ lb. raw, minced beef, season with salt and pepper—and mixed herbs or chopped parsley and onion, if liked—add knob of margarine and put under grill. Cook gently until meat changes colour and loses raw appearance and feels tender when speared with a fork. Now top with sliced tomatoes (or mushrooms if you are feeling extravagant) and grill again for a minute or two until these are cooked. A delicious dish, and all the gravy is caught in the toast.

Mixed Grill.—According to appetite, fry or grill one or more sausages, bacon rashers, halved tomatoes, and any left-over mince. Arrange all on a warmed plate and add watercress, if liked, add snippets of dry toast.

Meat Fritters.—Make a simple batter (see Puddings chapter). Cut thickish slices of pork luncheon meat loaf, dip in batter and roll in crumbs, fry in smoking hot fat to cover. Drain on kitchen paper before serving.

NOTE: Rolls of kitchen paper towelling can be bought at good stationers and are most useful for cooking and other purposes. Drums of ready-prepared brown crumbs can also be bought and last well.

Main Course Soup.—Open a can of concentrated soup—tomato, celery, mushroom, pea, for instance—dilute with a canful of half milk, half water, and heat through. Pour off a helping and the rest will keep for a day or two for another meal. Reinforce the soup with diced left-overs of meat and vegetables, and, if you feel luxurious—and in funds—stir in a spoonful of fresh cream just before eating.

Savoury Pasty (for those with an oven). —Buy $\frac{1}{4}$ lb. ready-made pastry. Roll out $\frac{1}{4}$ in. thick and cut out two rounds, using a small saucer. Milk the edges and fill one round with cooked meat, fish or chicken, bound with a little egg or well-seasoned thick white sauce. Place second round on top, pinch edges together, brush with beaten egg or milk and cut two air slits on top. Bake in a hot oven until nicely brown.

Kedgeree.—If you have enjoyed Finnan haddock for dinner one night and have about ½ lb. left, use up as follows: put 2 tablespoonfuls rice in boiling salted water and hard-boil a shell egg. Flake fish, remove bones, and heat in a separate pan (on top of double boiler) with 1 oz. butter or margarine. When rice is cooked and drained, add to fish and season. Pile on a dish and decorate with hard-boiled egg rings and chopped parsley.

Mock Kedgeree.—An excellent emergency meal when the larder is low. Wash and cook 2 tablespoonfuls rice in boiling salted water until tender. Drain and, while still hot, work in a teaspoonful of butter or margarine, two skinned and mashed tomatoes, and 1 tablespoonful or more of grated cheese, also curry powder to taste and a few raisins if liked. Stir well, reheat if necessary, and eat with lightly buttered crisp brown toast.

Dutch Oven Cookery

This is a grand appliance if you have no grill; after a little practice you can produce succulent grilled chops and grilled steaks and sausages nicely chippy outside and soft inside. You will also be able to do:

Kebabs. — These are skewerfuls of mouth-sized bites—for example, cubes of grilling steak or lamb, squares of bacon, button mushrooms and thick slices of tomato, threaded alternately on one skewer per person. Season with pepper and salt, brush with oil. Turn up the fire so that the inside of the oven is very hot and grill the kebabs for 10–20 minutes, turning once. If

nothing suitable is available, you may have to invest in an iron trivet on which to stand the oven in front of the fire, or an upturned large biscuit tin or box will sometimes do.

Vegetables

Serve yourself a vegetable with your evening meal, for health as well as variety; canned and frozen are excellent and quick to serve, and here are some tips on fresh vegetables:

Special Brussels Sprouts.—To make more digestible, soak for 5 minutes in cold water after preparing, put in a pan with a little milk and cook gently until tender. When possible, plan to have this vegetable with a main dish needing a sauce and use the milk from the sprouts for the sauce.

Five-minute Carrots.—To have these hot and reduce cooking time, wash, scrape

A baby cooker with two simmer controlled radiant rings, a thermostatically controlled oven and a full-size cooker grill, the G.E.C. Little Treasure has a matching base cabinet for storage

327

Smart enough to adorn any dinner table, with its copper-toned lid, the thermostatically heat-controlled Morphy-Richards Electric Skillet (right) stews, fries, roasts and bakes equally well

The Presto Cooker-Fryer (below) is another multiple-use appliance and it runs off the same control unit as the Presto Fry Pan and Pressure Cooker

and then grate finely. Put in a small pan with a good piece of butter or margarine, season, and stir over low heat until fat is melted and the vegetable is hot right through—literally a matter of about 5 minutes.

Potatoes.—If you are making a dish over a pan of hot water, potatoes can be cooked in the water, and to save trouble and give the best flavour and nourishment, scrub and boil in their jackets: as a change, finish them off in the Dutch oven if you acquire one.

Light Sweets

A useful item to have as part of your equipment is a vacuum jar. In this you can collect ice cream—on your way home, per-

haps—or a mousse, and keep it until your meal is ready.

If you are entertaining, an individual block of strawberry or coffee ice put between the carefully separated halves of a confectioner's meringue makes a festive and delicious sweet course.

Another simple and pleasant idea is to make up half a pint of packet custard, line the bottom of a small dish with, say, chopped apple, sliced banana and a sprinkle of raisins, and pour over the custard. Leave to get cold. And another fruity idea:

Grapefruit Salad.—Cut top off a small grapefruit and take out most of the inside. Fill the space with any fruit you may have —peeled and pipped grapes, pieces of the grapefruit and pieces of pear, a small can of mixed fruit salad, chopped bananas.

A quick, nourishing sweet is made as follows:

Baked Cup Custard.—Lightly beat an egg in a large, strong breakfast cup. Add milk to about 1½ in. from the top, and sugar to taste. Cover cup with a tight-fitting lid and place in a saucepan of water to come half-way up the cup. Bring to the boil and boil gently for 15–20 minutes.

You cannot improve on fresh fruit in

season for the last course if you feel disinclined to prepare a sweet.

More Substantial Sweets

Canned puddings need only to be heated as directed and a sweet white sauce made if you feel like it; or, for a change, run some Golden Syrup over the top instead.

Here is a recipe for an uncooked cake that makes a good after-dinner sweet:

Biscuit Cake.—$\frac{1}{4}$ lb. margarine; $\frac{1}{4}$ lb. block chocolate; 3 tablespoonfuls sugar; 1 egg; $\frac{1}{2}$ lb. biscuits of the oval rich tea or petit beurre type.

Break biscuits in small neat pieces and put into a fairly large basin. Break an egg into a small basin or cup and beat well until smooth. Now melt margarine, sugar and chocolate in a double saucepan until sugar is dissolved, chocolate melted and all are smoothly blended. Add beaten egg and continue cooking, stirring all the time, for about 7–10 minutes. The mixture must not boil. When cooked, pour mixture over biscuits and stir carefully to coat them thoroughly. Grease an oblong bread tin, press mixture into this and leave to get cold. Turn out and slice as required.

Sweet Rice.—Wash and cook 1 or 2 tablespoonfuls rice in boiling salted water. Drain and eat hot with moist brown sugar, honey or Golden Syrup, and butter.

A good sweet to make at week-ends when there is more time for preparation:

Tapioca Apples.—Take $1\frac{1}{2}$ tablespoonfuls of large tapioca and $\frac{1}{2}$-pint milk together with a sliver of lemon rind for flavouring. Place in double saucepan and cook for about $1\frac{1}{2}$ hours. Meanwhile, peel and core three medium-sized cooking apples, cut these in quarters and stew gently in a little water, with sugar added. When apples and tapioca are ready, put half the tapioca in a fireproof glass dish, add half the apples, remaining tapioca, and lastly, the remaining apples. Cover with a layer of apricot jam, and pop under grill or in oven, if you have one, before serving.

Batter Sweets.—Pancakes (see Puddings chapter) are always popular and can be eaten with sugar and lemon juice, or folded over jam or fruit.

Bananas, split lengthwise, apple rings and orange rings are delicious dipped in batter, fried and rolled in sugar before eating.

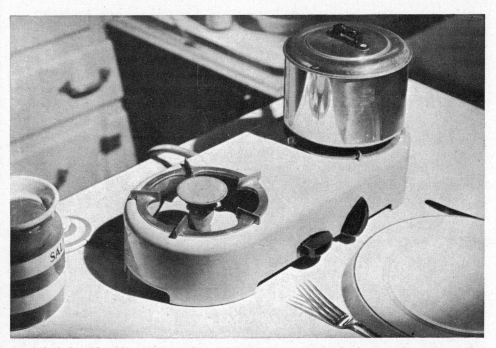

Specially designed for old people living alone, this double-burner cooking ring by Ascot Water Heaters Ltd. cannot light back, has easy flame control from simmering to boiling and is ideal for casserole cooking

JAMS, JELLIES, MARMALADE, PICKLES AND CHUTNEY

There is nothing quite so satisfying as a well-stocked store cupboard,
full of good things you have made—and maybe also grown—yourself

JAM MAKING

JAM MAKING is not difficult, provided certain rules are carefully followed, and does not take an unduly long time. For anyone who grows fruit in the garden, there is the special joy of "all my own work." Even those who have to buy the fruit will find it worth while and a saving to make jam when seasonable fruits are cheap.

Weighing and measuring must be absolutely accurate, and the jam must be boiled until a good set is secured. A common failing of home-made jam is that it is too runny, and preparations are on the market to make it set. But jams and jellies containing nothing but fruit, sugar and water should set perfectly. Certain fruits—such as strawberries, cherries and marrow, for example—are deficient in pectin (the acid which makes jams set), but it is easy to counteract this by adding the juice of fruit rich in pectin, such as lemon, gooseberry or redcurrant. The juice of the two latter can be extracted by boiling them with a little water until tender and then straining the juice.

The best sort of preserving pan to use is a strong aluminium one. Failing this, a copper pan can be used, but never in any circumstances use a galvanised container. Never fill the pan too full or the jam may boil over.

Either loaf or granulated sugar can be used for jam and jelly. For good results, 1 lb. of sugar should be used for every 1 lb. of fruit.

Here are a few special points which should be carefully noted:

(1) Always use firm, undamaged fruit, not too ripe, freshly picked (on a fine day, if possible). Wash the harder fruits. Go through the fruit carefully and remove bad ones or blemishes.

(2) Tough fruit should be simmered in a little water until tender before the sugar is added. Tender fruit can have the sugar added at once. Care must be taken that it does not burn before the juice comes out of the fruit.

(3) Jam must always be stirred once the sugar is in, and the sugar should be warmed first. Do not let the mixture boil until all the sugar has dissolved.

(4) When the sugar is dissolved, boil the jam rapidly. A large amount of scum will come to the surface. Wait until the jam is nearly done before removing it, as a large part of it will boil back into the jam; the rest can easily be removed with a fish slice or shallow spoon. A good way of using up jam skimmings is to make a Queen's Pudding with them (see Puddings chapter).

(5) As the jam thickens and the fruit becomes clear, test the juice, to see if it will set, by dropping a very little on to a china plate and putting it by the window for a minute. Touch the drops lightly with one finger. If the surface crinkles the jam is done.

(6) In some jam the fruit is apt to rise to the surface, leaving only syrup at the bottom of the jars. To prevent this, let the jam cool in the pan and give it a stir before pouring it out.

(7) The jars should be scrupulously clean, absolutely dry, and heated a little in the oven, otherwise they may crack.

(8) Fill the jars very full because jam sinks as it cools. Use a sauceboat or small jug and, if necessary, wipe the tops and sides of the jars while still hot. A jam funnel put in the neck of the jars will keep the top and sides quite clean.

(9) There are two schools of thought about when to cover jam, some people doing it when still hot, others leaving it to cool. The former method is probably preferable as the sooner the jam is covered the less likely are mould spores to enter. The difficulty about covering jam while hot is that

it sinks during cooling so that an inner paper put on at once either goes down with the jam or sticks to the sides of the jar, leaving a space between it and the jam. Cellophane covers applied dry the moment the jam is potted, and secured with rubber bands or strings, keep the jam in excellent condition. (There are one or two jams, such as strawberry, which it is advisable to leave for a time before potting, as otherwise the fruit tends to rise to the top of the jars.)

(10) Jam should keep perfectly for a year if stored in a cool, dry place.

Apricot Jam (Dried Fruit)

  3 *lb. dried apricots*
  9 *pints water*
  9 *lb. sugar*
  2 *oz. almonds*

Wash the apricots, cut in pieces and stand them in the water for 24 hours. Blanch the almonds and cut them to resemble kernels. Boil the apricots and water until the fruit is tender—40–50 minutes. Add the sugar, let it dissolve, and boil rapidly until the juice will nearly set. Add the almonds and boil until the juice will set, skimming if necessary. Pour into warm, dry jars and tie down at once.

Apricot Jam (Fresh Fruit)

  4 *lb. fresh apricots*   4 *lb. sugar*
  ¼ *pint water*   *Juice of a lemon*

Wash fruit, halve and remove stones. Crack a few stones and blanch the kernels. Put fruit, water, lemon juice and kernels into the pan and bring to the boil. Cook gently until fruit is tender, then add sugar, stir till boiling. Boil hard until a set is obtained.

Jam and jelly making is not at all difficult but, for success, the ingredients must be accurately weighed and measured. A strong aluminium or copper pan should be used

Blackberry and Apple Jam

  8 *lb. blackberries*   3 *lb. apples*
  Sugar   1 *pint water*

Remove stalks and put the blackberries in a pan with a gill of water. Simmer until tender, then put through a sieve. Peel, core and slice the apples coarsely, put with the rest of the water into the pan and cook until soft, then mash up with a fork, add the blackberry juice and weigh, allowing an equal weight of sugar. Heat slowly

331

while the sugar dissolves, then increase the heat and boil briskly until it will set when tested. Skim, if necessary, pour into warm, dry jars and tie down at once.

Blackcurrant Jam

6 lb. blackcurrants   7¼ lb. sugar
4 pints water

Remove the stalks and larger snuffs from the currants, place with the water in the preserving pan, and boil gently until the fruit is quite tender and the mixture considerably reduced. Add the sugar and let it dissolve. Boil until the jam will set when tested. Skim towards the end, if necessary. Pour the jam into warm, dry jars and cover at once.

Cherry Jam

12 lb. black cherries   Sugar
1 lb. redcurrants   Water

Stone and weigh the cherries. To every 1 lb. of stoned cherries allow 1 lb. of sugar. Boil the currants, adding a little water. When they have boiled for ½ hour, strain through a jelly bag and add the juice to the cherries. Boil the cherries with the juice for about ¼ hour until soft. Add the sugar and bring slowly to the boil, allowing the sugar to melt before it boils. Boil quickly until the juice is thick and not too runny, skimming if necessary, then pour into warm, dry jars and cover at once.

Gooseberry Jam

6 lb. gooseberries   1½ pints water
7½ lb. sugar

Wash, top and tail the gooseberries and place them in the preserving pan with the water. Simmer until the fruit is mashed and tender and the contents of the pan considerably reduced. Add the sugar and let it dissolve. Boil until the jam will set when tested, skimming if necessary. Pour it into warm, dry jars and tie down at once.

Marrow Jam

6 lb. marrow   3 lemons
6 lb. sugar   1½ oz. root ginger

The marrows must be quite ripe and almost woody, or they will boil pulpy. Peel them, remove all the soft parts and seeds, and cut into cubes of about 1 in. Put the marrow and sugar into a preserving pan with the juice and very finely cut rind of the lemons. Mix all together and let it stand for 24 hours. Then add the ginger, bruising it well and putting it into a muslin bag. Cook until the cubes of marrow are transparent and the juice is sticky but not runny. Remove the ginger. Skim, if necessary. Let the jam stand until nearly cold before pouring into the jars. Cover at once.

Nectarine Jam (Dried Fruit)

This can be made in exactly the same way as peach jam, substituting dried nectarines for the dried peaches.

Peach Jam (Dried Fruit)

3 lb. dried peaches   9 lb. sugar
9 pints water   Juice of 2 lemons

Wash the peaches and cut into pieces. Stand them in the water for 24 hours. Add the lemon juice and boil slowly until the fruit is tender. Add the sugar, let it dissolve, and then boil rapidly until the juice will set when tested, skimming if necessary. Pour into warm, dry jars and cover at once.

Peach and Raspberry Jam

2 lb. fresh peaches   3 lb. sugar
  (stoned)   2 lb. raspberries
¼ pint water

Skin the peaches and cut them into pieces. Crack the stones, take out kernels and blanch. Put the fruit, water and kernels into the preserving pan and cook gently until tender. Add the sugar and stir until it has dissolved, boil for 15 minutes, then test for set.

Pineapple Jam

1 large ripe pineapple   Juice of a lemon
  Sugar

Peel the pineapple and cut out the woody parts. Chop up the rest into neat cubes. Weigh it and place in a pan with an equal weight of sugar. Let it stand all night. Next day, add the lemon juice and boil until the cubes are transparent and the syrup thick. Skim, if necessary. Let it stand until nearly cold and then pour into warm, dry jars and cover at once.

Plum Jam

6 lb. plums   7½ lb. sugar
2½ pints water

Wash the plums and cook them in the water until quite tender and until the contents of the pan are considerably reduced.

(Remove any stones that come away easily —the rest can be removed after the sugar has been added, when they will come to the top.) Add the sugar, dissolve slowly over a low heat, then bring to the boil and boil quickly until the jam will set when tested. Skim, if necessary. Pour into warm, dry jars and tie down at once.

Raspberry Jam

Take freshly picked raspberries, look them over carefully and weigh them. Allow 1½ lb. sugar to every 1 lb. raspberries. Put the sugar and fruit into a preserving pan and heat until the sugar is dissolved, stirring well. Then bring to the boil and boil hard for exactly 3 minutes, skimming if necessary. Pour into warm, dry jars and cover at once.

Redcurrant Jam

To every 1 lb. of fruit put 1 lb. of sugar. Remove the stalks from the fruit. Bruise the currants first. Add the sugar to the currants, let the sugar dissolve slowly, stirring all the time, and then boil gently until clear and sufficiently stiff, skimming if

necessary. Pour into warm, dry jars and tie down.

Redcurrant and Raspberry Jam

| 6 lb. redcurrants | 8 lb. sugar |
| 2 lb. raspberries | A very little water |

Remove the stalks from the currants and put them with the raspberries in a very little water. Simmer the fruit until the currants are tender and cooked. Then add the sugar and let it dissolve, stirring all the time. Boil until the jam will set when tested, skimming towards the end if necessary. Pour into warm, dry jars and cover at once.

Rhubarb Jam

| 3 lb. rhubarb (cut up) | 1½ oz. root ginger |
| 3 lb. sugar | 2 small lemons |

Cut the rhubarb into small pieces and put into a preserving pan with the sugar. Heat slowly until the sugar is dissolved, stirring all the time. Add the lemon juice and finely grated lemon rind; bruise the ginger, tie it in a muslin bag and add. Boil until the mixture sets when tested, skimming if necessary. Remove the ginger and pour the jam into warm, dry jars. Cover at once.

Strawberry Jam

| 5 lb. hulled straw-
berries | 1 gill gooseberry
juice, or juice of 2 |
| 5 lb. sugar | lemons |

Place all the ingredients in preserving

Blackberry and Apple is one of the most delicious fruit mixtures for home-made jam—and you usually pick the blackberries in the hedgerows for nothing

pan and heat until the sugar is quite dissolved. Boil until the jam will set when tested. Skim towards the end, if necessary. Let the jam stand until almost cold and then pour it into the jars. Cover at once.

Strawberry Jam (Quick method)

2 lb. small straw-   ½ teaspoonful tartaric
berries   acid, or juice of 1
3 lb. sugar   lemon, or red-
     currant juice

Butter the preserving pan thoroughly, put in strawberries and mash them slightly. Add sugar and acid (or lemon or red-currant juice), stir until the sugar melts, then bring to boil and boil hard for 3 minutes. Remove from heat and *stir for 5 minutes*—this is absolutely necessary— skimming as required. (Yield: 5 lb. jam.)

Tomato Jam

9 lb. ripe tomatoes   6 lb. sugar
A little lemon juice

Pour boiling water over the tomatoes and remove the skins. Put the fruit, sugar and lemon juice in a preserving pan and bring it to the boil slowly, allowing the sugar to dissolve. Boil until the fruit is transparent and the syrup thick. Skim towards the end, if necessary. Let the jam stand until cold, then pour into the jars and cover at once.

JELLY MAKING

The prime essential is a good jelly bag. Various kinds can be bought, but it is quite easy to make one's own. Use strong butter muslin and make the bag wide at the top, tapering to a point. Sew on loops. A broom handle threaded through the loops can be balanced on two tables, or the backs of two kitchen chairs, over the basin.

Always scald jelly bags before using them.

Here are a few points to bear in mind when making jelly:

(1) The fruit, which need not have stalks or husks removed, should be put in the preserving pan with water and simmered until tender.

(2) The whole contents of the pan should then be put into the jelly bag. Let it drip all night into a basin. *Never* squeeze the bag or try to hurry up the dripping process. If you do, the jelly will be cloudy instead of clear.

(3) The next day, measure the juice and add the sugar, usually 1 lb. of sugar to each pint of juice. Let the sugar dissolve; then boil rapidly until the jelly will set, stirring all the time. Skim towards the end, if necessary.

(4) Test as for jam, but the drops should keep their shape, as well as crinkling on the surface.

(5) Pour jelly into jars as soon as it is done. Do not stir after it leaves the fire, or it will be full of bubbles.

Apple Jelly

Quarter the apples and cut away any bad parts. Put in the preserving pan with enough water to float them, and boil until they are soft but not pulpy. Put the mixture into a jelly bag and leave to drip through all night. Measure the juice and allow 1 lb. of sugar to every pint. Put juice and sugar into the pan and let the sugar dissolve before the mixture boils. Stir all the time. Then boil until it will set when tested, skimming if necessary. Pour into warm, dry jars and tie down.

Blackcurrant Jelly

6 lb. blackcurrants   Sugar
2 pints water

Put the fruit (which need not be stalked) and water into a pan and simmer until tender. Mash well and pour into a jelly bag. Leave to drip all night, then measure the juice and add 1 lb. of sugar to every pint of juice. Put the sugar and juice in a preserving pan and heat slowly until the sugar is dissolved, stirring all the time. Then bring it to the boil and continue boiling until the jelly will set when tested, skimming if necessary. Pour into warm, dry jars and tie down.

Bramble Jelly

6 lb. blackberries   Sugar
1 pint water

Pick the blackberries on a fine day. Remove the stalks, put with the water in the preserving pan and boil gently for about 20 minutes, until the fruit is tender. Mash well, then pour the pulp into a jelly bag and leave to drip all night. Measure the juice and add 1 lb. of sugar to every pint of juice. Put the sugar and juice into the preserving pan and let the sugar dissolve before it boils, stirring all the time. Boil quickly until it will set in a good jelly, skimming if necessary.

NOTE: Blackberries gathered early in the season make the best jelly.

Crab Apple Jelly

Make in the same way as apple jelly (see opposite), but instead of cutting up the apples put them in the preserving pan whole, just as they are. Do not on any account let them get mashed or the jelly will be too acid.

Gooseberry Jelly

Wash the gooseberries but do not top and tail them. Place them in a preserving pan with just enough water to cover and simmer until they turn to a pulp. Pour the mixture into a jelly bag and leave to drip all night. Remove the pulp, place in the preserving pan, cover with water and simmer for about 1 hour, stirring occasionally. Strain again through the jelly bag and mix both lots of juice. Weigh the juice and allow 1 lb. of sugar to every pint of juice. Let the sugar dissolve slowly, then bring the mixture to the boil and boil briskly until it sets. Skim, if necessary. Pour into warm, dry jars and cover at once.

Grape Jelly

6 lb. grapes   1 quart water
Juice of 2 lemons   Loaf sugar

Stalk and wash the grapes, put into the preserving pan with the water and bring slowly to the boil. Simmer until the fruit is a soft pulp, then turn into a hair sieve over a large bowl and allow the juice to drip through, stirring without squeezing. When dripping stops, add the juice of two lemons (for tartness) and for each pint of liquid allow $\frac{3}{4}$ lb. sugar. Put the juice in the preserving pan and boil quietly for 15 minutes. Add the sugar, stir until it dis-

solves and continue boiling until the liquid sets on testing. Pour into warm, dry jars, cover and store in the ordinary way.

Excellent as an alternative to Redcurrant or Crab Apple Jelly, or to "mask" an open fruit tart.

Loganberry Jelly

6 lb. loganberries   1½ pints water
         Sugar

Make in exactly the same way as blackcurrant jelly (see opposite page).

Quince Jelly

Make in the same way as apple jelly (see opposite), but remove the cores and pips before boiling the fruit.

Redcurrant Jelly

Make in exactly the same way as blackcurrant jelly (see opposite page).

MISCELLANEOUS RECIPES

Damson Cheese

Place the damsons in an earthenware pan. Sprinkle them with sugar to bring out the juice. Put them in the oven until quite soft, then rub through a hair sieve while still warm. Measure the pulp and add 1 lb. of sugar to every pint of pulp. Put the sugar and the pulp in a preserving pan and boil gently until it will set when tested. Pour into jars and cover when cold.

Lemon Curd

6 lemons   6 oz. butter
6 eggs   12 oz. castor sugar

Place the butter in a 7-lb. stone jam jar and stand it on the fire in a saucepan a quarter full of boiling water. Sieve the sugar on to a piece of paper. Grate the yellow part of the lemon rind on to a plate. Squeeze the lemon juice into a small basin. Beat the eggs together in another basin. When the butter is melted, add the sugar, then the lemon juice and rind and, finally, the eggs. Stir continuously over the boiling water until the mixture becomes thick (20–30 minutes). Pour into jars and tie down as soon as it is cold.

Orange Curd

This is made in exactly the same way as lemon curd, using 4 sweet oranges and 2 lemons or Seville oranges. If made with sweet oranges alone, it is apt to be rather sickly.

Mincemeat

1 lb. suet	1 lb. castor sugar
1 lb. raisins	4 oz. candied peel
1 lb. sultanas	1 lemon
1 lb. currants	1 teaspoonful salt
1 lb. apples (peeled	Cinnamon
and cored)	Nutmeg
1 gill rum or brandy	

Chop the suet very finely and put in a basin. Stone the raisins, chop them finely with the apples, sultanas, currants and peel, and add them, with the sugar, to the suet. Add the grated lemon rind and strain in half the juice. Lastly, add the brandy, salt and spices and stir the whole mixture thoroughly. Tie a piece of greaseproof paper over the basin and put it away for a few days. Then give the mincemeat another good stir and put it into jam jars, tie down the covers and store in a cool, dry place.

MARMALADE MAKING

Marmalade can be made very successfully and economically at home. Seville oranges can be bought in the U.K. from the beginning of January until the beginning of March. February is the best month to make marmalade, as the fruit is then at its best and cheapest.

For those who find the cutting up by hand too laborious, a special cutter is obtainable, but with practice one can do it very quickly by hand. The secret is to have a very sharp knife to begin with and to sharpen it from time to time.

Grapefruit Marmalade

3 grapefruit	1 sweet orange
3 lemons	6 lb. sugar
6½ pints water	

Boil the grapefruit whole for 2 hours in 6 pints of water, take out and allow to cool. Cut the lemons and orange in half and scoop out the insides. Break them up well and put to soak in the water the grapefruit was boiled in. Put the pips to soak separately in ½ pint of water. Peel the grapefruit and slice the peel very finely. Break up the insides and put in a separate basin from the other fruit, keeping out the pips, which are added to the lemon and orange pips.

Next day, add the grapefruit, and the water the pips were soaked in, to the other fruit and water. Bring to the boil and boil sharply for 10 minutes. Then add the sugar, heat gently until the sugar is dissolved, stirring all the time, then boil quickly until the juice will set in a jelly when tested. Skim if necessary, pour into warm, dry jars and tie down at once.

Ginger Marmalade

2 lb. crystallised	4 lb. sugar
ginger	1 teaspoonful ground
3 pints water	ginger

Chop the ginger up into small pieces. Boil sugar and water to syrup, add ground and crystallised ginger, and boil until it will set when tested. Put into warmed pots and cover at once.

Lemon Marmalade

Use equal weights of lemons and sugar. Wash and cut lemons in half, squeezing the juice and putting it on one side. Put pips in a little cold water. Peel lemons and cover the peel in the preserving pan with cold water. Cook until peel is tender, remove from heat, cut off the pith and slice the peel thinly. Put sugar, juice and water in which the pips have soaked into the pan and boil to a syrup. Add lemon peel and boil until it will set to a jelly when tested. Leave to cool and then cover.

Orange Marmalade (1)

Slice Seville oranges very thinly, taking out only the pips. To each 1 lb. of sliced fruit add 3 pints of cold water, and let this stand for 24 hours.

Then boil until the peel is quite tender and allow to stand until the next day. Weigh, and to every 1 lb. of fruit add 1½ lb. sugar. Boil the whole until it is clear, skimming if necessary. Let it stand for a little while before pouring it into warm, dry jars. Tie down at once.

The ever popular Piccalilli is particularly tasty when home-made from your own garden produce—or you can pickle the various vegetables separately

Orange Marmalade (2)

12 *Seville oranges*	12 *pints cold water*
2 *lemons*	12 *lb. sugar*

Peel the oranges and lemons; break up the insides into a large basin, taking out the pips and putting them into a small basin. Slice the peel as finely as possible and add to the large basin. Next, add the water, keeping back ½ pint which is poured over the pips. Let all stand for 24 hours. Strain the water from the pips through muslin and add it to the fruit. Boil the fruit for about 2½ hours until the peel is quite tender. Then add the sugar and let it dissolve, stirring all the time. Boil quickly until the juice is clear and will set into a good jelly. Skim, if necessary. Pour into warm, dry jars and tie down at once.

NOTE: To make a more bitter marmalade, put the pips in a muslin bag, bruise them well with a hammer and boil them with the fruit until the sugar is added. The peel should be cut rather more coarsely than for ordinary marmalade.

Orange Marmalade (3) (Quick Method)

5 *Seville oranges*	1 *lemon*
5 *pints boiling water*	6 *lb. sugar*

Cut oranges and lemon up small, removing pips and putting them into a muslin bag, and cover with the boiling water. Tie the bag containing the pips with string and put into the pan with the fruit. Boil hard until fruit is thoroughly tender. Remove pan from heat, take out pips, and add sugar. Bring to the boil and cook steadily until a little of the marmalade tested on a cold plate sets—probably about 1½ hours, according to how much the fruit was cooked first and how fast it has been boiling.

Tangerine Marmalade

12 *tangerines*	*Sugar*
3 *lemons*	*Water*

Remove the lemon rinds and slice up the insides. Pare the tangerines and shred the peel, then slice the insides and put them into a basin with the shredded peel and the insides of the lemons. Cover the fruit with cold water, allowing 2½ pints to every 1 lb. of fruit, and let it soak for 24 hours. Put all the pips in a separate basin with a little water. The next day, strain them and add the liquid to the fruit and water. Boil the mixture for $\frac{1}{2}$ hour and let it stand again for 24 hours. Then add the sugar, allowing $\frac{3}{4}$ lb. to every pint of pulp. Dissolve the sugar slowly, stirring well, and then boil quickly until the juice will set into a jelly when tested. Skim and pour into warm, dry jars. Tie down at once.

PICKLES AND CHUTNEY

These are very easy to make at home. Jars with screw tops, such as are used for bottling fruit, are excellent for storing pickles and chutney, but ordinary jam jars can, of course, be used.

Apple Chutney

6 lb. peeled and cored apples	3 oz. mustard seeds
3 lb. sultanas	3 lb. shallots
4½ lb. Demerara sugar	1 tablespoonful salt
	¾ oz. Cayenne pepper
4½ pints vinegar	

Chop the apples and shallots. Place all the ingredients in a pan together and boil until thick, about 2 hours. Pour the mixture into warm, dry jars and fix down the tops at once.

Green Gooseberry Chutney

2 pints gooseberries	2 pints vinegar
3 medium-sized onions	8 oz. brown sugar
12 oz. raisins	2 tablespoonfuls ground ginger
1 saltspoonful red pepper	A little salt
	A little mustard seed

Top and tail and chop the gooseberries; also chop onions and raisins, and place in a pan with all the dry ingredients. Mix well together. Add the vinegar and simmer for about 1 hour. Pour into warm, dry jars and screw the tops down immediately.

Green Tomato Chutney

3 lb. tomatoes	1 lb. sultanas
4 oz. mustard	2 tablespoonfuls salt
3 lb. apples	1 teaspoonful Cayenne pepper
1½ lb. moist sugar	
2 quarts vinegar	2 teaspoonfuls white pepper
3 lb. onions	

Skin the tomatoes and peel and core the apples, and chop them up finely with the onions. Place in a preserving pan with the sultanas and 1½ quarts of vinegar and boil until quite soft. Then mix the mustard with the rest of the vinegar and add it to the tomatoes, etc., with the sugar, salt and pepper. Boil until the mixture will set like jam. Pour into warm, dry jars and screw down the tops at once.

NOTE: To skin tomatoes easily, plunge them into boiling water for 2 or 3 minutes, then peel with a sharp knife.

Marrow Chutney

8 lb. ripe marrow	2 oz. turmeric
2 quarts vinegar	A little ground ginger
8 chillies	2 oz. mustard
12 shallots	12 oz. loaf sugar
Salt	

Peel and cut the marrow into small cubes. Cover with salt and leave overnight. Boil the vinegar, sugar, turmeric, chillies and shallots for $\frac{1}{4}$ hour. Add the marrow, first draining off the salt, and boil until very soft. Add the ground ginger and, finally, the mustard mixed with a little cold vinegar. Put into warm, dry jars and fasten down.

Tomato Chutney

3 lb. ripe tomatoes	2 lb. small onions
3 lb. peeled and cored apples	2 teaspoonfuls Cayenne pepper
1½ lb. sultanas	4 teaspoonfuls salt
1½ lb. raisins	24 cloves
2 lb. brown sugar	16 chillies
1 pint vinegar	

Place the tomatoes in hot water and remove the skins. Chop up finely the tomatoes, apples, raisins and onions. Put all the ingredients, except the vinegar, into a pan and simmer for $\frac{1}{2}$ hour. Add the vinegar and simmer for 3 hours. Pour the mixture into warm, dry jars and cover at once.

Piccalilli

Cauliflower	1 oz. flour
Cucumber	1 quart vinegar
Button onions ⎰ 4 lb.	1 oz. turmeric
French beans	1 oz. mustard
4 chillies	2 oz. loaf sugar
A little ground ginger	Salt

Prepare 4 lb. of vegetables. The cauliflower should be broken up into small branches, using only the flower. Choose small beans and string them only. Peel the onions but leave them whole. Peel the cucumber and cut it into good-sized pieces. Spread all the vegetables out on a large dish, sprinkle with salt and stand for 24 hours. Drain well and leave to dry. Mix the mustard and flour to a smooth paste with a little of the vinegar. Put the rest of the vinegar on to boil with the turmeric, chillies, sugar and ground ginger. Then add the mustard paste, stirring it well. When it boils, put in all the vegetables and boil gently for about 5 minutes. When cool, bottle the piccalilli, and tie down when cold.

Pickled Beetroot

Cook the beetroots and, when cold, cut them into thin, round slices. Place in jars and pour over them spiced vinegar.

For the spiced vinegar, allow ¼ oz. each of cinnamon, cloves, mace and allspice, and a few peppercorns to a quart of vinegar.

Pickled Cauliflowers

Cauliflowers   Mace
Vinegar   Peppercorns

Break the cauliflowers into sprigs and put into a pan of strongly salted water. Leave to soak all night. The next day, boil them in the salted water for 5–10 minutes. Drain, and put aside to cool. When cold, place in the jars.

Boil the vinegar, mace and peppercorns together, allowing ¼ oz. mace and ¼ oz. peppercorns to every quart of vinegar. Strain the liquid and pour it over the cauliflowers. When quite cold, screw down the tops of the jars.

Pickled Mushrooms

Use small button mushrooms. Rub each mushroom with salt, and put in a jar. Boil sufficient vinegar, with a little pickling spice, to cover the mushrooms. Let it cool, then strain it and pour over the mushrooms. Cover the jar and let it stand for a fortnight, when the mushrooms will be ready to eat.

Pickled Red Cabbage

1 large red cabbage   1 oz. whole black
Salt   peppercorns
2½ quarts vinegar   Saltspoonful Cayenne
½ oz. whole ginger   pepper
   (bruised)

Take off the outer leaves of the cabbage, cut it into four, remove the thick stalks, cut into thin slices and spread on a large dish. Sprinkle with salt, cover with another dish and leave for 24 hours.

Drain in a colander and pack the cabbage into screw-top jars.

Boil the vinegar with the spices and pepper, and strain it. Let it cool. When cold, pour over the cabbage. Screw up the jars. Let it stand for at least a fortnight before it is used.

NOTE: If kept too long, the cabbage becomes discoloured and soft.

Pickled Cherries

3 quarts cherries
   (whole, firm, tart
   cherries, not stoned)
1½ pints vinegar
½ cupful brown sugar
1 tablespoonful whole
   cloves
4 blades of mace

Stir the sugar, cloves and mace into the vinegar and bring it to the boil. Boil for 5 minutes and leave to cool. Place the washed cherries in the jars. Strain the vinegar, etc., when cold, and pour it over the cherries, filling the jars to the brim. Screw down the tops of the jars.

PUDDINGS TAKE WINGS...

Baked and steamed sponges are extra light if you replace 1 tablespoonful of the flour in the recipe with 1 tablespoonful cornflour. The same goes for cakes and biscuits if you want them to have a lovely, light, melt-in-the-mouth texture. Tested at the experimental kitchen of Brown & Polson Ltd.

Pickled Walnuts

Use green walnuts and test each one with a needle, removing any that have begun to form shells. Put into brine, made with ¾ lb. salt to every quart of water, for 9 days, changing the brine every third day. Drain, place on a dish and put into the sun until they turn black, then put into dry jars.

To every quart of vinegar allow 2 oz. peppercorns, 1 oz. allspice and bruised ginger. Simmer together for 10 minutes, strain, then pour hot over the walnuts. Tie down.

FRUIT BOTTLING

A simple, easy way to enjoy summer fruits in the depth of winter—and to take full advantage of your own garden crops

THE bottling or "sterilising" of fruit for the store cupboard is a simple process provided certain rules are followed. There are three main types of container suitable for the purpose:

(1) Vacuum jars with rubber rings, glass lids and metal screw caps.

(2) Vacuum jars with metal tops, rubber bands and clips.

(3) Ordinary jam jars sealed by metal snap closures, fitted with rubber bands, with clips to keep the closures in place; or by plastic skin which is available to fit any sized jar.

Fruit can be sterilised either in the oven or on the hot-plate. In either process the following points should be borne in mind:

(1) Use only perfectly clean, sound bottles —chipped or cracked ones should be discarded.

(2) Rubber bands should be pliable and fit tightly; if very stiff, put them in warm water for 15 minutes to soften. Never use bands that have been stretched and are beginning to perish and lose their shape.

(3) Metal screw tops or lids must not be rusty.

(4) Use only sound, just-ripe fruit picked when dry and pack it as tightly as possible into the bottles without bruising it. It shrinks in cooking, so have a spare jar from which to fill up the others. Hard fruit should be washed in cold water and then drained. Soft fruit should be handled carefully; put it into a colander and hold it under the cold tap with just a trickle of water flowing over it. Large fruit (pears and plums) may be cut in half.

(5) Fruit can be bottled either in plain water or sugar syrup. Sugar syrup undoubtedly gives more flavour and preserves the colour better. *To make the syrup.*—Bring 1 lb. sugar and 1 quart of water to the boil, cook for a few minutes, then skim. Use either hot or cold as directed.

(6) Never put hot bottles down on a cold

340

surface or they may crack and even break.

(7) Leave the bottles undisturbed for 24 hours, then test to make sure the vacuum is perfect. Remove the screw or clip and lift the bottle by the glass lid only. If it holds, the jar is sealed; if the lid comes away, the jar must either be re-sterilised or the fruit eaten quickly.

(8) Before storing your bottled fruit away in a cool, dry place, remove the screw caps, if used, and smear the insides lightly with Vaseline, then put back loosely.

The Hot-plate Method

For this you need a deep vessel, preferably with a lid of some kind and a false bottom on which to stand the bottles so that they do not come into direct contact with the heat. Thin pieces of wood nailed together do very well, or you can use a thick layer of old rags or an old blanket. Be careful to see that the bottles do not touch each other.

Fill your bottles with the fruit, then add the covering liquid *cold*, filling to the brim. Put on the rubber rings, lids and screw caps or clips. If screw caps are used tighten them, then give them a half-turn back. Otherwise, when the glass expands during the heating process, it may crack.

Stand the bottles on the false bottom, fill the vessel with cold water to cover them

The latest kind of bottling jar has a wide mouth so that fruit is easy to arrange inside, and one size of disc and screw band to fit all sizes. Use a disc only once for preserving

completely, put on the lid and bring the water very slowly to the required temperature (see next page). If you have no thermometer, bring the water up very slowly to a gentle simmer—it should on no account boil—and keep at that temperature for the time given in the table on the next page.

Remove the bottles one by one—it is best to bale out some of the water first as it is easier then to get hold of the bottles—and if screw caps are used tighten them at once.

Soft fruits need gentle handling to avoid damage. Remove red or black currants from their stalks with a fork

Apples, apricots, blackberries, damsons, gooseberries, loganberries, raspberries, rhubarb:

Bring the temperature up slowly to 165° F. in 1½ hours and maintain at this temperature for 10 minutes.

Black or red currants, cherries, plums, peaches:

Bring the temperature up slowly to 180° F. in 1½ hours and maintain at this temperature for 15 minutes.

Pears, quinces, tomatoes:

Bring the temperature up slowly to 190° F. in 1½ hours and maintain at this temperature for 30 minutes.

The Oven Method

The oven temperature should be round about 200–220° F. Fill the bottles with the fruit, but do not add any liquid. Cover them with their own lids or patty pans to prevent the fruit on the top from discolouring, then stand them on a piece of stiff cardboard in the oven. Do not let them touch each other.

When the fruit shrinks and the juice begins to flow, it is cooked sufficiently. Rhubarb, gooseberries, raspberries, loganberries, etc., will take about 45 minutes; plums, tomatoes, pears and quinces as long as 1½ hours or more; cherries, apricots, currants, peaches, damsons, etc., about 1–1½ hours.

Have ready the covering liquid (either water or sugar syrup) brought to boiling point and maintained at this temperature while you remove the bottles from the oven. Take out one at a time, remove the lid, add extra fruit from spare bottle if necessary, and fill to overflowing with the boiling liquid. Put on the rubber ring, lid and screw cap or clip. Be as quick as you can in filling and covering the bottles so as to make sure you get a vacuum.

Bottling with Preserving Tablets

This is a particularly suitable method for fruits that are peeled before bottling, such as apples and pears. The fruit is covered with cold water, the instructions on the packet should be carefully followed and, when the fruit is opened, it should be put, with the liquid, into an uncovered saucepan and boiled hard for a few minutes to remove the chemical.

Fruit Bottling in a Pressure Cooker

This is a very quick and easy way. (See Pressure Cookery chapter.)

Bottling Tomatoes

Tomatoes can be bottled most successfully in the same way as other fruit, but to get the full flavour, no liquid at all should be added. If liked, the tomatoes can first be skinned, after being well washed (plunging them into boiling water for a minute will loosen the skins). Sprinkle between the layers ¼ oz. salt to each 2 lb. tomatoes and, if liked, a teaspoonful of sugar. Press the tomatoes well down with the handle of a wooden spoon, then put on the rubber bands, etc., and proceed as for the hot-plate method. Bring the water round the bottles up to 190° F. in 1½ hours and keep at this temperature for 30 minutes.

Watch for Fermentation

Watch for fermentation, a sign that some form of bacteria is active. The signs of this are discoloration of the fruit, small bubbles and a distinctive taste rather like vinegar; the liquid will probably have begun to ooze from the bottle. The reason for fermentation is insufficient sterilising, so make a point never to try to hasten the process. It is advisable not to eat fermented fruit even if the vinegary taste is only very slight.

If you should find traces of mould on the top of bottled fruit, it is an indication that spores from the air have somehow found their way in while the fruit was cooling. To prevent this, see that the bottles are sealed quickly. Usually the mould can be removed easily and the contents are not affected, provided it is detected early.

Vegetable Bottling

The bottling of vegetables is a more difficult process than that of fruit, on account of the difference in their chemical composition. The acid contained in fruit actually helps the sterilising process, while in vegetables there is little or no acid present. Also, vegetables contain soil bacteria which are very resistant to heat, so that even if heated to boiling point and maintained at that temperature for 2 hours the spores may not be killed and, if the vegetables are stored for some time, may cause decomposition. So it is safer not to bottle vegetables.

USING UP LEFT-OVERS

"Waste not, want not" is sound advice, but how to make the odd scraps in the larder really appetising . . .? Here are some ideas

EVERY larder has its left-overs, and every cook her headache thinking up ways of using them. Here are some ideas: others will be found in the chapter on Cold Meat and Made-up Dishes.

MEAT

Savoury Mince

Remove the remains of the joint from its bone and put through mincer. Season well, moisten with gravy and add any, or all of the following: piece of bacon, chopped; one or two slices of tinned luncheon meat cut in cubes; one medium or two small tomatoes, peeled and chopped (or canned tomato or sauce or purée); one small, diced onion and a pinch of powdered mace.

Cook slowly for about 30 minutes, preferably in a covered casserole in the oven or on top of a double boiler. Serve in a ring of mashed potato or boiled rice.

Macaroni Mince

8 oz. minced cooked meat	Salt, pepper
½ pint stock	2 oz. grated cheese
8 oz. cooked macaroni	1 tablespoonful tomato purée

Put the macaroni and meat in a greased pie dish. Sprinkle with grated cheese. Mix stock, tomato purée, salt and pepper, and pour over the meat and macaroni. Cook for 15 minutes in a hot oven.

A Quick Supper Dish

½ lb. chopped cooked meat	1 small can peas
1 onion	6 oz. quick-cooking macaroni
1 apple	1 dessertspoonful
Salt, pepper	Tarragon vinegar
Fat for frying	

Diced cold meat takes on a new lease of life set in aspic jelly with a few peas and egg slices for colour

Cook the macaroni and drain well. Slice onion and apple, and fry in the fat for 5 minutes. Add peas, vinegar, salt, pepper, meat and macaroni. Simmer for 10–15 minutes.

Jellied Meat

Cut up meat into cubes and place in shallow dish. Make up packet aspic jelly according to instructions, pour over meat and set in moulds. When cold, turn them out and serve on a bed of salad. Sliced, hard-boiled egg and/or left-over cooked vegetables may be added to meat before setting in jelly. A few green peas or a sliced tomato add colour as well as flavour.

Meat in Batter

To make slices of a left-over joint go farther, dip in batter, drop into boiling fat and fry quickly on both sides. Drain, season and serve with a freshly cooked green vegetable or green salad.

343

Meat on Toast

A little left-over meat goes a long way if diced and stirred into a good thick, white sauce, well seasoned (see Sauces chapter). Serve on rounds of toast with grilled tomatoes or mushrooms as a supper dish.

VEGETABLES

Bubble and Squeak

Mix together equal quantities of cold, cooked, mashed potatoes and cold, cooked, chopped cabbage. Add salt and pepper. Heat a little bacon fat, put the mixture into it, smooth down and cook gently. When the underneath is brown, turn carefully and brown the other side. Be sure it is heated right through.

You will never have left-over mashed potato if you cook it as follows:

Baked Potato Puff (for 6)

6 medium-sized potatoes	1 teaspoonful baking powder
3 tablespoonfuls butter	1 shallot, finely minced
1 egg	2 tablespoonfuls fresh parsley, finely minced
3 tablespoonfuls milk	
½ teaspoonful salt	

Boil potatoes, preferably unpeeled, in enough water to cover. Drain and dry thoroughly Peel and mash potatoes. Add remaining ingredients and beat until creamy. Pile into a well-buttered baking dish. Bake 30 minutes in a moderate oven or until puffy and brown. Serve while hot.

Curried Vegetables

1 apple	½ oz. rice flour
1 onion	Curry powder to taste
A squeeze of lemon juice	Salt
1 teaspoonful chopped chutney	Cold potatoes, carrots, turnips, green peas, parsnips, etc., cut up small if necessary
½ pint vegetable stock	
1 oz. butter	

Fry the onion and the apple, sliced, in the hot butter until brown. Add the rice flour, curry powder and salt, stirring well, and cook for 5 minutes. Stir in the stock, and bring to the boil. Put the cold vegetables in, add the chopped chutney and re-heat. Remove from the fire and add a squeeze of lemon juice last thing.

NOTE: If uncooked vegetables are used, cook them all together first and use the vegetable water instead of stock to make the curry. Then add the vegetables as already described above.

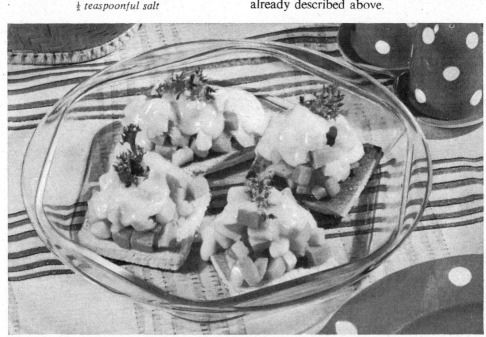

Macédoine of Vegetables makes a tasty savoury served on toast. Mask any cold cooked vegetables in velouté sauce and top with parsley

Serve Baked Potato Puff piping hot and straight from the oven in its baking dish— it's a sure family favourite

Macédoine of Vegetables

Cold carrots, green
* peas, turnips,*
* parsnips, cut into*
* small pieces*
½ pint velouté sauce
* (see Sauces chapter)*
* or mayonnaise*
* sauce (see Salads*
* chapter)*

Make a thin velouté sauce and warm the vegetables in it, or serve cold in mayonnaise sauce.

Parsnip or Artichoke Balls

Mash cold boiled parsnips or artichokes, season with salt and pepper, moisten with a little milk. Make into small round cakes, roll in flour and fry in a little butter until brown.

Parsnips (Fried)

Cut cold, boiled young parsnips into slices lengthways. Fry in a little butter until light brown, and sprinkle with pepper and salt.

Roman Pie (for 3)

4 oz. short pastry
½–1 oz. cooked
  macaroni
1 chopped tomato
½ gill cheese sauce
  (see Sauces chapter)

6 oz. mixed vege-
  tables
1 chopped mushroom
1 dessertspoonful
  grated onion
Brown breadcrumbs

As an alternative to Bubble and Squeak, fry up cold potatoes with a little chopped parsley for a change

Line with the pastry a 5-in. cake tin which has been greased and coated with brown breadcrumbs, saving enough pastry to make a lid. Fill with layers of vegetables, sauce and macaroni, and cover with the lid. Bake in moderate oven for 40–45 minutes.

PUDDINGS

Using Up Cold Sweets

Enough for several helpings can be made out of the remains of baked custard puddings, plain jellies, blancmange and trifle by adding fruit. Use fruits such as dates, stoned and chopped, sliced banana, raisins and cooked prunes, stoned and chopped. Carefully break up the pudding and mix in the fruit, fill into individual glasses and top with whipped cream or evaporated milk.

Oddments of stewed or canned fruit, if fairly firm, can be used up in a freshly made steamed sponge pudding. The fruit should be *well* drained of syrup to make it as dry as possible, and cut into small uniform pieces.

If the fruit is on the mushy side, press through a hair sieve and set in a plain fruit jelly or use for a mousse.

The oddment of rice pudding could be incorporated into a similar pudding on the lines of the following recipe, reducing the amount of macaroni proportionately and using a little less sugar. Break up the cold rice pudding finely, moistening with a little milk if stiff, and mix with the macaroni or beat it up with the eggs.

Macaroni Custard Pudding

4 oz. cooked macaroni	2 eggs
Grated rind of ½	1 tablespoonful
lemon	sugar
1 pint of milk	

Put macaroni in greased pie dish, beat eggs, and add sugar and milk. Scatter the lemon rind on the macaroni, pour over the milk and bake in moderate oven until top browns and custard has set.

Using Up Boiled Puddings

Sponge puddings and Christmas or other fruit puddings can be made fit to appear at another meal, as follows: Break up pudding in a basin, moisten with a little milk and mix well with a fork. If the pudding was first baked with a jam, syrup or other topping, see that this is well mixed through to distribute the flavour, add a handful of raisins and/or currants, if liked. Grease individual moulds or tiny basins, fill with the pudding, tie down with paper and steam for about 1 hour.

Suet pudding left-overs are good used up in this way: Slice pudding ¼ in. thick in small rounds or other shapes with pastry cutters, and fry in butter or good margarine. Drain and sprinkle with sugar before serving.

CAKES

Stale fruit or ginger cakes can be turned into individual fruit puddings if prepared in the same way as for left-over sponge puddings described above. No extra fruit should be necessary, but some finely chopped almonds or walnuts might be added to give extra flavour. To a ginger cake, add a little Golden Syrup or treacle.

Pieces of sandwich cake, filled or unfilled, and remnants of sponge cake make an even more delicious trifle than the more usual sponge fingers from a confectioner. Cut cake into thin fingers and stick any unjammed pieces together with fresh jam.

Lay in a glass dish, and if you have one or two stale macaroon biscuits, crumble and scatter over cake, or sprinkle over a little ground almond if you can spare it. Moisten with sherry, if possible, and pour over custard. A more elaborate trifle should be topped with whipped cream and include ratafia biscuits.

EGG-WHITES AND YOLKS

When a recipe calls for egg-whites or yolks only, the remainder sometimes presents a problem. The following suggestions provide ideas for using them up.

Whites, Sweetened

Meringues.—The obvious answer is: make meringues! These are handy as well as delicious, because they can be stored in an airtight tin. Put waxed paper between each layer and use with whipped cream or individual blocks of ice cream between the halves. For success, cook in a *really* slow oven, 200° F. or gas setting at ¼, for about 1½ hours. (See Puddings, page 138.)

Apple Snow.—One pound of cooking apples are washed, roughly cut up but not peeled or cored (just the damaged or bruised parts being removed), and cooked to a pulp with no more than about a tablespoonful of water. When soft enough, rub through a sieve. Stir in one stiffly whipped egg-white and Golden Syrup or sugar and lemon juice, as liked. (NOTE: Only very sour apples need sugar when cooked this way.)

Coconut Pyramids.—Fold approximately 2 oz. desiccated coconut and castor sugar (according to how much egg is sweetened) to each egg-white. Place small peaked heaps on rice paper in a baking tin and bake in a moderate oven for 10 minutes.

Supper Dish.—Beat together 1 egg-white, 1 grated sour apple and 3 oz. castor sugar. Use just as it is, uncooked, on crackers or other plain biscuits, or spread on thin pre-cooked pastry fingers and cook gently in the oven for about 10 minutes.

You can add a party touch to an open jam tart, fruit flan or baked custard pudding by using the egg-whites, beaten, to cover the top. Gently brown under the grill or in the oven.

Whites, Unsweetened

Cheese Puffs.—Season stiffly beaten egg-white with salt and pepper, fold in two tablespoonfuls finely grated hard cheese. Bake as for Coconut Pyramids; alternatively, drop dessertspoonfuls into smoking hot fat and fry until golden. Drain well and eat warm.

Yolks

Yolks only are needed for egg-and-breadcrumbing, and if 2 teaspoonfuls oil are added to each yolk, well beaten in, to mix thoroughly, the coating that results is light and fluffy.

An egg-yolk can very well be added to every $\frac{1}{2}$ lb. flour when making shortcrust pastry. If using plain flour, add $\frac{1}{2}$ teaspoonful baking powder for each yolk.

An egg-yolk can also be worked into mashed potato, making it rather richer but extremely good.

Zabaglione.—This Italian sweet takes care of egg-yolks nicely. Allow $\frac{1}{2}$ oz. castor sugar and just over 2 tablespoonfuls Marsala wine or Madeira to each egg-yolk. Put yolks and sugar in a basin and beat until almost white and very light. Add wine and mix thoroughly. Pour into saucepan, put over quick heat and beat incessantly without boiling or thickening. The moment it rises, remove pan, pour into warmed glasses and serve *immediately*.

NOTE: **Yolks** keep in good condition for several days if beaten up with 1 teaspoonful cold water to each yolk. **Whites,** for all purposes, must be beaten to a stiff froth to give successful results. Use an egg whisk rather than a rotary beater. Start slowly and steadily until whites become a loose globular mass, then a little quicker until globules close up, then as quickly as possible, but always steadily, until the consistency looks like whipped cream, and a mass comes away with the beater without a drop falling.

One or two egg-whites left over? Make some meringues and fill them with whipped or ice cream for a tea-time treat. If there are any left, they keep well in a tin

STALE BREAD

After parties, Christmas, any time of extra catering, bread is a frequent left-over, and sometimes bread and butter.

Breadcrumbs

Now is the time to cut off the crusts, dry and brown them in the oven, roll them fine with a rolling pin and store in an airtight tin for breadcrumbing. A mixture of brown and white bread crusts makes a good breadcrumb.

Plan a meal starting with soup and use some of the bread for fried croûtons to go with it.

A soup that will help use up the remains of a loaf is:

Onion Soup, French Style (for 6–8)

1 lb. chopped onions	2 oz. butter or mar-
1 teaspoonful curry	garine
powder	2 pints hot water
1 tablespoonful meat	6–8 slices buttered
extract	bread
3–4 oz. grated cheese	Salt and pepper

Cook onions and curry gently in margarine with the lid on till soft (about 15–20 minutes). Add hot water and meat extract. Simmer 5 minutes or till onion is quite tender. Season. Sprinkle cheese on bread, brown under the grill. Cut and put three or four small pieces in each serving of soup.

Supper Dish

Grease a pie dish, fill with alternate layers of breadcrumbs, grated cheese and sliced tomato, seasoning each layer. Moisten carefully with milk but do not make the mixture wet. Top with grated cheese and browned crumbs, add dots of butter or margarine, and cook for half an hour in a medium oven

Hot or Cold Sweet (also uses up egg-yolks)

Soak 2 teacupfuls breadcrumbs in 1½ pints boiling milk, add 2 oz. castor sugar, grated rind and juice of half a lemon or orange. Mix lightly, adding egg-yolk if available, and bake in a gentle oven for about 30 minutes.

Left-over bread and butter makes a delicious crispy topping on a baked custard pudding, and can also be used up in an apple charlotte. For the former, place carefully on top of liquid, butter side up, and scatter with sugar before baking. For the charlotte, line dish with the pieces, butter side down, follow with alternate layers of apple and bread and butter, finishing with a topping of bread and butter. Sprinkle sugar, grated lemon rind or nutmeg, and dots of butter between layers.

And of course there is always that delightful sweet, Bread and Butter Pudding (see Puddings chapter), which uses up milk and an egg as well. If made with stale bun loaf, no sultanas are needed.

There is no difficulty in eating up left-over sandwiches if they are put under the grill, toasted on both sides and eaten hot. Watercress is good with these.

MILK

Too much milk in the larder can be introduced into some soups, substituting milk for part of the quantity of water. When using canned soup, thin the contents of each can with a further canful of milk. And here are two unusual milk recipes:

Cream of Corn Soup

Put 5 cupfuls fresh or canned corn in a double boiler with a peeled onion and 2½ cupfuls milk. Cook until both are soft, then put all through a sieve. Heat 2 tablespoonfuls butter and stir in the same amount of flour and 2½ cupfuls milk, less 2 tablespoonfuls. Season with pepper and salt, stir until boiling. Cook for 5 minutes, add corn purée and bring to boil. Draw to side of stove, add 2 egg-yolks beaten in the 2 tablespoonfuls of milk, whisk well and serve very hot.

Almond Milk Soup

Put 2 pints milk in a saucepan with 2 oz. ground sweet almonds and 1 teaspoonful ground bitter almonds, 1 tablespoonful sugar and a pinch of salt. Bring to boil and simmer gently until well blended. Mix 1 tablespoonful flour to a smooth paste with a little cold milk and gradually stir in boiled milk. Return to saucepan and bring to boil, stirring all the time. Boil gently for a few minutes longer and serve.

To encourage the drinking of left-over milk, give it a fillip, such as 1 teaspoonful Virol or Marmite to ½ pint warm milk. A drop or two of flavouring essence, vanilla, almond, banana, coconut, etc., to ½ pint, well whisked with a rotary beater, a little

Quick and easy to make and an excellent way of using up an egg-white left over from some other recipe—Coconut Pyramids are popular tea-time favourites

sugar added if necessary, makes a milk shake that pleases children.

Sour milk, of course, helps to make excellent scones, and a very good home-made cream cheese. To do this, place a piece of fine linen in a basin, pour in the milk, pick up the corners of the linen and tie round with string, finishing the string off in a loop. Hang the milk directly over the basin and leave to drip until the next day. Season the resulting curds with pepper and salt and chopped chives, if liked, and pat into a neat shape.

PASTRY

Those oddments of paste left over from tart and flan-making can be finished up as follows: press together and roll out into as large a sheet as possible. Spread butter over one half and sprinkle thickly either with brown sugar or grated cheese. Fold over other half and pinch edges together neatly. Milk or egg the top and mark into thin finger-lengths before baking. Six, eight or more sweet or savoury fingers can be made for nibbling this way. The left-overs are also useful if rolled out and cut into plain fingers and small shapes, baked and stored in a tin: pleasant to eat with

cheese or as a basis for cocktail snacks. They may be warmed in the oven and allowed to cool, to crisp them before use if this is necessary.

NOTE: Uncooked pastry will keep for a week or more wrapped in a polythene bag in a refrigerator, ready for use when wanted.

JAMS

A spoonful or two of jam left in each of several jars is the sort of left-over that never seems to be finished up. One sure way is to blend them together and fill into individual pastry tartlet cases. Orange marmalade can be included—it adds interest to the flavour—and any large pieces of peel can be chopped into small bits first. Bitter marmalade is not recommended, but oddments of jelly marmalade and other fruit jellies are all usable in this way.

Oddments of jams and jellies may be added to 1 pint water, brought to the boil and boiled gently until dissolved by stirring. The liquid should be strained through a hair sieve or fine linen, and can then be used as a basis for fruit drinks, adding bottled lemon, lime or orange juice or barley water, and soda water if liked.

DICTIONARY OF
COOKERY TERMS

A brief guide to some of the commoner words and phrases in the language of the culinary art (see also chapter on Restaurant French)

ASPIC: Meat glaze or jelly.

AU GRATIN: Topping of breadcrumbs (*not* necessarily with cheese).

BAIN-MARIE: A pan of hot water in which a saucepan is stood to keep its contents nearly boiling.

BAKING: Cook in an oven. Meat and poultry usually at high temperature for 10-15 minutes to seal in juices; thereafter at reduced temperature with frequent basting.

BARDING: The process of covering the breast of poultry or game with strips of fat bacon, tied in position, to add flavour and juiciness. Bacon is removed about 10 minutes before serving and the flesh frequently basted to brown.

BASTING: When roasting foods, particularly meat or poultry, keep them moist by frequently spooning over them the juice from the pan.

BÉCHAMEL: The famous white sauce with foundation of milk or cream; the foundation of other sauces (see Sauces).

BINDING: To add sufficient liquid (usually eggs, milk or water) to make a mixture hold together.

BLANCHING: A method used to improve colour or reduce strong flavour of foodstuffs, facilitate cooking generally or as a help in cleansing or preparing vegetables. As a general rule, foodstuffs other than vegetables are placed in cold water and brought to the boil, then removed; vegetables are plunged into fast boiling salted water.

BLANQUETTE: A white stew, due to the white or pale-coloured flesh and sauce.

BOILING: A method of cooking food in liquid. Some foods are put into cold water and brought to the boil therein; others plunged into the water when it is boiling.

BOUILLON: Beef, veal or chicken stock.

BOUQUET GARNI: Herbs used for flavouring and removed before serving; either tied in a bunch or put in muslin bag. Where selection of herbs is not indicated, thyme, parsley and a bay leaf make a popular choice.

BRAISING: A method of stewing over a slow heat or in a slow oven in a vessel with close-fitting lid. Best results come from using the minimum of liquid in a utensil that holds the contents closely. Originally braising was done in iron pots on an open fire with hot coals piled on the lid to provide heat all round the pot. Hence modern braising is best done in an oven.

BROCHETTE: A savoury made by threading blended titbits (e.g. mushrooms and bacon) on a skewer and frying in butter.

BROILING: See Grilling.

CARAMELISE: To melt sugar slowly till it turns dark brown.

CASSEROLE: Glazed earthenware or ovenproof glass vessel. To cook in a casserole.

CLARIFYING: (1) *Butter*—put in small saucepan and warm over very low heat until froth rises and sinks, solidified, to bottom. Strain clear liquid butter through a thin cloth and it is ready for use. The object of this treatment is to remove impurities that might otherwise burn in cooking and appear as black specks. (2) *Other Fats*—bring to the boil with water. leave to cool, and remove fat and sediment. (3) *Soups*—when cold, put two egg-whites in a saucepan, beat lightly but not to a froth, add the crushed egg-shells and stock. Bring very slowly to boil, stirring and beating all the time. All scum rises to the surface on the boil and this should continue for about 15 minutes without stirring. Remove and strain soup into a basin through a jelly-bag.

CREAM: To work a mixture with a spoon or knife until it is smooth and creamy.

CROQUETTES: A method of serving minced, cooked meats or fish bound with sauce and formed into shapes, rolled in egg and breadcrumbs, and fried crisp.

CROÛTES, CROÛTADES: Large pieces of fried bread as a base on which to serve minced or other meats.

CROÛTONS: Small dice of bread fried and used to garnish or in soup.

DARIOLE: Minced meat entrée shaped in a mould—the name of such a mould; also small pastries.

DREDGE: To sift flour, etc., evenly over food.

ESPAGNOLE: The foundation brown sauce (Spanish) used as a base for other sauces; made with brown stock, vegetables and herbs, and white wine (see Sauces chapter).

FINES-HERBES: A mixture of finely chopped herbs.

FOLDING: Gently stirring in an ingredient without allowing the air to escape from the mixture. Cut downwards through the mixture with the spoon, run it across bottom of bowl, then up again so that part of the surface is folded under.

FRICASSÉE: A white stew of chicken or veal.

FRYING: There are two kinds: (1) deep frying, in which the food is completely covered with fat; (2) shallow frying (sauté), in which only a small quantity of fat is used. In either case, fat must be very hot, giving off a thin bluish smoke.

GALANTINE: A roll of cooked meat or boned poultry with a covering of its own jelly.

GLAZING: A garnish for a preparation such as galantine, or the sugar coating on cakes or buns. Meat glaze is made by reducing brown stock to the consistency of syrup and bottling in a glazing jar while still hot.

GNOCCHI: Small choux paste shapes flavoured with cheese and poached in boiling salted water.

GRILLING: A method, like roasting, of cooking food at a high temperature at first to seal, the time taken for cooking depending on the thickness of the meat, fish, etc. The grill should be pre-heated.

KNEADING: To work a dough by pressing it firmly with the hands.

LARDING: A method of adding flavour and juiciness to meat and poultry by "stitching" short, narrow strips of fat bacon through flesh in vertical rows, using a larding needle.

MACÉDOINE: A mixture of fruits or vegetables cut up in small dice.

MARINADE: See Marinating.

MARINATING: A method of preserving, flavouring or tenderising meat, in which it stands in a mixture of finely chopped flavouring vegetables, with wine and/or vinegar and oil. Meats for grilling are sometimes marinated for a short time by sprinkling with salt and pepper and moistening with oil and lemon juice.

MARMITE: A stew pot.

MASKING: A rich sauce covering meat, of which Béchamel is the base with grated Gruyère and Parmesan cheese added; or mayonnaise.

MULL: To warm ale or wine with spices and flavourings.

PANADA: A mixture of bread, flour or rice with milk, water or stock, boiled until thick and used with stuffing.

PARBOIL: To cook in boiling water until partially but not completely cooked.

POACHING: Cooking in hot liquid so as to keep shape.

POUND: To pulverise by beating.

PURÉE: Finely ground vegetables, fruit or other foodstuffs; obtained by pressing through a hair sieve with a wooden pestle made for the purpose.

RAGOÛT: A rich stew.

RAMEKINS: Small moulds for savouries.

RASP: To grate stale bread crusts.

RÉCHAUFFÉ: Indicates any dish reheated.

REDUCING: Evaporating moisture by fast boiling.

RENDERING: Fat is purified by slow heating so that it melts.

RISOTTO: A savoury rice dish served plain with grated cheese or with various additions, such as chicken giblets, mushrooms, etc.

ROASTING: Originally a method of cooking meat and poultry over or in front of a clear hot fire, on a spit or in a Dutch oven; close to the fire to begin with to form a thin crust quickly and seal in the juices, then drawn farther from heat for remainder of cooking: superseded by baking in the oven.

ROUX: Butter-and-flour thickening for sauces; may be termed (a) brown, (b) blond or (c) white, the colour depending on the length of time the butter and flour are cooked and the type of sauce for which it is to be used.

SALMI: A stew of game.

SAUTÉ: See Frying.

SEASON: To add salt, pepper and other seasonings.

SEPARATE: To separate the white from the yolk of an egg.

SHORTENING: Fat, butter, margarine, vegetable fat, lard.

SHRED: Cut into thin strips.

SIMMERING: Often wrongly interpreted as slow boiling. Simmering liquid should show no more than a faint movement or ripple.

SOUSE: To cover with vinegar and spices.

STEAMING: For best results a steamer should be used, or, failing that, a double boiler. Specially recommended for invalid diet.

STEWING: See Braising.

STOCK: The base of many soups, sauces and stews. Stock in which meat for a main dish has been cooked or stock prepared primarily for soup-making is not necessarily gelatinous enough for sauces and aspic jellies, and for good results a separate stock is usually prepared for these items.

SWEAT: To heat very gently to get the full flavour.

TERRINE: A small earthenware pot used for potting meats.

TIMBALE: A mould; a pie baked in it.

VOL-au-VENT: Round puff pastry crust holding a savoury filling bound with sauce.

WEIGHTS AND MEASURES

THE inexperienced cook is wise to rely on accurate scales for good results. However, there comes a time when everyone may need an alternative to scales, and the following tables will be useful though only approximate.

Measurements by Cup

Liquid Measures

1 breakfast cup equals ½ pint or 2 gills.
1 tea cup equals ¼ pint or 1 gill.
1 wine glass equals ½ gill.

Solid Measures

1 breakfast cup, heaped, moist brown sugar equals ½ lb.
1 breakfast cup, rounded, granulated sugar equals ½ lb.
1 breakfast cup, level, castor sugar equals ½ lb.
1 breakfast cup, heaped, icing sugar equals ½ lb.
1 breakfast cup, level, rice equals ½ lb.

1 breakfast cup, heaped, lard, butter or fat equals $\frac{1}{2}$ lb.
1 breakfast cup, heaped, chopped suet equals $\frac{1}{4}$ lb.
1 breakfast cup, level, stale breadcrumbs equals $\frac{1}{4}$ lb.
1 breakfast cup, heaped, sago, semolina, tapioca equals $\frac{1}{2}$ lb.
1 breakfast cup, heaped, flour or cornflour equals $\frac{1}{4}$ lb.
1 breakfast cup, heaped, raisins or currants, equals $\frac{1}{2}$ lb.
1 breakfast cup minced beef, pressed tightly, equals $\frac{1}{2}$ lb.

Measurements by Spoon
Liquid Measures
1 teaspoonful equals 55 drops.
4 teaspoonfuls equals 1 tablespoonful.
3 tablespoonfuls equals 1 wine glass or $\frac{1}{2}$ gill.
6 tablespoonfuls equals 1 tea cup or $\frac{1}{4}$ pint.

Solid Measures
1 tablespoonful, heaped, finely chopped suet equals 1 oz.
1 tablespoonful, heaped, flour or cornflour equals 1 oz.
2 tablespoonfuls, level, flour or cornflour equals 1 oz.
1 tablespoonful, heaped, moist brown sugar equals 1 oz.
1 tablespoonful, rounded, granulated sugar equals 1 oz.
1 tablespoonful, level, castor sugar equals 1 oz.
1 tablespoonful, heaped icing sugar equals 1 oz.
1 tablespoonful, level, rice equals 1 oz.
1 tablespoonful, heaped, sago, semolina, tapioca equals 1 oz.
1 tablespoonful, heaped, raisins, currants equals 1 oz.
1 tablespoonful, heaped, coffee equals $\frac{1}{2}$ oz.
1 tablespoonful syrup or jam equals 2 oz.
2 tablespoonfuls melted butter equals 1 oz.
1 tablespoonful solid butter equals 1 oz.

Smaller Quantities of the Above
1 heaped teaspoonful equals $\frac{1}{4}$ oz.
1 heaped dessertspoonful equals $\frac{1}{2}$ oz.

Measurements by Weight of Coins
These will be a guide if you have scales but find some of the smaller weights missing.

1 halfpenny weighs slightly under $\frac{1}{4}$ oz.
1 penny and 1 halfpenny, or 1 half-crown equals $\frac{1}{2}$ oz.
3 pennies, or 5 halfpennies equals 1 oz.
6 pennies equals 2 oz.

Fluid Measurements
3 tablespoonfuls equals $2\frac{1}{2}$ fluid oz.
1 breakfast cup equals 10 fluid oz.
6 tablespoonfuls equals 5 fluid oz or 1 gill.
4 gills equals 1 pint.
2 pints equals 1 quart.
4 quarts equals 1 gallon.

Conversion of Fluid Measure to Dry
1 pint equals 1 lb.

Miscellaneous Measurements
9 afternoon tea cubes of sugar equals 1 oz.
5 average size eggs equals $\frac{1}{2}$ lb.
2 eggs and their weight in butter, flour and sugar make an excellent basic recipe for a sandwich cake.

When you use cups and spoons for measuring, take care not to use different kinds for the ingredients of your recipe. For example, if you have one of those sets of measuring spoons, ranging from 1 tablespoon to $\frac{1}{4}$ teaspoon, use them for measuring *all* the ingredients. If you use these for some of the ingredients and, say, a tablespoon out of the cooking drawer for other ingredients, you may get a discrepancy in weight that might spoil your dish. When buying a set of measuring spoons, be sure it is one approved by the British Standards Institution and bears their mark.

If you need a level spoonful or cupful of some dry ingredient, first fill it to overflowing, then slide the back of a knife across the top of the measure to remove the surplus.

For greater accuracy, sift such items as flour, castor and icing sugar, and free salt, etc., from lumps, before weighing. Pack butter and fats solidly, so that no weight is lost through air pockets.

If you can, without offending your milkman, hang on to one half-pint and one pint milk bottle and keep as emergency measures; also the one-ounce drums in which pepper and spices are packed can be used as approximate measures. If they are thoroughly wiped and left to air, any spicy smell soon goes off.

CHILDREN'S MEALS

Some clever disguises are sometimes needed to persuade
youngsters to eat what's good for them

IN planning suitable meals for children of all ages, the important thing to remember is that the object of their food is to *build* as well as to *sustain*. Youthful bodies are growing all the time. Whether this progress goes on apace depends entirely upon us. For, as Walter de la Mare puts it,

> "It's a very odd thing—
> As odd as can be—
> That whatever Miss T. eats
> Turns into Miss T."

A WELL-BALANCED DIET

The chief constituents of a well-balanced diet are: proteins for growth and repair; carbohydrates (sugar and starch) for heat and energy; fats for heat, tissue-building, nerve-protecting, and, in the case of butter, egg-yolk, cod-liver oil, cream and other animal fats, for certain very valuable vitamins which prevent rickets. Add to these the vitamins that are found in fresh fruit and vegetables, which provide protection against infection, etc., and we have all the ingredients of a really well-chosen diet for any growing child.

How to balance these ingredients so that a small son or daughter does not get too much of one kind of food or too little of another is often a puzzle. A great many children, for instance, eat too much carbohydrate and not enough protein; others are overfed with fats, and their worried parents wonder why they haven't more appetite; a few children are given too much protein and suffer from over-taxed digestive organs.

A well-balanced diet is perfectly possible without any suspicion of the "faddiness" which makes school life difficult for a child. However, the wise mother must be ready to study and respect little variations in appetite even in infancy, and to help her children to look upon their meals as a pleasure rather than a duty. Despite this, she must not lose sight of the importance of milk in a child's diet and should make sure that, whether as a drink or in puddings, soups or egg or fish dishes, an average of 1 to 1½ pints is taken every day.

354

CHILDREN'S MEALS

As a rough guide, these are the approximate food requirements per day of the various age groups

CALORIES	1,000	1,250	1,500	2,150	2,550	2,700	2,000	2,900	3,000
Children: 1–2 years	☆								
2–3 years		☆							
3–6 years			☆						
8–10 years				☆					
10–12 years					☆				
12–14 years								☆	
Girls: 14–18 years							☆———		☆
Boys: 14–18 years									☆ to 3,400
Man doing hard manual work								4,000	
Man doing light work									☆
Woman doing hard work									☆
Woman doing light work (housewife)						☆			

A man and woman of approximately equal size doing equal work require the same number of calories

Milk is not enough

Though milk is the nearest approach to a complete food, it is deficient in Vitamin C and iron, and does not contain sufficient Vitamins A and D for a growing child. Hence the necessity to supplement a baby's diet of cows' milk with orange juice or rose-hip syrup (for Vitamin C), cod-liver oil (for Vitamins A and D) and to start sieved greens and lightly cooked eggs at an early age. Both these contain iron, and eggs are rich in animal protein and Vitamins A and D.

The schoolchild's great need is for protein, calcium, Vitamins A, D and C. The best source of all these is milk. Cheese, meat, eggs, fruit and green vegetables are also essential; and bread and home-made cakes (which contain fat, sugar, milk and eggs) will supply extra calories. Adolescents, too, should take plenty of milk and proteins.

The Toddler's Breakfast

When the toddler is about 1 year old his breakfast should contain some protein and not be confined to carbohydrates only. Most children can have eggs three times a week quite safely—either coddled, poached or scrambled. If a child really dislikes eggs or they cause biliousness, a little fish or crisp bacon can be given instead. Cereal should be omitted entirely or very much reduced in quantity when the child is having egg, bacon or fish for breakfast; if not, there is always a danger that he will eat a large amount and leave no room for the protein dish that follows.

The most suitable kinds of fish for small children are whiting, plaice, sole (lemon or witch are lighter than Dover soles, as well as cheaper), fresh haddock, Devon hake. Cod is heavy, halibut rather too close in texture. Small quantities of kipper or bloater can be spread on toast for the toddler and are very nourishing. Sardines, also spread on toast or in sandwiches between brown bread and butter, are excellent and usually very popular; the bones and skin should be removed.

Cheese—one of the most highly concentrated protein foods there is—is recommended by doctors and clinics for children from 9 months onwards because it is rich in calcium, which is essential for forming strong healthy teeth and bones. At 9 months a child should have his cheese grated and sprinkled on bread and butter at tea-time. From 18 months onwards, it is quite safe to give a finger of cheese to chew, provided he chews it well.

Some children prefer savoury to sweet dishes, and here a cheese-flavoured white sauce often transforms an otherwise unpopular meal into a favourite; it is also a good way of getting more milk into the meals.

Food unsuitable for Children under 5

Pork, veal, tea, coffee, over-ripe or under-ripe fruit, fruits with seeds or pips, cakes containing currants, and fried foods generally are unsuitable for small children. Some cannot take bananas, pears or plums; sweet oranges and ripe grapes are the safest fruits for little people; even apples (in most cases so wholesome) sometimes prove indigestible. It is most important to peel oranges and other fruits before

letting children handle them; the peel is very unlikely to be free from dust and germs, and cases of thread-worm trouble (and possibly worse infections) are often due to children holding unwashed and unpeeled oranges, bananas, apples, etc., and then sucking their fingers. Ripe bananas are excellent.

Those who do not like Milk

Children aged 2 to 5 are growing very fast and plenty of "growth" foods are needed. It is rather a temptation to let them "fill up" with lots of bread and butter, but unless proteins are also given they will lack muscle and stamina. Those who do not care for milk as a drink will often take it at their tea-supper meal in the form of junket (coloured pink with a cherry on the top for preference), or milk jelly or blancmange in an attractive colour and turned out of a pretty mould. Some of the nicest moulds in which to make puddings can now be bought with animals, fish, flowers, etc., on top. One of these has two rabbits on the top: you make a little chocolate-coloured custard or blancmange (just enough to fill in the shapes of the rabbits), then fill up the rest of the mould with another coloured pudding. When you turn it out, there are two brown bunnies sitting on top, just inviting a child to eat his pudding.

A Week's Sample Dinners for a 5-year-old and over

Sunday: Roast beef or mutton, potatoes and vegetables. Stewed fruit and custard. If the adults are having fruit tart, a small portion of pastry, but not too much.

Monday: Vegetable soup (lentil, pea, artichoke, tomato), with sippets of toast or light suet dumpling, according to time of year. Baked apple and custard.

Tuesday: Fish baked in oven with a little milk and buttered paper over it, with potatoes and/or cauliflower. Stewed prunes and sponge fingers.

Wednesday: Irish stew (neck of mutton, onions, carrots, potatoes, rice or pearl barley). Junket and jelly.

Thursday: Steamed chicken, rabbit or tripe, with potatoes and vegetables (onions, in the case of tripe, but remember to bring them to the boil and throw away the first water after five minutes:

this makes the onions more digestible and less likely to spoil the colour of the tripe). Sponge pudding (steamed) with jam.

Friday: Fish, steamed or made into a fish pudding, with brown bread and butter as a change from potatoes. Apple charlotte.

Saturday: Fresh minced beef (cooked in a double saucepan for 1½ hours and the gravy thickened slightly before serving), with potatoes and green vegetables. Treacle pudding.

In planning dinners it is important that the first and second courses should supplement and not echo one another. For instance, a steamed pudding should not be given after a meat course containing suet or starch; and custard should not be given after a first course containing eggs or milk.

Milk puddings may be served with fruit instead of custard; taken alone they are apt to be constipating.

SPECIAL DIETS

Children who tend to constipation need careful feeding. They should have very little white bread, solid cake, pudding, rice, etc. They need plenty of wholemeal bread, fruit, honey, black treacle, green vegetables, onions, leeks and fats such as butter and dripping. Very often they do better on diluted than on whole milk. Plenty of water should be drunk between meals and everything must be thoroughly chewed.

The bilious child should be kept off all fatty and greasy foods (such as dumplings, pastry, suet puddings and rich iced cakes) and should take a little barley sugar after meals.

Ideal for children, this PVC "embroidered" plastic mat will sponge easily, won't stretch or break, comes in cream, pastel blue or green in the Bex range of household equipment

The child who is subject to diarrhœa should never be given food containing "roughage," such as husks, seeds, pips or currants. His diet should be as bland and as unirritating as possible. But the mere appearance of certain foods (such as spinach or carrot) in a child's motions does not mean that it disagrees with him; so long as the motions are otherwise healthy-looking, it only means that this particular food has helped to carry off waste products of the bowel, as it was meant to do.

CHILDREN'S RECIPES

Most of the simpler dishes for which recipes are to be found in the various chapters of this book are perfectly suitable for children, but here are a few very simple "nursery specials" which may be helpful.

Oat Jelly is very useful for babies when first introduced to cereals. Mix 2 level tablespoonfuls of Robinson's Patent Groats to a smooth paste with cold water, add a pinch of salt, make up to ½ pint by stirring in boiling water. Boil gently for ½ hour or cook in double saucepan for 1 hour. Serve warm with a little milk poured over it.

Barley Jelly.—Make in the same way, using Robinson's Patent Barley instead of Groats. This can be given alternately with Oat Jelly, and in summer weather is rather less heating.

Raw Beef Juice (useful as a pick-me-up

The smiling pastry faces on these Jack o' Lanterns just invite young people to taste and see what's inside—a nourishing vegetable and cheese mixture

in children's ailments or for delicate or anæmic babies and toddlers).—Cut ¼ lb. steak into small pieces, place in a cup, just cover with cold water and leave for an hour. Then squeeze out the juice through a piece of clean boiled muslin, add salt and serve warm. If made hot, the albumen in the beef coagulates, and the appearance as well as the value of the raw beef juice will be spoilt.

Steamed Custard.—Heat ½ pint milk and beat it up with 1 egg and a dessert-spoonful sugar. Pour into a deep soup-plate and stand over a saucepan of boiling water until just set. Don't shake or stir it while it is setting. This is a good dish to make while boiling potatoes or vegetables, as it can cook over the saucepan.

Chicken (Steamed).—Pour a breakfast-cupful of water into a saucepan, add chopped carrot and onion and a little salt. Bring to the boil, then gently lay the chicken on top of the vegetables, cover closely and simmer for about 1½ hours for a small chicken or until the breast begins to split. Care must be taken that the liquid

does not boil too quickly or the pan may burn dry; the juices of the chicken and vegetables should combine with the small quantity of water to make a nourishing broth and the chicken itself, cooked in the minimum of water, will have a special flavour and food value.

Jack o' Lanterns.—This is an attractive way of presenting vegetables and cheese to children:

4 oz. flour	½ lb. mixed cooked
Pinch of baking	vegetables
powder	Cheese sauce (see
1 oz. margarine	Sauces chapter)
1 oz. lard	

Make the flour, baking powder and fats into pastry (see Pastry chapter). Mix the vegetables with the cheese sauce, season well and place in individual fireproof dishes. Roll out the pastry and cut into circles the size of the dishes, then make them into faces with holes for eyes, nose and mouth. Put the pastry faces on top of the vegetable mixture, brush lightly with milk or egg, and bake in a moderate oven until pastry is crisp and golden.

Banana Chocolate Pudding combines two of
most children's favourite flavours and looks
as good as it tastes

Wholemeal Cheese Biscuits (20–30 biscuits)

2 oz. wholemeal flour	4 oz. finely grated
Good pinch of salt	Cheddar cheese
Pinch of Cayenne	Approximately 1
pepper	tablespoonful cold
½ oz. margarine	water

Sieve the flour and seasonings into a
bowl and rub in the margarine. Add the
Cheddar cheese and mix well. Add sufficient cold water to bind, and knead the
dough firmly. Roll out to ⅛-in. thick on a
lightly floured board, prick with a fork and
cut into fancy shapes. Place on a lightly
greased baking sheet and bake towards the
top of a hot oven for 6–8 minutes until a
golden brown. Cool on a wire tray. These
biscuits will keep well in an airtight tin.

Banana Chocolate Pudding (for 4–6)

2 oz. self-raising flour	1¾ oz. shredded suet
1 oz. cocoa	4 bananas
½ teaspoonful golden	1 egg
raising powder	3 teaspoonfuls coffee
2 oz. castor sugar	powder
1½ oz. One-Minute	¾ tablespoonful milk
Quaker Oats	

Try Wholemeal Cheese Biscuits with milk
for nursery supper and see how quickly they
disappear

Sift flour, cocoa and raising powder. Stir in sugar, Quaker oats and suet. Mash 2 bananas and mix with the coffee powder. When blended, beat in the egg and the milk. Stir into the dry ingredients.

Put the mixture into a greased basin and cover with a piece of greased paper and a pudding cloth. Put basin into a saucepan with boiling water, cover and boil for 3 hours. Turn out on to a hot dish and use the two remaining bananas for decoration.

FOOD PREJUDICES

Most children have a strong prejudice against fat and greens. Even those who eat them up without complaint at home will start leaving them on their plates when they have meals at school and see other children doing it. In contrast, most youngsters like anything crisp.

It therefore pays, when planning nursery meals, to try to disguise the unpopular foods and make everything as crisp as possible, so that it will be eaten and enjoyed. A pastry crust makes meat much more attractive to children, and steak pie is therefore a popular dish. A crumbly top has the same effect in making the less-favoured types of stewed fruit acceptable. Fat will often be eaten with gusto in the form of dripping spread on hot toast or when used to fry bread.

TEMPTING A SICK CHILD

A single flower in an egg-cup or glass makes a bedtime tray more interesting. Always see that the cloth is speckless, even if it involves frequent washing. Many plastic cloths are now available. Small children appreciate attractive china with familiar nursery figures on it. To reach the picture at the bottom of a plate a child will often eat everything on it, even if he is not hungry.

Many ordinary dishes are more attractive if disguised thus:

Egg Flip (a raw egg beaten up in a glass of milk with sugar) can be served with straws to help it down. Given a special name, such as Creamade, its contents can be disguised.

Scrambled Egg is easier to eat served on thin bread and butter instead of toast.

White Fish is more interesting if pressed into a small mould and steamed lightly, served with white sauce or butter.

Potatoes should be mashed, rather than plain boiled, unless new, with butter.

Jellies dissolved in a little boiling water and then made up to round quantity with whipped evaporated milk are nourishing and different. Fruit juice may be added in the case of such flavours as orange and lemon.

Black Currant Purée whipped up with white of egg and served on a little sponge cake in the bottom of a small glass dish is light and easy to eat.

Soups can be made more nourishing by the addition of milk.

Vegetables.—Sieved vegetables are far easier to digest when a patient is ill. If there is no time to sieve fresh ones, excellent varieties can be bought ready in small tins.

Helpings.—Never serve too much on a plate at a time. There is nothing more calculated to put a patient off eating anything at all. Second helpings can always be provided if they are wanted.

A sick child will eat his meals if you serve them daintily and make them look and taste exciting and unusual

CHILDREN'S PARTIES

*Festive fare to delight the young and ideas for entertaining
boys and girls of all ages*

A SUCCESSFUL children's party depends, not on the amount of money it has cost, but on the ingenuity and thought that have gone into its preparation.

Whether you decide on a film show, conjurer or well organised games, the first item to be considered is, obviously, party fare. For the very young this will have to be a sit-down tea, but for the 8–12 age-group, try a 5.30 to 8.30 evening party, with a help-yourself buffet meal.

Tastes seem to have changed and modern children of all ages often prefer savouries to too many cakes and sweet dishes. Cold drinks are much more popular than hot ones and you cannot go wrong if you offer a choice of orangeade (with ice cubes chinking in the jug if possible), Coca-cola, milk or tea. Drinking straws should be provided and much of the danger of breakages is eliminated if drinks are served either in plastic washable beakers or cardboard picnic cups that can be thrown away after use.

Sandwiches should be varied, made with thinly sliced bread, preferably with the crusts cut off, and be labelled with flags describing the fillings. If there is an amateur artist in the family, little drawings of a chicken, an egg and so on, on the sandwich flags, will add to the fun.

SANDWICH FILLINGS

The old favourites—egg, sardine, chicken paste, cheese grated and mashed with butter—are still popular. And here, in addition, are some other ideas for fillings:

Peanut Butter—a great favourite with some children.

Bacon—small thin rashers grilled and put, when cold, into brown bread.

Cream Cheese and Pineapple—Mix well

361

together a small cream cheese and a small can of pineapple cubes chopped small.

Tomato and Egg—Skin the tomatoes by placing them for a moment in boiling water. Mash with hard-boiled eggs and beat with a wooden spoon to a soft paste.

Mashed Banana, either by itself or on buttered bread on one side only, the other half of the sandwich being spread with strawberry jam or clotted cream.

A bumper sandwich can be made like this: Remove the crusts from a sandwich loaf. Slice lengthwise in six. Butter each slice. Spread two slices with mashed banana, two with strawberry jam and two with clotted cream. Sandwich together alternately. Slice in the normal way fairly thickly and serve.

This method can also be used with savoury fillings: Sardine, egg and tomato. Lettuce, cheese and tomato. Marmite, lettuce and cheese. Sandwich spread, tomato and egg.

For very small children, cut the sandwiches into animal shapes, etc., with a sharp cutter. Small bridge rolls make an attractive alternative to bread.

Open Sandwiches are much too difficult for small children to manage. but they make a pleasant novelty for older ones. French bread, a round loaf or fingers of toast may be topped with: Lettuce, cheese, egg and tomato Lettuce, banana and cheese. Thinly sliced cheese, beetroot and tomato. Sardine, egg and tomato. Grilled bacon (cold), egg and cheese. Finely chopped celery and Dutch Edam cheese spread lightly with salad dressing. Scrambled egg topped with a few fragments of flaked, cooked kipper. Gouda cheese and split date. Chopped hard-boiled egg on slices of tomato. Ham and tomato. Date and banana or date and raw eating apple.

Small sausages, heated and speared on cocktail sticks; potato crisps and cheese croquettes piping hot from the oven, and savoury (salt or cheese-flavoured) biscuits all introduce a very grown-up air to a children's party and are all the more popular for that.

Along with your cakes, give them some petits-fours and dates stuffed with chocolate truffle.

Chocolate Truffle

Whip $\frac{1}{4}$ pint evaporated milk till it doubles its quantity. Stir in 3 oz. melted chocolate, $\frac{1}{4}$ teaspoonful vanilla essence, $\frac{1}{4}$ teaspoonful strong coffee or coffee essence. Make into a creamy paste by adding icing sugar gradually—probably about 3 tablespoonfuls. Stuff dates with the paste.

For a **Fruit Salad** it is surprising how far a sliced fresh peach or two or even a small fresh pineapple will go, with sliced fresh apricots, pears or plums, bananas, grapes, orange segments, all steeped in castor sugar to make a syrupy juice.

CAKES

Cakes depend for their success upon novelty of appearance rather than richness, so it pays to devote a little extra time and thought to the icing and decoration.

Named Cup Cakes

2 oz. self-raising flour	Pinch of salt
1 small dessertspoon-	2 oz. margarine
ful cocoa	2 oz. sugar
1 egg	Vanilla essence
	Little liquid to mix

Arrange a dozen cake cases on a baking tray. Cream the margarine and sugar until light and fluffy. Beat in the egg gradually, then fold in the sieved flour, cocoa and salt. Add vanilla essence and then liquid as necessary to make a soft dropping consistency. Place spoonfuls in cake cases so that they are not more than two-thirds full. Bake in moderately hot oven for 10–15 minutes. Ice some with chocolate icing, others with icing in different colours, and write the names of the small guests in contrasting icing on the tops of the cakes (see Icings chapter).

Cactus Cakes

2 oz. self-raising flour	2 oz. sugar
1 small dessertspoon-	1 egg
ful cocoa	Pinch of salt
2 oz. margarine	Vanilla essence
	Liquid to mix

Chocolate butter cream	
2 oz. margarine	3 oz. icing sugar
1 tablespoonful cocoa	

For the Cactus (Almond Paste)	
2 oz. ground almonds	A few drops green
2 oz. castor sugar	colouring
	Little egg to mix

Make as Named Cup Cakes (above)

Bananas are favourites with most children. Serve them sliced on peanut butter; mixed with chopped ham, celery and onion; spread sliced on chopped raisins and mayonnaise

and then, when cool, spread with chocolate butter cream made by beating the ingredients together.

For Cactus, mix almonds and sugar and bind with egg. Add a very little colouring. Making sure paste is not too soft, mould into various c a c t u s shapes and place on top of butter cream.

Here is a wonderful individual party cake that will thrill every boy or girl from 6 to 16.

Banana Candlestick Cake

Plain sponge cake   Orange slices cut in
Lemon butter icing   half
        Bananas

Cut cake in ½-in. slices—one for each child—and then in 3-in. rounds with biscuit cutter or large glass. Cover each round with lemon butter icing made by creaming 2 oz. butter with ½ lb. icing sugar, the grated peel of ½ lemon and enough lemon juice to make icing spread easily. Place iced rounds on plates for individual service. Slice oranges across and put half a slice against each round of cake to form candlestick handles. Immediately before serving, peel bananas, one for each two servings, cut across and place each half, cut side down, in centre of round to represent candles. For very small children, place candied cherry on top of banana to look like flame. For older children, put small candle in top of banana, light and serve.

Cook's tip.—Cake trimmings can be used for fruit trifle or, as crumbs, they make an excellent base for fruit flan.

The one cake that never loses its appeal to children is Chocolate. The following cakes will keep fresh for at least a week.

The quantities given are ample for 20 children.

Chocolate Cake

1 lb. flour	1 teaspoonful
8 oz. butter or mar- garine	bicarbonate of soda
	¼ teaspoonful salt
14 oz. castor sugar	½ pint milk
4 eggs	1 teaspoonful coffee
8 oz. grated chocolate	essence

Chocolate icing and coffee butter icing
(see next page)

Grease three 9-in. (or four 7-in.) sandwich tins and line with greased paper. Warm the grated chocolate in the milk until it has dissolved and leave on one side to cool. Cream the butter or margarine with the sugar and beat until it is white and very soft. Sieve the flour with the bicarbonate of soda and salt. Beat the eggs, one at a time, into the butter and sugar, adding a little of the flour if it shows signs of curdling. Then stir in the remainder of the sieved ingredients, alternately with the milk and chocolate. Add the coffee essence. Divide between the tins and bake in a moderately hot oven for 30 minutes or until cooked.

When the cakes are cooked, cool on a cake rack and sandwich together with coffee butter icing. Coat top with chocolate icing and sides with coffee butter icing. Decorate in any way.

Suggestions.—Divide cake into equal portions with piped line of coffee butter icing and write name of one child on each piece. Make a bunch of violets or mimosa, with crystallised violets or mimosa balls and angelica cut into strips. Pipe any design with the coffee butter icing.

Coffee Butter Icing

8 oz. butter or mar-	Coffee essence as
garine	required
12 oz. icing sugar	

Cream the butter and sugar, and beat until creamy. Add the coffee essence.

Chocolate Icing

8 oz. icing sugar	2 tablespoonfuls
Vanilla essence	cocoa
Hot water as required	

Sieve together the icing sugar and cocoa. Add vanilla essence and enough hot water to give a smooth coating consistency. Use immediately.

Another popular cake:

Rainbow Gâteau

9 oz. butter or mar-	Milk to mix
garine	Cochineal
9 oz. sugar	Cocoa
4–5 eggs (depending	Saffron or other
on size)	yellow colouring
13 oz. flour	Vanilla glacé icing
1½ teaspoonfuls	(see chapter on
baking powder	Icings and Fillings)

For vanilla butter cream icing

6 oz. butter or mar-	12 oz. icing sugar
garine	Vanilla essence

Grease and flour four 7-in. sandwich tins. Sieve together the flour and baking powder. Cream the butter or margarine and sugar together until white and creamy. Beat in the eggs, one at a time, adding a little of the flour if there is any sign of curdling. Add the sieved ingredients and mix with a little milk to a soft dropping consistency.

Put a quarter of the mixture into a sandwich tin. Colour one quarter with a few drops of cochineal, one quarter with the yellow colouring and the other chocolate colour with a little cocoa. Bake in a moderate oven for 25 minutes or until done. Cool on a cake rack.

To make butter cream icing, cream fat until soft and beat in the sieved sugar slowly. Add the vanilla essence. Use this to put the cakes together when cold.

Coat cake with vanilla glacé icing, leaving a little to which add a drop of cochineal. Drop this from a spoon on to the top of the cake whilst the white icing is still soft, and spread with a palette knife so that it forms a marbled effect on top.

Another favourite cake is—

Sponge Sandwich

4 oz. flour	4 eggs
4 oz. castor sugar	

Prepare two 7-in. sandwich tins by greasing and flouring. Sieve the flour. Break the eggs into a basin and whisk. Add sugar, and whisk over pan of hot water on low flame until the mixture is thick and creamy and will retain the impression of the egg-whisk. Remove from heat. Beat for a few minutes until cool. Fold in flour quickly and put into sandwich tins.

Bake in quick oven for 10 minutes or until cooked. To test, press gently with finger. If impression remains, the cake is not ready.

Suggested Fillings

Coffee butter cream and raspberry jam.—Spread one cake with thick layer of raspberry jam and the other with coffee butter cream (made as vanilla butter cream in Rainbow Gâteau recipe above).

Orange and cream.—Whip small-size carton of double cream. Add grated rind of 1 orange. Spread half on each cake and sandwich together.

Chocolate and cream.—Whip small-size carton of double cream. Add 2 oz. grated chocolate. Spread half on each cake and sandwich together.

Orange and lemon cream.—Make butter cream as for vanilla butter cream icing (see Rainbow Gâteau recipe), but substitute grated rind of ½ lemon and ½ orange instead of vanilla essence. Spread and sandwich cakes together.

A plain fruit cake which can be iced or not, according to taste, is a good stand-by and may be popular with older children.

Sultana Cake

12 oz. flour	¼ teaspoonful salt
1 teaspoonful baking	8 oz. sultanas
powder	6 oz. sugar
6 oz. butter or mar-	2 eggs
garine	Milk to mix

Prepare a 6-in. cake tin by greasing and

flouring. Clean sultanas by rubbing in a floured cloth.

Sieve flour, salt and baking powder into a basin. Rub in the butter or margarine until the mixture is of the consistency of breadcrumbs. Add the sugar and sultanas, and mix well.

Beat the eggs thoroughly: make a well in the centre of the dry mixture and stir in the eggs with enough milk to make the mixture moist and of a dropping consistency. Pour into the prepared tin. Bake in moderate oven for 20 minutes. Then reduce heat slightly and cook until the cake is done—approximately 1 hour 15 minutes.

Dominoes

For the chocolate sponge

2 *eggs*	2 *oz. plain flour*
2 *oz. sugar*	1 *oz. cocoa*
	Pinch of salt

For the white sponge

2 *eggs*	3 *oz. plain flour*
2 *oz. sugar*	*Vanilla essence*
	Pinch of salt

Line and grease two Swiss roll tins. Make each sponge separately by whisking the eggs and sugar together until thick and foamy, then lightly folding in other ingredients. Pour into prepared tins, spread evenly and bake in a hot oven for 7 minutes. Cool. Ice chocolate sponge with white icing and white sponge with chocolate icing (see chapter on Icings and Fillings). When cold, cut into slices. Pipe domino numbers in contrasting colours.

Chocolate Biscuit Characters

All you need is a packet of chocolate biscuits in various shapes, a tube of ready-made icing (available in various colours) or some made yourself (see chapter on Icings), a few almonds, glacé cherries and angelica. You just "ice" the features on, using round biscuits for the faces. Cut hats out of rice-paper and stick them on with a dab of icing. Incidentally, a pin stuck in the back will hold the biscuits together while the icing sets—but don't forget to remove the pins before serving!

"Poached Eggs"

Cut as many squares of sponge cake as there are guests. Put a teaspoonful of straw-

These quaint party characters are made from Cadbury's chocolate biscuits in various shapes, the faces "made up" with coloured icing, cherries and angelica—the hats are rice-paper

berry jam in the centre of each square. Place half a tinned peach on top, the stone cavity over the jam. Mask with whipped cream.

Fruit and Sponge Delight

Line a mould with sponge fingers. Make packet jelly in any fruit flavour according to directions on packet. Pour one quarter into mould and leave until cool but not set. Put in prepared grapes, tangerine sections, pear or any other fruit and add remainder of jelly, which should be kept just warm over hot water. Leave to set. Turn out and serve with border of fruit.

Jelly Soufflé

Boil a tin of evaporated milk and leave in cold place (preferably refrigerator) overnight. Put orange or lemon jelly in a basin and melt in a very little boiling water. Leave to cool. Whisk evaporated milk until it has greatly increased in bulk and is so thick that it will retain the impression of an egg whisk. Add juice and grated rind of 1 lemon and 1 orange to jelly. When cool but not setting, add to milk and mix thoroughly. Pour into glass dish and leave until set. This mixture sets very quickly and can be used within an hour or so.

Bon-bon Jelly

Make strawberry or raspberry jelly as directed on packet. Pour one quarter into mould rinsed in cold water and leave until almost set, keeping the remainder of the jelly tepid over hot water. Press fondants and other soft sweets top downwards into jelly and add remaining jelly. Leave until set and turn out.

Meringues are another popular favourite. See chapter on Puddings and Sweets.

Trifle

Cut 16 sponge cakes in half and spread with strawberry or other jam. Sandwich together and cut in half. Line a large glass bowl with the pieces, fitting them together and adding layer after layer until all are used. Pour over $\frac{1}{2}$ pint of fruit juice. The syrup from canned fruit is suitable, diluted black-currant purée, or juice from any stewed fruit. Make $1\frac{1}{2}$ pints custard. Cool for a few moments, pour over and

leave trifle overnight. Decorate next day with whipped cream, glacé cherries, almonds—these should be omitted where the party is for very young children—and glacé fruits or crystallised violets and rose leaves.

Ice cream can be purchased locally or made at home. The Neapolitan variety is a great favourite and it is much more economical to buy family-size bricks, cut them into portions and serve in cornets which you can get from your retailer. The best time for the ice cream is just before parents come to fetch their children, rather than at the end of a big tea.

If you have a refrigerator, you can also make those top favourites—iced lollies. Freezing containers the right shape can be bought in most shops and you only need to make a good strong fruit drink and freeze it (see also Chapter on Ices).

BUFFET FOR OLDER CHILDREN

As well as the savouries and sandwiches already suggested, it is a good plan to have one or two hot dishes at a buffet meal for the older children. Hot Dogs, Hamburgers and Cheeseburgers are great favourites. So are potatoes baked in their jackets.

For the twelve-year-olds and above you can provide quite sophisticated hot food. Here are two simple, inexpensive hot dishes:

Spanish Rice with Frankfurters

1 large sliced onion	8–10 split frankfurters
3 tablespoonfuls bacon fat or oil	1 tablespoonful sugar
	1½ teaspoonfuls salt
3½ cups canned tomatoes	Pinch ground cloves
	1 bay leaf
1 green pepper, finely chopped	½ lb. uncooked rice

Fry onions in fat until tender, add tomatoes, green pepper and seasonings. Simmer for 10 minutes. Stir in the rice, cover and simmer for about 45 minutes, adding a little water if necessary to keep moist. Arrange alternate layers of the rice mixture and frankfurter halves in a greased casserole and cover, then bake in a moderate oven for about half-an-hour.

EAT YOUR EASTER BONNET

Specially photographed in the Brown & Polson kitchens

No little girl will be able to resist these coloured biscuits that look like hats

TO MAKE THE HATS:

6 oz. plain flour
2 oz. cornflour
1 level teaspoonful baking powder
Marshmallows
3 oz. butter
3 oz. sugar
1 egg

Sift flour, cornflour and baking powder together. Cream the butter and sugar, add flour mixture and beaten egg alternately, kneading the mixture lightly with the hand and making a smooth firm dough. Roll out thinly and cut into rounds with a 3-in. plain or fluted cutter. Bake some on a lightly greased baking tin and some in shallow patty tins—to make flat and curved brims. When cold, put half a marshmallow in the centre of each biscuit for the crown of hat, and cover the whole with glacé icing in different colours. Decorate the hats by piping with a contrasting coloured icing or with tiny feathers or hat pins made from cocktail sticks.

To make the icing: Sift 1 level teaspoonful flavoured cornflour with 4 tablespoonfuls icing sugar and add enough milk or water to make a stiff icing. Flavoured cornflour is obtainable in six flavours—banana, raspberry, caramel, strawberry, pineapple and chocolate—and has the added advantage of providing icing of different colours as well as taste!

When made and decorated, the tiny hats can either be arranged on a plate for the tea table, perched on miniature glass vases as in a milliner's shop window for the centre piece of the table—or one can be placed at each girl's place.

CHOCOLATE GOLLIWOGS

1 orange jelly
2 bananas
2 level tablespoonfuls custard powder
1 level tablespoonful cocoa
1 pint milk
¼ pint coffee
3 oz. sugar
A little whipped cream

Make up the jelly to just under 1 pint, and set in individual dishes with two-thirds of the bananas, cut into slices. Allow to set. Mix the custard powder, cocoa and sugar together and blend with a little cold milk. Mix the rest of the milk and coffee together, bring to the boil, pour on to the blended custard, return to saucepan and boil 1 minute. Allow to become almost cold, then pour on to the set jelly. Set aside until quite cold.

Cut the rest of the bananas into slices to form eyes, pipe cream on top and place a currant in the centre to complete eye. Use the rest of the cream to make the nose and mouth. Serve quite cold.

Photograph by Alfred Bird

Sauerkraut with Apples and Bacon

1 lb. unsmoked bacon (flank, collar, fore-end) or streaky rashers	Cloves
	1 tin sauerkraut
	3 tablespoonfuls butter
3 or 4 tart cooking apples	3–4 tablesp...

Simmer ... half an hour. Peel ... apples and cut into eight, and ...g each segment with a whole clove. ...rrange alternate layers of saukerkraut and apples in a saucepan. Barely cover with water, heat to boiling point, cover and simmer until the apples are tender (20 to 25 minutes). Most of the liquid should have evaporated. Add butter and sugar, stir in well and continue cooking carefully until all the liquid has evaporated. Turn into a hot dish and serve with slices of the boiled bacon or cooked rashers.

All these dishes go well with lots of hot French bread.

Some of the older girls will probably be worrying about their figures, so do provide a tasty, non-fattening salad. Plain or savoury hard-boiled eggs go well with Apple Slaw and are very low in calories. Make the Slaw from thinly sliced unpeeled sharp red apples and shredded white cabbage, dress with sour cream flavoured with lemon juice, sugar, salt, pepper and a pinch of ground cloves.

Coffee is the most popular teenage drink, so serve it in large quantities—either iced or steaming hot, with piping (but not boiled) milk and big bowls of soft brown sugar or multi-coloured coffee sugar crystals.

Later on in the evening, when they want to cool down after dancing, you might serve coke, a cider cup or a mixture of soft drinks. Lime and Ginger Beer go well together: just shake a dash of lime juice with ice and top up with ginger beer—or even soda water.

If your table has eye-appeal, your party is already well on the way to success. Here a gift for each guest is individually and colourfully wrapped and the festive tea served on lovely old Willow Pattern china, with a charming old kettle to match. Nowadays tea is seldom a sit-down meal, except for the very young. Older children and teenagers will enjoy themselves more if you display your home-made cakes, biscuits and gateaux on the table and let them help themselves, buffet style.

ALL-ON-A-LEVEL KITCHEN

Gone are the days when the housewife had to stoop to get at her oven. The new split-level cookers, as seen in this charming and efficient modern kitchen fitted with Credaplan, bring the oven as well as the hot-plates to waist-level. And what a convenience to be able to slide your saucepans straight off the hob on to the working surface, with shelves and cupboards all close at hand.

TYPE OF FOOD	CENTRE OVEN TEMP. °F	THERMO-STAT SETTING	HEAT OF OVEN
Fruit Bottling	240°	¼	Very Cool
Stews	260°	½	Very Cool
Custard and Egg Dishes Milk Puddings	280°	1	Cool
Rich Fruit Cake	300°	2	Cool
	320°		Warm
Slow Roasting Shortbread	340°	3	Warm
Plain Fruit Cake, Madeira Cake, Biscuits	360°	4	Moderate
Queen Cakes, Sponges	380°	5	Fairly Hot
Plain Buns, Plate Tarts, Short Pastry	400°	6	Fairly Hot
Scones Roasting	420°	7	Hot
	440°		Hot
Puff and Flaky Pastry		8	Very Hot
	460°	9	Very Hot
	480°		Very Hot

TURNING ON THE HEAT

Nothing is more vital to successful cooking
than the right temperature for the job

ABOVE is a handy and comprehensive guide to the right oven temperature at which to cook various foods, prepared by the North Thames Gas Board.

WHEN a recipe says "bake in a hot oven," you have only to turn to this chart to see that this will mean 420° F. on an electric cooker, Thermostat Setting 7 if you use gas. But do be sure also to follow the instructions provided by the makers of your cooker as to the best place in the oven in which to cook different things.

CHOOSING your cooking stove is a momentous event, second only to choosing your life partner. For you and the cooker you finally select from to-day's dazzling array will doubtless have to work together in harmony for many years to come. Whether you choose gas, electricity or solid fuel—or the decision is made for you by circumstances—standards of efficiency vary very little these days, and all leading manufacturers produce a first-rate article. The choice is therefore largely a matter of personal preference.

CHOOSING THE COOKER FOR YOU

Whether it is powered by gas, electricity or solid fuel, it can be a streamlined, labour-saving piece of modern equipment

GAS COOKERS

The gas cooker has what many women consider a definite advantage over all others in that it is the only means of cooking which gives a visible flame with instantaneous control. This means that it can be adjusted at once to ensure exactly the necessary heat for whatever is cooking on the hot-plates or in the oven, with, in many cases, a corresponding economy in gas consumption.

In step with the general trend among manufacturers of cooking appliances, the makers of gas cookers have carried out extensive research to effect (1) the utmost economy in the use of gas; (2) streamlined, easy to clean models with a pleasing, modern appearance; (3) high-grade efficiency in operation.

The introduction of simple automatic controls has revolutionised gas cooking in recent years. The principle of the thermo-static oven control, now standard equipment that is taken for granted, has been applied to the hot-plate burners as well. You simply light the gas, set a numbered dial at the temperature you need and the gas flame adjusts itself automatically. Thus milk can be heated in a saucepan without boiling over or fat be melted in a frying pan without becoming overheated.

Pre-set automatic oven control, either by an electric or clockwork device, enables the housewife to put an evening meal in her gas oven in the morning and set a time control dial to the times when she wants cooking to begin and end. She can then go off to work or out for the day, confident that at the pre-set time the gas will turn itself on—and off again just as punctually and automatically when the meal is cooked.

There is no need to fear that this method will not be successful because the food has to start in a cold oven, instead of being put into a pre-heated one. Experience has proved that most dishes, including meats, cook just as well, if not better, starting from cold. (For methods, see page 374.)

Designed as two independent units — hot-plate and grill with a separate oven — the Radiation New World 72 gas cooker can be built into standard 21-in. deep fitted kitchen furniture. The oven has a drop-door and is at waist-level

The latest safety device on the Cannon gas cooker consists of stainless steel rings that hold saucepans firmly in place. No amount of tugging or pulling will tip the pan or its contents over

The Main Melfort gas cooker (right) has two interesting features; a smooth glide-over hot-plate with tap supports consisting of stainless steel rods, quick and easy to remove, and fully automatic press-button lighting instead of the usual gas-match attachment at the side

Many of the cheaper gas cookers as well as the luxury models now have eye-level grills and for some you can also get a mechanical spit-roaster (no electricity required, as it winds up by hand) which is inserted in the grill.

All gas burners now have automatic ignition to hot-plate burners, some to the oven and high-level grill as well. All taps are of safety pattern so that clothing cannot catch and turn the gas on accidentally, and they are clearly marked so that there is no possible doubt which burner is served by which tap.

The most important current development in gas cooker design is the trend towards greater flexibility of cooking components. Instead of a cooker all in one piece, you now build into your kitchen units a separate oven and hot plate which may be side

by side or on opposite sides of the kitchen, according to the design of your working surfaces.

That means that the oven can be put in at waist-level, thus saving stooping, and some of the luxury models have their hot-plate burners sunk into a working top. Other interesting features include an automatic spit-roaster in the oven so that it can be used for automatic timer-control cooking, a meat thermometer which buzzes when your joint is cooked exactly as you like it, and a glass panel in the oven door for those who like to see what's going on inside.

Many cookers have glide-over tops on which heavy pans can be slid over the sur-

face very easily, without having to be lifted. Pan supports on the new Radiation models are composed of stainless steel rods which give a completely flat surface and are removable for cleaning.

There is a particularly good safety device, specially valuable in homes where there are young children, on the Cannon cooker. Each burner has a stainless steel ring which holds the saucepan rigid so that even the most determined youngster could not possibly pull it over. The rings are easily removed when not required.

There is a cooker with a built-in panel on the splashplate listing all the commonest dishes with the appropriate gas mark number, oven shelf position and cooking time; one with an eye-level grill that has a "glide-away" door and a warming rack big enough for six dinner plates.

Cleaning the cooker is no longer the unpleasant task it once was. Oven ceilings can be removed or let down. Burner heads, many of which are made of stainless steel, take out easily and drop into place with a protective surround that prevents liquids seeping down below the spillage tray. Hot-plate tops are curved to take any spillage and the designers have eliminated sharp corners and crevasses, enabling the housewife to wipe her cooker clean with a damp cloth.

Storage drawers or compartments are fitted beneath the oven, some being separately heated, others heated when the oven is in use. They will take plates and dishes for warming, or food that is to be kept hot without drying up and they also provide valuable storage space for cooking utensils.

Drop-down oven doors provide a good firm place on which to rest hot dishes or baking tins while basting and dishing up and many of the new cookers have been designed without the customary lighting device attached to the side, thus making it possible for them to fit flush up against the kitchen wall or other units.

The individual needs of your particular family must be carefully considered when buying a cooker. Gas cookers range from good-sized "family" models to huge luxury types, while at the other end of the scale there are some splendid little portable cookers suitable for the person living in a small flat or bed-sitting room (see chapter, "One-Room Chef").

ELECTRIC COOKERS

Electricity now rivals gas for cooking and the chief reason is that it has at last achieved high speed and flexibility comparable with other cooking methods—and a way of showing the housewife what it is doing!

The old solid type hot-plates were often terribly slow to heat up and, when they got hot, there was no visible means of knowing. It was also very difficult, if not impossible, to regulate the heat for slow cooking.

Now all that is changed. The electric cooker of today has very fast radiant rings or high-speed enclosed boiling plates set in spill-proof hobs. Multi-heat controls have five or more marked settings and the heat can be varied as accurately and easily as by gas. No matter how small the quantity of liquid in the pan, you can, with a multi-heat switch, obtain perfect simmering.

Most cookers have four of the new high-speed hot-plates and some manufacturers are making them in different sizes, from $6\frac{1}{2}''$ to $8''$ in diameter, to fit various sized pans and so eliminate

This luxury separate-unit cooker by Moffat boasts a waist-level oven with glass picture window, self-basting rotisserie, automatic roast-meter which buzzes when the meat is cooked just as required and burners controllable from fast boiling to gentle simmer

waste of electricity. On many of the latest models one of the hot-plates is equipped with a special heat-sensitive thermostatic device. You pre set it to any heat you want and can then leave it for hours, with no fear of anything boiling over or burning.

The housewife no longer has cause for complaint that, with an electric cooker, she cannot see what is going on. Most radiant rings glow red as they get hot and a further refinement on one model is a row of Heat-View controls. These are little windows on the splashback, one corresponding to each hot-plate. When you turn on the heat (by means of a knob on the *top* of the splash-back, right out of children's reach) a red marker instantly appears in the appropriate window. The higher the little red "flame" in the window, the more heat you know you have in the ring. When the "flame" dies down, you are at the lowest heat setting possible; when there is no "flame" at all, no electricity is on.

The grill, one of the most constantly used parts of the cooker since electric grilling is second to none, may be combined with one of the boiling rings, at eye-level, in the top of the oven or (currently the most popular position on electric cookers) in its old place below the hob. Wherever it is, the electric grill has one inestimable advantage—it is self-cleaning, spots of fat simply burning off the element. Grill chambers have increased in size and grills are heat-controlled, from gentle warming to high-speed grilling. Often there is ample room to grill six chops or six slices of toast at a time, or there are two-part grills. When you want to cook a small snack, you only switch on half the grill, another electricity saver.

Large single or double ovens heat evenly and quickly, those in many of the bigger cookers being capable of taking a 35-lb. turkey and all the trimmings without trouble. Many ovens have flap-down doors, providing a convenient surface on which to pull out pans or dishes for basting, others inner glass doors. The new non-tilt rod shelves are made of rust-proofed metal. Auto-timers enable a meal to be left to cook by itself, switching on and off at preset times.

The modern trend in electric, as well as gas cooking, is towards the built-in unit—the oven and the surface unit being separ-

An electric cooker on which the heat can be seen! Hotpoint's luxury 4-ring model has Heat-View control. The red markers indicate just how much heat is being produced by the radiant rings and grill. Panguard prevents liquids boiling over, the oven has a light

ate and specially designed for installation anywhere in the kitchen to suit the owner's personal taste. A hob with four fast plates can be dropped into an aperture cut in the counter top of a kitchen unit, with the switches on the horizontal surface (well out of children's way), or located in a "countersunk" recess in a run of kitchen cabinets, its switches mounted on a vertical panel. The separate oven is at waist level, with a capacious grill below.

One of the long acknowledged advantages of electric cooking is its cleanliness. As there is no product of combustion and no fumes, oven interiors are maintained in a perfectly clean condition and no deposit is caused on surrounding walls and ceilings. Vitreous enamel surfaces, both inside and out, need only to be wiped over with a damp cloth immediately after use. Moreover, an electric stove—unless built in—can always be moved for easy cleaning underneath and behind. The sides, top, floor and back of most electric ovens can be removed for cleaning and the oven lining of one cooker comes out all in one piece, which is easier still.

Finally, there are the Infra Red Grills which cook chops, steaks, fish, chicken and similar dishes at great heat and fantastic speeds. Grills cooked by infra red radiation are more tender and juicy because the pores of the meat are sealed instantaneously, so that none of the juices or the flavour escape. There is automatic control to prevent the food from burning and both sides are cooked at the same time. Sausages can be grilled in 90 seconds, a chop in 3 minutes, bacon in 20 seconds. Some models are equipped with a revolving spit, enabling the hostess to roast a chicken or joint on the dinner table in full view of her guests.

Cooking by Time Control

Almost everything usually cooked in the oven is suitable for time-controlled cookery and the fact that the cooking starts in a cold oven is economical, as it saves a certain amount of cooking time and fuel.

No special utensils are needed for automatic cookery. Oven-proof glass, enamelled ware, tin and earthenware, all are suitable, provided that any dishes that might tend to dry up during the waiting period are properly covered with a lid, greased paper or aluminium foil.

When you are working out a complete meal to cook in your absence, it is important to choose dishes which take the same time to cook.

SOLID FUEL COOKERS

Solid fuel cookers fall into four main classes: (1) heat storage, (2) thermostatically controlled free standing, (3) free standing, and (4) combination grates, which combine an open fire with an oven at the side, over or at the back of the fire.

The cookers are designed to burn continuously and can "idle" for at least ten hours without attention, providing cooking facilities at all times. Ovens are evenly heated and usually have a heat indicator and there are hot-plates for boiling and simmering. Some cookers have a second oven for slow cooking or a hot cupboard for keeping food hot or warming plates.

When choosing a cooker, be sure it is going to be large enough for your requirements and has a boiler big enough to provide adequate hot water for your needs; it is more economical to run a fire slowly than race it to provide adequate heat. Have your cooker installed, according to the manufacturer's instructions, by a competent builder and insulate the hot water cylinder.

As the name implies, with the Heat Storage Cooker, heat is stored up and released to oven and hot-plate. This is achieved by means of a "heat storage" unit—a thick metal casting placed next to the fire, which has the power to absorb and retain heat for long periods. The whole cooker is heavily and thoroughly insulated, and the hot-plate has a thick insulated cover which is kept down when the cooker is not in use.

Heat storage cookers of this type are more expensive than other kinds of solid fuel cookers, but over a period of years the initial cost is redeemed by saving in fuel.

Weekly consumption of fuel should be about $1\frac{1}{4}$ cwt. of anthracite, or $1\frac{1}{2}$ cwt. of coke. Rate of burning can be adjusted by thermostatic control, and stoking is normally only necessary twice in every 24 hours.

A boiler is incorporated with a number of cookers of this kind, and there are often two ovens, which are constantly maintained at different temperatures.

Smokeless fuels—coke, phurnacite or anthracite—are used for most solid fuel heat storage cookers, but one model has now been adapted to burn coal as well. To obtain the best results, flues should be cleaned about once a month.

A thermostatically controlled free standing cooker, with numbered thermostat for controlling the oven heat, can also have a boiler and, under average conditions, fuel consumption is $1\frac{1}{2}$ to $1\frac{3}{4}$ cwt. per week, though faulty operation increases this consumption.

All these cookers are more efficient and convenient if burnt continuously and the manufacturer's instructions for operation should be followed carefully.

The free standing cooker, which may have an open or closed fire, can also have a boiler and many have a left- or right-hand oven heated by hot air circulating

The family-size grill on the G.E.C. Treasure electric cooker (right) is at eye-level, there are four 7-inch radiant boiling plates and the oven has an inner glass door and automatic light

The Belling Classic Fifty electric cooker (above) has a giant double grill and, for economy, you can use half at a time with separate grill pans. Note eye-level controls and spacious hot cupboards

Another version of the "separates" story—above, Jackson "High-line" built-in electric units. The four plates are sealed on to the hob so that spillage cannot seep through. The oven is at waist-level

A coloured splash panel of toughened glass is an eye-catching feature of the Creda Carefree electric cooker with wide grill below hob

No more difficulties about which bit goes back first! The oven lining on the Belling Classic Fifty electric cooker comes out in one piece for easy cleaning. On rollers too, so that you can push it out to clean behind

inside or round the oven or by flue gases passing round the oven. With correct operation, which varies with different makes, this type of cooker uses between 1¼ and 2 cwt. of fuel a week.

The modern combination grate is a very suitable appliance for a living-room kitchen, with its cheerful open fire and a fire-box which can be controlled for continuous burning. All such grates can also have boilers.

Some models have the oven over the fire, some at the back, but in a normal family house the side oven combination grate is usually the most satisfactory. As the heat is taken round the oven in the form of flue gases, good results are obtained by using coal, but smokeless fuels can also be used and with correct operation, fuel consumption will be 1½ to 2½ cwt. a week.

Briefly, the advantages of the solid fuel cookers can be summed up as follows:

(1) The majority are designed to provide hot water as well as cooking facilities, doing away with the necessity for a separate domestic boiler.

They will provide up to 350 gallons per week, if the hot water system is compact and is well "lagged."

(2) Continuous burning supplies a regular, steady warmth to the room in which the cooker is installed, and does away with the need for any other heating.

(3) Hot-plate and oven are both fully heated by the one fire, so that no extra cost is involved when full use is made of both of them.

(4) As a heat storage cooker is storing up heat all the time, it is always ready for full use.

While many households will find the advantages of the solid fuel cooker far outweigh its disadvantages, others will need to bear in mind the following points:

(a) the need for fuel storage space;

(b) the fact that boiling water is not so quickly available first thing in the morning;

(c) the solid fuel cooker cannot be so finely and immediately regulated as the cooker operated by tap or switch;

(d) neither is toast so quickly made nor so crisp;

(e) the kitchen, which will be kept pleasantly warm in winter, may become a trifle over-heated for comfort in the event of real summer weather.

(f) there must always be a certain amount of dust and dirt where a fire has to be made up with solid fuel and ashes removed.

Where you want to keep the kitchen warm too, the answer is a freestanding cooker with open fire and boiler—like the Sofono

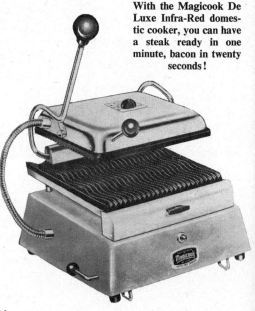

With the Magicook De Luxe Infra-Red domestic cooker, you can have a steak ready in one minute, bacon in twenty seconds!

MAKING THE BEST OF WHAT YOU HAVE

Many people have to make the best of the cooker already installed, even when moving into new premises. If, for instance, it also provides domestic hot water and central heating and is quite effective for cooking, it would obviously be an unjustifiable expense to replace it, simply because of a preference for one kind of cooking over another.

The most practical alternative under such circumstances is to learn to get the best out of the existing cooker and supplement it with one of the new electric "cook at the table" portable appliances. There are frypan/cookers, cooker/boilers, griddle/hot plates, pressure cookers, all made of heavy

A continuous burning heat storage cooker provides excellent cooking facilities at all times. Above is the Aga CB De Luxe Model

Solid fuel cookers will roast or bake at all temperatures and the hot-plates provide graded heats. Below is a Rayburn Royal freestanding cooker

Suitable for a room doing double duty as kitchen and living-room is the Yorkist 12, a combination grate with side oven and boiler

aluminium and quite smart enough to come to the dinner table.

Cooking is simplified to positively mathematical precision, there being a thermostatic setting and time for every dish. Best of all, the hostess has only to prepare the raw materials for the meal beforehand and the guests sit round the table and watch the food cook. There is even a portable Rotisserie for spit-roasting, the fat-free method of cookery that really does preserve all the flavour.

KEEPING FOOD FRESH

For absolute safety, particularly in summer, many foods must be stored at low temperatures, and that means some form of refrigeration

One of the cheapest fridges on the market, the 2·7 cubic feet capacity Gascold has 5·4 square feet of shelf space. Absolutely silent, it's white, lined turquoise green

THE safe storage temperature for most perishable foods is below 45° F. Uncooked meat and poultry require a still lower temperature, a few degrees above freezing point. This means that, however good the larder accommodation, all homes should, ideally, have a refrigerator to ensure safe food storage during summer months.

REFRIGERATORS

Apart from the safety angle, a refrigerator is a most useful piece of household equipment. It

You can fix the Electrolux 16 to the wall or have it as a freestanding model. White or cream, lined in blue, it has a thermostat knob on the back panel

saves food spoilage, thus reducing costs; cuts out the need for very frequent shopping and makes it possible to use left-overs appetisingly. It also permits an increased repertoire of interesting dishes without adding to catering costs, enables frozen foods to be stored for from a week to three months, according to the Star Rating of the freezer, and provides ice for drinks.

Domestic refrigerators are of both the absorption and motor compressor type. The former can be operated by mains (gas or electricity) or bottled gas or paraffin as well as by electricity. Motor compressor types are electrically driven.

In appearance the two types are practically indistinguishable, though each make differs slightly in styling and detail. A five-year guarantee of the unit (absorption or compressor) and one-year of the cabinet is usual. Neither kind should cause radio or television interference.

Absorption Refrigerators

Absorption refrigerators have the advantage of being permanently silent and free from vibration. Due to the absence of any moving parts, mechanical wear is non-existent and the potential life of the cooling unit long. Also electric models can be operated on D.C. as well as A.C., and voltage changes can be easily and inexpensively carried out. Conversion from one system (paraffin, gas or electricity) to another can also be effected quite inexpensively. An ab-

in the smallest kitchen. There is a specially slim free-standing model which is only $19\frac{3}{8}$ ins. high with a storage area of $5\frac{1}{4}$ square feet; and another small, versatile model that can be stood on a table, on its own legs or be mounted on the wall. You can have a built-in refrigerator installed at waist height or tucked away under a working top or the draining board.

There are doors to open within the width of the cabinet and they can be provided with either right- or left-hand opening, so that the refrigerator can, if kitchen space is limited, be pushed up tight against other units. For ease of movement when cleaning, there are models mounted on rollers or equipped with wheels which brake automatically.

Extra storage space has been provided by door interiors which are recessed and

On top of a normal fridge the English Electric Slimline "Fresh and Freeze" has a zero-temperature compartment to hold 50 pounds of frozen foods and 2 ice trays. Automatic defrosting too

The Frigidaire "Sheer-Look" (right) has an evaporator concealed by a blue and white filigree patterned door, with a storage space for $12\frac{1}{2}$ pounds of frozen foods and ice cream

sorption unit can be made as small as desired and therefore refrigerators of $1\frac{1}{2}$ to $2\frac{1}{2}$ cu. feet at low prices are available.

Motor Compressor Refrigerators

Star features of compressor refrigerators are high freezing speeds and specially low running costs. Modern units are enclosed and hermetically sealed, which cuts down running noise considerably and minimises wear.

Full Use of Space

The modern refrigerator has been specially designed to combine or be built in with other kitchen units and to find a place even

fitted with shelves to take eggs, milk and wine bottles (some have compartments tall enough for hock bottles), butter and other dairy produce. This, incidentally, is the ideal spot for these items, being the least cold part of the refrigerator.

Plastic or polythene is much used for shelf coverings, thus making the shelves smooth and quiet in use. Adjustable shelves help to increase storage space and one model has white, gold-trimmed shelves that glide out smoothly and are also self-supporting even when partially pulled out

Egg rack, dairy compartments and bottle space tall enough for hock bottles are all to be found in the door of the Creda 475. The ice-tray comes with quick service containers for making ball ice, shelves glide out easily, there's a crisper drawer for salads and an automatic light

—a great boon when getting out food stored at the back.

Design and Star Marking

The discovery of polyurethane foam as a thin but highly efficient insulator has enabled designers to create 4 cubic feet of space where before there was only 3, without altering the outside dimensions of the refrigerator. All the new fridges have these new slim walls and doors and this form of insulation.

Most British refrigerator freeze compartments now carry a One, Two or Three Star marking. One Star means that the temperature of the compartment is below 21° F. and packets of frozen food may be kept for up to one week. Two Stars means that the temperature is below 10° F. and frozen food packets may be kept for up to one month. Three Stars means that the temperature is below 0° F. and frozen foods may be kept up to three months. It is only in Three Star freeze compartments that fresh garden or bought produce (up to three pounds per cubic foot) may be home-frozen.

Other improvements include automatic de-frosting, automatic interior lighting, silent self-closing doors and such luxury touches as special containers for making ball-ice in the ice tray.

You can choose a refrigerator with a colourful worktop to add to your working space or with a removable coloured top that makes a useful tray for carrying food and drinks from the cabinet to the table.

In colour, white and cream are top favourites and cool cleanliness is suggested by interiors in pale and crystal shades—turquoise, ice-blue, beige, pearl grey and pale green.

The refrigerator is no longer necessarily confined to the kitchen. There is one specially "dressed" for the dining-room, hall or lounge, with a veneered cabinet that blends in unobtrusively with most furniture. An excellent idea this where the kitchen really *is* too small to take even the smallest fridge.

There are also smaller ones which are completely portable—you just plug them into the mains.

There is even a portable Thermoelectric refrigerator that goes everywhere—in the car or boat, on to the beach or camping, as well as around the house. Expensive at the moment at £70, it is quite silent, weighs only 22 pounds, operates on 115-volt A.C. at home, on 12-volt D.C. in car or boat, and on its own rechargeable Power Pak when picknicking or camping.

How to Choose

It is most important to choose a refrigerator made by a manufacturer of repute and to buy it from a reputable retailer or a Gas or Electricity Showroom. An electric model should carry the BEAB approved label, which shows that it has been tested for electrical safety.

Prices

Styling and detail do affect price a little, but generally speaking, it is usually commensurate with capacity, irrespective of type. Smallest and cheapest model costs as little as 22 guineas.

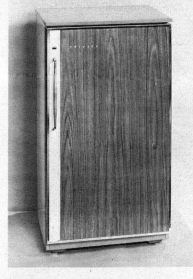

A fridge that looks smart enough for the dining-room, hall, lounge or office—the Tricity "Tatler" 4·3 cubic feet is bronze finished with a richly grained door opening within its own width and a copper trimmed laminate working top.

Care and Servicing

Beyond keeping scrupulously clean, remembering always to close the doors firmly and to defrost periodically, refrigerators need little attention from the housewife. Any spilt liquids should be wiped up immediately and the interior washed regularly with warm water in which a little bicarbonate of soda is dissolved. Soap or detergent is not recommended. Detailed instructions for defrosting are supplied with each machine. There is now a compact little unit, the Smiths-Waldy Defromatic, as easily wired as an ordinary plug-top, that will automatically de-frost any electric refrigerator during the night. Instructions as to loading the cabinet to best advantage and to regulation temperatures are also given. Electric and gas models are thermostatically controlled. Any make of machine is liable to need expert servicing periodically and most manufacturers send out their own service engineers.

Meet the Wright Holiday portable fridge, the most versatile ever—it operates at home on 115-volt A.C., in the car or boat on 12-volt D.C.—runs off its own recharging power pack for picnicking or camping

HOME FREEZERS

Home freezers are a form of cold store operating at much lower temperatures than the ordinary domestic refrigerator. They have a dual purpose: first, to freeze specially prepared fresh food and secondly to store the food at a very low temperature for periods of months. Summer fruits and vegetables can be frozen as they ripen and kept, ready to serve in fresh condition in the depth of winter. The same applies to poultry, meat, game and fresh-caught fish.

All food frozen and stored in a home freezer has to be correctly prepared. Vegetables require blanching and fruit sugaring, or putting into syrup. Poultry must be drawn and cleaned. Packing in special boxes, cartons or bag containers with heat sealing, sealing with special tape or with a bag fastener is advisable. Home freeze cabinets are more expensive than the largest size domestic refrigerators.

Dairy produce may also be frozen and stored at 0° F., and baked or unbaked cakes, bread and pastry can also be cooled, packaged and kept until required.

PRACTICAL FOOD STORAGE

*Perishables, dry goods, even cans and jars only remain
at their best if kept under the proper conditions*

**Defrost your refrigerator regularly. Stains will come
off easily if shelves are wiped with a mild sudsing cleanser
and a damp cloth. Specially photographed at the Hedley
Home & Beauty Information Service**

WITH A REFRIGERATOR

STORING food the right way when you
get it home is just as important as buying it wisely and economically.

A refrigerator does, of course, solve
more than half the problem. The next best
thing—and still valuable even if you have
a "fridge"—is a good airy storage cupboard in a cool, dry place, preferably
facing north, where it will not be subjected
to drastic changes of temperature. Instead
of having the cupboard in the kitchen,
which gets hot, then cools down suddenly,
it is far better to choose a spot where
the temperature will remain constant.

Otherwise the condensation will
produce damp, dry goods will go
lumpy, packets get limp and
soggy, and canned foods be in
danger from rust.

Choose a lot of shallow shelves
in preference to a few deep ones,
fix up a good light so that you can
see what you are looking for without fumbling, label everything
clearly—and also write the date of
purchase on all tins, jars, packets,
etc., as well as the date on which
jams were made or fruits bottled.
This will help you to use up the
older ones first.

At least four times a year—
more often if you have the time—
a food cupboard should be turned
out, thoroughly cleaned and the
contents inspected. Dry goods
need very careful watching because of the various forms of tiny
mites that sometimes flourish in
them. Anything contaminated by
these should be thrown away before it infects the other contents of
the cupboard. Canned goods need
wiping with a dry cloth and should
be watched for the appearance of
pin-points of rust. It is advisable
to open and use the contents of a
can beginning to rust rather than risk
further damage. Tins of liquid should be
turned upside down when the cupboard is
cleaned, so that the liquid runs to the other
end of the can.

A food can with an inward dent in it
need not worry you; the chances are that
it has been dropped in the shop or factory.
But an outward bulge indicates the presence of air and is a serious danger sign.
Such a can and its contents should be
thrown away forthwith.

Some foods like extreme cold, others
keep better at a more moderate temperature. Here is a guide, starting with those
requiring very low temperatures.

Frozen Foods

If frozen foods are to be stored for any length of time—that is more than a few days—they require a constant temperature of 0° F. or less and this is only found in a freezer with a Three Star marking. Under these conditions frozen foods will maintain their freshness, bright colour and peak condition for lengthy periods—of up to three months. At a temperature of 20° F. or less they are perfectly safe, but will suffer some loss of quality. Therefore, if you are going to take full advantage of these valuable convenience foods, make sure when buying a refrigerator that you choose one with a Three Star marking in which ice-cream can also be kept for considerable periods.

The best method is to date your frozen foods and always put the new ones in at the bottom, so that they get used in date order. It is not necessary to use up a whole packet of frozen vegetables at one time. Loose packed peas and beans are particularly handy when only small quantities are wanted at once. You just shake out as many as you require, then close the packet and re-store the remainder. Even part of a frozen block of vegetables can safely be wrapped tightly in aluminium foil and re-stored.

It is not advisable to re-freeze meats, chicken livers, fish, shell fish and similar perishables, once they have been thawed.

The best thing to do with frozen foods while defrosting is to empty the ice cubes out of the ice tray into several layers of newspaper, then wrap the frozen foods and the cubes together in the paper until the freezer is ready for them to be put back. In the event of a power failure or breakdown, avoid opening the fridge door more than absolutely necessary, as this lets in the warm air.

Store in the coldest part of the refrigerator, or in the coolest available spot:

Uncooked Fish—no need to cover it, and it will not contaminate other foods if stored in the tray just below the freezing unit, the coldest part of the refrigerator.

Uncooked Meat and Poultry need dry cold, as close to freezing as possible. May be uncovered in a refrigerator, but need protection from flies elsewhere.

Store lower down the refrigerator, in the cool but not freezing:

Cooked Meat, Fish, Left-overs, Soups and Stock can all go, uncovered, into the refrigerator, but must be covered if kept in a cupboard. Cold meat can be wrapped in greaseproof paper to prevent hardening on the outside due to the cold in the fridge.

Raw Vegetables, such as cauliflower, asparagus, new carrots, tomatoes and radishes, keep best, uncovered, at the bottom of a refrigerator or in a cool place. Vegetables and fruits want a cool, moist atmosphere to keep them fresh and crisp.

Salads—lettuce and other salad greens should be washed and dried, then stored in the special salad drawer or low down in the refrigerator in covered containers or plastic bags so that they retain their moisture.

Soft Fruits, both cooked and raw, may be kept in the refrigerator. Low temperatures prevent them from ripening too soon.

Bacon, so long as it is well wrapped in

Maximum Storage Times for Various Types of Food

	In freezer at 0° F.	In fridge at 10°–20° F.	On fridge shelf
Cooked Dishes (Pies, Dinners)	1 year	1 month	2 days
Fish, Shellfish	6 months	1 month	2 days
Fruits	1 year	2 months	3 days
Fruit juices	1 year	2 months	6 days
Meats—Pork	6 months	1 month	6 days
Others	1 year	2 months	6 days
Poultry	6 months	1 month	3 days
Vegetables	1 year	1 month	4 days

greaseproof paper to prevent it becoming hard, may be kept in the refrigerator or any cool place.

Store on the inside of the door, the least cold place in the refrigerator:

Milk is at its best at a temperature of 50° F. Remember always to cover milk, in or out of the fridge and even when standing on the table for more than a few seconds, because it is so susceptible to flies and dust. You can either replace the dairy's bottle top or cover bottle or jug with a washable plastic cover. These can be bought in assorted sizes to fit anything from a milk bottle to a mixing bowl—and some have elastic round the base to make them fit tightly.

Butter, Margarine, Cooking Fats and Cream require the same conditions as milk. They tend to absorb the taste of stronger flavoured foods with which they come in contact, so should always be well wrapped in greaseproof paper.

Eggs need a good current of cool air and may be put in a bowl or basket and kept low down in the refrigerator.

Do not store these foods in the refrigerator:

Cheese gets hard on the outside in intense cold and also tends to contaminate other foods. Cheeses, particularly the strong kinds, keep best if they are wrapped in muslin steeped in vinegar and water and put in a cool place.

Bananas, Pineapple and Melon have a habit of contaminating everything else in a refrigerator with their own flavour, so keep them out.

Cucumber can be chilled for a short time, but will not keep if stored in the refrigerator.

A good free circulation of air, both inside a refrigerator and in a cupboard, is essential if food is to be kept fresh and good. It is therefore unwise to pack too many things in on top of one another. If the refrigerator gets overcrowded, you will find that plastic food bags, being soft and pliable, take up less space than solid containers.

Bread, of course, comes into a category of its own from the storage point of view. It likes a ventilated bread bin, preferably on a ledge or shelf in a cool spot where there is a good current of air. Lacking these conditions, it may go mouldy.

Canned Goods

Remember, too, that even canned goods, those standbys of the emergency cupboard, have a life span which should not be exceeded and which varies between 6 months and 5 years. That is why it is so important to write the date of purchase on cans. Then you can be sure to eat up:

Canned Fish in Oil and *Canned Meat* before it is more than 5 *years old*.

Canned Jam and *Honey* within 3 *years*.

Canned Vegetables in under 2 *years*.

Canned Fruits and *Milk* and *Canned Fish in Tomato Sauce* within 12 *months* at the very most.

Condensed Milk in 6 *months*.

Dry Goods

Amongst the dry goods in your store cupboard, you will find that cornflour lasts almost indefinitely, provided you keep it screwed up and in a dry place: barley, peas and beans keep for about 6 months before becoming hard; custard powder stays good

This Insulex box of lightweight polystrene keeps pre-chilled food and drink cold for 24 hours—excellent for kitchen storage in hot weather

POTS AND PANS GO GAY TOO

Cooking utensils, like everything else in the well-planned modern home, are now decorative and colourful as well as practical and labour-saving.   From the Mirroware range, with their gay red and white handles, come the selection shown here—top, the saucepan available in three sizes; centre, the Tallboy Dial-o-matic pressure cooker; right, the Mirromagic "can't boil over" milk pan with its unusual shape; and below, the fish fryer with basket and lid.

OVENWARE COMES TO TABLE

It's smart enough for any occasion—
and keeps the food really hot, too

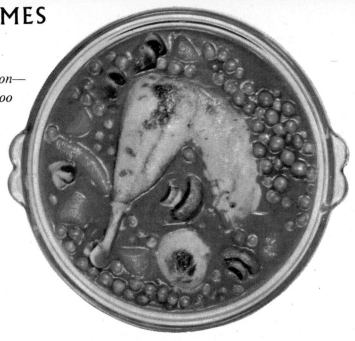

Decorative ovenware has brought a new interest to the twin arts of cooking and entertaining. Nowadays you prepare the food for the table, arranging it with an eye to shape, colour contrast and general appearance, when you get it ready for the oven. At the appointed time, cooking completed, out it comes ready, after the slightest attention, for transport to table.

There is a variety of shapes—and colours, too—obtainable in oven-glass. Two from the Phoenix Gourmet range are seen on this page with their lids removed. The round one (above) contains chicken cooked with mushrooms and green peas in a rich sauce; the square one (left) a round of beef roast with new potatoes and baby carrots.

Top left, a delicious breakfast menu of chipolata sausages and fried eggs served in Rorstrand Gratina ovenware from Sweden, with its ruby-red exterior and soft bluish-green inside.

Remember: even the best ovenware doesn't like being exposed to sudden drastic changes of temperature—from oven to sink, for instance!

When you can't keep dairy produce on ice, keep it in the coldest possible conditions—standing in a little cold water in these covered coolers, for instance

The Osokool Twenty works by evaporation—no gas or electricity, just fill the top with water! Milk, butter and other foods will stay fresh in the hottest weather

for at least 1 year, cocoa for 6 months, flour for 3 months, oatmeal for 2 months and dried fruits for 6–12 months. Coffee and all ground spices (except pepper, which lasts indefinitely) lose their strength quickly and should always be bought in small quantities and used promptly. Even if kept in an airtight container, coffee loses its flavour within a day or two of grinding. It is therefore much more economical to invest in a grinder and buy coffee beans for grinding at home as required.

WITHOUT A REFRIGERATOR

Compiled by the National Institute of Houseworkers

Making a Larder

IT is essential to have a larder, a ventilated food cupboard or a food safe to store perishable foods in the absence of a refrigerator. Food will go bad quickly if it is shut up in a cupboard without any air, but it should not be left about, as it will encourage mice and flies.

If there is nowhere suitable for food storage in your house it is quite simple to make a food safe if you are handy with hammer and tacks. Take a strong wooden box (an apple box with a division in the centre which can act as a shelf is excellent), make a door, using a sheet of wire gauze and the wood from the lid to form a frame. Fix on with hinges and fasten with a turn button. Place this safe in an airy place and use for the storage of all perishable foods.

A shelf with a cool surface is a great asset in a larder or food cupboard. A marble top from an old washstand, a piece of slate or plate glass, or even a couple of butcher's trays, are excellent for the storage of perishable goods.

Care of the Food Safe

Put food left over after a meal on clean dishes. Never put steaming hot food into the larder or food safe as it may turn the existing contents bad. Every day see what food is left over and use it up. Wipe up any food that has been spilt. Once a week scrub out with a good soap; if bothered with flies, spray the inside of the larder or safe with a D.D.T. atomiser, first making sure that there is no food about. Keep food covered, using pieces of clean muslin, talc or wire covers, Cellophane or metal foil paper. Wash these covers once a week.

Some foods need special care if they are to be kept in good condition, especially in warm and thundery weather.

Meat.—Wipe raw meat with a cloth wrung out in vinegar and water. Place on a grid over a clean plate and keep covered. If any portion of a piece of meat gets contaminated by flies, that piece must be cut off. Cooked meats or the remains of the joint can be wrapped in greaseproof paper. Keep bacon in clean greaseproof paper, and use rashers where a bone has been removed first, as these go bad quickly.

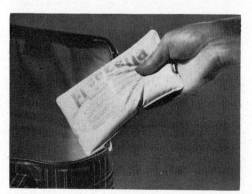

Raw Fish is not a good food to keep, so buy and use up as soon as possible. If it has to be kept, place on a clean dish and sprinkle liberally with salt. A whole fish will always keep better than fillets.

Milk.—Never leave milk standing on the doorstep for any length of time; it may well be in the blazing sun, where dogs and cats can lick round the bottles and birds often remove the caps and drink the cream. If you are out when the milk is delivered, arrange with the milkman to leave it in some shady safe place. If there is no alternative, leave a covered tin on the doorstep for the milk to be put in.

Milk keeps best in bottles. Special milk coolers are available, which have to be soaked in cold water and then put over the bottles; alternatively the bottles can be stood in a vessel containing salt and water (2 teaspoonfuls to the pint) and covered with a piece of muslin, the ends of which must dip down into the water so that the muslin always keeps wet.

Never mix the previous day's milk with the new supply, as the old milk may turn the new milk sour very quickly, and do not use dirty milk jugs for fresh milk. If, despite all your efforts, milk goes sour, use it for mixing scones, cakes or puddings.

In hot weather it may be necessary to scald milk to keep it fresh. To do this, bring the milk to the boil quickly, pour it into a jug and stand it in a basin of cold water to cool quickly.

Fats must be kept on the cool shelf in your safe or larder. They can also be treated like milk—that is, placed under a cooler or in a bowl which stands in another with salt and water in it and covered with muslin.

Lettuce and Green Vegetables.—Keep in a dark place, wrap in newspaper or keep in an old saucepan with the lid on.

Apples and Root Vegetables.—Look over and use first any that are bruised. A damaged apple or vegetable will cause others to decay unless removed.

Soft fruit.—Look over, remove stalks and place in a basin with sugar.

Freezella, a chemical cooler in a sachet, only has to be frozen in the ice compartment of the fridge and your picnic drinks will be really cold

HOME PRECAUTIONS AGAINST FOOD POISONING

For the protection of your family, watch for the
unsuspected dangers that lurk in your kitchen

"THE standard of food hygiene in this country must be raised." That statement has been voiced in the press, on the radio, in Parliament, even on the village green, with increasing frequency during the past few years. And rightly so, for it concerns us all. But it is the housewife particularly who has it in her power to see that the standard *is* raised.

She can start off by boycotting shops that are obviously dirty; ones where food is handled unnecessarily by assistants who do not appear to be clean in their personal habits, who blow in paper bags to open them or lick their fingers to get a better hold on a piece of greaseproof paper and, in between whiles, dangle a cigarette from their lips.

Having made sure that she has bought her foodstuffs from the cleanest possible source, it is up to the housewife to practise what she preaches in her own home. And this includes setting a high standard of hygiene for the rest of the family to follow.

The word hygiene, often thought of as being synonymous with "extra" cleanliness, is, in fact, open to the widest possible interpretation. Some people consider food-handling hygiene almost as a religion, while others regard it as rather a fad. However, since hygiene is a system of rules for promotion of health and the prevention of disease, it naturally follows that food-handling hygiene is a system of rules for the promotion of health by the prevention of food poisoning; and as most food poisoning is infectious, it must be preventable.

"Food poisoning" is the term used to describe any illness caused by eating or drinking anything unfit for human consumption. There are two principal causes of food poisoning, namely: chemical and bacteriological.

Direct Chemical Causes

Food poisoning due to contamination of food with metals is occasionally reported. Antimony poisoning can arise from food cooked in cheap grey-enamelled pots; cadmium poisoning has been reported when acid fluids such as wine, fruit drinks and jellies have been stored in cadmium-lined containers; and zinc poisoning when acid fruits, such as apples, have been cooked in a galvanised iron kettle. Barium carbonate and sodium fluoride have been mistaken for flour or baking powder and put into pastry and tarts.

Certain mushrooms and toadstools have well-known toxic properties, and occasionally rhubarb leaves, eaten as greens, have caused oxalic acid poisoning. Rye meal or fungus-infected rye bread can cause ergot poisoning. Certain mussels may contain an excess of complex alkaloids which can be toxic. Most fish food poisoning, however, is the result of microbic infection.

Indirect Chemical Causes

If certain bacteria infect food they will grow rapidly in it, especially if warm, moist conditions prevail, and as these germs multiply they excrete a poison which can be toxic to man when the food is eaten.

Here are two examples:

(1) Botulism (botulus, a sausage) is caused by the toxin produced in food by the anærobic soil bacterium, clostridium botulinum. This infection is found principally in canned foods, such as sausage, fish, meat and vegetables, and arises where heat treatment at the canning factory has been insufficient. Ordinary warming does not destroy the toxin, but thorough boiling does. Owing to excellent canning factory control, botulism is very rare indeed in the U.K. to-day.

(2) Staphylococcal food poisoning is caused by a toxin produced in food by the microbes known as staphylococci. Foods that may be affected include meat pies, cakes, sandwiches, meats, pastries, gravies, trifles, bread puddings, fish cakes, tarts, brawn, salad cream and synthetic cream. Unlike those affected with Cl. botulinum, foodstuffs affected with staphylococcal enterotoxin in amounts sufficient to cause food poisoning very rarely have any untoward odour or taste. Only prolonged boiling will break down this toxin. Many food poisoning cases are due to staphylococci, and these germs are frequently found in the noses, throats and hands of food handlers, and in skin infections such as boils and pimples.

Infection

Certain food poisoning bacteria other than staphylococci can infect food and grow in it without detectable taste or smell. Then, when the food is eaten, these germs gain access to the gut of the consumer, multiply there and cause a typical gastro-enteric form of poisoning.

An example of this type of infection is that caused by the Salmonella group of bacteria. These germs are normally carried in the gut by pigs, poultry, cows, bullocks, sheep, domestic animals and rodents, and, to a lesser extent, human beings. Eggs (especially duck), egg powder and milk can also be affected.

These three examples briefly outline the main chemical and microbic causes of food poisoning.

The hygiene hazards in the kitchen run by the housewife with a comparatively small turnover of meals and utensils will, of course, be generally far less than those in large kitchens with a huge turnover and attendant staff problems. But there can be very real problems in the home, and the first of these concerns personal hygiene.

For the housewife this not only affects herself but also everyone else in the home, since she is the common link between them all. Obviously she will be aware of the risks of transferring any possible infection from her own person into food through handling, hair and clothing; and there is also the possible transmission of infection

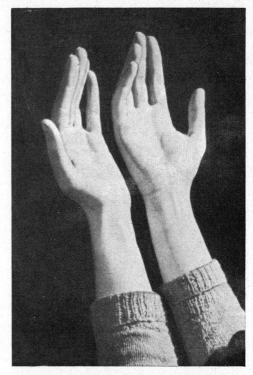

Always wash the hands in hot water with soap after going to the toilet and before preparing food

via similar sources from other members of the household. Undoubtedly, the most important vehicles for carrying infection to food in the home are the hands.

Hands

Staphylococcal food poisoning can start from infected hands. Hands in contact with food must be free of any septic spots, cuts or rashes. Sodden or dirty linen bandages do not provide adequate protection, and if someone with a hand or finger lesion has to go on handling food, waterproof dressings must be used.

After using the lavatory, hands must always be carefully washed in hot water with soap. After handling and preparing vegetables, which are often soiled with manured earth, the hands should be washed (see also next chapter).

The Kitchen

Obviously the better planned and equipped a kitchen is, the easier work becomes and the simpler it is to keep clean

It does not follow, however, that good hygiene cannot be achieved in an old-fashioned kitchen or that eye-appeal modernity will automatically ensure good hygiene. The questions most housewives will want answered are these:

How much scrubbing down is necessary in a kitchen?

Do tea towels need boiling every day?

Do food utensils actually hold any contamination?

To the bacteriologist all these questions centre on cleaning and the answer is: All surfaces with which raw food has been in contact require thorough cleaning and so do all utensils which have been used for the preparation and cooking of food.

Dishcloths

Before cooking, meat is freely handled and placed upon or cut up on surfaces. Cooking sterilises, but what of the cook's hands, and the cloth which may have been used to wipe over the meat and also to mop over any surfaces with which the meat came into contact? Here, obviously, are ways of spreading infection.

Vegetables are often soiled with mud and manure, yet they are introduced right into the kitchen, often on to a table or draining board. After they have been prepared, the surface on which they have been may get a quick wipe with the dishcloth—again a possible means of spreading infection.

On some days the pots and pans may get particularly sticky and require a lot of rubbing around during cleaning. The hot water supply may not be all that one might desire, so the dishcloth will pick up food residues. Then, possibly, flies from the dustbin outside alight on the dishcloth left on the side of the sink—it can happen. Suddenly a basin is wanted quickly in which to make a custard, or artificial cream. Perhaps this particular basin has not been used for some time and is dusty. The dishcloth is rapidly wiped round the inside of the basin, and then warm custard or synthetic cream is put into it. This may happen in the morning and the custard or cream will not be eaten until evening. So, any infection which may have been transferred from the dishcloth to the basin now has a good medium in which to grow for perhaps as long as eight hours.

Under such conditions, disease germs can flourish and food poisoning may be the result. Also, sometimes cutlery is hastily wiped over with a dishcloth that may not be too clean—another way of transferring disease germs.

The dishcloth should always look white and clean, never greasy and stained, for in that condition it is certain to carry infection. To keep dishcloths in a satisfactory

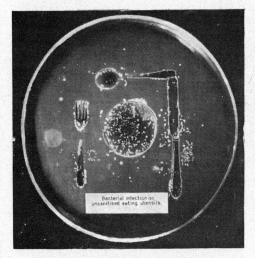

Cutlery washed up under insanitary conditions reveals extensive bacterial infection and could very easily cause illness

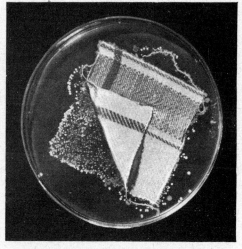

That stained, greasy dishcloth that lives on the edge of the sink and is used for all sorts of jobs is a source of extensive bacterial infection

condition, they can be boiled in soda water, or, better still, soaked in a hypochlorite solution which will free them from infection, deodorise them and keep them white.

Airborne Infections

Apart from infections that can be brought into the kitchen by the food itself and spread by careless washing and handling, there is the possibility of airborne infections. These may be caused by coughing and sneezing, dust

Dirty sinks and dishcloths (above) and greasy washing-up water always harbour infection. Plates washed like that are dangerous to all who eat from them

A clean grease-free sink and plenty of hot water softened with soap or detergent (above) spell good hygiene in the kitchen

and flies. It is obvious that if a person has a bad cold, the way to spread the infection around is to sneeze and cough about the place. In this way, many thousands of droplets are expelled from the nose and throat. These carry potential disease germs not only of the common cold, but, in certain circumstances, also certain types of staphylococcus germs which, if they

alight on cold meat or custards or creams, can grow and cause food poisoning.

Some housewives are not too particular when sweeping up in a kitchen, shaking mats or dusting. Raising clouds of dust in these ways may have an effect similar to that of coughing and sneezing and be the means of disseminating disease germs in a kitchen. Reasonable care is all that is necessary, coupled with damp dusting—if dusting is required.

One of the things which strikes an American housewife on entering the average kitchen in the U.K. is the almost universal lack of wire screening over windows and doors to keep out flies. Curiously enough, at the turn of the twentieth century, wire screening of pantries was common in Britain but is rarely seen to-day, perhaps because of the growth of refrigeration and the good supply of fly-sprays now available. Flies usually breed outside in rubbish, garbage and dung, and then gain entrance into the house as adult winged specimens; they are a disease menace which must be seriously considered when discussing food hygiene.

The Human Hazard

It sometimes happens, as is well known, that a perfectly healthy person can carry disease germs in the gut, nose and even on the skin without being aware of it. Those who have recently suffered such diseases as dysentery can carry the germs for several months after recovering completely from the original infection. Indeed, a famous case was that of "Typhoid Mary," an American cook, a typhoid carrier, who was paid a pension by the U.S. Government for nearly fifty years in order to keep her away from the kitchen. She was, of course, an exceptional case.

Any such hazard from a housewife would best be met by her own fastidiousness in the matter of handwashing and personal hygiene. For good kitchen habits add up to good food hygiene, and this is especially important in the training of children.

In the home kitchen a good housewife can maintain a high standard with elbow grease, sufficient hot water and her own homely methods properly done. Experience and common sense prove this every day. On the other hand, a filthy, soaking tea towel is obviously wrong. So is a dirty brown, greasy dishcloth or a stained sink. All these things speak for themselves—and are not seen in any decent household. But if there is contagious illness in the home, there is an added hazard present which demands added precautions. Food utensils, linen, thermometers, everything used by the sick person should be disinfected after washing.

In the country, or when travelling abroad, there may be the hazard of infection in the water supply through lack of chlorination. This risk can be easily overcome by the use of a chlorine compound such as Milton, which can also be used for sickroom disinfection.

Washing-up

Is there any proof that dishes which have been washed and air-dried are less contaminated than those which have been dried with cloths?

This is a question often asked of the bacteriologist concerned with food hygiene. It all depends on the state of the dishwater, the surface of the dishes and the conditions of the drying cloth. In a well-run home kitchen, either rack-drying or cloth-drying is satisfactory. In a communal meal kitchen there is usually less contamination after air-drying utensils because cloths get wet over and over again.

Food covers present another problem. Though the type of cover used is entirely a matter of taste, badly designed ones covered with nooks and crannies should be avoided, also metal covers which go rusty. Food covers should be thoroughly washed in very hot water, or given a sterilising chemical rinse, the best method for plastic.

To sum up, the climate of opinion on the subject of food-handling hygiene swings violently from fadism on the one hand to *laissez faire* on the other. Between these two extremes, common sense and experience must operate. And to-day, with the aid of science, simple rules of hygiene can be drawn up and systematically applied:

(1) Scrupulous cleanliness required for: sinks, draining boards, chopping boards, table tops, dishcloths, tea towels, mincers, cream bags, crockery, cutlery, basins, pots and pans.
(2) Protect all food from dust, flies and unnecessary handling.
(3) Especially in hot weather, use all perishable foods on the day they are prepared; or use a refrigerator.
(4) Keep hands and nails in good trim. Wash thoroughly after toilet or housework and before handling food.
(5) Do not sneeze or cough over food.

The common house fly is a menace to health. He lives outside on dung or refuse, then, if you let him, comes into the house and walks all over uncovered food

HANDLE WITH CARE

These foods may be a source of danger

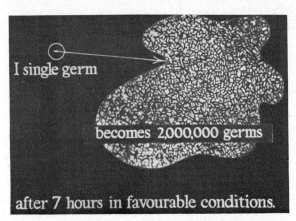

I single germ

becomes 2,000,000 germs

after 7 hours in favourable conditions.

Suppose a single germ gets into a basin of custard at 10 a.m.—by teatime there are 2,000,000 germs to set up acute food poisoning

THE efforts of the Public Health Authorities to improve food hygiene are aimed at reducing the high number of cases of food poisoning which occur every year. Quite apart from the mass outbreaks after outings or parties, or in schools or resident institutions, odd food poisoning cases occur every day in our homes. Often they are the result of some mistake in food handling in the household kitchen. It may be no more than just the occasional case of diarrhœa and possibly vomiting among the children. Nevertheless, the risks of such infections are avoidable; and my purpose is to describe the possible causes and outline methods of prevention with regard to particular foodstuffs.

Meat

Most women hate the thought of an abattoir. Such places are necessary but not pleasant. In them, blood and fæces of animals are splashed about and, although hygiene conditions are improving, the slaughtermen, as a rule, do not pay much heed to such niceties as the sterilisation of their knives or wiping-down cloths. Then follows the journey the carcases must make in the (sometimes not too clean) meat lorry, after which they are humped on the back of a meat porter into the butcher's shop. The butcher usually displays and finally handles the meat while cutting and serving it to his customer, who leaves the shop with the purchase quite possibly wrapped rather inadequately. So, from the time the living beast passes into the abattoir, until it reaches the kitchen table as meat, its surface, at least, is exposed to a number of infection hazards.

The degree of surface infection varies, but the risk is always there. When the meat reaches the kitchen, it will either be used straight away or stored. As soon as possible after reaching the kitchen, the meat should be carefully inspected for fly ova deposits. Joints should be quickly washed under the cold running tap and any discoloured portions cut away. If a refrigerator is available, cold storage will not permit any surface infection to increase. If stored at atmospheric temperature in the kitchen or larder, then infection can multiply on the meat surface according to season, humidity and length of time before cooking.

Such hazards have been recognised for centuries by cooks and housewives, and all over the world different methods of meat preservation are to be found, such as sprinkling with salt and soaking in brine or vinegar. To-day, particularly in hot weather, many housewives wipe over meat with a clean cloth previously wrung out in a solution of electrolytic sodium hypochlorite (such as Milton) for the purpose of destroying surface infection.

Cooked Meat

The act of cooking meat is, in most cases, equivalent to sterilising it. Indeed, some historians believe that cooking was evolved as a primitive method of keeping meat. In the oven, in the pan or on the grill, the meat is heated at a sufficiently high temperature for long enough to kill any growing germs which might be present on or in it. But it does not follow that once meat or meat products have been cooked they are safe from contamination. This applies particularly to stock, gravies, soup and meat jollies, which may be allowed to stand about from one day to the next in a hot kitchen. Such foods can pick up infection from dust and utensils (as explained in the previous chapter) and food poisoning bacteria can grow rapidly in them. Reheating is not usually sufficient to kill any infection or toxin which may have been generated. Food poisoning therefore can and does arise.

The housewife may wonder why it is she needs to be so particular to prevent infection in most meats, but is encouraged to allow certain feathered game, hare and venison to hang before cooking until it gets high. The reason is that the birds and animals concerned are killed out of doors and in the wild state. The kinds of bacteria peculiar to high meats are similar in one respect to those which produce cheeses like Stilton, Blue, Gorgonzola and Camembert, in that they do not produce toxins injurious to man. Further, the conditions under which these peculiar types of germs grow do not normally permit disease germs to multiply. In any case, cooking renders all high meats quite safe. Nevertheless, if any meats, high or otherwise, are left about too long after cooking, especially if remaining in their own gravy or jelly, then food poisoning germs may grow in them.

Meat Products

All meat products, brisket, brawn, pies, mince and sausage, which may be bought pre-cooked may be open occasionally to some food poisoning risks during manufacture and transport. Against such risks the housewife is powerless unless the meat or meat product shows some obvious sign, such as greening, or has a detectable smell or unpleasant taste. However, she usually knows the origin of such foodstuffs and will take all reasonable precautions at the time of purchase. But once these meats or meat products are in her kitchen, the same hygiene rules apply to them as to any other meat. Briefly, all meat products should be kept cool and free from dust and flies; if not refrigerated, they should be eaten as soon after purchase as is reasonably possible.

Vegetables

Vegetables intended for cooking carry only one risk: they bring soil and perhaps particles of manure into the kitchen. After suitable preparation and cooking, vegetables are rendered both palatable and safe. So it only behoves the housewife to be careful in cleaning all surfaces or utensils with which the raw vegetables have been in contact.

But vegetables to be eaten raw in salads are different. Apart from washing, they pass direct to the eater from the ground, or, in the case of watercress, from bed or river which may carry sewage contamination. Anyone who has lived in the tropics knows well the risk of contracting enteric diseases after eating uncooked salads. Formerly, in hot countries, such salad vegetables were disinfected by soaking them in Condy's fluid, but recent research has proved even this to be unsafe and hypochlorite has taken its place. In temperate zones there is nothing like so great a danger arising from salad vegetables, but there are on record outbreaks of enteritis traced from this source in England, France, Germany, the United States, Scandinavia and other countries. The poliomyelitis virus is passed in human excreta and will live in water for several weeks. It is thought by some research workers that the virus may be passed on via sewage-contaminated vegetables, particularly, in some places, watercress and celery.

The disinfection of salad vegetables of both bacteria and viruses has been carefully studied and a very simple method evolved. All that is necessary is to immerse the washed vegetables for 15 minutes in a dilute hypochlorite solution (2 tablespoonfuls Milton to 2 quarts water). No taste or discoloration results from this treatment, which makes the vegetables perfectly safe to eat. Fruit, if desired, can be similarly treated but, broadly speaking, the food poisoning hazards with fruit do not loom large.

Eggs

Any egg, either fresh or preserved, which is considered suitable for eating should, when opened, have a pleasant smell, a yellow yolk free from spots, surrounded by a clear "white." Normally the contents of an egg are sterile, but just occasionally a diseased bird lays infected eggs. Some eggs are produced under dirty conditions and may thereby become infected. Hence the housewife should be suspicious of dirty eggs unless she knows where they came from. Ducks, if not kept under close supervision, often wander into all kinds of excreta and garbage and pick up infection which cannot be detected by the ordinary tests of sight and smell.

So, for safety, all duck eggs should be hard-boiled for 10–15 minutes. Before the war, in Germany, all duck eggs were labelled with such an instruction. Mayonnaise made from raw eggs, and also whipped raw-egg dressing, have been the cause of outbreaks of food poisoning. Both dried egg powder and frozen liquid egg

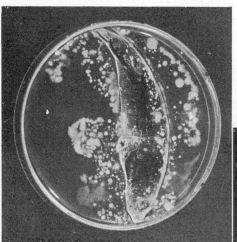

Invisible to the human eye, unfortunately, but just look at the bacterial infection on the uncooked fish (above)

have been shown to be potential carriers of food poisoning germs. For that reason, they should be used only for dishes or cakes which are to be cooked at a high temperature.

Generally speaking, in the home it is unwise to use egg powder or liquid egg for anything to be served uncooked or lightly heated. These products are used on a large scale, however, in industry, where they are under close supervision.

Fish

Fresh, cured, pickled or smoked fish sold in the fishmonger's is remarkably safe from food poisoning. Every housewife knows by smell and appearance if the fish is good, and very rarely indeed is it otherwise. But once it reaches the kitchen, the food hygiene rules already described apply, whether or not the fish has been cooked. So often fish heads and tails are put outside for the cat, and it is forgotten that what the cat leaves makes excellent breeding rubbish for flies.

Shell-fish such as crabs, lobsters, crayfish, prawns and shrimps, if not fresh, usually tell their own tale. The following characteristics indicate staleness: limpness, faded appearance, wet or sticky claws, offensive smell under shell, and a limp tail which, if pulled back, fails to spring forward again. In shell-fish such as oysters, mussels, cockles, scallops, periwinkles and whelks, other signs must be looked for. In former times, oysters were often responsible for food poisoning because they were grown in sewage-polluted water. Now,

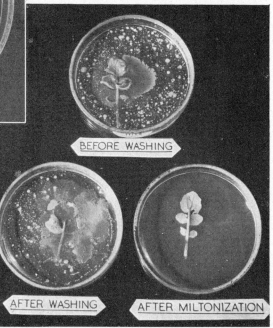

BEFORE WASHING

AFTER WASHING

AFTER MILTONIZATION

Watercress comes direct from bed or river which may carry sewage contamination. Ordinary washing is not enough. For absolute safety, immerse in a Milton solution for 15 minutes

however, they are carefully cleansed in chlorinated water and have become very safe indeed. One point, however, needs attention. When a housewife asks the fishmonger to open oysters for her, he should do this under the slow-running tap and not in a bowl of static water which may be infected with fæcal bacteria.

Mussels, cockles, scallops, periwinkles and whelks are all cooked before being eaten and very rarely cause any trouble, provided they are fresh. Occasionally, cockles which have been badly handled before reaching the fishmonger have caused food poisoning, but this is quite rare.

Sometimes, when on holiday, children gather mussels and cockles and like to cook them for home consumption. Such shell-fish should be inspected before cooking for gaping shells or offensive smell, which will indicate that they are unsound.

Fish cakes are usually made mainly from cooked fish and potatoes, and should contain at least 35 per cent. of fish by weight. These should be cooked and eaten as soon as possible and not stored at room temperature.

Canned fish should be turned out of the can when opened, but otherwise can be treated like any other foodstuff. Fish pastes are made from cooked fish, fat and cereal fillings, plus seasoning, flavours and colourings. The whole is crushed to a paste and packed into jars which are sealed and sterilised. Such pastes must contain at least 70 per cent. of fish. They are so manufactured that they keep well, especially if refrigerated, and when opened, if kept with the lid on when not in use, rarely, if ever, become infected except with harmless moulds. These, however, usually indicate to the housewife that it is time to throw the pot away.

Cream

Fresh cream is usually pasteurised before being offered for sale and so, when purchased, is safe from food poisoning germs. If stored in a refrigerator, pasteurised cream will remain fresh for several months. The practice still persists in some places of selling unpasteurised cream direct from an uncovered bowl on the dairy counter. Unless the producers and the retailers are scrupulously clean, such cream is wide open to infection from several points, especially as preservatives are forbidden by law. The methods by which clotted creams are produced usually ensure a safe product, but contamination may occur during packing. So, if clotted cream is received by post, especially during very hot weather, it should be carefully examined before eating. If it is incorporated into whipped decorations for fruit salad and so on, cream should never be left exposed to dust. Even so, by the ordinary tests of sight and smell, it may not be possible to detect infection. However, if the cream was packed under unsatisfactory conditions it will probably show some signs of souring, which will put the housewife on her guard. Canned cream is quite safe and should be treated like any other canned food, but should be used soon after being turned out of the tin.

For decorating and filling pastries, artificial or "synthetic" cream is widely used in the catering and baking industries, but relatively little in the home. Such artificial creams have frequently been associated with outbreaks of food poisoning and should be used only strictly according to the maker's instructions.

Ice Cream

Ice cream is looked upon as a modern product. As an item of food it is, but as a rare luxury it has been eaten at least since the seventeenth century. At the everyday consumer level, ice cream was introduced in the United Kingdom by an Italian called Gatti about 1860. Until relatively recent times ice cream had been frequently associated with food poisoning, but better methods of manufacture and control have made it safe during production, except for rare accidents. However, the manner in which, after manufacture, it may be served is still often open to question. Wafers and cornets are dispensed with unsterile utensils taken from a milky and possibly infected jar of water, and the server may be handling wafers and cones with anything but clean hands. The housewife should watch these points before allowing her children to purchase ice creams. She would be wise to insist on buying only from vendors with a clean hygiene service. There are cases, however, where ice cream, badly handled, has become infected in the home. It has been placed on infected surfaces or cut with infected knives. Some people think that

After piping cream from savoy bags, the bags must always be boiled.   Mock cream should only be used in accordance with maker's instructions and not kept too long

the low temperature of ice cream kills germs, but it does not.

Water ices, or iced lollies, so much favoured by children, have little or no nutritive value, and therefore cannot truly be said to be responsible for food poisoning. These products are not processed—only frozen—and no outbreak of food poisoning has been traced to them. Some criticism has been directed against them because minute traces of metal from the moulds have been found in them, but no marked untoward results have been reported.

Milk

There is little comment to pass on milk, provided it is pasteurised and properly stored. In raw milk, however, disease germs of several kinds, as well as those of food poisoning, can be passed to the drinker. Everything depends on the conditions under which the milk is collected, distributed and stored. Considering the possible hazards, there is no doubt that pasteurised milk is safest, but considerable quantities of raw milk are still consumed daily.

The growth of the T.T. herds, the use of abortus vaccines and the help given by the National Agricultural Advisory Service represent great strides in making raw milk safer, but housewives still need to be careful about using it and really ought to know the conditions under which it is produced. Special care needs to be exercised in the case of babies, and naturally the doctor, midwife and health visitor will advise on infant feeding. For bottle-fed babies it is wise to use a regular routine of sterilisation of the bottles and teats such as the well-known Milton method.

Home Care

In a comparatively short space it is impossible to mention all the points about prevention of food poisoning. But this is intended merely as guidance for the housewife, whose standby must be common sense and experience. The fact remains, however, that in the United Kingdom to-day there is still far too high an incidence of food poisoning, a certain percentage of which arises in the home. These cases could be almost completely eliminated if the simple points described were generally understood and the food hygiene rules followed by all.

The tummy upset is too common to be ignored—its prevention starts in the rules of the kitchen.

EQUIPPING A KITCHEN

How to choose the domestic utensils which really are essential for cooking

A set of food storage containers is a "must." Those above are in clear polystyrene with red, white, blue or lemon lids. Bex

Right, the Prestige wall type can opener is magnetised so that the lid does not fall into the can as it comes off

CHOOSE the equipment for your kitchen with care and forethought. Kitchen utensils get used more than anything else in the house and there will be many an occasion to be grateful for the article that pleases you and saves labour, while ill-chosen or badly made equipment will often cause annoyance.

A young married couple should choose a gas or electric cooker that will allow for an increase in the size of the family. The extra cost is not great when spread over the years in hire purchase, but if you should want to change a stove in a few years time you will find that little is allowed for a second-hand cooker.

Easily Cleaned Surfaces

See that the working surface in the kitchen is covered with some easily cleaned material rather than wood that needs scrubbing. There are plenty of wonderful laminated plastic table coverings obtainable in sheet form that will withstand very hard wear. Easier still for an amateur to apply are the stick-on plastic surfaces such as Fablon and Contact, which come in good colours and designs.

Good saucepans are expensive but they last for years and save fuel. The best saucepans are the heavy aluminium ones, and special ones with cast bases are required for electric stoves. There is no need to buy a lot of saucepans. It is usually better to buy individual ones rather than sets, as you then obtain the sizes you really need for the requirements of your family.

Saucepans

The following should meet the basic needs of a small family:

Two medium-sized saucepans for potatoes and a second vegetable.

A large pan that will take a steamer and will also do for making soup or boiling a piece of bacon. A steamer to fit this saucepan.

A small pan for custard or sauce.

A milk saucepan. Those with a slightly turned-over edge all round are much better for pouring than those with lips.

A cheap enamel saucepan for boiling eggs.

A frying pan. Before buying a frying

pan, see that it will stand level, as so often the handles are too heavy. Choose a fairly heavy frying pan because thin ones burn and buckle so easily.

A kettle. If you only have one, make it a good-sized one, say to hold 6 pints, and only half fill it when making tea for two or three.

Additional pans can be added as circumstances permit and according to the amount of cooking you do.

For the Oven

A roasting tin is usually provided with the cooker, but it is wise to buy a smaller one for cooking a small piece of meat or making Yorkshire pudding.

Flat baking tins are also often provided with the cooker. These are useful for scones, biscuits, etc., or for placing under a fruit tart that may boil over. If none are available, a couple of swiss-roll tins will answer the purpose. For making cakes or jam tarts, two sets of bun tins are required, and for a large cake a 7-in. cake tin with a removable bottom. Two sandwich tins are very useful for making jam sponges and for tarts or flans.

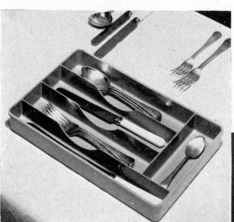

A cutlery tray (above) in red, white, lemon, or blue, with an extra long compartment for carvers, bread knives, etc., from Bex

An open frypan, a non-stick omelet pan (with its own coated metal turner) and a covered stewpan, all in aluminium, with matching handles in red, blue or yellow, by Prestige

Cooking Bowls and Casseroles

You will need a large bowl for mixing pastry, puddings or cakes—either oven-glass or pottery—and one or two pudding basins of varying sizes, one large enough for a family-sized steamed pudding.

At least one casserole is an indispensable kitchen item. Have one big enough for a stew and vegetables for the family. An oven-glass one, the lid of which also serves as a dish, is a good investment. A collection of varying sized casseroles is a great asset to any kitchen.

A glass pieplate is a good buy: it can be used for making pies, for baking tomatoes or apples and for re-heating food. An oven-glass pie dish is also useful, as it will do duty for a fruit dish as well as for pies or milk puddings.

Wooden Articles

If there is a good cool working surface in the kitchen, there is no need to have a pastry board, but a small chopping board is very necessary. Choose a rolling-pin of simple design and with a cool exterior, or failing this, you can manage very well indeed with a well-washed milk bottle.

Kitchen Tools

The following are essential:

A tablespoon, dessertspoon and teaspoon kept for cooking.

A wooden spoon.

A sharp vegetable knife; a sharp steel, fair-sized knife.

A palette knife or large flexible round-ended knife.

A good covered roasting pan is essential—this is the Nevastik Double Roaster by London Aluminium Co.

A hygienic waste disposal unit that takes no floor space—right, the Garbina fits on any door, wall or cupboard, takes wet and dry refuse. When the bag is full, just replace with a clean new one

A potato peeler. A tin opener. A master key for sardines, etc.

A fish slice. A wire or rotary whisk.

Miscellaneous Articles

A plastic bowl for washing up.

A plate rack for draining plates.

A colander for straining vegetables.

Some jars for storing dry goods.

In addition, these items are practically indispensable:

A round strainer, to serve also as sieve.

A pint measure for measuring liquids.

A cheese grater.

A pair of kitchen scissors to cut rind off bacon or chop parsley.

A mincer.

A wire cake rack.

Care of Equipment

Saucepans. — Soak all pans immediately they are empty; greasy ones in hot water and those that have been used for starchy foods, such as custard or porridge, in cold

Three useful accessories (above) in various colours — Hi-Speed chromium plated beater, potato peeler with finger rest, and Tapmaster rubber fitments for taps

The Bex 1½-pint measuring jug (below) is robust and more stain resistant than many other materials, with clear markings

A chicken casserole (above) in Pyrex clear oven glassware is big enough for poultry or a large joint, can also be used as two separate dishes

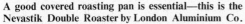

The Swedish cook's knife (above) is angled for an easy rocking action when chopping vegetables. From the Prestige range

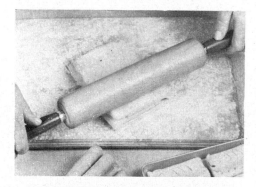

The wood rolling pin, from the Skyline range, has hardwood handles enamelled red and white, holes for hanging, grooves for your thumbs

On the wall rack hang a spatula, bowl ladle, 3-prong fork, potato masher, straining spoon and fish slice. Skyline, in stainless steel

water. It is best not to use soda for aluminium pans. Use steel wool or a nylon scourer and dry well before putting away.

Or bring a little water and detergent powder to the boil in the pan and leave to soak for a few minutes to remove obstinate marks and stains. Non-stick pans should be rinsed in hot water only and then dried.

One exception to the soaking rule is the omelet pan. Many people have very strong views on its treatment and only wipe it clean with kitchen paper after using, *never* washing it or allowing water to come into contact with it at all. Wipe the pan while it is still hot after use and it will come quite clean without difficulty.

Tins.—After making gravy in a roasting tin, place a lump of soda in the tin, fill with water, put back on the stove, and bring to the boil, clean with steel wool or saucepan cleaner, rinse, dry, and then place in the oven, which will still be warm, to dry off. Cake tins can be rubbed clean with newspaper or a dry cloth while still hot; if washed, dry completely in a warm oven.

Casseroles.—After using a casserole or pie dish, it is best to leave it soaking for a little while and then clean with steel wool or a nylon scourer that will remove the brown marks. Rinse and dry.

Wooden Utensils.—Pastry and chopping boards, rolling pins, etc., should be scrubbed well with soap and warm water, rinsed, dried, then stood in a current of air.

Kitchen Cloths

Choose linen teacloths if possible; they dry up better, last well and do not leave fluff on the dishes. Keep these for drying dishes only, and have an oven cloth or oven gloves for taking things from the oven and a dry dishcloth for drying pans. Wash all kitchen cloths frequently and spread the dishcloth out between washing-ups to become dry—it will be much sweeter than if left wet.

Kitchen paper is invaluable; it will absorb surplus grease if chips, fried fish etc. are dished up on to it and you can also use it to wipe up spills and take the grease out of cooking pans.

For easy washing-up use the special little sponges that come in a variety of colours and fit into a long handle—and a Wettex dish cloth that does not get slimy.

SHOPPING TO ADVANTAGE

*How to buy economically and how to choose
fruit and vegetables that are really fresh*

LET it be a comforting thought to all new housewives that even those of long experience can sometimes fall down on food purchases. Certainly there is much for the beginner to learn about wise buying of food; all the different cuts of meat, varieties of fish, fruit, vegetables and dry goods, and whether or not they are as fresh as they should be, in season or out of it.

To graduate as a good food shopper, over whom no salesman can pull a fast one, you will need to "pass" in three aspects of the job: knowing (a) what you want; (b) the right price for the goods and for your housekeeping budget; and (c) whether what you buy is fresh or not.

You can, and should, take your time over (a). It is not possible to learn all the cuts of meat and kinds of fish until you have cooked and tried different recipes for some little time. Included in the Meat and Fish chapters of this book there is plenty to guide you initially. Seek advice on the shops with the best reputation and shop there. Goods may cost a penny or two more, but this is not lack of economy when it ensures quality and freshness. Also you can ask for advice, and get it. You may learn a lot from experienced shopkeepers.

Turning now to (b) price, and (c) freshness, you need to gain knowledge on these aspects as quickly as possible. Once you have memorised the average prices of meat, fish, fruit and vegetables, and which prices suit your budget best, you can shop by price, asking for something at so much.

The radio and some newspapers give weekly food bulletins for the housewife. If you note these down for two or three weeks, you can make yourself a useful guide to average prices.

CHOOSING VEGETABLES

Artichokes (Globe).—When you cut the stems they should be white and moist, leaves should be very firm.

Artichokes (Jerusalem). — Should be hard. They quickly soften if kept.

Asparagus.—Sticks should be straight and stiff, tips close packed, no leaf sprouts.

Aubergines.—Stems should be firmly fixed to skins, deep violet-purple in colour. Pips and pulp creamy, free from blemishes.

Beetroots.—These must be firm and skins absolutely whole and undamaged, otherwise they will "bleed" in cooking.

Broad Beans.—Buy when young and pale apple green; indigestible when large.

Broccoli.—Stalks should be short and crisp.

Brussels Sprouts.—Best when small and tightly closed.

Cabbage.—Hearts should be firm and closely packed. Watch out for holes which may indicate caterpillars inside.

Carrots.—Buy firm and bright coloured with no splits and only a tiny circle of green at the top.

Cauliflower.—Leaves should be crisp and green, flower white, closely packed and unblemished.

Celeriac.—Choose these small and hard.

Celery.—Small, closely packed heads.

Chestnuts.—Skins tightly filled.

Chicory.—See that leaves are crisp and silvery and heads tightly packed.

Corn on the Cob to be fresh should be greenish, turning golden.

Cucumber must be firm with a shiny green skin.

French Beans.—These should be a soft, clear green, plump with a smooth skin.

Kale or Turnip Tops.—Buy if crisp and bright coloured.

Kohl Rabi.—Should be firm, medium-sized and unblemished.

Leeks.—Choose snowy-white and small.

Lettuce should be bought only when crisp and with a faint shine on the leaves.

Marrows should look like sausage-shaped balloons, lightly polished, and very firm.

Mushrooms are heavy when fresh and the underside pinkish brown.

Parsnips are at their best after frost.

Peas (Green).—The pods should be a good green without blemish, juicy when pressed, not too tightly packed.

Potatoes.—The point here is to ask for a floury kind (Arran, British Queen and Epicure are some) for plain boiled and mashed potato dishes; a waxy kind (Sharp's Express, King Edward and Gladstone when small) for frying and sauté potatoes, because they do not readily absorb fat.

Runner Beans.—Pods should be bright green and fine textured, and they should snap sharply when bent in two.

Salsify should be firm and unblemished.

Sea Kale should be crisp and creamy white.

Spinach.—This is fresh when the leaves are straight and lightly glossed.

Swedes and Turnips, like all roots, should be firm with undamaged skins.

Tomatoes.—Buy when firm and of a uniform redness and without blemish.

FRUITS

On the whole, fruits are easier to choose well than other perishables. Colour should always be good and skins undamaged. Oranges and lemons particularly should have brightly coloured, clean skins, and should be soft when squeezed, to be juicy. Bananas should be firm with clear, soft yellow skins and only light touches of brown; too much brown may mean pulpy patches under the skin. Feel the stem end of a pear; it should be just soft to be ready to eat. Soft fruits should *not* be soft when bought. They should hold their shape well, be true coloured and dry. Strawberries should look lightly polished. To test if a pineapple is ripe, lightly pull out one of the green leaves, which should come out quite easily.

ECONOMICAL BUYING

This may sound ironic these days when prices remain high for most of the year, but you can still beat the price rises if you time your bulk shopping wisely.

Canned goods are one of the most helpful items, and a wise plan is to lay in a small stock of fruit and vegetables in the summer for use in winter. The same can be done with dried fruits, which should be washed at the time of purchase, thoroughly dried and stored in clean storage cans in a cool, dry place.

Egg prices are very variable, but whenever they drop a little, buy as many extra as you can afford and preserve them. Date them all in pencil so that you use them in rotation.

EXOTIC FRUITS

Introducing some lesser-known delicacies and how to serve them

A selection specially photographed at Shearn's of London: at the back, a Pineapple; in front and just to the left, an Avocado Pear; far left, a Custard Apple. Next to it, the pale smooth fruit, seen also sliced on the plate, is an Ortanique, with several Passion Fruit to its right and, far right, an Ugli. The little things in front are Lychees

EXOTIC fruit, so new to many of us, is now to be bought in the shops, and such delicacies as pineapples, custard apples, avocado pears, persimmons and pomegranates are to be seen on the barrows in street markets.

Some of these, which I have tried myself, are exciting to eat. The **Avocado Pear** (wrongly called Alligator Pear by some people) is a native of Mexico, but now grows in the West Indies, Madeira, and parts of the U.S.A. It does not really taste like a fruit and is served as a first course or savoury. You cut it in half, remove the large stone and then spoon out the soft pulp and eat it as it is, or add salt and white pepper, lemon, lime juice or French dressing. This fruit is rich in oil and Vitamin B and grows very well indoors when planted in a large pot and given plenty of light. The large, laurel-shaped leaves make it an interesting plant, suitable for modern interiors.

Cape Gooseberries, or Cape Golden Berries, originally came from tropical America. In India, where they also grow, they are called Brazil Cherries. As the name indicates, they are now grown also in South Africa. In France, where they are very popular, they are called Physalis or Coqueret. This fruit is eaten without its covering, and its acid flavour is very refreshing. It is also most suitable for fruit cheese, prepared in the same way as quince or damson cheese.

When I saw **Custard Apples** for the first time, I admired the green, quilted-looking skin, but when I tasted them, I realised that my palate had met with a new experience. They are creamy and sweet, and deliciously flavoured. They, too, are spooned out, and taste wonderful with a little cream and brown sugar.

Lychees are another exciting fruit: the thin, prickly shell is removed and a moist, white fruit remains, tasting like a cross between a large, skinless grape and a gooseberry. The kernel is comparatively large and has to be discarded. Lychees, which originally came from China, are now quite extensively cultivated in the West Indies, South Africa and the Philippines.

The best fruit, according to many connoisseurs, is the **Mango,** eaten when really fresh. It is imported from the West Indies and Malaya. The Mango is a versatile fruit, used when still unripe as an addition to salads. There are also curries whose main ingredient is the Mango. It is pickled with salt, oil and chillies, used in jellies and preserves, boiled with milk and sugar to make Mango Fool, and also used dried.

One day I saw a large green cone at the fruiterer's, and when I heard that this was the **Monstera Deliciosa,** I had to try it out. This fruit has to lie in a sunny place until its skin—or, better, its shell—bursts. It has a most puzzling and unusual flavour, like a banana and pineapple mixture. The only disadvantage is that the black, rather prickly seeds are slightly irritating to the tongue. In Mexico, where this plant grows as a climber, people are so used to it that they do not notice the seeds at all.

Passionfruit (or Grenadilla) is a fruit similar to the Pomegranate. The moist pulp, which is full of pips, should be scooped out with a teaspoon. It is greatly improved when served with a mixture of cream, sherry and sugar.

The small, olive-like fruit of the date plum, called **Persimmon,** grows wild in Japan and the southern parts of America. It needs frost to turn the sour, unripe fruit into a sweet and soft dessert fruit. The wood from the date plum tree, which is related to the ebony, is a very strong timber used for many purposes.

One of the earliest fruits imported into Europe is the **Pomegranate.** It is the size of an orange and has pockets, full of soft and slightly acid grains, though almost seedless varieties are now grown in Spain and Tunisia. It is a refreshing fruit, but has very little flavour.

Ugli fruit looks like a grapefruit gone wrong. It is one of the most palatable citrus fruits and very popular in the U.S.A., where it is called Tangelo. It can be eaten like an orange or used for the same purposes—i.e. in fruit salads, for flavouring, etc. It is extensively grown in Jamaica.

A reddish fruit, looking like an outsize Victoria plum, is called **Winepods,** or Tree Tomato. It comes from Madeira, and though the first impression is disappointing, the taste for this fruit can be acquired. The skin has a bitter flavour and the juicy pulp is bitter-sweet.

QUICK GLACÉ FRUIT

Glacé Fruits are very expensive to buy, and the usual process of making them is fairly complicated and laborious. However, there is a simplified version which tastes good, its only disadvantage being that it has to be eaten the same or the next day, before the covering dissolves.

Preparations can begin the previous day. The fruit must be stoned, marzipan for stuffing can be either made or bought and, if canned fruit is used, it should be drained overnight.

You will need the following ingredients: Various kinds of fruit, such as white and black grapes, large prunes, dates, figs, orange slices, etc. *For stuffing:* Nuts or almonds, marzipan. *For glacé icing:* 2 lb. sugar, preferably lump, 2 tablespoonfuls vinegar, $\frac{3}{4}$ pint and 5 tablespoonfuls water. Thin wooden skewers or toothpicks for dipping the fruit. Oil or melted butter for greasing plates.

When using marzipan, add a few drops of edible colour and half the amount of icing sugar in weight (to $\frac{1}{2}$ lb. marzipan add $\frac{1}{4}$ lb. sugar). Form marzipan into small sausages, the size of a prune or date stone, and insert it so that it shows. Grease baking sheets or plates with either oil or melted butter and dip the ends of toothpicks or skewers in fat. Pour water and vinegar over sugar and let it stand for $\frac{1}{2}$ hour. Bring to the boil, and boil briskly until the sugar thermometer shows 310° F. If no thermometer is available, dip a wooden skewer into cold water, then into the boiling syrup and back into cold water. Break off sugar, which should be brittle. If it draws a thread, it is not yet ready.

Insert greased end of skewer into fruit and dip into syrup, let drip for a moment and put fruit on greased sheet or plate.

Remove toothpicks or skewers as soon as the fruit dries (in a few minutes). Put each fruit into a paper case before serving.

As the sugar darkens quickly, it is advisable to dip the light-coloured fruits first and the darker ones later. This quantity of sugar will be sufficient for about five dozen fruits.

CATERING HINTS

How much for how many—and how to tell the good from the bad

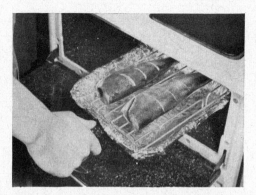

Ice Cream Brandy Punch (above) is a party winner. Left, an economy idea: when grilling, line the pan with Mirap aluminium foil—its shiny surface reflects the heat, speeds cooking and protects the pan from grease

IN the initial stages of housekeeping it is a little difficult to know how much to buy of this and that commodity, especially the perishables.

Here is an approximate guide: allow 4–6 oz. of meat or fish per person, including active children; 4 oz. vegetables and 2–3 medium-sized potatoes; when soup starts the meal, allow two-thirds of a soup *cup* per person of thick soup, rather more of thinner soups.

For sweet courses, reckon that a pint pudding basin (steamed puddings) or a pint dish (trifle, rice pudding, etc.) will serve four.

For such items as dressed crabs, allow one large one for four persons, a medium one for three; in the case of small fish such as sprats, allow about 1 lb. for three people. Salmon is a rich, solid fish, so allow a little less.

Catering for Large Numbers.—Allowing for waste and loss of weight in cooking, a 12-lb. turkey will serve about 14 people; the same weight of goose serves about 10 people; one good-sized, plump duck, or two smaller ones, will serve 6–7 people. Reckon on a joint of 10 lb. for about 12 persons.

Larger Numbers: Party Items.—Allow 1 pint of ice cream for about 7 people; 3 sandwiches, 3–4 cocktail sausages, 2 pastry savouries per person. Sweets are most easily managed served in individual glasses or dishes—about half-full, for at a party both children and adults are inclined to eat a little of a fair variety of eatables, rather than a lot of one kind.

Here is a very good party recipe:

Ice Cream Brandy Punch

1 *family brick vanilla*	1 *pint milk*
ice cream	1 *egg (optional)*
½ *gill brandy*	

Add ice cream, cut into small pieces, to other ingredients in a large mixing bowl, whisk till frothy. Serve from a punch bowl. Makes 6 to 8 glasses.

HOME GOODNESS TESTS

There is always a certain amount of worry about mushrooms. If you have any doubt at all, put a real silver spoon or coin in the pan. If it turns black, the mushrooms are dangerous.

Eggs too are sometimes unknown quantities, but here are some tests: put the doubtful one into a bowl of water when it will (*a*) sink to the bottom if fresh; (*b*) rise slightly, broad end up, if two or three weeks old; (*c*) come to the surface or above it if really stale. You can apply a further test by holding the egg against a strong light. If it looks unclouded, it is fresh; if it is bad, it will look dark-coloured.

Among dry goods, flour and floury items are not always good keepers. If you feel uncertain of them, grasp a handful and squeeze for half a minute. If the substance is pure, it will hold its shape; if not, it will break up and fall.

ENGLISH COUNTIES

Some traditional recipes from all over England,
compiled by Whitbread & Co. Ltd.

BEDFORDSHIRE

Apple Florentine Pie (an 18th-century Christmas dish)

4 *good cooking apples*	*Grated lemon peel*
Short pastry (see	2 *tablespoonfuls*
Pastry Chapter)	*sugar*

For the hot spiced ale

1 *pint ale*	*A little nutmeg and*
1 *tablespoonful sugar*	*cinnamon*
	1 *clove*

Core the apples, wash them and place in a deep pie dish. Put sugar over them and lemon peel, and cover with short pastry. Bake in a moderate oven for 30 minutes. Remove the pastry, pour the spiced ale over, cut pastry into required pieces and put back on the dish. Serve hot.

Spiced Ale.—Heat the ale very gently with the spices and sugar. Do not let it boil. It used to be served in a very large pewter dish.

Catherine Cakes (or Kattern Cakes)

So-called after Catherine of Aragon, the Queen who used to live at Ampthill Castle. Ampthill was a favourite lace-making district, and Catherine was very interested in it. Catherine Cakes were specially made for November 25th, St. Catherine's Day.

2 *lb. dough (see*	2 *oz. sugar*
Bread Chapter)	*A few caraway seeds*
1 *egg*	2 *oz. butter*

Dough made with yeast, as for bread. Knead well with butter, caraway seeds, sugar and egg. Leave to rise in a warm place for 2 hours. Place on floured baking tin and bake in a moderate oven for 2–3 hours.

BERKSHIRE

Bacon Pudding

1 *lb. flour*	6 *oz. suet*
6 *oz. fat bacon*	2 *onions*
A little sage	*Salt and pepper*

Make a stiff paste with flour, shredded suet and water. Roll out ½ in. thick. Cover with bacon and chopped onions mixed with sage and seasoning. Roll up pastry and secure at both ends, wrap up in cloth and boil for 2 hours.

Poor Knights of Windsor

8 *slices of bread* ½ *in.*	*A little butter or lard*
thick	*A little jam, sugar*
A little white wine or	*or cinnamon*
milk and sugar	

Put white wine or milk and sugar into a dish; dip the bread in it on both sides. Then fry bread gently, on both sides, in a little hot fat. Dish up on a hot plate and spread a little jam or sugar or cinnamon over it.

BUCKINGHAMSHIRE

Stokenchurch Pie

1 *lb. flour*	1½ *lb. meat (any*
8 *oz. lard*	*cooked meat or*
4 *oz. macaroni*	*scrag)*
A little stock	3 *hard-boiled eggs*
	A little salt

Mince the meat and add to a little thickened stock. Boil the macaroni in salt water until tender, cut up and mix with meat. Cut up the eggs in quarters. Make a good pastry with flour and lard (see Pastry chapter), roll out and line a well-greased tin. Put in half the meat, the eggs, and then the rest of the meat on top. Cover with pastry. Make a hole in the centre, decorate the top with bits of pastry, and brush over with milk. Bake in a hot oven for 30 minutes.

Old Bucks Custom for Baking a Joint of Beef

Use brown sugar for sprinkling instead of salt; the result is extra rich gravy and a fine flavour to the beef.

CAMBRIDGESHIRE

Cambridge Sauce

Cambridge sauce is similar to mayonnaise, served cold with cold dishes. The ingredients are oil and vinegar, yolks of hard-boiled eggs, tarragon, chives, chervil and a little cayenne.

CHESHIRE

Cheshire Pork Pie

> Pork
> Salt, pepper and nut-
>   meg to taste
> Shortcrust pastry
> A little white wine or cider
> Apples
> Sugar
> A little butter

Layers of pork and apples seasoned with salt, pepper, nutmeg and sugar. Add a little white wine or cider and a little butter on top. Cover with pastry and bake in a moderate oven for 45 minutes.

Chester Pudding

> 4 oz. breadcrumbs
> 4 oz. flour
> 4 oz. shredded suet
> 4 oz. black currant jam
> 2 oz. castor sugar
> A little bicarbonate of soda
> A little milk
> A little salt

Mix flour, breadcrumbs, suet, salt and sugar. Make a well in the centre and put in the jam; warm the milk, add the bicarbonate of soda to it and pour over the jam. Mix everything together. Place in a well-greased basin or mould and steam for 3 hours. Serve with black currant jam sauce.

Flummery

The name is now applied to any starch jelly made from cereals, wheat flour, rice, sago, etc. It used to apply to oatmeal only, eaten with honey, wine, sack, claret, strong beer, ale or milk. It is like porridge, but when the oats are cooked, they are passed through a sieve, sugar is added and orange flower water. It is then put into shallow dishes and served with one of the beverages mentioned above.

A tea-time treat with happy holiday memories—
Cornish Splits with jam and cream inside

CORNWALL

Cornish Pasty (or Hoggan)

The great distinction between the Cornish pasty and any other kind of pasty is that the ingredients are raw, not previously cooked remains. The pasty is joined at the side, but the Cornish hoggin is joined at the top.

> ½ lb. flour   Water to make fine
> 3 oz. dripping or lard   dough—about 1 gill
> Pinch of salt

For the filling

> ½ lb. beef steak   ¼ lb. calf's liver
> 2 uncooked potatoes   1 large onion
> 1 medium-sized turnip   1 large or 2 small
> Pepper and salt   carrots
> A little egg-white

Time to bake.— 1 hour; at first in a good oven to raise the pastry, and then in a moderate oven to cook the meat and vegetables.

Roll out the dough fairly thin, cut in squares. Chop the steak and liver finely, mix together and season. Peel or scrape, and slice the potato, onion, turnip and carrot. Mix and season the vegetables. Put a layer of vegetables on half of each square of pastry and some of the chopped meat on top. Brush the edges of the pastry with egg-white, fold the plain half over the meat and pinch the edges well together. Bake as above.

NOTE: It is important to close the edges neatly and closely so that no steam escapes, and to use uncooked meat and vegetables. The contents cook in their own juices, so after the first few minutes require a very moderate oven. The amounts given make 2 large or 3 medium pasties.

It has been said that Cornishwomen put everything into a pasty. Variations include:

Apple Pasty

Peel apples, slice thinly and lightly sprinkle with brown sugar. In summer time blackberries are usually mixed with the apple.

Chicken Pasty

The chicken is cut up into small pieces.

Eggy Pasty

Bacon cut in dice, parsley and one or two eggs, according to size of pasty required.

Herb Pasty

Pastry	Parsley
Chopped shallots	Bits, a North Cornish
Cut-up spinach	herb (optional)
1 egg	Slices of bacon

Prepare pastry as for pasties. Take equal quantities of parsley, finely chopped shallots, bits, spinach, some finely cut slices of bacon and a well-beaten egg. Pour boiling water over the herbs, leave to stand a little, squeeze all moisture out of the herbs. Mix all together except the egg, and put into the pastry. Before quite closing it, add the egg, finish pinching and bake in quick oven.

Jam Pasty

These are usually made smaller than a savoury pasty and any kind of jam may be used.

Mackerel Pasty

Allow one or two mackerel to each pasty and clean and boil them in the usual way; remove skin and bones and lay on pastry. Fill up with washed parsley and add pepper and salt. Finish as above.

Parsley Pasty

These are made with parsley and lamb or mutton.

Pork Pasty

Fresh pork and potatoes, flavoured with onion, sage or thyme.

Rabitty Pasty

Use fleshy part of rabbit, cut up fairly small, in the same way as other meat.

Cornish Splits

1 lb. flour	1 oz. butter
½ oz. yeast	½ oz. castor sugar
¼ pint tepid milk	1 teaspoonful salt

Cream yeast and sugar until liquid, then add milk; sieve the flour and salt into a basin. Melt the butter; add milk and salt with the butter to the flour and mix into a smooth dough. Let the dough rise in a cool place for 45 minutes. Then shape into round balls and bake in a floured baking tin in a hot oven for 15–20 minutes. Split them, cover with butter and serve hot, or let them get cold and serve with jam and cream or Golden Syrup.

Eel Pie

Eels	Handful of currants
Suet pastry to cover	A little butter
	Sweet herbs

Cut the eels into 2-in. lengths, place them in a pie dish, add sweet seasoning, a handful of currants and a little butter, cover with suet pastry and bake in a moderate oven for about 40 minutes.

Heavy Cake

1½ lb. flour	A little grated lemon
4 oz. beef dripping	peel
2 dessertspoonfuls	4 oz. butter
sugar	12 oz. currants
	1 teaspoonful salt

Mix butter and dripping roughly into the flour. Mix in the other ingredients, add a little water and make into a stiff dough. Roll out on a board, then roll it up again and put aside for 1–2 hours. Roll out again. Cut across with a knife. Bake for 20–30 minutes in a fairly hot oven.

Saffron Cakes

1 lb. 2 oz. flour	2 oz. mixed peel
4 oz. butter	3 oz. sugar
4 oz. lard	Pinch of saffron
½ oz. yeast	A little milk and salt
Pinch of nutmeg	

Mix the ingredients together well, add the yeast, leave till the dough rises and bake in a moderate oven for 50–60 minutes.

Star-gazy Pie

6 herrings, mackerel or pilchards	3 or 4 eggs or cream
	A little pepper and
Tarragon vinegar	salt
Pastry	A little parsley
Breadcrumbs	A little fat
2 uncooked potatoes	

Clean and bone the fish well, and season with salt, pepper and chopped parsley. Do not cut off heads. Place in a pie dish lined with fat and breadcrumbs, with heads facing inwards. Pour the eggs beaten in Tarragon vinegar, or cream over them Put a pastry over the dish (with potatoes as for pasties), leaving a hole in the middle for the heads of the fish to stick out. Bake for about 1 hour in a moderate oven. Place parsley into the mouths of the fish before serving.

CUMBERLAND

Almond Pudding

2 oz. butter	4 oz. rice flour
2 eggs	2 tablespoonfuls
2 oz. castor sugar	ground almond
Raspberry jam	Short pastry (see Pastry Chapter)

Line 3 saucers with short pastry and prick with a fork. Spread a thin layer of raspberry jam over them. Cream butter and sugar, add eggs, and work in rice flour and almonds. Spread over jam, bake in a moderate oven for 30 minutes. Serve hot.

Clipping-time Pudding

8 oz. rice	3 oz. sugar
Beef marrow bones	4 oz. currants
4 oz. stoned raisins	A little cinnamon
1 pint milk	1 egg
A little salt	

Blanch the rice in a little salt water, cook slowly in milk, then add cinnamon and sugar, and boil for a while longer until the rice is tender. Beat the egg and add, with currants and raisins, and stir well together. Then add the marrow cut in small pieces. Bake for 20 minutes in a moderate oven.

Sandcake

2 oz. butter	A little lemon essence
4 oz. cornflour	4 oz. castor sugar
1 teaspoonful baking powder	1 oz. plain flour
	2 eggs, lightly beaten

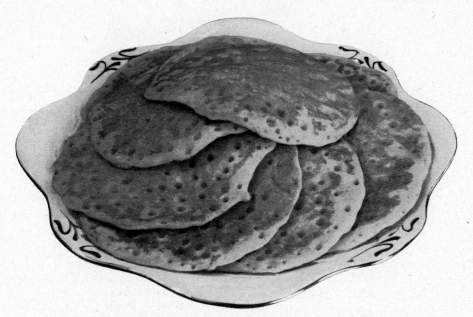

Pikelets come from Durham and are eaten piping hot and spread lavishly with butter

Cream butter and sugar, add lemon essence, eggs, cornflour, plain flour and baking powder. Mix well and bake in a moderate oven in a well-greased, lined tin.

Vanilla Jelly

2 tablespoonfuls sugar	2 eggs
½ oz. powdered gelatine	A little vanilla essence
1 pint milk	

Warm the milk and add egg-yolks beaten with sugar and vanilla essence. Stir over gentle heat until creamy; pour into basin. Dissolve the gelatine in a little water. Add to the milk and pour in the beaten egg-whites. Pour into wetted mould and leave to set. Turn out and serve cold.

DERBYSHIRE

Bakewell Tart

2 eggs	8 oz. sugar	1 heaped table-
4 oz. butter	8 oz. jam	spoon ground
Puff pastry (see Pastry		almonds or
Chapter)		cake crumbs

Line a patty tin with pastry. Cover with a layer of jam. Melt the butter, and stir eggs, sugar and ground almonds or cake crumbs into it. Beat well together. Place a thick layer on the jam-covered pastry. Bake until delicately brown in a moderate oven.

Steamed Batter Pudding (a speciality of Duffield)

3 eggs	3 tablespoonfuls flour
1 pint milk	1 oz. butter
A little salt	

Mix flour with sufficient milk to moisten it, add more milk very gently, stirring all the time. Melt the butter, and stir into the mixture; add salt, beat in the eggs and stir well. Pour into a well-greased pudding basin, seal tightly, place in boiling water and move the basin about for 1 minute to prevent the flour from dropping to the bottom. Boil for 1 hour and 35 minutes. Serve with fruit, jam or wine sauce.

DEVONSHIRE

Devonshire Cream

Pour fresh milk (straight from the cow, bottled milk is no good for it) into a large shallow pan. Leave to stand for at least 6 hours until the cream has risen to the top.

Heat the milk very, very slowly (on no account must it boil) for 1 hour. Do not skim the cream off the milk until it is quite cold, preferably the next day.

Devon Flats

8 oz. Devonshire cream	A little milk
	1 lb. flour
1 egg	8 oz. sugar

Rub the cream into the flour, beat the egg in and add the sugar. Mix well and make into a smooth dough with milk. Roll out very thinly on a board and cut into rounds. Sprinkle with a little sugar and bake in a hot oven for 10 minutes.

Junket

1 pint milk	1 large teaspoonful
A little rum or brandy	essence of rennet
A little sugar	

The milk should be "blood" warm. Mix sugar, milk, rum and rennet, in that order; stir well, then leave to set and do not disturb. Use a pretty dish for making the junket, or individual small pudding dishes.

Squab Pie

1 lb. neck of mutton chops	2 lb. sour apples
	Short pastry to cover
1 onion	(see Pastry Chapter)
Ground allspice	Pepper and salt
¼ pint gravy or water	

Fill a pie dish with a layer of chops and slices of onion and peeled and cored apples. Season well and repeat until the dish is full. Pour in gravy or water and cover with pastry. Bake for 2 hours in moderate oven. Squab is also the name given to a young pigeon, weighing just under 1 lb.

Sally Lunns

1¼ pints milk	1 oz. yeast
4 oz. butter	2 lb. flour
2 oz. lump sugar	Cream
A little castor sugar	

Make a thick batter with 1 pint of warm milk, yeast, flour and a little sugar. Cover and leave to rise in a warm place for 2 hours. Add lump sugar dissolved in ¼ pint warm milk. Rub butter into a little of the flour. Mix with the batter and knead lightly; leave to stand for ½ hour. Make into round cakes and place on tins. When they have risen, bake in a hot oven for 30 minutes. Split and spread with cream.

Widecombe Fair: Spiced Ale and Gingerbread

For the gingerbread

5 oz. butter
1 teaspoonful ginger
6 oz. sugar
6 oz. flour
6 oz. treacle

Rub butter into flour, and add sugar and ginger. Warm the treacle and mix in well. Drop small pieces on a well-greased tin and bake in a moderate oven for 30–40 minutes.

For the spiced ale

1 quart ale
A little mixed spice
1 teaspoonful nutmeg
4 cloves
2 apples
1 teaspoonful sugar

Heat the ale very slowly until very hot, but on no account must it boil. Cut up the apples in slices and add all ingredients. Stir well, strain and serve hot with a slice of apple floating in the glass or tankard.

DORSET

Roast Cygnets

Cygnets (young swans) used to be served at official banquets as far back as the fourteenth century. Cygnets are still eaten once a year at the Vintners' Hall in the City of London, in the traditional manner, covered with a flour-and-water paste.

Stuff the cygnet, trussed the same way as a goose, with minced rump steak well seasoned with grated nutmeg, salt and pepper and finely chopped onions. Sew up, cover the bird with greased paper and roast for about 2 hours, according to size, basting frequently. Serve with gravy and port wine sauce. In former days the birds were wrapped up in a flour-and-water paste and roasted for 4 hours.

DURHAM

Buckwheat Cakes

1 teaspoonful brewer's yeast	A little salt
	3 pints warm water
Buckwheat meal	A little butter

Eccles Cakes, a famous Lancashire delicacy that can easily be made at home

Mix the yeast with water in a basin and stir in buckwheat meal to make a good batter, add salt, cover the basin and let it stand in a warm place to rise. When full of bubbles, pour a spoonful of the batter into a buttered frying pan and cook as for pancakes. Butter the cakes while hot and serve.

Pikelets

8 oz. flour	A little bicarbonate of soda
Buttermilk or sour milk to mix	A little salt
1½ oz. sugar	Lard for frying

Mix flour, sugar and salt. Make a well in the centre and pour in enough buttermilk to make a nice batter. Add bicarbonate of soda, dissolved in a little water. Beat the batter well and fry on a girdle or frying pan in a little lard until golden brown on both sides. Spread with butter and serve hot.

Stanhope Firelighters

4 oz. sugar	4 oz. oats
4 oz. margarine	

Mix all ingredients together and put in a dripping tin. Bake for 30 minutes in a moderate oven. When done, cut into squares.

411

ESSEX

Epping Sausages

1 lb. pork	1 lb. suet
A little sage, thyme, savoury marjoram, lemon, nutmeg	Pepper and salt 1 egg

Mince the pork and shred the suet. Mix all the ingredients together. Make into shape of sausages and fry or grill.

Samphire Pickle

Samphire is common on rocks along the coast (not in the north of England or Scotland). It has fleshy leaves, yellow flowers, and a resinous taste.

1 pint samphire	A few elder buds (or
A few peppercorns	nasturtium seeds)
A little horseradish	A little salt
½ pint cider	½ pint vinegar

Wash the samphire and elder buds, and place in a jar with peppercorns and horseradish and pour boiling vinegar and cider (or wine or water) over them with a little salt. Put the jar into a warm oven for 1 hour to infuse. Seal and store.

GLOUCESTER

Cheese-and-Ale

8 oz. Gloucester cheese	½ pint ale A little mustard
Brown bread	

Cut some Gloucester cheese into thin flakes. Place in a fireproof dish. Spread some mustard over the cheese and cover with ale. Cook in the oven until the cheese is dissolved. Make some toast with thick slices of brown bread, and moisten with hot ale. Pour the cheese over the toast and serve very hot.

Gingerbread Husbands

Figures of men made of gingerbread pressed into wooden moulds, baked and gilded.

HAMPSHIRE

Isle of Wight Doughnuts

2 oz. butter	Pinch of salt
½ oz. yeast	1 lb. flour
Lard	2 eggs
Raspberry jam	1 oz. castor sugar
1½ gills of warm milk	

Mix flour, salt and sugar, and divide into two basins. Rub butter into one, yeast and milk into the other. Let batter mixture rise for ½ hour, then mix both together and beat in the eggs. Let the batter stand for 1 hour to rise. Knead and make into 24 round balls; make a hole and put a little jam in the centre of each. Close up securely. Leave to stand for a little on a floured tin to prove. Drop into a deep bath of boiling fat and fry until a golden brown; then roll in castor sugar.

Friar's Omelet

6 good cooking apples	3 oz. butter
2 oz. sugar	4 egg-yolks
Grated lemon rind	Cloves or nutmeg to
4 oz. breadcrumbs	flavour

Bake the apples till tender. Scrape out the pulp. Cream butter and sugar, add lemon rind, pulp and grated cloves or nutmeg. Grease a pie dish and sprinkle with breadcrumbs. Beat the yolks into the apple in the pie dish, pour the mixture over, cover with breadcrumbs, put small pats of butter on top and bake in a moderate oven for 1½ hours till firm and set.

Hampshire Drops

4 oz. flour	4 oz. castor sugar
1 egg	4 oz. cornflour
4 oz. butter	A little baking
A little jam	powder

Beat butter and sugar until creamy, add egg and beat well, then mix in the other ingredients except jam. Put in teaspoonfuls on a greased tin. Put two together, when all are baked, with a little jam in the middle. They take 10 minutes to bake in a moderate oven.

Mothering Sunday Wafers

2 tablespoonfuls cream	2 tablespoonfuls sugar
2 tablespoonfuls flour	1 tablespoonful orange flower water

Beat all together for 30 minutes, spread very thinly on a flat greased tin, about 6 in. diameter. Bake in a hot oven. Roll over a stick as soon as they are a light golden colour. They are very crisp when dry, and are served with jelly.

HEREFORDSHIRE

Love in Disguise

A calf's heart	4 oz. breadcrumbs
2 tablespoonfuls shredded suet	2 oz. minced ham 4 or 5 slices of fat
A little mustard	bacon
2 teaspoonfuls chopped parsley	1 teaspoonful marjoram
A little lemon rind	Salt and pepper
1 oz. broken-up vermicelli	Gravy made with tomatoes
1 egg	

Cook the vermicelli, drain and leave to get cold; remove all the pipes from the inside of the calf's heart, wash and put in cold water for 1 hour. Make a stuffing from breadcrumbs, suet, a little of the egg, herbs, mustard, salt and pepper, ham and lemon rind. Dry the calf's heart, fill it with the stuffing, wrap the bacon round it and fasten with small skewers. Wrap up in greaseproof paper and cover with fat. Bake in a baking tin for 1½ hours. Remove the paper and brush over with egg-yolk. Then roll in breadcrumbs mixed with vermicelli. Put back in the tin and bake in the oven till nicely browned. Serve with tomato gravy.

HERTFORDSHIRE

Pope Lady Cakes

1 lb. flour	A little baking
12 oz. butter	powder
2 oz. cornstarch	Lemon or almond
1 lb. sugar	extract or rose
16 egg-whites	water

Cream butter and sugar with 8 egg-whites. Sift flour, cornstarch and baking powder, and add to mixture. Beat the remaining egg-whites very stiff and fold in gently. Add the flavouring. Grease two baking tins, pour in the mixture and bake in a slow oven for about 1½ hours.

HUNTINGDONSHIRE

Huntingdon Pudding

8 oz. flour	1 egg
3 oz. castor sugar	A little baking
5 oz. suet	powder
1 pint gooseberries	¼ pint milk

Mix the flour and shredded suet, add sugar, baking powder and gooseberries. Stir well. Beat up the egg in milk, and add to the mixture gradually. Steam in a greased basin for 3 hours and serve with Golden Syrup.

KENT

Huffkins

1 lb. flour (plain)
2½ gills warm milk
and water
1 teaspoonful sugar
1 oz. compressed yeast
½ teaspoonful salt
1 oz. lard

Warm the mixing bowl. Sift flour and salt, and rub in the lard. Cream yeast and sugar in another basin. Add milk and water. Then pour into the flour and make a light dough. Stand in a warm place for 1 hour to rise. Knead well. Then divide into three oval cakes about ½ in. thick. Make a hole in the middle. Flour the cakes and place on a warm tin. Leave in a warm place to prove until well risen. Bake in a hot oven for about 10–20 minutes, according to size. Take out and wrap the cakes in a warm cloth until cool. This will keep the crust soft and tender.

Kentish Cheese Pasties

1 lb. flour	Cayenne pepper and
4 oz. lard	salt to taste
4 oz. butter	12 oz. cheese, cut in
1 egg	- very thin flakes,
	mixed with butter

Make some flaky pastry (see Pastry chapter) with flour, butter and lard. Roll out very thin on a board and cut into circles the size of a saucer. Put a tablespoonful of the cheese in the centre and sprinkle with salt and Cayenne pepper. Moisten the edges of the pasties and fold up. Brush over with beaten egg. Bake in a hot oven for about 15–20 minutes and serve hot.

Oast Cakes

1 lb. flour	2 oz. sugar
4 oz. lard	A little lemon juice
6 oz. currants	1 teaspoonful baking
A little salt	powder
A little water to mix	Lard for frying

Lancashire's traditional Hot Pot is a nourishing and tasty dish for a cold wintry day

Mix dry ingredients and rub in the lard, add currants. Make a light dough with a little water and add lemon juice. Shape the dough into small pieces and roll out on a board. Fry in lard until golden brown. Serve hot.

Twice Laid

Codfish	A little fat
A little milk	Mashed potatoes
Salt and pepper	1 egg
	Breadcrumbs

Divide the remains of codfish or cold salt fish into flakes. Mix in twice as much mashed potatoes. Add a little milk. Season with salt and pepper and make into balls. Dip into the egg, roll in breadcrumbs and fry in fat until brown.

LANCASHIRE

Eccles Cakes

Shortcrust pastry (see Pastry Chapter)	1 oz. ground almonds
A little nutmeg	4 oz. Golden Syrup
4 oz. currants	A little lemon juice
	1 oz. ground coconut

Line some patty pans with shortcrust, put in each a layer of syrup, then currants, spice, lemon juice, coconut and almonds. Cover with pastry. Roll over with the pin very gently. Bake in a moderate oven for about 30 minutes.

Brawn

1 pig's head	A little lemon rind,
1 tongue	cloves, mace,
1 heart	pepper and salt
	¼ pint vinegar

Simmer the meat very gently in a saucepan with enough water to cover. When tender, remove the bones and cut the meat into small pieces. Return to the water, add seasoning and vinegar. Boil up once and pour into a mould and leave to set in a cool place. Turn out when cold.

Lancashire Hot Pot

2 lb. mutton chops	Cayenne pepper and
2 lb. potatoes	salt to season
8 oz. mushrooms	1 lb. onions
2 oz. ham (or bacon)	2 oz. butter
3 sheep's kidneys	½ pint stock (or water)

Cut the kidneys, peel and slice the onions and potatoes, and chop the ham. Place a layer of chops in a casserole, then the kidneys, mushrooms, ham, onions and potatoes, and season every layer; the last layer must be potatoes. Pour over the stock and put little pieces of butter on top. Cover the casserole and cook *very* slowly for about 3 hours. Take the lid off and brown the top before serving.

Manchester Pudding

Shortcrust pastry (see Pastry Chapter)	Jam (stoneless)
2 oz. butter	2 eggs
1 oz. castor sugar	1 tablespoonful
Rind of 1 lemon	brandy
	½ pint milk
2 oz. breadcrumbs	

Boil the lemon rind in milk and pour over the breadcrumbs. Take the rind out and beat in the egg-yolks after 5 minutes with butter, sugar and brandy. Line a pie dish with pastry and spread some jam over it. Cover with the breadcrumbs mixture and bake in a moderate oven for 45 minutes. Whip the egg-whites with some castor sugar and lay over the dish. Return to the oven for 1 minute to set. Serve cold.

Parkin

1½ lb. oatmeal	1 teaspoonful ground
8 oz. brown sugar	ginger
1 lb. treacle	8 oz. butter
1 teaspoonful allspice	

Mix the dry ingredients. Heat treacle and butter; add to the dry mixture and leave to stand overnight. Place in a well-greased shallow baking tin and bake in a moderate oven for about 2 hours. It is done when the parkin springs back when touched.

Potted Shrimps

1 pint shrimps	4 oz. butter
1 blade ground mace	A little Cayenne
A little ground nutmeg	pepper

Only the freshest shrimps should be used. Melt the butter, add seasoning and shelled shrimps. Heat through gently, but do not boil. Pour into small pots and eat when cold.

Tripe and Onions

1 lb. tripe	½ pint milk
½ pint water	A little flour
2 onions	Salt and pepper

Wash the tripe well, cut into square pieces and bring to the boil in water. Throw the water away and add water and milk, chopped onions, salt and pepper. Thicken with flour, after having boiled the tripe for a good 3 hours, by stirring it in with a little milk. Bring to the boil again and serve.

414

From Grantham, Lincolnshire, comes the unusual White Gingerbread (above), which is baked very pale. Below, Parkin from Lancashire

off after a short while; leave for 24 hours. By that time the husks should have burst and the wheat set to a thick jelly This process is to "cree" or stew the wheat, and is then called "frumenty wheat." It can be eaten as a breakfast food with milk and sugar, or with eggs beaten in with it, or as a sweet with fruit and cream.

Melton Mowbray Pie

> 2 lb. pork cut in small
>   dice
> 1½ lb. flour
> 1 egg
> 1 lb. lard
> A little milk and
>   water mixed
> Salt and pepper to
>   taste

Rub half the quantity of lard into the flour with a little salt. Boil the rest of the lard with the milk and water. When boiling, pour half over the flour and stir well, then add the egg (beaten well) and pour over the rest of the liquid. Knead the mixture and leave to stand for a few minutes. Line a mould or tin, and put in the pork with a little pepper and salt and a little water. Roll out the rest of the pastry and cover the top of the pie and decorate the edge. Brush over with a little egg and bake for 2 hours, starting with a very hot oven and reducing the heat. Make a stock of the bones and trimmings of the meat until it jells. Pour into a hole in the centre of the pie with a funnel when lukewarm. Serve cold.

LEICESTERSHIRE

Bosworth Jumbels

8 oz. flour	6 oz. butter
1 lb. sugar	1 large egg

Beat the sugar and butter, and stir in the egg. Add flour and mix thoroughly. Shape pieces of the mixture into the form of an S and place on a hot greased tin. Bake in a moderate oven until brown.

This recipe is said to have been picked up on the battlefield of Bosworth, having been dropped by Richard III's cook.

Frumenty (see also under Lincolnshire)

Wash wheat. Place in a stone jar and fill with three times the wheat's measure of water. Put in a hot oven, but turn the oven

LINCOLNSHIRE

Apple Pudding

9 apples	2 eggs
½ lemon	Puff pastry (see
2 oz. Demerara sugar	Pastry Chapter)
A little cinnamon	8 oz. butter
Cloves and nutmeg	

Peel, core and slice the apples. Stew in a little water until soft, add cloves, nutmeg and cinnamon. Pass through a sieve and mix in butter, egg-yolks, one egg-white and sugar; add lemon juice and mix well together. Line a pie dish with puff pastry, decorate the edges and pour in the mixture. Bake in a moderate oven for 20 minutes.

Frumenty (see also Leicestershire)

1 quart frumenty wheat	Sugar to sweeten
2 oz. raisins	1 quart milk
	A little nutmeg
A little flour	

Boil the frumenty wheat in milk for about 15 minutes, add the other ingredients and when it begins to thicken, stir in a little flour made into a cream with a little milk. Boil up and serve.

Grantham Gingerbread (White)

8 oz. flour	A little baking
4 oz. sugar	powder
1 oz. ground ginger	4 oz. butter
1 egg	

Cream butter and sugar, beat in egg-yolk, add flour, baking powder and ginger. Whip the egg-white and fold into the mixture. Bake on a greased paper in a moderate oven for 30–40 minutes, but keep pale in colour.

Mock Goose

Sage and onion stuffing	Leg of pork

Parboil the pork. Take off skin and bone. Fill the void with the stuffing. Press into the shape of a goose and roast until golden brown. Serve with apple sauce and brown gravy.

LONDON

Chelsea Buns

12 oz. flour	¼ oz. yeast
4 oz. sugar	4 oz. butter
1 lemon	2 eggs
A little milk	

Warm the milk and add the yeast creamed with a little sugar. Rub half the butter into the flour and add half the sugar. Beat in the eggs and yeast, a little lemon rind and juice and leave to rise in a warm place for about 2 hours. Knead the dough and roll out on a board about ¼ in. thick. Spread the other half of butter and sugar over the dough. Fold in three, roll out

again into a square. Roll up the dough and cut into thick slices. Leave to stand for about 20 minutes to prove. Bake in a moderate oven for 20 minutes.

Johnny Cakes (or London Buns)

2 lb. flour	1 oz. candied orange
4 oz. castor sugar	peel
1 pint milk	1 egg
1 oz. yeast	3 oz. butter

Sift flour and sugar into a basin. Melt butter in a saucepan and add milk. Dissolve the yeast in the milk. Pour into centre of the flour, mix well; add finely cut orange peel. Leave the dough to rise in a warm place for about 2 hours. Knead and make into 24 round buns. Place on a greased baking sheet and let them prove. Bake in a hot oven for 30 minutes. Brush over with a little egg and sugar mixed, to glaze the buns.

MONMOUTHSHIRE
Backstone Cakes (Baxton, Bakestone)

8 oz. flour	Cream to mix
2 oz. butter	

Rub the butter into the flour and make into a stiff paste with cream. Roll out very thin and cut into small rounds. Bake on a backstone or girdle; turn once or twice until lightly browned. Split, butter and serve hot.

Treacle Posset

2 pints ale	2 teaspoonfuls grated
4 oz. treacle	nutmeg
1 pint milk	

Heat the ale and melt the treacle in milk and mix together. Add nutmeg and serve very hot.

NORFOLK
Biffins

Take some Norfolk biffins (red-cheeked apples), choosing the clearest without any blemishes, lay them on clean straw on baking wire and cover well with some more straw. Set them in a very slow oven for about 4 or 5 hours. Draw them out and press them very gently, so as not to burst the skins. Put back in the oven for another hour, and press again. Rub them over with clarified sugar when cold. These are the dried biffins sold in Norwich.

Norfolk and Suffolk are the counties for dumplings, which are either eaten as a separate dish or added to a stew

Dumplings

1 lb. flour	1 teaspoonful castor
¼ pint hot water	sugar
½ oz yeast	A little milk

Cream yeast and sugar. Pour milk and water over the yeast. Put flour into a basin and pour milk and yeast into it, making a well in the centre. Mix well and allow to rise for about 2 hours. Knead the dough well and form into dumplings. Allow these to stand for 10 minutes. Have ready a saucepan with boiling water, throw in the dumplings and boil for 20 minutes. Serve hot with a little melted butter and a sprinkling of sugar, or omit the sugar when preparing the dumplings and serve hot with meat and gravy.

Pork Cheese (Brawn)

A hock of salt pork	Pepper and sage to
	season

Stand the hock in cold water for 12 hours. Place in a saucepan with enough water to cover. Boil until the meat comes off the bone. Lift out and remove the bones. Put the bones back into the saucepan and simmer. Rub a little pepper into the meat and add finely chopped sage. Cut up the meat very finely. Strain the stock over the meat (there should be ½ pint left). Pour into wetted basin. Turn out when cold.

NORTHAMPTONSHIRE

Cheese Cakes

Some short or flaky	A little grated nutmeg
pastry (see Pastry	2 oz. currants
Chapter)	1 egg
1 oz. butter	1 pint sour milk
1½ oz. sugar	A little grated lemon
A little almond	rind
essence	

Stir butter, egg and sugar in a saucepan over a low fire until thick; do not allow to boil. Boil the sour milk until it separates into curds and whey. Strain off the curd, press well. Add it to the mixture when cold, with currants, spice, flavourings. Line some patty pans with pastry, fill them with the mixture and bake in a hot oven for about 10 minutes. Cheese cakes and frumenty were eaten at sheep-shearing.

Fig Pudding

8 oz. dried figs	A little salt
2 eggs	4 oz. flour
4 oz. sugar	6 oz. grated suet
½ pint milk	

Chop the figs and mix with suet, flour, salt and sugar. Beat eggs and add. Make into a dough with milk, place in a greased pudding basin and steam for 3½ hours.

Dried figs were sold in quantities for fig pudding on Fig (Palm) Sunday.

Seed Cake

1 lb. flour	1 lb. butter
1 lb. sugar	8 eggs
2 oz. caraway seeds	1 grated nutmeg

Separate the egg-yolks from the whites. Beat the butter to a cream, add the sugar, and then beat the egg-whites and add, beat the egg-yolks and add. Beat in the flour, spice and seeds, turn into a greased cake-tin and bake in a hot oven for 1½ hours.

Seed cake was eaten at sheep-shearing.

Venison Pasty

1 lb. venison	A few herbs
¼ pint port wine	Pie crust (see
Salt and pepper to	Pastry Chapter)
taste	Redcurrant sauce
2 onions	

Chop the meat and onions very fine. Boil for 3 hours, add port wine, herbs and seasoning, and simmer until the meat is quite tender. Strain the meat and put in a pie, when cold, and add as much of the gravy as desired. Bake in a moderate oven for 1 hour. Serve hot or cold, with redcurrant sauce.

NORTHUMBERLAND

Felton Spice Loaf

4 oz. butter	A little milk
2 eggs	4 oz. sugar
2 oz. ground almonds	8 oz. currants
4 oz. plain flour	2 oz. shredded peel
4 oz. self-raising flour	

Sieve almonds and flour. Mix peel and currants in a separate basin. Cream butter and sugar, and add eggs, beating all the time. Add flour and milk, then mix in the fruit. Turn into a well-greased dripping tin and spread level. Bake in a fairly hot oven for about 30 minutes, turning the heat down half-way through.

Pan Haggerty

1 lb. potatoes	Pepper and salt
A little dripping	8 oz. onions
4 oz. grated cheese	

Peel potatoes and onions, cut in very thin slices and dry the potatoes in a cloth. Make the dripping hot in a pan, put in a layer of potatoes, then of onions, then cheese and another layer of potatoes. Season each layer with pepper and salt. Fry gently until nearly cooked through, then either turn in the pan or brown the haggerty under the grill.

Pickled Salmon

Salmon	A little mace, cloves,
Vinegar	pepper and salt
White wine	

Boil the salmon in salt water, sufficient to cover. Drain off the liquor when cooked and place the salmon in a deep dish, pour over it equal quantities of the liquor, vinegar and white wine, seasoned with a little mace, pepper and some cloves. Leave to stand in a cool place until next day. Warm the salmon in the liquor and serve hot.

Singin' Hinnies

Singin' Hinnies get their name from the fact that they are so rich that they sing and sizzle while they cook.

1 lb. flour	½ teaspoonful cream
¼ teaspoonful bicar-	of tartar
bonate of soda	6 oz. currants
4 oz. lard	A little mutton fat
A little milk	4 oz. butter
A little salt	

Rub the lard and butter into the flour. Add the cream of tartar, bicarbonate and salt. Add the currants. Make into a stiff dough with the milk. Shape into a round and roll out to ½-in. thickness. Rub the girdle with a little mutton fat. Place the cake on it and cook until the underside is brown. Turn carefully with a palette knife. Turn again when cooked, to have it quite hot. Cut into pieces, split, butter and serve hot.

Snails

Snails are best from spring to autumn.

Drop them into boiling salt water and boil for 30 minutes. Take off the shells and cut away the hard bits. Put the meat into a fireproof dish with a little butter, garlic, pepper, salt and chopped parsley. Cover, and bake in a hot oven for 10 minutes. Serve with brown bread and butter and lemon.

Snails used to be the traditional fare at the Glassmakers' Feast.

NOTTINGHAMSHIRE

Cowslip Vinegar

2 *pints cowslip "pips"*	1 *pint white wine*
Soda water	*vinegar*
Brandy	*Lump sugar*

Gather the cowslips on a dry day. Pick all the flower "pips" from the stalks. Put them into a basin. Pour on white wine vinegar and leave to stand in a cool place for 3 days to infuse. Wet a piece of muslin with vinegar and strain the liquor from the pips into a stone jar; add 1 lb. lump sugar to every pint of liquor. Stir until the sugar is dissolved. Cover the jar, set in a saucepan of boiling water and boil for 1 hour. Add 1 wineglassful of brandy to each pint. Bottle when cold and seal the corks. Dilute with soda water as a cooling drink.

Pork Pie

4 lb. pork
4 oz. suet
8 oz. butter
Salt, pepper and sage
   to taste
8 oz. lard
4 lb. flour
Stock for the gravy
   made from 2 pig's
   feet and 1 pint water

Rub fats into flour and knead into a stiff dough with water. Roll out 1 in. thick and line a greased tin with it. Cut up the pork very fine, put into the tin and season. Pour stock from the pig's feet over it (this will jelly when cold). Cover the pie, but leave a little opening. Bake in a moderate oven for 2½ hours. When cool, add more stock through the opening. Serve cold.

OXFORDSHIRE

Banbury Apple Pie

5 good-sized cooking
   apples
3 oz. sugar
4 oz. currants
Shortcrust (see
   Pastry Chapter)
2 oz. candied peel
3 oz. butter
A little ground ginger
   and cinnamon
A little milk

Peel and slice the apples. Place a layer in a greased pie dish, then the chopped peel, spices and currants. Pour a little melted butter on top. Place another layer of apples and chopped peel over it. Boil ½ pint of water, melt some sugar in it and pour over the apples. Cover with short pastry and bake for 30 minutes in a moderate oven. Glaze with a little sugar and milk.

Brasenose Ale

6 *quarts of ale*	*Sugar*
Nutmeg and cloves	6 *roast apples*

Heat the ale, season with nutmeg and cloves, add sugar to taste and float the apples in it.

This is served in Brasenose College hall, in an enormous silver tankard, after dinner on Shrove Tuesday.

Tripe and Onions, as cooked in Lancashire—long and slowly in milk

Carrot Pudding

2 lb. carrots	2 tablespoonfuls flour
1 egg	A little butter
A little milk	Salt and pepper

Boil the carrots until soft, then mash. Melt butter and brown the flour in it, add milk and seasoning, and mix well. Add egg-yolk and carrots. Beat the egg-white and fold into the mixture. Put in a greased pudding basin, tie up and steam for 15 minutes. Turn out, pour a little melted butter over it and serve hot.

Oxford Pudding

6 apricots	2 egg-whites
A little cream	Puff pastry (see
Sugar to taste	Pastry Chapter)
4 eggs	

Steam the apricots until tender. Cut up and add a little sugar to taste. When cold, beat in the whole eggs and cream. Butter a pie dish and line with puff pastry. Place the mixture over it and bake for about 30 minutes in a hot oven; turn the oven down for the last 15 minutes. Beat up the 2 egg-whites, add a little sugar and place over the dish. Bake in a hot oven for 10 minutes.

RUTLAND

Plum Shuttles or Valentine Buns

Buns of an oval shape like a weaver's shuttle, carried round on Valentine's Day. They have currants and caraway seeds.

SHROPSHIRE

Fidget Pie

1 lb. potatoes	8 oz. onions
8 oz. bacon or ham	Pepper and salt to
½ pint stock	taste
Sugar or Golden	Shortcrust to cover
Syrup to taste	(see Pastry Chapter)
1 lb. apples	

Peel and slice the potatoes, apples and onions. Cut the ham or bacon into small pieces. Place a layer of the potatoes in the bottom of the dish, then the bacon and apples (add sugar or Golden Syrup if sour). Repeat until the dish is quite full. Season each layer with a little salt and pepper, and sprinkle with onions. Pour the stock over it all. Cover the dish with the shortcrust and bake for 1½ hours in a moderate oven.

Shrewsbury Biscuits (see also Biscuits chapter)

4 oz. butter	1 egg
A little baking powder	8 oz. flour
	4 oz. sugar

Beat the butter to a cream, add sugar, beaten egg, baking powder and flour. Mix well and roll out on a board to ¼ in. thickness. Cut into rounds and prick. Bake in a moderate oven. Sprinkle sugar over them while still hot.

Shrewsbury Cakes

8 oz. butter	8 oz. castor sugar
¼ gill cream	½ lemon
1 egg	8 oz. flour

Cream butter and sugar, add the egg, then the flour, grated lemon rind and juice and, lastly, the cream. Turn out on a board and knead well. Leave to stand for ½ hour. Roll out thinly, cut into small rounds and place on a greased baking sheet. Bake in a moderate oven for about 10 minutes. Sometimes a little sherry, rose water, caraway seeds or nutmeg are added.

SOMERSET

Bath Buns

1 lb. flour	A few caraway seeds
4 oz. butter	½ oz. yeast
2 oz. crushed lump sugar	3 oz. castor sugar
	3 eggs
2 oz. sultanas	3 oz. candied peel
1 gill milk	

Cream the yeast with a little sugar, add milk, strain into half the flour and mix well. Leave to stand until risen. Rub butter into other half of the flour, and add sultanas, castor sugar, candied peel and yeast mixture. Beat in the eggs well and leave to rise again. Form into 12 rocky buns, sprinkle with crushed lump sugar and caraway seeds. Let them "prove," and bake in a moderate oven for about 15 minutes.

Plovers' Eggs

Plovers' eggs are a great April delicacy. They should be semi-hard-boiled by simmering gently for 5 minutes. It is, however, now legally forbidden to take all the eggs from the nests. Each nest always has four eggs; only two eggs should ever be taken from each nest at a time; the hen then lays another and the process is repeated. This has the indirect result of giving the young plover a better start in life, since the last batch of four eggs will hatch out in May when the weather is milder. Gulls' eggs are very similar to, and are often sold in place of, plovers' eggs.

Singin' Hinnies hail from Northumberland and get their name because they are so rich they sizzle as they cook

STAFFORDSHIRE
Whip Syllabub

½ gill brandy
½ gill sweet wine
¼ lb. sugar
1½ pints cream
1 lemon (juice and
    grated rind)

Whisk all the ingredients well, take off the froth as it rises and put on a sieve. Fill some custard dishes with the mixture and cover with froth.

Yeomanry Pudding

4 eggs (4 yolks, 2 whites)
Some raspberry jam
1 oz. ground almonds
8 oz. butter   Rich pastry to cover
8 oz. castor sugar   (see Pastry Chapter)

Grease a pie dish and line with some of the pastry. Spread a layer of jam over the bottom of the dish. Beat the yolks and whites together. Cream the butter, and add sugar, almonds and beaten eggs. Pour over the jam and bake in a hot oven for a little, then reduce heat and bake for about 50 minutes.

SUFFOLK
Almond Pudding

4 oz. ground almonds   2 egg-whites
¾ pint cream   2 oz. castor sugar
4 egg-yolks   A little rose or orange
1½ oz. breadcrumbs   water
        A little butter

Warm the cream and pour over the breadcrumbs, stir in sugar, almonds and flavouring. Beat up egg-yolks and egg-whites. Mix well with the other mixture and place in a pie dish. Put a little butter on the top and bake in a moderate oven for 30 minutes.

Suffolk Dumplings

Dough made with yeast and milk as for bread (see Bread chapter) left to rise 1 hour in a warm place. Make into balls the size of an apple. Throw in boiling water and boil for 20 minutes. Test by sticking a fork into the dumplings; if it comes out clean, they are done. Serve immediately with gravy, butter or meat.

SURREY
Maids of Honour Cakes

These cakes are said to derive their name from Queen Elizabeth's maids of honour when she lived at Richmond Palace. The recipe is taken from a cooking manuscript of the period.

4 oz. butter   Grated rind of 1
1 oz. sugar   lemon
½ pint milk   2 tablespoonfuls
3 eggs   breadcrumbs
2 oz. ground almonds   Puff pastry (see
                         Pastry Chapter)

Boil the milk with breadcrumbs, and let the mixture stand for a few minutes; then add butter, sugar, almonds and lemon rind. Beat in the eggs, one at a time; line some patty pans with puff pastry and place the mixture in them. Bake in a hot oven until they are golden brown.

SUSSEX
Arundel Mullets

Mullet   2 onions
A little lemon juice   Salt and pepper to
2 wineglassfuls red   taste
  wine   A bunch of sweet
A little nutmeg   herbs
        A few anchovies

Boil the mullet very gently in salt water for about 15 minutes. Pour away half the water and keep the fish warm. Add the wine, with finely chopped onions and the other ingredients, and cook gently until done. Serve the fish in a shallow dish and pour the sauce over. Shrimp or oyster sauce may be used as well. Mullet is also very good fried in butter and served with lemon and anchovies.

Chiddingly Hot Pot

1 lb. beef	8 oz. celery
8 oz. olives	A little tarragon
A little allspice	vinegar
1 lb. potatoes	A little malt vinegar
A few cloves and	1 lb. onions or
black peppercorns	shallots

Place a layer of chopped onions on the bottom of a large casserole dish with chopped olives and celery. Put thin slices of beef over them and sprinkle with spices and vinegars. Cut potatoes into thin slices and place over the meat with some more chopped olives. Repeat until all the ingredients are used up. Pour enough water into the casserole nearly to cover. Cook in a low oven for about 3–4 hours according to quantities used. The vinegar renders additional salt unnecessary.

Ifield Vicarage Hog's Pudding

1 lb. pork	A little allspice
A little baking powder	1 lb. currants
1½ lb. flour	Some sausage skins
	1 lb. lard

Cut the meat into small pieces and put on to boil gently for about 1 hour. Mix the flour and baking powder with the meat, currants and spice, and rub in the lard. Fill sausage skins and tie up in bunches. Prick the sausages with a fork and drop into boiling water. Boil them for 1½ hours. Take out and hang up to dry. They will snap when broken in two. Hog's pudding is usually the size of an egg and irregular in shape, and is generally eaten as a savoury, either hot or cold.

Lardy Johns

4 oz. flour	A few currants
A little baking powder	2 teaspoonfuls sugar
2 oz. lard	

Rub all the ingredients together and make into a stiff dough with a little water. Roll out thinly and cut into squares. Bake for 10 minutes in a hot oven.

Sussex Blanket Pudding

12 oz. flour	2 eggs
A little pepper and	12 oz. suet
salt	8 oz. breadcrumbs
A little milk	

Mix dry ingredients together and fold in the eggs. Make into a light dough with a little milk. Roll out and spread one of the fillings (see below) over the dough. Roll up in a floured cloth and boil for 2–3 hours.

Fillings.—(1) Liver and bacon, minced, with parsley and onion; (2) sausage meat; (3) any scraps of minced meat.

Sweet fillings.—(1) Jam or Golden Syrup; (2) mincemeat; (3) chopped apples, a little butter, and orange marmalade or quince jam; (4) finely chopped peel, currants, raisins and sugar.

Sussex Heavies

2 breakfastcupfuls	1 teacupful milk
flour	soured with the
1 oz. castor sugar	juice of half a
2 oz. currants	lemon
2 oz. lard	

Rub lard into flour, add sugar and currants and make into a stiff pastry with soured milk. Roll out on a board to 1-in. thickness, cut into small rounds, brush over with a little soured milk, place in a moderate oven and bake for 15 minutes.

WARWICKSHIRE

Baked Apples and Caraway Comfits

1 tablespoonful icing	1 tablespoonful
sugar	caraway seeds
6 baking apples	A little gum arabic
A little starch	

Clean and core the apples, place in a pie dish and bake in the usual way. Clarify the sugar. Dissolve the gum arabic in a little hot water. Put a sixth part of the sugar, starch and gum in a small saucepan, boil the mixture and add the caraway seeds. Add a little more gum and stir the pan until the seeds are dry. Take the comfits out of the pan and place in a sieve. Repeat the process 5 times, cleaning out the pan each time. Dry the caraway comfits in a low oven. Sprinkle over the baked apples.

Crayfish and Bacon Savoury

3 freshly boiled cray-	A little salt and
fish	pepper
6 pieces of buttered	6 rashers of bacon
toast	

Cut the bacon into small pieces and fry gently in a frying pan. Cut up the crayfish into small pieces and add to the bacon when there is enough fat in the pan for them not to stick. Fry for a few minutes, season, pour on to hot buttered toast.

WESTMORLAND

Easter-ledge, Dandelion or Nettle Pudding

Easter-ledge leaves (Persicaria)
1 egg
A little butter
Pepper and salt to taste
Boiled barley

Take young Easter-ledge leaves, or nettle. Wash, drop into boiling water and cook for about 20 minutes. Strain and chop. Add a little boiled barley, hard-boil the egg, chop up and add to the leaves with a little butter and pepper and salt. Put the mixture into the saucepan and heat through, turn into a pudding basin and press well down; then turn out on a plate and serve with meat.

WILTSHIRE

Devizes Pie

A few slices of cold calf's head, cold lamb, calf's brains, tongue and bacon
Pastry to cover (see Pastry chapter)
3 hard-boiled eggs
Spice
Cayenne pepper and salt to taste
Gravy

Season the meat and place in a pie dish in layers with the eggs cut in rings. Fill the dish with a rich clear gravy, made from the calf's head. Cover the pie with pastry and bake in a moderate oven for about 1 hour. Turn into a dish when cold. Garnish the edge with parsley and serve.

YORKSHIRE

Doncaster Butterscotch

1 lb. brown sugar
6 oz. butter
½ pint milk
A little cream of tartar

Melt the sugar in milk over a low heat, add butter and cream of tartar. Boil until a little dropped into cold water hardens. Pour into greased tins and leave to set.

Solomon Gundy

6 herrings
A few capers, mushrooms and pickled oysters
1 large apple
4 oz. anchovies
Peel of 2 lemons
1 onion, shredded

Boil the herrings as gently as possible. Take the fish from the bone, without removing head and tail. Do not break the bones. Shred and mix the herring meat with anchovies, apple, onion and a little grated lemon peel. Lay the mixture over each of the bones in the shape of a herring. Garnish with lemon peel, capers, mushrooms and pickled oysters.

Yorkshire Pudding (see Puddings chapter)

ISLE OF MAN

Sollaghan (served on Christmas Day)

Put some oatmeal in a pan over a low heat and stir until crisp and dry. Then skim the top of the stock pot on to it and stir well. Eat with pepper and salt.

Maids of Honour come from Richmond, Surrey, and were named after the first Queen Elizabeth's ladies when she lived at Richmond Palace

423

SCOTLAND

*Many a world-famous dish, from haggis to porridge,
hails from North of the Border*

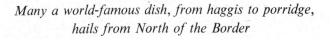

SOUPS

Cock-a-Leekie Soup (for 10)

2–3 *bunches of leeks*   5 *quarts of stock*
1 *boiling fowl*   *Seasoning*

Wash the leeks well (if old, scald them in boiling water). Take off the roots and part of the heads, and cut them into 1-in. lengths. Put half the quantity into a pot with the stock and the fowl and simmer gently for ¼ hour. Add the remaining leeks and simmer for 3–4 hours. Skim carefully and season to taste. Before serving, carve the fowl, place the pieces in tureen or plates and pour the soup over.

Hare Soup

1 *hare*	4 *peppercorns*
3 *carrots*	1 *stick celery, or 1*
½ *turnip*	*teaspoonful celery*
4 *onions*	*salt*
Small bunch thyme	*Butter for frying*
and parsley	*Flour*

After the hare has been skinned, cleaned and cut up, put into a basin of cold water for a few minutes. Then take the pieces out, dip in flour and fry in butter. The blood should have been retained. Add to the water in the basin and strain in with the meat; stir till it boils. Season and simmer for 6–8 hours, adding the vegetables about 2 hours before the cooking is done. Take out the back when cooked and save for cutting in dice when the soup is served. If not thick enough, add a little flour and butter thickening.

FISH

Baked Stuffed Haddock

1 *large fresh haddock*	1 *teaspoonful*
3 *oz. breadcrumbs*	*chopped parsley (or*
1 *oz. chopped suet*	*other herbs if*
Pepper and salt	*preferred)*
	A little milk

Mix the breadcrumbs, suet and seasoning well together with a little milk. Wipe the fish, cut off fins, scrape a little to remove scales. Wipe the inside with a moistened cloth dipped in salt. Stuff and fix with a skewer or by sewing, which can be easily undone after cooking.

Sprinkle with breadcrumbs and put small bits of suet or butter on top. Bake in moderate oven for 25–30 minutes. Serve with egg or brown sauce (see Sauces).

Fillets of haddock may also be stuffed in this way, rolled up and cooked in casserole or a pie dish for 20–25 minutes.

Baked White Fish

Brill and halibut are the usual fish used in this recipe, but haddock, monkfish and cod are also very tasty done this way.

Cut the fish in neat pieces and place flat in a pie dish. Sprinkle freely with soft breadcrumbs seasoned with salt, pepper, chopped parsley and grated nutmeg to taste. Just cover with milk, and place on each piece of fish a small piece of butter. Bake in a quick oven until nicely browned —about 15 minutes. A little grated cheese may be added on top, if liked.

Fish Custard (for 2)

¼ *lb. filleted white*	1 *egg*
fish	*Salt and pepper*
½ *pint milk*	*Nutmeg if liked*
	A little flour

Cut the fish into neat pieces and dip in seasoned flour. A little nutmeg, if liked, much improves the seasoning. Place in a greased pie dish. Beat the egg, add milk, pour over the fish and bake carefully in a moderate oven until nicely browned and set.

Fried Trout

Mushrooms	*Trout*
Truffles (if available)	*Salt*
Tomato sauce	*Pepper*
	Egg and breadcrumbs

Prepare a stuffing of well-minced mushrooms, truffles, salt and pepper. Clean and empty trout, allowing one per person. Fill with stuffing. Sew the fish up and

Herrings fried in oatmeal, garnished with lemon and parsley, are good for breakfast or supper and full of nourishment

cook gently in Court Bouillon, made as under. Leave to get cold, drain well, dip in beaten egg-yolk and breadcrumbs. Fry and serve with tomato sauce.

Court Bouillon.—Water, salt, pepper, carrots, onion, thyme, bay leaf, clove, vinegar, white wine (or half wine, half water). The fish must be entirely covered whilst cooking.

Haddock Cases

1 *smoked haddock*	1 *gill thick cream*
(cooked)	1 *oz. butter*
A little Cayenne	*Bread*
pepper	1 *egg-white*

Pound the butter and cooked haddock. Pass through a sieve. Add the cream and flavour with pepper. Beat to a rich purée. Meanwhile, prepare some tiny cases of fried bread. Fill with the mixture and cover them with stiffly whipped egg-white. Bake in a slow oven till the white is crisp and pale brown in colour.

Herrings Fried in Oatmeal

Wash and clean herrings in usual way. Roll well in fine oatmeal and fry in boiling fat from which the smoke is rising.

Partan (Crab) Pie

Take the meat from the claws and body of the crab. Then clean the shell thoroughly. Season the crab meat with salt, white pepper and nutmeg, adding some pieces of fresh butter and breadcrumbs. You may add to it also a wine-glassful of vinegar, seasoned, if liked, with a little mustard. Alternatively, salad oil can be substituted for the butter. Then return the crab meat to the shell and brown under the grill.

Pickled Herrings

Herrings	*Mace*
Pepper and salt	*Butter*
1 *bay leaf*	*Vinegar*

Wash the required number of herrings in cold water and a little salt, remove the heads and tails, split them down the back and take out the backbones: then dry well in a cloth, sprinkle with a little pepper and salt, and lay on each herring a piece of butter the size of a filbert. Then roll the herring up, beginning at the head, and place in a dish with the bay leaf and mace. and vinegar to cover. Cook in a slow oven for 1 hour or until done.

Scotch Potatoes

Bake some large potatoes in their jackets (one or more for each person), break them in half with a fork and scoop out the insides and beat up in a bowl with plenty of margarine, salt, pepper, a little anchovy or Worcester sauce, and some chopped cooked fish. Stuff the potato shells with the mixture. Sprinkle each one generously with grated cheese, dot with margarine and brown under grill.

Whiting in the Scots Way

Choose small fish if you can, and be sure they are quite fresh. Then rub them in flour until it adheres. They should, traditionally, be fried in butter, but the best cooking fat may have to suffice. Sauté them very slowly—they should *not* be dry or coloured. Mince some parsley and chives (or small green onions) very finely; put them into some good broth with 2 tablespoonfuls of top of the milk, mix well together and pour over the whiting before they are quite cooked. Move the fish about gently so as not to break them until they are done. A simple method, but great care is required in the frying.

MEAT DISHES

Beef Soufflé (for 2–3)

¼ lb. lean roast beef	3 egg-yolks
Pepper	4 egg-whites
Salt	Shallot

For the sauce

1 oz. butter	1 teacupful beef gravy
½ tablespoonful flour	Worcester or anchovy
1 tablespoonful	sauce
mushroom ketchup	Pepper and salt

To make the sauce.—Melt the butter, add flour and cook for 1 minute. Stir in gravy, ketchup and sauce, and add pepper and salt. Boil until it thickens.

Mince and pound the beef with the sauce, season well with pepper and salt. Add the egg-yolks. Put through a sieve and mix in chopped shallot to taste. Fold in lightly the stiffly beaten egg-whites. Pour into a soufflé dish, lay a paper over the top to prevent burning, and bake for 20 minutes.

Galantine or Bassamore (for 5–6)

2 lb. fillet of veal	Breadcrumbs
¼ lb. ham	Pepper, salt, nutmeg
3 egg-yolks	A pinch of mace
2 egg-whites	Grated rind of 1
A little cream	lemon

Chop all but the eggs and cream very finely. Mix with eggs and cream. Tie up in a cloth and boil for 1½ hours. Glaze (see chapter on French cookery) and serve cold.

Haggis

Sheep's bag and pluck	½ teaspoonful
½ lb. minced suet	powdered herbs
½ lb. oatmeal	Pepper and salt to
4 small onions	taste

Wash bag in cold water, scrape and clean well. Leave in cold water with salt overnight. Wash the pluck. Put it into a pan of boiling water with a tablespoonful of salt. Boil for 2 hours, letting the windpipe hang out of the saucepan. When cold, cut off the windpipe, grate half the liver, mince the heart, lights, suet and onions very small. Add the oatmeal, which has been toasted to a golden brown, the pepper, salt, herbs and a cupful of the liquor in which the pluck was boiled. Mix well, fill the bag rather more than half with the mixture, and sew it up. Place in a saucepan of boiling water and boil for 3 hours, pricking it occasionally to keep it from bursting.

Quenelles

Equal quantities fresh	Butter
or cooked meat	1 well-beaten egg
and breadcrumbs	A little cream
soaked in milk	Seasoning

Pound well in a mortar the meat, breadcrumbs and butter. Add the other ingredients and mix to a firm paste. Pound all well again. Pass through a fine sieve. Shape with a large spoon, or put in small moulds. Poach in a pan of hot water for 10 minutes.

Scotch Collops (for 4–5)

2 lb. tender side of a	1 slice bread, grated
round of beef	1 apple, minced
Pepper and salt	1 small onion, minced

Mix bread, apple and onion. Beat the beef with a rolling pin, then cut it in pieces. Rub the saucepan with beef suet, put a layer of the beef in the bottom. Shake some of the bread, apple and onion mixture over it, also pepper and salt. Then put another layer of beef and another layer of bread, apple and onion. Continue with alternate layers, cover with a lid and cook in a slow oven till done.

Sheep's Head

1 *sheep's head*	*Parsley*
2 *tablespoonfuls pearl*	*Thyme*
barley (or rice)	*Bay leaf*
2 *onions*	10 *peppercorns*
2 *small carrots*	*Salt*
1 *small turnip*	*Pepper*

Cut the head in half, remove the brains, wash them and put them into cold water with a little salt. Wash the head in several waters, carefully remove any splintered bones and soak in salt and water for 1 hour. Put it in a saucepan and cover with cold water. Bring to the boil, pour away water and refill with fresh water. Add parsley, thyme, bay leaf and peppercorns. Season with salt and pepper. Boil up and skim well. The head must be cooked slowly for approximately 3 hours; 1½ hours before serving, add the vegetables (sliced) and barley (or rice). The liquor in which the head is boiled must be retained for the sauce.

Sauce for sheep's head

1½ oz. butter	1½ oz. flour
Brains	Seasoning

Remove skin and fibre from brains. Tie them in muslin and boil for 10–15 minutes in the liquor in which the head was cooked. Chop coarsely. Heat the butter, add flour, stir over flame for 2 or 3 minutes. Add ¾ pint liquor from the sheep's head. Simmer for 10 minutes. Add brains. Season to taste.

Serve the head garnished with parsley, carrots and other vegetables and masked with the sauce.

Sheep's Head Mould

A good-sized sheep's	*Hard-boiled egg*
head, scalded	*Pepper and salt*

Boil the head till the meat leaves the bones easily. Remove from heat and leave until cold. Boil down the liquid to a pint. Cut the meat up in small pieces. Slice the tongue. Line the bottom of a bowl with sliced hard-boiled egg, then a layer of meat. season well with black pepper and salt, and, as you fill up, pour the liquid over. Leave standing in a cool place all night to set. Turn out.

Pickled or "soused" herrings, eaten either hot or cold, are very popular in Scotland

Sheep's Head Pie

1 *sheep's head*	2 *or 3 eggs (hard-*
Ham or bacon	*boiled)*
(cooked)	*Pepper, salt, mixed*
Short pastry	*spice*

Wash the head thoroughly and boil till the bones shake out. Strain the stock from the head and cut slices of ham or bacon. Cut the meat from the head in small pieces and put layers in a pie dish alternately with the ham or bacon and eggs. Season with pepper, salt and spice. Pour in the stock and cover with a good short pastry. Bake for ¾ hour in a hot oven.

GAME

Grouse Soufflé

Cold grouse	1 *tablespoonful meat*
Two handfuls boiled	*glaze, dissolved in*
rice	*a little stock*
1 *oz. butter*	*Seasoning*
	3 *eggs*

Remove the meat from the bones of the grouse, pound well with the rice, butter and glaze, season well and rub all through a wire sieve. Mix in the egg-yolks, then add the whites beaten very stiff. Steam gently for 1 hour and serve with brown sauce.

To Cook Tough Blackgame, etc.

Remove the meat from the breast, leaving the skin. Pound well with a very little butter. Put back on the bird, shaping it to the correct shape. Cover with the skin and cook as usual.

To Cook Old Game (Game Mould)

Prepare the bird for cooking as usual. Then cut off the legs at the knees, and the wings at the pinions. Rub the bird inside and out with 2–4 oz. butter, according to size of bird, Add a small pinch of pepper and salt. Put the bird in a pie dish with plenty of good gravy. Fill up with water. Turn another pie dish over the first. Put the whole into a slow oven and stew for 3 hours. Then add a very little gelatine to set the gravy. Leave until quite cold. Turn out on to a meat dish. It will have set into a Game Mould.

PUDDINGS

Baked or Boiled Carrot Pudding (for 4–5)

½ *lb. breadcrumbs*	¼ *lb. currants*
4 *oz. suet*	3 *oz. sugar*
¼ *lb. raisins (stoned)*	3 *eggs*
¼ *lb. carrots*	*Milk*
	Nutmeg

Boil carrots until tender enough to mash to a pulp. Add the remaining ingredients and moisten with sufficient milk to make a thick batter. If the pudding is to be boiled, put the mixture into a greased basin, tie down with a cloth and boil for 2¼ hours. If to be baked, put it into a pie dish and bake for about 1 hour. Turn out on a dish and dredge with castor sugar.

Potato Pudding (for 4–5)

1 *lb. old potatoes,*	3 *eggs*
boiled and mashed	1 *lb. sugar*
2 *oz. butter*	*Brandy or sherry*
1 *doz. sweet almonds*	*(optional)*
	1 *tablespoonful cream*

Mix all the ingredients well. A glass of either brandy or sherry is a great improvement but is not essential. Turn mixture into pie dish and bake for 1 hour in a moderate oven.

Red Grout

1¾ *lb. juice of*	¼ *oz. minced bitter*
currants	*almonds*
1½ *pints water*	½ *lb. sago*
½ *oz. minced sweet*	½ *oz. cinnamon*
almonds	*Sugar to taste*

Put all the ingredients except the sago into a saucepan and bring to the boil, then add the sago (which has first been well rinsed in cold water). Boil for ¼ hour, stirring frequently. Turn the mixture into moulds or cups rinsed with cold water and leave to get cold. Turn out and serve with cream and sugar.

Snow Cheese

1 *pint cream*	*Wineglassful sherry*
Juice of 2 lemons	*Sugar to taste*

Mix cream, lemon juice, sherry and sugar. Beat well until quite thick. Put into a cloth and leave to drain overnight, when it will be ready to serve.

Sweet Potato Soufflé (for 3–4)

3 *oz. potatoes (boiled*	3 *oz. butter*
and put through a	3 *eggs*
sieve)	*Juice of 2 lemons*
3 *oz. castor sugar*	*Jam or apple purée*

Put the potatoes, lemon juice, sugar and butter into a basin and whip them together with a fork until they are creamy. Separate the yolks of the eggs from the whites and stir them in. Butter a soufflé dish and bake mixture in it for 10 minutes. Remove and put a layer of jam or apples on the top. Whip the whites of the eggs with a little castor sugar until quite stiff. Place on the

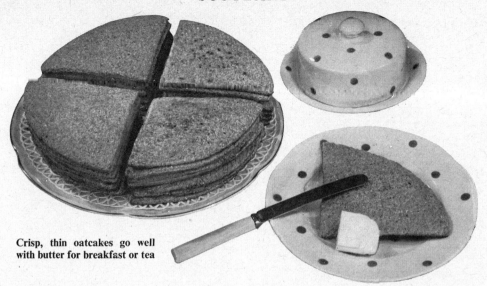

Crisp, thin oatcakes go well with butter for breakfast or tea

top, return to the oven and bake until the meringue is firm and light brown in colour.

CAKES AND SCONES

Brandy Wafers

2 oz. syrup	1¾ oz. sugar
1¼ oz. flour	½ teaspoonful lemon
½ teaspoonful ground	rind
ginger	½ teaspoonful brandy
	2 oz butter

Melt butter, syrup and sugar in a saucepan. Stir in flour, ginger, lemon rind and brandy. Mix well. Drop in small teaspoonfuls on a greased tin. Bake 5–10 minutes in hot oven. Roll quickly round a wooden roller.

Drop Scones (1)

6 tablespoonfuls flour	½ teaspoonful cream
1 tablespoonful sugar	of tartar
½ teaspoonful	2 eggs
bicarbonate of soda	4 teacupfuls of milk

Beat the eggs and milk together. Sieve the dry ingredients, and add egg and milk. Grease the girdle and, when hot, drop on about a tablespoonful for each scone. Turn with a knife when done, and cook the other side.

Drop Scones (2)

6 teacupfuls flour	3 tablespoonfuls
2 teaspoonfuls	sugar
bicarbonate of soda	Buttermilk (sour or
1 teaspoonful cream	fresh milk may be
of tartar	substituted)

Sieve flour, soda, cream of tartar and sugar. Mix to a stiff batter with the buttermilk. Grease the girdle and, when hot, drop about a tablespoonful for each scone. Turn with a knife when done and cook on the other side.

Girdle Cakes

½ lb. flour	½ lb. butter or mar-
Salt	garine
	Milk

Sieve the flour with a little salt. Rub in the butter or margarine and mix to a stiff dough with the milk. Roll out to ¼ in. thick. Cut in small rounds. Grease girdle (a heavy frying pan will do instead if no girdle is available) and, when hot, put the cakes on. When cooked on one side, turn. They should be served very hot, split and buttered.

Girdle Scones

2½ breakfastcupfuls	Pinch of salt
flour	1 oz. butter
1 teaspoonful cream	1 teaspoonful Golden
of tartar	Syrup
1 teaspoonful	Buttermilk (sour or
bicarbonate of soda	fresh milk may be
	substituted)

Sieve the flour, cream of tartar, soda and salt. Rub in the butter. Add the syrup and mix to a soft consistency with buttermilk or milk. Turn out on a floured board and roll quickly. Cut into shapes. Grease and heat a girdle (or heavy frying pan) and bake scones on both sides. Cooking time: 10 minutes.

Oatcakes

2 *large breakfastcupfuls fine oatmeal*
A pinch of bicarbonate of soda
A pinch of salt
1 *tablespoonful fresh lard or beef dripping*
1 *teacupful hot water*

Put meal in large bowl, adding soda and salt. Rub in the dripping or lard. Mix with the water to pastry consistency. Roll out on pastry board well dusted with oatmeal. Cut in rounds or squares and cook on a hot girdle.

Petticoat Tails

This is an old Scotch recipe.

6 *oz. butter*   1 *lb. flour*
6 *oz. sugar*   *A little water*
          Castor sugar

Rub butter and sugar into the flour. Add water and work to a smooth dough. Divide into two. Roll into two round cakes about the size of a large dinner plate. Cut a round from the centre of each with a cutter 4 in. in diameter. Then cut the outside of each into eight pieces. Prick the tops, dust over with castor sugar and bake in a moderate oven for ½ hour. Lay the rounds on separate plates, with eight petticoats round each.

Plum Cake

2 *oz. currants*   1 *teaspoonful*
2 *oz. raisins*   *bicarbonate of soda*
4 *oz. brown sugar*   2 *large teacupfuls*
4 *oz. butter or mar-*   *milk*
  garine   2 *teaspoonfuls mixed*
8 *oz. flour*   *spice*
2 *oz. peel*

Wash fruit. Mince raisins. Chop peel. Dissolve soda in milk and add spice. Cream fat and sugar until soft. Sieve flour, add fruit and peel, and stir into fat mixture alternately with milk. The mixture must be very moist. Add further milk if necessary. Bake in a very hot oven for 1¼ hours, reducing heat slightly after 30 minutes.

Plain Scones (1)

1 *pint milk*   *Flour*
          Pinch of salt

Bring the milk to the boil and then sprinkle in sufficient flour to make the mixture the consistency of thick porridge. Add a little salt. Remove from pan and roll out on a well-floured board, fairly thin. Cut into rounds and cook on a well-greased girdle or thick frying pan until brown. Turn, and cook on the other side.

Plain Scones (2)

1 *lb. flour*   3 *teaspoonfuls baking*
1 *oz. butter or mar-*   *powder*
  garine   *A little salt*
          Milk

Sieve the flour, salt and baking powder. Rub in butter. Mix to a light dough with milk. Roll out on a floured board and cut with round or fancy cutter. Bake in a hot oven.

NOTE: It is always easy to see if scones are cooked. Pick one out, pull gently, and if it parts in the middle it is done.

Potato Scones (1)

1 *lb. flour*   ½ *oz. butter*
½ *teaspoonful baking*   *Pinch of salt*
  soda   *Buttermilk (sour or*
3 *potatoes, cooked*   *fresh milk may be*
  and mashed   *substituted)*

Sieve the flour into a basin, add the mashed potatoes, soda and salt. Rub in butter and mix well with buttermilk or milk. Roll out thin, cut into rounds and place on a hot, greased girdle (or thick frying pan). Turn when brown and cook on other side. Serve hot.

Potato Scones (2)

½ *lb. flour*   3 *oz butter*
6 *oz. mashed potatoes* *A little water*

Rub the butter into the sieved flour. Add the potatoes. Mix with a little water. Roll out on a floured board about 1 in. thick, or thinner, as preferred. Cut into rounds and bake in a hot oven.

Potato Scones (3)

1 *pint mashed*   ½ *teaspoonful salt*
  potatoes   1 *tablespoonful butter*
1 *teaspoonful baking*   2 *tablespoonfuls flour*
  powder   *Water to mix*

Sieve flour, salt and baking powder. Rub in butter and add potatoes. Mix with a little water. Roll out on a floured board to ¼ in. in thickness, cut into rounds and bake in a hot oven. Split and butter.

Shortbread (1)

1 *lb. flour*   ½ *lb. fresh butter*
          4 *oz. castor sugar*

Mix the flour and sugar. Work in the butter. Divide the dough in half. Knead it into two rounds. Nick round the edges with thumb and prick with fork. Divide the rounds in four and bake in a moderate oven.

Shortbread (2)

1 lb. butter (prefer-
  ably half fresh and
  half salt)
1¼ lb. flour
6 oz. sugar
4 oz. rice flour

Beat the butter to a cream. Mix in flours and sugar. Knead into rounds. Nick round the edges with thumb and prick with fork. Mark each round in four divisions and bake in a moderate oven. The shortbread may be ornamented with orange peel before baking if desired.

NOTE: Margarine may be substituted for butter, but for shortbread butter is infinitely better.

Soda Scones

½ lb. flour (sieved)
½ teaspoonful salt
½ teaspoonful baking
  soda
½ teaspoonful cream
  of tartar [1]
Pinch of sugar
Nut of butter
Milk to mix

[1] Sour milk makes a very light mixture. If using sour milk, add very little cream of tartar.

Drop Scones, one of the many varieties for which Scotland is famous, are cooked on a girdle

Sieve all dry ingredients, rub in butter, add enough milk to make a stiff dough (the right consistency leaves the bowl clean when you turn it out). Roll out very lightly and cut into rounds, or leave in one large round and cut in triangles. Bake in a very hot oven. *The oven can scarcely be too hot for scones, which should cook in 5–10 minutes.*

Parkins (1)

1 lb. oatmeal
12 oz. syrup
½ lb. sugar
6 teaspoonfuls ginger
3 teaspoonfuls baking
  soda

1 lb. flour
½ lb. lard
6 teaspoonfuls
  cinnamon
3 teaspoonfuls mixed
  spice

2 eggs

Sieve all the dry ingredients together thoroughly. Rub in fat. Melt sugar and syrup, and mix with dry ingredients and fat. Beat eggs and add. Roll into small balls in dry oatmeal and bake in a slow oven until brown.

Parkins (2)

1 lb. oatmeal
5 oz. lard
1 oz. bicarbonate of
  soda
Egg

½ lb. sugar
1 lb. flour
1 lb. syrup
Almond essence
Almonds

Sieve dry ingredients. Rub in fat. Melt sugar and syrup, and mix in. Add almond essence and a little milk. Roll into small balls, set well apart on a well-buttered sheet. Brush over with egg. Put half an almond (blanched) on top of each and bake in a very cool oven for about ½ hour.

SCOTLAND

BEVERAGES

Atholl Brose

1 lb. honey   1½ pints whisky
About a cupful of cold water

Put honey in a basin. Add sufficient cold water to dissolve it. Stir with a silver spoon and, when honey and water are well mixed, add the whisky by degrees. Stir briskly till a froth begins to rise. Bottle, and keep tightly corked.

Highland Bitters

This is a very old recipe.

1¾ oz. gentian root   ¼ oz. camomile flower
½ oz. bitter orange   ¼ oz. cinnamon stick
  peel   ½ oz. cloves (whole)
1 oz. coriander seed   Whisky

Bruise the coriander seed, camomile flower, cinnamon stick, cloves, gentian root and bitter orange peel. Cut the root and peel in small pieces. Add as much whisky as desired. Leave to soak for about 10 days. Strain off. Put more whisky on. The ingredients are sufficient for two bottles of whisky at a time, and may be used a number of times.

Rowanberry Liqueur

1 pint brandy   1 pint syrup
  1 handful picked rowanberries

Dry the berries until they shrivel. Place in the brandy and leave for a week or 10 days. Strain and mix with an equal quantity of thick, very clear, syrup, made with loaf sugar in a brass pan.

MISCELLANEOUS

Aberdeen Toast

4 oatcakes   2 egg-yolks
Bloater paste   1 oz. butter
1 egg-white   Cayenne pepper

Make the oatcakes quite hot. Melt the butter, add the eggs, the bloater paste and Cayenne. Stir till thick. Pile on hot oatcakes, sprinkle with browned crumbs and serve at once.

Bignon's Sauce for Cold Lamb

Take equal quantities of capers, parsley, chives, gherkins and tarragon. Mince all very finely. Mix. Season with pepper, salt and cayenne, and put into a jar with tarragon vinegar. When required, add plenty of finely minced chervil, a little French mustard and salad oil to taste.

Oatmeal Porridge (for 4)

4–5 handfuls oatmeal   2 pints boiling water

Into 2 pints boiling water sift a handful of oatmeal through the fingers of the left hand, stirring all the time with a wooden spoon. Repeat this until the porridge is fairly thick. About 4 or 5 handfuls to this quantity of water. Draw the pan to the side of the fire or put on a low flame, preferably with an asbestos mat underneath. Add salt, put the lid on and cook steadily for about 1 hour, stirring well at intervals.

Rowan Jelly

Gather the berries just as they are on the point of ripening. Rinse in water and put them in a jelly pan with enough water to cover. Boil till the berries are soft. Strain the liquor through a jelly bag and return it to the fire. Add 1 lb. of loaf sugar to every pint of juice and boil rapidly for ½ hour, simmering carefully. Test on a saucer for setting and, when ready, bottle in warm jars and cover immediately with air-tight tops.

Scotch Marmalade (Thick)

2 lb. bitter oranges   9 lb. sugar
  and 2 sweet oranges   2 lemons
          6 pints water

Wipe the fruit with a damp cloth and pare the yellow rind thinly off 3 or 4 of the oranges. Cut it with scissors into fine shreds and soak in a little of the water.

Peel the fruit, taking off all white pith. Quarter and cut the fruit up finely, removing pips. Soak the pulp for 24 hours in the water, also the pips tied in a muslin bag. Put the shreds and the pulp into a preserving pan. Squeeze the liquid from the pips and throw the pips away. Boil slowly for ¾ hour.

Remove from the fire, add the sugar, and boil until a little will set on a plate—about ½ hour. Skim and put into jars.

Sugar Tablet

2 lb. sugar   ¼ lb. butter
3 cupfuls water   Flavouring to taste

Dissolve the sugar in the water. Add the butter, but do not boil as fast as for toffee. Test in cold water, and when a little rolls into a soft ball, take it off. Add flavouring to taste. Stir quickly with a spoon. It will begin to solidify round the edge. Scrape this off repeatedly and keep stirring until it is all of a soft, creamy consistency. Pour into a buttered slab or tin. Leave until set, then cut.

WALES

Welsh Rarebit is not by any means the only national dish; most of these recipes are by courtesy of the Whitbread Library

Bara-Brith (the national bun loaf of Wales) with yeast (makes 2 loaves).

(There are 60 varieties of bread, buns, etc., in the Welsh-English dictionary, all starting with Bara, meaning eat, sustenance.)

½ oz. yeast	1 heaped teaspoonful
4 oz. sugar	mixed spice
½ pint and 4 table-	1 large egg
spoonfuls milk (or	4 oz. sultanas
milk and water)	4 oz. raisins
1½ lb. flour	4 oz. currants
½ level teaspoonful	1 oz. chopped
salt	candied peel
2 oz. margarine	

Glaze

1 heaped tablespoon-	2 tablespoonfuls
ful brown sugar	water
A squeeze of lemon juice (optional)	

Cream the yeast and sugar together. Heat the milk until just lukewarm, and blend with the yeast. Sieve the flour, salt, and mixed spice together into a warmed basin. Make a well in the centre and pour in the yeast mixture. Stir, cover with a damp cloth, and set in a warm place for 30 minutes to rise (the bars over the cooker are very suitable when the oven is on, or when the heat is low on top).

Melt the margarine gently, add to the risen yeast mixture, stir in, sprinkle with flour, and knead for 3 minutes. Again cover with a damp cloth, and leave for a further 30 minutes in a warm place to rise. Beat the egg, add to the dough, mix in, knead well, then stir in the fruit and peel. Turn the mixture on to a floured board, divide in half, mould each into an oblong, and place in two 2-lb. bread tins, well brushed inside with melted margarine. Leave to prove in a warm place until the

Bara-Brith, the national bun loaf of Wales, right, and Huish Cake are two characteristic national dishes. Made and photographed specially by the Stork Margarine Cookery Service

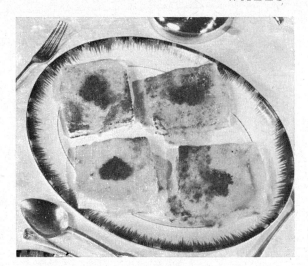

A real Welsh Rarebit, served lightly brown, contains ale in its ingredients

the eggs and beat the yolks into the creamed mixture. Add flour and ground rice, sieved together. Beat the egg-whites stiff and add them and the yolks (well beaten) and caraway seeds. Stir well, place in a 7-in. greased baking tin and bake in a moderate oven for about 1 hour 10 minutes.

Leek Porridge

Wash, skim and trim the leeks and put on to boil in a little cold water. When done, cut the leeks into thin slices and place in porridge or soup plates, pouring a little of the water over them. Serve with toast cut into fingers.

Welsh Mutton Cowl (for 4)

1½ lb. scrag or best end neck of mutton	
Piece of turnip	
Parsley	Bunch of leeks
2 oz. pearl barley	1½ pints of cold water
Carrot	Salt and pepper to
Potatoes	taste

Wash and joint the meat and put it into a saucepan with the cold water. Bring to the boil quickly and skim the top. Add whole potatoes, diced carrot and turnip, pepper and salt, and pearl barley. Chop the parsley finely. Wash the leeks well in salted water, and cut them into rings, discarding the green part unless they are very young. Add parsley and leeks to meat and simmer for 1½ hours. Serve at once without thickening while the leeks are almost crisp, in small bowls with bread cut into dice.

Snowdon Pudding (for 4)

8 oz. suet	Grated rind of 2
6 eggs	lemons
Pinch of salt	4 oz. stoneless raisins
6 oz. lemon mar-	1½ oz. rice or corn-
malade	flour
8 oz. breadcrumbs	6 oz. brown sugar

Butter a quart mould or basin thickly and ornament with raisins. Mix all the dry ingredients together, beat the eggs and add to the mixture. Pour into the basin carefully, tie up and boil for 1½ hours. Serve with wine sauce.

Wine Sauce

Rind of ½ lemon	1 oz. butter
Water	1½ wineglassfuls
½ teaspoonful flour	sherry, madeira or
1½ oz. sugar	white wine

dough is even with the rim, with a nicely domed centre. Bake side by side on the middle shelf of a hot oven for 15 minutes. Turn the heat down to moderate and bake for 30–35 minutes longer until golden brown and firm. Cool on a wire tray.

To make the glaze, place the ingredients all together in a pan, stir until the sugar is dissolved, and boil for 1–2 minutes, but do not allow to caramelise. Cool a little, and brush evenly over the tops of the loaves. Leave until set before cutting. (Halve all ingredients for one loaf.)

Boiled Salted Duck

1 duck	1 lb. onions
A little butter, flour and milk	Salt and pepper

Salt the duck the day before. Put in a saucepan with enough water to cover and simmer for 1½ hours. Make onion sauce by boiling the onions in milk and water with salt and pepper, melting the butter in another saucepan, stirring in flour and gradually adding boiled milk and onions. Dish up the duck and pour the sauce over it.

Huish Cake

4 oz. ground rice (or semolina)	4 oz. margarine
8 oz. castor sugar	4 oz. flour
	4 eggs
A few caraway seeds	

Cream margarine and sugar. Separate

Boil sugar and lemon rind in a wine-glassful of water for about 15 minutes. Remove lemon peel and stir in butter into which flour has been kneaded. Add the wine, stir, and serve when quite hot.

Spiced Beef

10 *or* 12 *lb. silverside*	8 *oz. salt*
of beef	2 *oz. saltpetre*
2 *oz. black pepper*	2 *oz. allspice*

Rub the saltpetre into the beef and leave for 24 hours. Then rub the other ingredients in, having mixed them well previously. Put the beef into an earthenware pan and leave there for a fortnight, turning it every day. Put it into a clean pan, pour melted suet over it and cover the top of the pan with a paste made from flour and water. Bake in a very slow oven for 12 hours. Then place the meat between two plates and put a weight over it. The meat should be eaten cold and will keep for some time.

Welsh Pikelets

8 *oz. flour*	1 *teaspoonful bicar-*
A little lard	*bonate of soda*
½ *gill boiling water*	2 *oz. castor sugar*
4 *oz. buttermilk*	*Pinch of salt*

Mix flour, salt and sugar into a thick batter with buttermilk. Dissolve bicarbonate of soda in boiling water and add to the mixture. Take a tablespoonful of the batter at a time and fry on both sides in a little hot lard. Serve hot and buttered.

Welsh Rarebit (for 2)

4 *oz. grated cheese*	1 *oz. butter*
2 *large tablespoonfuls*	*Pepper, salt and*
ale	*mustard to taste*
	2 *slices toast*

Put the ale into a saucepan and melt the cheese in it slowly. Add the pepper, salt and mustard, and the butter. When thoroughly hot, pour the mixture on the freshly made toast, place under a grill until lightly browned and serve.

COOKERY AT HOME AND ABROAD

IRELAND

Good eating has for long been associated with the Emerald Isle. Recipes compiled from the Whitbread Library

Colcannon (for 4)

1 *lb. boiled cold*	8 *oz. boiled cabbage*
potatoes	*Salt and pepper to*
2 *oz. bacon fat*	*taste*
	1 *onion*

Mash the potatoes. Chop the onion fine and fry gently in the bacon fat. Add the potatoes and cabbage, season, mix well together and turn into a greased pudding basin. Reheat in the oven, turn out on a dish and serve.

Hunter's Pie (for 6)

6 *mutton chops*	2 *dozen potatoes*
A little butter	*Pepper and salt to*
A little gravy	*taste*

Braise the chops. Boil and mash the potatoes and add pepper and salt. Butter a large pie dish, line with potatoes, put in the chops and cover with the remaining potatoes and bake in a moderate oven for 30 minutes. Cut a hole in the top and pour in the gravy (made by thickening the water in which the chops were cooked).

Irish Apple Baskets (for 4–6)

Filling

1 *lb. cooking apples*	*Pinch of nutmeg,*
3 *heaped tablespoon-*	*mixed spice or cin-*
fuls sugar	*namon, or 1–2*
3 *tablespoonfuls*	*heaped tablespoon-*
water	*fuls sultanas or*
½ *oz. margarine*	*stoned raisins*

Short pastry

6 *oz. flour*	3 *dessertspoonfuls*
Pinch of salt	*cold water, milk or*
3 *oz. margarine*	*water, and castor*
	sugar to coat

Turn on the oven heat, and set to fairly hot.

Peel, core, and slice the apples, and place in a saucepan with the other ingredients. Simmer gently until soft, and mash smoothly with a fork. Cool.

Make short pastry (see Pastry chapter),

using the ingredients listed, roll out thinly, cut into rounds, and line 9–12 bun tins. Using the scraps of pastry to make narrow strips, put in the apple filling and arrange the strips in star or lattice patterns over the apples. Brush with milk or water, sprinkle with castor sugar, and bake for 20–25 minutes in a pre-heated oven on the second shelf from the top. Serve either hot or cold. (Makes 9–12 tartlets, according to size.)

Irish Cheesecakes

4 oz. sweet almonds	A little lemon juice
3 oz. sugar	and grated lemon
A little rose-water	peel
2 oz. butter	3 bitter almonds
Pastry as for Irish	3 eggs
Apple Baskets	

Blanch and chop the almonds very fine. Mix in the rose-water. Beat the eggs and add with melted butter, lemon peel, juice and sugar. Line 12 patty pans with pastry and fill with the mixture. Bake in a hot oven for about 15 minutes.

Irish Delight (for 4)

1½ oz. cornflour	1½ pints milk
2 eggs	A little fat
A little vanilla	1 dessertspoonful
essence	castor sugar
3 oz. breadcrumbs	

Mix the cornflour to a smooth paste. with a little of the milk. Bring the rest of the milk to the boil and stir gently into the cornflour, boil for 10 minutes, stirring all the time. Add the vanilla and sugar, and pour into a shallow flat tin or dish. When quite cold, cut into oblong slices, dip in beaten egg, roll in breadcrumbs and fry a golden brown in a little hot fat. Salt,

pepper and grated cheese can be used instead of sugar and vanilla.

Irish Soda Cake

1 lb. plain flour	4 oz. margarine
1 rounded teaspoonful cream of tartar	4 oz. sugar
	4 oz. sultanas, or
1 rounded teaspoonful bicarbonate of soda	stoned raisins
	2 oz. mixed chopped peel
1 level teaspoonful salt	½ pint and 6 table-spoonfuls sour milk

Turn on the oven heat, and set to fairly hot. Brush a 7-in. cake tin all round inside with melted margarine. Sieve the flour, cream of tartar, bicarbonate of soda, and salt together into a mixing bowl. Cut the margarine into pieces, add, and rub in until the mixture looks crumbly. Stir in the sugar, fruit, and peel. Add the milk and mix with a knife to a fairly soft dough. Turn out on to a well-floured board, sprinkle with flour, knead very lightly, and form into a round. Put into the prepared tin; press out with the knuckles to the sides; mark a cross, or squares, etc., on the top with a knife, and bake for 1 hour on the middle shelf of the prepared oven. Turn the heat down to moderate and bake for a further half-hour.

NOTE: 2 heaped tablespoonfuls caraway seed may be used instead of fruit.

If bicarbonate of soda and cream of tartar are not available, use 4 heaped teaspoonfuls baking powder instead.

If sour milk is not available, use ½ pint and 5 tablespoonfuls fresh milk and 1 tablespoonful vinegar, mixed together, and if necessary, heated very gently until the milk curdles. Cool before using.

Irish Pancakes

4 eggs	⅛ pint cream
1½ oz. butter	3 oz. plain flour
A little grated nutmeg	A little castor sugar

Beat 2 egg-whites with 4 yolks and mix in the cream, slightly warmed. Then add melted butter, mix to a smooth batter with flour and add nutmeg. Fry the pancakes in a little butter. They should be very thin. Roll, sprinkle with a little sugar and serve hot.

Irish Stew, made from scrag or neck of mutton with onions and potatoes, needs to simmer slowly

436

Irish Apple Baskets and Irish Soda Cake are two favourite tea-time recipes from Ireland, here seen tested and photographed by the Stork Margarine Cookery Service

Irish Stew (for 6)

2 lb. scrag or neck of mutton	½ pint water
1 lb. onions	Pepper and salt to taste
3 lb. potatoes	

Cut the meat into neat pieces, slice the potatoes and the onions and put into a good saucepan, the meat first, then the potatoes and onions, sprinkling each layer with pepper and salt. Repeat, then pour on the water and simmer for 3 hours.

Pig's Face

Half a pig's head   Cabbage

Singe off all the hair from the head and soak in a basin of water for 12 hours. Wash well and boil in cold water, allowing 25 minutes for each pound. When cooked, lay the head on one side, score the skin and grill a golden brown in front of an open fire or in the oven. Cabbage should be put all round the pig's face to garnish and the liquor in which the head was boiled served as soup.

Potato and Apple Cake (for 4–6)

6 good-sized mashed potatoes	1½ lb. flour
8 oz. dripping	6 good-sized apples
	3 oz. sugar

Rub dripping into flour, mix with potatoes into a stiff dough and roll out on a board about ½ in. thick. Grease a fireproof dish and line with some of the pastry. Cover with peeled, cored and sliced apples and sprinkle with sugar. Cover with another layer of pastry, and then apples and pastry again. Bake in a moderate oven for 1 hour. Serve hot.

Potato Cakes

6 boiled potatoes	2 tablespoonfuls flour
Butter	
A little salt	

Mash the potatoes, and add the salt and sufficient flour to make into stiff dough. Roll out on the board ½ in. thick, cut into squares and bake on a griddle. Split and butter immediately and serve hot.

★ **TO DISCOVER THE REAL POSSIBILITIES OF THE POTATO, TRY IRISH COOKERY** ★

ELIZABETHAN RECIPES

Authentic traditional fare from the days of Good Queen Bess,
as served in the Elizabethan Room at the Gore Hotel, London

Lobster Pie

MAKE a good crust, boil two lobsters, take out the tails, cut them in two, take out the gut, cut each tail in four pieces, and lay them in the dish. Take the bodies, bruise them well with the claws and pick out all the rest of the meat. Chop it all together, season it with pepper, salt and about two or three teaspoonfuls of vinegar, melt half a pound of butter, stir all together, with the crumb part of a bread roll rubbed in a small, clean cloth, lay it over the tails, put on your pastry cover, and bake in a slow oven.

Artichoke Pie

Boil your artichokes well, then take the bottoms from the leaves, and season them with a little beaten mace, and put to them a pretty quantity of butter, lay a layer in the bottom, then lay in the artichokes, sprinkle them with a little salt, put some sugar over them, put in grated pieces of marrow rolled in egg-yolks, then put in a few gooseberries or grapes, and lay upon it

large mace and dates stoned, some yolks of hard-boiled eggs, lettuce stalks, and citron (lemon), cover it with butter, and when it is baked, put in scalded white wine and shake it together and serve it up.

Syllabub

Take a pint of canary or white wine, a pint of raspberry juice, a sprig of rosemary, a nutmeg quartered, the juice of a lemon, and some of the peel with sugar, put these together in a pot all night and cover them. In the morning take a pint and a half of cream, and a pint and a half of new milk. Then take out the lemon peel, rosemary and nutmeg, and squirt your milk and cream into the pot. With a wooden cow, fold at the corners. (The nearest modern equivalent of a wooden cow is a grooved wooden butter pat; the proper thing is to turn out the mixture and fold it in at the edges with the pat, but this part of the recipe can be omitted without damage to the resulting dish.)

Peacock

Roast a peacock exactly as you would any other bird of the same size, then place it on the mounted model.

Sturgeon

Cook a centre cut of sturgeon in the same way as salmon, boiling or grilling it.

Roast Swan

Roast a swan just as you would any other bird of the same size and weight.

Hare in Coffin

First remove the head, legs and tail from a hare. The body may either be roast whole, minced or turned into a paté and then encased in pastry, leaving openings for the insertion of head, tail and legs. Bake.

Colour page, (top) shows a sucking pig, boar's head, centre cut of sturgeon garnished, lobster pie, a peacock with tail erect and a roast swan. In the lower picture, syllabub is seen in small wooden bowls

Photographs taken by McCall's of New York

A TYPICAL FEAST AS IN THE DAYS OF THE FIRST QUEEN ELIZABETH

Whether you are entertaining on the grand scale, giving a small family party or just cooking for two at Christmas, some kind of poultry will probably be the main dish. But even with such traditional fare, you can ring the changes and display your originality with the trimmings. There is an infinite variety of accompaniments and garnishes for the Christmas bird. Cranberry sauce is particularly appetising. To add a touch of colour to the dish, garnish with fresh green watercress and cranberry sauce—or whole cranberries—in tinned peach halves. For a different vegetable accompaniment, try a mixture of frozen peas and sweet corn, with a slice or two of tinned pimento for a touch of red.

PLANNING THE
CHRISTMAS DINNER

It should be done with the precision and advance preparation of a military operation—if the cook is going to enjoy it too

WIFE, mother, sister, whoever does the Christmas catering, must be able to enjoy herself with the others, without giving too much time to the stove and the kitchen. A strict time-table is the best answer, both before-hand as well as on the day itself.

ORDERING

All the extra items needed for Christmas cooking should be thought of well ahead. First, sit down and choose your recipes for cake, puddings and mincemeat, and list the ingredients you will need for all these items. Start at the beginning of November and lay in these stocks during the month.

Help yourself when it comes to cooking, by washing all dried fruit as you buy it. Mop it in a clean towel, and spread out on kitchen paper over wire trays to dry off. Store in airtight tins.

At the appointed time, the bird, vegetables and trimmings are on the table and the most festive meal of the year can begin

At the beginning of December, make a preliminary decision on the kind of bird you would like, and start enquiries as to price and availability. As soon as your final decision is made, and the bird ordered, list the accessories you will need for it—bacon, sausages, kind of stuffing, vegetables — and quantities, according

439

to the weight of the bird and number of people for Christmas dinner. If you have groceries, bread and vegetables delivered, mark on your list the day on which you must order all these items for delivery in time for the holiday.

If you shop personally, you will not want to be carrying extra heavy loads, so buy bread (for stuffing and bread sauce) four days before Christmas Eve, vegetables the day before, and sausages, bacon and any other garnishes on Christmas Eve. Spread potato buying over the other days of Christmas week, as the total weight needed will be the heaviest.

At the beginning of Christmas week, order the joint you are likely to need to help over the rest of the holiday, and also the fresh bread for the whole holiday period. If collecting this yourself, do so as late as possible on Christmas Eve.

Spread the buying of soft drinks, wines and spirits needed over the month of December, aiming at having your supply complete by the beginning of Christmas week.

Flour cannot be kept too long, but if you have cool, dry storage space, you can get in your quantity a fortnight ahead.

COOKING BEFOREHAND

Mincemeat, puddings and cake can all be made a matter of weeks before the festive holiday.

Mincemeat.—When this contains wine or spirits, it can be made in early November, as soon as you have all the necessary ingredients. Otherwise, make it two or three weeks before Christmas Day.

Puddings.—These may be made one month before needed.

The Cake.—Make the cake itself one month beforehand. When quite cold, wrap in greaseproof paper and store.

The Almond Paste should be put on the cake at least one week before Christmas, and must be left for two or three days at least to dry out completely before the white icing is put on.

The Icing and Decoration.—Accomplish this task two or three days ahead.

JOBS FOR THE 24th

Try to get all shopping done as early as possible, leaving you free to carry out the following preparations:

Make mince pies, also make a batch of pastry and store in a tin or in the refrigerator. This will be useful for making additional mince pies or other sweet or savoury pastry items over the holiday.

Make stuffing, and prepare and stuff the bird (but do not put in sausage meat). Put the bird ready in its tin to go in the oven the next day.

Make the necessary quantity of breadcrumbs ready for the bread sauce; and, if hard sauce is on the menu for the pudding, make this.

Prepare sausages for the bird, rind the bacon and do all vegetable preparation.

See that the pudding is in order, ready for reheating the next day.

CHRISTMAS DAY

Aim at a definite time for the meal. The housewife can then feel confident and happy over a careful schedule for dinner at 1.30 p.m., which is worked out as follows:

8.45 a.m.—Preheat oven. Add sausage meat stuffing to the turkey.

9 a.m.—Put turkey in oven, baste half-hourly. Put the onion to infuse in the milk for bread sauce.

10 a.m.—Lay table and put wines ready. If a white sauce is preferred to a hard sauce for the pudding, make it now and put to heat when you dish up the pudding.

11 a.m.—Put giblets to simmer for gravy.

11.15 a.m.—Pudding on to reheat in saucepan of boiling water.

11.30 a.m.—Potatoes on to boil for 5 minutes.

12 noon.—Potatoes round turkey to roast.

12.50 p.m.—Celery on now, if on menu.

1.5 p.m.—Sprouts on to boil. Finish the bread sauce and keep hot.

1.10 p.m.—Mince pies to warm.

1.15 p.m.—Sausage and bacon on to grill, turn after 5 minutes. Put potatoes to pan roast if they cannot be cooked round turkey. Make gravy and dish up turkey and vegetables.

Pudding should be left on a pin-point of gas while first course is being eaten, and dished while one or two of the diners clear away the first course.

INDIA

Described by J. R. MODY,
*proprietor of Jamshid
Restaurant, London*

*All kinds of spices are much used—but there are
many other dishes besides curry!*

From top down-
wards: dried French
beans, yellow lentils,
almonds, dried peas,
green lentils

THERE are three main characteristics
of Indian cookery, which does *not* consist entirely of curries.

(1) Everything contains spices of one
kind or another.

(2) Rice is extensively used.

(3) The basis of most dishes is ghee or
clarified butter.

Ghee can sometimes be obtained in
the U.K., but it is very simple to make.
Boil the butter over a very gentle heat, constantly skimming off the froth as it rises to
the top, for between 1 hour and 1½ hours,
then strain it. The resulting fat is less solid
and easier to use for cooking than butter,
and will keep for about 6 to 9 months.

How to cook Rice

Fill the largest available pan with water
to within an inch of the top and bring to
the boil. When boiling really vigorously,
add the rice and boil for 10–12 minutes.
After 10 minutes, examine a few grains,
pressing between finger and thumb, to see
if they are done. Strain rice in a colander
and pour plenty of cold water over it. Then
reheat dry in a moderate oven for about 10
minutes. The rice should then be perfect
and ready to serve.

Lamb Curry (for 4)

1 *lb. lean lamb (pref-*	¼ *lb. ghee or cooking*
erably leg)	*fat*
4 *green chillies*	3 *tablespoonfuls*
4 *large onions*	*curry paste*
2 *cloves of garlic*	1½ *pints stock*
Salt to taste	

Chop the onions finely and fry till golden
brown in the ghee. Add the garlic
(crushed) and the chillies (sliced), and
cook for a few minutes. Add the curry
paste and allow to simmer for 10 minutes,

making sure there is enough fat in the pan to prevent the onions from burning—they must remain golden brown. Wash meat, cut into 1-in. squares, put into the mixture and cook for 10 minutes. Add the stock and cook slowly over a gentle heat until the gravy is thick and the meat tender (about 1¼ hours), adding salt to taste.

Curry Powder needs to be as freshly roasted and ground as coffee, so it should be bought only in small quantities at a time. If it is then carefully kept in a tin, it should last for 2 to 3 months. A good curry paste which contains oil will last 4 or 5 months.

Curried Eggs (for 4)

6 *hard-boiled eggs*	1 *dessertspoonful*
1 *oz. curry powder or*	*tamarind*
paste	¼ *lb. ghee or cooking*
½ *fresh coconut*	*fat*
2 *cloves of garlic*	2 *medium onions*
½ *teaspoonful cinna-*	*Salt to taste*
mon powder	

Soak the tamarind in half a cupful of warm water, stand for 15 minutes, then squeeze through muslin. Pour boiling water over grated coconut and let it stand for 15 minutes, then squeeze that through muslin. Chop onions and fry in the ghee till golden, adding crushed garlic, curry powder or paste, stirring all the time, then add the cinnamon, coconut milk, tamarind water and salt. Simmer until the mixture thickens. Drop in the eggs, and bring slowly to the boil. Serve with boiled rice.

Straw Potatoes and Chicken (Sali moorgi) (Parsee speciality) (for 4)

1 *medium roasting*	1 *pint cooking oil*
chicken	*Salt to taste*
1 *lb. peeled potatoes*	*A piece of fresh*
4 *cloves of garlic*	*ginger or ½ tea-*
1 *medium onion*	*spoonful ginger*
1 *tablespoonful ghee*	*powder*
or cooking fat	

Wash, clean and cut the chicken into convenient joints. Crush the ginger and garlic together and rub the mixture over the chicken, then leave it for 1 hour. Cut the potatoes into thin straws, sprinkle them with salt and leave. Slice the onion thinly and fry in the ghee. When golden, add the chicken and fry lightly; then 5 teacupfuls of water and salt to taste, and cook on a low heat until the chicken is tender and only a cupful of gravy remains. Then fry the potato straws in very hot oil (they should be cream-coloured and very crisp). Dish up the chicken and cover with the potato straws. This is an excellent dish for children because, unlike nearly all Indian dishes, it contains no spices.

Fish Curry (for 4)

6 *medium cutlets of*	3 *dessertspoonfuls*
turbot or halibut	*vinegar*
3 *medium onions*	*Juice of 2 lemons*
7 *green chillies*	4 *tablespoonfuls*
5 *cloves of garlic*	*cooking oil*
1 *teaspoonful tur-*	1 *tablespoonful flour*
meric powder	*A piece of fresh*
2 *cupfuls coconut*	*ginger or ½ tea-*
milk	*spoonful ginger*
1 *dessertspoonful*	*powder*
brown sugar	

Wash and salt the fish. Chop onions and chillies and crush garlic. Fry onions in oil till golden, add chillies, garlic and ginger (ground, if in the piece), turmeric and flour. Keep on low heat for 5 minutes, stirring all the time. Add coconut milk and boil gently for 10 minutes. Add fish, simmer gently until cooked. Mix vinegar, lemon juice and sugar together, and pour over fish. Keep on low heat until the liquid thickens.

Vegetable Curry (Mixed vegetable salad) (for 4)

3 *medium potatoes*	¼ *teaspoonful mustard*
1 *large aubergine*	¼ *teaspoonful fenu-*
1 *small cauliflower*	*greek seeds*
3 *large onions*	1 *small piece cassia*
1 *parsnip*	½ *level teaspoonful*
5 *cloves of garlic*	*cummin grey*
1 *heaped tablespoon-*	*powder*
ful grated coconut	½ *level teaspoonful*
1 *level teaspoonful*	*turmeric powder*
chilli powder	*Juice of 1 lemon*
2 *tablespoonfuls ghee*	1 *level teaspoonful*
3 *green chillies*	*chopped parsley*
Salt to taste	1 *small piece fresh*
½ *level teaspoonful*	*ginger*
coriander powder	

Slice onions, chop chillies, crush ginger and garlic, fenugreek and cassia. Cut all the other vegetables into small pieces and boil till tender. Fry onions in ghee till golden, add mustard, fenugreek and cassia, stirring all the time. When it bubbles, add the rest of the spices, chopped parsley, ginger and coconut. Stir over low heat for 5 minutes, add all the vegetables, more salt if needed, and mix together, adding a little water if required. Simmer for 10–15 minutes. Add lemon juice and remove from heat.

Dhal (for 4)

¼ lb. red lentils	½ teaspoonful
2 small onions	coriander powder
¼ lb. tomatoes	½ teaspoonful cummin
2 green chillies	grey powder
½ teaspoonful	Salt to taste
turmeric	3 oz. ghee or cooking
1 teaspoonful chilli	fat
powder	

Chop chillies, tomatoes and onions. Wash lentils, put them in a pan with 1½ pints of cold water, the turmeric and salt, and cook for ½ hour on medium heat, when they should have absorbed all the liquid. Meanwhile, fry the onions till golden, add chillies, spices and tomatoes, and mix well with the lentils. Add small cupful of water and bring to the boil. Stir continuously and remove from heat when well mixed and of the required thickness (it should be about the consistency of thick soup). Pour over boiled rice. Alternatively, it may be cooked until very thick, like paste, and eaten with chapatis.

Chapatis (Indian bread) are with dhal and rice the staple diet.

1 oz. ghee	1 lb. atta (Indian
Pinch of salt	wheat flour)

Rub the ghee into the atta and salt, and mix to a stiff dough with a little warm water. Leave for ½ hour, then knead well with a little warm water to a fairly soft dough. Divide into ten equal-sized balls, roll each one out thinly into a circle about 6 in. in diameter. Get a griddle plate very hot, then drop the chapati on to it, moving it round until it puffs up but does not turn brown. Turn over and cook on the other side—about 1 minute each side. Finally, put the chapati over a bare gas flame for a second till it puffs up like a balloon, repeating on the reverse side. Serve hot or cold with the main dish. In India, chapatis are eaten with vegetable dishes or a dry meat dish, but not with rice.

Savoury Biscuits (Pappadams)

These are bought in tins and cooked by bringing plenty of oil to the boil in a deep frying pan. When the oil is smoking, slide in the pappadams, one at a time, turning

A curry, hot and spicy, as made in India and Pakistan, often served with Chapatis (Indian bread), which are eaten with everything except rice

Sali moorgi, or Straw Potatoes with Chicken—an excellent Indian dish for children because it is one of the few that contain no spices

them instantaneously and removing them—all in a split second. Drain them, preferably vertically. Serve cold as a cocktail savoury.

Capsicums

These vegetables are obtainable fresh in the U.K., usually between July and the end of October.

1 lb. capsicums
2 onions
½ lb. fresh peas
½ teaspoonful turmeric powder
3 tablespoonfuls cooking oil
½ teaspoonful chilli powder
¼ teaspoonful coriander powder
¼ teaspoonful cummin grey
Salt to taste

Wash and cut tops from capsicums. Then cut them lengthwise into four or six pieces each. Slice onions and fry in oil till golden. Cook peas separately, add them with capsicums, salt and spices, cover and simmer on low heat, stirring occasionally, for about 15 minutes. Serve as a side dish with meat or with dhal and chapatis.

Finally a sweet dish:

Barfi (for 4)

2 pints milk
1 oz. blanched almonds
2 teaspoonfuls vanilla essence
Juice of 2 lemons
2 oz. ground almonds
1 lb. granulated sugar
1 tablespoonful butter

Boil the milk, then add the lemon juice as required to curdle it. Tie up in muslin till all the liquid has run out, then pass the "curds" through a sieve. Put into a pan with the vanilla, sugar, ground almonds and butter over a low flame, stirring all the time and taking great care that it does not burn. It is ready when, on tilting the pan towards you, the mixture comes clear away from the bottom. Butter a dish and spread the mixture about ½ in. thick. Slice and very lightly fry the blanched almonds and decorate the top of the mixture with them. Cool, shape into diamonds and cut.

*   *   *   *   *   *

NOTE ON SUPPLIES: All spices used throughout this chapter, also cereals such as atta (Indian wheat flour), pappadams, etc., are obtainable from Lal Jolly, 70, Warwick Road, London, S.W.5.

PAKISTAN

*Rice is a staple item of daily diet, and the housewife really
knows how to cook it perfectly*

Compiled exclusively by the BEGAM AHMAD ALI KHAN

PAKISTAN is largely a Muslim country, so our foods are mainly Middle Eastern, with the addition of the spices used so much in India.

Wheat and rice are the staple items of our daily diet, and the three spices most used in our dishes are turmeric, coriander and chilli powder. We vary our flavours by using more of one or less of another and sometimes leaving out one of the three. All three spices—and also cummin grey, which we use in cooking nearly all our vegetables—can be obtained in London (from Selfridges Ltd., Oxford Street) or Lal Jolly, 70, Warwick Road, London, S.W.5.

RICE DISHES

On Choosing Rice

European housewives often ask how they can tell a good rice from an inferior one. We test the quality by cooking a number of samples in little muslin bags, but the chief point to look for in uncooked rice is a long, thin grain. Patna rice, now easily obtainable, is quite a good average quality and much better than the little roundish grains. Do not be put off by rice of a darker colour. It usually means that it is older and should be better than the very white varieties.

To Prepare Boiled Rice (1st method)

Soak for about 2 hours or less (this applies to Patna rice, but the time varies according to the quality of the rice). Boil in plenty of salted water in a large pan until, when you take out a grain to test it, it feels almost but not quite soft. Strain. Pour cold water over the rice, shake well to get out the water, return to the pan, which must be tightly covered by a well-fitting lid (a little butter melted in the pan before the rice is put back will prevent it from stick-

ing), and cook for about 20 minutes over a low heat.

To Prepare Rice (2nd method)

Soak the rice for about 2 hours. Fry an onion till lightly coloured in about 2 oz. fat, add the rice and double the quantity of warm water (two teacupfuls of water to one teacupful of rice), and cook fast for 10 minutes, then simmer for 20–30 minutes or until the rice grain is tender when pressed between finger and thumb and the rice is dry.

Lamb Pullao (for 4)

1 *lb. rice*	4 *oz. butter or cook-*
1 *lb. lamb*	*ing fat*
	½ *lb. onions*

Soak the rice for about 2 hours. Fry sliced onions until golden brown, add the lamb, cut into small pieces, and about ½ pint water and cook until tender and almost dry. Put in the rice, twice as much water and cook as for rice—2nd method—given above.

Chicken Pullao (for 6)

Medium-sized boiling	½ *teaspoonful saffron*
fowl	¼ *lb. butter or cook-*
1½ *lb. rice*	*ing fat*
1 *bottle yoghourt*	

Boil the chicken in a little water until tender enough to break easily into joints. Break into convenient pieces, put in a bowl, spread thickly with yoghourt and leave for about 2 hours so that the yoghourt is absorbed.

Prepare the saffron by placing it under the grill for 1 minute so that it becomes dry and crisp, powder it with the fingers, then pour over it a tablespoonful of boiling water and leave it to dissolve.

Prepare the rice by the 1st method given above, but before returning it to the pan melt the butter with ¼ cupful of water, then take out half for use later on. Strain the cooked rice and place half in a saucepan, put the chicken on top and then the remainder of the rice mixed with the saffron. Cover with a tight-fitting lid, cook fast for 7 minutes, add the remaining water and butter, and cook slowly for another 15 minutes.

Curry (for 4)

1 lb. lean stewing lamb or mutton	Potatoes
1 onion	1 teaspoonful turmeric
¼ lb. butter or cooking fat	2 teaspoonfuls coriander
Chilli powder to taste	

Fry the chopped onion in the fat until golden, add the spices and a little water gradually, stirring all the time to get the full flavour out of the spices. Add the meat, washed and cut into small pieces, and enough water to cover. Simmer slowly for 1 hour, or 1½ hours (depending on the quality of the meat), and, when tender, add sliced potatoes and continue simmering until they are cooked. (This curry should not be very dry.)

Marrow, turnips, peas, etc., can be used instead of potatoes. If using spinach or tomatoes, cook until nearly all the water has disappeared.

SWEETS

Halva (made from carrots) (for 4)

1 lb. carrots	1 pint milk
Sugar to taste	Seedless raisins or
2–3 cardamoms	chopped almonds
½ lb. butter	

Peel, wash and finely grate the carrots. Melt the butter and put into it 2 or 3 cardamoms and the carrots, and cook gently with the lid on until all the butter has been absorbed. Add the milk and simmer on a medium heat, stirring occasionally, until all the milk has dried up and the butter begins to show again at the bottom of the pan (the mixture should be the consistency of rice pudding), add sugar and chopped almonds or seedless raisins, according to taste. Serve either hot or cold.

Gujrela (for 4)

½ lb. carrots	Almonds, pistachios
1 pint milk	and angelica for
1 tablespoonful rice	decoration
Sugar to taste	

Peel, wash and grate the carrots, cook with the rice in a pint of milk slowly until

thick. Add sugar, decorate and serve ice-cold.

COOKING VEGETABLES

In Pakistan we cook all the vegetables in butter flavoured with cummin grey, usually two or three vegetables being cooked together. To cook 1 lb. potatoes, melt 2 oz. butter or cooking fat with ½ teaspoonful cummin grey. When the cummin grey is golden brown, put in the sliced potatoes, salt and pepper, ⅓ cupful of water and cook over a low heat for about 10 minutes with the lid on—or until the potatoes are a little soft—add sliced tomatoes and cook for another 5 minutes. Beans, peas or spinach may be cooked with the potatoes.

SAVOURIES, Etc.

Pouri

4 oz. white self-raising or wholemeal flour	½ oz. butter or cooking fat
Salt	Fat for frying

Shred the fat into the flour, add salt, then, with a little water, mix to the consistency of pastry. Divide into six equal portions, roll each out thinly into a circle about the size of a coffee saucer and fry in hot deep fat until it turns golden brown and becomes puffy.

Paratha

4 oz. plain flour	Butter for "spread-
2 oz. butter or lard for dough	ing" and frying
	Salt

Make a dough with the flour, butter or lard, salt and a little water, divide into four equal portions and roll each out into an oval. Spread lightly, or brush over, with butter, then fold over one long side of the oval, brush over with butter and roll, fold over the other side, brush with butter and roll again (the dough is now the shape of a rolled pancake); fold up one narrow end half-way, brush with butter, roll, then fold over the other end so that you have a small square. Roll this out thinly, still keeping it square, prick in two or three places with a fork; then fry in a very little butter until golden brown and like a pancake. Repeat with the other three portions.

Samosas

These are stuffed savoury pouri filled either with a meat or vegetable stuffing.

For the pouri

4 oz. white self-raising flour	1 oz. butter or cooking fat

A typical meal as served in India or Pakistan. The main dish (right) is Chicken Pullao, with Samosas (left) and Halva just behind as a sweet

For a meat filling

½ lb. minced meat	¼ teaspoonful
1 medium onion	turmeric
Chilli powder to taste	½ teaspoonful
Fat for frying	coriander

For a vegetable filling

½ lb. potatoes	1 oz. butter or cook-
½ teaspoonful cum-	ing fat
min grey	1 teaspoonful lemon
Salt and chilli powder	juice

Make the pouri as already described, roll out into circles and cut each circle in half. Fold the half-circle across in half again, and stick the two halves of the straight side together by damping with water, thus forming a cone shape.

The filling.—If using meat, fry the chopped onion till golden brown, add turmeric, coriander and chilli powder to taste, stirring all the time. Add the meat and cook slowly for about 20 minutes.

For the vegetable filling, peel and slice potatoes into tiny pieces about the size of large peas, cook in melted butter or cooking fat with cummin grey, salt and chilli powder until golden brown, adding lemon juice.

Fill the little cones with the mixture, fastening their tops by damping and pressing edges together. Fry in deep fat until golden brown. Serve hot as an afternoon tea dish or with cocktails.

Pakoras (Cocktail or teatime snacks)

4 oz. Gram flour	1 cupful water
(Basan Atta)	Pinch of salt
Chilli powder to taste	Spinach or lettuce
½ teaspoonful cum-	leaves or potatoes
min grey	sliced as for chips
Fat for frying	

Make a batter, using the flour, chilli powder, salt, cummin grey and water, and beating well. Take separate leaves of spinach or lettuce, or a slice of potato, dip in the batter and fry in deep, very hot fat. Serve piping hot, with chilli sauce if desired.

FRANCE

The paradise of the gourmet, where every housewife
brings a touch of true inspiration to her cooking

Some recipes, classical and regional, of specialities served à l'Ecu de France,
London, and compiled by EUGÈNE HERBODEAU

THE pre-eminence of French cookery derives from the four duchies or provinces, each as delectable as the rest, into which the culinary realm is divided. These are:

First, *La Haute Cuisine*, the aristocracy of the Art, the triumph of our great chefs, our renowned practitioners, who have set up, for every country in the civilised world to follow, a model and exemplar of cookery in perfection.

Then, *La Cuisine Bourgeoise*, that home or family cooking which is the pride and glory of the first-rate cooks and the housewives of France.

Next, *La Cuisine Impromptue*, that is to say, "unpremeditated," "pot luck," none the less exquisite for being spontaneous, "the perfume and suppliance of a minute."

And finally, *La Cuisine Régionale*, which epitomises, so to speak, the taste, the character, the individuality of each separate French province.

Of the four schools of French cookery, it is the regional school which, from the nature of the case, has hitherto been the least widely known. And judging by the success of l'Ecu de France, London, where genuine French regional dishes are served, the English public appreciate the merits of this method of cooking, the distinctive characteristic of which is its delightful originality.

In addition to our Regional Recipes, we have also included a number of Classical Dishes and Fonds which, we venture to think, every housewife who takes a pride in her table will be glad to have for reference. We mean no disrespect to Classical Cookery when we say, as we do without hesitation, that in the Regional Cookery the soul and expression of typical French cooking is really and most completely to be found.

**A chef in the Dordogne department of France prepares one
of the famous specialities of the region**

COOKERY AT HOME AND ABROAD

TWO DISHES FROM ITALY

Selected by P. G. Leoni of Leoni's Quo Vadis Restaurant, London

SUPREME DE VOLAILLE YOLANDA (above). Cut white meat from breast of a chicken with the wing bone, beat out flat. Pass through flour, beaten egg, and grated Parmesan cheese. Fry in oil until golden, arrange three spears of asparagus on top, sprinkle with grated cheese, add a walnut of butter and grill for a few minutes.

CANETON NOEMI (FROID) (below). Prepare a roast duck and serve cold with this sauce: Sieve contents of a small tin of tunny fish. Add 3 tablespoonfuls each of mayonnaise and cream and enough tomato ketchup to tint pink. Mix, season with pepper and salt. Mask the duck with cold sauce, decorate with a border of cherries. Garnish with triangles of chopped cooked tomatoes, aubergines, courgettes bound with mayonnaise and covered with sauce and gelatine.

COOKERY AT HOME AND ABROAD

NORWAY

Typical Scandinavian cold table (above): Ham, sliced thin and rolled with lettuce; roast lamb, also rolled; Italian salad; beetroot; salami with cauliflower; egg and tomato boats with cucumber; mixed vegetable plate— and to finish with, a whole gorgonzola cheese with biscuits

POLAND

Chlodnik is a Polish cold soup (right). Its rich red colouring comes from the beetroot it contains. It is served chilled with fresh cucumber, lettuce, etc., and sour cream added at the last moment. Served hot with different accompaniments, this soup is the famous Barszcz

One sure way to recapture happy memories of a holiday in Paris, with its gay cafés, is to try making some of the French dishes in this chapter

(In the following recipes the quantities have been reduced, as far as possible, to come within the scope of ordinary households. One or two, including the Fonds, have had to remain unchanged. If they were made with smaller quantities of the various ingredients, they would, due to the long cooking, simply reduce themselves to nothing.—EDITOR.)

The White Fonds

8 lb. knuckle of veal	1 stick of celery
1½ lb. fowl	1 oz. parsley stalks
12 oz. carrots	1 sprig of thyme
6 oz. onions	1 bay leaf
1 small leek	4 quarts water
½ oz. salt	

Break the veal knuckles into small pieces and put them into a casserole or stock pot with the fowl. Cover with water and add salt. Simmer gently. Remove the scum carefully as it forms. Add the vegetables. Boil for 4 hours, strain through a cloth. Keep in cool place for use when required.

Clear Fonds of Veal

6 lb. veal shoulder and knuckle	6 oz. onions
4½ lb. crushed veal bones	1½ oz. parsley stalks
	1 bay leaf
12 oz. carrots	1 sprig thyme
	4 quarts water
½ oz. salt	

Put meat and bones into the oven until browned, then place in a casserole or stock pot with the carrots and add seasonings; put the lid on and simmer for 15 minutes. Add the water, little by little, and bring to boiling point, skimming carefully. Add rest of vegetables and boil slowly for 6 hours. Strain through a cloth.

Thickened Veal Fonds

3½ pints veal fonds	½ oz. arrowroot

Boil the veal fonds until reduced to 1 pint. Mix the arrowroot with a few spoonfuls of cold fonds until smooth. Add to the reduced fonds and boil for 1 minute. Strain through muslin.

Meat Jelly

2 lb. knuckle of veal	1 oz. leek
2 lb. veal bones	1 stick celery
1¾ lb. lean beef	1 bouquet garni (bay
1 calf's foot, boned	leaf, parsley stalks,
and scalded	sprig chervil, sprig
3 oz. fresh bacon rind	tarragon, thyme)
3 oz. carrots	4 quarts water
3 oz. onions	1 egg-white

Put the knuckle, bones, calf's foot and 1 lb. lean beef with vegetables, bouquet garni, bacon rind and water in a stock pot. Bring slowly to the boil, skim carefully, and simmer for 6–8 hours. Pour through a strainer, and carefully take off the fat.

Put in a stew pan the remaining ¾ lb. minced lean beef and the egg-white. Pour the fonds on the minced meat and stir with a whisk. Bring slowly to boiling point, whisking all the time. Simmer for 15 minutes and strain.

Preparation of Glazes

Glazes are concentrated extracts of meat, poultry, game or fish, reduced to the consistency of jelly.

The fonds intended to be reduced to glaze require the use of very fresh meat and a slow and regular cooking. Great care must be taken to get perfectly transparent glazes. A large proportion of bones and meats rich in gelatinous elements, such as knuckles of veal, are indispensable. Season with great discretion, especially as regards salt. Beware of reducing the fonds too much and so destroying the delicacy of their flavour. The glaze should have the consistency of a thick syrup with a sound and clean savour, free from any bitter taste.

Court Bouillon for Fish

1 quart water	1 oz. parsley stalks
1 quart white wine	1 sprig thyme
¾ lb. carrots and	½ bay leaf
onions, cut in	1 oz. salt
round slices	¼ oz. peppercorns

Mix the liquids and seasonings in a stock pot and boil slowly.

Put the fish into cold court bouillon if whole, or into hot court bouillon if sliced. In both cases cook very slowly, simmering, not boiling.

Souse (Marinade)

4 oz. carrots	1 bay leaf
4 oz. onions	1 sprig thyme
1½ oz. shallots	2 cloves
1 oz. celery	A few peppercorns
2 cloves of garlic	2 pints white wine
3 parsley stalks	1 pint vinegar
½ pint olive oil	

Mince the carrots, onions and shallots. Put them all together, with the flavourings, into a vessel and pour in the wine, vinegar and oil. Keep in a cool place.

The meat must be seasoned with salt and pepper before being soused. This souse can be boiled, but then all vegetables and spices should be covered in oil first before adding wine and vinegar. Boil slowly for 25 minutes and let it cool before pouring it over the meat in the vessel.

SAVOURY BUTTERS

Anchovy

Pound 2 oz. fillets of best anchovy, well washed and dried; add ¼ lb. butter. Continue pounding together and pass through fine sieve.

Maître d'Hôtel

Cream ¼ lb. butter and blend with a tablespoonful of chopped parsley and the juice of ½ lemon. Season with salt and pepper.

Colbert

Same process as for Maître d'Hôtel butter, to which is added ½ teaspoonful of chopped tarragon and 1 tablespoonful of dissolved chicken glaze.

Escargot

6 oz. butter	2 teaspoonfuls
½ oz. minced shallot	chopped parsley
½ crushed clove of	1 ground peppercorn
garlic	¼ oz. salt

Mix well and keep in a cool place.

SAUCES

Les Roux

2 oz. butter	2¼ oz. flour

Melt the butter, sprinkle in the flour, and stir over low heat until it has become a flaxen colour. To have it a deeper colour, cook a little longer until it becomes hazel brown. If a roux is to be used for a Béchamel sauce, great care must be taken that it does not get coloured at all.

In order to make a sauce, add to the roux 2 pints of liquid, either clear veal fonds for a velouté or milk for a Béchamel.

Le Velouté

2½ oz. roux blond   1¼ pints white stock

Dilute the roux with the white stock. Stir while bringing to the boil, then boil steadily for ½ hour. Skim carefully. Strain with tammy and stir until cold.

Tomato Sauce (La sauce tomate)

1¼ oz. streaky bacon, cut in dice	¾ pint white stock
3¼ lb. fresh tomatoes	Small sprig thyme
2 oz. diced carrots	¼ bay leaf
1¼ oz. onions	½ clove garlic
1¼ oz. flour	¼ oz. salt
	¼ oz. sugar
Pinch of pepper	

Fry the bacon lightly in a casserole. Add carrots and onions, sliced. Fry gently and add the flour. Cook until lightly browned. Add the tomatoes, which should be crushed, the stock, herbs, garlic, salt, sugar and pepper. Bring to the boil while stirring, cover the casserole and cook slowly in the oven for ¾ hour. Pass through a strainer.

White Sauce (La sauce Béchamelle)

2½ oz. white roux
1 pint milk
½ small onion, minced
1 teaspoonful salt
1 small sprig of thyme
1 pinch of mignonette pepper

Mix the white roux with the milk, brought to boiling point. Stir until it reaches the boil. Add seasoning and cook very slowly for 30 minutes. Pass through tammy.

La Sauce Bordelaise

½ gill red wine
1 tablespoonful chopped shallots
2 oz. beef marrow
1½ gills thick veal fonds
A pinch of mignonette pepper

Add shallots and pepper to red wine and reduce to half. Add the veal fonds and simmer for about 30 minutes. Strain and add the marrow, previously poached in boiling water and cut in dice.

La Sauce Hollandaise

2 egg-yolks   6 oz. butter
Lemon juice

Put in a casserole or bowl 2 tablespoonfuls of water and the egg-yolks. Melt the butter separately in advance. Place the casserole or bowl over a pan of boiling water, add the butter and whip lightly. From time to time add a little water to make the sauce light. Season and add a few drops of lemon juice. Pass through tammy.

Mayonnaise

3 egg-yolks	½ teaspoonful salt
⅞ pint of olive oil	¾ tablespoonful vinegar or lemon juice
Pinch of white pepper	

Whip the egg-yolks with salt, pepper and a few drops of lemon juice. Add the oil drop by drop to begin with, then as a

The French housewife has an abundance of foods to choose from and likes to buy her fish, vegetables, meat and fruits from the market

thin trickle; from time to time break into the body of sauce with a dash of vinegar.

Add 3 tablespoonfuls of boiling water to ensure the cohesion of the sauce and prevent its disintegration.

La Sauce Béarnaise

6 tablespoonfuls vinegar	1 teaspoonful chervil
2 tablespoonfuls chopped shallot	Pinch of mignonette pepper
½ oz. tarragon	Pinch of salt
	3 egg-yolks
½ lb. butter	

Put into a casserole the chopped shallots, tarragon crushed, the chervil, pepper, salt and vinegar, and reduce to two-thirds. Leave for a few minutes to cool, then add the egg-yolks. Place the sauce on a low fire with the butter and whip gently until it thickens. Pass through a tammy and add 1 teaspoonful of chopped tarragon and ½ teaspoonful of chopped chervil.

CLASSICAL SOUPS

Le Pot au Feu

3½ lb. beef	1 leek
1 knuckle veal	½ stalk of celery
1½ lb. fowl	Small sprig of thyme
1 oz. salt	1 bay leaf
2 large carrots	1 small onion with
1 large turnip	clove stuck into it
1 clove of garlic	

Cover the meat in cold water. Bring slowly to boiling point and skim thoroughly. Add vegetables and herbs. Simmer slowly and evenly for 6 hours. Skim the fat off, strain, and season to taste. This stock can not only be used for soup, but it will be the basis of numerous sauces.

Potato Soup (Potage parmentier) (for 8)

1½ lb. potatoes	1 gill cream
3 whites of leeks	3 pints stock
3½ oz. butter	

Chop the leeks and cook in butter. Add potatoes, peeled and cut in large pieces. Cover with stock and bring to boil rapidly. Simmer until vegetables are tender. Whisk into a purée and pass through tammy. Reheat, adding finally butter and cream.

NOTE: This purée is the basis of numerous soups, such as:

Watercress Soup

Add to the purée ¼ lb. leaves of watercress cooked 5 minutes in salted water.

Potage Santé

Add to the purée ¼ lb. sorrel chopped finely and cooked in butter.

Lettuce Soup

Scald the lettuce in salted water, and then put it under cold water. Chop finely and cook in butter. Add to the purée.

Potage à la Reine (for 6–8)

1 3-lb. fowl	3 egg-yolks
2½ pints stock	½ lb. butter
¼ lb. rice	1 gill cream

Cook the fowl in the stock until tender. Remove the fowl. Add rice and cook thoroughly. Bone fowl, retain the breast in fillets. Pound the rest of the flesh, then add the cooked rice and continue to pound into a fine purée. Pass through tammy, diluting with stock. Replace on fire and bring to boil. Withdraw from fire and add butter, cream and well-beaten egg-yolks. Garnish the soup with the breast cut into very small dice. Season to taste.

Green Pea Soup (Potage St. Germain) (for 6)

1 pint large shelled green peas	1 lettuce
	1 green top of leek
Cream and butter	

Cook in salted water the peas, lettuce and leek chopped finely. Strain in colander and retain the stock. Pound in mortar to reduce to a purée and pass through tammy. Dilute with the stock and bring to boiling point. Remove from the fire and add about ½ oz. butter and a little cream.

For a garnish, add a few whole peas previously boiled in water, a few leaves of chervil and small croûtons of bread fried in butter and served separately.

Potage Bonne Femme (for 8–10)

5 whites of leeks	½ oz. salt
1 lb. potatoes	2½ oz. butter
2 quarts tepid water	

Chop leeks and cook in butter. Add the water, potatoes and salt, and cook gently. Before serving, add the butter. Serve with small rounds of toasted bread.

Consommé à la Minute (for 6)

2 lb. beef with all fat removed, and hashed	2½ pints cold water
	Salt to taste

Place meat and water in a casserole and bring very slowly to boiling point. Skim thoroughly. Add salt. After boiling slowly for another 10 minutes, pass through a fine cloth.

Another Method. — Bring the water to the boil with a little salt. Add a stick of celery, a grated carrot, a small chopped onion and a sprig of chervil.

After a few minutes of boiling, add the meat.

Boil very slowly for 10 minutes and pass through a wet cloth.

Lobster Soup (Bisque d'homard) (for 8)

2 *lb. small lobsters*
2 *oz. carrots*
2 *oz. onions*
1 *sprig thyme*
1 *small bay leaf*
Few sprigs of parsley
5 *oz. fresh butter*
5 *oz. rice*
1 *small glass brandy*
1 *gill white wine*
2½ *pints of stock*
½ *oz. salt*
½ *gill cream*
Pepper

Cut the carrots and onions into small dice and brown in butter. Remove the shells from the lobsters, well washed and cut up in small pieces, and chop the flesh finely. Season with salt and a little freshly ground pepper. Add the herbs, brandy and the white wine. Cover with ½ pint of stock and cook for 15 minutes.

Cook separately the rice with the remainder of stock. Add all ingredients and the cooked rice, and pass the whole through tammy. Dilute this purée with ⅛ pint of stock, ⅛ pint of cream, and add the butter. Correct seasoning, adding a pinch of Cayenne pepper.

Only in Marseilles can you obtain all the varied ingredients needed for the authentic Bouillabaisse, including many kinds of shell fish and other sea food

and cover with white or rosé wine. Put on a brisk fire until cooked, remove the fish and keep it warm; strain the stock and pour it over small browned onions and mushrooms; bind this roux with two egg-yolks (no flour) and 3 or 4 tablespoonfuls of cream, whipping it gently without letting it boil; then, in what remains of the stock, warm up the fish on a hot fire; place it in a deep dish upon slices of toasted bread, and pour the whole of the stock over it.

FISH DISHES

Stewed Eels Meusienne (La matelote d'anguille Meusienne) (Nancy)

The Matelote Lorraine is made with carp, pike, large and small barbel or, failing that, eel. Cut the fish in pieces and put in a casserole with salt, pepper, bay leaf, thyme, a minced onion, parsley, 2 cloves,

Fillets of Pike in White Butter (Le brochet de Loire au beurre blanc) (Tours)

The pike can be boiled in a court bouillon (see p. 450) or else baked in the oven on a bed of carrots, onions, parsley, thyme, bay leaf, peppercorns, a spray of fennel and moistened with a glass of good white Anjou wine. Once cooked and drained, cover with melted butter, sprinkle with chopped parsley and serve at once.

Beurre Blanc (White Butter) (for 6)

2 tablespoonfuls white vinegar	1 chopped shallot 6 oz. fresh butter
Salt and pepper	

Reduce to half the vinegar with the chopped shallot, salt and pepper; before the reduction is complete, and while still over a hot fire, add 2 oz. butter. When it begins to bubble, remove the saucepan from the fire and add, in small quantities, remainder of butter, shaking the pan constantly without whipping.

Pike cooked in Chablis (Le brochet des settons rôti au Chablis) (Dijon)

Thickly butter a flat gratin dish; sprinkle over it 2 or 3 finely cut shallots; moisten with ½ pint Chablis wine and add 2 or 3 crushed tomatoes. Cut and clean the pike, season with salt and pepper, and place in the middle of the dish. Put in a hot oven, baste every 5 minutes. After cooking for 25–30 minutes it should be well browned.

Serve on a long dish, garnished with slices of lemon and chopped parsley placed round the fish. Add to the sauce about 2 oz. butter. Beat in without boiling. Pass through a sieve and pour over the pike.

Le Saumon Braisé au Vin du Rhin (Strasbourg) (for 4–6)

1 lb. fresh salmon	Sprig of thyme,
½ bottle of Sylvaner	parsley and chervil
1 carrot	1 bay leaf
1 onion	Salt and pepper
2 oz. butter	Cream and lemon juice

Cut the carrot and onion into slices and fry slightly in a casserole. Add the seasoning and Sylvaner. Place the salmon in the casserole and braise in the oven. When cooked, skin and dress on the serving dish. Reduce the sauce slightly, add 2 tablespoonfuls of cream, a tablespoonful of lemon juice and bind with Hollandaise sauce (see p. 451). Cover the fish with the sauce, and garnish with a few mushrooms, pieces of puff pastry and slices of truffle.

Le Sole au plat à la Rochellaise (Bordeaux)

Cover the soles in dry white wine, with chopped shallots, mushrooms cut in small pieces and crushed tomatoes; season strongly with salt, pepper and paprika.

Poach on a low fire for about 10 minutes. When cooked, drain and keep them warm. Add to the sauce half a glass of white vinegar and some cream and reduce. Add Hollandaise sauce (see p. 451) and heat slightly on a corner of the fire. Garnish with shelled shrimps; add lemon juice in suitable quantity to flavour.

Cover the soles with this sauce, brown under the grill and place a large slice of truffle on each sole before serving.

Les Filets de Sole à la façon du pêcheur Cauchois (Rouen) (for 6)

12 good-sized sole fillets	2 glasses well-flavoured stock
2 carrots and an equal amount of parsley root	2 oz. butter Juice of 1 lemon 1 tablespoonful
2 sticks of celery	chopped parsley
6 mushrooms	Few small heads of
2 glasses of white wine	blanched mushrooms
Few shelled shrimps	

Chop into dice the carrots, parsley root, and celery, and blanch well. Chop the mushrooms and keep them aside. Put the fillets of sole in a well-buttered pan, add the wine, stock, carrots, parsley root, celery and mushrooms. Place over a hot fire and bring to the boil. When cooked, remove fillets and arrange them on a dish diagonally. Drain the vegetables and arrange around the dish.

Stir the sauce and cook gently until it reduces and thickens. Remove from the fire and add butter, lemon juice, chopped parsley, small heads of mushrooms and shelled shrimps. Cover the fish with the sauce and serve very hot.

Le Turbotin Braisé au Champagne Brut (Rheims) (for 6–8)

1 chicken turbot	Parsley
1 bottle Brut Champagne	Cream 4 oz. butter
¼ lb. shallots	Juice of 1 lemon
2 onions	Few braised mushrooms
Chervil	rooms

Slice the onions and shallots, and add chervil and parsley to form a bed in a casserole. Add champagne. Butter the turbot and place in the casserole. Braise in a moderate oven, basting frequently.

When cooked, strain and place on the serving dish. Reduce the liquor, add butter, juice of a lemon and a little cream. Place over the fish a few braised mushrooms and pour the sauce over it.

Homard à l'Américaine
(Classical Modern) (for 6)

1 lobster (about 2 lb.)
4 tablespoonfuls
    olive oil
2 tablespoonfuls
    butter
5 tablespoonfuls
    brandy
4 oz. butter
1 gill dry white wine
2 chopped shallots
6 peeled, pipped,
    chopped tomatoes
1 clove garlic
Pinch of parsley
½ lemon.
Salt and pepper
Chopped parsley and chervil

Split the lobster down the middle. Remove the pocket at the top of the head. Put on one side the creamy part which will be found at the side of the pocket, crush with a fork on a plate and mix in a spoonful of butter. Remove the claws, crack the shell to remove the meat after it is boiled; cut each half of the lobster in three pieces; season with salt and pepper.

Heat the oil with a tablespoonful of butter. Place the pieces of lobster in the boiling sauce. Toss over the fire until they take on a bright red colour; sprinkle in the brandy and wine; add the shallots, garlic, tomatoes and parsley; cover the saucepan, cook for 20 minutes.

Place the pieces in a deep dish; mix with the liquid the creamy part removed from the pocket at the top of the head. Keep warm, without cooking, and add in small pieces the ¼ lb. butter and the lemon juice. Sprinkle with parsley and chervil finely chopped.

The culinary art goes really gay—a roast is intricately and beautifully decorated with a flower design by a Paris chef

MEAT AND POULTRY

Braising (L'estouffade) (Classical) (for 6)

2 lb. ribs of beef	½ oz. salt
½ lb. lean bacon	Pinch of pepper
3 medium-sized onions	½ lb. mushrooms
1 clove garlic	1 quart red wine
1 bouquet garni	1 quart veal fonds
	Butter

Cut the beef in small squares of about 4 oz. Cut the bacon in large dice. Blanch, fry and drain it. In the same fat, fry lightly the pieces of beef and the onions cut in quarters. Drain the fat and pour in the red wine and the veal fonds thickened. Add the garlic crushed, the bouquet garni, salt and pepper, and cook in a covered saucepan in a slow oven for 4 hours. Add the bacon and the mushrooms fried in butter. Remove any fat from the sauce and simmer for another 30 minutes.

Truffles (Le filet de bœuf à la Sarladaise) (Périgueux) (for 12)

4 lb. fillet of beef	Truffles

For the marinade

½ bottle white wine	1 tablespoonful chopped thyme
2 tablespoonfuls brandy	Bay leaf
Sliced onion	Clove of garlic
1 tablespoonful chopped parsley	Salt and pepper

455

Lard the beef and stick with truffles. Souse it overnight in the marinade. Remove the fillet and place the marinade on one side. Cover the fillet well with butter and roast, basting frequently with the marinade mixture. Remove the fillet, which should be blood-red when cut. Use the remainder of the marinade to drain the dish and obtain a thick, well-flavoured gravy. Serve with potatoes and truffles cut into rounds and sautéd in butter. Serve the gravy separately.

Stewed Oxtail (La queue de bœuf en hochepot à la façon du Cambrésis) (Amiens) (for 5)

1 oxtail	Salt and pepper
2 boned calves' feet	10 small chipolata
Carrots, onions,	sausages
thyme, bay leaf,	1 lettuce
garlic	Dry white wine and
Bacon rinds	stock
Few mushroom tops	

Slice the carrots and onions and add thyme, bay leaf, and garlic to form a bed in a casserole. Joint the oxtail and place the pieces on the bed of vegetables. Add bacon rinds, boned calves' feet, and leave in the oven for ½ hour. Steep all the pieces in dry white wine and stock mixed. Season with salt and pepper, cover with a buttered paper and cook for 4 hours in a gentle oven.

When the pieces are cooked, remove them into a sauté pan, skim the sauce well and strain. Cut the bacon rinds in coarse shreds and put them back with blanched mushroom tops, braised carrots, chipolata sausages, small onions and lettuce braised in butter. Simmer for ½ hour.

Serve very hot with baked potatoes.

Leg of Lamb with Vegetables (La gasconnade de fins-gigots aux légumes nouveaux) (Bayonne) (for 8)

Thickly butter a nice plump leg of lamb, graft a good clove of garlic in the knuckle and roast on a flat dish. Brown on the dish a few small slightly smoked lardons (strips of fat bacon) and cook in a slow heat, basting frequently.

Separately, sauté in a pan a few chopped shallots, with very finely cut celery. Prepare carrots and turnips, 2 pints of green peas, a few tops of mushrooms and small spring onions, and sauté in butter. When this garnish becomes mellow and light brown, add it to the leg a short while before serving.

Serve the meat, which must be pink under the knife.

Rinse the meat dish with a dash of Madeira and a few tablespoonfuls of white fonds (see p. 449). Simmer for a few moments. Sprinkle with chopped parsley.

Poulet à la Crème (Classical) (for 6)

1 3-lb. chicken	2 egg-yolks
6 small onions, peeled	2 oz. butter
2 cloves of garlic	Bouquet garni
1 oz. lean bacon	1 glass of very dry
1 pint fresh cream	white wine

Into a casserole put the butter, the bacon diced and blanched, the onions, bouquet garni and garlic. Melt on a low fire. Put in the chicken cut in pieces, salt, and stir with a wooden spoon so that nothing sticks to the bottom of the casserole. Cook until a light brown. Put the casserole on a very low fire. Cover and cook for 20 minutes. Remove the pieces of chicken and keep them warm; drain off all the grease. Add the glass of white wine and reduce.

In the meantime, mix the yolks with the cream and add this to the mixture in the casserole, stirring all the time, but do not let it boil again. Add the portions of chicken to the sauce, warm it up, and season.

La Poulet Sauté comme à Chambéry (Grenoble)

1 tender chicken	Few lardons (strips
2 oz. butter	of fat bacon)
½ pint Chambéry	½ lb. artichokes
vermouth	¾ pint cream
Few small mush-	Paprika
rooms	Chopped parsley

Cut the chicken in pieces and brown in the butter. Add the Chambéry vermouth, small tops of mushrooms, lardons, artichokes blanched and cut in four, cream, and a dash of paprika. Continue cooking for about 20 minutes.

Serve the chicken; season and complete the sauce with a few spoonfuls of cream. Serve very hot with a sprinkling of chopped parsley.

A dish to make a hostess famous in a night—Pancakes in the French manner, flavoured with brandy

La Poularde Sautée à la Nantaise (Nantes)

1 young chicken	1 glass white
1 onion, minced	Muscadet wine
1 carrot, minced	Vinegar
2 oz. butter	1 shallot, chopped
Bouquet garni	Hollandaise sauce
Salt, pepper and	(see p. 451)
paprika	

For the garnish

Mushrooms	Carrots
Small onions	Artichokes

Put into a casserole the onion, carrot, bouquet garni, salt and pepper, butter and chicken. Cook over a moderate fire for a few minutes, add the wine, dash of vinegar, and continue cooking for 30–40 minutes, according to size of the chicken. Place the chicken in an earthenware dish.

To the juice remaining in the casserole add the chopped shallot and reduce strongly. Add vinegar to taste, and increase with the Hollandaise sauce. As a garnish, add mushrooms cut in quarters, small onions, carrots cut in four, and a dice of artichoke bottoms, all blanched. Season to taste, use paprika lightly, in order that the sauce may retain a golden tint; cover the chicken with the sauce and garnish.

Sprinkle with finely chopped herbs.

Le Poulet Sauté à la manière des Vignerons Tourangeaux (Tours)

Brown in good butter a handful of small onions, a generous helping of small leeks cut in strips, lardons (strips of bacon), small heads of mushrooms and crushed tomatoes. When this garnish has taken a good colour, add a bottle of Vouvray, a tablespoonful of cream; season with salt, pepper and paprika. In a separate pan cook in butter some quarters of chicken and, when nicely coloured, simmer with the sauce until quite cooked. If necessary, finish the binding with double cream. Just before serving, sprinkle with chopped parsley and serve very hot.

La Fricassée du Poulet à l'ancienne
(Classical) (for 6–8)

1 4-lb. chicken	½ gill stock
2 oz. butter	½ gill cream
½ lb. small onions	3 egg-yolks
½ lb. white mush-	2 tablespoonfuls flour
rooms	Bouquet garni
Lemon juice, salt and pepper	

Cut the chicken in pieces, season with salt and pepper; fry lightly with the butter in a pan without browning. Sprinkle in the flour. Cook for a few minutes without browning. Pour in the stock and cook for 15 minutes. Drain out the pieces of chicken and place in a fresh pan, adding the onions partly cooked and the raw mushrooms. Pour over all the sauce passed through a pointed strainer. Add the bouquet garni and cook very slowly for about 40 minutes. At the last moment, give body to the sauce with the yolks mixed with the cream and a little lemon juice.

Le Caneton farci et mijoté à l'ancienne mode de Provence (Marseilles)

1 duckling	A few stoned green
Périgueux or Brown	olives
Sauces (see Sauces	¼ lb. artichoke
Chapter)	bottoms
Madeira	Tops of mushrooms

For the stuffing

½ lb. streaky bacon	Egg-yolk
Duckling liver	20 black olives
2 or 3 chopped onions	20 white mushrooms
½ teaspoonful fried	Few Jamaica peppers
shallot	Truffles
Pepper and salt	Armagnac

To make the stuffing.—Boil the bacon until almost cooked, then mince finely. Add the liver, chopped onions, shallot, salt and pepper and mix well. Bind with the egg-yolk. Stone the olives and chop with the mushrooms, Jamaica peppers, and mix with the hash. Add a few dice of truffles, moisten with a good dash of Armagnac.

Stuff the duckling with this, 24 hours before cooking. Braise, adding a rich Périgueux sauce well moistened with Madeira, quarters of artichoke bottoms, tops of mushrooms, and a few stoned green olives. Allow 20 minutes per lb. for cooking.

Jugged Hare (Classical) (for 6–8)

1 4-lb. hare	7 oz. streaky bacon
20 small peeled	cut into dice and
onions	blanched
5 crushed cloves of	Bouquet garni
garlic	4 oz. butter
5 minced shallots	3 tablespoonfuls flour
2½ pints red wine	1 glass brandy
Salt and pepper	

Skin and clean the hare, taking care to collect all the blood, and the liver. Carve the hare into equal portions of 1½–2 oz. each. Place the butter in a sauté pan and lightly brown the bacon. Drain and spread on a plate. In the same butter, brown the small onions, drain, and keep on one side with the bacon.

Season the hare with salt and pepper, place in the pan and brown on a quick fire. Add the shallots, garlic and the flour. Cook for a few moments, add the wine and brandy, bring to the boil, skim, add the bouquet garni, the bacon and the small onions. Cover, and cook on a slow fire.

Chop the liver finely, mix with the blood and, when the hare is cooked, blend the sauce with this mixture but do not allow it to boil.

Le Civet de Lièvre de Diane de Château-morand (Belley) (for 6–8)

1 hare	¼ pint stock
1 oz. fat pork	1 tablespoonful
2½ oz. butter	olive oil
1 oz. flour	¼ pint good red wine

For the marinade

1 wineglassful	2 onions
wine vinegar	Pepper and salt
½ wineglassful	Thyme
olive oil	

Skin and gut the hare, carefully preserving the blood and the liver. Place the hare in a tureen large enough to hold it whole, pour over it the vinegar and olive oil. Season with pepper, salt and thyme, and 1 onion cut in rounds. Turn the hare frequently in this marinade and leave for 12 hours at least before cooking.

Chop together the onion and pork, cut the hare in pieces and cook the whole in butter for 20 minutes, when the flesh will have taken on a white-grey colour and exuded its moisture. Sprinkle with the flour and cook slowly for 25 minutes, stirring frequently. Pour in the stock and red wine. Add seasoning and cook for another 35 minutes.

Pound the black liver to a fine purée and dilute with the marinade after removing the onion and thyme. Mix the blood with it and pass through a sieve. Pour the whole preparation over the hare 5 minutes before serving, and bring to the boil. Try the sauce and, if it is insipid, season with a dash of vinegar. Finish by adding a tablespoonful of olive oil.

This can be made on the eve of the day when it is to be eaten, as it is better when warmed up. Its succulence depends on the quality of the hare and on the quantity of blood gathered: the colour of the ragoût must be like chocolate boiled in water. (*After Lucien Tendret.*)

In Brittany they wear their colourful national costumes (above) to serve their famous regional dishes

A Soufflé (right) is not an extravagant or a difficult dish to make—and what a thrill when it comes out of the oven looking like that

Rice Pilaw (Pilaff de riz)

9 oz. Patna rice	1 tablespoonful
4 oz. butter	chopped onion
1 pint stock	Pinch of salt

Cook the onion in 2 oz. butter in a casserole until golden brown. Mix in the rice with a wooden spoon until it is well blended with hot butter and add salt. Have boiling stock ready and pour over it. Cover the casserole with a tight-fitting lid and put it in the oven for 18 minutes. When

Soufflé by Creda. All other photographs in this chapter: French Government Tourist Office

cooked, mix in quickly 2 oz. butter in small pieces.

Artichokes à la Greque

15 *small artichokes*
1¼ *pints water*
¼ *pint olive oil*
⅓ *oz. salt*
Juice of 3 lemons
Sprig of thyme
1 *bay leaf*
*Few whole pepper-
corns*
1 *stick of celery*

Trim the artichokes, cut into four, remove fibrous part, blanch in boiling water with lemon juice, strain and cool. Boil together all the other ingredients, which will constitute a marinade. Cook the artichokes in the marinade. Take the pan off the fire and let them cool down in the marinade. This same marinade may be used for cauliflowers, small onions, leeks, squash, celery, etc.

CLASSICAL PASTRY RECIPES

Short Pastry (La pâte à foncer)

1 *lb. flour*	⅓ *oz. salt*
10 *oz. butter*	1 *egg*
2 *oz. sugar*	¼ *pint water*

Cream the butter, spread the flour in a circle, making a well. Mix the butter with the sugar, egg and salt, and place in the middle, incorporating flour and water. Do not knead, but beat and shape into a ball, and keep in a cool place.

Noodles (La pâte à nouilles)

1 lb. flour	5 egg-yolks
4 whole eggs	½ oz. salt

Mix the flour and salt with the eggs. Knead several times to obtain a well-mixed paste, and let it rest for 1 hour. Cut it in long thin strips, and lightly dry, spread over a cloth.

Poach the noodles for 10–12 minutes.

Pancakes (La pâte à crêpes) (for 6–8)

½ lb. flour	1¼ pints milk
3 oz. sugar	1 glass of brandy
Pinch of salt	2 tablespoonfuls of
6 eggs	orange flower water

Put the flour, sugar and salt in a bowl and add the eggs. Mix until smooth and thin out with the milk. Add the brandy and orange flower water at the last moment before cooking.

Batter (La pâte à frire)

¼ lb. flour	⅓ pint lukewarm
Pinch of salt	water
2 tablespoonfuls	2 egg-whites
olive oil	

Place all except the egg-whites in a bowl. Mix well without working the paste. Just before using, add the egg-whites whipped to a snow.

Les Madeleines

5 eggs	½ teaspoonful
½ lb. castor sugar	lemon-flavoured
½ lb. clarified butter	sugar
7 oz. flour	Pinch of salt

Mix in a bowl the sugar, salt and 2 eggs. Whip the mixture until it is quite white. Add the other 3 eggs, one at a time, always whipping. When the mixture is a stiff froth, add alternately the flour, passed through a sieve, and the clarified butter, folding it carefully into the mixture.

Put the mixture into special tins of "madeleine" shape and cook in a moderately hot oven.

Le Soufflé (for 4)

1 gill milk	1 oz. potato flour
2 oz. sugar	3 egg-yolks
Pinch of salt	½ oz. butter
4 egg-whites	

Mix the flour with 2 tablespoonfuls of cold milk. Boil the rest of the milk with the sugar and salt, and pour over the flour paste. Cook the mixture for 2 minutes and, while still stirring, remove from the fire and add the egg-yolks and the butter. Mix well and add suitable flavouring to taste. At the last moment, add the whites whipped to a stiff froth. Cook in a moderate oven.

Custard (La crème Anglaise) (for 4)

1 pint milk	4 oz. sugar
½ pod vanilla	8 egg-yolks

Boil the milk with the vanilla; whisk the egg-yolks and sugar and pour the milk over them. Cook this cream over the fire, stirring constantly until nearly boiling.

To keep this mixture a really creamy texture, add, if liked, ½ oz. of arrowroot to the yolks when beating.

Fritters (Les beignets soufflés) (for 6–8)

½ pint water	¼ oz. sugar
1¾ oz. butter	4 eggs
Pinch of salt	6 oz. flour

Put into a saucepan the water, butter, salt and sugar, and bring to the boil. Shake in the flour, previously passed through a sieve. Work it into a paste until it forms a thick cream and will easily leave the sides. Remove from the fire and add the eggs one by one, continuing to knead the paste. Flavour to taste with lemon, vanilla, etc.

To cook.—Place in moderately heated fat, pieces of the paste the size of a walnut. Heat gradually until a golden brown. Remove and drain. Sprinkle with soft sugar.

Soufflé Surprise du Château Trompette à Bordeaux (Bordeaux) (for 6–8)

5 egg-yolks	1 lb. castor sugar
8 egg-whites	

Whisk the egg-yolks and castor sugar until thick and creamy. Whip separately the egg-whites until stiff and mix all together, using a butter pat.

Set out in a silver dish, finger-biscuits steeped in a liqueur (preferably Grand Marnier). Cover with a vanilla ice. Pour out the egg mixture in a tall heap. Smooth with the butter-pat to give it a regular shape, and decorate.

Glaze in a hot oven for 2 or 3 minutes. Serve at once. Flame.

To flame.—Place over it 2 or 3 egg-shells containing the liqueur. Set fire to it and shake the shells so that the burning liqueur runs over the sides of the soufflé.

RESTAURANT FRENCH

A handy guide to some of the French terms you may find
on the menu and with which you may not be quite familiar

Abricot: Apricot.

À la carte: Indicates choice of any dish shown.

Aloyau de bœuf: Beef, sirloin of.

Ananas: Pineapple.

Anchois: Anchovy.

Anguille: Eel.

Asperges: Asparagus.

Bœuf: Beef.

Bombe: A moulded ice cream, probably including a richer ice cream, fruit and nuts.

Bouchées: Very small patties of puff paste with savoury fillings.

Café au lait: Coffee, white.

Café noir: Coffee, black.

Canapés: Small savouries; various shapes of fried or toasted bread with savoury toppings.

Canard rôti: Duck, roast.

Canard sauvage: Duck, wild.

Carrelet: Plaice.

Champignons: Mushrooms.

Chaudfroid: A sauce, of which Béchamel is the base, for masking cold, cooked meats. A cold entrée.

Chou-fleur: Cauliflower.

Consommé: Clear meat soup, served hot, or cold and jellied.

Consommé de volaille: Chicken soup.

Côte de bœuf rôtie: Beef, roast of.

Côtelettes d'Agneau: Lamb cutlets.

Crêpes: Pancakes.

Entrecôte: A steak cut from the sirloin.

Entrée: A hot or cold side dish.

Entremets douceurs: Sweets.

Escalopes: Thin steaks cut from fillet or leg of veal, usually egg and breadcrumbed and lightly cooked in sauté pan.

Faisan: Pheasant.

Foie-gras: A savoury paste of goose liver and herbs served with thin toast.

Fraises: Strawberries.

Framboises: Raspberries.

Fricandeau: Fillet of veal, larded and braised.

Fromage: Cheese.

Fruits confits: Preserved fruits.

Gigot de mouton: Leg of mutton.

Haricots verts: French beans.

Hollandaise: Well-known sauce of which butter is the base.

Homard: Lobster.

Jambon: Ham.

Légumes: Vegetables.

Lièvre en casserole: Hare, jugged.

Maître d'hôtel: Well-known garnish of chopped parsley pounded with butter, seasoned with salt, pepper and lemon juice.

Maquereau: Mackerel.

Marrons glacés: Chestnuts, glazed.

Mornay: Well-known sauce, Béchamel base with finely grated Gruyère or Parmesan cheese added.

Navarin: Haricot mutton.

Nouilles: Noodles.

Oie rôtie: Goose, roast.

Oignons: Onions.

Pêche: Peach.

Perdrix: Partridge.

Petits pois: Green peas.

Poire: Pear.

Poisson: Fish.

Pommes-de-terre: Potatoes.

Potage: Soup.

Potage lyonnais: Onion soup.

Potage parmentier: Potato soup.

Poulet rôti: Chicken, roast.

Poussin: Baby chicken.

Prunes: Plums.

Purée de lentilles: Lentil soup.

Ragoût: Meat stew.

Raisins: Grapes.

Ris de veau: Sweetbreads.

Rognons: Kidneys.

Saumon: Salmon.

Selle de mouton: Saddle of mutton.

Soufflé: A very light egg dish, sweet or savoury.

Table d'hôte: A set meal, usually consisting of Soup or Hors d'œuvres; Meat or Fish; Sweet or Biscuits and Cheese.

Tête de veau: Calf's head.

Tournedos: Small, thinly sliced fillets of beef.

Veau: Veal.

SWITZERLAND

Some typically simple peasant dishes described by the proprietors of Maison Suisse and Bartholdi's Restaurant and Stores, London

THEY eat well in Switzerland. The Swiss as a nation are interested in good food and their fare is distinguished by a glorious variety—not surprisingly, when one considers the geography of the country. The best dishes of three neighbouring lands go to make up those wonderful meals which impress the tourists in Switzerland. But the cuisine in the hotels is too international to be characteristic. The dishes given here, often very simple and peasant in origin, are those found in the homes of the Swiss people—in town homes as well as in remote mountain châlets. They represent the traditional fare of Switzerland, influenced by French cuisine in the south-western region, Italian in the southern, and German in the northern and eastern parts.

The geographical position of a region, the Swiss dairy produce—the plentiful milk, butter, eggs and well-known cheeses, such as Gruyère, Emmenthaler, Appenzeller and Vacherin—and the mountain air (whetting the appetite!) determine the type —and quantity—of the food.

The famous **Fondue** is a truly Swiss national cheese dish, made all over the country and particularly in the French-speaking parts.

It is a fine dish to return to on a cold winter's night, and its method of serving and consumption is very much a family, domestic affair.

To make it, the Swiss housewife allows about 6 oz. of Gruyère or Emmenthaler cheese and a wineglassful of white wine (preferably a dry wine) for each member of her family. She rubs garlic around the inside of an iron pot or fireproof earthenware dish or heavy saucepan, and puts in a piece of butter to keep the cheese from sticking. She then adds the cheese, grated, with half the quantity of wine, and puts it on a very low heat to melt and come to the boil, stirring it constantly. After about 20 minutes, she adds the rest of the wine. It should now have a batter-like consistency.

Meanwhile the family has gathered round the table, each member armed with a piece of bread impaled on a fork (preferably French bread with a strong crust). The housewife puts the pot or dish on the table over a spirit flame to keep the cheese at boiling point, with just a bubble now and then working up. The family then gets to work. Each member dips his or her piece of bread in the dish, twisting the fork to wind the strands of cheese safely round the bread—and then just eats it off the fork, dipping in more bread until the pot is empty. That is all—except that Kirsch should be drunk with it. In some districts a liqueur glass of Kirsch is added to the pot, but this is frowned on elsewhere as confusing the flavours. No other course to the meal is needed—the *fondue* is enough to satisfy any appetite.

There are several variations. Some people, for instance, add onions, cut into large pieces, to the pot, and some add a little cornflour. Strong-flavoured local cheeses are often used, and gherkins eaten with the *fondue*. Cider can be used instead of wine.

Raclette is another favourite cheese dish of great simplicity—to make a snack meal. A slab of Gruyère is held against the fire or put under the grill. As the cheese melts it is scraped off with a knife, put on a plate, and eaten with crusty bread and gherkins.

Dishes from the Northern and Eastern Regions

These dishes are made everywhere, but are mainly characteristic of the German-speaking areas (the larger part of Switzerland).

Bernerplatte is a well-known Swiss dish

turnips, *Sauerkraut*, potatoes.... A little of the meat liquor is served also.

Rippli is smoked and salted loin of pork cooked on a layer of *Sauerkraut*. To make this for 4 persons, put about 1½ lb. of *Sauerkraut* and 2 lb. of pork in a big saucepan, with just enough water not to have to throw any away at the end. Simmer until the meat is ready and

With appetites whetted by the mountain air, visitors to Switzerland enjoy a meal served by waiters on skates. Below, a typical home scene—serving the famous Fondue is a very domestic affair

Photos: Swiss National Tourist Office and Swiss Federal Railways

Everyone comes to the table armed with a piece of bread impaled on a fork—and dips in the Fondue that bubbles merrily in a fireproof bowl over a lighted spirit lamp

only a little juice left. Potatoes are sometimes cooked in the same saucepan.

Speck und Bohnen is another popular dish in Swiss homes. Fry onions in a big pan, add runner beans and toss them in the fat, then add a piece of bacon and water to cover it. Simmer until the bacon is cooked.

Sausages of all kinds and smoked ham are much in evidence. Among the sausages, **Cervelat** is a favourite, composed of beef and pork. The Swiss take the skin off, cut it into very thin slices and serve it with "heaps of onions," sliced and dressed with oil and vinegar.

—and an elaborate one when it appears in its full glory. It consists of an assortment of boiled meats, served hot. As many as ten kinds of meat can be used—fresh beef, salt beef, streaky bacon, tongue, Frankfürter and other boiled sausages, perhaps a piece of boiled calf's head, and so on. With this noble array a variety of vegetables is served—cabbage, celery, leeks,

Bratwurst, a veal sausage made with milk, is fried and eaten with a salad—perhaps a cabbage salad (white cabbage shredded very finely and dressed with oil and vinegar). And it may be accompanied by *roesti*.

Roesti is a simple dish, found everywhere in Switzerland. To prepare this, boil potatoes in their jackets, peel and let them go cold before using. Then slice or shred them. Fry some sliced onions in shallow fat, add the potatoes, and fry to a golden brown. This must be done quickly and the *roesti* served as soon as ready. If the potatoes are shredded, it can be turned out like a pancake. This is eaten with a meat dish or on its own. Swiss farmers like it for breakfast.

Knoepfli is a favourite dish in Swiss homes. For this, make a thick dough with $\frac{1}{2}$ lb. of plain flour, two eggs, milk and salt. It must be well beaten. Let it stand for an hour or so, if possible. Have a large saucepan ready with boiling salted water. Put some of the dough on a small board and, from this, cut thin strips straight into the water. Do small quantities at a time. When the strips come to the top (after about 2 minutes), they are cooked. Put them into a dish with grated cheese on top and melted butter or breadcrumbs fried in butter.

Dishes from the Southern and Western Regions

Swiss dishes from these parts naturally show French and Italian influences. Spaghetti and other *pasta* are used a great deal.

Croûton au Fromage.—Make a pancake batter with milk and egg. Cut pieces of Emmenthaler cheese about 1 in. square and $\frac{1}{4}$ in. thick. Put them into the batter and lift them out again, well coated, with the help of two forks. Fry them in deep fat.

The following is a popular variation of the Italian **Gnocchi**, using potatoes, which give lightness to the dish.

Mix $\frac{1}{2}$ lb. of flour with $\frac{1}{2}$ lb. of boiled and mashed potatoes; make into a paste with two beaten eggs and a little milk. Roll it out, then roll it up and cut it on the slant into pieces about the size of a nut. Press each piece with a fork into a cockleshell shape. Then let them dry for a time,

with a little flour sprinkled under and over them. Drop them into a pan of boiling salted water, and boil for about 20 minutes. Lift them out and cook in butter until golden. Serve with a sauce made with chopped onion, garlic and well-fried tomatoes, and sprinkle with grated Parmesan cheese.

Ricotta is found in the Ticino district. After cheese is made, the residue is treated to produce a curd. This curd, when fresh, is beaten up with eggs, salt and pepper, and fried in butter.

The Italian **Polenta** is made in Switzerland as follows: Boil maize flour in a copper pan of boiling salted water for about 20 minutes to make a stiff paste. Work a piece of butter into it. Let it cool, then cut it up and sauté in butter, or serve as it is with a brown sauce. Or press the *polenta* into buttered moulds lined with plenty of grated cheese. Turn out and eat with meat dishes.

Morilles.—Mushrooms are a favourite food in Switzerland, and people climb the slopes gathering them. Here is a dish popular in Lausanne and Geneva, using the wild mushrooms, *morilles* (obtainable in tins in the U.K.). Sauté the mushrooms in butter with chopped shallots, according to taste, and a very little garlic. Add fresh cream, salt and pepper, and simmer. Add a little butter when cooked. Dish up and keep hot. Thicken the sauce with cornflour and pour over. This is served as a separate dish. The ordinary field mushrooms are also cooked in this way, but *morilles* give a finer flavour.

Soup is a very regular feature of Swiss fare, but there is none specifically Swiss. Vegetable soup with a meat base is the most common.

Similarly, the sweets, cakes and pastries which delight the visitors in the hotels are mostly French and Austrian in origin. Switzerland does not even claim the familiar "Swiss Roll." (This is said to have been invented by a Swiss chef.) In Swiss homes, cheese and fruit tend to take the place of a sweet course.

The celebrated Swiss black cherry jam is, however, a national speciality and is exported as such. The fruit is kept whole in the syrup. It is served at breakfast.

Italian table-ware, hand-painted by Mancioli, in olive green and black on white, from Bentall's

ITALY

Where cooking is infinitely varied and even spaghetti is served differently in each province

"*A TAVOLA non s'invecchia*"—"at table one does not grow old." This is an old Italian proverb which is also a most appropriate one. In Italy a good deal of time is spent at the table, and the preparation of good food is a natural pride of every Italian housewife.

Italian cooking is most varied. Each region—indeed, each province—has its own specialities, and even dishes which might loosely be termed national vary considerably from place to place. Thus, when talking of Italian cooking, we must visualise a whole series of regional cuisines rather than, as in most other countries, a mass of national dishes with here and there a leavening of local specialities.

Spaghetti—most popular and best known of all Italian dishes—is a case in point. In Bologna it would be served with a rich sauce of minced meat and mushrooms, whereas in Naples it would be eaten with a thin watery sauce or perhaps with *vongole*. These are small Mediterranean shell-fish something like cockles.

Vegetables play an important part in the Italian menu. These, when in season, are plentiful, varied and cheap. Not only are they cooked in a great variety of ways, they are also used raw in salads with olive oil, vinegar or lemon juice, salt and pepper. In this way they are usually eaten as an *antipasto*—hors d'œuvres. The most popular are perhaps sweet peppers or capsicums—yellow, red and green—but celery, fennel, globe artichokes and cardoons are among the vegetables eaten in this way. Green salads, too, are served every day in most households. Potatoes are not as popular as they are in the U.K., and certainly do not appear at every meal. They are used fairly extensively in soups and gnocchi, but only occasionally as a vegetable.

Italy, being an agricultural country, produces a great variety of cheeses. Because of this, cheese is used as a condiment in a large number of dishes. In Southern Italy, Peccorino cheese, made from goats' milk, and Mozzarella, a soft creamy cheese made of buffalo milk, are very popular. Northern Italy, and especially the Lombardy plain, produces lovely cheese in great variety—Gorgonzola, Parmesan, Bel Paese, Fontina, Stracchino, Mascarpone are just a few of the most popular and have become world famous.

Puddings are hardly ever served. A meal usually ends with fresh fruit, which is varied, plentiful and cheap. Particularly delicious are the famous *pesche di vigna*—

large, luscious peaches grown between rows of grape vines—but there are also figs, both mauve and white, dripping with syrup, apricots, cherries, Palermo blood oranges from Sicily, walnuts from Sorrento, to mention only a few.

Margarine and dripping are rarely used. Instead, the Italian housewife turns to butter, olive oil and, in Southern Italy, lard.

Italy also produces wines in great variety, both red and white, among which Chianti, Barbaresco, Barolo, Asti spumante and Marsala are perhaps the best known.

HORS D'ŒUVRES (Antipasto)

One of the most popular ways of beginning a meal is with a large dish of *affettato*, which consists of thin slices of mixed salami, cooked and raw, such as Coppa (salted loin of pork), Mortadella and Parma Ham. This is a delicious specially cured unsmoked ham, which is sliced very thinly and eaten with fresh figs or iced melon.

Tunny Salad (Insalata di tonno)

1 *can tunny fish*	1 *Spanish onion*
Olive oil	*Vinegar*
Salt and pepper	*Parsley (optional)*

Break tunny fish into small pieces and add finely sliced onion. Mix with olive oil, vinegar, salt and pepper. A little chopped parsley can be added, but this is optional.

Poached Eggs with Green Sauce (Uova in camicia con salsa verde)

1 *egg per person*	1 *small tomato*
2 *fillets of anchovies*	½ *clove of garlic*
1 *small onion*	*Olive oil*
Salt and pepper	*Parsley*
1 *tablespoonful vinegar*	

Poach the eggs in salted water to which the vinegar has been added, drain well, and when cold cover with the following sauce: Chop very finely the parsley, tomato, anchovy fillets, garlic and onion, put into a basin and mix with olive oil, vinegar, salt and pepper. The sauce should be quite thick, so plenty of parsley must be used.

Calf's Head Salad (Insalata di testina di vitello)

½ *calf's head*	2 *onions*
1 *clove of garlic*	2 *carrots*
1 *bay leaf*	1 *stick of celery*
Olive oil	*Vinegar*
Salt, pepper and	*A little dry mustard*
peppercorns	*Lettuce*
Chopped parsley	

Wash the calf's head thoroughly, put into a saucepan, cover with cold water and bring to the boil. Skim well, add celery, carrots, one onion, garlic, salt, peppercorns and bay leaf. Boil again. Lower heat and cook slowly until tender. Allow to cool slightly, then cut into small pieces, add a finely sliced Spanish onion and a tablespoonful of chopped parsley and cover with a salad dressing of olive oil, vinegar, dry mustard, salt and pepper.

One of the many variations of the famous savoury, Pizza, specially made at Forte's

Each province of Italy has its own particular Fritto Misto. In Florence it is cooked in olive oil, in Milan in butter—but it always contains a variety of ingredients

Sliced Tomatoes with Anchovies (Pomidori affettate con acciughe)

3 large firm tomatoes   *Lettuce*
Vinegar   *Fillets of anchovies*
Pepper   *Olive oil*
     Chopped parsley

Cut the tomatoes into fairly thin slices and place on a dish lined with lettuce leaves. On each slice place a rolled fillet of anchovy, then pour on a salad dressing of olive oil, vinegar, pepper, and sprinkle with chopped parsley. A little salt can be added, but be sparing with it as the anchovies are salty.

SOUPS (Minestre)

Minestrone (for 6)

This is the best known and most popular of all Italian soups and, although it is really a speciality of Milan, it is eaten all over Italy. It can be made either with stock or water, and served either hot or ice cold.

4 oz. butter or haricot beans (previously soaked for at least 12 hours)	2 large carrots
	3 potatoes
	1 onion
2 celery stalks	2 oz. streaky un-
2 oz. French beans (cut into small pieces)	smoked bacon
	1 clove of garlic
	(optional)
½ small white cabbage	3 pints water (or
1 oz. butter or olive oil	stock)
	2 oz. rice (or cut
Grated Parmesan cheese	macaroni)
	Bay leaf
	Salt to taste

Chop the bacon and garlic very finely and put into a saucepan with the butter or olive oil, add the chopped onion and fry together lightly. Next, add all the other vegetables, except the cabbage, cut up small and toss them in the saucepan; add water or stock, bay leaf and salt to taste and bring to the boil; add shredded cabbage, simmer for another hour, add either rice or macaroni, according to taste, and cook until tender. Serve piping hot or ice cold, with a sprinkling of grated Parmesan cheese.

Fish Soup (Zuppa di pesce) (for 5–6)

½ lb. turbot (cut near the head)	2 tablespoonfuls olive oil
½ lb. rock salmon	1 wineglass white
½ lb. mackerel	wine
1 medium-sized red mullet	½ teaspoonful
	chopped garlic
12 prawns	4 peeled and crushed
1 celery heart	tomatoes
½ teaspoonful chopped parsley	Pinch of saffron
	Salt and pepper
1 onion	Slices of French bread
A little thyme, sweet basil and a bay leaf	(either toasted or fried in olive oil)
2½ pints water	

Put olive oil into a fairly large saucepan and lightly fry the onion, garlic and bay leaf, add turbot, mackerel and rock salmon, cut in pieces, prawns and chopped celery and cook briskly for a few minutes. Next, add the wine and let it reduce for a few minutes on a strong heat, then add the red mullet, cut into pieces, tomatoes, salt and pepper, cover and simmer for 5 minutes. Pour in the boiling water, add a

pinch of saffron and boil briskly for about 10 minutes. Lastly, add the parsley, thyme and sweet basil. Put slices of fried bread in individual soup plates and pour the hot soup over them.

Married Soup (Miniestra maritata) (for 4)

For this soup a good chicken or meat stock is needed.

1 egg	2 tablespoonfuls
2 tablespoonfuls fresh white bread-crumbs	grated Parmesan cheese
	2 tablespoonfuls
2 pints of good stock	cream
Salt and pepper	

Beat egg in basin, add to it the cheese, breadcrumbs, cream, a little salt and pepper, and mix together thoroughly. Bring stock to the boil, add a little to the mixture, stir well, return to saucepan, bring to the boil again and serve.

This is a very good nourishing soup and very simple to make.

FISH (Pesce)

Baked Fish (Pesce al forno)

Bream lends itself well to this special way of preparing fish as it is a nice white "meaty" fish, but other white fish, such as halibut, turbot, etc., can be used.

1 large bream (about 2 lb.)	A little flour
	2 tablespoonfuls fresh
1 tablespoonful chopped capers	breadcrumbs
	3 tablespoonfuls
2 fillets of anchovy (finely chopped)	chopped parsley
	1 clove of garlic
6 tablespoonfuls olive oil	(finely chopped)
	Salt and pepper

Fillet and skin the fish, coat with flour, salt and pepper, and place on a fireproof dish. Mix all the chopped ingredients with a little olive oil, cover the fish with this mixture, pour the rest of the olive oil on top and bake in a slow oven for about 1 hour.

Red Mullet as eaten in Leghorn (Triglie alla Livornese)

1 red mullet per person	Pinch of thyme
	2 cloves of garlic
Olive oil	1 tablespoonful
Peeled and chopped tomatoes	chopped parsley
	A little chopped onion
Bay leaf	Flour, salt and pepper

Scrape the mullet and pull out its gills, wash, and dry well in a cloth. Rub the fish in flour seasoned with salt and pepper, and fry in olive oil. When cooked, place care-

Ravioli served as a main dish. They can also be boiled in stock and served as soup

fully on a fireproof dish and keep warm while preparing the sauce. Put 2 tablespoonfuls of olive oil in a saucepan and, when warm, add the onion, finely chopped garlic, parsley, bay leaf, with salt and pepper and thyme. Lastly, add the tomatoes and cook for about 20 minutes. Pour over fish and serve at once.

Fried Scampi (Scampi fritti)

Take as many scampi (or Dublin Bay prawns) as needed, wash and dry thoroughly in a cloth. Toss in flour and fry in fairly deep smoking-hot olive oil. Serve with quarters of lemon or mayonnaise.

Mayonnaise

1 egg-yolk	Juice of half a lemon
Salt, pepper, dried mustard and vinegar to taste	1 teacupful olive oil or refined tea-seed oil

Place the yolk in a basin and break with a hand whisk or fork; add lemon juice and a good pinch of salt. Stir together before adding oil, drop by drop, beating steadily. When all the oil has been added, the mayonnaise should be of a nice thick consistency. Add vinegar, etc., to taste.

MEAT (Le Carni)

Braised Beef (Manzo stuffato)

NOTE: This dish needs a thick solid piece of meat of at least 3 lb.—preferably more.

A nice thick piece of lean beef	2 tablespoonfuls olive oil
4 mushrooms	2 carrots
1 clove of garlic	1 onion
1 glass dry red wine	4 peeled and chopped tomatoes
1 tablespoonful Italian tomato paste	1 stick of celery
Salt and pepper	Bay leaf
A little water	

Put the oil into a saucepan that will just take the meat but is not too large. When the oil is warm, put in the chopped onion and garlic, then add the meat, well seasoned with salt and pepper, and fry it on all sides, turning round continually for about 10 minutes. Pour in the wine and let it reduce by cooking uncovered on a fairly strong heat. Add all the other ingredients, including the finely chopped mushrooms and about half a teacupful of water, and cover tightly. Cook slowly, allowing about 35 minutes per lb. of meat.

When meat is cooked, remove from saucepan and keep in a warm place. Next, take out the vegetables, pass them through a fine wire sieve and return them to the sauce remaining in the saucepan, stirring well. If the sauce seems a little thin, reduce it by boiling quickly for a few moments with the lid off. Slice the meat thickly, place on a large dish, pour the sauce on top and serve with a border of creamed potatoes.

Cutlets Milanese (Costolette alla Milanese)

1 cutlet per person (cut from best end)	Butter
Flour	Fresh breadcrumbs
Salt and pepper	Egg
	Lemon

Beat and trim the cutlets, season them and coat with flour. Dip into well-beaten egg and, lastly, coat with fresh breadcrumbs, patting well so that the breadcrumbs stick to the egg. Put butter into a frying pan and, when hot, add the cutlets. Fry well on both sides, then place on a dish. Put another piece of butter in the pan and, when foaming, pour over cutlets and serve them still sizzling. Quarters of lemon and sauté potatoes should be served with the cutlets.

Fritto Misto (for 4–6)

Each province of Italy has its own particular Fritto Misto. The difference is in the fat used for cooking, as the basic ingredients are usually the same. In Florence, for instance, it is cooked in deep olive oil, in Milan it is cooked in butter. The following is the Milanese recipe:

1 set of calf's brains	6 slices of calves' kidney
6 thin slices of veal	
6 small sausages	6 pieces of cooked cauliflower
6 slices of tomato	
2 oz. butter, or more if necessary	Egg, flour and fresh breadcrumbs
6 slices of calves' liver	Lemon to garnish

Soak and wash the brains in cold water and cut into six pieces. Coat the brains and cauliflower, with flour, egg and breadcrumbs, prick the sausages, and coat all the other ingredients in flour only. Put about 2 oz. butter in a frying-pan and, when hot, cook all the ingredients carefully, taking care not to break them. Add more butter if necessary. Place on a very hot dish, pour foaming butter on top and serve with quarters of lemon.

Fried Red Peppers (Peperonata) (for 4)

(Red, yellow or green peppers can be used, but the yellow or red are usually much meatier.)

4 large peppers	3 tomatoes
2 onions	Olive oil
Salt and pepper	

Wash the peppers and cut into strips about 1 in. wide. Put 2 tablespoonfuls of olive oil into a large frying pan and, when warm, add the finely chopped onions. Cook until golden, then add peppers, peeled and crushed tomatoes, salt and, if capsicums are sweet, a little pepper. Cover the pan and cook slowly for about 35–40 minutes, stirring frequently to prevent sticking.

Peas with Garlic and Ham (Piselli alla toscana) (for 4)

8 tablespoonfuls fresh or quick-frozen peas	1 clove of garlic (chopped)
	2 tablespoonfuls olive oil
1 slice unsmoked lean bacon cut into small pieces	3 tablespoonfuls cold water
Pinch of sugar	Pinch of salt

Put all the ingredients into a small saucepan, bring to the boil, cover and cook slowly for about 25 minutes, or until peas are cooked. The time, of course, will depend on the quality of the peas, which really should be young and tender.

Potatoes with Rosemary (Patate al Rosmarino)

Potatoes	Rosemary
Olive oil	Salt

Cut the potatoes into any desired shape. (Many people like to make them into little balls with a special gadget which can be bought at any good kitchen equipment shop.) Put the olive oil into a frying pan and, when hot, add potatoes. Add salt while cooking and scatter enough rosemary over them to give a good flavour. Cook until potatoes are golden brown and soft, and serve piping hot.

Ravioli with Tomato Sauce (Ravioli al sugo)

There are several methods of making ravioli. The following is a practical and good recipe.

For the paste:

3 eggs	8 heaped tablespoonfuls plain flour
¼ teaspoonful of salt	

For the filling:

A little cooked chicken	½ small onion
½ calf's brain	2 heaped tablespoon-
1 egg	fuls grated
2 tablespoonfuls stock	Parmesan cheese
1 oz. butter	2 tablespoonfuls
2 slices lean ham	cooked chopped
1 bay leaf	spinach
	Salt and pepper

Make a dough with the flour, eggs and salt. Knead firmly on a floured board until smooth and even. Let the dough stand covered with a cloth for about 30 minutes, then cut in half and roll out into two thin sheets. This takes a little time, but the results are well worth the effort.

For the filling.—Soak and wash the brain in cold water, drain and dry. Slice the onion and fry it lightly in the butter, add ham, brains, chicken, bay leaf, spinach salt, pepper and stock, and cook gently for about 30 minutes. Remove the bay leaf and pass the mixture through a fine mincer, place it in a basin, add the egg-yolk and Parmesan cheese, season to taste and mix well into a thick paste.

With a plain round cutter, 2½–3 in. in diameter, cut the paste into rounds. Place about ½ teaspoonful of stuffing on each round, damp edges with a little beaten white of egg and fold over, pressing edges firmly together so that ravioli do not open while cooking. Boil for about 20 minutes, or longer if liked very soft, in a large saucepan of boiling water. Drain well, serve with either tomato or Bolognese sauce (see page 472) and sprinkle grated Parmesan cheese on top.

Ravioli are also good as a soup. Just boil them in a good stock and serve about 6 per person floating in a bowl of hot stock.

Risotto Milanese (for 4)

6 tablespoonfuls Italian rice
1 oz. butter
3 tablespoonfuls grated Parmesan cheese
1 small onion
1 oz. beef marrow fat
2 pints good chicken stock
Pinch of saffron
Salt and pepper

Melt the marrow fat and add chopped onion. When onion is cooked to a golden brown, add rice and saffron, stir well and gradually add stock. Simmer for about 20 minutes, or longer if you like it very soft, stirring often to prevent rice from sticking. Add butter, seasoning and cheese, stir well and leave covered for a few minutes before serving.

Risotto with Mushrooms (Risotto con funghi) (for 4)

6 tablespoonfuls Italian rice	3 tablespoonfuls grated Parmesan cheese
2 oz. butter	2 pints good stock
2 oz. sliced mushrooms	1 small onion

Put 1 oz. butter in a saucepan and, when warm, add the finely chopped onion. Fry lightly, then add sliced mushrooms and mix well together. Wash and dry the rice thoroughly and add to the saucepan. Stir well and add boiling stock. Simmer for about 20 minutes or until all the stock has been absorbed by the rice. Reduce the heat, add the rest of the butter and grated cheese, stir well, cover and leave for a few minutes before serving.

Rice with Peas (Riso e piselli) (for 4)

6 tablespoonfuls Italian rice	Small onion
2 oz. butter	4 tablespoonfuls new peas
3 tablespoonfuls grated Parmesan cheese	2 pints good stock
	Salt and pepper

Proceed as for Risotto with Mushrooms, adding peas just after stock so that they will retain their colour.

COOK'S TIP

TO FRY WITHOUT SPLASHING—
dry all foods thoroughly before putting them into the hot fat. It's water that causes the spluttering.

Spaghetti with Tomato Sauce (Spaghetti al pomidoro) (for 4)

1 lb. long spaghetti
1 tablespoonful Italian tomato paste
1 oz. butter
1 clove of garlic
Grated Parmesan cheese
2 tablespoonfuls stock
8 oz. Italian peeled tomatoes
2 tablespoonfuls olive oil
1 small onion
1 bay leaf
Salt and pepper

Chop the onion and garlic very finely and

fry to a light golden brown in a small saucepan with the olive oil. Add bay leaf, tomatoes, tomato paste, salt and pepper, and stock. Bring to the boil and cook very slowly for about 30 minutes. Meanwhile, cook the spaghetti (left long and *not* cut into small pieces) in a large saucepan of boiling salted water for about 20 minutes. Drain well, put on a hot dish, add butter and sauce, and mix well. Sprinkle with a good portion of grated Parmesan cheese and serve very hot.

Spaghetti Bolognese (Spaghetti alla Bolognese)

To make a Bolognese sauce, the method is the same as in the previous recipe, but before adding tomatoes, add 4 oz. peeled and chopped mushrooms and about 6 oz. lean minced beef, preferably fillet.

Stuffed Peppers or Capsicums (Pepperoni ripieni) (for 4)

4 *large red or yellow*	*Salt and pepper*
capsicums	1 *aubergine*
2 *slices white bread*	1 *tablespoonful*
soaked in milk	*capers*
¼ *lb. black olives*	4 *fillets of anchovy*
Olive oil	

Wash, dry and remove stalks and seeds from capsicums, taking care not to break them. Peel and cut aubergine into small slices or pieces and fry in about 2 tablespoonfuls of olive oil, add salt and pepper, cover saucepan and cook over a low heat until tender, stirring now and again to prevent sticking. Leave to cool. Squeeze the bread free from milk and put into a basin, add chopped capers, anchovies, stoned olives, salt and pepper and the aubergine, and mix well together. Stuff the capsicums with the mixture, place in a fireproof dish, pour on top about 2 tablespoonfuls of olive oil and cook in a moderate oven for about 1 hour. They can be eaten either hot or cold.

Tagliatelle with Bolognese Sauce (Tagliatelle alla Bolognese) (for 4)

3 *eggs*	8 *heaped tablespoon-*
½ *teaspoonful salt*	*fuls plain flour*

Put flour and salt in a bowl, make a well in the centre and break in eggs. Mix together thoroughly, then knead on a floured board until smooth and even. Cover with a cloth and let the dough rest for about 30 minutes. Cut into two and roll into sheets,

the thinner the better. Again let the sheets rest on a floured board until they dry a little, then fold over several times (as a newspaper would be folded). With a sharp knife, cut into thin strips about ⅛ in. wide. (The width is a matter of taste. Some people like their noodles cut into much thicker strips.) Shake the strips well and leave on a floured board until needed.

Boil in a large saucepan of salted water as for spaghetti, drain well and serve with a Bolognese sauce (see previous column).

SWEETS (Dolci)

Rich Shortcrust Tart (Tarta di pasta frolla)

6 *oz. butter*	½ *lb. plain flour*
4 *oz. castor sugar*	1 *egg*
Grated rind of a lemon	

Put all the ingredients, including the lemon rind, in a bowl and knead into a smooth dough. Put on a floured board and roll out to about ¼ in. thickness. Well grease a tart tin with butter, sprinkle with flour, and line with the pastry.

In Italy, either jam or cooked fruit is put in the tart and strips of pastry about ¼ in. wide are laid crossways on top, the whole being then brushed with beaten egg and baked in a fairly hot oven for about 1 hour.

If fruit is used, it is usual to slice either apples or ripe pears rather thinly and put into a frying pan with about 1 oz. melted butter. Sugar to taste, and cover until cooked. It is advisable to stir now and again to prevent fruit from sticking. If liked, a thin slice of lemon or orange peel can be added to flavour the fruit. Allow fruit to cool before putting it on the pastry.

Stuffed Peaches (Pesche ripiene)

Sponge cake	*Marsala wine, sherry*
Chopped almonds and	*or liqueur*
whole almonds	2 *whole peaches cut*
2 *oz. ground almonds*	*in half*
Raspberry jam	1 *egg-yolk*
2 *oz. castor sugar*	

Cut 4 rounds of sponge about ¼ in. thick with a fancy cutter. Spread with hot sieved jam, roll in chopped almonds, place on a plate and put half a peach on each piece of cake. Mix together the ground almonds, sugar, egg-yolk and wine or liqueur, put mixture into a forcing bag and fill the halved peaches, then put a whole blanched almond in the centre of each. Pour on top

Among the most popular ways of serving spaghetti in Italy are with Tomato or Bolognese Sauce

a sauce made from sieved jam diluted with water and flavoured with wine or liqueur.

Zabaglione al Marsala

2 egg-yolks	4 tablespoonfuls
2 teaspoonfuls castor	Marsala wine
sugar	

Put all the ingredients into the top part of a double saucepan, beat well with a whisk and place over the bottom part of the saucepan, which should be half-full of boiling water. Continue beating, without stopping, until the mixture becomes creamy and frothy, taking care not to let it curdle. Serve in individual glasses, with sponge fingers.

SAVOURIES

Pizza

There are several kinds of Pizza, but this is the most popular and best known all over Italy:

Bread dough, flaky or	5 tablespoonfuls
unsweetened short	olive oil
pastry	¼ lb. black olives
6 fillets of anchovies	3 skinned and seeded
¼ lb. Bel Paese or	tomatoes
Mozzarella cheese	1 clove garlic
1 teaspoonful oregano	(chopped)

NOTE: Oregano is a very popular herb in Italy and is always used in Pizza.

Well grease a round tart tin with olive oil and line with a thin layer of one of the pastries suggested. Stone the olives, cut in pieces and place neatly in a straight line across the tart. Do the same with the tomatoes, cheese and anchovies until the whole tart is covered, varying the colours so that the pizza looks really attractive when cooked. Pour on the rest of the olive oil, sprinkle with chopped garlic and oregano and bake in a moderate oven for about 40 minutes. It should be eaten hot, although some people like it cold.

Mozzarella in Carozza

NOTE: Mozzarella is a fresh cream cheese made from buffalo milk.

Thin slices of bread	A little flour
Beaten egg	Deep olive oil for
Thin slices of	frying
Mozzarella	Cocktail sticks

Cut the bread and mozzarella into squares of about 2 inches, put together alternate layers of bread and cheese to make a thick sandwich, beginning and ending with bread (3 squares of bread and 2 of cheese is the usual size), and hold together with wooden cocktail sticks. Dip in flour, then in beaten egg and fry in deep oil. Serve very hot—straight out of the pan.

SPAIN

*Rich, colourful and highly seasoned, Spanish food
makes you think of hot golden sunshine*

Described by G. NEGRI, *of Martinez Spanish Restaurant, London*

YOU really need the climate of Spain to enjoy Spanish cookery in all its rich, colourful and highly seasoned glory.

Like all European countries, it has borrowed a little from the French, but, nevertheless, Spanish cookery remains highly individual. Because butter is expensive, nearly everything is cooked in oil and the (to us) most unlikely ingredients are used together. Chicken, shellfish and rice combine with a number of vegetables to create the famous national dish, Paella.

In Spain, sweet dishes are seldom made, and the most popular sweet course is Turron, a kind of very sweet nougat.

Arroz à la Valenciana (Paella) (for 4)

2 *teacupfuls rice*	1 *small chicken*
1 *small cooked lobster*	6 *teacupfuls chicken*
1 *dozen mussels*	*broth*
¼ *lb. Chorizo*	*A handful of shelled*
(Spanish sausage)	*peas*
½ *small packet*	*A smaller handful of*
shredded saffron	*pimentoes*
(or a pinch of	¼ *pint best oil for*
powdered saffron)	*frying*
Salt and pepper	

Cut chicken into pieces. Make the oil very hot and cook the raw rice in it until it becomes a golden colour. Add the cubed chicken and cook until that too turns golden, then in turn the peas, the sliced sausage, the sliced pimentoes, lobster, mussels and, finally, the chicken broth, stirring well. Season with salt and pepper, and add saffron. Simmer all together for 25 minutes, when the rice should have absorbed all the liquid.

The Spanish housewife makes infinite variations on this theme, using eels and veal, for instance, instead of lobster and chicken, but the important thing is the mixture of meat, fish and rice.

NOTE: Spanish sausage (Chorizo) is not easy to find in the U.K., but can sometimes be bought in continental shops, particularly in London's Soho. It is smaller than salami, about 5 in. long, and a deep red colour from the pimentoes it contains.

Spanish Omelet

As served in Spain, this is a very simple dish. Just fry in oil a few diced cold boiled potatoes and a little onion chopped fine, then pour in the lightly beaten eggs and make the omelet in the usual way (see Egg Dishes), the only difference being that a Spanish omelet is served flat, instead of folded in two, and is usually finished off under the grill.

As served at Martinez Restaurant, London.—Diced cold boiled potatoes, finely sliced onion; chopped pimentoes and tomatoes are added to the eggs before the omelet is made in the usual way—and served flat, not folded.

Huevos à la Flamença

Put a thin slice of ham into a well-buttered or oiled individual chafing dish or casserole, add a few cooked peas, two or three thin slices of Chorizo (Spanish sausage), some chopped tomatoes and pimentoes, and then break one or two eggs on top. Put under a hot grill, or into a quick oven, until the eggs set, when the dish is ready for serving.

If serving Huevos à la Flamença before the main course, one egg per person is sufficient; if it is the main dish, use two eggs each.

Sole (Lenguado) Alfonso

Cook the sole in butter as for Sole Meunière (see chapter on Entertaining) and serve with finely chopped tomato and onion fried in oil and lightly fried sliced bananas.

Cocido (for 4)

This is the national dish and is served all over Spain, particularly on Sundays.

Paella, the famous Spanish national dish, in which chicken, shellfish and rice are mixed with a number of vegetables. The Spanish housewife makes many variations on this theme

1 *small boiling chicken*	1 *small cabbage*
½ *lb. potatoes*	1–2 *lb. boiling beef*
½ *lb. Spanish chick peas*	1 *lb. pork*
	2 *or* 3 *Spanish sausages*

Boil separately the chicken, the meats, the potatoes, cabbage, chick peas (previously soaked) until all are done. Dish up on one large dish and keep hot.

Serve the broth first, thickened with rice or vermicelli, and the meat as a separate main course with the vegetables. Many Spaniards like oil and vinegar or tomato sauce with the meat.

Fabada (for 4)

4 *pork chops*	*Olive oil for frying*
2 *large slices cooked ham*	1 *lb. haricot beans*
	4 *slices black pudding*
4 *slices Spanish sausage*	*Garlic*
	Tomato sauce

Heat the olive oil in a pan with just a touch of garlic. Remove the garlic, then quickly fry the pork chops until they are golden on both sides. Boil the haricot beans (previously soaked overnight) and put them into a deep casserole, moisten with a little tomato sauce (made from fresh tomatoes, *not* bottled, then add the chops, ham, black pudding and sausage. Cover and cook in a moderate oven for about 15 minutes.

Fish Soup

There are various Spanish fish soups very much like the Bouillabaisse of Marseilles. What kind of fish goes into them depends on what is caught in the locality, but they can be made with practically any good mixture of white and shellfish, such as Red Mullet, Mussels and Turbot, plus some good fish stock. First wash and cut up the fish, then fry it gently in boiling oil till golden. Add fish stock and a touch of saffron. Serve with croûtons.

Andalusian Gaspacho (for 6)

Pound 3 cloves of garlic, with salt and green pepper to taste, in a mortar, then gradually add a handful of crumbled dry bread and after that, a little at a time, olive oil, stirring continuously until the bread has dissolved. Add two skinned tomatoes, vinegar to taste and sufficient water for six plates. Chill in the refrigerator and serve ice cold, garnished with cubes of cucumber and bread.

Huevos à la Cubana, eggs fried in deep fat and served with fried bananas on a bed of onions and rice

Gaspacho as served in Majorca (for 10)

5 *green peppers*	2 *medium-sized fresh*
7 *or 8 large tomatoes*	*cucumbers*
(seeded)	1 *clove garlic*
4 *oz. bread with the*	3 *tablespoonfuls best*
crusts on, soaked in	*white vinegar*
water	1 *tablespoonful*
3 *tablespoonfuls*	*mayonnaise*
olive oil	1 *teacupful cold water*
4 *medium-sized*	*Salt to taste*
onions	

Pound the garlic and peppers in a mortar. Mince the other solids into a large bowl, then add the rest of the ingredients, mix well and strain through a cloth or fine strainer. Put the liquid in the refrigerator to chill. Serve the soup very cold, accompanied by separate little dishes of sliced green peppers, cucumbers, tomatoes, raw onion and toasted bread.

Garlic Soup

1 *thin slice of bread*	*Stock*
per person	*Oil for frying*
1 *clove garlic*	*Salt and pepper*
	to taste

Fry the garlic in the oil, then remove it and put in the bread and seasoning. Cover with the hot stock, bring to the boil, boil for a minute or two, then serve.

Garlic soup is improved out of all recognition with this addition: Drop one raw egg per person into the boiling soup, sprinkle generously with grated cheese and put under a very hot grill just long enough to set the egg and melt the cheese.

Trout in Oil

Fry the trout in olive oil with some herbs and finely sliced onion, until it is 90 per cent. cooked. Then dish it up and cover it with vinegar and leave for 4 or 5 days. At the end of that time it will be delicious for hors d'œuvres.

Asparagus with Egg and Cheese

Boil the asparagus in the usual way (till tender), put into a flat dish, pour over some melted butter, then add a generous sprinkling of grated cheese and a fried egg per person. Put under a hot grill to melt the cheese. (Alternatively, raw eggs may be dropped on to the layer of grated cheese and set under the grill.)

Globe Artichokes à l'Espagnole

Boil the artichokes till tender with a little lemon juice to preserve their colour. Strain and dry, then separate the leaves and fill with a mixture of grated cheese and breadcrumbs, salt and pepper. When the cavities have been well filled, close the leaves again, put the artichokes into a casserole with a little oil in the bottom, cover and cook gently over a very low flame for about 10 minutes (or until the cheese melts inside the leaves).

Chick Pea Salad

Soak the chick peas for 24 hours, boil for 10 minutes before salting—if you put the salt in sooner, the peas will not absorb it—and simmer gently till tender. When cold, mix with finely sliced onion, add a fairly hot and vinegary French dressing an hour before serving. (This is an excellent way of using up left-over cooked chick peas.)

Tunny Salad

Thoroughly mix together a shredded lettuce, some flaked tunny fish and a shredded onion. Dress with oil and vinegar and seasoning.

Eggs Otero

For each person bake one good-sized potato in its jacket until soft. Split each potato in half lengthwise, scoop out the contents, mix with peeled shrimps, Béchamel sauce (see Sauces chapter), salt and pepper and an egg per person, then put back into the skins, sprinkle with grated cheese and brown under a hot grill for a minute or two (or until the cheese melts nicely).

Bacalao à la Vizcaina (for 6–8)

The traditional Dry Salt Cod served on Good Friday.

1 salt cod	Ordinary ground
1 oz. bread	pepper
10 oz. tomatoes	Chopped parsley
3 Spanish red peppers	2 oz. flour
1 clove garlic	7 oz. olive oil
Ground Spanish red	10 oz. onions
pepper	Salt

Soak the fish for 24 hours, then remove the bones and cut in pieces 1½ in. × 3 in. Dip in flour and fry in oil. Place in a baking pan with the bread, cut up and fried, on top. Thinly slice and fry the onions in the oil and, when golden brown, add the garlic, chopped very finely, the chopped parsley, Spanish peppers and peeled, chopped tomatoes. Season with salt and pepper. Pour this sauce over the cod, garnish with a few strips of Spanish pepper and cook in the oven for 30 minutes.

Bacalao Omelet

To use up left-over Bacalao, make an ordinary soft plain omelet and warm the Bacalao with a little cream. When the omelet is done, fold the Bacalao mixture into the middle, before folding it over. Top with grated cheese, putting the omelet under the hot grill for a minute or two to melt the cheese.

Huevos à la Cubana

Into very hot deep oil drop the eggs, one at a time, so that they cook like poached eggs, forming a coating of white. Dish them up on to a bed of plain boiled rice. Sauté in a little oil some very finely chopped onion and the faintest trace of garlic. Top the rice with this and some fried bananas.

Suprême Hortelana—fried breast of chicken with young vegetables—is another favourite dish on the menu at Martinez Restaurant

PORTUGAL

*Monday is the national wash-day here too, and everyone eats Boiled Salt
Cod for midday dinner to save a lot of cooking*

by JOAN CROFT DE MOURA

PORTUGUESE cookery has much in common with Spanish, but it is generally simpler, less exotic and exaggerated. Nearly everything is cooked in oil, which is used both for frying and baking; food is seldom served boiled. All the meats are marinaded, even steaks and chops, for a few minutes, and all fat removed from the meat. Soup, usually a thick vegetable soup, is generally served at lunch and dinner, often followed by fish, meat, an egg dish and fresh fruit. In the north, the soup comes *after* the fish and meat courses.

The average Portuguese housewife has no packaged cereals, jams or canned goods in her store cupboard. Milk in Portugal is not good. Meat is not abundant, with the exception of pork, which is plentiful, most families in the country, even the poorest, owning a pig. Those who live on the coast eat plenty of fresh fish, including grilled sardines (which taste much better than the canned variety), but inland, with the exception of large towns, the only fish available is dried salt codfish, which is therefore much used.

Eggs are cheap and plentiful, so the Portuguese housewife uses them lavishly, thinking nothing of using eight eggs for a cake. Favourite dishes are eggs fried in oil, scrambled eggs and omelets.

Every meal ends with fresh raw fruit, which is eaten in tremendous quantities all day and every day, as dessert and between meals. There are oranges in winter, and in summer sixty or seventy kinds of grapes to choose from, as well as water-melons and all the other summer fruits. Vegetables, which are much the same as those available in the U.K., are usually served with oil and vinegar. The Portuguese eat a lot of bread—and cook with it, too—but not much butter, which is very expensive. If they do have jam, they do not spread it on bread and butter, but eat it by itself in a spoon; cheese (mostly made from goats' milk) is also eaten alone.

Boiled Salt Codfish

This is the national Portuguese dish, which you will find served all over the country on Mondays when housewives are too busy with their washing for much cooking. Everybody eats codfish, from the poorest peasant to the Duke of Palmela. Soak the codfish overnight. Boil it with onions and potatoes, and serve hot with oil and vinegar.

Braised Tunny

Tunny fish	Cream
A little lemon juice	Fillets of anchovies
Slices of fat bacon	Mixed vegetables
Herbs and spices as	Port wine
liked	Mashed sorrel
1 egg-yolk	

Interlard a slice of tunny with fillets of anchovies, the quantity depending on individual taste. Boil in salted water to which some lemon juice has been added. After a few minutes, place the tunny in a flat pan on a bed of vegetables and slices of fat bacon. Cover with equal parts of port wine and the liquid in which the fish was boiled. Simmer for 45 minutes with herbs and spices as liked. Place the tunny on a purée of fresh cream, egg-yolk and mashed sorrel. Skim the fat off the stock and make demi-glacé sauce (see Sauces chapter) reduced to the consistency of thick syrup and pour it over the tunny. Serve hot.

Caldeirada a Fragateira de Lisboa (for 6–8)

2 lb. fish (mullet, bass, hake, eel, sole, red mullet or skate)	1 lobster
	A few shrimps, mussels or cockles
3 onions	3 tomatoes
3 pints water	Sprig of parsley
Juice of ½ lemon	Wineglassful of port wine
Salt and pepper	
Coriander	Clove of garlic
Bay leaves	Olive oil for frying

Remove heads and bones from fish and

Sweet Rice (right) patterned with cinnamon is the Portuguese version of rice pudding. On the left are Coconut and Almond Balls, and, above, Golden Threads

make them into a stock by simmering slowly for 30 minutes in the water and wine, with one finely minced onion, parsley and bay leaves, salt and pepper. Stir, and remove froth as it rises. Put through a fine sieve, then pour into an earthenware cocotte with 2 sliced onions, a clove of garlic (mashed), the tomatoes (with pips removed), and a little coriander. Bring to the boil, and boil for 10 minutes. Then put in the fish and shellfish, and boil again for 15 minutes. Serve hot with sippets fried in olive oil.

Codfish Cakes (Pasteis de bacalhau)

Equal quantities of   *1 or 2 eggs*
dried salt cod and   *Olive oil for frying*
mashed boiled
potatoes

Soak the cod overnight in cold water. Next day, boil it, then shred it as finely as possible. Prepare an equal quantity of very well mashed boiled potatoes, mix with the fish, binding with one or two egg-yolks

and mixing thoroughly. Beat the egg-whites till stiff and fold them into the fish mixture. Drop tablespoonfuls of the mixture into very deep frying fat (preferably olive oil) and fry to a light golden brown. Serve with a crisp green salad and black olives. These fish cakes, which should be the shape of the spoon, are equally good eaten hot or cold.

Left-over Fish

Left-over salt codfish can be flaked, and added, with a little fried onion and chopped black olives, to scrambled eggs. Or flake the fish into a casserole, slice some boiled potatoes, onions and olives, and bake in the oven with a little oil.

Liver Slices (Iscas a Portuguesa)

Slice the liver very thinly, marinade overnight in white wine vinegar with garlic, bay leaf and a few peppercorns. Fry the liver very quickly in a little lard in a frying pan (preferably of earthenware).

Into the remainder of the lard pour a little of the vinegar with the garlic and bay leaf, boil quickly to reduce and pour over liver. Serve at once with sliced boiled or fried potatoes.

Pork Roast in White Wine

Marinade a loin of pork overnight in white wine, with garlic, salt and bay leaves, having first removed all the fat. (In Portugal pork is not served with crackling.) Next day, place plenty of pork fat on the joint and roast it. Bake little potatoes in their jackets until they are soft, then squash them up and finish them off in the pan with the pork, so that they absorb the gravy. Serve with lemon juice and sugar mixed.

Alternatively, the pork may be served with baked apples and chestnuts. For this, first boil and skin the chestnuts, then bake them and the apples (cut in halves) in the meat tin with the pork.

Sauté de Veau au vin de port (for 4)

2 lb. veal	1 tablespoonful lard
½ glass of port wine	A little flour
¼ pint hot water	Seasoning

Cut the veal into strips about 1½ in. long. Melt the lard in a cocotte and fry the meat in it to a golden brown, turning it on all sides. Remove the fat, sprinkle a little flour over the meat and fry till brown; then add water. Season. Leave to simmer for 1 hour, watching that the gravy does not catch or become too thick. Add the port wine ½ hour before serving.

Almond Pudding à la Portugaise

6 oz. almonds (whole)	6 oz. sugar
3 eggs	Wineglassful of port
1 pint milk	wine

Soak the almonds in a mixture of boiling milk, sugar and a small glass of port wine, red or white; stir carefully and add the beaten egg-yolks and then the whites. Put the mixture into a mould in which you have previously melted some sugar to a caramel, and steam. Cool and serve with cream flavoured with vanilla.

Coconut and Almond Balls (Bolas de Coco e Amendoa)

These are made in three parts:

(1)	8 oz. ground almonds	3 egg-yolks	
		8 oz. sugar	
(2)	4 oz. chocolate	4 oz. sugar	
	4 oz. ground almonds	A little water	
(3)	4 oz. shredded coconut	3 egg-yolks	
		4 oz. sugar	

(1) Boil sugar with a little water, stir in ground almonds and egg-yolks, mix well, and leave to cool.
(2) Grate the chocolate, add sugar and mix with a little water, then add ground almonds and knead well.
(3) Mix the coconut with the sugar, add egg-yolks and knead well.

Take a little of each mixture, in the order given above, form into cigar shape and press well together, using a little syrup or egg-white to make them stick. Roll in castor sugar.

Golden Threads (Fios de Ovos)

5 or 6 egg-yolks	½ lb. sugar
A little port or Madeira	Glacé cherries (for decoration)
Cream (optional)	Water (about ¾ pint)

Break up the egg-yolks with a fork and strain through a fine sieve. Heat the sugar in a frying pan with sufficient water to make a fairly liquid syrup. Keep the flame low so that the syrup is very hot but not boiling. Pipe egg-yolk through an icing bag into the syrup, making long threads. Leave threads in syrup for 3 or 4 minutes, then lift out with a fork and pile on a dish. When cold, pour a little port or Madeira on top and decorate with glacé cherries. Serve with cream if liked. Golden Threads can also be used for decorating other sweets.

Sweet Clouds (Nuvens or Farofias)

Make a boiled or steamed (not baked) custard with several egg-yolks and plenty of sugar. Beat the egg-whites till stiff. Drop spoonfuls of them into boiling milk. They will poach quite quickly. Remove from milk and drain. Serve the custard cold in individual cups and cap with the poached whites.

Sweet Rice (Arroz Doce)

This is the Portuguese version of rice pudding.

1 cupful rice	2 or 3 egg-yolks
2 cupfuls milk	A little lemon peel or
Cinnamon	vanilla pod

Bring the rice, milk and lemon peel or vanilla *very* slowly to the boil and cook gently till the rice is quite soft. Then stir in, little by little, the egg-yolks, stirring till it thickens. After the eggs have been added, the mixture must not boil. Pour into a flat dish to cool; sprinkle with cinnamon in a criss-cross pattern.

THE NETHERLANDS

*The Dutch have many delicious ways of cooking
and serving vegetables, usually with spices*

Compiled by MIA VAN DEN BERG

**Asparagus with hard-boiled eggs, melted butter and grated nutmeg, is served
elegantly garnished as a main dish**

THE Dutch like to eat well, and they do eat well every day of the week.

The Dutch housewife takes pride and pleasure in preparing meals of great variety, using to full advantage the abundance of inexpensive but high quality food —dairy products, vegetables and meat— that Holland produces.

Yet the Dutch menu is, as an everyday rule, simple, straightforward and easy to prepare. It does full justice to the food values, such as mineral salts and vitamins, and takes little time to prepare.

It is customary to have one main cooked meal a day, mostly in the evening. Breakfast consists usually of cheese, an egg, bread and tea; lunch of bread with cold meat and coffee; and tea of a cup of tea and a biscuit. The evening meal is therefore a substantial one, beginning with soup, followed by meat, vegetables and potatoes, and ending with a sweet. At each course the helpings are hearty.

Vegetables in Holland can all be bought cleaned and cut up ready for cooking. Even the smallest greengrocers have machinery to do this, and it is a tremendous boon to the busy housewife and especially the businesswoman who also runs her own home. You pay a few cents more to have the vegetables prepared, but even potatoes can be peeled while you wait.

Most of the vegetables are steamed in plenty of butter and very little water, and flavoured with spices, nutmeg being a favourite.

Rye-bread sandwiched with Dutch cheese
makes an attractive cocktail savoury

liked), and serve with chopped parsley.

Sprouts

Cook in the same way as French beans, or with chestnuts.

Asparagus

Cook in the usual way in boiling water until tender, then serve as a main dish with hard-boiled eggs, melted butter and grated nutmeg.

NOTE: Dutch rusks and Dutch dried vegetables for soup are obtainable from many continental shops and the provision departments of large stores.

VEGETABLE COOKERY

At the main meal it is usual to serve two or three different vegetables and perhaps lettuce with a French dressing into which a hard-boiled egg has been grated. The following are characteristic methods of cooking and serving ordinary vegetables.

French Beans

Wash and string the beans, leaving them whole. Put into a *very* little fast-boiling water and cook till just tender but *not* mushy. Drain. Put a good big pat of butter or margarine into the bottom of the pan, melt over a medium flame, put back the beans and simmer in the butter for 2 or 3 minutes, shaking the pan to prevent them from sticking. Serve with grated nutmeg.

Cauliflower

Boil in the usual way until tender, and serve with a white or cheese sauce and grated nutmeg.

Young Green Peas

Cook in the same way as French beans, in butter, and serve with chopped parsley.

Carrots

Cook in the same way as French beans, with a little sugar added to the butter (if

Red Cabbage

Wash and cut up the cabbage and plunge into a *small* quantity of fast-boiling water, with 2 or 3 cloves and 1 grated apple, a dash of vinegar and sugar to taste. Cook until the cabbage is tender but still reasonably crisp. Drain well, simmer with pat of butter and thicken with cornflour.

Hot Beetroot is a delicious dish which is very popular in Holland. Cooked beetroot is sliced, then gently heated in a little water, with a dash of vinegar, salt, sugar and 1 or 2 cloves. Simmer with a pat of butter.

Endive

Cook in the same way as French beans and serve with white sauce and nutmeg.

Mashed Potatoes

Using a wooden spoon, mash boiled potatoes to a really smooth cream with milk and butter, beating in a little nutmeg at the last minute.

Spinach (Spinazie) (for 4)

4 lb. spinach	3 or 4 Dutch rusks
2 eggs	Some stale bread
Salt	1 oz. margarine

Wash and clean the spinach, add a pinch of salt and cook in a little hot water, with the lid on the pan, for 5–10 minutes. Drain thoroughly and chop. Add the margarine and finely crushed Dutch rusks, and simmer for another 5 minutes. Boil the eggs hard, shell and divide them in quarters. Fry strips of bread in margarine until golden brown.

Serve the spinach with the egg and fried bread-strips on top.

MEAT DISHES

Vegetable Soup with Small Meat-balls
(Groentesoep met balletjes) (for 4–6)

2 pints stock (or water with 4–5 meat cubes)	½ lb. minced meat
	Dutch dried
Milk and bread-crumbs	vegetables for soup
	2 oz. vermicelli
	Salt and pepper

Boil the stock (or water with meat cubes) for about 5 minutes, add dried vegetables and salt to taste, boil for about 15 minutes. Meanwhile, mix minced meat with bread-crumbs and milk, add salt and pepper to taste, and form the mixture into small meat-balls the size of marbles. Add meat-balls to the boiling soup, cook for 15 minutes, add vermicelli and boil slowly for 15 more minutes.

Hotchpot with Stewing Steak or Pork
(Hutspot met klapstuk) (for 4–6)

1 lb. fat stewing steak or Pork	1 lb. onions
3 lb. carrots	2 oz. fat
4 lb. potatoes	1½ pints water
	Salt

Wash meat and add water and salt. Bring to the boil and simmer for about 2 hours. Peel and mince carrots and add them. In ½ hour, add peeled potatoes and chopped onions and simmer for ½ hour more until the vegetables are very tender. By this time the water should have evaporated completely. Take out the meat, mash the vegetables with a wooden spoon, add fat and serve.

Veal Escallops with Bacon and Minced Meat (Blinde vinken) (for 4)

4 thinly cut veal escallops (about 3 oz. each)	4 oz. butter
	Salt and pepper
4 oz. minced meat	1 egg
4 rashers bacon	Breadcrumbs

Rub salt and pepper into both sides of the veal escallops. Put one rasher of bacon

Two stages in the preparation of Veal Escallops with Bacon and Minced Meat—right, the stuffing is put on the escallops ; left, they are rolled up and tied for cooking

on top of each escallop. Mix the minced meat with the egg and some breadcrumbs until smooth, adding pepper and salt to taste.

Divide the minced meat between the escallops, roll them round it, tying together with a piece of thread around each little roll. Fry the "blinde vinken" quickly in butter until golden brown, then put on a low flame, add some water and simmer for about ½ hour.

Cut the threads and serve very hot.

Calf's Tongue in White Sauce, Runner Beans, Haricot Beans and Potato Croquettes (Tong in zure saus, snijbonen, witte bonen en kleine aardappel-croquetjes) (for 4)

1 calf's tongue (about 1 lb.)	Margarine, milk, breadcrumbs
2 oz. butter or margarine	1 beaten egg
1 oz. flour	Salt, onion, carrot, parsley, herbs
Salt, vinegar or lemon juice	1 pint water
½ lb. haricot beans	1 lb. runner beans
	2 lb. potatoes
Deep frying fat	

Clean the tongue and boil for about 1½ hours in water with a pinch of salt, onion,

Cinnamon Bread Turnovers are a delicious, inexpensive and quickly prepared sweet

carrot and herbs. Skin the tongue, cut into thick slices and cover with a sauce made as follows.

For the sauce.—Melt the butter, stir in the flour and then the water, stirring all the time. Finally, add vinegar or lemon juice to taste. Boil runner beans and haricot beans (soaked beforehand for 12 hours) separately until tender. Boil potatoes, mash with margarine and milk and make them into small croquettes, cover with breadcrumbs, beaten egg and again with breadcrumbs, and fry in deep fat until golden brown. Serve everything piping hot.

Dutch Steak, Peas, Carrots, French Beans, Sprouts and Fried Potatoes (Hollandse biefstuk, erwtjes, worteljes, princessebonen, spruitjes en gebakken aardappelen) (for 4)

2 lb. tender round steak (1½ in. thick)	2 tablespoonfuls vinegar
1 teaspoonful pepper	¼ lb. butter or margarine
½ to 1 cupful water	(for frying)
1 lb. peas	or packets of frozen vegetables
1 lb. carrots	
1 lb. French beans	
1 lb. sprouts	
Parsley	2 lb. potatoes
Pats of butter or margarine	Salt

Pound the meat on both sides and cube it. Mix vinegar with salt and pepper and rub this on both sides of steak. Leave for ¼ hour. Fry steaks just before serving. Brown butter or margarine in heavy frying pan, place steaks in pan and fry for about 1 minute each side—or a little longer if you prefer them well done—moving them backwards and forwards continually. Add hot water to the fat in the pan and serve this in gravy boat.

Boil the vegetables separately in a very little water, add a pinch of salt. Drain, and simmer with a pat of butter or margarine. Cut the potatoes in flat slices and fry in ample butter or margarine. Sprinkle chopped parsley over peas and carrots, and serve everything on a flat dish piping hot.

HOT CHEESE DISHES
Cabbage and Dutch Cheese (for 4)

1 large cabbage	½ lb. Dutch Gouda or Edam cheese
Salt	
Breadcrumbs	Butter

Clean the cabbage. Cut the outer leaves off very carefully and boil them in water

To serve with cocktails, these little Cheese Puffs are made of choux pastry with a delicious savoury filling of butter and cheese

with a pinch of salt until they are nearly cooked. Drain the cabbage leaves and roll a piece of Dutch cheese, about ½ in. thick and 3 in. long, into each cabbage leaf. Put these into a greased fireproof dish, cover with breadcrumbs and pats of butter, and put the dish in a fairly hot oven until golden brown.

Spinach with Dutch Cheese (for 4)

2 oz. grated Dutch Gouda or Edam cheese	2 lb. spinach (or 1 lb. canned chopped spinach)
4 tablespoonfuls milk	4 eggs
2 oz. butter	Pepper and salt

Clean the spinach (if fresh) and cook in little or no water and a pinch of salt until done. Chop, add salt and butter to taste and keep warm. Beat the eggs with a pinch of salt and pepper, add milk, fry four small omelets made from the mixture. Cover each omelet with spinach, roll it up and put into a greased fireproof dish. Cover with grated cheese and leave the dish in a moderately hot oven for 2 minutes.

SWEET DISHES

Cinnamon Bread Turnovers (Wentelteefjes) (for 4)

8 slices stale bread	½ pint milk
2 oz. sugar	1 teaspoonful ground cinnamon
Margarine for frying	
Pinch of salt	1 egg

Beat the egg with 1 oz. sugar, pinch of salt and some cinnamon. Soak the bread in a mixture of milk and the beaten egg until the slices are quite soft. Fry in a shallow pan in margarine until golden brown on both sides. Sprinkle with the remainder of the sugar and cinnamon.

Dutch Rusks with Currant Sauce (Beschuit met bessensap) (for 4–6)

12 Dutch rusks	1 pint red currant juice (or diluted red currant jelly
1 pint water	
½ lb. sugar	
1 piece spiced cinnamon	1 tablespoonful cornflour
Peel of 1 lemon	

Soak the rusks, each one separately, in half the red currant juice in a large dish,

Slowly heat the rest of the juice with the sugar, water, cinnamon and peel. Mix the cornflour with a little water and add this to the hot juice when almost boiling. Keep on stirring and let the sauce boil for several minutes. Then pour over the rusks in a dish and serve hot or cold.

Butter Cake (Boterkoek)

1 *egg*	*Salt*
½ *lb. butter or*	½ *lb. flour*
margarine	½ *lb. Demerara sugar*
Grated lemon rind	

Beat the egg, saving some of it in a separate dish. Cut butter or margarine into small pieces and add with flour, sugar, pinch of salt and, if desired, grated lemon rind, to the egg.

Put into a greased 8-in. or 9-in. cake tin. Cover the top with the remainder of the egg. Bake the butter cake for 45–60 minutes in a fairly hot oven until light brown. Cool before serving.

COLD DISHES—COCKTAIL SAVOURIES

Rye-bread and Dutch Cheese

1 *packet "Pumpernickel" rye-bread*
1 *packet Dutch cream cheese (or a mixture of butter and grated Dutch Gouda or Edam cheese in equal quantities*

Put a thick layer of Dutch cream cheese, or cheese mixture, in between three or four slices of rye-bread. Cut into thin strips, then into squares, and you have a cocktail savoury which looks interesting and tastes even better.

(It is easier to cut the squares after the rye-bread with the cheese filling has been in the refrigerator for about 1 hour.)

Cheese Puffs (enough for 25–30 puffs)

4½ *tablespoonfuls*	1 *oz. butter or*
water	*margarine*
Pinch of salt	1 *oz. flour*
1 *egg*	

For the filling

4 *oz. Dutch Edam or*	4 *oz. butter or*
Gouda cheese	*margarine*
French mustard to taste	

Bring the water, margarine and salt to the boil, then add all the flour at once, stir for a short while until the mixture sticks together and remove from heat. Add, still away from heat, the egg and beat into the mixture. This will take some time. With

two teaspoons, form into small balls the size of marbles and put them on a greased baking tin, about 1–2 in. apart. Bake in a hot oven for 10–15 minutes. Do *not* open the oven door during the first 10 minutes or the puffs will go flat.

Filling.—Put the butter or margarine in a warm place for a while and add the grated cheese. Flavour with a pinch of salt and some French mustard to taste, and stir well.

Cut the puffs open at the top and fill them with the cheese and butter mixture, close them again, or top them with some grated cheese.

Cheese Fritters

1 *oz. margarine*	1 *oz. flour*
2 *oz. water*	1 *egg*
2 *oz. old Dutch*	*Pinch of salt*
cheese, grated	

Bring water, margarine and salt to the boil, then add all the flour at once, stir for a while until the mixture sticks together, then remove from the heat. Add the egg and grated cheese and mix thoroughly. Put the mixture into a piping bag; from it drop small quantities into hot deep fat, and fry very quickly until golden brown.

Cheese Biscuits

6 *oz. flour*	4 *oz. butter*
4 *oz. grated Dutch*	*Pepper and salt*
Gouda or Edam	1 *egg-yolk*
cheese	

Mix the flour with the butter and nearly all the grated cheese, add salt and pepper to taste. Roll out the dough about ¼ in. thick, cut into 2-in. squares, or into biscuit shapes. Cover the biscuits with egg-yolk, sprinkle the remainder of the grated cheese over them, and bake for about 10 minutes in a fairly hot oven.

Asparagus Tips in Bread

Cut very thin slices of white or brown bread and butter, cover with grated Dutch Gouda or Edam cheese. Roll each slice of bread round an asparagus tip and fix with a cocktail stick.

Tomatoes filled with Cheese and Butter

Cut each tomato into the shape of a basket by cutting two sections away at the top. Remove the seeds. Fill tomatoes with a mixture of butter and grated Dutch Gouda or Edam cheese. Sprinkle some chopped parsley on top.

RUSSIA

Exciting foods full of unexpected flavours and strange contrasts are a legacy of the Czars

Niki, who serves dishes à la Russe at Chez Luba Restaurant, London, describes some of his specialities below

FOR a typical Russian main meal, begin with Bortsch, served with Piroschki or Blinys and caviare washed down with vodka, follow that by Chicken Kieff, and finish with Sernik, a pancake stuffed with sour cream and sultanas. Unusual, yes, but delicious. . . .

Bortsch (for 4)

2 onions	½ cabbage
1 leek	6 uncooked beetroots
1 stick celery	2 oz. margarine
Clove of garlic	Bay leaf
Dried mushrooms	Thyme
Lemon juice	4 oz. uncooked lean
1 carrot	pork or beef

Shred the onion, leek, celery, carrot, cabbage and five of the beets very fine, and sauté them in a covered pan in the margarine for 10–15 minutes. Add 2 quarts of cold water, bring to the boil and simmer gently for 20 minutes. Then add the bay leaf, garlic, thyme, three or four little pieces of dried mushroom and the meat cut up small. Cook for 20–25 minutes. By this time the Bortsch will have lost its colour so, just before serving, shred the last beetroot, previously boiled by itself, sprinkle it lavishly with lemon juice and drop it into the soup to restore the colour. After this the Bortsch must not be brought to the boil again. It is now ready to serve and is a good deep red. It should be accompanied by Piroschki, which is served in Russia instead of bread.

Piroschki (for 4)

About 2 oz. each of	1 hard-boiled egg
cooked lean beef	1 onion
and veal	4 oz. puff pastry
2 oz. margarine	Sage, parsley, salt
1 teaspoonful cream	and pepper to taste

Mince the meat. Chop the onion finely and fry till golden in margarine. Add the meat, sage, parsley, salt and pepper, the shredded hard-boiled egg and the cream, and mix thoroughly but do not cook any more. Roll out your puff pastry and fill it with the prepared stuffing like a large sausage roll. Cut the roll into four slices (one for each person), brush with egg and bake in a moderate oven for 15–20 minutes. Serve hot with Bortsch.

Russian Pancakes (Blinys)

2 oz. buckwheat flour	¼ oz. yeast
4 oz. white flour	Pinch of salt
1 egg	1 gill of milk

If buckwheat flour cannot be obtained, white flour can be used.

Warm the milk slightly. Put the yeast in the warmed milk and leave for 10 minutes. Put the flour and salt in a basin, add the egg, the milk and yeast, and make a thick pancake mixture. Then fry like ordinary pancakes in a small pan. Keep them in the oven, hot and dry, till served.

Blinys are best served with smoked salmon and caviare, but some people like them with sour cream.

Chicken Kieff (for 2)

1 chicken	2 oz. butter
2 oz. mushrooms	Clarified butter for
Egg and breadcrumbs	frying
Salt and pepper	

This is an extravagant dish. As only the breast of the chicken is used, you need one bird for every two people, but it's worth it!

First carefully remove the two breasts from the chicken, cutting the meat away from the carcase with a very sharp knife and leaving only the top of the wing bone attached. Next, slice a little thin fillet, about 4 in. long and 2 in. wide, off the inside of the breast and put this aside. Then run a sharp knife into the flesh of the breast and right round it to make a little envelope. Now take the little fillet and wrap it firmly round a rectangle of butter (about 1 oz.). Put this inside the opening in the "envelope," together with the chopped mushrooms and salt and pepper and close firmly.

Sprinkle the stuffed breast with flour, dip first in egg and then breadcrumbs and fry in very hot clarified butter for about 5 minutes or until golden brown. It is advisable to test the hot clarified butter by dropping in a piece of raw potato; if it quickly fries into a perfect chip, the temperature is right for the chicken.

Having used the breasts of chicken, what do you do with the rest of the bird or birds? Here is the solution.

Forschmak Dragomiroff

Boil the chicken legs for 15 minutes. Remove all the skin and meat from the bones. Dice it, add equal quantity of diced cooked ham and half the quantity of diced mushrooms. Mix this into a plain white sauce to which has been added either the yolk of one egg or grated cheese to taste. Top with grated cheese and bake in a fireproof dish for 15 minutes. Serve with baked rice.

Baked Rice

4 oz. margarine	Bay leaf
1 cupful washed rice	Teaspoonful salt
Garlic to taste	2 cupfuls chicken
Pepper	stock or water
1 onion	

Fry the chopped onion in the margarine till golden. Add the rice and fry with the onion for about 5 minutes or until quite dry, stirring to prevent it sticking to the pan. Then add 2 cupfuls of chicken stock or water, the bay leaf, salt, pepper and a touch of garlic; bring to the boil, then cook in the oven for 15–18 minutes. Remove from the oven and stand on one side for at least 10 minutes, being careful not to shake it, or the rice will not dry thoroughly and may be sticky.

Zrazy à la Nelson (for 4)

1 lb. fillet steak	1 teaspoonful tomato
2 medium onions	purée
1 oz. flour	4 small tomatoes
4 oz. margarine	4 or 5 mushrooms
½ pint stock or water	1 teaspoonful cream
Parsley	Croûtons

Fillet steak *must* be used for this dish. Cut it about ½ in. thick into circles approximately 1 in. in diameter, grill or fry according to taste. Meanwhile, fry some croûtons in deep fat and place the steaks on top of these, then cover the whole with the following sauce.

Fry chopped onions in margarine till golden, add flour to make a roux. Add a teaspoonful of tomato purée and enough stock or water to make the sauce a creamy consistency. Fry four or five mushrooms separately and add these to the sauce, with a little gravy browning to darken the colour and the cream to make it richer.

When this sauce has been poured over the steaks, top each one with a blanched and lightly fried tomato and a sprinkling of fresh parsley.

Sole à la Russe

This consists of a fillet of sole cut into tiny fingers, floured, rolled in egg-yolk and breadcrumbs, then fried in deep fat and served on a doyley with lemon.

Sernik

For the pancakes	
4 oz. flour	1 egg
½ pint milk	Pinch of salt

For the filling	
4 oz. sour milk (made	Icing sugar
from about 1½	Pinch of cinnamon
pints)	1 level dessertspoon-
1 oz. sultanas	ful sugar
Grated rind of	Squeeze lemon juice
1 lemon	Pinch of salt
1 dessertspoonful	1 egg-white
cream	2 oz. butter for frying

Make an ordinary pancake batter (see Puddings chapter) and fry one good-sized pancake for each person. For the filling, leave about 1½ pints of milk in a really warm atmosphere for 24 hours, till it begins to separate, then pour it into a muslin bag and leave to drip; this will provide approximately 4 oz. of sour milk cheese, but the amount varies with the quality of the milk. (The cream cheese sold at delicatessens for cooking purposes can be used but is not so good.) Mix all the filling ingredients together, using a wooden spoon, and the egg-white to bind them. Place some of the mixture on half of each pancake, fold over, seal the edges with egg-yolk to close like an envelope. Fry in butter for 2–3 minutes until golden, then turn over and do the other side. Sprinkle with icing sugar and serve, either as a first or last course.

Chicken Kieff is an extravagant dish, using one whole breast of chicken per person, but it's worth it

Sernik—pancakes with a filling of sour milk cheese— are served either first or last

Potato Cakes

> 2 medium potatoes
> Salt and pepper
> 1 egg
> Olive oil for frying

Peel and shred the potatoes finely, add salt and pepper, half the egg-yolk and all the white, and stir together. Fry the mixture, dropping it in little dollops off a spoon into hot, half-deep olive oil, for about 5 minutes until golden brown and crispy. Serve hot with sour cream, jam or marmalade, according to individual taste.

Turbot Caucasien

> 1 thick cutlet of tur-   8 oz. margarine or
>   bot per person   olive oil
> 1 onion   Clove of garlic
> Chopped mushrooms Paprika to taste

Skin, flour and fry the cutlets in the margarine or oil. Meanwhile, chop the onion into half-rings and fry separately until golden. Add the chopped mushrooms, garlic and paprika to the onion. Cover and fry for about 10–15 minutes. Pour over the cooked fish and serve hot or cold—preferably cold.

Russian Herring Salad

Cut cooked turnip, carrot, peas and pimento into little squares in equal quantities, mix with salt and pepper and a home-made mayonnaise, flavoured with lemon juice, tomato ketchup or Worcester sauce. Top with slices of herring fillet (obtainable from delicatessens) and decorate with lemon and parsley.

Beetroot as a Vegetable

For this dish you must boil your own beetroots, adding lemon juice to keep the colour, then mince finely. Fry two or three little pieces of pork or a rasher of bacon cut up small, add the minced beetroot and a dessertspoonful of white sauce, lemon juice or vinegar to taste, and serve hot.

HUNGARY

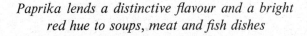

*Paprika lends a distinctive flavour and a bright
red hue to soups, meat and fish dishes*

Recipes by L. RODESINO, *Chef de Cuisine, Hungaria Restaurant, London*

BRILLIANT red dishes, coloured and distinctively flavoured with paprika, are typical of Hungarian cookery. Paprika, which is not hot like Cayenne, goes into Hungarian soups, fish and meat dishes, and gives its name to one of Hungary's two most famous national dishes: Chicken Paprika. The other, of course, is Goulash.

Yellow Split Pea Soup

4 oz. dried yellow split peas	3 oz. lard
1 onion, finely chopped and fried in lard	1 piece of lean smoked pork A little cream, salt and pepper

1 tablespoonful flour

Wash the dried peas well and soak overnight in cold water. Drain; add fresh cold water; bring to boil; skim; add the smoked pork and cook till very tender. Melt lard; add flour and cook, stirring till it becomes a yellow colour. Remove from fire and mix gradually with stock and peas. Boil and strain. Boil again; add salt and pepper to taste, the chopped onion, the meat from the pork cut into small dice and a little cream. Serve with fried croûtons.

Carpe à la Racz

This excellent recipe for Carp can be used for any salt- or fresh-water fish, other countries not being as abundantly supplied with fresh-water fish as Hungary.

1 medium-sized carp	A little chopped garlic
2 oz. lard	1 coffeecupful sour
2 oz. diced bacon, partly fried	cream, 1 teaspoonful flour (well
3 tomatoes (quartered), not skinned	mixed together) 3 cooked potatoes cut
2 green pimentoes, cut in squares	in thick slices ¼ lb. finely sliced
1 dessertspoonful paprika	onions Salt

Scale and clean the carp. Remove head. Divide in two, lengthwise; cut each side in three. Salt and leave to stand for 30 minutes. Fry onions in lard to a golden colour; add paprika and garlic and stir; pour in two cupfuls of water; bring to boil.

Lay pieces of fish in shallow saucepan; place tomatoes, pimentoes, potatoes, bacon and paprika on top; cover with the prepared mixture; bring to boil and finish cooking in moderate oven for about 10 minutes.

Remove from oven, pour in gradually the flour and cream; mix by shaking the saucepan while bringing it to the boil; add salt, if needed, and simmer for a few minutes.

Stuffed Pimentoes

Stuffing for 6 fresh pimentoes

¾ lb. chopped pork	Freshly ground peppers
1 small chopped onion	Garlic (very little)
2 tablespoonfuls cooked rice	Salt Lard for frying

1 egg

For the sauce

1 oz. flour	1½ pints water or
1 oz. lard	stock
1 dessertspoonful sugar	Salt and pepper 1 cupful tomato purée

Fry onion lightly in lard; add garlic and rice and mix well with meat, egg, salt and peppers. Open pimentoes from the stalk side; remove seeds and dip the pimentoes in boiling water for 1 minute. When cold, stuff with the mixture.

For sauce, heat lard; add flour and fry without browning; add water or stock and tomato purée. Season with salt, pepper and sugar, and mix. Bring to boil; add pimentoes and cook for 30 minutes.

Veal Goulash (for 4)

1 lb. stewing veal	1 dessertspoonful
1 dessertspoonful paprika	tomato purée 1 green pimento
6 oz. chopped onions	(shredded) if
3 oz. lard	available
1 clove garlic (chopped)	2 tomatoes (cut in quarters)

1 tablespoonful flour

Cut meat into cubes and wash well. Fry onions in lard till they begin to brown; stir

Veal Goulash, one of Hungary's most famous national dishes, is flavoured with paprika and can be served with spaghetti, rice or potatoes

in paprika; add 1 cupful of water, garlic, meat and tomato purée. Bring to boil and stew slowly with lid on till tender, adding a little water during cooking if necessary.

When cooked, sprinkle the flour on the meat and stir; add more water to cover; bring to boil and simmer for a few minutes, adding the pimentoes and the tomatoes.

Serve with spaghetti, rice or potatoes.

Chicken Paprika

2 2-lb. chickens	¼ pint milk, ¼ pint
2 oz. lard	cream, 1 tablespoon-
1 medium onion	ful flour (mixed
(chopped)	well together)
Salt	1 oz. paprika
¼ lb. tomatoes	1 pimento
1 cupful water	(if available)

Remove legs from chickens, split breasts into two, removing all small bones. Fry the onion in the lard until it begins to brown, stir in paprika, add water, salt and the chickens. Bring to the boil and cook with lid on until tender (about 20–30 minutes). Add a little water during cooking if necessary. Add the tomatoes and pimento during the last five minutes. When cooked, pour in the mixture of milk, cream and flour, stir while bringing to the boil and simmer for a few minutes. Add salt if required and serve with rice, spaghetti or boiled potatoes.

Cherry Strudel

1 lb. flour	¼ lb. sugar
1 egg	Lard
3 lb. cherries (stoned)	Dried breadcrumbs
	Cinnamon powder

Make a fairly soft dough with flour, egg and tepid water; work it and beat it till it comes clean off the table; lay it on floured board; cover with serviette and leave for 1½ hours. Place dough on a well-floured large cloth; pull and stretch it carefully in all directions until it is very thin and transparent. Trim off odd pieces outside the cloth. Spread on the top breadcrumbs, cherries, sugar and cinnamon powder, and sprinkle with melted lard. Lift the two corners of the cloth and roll till completely folded. Lay the rolled pastry on buttered pastry tray; brush with melted lard and cook in moderate oven for about 20 minutes.

Cut into portions and sprinkle with sugar.

GREECE

*Traditional Greek Dishes
as served at the White
Tower Restaurant, London*

To prepare the aubergine for Aubergine Imam Bayeldi the vegetable is peeled thinly in strips, leaving three or four of the strips on, above, and then slit with a knife to take the stuffing, right. Below, the finished dish

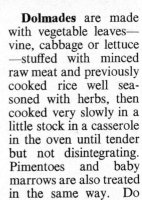

Dolmades are made with vegetable leaves—vine, cabbage or lettuce—stuffed with minced raw meat and previously cooked rice well seasoned with herbs, then cooked very slowly in a little stock in a casserole in the oven until tender but not disintegrating. Pimentoes and baby marrows are also treated in the same way. Do

G REEK cookery owes its inspiration to many lands, the strongest single influence being that of the Ottoman Empire. Stewy dishes are popular and there is an interesting method of cooking vegetables, not separately in water but with the meat they are to accompany, and usually "dolmadised." That delicious, mouth-watering word simply means stuffed, but in a very special way.

not skin pimentoes, but remove pips. Baby marrows should be partly skinned (for method, see Aubergine Imam Bayeldi and pictures on this page) if they are on the large side, and the pips removed.

This dish is served hot. A variation, consisting of vine (or cabbage or lettuce) leaves stuffed with rice and herbs only, without meat, makes a delicious hors d'œuvre and should then be served cold.

*Stuffed vine leaves, lamb grilled on a skewer, a gourmet's dream soup—
the Greeks have a word—and a recipe for them all*

Shashlik, a famous dish in all the Balkan countries, consists of small pieces of lamb, with various accompaniments, grilled over a charcoal fire and served with boiled rice

Taramosalata

This is a delicious Pâté of Smoked Cod's Roe which is easily and quickly made by adding chopped parsley, lemon juice, breadcrumbs and olive oil until it is a soft consistency for spreading. Serve hot on buttered toast.

Aubergine Imam Bayeldi
(for 4)

This dish, which is a stuffed aubergine, got its name because a famous Imam, a great gourmet but exceedingly greedy, ate so much of it that he "bayeldied," i.e. fainted away!

4 medium (or 2 large) aubergines
1 clove of garlic   Olive oil for frying
4 onions   4 tomatoes

To prepare your aubergine, remove the hard stalky end, then peel it fairly thinly lengthwise, in strips, leaving three or four strips of the skin on. This prevents the aubergine from falling to pieces during cooking. Finally, make about half a dozen lengthwise slits right through to the centre (see photos opposite). Now gently fry the aubergine in olive oil till golden. In another pan, fry to a golden brown the finely chopped onions, tomatoes and garlic (you need about twice as much as required to stuff the aubergine). Fill the slits with half this stuffing, lay the aubergines in a neat row in a casserole and pour the remainder of the stuffing over them. Bake slowly in a moderate oven until the onion is thoroughly done and the aubergine feels soft but still holds together. Leave to cool and serve cold with baked beans or cold stewed French Haricots Blancs.

NOTE: If using one large aubergine between two, always divide it lengthwise. This is because the thin stalky end has less goodness and flavour, and thus you equally divide the good and the not-so-good.

493

Fish Flaki

This is usually made with mackerel, but other fish could be used. It is baked in the oven for about an hour, smothered with sliced tomatoes, onions and garlic which have first been fried to a golden brown in olive oil. Can be served hot, but is even better cold.

Potage Avgolemono (for 4)

This is the Greek national soup, expensive but worth it.

1 *small to medium boiling chicken*	3 (*or, if possible,* 5) *new-laid eggs*
½ *lb. Patna rice*	*Lemon juice*

Boil the chicken very slowly, until it is practically falling to pieces, with the rice. Beat the eggs in a large bowl with the lemon juice, then, when the chicken broth is ready, begin to pour it into the bowl *very slowly*—the tiniest quantity at a time—without stopping beating for a moment. (Obviously, this is much easier if there are two of you in the kitchen.) When the quantity in the bowl is about double that of the original beaten eggs, pour it back into the broth, mix together and serve. Be sure to have a peppermill filled with black pepper on the table, as this is essential to bring out the full flavour of the soup. Or you can do as they do in some parts of Greece and serve with a little cinnamon sprinkled on top.

Fonds d'Artichaut à la Polita (for 4)

4 *globe artichokes*	½ *lb. green peas or*
1 *lemon*	*French beans*
½ *lb. young carrots*	*Olive oil and lemon*
½ *lb. young pickling onions*	*juice for dressing*

Always, when preparing an artichoke, squeeze lemon generously over it to keep it white; otherwise the artichoke, the knife and your hands will all blacken rapidly. Boil the base of the artichoke with the remains of the lemon (lime will not do) and cook until soft. Meanwhile, boil baby carrots, young pickling onions, green peas or young French beans (you need something green and the red of the carrots to make this otherwise colourless dish look appetising). Arrange round the artichokes and serve cold, garnished with a dressing of olive oil and lemon juice to taste.

Mussaka (for 4)

4 *medium aubergines*	*Mixed spice, garlic,*
Olive oil for frying	*onions and bay*
¼ *lb. minced beef*	*leaves to season*

For the sauce

1 *oz. flour*	4 *oz. grated*
2 *oz. butter*	*Parmesan cheese*
	¼ *pint milk*

This pie, made with layers of aubergines and minced meat, is a famous Greek national dish. First, peel the aubergines and slice them, removing all the skin, then fry in olive oil until pale golden in colour. At the same time, fry minced beef, well seasoned, also in olive oil. Put aubergines and meat in alternate layers in a casserole, cover with a rich cheese sauce and bake in the oven for about an hour. Serve hot.

Shashlik is a very famous dish in all the Balkan countries and consists of little pieces of lamb grilled on a skewer, with various accompaniments, over a charcoal fire.

Choose lean lamb, cut it into small neat squares and marinade it in olive oil with bay leaves, onion and lemon juice. Skewer the meat squares through their centres, alternately with slices of tomato and onion, small rashers of bacon and mushrooms. Grill (preferably over a charcoal fire) very fast in intense heat, turning the skewers frequently, until the lamb is done. Sprinkle with chopped parsley and serve on a bed of boiled rice.

Loukmades (for 4)

6 *oz. flour*	*Cinnamon, castor*
½ *teaspoonful yeast*	*sugar and honey*
Olive oil for frying	*for garnish*

Mix thoroughly well together the flour, water and a very little yeast and leave to stand. This must be done in the morning if you wish to make the Loukmades that evening. Make a little olive oil really hot in a frying pan. Then, with your bare hand, take a small handful of the dough, close your fist tightly so that a little squeezes through your first finger. With a teaspoon dipped in water, nip off a tiny little blob of the dough no bigger than a small fried potato. Drop it into the hot olive oil and fry on both sides until golden brown in colour and swollen and puffy. They should swell up but be "full of nothing." Sprinkle with cinnamon and castor sugar and serve hot with honey.

494

POLAND

*Here is a cuisine that avoids dullness, displays imagination,
tastes excellent—and makes even cabbage seem exciting*

by HALINA WUDZKA

IT is not generally realised how deeply
Polish literature and art were influenced
by the romantic period in English literature
at the beginning of the nineteenth century.
This, indeed, is regarded as the classical
period in Poland's literature and it owes
its origin directly to Byron, Wordsworth
and their contemporaries, just as Chopin's
music owed so much to the influence of
John Field.

Ever since then there has been a streak
of romanticism in the Polish national character, and so Polish cooking is, in its own
way, romantic too. It successfully avoids
dullness, it displays imagination and it
tastes excellent. Good restaurants in pre-
war Warsaw were among the best in
Europe, and Polish sausages were the best
on the Continent.

In addition to the good
restaurants, the dairies or
"milk shops" were a fea-
ture of Warsaw. These
were little places with
perhaps half a dozen
small tables where one
could drink a glass of hot
or cold milk or get the
most popular snack, "set
milk with potatoes."
This was fresh-set sour
milk (not yoghourt) set in
individual bowls and
cooled or chilled, accom-
panied by a plateful of
hot boiled potatoes with
crisply fried onions
sprinkled on the top. It
was eaten with a spoon,
alternate mouthfuls of the
milk and the potatoes.

Try some of the Polish
recipes and discover what
an exciting thing, for instance, cabbage can be—a vegetable not
generally regarded as likely to stir up
strong emotions.

Polish Beetroot Soup (Barszcz)

2–3 *pints clear beef* *stock or freshly* *made beef bouillon*	1 *bay leaf*
1 *grated raw beetroot*	1 *or* 2 *beetroot,* *cooked, peeled, cut* *into thin strips like*
½ *teaspoonful vinegar* *or lemon juice*	*noodles*
1 *tablespoonful butter*	½ *lb. tomatoes*
	½ *cupful flour*
Salt and pepper	

For beef bouillon.—1½ lb. beef, 1 carrot,
1 onion, a bouquet garni, cooked together
and skimmed clear.

Cook the tomatoes separately in 3 tablespoonfuls of water until soft, then rub
through a sieve. Add the tomato purée, the
cooked beetroot and the vinegar or lemon

**Chicken Cutlets may be topped with a fried egg and served with
potatoes, mushrooms and new peas, or eaten cold as a picnic dish**

juice to the stock or bouillon, and bind the soup by slightly browning the flour in the butter and gradually adding a little of the broth until it is smooth and thin, then stirring into the soup. Simmer gently for at least 1½ hours, adding salt and pepper to taste and a bay leaf. Just before serving, colour with grated raw beetroot and bring just to the boil; if cooked any longer, the colour will fade. Serve with finely chopped dill (or fennel) or parsley and sour cream; these are usually served in side dishes so that each person can suit his individual taste. For variation, small Frankfurter-type sausages or little cubes of ham may also be added to the soup.

Polish Cold Soup (Chlodnik)

Prepare beetroot soup as above. When ready, add 1 or 2 cupfuls of diced boiled beef (from the freshly made beef bouillon), some diced ham or Frankfurters, or both, some diced fresh cucumber, a couple of sliced radishes, a little shredded tender lettuce or spinach or sorrel and a cupful of sharp cider or red wine. Chill thoroughly. Just before serving, add at least ¼ pint sour cream.

Dressed Herring

1 herring, salted or cured in brine	Vinegar, olive oil and black pepper
Milk	Onions

Soak herring for at least 24 hours in milk; drain; cut off head and tail; scrape off skin; remove all bones.

Cut across in ¾-in. strips, lay them on a flat dish, keeping the shape of the fish, and make it more attractive by appropriately placing the head and tail. At least 1 hour before serving, cover with a dressing of 1 part vinegar to 2 parts olive oil and a good sprinkle of pepper, preferably black.

Serve surrounded with onions, either raw mild onions cut in thin slices or rings, or onion salad.

To make onion salad.—Slice 3 or 4 onions in thin rings, parboil for a few minutes until they become transparent, drain well and, while still warm, mix with basic dressing: ½ teaspoonful salt, ¼ teaspoonful pepper, ½ teaspoonful mustard, 2 tablespoonfuls vinegar (preferably malt vinegar), 2 tablespoonfuls olive oil.

Stuffed Herring

1 herring, salted or cured in brine	
½ lb. cooking apples, raw, peeled and cored	Cold boiled potatoes, of bulk equal to the quantity of apples

Begin as for dressed herring, again keeping aside the head and tail. After removing all bones, put the herring, apple and potatoes twice through a fine mincer to ensure that it is finely minced, then mix with a dressing as for dressed herring, adding salt to taste.

Serve on a flat dish, making the mixture into the shape of a fish (with a fork) and adding the head and tail. Surround with raw onion rings or onion salad, as already described.

Meat and Cabbage (Bigos) (for 4)

1–2 lb. fresh cabbage or Sauerkraut, and approximately the same quantity of ham or gammon cut in small chunks or salt pork or bacon	
A few pieces of smoked sausage	1 or 2 Frankfurter sausages cut in pieces
A few pieces of garlic sausage	Bacon or pork fat
Salt and pepper	1 wineglassful red wine
2 tablespoonfuls flour	
Several sliced onions	

Finely shred the cabbage or Sauerkraut, cover it with water and bring to the boil, then drain thoroughly, to remove any traces of bitterness. Add the meat, sausage and sliced onions to the prepared cabbage, season well with salt and pepper, add a little water and simmer very gently for at least 1 hour, adding a little more water if necessary but only just enough to keep it moist. When the cabbage and onions are thoroughly cooked and tender, make a gravy separately by melting some bacon or pork fat, stirring into it the flour and browning slightly, then adding a little water. Pour this over the meat and cabbage, and at the last minute add the wine. Heat, but do not cook any longer. Serve at once.

This dish may be served with boiled potatoes and should be accompanied by a good red wine and rye bread.

Chicken Cutlets (Pożarski)

1 boiling fowl	Milk
Flour or fine breadcrumbs and butter for frying	1–2 cupfuls white bread and 1 or 2 eggs, according to size of fowl
Salt and pepper to taste	

Photographs of Polish food taken at the Polish Air Force Club, London

There are many ways of cooking Stuffed White Cabbage. Sour cream or sour cream cheese and rye bread are served with most main dishes

Remove skin and mince finely all the white meat from a boiling fowl. Add the bread soaked in milk and mince again. Season with salt and pepper. Mix well with the eggs, lightly beaten, and shape into small flat cakes about 1 in. thick. Coat with flour or egg and breadcrumbs and fry in butter, quickly browning the outside first, then cooking slowly to keep the cutlets juicy while cooking right through. Serve hot with mashed potatoes, carrots, little peas, button mushrooms, asparagus tips; or eat cold with salad as a picnic dish. A fried egg may be served on each cutlet, if liked.

Pirogi

Pirogi are a mainstay of Polish and Russian home cooking. They are a kind of small turnover, boiled in water, with various fillings, both sweet and savoury.

For the dough

12 oz. plain flour	1 egg
A knob of fat	Salt

Make a not too soft dough, knead well and roll out to $\frac{1}{8}$ in. in thickness. Cut into rounds, about $2\frac{1}{2}$ in. diameter, and put a teaspoonful of filling in the middle of each. Close them up very firmly—this is essential, otherwise the filling will cook out—and boil for 3 minutes in salted water.

These are some popular fillings:

Sour Milk Cheese Filling

$\frac{1}{2}$ lb. sour milk cheese	Butter or margarine
$\frac{1}{2}$ lb. boiled potatoes	1 oz. Danish blue
1 tablespoonful	cheese
semolina	Salt and pepper to
1 small onion	taste

Fry the chopped onion in butter or margarine until golden brown, then add all the other ingredients and mix together very thoroughly.

Serve with chopped onions fried in butter or margarine until golden brown.

Morella Cherry Filling (a summer dish)

Stone the cherries and put 3 or 4 on each round of dough. When the Pirogi are cooked, brush them over with melted butter and serve cold with yoghourt poured on top and plenty of sugar.

Curds or Curd Cheese mixed with an egg to a smooth paste and very slightly salted. When Pirogi are cooked, brush generously with melted butter, serve hot with sour cream and sugar or sugar mixed with nutmeg or cinnamon to taste.

Polish Roast Chicken

One small chicken or Poussin per person is stuffed with breadcrumbs and plenty of chopped dill bound with a beaten egg, or simply with branches or sprigs of dill. Roast in butter, basting frequently. Make gravy in the roasting pan by lightly browning a little flour and adding sour cream at the last minute and just heating through. Serve with fresh cucumber salad and new potatoes.

"Selyanka" Meat and Cabbage

Approximately 1 lb. of various meats: bacon or gammon or ham; smoked and well-spiced pork sausage or garlic sausage or ham sausage.	*1 or 2 lb. Sauerkraut, squeezed dry of its liquid*
	1 or 2 lb. onions, sliced
	Garlic
Breadcrumbs and/or grated cheese	*Cooking fat and olive oil*
	Salt and pepper

Fry the meats, cut in small strips, very gently until well done in a large frying pan, then remove to a good-sized mixing bowl. There should be plenty of fat left in the pan. Add cooking fat (or good dripping), if necessary, and a dash of olive oil, and fry the onions, gently, until transparent; also a whole bud of garlic, which should then be removed. When the onions are done, take them out of the frying pan and add to the meat. Then fry the drained Sauerkraut, stirring constantly until well browned, and adding more fat as required to prevent sticking or burning. Season well with salt and pepper. Mix all the ingredients thoroughly, put into ovenproof dish, sprinkle the top with breadcrumbs and/or grated cheese. Before baking, add about a teacupful of boiling water (or perhaps a little more), so that the cabbage is quite moist. Bake in the oven until brown. Serve with boiled potatoes.

Tripe à la Polonaise (Flaki) (for 3–4)

1 lb. tripe	*3 oz. butter*
2 oz. flour	*A little ground ginger, nutmeg, cloves, salt, pepper and Cayenne to taste*
2 carrots	
2 sticks celery	
A little more than 2 quarts stock	*1 onion*
Mixed herbs	

Clean the tripe and wash several times, then blanch in boiling salted water, wash again in cold water, then put into boiling water and simmer very slowly for 5–6 hours. Take out and cut into narrow strips like noodles. Melt the butter, stir in the flour and brown it, then make a roux with a little of the stock. Add this to the stock with the sliced vegetables, herbs, seasoning and spices. Bring to the boil and simmer for 20 minutes. Add the tripe, cover and simmer until all is tender.

NOTE: As a rule the sauce is only lightly spiced, this dish always being served in Warsaw accompanied by a whole array of little separate dishes containing an assortment of spices from which one helps oneself, according to taste. The spices should include mixed herbs, ground ginger, grated nutmeg, red pepper, chopped marjoram, grated cheese, salt, and black pepper in a mill.

Cabbage Pie

Line a deep baking dish with pastry or yeast dough. Scald a white cabbage for a minute or two, drain, cut up in 1-in. squares, mix with a lightly beaten egg, season with salt and pepper, and fill the baking dish with these ingredients. Cover the cabbage with a lid or plate to keep in the steam and prevent it from browning, and bake in a moderate oven until tender. Serve very hot, adding several knobs of butter at the last minute so that they just melt on top.

Mushrooms with Eggs

This very popular Polish dish can be made either with fresh mushrooms or—this is well worth trying—with dried ones. Dried mushrooms from Italy can now be bought by the ounce in many shops.

½ lb. mushrooms	*2 oz. butter*
5–6 tablespoonfuls fresh-set sour milk	*1 tablespoonful semolina*
1 medium-sized onion, chopped	*Fried eggs as required*
	Salt and pepper

Wash, but do not peel, the mushrooms and slice them finely. Fry the onion in the butter until transparent, then add the mushrooms and fry together for 1 minute. Add water to cover and simmer for ½ hour, add semolina and sour milk, salt and pepper to taste and serve with fried eggs.

If dried mush-rooms are used, wash them and let them soak for a few hours in warm water, then proceed as above, cooking in the water in which they were soaked.

Stuffed White Cab-bage (A dish from East Poland, some-times called Gol-ubtsy or Little Pigeons)

1 *lb. minced beef*
(raw)
1 *tablespoonful rice*
1 *large white cabbage*
1 *medium-sized*
onion, finely
chopped
Salt and pepper
Finely chopped
mushrooms

Babka is a famous national cake, always made in a fluted tin like a jelly mould and lightly iced

For the gravy

1 *oz. dripping*
1 *tablespoonful*
  Golden Syrup
1 *medium-sized onion*
  ½ *pint stock or water*

1 *oz. flour*
1 *tablespoonful*
  vinegar
Salt

Peel off the outer leaves of the cabbage, cut off the protruding parts of the stalks and plunge into boiling water for 1 minute to make them pliable. Mix all the other in-gredients together and put 1 tablespoonful in each leaf, fold up neatly and tie with string. Pack tightly into a fireproof dish. *For the gravy.*—Cut up the onion and fry it in the dripping until golden brown, add flour and fry until flour is brown too, then add boiling water or stock, Golden Syrup, vinegar and salt, and boil for a few minutes. When smooth, pour over the stuffed leaves and put into a slow oven. Cook until the leaves are dark brown on one side, then turn them over and brown the other side. This dish should simmer in the oven for several hours—in fact, it im-proves considerably if it is cooked on two successive days, as the slowly roasted cab-bage leaves give a distinctive flavour.

Babka

A cake with a texture between a fine-grained Angel Cake and a porous Sponge Cake.

1½ *lb. flour, well*
  sifted
6 *egg-yolks*
1 *cupful melted*
  butter
1¼ *to* 1½ *oz. yeast, dis-*
  solved in ½ *cupful*
  warm milk

Pinch of salt, handful
  of Sultanas, tea-
  spoonful vanilla
  flavouring
2 *to* 3 *tablespoonfuls*
  white icing, a little
  rum or lemon juice
¾ *cupful sugar*

Beat egg-yolks thoroughly, mix well with melted warm (not hot) butter, add yeast dissolved in milk, mix thoroughly, add flour, beat well, put into warm place to rise for ½ to ¾ of an hour. Add sugar, salt, flavouring and sultanas, and knead or beat again, the longer the better, until dough shows bubbles and no longer ad-heres to the hands. Let it rise again in a warm place, and be sure always to cover it and protect it from draughts, for 1½ to 2 hours. Knead or beat for another 10 minutes, put into greased baking tin shaped like a jelly mould, filling only one-quarter to one-third, let it rise again till tin is about three-quarters full. Bake in hot oven for about an hour.

While still warm, spread over the top a little white icing, flavoured with a few drops of rum or lemon juice, letting it trickle down the sides.

AUSTRIA

From Vienna comes a cuisine that is good and gay, with a sublime disregard for slimming rules

by CAMILLA KAPRALIK

OLD Austria was a country of many nationalities. They met and mixed in its splendid capital, Vienna, and so did their respective cuisines. Thus the famous Viennese cuisine is in reality a happy mixture of Austrian, Czech and Hungarian dishes, with a dash of Italian and Polish cooking for good measure. It is good and gay, and displays a sublime disregard for slimming rules—which may be the secret of its attraction for all those who visit the country. The following typical Austrian dishes exemplify the deep-rooted national belief in eating well.

Beef Broth with Liver Dumplings (for 4)

The centrepiece of the Austrian middle-class family's regular midday meal on weekdays is boiled beef, with vegetables or horseradish sauce, preceded by a beef broth, sometimes with vermicelli, etc., in it, but more often with liver dumplings.

For the broth

1½ lb. beef (prefer-ably chuck steak)	1 onion
Parsley	Peppercorns
	A few sticks of celery

Boil the beef slowly in salted water with the other ingredients. When the meat is tender, strain off the soup and cook the dumplings in it.

For the dumplings

¼ lb. calf's liver	1 clove of garlic,
1 calf's milt (spleen)	crushed (optional)
1 crisp roll (or bread)	1 oz. dripping
1 egg	White breadcrumbs
	Pinch of salt

Cream the fat and salt, mix in the egg, soak the roll or bread in water and squeeze out all the liquid. Mince the liver and milt, and mix with the other ingredients, add about 2 tablespoonfuls of breadcrumbs, and let the mixture stand for a while. It should be of such a consistency that it can be formed into little dumplings. Boil for about 5 minutes in the broth.

Beef Gulasch (for 4)

Although of Hungarian origin, the Austrian version is a great favourite.

1½ lb. beef (prefer-ably back-rib)	1–2 oz. beef dripping or lard
½ lb. onions	1 heaped teaspoonful
½ teaspoonful paprika (not red pepper)	flour
Salt to taste	½ teaspoonful cara-way seeds

Chop the onions finely and fry in the fat in a heavy saucepan until they are a rich golden brown. Cut the meat into 1-in. squares and add it, with all the other ingredients, to the onions, and fry, stirring frequently, until the flour is dark brown. Cover with a lid and simmer until the juice is extracted from the meat. When all the liquid has evaporated (this is a critical moment; if left too long the meat will burn), add a little water and continue to simmer until the meat is tender. Serve with boiled potatoes.

Veal Gulasch

This is made in the same way as Beef Gulasch, using stewing veal in place of the beef, one ripe tomato instead of the caraway seeds and omitting the flour when frying. The onions should be fried only to a pale golden colour. Stir 1 teaspoonful of flour into about half a bottle of yoghourt, or top of the milk with a few drops of lemon juice, until quite smooth and free from lumps, and when the meat is tender add this to the gravy and let it simmer for a while.

Weiner Schnitzel (for 4)

This is the favourite Austrian Sunday dinner dish and, when served cold, is also popular for picnics.

4 slices of leg of veal or pork	Breadcrumbs and flour
Pinch of paprika	2 tablespoonfuls milk
Lard for frying	2 eggs
	Salt

NOTE: To make authentic Schnitzel, as

eaten in Vienna, here are three important rules:

(1) Prepare the breadcrumbs yourself—bought o n e s will not do! Buy two French loaves and put them in a very cool oven until they are quite dry but not brown, then grate them and finally rub them through a sieve.

(2) Use lard for frying, NOT dripping or any fat that has been used before.

(3) Do not let the meat stand for any length of time after it has been coated, as the breadcrumbs will become soaked and the schnitzels will not crisp. Prepare the second piece of meat while the first is frying.

Beat out the meat until it is ⅓-in. thick and salt slightly on both sides. Mix the eggs with the milk, paprika and salt. Roll the meat in flour, shake off surplus, then dip in the egg mixture, drip off any excess, coat with breadcrumbs, dabbing the crumbs on lightly and shaking off the surplus. (Make sure that all the meat is evenly covered with all the ingredients.) Get the lard smoking hot in a heavy pan and deep-fry the schnitzels. Serve with potatoes and slices of lemon but, please, NOT with tomato sauce and macaroni.

Spring chicken (*poussin*) prepared in the same way, but fried more slowly, makes another famous Austrian dish, and so does fish—carp being a particular favourite.

In summer it is the thing to serve Weiner Schnitzel with new potatoes tossed in butter and finely chopped parsley and a cucumber salad.

Cucumber Salad

Slice the cucumber very thinly, salt and cover it for ¼ hour, then squeeze out the liquid. Make a dressing of French vinegar,

To be really extravagant, serve Stuffed Rumpsteak with puff-pastry crescents, or vol-au-vents filled with creamy potatoes and diced ham

diluted to taste, a pinch of sugar and a pinch of pepper, and pour it over the cucumber. If liked, a little olive oil may be added and a small piece of crushed garlic.

Boiled Ham, Sauerkraut and Dumplings
(Geselchtes, kraut und knödel) (for 4)

1½ lb. bacon (gammon or shoulder)	½ teaspoonful sugar
2 bay leaves	1 or 2 cloves
Sauerkraut	½ teaspoonful caraway seeds
1 large raw potato	

NOTE: Very good tinned sauerkraut—either Dutch or Israeli—is obtainable in the U.K.

Simmer the bacon until tender, with the sugar, bay leaves and cloves. Simmer separately the sauerkraut with the caraway seeds for $\frac{1}{2}$ hour, then grate the raw potato into it and simmer for another $\frac{1}{2}$ hour.

For the dumplings

1 French loaf	2 oz. dripping or
1 egg	margarine
$\frac{1}{2}$ teaspoonful salt	$\frac{1}{4}$ pint milk
4 tablespoonfuls plain flour	

Cut the bread into small cubes and pour over it the melted fat. Mix together the egg, milk and salt, add to the bread and leave for at least 1 hour, stirring occasionally. Add the flour, mix thoroughly, form into four balls, roll them in flour and boil for 10 minutes in salted water.

NOTE: Roast pork is also served in Austria with sauerkraut and dumplings. When roasting pork, the Austrians add an onion and sprinkle the joint generously with caraway seeds, which gives it a distinctive flavour.

Minced meat fritters are in the luxury class made this way, as served in Vienna

Stuffed Rump Steak (for 4)

2 oz. dripping or lard	4 good-sized rump
$\frac{1}{2}$ lb. onions	steaks
8 fillets of anchovy	4 bacon rashers
1 oz. capers	$\frac{1}{2}$ bottle Yoghourt
1 teaspoonful French	1 or 2 pickled cucum-
mustard	bers (not gherkins)
$\frac{1}{2}$ teaspoonful paprika	Flour

Beat the steak to $\frac{1}{2}$-in. thickness, sprinkle with paprika, spread with finely chopped anchovy, capers and mustard. Put the bacon rashers into boiling water for a minute or two, then put one on each steak and add half or quarter of a pickled cucumber, according to size, roll up and tie with white sewing cotton. Chop the onions and fry in the dripping or lard until golden brown. Roll the meat in flour and fry with onions until a rich brown on all sides, then proceed as for Beef Gulasch (page 500). When the meat is tender, add half a bottle of yoghourt with 1 teaspoonful flour and simmer for 20 minutes. Remove cotton and serve with boiled potatoes or, if you want to be really extravagant, with pastry crescents or vol-au-vents filled with creamed potatoes and diced ham.

Minced Meat Fritters (for 4)

1 lb. beef (topside)
1 crisp roll (or white bread)
Breadcrumbs
1 clove garlic, crushed
$\frac{1}{2}$ lb. pork
1 egg
Salt and pepper
Lard for frying

Mince the raw meat (or get the butcher to do it for you). Soak the bread in water, then press out all the liquid and add the egg, garlic, salt and pepper and mix together very thoroughly, adding 1 tablespoonful of breadcrumbs. Form the mixture into oblong fritters, dip them in breadcrumbs and fry in medium deep fat (preferably lard) until a rich brown on both sides. Serve with mashed potatoes, potato salad, pickled cucumbers or cucumber salad

Viennese Guglhupf, a typical Austrian delicacy, is delicious served with coffee or chocolate topped with sweetened whipped cream

Lights and Heart with Dumplings (Beuschl mit knödeln) (for 4)

This competes in popularity with Gulasch.

1 *set of calf's (or*	1 *onion*
pig's) lights with	*A few peppercorns*
the heart or 2 *hearts*	1 *clove of garlic*
A sprig of thyme	1 *tablespoonful*
2 *sticks of celery*	*French vinegar*

For the gravy

1 *oz. flour*	1 *oz. dripping*
Meat broth as required	

Cook all the ingredients together until tender, then leave to cool (preferably overnight). Make a fairly thick gravy, using the flour fried in dripping until golden brown, and some of the broth in which the meat was cooked. Bring to the boil, stirring all the time, then add the finely sliced meat and reheat, but do not boil. Serve with slices of lemon.

This dish is also served with bread dumplings (see boiled ham, sauerkraut and dumplings, page 501).

SWEET DISHES

Dough made with yeast is typically Austrian and is used in many different ways. It is made as follows:

12 *oz. plain flour*	*A pinch of grated*
1 *oz. yeast*	*lemon rind*
4 *oz. butter or mar-*	2 *egg-yolks*
garine	½ *pint milk (approx.)*
3 *oz. castor sugar*	

Warm the milk, pour off one-third and add to it 1 teaspoonful sugar and the yeast, cover and put in a warm place to rise. Work the butter or margarine into the flour (as for short pastry), add egg-yolks, sugar, lemon rind, risen yeast and—slowly—the rest of the milk, to make a fairly soft dough. Beat with a wooden spoon until it no longer sticks, is quite smooth and shows little bubbles. Cover it up and keep in a warm place until it has risen to twice its size.

This yeast dough is the basis for the following sweet dishes and cakes:

(a) Viennese Guglhupf (the famous tea-time cake)

Before the dough has risen, add 1 oz. sultanas. Grease a fluted baking tin (special Guglhupf tins can be bought in big cities) thickly with melted butter or margarine and let it cool, then sprinkle the sides of the tin with thinly sliced blanched almonds. Fill the tin with the dough and leave covered in a warm place until the dough has risen to double its original size, Bake for ¾ hour in a cool oven until golden brown, turn out on to a plate and, while still hot, sprinkle freely with vanilla sugar.

This Guglhupf is served with coffee or chocolate, topped with sweetened whipped cream.

Vanilla Sugar

Place a vanilla pod, cut into two or three pieces, in a screw-top jar full of icing sugar. In about 10 days the sugar is delicately flavoured.

(b) Steam Noodles

Sprinkle a warmed pastry board with flour and place the dough on it in tablespoonfuls. Make a small well in the centre of each little piece of dough and fill with ½ teaspoonful plum jam mixed with grated lemon rind and a pinch of cinnamon. Fold the dough over the jam and close tightly. Put into a well-greased oven-glass dish and grease each bun on the sides or they will stick together. Leave in a warm place until risen to double size, bake in a cool oven for about 30 minutes, then, before the buns begin to show any colour, sprinkle them with about ¼ pint boiling water, and keep them in the oven for about 20 minutes longer. The buns should not have any colour. Serve hot with melted butter and ground walnuts mixed with vanilla sugar (see above).

NOTE: A pure jam should be used. Jams made with special pectin preparations may start to run and so spoil the dough.

(c) Viennese Buns (Wiener buchteln)

These are made in exactly the same way as Steam Noodles, but filled with any jam you fancy and baked, without adding water, until they are a golden brown. While still hot, sprinkle with vanilla sugar. They are served at tea-time or as a sweet dish after a main meal.

(d) Viennese Sparrows (Wiener spatzen)

After the dough has risen, cut off pieces with a tablespoon and drop into a frying pan containing deep hot lard. Fry until golden brown on both sides, then put on to blotting paper for a minute or two, sprinkle with vanilla sugar and serve hot with raspberry jam.

NOTE: If a tablespoonful of rum is mixed with the dough for this recipe, it will absorb less fat.

Apfelstrudel

To make an Apfelstrudel (the real thing) you need a fairly large table, say about 2 ft. 6 in. by 3 ft. 6 in. Also, as flour in the U.K. is completely different from flour in Austria, I would strongly suggest using McDougall's self-raising flour, with which I personally have obtained the best results.

For the dough

12 oz. flour	2 oz. lard

Use lukewarm water to make a soft dough which must be kneaded until it shows little bubbles. Now warm a bowl, cover the dough with it and let it stand for ½ hour.

For the filling

2 lb. cooking apples (Bramleys or Blenheims, peeled and sliced)	5 oz. breadcrumbs
	Lemon juice
	4 oz. castor sugar
	6 oz. margarine
A pinch of cinnamon	3 oz. sultanas

Fry the breadcrumbs in 2 oz. margarine until golden brown, melt the rest of the margarine. When all the ingredients have been prepared, put a cloth on the table and sprinkle it with flour, then pull out the dough on the cloth until it is nearly as thin as tissue paper. Cut off the thick edges, sprinkle with the 4 oz. melted margarine, put the sliced apples and sultanas on only a quarter part of the dough along the wide side of the table, and sprinkle the apples with lemon juice. Scatter the breadcrumbs and the sugar mixed with cinnamon all over the dough. Pick up the ends of the tablecloth and, by moving the cloth, roll the strudel up very tightly. Grease all over with melted margarine, put on a greased baking-tin and bake in a moderate oven for about 1 hour until golden. Immediately it comes out of the oven, cut it in pieces, put on a plate and sprinkle with vanilla sugar.

NOTE: The pulling out of the dough needs practice. Do not be discouraged if you do not succeed the first time—try again.

Viennese Chocolate Cake

6 oz. sugar	6 oz. ground plain
3 oz. margarine	chocolate
1½ oz. breadcrumbs	6 eggs
3 oz. ground almonds or cobnuts	A dash of rum

504

Cream the margarine with the sugar and the egg-yolks, add breadcrumbs, rum, almonds or cobnuts (ground with their skins), chocolate and, finally, the stiffly beaten egg-whites. Put the mixture into a loose-bottomed cake tin well greased with butter and lightly covered with breadcrumbs (shake off the surplus). Bake in a cool oven for about $\frac{3}{4}$ hour. When cold, split and fill with the following cream:

4 oz. chocolate	3½ oz. margarine or
4 oz. sugar	butter
1–2 tablespoonfuls rum	1 egg-yolk

Melt the chocolate with a little water and leave to cool. Cream the butter or margarine with the sugar and egg, and add the chocolate and rum. Cover the cake with chocolate icing (see Icings chapter).

Emperor's Omelet (Kaiserschmarrn)

3 oz. plain flour	4 oz. castor sugar
3 oz. margarine	1 oz. sultanas
Milk (about ¼ pint)	¼ pint whipped cream
3 eggs	A pinch of salt

Mix the flour to a thin paste with the milk, add the egg-yolks, sugar and salt, Whip the egg-whites very stiffly and mix into the paste very carefully. Add the whipped cream. Put the margarine in a baking tin and let it get hot, pour in the mixture and cook in a moderate oven until golden brown, then pull to little pieces with two forks (if not quite done, put back into the oven for a few minutes) and add the sultanas, sprinkle with vanilla sugar and serve with stewed plums.

Linzer Torte

6 oz. sugar	6 oz. margarine
6 oz. breadcrumbs	6 oz. ground almonds
1 egg (whole)	1 egg-white
½ teaspoonful mixed ground spice	Grated lemon rind Strawberry jam

Make a dough, using all ingredients except egg-white and jam, and put three-quarters of it into a baking tin with a loose bottom. Moisten the 1-in.-thick dough with the egg-white. Make the rest of the dough into long thin strips and with these make a rim round the bottom layer of dough and a lattice-work pattern on top. Paint with white of egg. Bake in a cool oven until well browned, then fill the spaces with strawberry jam.

Another famous national sweet dish is Linzer Torte, a lattice-patterned tart tasting of almonds and topped with strawberry jam

GERMANY

*Where the food reflects the national
character and good rye bread is plentiful*

IT has been said that a nation's cuisine reflects that nation's basic characteristics.
Germany is a country of many tribes, and
just as north Germans differ from Rhinelanders and Bavarians, so does their way
of cooking. Food in north Germany is
rather stern and robust, in the south it is
more akin to the rich Austrian fare.

Good bread, and plenty of it, is an essential part of a German meal. Praise is due to
the quality of German bread, especially to
the dark grey rye bread which can be
bought in the U.K. This is wholesome and
an excellent help to digestion. The pumpernickel type of bread is also worth trying;
it is delicious with butter and cheese.

Visitors to Germany will probably have
come across some of the following dishes.

Cold Cherry Soup (for 4–5)

2 lb. black cherries	½ lb. sugar
1½ pints water	Cinnamon
Cloves	1 egg-white
Cornflour	

Stone the cherries and cook in water with
the sugar and spices; thicken with cornflour. Pour into soup bowls and leave to
cool. When cold, put in the centre of each
bowl a blob of slightly sweetened whipped
egg-white.

Pea Soup with Sausage (for 4)

½ lb. dried peas	Frankfurters (or other
1 oz. dripping	continental cooking
1 tablespoonful flour	sausages)
Water or stock	

Soak the peas (the wrinkled green variety
are the best available in the U.K.) for
about 12 hours, boil in water or stock
until quite tender, pass through a sieve and
add sufficient stock or water to make four
helpings. Fry the flour in the dripping until
golden brown, add to the liquid and simmer for about ½ hour. Before serving, add
some continental cooking sausage or
Frankfurter cut in small pieces. Serve with

small cubes of fried bread. This is a very
tasty, substantial and nourishing dish.

Herring Salad (for 4)

3 salted herrings	Yoghourt
A little vinegar	1 sprig of thyme
1 bay leaf	A pinch of sugar
1 onion (cut into thin	½ teaspoonful French
rings)	mustard

Soak the herrings in water for 48 hours,
changing the water once or twice, then bone
the fish and cut into small pieces. Cook the
onion in the vinegar, diluted to taste, with
the herbs and sugar. When cold, add the
yoghourt and mustard, and pour over the
herrings. Leave to stand for 2 days, then
serve with potatoes boiled in their jackets.

Stuffed Herrings

Pickled herrings	Vegetable salad
1 apple	Mayonnaise
Pickled cucumber	Tomatoes
Parsley	

Pickled herrings can be bought in jars.
Remove them from the brine and drip dry,
then split open and stuff with a mixture of
vegetable salad, mayonnaise and sliced
apple. Serve garnished with cucumber,
tomatoes and parsley.

Macaroni with Boiled Bacon (for 4)

½ lb. macaroni or	4 tablespoonfuls
noodles (real egg	yoghourt
noodles are the	½ lb. cooked bacon
most suitable)	2 oz. margarine
3 eggs	Breadcrumbs

Cook macaroni or noodles in boiling
salted water until tender, and rinse in cold
water. Separate the egg-yolks from the
whites, and cream the margarine with the
yolks. Mix with the cold macaroni or
noodles, chopped bacon and yoghourt.
Add the very stiffly whipped egg-whites.
Grease a fireproof dish, sprinkle with
breadcrumbs, pour in the mixture and bake
in a moderate oven until golden brown.
Serve with lettuce, white cabbage salad

Pickled herrings, stuffed with mixed vegetable salad and garnished with
cucumber, tomato and parsley

dressed with vinegar and oil, or with a rich tomato sauce.

Boiled Chicken with Lemon Sauce and Rice

1 *boiling fowl*	*Parsley*
2 *sticks of celery*	*White sauce*
Lemon juice	1 *small onion*
Rice	1 *egg-yolk*
1 *or* 2 *cloves*	*Peppercorns*

Boil the chicken with the onion, peppercorns, celery and parsley until tender. Serve with white sauce, to which lemon juice and egg-yolk have been added.

Rice is boiled in the chicken broth, in the proportion of 1 teacupful of rice to **2** teacupfuls of broth. Add the onion, whole, with the cloves stuck firmly in it, and cook in a slow oven until tender.

Reibe Kuchen (Potato pancakes)

1 lb. potatoes   Salt and pepper
3 tablespoonfuls plain   1 egg
    flour   1 onion (optional)
      Oil for frying

Grate the raw potatoes and let them drip off; mix in the egg, flour and salt and pepper, and grated onion (if liked). Make into thin fritters and fry, preferably in oil, until golden brown on both sides.

Hackbraten (Minced meat loaf with savoury sauce) (for 5—6)

1½ lb. raw beef (top   Breadcrumbs
    rib)   ½ lb pork
2 eggs   2 oz. white bread
Salt and pepper   1 medium-sized onion
2 hard-boiled eggs for   1 oz. dripping
    stuffing

For the sauce
2 oz. capers
About 4 tablespoonfuls of sour cream or
yoghourt   Four

Soak the bread in water, then squeeze out all the liquid. Mince the raw beef and mix it very thoroughly with the eggs and soaked bread; add salt and pepper to taste. Form into an oblong loaf, with the hard-boiled eggs in the middle and completely covered by meat. Roll in breadcrumbs and put into a roasting tin with a little dripping and the onion, peeled and cut in half. Roast for about 1½ hours, then add the capers, sour cream and a little flour for thickening. Keep in the oven for another ½ hour. Serve with very creamy mashed potatoes.

Cheese Cake

Short pastry   ½ lb. sour-milk cheese
2 oz. margarine   4 oz. castor sugar
3 egg-yolks   2 oz. sultanas
Grated lemon rind   ½ teaspoonful baking
Blanched almonds   powder

Line a loose-bottom sponge cake tin with the pastry. Cream the margarine with the sugar and the egg-yolks, add the cheese, baking powder, sultanas and lemon rind. Put this mixture on the pastry, sprinkle with thinly sliced blanched almonds and bake in a moderate oven until golden brown.

Pancakes with Asparagus

10 oz. plain flour   3 eggs
Milk   Salt and parsley
Asparagus   Margarine

Wash, peel and trim the asparagus, and braise until tender in margarine and water with finely chopped parsley and salt. Meanwhile, make pancakes (see Puddings and Sweets) wrap sticks of asparagus in

One of the most typical of all German dishes—Frankfurters are served hot with sauerkraut and boiled potatoes or cold with potato salad

Whole pears served in a dish of chocolate sauce

them, and serve hot. Put a slice of beetroot on each pancake and fix with a cocktail stick.

Cold Rice with Rhubarb Jelly (for 4)

> 2 teacupfuls rice
> 5 teacupfuls milk
> Pinch of salt
> 6 oz. sugar
> ¼ vanilla pod
> 1½ lb. red rhubarb
> ½ pint water
> ½ lb. sugar
> Cinnamon
> 1 oz. gelatine
> 1 orange
>
> For decoration
> 1 tablespoonful straw-
>   berry or raspberry
>   jam
> Whipped cream

Cook the rice in the milk with the sugar and vanilla pod. Remove the vanilla pod and press half the rice into a mould, rinsed out with cold water. Leave until quite cold. Cut the orange in half and carefully scoop out the fruit, taking care not to cut the skin. Cook the rhubarb with sugar and

A party sweet, Cold Rice with Rhubarb Jelly set in orange skins and decorated with whipped cream

cinnamon until tender, then pass through a sieve, dissolve the gelatine in the hot liquid, fill the orange skins, and leave to set. When the remaining jelly is nearly set, put it on top of the rice in the mould and leave to set. Press the remainder of the rice firmly down on top of the jelly and turn on to a plate. Cut the jelly-filled orange into thin slices, cut each slice in half and place round the foot of the mould. Mix the jam with the cream and pipe a decoration on the top.

Kirschenblotzer (Cherry soufflé)

3 oz. butter	2 oz. sugar
4 eggs	6 oz. flour
Black cherries and	Cream
sugar	

Stone the cherries, sprinkle well with sugar and leave to stand. Cream the butter, add sugar and egg-yolks and then the flour, gradually, and some fresh cream. When well mixed, add stiffly-beaten egg-whites. (The mixture must not be too hard.) Prepare a soufflé dish and fill with alternate layers of mixture and cherries, beginning and ending with the mixture. Cook in a moderate oven for about 1 hour.

NOTE: If desired, 2 stiffly-beaten, sweetened, egg-whites can be put on top of the soufflé 15 minutes before serving.

Marmorkuchen (Marble cake)

14 oz. flour	1 teaspoonful baking
8 oz. sugar	powder
3 tablespoonfuls	4 eggs
cocoa or chocolate	Small cupful of warm
powder	milk
6 oz. butter	

Beat butter and sugar to a cream, add egg-yolks gradually, then flour and baking powder. Lastly, add the milk and the well-beaten egg-whites. Divide the mixture in half, and add to one half the cocoa or chocolate powder. Fill cake tin with alternate layers of plain and chocolate mixture and bake in a hot oven for 1 hour.

Chocolate Cream with Pears

¾ pint milk	1 oz. cornflour
2 tablespoonfuls	2 oz. sugar
cocoa or chocolate	1 egg
powder	Cream
Vanilla essence	Pears

Heat the milk, sugar and vanilla essence, and stir in cocoa or chocolate powder. When boiling, add cornflour (previously mixed to a paste with a little milk) and,

lastly, egg-yolk. Place in a dish to cool. Place pears on top (drained tinned ones will do if fresh are not available), decorate with glacé cherries and piped whipped cream.

Schnee Eier (Snow eggs)

½ pint milk	2 egg-whites
2 tablespoonfuls	Thick custard
sugar	

Beat the egg-whites with sugar until very stiff. Heat the milk in a shallow pan and, when boiling, put in the egg-whites, shaping with a tablespoon to look like eggs. Leave for a few minutes, turn once, then take out and place round the custard in a shallow bowl.

Apple Soufflé

1 lb. cooking apples	2 eggs
4 oz. sugar	4 oz. flour

Peel and core the apples, cut into thin slices and place in a soufflé dish. Beat eggs and sugar together, add flour, and mix well. (If too stiff, use a little milk, or another egg.) Pour over apples and bake slowly in a moderate oven for about 1 hour.

Rote Grütze (Red sago mould)

1 lb. red-currants and	6 oz. sugar
raspberries (or red-	2 oz. sago
currants only)	

Place fruit in pan with sufficient water to stew. Cook very slowly to preserve flavour. Drain off the fruit juice, add sugar to it and bring to the boil. Stir in sago and cook until tender. Place in prepared mould, leave to cool, and serve with fresh cream or custard.

Sandkuchen (Sand cake)

6 eggs, and their weight in flour, sugar and butter

Beat eggs and sugar to a cream. Add flour gradually, then the butter. Bake in a moderate oven for about ¾ hour.

Creamed Potatoes

Steam the required amount of potatoes, then peel them and leave to cool. Cut into fairly thick slices. Make half a pint of white sauce, using 1 oz. margarine, 1 oz. flour, and add the potatoes to it. (More milk can be added if needed.) Chopped parsley should be added just before serving.

NOTE: This dish is generally eaten without a second vegetable; lettuce or beetroot make good additions—suitable for meat without gravy.

NORWAY

*In the land of the midnight sun, where the climate is
cold, they eat lots of fish caught around their coasts and
cook it in many interesting ways*

NORWEGIANS lead a very active life in a very cold climate. The Norwegian housewife therefore provides sustaining though plain meals, and since the sea lies all about her, she relies on fish as a staple item of diet, cooking and preparing it in many different ways, preserving, smoking and pickling the fish harvest in even greater variety than her Danish and Swedish neighbours.

Norwegians like their fish to be really fresh, so the housewife buys it alive from tanks in the fishmarket. She broils, bakes or fries it by itself, mixes it with vegetables and also makes fish soups and puddings. Cauliflower with shrimps, garnished with a cream sauce, is a delicious and favourite dish.

Smoked meat is popular, smoked mutton and reindeer in particular, and smoked reindeer tongues are a great luxury. Meat is usually served in "made up" dishes, and very often in aspic.

In the autumn there is plentiful game, and roast ptarmigan is a national delicacy. Poultry, too, is popular and chicken (*kylling*) is often served roast with a cream sauce. Duck stuffed with prunes is another Norwegian speciality.

Although Norway has to import fruit and green vegetables to balance her diet, the housewife has plentiful supplies of potatoes, root vegetables and many berries. She uses quantities of potatoes at each meal, and serves her vegetables with a cream sauce. Salads she dresses with sour cream and garnishes with chopped dill or parsley.

Like most Scandinavian housewives, she uses dairy produce and grain for nourishing and filling dishes. Oats, barley and rye are baked into thin bread wafers called "Flatbröd," while milk soup with barley groats is the prelude to many a country family's main meal.

Fruit soups are popular for dessert as well as the usual Scandinavian berry puddings and pies. Often the meal ends without a sweet dish, and then sometimes there will be waffles served with the coffee or a delicious nut coffee layer cake.

Fish Soup (for 4)

1 *tablespoonful butter*	*Chopped chives and salt*
1½ *pints fish stock*	2 *tablespoonfuls wheat flour*
½ *pint milk*	½ *gill sour cream*
1 *egg*	

To make the stock

Skin and bones of fish	1 *large teaspoonful salt to each quart of water*
Water	

Put the skin and bones into a saucepan with enough cold salted water to cover them. Cook very slowly, with the lid on, for ½ hour and skim carefully. Take out bones and strain the stock.

Lapskaus, or Norwegian Stew, is made from a mixture of beef and pork, served with a crisp salad or mashed turnips

To make the soup.—Put butter and flour in a pan and stir until well mixed. Add stock, then milk, a little at a time, stirring continually, and bring to the boil after each addition of liquid. Boil for 5–10 minutes and salt to taste. Beat the egg and cream in the tureen and pour on the soup, stirring steadily. Add chives. This is often garnished with small fishballs.

Exquisite Fishballs (Fiskeballer) (for 4)

1 lb. fresh haddock
1 dessertspoonful potato flour
½ gill cream
2 teaspoonfuls salt
¼ teaspoonful mace
¾ pint milk

Scrape the fish and rinse several times in cold water. (Always scrape from tail to head.) Dry well and fillet. Skin and take away membrane and bones, rub with salt until fillets are leathery. Stir well for about 10 minutes in a basin with potato flour and mace. Mix in the cream and milk, cold, one tablespoonful at a time, doubling the quantity when half the cream and milk has been used, and stirring all the time. This paste can be used for:

Fishballs.—Form into small balls, using a spoon dipped into cold water, put into boiling fish stock and cook gently for about 5–10 minutes.

Pudding and timbales.—Put the paste into a tin, or into timbale moulds, greased with melted butter. Stand the tin in a larger pan half-filled with boiling water and cook in a moderate oven. Cook timbales for 20 minutes, pudding ¾–1 hour. The water must not boil hard enough for the pudding to rise too high. Serve with shrimp sauce (see Sauces chapter).

Herring Salad (Sildesalat) (for 4—6)

10 salt herrings
¾ lb. boiled potatoes
½ lb. pickled beetroot
6 oz. apples
A thin slice of onion
2 oz. pickled gherkin
4 tablespoonfuls vinegar
2 tablespoonfuls water
1 oz. sugar
½ pint cream (whipped)
1 sliced hard-boiled egg
Pepper to taste
Parsley

Clean the fish, removing the heads, and soak overnight in cold water. Drain, skin and fillet, then dice the fillets, potatoes, beetroot, apple, onion and gherkin and mix thoroughly. Blend vinegar, sugar and water well, season with pepper and add, stirring gently. Add the whipped cream.

Rinse a mould in cold water, put the mixture in and chill in the refrigerator. Turn out of the mould to serve, garnish with the egg and chopped parsley. To be really Norwegian, this dish should be eaten with sour cream.

Salad Dressing (Römmesalat)

¾ pint sour cream
¼ oz. sugar
2 teaspoonfuls vinegar

Mix the ingredients together, adding the vinegar by drops. When smooth, use for dressing on lettuce.

Duck with Prune Stuffing (for 4–6)

1 duck (3–5 lb.)
White pepper
2 teaspoonfuls salt

For the stuffing

5 peeled and sliced apples
10–15 prunes

For the sauce

3 tablespoonfuls flour
1 gill cream
Blackcurrant juice if liked
3½ gills gravy

Prepare and season the duck as usual. Stuff with the fruits, sew up, and roast in oven for 1¾–2½ hours.

Skim the fat from the gravy, add a little water and stir in flour to thicken. Add the cream and, if liked, a little blackcurrant juice. Serve with fried potatoes and more cooked prunes and apples.

Norwegian Stew (Lapskaus) (for 4–5)

¾ lb. diced raw beef
½ lb. diced fresh pork
½ teaspoonful pepper
2 lb. raw potatoes
1 onion
Salt

Cover raw beef and fresh pork with water and boil slowly for ½ hour. Peel and cut the potatoes in pieces, add to the meat, together with sliced onion and pepper. Simmer for another ½ hour, or until tender. Add salt if desired. Serve with a crisp salad, boiled carrots or mashed turnips.

Ptarmigan with Brown Sauce (for 4)

2 ptarmigan
2 tablespoonfuls butter
2 oz. lard
1 gill water
¾ pint milk
1 teaspoonful salt

For the sauce

1 tablespoonful butter
3½ gills gravy
2 tablespoonfuls flour
1 gill sour cream

Clean the birds well in water, dry carefully. Cut lard into thin strips, slit the breast skin and put lard on both sides of the

A delicious cold buffet dish—
finely sliced salami surrounds a
cauliflower, cooked whole and
garnished with hard-boiled egg,
gherkin and beetroot

breastbones, then put
skin back in place. Tie
wings and legs to-
gether. Melt the but-
ter in a warm pan until
golden, put birds and
the entrails into pan
together with boiling
milk and water and a
little salt. Cook the
birds gently in the
oven until tender (1½–
2 hours), basting them
frequently. K e e p
warm, and use the
gravy from the pan for the sauce.

Brown Sauce.—Stir butter and flour in
warm pan until light brown. Pour in
gravy, little by little. Stir well and bring
to the boil. Add cream and boil for 5–10
minutes. Salt to taste. Chop entrails and
hearts up small and put into the sauce.

Loganberries with Rice (Tyttebaer med ris)

1 lb. cold boiled rice	¼ pint whipped cream
1 quart loganberries	1½ oz. sugar (omit if
(or 8 oz. jam)	jam is used)

Place a layer of rice in a round baking-
dish, then a thin layer of jam or loganberries and a little sugar, and so on alternately, ending with a top layer of berries.
Whip the cream with sugar and spread on
top. Chill and serve.

NOTE: This recipe is equally suitable
for raspberries.

Waffles (V*ffler)

4 eggs	½ lb. flour
2 oz. sugar	1 pint sour cream

Beat the eggs, sugar, flour and cream together until light. Cook in waffle irons in
the usual way. Often eaten with coffee for
breakfast.

Norwegian Dessert-cake (Dessertkake)

Weigh 3 boiled potatoes and take the
same weight in butter and flour. Rub butter well into the flour and mash the pota-

toes. Mix together, then put into the
refrigerator for ½ hour or until thoroughly
chilled. Roll out very thinly, cut into
circles, using a saucer or small plate, and
bake in a slow oven until light brown.
Sandwich with jam, preferably rhubarb,
and top with whipped cream.

The Prince's Cake (Fyrstekake)

3½ oz. butter	7 oz. flour
1 egg-yolk	2–3 tablespoonfuls
3½ oz. sugar	water
1½ teaspoonfuls baking powder	

For the filling

5½ oz. almonds	5½ oz. icing sugar
½ teaspoonful vanilla	½ teaspoonful carda-
essence	mom
½ oz. baking powder	3 egg-whites

Grease a round tin with butter. Cream
sugar and butter until white, add egg-yolk
and water. Sift in flour and baking powder, and mix well. Leave in a cold place.
Scald, blanch and dry almonds, and mix
with the icing sugar, spice and baking
powder. Beat egg-whites until stiff and add,
with essence, to almond mixture.
Roll out the cake dough and put two-
thirds into the tin, making it about ½ in.
higher at the edge. Spread the filling all
over it, then cut the remaining dough into
½-in. strips and put them on in check pattern. Brush strips with beaten egg and
bake in a moderate oven until it rises
nicely, is golden brown and the filling a
little leathery.

SWEDEN

*A land of modern design
and up-to-date equipment
where the favourite dishes
are traditional*

BOTH Swedish kitchens and Swedish cooking have changed considerably since the Second World War. Modern domestic equipment and time-saving methods, largely of American origin, have brought the Swedish housewife much precious leisure time. Deep frozen foods, such as meat, fish and vegetables, are available in almost every country shop all over Sweden. But in spite of modern methods, traditional and local customs are still observed in most Swedish homes.

Most famous dish of all—known, indeed, all over the world—is the Swedish Smörgåsbord, a rich variety of hot and cold dishes, sometimes amounting to thirty different kinds. This Smörgåsbord is set out on a special table and everybody is invited to serve themselves as often as they like—or can! This is a practical expedient, since no plate is large enough for more than samples at one time of bread, butter, cheeses, different kinds of ham and sauces, omelets, meatballs, crabfish, salads and, most important, the herring dishes, the fish being served in various ways—in vinegar, with leeks and spices, salted, smoked, fried, and in marinade.

Fish does, in fact, play an important part in the Swedish diet, and the herring is a basic food. Although it can always be bought fresh, the Swedes are extremely fond of eating fish pickled and smoked. Dried cod, called "lutfisk," is served traditionally at Christmas. Its flavour is unusual, perhaps, to the outsider, since it has been soaked for over three weeks in a mixture of wood-ash, lime and soda.

Shellfish is also popular and is excellent in Sweden. From August 8th, when the crayfish season is in full swing, crayfish suppers are a great attraction all over the country, and special table linen, decorated with crayfish designs, is used. It is an old custom to drink a glass of schnapps with every claw—and you are expected to eat at least ten crayfish.

The climate doubtless makes the Swedes great meat-consumers. The meat is nowadays extremely good, and for Sunday dinner you will often find either a so-called "Slottsstek" (Steak of the Castle) or a steak of veal. But for everyday, joints are cooked and served with various sauces and spices (dill mutton and collops, for example).

Salads have become more and more popular now that vegetables are available throughout the year, even in the far north. Consequently, potatoes are no longer the mainstay of the household as in the old days. Vegetables are often served as a stew, a relic of the time when they were scarce and so had to be made into a substantial main dish.

Milk and cheese (also Filbunke, or sour milk) are nearly always on the table, but there are also soups made from vegetables, fruit and milk. Many of the sweet dishes are made of fruit and berries. Puddings, pancakes and lots of sweet cakes are also served, usually with jam. A typical Swedish jam is made from "lingon," a Nordic kind of cranberry.

Swedish housewives like to bake at home, chiefly white sweet bread and the famous "Seven Assorted Cakes" for their coffee. Another type of everyday·bread is the famous "knäckebröd," once baked at home in bulk and strung on a pole near the ceiling. Very good for the teeth and the

Ideal both for cooking and serving Swedish dishes, colourful Rorstrand ovenware is obtainable in the U.K.

digestion, highly recommended for children and served at school breakfasts, this bread has become an important Swedish export. It is found all over the world as "Rye-King."

No chapter on Swedish cooking would be complete without a mention of the Swedish Pea Soup, the "Arter med fläsk," which is served every Thursday in almost every Swedish home, including the Royal Palace. The soup is accompanied by a glass of hot Swedish punch and always followed by pancakes. Similarly, Fettisdagsbullar is the dessert served on Shrove Tuesday. It is rather like cream buns filled with whipped cream and marzipan, and eaten in a soup-plate with hot milk flavoured with cinnamon.

Christmas is, of course, the time for traditional dishes in Sweden as elsewhere. The main meal is usually served in the kitchen, already decorated, at midday on Christmas Eve. This consists of Smörgåsbord, with special extra dishes. To start with, there is the "Doppigrytan," a simple,

symbolic ceremony in which various types of bread, such as Limpa (sour) and Vörtbörd (sweet), are dipped into the decorated copper pot full of stock in which the traditional ham and pork sausages have been boiled. At this meal everyone serves himself. Dishes typical of Sweden as a whole include ham, up to five different kinds of sausages, meatballs, brown beans, red cabbage, salads. A pig's head is smoked and decorated, a memory of pagan times. Later in the day there is a Christmas coffee

Informal buffet supper in Swedish style, laid with Rorstrand earthenware and ovenware

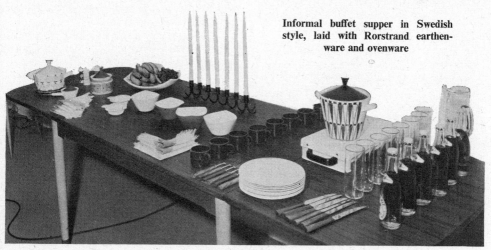

table with cakes and biscuits of different kinds, such as Peppercakes and bread shaped into figures.

Later on in the afternoon there is a sit-down meal with Lutfisk, Christmas porridge (Risgrynsgröt), and then many families start all over again with Christmas Smörgåsbord!

SMÖRGÅSBORD

Anyone wishing to cook in the Swedish way will, of course, start with Smörgåsbord, a few suggestions for which are:

1. Cut hard-boiled eggs in half and arrange strips of anchovy fillets across them.
2. Slice cold roast beef wafer thin. Decorate each slice with a whirl of mayonnaise or horseradish cream, or, alternatively, roll a slice of cooked ham round a stick of asparagus.
3. Cut very thin slices from the cold joint. Garnish with sliced gherkins or cucumber. If you are using veal, make the gravy into a jelly and use to garnish, decorating with parsley.
4. Cover halves of hard-boiled eggs with mayonnaise. Surround with cooked shrimps and garnish with parsley.
5. Arrange three or four different kinds of cheese, each in a small glass dish, garnished with radishes, parsley or chopped chives.
6, On a bed of lettuce arrange sliced tomatoes, cold rice flavoured with chopped pimento and slices of hard-boiled egg. Garnish with olive.

No Smörgåsbord would be complete without these two special herring dishes:

The Glazier's Herring (Glasmästarsill)

2 lb. salted herrings	2 teaspoonfuls whole
2½ coffee cupfuls	Jamaica pepper
sugar	1 pint vinegar
½ carrot	dressing (made of ⅓
A piece of gherkin	vinegar and ⅔ water)
(salted if available,	4 leeks (red)
otherwise pickled)	½ horseradish

Skin the herrings without removing the bone and soak them in water overnight. Mix the dressing with the sugar, and warm, then chill it. Dry the herrings on paper, cut them in pieces straight across the big bone, and put in a pot with pounded pepper and the vegetables cut in thin slices between the layers. Cover with the dressing and leave for at least 3 hours (it can be left for a week).

Another delicious hot fish dish on the Smörgåsbord is:

Mr. Janson's Temptation (Janson's frestelse)

5–6 raw potatoes	2 leeks
2–2½ gills cream	6–8 anchovies
1 tablespoonful	Breadcrumbs
margarine or butter	

Cut the potatoes in fine strips, the leeks into thin slices and fillet the anchovies. Into a buttered fireproof dish, put layers of potatoes, then anchovy, then leek and so on, ending with potatoes. Pour on the cream and, if possible, some of the juice from the anchovies. Dot with pieces of margarine and sprinkle breadcrumbs on top. Cook in a moderate oven until the potatoes are tender (about 45 minutes). Instead of anchovy you can use 4–6 smoked herrings.

OTHER DISHES

Swedish Pea Soup (Arter med fläsk) (for 4)

½ lb. split peas	Salt to taste
1½ quarts water	1 lb. pork (fresh or
1 leek or onion (or	slightly salted)
ginger if preferred)	Sweet marjoram

Wash the peas and soak them overnight in salted water. Cook them in the same water, together with marjoram and onion, bringing them quickly to the boil and skimming off the shells as they float to the top. When all shells have been removed, add the pork and season. Cover the pan and simmer gently until both pork and peas are tender. Remove the pork, slice it and place on a dish. Pour the soup into individual bowls and serve with the sliced pork and mustard. The pork can also be cut in cubes and served in the soup.

Nettle Soup (for 4)

3 pints very young	Poached or hard-
nettles	boiled eggs
A few sprigs of chive,	2 oz. butter
chervil or fennel	3½ pints rich stock
seed	3½ oz. flour
Pepper and salt	

Clean and rinse the nettles well. Plunge them into boiling salted water and simmer for 15 minutes. Drain, rinse in cold water and drain again. Chop finely together with the chives, chervil or fennel seed. Sprinkle

For gracious dining, a Rorstrand porcelain dinner service, "Ice Crystal," patterned in misty blue-grey on white, with salt and pepper pots in cobalt blue

with flour. Heat in melted butter, add stock gradually, stirring all the time. Simmer with lid on for ¼ hour. Skim well and season. Serve with hard-boiled eggs cut into sections, or poached eggs.

NOTE: The nettles are picked in the spring. They can be dried in the open air and stored in paper bags so that it is possible to have nettle soup all the year round. Alternatively, spinach may be used instead of nettles.

Mashed Turnips (Rotmos) (for 4)

1 lb. turnips	½ gill cream or 2 oz.
1 lb. potatoes	butter
1 pint stock (prefer-	1 rounded teaspoonful
ably made from	sugar
shank pork)	Salt and pepper

Wash, peel and cube turnips and potatoes. Cook turnips in stock for ½ hour, add potatoes and cook until soft (about 20 minutes). Drain and mash, adding cream or butter and seasoning. Beat until quite smooth. Serve with the pork shank, or salt beef, or sausages.

Swedish Hash (Pytt i panna) (for 4)

1 lb. left-over cold	2 medium-sized
meat	onions
1 lb. cold boiled	2 oz. butter
potatoes	Salt and pepper
4 fried eggs	Chopped parsley

Dice the meat and potatoes and chop the onions. Using half the butter, fry the onions until golden brown. In the remaining butter, fry first the potatoes and then the meat until both are nicely browned. Mix with the onions and add the seasoning. Arrange on a hot dish and garnish with chopped parsley. Serve with fried eggs, similarly garnished, placed on top of the hash.

Meatballs (Köttbullar) (for 4)

1 lb. finely minced	2 medium-sized
meat (¾ lb. beef	onions
and ¼ lb. pork)	1½ oz. butter
1 oz. breadcrumbs	Salt and pepper to
½ pint milk	taste
1 egg	A little cream
½ oz. flour	

Soak the breadcrumbs in milk. Add the meat, the grated onion, raw egg, salt and pepper, and mix thoroughly. Shape balls in the left hand with a spoon and fry them in butter. Keep hot. Whip up the butter with a little water and make into a gravy with the flour. Season the gravy to taste and, if too thick, add a little cream. Serve with boiled potatoes and sliced gherkin and cranberry jam. (Instead of potatoes, cooked marcaroni can be served.)

Stuffed Herrings (Sill i krappock) (for 4)

4 *large fresh herrings*　6 *oz. each chopped*
2 *oz butter.*　　　　　*parsley, chives and*
2 *teaspoonfuls salt*　*onions*
1 *tablespoonful lemon*　*Waxed paper*
　juice

Slit the underside of each fish, remove bones and intestines, and wash well under running cold water. Dry, and sprinkle with salt. Stuff with a mixture of parsley, chives, onion and lemon juice. Put each fish in buttered waxed paper, each piece large enough to form an envelope for one fish. Cook on a baking sheet in a moderately hot oven for 10—15 minutes. Serve, still in their paper envelopes, with boiled potatoes.

NOTE: Trout may also be cooked in this way.

Baked Eel (Ungstekt äl) (for 4)

1 *fat eel (about 2 lb.*　1 *egg*
　weight)　　　　　3 *oz. breadcrumbs*
2 *oz. butter*　　　*Juice of ½ lemon*
　　　Salt and pepper

Loosen the skin round the eel's neck with a sharp knife and draw off with a piece of cloth held in the hand. Remove the head and backbone, split open and clean thoroughly, taking care not to pierce the flesh. Dry, then rub with salt and lemon juice, and brush with beaten egg and sprinkle with seasoned breadcrumbs. Place in a well-buttered baking dish or fireproof oven dish and dot with remaining butter. Bake in a hot oven, basting frequently and adding a little hot water if needed, for about 40 minutes. Serve hot, with boiled potatoes, or cold, with salad.

Swedish Brown Beans with Pork (for 4)

12 *oz. brown beans*　　1 *tablespoonful*
2½ *pints water*　　　　*Golden Syrup*
2 *saltspoonfuls vinegar*　*Pinch of salt*

Rinse the beans, put into cold water, bring to the boil and simmer until tender (about 3 hours), adding hot water occasionally if necessary. When cooked, add syrup, vinegar and a pinch of salt. Serve with fried bacon or pork.

Swedish Christmas Porridge (Julgröt) (for 4)

1 *teacupful Carolina*　3½ *oz. butter*
　rice　　　　　　　½ *pint cream*
1¾ *pints water*　　　1 *teaspoonful salt*
　　　1 *tablespoonful sugar*

Rinse the rice, cook in boiling water until soft and strain. Add the butter and the cream whipped stiffly. Reheat the porridge, but do not let it boil. Add salt and sugar, and serve with cold milk.

NOTE: An almond is always hidden in the porridge. The person who finds it will be the first to get married!

Steak of the Castle (Slottsstek—a typical Swedish Sunday dish)

2 *lb. rump steak*　　2 *teaspoonfuls salt*
2 *oz. butter*　　　　8 *grains of Jamaica*
1 *bay leaf*　　　　　*pepper*
1 *red leek*　　　　8 *grains of white*
3 *anchovies*　　　　*pepper*
2 *tablespoonfuls*　　1 *tablespoonful*
　cream　　　　　*vinegar*
Water　　　　　　½ *tablespoonful syrup*
　　　2 *tablespoonfuls flour*

Roast the meat in a braising pan until it is brown on the outside, add all the other ingredients and cook in the oven until done (about 2 hours).

Berry Cream (for 4)

1 *quart mixed berries*　1 *pint water*
1 *oz. potato flour*　　5 *oz. sugar*

Wash the berries. Bring the water to the boil, add the berries and the sugar, and boil for several minutes. Mix the potato flour with a little cold water, stir in with the fruit and bring the mixture to the boil. Serve cold, with cream or milk.

Sour Milk (Filbunke) (for 4)

2 *tablespoonfuls sour*　*Sugar, cinnamon and*
　cream　　　　　　*ginger to taste*
　　　1 *pint fresh milk*

Spread the sour cream in the bottom of a bowl and add the milk. Cover the bowl and leave in a warm place until the milk becomes thick as custard. Then chill and serve with sugar, ginger and cinnamon.

Swedish Peppercakes (225 cakes)

3½ *oz. white sugar*　　5½ *oz. butter*
3½ *oz. Demerara*　　3 *teaspoonfuls cinna-*
　sugar　　　　　　*mon*
½ *teaspoonful cloves*　½ *teaspoonful*
1 *gill thick cream*　　*cardamon*
Bicarbonate of soda　1 *lb. 3 oz. flour*
7½ *oz. syrup*

Beat together the two sugars, the syrup, butter and the powdered spices for about 15 minutes. Whip the cream and add. Finally, add the flour mixed with the bicarbonate of soda, keeping back a little of the flour for rolling. Knead the dough well and leave for 24 hours (well covered), then knead again. Roll it out thin and cut with fancy cutters. Bake in a hot oven for 8-10 minutes.

A typical dish of Smørrebrød, fish, meat, eggs and vegetables all appetisingly arranged on slices of thickly buttered rye bread

COOKERY AT HOME AND ABROAD

DENMARK

The home of Smørrebrød—open sandwiches in infinite variety—is full of good ideas for home entertaining

THE Danes do enjoy food, have immense appetites and take their meals seriously. The Danish housewife is extremely house-proud, most particularly of her kitchen, and can draw on plentiful supplies of homegrown dairy produce, meat and fresh fish.

"Smørrebrød," the traditional open sandwich, is perhaps the best known of all Danish dishes, and forms the midday meal for children and the majority of workers. Generally, these tasty snacks, each almost a meal in itself, are made on a foundation of rye bread, the butter smeared on thickly and the filling so generous that it hangs over the edges. With the midday "smørrebrød" the children drink milk. Grown-ups usually prefer Danish beer.

The evening meal is taken at six o'clock, sometimes earlier, as soon as all the family have arrived home. The first course is often

a fruit soup, a typical Danish speciality, or one of the sustaining beer-flavoured gruels that taste a great deal more pleasant than they sound. The main course is usually a meat dish.

The Danes love entertaining in their homes, and no housewife feels that time spent on preparation and decoration is wasted. As a result, the food is beautifully served and appetisingly garnished, the tables laid with fine china and silverware and massed with flowers and candles.

As in most countries, entertaining reaches its peak at Christmas. At six o'clock comes the traditional Christmas Eve dinner, which begins with a sweet rice pudding, continues with roast goose stuffed with prunes and apples, served with stewed red cabbage and caramel potatoes, and finishes with a sweet red-berry pudding. After that, one is served with coffee and

Christmas biscuits, home-baked and in infinite variety, not to mention cherry brandy, a favourite drink with the Danes, which invariably follows.

Beer and Bread Soup (Øllebrød) (for 4)

10 *oz. rye bread*	1 *stick cinnamon*
1 *gill water*	(¾ *in. long by* ½ *in.*
2 *pint bottles pale ale*	*thick, approx.*)
Lemon peel	2½ *oz. sugar*

Cut bread into small dice and soak for 12 hours in water and one bottle of ale. Then simmer for 20 minutes, rub through a sieve and cook the purée with the cinnamon over slow heat, thinning gradually with the second bottle of ale. Add the lemon peel and sugar and serve in soup plates with whipped cream.

NOTE: This dish is served in Denmark as a porridge in the morning, as a soup to start a meal, as a sweet or supper dish.

Giblet Soup (Kraasesuppe) (for 4)

1–2 *sets of giblets*	3 *small apples*
3 *carrots*	2 *or* 3 *prunes*
2 *small sticks of*	½ *oz. sugar*
celery	1 *tablespoonful*
1 *leek*	*vinegar*
	Salt to taste

Soak the prunes overnight. Slice the carrots and apples into small pieces. Wash the giblets thoroughly, cover with cold salted water and bring gradually to the boil. Skim, and simmer for 30 minutes. Add the vegetables and fruit, and simmer until quite tender. Add sugar and vinegar, and serve hot with Flour Dumplings. Alternatively, thicken the soup with 3 tablespoonfuls cream and an egg-yolk.

Flour Dumplings (for 4)

2 *oz. butter*	2 *eggs*
2 *oz. flour*	*Pinch of salt and*
¼ *pint boiling water*	*cardamom*

Melt butter and stir flour into it. When well mixed, add boiling water and stir until the mixture comes away from the sides of the pan. Leave to cool. Add egg-yolks, salt and cardamom, and finally the egg-whites, beaten stiff. Form into small balls, drop into boiling salted water or soup and cook for 5–10 minutes. Lift out the dumplings, using a perforated ladle. Serve with meat or fruit soups.

Copenhagen Codfish

The Danes have an unsurpassed reputation for fish cookery, and in Copenhagen restaurants it is usual to offer four or five different sauces with each dish. Copenhagen Codfish can be served with one of the four milky sauces suggested below.

½ *lb. raw cod fillet*	1 *rounded tea-*
(skin removed)	*spoonful chopped*
1 *oz. breadcrumbs*	*parsley*
2 *oz. suet*	1–2 *tablespoonfuls*
1 *egg*	*lemon juice*
¾ *gill milk*	*(strained)*
Pepper and salt	*Parsley for decora-*
Flour	*tion*

Shred cod finely; chop suet with about 1 teaspoonful of flour (this makes chopping easier). Mix all ingredients well together to a dropping consistency. Season well.

Turn mixture into a greased pudding bowl, cover with pudding cloth or greaseproof paper, and steam gently for ¾ to 1 hour. Turn out and coat with either Dutch Cream, Anchovy, Egg or Shrimp Sauce.

Dutch Cream Sauce: Cook ¼ pint of white sauce slightly, add one raw egg-yolk and stir over a moderate heat till the yolk thickens. Do not boil. Add a few drops of lemon juice and vinegar to give a sharp flavour.

For Anchovy, Egg and Shrimp Sauces, see Sauces chapter.

Minced Fish (Fiskefars) (for 4)

2½ *lb. cod (middle*	¼ *pint cream*
cut) to give about	1 *oz. potato flour*
1½ *lb. fish when*	1 *oz. butter*
skin and bones are	*Salt and pepper to*
removed	*taste*
Breadcrumbs	1 *egg-white*

Remove skin and bones from the fish, and mince finely three or four times at least. Add flour, and mix with the egg-white and cream. Season, and put in a tin buttered and spread with breadcrumbs. Stand this tin inside another one containing boiling water and cook in a moderate oven for ¾ hour, or until it is a nice golden brown.

Egg and Bacon Cake (Aeggekage) (for 4)

8 *rashers streaky*	1 *oz. flour*
Danish bacon	1 *oz. butter*
4 *eggs*	*Salt and pepper to*
¼ *pint milk*	*taste*
	Chopped parsley or chives

Fry or grill the bacon rashers and keep hot. Beat the eggs, flour and milk together, seasoning with salt and pepper. Melt butter in a heated omelet pan, pour in the mixture and cook quickly until nearly set, shaking the pan from time to time. Turn on to a hot dish, place the cooked bacon on top and garnish with chopped parsley or chives.

Cucumber Salad (easily digested)

Cut cucumber into paper thin slices, put into a shallow bowl or soup plate with plenty of salt, cover with a plate and put a really heavy object (such as an iron) on top. This helps to squeeze the juice out of the cucumber. Leave for an hour, then put cucumber into a clean cloth and squeeze hard to get out the rest of the water. Serve in a glass bowl in ¾ cupful vinegar with ¼ cupful water and a tablespoonful of salt. Sprinkle with black pepper.

Herring Salad (Siddesalat) (for 4)

2 soused herrings	2 tablespoonfuls
3 large cooked pota-	olive oil
toes	2 tablespoonfuls
1 cooked beetroot	vinegar
1 pickled cucumber	Salt and pepper to
2 dessert apples	taste
2 hard-boiled eggs	Chopped parsley

Flake the fish, or cut them into small pieces. Dice the potatoes, beetroot and cucumber. Core apples, but do not peel them. Cut them into pieces. Blend the oil and vinegar together in a large bowl, add the other ingredients and the seasoning. Mix thoroughly. Serve in a glass dish or wooden salad bowl, garnished with sliced hard-boiled eggs and chopped parsley.

Caramel Potatoes
(Brunede kartofler) (for 4)

> 1½ lb. potatoes
> 2 oz. sugar
> 2 oz. butter

Wash, boil and peel the potatoes. Cut them into pieces. Melt the sugar in a pan, add the butter and heat until light brown. Rinse the potatoes in cold water, then dip them in the caramel mixture, thoroughly coating each piece. Serve hot.

Fruit Jelly (Rødgrod med fløde)

1 lb. berries (equal	1 pint water
parts strawberries,	4½ oz. sugar
currants and black-	1½–2 oz. potato flour
berries, or red-	to every quart of
currants, rasp-	juice
berries and cherries	
are good mixtures)	

Wash the berries and remove stalks. Cook them in the water until they are soft. Press through a fine sieve. Measure the juice before you put it back into the saucepan and add the sugar. Mix as much flour as you need with cold juice and stir thoroughly in the saucepan. Cook until thickened. Pour it into a glass bowl and sprinkle with sugar to prevent the formation of skin. Serve hot or cold with cream, garnishing with chopped almonds.

Peasant Girl with Veil (Bondepige med slor) (for 4)

8 oz. rye-bread-	2 oz. butter
crumbs	1½ lb. cooking apples
3 oz. brown sugar	2 oz. grated chocolate
Lemon juice and	¼ pint double cream
sugar to taste	(whipped)

Mix the crumbs and sugar together and fry in the butter until crisp. Peel, core and cut up the apples, and cook them until soft in a very little water with a good squeeze of lemon juice and sugar to taste. Into a glass dish put alternate layers of the fried crumb

Cheese is eaten at breakfast-time in Denmark with rolls or rye bread and milk or coffee

mixture and apple pulp, finishing with a layer of crumbs. When the pudding is quite cold, spread the whipped cream on top and sprinkle with grated chocolate.

SMØRREBRØD

These open sandwiches provide infinite scope for the housewife's originality in devising mixtures that both look and taste delicious. They also enable left-overs to be used up. Here are a few popular varieties:

Sunrise at Bornholm (Solopgang paa Bornholm)

In the middle a raw egg-yolk, with pieces of smoked herring (previously boned) in a circle round it, then another circle of chopped beetroot (cooked and in marinade) and another of chopped leek. Finally, sprinkle the sandwich with capers.

Shrimps in the Crush (Reier i traengsel)

Pile a lot of shrimps high on the bread and sprinkle over them a little Jamaica pepper mixed with white pepper.

The Vet's Nightsnack (Dyrlaegens natmad)

On the buttered bread put a thick slice of foie gras with a slice of salt beef on top.

Hans Christian Andersen's Sandwich

On a thickly buttered slice of bread put a rasher of crisp grilled bacon, then a thick slice of raw tomato and one of liver sausage with a pat of horseradish cream and/or a little meat jelly.

Fillets of Plaice with Remoulade

Fillets of plaice, rolled in egg and breadcrumbs, are fried in butter and served hot on slices of rye or white bread with a remoulade sauce garnish. (Remoulade is a mayonnaise flavoured with chopped parsley, fennel and tarragon leaves, shallots and made mustard. See Salads chapter for method.)

Cod Roe Salad

Boil the roe in salted water for about 30 minutes, depending on size. Leave in water to cool, then skin and pass through a sieve. Add lemon juice, a little curry powder and other spices according to taste. Spread on buttered bread and garnish with slices of lemon and cress.

Meat Salad

This is a good way of using up left-overs of cooked meat. Remove fat and cut meat into small squares and cover with mayonnaise to which are added some diced gherkins or cucumber. Pile on well-buttered bread.

Salami

On a thick slice of buttered bread put a slice of salami sausage, then a thick slice of tomato and a slice of hard-boiled egg, with an olive or a dab of tomato ketchup on top.

Another very popular sandwich is just a slice of salami on a slice of thickly buttered bread, but its name is poetic—"The Roskilde Turnpike."

DANISH CHRISTMAS BISCUITS

These small cakes are extensively served at Christmas-time in Denmark, and made in large quantities ready for the festive season's entertaining.

Brown Cakes (Brune Kager)

1 lb. black treacle	$\frac{1}{4}$ lb. butter
$\frac{1}{3}$ oz. ground cinnamon	$\frac{1}{2}$ lb. brown sugar
	$\frac{1}{6}$ oz. ground cloves
1 teaspoonful bicarbonate of soda	$\frac{1}{6}$ oz. ground ginger
	$1\frac{1}{2}$ lb. flour

A little grated orange peel

For decoration
Blanched almonds and candied peel

Heat together in a strong pan the treacle, sugar, butter, cloves, cinnamon, ginger and orange peel and, when hot, add the bicarbonate of soda. Remove from the stove and stir in the flour. Leave the dough for 3 or 4 days, then roll it out very thin, using a little flour if it sticks. Cut into oblong cakes, place on a greased baking sheet, decorate with almonds and candied peel, and bake in a brisk oven until brown and crisp.

Flead Cakes (Klejner)

3 eggs	$1\frac{1}{4}$ lb. flour
5 oz. sugar	$\frac{1}{4}$ lb. butter
$\frac{1}{2}$ pint cream	A little cardamom
A little grated lemon rind	Lard for frying

First, stir together the eggs, sugar, butter (just slightly warmed), cardamom and lemon rind, then work in the cream and flour. Roll the dough out very thin and cut into strips. Make an incision in the middle of each strip and draw one end

The Danes like elegant table-settings. Here the national colours have been cleverly used, red mats set-off by white china, napkins and candles

through. Heat the lard in a strong, deep pan until very hot, drop in the biscuits and cook to a nice brown colour, then spread them on brown paper to drain. Next day, place in a cake tin, where they will keep fresh for a long time.

Jewish Cakes (Jodekager)

1 lb. flour	½ teaspoonful salt of
10 oz. sugar	hartshorn
A little grated lemon	1 egg
rind	A small glass of
¼ lb. butter	Danish Akvavit

For decoration
Sugar, chopped almonds and pounded vanilla

Mix all the ingredients together and roll out the dough very thinly. Cut into small rounds with a biscuit cutter or wineglass, place close together on a baking sheet, brush over with beaten egg, then sprinkle with sugar, vanilla and almonds. Bake in a quick oven until light brown.

Peppernuts (Pebernodder)

4 eggs	1 teaspoonful salt of
2 teaspoonfuls grated	hartshorn
lemon peel	Small equal quantities
A little lemon juice	of cardamom and
1 lb. flour	ground ginger
10 oz. sugar	

Beat the eggs well and with them mix the sugar, cardamom, ginger, lemon peel and salt of hartshorn diluted in water and a little lemon juice. Work in the flour and form into thin sticks. Roll into balls and bake in a hot oven.

Vanilla Rings (Vaniljhekranse)

1 lb. flour	½ lb. sugar
¾ lb. butter	1 egg
1 vanilla pod	¼ lb. almonds

Blanch and peel the almonds and chop them up finely, then work all the ingredients together to a firm dough. Make into long thin rolls, cut off 4-in. lengths, form into rings. Bake in a hot oven until light brown.

BELGIUM

A country of nine provinces, each with its own customs, folklore and traditional dishes

described by FLEUR VAN ACKER

BELGIUM is divided into nine Provinces, partly Flemish, partly Walloon, and each with its own characteristics, customs, folklore and traditional dishes. On the coast is *West Flanders*, the capital of which is Bruges. Here, every year on the first Monday after May 3rd, the traditional Procession of the Holy Blood passes through the main streets. This ceremony dates back to the twelfth century when, after the Second Crusade, Derrick d'Alsace brought back a few drops of the holy blood from the Holy Land. The traditional dish served on this day is roast veal and spinach, while no visitor ever leaves Bruges without some of the famous "Nœuds de Bruges."

Spinach

1 *lb. spinach per*	1 *egg-yolk*
person	1 *oz. butter, dripping*
Pepper and salt	*or margarine*
Nutmeg	

Remove stalks from spinach, wash thoroughly and put into a colander to drain for a few minutes. Rinse out a saucepan with water, but do not dry it, and put in the spinach. Cover, and bring to the boil. When boiling, remove lid and boil until tender. Pour spinach into a colander and leave to drain for about 5 minutes, then rub through the colander and return to saucepan, adding fat and seasoning. Heat, stirring all the time, and immediately before serving stir in the egg-yolk.

Nœuds de Bruges

¼ *lb. flour*	¼ *lb. butter*
¼ *lb. dark brown*	*Salt*
sugar	½ *pint water*

Sieve the flour into a basin, add salt, sugar and mix well. Melt the butter in the water, leave to cool and, when just lukewarm, pour into the centre of the flour mixture. Mix lightly to a stiff consistency, then, on a floured pastry board, roll out to ½-in. thickness and leave for 1 hour.

Next, divide the dough into four pieces, and each piece into ten. Roll the pieces in brown sugar and shape either into figures of eight or little bows. Put them—½ in. apart—on a buttered baking tin, flatten out slightly and sprinkle with brown sugar. Leave overnight and cook in a very hot oven until the sugar has turned to caramel (about 20 minutes). Cool on a wire tray or on greaseproof paper.

All along the coast during the summer months, the Blessing of the Sea takes place, starting at Ostend on the first Sunday after June 29th (Saints Peter and Paul, Patron Saints) and ending at Zeebrugge at the end of August. Two dishes invariably eaten during this period are "Tomates aux Crevettes" and "Croquettes aux Crevettes." Both are delicious and frequently served at public dinners.

Tomatoes with Shrimps (Tomates aux Crevettes)

To serve as an hors d'œuvre, allow for each person:

2 *firm, medium-*	3 *oz. fresh shelled*
sized tomatoes	*shrimps*
1 *tablespoonful*	*Seasoning and lemon*
mayonnaise	*Chives or parsley*
Lettuce	*for decoration*

Wash the tomatoes and wipe them dry. Cut off the tops and scoop out the pulp with a teaspoon, taking care not to split the tomatoes. Sprinkle the insides with salt and pepper, then turn them upside down and leave. Add 1 tablespoonful of mayonnaise to the shrimps, mix well, and put into the tomato cases. Squeeze a few drops of lemon over the filling and replace the tomato tops. Decorate with chopped chives or sprigs of parsley and, if liked, serve on a bed of lettuce.

East Flanders.—The capital is Ghent, a town with many attractions for the tourist, including the famous Van Eyck paintings in the Cathedral of St. Bavon (Sint Baafs), medieval streets and buildings, among which is the Petit-Beguinage Notre Dame, founded in 1234, and museums. July 21st, when Ghent holds its Kermesse (Gentse Feeste), is also the Belgian National Day, and feasting continues for three days with music and dancing in the streets. The main attraction is on the Place d'Armes, or Kouter, where dancing goes on all night.

The dish served everywhere at this time is Waterzooi—chicken in hot broth.

Waterzooi (for 4)

Foundation (Broth)

2 lb. chicken giblets   A few chicken heads,
1 large knuckle of veal   necks and feet
1 large head of celery   (well-washed)
1 leek   A few carrots

1 saltspoonful pepper   1 slice of bread, 1 in.
4 pints cold water   thick
            2 doz. parsley roots

Chicken

1 fair-sized chicken or   4 oz. butter
2 spring chickens   1 pint stock or boiling
1 teaspoonful salt   water
      Chopped parsley

Put all the broth ingredients into a deep saucepan, bring to the boil and simmer until all are tender, then pass through a colander.

Melt the butter in a saucepan and, when very hot, put in the chicken, turn it so that it is lightly fried on all sides, but do not let it get brown. Add stock (or water) and salt, and boil gently until tender. When ready, add the foundation and serve. Chopped parsley can be added before serving and the chicken can be cut up if desired.

Fresh cream, bread and butter, and pieces of lemon should be handed round with this dish.

Tarte au Riz Liegeoise

This is the great speciality of the *Province of Liege* and is served with coffee between 3.30 and 5 p.m.

About 8 oz. short or
  flaky pastry
1½ pints milk
6 oz. sugar
1 tablespoonful cornflour
¼ lb. rice
Pinch of salt
Pinch of cinnamon
3 eggs

Roll out the pastry to ¼-in thickness and line a tart tin with it. Wash the rice well, drain it and bring to the boil in the milk with salt, stirring with a wooden spoon. When boiling, add cinnamon and sugar and cook for ½ hour or until tender (and the rice must be *really* tender). With a little milk mix the cornflour to a smooth paste, add the whisked eggyolks, pour into the rice

Photo: Robelus, by courtesy of the Belgian State Tourist Office

All along the coast in summer the Blessing of the Sea takes place, and the dish popularly eaten is Tomatoes with Shrimps

and continue stirring until it thickens, then remove from heat and add the whipped egg-whites. Pour evenly on to the pastry, brush over with beaten egg and sugar, and cook in a hot oven until golden brown (about $\frac{1}{2}$ hour). When cool, sprinkle icing sugar on top.

Gâteau de Verviers

This is a kind of bun-loaf.

> 2¼ lb. flour
> ¼ lb. butter or margarine
> 1 tablespoonful castor sugar
> 2 oz. yeast
> ½ lb. candy (or small pieces of lump) sugar
> 4 eggs
> 1 teaspoonful salt
> 1 pint water
> Pinch of cinnamon

These little brown biscuits in animal shapes and iced are called Speculaus, and belong to the Feast of St. Nicholas. Tea service is Royal Doulton's "Desert Showers" in green on a cream background

Make these ingredients into a smooth paste and leave for 1 hour, to rise, in a very warm place, adding the lumps of sugar when ready. Divide into two or four pieces and place on buttered baking sheets or tins. Bake in a warm oven, as for bread.

The Province of Hainault is famous for the Carnival de Binche, which is held on Shrove Tuesday (Mardi Gras). All the men of the town join in this, wearing a special costume which has humps and bells both front and back. They wear clogs and carry wicker baskets full of oranges which they throw or hand to the spectators. But most striking are their hats, made of curled ostrich feathers and more than 3 ft. high. The men also perform a dance, shaking the bells in rhythm to the strains of a brass band.

A special soup is served in all the restaurants and beer-houses during the Carnival Season:

Soupe à l'Onion (for 6)

> 4 pints stock
> 2 oz. butter, margarine or dripping
> 2 oz. Gruyère and Parmesan cheese mixed
> 2 lb. onions
> 1 lb. potatoes
> 1 bay leaf
> Seasoning
> Fried bread

Cut ¾ lb. onions into thin slices and cook in the butter, margarine or dripping, until very pale golden brown, then add 1 pint of stock and bring to the boil slowly. Simmer until tender, taking care that they do not break up too much. In another saucepan, boil the potatoes and the rest of the onions with the bay leaf and 2 pints of stock. When tender, put through a hair sieve, return to saucepan, add the onions and remainder of the stock, season and bring to the boil. When serving, add to each plate or bowl a round of fried bread, and top with grated cheese. This is a delicious and very nourishing soup.

Belgian Ardennes.—The chief specialities in this Province are dishes using wild boar, venison, hare and rabbit. One that is extremely popular.

Rabbit with Prunes (Lapin aux Pruneaux) (for 6)

> 1 rabbit
> Small piece of unsalted pork fat (2 in. square)
> Sprig of thyme
> 1 teaspoonful cornflour
> 2 oz. butter
> ¼ lb. finely chopped onions
> 2 bay leaves
> ¼ lb. prunes
> 1 wineglassful red wine or ½ wineglassful vinegar

Cut the rabbit into fair-sized pieces, wash, dry thoroughly and dust lightly with flour. Melt the butter and let it get brown, then put in the pork fat. Brown in it the pieces of rabbit until they are dark brown on all sides (but take care not to let them burn). Take out the rabbit and put in the onions and brown them, stirring all the time. Return the rabbit to the pan, add $\frac{1}{2}$ pint water, herbs and seasoning, bring to the boil and simmer for $\frac{1}{2}$ hour before adding prunes. Continue simmering until the rabbit is tender (but the pieces should still be whole). Some people put the sauce in which the rabbit was cooked through a hair sieve, but others prefer to leave the pieces of onion and prune as they are. The sauce should be thickened with cornflour and a wineglass of red wine or a $\frac{1}{2}$ wineglass vinegar added just before serving.

NOTE: If wild rabbit, or hare, is used, it should first be left overnight in a marinade made from one-third wine vinegar and two-thirds wine, well seasoned.

Tarte au Fromage Blanc

This is served either as a dessert or at 5 o'clock coffee, and is a favourite in the Walloon country.

Flaky pastry	2 tablespoonfuls
2 oz. sugar	melted butter
$\frac{1}{2}$ oz. flour	Pinch of salt
Fresh cottage cheese	2 eggs

Roll out the pastry and line an open tart tin with it. Separate the egg-yolks from the whites, put aside the whites and mix all the other ingredients together, then whip the whites stiffly and add them, stirring well. Fill the tart with the mixture and bake in a hot oven. When cooked, sprinkle with sugar and return to oven for 1–2 minutes until the sugar is nicely browned.

Limbourg.—Every seventh year on the Sunday before the Assumption, the Marian procession of the Virgin Jesse takes place in Hasselt, the capital of Limbourg. Great crowds flock to the town and there is much feasting when, among the many excellent dishes served, there is always a large Vol au Vent.

Vol au Vent (for 4)

2 pints stock (or water)	Juice of 1 lemon
	$\frac{1}{2}$ boiling fowl
1 small pigeon (duck is sometimes used)	1 small knuckle of veal
2 oz. forcemeat (pork and veal)	$\frac{1}{4}$ lb. sweetbreads
	2 egg-yolks
Seasoning	

Flaky or puff pastry vol au vent case the size of a 2-lb. cake tin

Soak the sweetbreads in milk for 12 hours. Bring the stock or water to the boil, put in the meat and poultry and boil until almost tender, then add the sweetbreads and continue boiling until tender. Remove all the meat from the broth and cut it into fair-sized pieces, taking away any skin, bone and gristle.

Make very tiny balls of forcemeat, drop them into the boiling broth for about 1 second, and then add them to the meat.

Make a roux, using broth instead of milk, add lemon juice, season to taste and bring to the boil. Stir in the beaten egg-yolks and remove immediately from the fire. Stir in all the meat and pour into the pastry case. Decorate with parsley and serve piping hot. Mushrooms can be added.

Saint Nicholas (December 6th).—By tradition this is the children's day and a school holiday. The good Saint rides through the night in a sledge drawn by reindeer and visits every home, bringing sweetmeats and presents, among which is always the traditional "Speculaus." This is a kind of dark brown biscuit (looking like a ginger biscuit), decorated with white and pink sugar and cut into various shapes —horses, elephants, clowns, milkmaids and even St. Nicholas himself. These biscuits measure anything from 3 in. to 1 yd. in length. When they are more than $\frac{1}{2}$ yd. long, they are tied down on to a piece of wood covered with white paper. They should be made about a week, or even longer, before they are needed, and kept in a tin or in a very dry place.

Speculaus

1 lb. plain flour	1 oz. ground cinnamon
6 oz. fresh butter or margarine	$\frac{1}{2}$ teaspoonful baking powder
Pinch of salt	Water to mix
6 oz. dark brown sugar	

Mix the dry ingredients together, knead in the butter and enough water to make a pliable dough. Roll out and leave for 1–2 days. Place on a lightly floured pastry board and roll out to $\frac{1}{2}$–1-in. thickness, according to size and depth required, and cut in fancy shapes. (These can be bought in the U.K. as well as on the Continent.) Put on a baking sheet and bake in a fairly hot oven until an even golden colour. Cool on a wire tray and, when quite cold, store in an airtight tin—they improve in flavour with keeping. Decorate with white and pink icing sugar.

Namur.—There has recently been a revival of a Fête Folklorique called "Le combat des Echasseurs" (The Battle of the Stiltrunners) which dates back to a visit made by Napoleon I. There are two Stilt Societies, the Melans and the Avresses, exclusive to Namur. They wear special outfits in the colours of their societies and are perched on stilts also in the societies' colours. In the "battle" each society tries to dislodge its opponents from its stilts, and there is a prize for the winners. A special dish is served at this time, but it has become so popular that it can often be obtained at other times as well.

Meuse Fish in Jelly (Poisson de Meuse à l'Escaveche)

| Fish | Butter and a little |
| Onions | olive oil for frying |

1 lemon

For the sauce

| ⅓ white vinegar to ⅓ water | 1 teaspoonful salt |
| A few cloves and peppercorns | A few sheets of gelatine, broken into small pieces |

Fry the fish in butter and olive oil until deep brown, but not broken up or burnt. Place in a fairly deep earthenware dish and put on top thinly sliced onion and slices of peeled lemon. Prepare the sauce by boiling all the ingredients together. Boil for 2–3 minutes and pour immediately over the fish. Leave for a few days in a cool place before serving. Bread and butter is always served with this dish.

Province of Brabant.—Brussels, the capital of Belgium, is also the capital of this Province. Here there has now been revived the famous Omegang, a procession including the Town Magistrates, surrounded

One of the most popular dishes throughout Belgium is Chicons à la Portugaise—chicory in cheese and tomato sauce with eggs. Specially photographed in a Pyrex dish, with ovenware and cruets in yellow and grey Denby Dovedale

by all their colourfully dressed attendants, military detachments and decorated wagons depicting the Legend of St. Michele and St. Gudule, patron saints of Brussels, and other legendary and historical subjects. Thousands of people flock to the capital to see the procession, and the favourite dish at this time is Sweetbreads in Madeira Sauce (Schoesels au Madère).

Sweetbreads in Madeira Sauce (for 4–6)

2 ox sweetbreads	½ lb. breast of veal
1 lb. onions	1 kidney (ox)
½ lb. lamb (lean)	1 glass of beer
Butter for frying	1 wineglass vinegar
Sprig of thyme	2 bay leaves
2 parsley roots	Salt, pepper and nut-
½ lb. mushrooms	meg
2 wineglasses Madeira	1 dessertspoonful
Minced pork and veal	cornflour
1 oxtail	A few lumps of sugar

Cut the onions into thin rounds and brown them in butter in a saucepan, then add the oxtail, cut into small pieces, and brown. Cover the pan and simmer for about 1 hour, then add the veal, sweetbreads, kidney and lamb all cut into medium-sized pieces. Add the beer, sugar, herbs, vinegar and seasoning, cover and simmer for 2 hours. Make the pork and veal into small meatballs, clean and slice the mushrooms and add to the other ingredients. Mix the cornflour to a smooth paste with the Madeira and, when all ingredients are tender (about 2½–3 hours altogether), remove herbs and add cornflour mixture, stirring it in very lightly and taking care not to break up the pieces. Serve with boiled or mashed potatoes.

From October until the end of March, Brussels chicory (Witloof) is served all over Belgium, both in the home and in the restaurants, either raw or cooked in various ways.

Chicons à la Portugaise

1 lb. Brussels chicory	1 oz. flour
(Witloof)	2 oz. grated Gruyère
1 oz. butter	cheese
1 oz. tomato purée	1 large cupful milk
Seasoning	Juice of ½ lemon

Boil the chicory for 20 minutes in salted water with the lemon juice. Pour into a colander, rinse under the cold tap and leave to drain. Meanwhile, make a white sauce with the butter, flour, milk and seasoning, bring to the boil, then add the cheese and stir until it has melted. Dilute the tomato purée with a little water and add to the sauce, then bring to the boil. Arrange the chicory on a dish and pour the sauce on top, covering completely. Garnish with halved hard-boiled eggs and chopped parsley.

Chicory in Melted Butter

Cook and drain chicory (see Vegetables chapter). Melt butter or margarine in a frying pan. When it is golden brown, put in the heads of chicory and brown them on all sides, then arrange them on a dish, pour on the melted butter and sprinkle with chopped parsley.

Province of Antwerp.—This Province has two special dishes—Asparagus and Eels in Sorrel. Malines is famous for its asparagus, which is exported all over the Continent.

Asperges à la Flamande

1 bundle asparagus	Chopped parsley
White sauce	Hard-boiled eggs

Wash the asparagus, cut off coarse end of stalks (about 1 in.) and place in salted water in a large saucepan (a special tray which hangs from the side of the saucepan can be used). Bring to the boil and boil until tender (about 15–20 minutes). Take out asparagus, keeping the water for sauce, place on a long dish and garnish with halved hard-boiled eggs and parsley. Make a white sauce, using half milk and half asparagus water, and either serve separately or pour over half the asparagus.

Eels in Sorrel (Anguilles au Vert)

This dish can be eaten all the year round and many restaurants in Antwerp are famous for it.

2 lb. eels	¼ lb. sorrel
A little parsley	A few small onions
Sage	2 oz. melted butter
Juice of 1 lemon	Pepper and salt
1 teaspoonful corn-	1 egg-yolk
flour	

Chop up finely the sorrel, parsley, onions and sage, put into saucepan with the butter and simmer. Cut the eels into medium-sized pieces and add, with the lemon juice, pepper and salt and cook for 10 minutes. Before serving, bind the sauce with the cornflour and egg-yolk.

JEWISH

Some typical dishes selected from a rich and varied tradition

by FLORENCE GREENBERG, *author of "The Jewish Chronicle Cookery Book" and*
"Florence Greenberg's Cookery Book"

JEWISH cookery characteristics are derived from two main sources—religious tradition and the wanderings of the Jewish people.

Traditional Jewish laws impose bans on the consumption of animals that do not chew the cud and have cloven hooves, such as pigs and rabbits, and on sea food that does not have fins and scales, such as shellfish. Scavengers, birds of prey, and hindquarter meat are also forbidden. Indeed, because consumption of blood is not allowed, all animals must be slaughtered by a "shochet," a man specially trained to kill them by severing the jugular vein, a method which permits the maximum flow of blood. All blood remaining on the meat is removed by the housewife by the process of soaking in cold water and salting, known as Koshering. Finally, traditional religious laws state that milk and meat must not be cooked together, nor, generally speaking, consumed at the same meal.

As a result, Jewish housewives are limited in the foods they may utilise for cooking, and the limitation has often been magnified in the past by the privations and poverty that the Jews have suffered in their wanderings in many countries of the world. Thus prevented from gaining variety by using different kinds of food, the Jewish housewife developed the art of cooking the same foods differently. It is, perhaps, because Kosher meat was not always available that she developed particular ability in preparing fish dishes and in chopping the fish, as in "Gefillte Fish," to make the food go farther when it was in short supply.

Many dishes prepared by Jewish housewives are derived from the countries in which their forebears sojourned. Thus, for example, it was in Spain and Portugal that they learned to fry fish in oil, in Germany

that they learned to make sweet and sour stews, and in Russia that they learned to make blintzes and borsch.

At the same time there has grown up a specifically Jewish tradition in which particular dishes are associated with particular festivals. For Jews, each festival, including the Sabbath, lasts from sunset to sunset and the festive meal is taken on the eve of the holy-day to usher it in.

On the Sabbath eve it is customary to eat cold fried fish or gefillte fish. And because on the Sabbath all work, including the lighting of a fire, is forbidden, a special stew called "Cholent" is prepared before sunset on Friday, then left simmering in a very cool oven until midday dinner the following day.

On New Year's Eve (which falls in the autumn, according to the Jewish calendar) honey cake and apples dipped in honey are consumed, to signify the hope of a sweet and fruitful year to come. At Tabernacles, the harvest festival, stuffed cabbage leaves, sweet and sour, are traditional. The Feast of Purim commemorates the exposure by the Jew Mordecai of the conspirator Haman, and "Haman Taschen," a three-cornered bun said to represent the "ass-like" ears of the rogue, are eaten. At Shevouoth, celebration of the gleaning of the firstfruits, cheese dishes, especially blintzes, are the festive fare.

During the Festival of Passover, when Jews commemorate the liberation of their ancestors from Egyptian bondage, only unleavened bread may be eaten, as a reminder that the Israelites left in such a hurry that they had no time to leaven their bread, which they baked on their backs as they went. From the injunction to use only unleavened flour during this festival has arisen a whole galaxy of special

One of the dishes customarily eaten on the Sabbath eve is cold fried fish

recipes, some examples of which are given here.

In the course of the following pages it has been possible to give a few samples only from a rich and varied tradition. But I think that those who taste will find them good.

PASSOVER DISHES

Almond Biscuits

6 oz. fine motza meal	3 oz. castor sugar
4 oz. margarine	1 egg
Almond essence	Chopped almonds

Cream the margarine and sugar. Reserve a little of the egg-white to brush over the top of the biscuits, beat up remainder and add to the creamed margarine together with the motza meal, flavour with almond essence and knead thoroughly. Press on to a greased baking sheet to a thickness of about $\frac{1}{4}$ in., brush over with white of egg and sprinkle with chopped almonds. Bake in a moderately hot oven till lightly browned—about 20 minutes. Cut into squares or fingers, then remove from tin and cool on a cake tray.

Wafer Biscuits

1 oz. potato flour	2 oz. margarine
1 oz. fine motza meal	1 egg
2 oz. castor sugar	Vanilla essence

Melt the margarine, but do not let it boil.

Whip the egg and sugar till light and frothy, add the melted margarine and a few drops of essence of vanilla, whisk again, then stir in the meal and potato flour.

Grease some baking-tins very thoroughly with cooking fat and put on teaspoonfuls of the mixture, with a good space between each, as they spread considerably. Bake in a hot oven till set and the edges lightly browned. Remove from tins immediately and cool on a cake tray.

Savoury Balls for Soup or Stew (Motza-kleis) (for 4–5)

1 motza	Fine meal
1 small onion	Seasoning (pepper,
1 egg	salt and ginger)
1 oz. chicken fat	

Soak the motza in cold water till soft, then drain and squeeze dry. Put in a basin and beat up with a fork. Chop the onion finely (there should be about 1 tablespoonful) and fry in the fat till lightly browned, then add it to the soaked motza together with the fat in which it was fried, season with salt, pepper and ginger, add the beaten egg and sufficient fine meal to bind the mixture. Roll into tiny balls and coat with fine meal. Drop into fast-boiling soup or stew, and after 2 minutes reduce the heat and simmer for 20 minutes.

These are best made in advance and left

for a few hours in a cool place or refrigerator before cooking.

Steamed Fruit Pudding (for 4–5)

6 oz. dried fruit	2 oz. brown sugar
1 oz. chopped peel	2 motzas
3 oz. shredded suet	½ teaspoonful mixed
2 tablespoonfuls	spice
motza meal	2 eggs

Soak the motzas in cold water till soft, drain in a colander and press out all moisture, then put in a mixing bowl and beat up with a fork. Add the remaining ingredients and mix thoroughly. Turn into a greased basin and steam for 2–2½ hours.

This pudding can also be baked. Turn the mixture into a greased baking dish and bake about 1 hour in a moderate oven.

Apple Charlotte (for 5–6)

6 oz. medium motza	3 oz. margarine
meal	2 oz. sultanas
1½ lb. apples	Sugar
4 tablespoonfuls	½ lemon
water	

Peel the apples and cut into small pieces. Rub 2½ oz. margarine into the meal and add 2 tablespoonfuls of sugar. Grease a baking dish and put in one-third of the meal, cover with half the apples, sprinkle with sugar, sultanas, grated lemon rind and juice. Repeat the layers and pour over the water. Put the remaining meal on top, sprinkle with sugar and dot with remaining margarine. Bake in a moderate oven 1–1¼ hours.

Stuffed Chremslach (for 4–5)

2 motzas	¼ teaspoonful cinnamon
2 oz. motza meal	mon
1 oz. sugar	Fruit filling
1 egg	Cooking fat for
	frying

Soak the motzas in cold water till soft, drain, squeeze dry and beat up with a fork. Add the meal, beaten egg, sugar and cinnamon, and mix thoroughly. Form into small flat oval shapes, cover half with the fruit filling and place another on top. Shape neatly, coat with motza meal and fry a golden brown on both sides in hot fat. Serve hot, sprinkled with sugar.

Fruit Filling.—Mix together 6 oz. dried fruit, 1 oz. sugar, ¼ teaspoonful cinnamon and 2 teaspoonfuls lemon juice.

OTHER DISHES

Bream with Sweet and Sour Sauce (for 4–5)

2 lb. bream	Salt
1 small onion	1 oz. sultanas
1 bay leaf	1 oz. sugar
4 tablespoonfuls	2 oz. margarine
vinegar	1½ oz. flour
Pepper	

Cut the fish into convenient-sized pieces for serving, place in a saucepan with the sliced onion and bay leaf, sprinkle with salt and pepper, and pour over sufficient hot water to cover. Put the lid on the pan and simmer gently until the fish is cooked—about 15 minutes. Then remove the bay leaf and lift fish on to a serving dish.

Melt the margarine, stir in the flour, then gradually add ¾ pint of the liquor in which the fish was cooked and the vinegar, stir till boiling, add the sugar and sultanas, season with salt and pepper, and simmer for 5 minutes. Pour over the fish and serve either hot or cold.

The amount of vinegar and sugar can be varied according to taste.

Cod or haddock can be cooked in the same way.

Fried Fish (for 5–6)

2–3 lb. fish	Frying oil
2–3 oz. flour	Parsley
2 eggs	Salt

Any kind of fish can be used. Small fish can be fried whole, larger ones can be filleted or cut into steaks.

Wash the fish, put it in a bowl, sprinkle with salt and leave for 15 minutes, then dry thoroughly. Coat the pieces of fish with flour seasoned with salt, then with beaten egg. Heat sufficient frying oil in a frying pan to half-cover the fish and, when really hot, fry the fish a golden brown, first on one side, then the other. Drain thoroughly on soft paper and serve cold, garnished with parsley.

Gefillte Fish (for 5–6)

2–2½ lb. fish (bream,	2 sticks of celery
cod or haddock)	1 tablespoonful
2 eggs	chopped parsley
2 onions	1½ pints water
1 large carrot	Fresh breadcrumbs
Salt and pepper	

Remove the skin and bones from the fish and put them in a saucepan with one cut-up onion, the celery and a small piece of carrot, pour over the water and season with salt and pepper. Cover and simmer gently for $\frac{1}{2}$ hour, then strain.

Put the fish and remaining onion through the mincing machine, add the parsley and beaten eggs to the minced fish and sufficient fresh breadcrumbs to bind, season with salt and pepper. With floured hands, roll into balls. Slice the carrot, add to the fish stock and bring to the boil, then lay in it the fish balls, cover and simmer very gently for 1 hour. Lift the balls on to a serving dish and place a slice of carrot on top of each. Spoon over a little of the fish stock and serve cold, when the stock should have set in a jelly.

Cholent (for 5-6)

This is the traditional dish served on the Sabbath when a hot meal is required. It is prepared on Friday and cooked till midday dinner the following day.

2 lb. fat brisket or	Dumpling
short rib of beef	1 onion
$\frac{1}{2}$ lb. butter beans	1 oz. sugar
2 lb. medium-size	Salt and pepper
potatoes	Water

Use a short-handled saucepan with a tightly fitting lid, or a large casserole.

Peel the potatoes and leave them whole. Put the beans in the bottom of the pan, add the chopped onion and half the potatoes. Place the meat and dumpling on top and fill up with remaining potatoes. Season each layer with salt and pepper, sprinkle over the sugar and pour over sufficient boiling water to cover. Place greaseproof paper over the top before putting on the lid. Place in a very slow oven till required the following day.

For the dumpling

4 oz. flour	1 large potato
1 small onion	2 teaspoonfuls
1 oz. suet or raw	chopped parsley
chicken fat	Salt and pepper

Peel and grate the potato and onion, chop the suet or chicken fat finely, mix all ingredients, seasoning with salt and pepper, then form into a roll.

Calves' Feet with Prunes and Chestnuts (for 4-5)

2 calves' feet	1 small onion
$\frac{1}{2}$ lb. prunes	2 sticks celery
$\frac{1}{2}$ lb. chestnuts	2 or 3 olives
2 tablespoonfuls	Stock or water
sherry	Salt, pepper, paprika

Soak the prunes in cold water overnight. Boil the chestnuts for 15 minutes, then remove outer and inner skins. Cut up the onion and celery. Joint the calves' feet and put them in a stewpan with sufficient stock or water to cover well. Season with salt, pepper and $\frac{1}{2}$ teaspoonful of paprika, cover and cook very gently for 2 hours.

Gefillte fish is one of the best known of Jewish dishes. Minced fish is made into balls which are then boiled, decorated with carrot and served cold

Then add the prunes, chestnuts, onion and celery and continue to cook gently for another hour. Before serving, add the sherry and the chopped olives.

Stuffed Cabbage Leaves, sweet and sour (Holishkes) (for 4–6)

¼ lb. raw minced beef	1 oz. sugar
1 teacupful cooked rice	Cabbage leaves
	½ pint water
1 tablespoonful grated onion	2 oz. sultanas
2 tablespoonfuls con-	2 tablespoonfuls
centrated tomato	vinegar
purée	Salt and pepper

Use a white cabbage. Remove twelve of the largest leaves, place them in a bowl, cover with boiling water, leave for 2 or 3 minutes, then drain, dry with a cloth and cut away the tough stem ends. Mix the meat and rice, add the grated onion and ½ teaspoonful of tomato purée, and season with salt and pepper. Put a portion in the centre of each cabbage leaf, fold over the sides, roll up like a parcel and fasten with thread. Line a large saucepan with a few more scalded leaves and place the rolls close together on top. Pour over the tomato purée and water, add the vinegar, sugar and sultanas. Cover, and cook over a very gentle heat for 2 hours. If the liquid boils away, add a little more water.

If preferred, these can be cooked in a covered casserole in a slow oven.

Poppy Seed Buns (Haman Taschen)

1 lb. flour	½ oz. yeast
2 oz. castor sugar	2 oz margarine
½ pint milk	1 egg
Poppy-seed filling	Honey

Cream the yeast with a teaspoonful of sugar. Melt the margarine in the milk and, when just lukewarm, pour it on to the creamed yeast. Sieve the flour with a pinch of salt into a warmed basin, make a well in the centre and pour in the yeast mixture, gradually work in the flour from the sides and knead to a smooth dough. Cover and leave in a warm place to rise for 1½–2 hours, then add the sugar and beaten egg, and knead thoroughly.

Roll out the dough ¼ in. thick and cut into 4-in. squares. Put a heaped teaspoonful of the filling in the centre of each and fold across into triangles, pressing edges well together and folding them under. Place well apart on greased baking tins and leave in a warm place to rise for 1 hour,

then brush the tops lightly with warm honey and bake in a moderate oven till golden brown—about 20 minutes.

Poppy-seed filling

1 teacupful ground poppy seeds	1 oz. sugar
	2 oz. margarine
1 teacupful milk or water	2 tablespoonfuls honey
1 oz chopped peel	1 oz. sultanas
1 oz. chopped nuts	

Put all ingredients into a saucepan, bring to the boil and cook over a gentle heat until the liquid is absorbed, keeping it well stirred.

Filled Pancakes (Cheese blintzes) (for 4–5)

4 oz. flour	2 eggs
¼ pint milk	6–8 oz. curd cheese
¼ pint water	Grated lemon rind
1 teaspoonful sugar	Salt
	Fat for frying

Add the sugar and a little grated lemon rind to the cheese. Make a smooth batter with the flour, eggs, milk and water, adding salt to taste.

Grease a heated omelette pan with cooking fat and pour in just sufficient batter to cover the bottom of the pan with a very thin layer. Cook over a moderate heat until the pancake is firm, frying on one side only, then invert on to a clean cloth, cooked side uppermost, and fry remaining batter in the same way. Put a little of the cheese in the centre of each and fold over in the shape of an envelope. Fry a golden brown on both sides.

Purim Fritters (Fritlach) (for 5–6)

2 eggs	Flour
3 tablespoonfuls oil	Castor sugar
	Oil for frying

Beat up the eggs, stir in the oil, then mix in enough flour to make a soft dough. Knead very thoroughly, break off small pieces and roll out wafer thin into circles about 8 in. across, then cut each into four sections. Leave for an hour or longer till quite dry, then fry in hot oil a very light brown. Drain and sprinkle with castor sugar. These need careful handling, as they break very easily.

Apple Steffon (for 5–6)

1½ lb. apples	10 oz. flour
2 oz. currants	1 teaspoonful baking
1 oz. chopped peel	powder
1 oz. margarine	Brown sugar
Pinch of salt	Cinnamon
Cold water	½ lemon
4 oz. shredded suet	

Lockschen Pudding is made with either noodles or spaghetti and sultanas

Sieve flour, baking powder and salt, add the suet and water to make a soft dough.

Spread the margarine thickly over the bottom and sides of a 2-pint pudding basin, then sprinkle liberally with brown sugar.

Roll out three-quarters of the pastry $\frac{1}{3}$ in. thick and line the basin with it. Peel, core and cut up the apples, put half in the lined basin, sprinkle over the peel, currants, grated rind and juice of half a lemon, and dust of cinnamon and sugar to taste, then add the remaining apples, a little more sugar and pour over $\frac{1}{2}$ teacupful of cold water. Cover with remaining pastry, twist a greased paper over the top and bake in a moderate oven about $1\frac{1}{4}$ hours.

Stuffed Monkey

6 oz. flour	$\frac{1}{2}$ teaspoonful
4 oz. margarine	cinnamon
4 oz. soft brown	1 egg
sugar	Filling

Sieve the flour and cinnamon, rub in the margarine, add the yolk of the egg and the sugar, and knead to a pliable dough. Roll out the paste into two rounds to fit an 8-in. shallow cake tin (about 2 in. deep). Grease the tin and put in one round, spread with the filling and cover with the other round. Brush over with white of egg and bake in a moderate oven about 30 minutes. Cool in the tin.

For the filling

2 oz. chopped peel	2 oz. ground almonds
1$\frac{1}{2}$ oz. margarine	1 oz. castor sugar
1 egg-yolk	

Melt margarine, mix all ingredients.

Honey Cake (Lekach)

$\frac{1}{2}$ lb. honey	$\frac{1}{2}$ teaspoonful mixed
12 oz. flour	spice
4 oz. castor sugar	$\frac{1}{2}$ teaspoonful
2 eggs	bicarbonate of soda
$\frac{1}{4}$ pint warm water	3 tablespoonfuls
1 teaspoonful ground	cooking oil
ginger	Shredded almonds

Grease a shallow cake tin about 9 in. across. Sieve the flour, ginger, spice and bicarbonate of soda, warm the honey. Beat the eggs and sugar till light and frothy, add the oil and warmed honey, then the dry ingredients alternately with the water and mix to a smooth batter. Turn into greased tin, sprinkle with shredded almonds and bake about 1 hour in a moderate oven.

Lockschen Pudding (for 4–5)

1 pint cooked noodles	2 oz. sugar
or spaghetti	2 oz. margarine
4 oz. sultanas	$\frac{1}{4}$ teaspoonful
1 oz. chopped peel	cinnamon
2 eggs	

Melt the margarine, beat eggs lightly. Mix all ingredients. Turn into a greased baking dish and bake in a moderate oven about 40 minutes.

CHINA

*Compiled by T. W. Chen Hsu
from the classical Chinese
cuisine of the Great Wall
Restaurant, London*

Snow on the Meadow, like all Chinese
dishes, can be eaten with chopsticks or
spoon and fork. A knife never comes to a
Chinese table

IN Chinese cookery, rice is used extensively, so are chicken, pork and eggs, but Chop Suey, so often served as a national dish, is never seen in China. Spices and herbs are not used, the only strong flavours being garlic and onion. At least four or five dishes are always served at the same time and all the food can be eaten either with chopsticks or a spoon and fork. A knife never comes to a Chinese table, because everything is cut up beforehand.

The following is the kind of meal that would be served to guests in China:

First: *Hors d'œuvres*, a number of different dishes arranged daintily around a plate and including, for instance, chopped roast pork; Soochow fish; chicken gizzard stewed in soya sauce; bean sprout salad with sweet-sour sauce; sweet and sour cucumber; tea-flavoured eggs.

Second: *Four Hot Dishes*, such as fried lobster or other sea foods.

Third: *Two Dessert Dishes*, one sweet, such as Snow on the Meadow; one savoury, such as Bao-Tse (Steamed Meat Buns).

Fourth: *Four Stewed Dishes*, a whole stewed duck or chicken; stewed beef; a vegetable dish; stewed fish, the fish always being eaten last. This served with plenty of boiled rice.

And, finally, tea to drink.

The reason for the four courses goes far back into Chinese history when it was the custom to give the whole day to entertaining a friend. When entertaining was telescoped into a few hours, all the meals for the day were served at once and in the right order. Thus the hors d'œuvres represent the cold first meal or breakfast; the four hot dishes, lunch; the dessert, afternoon tea, and the four stewed dishes with rice, the evening meal.

The following recipes have been specially chosen because they are all made from ingredients obtainable in the U.K. Chinese mushrooms (which are quite different from British ones—black all over and bigger) are obtainable dried, by the ounce; bamboo shoots, sweet lychees and water chestnuts in tins; green Chinese beans by the pound and Chinese vermicelli by the bundle, from Oriental shops, such as Lal Jolly, 70 Warwick Road, London, S.W.5, or the Hong Kong Emporium, 53 Rupert Street, London, W.1.

NOTE: Bean shoots can be grown in any kitchen. Scatter a pound of green Chinese beans on a large piece of flannel, cover with a second piece of flannel and sprinkle gently with water every day. The shoots will begin to appear in about ten days in winter, four or five days in summer weather, and will go on shooting.

Shallow Frying

Most Chinese frying is "shallow-frying," which means that only a very little fat is used, just to grease the pan (as for frying

The Chinese serve several dishes at once. Here, from left to right, are Steamed Meat Buns, Sweet and Sour Pork and mixed vegetables

pancakes), which must be very hot, with a little water added as required. In China, soya bean or peanut oil is chiefly used, but the best substitute easily obtainable outside China is tea-seed oil.

Three Sisters Soup (for 4)

The three sisters are Chicken, Chinese Mushrooms and Bamboo Shoots.

1 quart chicken broth	Salt to taste
4 pieces of dried	1 oz. bamboo shoots
mushroom	Breast of one chicken

Slice the bamboo shoots, dried Chinese mushrooms and breast of chicken very fine, and drop into the boiling chicken broth. Cook gently for about 3 minutes and serve—in little round bowls (not soup plates) if you want to be really Chinese.

Dan Jiao (Stuffed Egg Rolls) Soup

For soup

Stewing meat	A bundle of Chinese
½ lb. fresh watercress	vermicelli

For dan jiao

4 eggs	Oil or fat
¼ lb meat (pork or	½ oz. spring onion
veal)	Salt to taste

Beat up the eggs and add a pinch of salt.

For the stuffing, mince the meat and cut the onion into tiny bits; mix them together and add salt to taste.

Rub the oil or fat on a hot ladle, place over a low flame, so that a thin film of fat forms on the ladle's surface, and pour in half a tablespoonful of egg. Shake the ladle so that the egg forms a circle and immediately put on to it a little of the stuffing mixture. Fold the circle carefully in two, close it up and turn it over, and one dan jiao is thus formed. Repeat the process. 4 eggs make roughly 30 rolls.

For the soup, soak vermicelli in boiling water for 10 minutes, cut into lengths of 6–8 in.; boil the meat on a low flame for 1 hour, then add vermicelli.

Put the dan jiao and watercress into the soup and simmer for 1 minute. It will then be ready for serving.

Sliced Chicken

1 clove of garlic	½ lb. white meat of
¼ lb. mushrooms	chicken (uncooked)
A little cornflour	¼ lb. French beans
1 medium onion	Oil for frying
Cooking sherry to taste	

Slice chicken into thin pieces and mix it

in the cornflour, made into a paste with a little water, to prevent the pieces sticking together. Slit the beans in halves and cut them into inch-long pieces. Skin the mushrooms and cut into pieces the same size as the chicken slices. Slice the onion in the same way.

Fry the crushed garlic in hot oil and shallow-fry it with the onion until just cooked. Add salt to taste. Then shallow-fry the French beans and mushrooms. When cooked, dish up. Wipe the pan with a clean cloth or use a fresh pan. Put in some fat or oil and shallow-fry the chicken slices until they are almost cooked. Add other ingredients and a little cooking sherry, and stir the whole thing until the chicken slices are fully cooked.

To Cook Rice

4 *teacupfuls rice*   6 *teacupfuls of water*

Experiment is advisable. Those who prefer soft rice may, for instance, add a little more water.

Wash the rice thoroughly four or five times, then put in a pan with the cold water. Bring quickly to the boil and cook gently for a further 20 minutes, when the rice will be ready to serve.

Fried Rice with Ham and Egg

5 *teacupfuls of rice*   2 *eggs*
  (cooked as above)   1 *oz. spring onion*
2 *oz. ham*   *Lard or oil for frying*
      Salt to taste

Cut the ham and spring onion into tiny pieces. Beat the eggs, and add salt to taste. Put some lard or tea-seed oil in a frying pan and fry the rice for about 5 minutes. Scramble the egg in a similar way in another frying pan for about 2 minutes. Mix the cooked egg and chopped ham with the rice and fry again for about 3 minutes.

Sweet and Sour Pork

½ *lb. pork (or veal)*   1 *egg*
2 *tablespoonfuls self-*   *Fat for deep frying*
  raising flour
      For the sauce
1 *teacupful vinegar*   2 *tablespoonfuls oil*
1 *desertspoonful*   1 *sliced tomato and*
  cornflour   *some boiled green*
A clove of garlic   *peas*
      6 *tablespoonfuls sugar*

Cut the pork into pieces (half-domino size). Beat the egg and mix with flour. Dip the pieces of meat into this batter and fry in deep fat until brown. Serve hot with the sauce made as follows:

Mix the cornflour with the vinegar and sugar in half a cupful of water. Fry the crushed garlic in hot oil, add the cornflour and boil the mixture. Add the sliced tomato and simmer for 3 minutes. Lastly, add the boiled green peas.

Fried Lobster

Cut cooked lobster into domino-sized pieces, dip in batter (made from 1 egg and 2 tablespoonfuls self-raising flour as above) and deep-fry until golden.

Meat Balls

These are made from minced raw pork mixed with a little celery and onion to taste and minced very fine. Add salt and shape into balls, sprinkle with flour, dip in batter (made from 1 egg and 2 tablespoonfuls self-raising flour) and deep-fry until golden. Serve with sweet and sour sauce (see under recipe for Sweet and Sour Pork).

Mixed Vegetables

Use any or all of the following: onion, leek, Chinese mushroom (this should be included if possible), tomato, bean sprouts (or bamboo shoots or water chestnuts), celery, green peppers, spring greens.

Wash and clean all the vegetables, then slice them up into very thin strips and shallow-fry them all in very little oil in a hot pan. Add a little water and simmer for 5 minutes. The dish is then ready to serve in its own juice.

NOTE: This dish can be served as Vegetable Chop Suey.

Tea-flavoured Eggs

Hard-boil the required number of eggs, remove the shells and stand them in a bowl, covered in tea and a little salt for ½ hour. They will be chocolate-coloured and slightly flavoured with tea.

Snow on the Meadow

1 *large packet frozen*   2 *or* 3 *egg-whites*
  green peas   *Plenty of lard for*
6 *tablespoonfuls*   *frying*
  castor sugar

Cook the peas in the usual way in boiling salted water until tender, then put them through a mincer and mix in the sugar. Melt a large knob of lard (about 2 oz.) in a very hot pan and fry the minced peas for 10 minutes. Put on to a plate, keep hot and top with stiffly beaten cold egg-white.

Chopped vegetables and prawns are included in this salad. On the right are delicately flavoured lychees, often served as a dessert, either fresh or canned

Steamed Meat Buns (Steamed bao-tse)

For the pastry

1 *lb. self-raising flour*   1 *oz. yeast*
1 *teaspoonful sugar*   *Water to mix*

For the filling

Minced raw pork   *Soya bean sauce*
1 *minced spring*   *Salt to taste*
  onion

Dissolve yeast in a teacupful of warm water. Stir thoroughly, then mix with the flour and sugar into a dough. Leave for 10 minutes, then roll out and cut into circles about 2½ in. in diameter. Put about half a tablespoonful of filling into the centre of each circle, wrap the edges over the meat and leave for 20 minutes. Steam for 20 minutes.

Stewed Duck or Chicken

(This is a very popular dish in Southern China.) First remove *all* the bones from the bird (including the wing ones), stuff with a mixture of minced chestnuts, mushrooms, chopped ham and boiled rice, and stew in a very little water and about 3 tablespoonfuls of soya bean sauce for about 3 hours. Serve with rice. It can be done, though not *so* well, with a duck or chicken that still has its bones.

General Hints

As a dessert course at a Chinese meal, serve either preserved ginger or lychees, which can be bought in tins and are absolutely delicious with a flavour all their own. Bamboo shoots may be served as a separate vegetable—finely sliced and shallow-fried in oil with a little water added. Soya sauce is served with practically all meat, fish and vegetable dishes and with rice. Like the bean sprouts, it is full of vitamins.

INDONESIA

by S. F. RUNTUWENE

*No meal is complete without lots of rice and at least
one savoury dish fiery with chillies*

THE chief characteristics of Indonesian
cooking are the extensive use of rice and
the fact that most dishes contain chillies
and are therefore very hot.

A typical Indonesian main meal consists
of rice with four subsidiary dishes—one
containing chicken or meat, one fish, one
vegetables, and the fourth very hot and
spicy, called Sambel. After that, fresh fruit
is eaten and sometimes a savoury. But
whatever else is served at a meal, the rice is
of the greatest importance and is eaten first.

To Cook Rice—Indonesian Style

Allow 1 lb. of Patna rice for 4 people.

Put the rice into a pan and cover it with
cold water to a depth equal to two joints of
the middle finger. Bring to the boil, stir
once to prevent it sticking to the bottom,
then cover and cook slowly for ½ hour or
until the grains feel soft. Strain and serve.

Yellow Rice (Nasi kuning) (for 4)

1 lb. Patna rice	1 teaspoonful tur-
1½ pints coconut milk	meric powder
(or milk)	½ teaspoonful salt

Decoration

2 eggs	Red chillies
1 onion	Black soya beans
Celery leaf	½ cucumber
Carrots or radishes	

Bring to the boil the coconut milk (made
by soaking for 15 minutes and squashing
well half a grated fresh coconut or ½ lb.
desiccated coconut with 6 of 7 tablespoonfuls of water, then passing through a sieve),
add the rice and seasonings, cook until
milk is absorbed, stirring to prevent burning; leave on a low heat for about 5 minutes.
Finish by steaming the rice until cooked.
Make an omelette with the eggs, cut it into
strips and use for decoration with the other
ingredients listed above. Serve with roast
chicken.

FISH DISHES

Pindang Serani (for 4)

2 mackerel	¼ teaspoonful tur-
5 red chillies	meric powder
5 green chillies	1 teaspoonful ground
1 bay leaf	ginger
Salt	Lemon juice
1 onion	Margarine or oil for
3 cloves of garlic	frying

Slice the onion, garlic and chillies. Fry
a golden brown, and add salt, turmeric
powder, ginger and bay leaf. Add 6 teacupfuls of water and bring to the boil.
Wash and clean the fish, add with the
lemon juice and cook gently for about 5
minutes until the fish is cooked but not
falling to pieces.

NOTE: This dish is vastly improved if
made 2 or 3 days beforehand and the fish
left to soak in the liquid until required. If
this is done, an aluminium pan must NOT
be used.

Pickled Fish (for 4)

2 mackerel or whiting	3 cloves of garlic
1 onion	2 almonds
½ pint frying oil	1½ teaspoonfuls sugar
1 teaspoonful tur-	6 red chillies
meric powder	½ pint vinegar
Salt	8 shallots or spring
½ pint water	onions

Wash and clean the fish, mix with salt
and a little vinegar, and fry a golden brown
in the oil. Put dry seasonings, garlic and
onion through a mincer. Fry for about 2
minutes. Add water and vinegar. Bring
to the boil. Add shallots or spring onions,
sliced chillies and fried fish. Continue to
cook for a few minutes.

Roast Fish (for 4)

2 mackerel	6 red chillies
½ lemon	¼ teaspoonful ground
1 tablespoonful mar-	ginger
garine	Salt

Clean and wash the fish. Chop the
chillies finely, add ginger, salt and lemon

juice. Melt margarine, add the fish and seasoning. Slowly simmer until cooked.

MEAT AND POULTRY DISHES

Orak-Arik (for 4)

 ½ lb. cabbage
 Breast of 1 chicken
 Margarine
 ½ teaspoonful pepper
 Celery leaves
 5 shallots
 2 eggs
 Sugar and salt to taste

Chop the shallots, mix with pepper and fry in margarine. Add sliced chicken, celery leaves and mashed cabbage. Beat the eggs and pour into the mixture; add salt and sugar and cook for about 5 minutes, or until cabbage is sufficiently cooked. Serve with fried onions.

Abon (for 4)

 1 lb. beef
 ½ pint oil
 2 cloves of garlic
 1 teaspoonful lemon
   juice
 Salt and sugar to taste

Cook the beef in ½ pint

At the main meal rice is accompanied by subsidiary dishes containing chicken or meat, fish and vegetables, as well as a spicy Sambel

of water until it is so soft that it falls apart in strings. Chop garlic fine, mix with salt, sugar, lemon juice and the meat and leave for about 5 minutes. Heat the frying oil and fry the beef mixture until a golden brown. Eat with rice.

Nasi Gurih Ajam (for 4)

1 lb. rice	4 teaspoonfuls coco-
1 onion (or 10	nut milk (made
shallots)	from 2 lb. coco-
1 bay leaf	nut. See Yellow
1 young chicken	Rice recipe)
Salt	

Decorations

¼ lb. cabbage finely shredded, cucumber, omelet (1 egg) cut into strips, young celery leaves, radishes.

Wash the rice. Clean the chicken and cut in pieces. Put half of the rice into a stewpan with chicken, sliced onion (or shallots), bay leaf and salt. Put the rest of the rice on top, pour coconut milk over the rice and chicken and bring to the boil. When boiling, stir and mix everything well together. Continue cooking over a low heat for about 40 minutes. Garnish with decorations listed above.

Liver Dish (Sambel goreng ati) (for 4)

1 lb. liver	3 cloves of garlic
2 tomatoes	½ lb. desiccated
½ teaspoonful	coconut
paprika powder	1 teaspoonful chilli
½ lb. fresh green peas	powder
2 tablespoonfuls	2 tablespoonfuls
sliced onion	margarine
2 bay leaves	

Cut the liver into squares of about 1 in. Slice the garlic and fry with the onion, chilli powder and paprika powder. Add the liver, the bay leaves, and then the tomatoes and peas. Place the lid on the pan and switch to a low heat. Stir occasionally and, when nearly cooked, add 1 teacupful of coconut milk (made from ½ lb. desiccated coconut, see Yellow Rice recipe). Continue to cook until the liver is ready, stirring constantly to prevent curdling.

Roast Meat Balls (for 4)

1 egg	½ clove of garlic
4 potatoes	½ lb. minced meat
1½ tablespoonfuls	1 onion
margarine	¼ teaspoonful ground
3 tablespoonfuls	nutmeg
breadcrumbs	½ teaspoonful pepper

Peel the potatoes and boil them. Slice and fry onion and garlic in 1 tablespoonful

margarine for about 2 minutes. Mash the potatoes, mix with the fried onions, garlic and minced meat, egg and rest of the seasoning. Spread the breadcrumbs and ½ tablespoonful margarine in a fireproof pie-dish and add the mixture. Heat well in moderate oven. Serve hot.

Roast Chicken (Ajam panggang) (for 4)

1 small roasting	¼ teaspoonful
chicken	coriander
2 cloves of garlic	1 lb. shallots
2 almonds	1 teaspoonful
1 tablespoonful	granulated sugar
margarine	2 tomatoes
½ lb. desiccated coco-	2 bay leaves
nut or coconut milk	

Clean and wash the chicken. Melt the margarine. Put all the other ingredients, except the bay leaves and tomatoes, through a mincer and fry the mixed ingredients. Add the chicken and cook for about 3 minutes. Add about 2 teacupfuls of coconut milk (made with the desiccated coconut, see Yellow Rice recipe) and cook until it thickens. Place the cooked chicken in the grill pan and grill for about 5 minutes.

Grilled Lamb (Sate kambing) (for 4)

1 lb. lamb	¼ teaspoonful
1 onion	coriander
Salt and pepper to	1 clove of garlic
taste	Lemon juice

For the sauce

1 teacupful peanuts	½ teaspoonful ground
3 red chillies	ginger
1 clove garlic	1 onion
Lemon juice	

Cut the meat into squares of about 1 in. Mince the coriander, onion and garlic, mix this with the meat, pepper, salt and lemon juice. Thread on skewers, about four or five pieces to each, and grill. Serve with fried onion rings, a little vinegar and sauce made as follows: Put the peanuts through a mincer, fry with chopped onion, garlic, chillies and ginger, and add a little water. Finally, add lemon juice.

VEGETABLE DISHES

French Beans (Sambel goreng boontjes)

½ lb. meat or 1 pint	2 onions
shelled prawns	Salt
½ lb. desiccated	1 lb. French beans
coconut	3 chillies
1 bay leaf	Fat for frying

Mix the coconut with 6 or 7 teacupfuls of water, squash well and sieve. Cut up the meat into pieces about 1 in. square. Fry the onions a light brown, add the rest of the seasoning and the meat or prawns, fry, add the beans and the coconut milk. Bring to the boil and cook for a few minutes.

Urap (for 4)

Vegetables

¼ lb. French beans	¼ lb. soya bean
¼ lb. cabbage	sprouts
2 carrots	¼ lb. spinach
Cos lettuce	

NOTE: To obtain bean sprouts, put a cupful of soya beans in a damp sack in a damp atmosphere for 3 days and 3 nights. They should then be sprouting well and ready for use.

Seasoning

¼ lb. desiccated	1 teaspoonful sugar
coconut	4 red chillies
½ onion	2 cloves of garlic
1 bay leaf	Salt

Wash the vegetables, cut into pieces about 1 in. long, except carrots, which are cut into slices, and the spinach. Steam

vegetables together until three-quarters cooked. Put all seasoning through mincer, except coconut. Fry coconut in a little oil and then mix it with the minced seasoning and steamed vegetables and put in a fireproof dish. Heat through in a moderate oven. This dish is eaten as a savoury after the main course.

Mixed Vegetable Salad (Gado-gado) (for 4)

2 or 3 cabbage leaves	½ lb. bean sprouts
2 tomatoes	(see Urap recipe)
2 boiled potatoes	½ cucumber
½ lettuce	2 onions
Prawn crackers	2 hard-boiled eggs
A little margarine	

For the sauce

½ jar peanut butter	1½ tablespoonfuls
2 tablespoonfuls sugar	lemon juice
1 teaspoonful	1½ teacupfuls water
chilli powder	Salt to taste
½ tablespoonful margarine	

Wash and cut up cabbage. Cook it and bean sprouts separately. Slice tomatoes, cucumber, washed lettuce, boiled potatoes and eggs. Fry prawn crackers and sliced

A favourite Indonesian meat dish is Abon, made by first boiling beef until it is so soft it falls apart, and then frying it

onion separately. Arrange as follows. First put the cabbage on a plate, and on it the lettuce and bean sprouts, cucumber, potatoes, tomatoes, eggs, prawn crackers and fried onions. To make the sauce, fry chilli powder in margarine, add 1 teacupful of water, mix in sugar, salt and peanut butter, and stir until well mixed. Add ½ teacupful water with lemon juice. Boil for a few minutes.

HOT DISHES (containing Chilli)
Hot Tomato Dish

¼ onion	2 tomatoes
2 chillies	1½ tablespoonfuls
Juice of 1 lemon	water
Salt	

Slice onion, tomatoes and chillies very finely. Mix, add salt, lemon juice and water. Serve with rice, meat and a vegetable dish, and eat in *very* small quantities.

Hot Fried Tomato Dish

½ onion	4 red chillies
2 tomatoes	2 tablespoonfuls
Salt	margarine

Fry the sliced onion a golden brown in the margarine and add the finely sliced chillies. Add the sliced tomatoes and salt and fry for about 7 minutes.

EGG DISHES
Stuffed Omelet (for 4)

1½ lb. minced meat	2 cloves of garlic
1 onion	4 eggs
Pepper and salt	Margarine for frying

For the stuffing.—Slice onion and garlic and fry till golden brown in margarine, add pepper and salt. Put the minced meat in with the fried onions, etc., and keep frying until meat is cooked.

For the omelet.—Beat up the eggs with a pinch of salt. Melt a little fat in frying pan and pour in just enough of the beaten eggs to cover the bottom of pan. Cook until set, then toss over on to other side and spread with a portion of the filling and roll up. Repeat until eggs and filling are used.

Fried Eggs (for 4)

4 hard-boiled eggs	2 tablespoonfuls
1 onion	chillies
Margarine	3 tomatoes
Salt	

Peel the eggs and cut each egg in two. Slice onion, chillies and tomatoes, and fry in melted margarine, add the eggs and salt, and fry till vegetables are done.

Boiled-egg Dish (Sambel goreng telor) (for 4)

4 hard-boiled eggs	1 clove of garlic
2 tomatoes	½ onion
2 teacupfuls coconut	1 bay leaf
milk (see Yellow	½ teaspoonful sugar
Rice)	Salt
3 chillies	Margarine

Put the onion, garlic and chillies through the mincer and fry in a little margarine. Slice tomatoes into the frying pan, add seasoning and coconut milk, bring to the boil and cook until it thickens. Keep stirring to prevent curdling. Add the hard-boiled eggs and cook for about 2 minutes.

Egg Dish (Tjeploh asem) (for 4)

4 eggs	Salt and pepper
1 teaspoonful chilli	4 sliced tomatoes
powder	½ teaspoonful sugar
3 tablespoonfuls	3 tablespoonfuls
sliced onions	margarine
2 cloves of garlic	½ teacupful water

Fry the eggs in 1 tablespoonful of margarine. Add salt and pepper.
For the sauce.—Fry the sliced onion and garlic in 2 tablespoonfuls of margarine. Add chilli, tomatoes, water and sugar. Pour this sauce over the fried eggs.

MISCELLANEOUS
Fried Corn Fritters (Prekedel djagung) (for 4)

1 large can sweet	Salt and pepper to
corn	taste
5 stalks of spring	2 eggs
onions	2 tablespoonfuls
2 tablespoonfuls	sliced onions
margarine	Celery

Beat the eggs and mix with salt, pepper, onions, chopped spring onions, sliced celery and corn. Fry as for fritters.

Soya Bean Drink (Katjang idjo)

½ lb. soya beans	2 teacupfuls thick
½ teaspoonful ground	coconut milk (see
ginger	Yellow Rice)
A pinch of salt	4 tablespoonfuls
	sugar

Soak the soya beans for 1 hour in 3 teacupfuls of water. In the same water bring to the boil. Add sugar, salt and ginger, cook until thick. Add the coconut milk and stir to prevent curdling. Cook for about 10 minutes and serve hot.

Sosaties are generally eaten at a braaivleis, a kind of night-time picnic, cooked over an open fire

SOUTH AFRICA

*Including dishes of Afrikaans origin and
others brought from Malaya, described by
Mrs. Wrightson, author of "The Royal Hostess"*

Sosaties

1 *small fat leg of lamb or 2 lb. cut from fatty leg*	1 *tablespoonful curry powder*
1 *teaspoonful salt*	1 *tablespoonful sugar*
¼ *teaspoonful pepper*	2 *cupfuls vinegar*
2 *medium-sized chopped onions*	1 *tablespoonful fruit chutney*
2 *or 3 tablespoonfuls dripping*	1 *cupful cold water*
	6 *lemon or orange leaves coarsely chopped*

Cut the meat into small squares, season with salt and pepper, and put on to small wooden skewers, alternating meat and fat. Prepare a marinade as follows: Slice and chop the onions and brown them in a pan with dripping. Sprinkle in the curry powder and stir. Add the sugar, salt, pepper, vinegar, fruit chutney, water and lemon or orange leaves. Stir well. Put the skewered meat into a deep bowl and pour over it the marinade. Stand overnight, or longer, and stir so that all the meat is impregnated with the sauce. Remove the meat from the marinade and drain it. Grill over a hot fire (barbecue) or under an electric or gas grill for 10–15 minutes. The sauce should be heated, strained and served as gravy.

Robotie

A dish brought to South Africa by the Malays, who settled in the Cape in the early days.

2 *medium-sized sliced onions*	1 *teaspoonful salt*
2 *tablespoonfuls butter or dripping*	1 *tablespoonful vinegar*
1 *tablespoonful curry powder*	1 *lb. minced cooked beef or mutton*
1 *dessertspoonful sugar*	1 *thick slice bread*
	½ *pint milk*
	2 *eggs*

Fry the sliced onions in the butter or dripping until lightly browned. Sprinkle the curry powder over the onions, add salt, sugar, vinegar and meat, and mix well together. Soak the bread in the milk, then drain off the milk, mash the bread with a fork and add it to the meat mixture, together with 1 beaten egg. Turn into a buttered pie dish. Add sufficient milk to the milk drained from the bread to make up to ¾ cupful. Beat the remaining egg and mix it with the milk. Season with salt and pepper, and pour this over the meat mixture in the pie dish. Dot with small pieces of butter and stand the pie dish in a pan of water. Bake in a moderate oven for 30–40 minutes.

Pork with Sweet-Sour Sauce

1½ lb. belly of pork	Apples
Spinach	Pineapple
Tomatoes	Cucumber
Green peppers	Spring onions (or
Garlic and chillies to	other onions)
taste	Fat for frying
For the batter	
2 eggs	3 tablespoonfuls flour

Cut the pork into ¾-in. squares, dip in batter made with the eggs and flour (do not use any water or milk), and fry in deep hot fat until dark golden brown; drain and place on a large meat dish. Chop up coarsely all the vegetables and fruit, and put into a pan with about 2 tablespoonfuls of hot fat and cook for about 4 minutes; then pour over the meat. Finally, pour over the whole dish sauce made as follows:

1 tablespoonful corn-flour	1 tablespoonful sugar
1 tablespoonful malt vinegar	1 tablespoonful soya sauce (dark)
1½ cupfuls water	1 tablespoonful tomato sauce

Place all the ingredients except the tomato sauce in a pan and cook over a slow heat, stirring all the time, until the sauce has the consistency of treacle; add the tomato sauce.

NOTE: The sauce can be made first and reheated when needed.

Mos-bolletjies

These were originally made from fermented grape juice (mos) and are still fairly common in the wine-growing districts of the Western Cape. Because fermented grape juice is not easy to come by, raisins have been substituted.

¼ lb. raisins stoned and chopped finely	2 teacupfuls milk, scalded and cooled to blood temperature
2 cupfuls warm water (blood temperature)	
1 cake yeast	1 teaspoonful cinnamon
5 lb. flour	1 tablespoonful aniseed or grated nutmeg
6 oz. lard or good dripping	
1 tablespoonful salt	6 oz. butter
3 eggs	1 cupful sugar

Put the chopped raisins into a quart screw-topped jar, together with warm water. Cream the yeast cake with 1 tablespoonful of the sugar and add this to the raisins and water. Screw on the lid and place the jar in a warm place overnight for the mixture to ferment. Next morning, strain the yeast (which should be well risen) into a warmed bowl and add 1½–2 cupfuls of flour, beating into a smooth batter. Cover this sponge and stand in a warm place until bubbly and light. Mix the spices, salt and sugar with the remaining flour, and rub in the butter and lard finely. (All butter can be used if preferred.) When the sponge is nice and light, add the well-beaten eggs. Mix, and gradually add the flour mixture alternately with the scalded and cooled milk to blend into soft dough. A little more warm water can be added if necessary. Knead the dough for 10 minutes, cover and stand in a warm place until more than doubled in bulk. Turn on to a floured board, cut small pieces and form into balls. Place the *bolletjies* on a greased baking tin, close together, greasing lightly between them with a little cooking oil so that they will break apart easily when baked. Leave to rise in a warm place until very light, and bake in a hot oven for 20–25 minutes.

Koeksusters

1 lb. flour	4 teaspoonfuls baking powder
¼ teaspoonful salt	
Deep hot oil or fat for cooking	2 beaten eggs
	¼ lb. butter
A little milk	
For the syrup	
4 cupfuls sugar	3 cupfuls water

The syrup should be prepared a few hours before using and chilled thoroughly in a refrigerator.

Bring the sugar and water to the boil in a saucepan, stirring until the sugar is dissolved. Cool, then chill in refrigerator. The syrup can be flavoured with 1 teaspoonful cinnamon or 1 teaspoonful lemon essence if desired.

Sift the flour, salt and baking powder into a bowl, rub in the butter finely, then add the beaten eggs with a little milk to blend into a stiff dough. Roll out to ¼ in. thick and cut into strips approximately 4 by 2 in. Divide the strips into three tails, leaving the dough joined at one end. Plait the strips and press to join at the ends. Drop a few of the *koeksusters* at a time into the hot oil or fat, and cook until lightly browned and puffed. Lift out of the fat and drain for 1 minute on crumpled grease-proof paper, then drop at once into the chilled syrup. Turn over in the syrup, then lift out and drain on a sieve until dry. Store in a tin.

Melktert

For the pastry

¾ *lb. flour*	3 *tablespoonfuls*
¼ *teaspoonful salt*	*castor sugar*
2 *teaspoonfuls baking*	6 *oz. butter or mixed*
powder	*shortening*
¼ *teacupful milk*	1 *egg*
½ *teaspoonful vanilla essence (optional)*	

For the filling

1 *tablespoonful flour*	3 *tablespoonfuls*
1 *tablespoonful corn-*	*sugar*
flour	1 *teaspoonful cinna-*
4 *eggs (separated)*	*mon*
2 *pints milk*	

Sift the flour, salt and baking powder into a bowl; add the sugar and rub in the shortening until the mixture is the consistency of fine breadcrumbs. Beat the egg and mix with the milk; add vanilla essence if desired. Pour the liquid gradually into the dry mixture, stirring with a fork to blend it to a soft dough. The texture of the dough must be firm enough to roll out, but not dry.

For the filling.—Blend the flour and corn-flour into a thin paste with a little of the milk, then put the remaining milk on to boil with the sugar. Separate the eggs, beating the yolks well and adding them to the flour and cornflour mixture. Pour the hot milk on to this mixture, stirring vigorously all the time, then return to the pan and cook, stirring constantly, until thickened. Remove from heat and cool a little. Beat the egg-whites until stiff and fold them into the mixture.

Lightly grease two deep tart-plates and line them with the pastry rolled out to ¼ in. thick. Pour in the cooked filling and bake in a moderate oven for about 20–25 minutes. Sprinkle the cinnamon over the tarts just before baking.

Photo: *Royal Baking Powder*

It is said that Melktert (the Afrikaans for milk tart) was a favourite of Queen Elizabeth, the Queen Mother, during the Royal Tour of South Africa

AUSTRALIA

*A fascinating cuisine full of exciting flavour contrasts
that will appeal to all lovers of good food,
described by Nancy Gepp*

FISH

FISH is plentiful in Australian waters, but of different varieties from those found in the sea surrounding the United Kingdom. Some of the salt-water fish are as follows:—

Whiting—has a very delicate flavour and is one of the more expensive fish.

Mullet—similar in shape and texture to whiting, but not so delicate in flavour.

Flounder—can be found in the shallows of the bay beaches and is often caught by spearing. On a summer's night it is quite usual to see bathers with a torch attached to a stick walking along at the edge of the water. The light attracts the flounder and then it is speared. It is a flat fish somewhat similar in shape to plaice.

Schnapper—is a larger fish with a distinctive flavour and is very popular, usually sold in cutlets.

Flathead—as its name suggests, has a flat head. It has a very nice flavour and is often baked.

Bream—has a slightly coarser flesh than whiting and is usually baked whole, coated in breadcrumbs and stuffed.

Garfish—is a small thin fish with a long, hard, pointed nose. It is usually coated in flour, egg and breadcrumbs after the nose has been pushed into the tail, forming a circle. Shallow-frying is the usual method of cooking.

Turbot—is similar in size to schnapper and is also mainly sold in cutlets.

Pike—is a large fish with a pointed nose and may be cooked whole or in cutlets.

Other fish include: Kingfish, Barracouta, Barramundi, Trumpeter, Nannygai or Pearl Perch, John Dory, Gummy Shank, Perch, Jackass Fish, Tuna, Mackerel.

Crayfish—vary from lobster in that they have a long fat tail with a lot of flesh in it, but the claws are small in comparison.

Oysters.—These are commercially "grown" in some places around the Australian coast. They are quite large and juicy and much cheaper than in Britain.

Freshwater Fish

Murray Cod—is found only in the Murray River, which is over 1,000 miles long and is Australia's longest river. Some have been caught weighing up to 100 lb. For eating they must be over 18 in. long.

Rainbow and Spotted Trout—are caught mainly by amateur fishermen and rarely appear in the shops. They can be caught only in the appropriate season. The flesh is white and the skin is either spotted or multi-coloured.

Salmon Trout—are also seasonal and have pale pink flesh.

Fish Puff (for 6)

6 slices of stale bread, buttered and cut into cubes	4 oz. finely grated cheese
2 eggs	8 oz. flaked, cooked fish
½ teaspoonful Worcester sauce	Salt and Cayenne pepper
½ pint milk	

Place layers of bread cubes, cheese and fish alternately in a greased dish, the top layer being bread. Beat the eggs, add milk, sauce and seasonings, and strain over the contents of dish. Bake in a slow oven for 1 hour.

Oyster Pie (for 6)

½ pint thick white sauce (see Sauces chapter)	1 teaspoonful lemon juice
1 tablespoonful white wine (Chablis or Sauternes)	8 oz. rough puff pastry
1 dozen oysters	Salt and Cayenne pepper

Beard and blanch the oysters, then add them to the white sauce with the lemon juice, seasonings and wine. Allow the mixture to get cold. Roll out half the pastry and line a deep 7-in. tart plate. Add the filling and cover with remainder of pastry. Make a slit in the top, brush with egg glaze and bake in a hot oven for 30–35 minutes.

Schnapper with Mushroom Sauce (for 6)

6 schnapper cutlets
Salt and pepper
½ pint milk
Sprigs of parsley

For the sauce
1 oz. butter
½ pint water
2 tablespoonfuls
  cream
Salt and pepper
¼ lb. mushrooms
1 tablespoonful corn-
  flour
½ gill sherry

Wash the cutlets and place in a baking dish with the milk, seasoning and parsley. Bake gently for 40 minutes, turning the fish over after 20 minutes. Melt the butter in a pan, and add the peeled and chopped mushrooms. Cook for 5 minutes. Blend the corn-flour with a little of the water and add the rest to the mushrooms with the sherry. Cover the pan and cook gently until the mushrooms are tender. Pour some of the boiling liquid on to the corn-flour, return to the pan and stir until boiling. Cook for 2 minutes. Season well, add the cream and do not allow the sauce to boil. Lift on to a hot dish and add the sauce.

For a main meal Garden Salad with slices of luncheon meat and home-made mayonnaise in the centre

MEAT DISHES

Crown Roast of Lamb with Accompaniments (for 6–8)

A loin of lamb con-
  sisting of about 12
  chops
1 lb. potatoes
Gravy

2 tablespoonfuls fat
1 lb. new carrots
1 lb. peas
12 1-in. cubes of
  bread

Trim the fat from the meat and scrape the flesh from the top 2-in. of the bones. Bend the joint round to form a circle, having the skin side inwards. Secure with skewers and string. Place a bread cube over each bone. Weigh the meat and calculate cooking time. Roast until tender, adding the potatoes ¾ hour before serving.

Cook carrots and peas separately. When joint is cooked, remove string and bread, and place on hot serving dish. Fill the centre with some of the carrots and peas (serve the rest separately), put the potatoes round the meat and place a cutlet frill on each chop bone. Serve gravy separately.

Inside-out Pie (for 6–8)

For the case

1 lb. minced steak
1 tablespoonful
  chopped parsley
Tomato halves

1 egg
2 oz. soft white
  breadcrumbs
Bacon rolls

Salt and pepper

For the filling

½ pint medium white
  sauce (see Sauces
  chapter)
½ cupful cooked peas

4-oz can sweet corn
  kernels
½ cupful cooked diced
  carrots

Mix the steak, crumbs, parsley, seasonings and egg together and press it evenly on to the bottom and sides of a deep 8-in. diameter oven-ware plate. Combine the sauce and vegetables, season well and put into the uncooked meat case. Cover with a piece of greased paper and bake in a moderate oven for 30 minutes. Garnish with grilled tomatoes and bacon.

Liver Patties with Pineapple (for 6)

1 lb. calf's liver	1 can pineapple slices
½ level teaspoonful	(6 rings)
salt	4 oz. soft white
1 egg or 3 table-	breadcrumbs
spoonfuls milk	6 bacon rashers
A little pepper	½ oz. fat

For the garnish

Green peas	Brown gravy made
Potato purée	with pineapple
	juice

Wash and dry the liver, then pass it through the mincer. Mix in the breadcrumbs, salt, pepper and egg or milk. Form into 6 patties, wrap a piece of bacon round each and secure with a cocktail stick. Stand a patty on each pineapple ring. Heat the fat in a baking tin and bake the patties for ½ hour in a moderate oven. Serve with vegetables and gravy.

Pork and Prune Casserole (for 6)

1 lb. pork fillets	4 oz. cooked prunes
Salt and pepper	1 oz. flour
1 large onion, peeled	1 oz. fat
and cut into rings	1 lb. potatoes, peeled
Green vegetables in	and sliced, or tiny
season	new potatoes
½ pint prune juice	

Cut the meat into neat pieces. Add the seasonings to the flour and toss the meat in it. Melt the fat and fry the meat until browned. Place a layer of potatoes in a casserole, then onion, pork, prunes, onion and finish with potatoes. Season each layer. Pour in the prune liquor. Put the lid on tightly and cook in a moderate oven for 1–1¼ hours. Serve green vegetables separately.

VEGETABLE DISHES

Cauliflower Pie

1 large cauliflower	1 large onion
2 oz. cheese (grated)	Salt and pepper
1 dessertspoonful	4 tablespoonfuls
chopped parsley	milk
2 oz. butter or mar-	1 lb. tomatoes
garine	1 lb. potatoes, boiled

Cook the cauliflower until tender, then beat it until creamy with the butter, cheese, seasonings, parsley and half the milk. Line a deep casserole with the mixture and place on top the peeled, sliced tomatoes, and peeled and finely chopped onion with seasoning. Mash the potatoes with the rest of the milk and spread on top. Mark the top with a fork, dot with butter and bake for 20–30 minutes in a moderate oven.

Vegetable Cheese Shortcake

For the shortcake

8 oz. self-raising flour	½ teaspoonful salt
¼ teaspoonful dry	Pinch of Cayenne
mustard	pepper
2 oz. butter	3 oz. finely grated
1 egg	cheese
4 oz. milk (approx.)	

For the filling

½ pint medium white	Salt
sauce (see Sauces	1 onion, diced and
chapter)	cooked without
½ cupful cooked peas	browning
½ cupful cooked	½ cupful tomato pulp
diced carrots	Cayenne pepper

For the garnish: Bacon rolls

Sift the flour and seasonings together. Rub in the butter, add the cheese and mix to a soft dough with the beaten egg and as much milk as is necessary to obtain the correct consistency. Knead on a lightly floured board. Roll out to ½ in. thickness and cut with a 3-in. round plain cutter. Brush the surface with milk and bake in a hot oven for 10–12 minutes. Combine the vegetables with the white sauce and season well. Slit each shortcake in half. Put some of the filling on the base, cover with the top, and spoon extra filling over. Serve with grilled bacon rolls.

If desired, the shortcake can be made by baking the dough in two greased 7-in. sandwich tins, then sandwiching the cakes together with filling, and pouring the remainder of the filling on top.

Another variation is to use fish or meat fillings.

SALADS

Apple, Celery and Walnut Salad (for 6)

3 eating apples	1 lettuce
2 oz. chopped	2 tablespoonfuls
walnuts	salad cream or
Salt and pepper	mayonnaise
6 stalks of celery	

"Peaches" made from Queen Cake mixture baked in gem irons. Two cakes are put together with butter cream, brushed with warmed apricot jam and tossed in pink-coloured granulated sugar

Wash the apples and celery and cut them into small dice, leaving the rosy skin on the apples. Mix with the walnuts, salad cream and seasonings. Spoon into lettuce shells to serve.

This salad makes a nice accompaniment to cold meat.

For a variation, cut a slice from the top of the apples and scoop out the flesh. Make the salad and stuff the apples with the mixture, replacing the tops.

Garden Salad

In Australia this salad is varied according to taste, adding fruits as well as vegetables to the dish. It may be made up from the following selection, arranged attractively on a large platter:

Vegetables

Grated raw carrot	Cooked potato
Grated raw beetroot	Grated raw turnip
Radish roses	Celery curls
Spring onions	Lettuce
Sliced cucumber	Spiced beetroot slices
Cooked cauliflower sprigs	Raw tomato halves or slices
Cooked sweet corn kernels	Cooked French beans
	Cooked asparagus
Cooked garden peas	

Fruits

Apricot halves	Peach halves
Pineapple slices	Banana
Grated apple	Grapefruit sections
Orange slices	Grapes

The dressing to accompany these salad platters is often made with cream as a base and thinned down with juice from either the pineapples, apples, cucumbers or oranges. This gives an added "bite" to the salad.

Dressing for a Garden Salad

3 tablespoonfuls whipped cream	1 dessertspoonful white vinegar
Salt and pepper	1 tablespoonful fruit or cucumber juice
1 teaspoonful sugar	
Mustard	

Mix the seasonings, sugar and vinegar together, then stir them into the cream. Add the fruit juice and leave to stand for a while before serving. A tablespoonful of finely diced fruit or cucumber may also be added if liked.

Pineapple and Cheese Slouch Hats (for 6)

6 slices of pineapple (fresh or canned)	Salt and Cayenne pepper
2 tablespoonfuls mayonnaise	Thin strips of red pepper or tomato skin for the hat-bands
Lettuce leaves	
4 oz. grated cheese	

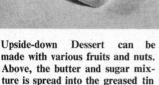

Upside-down Dessert can be made with various fruits and nuts. Above, the butter and sugar mixture is spread into the greased tin

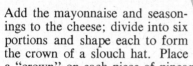

The fruit is arranged in patterns. Dates and walnuts are used here

Add the mayonnaise and seasonings to the cheese; divide into six portions and shape each to form the crown of a slouch hat. Place a "crown" on each piece of pineapple and finish with the red strip to form the hatband. Serve on a lettuce leaf.

This salad may be served on its own or as an accompaniment to cold cooked pork or other meat.

Stuffed Tomato Salad (for 6)

6 large round tomatoes	½ cupful cooked peas
½ cupful cooked diced carrots	½ cupful diced cucumber
Salt and pepper	2 tablespoonfuls mayonnaise
1 lettuce	Parsley sprigs

Wash the tomatoes and remove a slice from the stem end of each. Scoop out the flesh and cut it into dice. Turn the tomato cases upside down to drain. Mix the drained tomato pulp with the other vegetables, seasonings and mayonnaise. Spoon the mixture into the tomatoes, replace "caps" and serve on lettuce leaves garnished with parsley.

Summer Salad (for 6)

1 packet lemon table jelly	1 small lettuce
½ cupful finely diced cucumber	1 tablespoonful vinegar
½ cupful cooked peas	½ cupful finely grated carrot
½ cupful finely diced green pepper or celery	½ cupful drained crushed pineapple
4 oz. large cream crackers	½ teaspoonful salt
	4 oz. packet cream cheese triangles
⅛ teaspoonful pepper	

This is a very good dish for picnics or suppers on a hot evening.

Make the jelly, using the vinegar made up to 1 pint with hot water. Allow to cool until it begins to set, then add the vegetables and pineapple and season to taste. Pour into a plain mould and leave until firm. Turn out on to a bed of lettuce leaves, stand cheese wedges round the base and serve biscuits separately.

Triple Salad (for 6)

1 large Spanish onion	Sugar
1 lb. tomatoes	Salt and pepper
1 apple cucumber or ½ a long cucumber	2 tablespoonfuls white vinegar

Peel the vegetables and cut them all into very thin slices. Arrange them in a dish, keeping them separate. Sprinkle all with salt and pepper, and the tomatoes with a little sugar. Pour the vinegar over and allow to stand for at least 1 hour before serving.

HOT DESSERTS

Bananas in Raisin Sauce (for 6)

6 bananas	Juice of 1 lemon
3 oz. seedless raisins	2 level tablespoonfuls
3 level tablespoonfuls	cornflour
honey	¼ oz., butter
½ pint water	

Peel the bananas, cut them in half lengthwise, then across. Melt the butter in an oven-ware dish and place the bananas in it. Boil the raisins in ¼ pint water for 5 minutes, then add the honey and lemon juice. Blend the cornflour with ¼ pint water, add some of the raisin mixture, return all to the pan and stir until boiling. Cook for 2 minutes until the mixture clears. Pour it over the bananas and bake for 20 minutes in a moderate oven.

sugar gradually, leaving 1 teaspoonful until later. Pile the meringue on top of the apples, decorate with cherries and angelica, sprinkle the teaspoonful of sugar over and bake in a cool oven for 10 minutes until the meringue is a golden brown.

The remainder of the batter is spread on top (top right); the cake is turned out upside down (above) and decorated with whipped cream and more walnuts before cutting (right)

Hot Fruit Trifle

1 7-in. round of fat-	2 tablespoonfuls
less sponge cake	sherry
2 egg-whites	1 cupful stewed
3 oz. castor sugar	apple
Angelica	Pinch of salt
2 glacé cherries	

Stand the sponge in an 8-in. oven-ware pie plate and pour the sherry over. Spread the apple on top. Add salt to the egg-whites and beat them until stiff. Add the

This recipe may be varied by using any of the following fruits: 1 cupful drained stewed rhubarb; 1 cupful crushed pineapple; 1 cupful drained sliced peaches; 1 cupful drained preserved apricots; 1 cupful drained preserved or fresh mashed pears.

Peach Caramel Crumble (for 8)

1-lb. can sliced peaches	½ pint milk
2 oz. moist brown sugar	1 oz. butter
	1 oz. flour
	1 egg

For the crumble topping

2 oz. self-raising flour	1 oz. butter
1 oz. moist brown sugar	Pinch of salt
	2 oz. cake crumbs
1 oz. coconut	

Strain the liquid from the fruit and put the peaches into an oven-ware dish. Melt the butter in a pan, add the sugar and stir for 1 minute. Stir in the flour, cook for 1 minute, then add the milk and cook over the flame until the mixture boils. Allow to stand a little, then stir in the egg-yolk and cook, but do not boil. Beat the egg-white stiffly, then fold it in. Pour the sauce over the peaches.

Sift the flour and salt, rub in the butter, mix in remainder of the ingredients and sprinkle on top. Bake for 20 minutes in a moderate oven.

If the peach juice is thickened with a little cornflour, it can be used as an accompanying sauce.

Pineapple Upside-down Dessert (for 8)

2 oz. butter	2 oz. moist brown sugar
6 rings canned pineapple	A few walnut halves

For the batter

2 oz. butter	A little milk
Vanilla essence	3 oz. castor sugar
6 oz. self-raising flour	1 egg
Pinch of salt	

Melt the butter in a pan, add the sugar and cook for 1 minute. Spread it into a greased oblong tin 6 in. × 8 in. Drain the juice from the pineapple and place the rings on to the caramel mixture, putting the walnuts between. Cream the butter and sugar with the vanilla. Add the egg gradually and beat well. Fold in the sifted flour and salt alternately with the milk so as to keep the mixture the correct consistency. Spread the batter over the pineapple and bake for 35 minutes in a moderately cool oven. Turn out with the pineaple on top.

This recipe can be used hot as a dessert, or allowed to cool and served as a cake. It can also be made with other fruits—see photographs on previous page.

Pumpkin Pie (for 6)

½ pint pumpkin pulp	Shortcrust pastry made with 6 oz. flour (see Pastry chapter)
½ pint milk	
¼ teaspoonful grated nutmeg or mace	
2 oz. sugar	2 eggs

To prepare the pulp.—Cut a ripe pumpkin into thick slices. Pare off the skin and remove seeds. Cook gently with very little water until tender, then pass through a fine sieve and measure the pulp.

Separate the egg-yolks from the whites, beat the yolks and sugar together, add the spice, then the pumpkin pulp and milk. Fold in the stiffly beaten egg-whites. Roll out the pastry and cut a 1-in. strip to line the edge of the pie dish. Pour in the filling; cover with the pastry. Cut a slit in the top; glaze with milk and bake in a moderately hot oven for 20–30 minutes.

COLD DESSERTS

Apple Blossom Pie (for 8)

This recipe won first prize as Australia's National Pie in a nation-wide competition. 7-in. baked sweet pastry case.

1st layer

2 or 3 cooking apples	2 oz. sugar
½ cupful water	2 passionfruit

2nd layer

½ can sweetened condensed milk	1 egg-yolk
	Juice of 1 lemon

3rd layer

1 level dessertspoonful gelatine	1 egg-white
½ teaspoonful lemon essence	Juice from the cooked apples made up to ¾ cupful with water
Sweetened whipped cream	Red colouring

Peel, core and slice the apples. Place in a pan with sugar and water and cook until soft. Drain off the syrup and keep for third layer. Add the passionfruit pulp. Cool the mixture and put into pastry case.

Combine condensed milk with egg-yolk and lemon juice and beat until well mixed. Spread over the apple layer. Soak gelatine well in the cold apple syrup, then dissolve it over hot water, add the lemon essence and a few drops of red colouring. Allow to cool and become partly set. Beat until it becomes light and fluffy, then fold in the stiffly beaten egg-white. Pile on top of pie. Decorate with the cream by using a piping bag and tube.

Melon or Pineapple Fruit Salad

1 *large canteloup or*
  honeydew melon or
1 *large pineapple*

A bunch of mixed
  flowers or leaves
1-lb. can Australian
  tropical fruit salad

Wash and dry the fruit. Cut a slice from the stem end of the melon or from the top of the pineapple. Remove the pulp, discarding the seeds or the hard core. Cut the fruit into dice and mix it with the fruit salad. Return the fruit salad to the case and replace the cap. Stand it on a glass platter and arrange the flowers or leaves round its base. Chill before serving.

This makes a very attractive centre-piece for the table, and the top is removed when the fruit salad is required.

Passionfruit Flummery (for 6–8)

3 *eggs*
Juice of 1 lemon
1 *cupful water*
½ *cupful sugar*

3 *passionfruit*
1 *dessertspoonful*
  gelatine
¾ *cupful milk*

Separate the egg-whites from the yolks and put the yolks in a large bowl with the passionfruit pulp, lemon juice, milk and sugar. Soak the gelatine in the water for 10 minutes, then dissolve it over hot water and add to the other ingredients. Leave to become quite cold, then beat it to a froth. Fold in the stiffly beaten egg-whites and transfer to a glass serving dish to set.

Passionfruit Pavlova (for 8–10)

4 *egg-whites*
8 *oz. castor sugar*
1 *level teaspoonful*
  vanilla

1 *level teaspoonful*
  cornflour
1 *level teaspoonful*
  vinegar

A pinch of salt

For the decoration

3 *passionfruit*

¼ *pint whipped cream*

Add the salt to the egg-whites and beat them until stiff and fluffy. Gradually beat in half the sugar, then fold in the rest.

Apple Blossom Pie, the first prize-winner as Australia's National Pie in a nation-wide competition, has a three-layer filling

Next sift the cornflour over the surface and add the vanilla and vinegar. Fold these in, then transfer the mixture to an 8-in. well-buttered oven-ware dish. Bake in a cool oven for 1¼ hours. Turn out and, when cold, spread the underside with the cream. Cut passionfruit in half, scoop out pulp and put on top of the cream.

Peach Marshmallows (for 6)

6 rounds of fatless sponge cake	3 tablespoonfuls sherry
6 canned peach halves	¼ pint red table jelly

For the marshmallow

2 level teaspoonfuls gelatine	¾ cupful cold water
4 oz. castor sugar	½ teaspoonful vanilla essence

2 egg-whites

For the decoration

3 glacé cherries	Angelica

Sprinkle a dessertspoonful of sherry over each piece of sponge. Set a little jelly in the hollows of the peach halves, then place them, cut side down, on the sponge. Dry the rounded side of each peach with a soft cloth (this prevents the marshmallow from sliding off). Soak the gelatine in the cold water, then dissolve it over hot water. Beat the egg-whites stiffly and gradually beat in the gelatine, then the sugar and vanilla. Pour the marshmallow smoothly over each peach, completely covering the sponge as well. Decorate with a half-cherry and leaves cut from angelica.

Pineapple Whip (for 6)

1-lb. can crushed pineapple	1 level tablespoonful gelatine
A small strip of angelica	2 glacé cherries Whipped cream

Strain the juice from the pineapple and make the liquid up to ½ pint with water. Soak the gelatine in a little cold water, then dissolve it over hot water. Place the pineapple pulp, liquid and gelatine in a bowl and put in a very cold place until it begins to set. Whisk until it becomes light and frothy. Leave to set, then pile it into a serving dish. Decorate with whipped cream, cherry slices and thin strips of angelica.

SAVOURIES

Apple Bites (for about 48 savouries)

2 eating apples	1 oz. soft cream cheese
1 tablespoonful mayonnaise	1 oz. finely chopped walnuts
48 cocktail sticks	

Wash and dry the apples, leaving the skin on, and cut each into 24 cubes. Dry them well. Soften the cream cheese and mix in mayonnaise. Cover each apple cube with the cheese mixture, toss in the walnuts and roll into a ball. Impale each "bite" on a cocktail stick to serve.

Cheddar Cheesettes (for 24 savouries)

24 ½-in. cubes of fresh bread	2 oz. finely grated dry Cheddar cheese
1 oz. butter (melted)	1 egg
Salt and pepper	

Beat the egg well, add the butter and seasonings. Dip each bread cube into the egg mixture, drain off any excess, then toss in the cheese. Stand on a greased baking tray and cook for 10 minutes in a hot oven. Serve hot.

Curried Pineapple Titbits (for about 48 savouries)

1-lb. can of pineapple cubes or rings	4 oz. plain flour
	Pinch of salt
1 level teaspoonful curry powder	2 tablespoonfuls salad oil
1 egg-white	A little tepid water
	Fat for deep frying

Drain the liquid from the pineapple and dry each portion. If pineapple rings are used, cut each one into eight. Sift the flour, salt and curry powder together. Add the oil and stir it in, then add the water, keeping the batter fairly stiff. Allow it to stand for ½ hour. Fold in the stiffly beaten egg-white. Dip each piece of pineapple into the batter and deep-fry a golden brown. Serve hot. These savouries may be cooked before they are required and reheated.

Devilled Almond Croûtes (for 12 savouries)

2 oz. butter	12 rounds of bread
2 oz. finely grated cheese	1½ in. in diameter
1 heaped tablespoonful sweet chutney	2 oz. finely chopped almonds or almond nibs
1 dessertspoonful chopped parsley	Salt and Cayenne pepper

Melt the butter in a pan and brush one side of the bread with it. Sprinkle this side with some of the cheese and brown under a grill. Add the almonds to the remainder of the butter and cook to a golden brown. Add the cheese, chutney, seasonings and parsley, and heat until the cheese starts to melt. Spread on to the untoasted side of the croûtes. These savouries may be served hot or cold.

Open Sandwich Grill (for 4, or 16 pieces)

4 slices stale bread	4 oz. bacon rashers
4 small tomatoes	2 oz. sliced processed
Salt, pepper	cheese
Parsley sprigs	

Toast the bread on one side only. Cut the rind from the bacon and place the bacon on the untoasted side of the bread. Cook under the grill until the bacon fat is clear. Skin and slice the tomatoes and put them on top of the bacon, season well and cover with the cheese slices. Return to the grill until the cheese is brown and bubbly. Serve hot, garnished with sprigs of parsley.

This savoury may be served whole as an after-theatre snack, or cut into finger lengths for a buffet supper, etc.

SCONES, BISCUITS, CAKES

Anzac Biscuits (for 24 biscuits)

2 oz. butter
½ level teaspoonful
   bicarbonate of soda
1 teaspoonful Golden
   Syrup
4 oz. castor sugar
1 tablespoonful
   boiling water
3 oz. plain flour
4 oz. rolled oats

Melt the butter and Golden Syrup in a pan. Dissolve the soda in the water and add to the butter and syrup. Stir into the dry ingredients and mix well. Put on to a greased tray in small heaps, allowing room for the mixture to spread. Bake for 10 minutes in a cool oven. Lift on to a cooling tray before they become set.

Apricot and Walnut Loaves (for 2 loaves)

4 oz. dried apricots
Pinch of salt
2 oz. butter
1 egg
8 oz. self-raising flour
4 oz. castor sugar
2 oz. chopped walnuts
¼ pint milk

Wash the apricots and soak them for 1 hour. Drain and dry them, and cut into small pieces. Sift the flour, salt and sugar together.

Rub in the butter. Add the apricots and walnuts, and mix to a soft dough with the beaten egg and milk. Half-fill two nut-loaf tins; put the lids tightly on and cook in an upright position for 40 minutes in a moderately hot oven. Remove the loaves from the tins to cool and next day serve them sliced and spread with butter.

The mixture can be baked in two 1 lb. cocoa or baking-powder tins or in open loaf tins.

Date Slice (for 32 fingers)

12 oz. stoned dates	5 oz. butter
1 teaspoonful	1 teacupful water
bicarbonate of soda	8 oz. flaked oats
Pinch of salt	6 oz. self-raising flour
4 oz. castor sugar	

Place the dates, water and soda in a pan,

Gem irons—used here to make Gem Scones—can also be used for Snowballs and other fancy cakes

and cook until the dates are soft. Mash them well and keep the mixture warm. Sift the flour, salt and sugar together, add the oats. Rub in the butter. Press half into a greased baking tray 10 in. × 9 in. Spread the date mixture over, then sprinkle on and press down the remainder of the oats mixture. Bake for 25 minutes in a moderate oven. Allow to cool a little, then cut into finger lengths and leave until quite cold before storing.

Eggless Spicy Apple Cake

4 oz. butter	6 oz. self-raising flour
¾ cupful stewed apple	4 oz. sugar
¼ level teaspoonful ground nutmeg	1 level teaspoonful bicarbonate of soda
½ level teaspoonful ground cinnamon	1 level teaspoonful cocoa
3 oz. seedless raisins	

Cream the butter and sugar. Add the warm apple with the soda mixed in. Stir in the sifted flour, cocoa and spices mixed with the fruit. Transfer to a lined 7-in cake tin. Bake for 1 hour in a cool oven. Remove from tin and, when cold, ice with lemon water icing and dust the surface with ground cinnamon.

Gem Scones (for 24 scones)

2 oz. butter	3 oz. milk (approx.)
Vanilla essence	3 oz. castor sugar
8 oz. self-raising flour	1 egg
Pinch of salt	

A gem iron is a set of twelve deep semicircles joined together. As the cake batter rises to a dome, a round cake is the result. Deep bun tins are the next best thing to use.

Put the greased gem irons to heat. Cream the butter and sugar with the vanilla added. Add the egg gradually and beat well. Fold in the sifted flour and salt alternately with the milk to make a very soft mixture, similar in consistency to a cake batter. Quickly half-fill each container of the gem irons. Return to the hot oven and bake for 12–15 minutes. Turn out to cool and, when quite cold, serve slit in half and buttered.

In Australia the gem irons are also used for the baking of cake batters to be made into snowballs, peaches (like those made from Queen Cake mixture and shown on page 551) and other fancy cakes.

Jelly Biscuits (for 24 biscuits)

4 oz. butter	2 oz. cornflour
A little lemon essence	1 oz. castor sugar
1 packet (4 oz.) strawberry or raspberry jelly crystals	1 small egg
	2 oz. coconut
	4 oz. self-raising flour
Pinch of salt	

Cream the butter and sugar with the lemon essence. Add the egg gradually and beat well. Stir in the jelly crystals and coconut, then the sifted flour, cornflour and salt. Roll into 24 balls, place on a greased tray and flatten with the blade of a knife. Bake in a cool oven for 15 minutes. Allow to get quite cool before storing.

Lamingtons (for 12 or 16 cakes)

These are a favourite with Australians.

For the cake batter

4 oz. butter	A little milk
Vanilla essence	6 oz. castor sugar
10 oz. self-raising flour	2 eggs
	Pinch of salt
Raspberry jam	

For the coating

7 oz. sifted icing sugar	1 oz. cocoa
3 tablespoonfuls boiling water	4 oz. desiccated coconut

Cream the butter and sugar with the vanilla. Add the eggs gradually and beat well. Fold in the sifted flour and salt alternately with the milk to keep the mixture the correct consistency. Spread it into a prepared 8-in. square or 6-in. × 8-in oblong cake tin and bake for 50–60 minutes in a moderately cool oven.

Next day, slit the cake through the centre and spread with the raspberry jam. Place the two layers together again and cut into 2-in. squares.

Put the icing sugar in a bowl, make a well in the centre and add the cocoa. Pour the boiling water slowly on to the cocoa and at the same time stir with a wooden spoon, gradually working in the icing sugar. Add more water if necessary. Keep the icing thin by standing it over a bowl of hot water.

Put a square of cake on the prongs of a fork and dip it into the chocolate icing. Allow any excess to drip off, then toss the cake into the coconut.

When quite set, store in an airtight tin.

A national favourite, Lamingtons are coated with chocolate icing and desiccated coconut

Puffed Wheat Cookies (for 36 biscuits)

4 oz. butter	Pinch of salt
Vanilla essence	3 oz. castor sugar
5 oz. plain flour	1 egg
3 oz. puffed wheat	

Cream the butter and sugar with the vanilla. Add the egg gradually and beat well. Stir in the sifted flour and salt, then the puffed wheat. Place in dessertspoonfuls fairly well spaced apart on a greased baking tray. Bake for 10 minutes in a moderately cool oven, when they should be golden and crisp.

Pumpkin Sultana Cake (Eggless)

3 oz. butter	⅔ cupful castor sugar
Vanilla essence	1 cupful cooked
2 cupfuls self-raising	mashed pumpkin
flour	Pinch of salt
½ cupful milk	½ cupful sultanas

Cream the butter and sugar with the vanilla added. Stir in the pumpkin and mix well. Fold in the sifted flour and salt alternately with the milk, to keep the mixture the correct consistency. Lastly, fold in the sultanas. Transfer to an 8-in. square papered tin and bake in a cool oven for 1½ hours. Allow to stand for 15 minutes before turning out. When quite cold, ice with lemon butter icing (see chapter on Icings for method) and top with chopped peel.

Raisin-and-Walnut Slice

4 oz. butter	8 oz. plain flour
3 oz. castor sugar	Pinch of salt
1 egg	1 level teaspoonful
4 oz. raisins	baking powder
2 oz. chopped walnuts	2 tablespoonfuls milk

Cream the butter and sugar, add the egg and beat well. Stir in the raisins and walnuts, then the sifted flour, salt and baking powder, adding sufficient milk to make a soft mixture. Spread into a greased tin 8½ in. by 11 in., and bake for 25 minutes in a moderate oven. Allow to cool a little, then cut into 24 pieces. Leave in the tin to become cold before storing in an airtight tin.

NEW ZEALAND

Cake-making is a special national skill, and recipes brought out by pioneering ancestors are still used

THE New Zealand woman is a very skilled cake-maker. She can be ranked as an equal with the famous Belgian *pâtissiers*.

It is at tea and supper parties that she displays her special skill. A New Zealand tea table is something very special. It will include such items as scones made with butter and spread thickly with it; a home-made fruit or nut loaf also spread with butter; sandwiches such as oyster and brown bread, and asparagus rolls; pikelets or drop scones made with butter and spread with it, and biscuits and large cakes in great variety.

Women vie with each other in the quality and variety of food provided at these teas, and this is probably responsible for the development of a number of their excellent recipes. While many of these have been invented by present-day New Zealanders, others are treasured family recipes brought out by pioneer grandmothers and great-grandmothers over a hundred years ago.

The most popular cake of all is a light sponge made with fresh eggs and butter and filled with a mixture of whipped cream and passionfruit pulp or with a butter cream.

Nuts and dried fruits are used liberally in New Zealand cakes, and much wholemeal flour, giving variety in flavour and texture. The combination of flavours when butter and nuts or butter and brown sugar are used together is particularly pleasant.

The following typical New Zealand recipes are supplied by the Butter Information Council.

Anzac Nutties (enough for 24 small biscuits)

2 oz. wholemeal flour	2 oz. butter
4 oz. brown sugar	2 oz. white flour
2 oz. desiccated coconut	1 level tablespoonful Golden Syrup
1 tablespoonful hot water	½ level teaspoonful bicarbonate of soda
1 oz. chopped nuts	

Mix all the dry ingredients in a bowl. Melt the butter and syrup until hot but not boiling. Mix the water and soda and add both liquids to the dry ingredients. Mix well. Roll in small balls and place on baking trays, leaving plenty of room for spreading. Bake in a moderate oven for about 20 minutes. Leave on the trays to cool, when they will become quite crisp.

Fudge Fingers (no baking needed)

½ lb. sweet biscuits	4 oz. butter
4 oz. granulated sugar	3 level tablespoonfuls cocoa
Pinch of salt	2 tablespoonfuls milk
4 oz. chopped walnuts	Vanilla essence or rum or brandy
Chocolate icing	Desiccated coconut

Put the biscuits through the mincer or crush them to coarse crumbs with a rolling pin. Put butter, sugar, cocoa, salt and milk in a saucepan and bring to the boil. Add walnuts and flavouring, mix well and press into a greased tin about 9 in. × 6 in. Leave to set. Ice the top with chocolate icing and sprinkle with desiccated coconut. Cut in fingers to serve.

Shortbread Biscuits

4 oz. butter	Glacé cherries
6 oz. plain flour	2 oz. icing sugar
Pinch of salt	1 oz. cornflour
Vanilla essence	

Cream the butter and icing sugar until light and soft. Gradually work in the flour and cornflour with the salt and a few drops of essence. Knead well until quite smooth. Roll out about a quarter of an inch thick and cut in rounds or fancy shapes. Place a small piece of cherry in the centre of each. Bake on trays in a moderate oven for about 20 minutes. They should not be allowed to brown.

The following recipes are by Catherine Macfarlane, Lecturer (Foods) at the University of Otago, Dunedin, New Zealand.

DANISH DELIGHT

The Danes cook simple foods beautifully and serve them attractively. Dinner might begin with cold fillets of plaice garnished with shrimps, lemon slices and cucumber twists, go on to chicken (carved before coming to table) with new carrots and peas and a rich cream sauce flavoured with redcurrant jelly. Finally come crisp iced biscuits with a custard filling. A speciality is the famous Danish open sandwich, topped with cheese, cold meats or egg and all sorts of garnishes.

IDEAS FROM
THE EAST

Most people enjoy eating at
Chinese and Indian restaurants and many ideas from
the East can be adapted to
home cooking. Try serving
lots of tasty and colourful
accompaniments in little
dishes—like the chicken surrounded by pots of chutney
and other sweet and sharp
accompaniments. Rice dishes
are more appetising served in
Oriental dishes, with colourful garnishes—a slice of
tomato, a sliver of red
pimento or green pepper, a
sprig of watercress or parsley,
green peas, an onion ring.
Sweet and Sour Sauce, too,
makes many simple dishes
more interesting. Serve in a
centre dish with little pieces
of fried fish or pork or chicken
grouped around it.

LAMB WITH A DIFFERENCE

A Crown Roast of Lamb never fails to produce cries of admiration, yet the only difficult part of the job is the butcher's! Don't forget the paper cutlet frills from a stationers and, if you want to put the jewels on the crown, add *petits pois* and tiny carrots. Serve with new potatoes, a green vegetable and red-currant jelly. Fried Sweetbreads, too, go right into the luxury class served on a bed of mixed vegetables, with a rich mushroom sauce.

Kiwi Crisps (yields about 2 dozen biscuits)

4 oz. butter
6 oz. flour
2 tablespoonfuls sweetened con densed milk
4 oz. dark chocolate (broken into small pieces)
1 teaspoonful baking powder
2 oz. sugar

Cream the butter and sugar. Add the flour sifted with the baking powder alternately with the condensed milk. Add the chocolate. Shape the mixture into small balls; place them on oven trays, flatten the tops and bake in a moderate oven for 15–20 minutes.

Lemon Chiffon Pie

(for 4–6)

Crumb pastry
1 cup finely crushed wine biscuits
3 oz. butter

Lemon filling
1 tablespoonful gelatine
½ cupful lemon juice
8 oz. sugar
4 eggs (separated)
1 teaspoonful grated lemon rind
¼ cupful cold water
½ teaspoonful salt

Soften the butter and stir in the biscuit crumbs. Press the buttered crumbs evenly over the bottom and sides of a pie plate to make a layer ⅛-in. thick. Chill until firm.

For the filling, soak the gelatine in the cold water for 5 minutes. Add the lemon juice, egg-yolks, half the sugar and the salt. Cook over hot water, stirring constantly until the gelatine has dissolved and the mixture has thickened. Add the lemon rind and cool. When the mixture is beginning to stiffen, beat the egg-whites until stiff; add the remaining sugar gradually; fold in the lemon mixture. Place in the prepared crumb lining and chill. Garnish with cream.

FRUIT with LAMB

RIGHT, New Zealand lamb cutlets simmered in juice of 2 oranges, the liquid then made into sauce with 1 orange rind, ⅛ pint water, 1 tablespoonful flour. Below, boned shoulder of New Zealand lamb stuffed with a breadcrumb stuffing (see Poultry and Game chapter), containing chopped dried apricots. Delicious and different!

Scalloped Seafood

2 tablespoonfuls butter
8 oz. liquid (fish stock or milk)
1 dozen oysters
1 cupful flaked cooked fish
½ teaspoonful salt
½ cupful buttered breadcrumbs
2 tablespoonfuls flour
1 cupful chopped crayfish
2 teaspoonfuls lemon juice

Melt the butter in a saucepan, stir in the flour and salt and cook for a few seconds. Remove from the heat. Blend in the liquid and reheat until thick. Cook for 1 or 2 minutes; season with lemon juice. Butter individual heat-proof dishes. Place alternate layers of fish and sauce in the dishes, finishing with a layer of sauce. Sprinkle buttered crumbs over the top. Reheat in a moderate oven until the food is very hot and the crumbs are golden brown. Garnish with parsley and lemon. Serve very hot.

UNITED  STATES

Barbecued meats with pineapple exciting dishes . . . unusual ice of new ideas and combinations *slices . . . golden corn made into creams—American food is full*

MAIN DISHES

American Pot Roast

Joint of beef (allow ½ lb. per person)	Salt and pepper 1 cup hot water
Salad oil or fat for frying	

Melt the fat in a deep saucepan and brown the meat on all sides in it. Season with pepper and salt, add the hot water. Lift meat on to a rack, cover pan and simmer gently until tender, adding a little more water if necessary. A pot roast for six or more persons will take from 3–4 hours, according to size.

For Beef Pot Roast and Vegetables: Slice and brown 2 carrots, ½ turnip and 1 small onion per person, with several small potatoes, and add to the meat 1 hour before cooking time is completed.

Baked Ham with Pineapple (for 4)

1½ lb. smoked ham, cut about ⅛ in. thick	4 slices canned pineapple
1-in. piece stick cinnamon	½ cupful pineapple syrup
½ cupful light brown sugar	1 pint cold water
4 glacé cherries	Parsley or watercress to garnish

Cover ham with cold water and bring to boil to remove any excess salt. Drain. Place in fireproof dish, pour pint of water over, add cinnamon and bake in moderate oven until tender—about 1 hour or longer. Baste frequently with the liquid in the pan; turn over when half cooked. Drain, place the slices of pineapple on the ham, cover with the sugar and pour the pineapple syrup over the top. Bake 15 minutes longer, basting several times. Serve on hot dish, decorated with a cherry in the centre of each pineapple slice, and garnish with parsley or watercress.

Boston Baked Beans (for 4)

2 cupfuls haricot beans	½ teaspoonful dry mustard
1½ teaspoonfuls salt	2 tablespoonfuls finely chopped onion
2 tablespoonfuls brown sugar	
¼ cupful molasses	Salt pork (about ¼ lb.)
1 cupful boiling water	
1 bay leaf	

Wash beans; cover with cold water and leave overnight to soak. Drain. Cover well with boiling salted water and simmer gently for 1 hour; drain well. Mix together salt, sugar, molasses, bay leaf, dry mustard, chopped onion and cup of boiling water. Place all together with pork in covered pan and bake in slow oven for 4 hours, or until beans are tender. Remove cover of pan for last ½ hour.

Cover with a little additional boiling water if necessary during cooking.

Pan-broiled Porterhouse Steak

Grilling steak between ¾ in.–1½ in. thick (allow ½ lb. per person)	Fat Salt Pepper

Melt fat in a heavy saucepan and, when smoking, brown steak quickly on both sides. Reduce heat and cook slowly until done, pouring off fat if necessary; sprinkle with salt and pepper to suit taste.

Broiled Steak

Grilling steak at least 1 in. thick (allow ½ lb. per person)	2 tablespoonfuls melted butter Salt and pepper

First get the grill really hot so that the meat is seared quickly, or it may be tough and dry. Grease the meat rack and brush steak lightly with melted butter. If steak

A favourite American dish is Fried Chicken—at its best with dishes of piping hot skillet corn and strawberry sundaes to follow

is 1–1¾ in. thick, it should be about 2 in. below the heat.

Allow 7–8 minutes for a rare red steak; 8–9 minutes for medium done, and 10–12 minutes for well-done steak, if meat is 1 in. thick. For 1½ in. meat, allow 8–9 minutes for rare steak; 10–12 medium, and 12–15 well done.

Turn meat, seasoning with salt and pepper to taste, when half cooking time is completed.

Barbecued Ham

1 *slice gammon per person*	*Fat or salad oil*
3 *tablespoonfuls Worcester sauce*	2 *tablespoonfuls sugar*
	½ *cupful ketchup*
2 *tablespoonfuls vinegar*	1 *clove garlic*
	1 *medium-sized onion*
	¼ *teaspoonful tabasco*

Melt fat in frying pan and cook gammon gently, without browning. Mix together Worcester sauce, vinegar, sugar, ketchup and tabasco. Mash clove of garlic and chop onion; tie in muslin and add to sauce. Put gammon in deep pan or casserole, cover with sauce and cook for 1 hour. Remove muslin bag with onion and garlic before serving.

Corned Beef Hash (for 4)

2 *cupfuls corned beef chopped into cubes*	*Fat*
	3 *cupfuls cold cooked potatoes, chopped*
3 *tablespoonfuls finely chopped onion*	½ *cupful milk*
	Salt and pepper

Mix together corned beef, potatoes, onion and milk. Season with salt and pepper. Melt fat and cook mixture until well browned, turning frequently.

Fried Chicken

Jointed chicken	*Salt*
A little flour	*Pepper*
Fat	

Wash the jointed chicken and dry well. Roll in flour seasoned with salt and pepper. Melt fat (it should be about ¾–1 in. deep) and, when smoking, put in the chicken. Cover and cook slowly for about 45 minutes, turning frequently.

Hamburgers

1 lb. *finely minced beef (allow ¼ lb. per person)*
½ teaspoonful salt
¼ teaspoonful pepper
2 tablespoonfuls finely chopped onion
2 tablespoonfuls butter, or salad oil

Blend together meat, seasoning and finely chopped onion, mixing thoroughly, and shape into cakes. Melt the fat in a frying pan and cook for 10 minutes, turning carefully to brown both sides. The onion may, if liked, be cooked separately, and a little placed on top of each hamburger before serving.

Lobster Newburg (for 4)

2 lb. cooked lobster	3 egg-yolks
¼ cupful butter	2 tablespoonfuls
1 tablespoonful flour	sherry
1 cupful cream (top of	Salt
milk can be used)	A little paprika

Remove lobster meat from shell and dice it. Melt butter, add flour and seasoning and, when smooth, gradually blend in the cream, stirring well all the time. Bring to boiling point and stir in lobster meat. When this is thoroughly heated, add the beaten egg-yolks and the sherry. Transfer to a double saucepan and allow to cook gently until it thickens; it must not be allowed to boil.

Serve on toast.

Lobster Thermidor (for 4)

1½ lb. cooked lobster	1 cupful thin cream
2 tablespoonfuls	1 teaspoonful dry
flour	mustard
2 tablespoonfuls	¼ teaspoonful salt
butter	Dash of Cayenne
¼ cupful white wine	pepper
1 tablespoonful	Grated Parmesan
minced parsley	cheese

Cube the lobster meat and sauté in the butter for 5–7 minutes, then add the flour, salt, Cayenne, mustard, parsley and the cream, stirring continually while the mixture is heating. Add the wine; return the mixture to the lobster shells, sprinkle with the cheese and bake for about 10 minutes in a hot oven, or brown under a grill.

Shrimps á la Creole (for 4)

1 pint shrimps	1 bay leaf
1½ cupfuls stewed (or	2 level tablespoonfuls
canned) tomatoes	butter
1½ level tablespoon-	Salt and pepper to
fuls flour	taste
1 teaspoonful grated onion	

Melt the butter, add onion and flour and stir until smooth; add the seasonings, tomatoes and bay leaf, and bring to the boil, stirring all the time. Prepare the shrimps and add them to the sauce, stirring from time to time while they heat (about 7 minutes).

Boiled rice may be served as an accompaniment to this dish.

Southern-style Hash (for 4)

1 lb. minced veal	3 tablespoonfuls fat
2 onions	1 teaspoonful salt
2 cupfuls canned (or	Pepper
cooked) tomatoes	1 teaspoonful chilli
½ cupful rice	powder

Melt the fat in a deep saucepan, slice the onions and fry until golden brown. Add the meat and brown, then the tomatoes, rice, chilli powder, salt and pepper. Cover and cook for 35–40 minutes, or until the rice is tender, stirring from time to time.

Roast Stuffed Turkey with Cranberry Sauce

Turkey	2–4 oz. melted butter
Salt	or margarine

For the stuffing

12 cupfuls bread-	1 small level
crumbs	teaspoonful pepper
¾ cupful finely minced	1 heaped table-
onion	spoonful mixed
1 cupful bacon fat,	herbs
margarine, or	1 lb. pork sausage
clarified dripping	meat
1½ cupfuls finely	Hot water as
chopped celery	required
2 teaspoonfuls salt	

To make the stuffing.—Melt the fat and cook the minced onion over a gentle heat until golden brown. Add some of the breadcrumbs, stirring well to prevent burning. Turn into a large bowl and add the rest of the ingredients, with the sausage meat browned lightly over a gentle heat. Mix in just enough hot water to moisten sufficiently. Allow to cool before using.

Wash the prepared bird inside and out, drying well. Rub over inside with salt. Stuff bird, and brush well with melted fat. If cooking on rack in pan, place on one side, so that it roasts evenly, and can be turned when half cooked; cover with well-greased paper.

For a bird from 8–10 lb. allow 3–3½ hours
For a bird from 10–14 lb. allow 3½–4 hours
For a bird from 14–18 lb. allow 4½–6 hours

For the cranberry sauce

2 *cupfuls sugar*   2 *cupfuls water*
4 *cupfuls cranberries*

Boil sugar and water briskly for 5 minutes. Add cranberries and continue boiling for a further 5–10 minutes, or until the berries are cooked.

When Buying Duck

Allow at least ¾–1 lb. drawn duck per person. An easy way to tell if a duck is young or old is to pinch its windpipe. If it is rubbery, it is a young bird. If it cracks, it is too old.

Roasting Duck

The best results are obtained by placing the duck on a wire rack in a roasting pan. Do not prick, or brush with oil. Roast until thigh joint of bird moves easily. Another test is to press the drumstick meat between the fingers. If it is soft, the bird is done. The skin should be crisp.

When Buying Goose

Allow 1¼–1½ lb. drawn goose per person.

Roasting Goose

After stuffing goose, prick with fork through fat layers over back, around tail and into body around wings and legs. This helps draw out fat. Do not brush with fat or oil. Roast as for duck.

Roast Duckling (for 4)

1 *5-lb. duck*   *Hot water and butter*
Fruit stuffing   *for basting*
2 *oz. flour*   *Salt and pepper*

Wash bird and cut off neck. Fill cavity with apple stuffing. Fasten opening with skewers or sew it up with thick thread. Roast duck in very hot oven for 15 minutes. Reduce oven to moderate heat and continue roasting, basting often with hot water and butter. Remove excess fat as it accumulates in the pan. Season with salt and pepper when duck is half-cooked (25 minutes per lb.).

Pineapple is a popular accompaniment to many meat and poultry dishes. Here it is served grilled with chicken. It also goes with baked ham

Meanwhile, simmer neck and giblets for 45–50 minutes in sufficient water to cover, with one small onion and two or three sticks of celery.

To make gravy, drain stock from giblets and put on one side. Chop giblets and brown in 4 tablespoonfuls of fat from pan in which duck has been roasted. Add the flour. Stir till smooth and brown. Add 2 cupfuls of giblet stock and stir until thick. Cook for 5 minutes, season and strain.

Apple Stuffing (Suitable for duck or goose)

2 oz. butter or margarine	Salt and pepper
1 slice onion	4 oz. breadcrumbs
4 oz. chopped celery	4 oz. peeled chopped tart apples

Melt the butter or margarine and brown the onion. Add remainder of the ingredients, seasoning to taste and mix thoroughly. Heat through. Stuff the bird as directed. This is a sufficient quantity for a 5-lb. duck.

Goose with Prunes

1 goose	Clear stock
1 small onion, minced	Salt and black pepper
1 oz. goose fat	Pinch of sage
8 oz. soft breadcrumbs	1 tablespoonful minced parsley
½ lb. sausage meat	1 tablespoonful minced onion
1 egg, beaten	1 teaspoonful brandy
3 dozen small prunes, stoned	

Brown the onion in the goose fat. Add crumbs, sausage meat and beaten egg, and mix thoroughly over low flame. Soak the prunes for 3 hours in enough clear stock to cover. Add minced onion and seasonings. Mix well and add to crumbs and sausage meat mixture. Stuff goose and skewer or sew up. Baste frequently with fat from pan. Allow 25–30 minutes per lb.

Remove all fat from roasting pan and add 1½ pints clear stock, or meat essence melted in hot water. Cook until reduced to ½ pint. Add brandy and serve with goose.

Cantonese Duck

2 tablespoonfuls soy sauce	1 oz. cornflour
1 tablespoonful sherry	½ teaspoonful salt
1 chopped shallot	4 tablespoonfuls water
Breast and leg of duck	3 oz. lard or 3 tablespoonfuls vegetable oil
2 eggs	

Mix the soy sauce, sherry and chopped shallot. Put in the breast and leg of the duck and leave to marinate for 1 hour. Make a paste with the cornflour, eggs, salt and water. Remove the duck from sauce and roll in paste. Heat lard or vegetable oil in a large frying pan. Fry duck for 2 minutes on each side. Turn. Fry for further 2 minutes, then turn and fry for 10 minutes on each side or until skin is crisp. Serve the duck cut in ½-in. slices, accompanied by little bowls of 3 tablespoonfuls salt and ½ tablespoonful pepper mixed together.

Blade Duck

1 duck	2–4 oranges
Salt and pepper to taste	Juice of 1 orange
	½ lb. redcurrant jelly

Place duck in shallow roasting tin. Sprinkle with salt and pepper. Put in very hot oven and roast for 20 minutes. Reduce to moderate heat and cook until tender (25 minutes to the lb.). When the duck has cooked for a quarter of the allotted time, pour off most of the fat and add the juice of one large orange and the jelly. Cut remaining oranges into thick slices and place round the duck in the sauce. Baste frequently.

Duckling in Cranberry Sauce (for 4)

1 5–6-lb. duckling (whole or cut)	1 lb. fresh cranberries
4 cupfuls bread stuffing (optional)	½ pint water
½ oz. cornflour	¼ pint orange juice
4 oz. sugar	1 unpeeled orange, cut in 6 wedges

Stuff duckling, if desired. Roast in moderate oven for about 2 hours or until skin is light brown. Meanwhile, make sauce. Mix the cornflour and sugar in a saucepan, add the cranberries, water and orange juice and bring to the boil quickly, stirring constantly. Cook over moderate heat for 5 minutes or till liquid is syrupy and clear. Remove from flame and add orange. Take the duck out of the oven, put into a deep casserole, pour sauce over it and cover casserole. Return to oven for about 20 minutes or until the duck is tender when pricked with a fork. Baste the duck, or, if cut up, turn pieces once during the cooking.

Veal Orloff (for 6–8)

3 lb. shoulder of veal, boned and rolled	1 lb. chopped mushrooms, canned or fresh
2 oz. butter or margarine	4 oz. minced onion
1½ teaspoonfuls salt	

Succotash made from sweet corn and beans goes perfectly with America's traditional Thanksgiving Day turkey

For the Mornay sauce

6 oz. butter or margarine	¾ pint milk
	¼ pint roast veal juice
4 oz. flour	3 egg-yolks, beaten
½ teaspoonful salt	4 oz. shredded
Pinch of pepper	Gruyère cheese

If the veal is very lean, cover with bacon rashers. Roast in moderate oven, allowing 40 minutes to the lb. Remove from the oven and leave for about 15 minutes. Then slice in ½-in. slices almost, but not quite through. Keep hot. Save juice which flows during slicing.

The Stuffing should be made while the meat is cooking. Melt the butter in a large frying pan. Add mushrooms, onion and salt and cook for 7 minutes uncovered if canned mushrooms are used. If fresh mushrooms are used, simmer 10 minutes with pan covered. Take lid off and cook for a further 5 minutes.

The Mornay sauce can be made only when meat is roasted. Melt the butter in a pan, stir in flour, salt and pepper. Add milk and veal juice from slices gradually. Continue cooking until thickened, stirring constantly. Mix egg-yolks with 2 or 3 tablespoonfuls of hot sauce, then stir slowly back into remainder of sauce. Simmer for about 3 minutes, stirring all the time. Remove pan from the flame. Stir in cheese.

To finish.—Mix about 4 tablespoonfuls of the sauce with the stuffing. Spread between the slices of veal. Remove string from around the meat and tie back into oblong shape if necessary. Put the meat on serving dish, pour sauce over it and garnish with tomato decorations (see below) and parsley.

Tomato decorations.—Firm medium-sized tomatoes must be used. Peel each one as you would an apple, with a sharp knife, beginning at the flower end, peel round and round to stem end. Do not break peel. Wind the peel round finger. Place it down on stem end and fasten with cocktail stick or toothpick.

Steak Superb (for 6)

4 oz. soft butter or margarine	4 egg-yolks
1 tablespoonful lemon juice	1 tablespoonful Tarragon vinegar
¼ teaspoonful grated onion	¼ teaspoonful dried Tarragon
½ teaspoonful minced parsley	Dash of Cayenne pepper
Dash of paprika	6 fillets of beef, 1–1½ in. thick
6 rounds of toast	

First, make the Béarnaise sauce. Melt butter in the top of a double boiler over hot, but not boiling, water. Beat the egg-yolks, stir in lemon juice, vinegar, seasonings. Add to the butter. Stir constantly until the sauce is as thick as mayonnaise. This will take about 10 minutes. Remove from the hot water at once and place over lukewarm water whilst you prepare the steaks. Grill meat, allowing 5 minutes each side for under-done steaks, 6 minutes each side for medium and 8 minutes each side for well-done steaks. Place each steak on a round of toast, top with a spoonful of the Béarnaise sauce.

Pretzel Stuffing (for Turkey) (Sufficient for a 6–8-lb. bird)

¼ lb. coarsely crumbled pretzels	8 oz. diced celery
1 large onion, chopped	Pinch of pepper
1 teaspoonful mixed herbs	½ pint milk
	6 oz. butter or margarine, melted
	1 gill water

Mix the pretzel crumbs, celery, mixed herbs, onion and pepper in a bowl. Stir in the butter or margarine, milk and water. Mix well and stuff the turkey.

Barley Pilaff (for 4)

2 medium onions	14 oz. barley
½ lb. mushrooms	1½ pints clear or chicken stock
2 oz. butter	
Salt and pepper	

Heat oven to moderate. Chop onions coarsely and slice mushrooms thinly. Melt butter in a frying pan and cook the mushrooms and onions for about 5 minutes. Remove from pan. Put barley into fat in pan. Cook over medium heat until brown, turning frequently. Add mushrooms, onions and half the stock. Cover closely, put in oven and cook for ½ hour. Take off lid.

Add seasoning and remainder of stock. Cook for further ½ hour and, if the barley looks dry, add a little more stock. Bake for 10–20 minutes longer, until barley is cooked. Serve with roast duck or goose, or as a supper dish on its own.

Apple Ham Rolls (for 6)

8 oz. shredded raw apple	1 teaspoonful sugar
4 oz. fine or dry breadcrumbs	2 oz. melted butter or margarine
Pinch of salt	6 slices of cooked ham
Pepper	12 cloves
1 teaspoonful dry mustard	6 whole canned apricots

Mix the apple, crumbs, salt, pepper, mustard, sugar and butter in a bowl. Spread each slice of ham with a spoonful of this mixture and roll up. Fasten with cocktail sticks and put into a shallow casserole or pie dish. Pour syrup glaze (see below) over them. Bake in a hot oven for ½ hour, basting several times; 5 minutes before the rolls are done, push 2 cloves into each half apricot and put them round the ham.

Syrup Glaze.—Mix ¼ pint light corn syrup, 3 tablespoonfuls water, ⅛ pint cider vinegar, 2 teaspoonfuls grated orange rind, 6 whole cloves and a stick of cinnamon in a saucepan. Bring to the boil and simmer for 5 minutes.

Cucumbers with Tuna Fish (for 4)

4 cucumbers about 6 in. long	1 can of tuna fish, flaked
2 teaspoonfuls grated onion	2 oz. chopped celery
6 tablespoonfuls mayonnaise	6 oz. white breadcrumbs
2 tablespoonfuls lemon juice	½ teaspoonful salt
	2 oz. butter or margarine
Pinch of pepper	

Cut a thin slice from one side of each cucumber lengthwise. Boil cucumbers in sufficient salted water to cover for 10 minutes, then remove carefully from the water. Cool for a few minutes. Scoop out pulp and save, being careful not to break the shells. Drain and sprinkle inside with salt. Chop cucumber pulp and drain off liquid. Mix pulp with salt, pepper, lemon juice, mayonnaise, two-thirds of breadcrumbs, celery, onion and tuna fish. Put the mixture into the shells and sprinkle with rest of the breadcrumbs. Dot with butter. Bake in shallow dish with a little water in moderately hot oven until browned.

VEGETABLES

Orange Curry Cabbage

1 medium-sized cabbage	¼ teaspoonful curry powder
3 oz. butter	Grated rind and juice
1 teaspoonful chutney	of 1 orange

Shred cabbage and cook for 4 minutes in 1 quart salted boiling water. Drain well. Brown the butter and add chutney, curry powder, orange rind and juice. Pour over the cabbage, cover and leave to stand 10 minutes before serving.

Stuffed Egg-plant (for 2–3)

1 large egg plant or 2 or 3 smaller ones	Dash of Cayenne
1 clove garlic, finely chopped (optional)	3 oz. butter or margarine
4 oz. green pepper	4 oz. onion, chopped
Small can tomato purée	¾ lb. cooked rice
	1 teaspoonful salt

Cut off the top quarter of the egg-plant. Scoop out, leaving shells about ½ in. thick. Chop the pulp roughly. Melt the butter in a frying pan, add egg-plant pulp, onion, sliced green pepper and garlic (if liked). Cook until soft, then add rice, tomato purée, salt and Cayenne. Fill egg-plant shells with this mixture and bake in a hot oven for about 15 minutes.

Stuffed Turnips (for 4)

4 medium size turnips	8 oz. cooked peas
1 tablespoonful chopped parsley	2 oz. butter or margarine
Pinch of salt and pepper	

Peel the turnips and cook whole in boiling salted water until tender. Drain and scoop out centres, leaving shells about ½ in. thick. Keep these warm while making filling. Mix remaining ingredients in a saucepan. Heat until the butter melts and the peas are hot. Fill the turnip shells with the mixture.

Mint Potato Custard (for 4)

4 medium-size potatoes	½ cupful mint leaves, chopped
1 small onion, minced	1¼ pints milk
3 eggs	2 oz. butter
1½ teaspoonfuls salt	

Hamburgers topped with creamed mashed potato and grilled tomatoes, garnished with onion rings and parsley. These, the Devil's Food Cake and the Lemon Meringue Pie were specially made and photographed at the Spry Cookery Centre

Heat oven to moderate. Meantime peel, dice and boil the potatoes till tender but not too soft. Bring milk just to the boil. Remove from heat and add butter, salt and minced onion. Stir lightly beaten eggs into milk very slowly, a little at a time. Mix the chopped mint with the potatoes and add to milk and egg. Pour into casserole and place in a pan of warm water. Bake for 45 minutes.

CHOWDERS

Corn Chowder (for 4)

1 cupful water	4 cupfuls milk
1 small onion	1½ cupfuls canned
3 potatoes	(whole kernel) corn
¼ cupful margarine	Salt and pepper
Chives (optional)	

Peel and dice potatoes; peel and grate onion; add water and margarine and simmer gently until tender. Add corn and milk to this mixture and simmer a further 15 minutes. Season to taste with salt and pepper.

This dish may be garnished with finely chopped chives, if liked.

Manhattan Fish Chowder (for 3–4)

1 onion	1 cupful cooked,
1 potato	flaked cod
2 tablespoonfuls fat	Salt and pepper
1 cupful diced celery	1 slice bread per
1 cupful cooked	person
tomatoes	2 heaped tablespoon-
1 cupful (whole	fuls grated cheese
kernel) canned corn	

Chop onion very finely and cook in fat. Peel and dice potato. Add with celery, tomatoes, pepper and salt and simmer for 15 minutes. Mix in the corn and flaked fish, and heat well. Toast bread, or fry crisply in shallow fat. Place small slice or triangle on each portion and serve sprinkled with cheese.

Clam Chowder (for 4)

¼ cupful chopped	2 cupfuls boiling
onion	water
1 cupful diced potato	2 tablespoonfuls mar-
(raw)	garine
2 tablespoonfuls	1 cupful chopped
minced green	clams
peppers	1 cupful clam liquor
3 tablespoonfuls	Pinch of thyme
chopped celery	Salt and pepper
1 cupful canned tomatoes	

Melt margarine and brown onion and green pepper; then add celery, potato, and water, cover and cook for 15 minutes, when potato should be tender. Now add tomatoes, clams, and liquor, and salt, pepper and thyme.

Cover, simmer gently for a further 20 minutes to ½ hour, and serve.

SALADS

Waldorf Surprise Salad

2 cupfuls red-skinned,	½ cupful chopped
apples (unpeeled),	celery
cut in cubes	¼ cupful chopped
½ cupful chopped	walnuts
stoned dates	1 lettuce
Mayonnaise	

Mix together apples, dates, celery and nuts, and serve on prepared lettuce, with mayonnaise dressing (see Salads chapter).

Slaw Royal

½ cupful sliced apple	1 banana
(peeled)	½ cupful chopped
1½ cupfuls shredded	celery
red cabbage	Salad dressing to taste

Mix together salad dressing and slices of apple, and add sliced banana; mix in shredded cabbage and chopped celery.

Tomato and Lima Bean Salad

4 large tomatoes	1 small onion
1½ cupfuls cooked (or	1 cupful mixed nuts
canned) Lima	2 tablespoonfuls
beans	finely chopped
2 dessertspoonfuls	celery
finely chopped	Salt and pepper
parsley	Mayonnaise

Chop the nuts finely; grate the onion. Cut a slice from the top of each tomato and remove the pulp. Add celery, nuts, onion, parsley, salt and pepper to the beans, which should be well drained and cut in halves if large, and mix in a little mayonnaise.

Fill the scooped-out tomatoes with the mixture, and top with a little mayonnaise when serving.

Cheese and Grapefruit Salad

1 lettuce	Tomatoes
1 can grapefruit	½ cupful chopped wal-
3 large tablespoonfuls	nuts
cream cheese	Radishes to garnish
Mayonnaise or salad cream	

Mix chopped nuts into cream cheese, adding a little mayonnaise or salad cream, if necessary. Keep aside several nuts as garnish. Drain grapefruit, peel and slice tomatoes. Prepare lettuce. Arrange grapefruit, sliced tomatoes, and cheese on bed of lettuce. Garnish with radishes and the remaining walnuts. Serve with mayonnaise or salad cream.

Celeriac Salad

1 *small celeriac*	6 *walnuts*
1 *teaspoonful honey*	1 *sweet apple*
½ *cupful soaked sultanas*	1 *cup yoghourt*
	Pepper and salt

Peel and grate the raw celeriac and apple (or chop very finely). Drain the previously soaked sultanas and dry well. Chop the walnuts. Mix the honey with the apple and add to the grated celeriac. Finally, mix all together with the yoghourt and serve.

Coleslaw

3 *cupfuls shredded raw cabbage*	*Paprika to season*
	½ *cupful salad dressing*

For the salad dressing

2 *tablespoonfuls flour*
1 *tablespoonful salt*
¾ *tablespoonful dry mustard*
1 *tablespoonful sugar*
Pepper
Paprika
1 *egg*
1 *cupful milk*
¼ *cupful vinegar*
2 *tablespoonfuls margarine or butter*

To make the dressing mix together flour, salt, mustard, pepper, paprika and sugar. Beat the egg well and add, then gradually mix in the milk. Cook in a double pan over boiling water, stirring all the time until it thickens; add the vinegar very gradually and then the butter or margarine. Cover and allow to cool.

Mix the shredded cabbage with the dressing and sprinkle with a few grains of paprika. Serve at once.

Autumn Soufflé Salad (for 4–6)

1 *packet lime or lemon jelly*	2 *oz. chopped walnuts*
¼ *pint cold water*	½ *pint hot water*
¼ *pint mayonnaise*	2 *tablespoonfuls lemon juice*
6 *oz. seeded black grapes*	8 *oz. diced peeled apples*
Pinch of salt	

Dissolve jelly in hot water, then add mayonnaise, lemon juice, salt and cold water. Beat with egg whisk. Pour into freezing tray of refrigerator and freeze for 15–20 minutes or until firm at the edge but soft in the centre. Turn into a bowl and whip until fluffy. Fold in apples, grapes, and walnuts, and pour into a quart jelly mould or individual small moulds. Chill in the refrigerator, or leave overnight. Turn out and serve, garnished with fruit as desired

Pepper Salad Jelly (for 4–6)

1 *packet lemon jelly*	½ *pint hot water*
1 *tablespoonful vinegar*	½ *pint cold water*
1 *teaspoonful salt*	6 *oz. finely diced celery*
2 *oz. finely diced green peppers*	4 *oz. shredded or finely sliced carrots*

Dissolve jelly in hot water and add vinegar, cold water and half the salt. Mix thoroughly. Chill in the refrigerator until slightly thickened. Sprinkle remaining salt over vegetables and fold into jelly. Put into a quart mould or individual small moulds. Chill until firm or leave overnight. Turn out and decorate with tomatoes or other salad. Serve with lettuce and mayonnaise.

Fruit and Celery Jelly (for 8)

1 *packet lime jelly*	
1 *pint hot water*	
1½ *bananas, diced*	
3 *oz. diced celery*	
1 *packet lemon jelly*	
4 *oz. diced unpeeled apples*	4 *tablespoonfuls lemon juice*
1 *pint cold water*	1 *teaspoonful salt*

Dissolve lime and lemon jellies in hot water. Add lemon juice, salt and cold water. Chill in refrigerator until slightly thickened. Fold in celery, bananas and apples. Pour into 1½-quart mould or individual moulds. Chill in refrigerator until firm or leave overnight. Turn out and serve on lettuce with mayonnaise (optional).

CORN DISHES
Boiled Corn on the Cob

Prepare ears of corn by husking and removing silk. Cover the corn with salted boiling water and boil in a covered pan for 5–8 minutes.

Drain well and serve with melted butter, salt and pepper.

COOK'S TIP
STICKING CAKE

It won't stick to the tin if you stand the tin for a few minutes on a damp cloth when it comes out of the oven.

Sautéed Corn

1 *ear of cooked corn per person*	*¼ cupful cream*
2 *tablespoonfuls butter*	*Salt*
	A little sugar
	Pepper to taste

Remove corn kernels from cob, using sharp knife. Melt butter in saucepan and brown kernels lightly. Add cream, salt, pepper and sugar, and heat all together gently over a low heat until ready to serve.

Corn Fritters (1) (for 4)

4 *level tablespoonfuls flour*	*½ cupful milk*
2 *eggs*	*1½ cupfuls cooked or canned whole kernel corn*
½ teaspoonful salt	
Fat for frying	

Mix the well-beaten egg-yolks with the milk and add to the flour and salt to make a batter; beat until very smooth. Beat the egg-whites until fairly stiff and fold gently into the batter.

Melt the fat and, when very hot, drop in a little batter, pour a spoonful of the corn on to it before it sets, and press firmly down. Fry to a crisp golden brown, lift out on to a hot dish, and repeat until both batter and corn are all used.

Corn Fritters (2) (for 4)

1 *cupful cooked or canned whole kernel corn*	*½ teaspoonful baking powder*
2 *eggs*	*½ level teaspoonful salt*
½ cupful flour	*Pepper to taste*
Fat for frying	

Place corn in bowl with well-beaten eggs; sift and add dry ingredients and beat until smooth. Melt fat and drop mixture into it, one or two tablespoonfuls at a time. Dry on soft crumpled paper and serve piping hot.

Corn fritters are an ideal accompaniment to fried chicken, and may be served in place of potatoes.

Green Bean Succotash (for 4)

1½ *cupfuls cooked or canned green beans*	1½ *cupfuls cooked or canned whole kernel corn*
½ cupful cream	
Pepper and salt	

Mix together the beans and the corn, add the cream and season to taste with pepper and salt. Heat for about 10 minutes, stirring constantly.

Sage Succotash (for 4)

2 *cupfuls cooked or canned lima beans*	*½ cupful thin cream or top of milk*
1½ *cupfuls cooked or canned whole kernel corn*	*½ teaspoonful salt*
	2 *tablespoonfuls margarine*
½ eggspoonful sage	

Drain the beans well. Mix together with the corn, add sage, salt, cream or milk and the margarine. Heat for 10–15 minutes, stirring constantly.

WAFFLES

Plain Waffles

2 *cupfuls sifted flour*	*¼ teaspoonful salt*
2 *eggs*	1¼ *cupfuls milk*
6 *tablespoonfuls melted margarine*	2 *teaspoonfuls baking powder*

Separate the whites from the yolks of the eggs. Mix the dry ingredients together and make into a batter with the milk, beaten egg-yolks and melted fat. Beat the egg-whites until stiff, and fold lightly in.

Well grease the waffle iron, and cook the waffles on the preheated irons for 3 minutes.

Banana Waffles

2 *cupfuls sifted flour*	*½ cupful thin sliced banana*
2 *eggs*	2 *teaspoonfuls baking powder*
6 *tablespoonfuls melted margarine*	*¼ teaspoonful salt*
1¼ *cupfuls milk*	

Prepare and mix waffles as above, adding the sliced banana to the batter *before* folding in the egg-whites.

Nut Waffles

¾ cupful mixed finely chopped nuts	2 *eggs*
2 *cupfuls sifted flour*	2 *teaspoonfuls baking powder*
1¼ *cupfuls milk*	*¼ teaspoonful salt*
6 *tablespoonfuls melted margarine*	

Prepare and mix waffles as for plain waffles above, adding the finely chopped nuts to the batter *before* folding in the egg-whites.

Chocolate Waffles

2 *cupfuls sifted flour*	2 *teaspoonfuls baking powder*
3 *tablespoonfuls cocoa*	6 *tablespoonfuls melted margarine*
1¼ *cupfuls milk less ⅓ cup (replaced by black coffee)*	2 *eggs*
	¼ teaspoonful salt

Mix and prepare as for plain waffles, substituting 3 tablespoonfuls of cocoa for 3

Add the egg-yolks to the milk and beat well together, mixing gradually with the dry ingredients. Add flavouring essence. Beat the egg-whites until stiff, and fold lightly in.

Cook on preheated waffle irons, which have been well greased, until a crisp golden brown and serve at once with honey or Maple Syrup.

ICE CREAM DISHES

Vanilla Ice Cream

½ cupful condensed
  milk (sweetened)
½ cupful water
½ cupful cream
1 teaspoonful vanilla
  essence
Pinch of salt

Mix together all ingredients except the cream, and chill well. Whip cream slightly and fold into the mixture. Place in a refrigerator and freeze to a mush. Now turn out into a

Waffles come in all varieties—plain with maple syrup (above); or savoury, topped with grilled kidneys (right) or sausages (below)

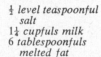

tablespoonfuls of the flour when making the batter, and replacing ⅓ cupful of milk by strong, freshly made black coffee.

Coconut Waffles

2 cupfuls flour	½ level teaspoonful
2 large eggs	salt
2 tablespoonfuls	1¼ cupfuls milk
sugar	6 tablespoonfuls
½ cup desiccated	melted fat
coconut	

Sift together flour, sugar, salt, and add coconut. Beat the egg-yolks and add to the milk, gradually mixing in the dry ingredients, and beat until smooth; add melted fat. Beat the egg-whites until stiff and fold them in gently.

Cook in well-greased waffle irons, which have been previously heated, until crisp and golden brown. Serve with melted butter and thin honey or maple syrup.

Oaten Waffles

1 cupful Quick por-	½ level teaspoonful
ridge oats	salt
1 cupful wholemeal	2 eggs
flour	1 teaspoonful vanilla
1 cupful milk	essence

Mix together the flour, oats and salt.

previously chilled bowl and beat well. Return to refrigerator and freeze firm.

This ice cream can be served with any sauce to suit individual taste.

Chocolate Ice Cream

1 oz. unsweetened	½ cupful water
chocolate	Pinch of salt
½ cupful sweetened	1 teaspoonful
condensed milk	vanilla essence
½ cupful cream	

Devil's Food, a rich dark chocolate cake with a crisp white icing, used on top and as a filling in the centre

Hot Chocolate Sauce

(To serve with ice cream)

> 3 oz. (*unsweetened*)
> *chocolate*
> ¼ *cupful sugar*
> *Pinch of salt*
> ¼ *teaspoonful coffee*
> *essence* (*optional*)
> ½ *cupful water*

Break up chocolate, add the water and heat together, stirring continually, until the chocolate is melted; then add the sugar, stirring well until it is dissolved. Remove from heat, add pinch of salt and coffee essence, if desired. Serve hot with ice cream.

Melt the chocolate in a double saucepan and add the condensed milk. Cook gently for about 5 minutes, or until thick, stirring continually. Gradually add the water and a pinch of salt; chill. Whip cream lightly and fold into mixture, adding the vanilla essence. Place in refrigerator and freeze to a mush. Then turn out into a previously chilled bowl and beat until smooth. Return to refrigerator tray and freeze until firm and ready to serve.

Banana Ice Cream

> 2 *egg-yolks*   ¼ *cupful water*
> ⅔ *cupful sugar*   2 *tablespoonfuls light*
> 1½ *cupfuls milk*   *corn syrup*
> ½ *cupful cream*   1 *teaspoonful vanilla*
> *Pinch of salt*   *essence*
> 2 *egg-whites*   1 *sieved banana*

Beat the egg-yolks well and add to half sugar, milk and pinch of salt. Cook slowly in a double saucepan until mixture thickens. Cool and set in refrigerator until it forms a mush. Meanwhile, boil together water, remainder of sugar and corn syrup until small quantity dropped from spoon forms a long thread. Beat egg-whites until stiff and add syrup gradually, beating all the time, and then the vanilla essence.

Turn out the mixture into a previously chilled bowl, and beat well until perfectly smooth, lightly folding in the two egg-whites and syrup mixture. Whip the cream and fold in together with the sieved banana pulp. Return to refrigerator and freeze till ready to serve.

Butterscotch Walnut Ice Cream

> 2 *eggs*   ½ *cupful cream*
> ⅔ *cupful brown sugar* 1 *teaspoonful vanilla*
> *Pinch of salt*   *essence*
> 1½ *cupfuls milk*   ½ *cupful shelled*
> ¼ *cupful water*   *chopped walnuts*
> 2 *tablespoonfuls light corn syrup*

Separate the whites and yolks of eggs; beat the yolks, adding half the sugar, milk, pinch of salt. Cook in a double saucepan, stirring well all the time, until mixture thickens. Cool, add chopped walnuts and set in freezing tray of refrigerator until mixture is mushy. Meanwhile, boil together water, remaining half of brown sugar and corn syrup, until mixture forms long thread when dropped from tip of spoon. Beat egg-whites stiffly, add syrup gradually, beating well all the time, then vanilla essence. Allow to cool; then turn first mixture out into previously chilled bowl, beat well until smooth and fold in egg-white mixture. Whip cream and fold in lightly. Return the completed mixture to refrigerator and freeze until firm and ready to serve.

HOT SANDWICHES

Hot sandwiches, which are more in the nature of quick hot "snacks" than sandwiches, are an important feature of American life. Here are some of the most popular:

Toasted Meat Rolls (for 4)

4 round soft rolls	4 eggs
3 tablespoonfuls margarine	1 cupful minced cooked meat
1½ tablespoonfuls minced onion	Salt and pepper to taste
Grated cheese (optional)	

Cut thin slices from tops of rolls and scoop out centres, making these into breadcrumbs. Melt 2 tablespoonfuls of margarine and brown onion, then add breadcrumbs and minced meat. Season with salt and pepper.

Melt remaining margarine and brush on to top of rolls, heat them for 10 minutes in hot oven; fill with hot meat mixture. Poach eggs and place one on top of each roll.

A little grated cheese may be sprinkled over, if liked.

Hot Roast Beef Sandwiches

1 slice of bread per person	A little gravy or horseradish sauce
Slices hot cooked roast beef	Salt and pepper

Toast the slices of bread, and top each one with slices of hot meat, sufficient to cover. Season with salt and pepper and cover with a little hot gravy, or garnish with horseradish sauce.

Hot Ham Sandwiches (for 4)

1 cupful finely minced cooked ham	2 tablespoonfuls margarine
	½ cupful milk
2 tablespoonfuls sweet pickle or chutney	1 egg
	2 slices of bread per person
3 tablespoonfuls ketchup	

Mix together the minced ham, sweet pickle and the ketchup, and spread on slices of bread to make sandwiches. Beat the egg well and add the milk. Dip each sandwich in the egg-and-milk mixture and brown quickly in the melted margarine. Serve hot.

Hot Cheese, Tomato and Bacon Sandwiches

1 slice streaky bacon per person	1 tomato per sandwich
1 slice bread per person	Parsley or watercress to garnish
Cheese	

Slice the cheese and place on the bread. Peel tomatoes by plunging in boiling water, then in cold, so that skin is easily removed, slice and place on the cheese. Cut each piece of bacon in half (lengthwise) and lay on top of the cheese and tomato.

Grill until bacon is cooked, turning it after a few minutes. Serve hot. Mustard may be put on the cheese under the bacon, if liked. Garnish with chopped parsley or a little watercress.

SWEET DISHES

Apple Mince Pie (for 4)

½ lb. flour	Hard-sauce apple rings (see below)
Water to mix	
1¾ lb. mincemeat	6 oz. butter, margarine or lard
2 medium-size tart cooking apples	Pinch of salt

Rub the butter or other fat into the flour and salt until the mixture resembles fine breadcrumbs. Mix to a soft dough with water. Roll out on floured pastry board to a round 12 in. in diameter. Cover 9-in. flan tin or plate with this. Trim until there is about ½-in. overlap. Turn this under flan so that it is flush with the edge. Decorate edge with knife or fork. Peel, core and finely chop the apples. Mix mincemeat and apples and put into prepared pastry. Spread evenly. Bake in hot

Angel Food Cake—as airy and light as its name suggests—is made in a specially shaped ring tin

oven for 30 minutes or until filling is bubbly and pastry is golden brown. Top with hard-sauce apple rings, put hard-sauce balls in their centres and serve.

Hard-sauce Apple Rings

2 medium-size apples 2 oz. sugar
½ teaspoonful   Few drops of red
  cornflour   vegetable colouring
1½ teaspoonfuls sugar dissolved in ⅓ gill water

Peel and core the apples, slice each into four rings. Mix the sugar, cornflour and sugar syrup in a frying pan and add enough red colouring to make the mixture deep red. Cook over medium heat, stirring occasionally until sugar is dissolved. Put the apple rings in the syrup and simmer for 10 minutes or until tender, turning frequently. Drain and cool.

Hard-sauce Balls

4½ oz. butter or   ¼ lb. sifted icing
  margarine   sugar
        ½ teaspoonful vanilla

Cream the butter or margarine, adding the sugar gradually and beating until soft and fluffy. Stir in the vanilla. Form with butter pats or fingers into eight large balls, chill in refrigerator and serve in the centre of hard-sauce apple rings.

Special Apple Pie (for 6)

2 lb. cooking apples   2 oz. butter or
1 tablespoonful   margarine (for
  lemon juice   filling)
½ teaspoonful nutmeg   6 oz. butter,
½ lb. flour   margarine, lard
Water to mix   or a mixture
1 teaspoonful grated   (for pastry)
  lemon rind   Pinch of salt
        ¾ cupful sugar

Peel, core and slice apples. Put them in a buttered pie dish. Sprinkle with lemon rind, juice, sugar and nutmeg. Dot with butter or margarine. Top with pastry made from the butter or other fat, flour, salt and water. Bake in a very hot oven for 10 minutes, reduce to moderate and bake for 30–40 minutes until crust is golden brown and apples tender.

Apple Pandowdy (for 6)

For the pastry

½ lb. sifted flour   4 oz. butter,
4 tablespoonfuls   margarine or
  water   shortening
        ¼ teaspoonful salt

For the fruit mixture

8 medium-size   ⅛ pint water
  cooking apples   ¼ teaspoonful salt
2 oz. sugar   Pinch of nutmeg
¼ teaspoonful   2 tablespoonfuls
  cinnamon   melted butter or
⅛ pint molasses   margarine
        2 tablespoonfuls milk

Make the pastry and then peel, core and cut apples into ½-in. wedges. Put in a shallow buttered pie dish and sprinkle with salt, cinnamon, nutmeg and sugar. Mix the molasses, melted butter or margarine and water, and pour over apples.

Cover completely with the rolled out pastry. Press edges down and brush with milk. Bake in hot oven for 10 minutes. Remove pudding from the oven and chop the crust into the apples until some pieces of crust stand on end. Reduce oven heat to warm and return pie to oven. Bake 1 hour or until the apples are tender.

Apple Chewies (for 8)

For the pastry

8 oz. sifted flour   2–3 tablespoonfuls
2¼ oz. shortening,   water
  butter or margarine ¼ teaspoonful salt
    Grated rind of half lemon

For the filling

4 medium-sized   2 oz. brown sugar
  cooking apples   6 oz. shredded
Pinch of cinnamon   coconut
1 oz. butter or   2 oz. granulated sugar
  margarine   2 tablespoonfuls
Pinch of salt   double cream
        1 egg, slightly beaten

Rub shortening, butter or margarine into sifted flour and salt until mixture resembles breadcrumbs. Add grated lemon rind. Mix to stiff dough with water. Roll out on lightly floured board to fit baking tin about 13 in. by 9 in. by 2 in. Line bottom of pan with the pastry. Peel, core and slice apples. Arrange in overlapping rows on pastry. Mix brown sugar and cinnamon. Sprinkle over apples. Dot with margarine or butter. Bake in a hot oven for 25 minutes. Remove from the oven. Reduce oven temperature to moderate. Mix coconut, granulated sugar, beaten egg, salt and whipped cream. Spread over apples and return to oven. Bake for about 15 minutes until the apples are tender and the topping is crisp.

Probably the most famous of all American sweet dishes — Lemon Meringue Pie is surprisingly quick and easy to make and always wins praise for a hostess from her guests

Apple Macaroon
(for 6)

4 medium-size
   cooking apples
8 oz. sugar
2 eggs
8 oz. flour
½ teaspoonful
   cinnamon
4 oz. chopped pecan
   nuts
4 oz. butter or
   margarine, melted

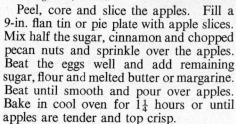

Peel, core and slice the apples. Fill a 9-in. flan tin or pie plate with apple slices. Mix half the sugar, cinnamon and chopped pecan nuts and sprinkle over the apples. Beat the eggs well and add remaining sugar, flour and melted butter or margarine. Beat until smooth and pour over apples. Bake in cool oven for 1¼ hours or until apples are tender and top crisp.

Lemon Meringue Pie (for 8)

1 oz. flour or corn-   2 eggs (separated)
   flour   ½ oz. butter
½ lb. sugar   Rind and juice of 1
8 oz. boiling water   lemon
      Short-pastry flan case

Mix sugar and flour in pan, add boiling water slowly and boil until clear, stirring all the time with a wooden spoon. Add butter gradually and the egg-yolks, lightly beaten. Still stirring, cook over boiling water until it holds its shape. Remove from heat and add lemon juice and rind. When cool, pour into baked short-pastry flan case, about 8 in. diameter (see Pastry chapter). Cover with meringue made by beating egg-whites stiff with 4 dessertspoonfuls sugar. Put in very cool oven until meringue is delicately browned in peaks, about 15 minutes.

Pumpkin Pie

2 cupfuls steamed   Uncooked pastry shell
   pumpkin   1 level teaspoonful
1 cupful sugar   ginger
½ level teaspoonful   1 level teaspoonful
   salt   cinnamon
2 eggs   ½ teaspoonful nutmeg
      ¾ pint scalded milk

Rub the pumpkin through a sieve, and add to it the sugar, spices, salt, milk and the well-beaten eggs. Allow to cool. Fill the uncooked pastry case with this mixture and bake in a moderate oven for 40–45 minutes.

CAKES

Angel Food Cake

1 cupful fine white   1¼ teaspoonfuls
   flour   cream of tartar
1⅓ cupfuls sugar   1 teaspoonful vanilla
10 egg-whites   essence
      ¼ teaspoonful salt

Sift the flour and ⅓ cupful sugar three times. Beat the egg-whites until foamy, and add the cream of tartar and the salt; beat until the mixture is stiff, but not dry. Sift the remaining sugar three times and gradually fold into the egg-white mixture, 2 tablespoonfuls at a time. Add the vanilla essence. Sift ¼ cupful flour and fold in lightly, continuing until all the flour is used. Pour into an ungreased border cake tin and bake in a moderate oven for 1¼ hours. Remove from oven and turn cake tin upside down on wire cake rack until cold—about 1 hour—before turning out cake.

Boston Favourite

4 oz. butter or mar-   1 gill milk
   garine   2½ teaspoonfuls
3 egg-yolks   baking powder
2 egg-whites   Flavouring or shelled
8 oz. sugar   walnuts
      14 oz. flour

Cream butter and sugar, add well-beaten egg-yolks. Mix and sift flour and baking powder, and add alternately with milk. Then add egg-whites, beaten stiff, nuts or essence, and bake in moderate oven for 45–50 minutes. Top with Boiled Frosting.

Boiled Frosting

8 oz. sugar
1 gill boiling water
1 egg-white

Flavouring—tea-spoonful vanilla or as liked

Boil sugar and water together until it threads with a little stirring. Pour syrup over beaten egg-white and beat until it reaches spreading consistency. Add flavouring, pour over cake and crease with knife.

Bride's Cake

8 oz. butter
1 lb. flour
1 lb. sugar
1 tablespoonful baking powder

8 oz. cornflour
5 egg-whites
½ teaspoonful almond essence
1 gill milk

Well cream butter and sugar together; sift dry ingredients and add, mixing thoroughly, alternately with the milk. Fold in stiffly beaten egg-whites and flavouring, divide between two sandwich tins and bake in moderate oven for about 25–30 minutes. Put together when cool with butter filling (see Icings chapter) or whipped cream flavoured to taste, ice with Boiled or Nut Caramel Frosting.

Nut Caramel Frosting

10 oz. brown sugar
2 oz. white sugar
1 gill water
4 oz. chopped walnuts

2 egg-whites
1 teaspoonful vanilla essence

Boil sugar and water until it threads, then pour, while beating, on to stiffly beaten egg-whites. Beat until lukewarm. Stand pan in larger pan of boiling water over heat and stir constantly until it becomes granular round the edges. Remove, and beat in with spoon the chopped walnuts and vanilla. Pour over cake, spread roughly.

Buckwheat Cakes

1 cupful buckwheat flour
1 cupful white flour
1 egg
1 level teaspoonful salt

1¾ cupfuls milk
4 level teaspoonfuls baking powder
2 tablespoonfuls molasses (optional)

Sift together the buckwheat flour, plain flour, salt and baking powder. Beat the egg well, and stir it in gradually with the milk. Beat thoroughly to remove any lumps and cook at once on a hot, greased griddle.

If desired, two tablespoonfuls of molasses may be added to the mixture before cooking. This helps to brown the cakes as well as to sweeten them.

Corn Bread

1 cupful plain white flour
1 cupful corn meal
3 teaspoonfuls baking powder

½ teaspoonful salt
1 egg
1 cupful milk
¼ cupful melted fat, or salad oil

Sift together the flour, corn meal, baking powder and salt. Beat the egg, and mix with the milk and melted fat. Add to dry ingredients. Pour into a greased pan and bake in a hot oven for ½ hour.

Cream Sponge

4 eggs
8 oz. sugar
3 tablespoonfuls cold water
1 teaspoonful lemon essence

1½ tablespoonfuls cornflour
8 oz. flour
1½ teaspoonfuls baking powder
¼ teaspoonful salt

Separate egg-yolks from whites, beat yolks until thick, add the sugar gradually, then water and essence. Mix and sift flour and cornflour with baking powder and salt, and add to egg-yolk mixture. Beat egg-whites until stiff and fold into the dough. Divide into two sandwich tins and bake in a fairly quick oven for 25–30 minutes. When cold, put together with whipped cream, sweetened and flavoured to taste.

Devil's Food Cake

2 eggs
1 lb. brown sugar
4 oz. melted butter
4 oz. plain chocolate, grated
1 gill sour milk

1 teaspoonful bicarbonate of soda
1 gill of boiling water
1 lb. flour
Vanilla essence to flavour

Dissolve chocolate in boiling water. Add sugar and melted butter, stir soda into milk and add with beaten eggs to chocolate mixture. Mix in sifted flour, add vanilla, beat well, divide between two sandwich tins and bake in moderate oven. When cold, put together and top with Boiled Frosting.

CANADA

Original salads and fish dishes, crisp and crunchy cookies, clever
ways with beans—they are all to be found in Canadian cookery

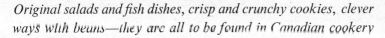

SOUPS

Bean Soup (for 4)

1 *pint black beans*	1 *teaspoonful meat*
3 *oz. butter*	*extract*
⅛ *teaspoonful paprika*	*Salt to season*
2 *tablespoonfuls*	*Hard-boiled egg*
sherry	2 *slices white bread*
1 *lemon*	*A little milk*

Soak the beans in cold water for 12 hours. Drain, cover with fresh cold water, bring to the boil and cook for about 1 hour, or until soft. Pass through sieve or fine strainer, stir in salt, paprika and meat extract. Add butter. Remove from the heat and stir in the bread, broken into small pieces and without the crust. If soup is too thick, add milk as necessary, and let it simmer gently for about 15 minutes, stirring well.

Stir in the sherry just before serving, and garnish each bowl with a thin slice of hard-boiled egg resting on a thin slice of lemon.

Crab Soup (for 4)

1½ *pints milk*	1½ *oz. cornflour*
½ *pint water*	14 *oz. cooked crab*
½ *teaspoonful*	*meat*
Worcester sauce	1½ *oz. butter*
1 *teaspoonful curry*	4 *hard-boiled eggs*
powder	1 *gill sherry*
2 *sticks celery*	*(optional)*
⅛ *teaspoonful mace*	*Twist of lemon peel*

Wash and trim celery stalks, cut into small lengths (about ¾ in.) and boil for 10 minutes in well-salted water. Drain. Mix the cornflour with enough cold milk to make a smooth paste; heat the rest of 1 pint and, when boiling, pour on to the paste, stirring well so that the mixture is smooth and free from lumps. Add the celery and allow to simmer very gently for a further 5 minutes, adding butter. Separate yolks and whites of hard-boiled eggs; chop whites finely and add to the soup, together with the Worcester sauce, mace, curry powder and crab meat. Remove from heat and gradually add the rest of the milk

mixed with the ½ pint of water, as necessary; you may not need to use quite all of it. Allow to simmer gently for a further 10 minutes, stirring from time to time.

Crumble the egg-yolks over the top of the soup after it has been put into individual bowls, just before serving.

If sherry is to accompany this soup, it should be well heated and handed round separately, with two thin coils of lemon peel in it, so that guests may help themselves, according to their taste.

French Canadian Chestnut Soup (for 4)

1 *lb. chestnuts*	2 *oz. fresh butter*
1 *onion*	1 *quart stock*
3 *tablespoonfuls*	½ *teaspoonful celery*
cream (optional)	*salt*
¾ *teaspoonful pepper*	

Boil the chestnuts for 20 minutes, then peel them and put them into a saucepan with the stock and the onion, peeled and chopped. Boil together for 20 minutes, then rub through a hair sieve.

Add the butter, celery salt and pepper and, if available, the cream.

FISH

Canadian-style Poached Fish (for 4)

1 *slice lemon*	1½ *lb. fresh haddock*
2 *teaspoonfuls salt*	*Few sprigs of green*
1 *bay leaf*	*celery top*
¼ *teaspoonful whole*	*Tablespoonful*
black peppers	*chopped parsley*
2 *slices onion*	2 *oz. melted butter*
1 *pint water*	

Put the lemon, salt, bay leaf, peppers, onion slices and celery sprigs into the water and boil for 10 minutes. Add the fish and simmer gently for 10 minutes, or until the fish flakes easily with a fork (time depends on its thickness).

Drain and serve hot with the melted butter poured over; garnish with the chopped parsley.

Montreal Tuna Fish Fritters (for 3 or 4)

6 oz. tuna fish	¼ teaspoonful pepper
2 eggs	4 oz. rice
⅛ pint milk	2 rounded table-
1 teaspoonful salt	spoonfuls flour
Salad oil for frying	

Bring the rice to the boil in a saucepan with ¾ pint of well-salted water. Cover and cook gently over a low heat for 15 minutes, then remove from the heat.

Separate the whites and yolks of the eggs; mix together the fish, milk, egg-yolks, flour and pepper and add to the rice, mixing well together.

Beat the egg-whites until stiff, and fold gently into the rice and fish mixture. Drop from a tablespoon into hot deep fat and fry until a crisp golden brown.

Oyster Stew (for 4)

1 pint oysters	1½ oz. margarine
Sprig of parsley	1½ tablespoonfuls
1 bay leaf	flour
1 slice onion	Salt and Cayenne
1 pint milk	pepper

Prepare the oysters, strain the liquor through a cheese cloth, cut the oysters in half and cook in the liquor for 3–5 minutes, or until the edges curl.

Add the parsley, bay leaf and onion to the milk and bring to the boil; strain. Melt the margarine and blend in the flour; add the milk gradually, and cook until slightly thickened, stirring all the time. Add the oysters and season with the salt and Cayenne pepper. Serve at once.

Tuna Chow Mein (for 4)

3 sticks celery	4 oz. cooked mush-
1 chopped onion	rooms
½ green pepper	6 oz. cooked or
1 oz. margarine	canned tuna fish
4 teaspoonfuls soy	1 tablespoonful corn-
sauce	flour
Salt and pepper to	4 oz. noodles
taste	2 teaspoonfuls lemon
½ pint mixed milk	juice
and water	

Chop the washed celery into short match-stick lengths, and cook in the margarine with the onion and finely chopped green pepper. Add mushrooms, cut into halves or quarters, soy sauce and fish; season with salt and pepper and mix in the milk and water. Bring to boil, cover and cook for 15–20 minutes.

Mix the cornflour to a smooth paste with

cold water, add to the mixture, stirring in carefully, and cook until it thickens; stir continually so that no lumps form.

Cook the noodles in boiling salted water for 15 minutes, or until tender; drain well.

Stir the lemon juice into the fish mixture, and turn out on to the noodles before serving.

MEAT AND POULTRY

Braised Pork Chops with Mushroom Gravy (for 6)

6 loin pork chops	1 bay leaf
1½ oz. bacon fat or	½ pint milk
margarine	Salt and pepper and a
½ lb. mushrooms	little flour for chops
1 tablespoonful flour	

Wipe the chops and trim away any excess fat. Sprinkle with salt and pepper, and roll in flour. Melt fat or margarine and brown chops lightly on both sides. Remove from the pan and keep hot. Prepare mushrooms and cut into quarters, cooking in the same fat. Season with salt and pepper.

When they are done, mix the flour to a smooth paste, using sufficient milk from the ½ pint, gradually add the rest of the milk, stirring all the time; pour over the mushrooms and bring all together to the boil; add bay leaf and simmer for 5 minutes, stirring from time to time.

Place the chops in a fireproof dish and pour the mushroom gravy over; cover closely and bake in a moderate oven for 45 minutes, turning the chops occasionally.

Cheeseburgers (for 4)

1 lb. finely minced	Fat for frying
beef	1 large or 2 small soft
Seasoning and	rolls per person
chopped onion	

For the Cheese Topping

¼ lb. grated Cheddar	2 tablespoonfuls
cheese or cheese	prepared mustard
spread	1 teaspoonful lemon
2 tablespoonfuls	· juice
mayonnaise	½ teaspoonful celery
	salt

Mix the meat, onion and seasoning thoroughly, shape into cakes to fit the rolls, then fry in melted fat until cooked to individual liking, either "rare," medium or well done. Split the rolls and put a hamburger into each, then top with:

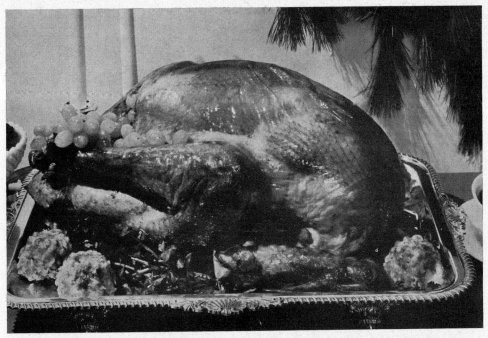

Small roast turkey is served with Chestnut Dressing. Simmer coarsely chopped cooked chestnuts with a little chopped onion and sliced apple, salt and sage, in butter for 10 minutes. Mix with breadcrumbs and pack lightly into the bird

Cheese Topping

Blend all ingredients thoroughly, spread cooked hamburgers with this and put under a hot grill until the cheese begins to bubble and brown slightly.

Chicken and Dumplings (for 4)

12 oz. cold cooked chicken	2 oz. margarine
1 oz. flour	Tablespoonful chopped parsley
1½ pints stock	

For the dumplings

1 egg	4 oz. flour
¼ teaspoonful salt	⅛ pint milk

Melt the margarine in a saucepan and blend the flour in carefully; add the stock gradually and cook until it thickens, stirring constantly. Add the pieces of chicken and bring the mixture gradually to the boil. *For the dumplings.*—Beat the egg well and add the milk. Mix together the salt and flour, and sift into the liquid; beat until smooth. Drop the dumpling mixture into the chicken soup by tablespoonfuls. Cover and simmer for 10–12 minutes.

Sprinkle with the chopped parsley and serve.

Ham and Mushroom Casserole (for 4)

4 oz. macaroni	1 tablespoonful flour
8 oz. ham	6 oz. grated cheese
1 tablespoonful minced onion	½ pint milk
	2 oz. margarine
Salt and pepper	4 oz. mushrooms

Cook the macaroni in boiling salted water until tender, drain and set aside. Melt the margarine in a frying pan and gently cook the mushrooms; when they are done, remove from pan, blend in flour with the fat and pour in the milk and about ⅛ pint of cold water. Bring gently to the boil, stirring all the time, and allow to simmer for 5 minutes.

Mix together the macaroni, ham, cheese, mushrooms and liquid from the pan, together with the minced onion. Season well with salt and pepper. Turn into a greased dish and bake in a medium oven for ½ hour.

Potatoes au Bœuf (for 4)

1 lb. minced beef	4 large potatoes
2 teaspoonfuls mixed herbs (thyme, marjoram, parsley)	1 oz. margarine
	¼ teaspoonful paprika
Salt and pepper to season	¼ pint milk

Scrub potatoes, prick once or twice with

a fork and bake in a fairly hot oven for between 1 and 1½ hours, according to size.

Melt fat in frying pan and brown the beef lightly, stirring with a fork, mix in the herbs, salt and pepper.

When potatoes are done, cut off the tops and scoop out the inside. Keep the skins. Whip up the potato, season with salt and pepper, and add enough hot milk to make the mixture light and fluffy. Fold the meat into the potato, and fill the skins with the mixture.

Sprinkle each potato with a little paprika and put under the grill until they are heated through and lightly browned on top.

Stuffed Shoulder of Mutton

Shoulder of mutton   Salad oil
        Salt and pepper

For the stuffing

1 small egg	2 heaped tablespoon-
2 teaspoonfuls finely	fuls breadcrumbs
chopped mint	Seasoning

Wipe the meat over with a damp cloth, and remove skin, using a sharp knife. Next, remove bone (or you can ask for this to be done at the butcher's).

Rub meat well with salt and pepper, and then with salad oil.

Mix together the breadcrumbs, minced or finely chopped mint, and salt and pepper. Beat up the egg and use just enough to bind the breadcrumb mixture. Insert the stuffing into the pocket left by the bone, and sew up.

Put into a hot oven for 10 minutes; then lower heat to moderate and cook till done, allowing 20 minutes for each pound and 20 minutes over for any remaining part of a pound.

VEGETABLE DISHES

Asparagus with Eggs (Asperges aux Œufs) (for 4)

1 bundle asparagus	4 eggs
3 oz. grated cheese	2 tablespoonfuls
(Parmesan or	salad oil
Gruyère)	Salt and pepper to
4 slices toast	taste
Small clove of garlic	

Wash the asparagus well and cook in boiling salted water for 10–15 minutes, or until barely tender; drain and put aside to keep hot.

Heat the oil, add the garlic and cook for about 1 minute, remove garlic, then fry eggs gently in a covered pan for about 3 minutes. Season with salt and pepper.

Divide the asparagus into four portions, top each with an egg and pour over a little of the hot oil. Sprinkle well with the grated cheese and serve with the toast cut into triangles.

Canadian Beans and Rice (for 4)

½ lb. lean salt pork or	2 teaspoonfuls
bacon	parsley, finely
6 oz. rice	chopped
6 oz. red kidney beans	Salt and pepper to
1 clove of garlic	taste

Wash the beans and boil in well salted water for 20 minutes, or until tender; drain and set aside. Cook the rice in boiling salted water until done; drain and set aside. Dice and fry the pork or bacon until brown and crisp. Remove from the pan, and cook the minced clove of garlic gently for about 2 minutes.

Add the rice and beans, salt and pepper, and mix well together, heating thoroughly.

Turn into a pre-heated dish, top with the diced pork cubes and sprinkle with the chopped parsley before serving.

Scalloped Asparagus (for 4)

1 bundle asparagus	1 pint milk
3 oz. margarine	2 oz. grated cheese
4 tablespoonfuls flour	(Cheddar or
¾ teaspoonful salt	Gruyère)
¾ teaspoonful pepper	½ teaspoonful paprika
3 oz. soft bread-	½ teaspoonful
crumbs	Worcester sauce
1 dessertspoonful	2 tablespoonfuls
finely chopped	sliced stuffed olives
parsley	

Wash and cut the asparagus into 2-in. lengths. Cook in salted water until barely tender—about 10–15 minutes; drain carefully and put in shallow fireproof baking dish.

Melt the margarine in top of double saucepan; take out a third (1 oz.) and mix with the breadcrumbs. Blend flour and seasonings carefully with the remaining margarine. Add the milk and cook over boiling water until the mixture thickens, stirring all the time. Add the cheese and cook until it melts, then the sliced olives. Pour the mixture over the asparagus and top with the margarined crumbs.

Bake in a moderate oven for 15 minutes —or slightly more—until the crumbs are golden brown. Garnish with finely chopped parsley.

Vegetable Hot-pot (for 4)

1½ oz. margarine
6 peeled potatoes
8 small carrots
6 spring onions
6 oz. shelled fresh
  peas
¼ lb. runner beans
2 tomatoes
1 tablespoonful
  chopped parsley
1 teaspoonful mixed
  herbs
Salt and pepper

Heat margarine in saucepan and prepare vegetables. Cut potatoes in half and brown in heated fat. Add carrots, sprinkle with salt and pepper, cover and cook for 5–7 minutes. Add onions, peas, beans, herbs and ½ pint of water; cover and allow to simmer gently for 30 minutes. Halve tomatoes and place them, cut side uppermost, on top of the other vegetables, cooking for a further 5–10 minutes.

Garnish with the chopped parsley and serve.

Cheeseburgers, hot and sizzling, are an ideal supper dish.
Serve them with spring onions and radish roses

SALADS

Canadian-style Country Salad

1 cucumber
4 tomatoes
Tarragon or herb
  vinegar
1 green pepper
2 sticks celery
Salt and pepper
1 tablespoonful
  minced or finely
  chopped onion
1 diced, unpeeled red
  apple, if liked

Wash and slice the tomatoes, peel and slice the cucumber; chop the green pepper and the celery into small pieces. Dice the apple and mix all together with the chopped or minced onion.

Season with salt and pepper to taste, and add the vinegar.

Canadian Tomato Salad

6 tomatoes
1 large clove garlic
1 tablespoonful
  chopped chives
2½ tablespoonfuls
  mayonnaise
1 tablespoonful finely
  chopped parsley
1 teaspoonful salt
1 teaspoonful mixed
  dried herbs
Pepper to taste

Wash the tomatoes and cut into large pieces, sprinkle the salt over and mix together lightly. Leave for 5 minutes, then drain.

Mix together the remaining ingredients and the garlic, cut into halves. Add this to the tomatoes and toss lightly. Cover and store in the refrigerator for 2–3 hours, if possible, before serving.

Montreal Chicken Salad

6 oz. cold cooked
  chicken
6 heaped tablespoon-
  fuls chopped celery
2 tablespoonfuls
  finely chopped
  green peppers
Lettuce
4 tomatoes
2 tablespoonfuls
  almonds
1 hard-boiled egg
Juice of ½ lemon
A few radishes
¼ pint mayonnaise

Chop the chicken into small pieces. Wash the lettuce. Blanch the almonds. Just slit the tomatoes into six portions, which remain joined together underneath. Prepare radishes.

Mix the chicken well with the celery, green peppers, blanched almonds and half the mayonnaise. Set the tomatoes out on a bed of lettuce, and fill each with the mixture; moisten with a little lemon juice and garnish with slices of hard-boiled egg and slices of radish.

Pile the remaining chicken mayonnaise in the centre of the dish and top with the rest of the mayonnaise.

Pear and Peanut Salad

1 lettuce	4 heaped tablespoon-
2 ripe eating pears	fuls diced celery
2 dessertspoonfuls	2 tablespoonfuls
salted peanuts	capers
½ lemon	Paprika to taste
	Mayonnaise

Peel and core the pears and cut them into dice. Add lemon juice and mix well; then stir in the celery, peanuts, capers and enough mayonnaise to moisten. Arrange on a bed of crisp, washed and thoroughly dried lettuce, and sprinkle lightly with paprika.

This salad is improved if the mixture is chilled in a refrigerator before it is placed on the lettuce.

Salade aux Olives

4 oz. olives	½ pint (10 oz.) frozen
1 spring onion	or fresh peas
2 heaped tablespoon-	(cooked)
fuls finely chopped	½ lemon
green pepper	Salt and pepper
6 heaped tablespoon-	Dash of paprika
fuls finely chopped	½ teaspoonful made
celery	mustard
¼ pint mayonnaise	½ teaspoonful
6 oz. processed cheese	Worcester sauce

Mix together the olives, finely chopped, the chopped onion, green pepper, celery, peas and cheese cut into dice. Mix together the mayonnaise, lemon juice, mustard and Worcester sauce and combine with first mixture, seasoning with salt and pepper. (Chill at this point, if possible.)

Sprinkle over very lightly with paprika before serving.

SWEETS, COOKIES, Etc.

Butter Fruit Tartlets (for 4)

2 eggs	6 oz. seedless raisins
8 oz. light brown	and sultanas mixed
sugar	1 oz. chopped walnuts
2 tablespoonfuls	Short pastry (see
vinegar	Pastry chapter)
4 oz. butter	1 teaspoonful vanilla
	essence

Beat eggs lightly, just sufficiently to blend yolks and whites. Add sugar, vinegar and vanilla essence. Stir in melted butter and add fruit and nuts.

Line tartlet tins with pastry and fill each case about two-thirds full with the fruit and butter mixture. Bake in a hot oven for first 7 minutes; then reduce heat to moderate for balance of baking time—about 20–25 minutes, or until filling is firm.

Coconut Pie (for 4)

2 eggs	4 oz. sugar
Pinch of salt	4 oz. desiccated coco-
Short pastry (see	nut
Pastry chapter)	

Line a flan ring or tin with pastry. Beat eggs, add sugar, pinch of salt and coconut, stirring well in.

Pour into pastry-shell and bake in moderate oven for about 25–30 minutes, or until mixture is firm and a golden brown.

Coconut and Walnut Cookies

4 oz. butter or mar-	6 oz. flour
garine	2 oz. brown sugar

For the nut mixture

8 oz. brown sugar	3 oz. desiccated coco-
3 tablespoonfuls flour	nut
½ teaspoonful vanilla	3 oz. finely chopped
essence	walnuts
	2 egg-whites

Rub the butter or margarine lightly into the flour. Add the sifted brown sugar and mix well. Pat this mixture well into a pan about 14 × 7 in. Bake in a moderate oven until a delicate golden brown, setting on a fairly high shelf so that it does not brown unduly on the bottom. Allow to cool.

For the nut mixture.—Mix together the flour and brown sugar, well sifted, and add the mixture gradually to the stiffly beaten egg-whites. Add the vanilla essence, and lightly fold in the coconut and walnuts.

Spread this mixture gently over the baked crumble crust, and return tin to oven, cooking in a slow oven until the nut méringue is delicately browned.

Remove from oven and, while still warm, cut into finger strips. Allow these to cool in the tin before removing.

Oatmeal Lace Cookies

7 oz. sugar	½ lb. flour
2 eggs	½ lb. quick-cooking
1 teaspoonful	porridge oats
powdered cinna-	2 oz. chopped nuts
mon	6 oz. mixed pure lard
4 oz. seedless raisins	and margarine
½ pint water	Pinch of salt

Stew the raisins in the water and set aside.

Cream the sugar and fats together, and add the well-beaten eggs. Fold in the flour, salt and cinnamon. Add porridge oats, nuts and stewed raisins. Use sufficient of the liquid in which the raisins were cooked to make a dough which will drop from a spoon.

Drop the mixture in spoonfuls on to a greased baking sheet and cook in a hot oven for about 10 minutes.

Party Sandwich Loaf (for 8–10)

1 unsliced sandwich loaf, one day old	Cheese frosting
	Cheese spread
Radishes	Parsley
Watercress	Tomatoes

Chicken Salad Filling:

½ cupful chopped cooked or canned chicken or turkey	¼ teaspoonful salt
	Grated rind of ½ lemon
¼ cupful minced celery	2 tablespoonfuls mayonnaise

Egg Salad Filling:

2 hard-boiled eggs, finely chopped	½ teaspoonful prepared mustard
2 tablespoonfuls minced olives	⅛ teaspoonful curry powder
½ teaspoonful salt	2 tablespoonfuls mustard

To make the fillings, combine the ingredients and chill until ready to use.

Cheese Frosting:

8 oz. soft cream cheese	¼ lb. grated Cheddar
	Single cream

Beat cream cheese until light and fluffy. Gradually blend in grated cheese with enough cream to make mixture light, fluffy and a good consistency for spreading.

Trim crusts from loaf and slice lengthwise into ½ in. slices. Spread alternate slices with different fillings. Frost top and sides of sandwich loaf with cheese frosting, garnish with sliced radishes, parsley and watercress.

The loaf will cut more easily and be easier to serve if prepared 6–12 hours in advance and stored in a refrigerator in a covered container.

No, not an iced cake but a party sandwich made by slicing a large loaf lengthwise, spreading with various savoury fillings and frosting all over with cream cheese

COOKING WITH WINE

It need not be in the least exotic or extravagant,
but what a difference it makes to the simplest food

LET'S first put it out of our heads that cooking with wine is (*a*) exotic, and (*b*) reserved for Continental types or the very rich. It can, of course, be exotic, but so can steak and kidney pudding with a dozen or so oysters added—you ask any connoisseur of this English classic. As for expense, you can buy extremely good wines for 5s. to 6s. a bottle, and since one uses it mostly by the tablespoonful, a bottle of wine will go a long way.

If you intend to try cooking with wine off your own bat, adding wine to your favourite dishes, remember that, generally speaking, fish and white wine go together, and meat usually calls for red wine. This is much too simple a division, but it is a good starting point.

You might also like to remember that lobster and crayfish have an affinity for sherry—and an even greater one for sherry and cream. And here is an "after the cinema" dish which has the double virtue of being made in about 10 minutes and tasting quite delicious.

QUICK DISHES

For two people you need one good-sized crayfish tail (out of season you can buy frozen ones), which the fishmonger will split for you, so that scooping it out of its shell is easy. You can use it either in its two halves or cut into smaller pieces. Make your very best white sauce (much nicer made with butter), add the crayfish, and then a glass of sherry, and let it get good and hot without reaching the boil. If there is a tablespoonful of thick cream available, or even the top of the milk, stir it in at the last moment. The cream is not essential, but it does add that touch. Dish up sprinkled with parsley and eat it piping hot with, or without, some crisp thin toast.

Alternatively, toast some thin bread on one side only, butter the untoasted side,

spread with Parmesan cheese (which *must* be the powdered kind) mixed to a paste with vermouth, clap two pieces together—and eat. Good for parties, too.

SAUCES

Perhaps the most familiar method of cooking with wine is the making of sauces. One of the best known is Sauce Espagnole, a sauce that was equally well known in France and England some three hundred years ago—and the only thing Spanish about it is its name.

Sauce Espagnole

Chop 2 oz. of bacon into tiny pieces and fry in 1 oz. of butter, adding a few sliced mushrooms, a carrot and an onion, both chopped. When the vegetables begin to brown, stir in 1 oz. of flour and cook till smooth, then add a gill of stock (the best stock for this sauce is made from veal bones), salt and pepper, and simmer very gently for half an hour. Then add 2 tomatoes cut into small pieces, 2 tablespoonfuls of sherry and cook for a further 10 minutes.

You can, if you wish, use Burgundy or Madeira for this sauce, or, if you feel that way about it, Champagne. With rather less stock added, it makes an excellent filling for omelets.

Madeira Sauce is another classic, and is particularly good with baked or grilled ham.

Begin by making a roux, using water instead of milk, and 1 oz. of butter to a tablespoonful of flour. To this add a wine-glass of Madeira and one of a good meat stock, and, of course, salt and pepper. The Madeira should be added gradually.

White Sauce—the only sauce the English can make, according to the French—*can* be so dull if it is badly made, but it can be very good, particularly when "dressed up." Our old friend parsley sauce, for instance, takes very happily to the addition of chopped chives, in small quantity, and a dessertspoonful of white wine. To go with fish, try adding a few shrimps or prawns, or some coarsely chopped hardboiled eggs, with some grated lemon and a dessertspoonful of white wine, preferably Chablis.

Hungarian Sauce—so useful because it goes with every kind of meat.

Brown 1 lb. of chopped onions in butter or lard (or, better still, kidney fat), add a large pinch of paprika, a glass of white wine, a pint of sour cream, bring it all to the boil, and serve. For variation, add chopped tomato too.

Old English Sauce is designed to mate with venison, but it goes equally well with mutton.

Boil 1 oz. of currants in water for a few minutes; add 3 tablespoonfuls of grated bread, a walnut-sized piece of butter, 4 cloves and a glass of port, and stir till it boils. Serve hot.

Sherry Sauce—for puddings, but equally happy with a lemon soufflé.

Put 2 egg-yolks, 5 tablespoonfuls of sherry and a teaspoonful of castor sugar into a double boiler (or a basin over a pan of boiling water) and beat until the mixture thickens, but do not boil. Remove from the stove and stir in 1 tablespoonful of thick cream.

SOUPS

The canning of soups has been brought to such a high art that it is no longer a heinous offence to own a can opener. But, good as they are (particularly when glorified a little by the cook), some proud

Any fairly large fresh- or sea-water fish is excellent stuffed with savoury rice or a vegetable mixture and cooked in wine

hostesses like to show that they can still make their own. Have a care, though, in adding wine to your soups: increasing the quantity recommended in a recipe does not necessarily improve the flavour. But for fun—*and* good flavour—let's start with a soup that comes from Belgium and is nearly all wine.

Wine Soup

Boil equal quantities of red wine and sweetened water with a stick of cinnamon. Pour it over toasted bread (or biscuits, if you prefer them), and there's your soup.

Mussel Soup (which sounds much more grandiose if you call it Moules Marinière).

Put 1½ pints of fish stock (or water with lots of fish bones) into a pan with 3 tablespoonfuls of white wine, and add a bouquet garni and a clove of garlic. Bring to the boil and simmer for 20 minutes. Make a thickening of 1 oz. of butter with flour and seasoning, and when smooth add to the stock. Stir till it boils, then simmer for 15 minutes.

Wash and scrub the mussels, and put them into another pan, with 3 tablespoonfuls of wine. Cover and bring to the boil, then shake over the heat for 2 or 3 minutes, and strain the liquor into the soup. Beard the mussels, but leave them in a half shell, and put them into the soup with some finely chopped parsley. Simmer for 5 minutes, add 2 tablespoonfuls of cream and serve.

Shrimp Soup

You need 1 onion, 1 leek, 1 carrot, cut into thin slices; put them into a pan with a bunch of mixed herbs and a clove and 2 wineglassfuls of white wine and bring to the boil. Then throw in the unshelled shrimps and cook for 10 minutes. Remove the shrimps and shell just a few of them, cutting up the flesh into small pieces. Grind the remainder into a paste (yes, the shells too) and return it to the pan with 1½ pints of fish stock (or water), 2 oz. of rice and 2 tablespoonfuls of tomato purée. Cook on a fairly low heat, with a cover on, for 1 hour. Then pass it through a sieve, forcing through with a wooden spoon any lumps of shrimp or vegetable, season, bring almost to the boil; add the cut-up pieces of shrimp and serve really hot.

Bean Soup

Soak ½ lb. dried haricot or butter beans overnight and cook them the next day in the same water until they are mushy, and beat them until smooth. Brown 2 oz. flour in 1 oz. of butter, mix with the beans and add 2 pints of white stock (or a mixture of water and milk), season and simmer for an hour. Add a gill of sour cream, 3 oz. grated cheese and a wineglassful of white wine. Reheat, but do not boil, and serve, preferably with croûtons.

Potato Cream Soup

Cook in 1 oz. of butter, 1 lb. of cubed old potatoes and some diced celery—do not brown. Add 1½ pints of stock and simmer till potatoes are cooked, then rub through a sieve and add an onion (into

which you have stuck several cloves), and a quart of fresh milk, and return to stove. Cook slowly for an hour, remove the onion and thicken with 3 oz. of flour, blended into a smooth paste before adding. Finally, add a gill of evaporated milk and 2 wineglassfuls of white wine and stir well.

Clear Game Soup

Simmer 2 rashers of diced bacon, 1 onion and a stick of celery, chopped, in about 2 oz. of butter with the giblets and carcase of any game bird. Broil all together briskly, add a quart of stock, stirring all the time, then simmer for a further half-hour. Add a few cooked peas, some small pieces of game if available, reheat and add a glass of sherry.

FISH

Take a look at the wondrous displays of fish on almost any fishmonger's slab in the U.K.—and think what a sorry sight it makes when it appears on so many family tables—slightly grey and almost invariably accompanied by a solid white sauce. We have some of the world's best fish, and we should treat it with the respect it deserves. Choose your sauces to enhance, and not to mask, the flavour of the fish itself, and at all costs avoid that soiled-looking pink dab which goes by the name of anchovy sauce.

There is a recipe which is usually given for the cooking of sole or plaice fillets, but it is especially good for the unfairly despised cod. Put pieces of cod (the pieces should be serving size) into a flat casserole with a good sprinkling of finely shaved onions and sliced mushrooms, pepper and salt, a generous glassful of white wine and a dab or two of butter. Cook in the oven until tender, and serve with a sauce made from the usual butter and flour, cooked with the liquid from the fish and thinned with milk, to which you should add shrimps or more mushrooms. Pour the sauce round, not on, the fish, and remember a touch of green—chopped parsley, or a few sprigs of watercress.

Sole Normande

Make a white roux with a dessertspoonful of flour, a tablespoonful of butter, half a glass of water, and a glass of white wine. Let it bubble a minute or two, then put in the prepared sole, and let it poach gently

Poached fish steaks are particularly good served with Sherry Sauce. Here the steaks are seen "sandwiched" together in pairs with savoury stuffing

for about 20 minutes. Clean a dozen mussels, cook them and remove from their shells, then put them to keep warm, saving the liquor from their cooking. Shell half a pound of shrimps. Cook in butter half a pound of mushrooms. *Now*, strain the sauce, very carefully, off the sole, add to it the liquor from the mussels and from the mushrooms, reducing a little if necessary —then add, away from the fire, the beaten yolks of 2 eggs and 3 dessertspoonfuls of double cream. Serve the sole surrounded with the shrimps, mushrooms and mussels and mask with the sauce. This sounds a great deal more complex than it really is, but the flavour is well worth any amount of trouble.

Baked Fish

This recipe is ideal for any large fresh-water fish, but can be very happily used for fresh haddock or cod. Chop finely a large onion, a stick of celery and a carrot and fry them lightly in olive oil or butter, adding when they are just getting tender a handful of finely chopped parsley and some peeled, chopped tomatoes. Stuff the cleaned fish (if you have a nice fishmonger, he will take out the backbone, which makes it very

much easier) with the vegetable mixture; put the fish into a fireproof dish, dot with butter, add the liquid from the vegetables, cover with red or white wine and simmer gently until it is cooked through.

A variation on this theme is to stuff the fish with a savoury rice—that is, rice (already cooked) mixed with chopped fried mushrooms, a very small quantity of herbs and an even smaller quantity of tarragon. If you are too generous with the tarragon, it covers every other flavour. For this dish dot with butter and allow to cook for a little while before adding the wine—white for preference. Bream is ideal for this method.

Poached Fish with Sherry Sauce

Make a sherry sauce by blending 1 oz. of melted butter with 1 oz. of flour and adding $\frac{1}{4}$ pint of fish stock and a tablespoonful of sherry. Stir all the time until it reaches boiling point, then add a bay leaf and a small shallot and reduce by simmering. Add 1 egg-yolk mixed with a tablespoonful of cream, and then a dessertspoonful of lemon juice, a little salt and some Cayenne pepper.

Serve the sauce with any white fish, preferably the kind you buy in steaks, such as turbot, which has been poached in boiling water with a teaspoonful of lemon juice and seasoning. Garnish with parsley.

MEAT

Recipes for cooking every kind of meat, poultry and game with wine are legion, but with a little experience a good cook will find her own moments for the addition of wine to a favoured dish. One small tip—if you are roasting wild duck, teal or widgeon, make the gravy (before you remove the bird) by pouring off most of the fat, leaving the delicious juices and adding a wineglassful of red wine. Put the dish back in the oven for a few minutes, and at the last squeeze just a few drops of lemon juice into it. Another tip is to add a glass of port to our old friend steak and kidney pudding (with a funnel inserted under the top crust) just before it is served.

Pork with Red or White Wine

Take 1 pork chop for each person, and even if they are quite fat, dot them with butter (though not lavishly), sprinkle with mixed herbs, add a tablespoonful or so of water and a glass of white wine. Cover the fireproof dish with greaseproof paper and put into a really hot oven for about 15 minutes, then reduce the heat and let the chops cook very slowly for at least $1\frac{1}{2}$ hours. About half an hour before they are ready, add some small mushrooms, which you should push *under* the meat, and just before you serve, take off the superfluous fat, but not all of it, add a little more wine and one gherkin to each person. The gherkins look prettier and heat through in the sauce more quickly if you slice them, like a fan, down to the stalk.

If you are using red wine instead of white, add when putting in the mushrooms. When properly cooked, you will find the meat is so tender that your greatest difficulty is serving it. It is wise, therefore, to cook it in a dish which can be taken to the table.

To vary this dish you can put in onions and/or tomatoes when the meat first goes in the oven, or use different herbs.

Beef Olives

These take quite a long time to prepare, but your reward comes with the appreciation of your guests.

Each olive requires a piece of really good stewing beef about 3 in. square, and you should allow 4 or 5 to each person. A good butcher will prepare the pieces for you, but see that they are *really* thin, something like $\frac{1}{4}$ in. Make a stuffing of herbs (as distinct from sage) and onions, as one does for pork, adding chopped hard-boiled egg if you like, and spread a little over each piece of beef. Then roll each piece up and secure with very fine string or thread, which must be removed before serving. Roll in seasoned flour and fry in a good beef dripping until they are a tempting brown, then put them either into a casserole or a good thick saucepan with meat stock or water and a generous glass of red wine. The liquid should cover them by about an inch. Simmer them for a minimum of 2 hours, but longer if possible.

Bœuf Bourguignon

Cut 1 lb. stewing beef into fairly small pieces and chop 2 or 3 rashers of bacon, and brown them in $\frac{1}{2}$ oz. butter with about 6 small onions. Drain off the butter, sprinkle a little flour into the pan and add two very finely chopped cloves of garlic. Pour in $\frac{1}{2}$ pint of red wine and a little water —just enough to cover the contents of the pan, and add salt and pepper. Cover the pan and simmer for 2 hours, but half an hour before the end add 4 oz. mushrooms cut into thin slices.

German Veal à la Minute

Cut some thin slices of veal about 4 in. long, pepper and salt them and lay them in a deep dish with nearly $\frac{1}{2}$ pint of white wine. Let it stand for 3 hours. Cover the bottom of a stewpan with butter, sprinkle both sides of the veal with flour, add a little more wine and enough white stock to cover it, together with the juice of a lemon. Simmer then for 5 to 10 minutes and serve.

Spanish Steak Stew

You need a thick piece of rump steak larded with fat bacon, and anchovies if you like them. Put it into a dish lined with fat smoked bacon, mixed herbs and spices to taste (*no salt*), 2 cloves of garlic, 2 shallots and a glass of white wine, and simmer very slowly for 5 to 6 hours. Strain the sauce, add a lump of butter with a little flour and some capers, thicken it over the stove and pour it round the steak.

Bœuf en Daube (for 4)

Cut up into small cubes about 1½ lb. of stewing steak, carefully removing the fat. Melt 1 oz. of lard or dripping in a large strong pan, add a couple of diced bacon rashers, two sliced onions, two sliced tomatoes and a calf's foot or pig's trotter cut in half (this is optional, but you will find it vastly improves the dish). Brown all these ingredients and the cut-up steak very gently. Then add mixed herbs, a bay leaf, two cloves of garlic, pepper and salt, a good wineglassful of red wine and sufficient stock (or, if you have none, water strengthened with a little Marmite) to cover the meat completely. Cover the pan and cook in a slow oven for about 5 hours.

Baked Chicken

Cut up a chicken and fry it in oil with some bacon, then lay it in a saucepan and on each piece place a slice of bacon and a slice of tomato. Season with salt and pepper, pour over the oil in which the chicken was cooked, add a little garlic, rosemary and parsley finely chopped, with a glass of white wine, and bake for half an hour in a moderate oven.

Braised Rabbit (or Chicken)

Joint the rabbit, roll each piece in seasoned flour, then put into a casserole or a thick saucepan with a tight-fitting lid. Cover with a good stock and a wineglassful of sauterne, and allow to simmer gently for about 2 hours. One can add vegetables, but they should be fried with the rabbit. Onions, sliced carrot or small new carrots left whole are the best, but you could also use celery.

SWEETS

Everyone knows about sherry and trifles, kirsch with pineapple, and maraschino with fresh strawberries—but the West Indians cook bananas with brown sugar, sherry and a dab of butter. Choose fairly firm bananas, and blanch them with boiling

Add a glass of port to a steak and kidney pudding just before serving—and taste the difference

water, so that they will keep their colour; but this is not vital. Put the dish low down in the oven (which should be medium hot) when you are dishing up the first course, and they'll be ready when you are.

A wineless variation (though it need not be) is to slice the bananas lengthwise, insert jam between the slices, put them in a dish with two or three tablespoonfuls of water (or a soft white wine) and a dab or two of butter, cover with greaseproof paper and cook for about 20 minutes. This is usually served with thick cream, and it is so good that no one seems to mind the richness.

Melon with Brandy is easy to prepare. Just cut out a small square, pour in a little brandy and chill for a couple of hours before serving.

Peaches in Claret for Impressive Occasions

You can use a cheap claret, but in this instance the better the wine, the more rewarding the dish. Allow about $1\frac{1}{2}$ peaches to each person, according to size of peaches, skin and stone them and cut them into what the Americans call "bite-size" pieces. Put them into fairly deep drinking glasses (not shallow dessert dishes), sprinkle liberally with sugar and more than cover with claret. Do this some time before you need them, preferably a few hours, so that the wine and the peaches take on something of each other's flavour. The best guests abandon their spoons with the last of the peach and drink the remaining nectar.

Brandy Pudding

One of the joys of this dish is that you can make it hours before you need it and have it well out of the way in the refrigerator while you are preparing the rest of the dinner.

Begin by whipping $\frac{1}{2}$ pint of cream. Then slice some sponge cake and lay it in brandy, after which you add a small glass of kirsch or maraschino. Over this put another layer of brandy-flavoured sponge, dabbed over with apricot jam, covered with a layer of cream, more sponge and finally another layer of cream—and freeze it for a minimum of 4 hours.

Stuffed Apples

Peel and core 4 medium cooking apples, and stuff the centres with a mixture of sultanas, currants and mixed peel moistened with a little sherry. Put them into a fireproof dish and pour over them 1 tablespoonful of melted honey. Add the rind and the juice of 1 lemon and about 4 tablespoonfuls of white wine (or just enough to cover the bottom of the dish). Bake in a moderate oven, basting well, and serve hot.

MADE WITH LIQUID APPLES

Now some dishes using the unfermented non-alcoholic juice of English apples, prepared by a famous Swiss process, instead of white wine

IN "Shloer" liquid apples, the natural fruit sugars are preserved and not converted into alcohol, as in cider. It is therefore excellent for children, and may be served, preferably cold, in a wineglass as a table drink or for breakfast, or used to make any of the following delicious dishes:

Apple Zabaione (Egg-punch) or
Sauce Cheaudeau

This should be served in large wine glasses, hot or cold, and eaten with a spoon.

1 *whole egg and 2* *egg-yolks*	$\frac{1}{2}$ *pint "Shloer" liquid apples*
	$1\frac{1}{2}$ *oz. sugar*

Put the whole egg, yolks and sugar in a basin. Beat till the mixture is almost white and very light.

Add the "Shloer" and mix thoroughly. Pour into a saucepan and put on a quick fire, beating incessantly, without allowing the mixture to boil or thicken. As soon as it begins to rise, remove from fire. Pour into glasses, and if to be served cold, keep in a cool place until required. Can also be used as a sauce for puddings or tinned fruit.

Apple Jelly

1 *pint "Shloer"* *liquid apples* *(20-oz. bottle)*	$\frac{1}{2}$ *to* 1 *oz. powdered* *gelatine* 1 *oz. sugar*
	Few drops lemon juice

Heat to just below boiling point. Put in a cold place to set. When serving, top with a glacé cherry or cream.

Apple Blanc-mange

2 tablespoonfuls
custard powder
1 pint bottle "Shloer"
liquid apples
A few drops of lemon juice

3-4 tablespoonfuls
sugar
1 or 2 eggs

Mix the custard powder with 6 tablespoonfuls "Shloer" to a smooth paste, and then pour in the rest of the bottle. Bring the liquid slowly to the boil, stirring all the time. Add sugar and a few drops of lemon. Take it from the heat and beat into the mixture the egg-yolks and the stiffly beaten whites.

Mix well and pour into a water-rinsed mould. Serve very cold.

Here are some excellent drinks, both alcoholic and non-alcoholic, made from "Shloer" liquid apples, to add to the drinks in our chapter on Cocktails, Cups and Punches.

NON-ALCOHOLIC DRINKS

Safety First

¼ "Shloer"
¼ ginger ale
Pineapple juice to
taste (optional)
Mint

A few drops of lemon
juice, twist of
lemon peel
Seasonal fruits

Mix all the ingredients together, put a twist of lemon peel on top, adding pineapple juice, if desired. Serve ice cold.

Mulled Liquid Apples

1 pint "Shloer"
A few cloves
A little sugar

A few drops of lemon
juice, some slices
of lemon

Heat the "Shloer" slowly, add the sugar and lemon juice to taste. Remove from the fire just before it reaches boiling point, garnish with cloves and lemon slices. Serve immediately while piping hot.

ALCOHOLIC DRINKS

Liquid Apple Hot Toddy (an excellent cold cure)

Make exactly the same as Mulled Liquid Apples (see recipe above under Non-Alcoholic Drinks), but add rum as required.

Hock Cup

⅔ Hock
⅓ "Shloer"
Sugar to taste

Some drops of lemon
juice and slices of
lemon or cucumber

Melon with brandy makes a wonderful sweet. You just cut out a small square, pour in a little brandy and chill

Mix hock and "Shloer" together with a little sugar and the lemon juice, add the lemon or cucumber slices on the top and serve ice cold.

Champagne Cup

⅔ Champagne
⅓ "Shloer"
A few slices of lemon

Chill the champagne and ice the "Shloer," mix, adding the lemon slices on the top.

Ace Cooler

Measure of gin
Measure of Dubonnet
Dash of cherry
brandy

"Shloer" to fill
Sliced apple and
cucumber rind
Cracked ice

Mix the gin, Dubonnet and cherry brandy, then fill up with "Shloer," garnish with sliced apples and cucumber rind. Add cracked ice.

Liquid Apple Highball

2 oz. gin, brandy or
rum
Cracked ice

8 oz. "Shloer"
Lemon peel, mint and
borage

Pour the gin, brandy, or rum into a 10-oz. glass with cracked ice. Fill up with "Shloer" and stir. Garnish with lemon peel, mint and borage.

THE KITCHEN STORE CUPBOARD

*Herbs, spices, flavourings, colourings and decorations are just as important
to good cookery as the basic ingredients*

THERE are a number of things, apart from basics like tea and flour, which everyone ought to keep in their kitchen. They crop up, as apparently minor ingredients, in countless recipes, but they are important. They are as vital, in their way, as the contents of a sewing basket, and a cook will need them to work on the basic materials. If you have not got them at hand, you must either forgo the dish you intended to make, or make it imperfectly.

Herbs

Chief of these are the cooking herbs. Most recipes for stews, and things cooked in a pot, demand a "bouquet garni," which is nothing more than a bunch of herbs. Generally it consists of 3 or 4 sprigs of parsley, a sprig of thyme and a bay leaf, but some dishes require rosemary, chives, cummin, mint, sage, sorrel, fennel or marjoram, and all these should be kept. In the summer many of them can be grown in the garden or, in the city, in flower pots or a window box on the kitchen sill. Fresh herbs are best, but out of season they can be bought dried. As well as the individual plants, it is useful to keep a packet of mixed herbs for omelets, etc.

Garlic is another essential. It comes in roots like a very small onion and, although supposed to be foreign to British palates, it is widely used in good cooking everywhere.

Spices

Next come the spices. Paprika, cinnamon, ginger, mixed spice, black peppercorns, curry powder, Cayenne, cloves, mustard, nutmeg, chillies, mace and allspice. Like the herbs and garlic, all these, except the curry, can be kept indefinitely, either in the neat matched jars with coloured tops which are everywhere available or, equally well, in the screw-topped bottles in which many liquids are sold.

NOTE: Allspice is known in some places as Jamaica pepper or pimento.

Sauces and flavourings are necessary too. Gravy browning, beef extract, horseradish, chutney, pickles and the favourite family sauce. Tomato purée (in tins or tubes), celery salt and always some cheese for cooking.

Olives are useful, and capers, gherkins and anchovies. There should be a bottle of olive oil and of vinegar, and with these, as with curry powder, it is best to stick to a chosen brand because strengths and flavours vary a lot.

Finally, before turning to sweeter things, there should be a bottle of cheap red cooking wine, and a bottle of dry cider which can often be used when the recipe calls for a white wine.

WHAT GOES INTO CAKES AND SWEETS

Cake- and sweet-making is an important part of good cookery, particularly to those who have children, and it is a good idea to devote one corner, however small, of the kitchen to the ingredients that may be needed at one time or another, for sponges or fruit cakes, fudge or peppermint creams. Perhaps you have a corner in your grocery cupboard or store-room, or, failing this, why not invest in one of those wonderful expanding contraptions which have a number of baskets made of enamelled wire on legs? It will sit or hang literally anywhere.

Basic Needs

Now for the stores required:

Flour—plain is essential; self-raising highly desirable; wholemeal a slight "extra," but it makes wonderful scones. Baking powder and cornflour, which is used in many cake and biscuit recipes and also for fillings.

Bicarbonate of soda has its place in many scone and other recipes, and cream of tartar is often wanted for scones, too, and also for some toffees and sweets.

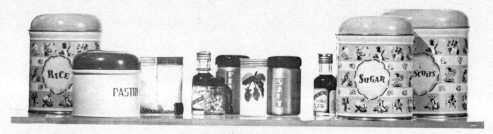

Oatmeal is obtainable — fine, medium and coarse. Usually the fine is required for biscuits and similar baking. Ground rice is wanted in such things as Sand Cake.

Sugars: castor, for light cakes; granulated for heavier cakes, puddings and many sweets; Demerara or Barbados (sometimes called "pieces") for fruit cakes, gingerbread and toffee; icing, for sweets and decorative purposes.

Condensed and evaporated milk should be available for sweet-making. Golden Syrup and treacle are useful for sweetening purposes and essential for such things as gingerbread. Jam and marmalade.

Dried fruits: currants, raisins, sultanas, peel (preferably ready chopped), prunes, dried apricots.

Other fruits: glacé cherries (tend to get sticky if kept too long) and canned fruits, such as pineapple.

Nuts: almonds, walnuts (cheaper in the long run to buy these shelled), ground almonds, desiccated coconut (which does not keep well for long periods).

NOTE: Hazelnuts make an excellent nutty flavouring for a cake if put through a Mouli-mincer.

Flavourings

Always buy a good brand of essence. It is cheaper in the long run than those of poor quality, which invariably taste horrible.

Vanilla pods give a very delicate flavour if you are using liquid in which they can first be soaked. They can be dried off after

A DOZEN LEADING QUESTIONS . . .

1. What is a bouquet garni?
2. Is sorrel a herb?
3. For what do you use mixed herbs?
4. What does garlic look like?
5. Know another name for allspice?
6. How long can you keep nutmeg?
7. Does curry powder last?
8. What can you use instead of white wine in cooking?
9. Which kind of sugar for fruit cakes?
10. Can you use vanilla pods a second time?
11. What gives yellow colouring?
12. How do you tint icing a pale pink?

use, ready for the next time.

Lemon: fresh lemon juice can now be bought and many people prefer it to the essence. Fresh lemon peel, finely grated and/or the juice of the lemon is, of course, excellent.

Almond essence.

Coffee flavouring: one of the coffee powders may be used in preference to the bottled liquid.

Powdered chocolate or cocoa: do not buy in large quantities as it quickly gets stale. Block cooking chocolate is also required sometimes. Incidentally, an excellent flavour results if you melt chocolate in black coffee instead of water.

Colourings

Cochineal colours from pale pink to deep red, depending on the quantity used. Saffron for yellow. There are also other vegetable colourings for special purposes.

Decorations

Most professional results are often achieved with decorations, and it is fun to add, as and when you can, to your jar or tin of "pretties," angelica for flower stalks, silver balls, violet and/or rose petals (crystallised), mimosa balls (available in several colours), hundreds and thousands, chocolate vermicelli. Marzipan also is useful for making your own decorations.

Always keep in stock a box of birthday cake candles with suitable holders. Father Christmas, a robin, snowmen and lots more will ultimately find their way into your collection. Clean them properly after use, and they will last for years.

WHAT MAKES A BALANCED DIET

How to translate the five chief nutrients into meals for a family

by DR. MARY LYMINGTON

THERE is a tendency in "civilised" countries and modern times to regard food as merely the excuse for a pleasant social occasion or for personal indulgence.

It is, however, most important that we should not forget the real function of food —to refuel and repair the body. The primary responsibility of the housewife is, indeed, to see that her family get a well-balanced diet.

Good balance is achieved only when the five chief nutrients are taken regularly in the correct proportions. If the balance gets upset, the result is malnutrition, as in the case of a child with rickets due to Vitamin D and calcium starvation, or a 'teenager who gets too fat owing to an excess of starch in the diet.

Food is composed of the following five nutrients:

(1) *Carbohydrates*, which provide the body with energy and, if unused, may be stored in the body tissues.
(2) *Fats*, which also provide energy and form body fat.
(3) *Proteins*, for growth and repair of body tissues.
(4) *Minerals*, which help in growth and repair, and are particularly important because of their function in regulating body processes. They include salt, calcium, phosphate, iron, iodine and a trace of copper.
(5) *Vitamins*, which have all kinds of important effects in regulating different processes.

What is a Normal Diet?

A diet for people trying neither to gain nor lose weight should contain 1 part protein to 1 part fat to 4 parts carbohydrates, calculated by weight.

The energy value of food is measured in terms of heat units called calories, a calorie being the amount of heat needed to raise the temperature of 1,000 grams of water by one degree Centigrade, from 15° to 16°. Obviously, the quantity of food a person requires depends very largely upon his expenditure of energy. In other words, a miner working hard below ground all day needs a great deal more nourishment than a lady of leisure, while a growing boy or girl in the 'teens requires more than a busy housewife because of the demands of physical development and growth.

A child from the age of ten up needs as many calories as an average adult, while from fourteen, the requirements of a boy or girl are *above* that of the average grown-up.

Where to Find the Nutrients

In order to produce a well-balanced diet, it is essential to know which of the common foods contain which of the nutrients. Many do, of course, contain more than one. Brown bread, for instance, is a source of protein as well as of carbohydrate, and milk contains some of practically everything needed in a diet. Listed opposite are the main sources of the five nutrients.

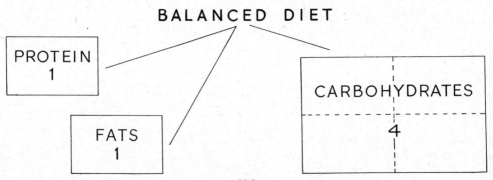

BALANCED DIET

PROTEIN
1

FATS
1

CARBOHYDRATES
4

Carbohydrates

Sugar, syrup, flour, oatmeal, jam, raisins, dates, currants, white bread, potatoes and, to a lesser degree, all fruits and vegetables.

Fats

Butter, margarine, lard, dripping, olive oil, nuts, bacon, cheese, fat meat, herring, egg, milk, canned salmon.

Proteins

There are two sources of protein:
(1) *Animal or First-class Protein*, found in all kinds of meat, game, poultry, fish (including shellfish), milk, cheese and eggs.
(2) *Vegetable or Second-class Protein*. The richest source is nuts, followed by dried peas and beans (though their protein value is reduced by the necessary process of soaking), and then fresh peas and beans and certain root vegetables. Potatoes contain more protein than carrots or turnips.

Minerals

The daily amount of *salts* required by an average person is more than accounted for by the common foods included in a normal diet and the salt added in cooking or taken at table. *Calcium*, essential for the formation of teeth and bones and therefore particularly important for expectant mothers and children, is found chiefly in milk, cheese and milk products, to a lesser degree in sardines and tinned salmon, bread and green vegetables. *Iron*, a deficiency of which produces anæmia, is found particularly in liver, kidneys, corned beef.

Vitamins

Vitamin A (essential to a child's growth, and also for good sight, healthy skin, bones and teeth, and for protection against infection) is found in animal foods, such as liver, dairy produce and eggs and in green and yellow vegetables (carrots). Halibut- and cod-liver oil are the two most concentrated sources.

The *Vitamin B* group has many subdivisions, including *Vitamin B₁* and *Riboflavine*, both of which contribute to the body's effective use of energy foods, help to maintain the muscular and nervous systems, and prevent undue fatigue. They are chiefly found in dried brewers' yeast, liver, wheatgerm; Vitamin B₁ also in peanuts, bacon, oatmeal, peas and beans, Riboflavine in milk and eggs. There is also in the Vitamin B group, *Nicotinic Acid*, a deficiency of which produces skin troubles, digestive upsets and mental symptoms. Main sources are meat extract, dried brewers' yeast, liver, kidney, meat and fish, wheatgerm. The other B vitamins, too numerous to describe in detail, are found chiefly in yeast, liver, cereals and pulses, some in green leafy vegetables.

Vitamin C (Ascorbic Acid) occurs mainly in fresh fruit and vegetables, but at least half is destroyed by cooking, even when the best possible methods are used. If Vitamin C is not contained in sufficient quantity in a diet, children's growth is checked, the gums and mouth are susceptible to infection, healing (of wounds) is slowed down and eventually scurvy results. Richest sources of Vitamin C are blackcurrants, then oranges, lemons, grapefruit and rose hips (which may be taken in the form of syrup).

Vitamin D is essential to good bone formation (and therefore of special importance to infants, children and expectant mothers); a deficiency leads to rickets. Our chief sources of Vitamin D are (*a*) foods such as cod-liver oil, sardines, herrings, canned salmon, margarine, and (*b*) sunlight on the skin.

Vitamin E, thought to affect fertility, is found chiefly in milk and wheatgerm; *Vitamin K*, which enables the blood to clot, in cabbage and green peas.

Value of Certain Foods

The chart following shows how many of the common items of a normal diet contain several of the essential nutrients and thus help the natural balance.

Notice the foods rich in all the essential components, particularly milk and, to a lesser degree, chocolate—and the value of eggs and certain fish. Try to build your family's menus around them, always bearing in mind the necessity for variety in stimulating the appetite. Although food fads should not be encouraged, particularly in children, there are some people who just cannot take milk, others with their own pet dislikes. For them, the problem is to find

BALANCED DIET SHEET — VALUE OF SOME FOODSTUFFS

	PROTEIN	FAT	CARBO-HYDRATE	SALTS	VITAMINS
MILK	+	+	+	} Phosphate and Calcium	A and D
BUTTER	—	+	—		A and D
MARGARINE	—	+	—		+
CHEESE	+	+	—	} Iron, Phosphate and Calcium	A and B
CHOCOLATE	+	+	+		
COCOA	+	+	+		
EGG	+	+	—	Iron and Phosphate	
SUGAR	—	—	+	—	
GOLDEN SYRUP	—	—	+	Iron	
HONEY	—	—	+	—	
JAM	+	—	+	Iron	
MARMALADE	+	—	+	Iron	
BREAD	+	+	+	} Iron and Phosphate	B
BISCUITS	+	+	+		
FLOUR	+	+	+		
MEAT	+	+	—	—	sometimes B
BLOATER	+	+	—	} Iron and Phosphate, some Calcium	
KIPPER	+	+	—		
HERRING	+	+	—		
SALMON	+	+	—		
COD	+	—	—		(Cod) B
HADDOCK	+	—	—		
VEGETABLES	+	—	+	+ all salts	+ especially A and C
APPLE, GRAPES, ORANGE	+	—	+	—	C
BANANA	+	—	+	—	A

small amounts (Protein column, JAM/MARMALADE)

small amounts (Fat column, BREAD/BISCUITS/FLOUR)

small amounts (Protein column, APPLE, GRAPES, ORANGE)

In the above chart a plus sign (+) indicates the presence of that particular nutrient, while a minus sign (—) means there is none. Thus, butter will be seen to contain no Protein or Carbohydrate, though it is a rich source of Fat, has some Salts (Phosphate and Calcium) and Vitamins (A and D). By using the Diet Sheet as a guide, you will be able to plan balanced meals for your family in the correct proportions for good health—1 part Protein and 1 part Fats to 4 parts Carbohydrates.

suitable alternatives. Children who will not drink milk or eat milk puddings will often take it in savoury form—turned into a tasty cheese sauce, for example, or as a white sauce served with fish or vegetables. They may also eat cheese and butter, which between them provide the next best thing to milk (see also chapter on Children's Meals).

Here is a specimen diet which provides good balance between all the components and upon which you can base your own menu planning:

BREAKFAST
Cereal or porridge and milk or fruit
Bacon, egg, fish, etc.
Toast and marmalade
Tea or coffee

LUNCH
Meat, fish, egg or cheese,
with salad or cooked vegetable
Pudding or fruit
Tea or coffee

TEA
(if desired)
A large tea meal usually results in too much starchy food, particularly in the case of the sedentary worker, who may, as a result, suffer from indigestion or tend to put on weight. Most people will be satisfied with a cup of tea and a slice of cake or two or three biscuits.

DINNER
Soup
Meat, fish, egg or cheese,
with vegetables or salad
Pudding or fruit
Cheese   Tea or coffee

BEDTIME
(optional)
Drink of some kind, preferably made with milk

The lunch and dinner menus are interchangeable according to circumstances. Generally speaking, children and old people should have their main meal at midday and a light supper; sedentary workers, on the other hand, are better with a big meal at night since it is bad to sit all the afternoon with a full tummy.

NOTE: *Liquids* should be taken, if possible, between meals, and their importance must on no account be overlooked. The need of the body for water is second in importance only to its need for air. *At least 1½ pints* of water or other fluid should be drunk every day; more if possible. Bear in mind that, if too little is drunk, dehydration occurs, whereas if too much is drunk, the body gets rid of the excess quite easily through the kidneys. So it is better to drink *more* than the daily minimum requirement than less. (This does not, of course, apply to alcoholic drinks.)

Effect of Cooking
The process of cooking nearly always directly improves the nutritional value of food, as well as improving its flavour and making it generally more attractive and appetising. The one great exception is Vitamin C, which is very easily destroyed by heat and a high proportion of which is invariably lost in the preparation of food for the table (see chapter on The Effect of Cooking and Storage on Vitamins).

When potatoes are peeled and then boiled, the loss of Vitamin C is 50 per cent.; when they are fried, 30 per cent. But bake them in their skins and the loss is reduced to 20 per cent., boil them in their skins and it is only 15 per cent.

Green vegetables lose more when they are put into cold water and then brought to the boil than when they are plunged into boiling water.

The best way to avoid this inevitable loss of Vitamin C in cooking is (1) to eat the vegetables raw in the form of salads, and (2) to cook them so that the loss is reduced to the absolute minimum. Essential cooking rules are:
(1) Choose absolutely fresh vegetables.
(2) Peel thinly or cook in their skins.
(3) Prepare just before cooking.
(4) Take care not to overcook them.
(5) Cook in a saucepan with a tight-fitting lid and in the smallest quantity of fast-boiling salted water, just enough to prevent them from burning.
(6) Never use bicarbonate of soda.
(7) Serve immediately.

A family who live on a well-balanced diet start off with a sound foundation of good health. But mealtimes should be pleasant, peaceful family occasions, not exercises in advanced dietetics. Food does people good in direct proportion to how much they enjoy it.

THE EFFECT OF COOKING AND STORAGE ON VITAMINS

SINCE we eat much of our food cooked, either in the home or before purchase, it is important to know whether we can do anything, by choice of method, to prevent loss of vitamins.

Methods of cooking are many and various: food may be cooked dry, in fat, in water or in steam; it may be exposed to air or enclosed in a pressure cooker; it may be cooked at high or low temperatures for short or long periods, and it may have been subject to some form of processing before cooking.

It is small wonder, therefore, that there is great variation in the nutritive value of foods as presented at the table.

Until recently, little research had been done on this subject, but by now we know a good deal about the effects of various cooking methods on vitamin retention.

MEAT

Meats are the chief sources of the vitamin B_2 group, riboflavine and nicotinic acid, and only to a lesser extent are they sources of vitamin B_1.

Riboflavine and nicotinic acid are relatively stable, and losses are usually less than 15 per cent. by roasting, grilling, frying, braising or stewing. Vitamin B_1 is more readily lost, especially by slow cooking. In stewing, as much as 50 per cent. may be lost, and 42–64 per cent. by roasting. But since meats are not the best sources of vitamin B_1 in any case, this is not as important as it might otherwise be.

Vitamin A is present in very high concentration in liver, and there is some, though less, in kidney, but this vitamin is not water soluble and is not reduced in amount by cooking.

EGGS

The chief vitamins of eggs are A, D and riboflavine. There is little B_1 or nicotinic acid and no vitamin C. Vitamins A and D are stable to cooking, but 10–15 per cent. of riboflavine may be lost when eggs are cooked either alone or as baked custard.

CEREALS

These are our chief sources of vitamins B_1, B_6 and E. Some contain also some nicotinic acid, and riboflavine is present only in small amounts.

Since most cereals are eaten cooked and some prepared foods are subjected to high temperatures, it is important to know what the effects are.

Vitamin B_1 is lost by oxidation. Hence in bread, less is retained in the crust than in the crumb, and toasting causes further loss. Any cereals browned throughout, like biscuits, or much charred, cannot be relied on to contain vitamin B_1. The use of baking powder, sodium bicarbonate and sour milk, unless used in excessive quantities in the baking of buns and cakes, seems to make no difference in the retention of vitamin B_1.

VEGETABLES AND FRUIT

Vegetables are the main sources of vitamin C and carotene, and, since vitamin C is one of the least stable of all vitamins, every possible measure should be taken to prevent loss.

Experiments have been done on the effects of various methods of cooking on the vitamin C content of a number of different vegetables. These included carrots, beets, potatoes, peas and leafy vegetables, such as cabbage, broccoli and spinach.

The retention of the vitamin was found to depend more on the method of cooking than on the type of vegetable, but there were wide variations from sample to sample. In general, it can be said that most vitamin is retained by pressure cooking and least when a large amount of water is used.

Vitamin C retention	Per cent. of fresh value
Pressure cooking	60–90 per cent.
Little water only	50–85 per cent.
Water to cover	40–70 per cent.

Storage after Cooking

Cooked vegetables rapidly lose their vitamin C if they are kept for the next day's meals. New potatoes cooked in their jackets retain their vitamin C well, but, if peeled, half the vitamin C may be lost by the next day. The type of utensil used for cooking—i.e. enamel, stainless steel, aluminium, glass—seems to make no difference.

Blackcurrants

Blackcurrants contain very large quantities of vitamin C, but the season for fresh fruit is short, so it is important to know the effects of preserving.

Very little vitamin C is lost by bottling, but much passes into the juice, which should always be used. There is progressive loss during storage. The best conditions are: low temperature, protection from light, and the use of glass or metal rather than plastic covers.

Jams

The following figures have been published:

Retention of ascorbic acid in:

	Freshly made	After 1 year storage
Blackcurrant jam	70 per cent.	30 per cent.
Gooseberry jam	66 per cent.	28 per cent.
Strawberry jam	55 per cent.	17 per cent.

THE STATE OF FOOD WHEN PUT INTO STORAGE

Some foods, such as hard fruits (apples and pears), root vegetables (potatoes, carrots, parsnips) and cereals (rice), are commonly stored for several months without special treatment; others are treated first, either by drying, salting, pickling, heat sterilisation or freezing, and are stored in special containers or sealed in tins or glass jars.

The vitamin content of the food when eaten depends on its state when put into storage and the conditions under which it is stored. The following are important factors for consideration: length of storage, temperature, access of light and air and moisture, both within the food and in its surroundings.

Vitamins, and especially water-soluble vitamins, occur within the living cells of plants. As long as the cells remain intact, the vitamin content is little changed, but mechanical damage as caused by bruising or cutting, or loss of water as caused by wilting, allows considerable deterioration.

Dried grass, finely divided, is now widely used by farmers as a source of vitamin A activity, and may lose as much as 40–50 per cent. of its potency during storage; or more if allowed to wilt before storage. Even so, it is a better source of carotene than hay. Vegetables and fruits which are little damaged by packing and handling hold their vitamins better than the more delicate varieties. As an example, cabbage bears the stress of transport better than spinach.

Vitamin C, being readily oxidised, is the vitamin most easily lost and the one about which most information is available.

Cabbage left whole and stored in the open but protected from rain loses very little ascorbic acid in a week and only about one-third of its content when stored for a month at room temperature.

On the other hand, minced or finely cut cabbage may lose much of its ascorbic acid in a matter of minutes.

Spinach, which wilts quickly, may lose 40 per cent. of its ascorbic acid in a day and nearly 80 per cent. in two days.

Asparagus may lose 80 per cent. in four days, from wilting.

Fruit similarly loses its ascorbic acid by cell damage. Apples and pears, when bruised, lose much of their ascorbic acid.

These examples show how important it is: (a) to handle all fresh foods so as to **avoid cell damage** and (b) to **prevent wilting.**

STORAGE

Foods stored in the home without special containers—e.g. fresh fruits and vegetables, bread and cereals, cheese—may lose some of their vitamins. The most vulnerable is vitamin C, then the B complex, and, to a lesser extent, vitamin A.

The following chart provides data on

EFFECT OF COOKING AND STORAGE ON VITAMINS

Vitamin C Loss	Fresh	1st day	2nd day	3rd day	4th day	5th day	6th day	7th day	Conditions
Blackcurrants . .	50 mg./oz.			45 mg./oz.	42 mg./oz.				Room temperature
Broccoli tops .	49				37		30		Room temperature
Brussels sprouts .	38				34				
Cauliflower . .	24						17		
Cabbage . .	14							13 / 11	0°–3° C. / 20° C.
Spinach . .	14							13 / 2	0°–3° C. / 20° C.
Asparagus . .	3	2·5			0·5				20° C.
Peas . . .	3						3 / 1·5		0°–3° C. / 20° C.

vitamin C losses in fruits and vegetables kept for short periods.

Green vegetables exposed to the air at ordinary temperatures may lose as much as half their vitamin C in a day and almost four-fifths in 2 days, but if fresh uncut cabbage is wrapped and kept at refrigeration temperature, it will retain its vitamin C for several weeks. Other green vegetables packed in ice retain their original vitamin C content for as long as 5 days, and tomatoes retain 90 per cent. when kept in a refrigerator for a week.

Root-type vegetables kept in a cool cellar retain their vitamin C well during the winter.

Potatoes, parsnips, onions and carrots contain relatively little of the vitamin but, as the quantities eaten are greater, they do contribute some vitamin C to the total amount consumed, and if these vegetables are taken in quantity, the amount is by no means negligible.

Vegetables are, in general, better stored at low temperatures, and where the texture is hard, vitamin retention is better. Potatoes, parsnips and carrots, for example, lose less during storage than do onions or celery. Onions lose from 50–80 per cent. in three months, while with potatoes the loss is progressive up to 50 per cent. or 60 per cent. in six months.

Fruits and vegetables are not good sources of the B vitamins. The small quantities of riboflavine present are not much changed with storage, but there is commonly a loss of 10–20 per cent. of vitamin B_1. The riboflavine of bread and rolls is protected by wrapping, even with translucent waxed paper.

Cereals are better sources of the B vitamins, and here freedom from moisture is important.

Bread, which contains about 50 per cent. of moisture, is usually kept only for a matter of days, but rice, oatmeal, pearl barley and packeted cereals may be stored for months. Although it is not customary to keep cereals indefinitely, Bemax, with a moisture content of about 5 per cent., will retain its vitamin B_1 without appreciable loss for many years, samples over twenty years old being as potent as those of contemporary manufacture.

Cheese, a food with a relatively low vitamin B_1 content, retains it well, only about 12 per cent. being lost in three months and 25 per cent. in six months.

PRESERVATION

The commonest process for the preservation of foods is **canning**, with which can be included **bottling**.

Exclusion of air is more efficient from canned than bottled foods, and this helps in the retention of vitamin C, which is lost by oxidation. Access of light is also prevented by canning.

Carotene and **vitamin A** remain relatively stable during both canning and subsequent storage, unless this is prolonged unduly. There is also little loss of vitamin D. This latter is important, since individuals other than infants may obtain their major supplies of vitamin D from canned fish such as herring and sardines.

Of the **B vitamins**, riboflavine and nicotinic acid are well retained in meat, fish and milk, but, during the prolonged heating needed for sterilisation, as much as 70 per cent. of vitamin B_1 may be lost. Little further loss occurs during storage, only up to 10 per cent. at refrigeration temperature, and up to 20 per cent. during one year at ordinary room temperature.

Vitamin C may be destroyed by the preliminary blanching of vegetables, but little is lost by the process of canning. From 30–50 per cent. may pass into the liquid portion of the contents. Even at relatively high room temperatures, the losses in fruit juices and sliced fruits are in most cases under 25 per cent.

The addition of ascorbic acid in not more than $0 \cdot 2$ per cent. of the weight of fruit stabilises the colour of canned fruit without affecting texture or flavour, and is retained for long periods in 30–60 per cent. sugar syrup.

CANNING

Non-acid foods, such as beans, peas, spinach and corn, retain only about half their original vitamins C and B; oranges and tomatoes much more. Fresh oranges vary widely, but canning losses in the juice are negligible.

Canned foods are best kept in a cool, dry place. It has been shown that storage at 50° F. causes only 5–15 per cent. loss of vitamin C, but at 80° F. this is increased to 20–35 per cent.

FREEZING

Freezing is looked upon as the most modern method of food preservation, although as early as 1865 slow freezing of fish and poultry was introduced, closely followed by the freezing of meat. Meat and fish preserved by this method lose little, if any, of their nutritive value after storage for long periods. During thawing, however, there is a tendency, particularly in the case of beef, to lose juices which will contain water-soluble proteins, minerals and vitamins.

The development of the quick method of freezing in 1929 has provided the most effective method for the preservation of vitamins in foods. Loss of water-soluble vitamins occurs during the preliminary processes; this is higher in vegetables than in fruits, fish, meat and poultry, since vegetables are subjected to blanching to destroy the oxidative enzymes. The storage temperature of foods preserved by these methods is of the utmost importance—28° C. being considered the maximum temperature for the effective retention of vitamins. Storage at –19° C. results in loss of one-third of the vitamin C in strawberries and beans. If the temperature is allowed to fluctuate between –19° C. and –17° C., loss is even greater, reaching 66 per cent. in strawberries and 8 per cent. in beans.

"Quick frozen" foods do not readily lose vitamins on thawing, but fruits allowed to stand for 12 hours at room temperatures lose a considerable amount of vitamin C.

SALTING

Salting, on the other hand, is the oldest method of food preservation and is still in use both domestically and commercially, either alone for the preservation of vegetables, or combined with saltpetre or smoking for the curing of meats and fish.

The domestic preservation of vegetables, such as beans, by packing in jars with salt is very destructive to vitamins. Little or no vitamin C can be expected to remain after 3 months' storage, and 47–80 per cent. of the original vitamin A is lost.

VITAMINS PRESERVED		VITAMINS DESTROYED	
	More vitamin B$_1$ in crumb than crust. Bemax retains it for years.		Any cereals toasted, browned or charred lose vitamin B.
	Pressure-cooking vegetables is the method retaining most vitamins.		Least vitamins are preserved when vegetables cooked in much water.
	Fresh uncut wrapped cabbage in a fridge retains vitamin C for weeks.		Green vegetables exposed to the air lose half their vitamin C in a day.
	Tomatoes retain 90 per cent. vitamin C in a refrigerator for a week.		Apples and pears, when bruised, lose much of their ascorbic acid.
	Quick-frozen foods do not readily lose vitamins on thawing.		Cooked vegetables kept till the next day rapidly lose their vitamin C.
	Cured hams contain a high percentage of their original vitamins.		Packing beans in jars with salt is very destructive of vitamins.
	Canned fish retains vitamins A and D; fruits most of their vitamin C.		Non-acid vegetables retain half their vitamins C and B after canning.

CURING

Curing and corning of meat are effective methods for the retention of the B vitamins. Hams prepared commercially by being placed in pickling solution for 12 days and then being smoked for 18 hours have been shown to contain 73 per cent. of their original aneurine, 92 per cent. of their riboflavine and 84 per cent. of their nicotinic acid. Corned beef retains 20–52 per cent. of its aneurine and 90–100 per cent. of its riboflavine. The nitrites and nitrates of cured meat rapidly destroy the vitamin C in vegetables when cooked with them in such dishes as stews.

PRESERVES

The making of jams is an effective method of preserving fruit without much loss of vitamin C, since the vitamin is resistant to the heat treatment of jam boiling. Commercially prepared jams which contain 30–40 per cent. of fruit may be said to contain approximately 30–40 per cent. of the vitamin originally present in the fruit from which they were made. The use of sugar for jam making is the most profitable way of using the amounts available when these are restricted.

PICKLES

Pickling is another method used both commercially and domestically for the storage of vegetables and fruits. The acetic acid present in vinegar penetrates the cells of vegetables immersed in it, particularly if these are sliced, and causes rapid oxidation of the vitamin C. Green walnuts are a very good source of vitamin C and when made into chutney at home retain 94 per cent.; when prepared commercially, the chutney retains only 40 per cent. of the vitamin C. Sauerkraut, which is prepared by fermenting cabbage, contains approximately the same amount of vitamin C as fresh cabbage, during and immediately after the fermentation process. Storage, however, results in rapid loss of the vitamin.

CHEESE

The manufacture of cheese is a method of converting surplus milk into a form in which it can be stored, to provide an excellent source of protein and calcium. Freshly made cheese contains 25–33 per cent. of the riboflavine, 9 per cent. of the aneurine and 85 per cent. of the vitamin A of the milk from which it is made. During the ripening process, the vitamin A remains stable, but further loss of 43–73 per cent. aneurine occurs. Riboflavine appears to increase in the surface layers of the cheese,

probably owing to synthesis by micro-organisms.

To summarise:

(1) Vegetables and fruit should be as fresh as possible when used either for cooking or preserving.

(2) If storage is necessary, they should be kept in as cool a place as possible.

(3) In cooking, the least quantity of water that is practicable should be used. Cooking should be rapid and for the shortest possible time.

(4) Vegetables should not be cooked one day for use the next.

(5) It should be noted that figures quoted in tables of vitamin values frequently refer to fruits and vegetables as freshly collected and may need considerable modification when used for calculations of the vitamin content of diets as eaten.

HIGH CALORIE DIETS

Increased physical activity, at work or play, demands extra intake

THE body does not distinguish between work and play. Increased physical activity, whether as a farm labourer or a mountaineer, a despatch rider or a fast swimmer, demands an extra intake of all the nutrients concerned in muscular activity.

All sorts of mistaken ideas are still current regarding the kind of food needed. It is said that high protein meals containing plenty of meat are necessary for strength and athletic achievement. In the animal world the elephant, though moving slowly, can pull down a tree, and the deer achieves a speed of 30 m.p.h., both on vegetarian diets. In man, provided the total protein intake is adequate in quality and quantity, there does not appear to be any need for additional amounts. Calories are needed in amounts increasing with the degree of muscular effort, and it has been shown that carbohydrate is the most satisfactory way of supplying the bulk of these extra calories. Excess fat may reduce muscular efficiency by loss of energy during its conversion.

The British Medical Association (Committee on Nutrition) gives six grades of activity for men and five for women as follows:

	Calories Men	Women
0. No work, almost basal (e.g. lying in bed) . .	1,750	1,500
1. Sedentary work and little travelling . . .	2,250	2,000
2. Light work and travelling	2,750	2,250
3. Medium work and travelling	3,000	2,500
4. Heavy work and travelling	3,500	3,000
5. Very heavy work and travelling	4,250	3,750
6. Extremely heavy work and travelling . . .	5,000	—

There is thus a 2–3-fold variation between the lowest and the highest calorie intake. In general, there is not such a wide variation in the size of the human stomach, and the weight of the food eaten varies from about 3½–5 lb. daily.

Hunger is experienced when the stomach is empty, satiety when it is relatively full, regardless of the calories available from the stomach contents. The problem is therefore to give the body the nutrients it needs in the bulk which it finds comfortable.

THE SIGNIFICANCE OF BULK

Individuals whose need for calories is low, must consume relatively bulky foods like green vegetables and fruits, whilst those whose need for calories is high must eat more highly concentrated foods of small bulk, e.g. chocolate or bread. The diagrams here show the relative weights of examples of foods, all of which supply 100 calories.

People doing heavy physical work or strenuous forms of athletics will need all the calories they can get without overloading the stomach with excess bulk. It may be necessary for some meals to contain relatively large amounts of fat. It has been recommended by the National Research Council (U.S.A.) that for those whose energy requirements are less than 3,000 calories daily, 20–25 per cent. of total calories should be supplied by fat, and for those with greater requirements 30–35 per cent. should be derived from fat.

Physical efficiency is lowest before breakfast and highest about an hour after meals.

TO SUPPLY 100 CALORIES YOU NEED

1. ¾ oz. butter, bacon or chocolate.

2. 1 oz. cereal, sugar or sardines.

3. 1½ oz. bread, beans or meat.

4. 2 oz. egg, herring or prunes.

5. 4–6 oz. potato, milk, banana or fish.

6. Right: 10–16 oz. apple, orange, onion or carrot.

7. Below: 20–25 oz. cabbage or tomato.

8. Over 30 oz. lettuce.

There is evidence that for heavy work and activity in cold or hot environments or at high altitudes, small frequent meals are better than larger ones at intervals.

EFFECT OF GLUCOSE

Glucose has long been looked upon as the best source of energy. Experiments show that there is no change in performance following the administration of a large dose of glucose. The liver and muscles of healthy adults contain glycogen ready for immediate breakdown. This process is hastened by the output of adrenaline in anticipation of approaching effort and for short sprints. The event is over before glucose or any other sugar taken just before the start can be absorbed and circulated to the muscles going into action.

THE DIET OF EXPLORERS

Men exploring new regions, whether polar or at high altitudes, have to carry heavy loads and at the same time be able to withstand extreme cold. They aim at reducing the weight of food to be carried to 2 lb. or less for each day's supply, but require a calorie intake of 4,000–5,000. This is achieved by carrying dehydrated or relatively dry foods to which water can be added when meals are prepared. A typical ration consists of dried meat or pemmican, biscuits, cereals, chocolate, dried vegetables and fruits, dried egg and dried milk.

Pemmican was originally made by Red Indians from dried buffalo or caribou meat made into cakes with fat. British pemmican is a modification in which beef is used.

An Actual Example used in Arctic Exploration

Food	Weight oz.	Calories
Pemmican	8	1,304
Butter	4	920
Milk chocolate	2	326
Fruit and nut chocolate	2	290
Sugar	4	464
Oats	3	357
Pea flour	1½	156
Biscuits	2	276
Bemax	1	104
Raisins	1	80
Cocoa/milk	1½	177
	30 oz.	4,454

PROTECTIVE FACTORS

Explorers have learned that the provision of calories in small bulk is not the only or even the most important consideration. The diet must be fully protective, and this means an adequate supply of good protein and all the necessary vitamins and minerals. The example given contains the necessary protein and factors of the vitamin B group, but is clearly short of vitamins A and C. On the expedition during which this was used, vitamin tablets were taken to compensate for these deficiencies.

In hot climates or during heavy work in a hot humid atmosphere, extra salt and vitamin C are needed.

For all athletes and heavy workers it is not sufficient to increase the intake of calories to the required amount. Extra calories will require extra B complex vitamins, particularly vitamin B_1, to effect their complete metabolism.

High Calorie Meals which can be carried by heavy workers or those engaged in outdoor activities

	Calories
(1) 8 buttered dry biscuits 2 oz. cheese 2 hard-boiled eggs 2 oz. chocolate	1,275
(2) 6 oz. corned beef 4 slices bread and butter/margarine 4 digestive biscuits	1,275
(3) 4 fried sausages 2 slices bread and butter/margarine 2 oz. stoned dates	1,140
(4) Pork pie 2 oz. nuts and raisins 4 buttered biscuits	1,100

The nutritive value of all these meals can be improved by the addition of tomatoes, oranges, etc., if these can be carried. If not, care must be taken to include in the breakfast or evening meal a good source of vitamin C. It is probably easier to ensure an adequate intake of the vitamin B complex, vitamin A and calcium either at breakfast or the evening meal eaten on returning. The appropriate quantities are provided by ½ pint of milk and 1 oz. Bemax.

SLIMMING WITH SAFETY

*Why we put on weight, the dangers of
obesity and a practical plan for healthy
and gradual reduction*

SINCE the slim figure has established itself as the æsthetic ideal of modern woman, much interest has centred on the problem of the putting on of fat and for the most part this interest has served the cause of health and fitness. Long-continued overweight can have serious repercussions upon all the systems of the body. Surplus fat is a burden upon all the tissues and organs, and statistics of Life Assurance Companies show that mortality rates rise steadily in proportion to the extent to which people are overweight.

There are still many men and women who accept increasing bulk with deplorable complacency, but they are a decreasing number. Obesity is a great handicap in the ceaseless competition of modern life.

A definition of obesity is difficult to give, for, while gross fatness is obvious, the insidious spreading of adipose tissue renders the frontier between normality and abnormality hard to detect. It is unfortunately the case that most people find themselves well in the toils of obesity before they awaken to the significant fact. Authorities have elaborated weight tables according to height and age and, although there is some divergence of opinion, they are for the most part reliable as guides. Naturally, there are individual variations, especially in so far as people differ in the compactness and weight of their bones. But a good rule is that adults, say over thirty-five years of age, should not vary much in their weight until middle age, when, after a *slight* temporary increase, there should be a slight decline in the elderly age period.

It is said with a good deal of truth that most men and women over forty are too fat. Again, it is usually agreed by doctors that there is some advantage in a slight degree of overweight in individuals under thirty-five. A small excess of fat seems to constitute a protection against infectious diseases which are the main causes of death in the early decades. It is equally agreed that there is an advantage in slight underweight after middle life, when degenerative diseases of the heart, blood vessels and kidneys take the prime place in the mortality figures.

It is the abdominal wall which suffers first. Fat develops between the muscle fibres, and these most important muscles are weakened and become ineffectual. Later, fat accumulates within the abdomen and further impedes organic activity. Briefly, the results are constipation, dyspepsia, liverishness, a tendency to gall stones, piles and a general lowering of vitality.

But the pathology of obesity does not stop there. A grave penalty of overweight is diabetes, which has a notoriously high incidence among the corpulent. Apart from the formation of fat round the heart, the heart muscle has extra labour to perform in maintaining a more extensive blood circulation. This in time leads to high blood pressure, hardening of the arteries and kidney inefficiency. Further, owing to the debilitated state of the heart muscle, the obese patient is a bad surgical risk. Overweight also produces adverse mechanical effects upon the skeletal tissues, the bones and joints.

All fat people eventually develop bad postures. They become round-shouldered, while the hip and knee joints creak under the strain. Osteo-arthritis is nearly always accompanied by obesity. The arches of the feet give way and this occasions much pain and distress.

Cause of Obesity

The fundamental cause of overweight is an excess of food intake over the body's requirements. Overweight is mainly the result of over-eating. Yet it is a remarkable

TABLE OF AVERAGE WEIGHTS OF WOMEN

HEIGHT ▶	4'8"	4'9"	4'10"	4'11"	5'0"	5'1"	5'2"	5'3"	5'4"	5'5"	5'6"	5'7"	5'8"	5'9"	5'10"	5'11"	6'0"
AGE 20	7.8	7.10	7.12	8.0	8.2	8.4	8.7	8.10	8.13	9.2	9.6	9.10	10.0	10.3	10.7	10.11	11.2
25	7.11	7.13	8.1	8.3	8.5	8.7	8.9	8.12	9.2	9.5	9.9	9.13	10.3	10.7	10.11	11.0	11.4
30	8.0	8.2	8.4	8.6	8.8	8.10	0.12	9.1	9.5	9.8	9.12	10.2	10.6	10.10	11.0	11.3	11.7
35	8.3	8.5	8.7	8.9	8.11	8.13	9.1	9.4	9.8	9.12	10.2	10.6	10.10	11.0	11.3	11.6	11.9
40	8.7	8.9	8.11	8.13	9.1	9.3	9.6	9.9	9.12	10.2	10.6	10.10	11.0	11.4	11.7	11.10	11.13
45	8.10	8.12	9.0	9.2	9.4	9.6	9.9	9.12	10.1	10.5	10.9	10.13	11.3	11.7	11.10	12.0	12.3
50	8.13	9.1	9.3	9.5	9.7	9.9	9.12	10.1	10.4	10.8	10.12	11.2	11.7	11.11	12.1	12.5	12.8
55	8.13	9.1	9.3	9.5	9.7	9.9	9.12	10.1	10.4	10.8	10.13	11.4	11.9	11.13	12.3	12.6	12.9

ALL WEIGHTS IN STONES AND POUNDS

physiological phenomenon how the healthy body maintains constancy in weight over long periods, in spite of great variations in food intake and in physical activity.

It is similar to the maintenance of body temperature under widely varying conditions. We know that the gourmand does not necessarily become obese and that the abstemious in food may remain plump. It is generally agreed that most of us eat more than our calorie requirements, but the excess in the normal person may not be absorbed or is easily dissipated. If it were not so, obesity would be a universal malady. We do not know all the factors which enter into the mechanism for regulating body weight, but there is the important factor of endocrine balance.

Our gland endowment to a large extent determines the rate at which our vital activities are carried out, whether the body furnace shall burn brightly or smoulder slowly.

These two factors, excess of food intake and the endocrine balance, are responsible then for overweight, but so far as *treatment* is concerned (except where there is obvious endocrine disturbance) *dieting* is the recognised, and, if properly carried out, the efficacious method.

It is often thought that hard exercise is a weight reducer, but one would consume only 60 extra calories by walking a mile (and this often increases appetite). Drastic methods such as purgation by salts, the production of severe sweating by Turkish baths, starvation diets, and the use of thyroid extracts and other drugs have had their vogue: their effects are likely to be short-lived and they are often most harmful to health.

Dietetic Control

In constructing a reducing dietary, the most important factor is the total *calorific value* of the diet. A calorie is the unit of food energy. There are three main kinds of food, carbohydrates (starches and sugar), protein (meats), and fat; and 1 gram of carbohydrate produces 4 calories, 1 gram of protein 4 calories, and 1 gram of fat 9 calories. Hence, if we know the composition of any food, we can calculate simply the calorie value of any given quantity: e.g. $3\frac{1}{2}$ oz. (half a glass) of milk contains 5 grams of carbohydrate, $3\frac{1}{2}$ grams of protein and $3\frac{1}{2}$ grams of fat. Therefore the total calorie value is $65\frac{1}{2}$. The daily calorie requirements of a healthy adult vary from about 2,000 for a sedentary worker to 3,000 for a heavy manual worker.

It is recommended that a dietary of 1,000–2,000 *calories* should be adopted for a steady and progressive loss of *two or three pounds* each week.

Since it is usually an excessive consumption of starchy and sugary foods which leads to overweight, such foods should be restricted. But excessive curtailment can lead to feelings of faintness, weakness and headache, so that not less than 100–130 grams of carbohydrate should be taken each day chiefly in the form of fruit and green vegetables, which give bulk and are low in calorie content. Moreover, they give a feeling of satiety and provide the roughage which prevents constipation, which low calorie diets may otherwise tend to produce.

With regard to fat, as the body calls upon its own reserves, this item can be reduced to a minimum. Some reducing diets exclude fats as such, only such fat being permitted which is inseparable from such foods as meat. Thus the daily intake may be as low as 20 grams. But extreme reduction of fats makes the diet unpalatable and would require the addition of the fat-soluble vitamins to maintain health. It is therefore considered that 40–50 grams of fat per day should be provided.

As protein is stimulating to the vital processes (metabolism), it is sometimes given in large quantities, but as this means a higher calorie intake and an unbalancing of the diet, it is not recommended. On the other hand, too low a protein intake will cause excessive destruction of tissue protein and will disturb the chemical balance of the body. Some 60–80 grams of protein is considered the best amount. It is not deemed wise to restrict fluids in a reducing diet, except for alcohol and sweetened drinks, but salt and salty foods are to be avoided.

Methods of Dieting

Those who would reduce, as already indicated, should aim at remaining on a dietary of 1,000–1,200 calories until such time as they have reached their ideal weight. Assuming a moderate degree of overweight, this should take from roughly four to six weeks. Thereafter, they should cautiously increase their dietary selectively to about 1,500–1,800 calories, carefully watching their weight. All the good will be undone if they return to their old diet, especially in those who tend to put on weight easily. Life for them becomes a series of "diet cures," and this is bad for health and morale.

It is possible progressively to reduce the amount of food per day by 50–100 calories and so reach the desired 1,000–1,200, and some may prefer to accustom themselves gradually to the low dietary in this way. But most people are anxious to achieve results as quickly as possible. Needless to say, this will involve a certain self-discipline and a degree of conscientiousness for success. The first few days may be difficult,

but once these are over, it should not prove unduly difficult to maintain the regime.

If one wishes to tackle a slimming diet in a strictly scientific way, then it is necessary to obtain scales and to weigh all the foodstuffs. Actually, this is not essential, provided the prescribed dietaries are followed intelligently and the approximate quantities are adhered to.

The following is a reducing dietary of 1,200 calories, containing 116 grams of carbohydrate, 70 grams of protein and 52 grams of fat.

BREAKFAST

One orange or half a grapefruit sweetened with saccharin NOT sugar

Tea or coffee with milk from ration *

One egg or one ounce of cold lean ham or tongue

One ounce of bread (equivalent of one thin slice) and quarter-ounce of butter (one small pat)

DINNER

Clear soup

Two to three ounces of lean meat, chicken, or white fish

A large helping of vegetables, excepting potatoes, dried peas, beans or lentils

Fresh salad (lettuce, cabbage, without oil or cream dressing)

Three-quarters of an ounce of cheese

Half an ounce (half-slice) of bread, or two plain biscuits

Fresh fruit, except bananas or plums

Coffee with milk from ration *

TEA

Tea with milk from ration * sweetened with saccharin, NOT sugar

Bread, one and a half ounces (one and a half slices)

Tomato, lettuce or cress for sandwiches

Quarter-ounce butter (small pat)

SUPPER

Clear soup

Three ounces (cooked weight) of fish, or egg, or one ounce lean meat

Vegetable salad and fruit as at dinner

Bread, half an ounce, or piece of crispbread

Milk from ration * for coffee, or for custard, using egg from breakfast

Butter, three-quarters of
  an ounce
Milk, half a pint
NO sugar

It should be noted
that most fresh fruits,
green vegetables, meat
extracts and clear soups,
tea and coffee without
milk can be taken freely,

The free foods which can be taken by
those feeling hungry between meals
while dieting

so that those who ex-
perience hunger between meals can find
comfort by taking such foods.

There it is then—a typical weight reducing dietary which can lend itself to a
great many variations to avoid a depressing
monotony. It is not a difficult dietary to
prepare and it is not expensive.

Here is a six days' guide:

EVERY DAY
BREAKFAST

Orange or half a grapefruit; one egg,
boiled, poached or scrambled; or one
ounce lean ham, or two ounces white
fish, baked or steamed, or one kipper or
one herring; one piece crispbread or
one thin slice of bread or toast; half
an ounce sugarless marmalade; tea or
coffee with milk, from **ration of half a
pint per day;** and butter from **three-
quarter ounce ration per day.***

FIRST DAY
DINNER

Tomato juice
One and half ounces lean grilled bacon,
  tomato and cauliflower
Three starch-reduced rolls or slices with
  butter from ration *
One apple
Coffee or tea with milk from ration *

SUPPER

Orange juice
One lean grilled chop,
  celery and sprouts
One piece crispbread with
  butter from ration *
One fresh pear with three
  tablespoonfuls junket

SECOND DAY
DINNER

Clear soup
Two ounces lean meat,
  cabbage and carrots
Fruit salad (orange,
  apple, grapes)
One slice bread with
  butter from ration *
Coffee or tea

SUPPER

Tomato juice
Three ounces steamed fish with lemon
  juice and celery
Three ounces stewed apricots
Two starch-reduced rolls or slices with
  butter from ration *
Three tablespoonfuls cornflour mould

THIRD DAY
DINNER

Half a grapefruit
Two ounces braised rabbit, cabbage and
  carrots
One piece crispbread and butter from
  ration *
Stewed rhubarb with tablespoonful rice
  pudding
Coffee or tea

SUPPER

Clear soup
Two ounces lean roast meat with cauli-
  flower
One slice fresh pineapple with three table-
  spoonfuls junket
One slice bread with butter from ration *

FOURTH DAY
DINNER

Vegetable broth (unthickened)
Two ounces grated cheese with lettuce,
  watercress and tomato
Three starch-reduced rolls or slices
  with butter from ration *
One orange
Tea or coffee

Rations for the day: Half a
pint of milk; three-quarters
of an ounce of butter

SUPPER

Lobster or crab salad

Stewed apples with three tablespoonfuls cornflour mould

One piece crispbread with butter from ration * and a small portion of cheese

FIFTH DAY

DINNER

Orange juice

One poached egg with spinach

Three starch-reduced rolls or slices with butter from ration *

Three ounces stewed apricots with three tablespoonfuls sago pudding

Coffee or tea

SUPPER

Clear soup

Three ounces haddock (steamed), tomato and lettuce

One slice bread and butter from ration * and small portion of cheese

One apple

SIXTH DAY

DINNER

Half a grapefruit

Two ounces cold lean meat with salad (lettuce, watercress, tomato)

Two starch-reduced rolls or slices with butter from ration * and small portion of cheese

Coffee or tea

SUPPER

Tomato juice

Two ounces lean grilled ham, tomatoes and spinach

Two starch-reduced rolls or slices with butter from ration *

Two and a half ounces figs with three tablespoonfuls custard

Finally, it must be again emphasised that successful dieting demands some special knowledge along with a reasonable self-discipline. Failure to achieve results nearly always arises from a loss of interest and enthusiasm, or from disappointment that the desired loss of weight is not achieved sufficiently rapidly. Patience is required, but the restoration of the body to its normal weight will assuredly improve the health of mind as well as body, and increase the joy of living.

FOOD TABLES

These tables show the number of calories given by convenient quantities of the common foodstuffs and their approximate content of carbohydrate, protein and fat. Reference to these tables will enable a person to diet with a considerable degree of accuracy.

Carbohydrate
CEREALS

	Oz.	Calories	C.	P.	F.
Arrowroot, uncooked	½	61½	15	0	0
Bread, average, white	1	74	15	3	0
Bread, average, brown	1	68	15	1½	0
Corn Flakes	½	45	10	1	0
Macaroni, boiled	2	58½	10	2	1
Oatmeal, raw	½	68	10	2	2
Rice, uncooked	½	51	12½	0	0
Sago, uncooked	½	51	12½	0	0

SUGARY FOODS

	Oz.	Calories	C.	P.	F.
Chocolate, average, milk	½	84	7½	1	5
Chocolate, average, plain	½	62	7½	1	3
Golden Syrup, as purchased	½	51	12½	0	0
Honey, as purchased	½	51	12½	0	0
Jam, average	¼	20½	5	0	0
Marmalade, ordinary	½	51	12½	0	0
Marmalade, sugarless, reliable make		Negligible			
Sugar, one large lump	½	20½	5	0	0

Carbohydrate (continued)

MILK

	Oz.	Calories	C.	P.	F
Buttermilk	$3\frac{1}{2}$	42	5	3	1
Milk, fresh	$\begin{cases} 1 \\ 3\frac{1}{2} \end{cases}$	19 / 67	$1\frac{1}{2}$ / 5	1 / $3\frac{1}{2}$	1 / $3\frac{1}{2}$
Milk, skimmed	$3\frac{1}{2}$	$41\frac{1}{2}$	5	4	$\frac{1}{2}$
Milk, condensed unsweetened	1	61	5	3	3
Milk, dried	$\frac{1}{2}$	67	5	$3\frac{1}{2}$	$3\frac{1}{2}$

FRUIT AND NUTS

	Oz.	Calories	C.	P.	F
Apple, with skin	2	$20\frac{1}{2}$	5	0	0
Apricots, fresh, with stones	3	25	5	1	0
Banana, average size	3	$61\frac{1}{2}$	15	0	0
Figs, green, raw	2	26	5	1	0
Grapefruit, with skin	6	22	5	$\frac{1}{2}$	0
Grapes, fresh	1	20	5	0	0
Melon, edible part	$3\frac{1}{2}$	23	5	1	0
Nuts, almond	$\frac{1}{2}$	78	$\frac{1}{2}$	3	7
Nuts, brazil	$\frac{1}{2}$	86	$\frac{1}{2}$	2	8
Nuts, chestnut	$\frac{1}{2}$	68	5	3	4
Nuts, walnut	$\frac{1}{2}$	74	$\frac{1}{2}$	2	7
Olives	1	$46\frac{1}{2}$	0	0	5
Peaches, fresh, with stones	$2\frac{1}{4}$	$22\frac{1}{2}$	5	$\frac{1}{2}$	0
Pears, fresh, with skin	3	27	6	$\frac{1}{2}$	0
Pineapple, fresh, edible part	$1\frac{1}{2}$	$20\frac{1}{2}$	5	0	0
Plums, ripe, Victoria (with stones)	2	$20\frac{1}{2}$	5	0	0
Rhubarb		Negligible			

VEGETABLES

	Oz.	Calories	C.	P.	F
Asparagus, fresh, boiled (edible part)	8	16	$2\frac{1}{2}$	$7\frac{1}{2}$	0
Beans, broad	$2\frac{1}{2}$	33	5	3	0
Beans, butter	2	56	10	4	0
Beans, haricot	2	56	10	4	0
Beans, french	8	16	$2\frac{1}{2}$	$1\frac{1}{2}$	0
Beans, scarlet runner		Negligible			
Beetroot, boiled once	$1\frac{3}{4}$	25	5	1	0
Brussels sprouts ⎫ Cabbage, spring ⎬ Cabbage, winter ⎭		May be considered negligible			
Carrots, boiled once	4	23	5	$\frac{1}{2}$	0
Cauliflower ⎫ Celery, raw ⎪ Celery, baked ⎬ Cress ⎭		May be considered negligible			
Cucumber, raw, without skin	5	14	$2\frac{1}{2}$	1	0
Cucumber, boiled	6	11	$2\frac{1}{2}$	0	0
Lettuce, raw		Negligible			
Mushrooms		Negligible			
Onions, boiled once	$3\frac{1}{2}$	14	$2\frac{1}{2}$	$\frac{1}{2}$	0
Peas, boiled once, green, fresh	2	70	14	2	$\frac{1}{2}$
Peas, tinned, green	2	57	10	4	0
Peas, green, dried	2	57	10	4	0
Potato, raw or boiled once	1	$22\frac{1}{2}$	5	$\frac{1}{2}$	0
Spinach, boiled once	6	46	$2\frac{1}{2}$	9	0
Tomatoes, raw, cooked or tinned	4	20	3	1	0
Watercress, raw	1	Negligible			

Protein

	Oz.	Calories	C.	P.	F.
Cheese	½	50–70 varies roughly			
Eggs, one average whole egg	—	76	—	6	5½

FISH

	Oz.	Calories	C.	P.	F.
Cod, boiled	3	61	0	15	0
Crab, edible part	2	58	0	10	2
Haddock, boiled	3	82	0	20	0
Halibut, boiled	1½	58	0	10	2
Herring, fresh	2	112	0	10	8
Kipper, boiled	1½	76	0	10	4
Mackerel, boiled	3	114	0	15	6
Plaice, steamed	2	50	0	10	1
Salmon, boiled	3	142	0	15	9
Skate, boiled	2	50	0	10	1
Turbot, cooked	3	60	0	15	0
Whiting, steamed	2	41	0	10	0

MEAT

	Oz.	Calories	C.	P.	F.
Bacon, fat, fried	1	160	0	5	15
Bacon, lean	1½	220	0	10	20
Beef, average roast	2	201	0	15	15
Beef, roast lean	2	87	0	15	3
Ham, boiled, lean only	1½	94	0	10	6
Kidneys, cooked	2	87	0	15	3
Lamb, roast	3	175	0	20	10
Liver, cooked	2	141	0	15	9
Mutton, roast	2	168	0	15	12
Mutton chop, lean, grilled	2	224	0	20	16
Pork, roast	2	229	0	15	18
Rabbit, stewed	2	89	0	15	3
Sweetbreads, cooked	1½	78	0	10	4
Tongue, ox, tinned	1½	162	0	10	13
Veal, roast	2	156	0	20	8

POULTRY AND GAME

	Oz.	Calories	C.	P.	F.
Chicken, roast or boiled	2	103	0	15	4½
Duck, roast or boiled	1½	134	0	10	10
Goose, roast	2	173	0	15	12
Turkey, roast	2	89	0	15	3

FATS

	Oz.	Calories	F.
Bacon	½	116	12½
Beef fat	½	116	12½
Butter	½	116	12½
Cream, average	1	46½	5
Dripping	½	139½	15
Lard	½	139½	15
Margarine	½	116	12½
Suet	½	139½	15

614

ROUTINE FOR PUTTING ON WEIGHT

Plenty of rest and exercise, a good diet of fattening foods and no worries—those are the essentials

PUTTING on weight is very much more difficult than taking it off. Even those few extra pounds which can make all the difference to the appearance, comfort and, no doubt, general health, can be quite a problem.

Before embarking on a diet, it is always advisable to seek the advice of your own doctor. This is particularly important if there has been a sudden or prolonged loss of weight for no good reason and without affecting normal appetite. Where loss of weight is the result of an illness or operation, it is usually quite quickly and easily regained after recovery. The routine to be described in this chapter will help in such cases, subject to the approval of your own doctor.

We are concerned here chiefly with that large army of men and women who are anxious to put on weight but who are the thin type by nature. Such people are born worriers, with excitable and energetic natures and over-active bowels, whose food does not remain in the intestines long enough to be properly absorbed.

Essential in the fattening process are:

Italian actress Pier Angeli gets through a huge plate of ice cream—an excellent fattening food

(1) **Keep calm and stop worrying.** That is obviously a counsel of perfection to those who easily get worked up, but it *can* be achieved by cultivating outside interests that take your mind away from the source of anxiety (it may be professional, domestic, financial, or all three).

(2) **Take plenty of rest.** A minimum of between 8 and 9 hours in bed at night, plus between 10 and 30 minutes after every meal.

(3) **Avoid rushing about, but take regular exercise.** On no account jump up immediately after a meal; take life at a leisurely pace. Strenuous games are good if you really enjoy them, because they create appetite; so does any form of outdoor exercise, however mild.

(4) **Eat well and regularly, and concentrate on the fattening foods** (list follows). But be careful not to stuff between meals or you will defeat the whole object and be unable to eat your main meals, which are far more important. You must also avoid *over*-eating, with the inevitable danger of indigestion and biliousness. Aim at three good meals a day, plus any extras (such as sweets, etc.) which you really fancy and a hot, preferably milk, drink last thing at night. The housewife should take as many meals out as she conveniently can because she will not have the worry of preparing them.

(5) **Cut down your smoking.** It diminishes the appetitite, so, if you must smoke at all, only after meals, please.

615

FATTENING FOODS

Sugar, sweets, jam, marmalade, fruits in syrup, treacle, honey, Golden Syrup.

Cakes, scones, pastry, cereals, bread, biscuits, puddings.

Thickened soups and gravies, sauces made from flour, butter and/or milk.

Fried foods, cream, salad dressings, butter, dripping.

Pork, duck, goose. All fat meat and bacon. Tinned fish in oil.

Sweet wines, beer, stout, spirits, sweet aerated waters.

Dried fruits. Bananas, grapes, plums.

Potatoes, peas, dried beans, parsnips, beetroot.

Cod-liver oil, Virol, olive oil.

Salt with food.

Foods with very little fattening value

Meat extracts. Marmite. Clear soups. Gelatine. Egg-white.

Green vegetables and salads. Vinegar. Tea. Coffee.

SPECIMEN DIET FOR PUTTING ON WEIGHT

Minimum: 1 pint of milk per day

On waking: Cup of tea, preferably with milk and sugar.

Breakfast: Cereal or porridge with milk and sugar or honey or syrup.
Bacon, egg, fish, etc.
Toast, butter and marmalade.
Coffee or tea.

11 a.m.: Coffee, cocoa or milk and a biscuit, or try this cocktail: One teaspoonful Spanish olive oil sandwiched between layers of orange juice in a wineglass. You can increase the quantity of olive oil gradually.

Lunch: Thick soup, if liked (if this makes it impossible to eat main course, substitute tomato or orange juice as an appetiser instead).
Meat, fish, game, poultry, etc.—both *fat and lean.* Serve with gravy, roast or fried potatoes and a green vegetable or salad with plenty of oily or cream dressing.
Pudding and/or cheese, butter and biscuits. Coffee.

Tea: Tea with cake or bread and butter or banana sandwich.

Dinner: Thick soup (see Lunch).
Fish, meat or poultry, with gravy, at least one vegetable from list of Fattening Foods; one green vegetable or salad with cream or oil dressing.
Steamed or boiled pudding or milk pudding or ice cream.
Cheese with bread or biscuits and butter. Coffee.

NOTE: Cocktails, wines, etc., may be taken as desired and obtainable. Stout or beer is good.

Bedtime: A hot drink, preferably containing milk.

Instead of rushing about just after eating, lie back in bed and enjoy your breakfast in leisurely fashion if you really want to put on weight

PASTE *YOUR* RECIPES HERE

PASTE *YOUR* RECIPES HERE

PASTE *YOUR* RECIPES HERE

PASTE *YOUR* RECIPES HERE

PASTE *YOUR* RECIPES HERE

PASTE *YOUR* RECIPES HERE

INDEX

INDEX

INDEX

INDEX